Crane Fruehauf have earned an enviable reputation for the competitive excellence of their container and semi-trailer models.

This aerial view of the CF container park illustrates the massive and successful scale of the company's operation. It shows some of the 8000 aluminium dry freight containers already in operation with OCL on their UK-Australia-UK run. Further major orders have been won from this leading UK container consortium for delivery during 1970. CF are also winning orders on a world-wide basis, including the world-record Export order for aluminium dry freight containers from Seatrain for their new trans-Atlantic services. Already Crane Fruehauf have supplied a wide variety of containers* to more than 50 home and overseas customers. CF are interested in every customer for containers and semi-trailers, large or small, whatever the requirement. Short and long-haul container market leaders are choosing CF container models—and proven performance is a vitally important factor in this overall success story.

*Models include: Smooth Skin or Exposed Post; Plastic Plywood; Dry Freight; Insulated, Refrigerated; Open-top; Tiltainers; Bulktainers; Tanker Containers; Hopper Containers. All to ISO recommendations.

Company facilities include the most modern and efficient foaming plant in the world for Insulated and Refrigerated Container manufacture.

Container and Semi-Trailer Market Leaders

Crane Fruehauf

Crane Fruehauf Containers Ltd., Head Office: Cromer Road, North Walsham, Norfolk. Tel: 069-24 3411

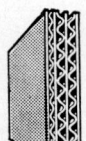

TRI-WALL PAK
the packaging that makes your exports more competitive

TRI-WALL PAK can cut packaging costs on a wide variety of products by as much as 25%! *Overall* packaging costs — not just material costs. So it helps to make your exports more competitive. This is why.

TRI-WALL PAK is very light so tare weight is reduced. It is also very strong so damage to goods is virtually eliminated. It is very simple to assemble and so it saves time and money on labour. It is clean and very easy to handle so packing, loading and unloading are speeded up.

TRI-WALL PAK is backed by an expert, international service. Tri-Wall packaging engineers are always at hand to advise you on the most efficient and economical design of packaging. And then if you want to try a test shipment to North America or Europe, Tri-Wall representatives can check it at its destination.

TRI-WALL PAK can be manufactured to your precise requirements by Tri-Wall Containers Ltd., or by one of their many fabricators who cover the whole of the UK.

TRI-WALL PAK is approved by US official organisations and in the UK by HM Ministries, British Rail, IATA, Shipping Conferences, and meets BoT Blue Book regulations governing hazardous cargoes.

TRI-WALL PAK is a lightweight, heavy-duty, triple-fluted fibreboard with high top-to-bottom compression. It is much stronger than twin-fluted boards and will not split or splinter. It is highly damp-resistant, and will not delaminate even when immersed in water for 24 hours!

For further information, please get in touch with :

Tri-Wall CONTAINERS LIMITED
ONE MOUNT STREET, LONDON W1Y 5AA. Tel. 01-493 4311. Telex 265382
USA : TRI-WALL CONTAINERS INC., One Dupont Street, Plainview, Long Island, New York 11803.
Europe : TRI-WALL CONTAINERS (EUROPA) NV, 5 J.C. van Markenlaan, Rijswijk, The Netherlands.

TRI-WALL PAK is the trade mark for triple-fluted corrugated board manufactured to the specifications of Tri-Wall Containers Inc. Manufacture, arrangement of fluting, fabrication, sale and use are protected by US Patents 2,759,523; 2,949,151; 2,969,170; 2,985,553; 3,096,224; 3,122,976; 3,199,763; 3,036,752 and UK Patents 805,320; 1,018,241; 1,053,095; 1,144,013. Other patents are pending.

S11

3

JANE'S FREIGHT CONTAINERS

Edited by Patrick Finlay

Order of Contents

World Sales Distribution

Jane's Yearbooks,
Paulton House, Shepherdess Walk,
London, N1, England

All the World
except

North, Central and South America:
McGraw-Hill Book Company,
330 West 42nd Street, New York, NY

and

Canada:
**McGraw-Hill Company of Canada
Ltd,** 330 Progress Avenue, Scarborough,
Ontario

Editorial communication to:

The Editor, Jane's Freight Containers
Jane's Yearbooks, Paulton House, Shepherdess Walk,
London N1, England
Telephone 01-251 0787

Advertisement communication to:

Jane's Advertising Department
Haymarket Publishing Group,
Gillow House, 5 Winsley Street,
London W1, England
Telephone 01-636 3600

ALPHABETICAL LIST OF ADVERTISERS.
1971 / 72 EDITION.

Crane Fruehauf produce more Skeletal and Platform Skeletal semi-trailers for container transportation than the rest of the UK semi-trailer industry put together.

As European market leaders in the design and manufacture of both semi-trailers and containers, Crane Fruehauf have proved to their customers that there can be no substitute for successful experience in this demanding field — a success which the Company is able to share with all its customers.

Highly competitive models, from the biggest semi-trailer range in the world, are readily available to meet any challenge.

Anyone in the market for semi-trailers or containers — standard models or specials, big orders or small — cannot be better advised than to consult Crane Fruehauf *now*.

Semi-Trailer and Container Market Leaders

Crane Fruehauf +Boden

Company facilities include the most modern and efficient foaming plant in the world for Insulated and Refrigerated Container manufacture.

Crane Fruehauf Trailers Ltd., Head Office: Hayes Gate House, Uxbridge Road, Hayes, Middlesex.
Telephone: 01-848 0225

NOW—A THROUGH
CONTAINER
SERVICE TO
JAPAN
WITH
OCL
SIMPLER, SAFER, SWIFTER
(we proved it on the Australian run)

The new OCL container service to Japan is the one with solid experience behind it.

Our Australian container route has given us millions of miles of know-how on delivering the goods half way round the world.

Co-ordinating a complex organisation of containers, road and rail transport, specially built ships, and capable of handling all the necessary export documentation is second nature to us now.

So when you are planning your next consignment to Japan, it makes sound sense to call in OCL.

OVERSEAS CONTAINERS LIMITED,
UK Marketing Headquarters, 17a – 18 Bevis Marks, London, E.C.3. Telephone 01-283 4242.

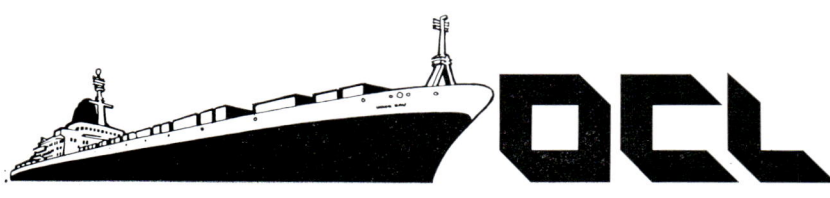

OCL *the containerway to Japan*

This container dock wasn't here yesterday.

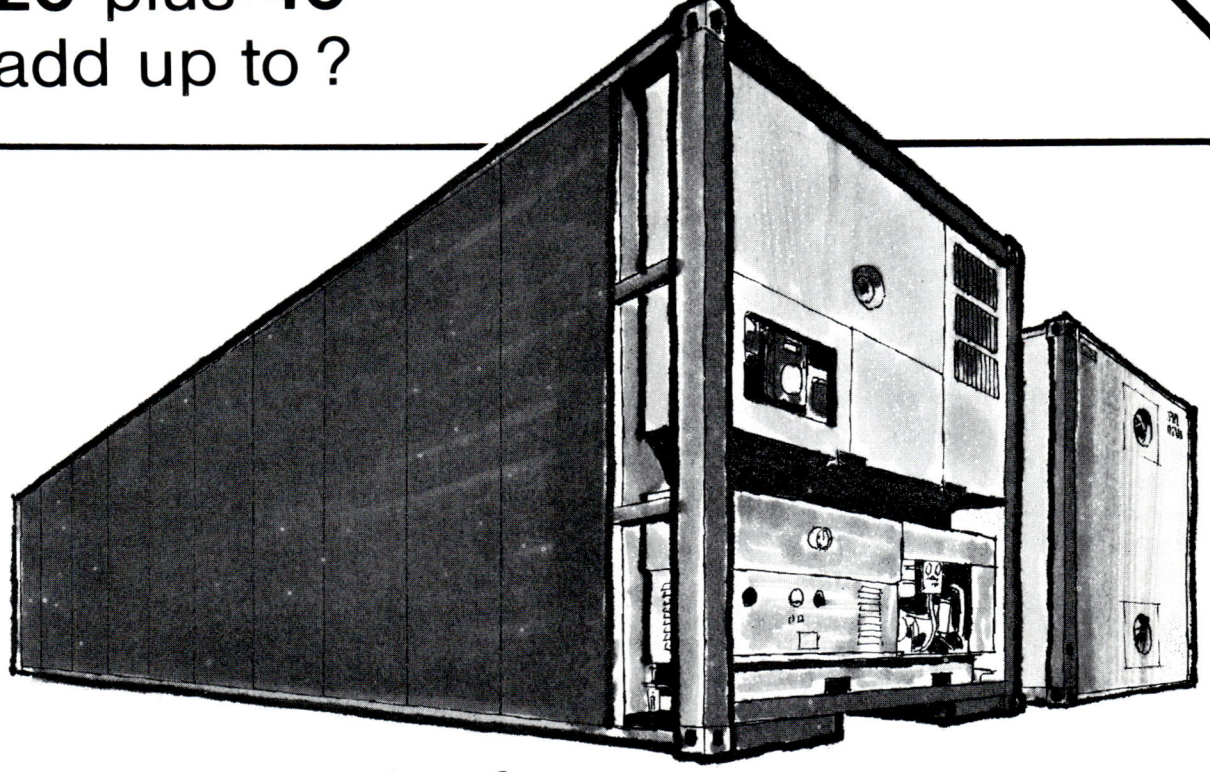

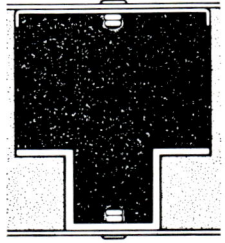

Now, the 250-ton P&H® Truck Crane...
Major breakthrough in container and cargo handling.

Load or unload containers. Minutes later, handle heavy machinery without twin lifts.

Or move over to a storage area and stack containers. The tremendous and mobile P&H 6250-TC does it all.

This work-anywhere giant is the largest production truck crane in the western hemisphere. It provides up to 250 tons of lift, close-in; over 30 tons at a 100 ft. radius. And it travels anywhere in the dock area with its boom fully rigged.

In smaller ports, the P&H 6250-TC can provide complete container-handling and heavy-cargo capability at a minimum investment. Initial cost is far below that of a limited-use container gantry. Or, consider leasing the 6250-TC and achieve immediate modernization without increasing bonded indebtedness.

Major ports can use the 6250-TC to back up gantry cranes and to provide extra cargo-handling capacity. Optimize your materials-handling investment with this P&H giant.

For full information, call 414-671-4400 Ext. 2509, Harnischfeger, Milwaukee, Wis. 53246.

P&H TRUCK CRANES

HARNISCHFEGER

Cable; Harninco

First of the 250-tonners, put in dock-side service by Hoffman Rigging and Crane Service, Inc. at the Port Elizabeth facility of the Port of New York. It loads 17 to 19 boxes per hour below deck, and over 25 boxes per hour on deck.

SEVERAL OF THE WORLDS LARGEST CONTAINER USERS BUY BN CONTAINERS

WHY?

SPEAKING OF

BELGIAN QUALITY!

OUR RANGE OF PRODUCTION INCLUDES

- ★ Light-alloy STRICK containers—Inner and outer skin
- ★ Steel box and Open-top containers
- ★ Plywood Box containers
- ★ Container-flats
- ★ Skeletal semi-trailers
- ★ Tilt-trailers

For further details please contact:

CONTAINER DEPT.
B-8200 - Brugge - Phone (050) 307-51-307.21 - Telex : BRGE 191.22 - Cable : Brunivel-Bruges
(Belgium)

S.A. LA BRUGEOISE - NIVELLES, N.V. — BRUGES / BRUGGE

MAT
serves Europe
completely

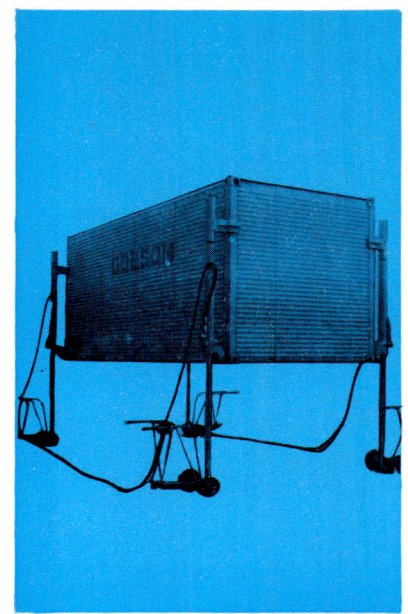

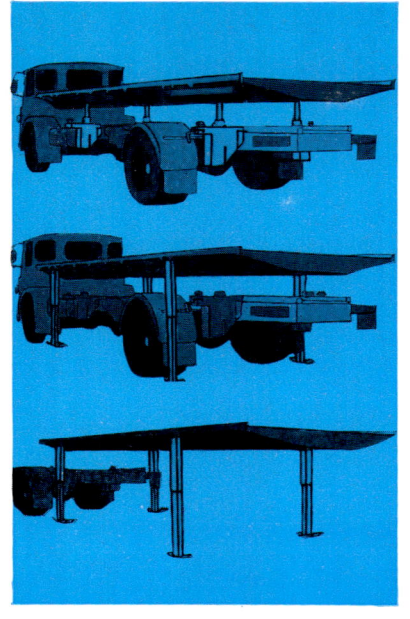

20 ton Mobile Corner Lifting Legs

Capable of off loading 20 ton loads to ground level. 35 ton heavy duty system also available.

Type 41 Demountable

Caters for all types of chassis, bodies and containers, and for any load carrying capacity applicable to the G.U.W. of the vehicle.

Fork Lift Trucks

Electric powered from 2000 lb. to 6000 lb. capacity. Cushioned or pneumatic tyred wheels.

DOBSON
the container handling people

Key: J.F.A.

Literature please on the Dobson

Hydraulic Corner Lifting Legs ☐
Demountable body systems ☐
Fork Trucks ☐

Name.. Position ....

Company .... Address ....

Tel:..

W.E. & F. Dobson Ltd., Colwick Industrial Estate, Colwick, Nottingham.
Member of Dobson Park Industries Ltd. Tel: 241341 Telex: 37132

CLASSIFIED LIST OF ADVERTISERS

A1. ALUMINIUM CONTAINERS

Crane Fruehauf
Fruehauf France

B1. BARS, SPRING LOADED SHORING

B. Dixon Bate Ltd.

B2. BLOCKS, HOIST PULLEY AND CHAIN BULK LOADING

Holt Williams & Co.
Port of New York

C1. CARGO CONTROL

B. Dixon Bate Ltd.

C2. CARTON CLAMPS

Coventry Climax

C3. CHISEL FORKS

Coventry Climax

C4. CLAMPS, SQUEEZE

Coventry Climax

C5. COMPREHENSIVE CONTAINER LEASING

Container Transport International
Rentcon

C6. COMPUTERIZED CONTAINER CONTROL

Container Transport International
Rentcon

C7. CONSOLIDATION SERVICES

Rentcon

C8. CONTAINERS

Container Transport International
Crane Fruehauf
Fruehauf France

C9. CONTAINER CLEANSING

Smith Bros. & Webb

C10. CONTAINER HANDLING LIFT TRUCKS

Coventry Climax

C11. CONTAINER LASHING SYSTEMS

Bromma Smides

C12. CONTAINER LINES

"K" Line
Tor Line

C13. CONTAINER LEASING

Container Transport International
Rentcon

C14. CONTAINERS, NON-STANDARD

Container Transport International

C15. CONTAINERS REPAIRS

Bromma Smides
Crane Fruehauf
Rentcon
Repcon Ltd.

C16. CONTAINER RESTRAINING (TWISTLOCKS)

Bromma Smides
Holt Williams & Co.

C17. CONTAINER SEMI-TRAILERS

Crane Fruehauf
Fruehauf France

C18. CONTAINER STUFFER TRUCKS

Clark Equipment Ltd.
Coventry Climax

C19. CONTAINER TERMINALS

Container Transport International
Irish Ferryways
Port of New York
Tor Lines

C20. CONTROL EQUIPMENT, CARGO & CONTAINER

B. Dixon Bate Ltd.

C21. COUPLABLE CONTAINERS

Container Transport International
Fruehauf France

C22. CRANE ARM FORK LIFT ATTACHMENTS

Coventry Climax

C23. CRANES, DOCKSIDE AND HARBOUR

The Harnischfeger Corp.

D1. DECKING, INTERNAL CONTAINER

B. Dixon Bate Ltd.

D2. DEMOUNTABLE VEHICLE BODIES

Dobson W. E. & F.

D3. DIESEL FORK LIFT TRUCKS

Clark Equipment Ltd.
Coventry Climax
Dobson W. E. & F.

D4. DRUM FORKS

Coventry Climax

D5. DRY FREIGHT CONTAINERS

Container Transport International
Crane Fruehauf

E1. ELECTRIC FORK LIFT TRUCKS

Clark Equipment Ltd.
Coventry Climax
Dobson W. E. & F.

E2. ELECTRIC TRACTOR

Coventry Climax

E3. EUROPEAN CONTAINER SERVICES

Container Transport International
Tor Line

E4. EXPORT SERVICE

Tor Line

E5. EXTENSIONS SLEEVES, FORK

Coventry Climax

F1. FERRY SERVICES

Irish Ferryways
Tor Line

F2. FIRE PUMP

Coventry Climax

F3. FORK LIFT LEASING

Coventry Climax

F4. FORK LIFT TRUCKS

Clark Equipment
Coventry Climax

F5. FORK TRUCK (New or reconditioned)

Clark Equipment

F6. FREIGHT CONTAINERS

Container Transport International
Crane Fruehauf
Luchaire

G1. GENERAL CONTAINER LEASING

Container Transport International
Rentcon

Irish Ferryways:

Trail-blazers in Ireland towards better exports/imports

Because Irish Ferryways pioneered in unit-loading in Ireland you can benefit by:—
* **Lower insurance rates**
* **More economical exports and imports**
* **Speedier transit**
* **Easier documentation**
* **Less pilferage**
* **Less breakage**

With a new terminal at Tolka Quay, Dublin, Irish Ferryways can put a really impressive range of unit-load equipment at your disposal.

And we take pride in being sufficiently versatile to handle all your traffic irrespective of size or shape. We can prove this to you if you contact us at:

FIF

Tolka Quay, Dublin. Phone: 47948. Telex: 5468 :: The Quay, New Ross. Phone: 21445. Telex: 6711 :: The Docks, Preston. Phone 726255. Telex: 67408 :: East Lock, Alexandra Dock, Newport, Mon. Phone: 51858. Telex: 49274 :: Containerway & Roadferry Ltd., Ripple Road, Berking, Essex. Phone: 592-7344. Telex: 263772 :: Harbour Street, Ardrossan, Ayrshire. Phone: 0294-61619. Telex: 778163.

G2. GENERAL PURPOSE CONTAINERS

Container Transport International
Crane Fruehauf
Fruehauf France

G3. GRAIN STORAGE

Port of New York Authority

H1. HANDLING CONTAINERS

Clark Equipment Ltd.
Dobson W. E. & F.
Rentcon

H2. HANDLING PLANT, MECHANICAL

Bromma Smides

H3. HIRE, FORK LIFT TRUCKS

Coventry Climax

H4. HOISTS, LEVER PULL

Holt Williams

H5. HYDRAULIC RAMS

Dobson W. E. & F.

H6. HYDRAULIC EQUIPMENT

Dobson W. E. & F.

H7. HYDRAULIC BODY HANDLING SYSTEMS

Dobson W. E. & F.

I 1. IMPORT CLEARANCE

Container Transport International

I 2. INSULATED CONTAINERS

Container Transport International
Crane Fruehauf

I 3. ISO CONTAINERS

Container Transport International
Crane Fruehauf

L1. LASHING STRAPS

Dixon Bate Ltd.

L2. LEASING FORK LIFT

Clark Equipment Ltd.
Coventry Climax

L3. LIFT TRUCKS

Clark Equipment Ltd.
Coventry Climax

L4. LIQUID STORAGE

Port of New York Authority

L5. LOADING DEVICES, CONTAINER

Bromma Smides
Clark Equipment

L6. LPG FORK LIFT TRUCKS

Clark Equipment
Coventry Climax
Dobson W. E. & F.

M1. MAINTENANCE, CONTAINER

Container Transport International
Crane Fruehauf
Rentcon

M2. MECHANICAL HANDLING PLANT

Clark Equipment

M3. MOBILE HYDRAULIC LIFTING LEGS

Dobson W. E. & F.

N1. NARROW AISLE FORK LIFTS

Coventry Climax

P1. PALLET STACKERS

Clark Equipment

P2. PAPER REEL STACKING TRUCKS

Coventry Climax

P3. PEDESTRIAN FORK LIFTS

Clark Equipment Ltd.

P4. PETROL FORK LIFT TRUCKS

Clark Equipment Ltd.
Coventry Climax

P5. PLATFORM TRUCKS, ELECTRIC

Coventry Climax

P6. PORT SERVICES

Port of New York Authority
Port of London Authority
Port of Singapore
Jacksonville Port Authority
Port of San Diego

P7. PUMPS, FIRE

Coventry Climax

R1. RAIL FACILITIES

Deutsche Bundesbahn
New Zealand Railways

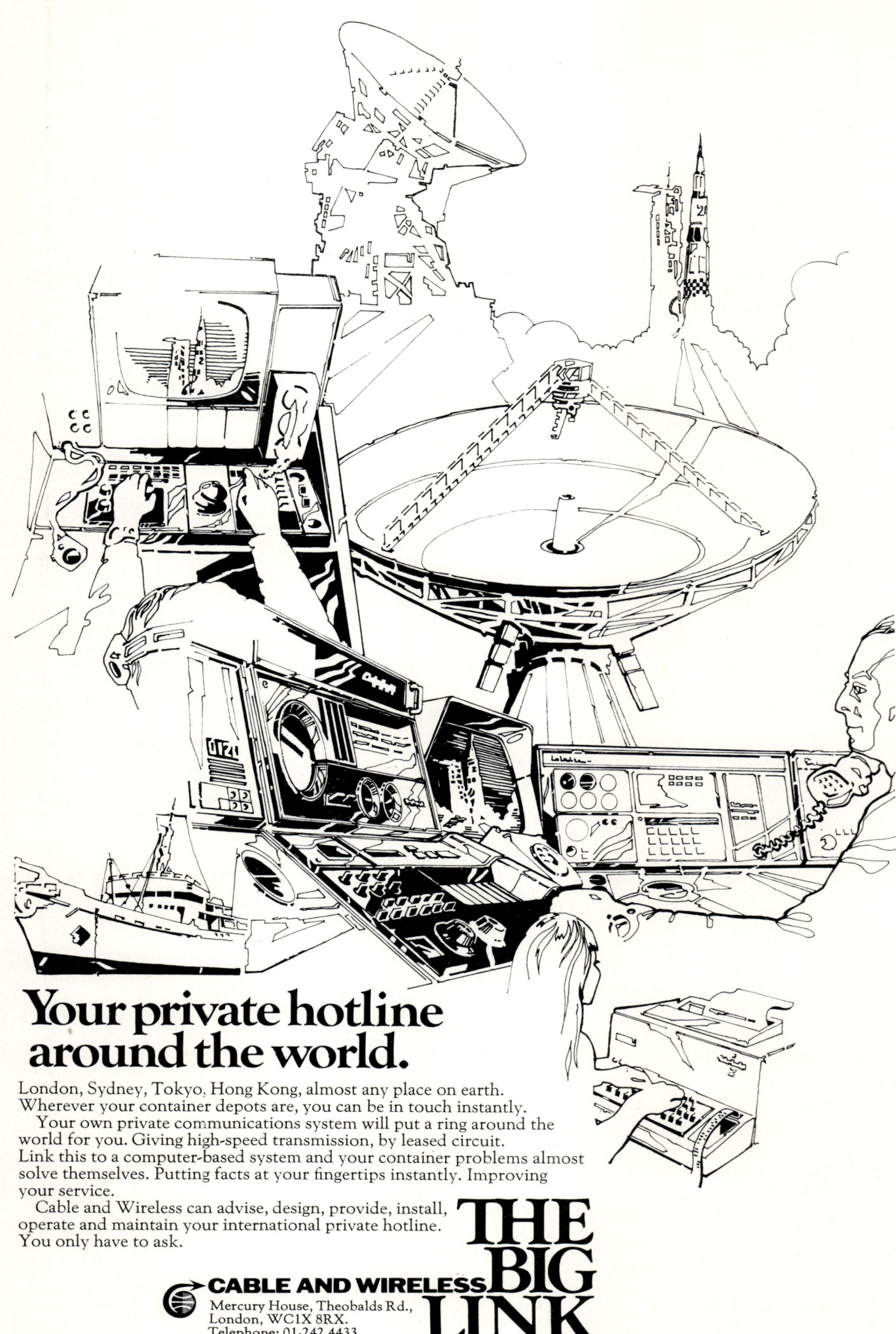

Your private hotline around the world.

London, Sydney, Tokyo, Hong Kong, almost any place on earth. Wherever your container depots are, you can be in touch instantly.

Your own private communications system will put a ring around the world for you. Giving high-speed transmission, by leased circuit. Link this to a computer-based system and your container problems almost solve themselves. Putting facts at your fingertips instantly. Improving your service.

Cable and Wireless can advise, design, provide, install, operate and maintain your international private hotline. You only have to ask.

CABLE AND WIRELESS
Mercury House, Theobalds Rd.,
London, WC1X 8RX.
Telephone: 01-242 4433

THE BIG LINK

R2. REACH TRUCKS

Clark Equipment Ltd.
Coventry Climax

R3. REFRIGERATED CONTAINER HIRE

Container Transport International
Rentcon

R4. REPAIRS, CONTAINER

Bromma Smides
Crane Fruehauf
Rentcon

R5. ROLL-ON ROLL-OFF CARGO, SERVICES USING TRAILERS, CONTAINERS, PALLETS ETC.

Container Transport International
Tor Line

R6. ROLL-ON ROLL-OFF PASSENGER/CARGO SERVICES

Tor Line

R7. ROTATING BALE CLAMP FOR FORKLIFT

Coventry Climax

S1. SHIPPING SERVICES, SCHEDULED

Tor Line
"K" Line
Irish Ferryways
Coras Iompair Eireann

S2. SHORING BARS

B. Dixon Bate Ltd.

S3. SKELETAL CONTAINER TRAILERS

Crane Fruehauf
Fruehauf France

S4. SLING ADJUSTER CHAIN

Holt Williams

S5. STEAMSHIP (CONTAINER SERVICES)

"K" Line
Tor Line

S6. STEEL CONTAINERS

Container Transport International

S7. STORAGE CONTAINERS

Container Transport International
Rentcon

S8. STRADDLE CARRIERS

Clark Equipment Ltd.

S9. STRAPS, LEASHING

B. Dixon Bate Ltd.
Bromma Smides
Holt Williams & Co.

T1. TANK CONTAINERS

Container Transport International
Crane Fruehauf

T2. TERMINAL DEPOTS, INTERNATIONAL FREIGHT

Tor Line

T3. TERMINALS, CONTAINER

Container Transport International
Port of New York Authority
Tor Line
Port of London Authority
Jacksonville Port Authority
Port of San Diego
Port of Singapore

T4. TILT CONTAINERS

Container Transport International
Crane Fruehauf
Rentcon

T5. THROUGH TRANSPORT OPERATORS

Overseas Containers Ltd.

T6. TOW TRACTORS

Coventry Climax

T7. TRACKING, CARGO CONTROL

B. Dixon Bate Ltd.

T8. TRACTORS, ELECTRIC

Coventry Climax

T9. TRAILERS

Crane Fruehauf

T10. TRUCKING FACILITIES

Rentcon

T11. TRUCKS, REACH

Coventry Climax

T12. TUGS

Coventry Climax

U1. UNIT LOAD SERVICE

Irish Ferryways
Tor Line

W1. WINCHES

Holt Williams & Co.

Great stuff, Climax!

Moving freight the modern way means containers and good container handling. But getting the best out of containers depends upon how cheaply and efficiently you "stuff" them. Manual "stuffing" is a dead loss, in time, money and efficiency. The good stuff begins and ends with Climax fork lift trucks.

Like the Climax 50–EC. 5,000 lb capacity, yet still complying with ISO floor loading requirements. Electric power with SCR'72 electronic control system for efficiency, economy, reliability and ease of maintenance. Available with high free-lift mast for operation both in and out of containers. And there's a wide range of models with capacities up to 18,000 lb for other applications.

Climax handling costs less

 *Climax*

Coventry Climax Engines Ltd., Widdrington Road, Coventry CV1 4DX Tel: Coventry 21424

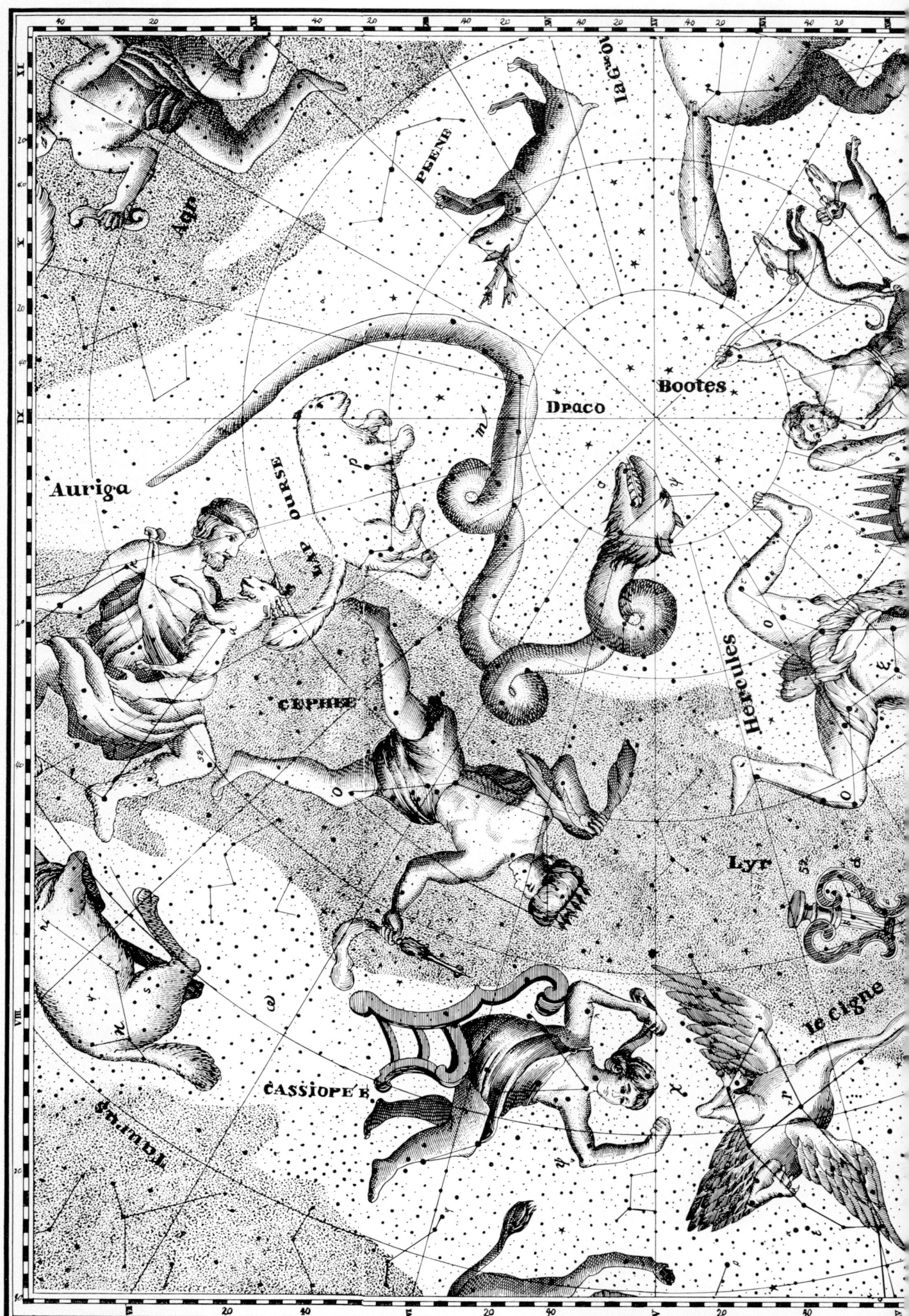

THE PORT

It's the container port of America.

The Port of New York has 16 container cranes. That's more than any other port in America.

The Port—it's a busy port—handled over 7 million long tons of containerized freight last year. No other U.S. port can match that.

The Port—it has 184 steamship lines, nearly every one offering some kind of container service. As a result The Port has more container services to more places than any other U.S. port.

And The Port keeps right on adding container facilities. This year. Next year. Every year.

So if you're shipping via container (or any other way), it's clear you should be shipping via The Port.

Elizabeth-Port Authority Marine Terminal — America's most advanced container facility.

The Port of New York Authority

London: Alan Bralower, Manager, Sam Notkin, Asst Manager,
130 Fenchurch Street, London E.C.3, England. Telephone: (01) 623-9131. Cable: Newthority, London E.C. 3M-5 E.D.

Engineered for Efficiency

Container cranes supplied by M. A. N. to Amsterdam and Le Havre: Single-box girder design, 50 tons capacity, waterside outreach 36 m, centre span 20 m and landside outreach 24 m, lifting height 25 m above rail level. Oblique position of containers during loading and unloading can be compensated by individual operation of the two hoists. Remote-controlled spreaders available for 20′ or 40′ containers, with 4 or 8 corner locks to handle one 40′ container or two 20′ containers, or telescopic spreaders. Locking to container is controlled from cab, eliminating the need for a slinger.

M·A·N
NUREMBERG WORKS

R 07 829/e

27

Special terminals provided for containers:

Container terminals

There are container terminals equipped with outstanding lifting facilities at

Basel, Bochum, Düsseldorf, Frankfurt (M), Hannover, Köln, Ludwigsburg, Mannheim, München, Nürnberg.

Of course you may also tranship containers in other important traffic centres. For further information apply to:

the regional D. B. headquarters (Bundesbahndirektionen), or the following D. B. offices: Zentrale Transportleitung at Mainz, Transfracht at Frankfurt (M), Bundesbahn-Auskunftei at Frankfurt (M), Karlstr. 4-6 (Telex: 412075),

the D. B. representatives in Austria, Belgium, Denmark, France, the Netherlands, Italy, Luxembourg, Sweden, Switzerland, and the U.S.A.:

Wien, Börsendorferstr. 2. Bruxelles 4, 23, rue du Luxembourg. København V, Vester Farimagsgade 1, Dør 472. Paris 9e, 24, rue Condorcet. Rotterdam 1, Rode Zand 34/III. Milano, Corso Vittorio Emmanuele 15. Luxembourg, 14, rue Duchscher. Stockholm C, Barnhusgatan 3 III. Basel, Schwarzwaldallee 200. New York, 36 N. Y. West, 42nd Street, Suite 446.

Traffic agencies in the following countries: Great-Britain, Jugoslavia, Spain:

London E. C. 2., Fa Schenkers Ltd, Royal London House, 13 Finsbury Square, Telex 22625. Jugoslavenske zeleznice Turisticnotransportni biro, Ljubljana, Titova 32. Madrid-3 Maudes, 51 (Edificio Minister), Telex 27767.

Deutsche Bundesbahn ‹‹‹TFG›››

Single sheet aluminium alloy roof for absolute weather-proofness

Roof bows in aluminium alloy

Steel frame carefully shot-blasted and then protected by special epoxy paint

Aluminium alloy or galvanized steel inside posts providing maximum useful width

Especially strong floor in laminated hardwood

Heavy steel sheet for protecting the roof

15.76 ton patented anti-racking device, simple and effective

Smooth riveted outside cladding of pre-painted steel or aluminium sheets

Door locking bars with new cam catches greatly increasing the liaison of the doors to the frame

it's the smallest details that go to make the greatest containers

View of one the container assembly lines in the FRUEHAUF-FRANCE factory at Auxerre (Yonne)

A container is a transportation tool called upon to work under especially harsh conditions.

To assure the necessary strength and resistance, FRUEHAUF-FRANCE, from the drawing board on, attend to even the smallest of details with the greatest of care, as it is these details combined which make FRUEHAUF containers the best in the world.

EDI-PUBLI MESSAGES   FR. 713-C

fruehauf-france

2, Avenue de l'Aunette, 91-RIS-ORANGIS • Tél. : 906-24-02
Télégr.: FRUEFRANCE-RIS-ORANGIS • Telex: FRUEHAUF-RISOR 69967

HOLTITE

ISO FREIGHT CONTAINER EQUIPMENT

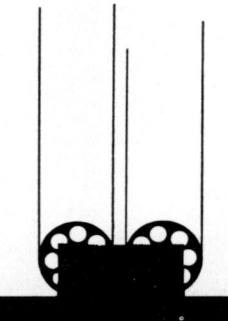

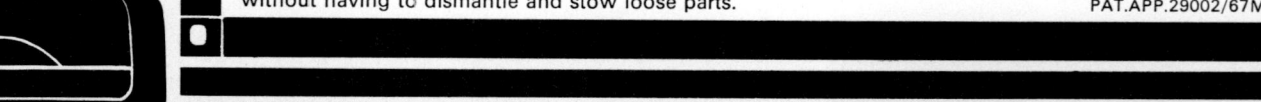

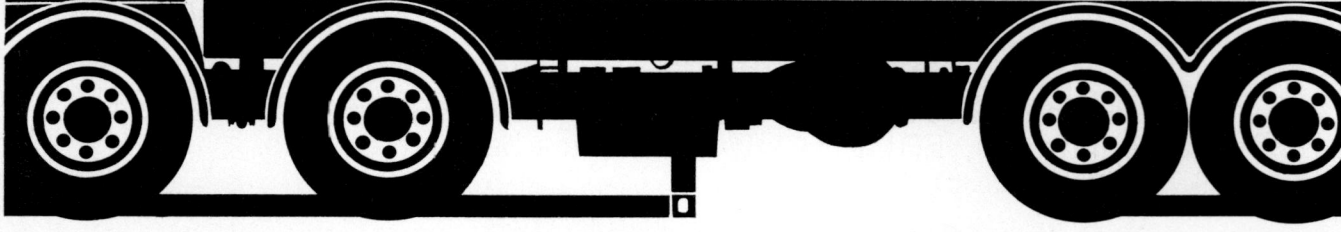

The only scheduled Transatlantic All-Cargo Airline...
IT MUST BE SEABOARD

We're unique – the only airline solely concerned with freighting to and from the States on a daily scheduled basis.

Twenty-seven times a week we send giant DC8 stretch jets with an 18 pallet capacity from Heathrow, Shannon and Prestwick to New York, Chicago, Detroit, Philadelphia or Boston.

10,642 cubic feet of nothing but cargo space – 40% more than regular jets because we freight freight and not passengers. This means guaranteed capacity – your shipments aren't split up.

Every facility for fast and careful handling of your cargo is on hand at our airports in the U.K. and the United States. Just get it to us within one hour before take off.

You won't get service like that from a passenger airline... after all, cargo is beneath them.

⟨SW⟩ SEABOARDWORLD
The freight people who _don't_ freight people!

CONTAINERISATION EFFICIENCY FROM
BROMMA - CONQUIP

The Bromma Automatic Telescopic Spreader handles any container size from 20 ft to 40 ft, both ISO and Sealand standards, in the one basic unit.

Weighing less than 7 tons, the unit has already been specified by the ports of London, Gothenburg, Glasgow, Copenhagen, Zeebrugge, Rotterdam and many others.

Available for fitting to any make of crane, the Bromma Spreader can be either electric or hydraulically operated. Optional extras include 360° rotation, retractable twist-locks, Twin-lift, etc.

CONLOCK

AUTOMATIC LASHING

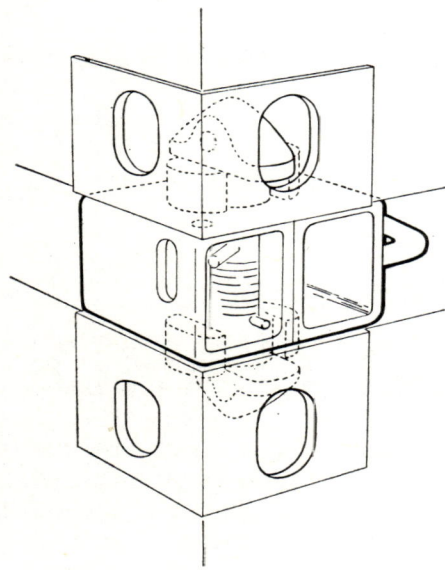

Container lashing with only one universal automatically locking fitting for all container loading and stacking combinations.

Save time, money, and space with Conlock—

Already specified for new services by leading ship-owners.

Up to 4-high stacking on weather-deck, eliminates climbing on container roofs as all fittings can be inserted on the quay if preferred.

Conventional Lashing Systems also supplied

What looks like a safe deposit box acts like a safe deposit box and flies?

THE FLYING SAFE DEPOSIT BOX

Our flying safe deposit box.

14 of them, each capable of carrying up to 2400 lbs. of cargo, are the first real containerization in air cargo history. They'll fly.

With them, air shippers get all the advantages of containerization plus one. They'll fly.

Inside our flying safe deposit box, air cargo has maximum protection from bad weather, pilferage and handling mishaps. And with these intermodal containers, world-wide door-to-door service can easily become a reality.

We'll let you have one free, for up to 48 hours, to pack yourself. And we can even arrange pick-up and delivery at home and overseas.

Yet, our 747 cargo load of 20 tons isn't just restricted to 14 containers. It can be divided up in a variable combination of containers and pallets. Plus, there's space for shipments smaller than container or pallet size.

Right now, our 747s and their flying safe deposit box system are serving London, New York, Paris, San Francisco, Brussels, Los Angeles, Amsterdam, Frankfurt, Rome, Lisbon, Barcelona, Tokyo, Hong Kong, Sydney, Honolulu, San Juan and Bermuda. And we'll be adding more cities.

So, if you want to unburden yourself, just call us. Pan Am's flying safe deposit box system is open for business all over the world.

The Pan Am 747 flying safe deposit box system.

Why does Oakland have the action?

Ask all the container lines that call here.

When it comes to container facilities, the Port of Oakland is second—worldwide—in *facilities, tonnage, and service.* The container lines calling at Oakland offer frequent service to Hawaii, the Far East, the Caribbean, the East Coast, and Europe. These lines know the value of Oakland's central location on the Pacific Coast and its ready access to inland areas via a network of freeways and three trans-continental railroads. They also know the Port of Oakland offers ample room for high-volume container storage yards and consolidation warehouses, and is served by more than 1,000 truck lines. Why does Oakland have the action? Because it has better facilities and offers better service.

See for yourself. Next time you're in a hurry to move goods, mark your Pacific Coast bills of lading "Ship via Oakland."

Now **OAKLAND** *has the action!*

 **Port of Oakland**

66 Jack London Square • Oakland, California 94607

Representatives in New York, Chicago, Tokyo, Brussels

Don't be rattled when they ask you about Seattle!

Don't just stand there the very next time (or the very first time, for that matter) someone asks you: "Why do you suppose imports moving through the Port of Seattle — that's in Western America, you know — have increased 294 percent in the past five years?" With this handy guide you can answer your questioner in a single sentence. Like this:

The Port of Seattle now has three container terminals, with two more on the drawing boards, the West's newest and fastest-loading grain terminal with dockside loading of ships up to 73 foot draft, more time-saving cargo cranes than any other Pacific Coast port, computerized inventories and other cargo controls, a new barge terminal, a thriving Foreign Trade Zone and a $124 million airport expansion program, all of which are directed by an experienced staff that includes cargo experts who will provide even the smallest shipper with free import-export rate studies and speed your cargoes to U.S. markets by three transcontinental railways or a network of truck and air routes.

That's why imports moving through the Port of Seattle have increased 294 percent during the past five years.

Now should we have lunch?

The Port of Seattle
Trade Development Department
Bell Street Terminal
Seattle, Washington, USA 98111

20' Open Top

20' Flat

20' Tank

20' Steel/Aluminium

20' Open Side

20' Steel

20' Steel

HUNGARIAN SHIPYARDS & CRANE FACTORY
Budapest, XIII. Vaci ut 202.
Address: Budapest 62, P.O. Box 280
Tel: 200-800
Cable: SHIPANCRANE Budapest
Telex: 3600

CTI's Container Pool Gives You:

More Types of Equipment
More Depots in More Places
More Flexibility in Leasing
More Years of Experience

40-Ft. Steel Side Door Container

20-Ft. Aluminum Dry Cargo Container

20-Ft. Frame with Coupleable Bogies

40-Ft. Gooseneck Container, Chassis, and Bogie

Write for our new catalog for details on this and many other types of equipment.

cti CONTAINER TRANSPORT INTERNATIONAL INC.

A Subsidiary of Leasco Data Processing Equipment Corporation

WORLD HEADQUARTERS 17 Battery Place, New York, N.Y. 10004, Phone: 212-425-2828, Telex: 222975, TWX: 701-581-2932
EUROPEAN HEADQUARTERS Eagle House, 109 Jermyn St., London S.W. 1, England, Phone: 01-930 0156/7/8, Telex: 24952

The new idea

Perishable goods. Non-stop flow: sea – rail – road – ports – stations – sidings – doorsteps. Cool, safe, value for money. Today in tomorrow's rolling stock: mechanically and ice cooled wagons, mechanically refrigerated containers.
Interfrigo – International Railway-owned Company for Refrigerated Transport. General Management: Wettsteinplatz 1, CH-4000 Basel 5, Phone (061) 33 07 50, Telex 62231.

the racing snowflake
la flèche du froid
der kühle Pfeil
la freccia del freddo

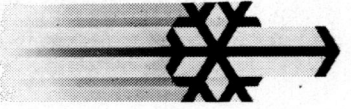

We'll wash if you'll drive

The Britannia Container Emaculator is specially designed to clean containers. For an immaculate result, the driver doesn't even need to leave his cab—just drives through on signal.

First stage is a dirt-dispersing chemical spray. The vehicle is held for the chemical to function, then passes on signal to stage two—a heavy clear-water spray which removes all traces of road dirt and chemical. And the complete wash cycle takes less than two minutes!

Fully guaranteed—leasing terms available. For full technical details on the Britannia Container Emaculator, write or phone:

Smith Bros. & Webb Limited,
Britannia Works,
Arden Forest Industrial Estate,
Alcester, Warwickshire.
Telephone: Alcester 3222
(STD 0789-71 3222)

41

Whatever it weighs in at, we'll take it on!

Being heavyweights, we'll tackle the lightest job.

The CIE Freight Service happily handles everything from a carton of eggs to cross-channel container traffic. Speedily and economically, we'll carry your goods by road, by rail, by air, and even across water. We've got the experience and we've got the equipment.

So let CIE take a freight off your mind. A phone call to any of our agents or area depots will quickly get things moving . . . quickly.

Contact our agents or CIE's Area Manager at Dublin, Cork, Limerick, Galway, or Waterford or Commercial Manager, Coras Iompair Eireann, Connolly Station, Dublin 1.

CIE **...the gentle heavyweights**

serving Irish industry for 25 years.

THE PAYLOAD PAY-OFF

Butterfield stainless steel tank containers for all purposes

Butterfield tank containers utilise 40 year's experience and the most stringent engineering standards to pay off *for you!* Their all-round quality ensures years of reliable trouble-free service, while the versatility of advanced design in stainless steel enables you to tackle a wide range of profitable payloads. Standard units include 4000 gallon stainless steel models, insulated or uninsulated for hazardous or non-hazardous loads. While special purpose designs can be quickly produced to customers individual specifications. All Butterfield tanks are to the relevant I.S.O. and Lloyd's standards, and free advice is available from a design team backed by 40 year's experience of liquid handling. Please 'phone or write for further information.

BUTTERFIELD

W. P. BUTTERFIELD (ENGINEERS) LIMITED
PO Box 38, Shipley, Yorks.
Tel: 0274 52244 (11 lines), Telex: 51583

A BUTTERFIELD-HARVEY COMPANY

© E.65

43

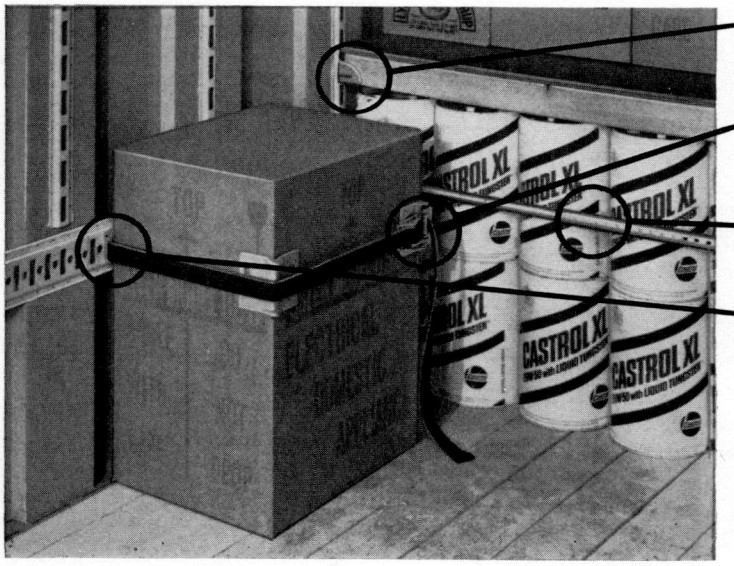

ACL

No.1 on the North Atlantic

We've got an unbeaten track record on the North Atlantic Container run. ACL carry more tonnage across the North Atlantic than any other container line afloat today. And there are many other features that give us a big lead over competition, too.

Datafreight

We introduced this revolutionary concept to streamline the paper work of exporting. It makes Bills of Lading unnecessary and out of date, speeds up transit times, eliminates waiting time at port of entry for customs clearance and generally clears the way for increased efficiency and increased customer satisfaction.

Roll on roll off

How ever big your load, we can take it. If it's too big to fit into a normal container, it's sure to fit our special handling equipment and Ro Ro can cut out crating, and packing. And we can ensure there's no possibility of damage in transit. Cranes, yachts, heavy machinery – we can take it all and more.

Regular reliable service

We run a weekly regular service, all year round, to the USA and Canada, and it takes us as little as 5 days to complete the crossing, which takes some beating. But when you're the biggest container line on the North Atlantic, like we are, it's no more than you'd expect.

ACL have the answer to your transatlantic needs. Contact our agent – he'll put you in the picture.

ACL CUNARD BROCKLEBANK

General Agents CUNARD–BROCKLEBANK LIMITED
Liverpool L3 1DY Tel. 051-227 3000 Telex 62343/4
London 01-480 7637 Telex 887884 & 887885
Bradford 0274-27134 · Birmingham 021-236 6745
Bristol 0272-293341 · Southampton 0703-29933
Telex 47638
Agents
Bigland Hogg & Co. Ltd., Middlesbrough 0642-43637
Telex 58488 · Anchor Line Ltd., Glasgow
041-221 9809 Telex 77594
Little Whiting & Tedford Ltd., Belfast
0232-24455/6
Irish Shipping Ltd., Agency Division,
Curran House, 11 Fleet Street, Dublin 2.
782277 Telex 5279.

Tilbury, Port of London – Britain's number one <u>container</u> port.

 The Port of London Authority, P.O. Box 242, Trinity Square, London EC3P 3BX. Tel: 01-481 2000 Telex: 885508.

ADAMSON

40′-0″ all steel container

. . . just one of the Company's expanding range of steel containers manufactured to ISO, TIR, Lloyds and other international standards. Continuous flowline production keeps prices competitive and deliveries on schedule.

Other containers in the Adamson range.

Adamson & Hatchett Ltd, Container Division, Dukinfield, Cheshire. Ashton-Under-Lyne 2822. One of the **ACROW** group of companies

Forward to France and through France by French Railways.

• Ferry trucks • Containers and transcontainers • Unit Loads
• Piggy-backs • Roll-on-roll-off • Parcels.   Through services for all the
above to and from France, Spain, Italy, Switzerland and countries beyond,
via Harwich/Dunkerque, Dover/Dunkerque and Newhaven/Dieppe.

Hauliers! If you have a permit problem, Kangaroo transport will solve it for you.

The latest method for the
handling of Kangaroo semi-trailers
by gantry crane.

FRENCH RAILWAYS Forward by rail!

Phone 01-493 1621 or write to French Railways Ltd. (Freight Dept.), 179 Piccadilly, London W1V 0BA.

WE BUILD CONTAINER SHIPS

SHIPYARD AND DIESEL ENGINE FACTORY - "SPLIT"
SPLIT - YUGOSLAVIA

Three Navigational Hazards:

(that you can do without)

Congestion

Bad Weather

Pilferage

Port congestion? Lack of dockside
warehousing? Pilferage? If they're costing you
time and money, you need a change of scene.
Pick a port where congestion is minimal, where
warehousing is ample, where pilferage
is no problem at all. And where wharfage
rates are the lowest on the Pacific Coast.
Such a port is San Diego. And we're
as near as your telephone. Why not call right
now? Ask how we can steer you clear of
costly, time-wasting shipping hazards.
Call today. The **toll-free** number:
800-854-2757.

Ship Safer
Ship
San Diego
MARKETING DEPARTMENT
3165 Pacific Highway
San Diego, CA 92112

New Zealand Railways can handle as many international containers as the world cares to send.

Today, all the ports, cities and industrial centres of New Zealand are rail-tainer linked to the major markets of the world. All we need are the containers.

For further information, contact our Advisory Engineer, c/o New Zealand Railways, New Zealand House, Haymarket, London, S.W.1. Phone 01-930 8422. He'll be pleased to help you.

Railways

11.4.1

Move 'em fast!

Where containers must move, you'll find a Clark Van Carrier.
Or three. As in the new Ocean Container Terminal at
Zeebrugge, Belgium, operated by Société Belgo-Anglaise des
Ferry-Boats. Clark Van Carriers move 20', 30' or 40' containers.
And stack them three high. Available with six or eight wheels
and capacities up to 40 tons.

That's why over 30 rail terminals and ports rely on more than
240 Clark Van Carriers.

For more information,
please write to
Clark International Marketing S.A.
Carrier Department
Pump Lane, Hayes, Middlesex,
England. Tel: 01-848 0111

CLARK
EQUIPMENT

Ivan Chernik at Tilbury, 1971

CP Voyageur at Quebec City, 1971

JANE'S FREIGHT CONTAINERS

Fourth Edition

EDITOR:
PATRICK FINLAY

1971-72

SBN 354 00088 8

JANE'S YEARBOOKS

LONDON
SAMPSON LOW MARSTON & Co., LTD.

Starporter®s DELIVER

JANE'S FREIGHT CONTAINERS
1971-72

EDITED BY: Patrick Finlay M.C.I.T., A.I.Inf. Sc.

COMPILERS:
SECTION ONE
SECTION TWO } The Editor

SECTION THREE
SECTION SIX } John Kinross
(and Container Repair, Testing & Cleaning Services)

SECTION FOUR
SECTION FIVE } J. Hyam, B.Sc. F.I.M.H.

SECTION SEVEN   Philip Robins

SECTION EIGHT   P. M. Bristow

SECTION NINE   Eugene M. Kolesnik

NORTH AMERICAN RAILROADS H. G. McClean

CONTENTS

THIS CONTAINER IS LOADED...

WITH REASONS
WHY YOU SHOULD TRY IT

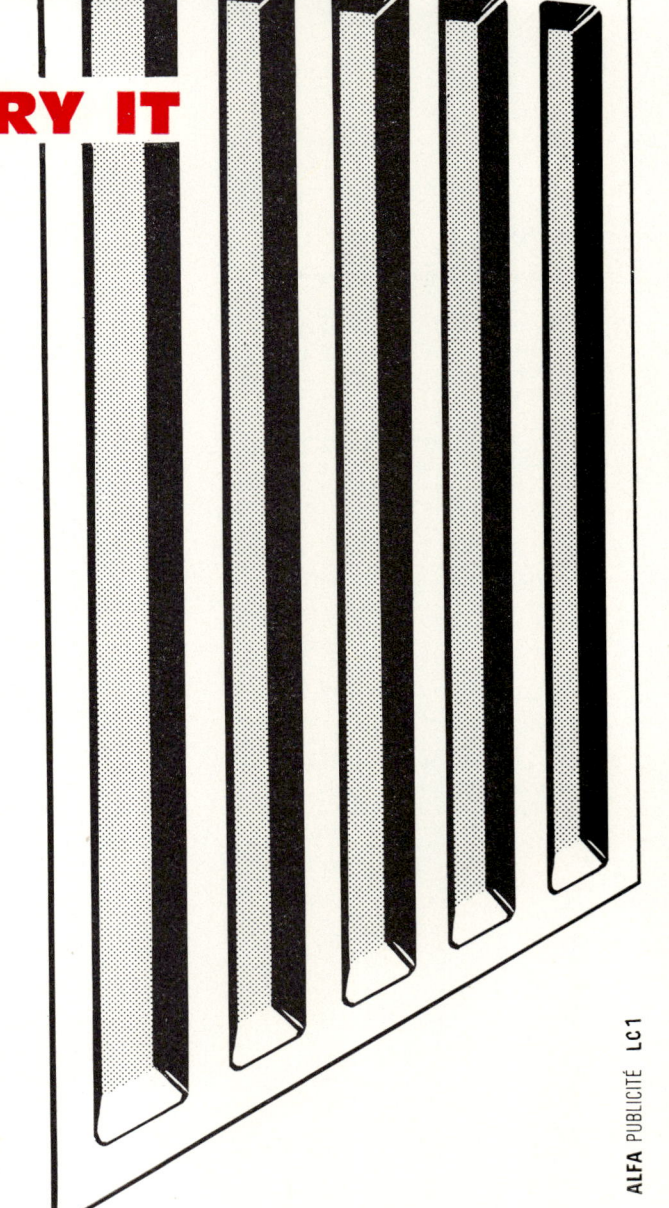

Pressed and corrugated pannels providing an unusual rigidity

Well tried welding techniques

Mass produced in one of the group's plants

20' to 40'

Early delivery at the most competitive prices

The new technology used by LUCHAIRE S. A. for this type of unit has been most filmed by our esteemed competitors during the last container show in PARIS

We are rather proud of this tremendous interest and we hope and look forward the imitations which shall appear on the market in the coming years

LUCHAIRE S.A.
METALLURGICAL SPECIALISTS SINCE 1720
CONTAINERS DEPARTMENT
180 Bd HAUSMANN - PARIS 8e
Telephon 924.63.44   Telex 65372 PARIS

ALFA PUBLICITÉ LC1

IN CONTAINERISATION ALWAYS ONE STEP AHEAD, A STEP FROM 20' to 40'

PREFACE

By R. P. Holubowicz, Executive Vice-President, International MacGregor Ltd.

In this the fourth year of issue of JANE'S FREIGHT CONTAINERS, many people in the marine industry are asking whether the container revolution has been a good thing or whether it is nothing more than a financial nightmare because of serious difficulties now being encountered in achieving operating profits. Whether one or the other is the case—and there are instances of both—there appears to be no question that the container as a way of life is here to stay in international transportation. What then are the major problems facing those who are committed for container operations, and what must be done to realise the profit potential there is in the container concept?

The box syndrome

Perhaps one of the most serious causes of the financial and operating problems caused by the container revolution has been the *box* syndrome that has affected and still affects many ship operators.

Before the advent of containers, the ship operator was concerned solely with the port-to-port aspects of international cargo movement. He was interested in getting the cargo from the quay shed into his ship, the movement of the ship to its port of destination, and the discharge of the cargo into a terminal transit shed. To this operator, the container naturally became a means by which he could consolidate small lots of goods into large units, thus improving his cargo handling productivity. As such, he viewed the container simply as a large *packing box* which he used to accomplish his purpose.

Even this limited application of the container by an operator affected by the *box* syndrome might have been economical but, alas, the container began taking on a life of its own and soon got out of control of the operator. He was faced with having to provide containers to shippers at points far distant from his terminal and having to allow the container to move far inland to the premises of consignees. The operator soon found himself continuing to get only his ocean freight rate and yet having to provide equipment for the land legs of the international movement.

It is obvious that the ocean transportation industry must rid itself of the *box* syndrome and begin to accept the fact that the container must be viewed as a *vehicle of transportation* and the ship itself only as an underlying carrier, or perhaps, more vividly, as merely a form of locomotion for the container. Only in this way will it be possible to use the container as a means of achieving an integrated transport system, with single carrier responsibility and a through tariff.

Integrated Transport

When thought of as a *vehicle of transportation*—as opposed to a method of packing—the container takes on equality of status with the lorry, the ship, the railroad van, and the aeroplane. The unique feature of the container is that it is physically capable of being moved on land, on sea, and in the air by using the existing modes of transport purely for locomotive power.

In a paper read at the Tenth Biennial International Conference of the International Cargo Handling Co-ordination Association, the United States Committee of ICHCA chose to give this quality of the container the name *transmodality*,—which connotes the ability to *pass over* all the modes of transport.

I am suggesting that the challenge in the coming decade is to adopt the concepts of and approach to the container that will bring about a true integration of transport and a time that will make international transport procedures no more difficult for shippers than is a trip to the local post office at the present time. I further suggest that the physical tools and technology are already in existence—as this issue of JANE'S FREIGHT CONTAINERS attests.

Indeed, the wide range of choice available to the container operator has the tendency to make him concentrate on technology rather than the real problem facing him in making container operators a success, and, that it is the need to think in terms of the wholly new concept of transport that is made possible by the existence of containers.

The international transporter's attention and main interest should be the intangible or invisible impediments for integration of transport, which, in turn, mean the need to make basic environmental changes, particularly in the organisation of his own company in relation to the modes of transport.

Perhaps the first *intangible* problem he needs to face is the resolution of the question of ownership and investment in containers, and the consequent responsibility for soliciting and generating cargo to fill those containers.

In the present stage of containerisation, for example, the steamship carrier has had very little choice but to provide steamship company-owned containers to shippers. This, in effect, is viewing the container as an extension but still an integral part of the ship. As a result, he is able to continue conducting business in the old manner, utilising freight forwarders and dealing with shippers as in the past. It is no wonder, therefore, that the ocean carrier is troubled by the staggering capital outlays required by his container operations which are making it increasingly evident that the smaller, privately owned companies cannot possibly survive this form of operation.

The most important step, it seems, is for the steamship carrier to divest himself of the ownership of containers—at least in his role as ocean carrier (as opposed to a subsidiary company taking on the role of a container operator transmodalist).

Another invisible or intangible factor that inhibits the integration of international freight movements is the problem of paper work. Some progress has been made however. The National Committee on International Trade Documentation (NCITD) who have produced a TCM Draft Convention containing suggested guide lines for an international agreement for developing a single-carrier, combined-transport responsibility. This document, which is being circulated for study, covers such issues as carrier liability, shipper responsibility, service, description of cargo, location of damage, and the effect of the agreement on existing carrier practices. The preparatory work thus performed by commercial interests should provide the basis for intergovernmental agreements. An international working committee sponsored by the United Nations has already voted to support and advocate a NCITD-designed format as a basis for a series of basic international shipping documents.

Another example of a basic structural change that would have to be made is the concept of the *ocean freight conferences* since the tendency is to go to single-carrier responsibility, the *conference* of the future, if it is to be useful, must take on an entirely different complexion. The new conference format must include all transportation interests in each trading area, including railroads, road transport, transmodalists, as well as the ocean carrier. The new broadened conference would be in a much better position to take advantage of containerisation and thereby encourage the growth of international trade.

There are, of course, many other such invisible or intangible impediments to the integration of transport which will have to be considered by the transportation industry and which will have to be resolved before containers can truly play a full role and achieve maximum benefits.

Port Facilities

Until the advent of the container revolution, ports, for the most part, served as marketing and distribution centres for the commerce carried in the ships calling at these ports. As a result, the traditional 19th and 20th century (the sailing and steamboat era) ports were beehives of activity, and the ports we see today are still manifestations of this now declining period of historial development. Even before the advent of containers, however, a dispersal of industry and commerce from the port areas was taking place as a result of rapid development of road and highway networks and improved railroad services. Further, rapid communications and rapid cargo delivery in recent years have brought about a further impact on the marketing and merchandising practices in international commerce. There is, for example, no longer a great need to maintain large inventories of goods to make up deficiencies of ocean transportation schedules and, accordingly, the warehousing function in ports has diminished very significantly.

With the advent of the container, the *steamboat era* can be considered at an end, and a new era in port accommodations, appearance, and requirements is upon us. In terms of the quay itself, for example, the major change promises to be the total elimination of the transit warehouse on the quay and the provision in its place of open space and equipment for marshalling containers for interchange between the ship and inland transport. No longer will the wharf be used as an assembly point for the thousands of individual shipments that make up a cargo in the liner trades, but rather the quay will merely perform the function of providing tie-up space for the container vessel and a point where the pre-assembled cargo of large container units is brought alongside for loading into the ship. What we must look forward to, therefore, is what the United States Committee of ICHCA has given the James Bond-like title of the *No port*. The question then might be asked: where, if not at the port, will the auxiliary port activities take place? The answer, simply, is "in the areas or regions to which most of the cargo is consigned or where most of the cargo originates." If a port region is also a large consumer or producer of international freight, it is logical for this port to contain cargo distribution centres located, not at the quayside, but most conveniently to the biggest concentration of shippers.

The port of the future, therefore, will be the port that least resembles a port as we have known it in the past, and will be one that specialises in and emphasises its facilities for rapid movement of the containers through the port area. There are a number of such ports now under construction or in operation, and this is already having the further effect of creating *load centres* in various parts of the world. These *load centres* are ports that will draw traffic from nearby ports and will eliminate the need for a multiplicity of smaller ports in the same coastal range. When it is considered that a berth for a ship can handle ten to fifteen times the volume of cargo handled in a conventional general cargo berth, one can easily see why load centre ports are developing and why life will become very difficult in the smaller ports unless these ports begin looking for and find some other use for their waterfront facilities.

Other Ocean Transportation Systems

Introduced into service in late 1970 and in 1971, is the LASH concept, which is a ship capable of carrying fully loaded barges. Because these barges are pre-loaded and pre-assembled they can be loaded quickly into the vessel and thus make possible a quick turn round of the ship itself.

The LASH system of ocean transportation is not a competitor to the container ship, in my opinion, since it does not afford or permit integrated transport, but it is a vast improvement over the conventional general cargo ship. In effect, therefore, the LASH system continues handling cargo in the conventional break-bulk fashion at quayside, but greatly improves the economics of ship operation by permitting the fast turnround of the ship and allows better planning and co-ordination of cargo handling into and out of the barges without holding up the ship itself.

The big challenge facing that portion of the industry committed to the LASH and Sea-Bee systems will be the need to adapt the port facilities, their own shore establishment and controls, and to work out the "bugs" that inevitably accompany any new technology. My own company, MacGregor International, is committed to the development of equipment and fittings for the LASH barges and ships that will ease some of the problems facing these operators, and we are looking forward to a large market as a result of the number of ships being built to the LASH concept.

At the same time we must not overlook the *unit-load* concept that has been pioneered by the Fred Olsen Company of Norway. Again, although this system cannot be considered as direct competition to a container operation—its proponents will dispute this—it too is a vast improvement over the conventional general cargo handling system. The ships that have been built or converted to accommodate the *unit-load* concept are marvels to see and some have characterised these ships as having a "swiss cheese" appearance. The objective of providing large openings in the sides and decks of ships is to permit cargo to move horizontally by using fork lift trucks as the principal cargo handling equipment. The net effect of the unit-load technique is to reduce very significantly the handling costs associated with general cargo. An additional advantage of the unit-load concept is that it can be married to both containerisation and to the LASH and Sea-Bee systems. While palletised unit-loads are an improvement in the handling of cargo into and out of containers, it is less important in truly integrated transport in view of the small number of handlings associated with cargo moved in the same container from origin to destination, or from shipper to consignee. In the case of the LASH system, however, it would appear to be absolutely essential and critical to the success of that operation that a marriage of the unit-load concept take place with the LASH concept.

Conclusion

The annual publication of JANE's FREIGHT CONTAINERS is a valuable and important service to the international transport community. Here, in one compilation, are all of the tools needed to make integrated transport through the use of containers a reality. JANE's FREIGHT CONTAINERS offers the reader the opportunity to "shop" and obtain the most advanced technology and the most economical hardware and to put together, for planning purposes at least, the equipment requirements for a total system of transport.

Patrick Finlay, the Editor, is to be congratulated on the splendid fashion in which he has prepared and presented the material contained herein. I am grateful to him, as well, for giving me this opportunity to express my views on what the future holds for the transport industry and what we all must do to achieve, at least partially, the great promise and potential that "awful beast" the container has offered to our generation.

The fourth edition of Jane's Freight Containers has the honour of including a preface by Ray Holubowicz, Executive Vice-President of MacGregor International. Mr. Holubowicz, a Master Mariner and a Master of Science, with considerable experience in port operations, ship operating and shipbuilding, was one of the earliest propounders of the intermodal transport system using containers. In the preface he suggests that all the physical tools and technology are now available and the challenge to the operators over the next decade will be to integrate them in such a way as to provide a simple international transport system for its users. He deals with the various problems which have to be overcome. The Editor acknowledges with thanks this most useful contribution.

The production of a book of this nature, which endeavours to report the state of the industry each year, involves keeping in touch with over 180 ports, some 250 container operators and about 200 manufacturers in over 50 countries as well as corresponding with and meeting numerous individuals and organisations throughout the world. The help received is gratefully acknowledged as without this co-operation the updating of practically all the entries contained in the book each year would be an impossible task.

This exchange of information brings in its wake a great deal of background knowledge and it is a consensus of this that the Editor tries to express in the foreword. In a fast developing industry future trends can often become fact or be discarded before the ink is dry. Where these ideas have been developed in theory they are included in Section Nine of the book which, this year, amongst other things continues the saga of the cargo airship and the catamaran surface carrier.

Intermodal Transport Developments

Four areas are of interest here:

Firstly, the awakening of public interest in containers in the USSR which took place in late 1969 with the publication of various discussion papers. This culminated in July 1971 with a policy announcement by the Comecon countries when it was stated that a single universal container transport system would be adopted and all forms of transport, including aircraft, would be modernised to carry boxes. The container lobby in the USSR is not altogether happy with the progress made and learned papers published from time to time have been fairly critical. The Ministry of Merchant Marine admitted in late 1970 that due to objections and difficulties from other agencies little had so far been achieved. However, the first half of 1971 saw further development of the Trans-Siberian service to Japan via Nakhodka which has had to face numerous difficulties including congestion and a lack of suitable port facilities.

Secondly, the Europe-Far East operational plans became clearer by mid-1971 with the announcements of the 'Trio' and 'ScanDutch' services although the French and also the Maersk-K alliance have yet to announce their plans. The total tonnage on the route should be sufficient to provide one service every four or five days and one service weekly; in all between 27 and 29 ships are now planned for the trade.

South Africa is now preparing for the advent of container services in that facilities are planned for major ports and rail terminals; coastal ship operators are also completing their arrangements. As yet the deep sea operators have not made their intentions clear.

Fourthly, there would seem to be a complete lack of interest in containers in South America and the barge carrier may well prove to be the solution for general cargo operations in this area.

Ports

In the beginning, ports secured container traffic on the promise of providing facilities. Later on they were judged to some extent on the quality and efficiency of ship turnround. To-day, when sophisticated handling gear is commonplace and the services offered are much the same, communication with the hinterland, settled industrial relations and the advantages of tidal, easily accessible facilities have taken on greater importance. Moreover, with berth throughputs becoming measurable, the true costs of container operations are doubtless being calculated.

Port and terminal operators may be faced with having to provide the faster handling equipment recently developed in order to remain competitive. They may also have to examine the need to provide vertical storage facilities to handle the greater throughputs being required for land restricted areas, particularly if packing and unpacking operations are carried out on the berth. One port is reported as carrying out advanced feasibility studies into vertical storage systems.

So far as is known only one terminal equipped with two container gantry cranes has to date achieved a throughput of close on one million long tons in a year. Others are reported to have worked at the hundred thousand twenty foot equivalent or million long tons per year rate for considerable periods and so the theoretical calculations made in the early studies are being shown as possible. It is perhaps worthwhile noting that only five short years ago twelve or more modern conventional general cargo berths would have been required to handle such a throughput.

Japan continues to dredge up container berths at a fast rate. At the latest count some 55 such facilities, each some 250/300 metres in length, equipped with two container gantry cranes will be operational by 1974/75. Additional land has been reserved for future general cargo handling facilities which are to be made available for 'whatever the form of sea vehicle designed'.

It is perhaps worthwhile recording that legal procedures have been adopted by individual United States ports to retain their container services and it will be interesting to see if protective legislation is attempted at Federal level if competition from Canadian ports on both the East and West Coasts continues.

Ship Operations

The 'third generation' container ships talked about to-day beg the question 'What is a third generation vessel?' The first generation, if they can so be called could be classed as the pioneer conversions and new tonnage of between 500 and 1,000 20 ft capacity. The second generation, purpose built with speeds of up to 33 knots and capacities of up to about 2,800 20 ft units, are constrained by the physical limitations of the Panama Canal. The largest are the 26 knot *Liverpool Bay* class, designed for the Europe Far East service, which could in theory lift over 3,000 boxes. Canal draught and practical operating restrictions could possibly preclude them from carrying this number.

Any larger design of vessel will therefore be employed on routes having high volumes of suitable traffic and which do not have to pass through the Panama Canal. The North Atlantic and Far East/North American Pacific ports routes are the two most likely. On the North Atlantic the recent pooling arrangements could pave the way for closer co-operation between some, if not all, of the operators to undertake a joint building programme for a small fleet of very large carriers. These could be operated on a space charter system when present tonnage, some of which has still to enter service, has used up its working life. Competition on the Pacific trades has still to develop and operators have yet to stake their claims to a percentage of the traffic. Again, vessels are only now entering service or under construction and it is unlikely that pooling will be resorted to for some time.

The third generation will undoubtedly come; it is the size of vessel and the time scale that are so difficult to estimate due to the gigantic capital investment required from an industry already fully committed to a programme which should be completed by 1973/74 but has still to show an adequate return. The early 1980's may see these vessels on order although the plans are probably already on the drawing boards.

Rail and Landbridge Operations

The Israel landbridge continues to expand and the progress made with the Trans-Siberian operation has already been mentioned. It should be noted that this latter route must be seen as a potential earner of foreign exchange for the USSR and accordingly it may well remain competitive in price as well as in time with the Europe Far East sea services. There are now four NVOC services using this route and if Japanese Railways base their container services on Niigata the transit time may be further reduced.

United States railroads have so far concentrated on domestic piggyback operations which offered relatively quick returns on investment. Overseas containerised exports after all, account for a very small percentage of industrial production and imports of general cargo are relatively unimportant when set against the total domestic consumption of commodities suitable for piggyback transport. Moreover, the review of piggyback operations at the beginning of the U.S. Rail Section explains that this traffic fell by 7 per cent over 1969. Results in 1971 will be worse, due to the economic situation, and this will not encourage the provision of co-ordinated through unit train services in a fragmented industry with little capital available for speculative investment.

Uses of the Container

Every day sees cargo being adapted to containers and containers being provided for special cargoes. Ore concentrates in Alaska, marble from Italy, cattle feeds etc. from the USA are some examples. The idea of equipping a research vessel with ISO containers fitted out as specialised laboratories to enable the vessel to undertake different types of oceanic research is reported on. The provision of hospital ships in times of national disaster or war by using the container vessels converted by the provision of operating theatre, ancillary medical equipment, etc. in modular ISO type units is also noted in the Future Developments section. Both these schemes are at the prototype stage and they could possibly lead to the use of container carriers, or even barge carriers, for other specialist purposes.

Air Freight

The current situation is reviewed fully in the introduction to the Air Freight Section where it is noted that the fleets of all freight configuration aircraft, so freely talked about a year or so ago, are further into the future than at first predicted. Only two B747 all-freight aircraft will be operational up to the mid-1970s. However, the airline operating one of these craft due to enter service in early 1972 is talking seriously of the 8 × 8 cross section for its containers. The aircraft is estimated to have a payload of 100 tons when operating between New York and Frankfurt and to offer a cargo volume equal to three times that of the B707.

The use of lighter-than-air craft may provide a real breakthrough for air freight by the end of the century; progress made in this field is recorded in the Future Developments Section.

Acknowledgements

Once again, thanks are due to those in the industry who have given their time to answer questions and have supplied comment and criticism on all aspects of the book. Every effort is made to ensure, where possible, that their suggestions are incorporated. If readers can provide additional information on any of the subjects covered, the Editor will be pleased to hear from them.

The acknowledgements would be incomplete without thanking the compilers for their work and without mentioning the patience and efficiency of the Jane's editorial and layout staff. The production of a book of this nature some thirteen weeks after the last entry has been completed calls for a great deal of organisation.

Finally, especially helpful guidance, which is keenly appreciated, was received from Christopher Wright of Jones, Bardelmeir and Clements, and Mike Fowler of 'K' Line.

PATRICK FINLAY

SECTION ONE

PORTS, INLAND TRANSPORT
and NON VESSEL OWNING OPERATORS
or FREIGHT FORWARDERS

CONTENTS

SECTION ONE—NATIONAL OPERATIONAL SERVICES

CONTENTS—*continued*

EUROPE

BELGIUM
ANTWERP

Port of Antwerp
General Management of the Port,
City Hall, B-2000 Antwerp
Telephone: 31 16 90
Telex: 31807
Directors:
Board comprises the Burgomaster and Aldermen of the City of Antwerp.
Principal Officials:
R. Vleugels (*General Manager*)
F. F. Suykens (*Assistant General Manager*)

Container Facilities at Churchill Dock

The terminal, situated in the Churchill Dock, comprises five berths equipped with seven gantry cranes and one equipped with two 28 ton cranes electronically coupled for container handling. All berths are privately operated, five by terminal operating companies, and are in close proximity to the rail container terminal of the Belgian Railway system. This terminal, in conjunction with Antwerp North rail shunting yard and the Intercontainer terminal links Antwerp with the great railway centres of Europe. Within two kilometres (2 miles) access can be gained to the new inter-European highways, R.E.3 (Lisbon—Stockholm) and R.E.10 (Paris—Amsterdam).

The container terminals are open 24 hours a day handling cargo for ship and inland transport operations.

'Intercontainer', the company formed by twelve European Railways, schedules special regular container train services from and to seaports and between some 160 railway terminals, equipped to provide road delivery to and collection from any address.

It is planned to construct a Public Bonded Warehouse next to the container terminal. It will have a total area of 10 hectares (nearly 25 acres).

Hessenatie Neptunus N.V. Berth

This terminal is located on the West Side of the southern quay of the Churchill Dock and covers 14 hectares (35 acres).

Behind a 1,025 m (3,362 ft) long docking-line with 15·25 m (50 ft) water depth, a 60,000 m² (14·8 acre) marshalling yard, including a warehouse of 2,000 m² (21,527 sq ft) is available, on the West side of which there is a consolidating shed of some 7,500 m² (80,730 sq ft). Auxiliary buildings are adjacent such as: offices, canteen, conveniences and a weigh bridge of 50 tons capacity. In addition there is a back up area behind the berth for car and trailer parking amounting to 100,000 m² (24·7 acres).

2 × 40 ton Boomsche Metaalwerken cranes, which operate at 35 tons with spreaders are provided. These have an outreach over water of 32·5 m (107 ft) and overland of 52·5 m (172 ft).

In order to be able to handle container roll-on/roll-off ships, such as those run by the Atlantic Container Line (ACL), there is a linkspan of 60 m × 20 m (200 × 65 ft) capable of carrying 120 ton loads, with berthing facilities on both sides.

Operator: Westerlund Corporation Ltd. Berth

On the southern quay of the Churchill Dock the Westerlund facility, 7·4 hectares (18 acres) in area, has a docking line of 200 m (656 ft). The quay-apron is 67 m (215 ft) wide. Behind it a 12,000 m² (3 acres) closed shed provides a useful space of 4·3 million cubic feet. In this shed a free height of 10 m (33 ft) allows the efficient stacking of unitised forest products.

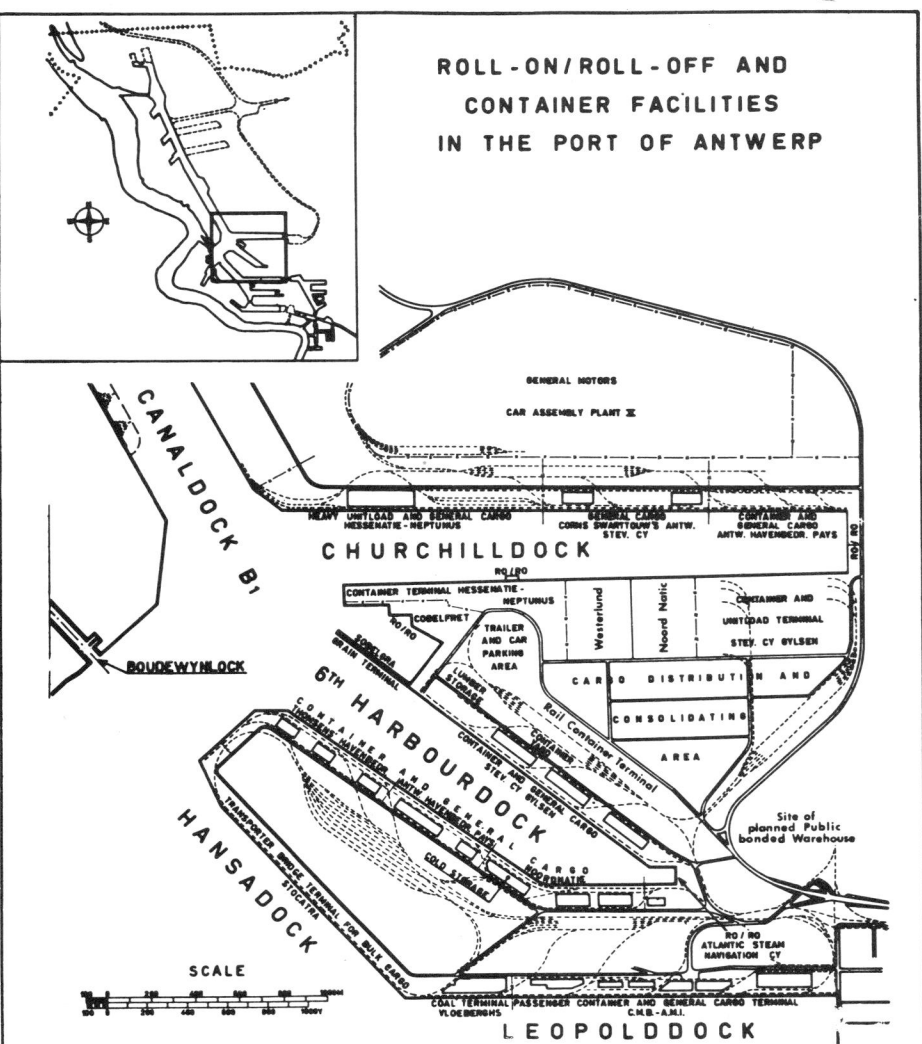

An ACL vessel at the Linkspan Roll-on/Roll-off platform in Churchill dock.

The company has planned for the construction of another warehouse in order to be able to cope with the expected increase of traffic.

A 60 ton weighbridge and two 40 ton straddle carriers have been provided.

There are further plans to fence an area of

18,000 m² (4·3 acres) for the parking of trailers.

A 45 ton Boomsche Metaalwerken container gantry-crane, capacity on automatic spreaders of 38 tons, is installed. It has an outreach of 32·5 m (107 ft) over water and 51·5 m (172 ft) on the landside.

Behind the gantry-tracks an open quay-apron of 13,400 m² (3·3 acres) is within the outreach of the gantry-crane.

Noord Natie Ltd. Berth

On the southern quay of the Churchill Dock, the Noord Natie facility, 13 hectares

TECHNICAL CHARACTERISTICS OF THE CONTAINER TERMINALS IN THE PORT OF ANTWERP

TERMINAL OF	AREA A Total B Covered	LENGTH OF QUAY	CONTAINER CRANES	SPECIAL EQUIPMENT
Hessenatie-Neptunus Ltd. Stijfselrui 20	A 18.5 hectares (45·6 acres) B 8,200 m² (88,264 ft²)	(3,362 ft) 1,025 m	2 of 40 t Outreach Water—32·5 m Quay—52·5 m	3 Clark Straddle carriers (1×16 t. 2×35 t.); 1 Demag 25 t sideloader; 2×18 t. Clark Forklifts; 5 fifth wheel tractors. Container repair shop, 50 ton weighbridge. Consolidation shed (984 × 69 ft)., where containers and flats are stuffed and unstuffed. For the handling of heavy loads and coils use can be made of a 35-ton travelling crane.
Westerlund Corporation Ltd. Oude Leeuwenrui, 8	A 7·4 hectares (18·2 acres) B 22,000 m² (236,800 ft²)	(656 ft) 200 m	1 of 40 t. Outreach—as above	2 × 23·5 ton Towmotor forklifts, 3 × 22·5 t. Clark forklifts.
Noord Natie C.S. Staadswaag 7-8	A 13·2 hectares (32·5 acres) B 6,500 m² (69,965 ft²)	(1,182 ft) 359 m	1 of 53 t. Outreach Water—32·50 m Quay—52·50 m	Two 40 t. Peiner straddle carriers; one Peiner 30 t. straddle carrier. Consolidation shed for stuffing and unstuffing of containers (395 ft × 164 ft) — Workshop for repair of containers. Mobile washing plant. 36 low loading chassis. 60 t. weighing bridge. Six 10 t. cranes and three 10 t. travelling cranes. Berthing facilities for roll on/roll off 60t. weighbridge.
Gylsen Stevedoring Company Ltd. Genuastraat 1-7	A 26·9 hectares (67 acres) B 11,250 m² (120,000 ft²)	(2,742 ft) 790 m	2 of 45 t. Outreach Water—37·50 m Quay—42·50 m	1 × 35 t. Le Tourneau Straddle carrier, 1 × 30 t. Peiner straddle carrier. 1 × 30 t. Clark straddle carrier. 1 × 30 t. forklift with top spreader. Several 25 t. forklifts, 3 fifth wheel tractors, 13 40 ft trailers, 64 refrigeration points, Container repair workshops.
Antwerps Havenbedrijf Pays Ltd. 6e Havendok 310, 312, 314	A 8·6 hectares (21·2 acres) B 20,000 m² (215,278 ft²)	(2,460 ft) 745 m	1 of 45 t. Outreach Water—32·50 m Quay—25·25 m	Roll-on ramp. Two electronically coupled cranes for the automatic handling of containers. Two 20 t. cranes — two 8 t. cranes — two 5 t. cranes — Two MAFI — a 60 t. weighing bridge. Consolidation centre with automatic conveyor system.
Corn Swarttouw's Antwerp Stevedoring Cy. Ltd. Steenborgersweert 18-20	A 7·5 hectares B 18,500 m² (199,130 ft²)	(2,460 ft) 750 m	—	Six 8 t. cranes. One crane for 40 ft containers.
Belgian Railways (S.N.C.B.)	A 23,200 m² (9·3 acres)	—	1 of 30 t. net on rail	Customs post open 0800-1700 hours daily. Weighbridge. Four loading tracks 400 m (1,312 ft) of useful length.

Antwerp-Churchill Dock

The rail terminal at Antwerp.

(32 acres) in area, has a docking line of
360 m (1,181 ft) and 6·5 hectares (16 acres)
have been reserved as a container parking
area.

A closed shed with an area of 48,000 m²
(395 × 164 ft) fitted with all facilities regarding the stacking and the handling of containers and heavy-units, has been built. It
is also designed to cater for the handling and
storage of forest products.

The lifting equipment of this terminal
consists of a Peiner gantry crane with a 53
ton capacity on the spreader and a span of
83 m (275 ft), (32·50 m overwater). Two
quay cranes (20 ton with 25 m reach and
10 ton with 45 m reach) have also been
provided.

Gylsen Stevedoring Co. Berth

At the eastern end of the Churchill Dock
southern quay, the Gylsen facility 26.85
hectares (66 acres) in area, provides container
and roll-on/roll-off berths.

There is a quay length of 836 m (2,743 ft)
including 136 m (446 ft) for the two roll-on/
roll-off berths situated at the end of the dock.

The container berth has a 370 m (1,085 ft)
wide apron providing 262,500 m²; the two
roll-on/roll-off berth aprons are 45 m (145 ft)
wide providing a total of 6000 m².

On the backland, an area of 1·5 hectares
(3·7 acres) has been provided for the stacking
of containers and the marshalling of trucks.

Two multi-purpose gantry cranes, capable
of lifting 45 tons on the spreader, have an
outreach of 37·5 m (138 ft) over water and
48·5 m (150 ft) over land.

The Gylsen berth is also equipped with six
10 ton cranes and three 10 ton travelling
bridge cranes.

Antwerps Havenbedrijf Pays Ltd. Berth

On the northern quay of the Churchill Dock
the Antwerps Havenbedrijf Pays Ltd has
erected a container-terminal with 754 m
(2,460 ft) length of quay including a 150 m
(492 ft) roll-on/roll-off berth. It comprises a
105 m (336 ft) wide wharf apron in front of
modern sheds. 71,000 m² (17·5 acres) marshalling areas for containers, trucks and other
cargoes. There are five sets of rail tracks and
easy road access.

Two closed sheds have been built in accordance with the latest handling and warehousing
techniques for general cargoes. They provide
20,000 m² (nearly 5 acres) of under cover
storage and are linked up by an open shed in
order to make the quay-apron more accessible to railway traffic.

Extension for marshalling, storage and
stuffing of containers will be possible on a
77,500 m² (19 acres) optional area behind the
terminal.

One container gantry crane with a 40
ton lifting capacity on the spreader has been
provided. The outreach is 32·5 m (106 ft)
over the water and 25·25 m (83 ft) over land.

Two electronically coupled quay cranes
for automatic handling of containers and six
other quay cranes varying from 5 to 20 tons
capacity are also available.

*Corns Swarttouw Antwerp Stevedoring Co., Ltd.
Berth*

The Corns Swarttouw's Antwerp Stevedor-

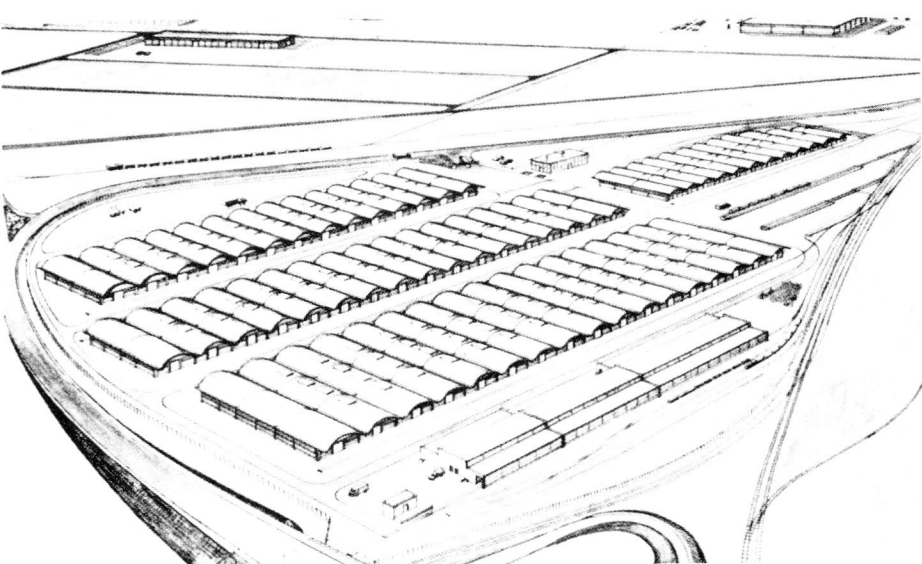

An artist's impression of the new Public Bonded Warehouse which is planned for construction next
to the Churchill Dock Container Terminal.

Antwerp—Transport Ferry Service Roll-on Terminal.

Antwerp—The Cobelfret-Wallenius Roll-on Terminal.

ing Co. Ltd. facility situated on the northern
quay of Churchill Dock has a total area of
about 7·5 hectares (18·5 acres) with an additional site of 4·5 hectares (11 acres) on which
an option has been taken.

Two extensive up-to-date warehouses are
available. Besides, there is a covered surface

of 17,200 m² and a large open trailer and
container-park of 18,800 m². Another shed
covering 60,000 m² is to be erected.

Alongside a 760 m (2,460 ft) long quay
wall, seven shore cranes are erected. Six of
them have following rates: 8-6-3 ton/25-32-40
m while a seventh one is rated 32-25-22 ton/
28-36-40 m.

Roll-on/Roll-off Berths other than those mentioned above:

Quays No. 366/372—Cobelfret/Wallenius
Situated in the basin south of Churchill Dock this facility has a quay length of 390 m (1,280 ft). The ramps are shore based and there is a marshalling area of 4 hectares (10 acres).

Quays No. 326/330—Transport Ferry Service
This facility is located at the eastern end of the Sixth Harbourdock. It has a quay length of 346 m (1,135 ft) and is fitted with shore ramps. The parking and marshalling area is 4·2 hectares (10·8 acres).

Belgian Railways Container Terminal:
In the centre of the triangular area situated between the VIth and the Churchill Dock, right at the rear of the Hessenatie Container Terminal and between the general cargo berth and the Container and Unit Load Terminal of the Gylsen Stevedoring Co., the Belgian Railways (Société Nationale des Chemins de Fer Belges) has built a four track marshalling yard, with 400 m (1,280 ft) sidings and surrounded with a fenced storing and stacking area for containers which are not to be stuffed or forwarded immediately. The total area is 3 hectares (7·4 acres). A travelling overhead crane with a 30 ton lifting capacity and 8·15 m (26 ft) lifting height operates in the sidings and yard. A tracking road, parallel to the total length of the yard, is connected with the road complex serving the nearby modern consolidating (groupage) installations. At the entrance there is a service building with Customs office and weigh-bridge.

CONTAINER AND ROLL-ON SERVICES WITH AGENTS:

Associated Antwerp Lines‡
London-2 sailings weekly.
Westcott Ltd. N.V.
Brouwersvliet 21, 2000 Antwerpen
Tel. 03/39.29.20
Telex: Westcott An 31343
Aug. Bulcke & Cie. Succrs. N.V.
Brouwersvliet 13-17, 2000 Antwerpen
Tel. 03/32.39.77
Telex: Bulcke Ant B 31.269

Associated Humber Lines*
12/15 sailings per month-Hull
Westcott Ltd. N.V.
(Humber Dept.)
Brouwersvliet 21, 2000 Antwerpen
Tel. 03/31.29.20
Telex: Westcott An 31343
Grisar & Velge S.A.
Keizerstraat 13, 2000 Antwerpen
Tel. 03/31.48.20
Telex: Grisarmar Antw B 31261

Atlantic Container Line**
Weekly to Canada and USA
Sasse & Co S.A.
Meir 24, 2000 Antwerpen
Tel. 03/31.36.70
Telex: Sasse Antw B 31622
Cobelfret N.V. (for cars only)
Mechelsesteenweg 150, 2000 Antwerpen
Tel. 03/38.78.50
Telex: Cobelfret Antw B 32645

Dart Containerline*
Weekly to Canada and USA
Agence Maritime Internationale S.A.
St.-Katelijnevest 61, 2000 Antwerpen
Tel. 03/33.88.90
Telex: Agenmarin An 31366

Cartainer Line‡
US Gulf Ports-Weekly
Cobelfret N.V.
Mechelsesteenweg 150, 2000 Antwerpen
Tel. 03/38.78.50
Telex: Cobelfret Antw B 32645
Phs. van Ommeren
(Antwerpen) N.V.
St.-Paulusstraat 42, 2000 Antwerpen
Tel. 03/32.79.70
Telex: Vanommeren An 31372

Cast Line‡
Montreal-Weekly
Cast Europe
Klipperstraat 15, 2030 Antwerpen
Tel. 03/41.68.55
Telex: 33153

European Unit Routes Ltd*
12/14 sailings per month to Tilbury
c/o Noord Natie Terminal
Churchilldok 416-418, 2030 Antwerpen
Tel. 03/41.37.30
Telex: EUR Antw 32984

Europe Canada Lakes Lines‡
Weekly to Canadian and Great Lakes Ports
Ahlers N.V.
Noorderlaan 139, 2030 Antwerpen
Tel. 03/41.69.50
Telex: Ahlers 31185-31186

Federal Atlantic Lakes Line‡
Fortnightly to Canadian and Great Lakes Ports
Cobelfret N.V.
Mechelsesteenweg 150, 2000 Antwerpen
Tel. 03/38.78.50
Telex: Cobelfret Antw B 32645

Hapag Lloyd‡
Monthly to US and Canadian West Coast Ports
Grisar & Velge S.A.
Keizerstraat 13, 2000 Antwerpen
Tel. 03/31.48.20
Telex: Grisarmar Antw B 31261

Hapag-Lloyd Nord Atlantik Containerfahrt*
Weekly to US East Coast Ports
Ahlers N.V.
Noorderlaan 139, 2030 Antwerpen
Tel. 03/41.69.50
Telex: Ahlers 31185-31186

Ibesca Containerline*
Weekly to Bremenhaven, Hamburg, Copenhagen, Malmo, Aarhus.
Weekly to Southampton, Le Havre, Bordeaux, Bilbao.
Agence Maritime Internationale S.A.
St.-Katelijnevest 61, 2000 Antwerpen
Tel. 03/33.88.90
Telex: Agenmarin An 31366

Johnson Line
*Weekly to US and Canadian Pacific Ports
‡Fortnightly to W. Coast, S. America
A. Durot S.A.
Tavernierkaai 2, 2000 Antwerpen
Tel. 03/32.78.50
Telex: Toruda Antw B 31155

Lykes Lines‡
Monthly to US Gulf Ports
Ahlers N.V.
Noorderlaan 139, 2000 Antwerpen
Tel. 03/41.69.50
Telex: Ahlers 31185-31186

Scanaustral‡
Australian Ports—Monthly
Best & Osterrieth S.A.
Frankrijklei 75, 2000 Antwerpen
Tel. 03/33.89.70

Short Sea Transport A.G.
Bremen and Bilbao—weekly
Agence Maritime A. Freyman & Van Loo S.A.
Cadixstraat 9-33, 2000 Antwerpen
Tel. 03/32.38.20
Telex: Freyloo An 31433

Swedish Atlantic—Wilhelmsen Line‡
Incoming cargo from Gulf Ports twice monthly
Best & Osterrieth S.A.
Frankrijklei 75, 2000 Antwerpen
Tel. 03/33.89.70
Telex: An 31244

The Transport Ferry Service†
12/14 sailings per month to Felixstowe
"A.M.A." Antwerps Maritiem Agentuur N.V.
Bordeauxstraat 8, 2000 Antwerpen
Tel. 03/31.16.36
Telex: AMA An 31291

Wallenius Lines†
14/18 sailings per month to Harwich.

Up to 4 sailings per month to US Ports and weekly to Helsingborg with new cars only.
Cobelfret N.V.
Mechelsesteenweg 150, 2000 Antwerpen
Tel. 03/38.78.50
Telex: Cobelfret Antw B 32645

*	Full Container Ships
**	Dual Purpose Ships
†	Roll-on Vessels
‡	Part Container Vessels

CONTAINER CARGO CONSOLIDATING COMPANIES

Ag. Mar. Charles Rantz s.a./n.v.
Korte Clarenstraat, 9, Antwerpen

Ag. Mar Defotanghe p.v.b.a./s.p.r.l.
Noorderlaan, 117, Antwerpen

Ag. Mar. Freyman & Van Loo s.a./n.v. (C.T.I.)
Cadixstraat, 9, Antwerpen

Ag. Mar. Internationale s.a./n.v.
St. Katelijnevest, 61, Antwerpen

Ag. Mar. Louis Schellen s.a./n.v.
Keizerstraat, 70, Antwerpen

Alpina Transports & Affrètements s.a./n.v.
Ankerrui, 2, Antwerpen

"A.M.A.", Antwerps Maritiem Agentuur n.v./s.a.
Bordeauxstraat, 8, Antwerpen

American Express
Meir, 87, Antwerpen

Antwerp Container Forwarding
Brouwersvliet, 25, Antwerpen

Antwerps Havenbedrijf Pays n.v./s.a.
6e Havendok nrs 310, 312, 314, Antwerpen

Antwerps Transport Kantoor n.v./s.a.
Ankerrui, 22, Antwerpen

Arthur Maes Transports s.p.r.l./p.v.b.a.
Meir, 24, Antwerpen

Associated Antwerp Stevedores n.v.
Rijnkaai, 20, Antwerpen

Atramef s.p.r.l./p.v.b.a.
Tavernierkaai, 4, Antwerpen

Edw. Bayet s.a./n.v.
Kipdorpvest, 40/42, Antwerpen

Beckmann & Jörgensen n.v./s.a.
Ankerrui, 13, Antwerpen

Belgian Container Company "BCC" p.v.b.a./s.p.r.l.
Veltwijcklaan, 54, Ekeren

Belgian Pakhoed n.v.s.a./
Oude Leeuwenrui, 25, Antwerpen

Belgian Rhine Transit n.v./s.a.
Oudaan, 18, Antwerpen

Belgo British Stevedoring Cy
St. Katelijnevest, 61, Antwerpen

B.K.S.I. n.v./s.a.
Gasthuishoevestraat, 50, Merksem

Fr. Bohner & Co s.a./n.v.
Schoenmarkt, 18, Antwerpen

Boschmans Thoumsin & Co.
Jordaenskaai, 25, Antwerpen

Aug. Bulke & Co Succrs s.a.n.v./
Italiëlei, 215, Antwerpen

Cobelfret n.v./s.a.
Mechelsesteenweg, 150, Antwerpen

Constant Lanoy p.v.b.a./s.p.r.l.
Lange Nieuwstraat, 27, Antwerpen

Corn Swarttouw's Antwerp Stevedoring Cy n.v./s.a.
Steenborgerweert, 18-20, Antwerpen

J. Couwels
Rijnkaai, 20, Antwerpen

Crowe & Co s.a./n.v.
Hanzestedenplaats, 3, Antwerpen

Daher & Cie s.a./n.v.
Meir, 44, Antwerpen

Deckers & Wirtz s.p.r.l./p.v.b.a.
Schoenmarkt, 31, Torengebouw, Antw.

Denning Freight Forwarders n.v./s.a.
Brouwersvliet, 21, Antwerpen

Edm. Depaire n.v./s.a.
Pourbusstraat, 25, Antwerpen

Dumanex n.v./s.a.
Kipdorp, 39, Antwerpen

A. Durot s.a./n.v.
Tavernierkaai, 2, Antwerpen

Erkelens Cooke & Marcus' p.v.b.a./s.p.r.l.
  Meir, 75, Antwerpen
Euro Road Transcontainer-ERT
  p.v.b.a./s.p.r.l.
  Statiestraat, 152, Berchem
Euro Shipping n.v./s.a.
  Jordaenskaai, 24, Antwerpen
Expeditiebedrijf Frans Mass
  p.v.b.a./s.p.r.l.
  Stijfselstraat, 10-12, Antwerpen
Expeditions Anversoises n.v./s.a.
  Fuggerstraat, 24, Antwerpen
Franbelti s.a./n.v. (United Cargo Corp-
  oration, U.C.C.)
  Ambtmanstraat 2 Antwerpen
Furness' Shipping & Agency Co s.a./n.v.
  Gramaystraat 4 Antwerpen
Gerlach & Co p.v.b.a./s.p.r.l.
  Meirbrug, 1 (Union Building), Antwerpen
Gondrand Frères n.v./s.a.
  Venusstraat, 18, Antwerpen
Goth & Co n.v./s.a.
  Korte Winkelstraat, 17A, Antwerpen
Grisar & Velge s.a./n.v. (Contrans)
  Keizerstraat, 13, Antwerpen
Halbart International Overseas
  s.p.r.l./p.v.b.a. (US Freight)
  Churchilldok-Noorderl. P.B. 464, Antwer-
  pen
R. Heinz n.v./s.a.
  St. Pietersvliet, 1, Antwerpen
Herfurth & Co s.a./n.v.
  Cassiersstraat, 17-19, Antwerpen
Hermann Ludwig
  Frankrijklei, 70, Antwerpen
Katoen Natie n.v./s.a.
  Van Aerdtstraat, 33, Antwerpen
Kennedy Hunter & Co Ltd s.a./n.v.
  (Reefer containers)
  Orteliuskaai, 2, Antwerpen
Kregspedi n.v./s.a.
  Grote Markt. 9, Antwerpen
Kühne & Nagel p.v.b.a./s.p.r.l.
  Van Eycklei, 14, Antwerpen
M. Lambertigts & A. Van Daelen
  p.v.b.a./s.p.r.l.
  Sint Laureiskaai, 9, Antwerpen
Louis Ghémar n.v./s.a.

Jordaenskaai, 24, Antwerpen
J. Luyckx & Co p.v.b.a./s.p.r.l.
  (North American Van)
  Italiëlei, 251, Antwerpen
Magemon s.a./n.v.
  Ankerrui, 22, Antwerpen
Natural (Belgique) s.a./n.v.
  Hanzestedenplaats, 3, Antwerpen
J. Nieberding & Fils p.v.b.a./s.p.r.l.
  Jezusstraat, 16, Antwerpen
Noord Natie s.v.
  Stadswaag, 7-8, Antwerpen
Omni-Trans p.v.b.a./s.p.r.l.
  Orteliuskaai. 2, Antwerpen
Henri Paës & Co p.v.b.a./s.p.r.l.
  Noorderlaan, 89, Antwerpen
Rhenus Belgë n.v./s.a.
  Ankerrui, 20, Antwerpen
Rijn-Schelde-Mondia n.v./s.a.
  Bordeauxstraat, 8, Antwerpen
Ruys & Co n.v./s.a.
  Britselei, 23-35, Antwerpen
Schenker & Co (België) n.v./s.a.
  Lange Klarenstraat, 23, Antwerpen
Simon Smits n.v./s.a.
  Albertdok-kaainr 131, Antwerpen
Safar n.v.
  Ankerrui, 20 (Tunnelbuilding) Antw.
Sogeco n.v./s.a.
  Italiëlei, 215, Antwerpen
Sogetrex n.v./s.a.
  Ankerrui, 13, Antwerpen
Thomas Meadows & Co (Belgique)
  n.v./s.a.
  Leguit, 23, Antwerpen
Müller Thomsen n.v./s.a.
  6de havendok, kaai nr 302, Antwerpen
Transintra s.a./n.v.
  Ernest Van Dijckkaai, 7, Antwerpen
Translloyd s.a./n.v.
  Hovenierstraat, 36-38, Antwerpen
Transtex p.v.b.a./s.p.r.l.
  (Tunnel Building), Ankerrui, 20 Antw.
F. Van Brée s.a./n.v.
  Lange Nieuwstraat, 47, Antwerpen

Edm. Van Dijck & Fils s.p.r.l./p.v.b.a.
  Sint Pietersvliet, 6, Antwerpen
van Gunsteren n.v./s.a.
  Groenplaats, 42. Antwerpen
Westcott Ltd n.v./s.a.
  Brouwersvliet, 21, Antwerpen
Westerlund Corporation n.v./s.a.
  Oude Leeuwenrui, 8, Antwerpen
West Friesland Eurotransport n.v./s.a.
  Ankerrui, 3, Antwerpen
Wetram p.v.b.a./s.p.r.l.
  Ankerrui, 13, Antwerpen
Zeigler & Co p.v.b.a./s.p.r.l.
  Kattendijkdok, 22, Antwerpen

CONTAINER REPAIRERS
Belgische Electro Laswerken p.v.b.a./s.p.r.l.
  Gebrs. Longueville,
  Trapstraat, 15, Antwerpen
The Cargo Securing Company
  Schaliënstraat, 36, Antwerpen
Continex p.v.b.a./s.p.r.l.
  St. Paulusstraat, 23, Antwerpen
Coppejans n.v./s.a.
  Kaai, 326, Antwerpen
Frama s.a./n.v.
  Indiënstraat, 17, Antwerpen
Henschel Engineering n.v./s.a.
  Boomsesteenweg, 604-606, Wilrijk
Fr. Lanslots & Co n.v./s.a.
  (Carl Tiedemann)
  Brouwersvliet, 30, Antwerpen
Hessenatie Neptunus n.v./s.a.
  Stijfselrui, 20, Antwerpen
Maretrail
  Veltwijcklaan, 50/52, Ekeren
Muylle & Co p.v.b.a./s.p.r.l.
  Lge Lobroekstraat, 250-252, Antwerpen
Pasec s.a./n.v.
  Natiestraat, 1, Antwerpen
Stevedoring Company Gylsen n.v./s.a.
  Genuastraat, 1-7, Antwerpen
Werkhuizen Verschueren p.v.b.a./s.p.r.l.
  Schaliënstraat, 32-36, Antwerpen

CONTAINER TRAFFIC:							
Year	Total				USA and Canada		
	Unloaded		Loaded		Unloaded		Loaded	
	Number	Metric Tons	Number	Metric Tons	Number	Metric Tons	Number	Metric Tons
1968	32,191	328,121	25,256	276,561	20,125	218,381	13,412	166,908
1969	51,000	594,065	49,073	601,511	22,442	272,370	16,408	213,653
1970	92,150	1,236,761	75,639	979,266	39,639	549,912	28,508	358,908

NOTE:
(i) The movement of empty containers or flats is excluded.
(ii) The tare weight of containers or flats is excluded.

ZEEBRUGGE

Zeebrugge-Brugge
Maatschappij der Brugsche Zeevaart Inrich
tingen N.V.
Louis Coiseaukaai, 2, Bruges
TELEPHONE: 330.65-31.402
TELEGRAMS: Ports Bruges
PRINCIPAL OFFICIALS:
L. Verboven (General Manager of the Port)
P. Beeken (Senior Harbourmaster)
R. Van Havere (Harbourmaster)
H. Hoorneart (Manager of Soc. Belgo-
  Anglaise des Ferry-Boats N.V.)
TERMINAL OPERATOR:
Société Belgo-Anglaise des Ferry-Boats, S.A.
Head Office: 21 rue de Louvain, Brussels 1
Telephone: 12.55.13-12.15.14
TELEX: 23584
Port Office: Loodswezenstraat, Zeebrugge
Train Ferry Terminal:
  Telephone: Brugge 547.91
  Telex: 19120
Container terminal:
  Telephone: Brugge 546.01/02

Zeebrugge—Short sea Container Terminal.

Telex: 19110
CONTAINER FACILITIES:

Short Sea Terminal

A quay 270 m (886 ft) long with an apron 53 m (174 ft) wide enables two ships to berth at the same time. It has a depth of water of 6·4 m (21 ft) at low water.

The quay is equipped with four railway-tracks and a road 12 metres wide. Two movable 30 ton Peiner gantry cranes with an outreach of 16 m (52 ft) over water and 50 m (164 ft) over the quay have a handling cycle of 30 containers per hour.

Adjacent to the container terminal, within port limits, there is a road vehicle parking area of 15 hectares (37 acres). In the rail marshalling area shunting operations have been speeded up by the installation of traction wagons running on small tracks between the rail tracks. These assist in positioning wagons and the operation is controlled by the crane driver.

Warehousing is under construction, with a storage capacity of about 30 acres. The container terminal is connected by road, by rail and by inland waterway to any destination in Europe.

Ocean Container Terminal

To be operated by Société Belgo-Anglaise des Ferry Boats s.a. this terminal came into service in June 1971 with an operational quay length of 400 m (1,312·3 ft). It is situated at the western head of the Zeebrugge outer harbour close to the existing container terminal.

The facility will have a quay length of 700 m (2,296·6 ft) with a width of 200 m (656·2 ft) and a minimum depth alongside of 13 m (42·65 ft). There will be a total area of 14 hectares (34·6 acres) of which 10 hectares (24·7 acres) is to be available for container operations after deducting the space taken up by the quay apron and buildings.

Initially there is an asphalted area of 3·5 hectares (8·65 acres) for Container marshalling and storage. Covered space of 2,500 m² (26,910 sq ft) with road and rail access is being provided.

The terminal is equipped with two 45 ton Munck container gantry cranes with an outreach of 32·5 m (106·6 ft). Four straddle carriers are in service.

The quay has been provided with four rail tracks on the quay linking the terminal with European railways which already provide services for the short sea container terminal to all European destinations.

Zeebrugge—Ocean Terminal.

The terminal is used by the Australia Europe Container service and negotiations are being conducted with operators of services to the United States and to the Far East.

EUROPEAN AGENTS:

Germany (Federal Republic):
Société Belgo-Anglaise des Ferry-Boats, S.A., 5 Köln, Am Hof 28
Telephone: 21.13.77 and 21.77.85
Telex: 888.1914

Austria and Central Europe:
Société Belgo-Anglaise des Ferry-Boats, S.A., Wien 1, Opernring 1
Telephone: 57.84.02
Telex: 12691

Italy:
Société Belgo-Anglaise des Ferry-Boats, S.A., Via Alberto da Giussano, 16, Milano
Telephone: 463.347
Telegram: Zeeboat Milano

Sweden:
Société Belgo-Anglaise des Ferry-Boats, S.A., c/o Aktiebolaget Svenska Godscentraler Strandvägen 7 A, Stockholm 14
Telephone: 67.08.80 and 67.97.20
Telex: 1343

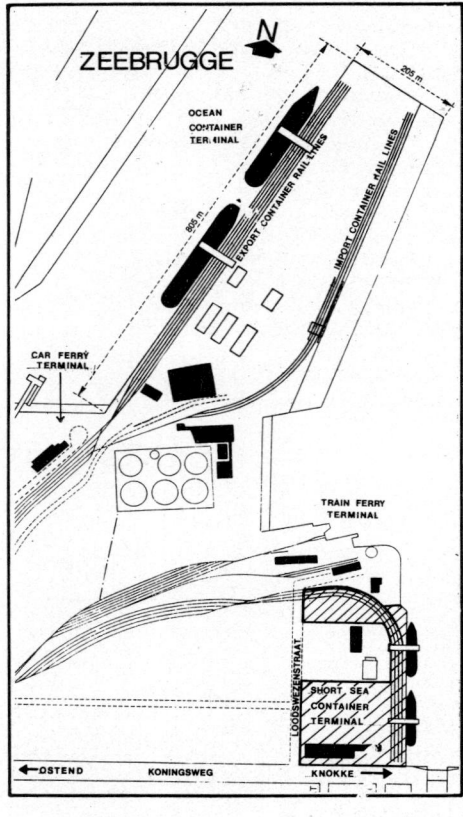

SHIPPING SERVICES:
Containers:

Name of Company	Berths used	Routes and Frequency
British Rail	Short Sea Terminal	Zeebrugge-Harwich. 15 sailings weekly.
Australia Europe Container Service	Ocean Terminal	Australia—Weekly.

Roll-on/

Name of Company	Berths used	Ships	Routes and Frequency
British Rail	Train Ferry Terminal.	Suffolk Ferry Norfolk Ferry Essex Ferry Cambridge Ferry	Zeebrugge-Harwich. Three to four sailings a day.
Townsend Car Ferries Ltd.	Townsend Terminal.	Free Enterprise I Free Enterprise II Free Enterprise III Auto-Carrier	Zeebrugge-Dover. From two to three sailings a day.

S.N.C.B.

Société Nationale des Chemins de fer Belges (SNCB)
Rue de Louvain 17 and 21
Brussels
TELEPHONE: 13.18.70
SERVICES:

At present trains are run daily to Great Britain (Harwich via Zeebrugge) Germany, Switzerland, Italy, France and Netherlands from Antwerp and Zeebrugge. In addition there are daily trains to the Ford and British Leyland factories from Zeebrugge.

WAGON AND CONTAINER FLEET

250 railcars type 3514 BO equipped with lateral guides are in service. No containers are owned by SNCB.

TERMINALS
Antwerp:

Storage under a 30 ton gantry crane amounts to 2,400 m² (25,800 sq ft). There is also a further 4,000 m² (43,000 sq ft) of storage area available.
Representative: M. Herremans
Telephone: 03/33-02-68

Zeebrugge:

See under Port entry.

Brussels:

A temporary 27 ton gantry crane has been provided for container handling.

Kortrijk Weide

A temporary 26 ton travelling crane is available for container handling
CONTAINER TRAFFIC

In 1969 the rail container traffic was as follows:
Zeebrugge:
Arrivals: 24,293 containers
Departures: 35,493 containers
Antwerp:
Arrivals: 20,008 containers
Departures: 15,371 containers

In 1970 SNCB handled a total of some 122,000 containers, in 1971 it expected that this figure will increase to 140,000 units.

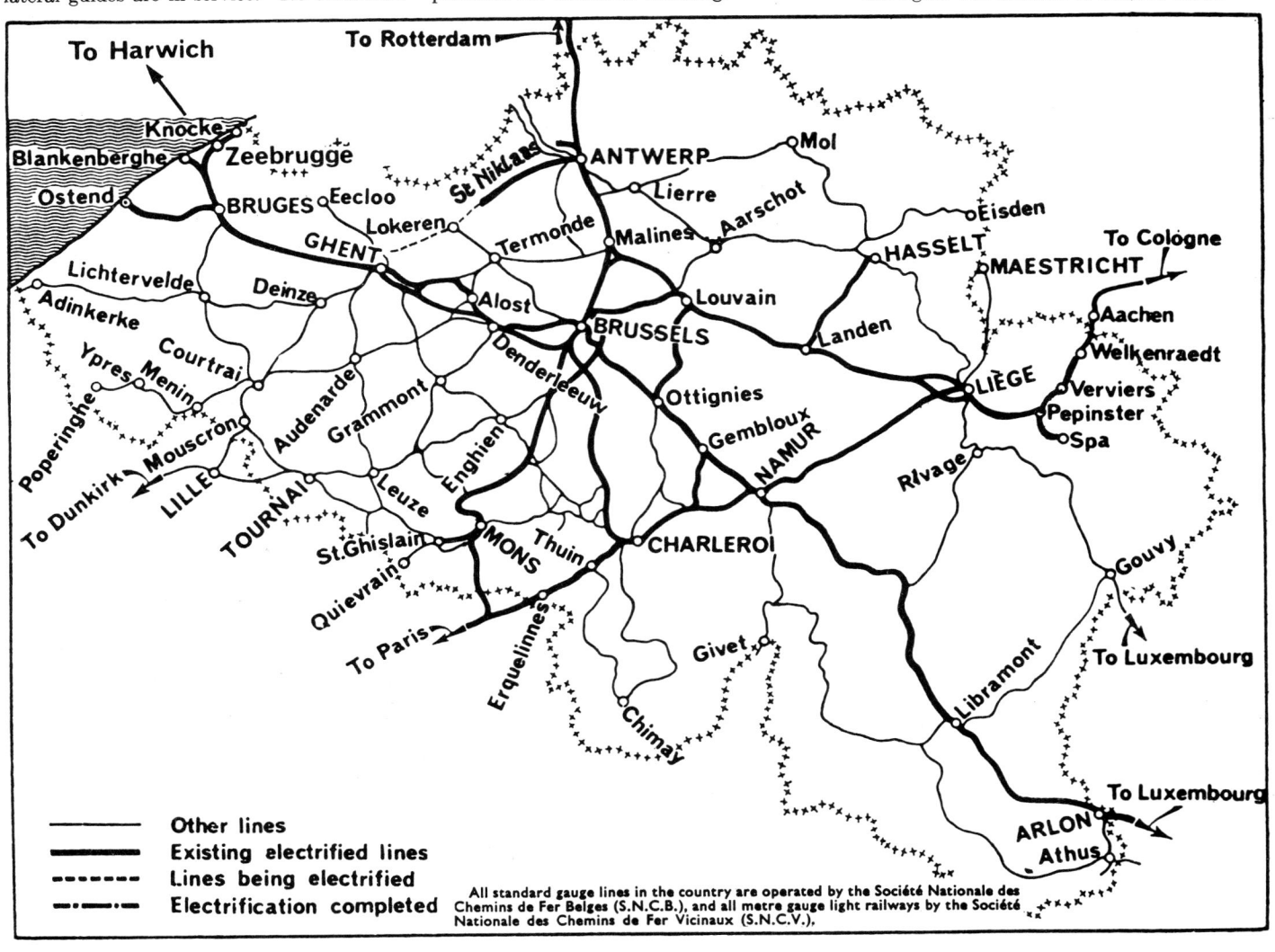

Other lines	
Existing electrified lines	
Lines being electrified	
Electrification completed	

All standard gauge lines in the country are operated by the Société Nationale des Chemins de Fer Belges (S.N.C.B.), and all metre gauge light railways by the Société Nationale des Chemins de Fer Vicinaux (S.N.C.V.).

DENMARK
ARHUS

Port of Arhus Authority
Europaplads 2, DK 8000 Århus C, Denmark
TELEPHONE: 06 13 33 33
PRINCIPAL OFFICIALS:
Bernhardt Jensen (Mayor of Århus) (*Chairman of the Harbour Board*).
A. Damkjær (*General Manager*)
K. Morbech (*Harbour Master*)
CONTAINER FACILITIES
No. 77/79 Berths, Pier 3
This facility, built for container operations, is capable of accepting vessels up to 300 m

Arhus—A model showing the terminal at 77/79 berths and the proposed development at Pier 4.

(984 ft) in length with a draught of 10 m (32·8 ft). The quay is equipped with a container gantry crane with an outreach of 33·22 m (109 ft) capable of handling 20, 35 and 40 ft units. There is also a 50 ton rail mounted luffing and slewing crane and the berth has a parking and marshalling area of 2·4 hectares (6 acres).

Pier 4

It is planned to develop a further quay length of about 325 m (1,066·ft) at the berths opposite Nos. 77/79 in Basin No. 7. The facility will be equipped with a container gantry crane.

ROLL-ON FACILITIES

The port has three berths, quays 47/49, 69/71 and 73/75, for roll-on/roll-off vessels. All can accept vessels of up to 7·5 m (24·6 ft) draught and 69/71 and 73/75, can accept vessels of about 130 m (426·5 ft) and 150 m (495·3 ft) respectively.

SHIPPING COMPANY SERVICES:

CONTAINERS:

Johnson Line, North Pacific and Canada every 10 days.
East Asiatic •Company, North Pacific—2 sailings monthly
Rotterdam Sont Line, Rotterdam—weekly
DA-NO Linien, Oslo—3 sailings weekly
KNSM, Holland—weekly
b-Line Container Service a-s, Immingham —weekly

Finland Steamship Co, Finland—weekly
ROLL-ON/ROLL-OFF:
DA-NO Linien, Oslo—3 sailings weekly
Veritas-Linien, Norway—2 sailings weekly.
Danish State Railways, Kalundborg—8 sailings daily.

PRINCIPAL CONTAINER FREIGHT FORWARDING COMPANIES:

Bergmann, Smith & Co., Pier 2
Telephone: 06 12 81 88
Telex: 4275
Knud Erichsen & Co., Havnegade 4
Telephone: 06 13 30 33
Telex: 4323
Schiøtt & Hochbrandt Århus A/S,
  Havnegade 24
Telephone: 06 13 00 88
  Telex: 4323
J. Gotfred Jensen A/S, Pier 3
  Telephone: 06 12 43 11
  Telex: 4545
Erik Aaen
  Mejlgade 10,
  Telephone: 06 124644
  Telex: 4422
b-Line Container Service a-s
  Gotlandsgade
  Telephone: 06 134733
  Telex: 4695

(map, right column)

PORT OF ÅRHUS.
1971   9531

COPENHAGEN

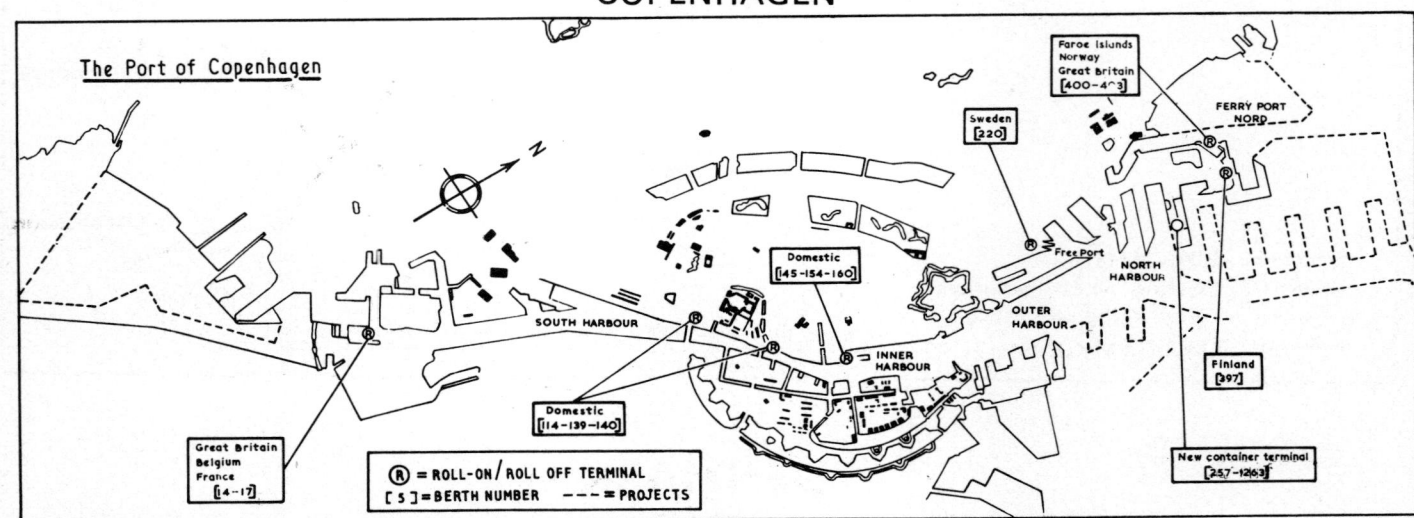

The Port of Copenhagen

Ⓡ = ROLL-ON/ROLL OFF TERMINAL
[S] = BERTH NUMBER   - - - = PROJECTS

Port of Copenhagen Authority
7. Nordre Todbod,
1259, Copenhagen, K,
Denmark
TELEPHONE: (01) 14.43.40
TELEGRAMS: Copenport
PRINCIPAL OFFICIALS
Eigil Andersen, (*General Manager*)
Carl Veng, (*Assistant General Manager*)
J. G. Rode, (*Chief Engineer*)
R. Hedegaard Jensen, (*Harbour Master*)
Poul Bøegh (*Public Relations*)

GENERAL:
Container transport is relatively new to Denmark and has only been used for international services. An effective Transit and Distribution Centre has now grown up. Copenhagen's 19 roll-on/roll-off berths serve

14 ports in Belgium, England, Finland, Germany, Holland, Norway and Sweden as well as to a number of Danish domestic ports. Special container trains have not yet been introduced, the containers being carried by sea, by truck or by regular fast freight trains.

To and from Germany and countries further east the border is crossed at the frontier stations of Padborg/Flensburg Weiche and Rødby Faerge/Puttgarden. For Sweden containers cross by train ferry between Helsingør and Hälsingborg, and between Copenhagen Free Port and Malmö.

Between the UK and Denmark (Harwich-Esbjerg) containers are carried in ships owned by DFDS.

Additional roll-on/roll-off berths are planned for the future.

CONTAINER FACILITIES:
Levantakaj

The container terminal, Berths 257/263, has a length of 600 m (1,968 ft) and a depth alongside up to 10 m (33 ft). A container gantry crane capable of lifting 32 tons with 20 cycles per hour became operational in 1970. This crane has an outreach of 30 m (98 feet). There is also a 50 ton crane with an outreach of 10·7 m (35 feet). The total parking area available for containers is 10 hectares (24·7 acres) and they are handled by straddle carriers and 'Jack Wagons'.

Containers are also handled at roll-on/roll-off berths and at conventional facilities.
TERMINAL OPERATING HOURS:

24 hours per day, if necessary for ship cargo handling operations. Inland transport operations take place between 0700 and 1630 hours.

ROLL-ON AND UNIT LOAD FACILITIES

Facility	Quay Length		Depth of Water		Ramps*	Open Space		Shed Space	
	m	ft	m	ft	No.	ha	Acres	m²	ft²
Ferry Port Nord	840	2,756	6·3-6·7	20·7-22	2 (1)	15	37·0	7,275	78,300
Kalkbraenderiloebskaj	618	2,027	6·3	20·7	3 (2)	11	27·2	4,610	49,600
Kulkaj	405	1,329	7·5	24·6	1	1·4	3·5	15,000	161,450
DSB Free Port	—	—	6·3	17·4	2	—	—	—	—
Kvaesthusbroen	740	2,428	6·2-6·9	20·3-22·6	7 (4)	1·3	3·2	4,500	48,450
Havnegade	637	2,090	6·2-6·9	20·3-22·6	1	(4,800 m²)	1·2	1,560	16,800
Christians Brygge	177	581	6·2	20·3	1	(200 m²)	(2,153 ft²)	—	—
S. Sluseholmen	387	1,270	7·0	22·9	2	4·2	10·4	11,125	119,500

*Numbers of Hydraulically operated ramps are shown in brackets

Tractors, trailers and mobile cranes are available for quay handling operations at all berths.

DIRECT UNIT LOAD SERVICES:
Lift-on
Antwerp-Sund Line
Agent:
　C. K. Hansen A/S
　Amaliegade 35, 1256 Copenhagen K
　Telephone: 11 72 72
　Telex: 2501
b-Line Container Service
Agent:
　b-Line
　Færgehavn Nord, 2100 Copenhagen Ø
　Telephone: 29 33 55
　Telex: 7242
Bugsier-, Reederei- und Bergungs A/G
Agent:
　Franck & Tobiesen
　Sølvgade 10, 1307 Copenhagen K
　Telephone: 15 00 55
　Telex: 2352
Currie Line Ltd.
Agent:
　C. K. Hansen A/S
　Amaliegade 35, 1256 Copenhagen K
　Telephone: 11 72 72
　Telex: 2501
Dart Containerline
Agent:
I.C.O.
　Færgehavn Nord, 2100 Copenhagen Ø
　Telephone: 29 68 88
　Telex: 6786
Johnson Line
Agent:
　Holm & Wonsild
　Amaliegade 36, 1256 Copenhagen K
　Telephone: 14 00 69
　Telex: 5269
Koninklijke Nederlandsche Stoomboot Mij
Agent:
　N. Schiøtt & Hochbrandt
　Amaliegade 45, 1256 Copenhagen K
　Telephone: 15 00 16
　Telex: 2538
Rotterdam Sont Lijn
Agent:
　C. K. Hansen A/S
　Amaliegade 35, 1256 Copenhagen K
　Telephone: 11 72 72
　Telex: 2501
Scandinavian Container Services
Agent:
　Samson Transport Co.
　Tuborg havn, 2900 Hellerup
　Telephone: 29 65 22
　Telex: 6752
Scanservice
Agent:
　The East Asiatic Company Ltd.
　Freight Department, Amaliegade 35,
　1256 Copenhagen K
　Telephone: 11 12 14
　Telex: 5300
USSR State Lines
Agent:
　Chr. Jensen A/S
　St. Kongensgade 77, 1264 Copenhagen K
　Telephone: 14 23 00
　Telex: 2249
Lift-on/Roll-on
Mountwood Shipping Co. Ltd.

Copenhagen—Part of the Container Terminal in the Free Port.

Copenhagen—Ferry Port Nord.

Agent:
　N. Schiøtt & Hochbrandt
　Amaliegade 45, 1256 Copenhagen K
　Telephone: 15 00 16
　Telex: 2538
Svea Line Syd AB
　I.C.O.
　Færgenhavn Nord, 2100 Copenhagen Ø

　Telephone: 29 68 88
　Telex: 6786
Wallenius Lines
Agent:
　Motorships Agéncies A/S
　Hornemansgade 36, 2100 København Ø
　Telephone: 29 68 00
　Telex: 2293

Roll-on
D/S På Bornholm af 1866
Agent:
  D/S på Bornholm af 1866
  Havnegade 27, 1058 Copenhagen K
  Telephone: MI 1868
  Telex: 5766

Finnlines OY
  Lehmann Junior
  Malmøgade 3, 2100 Copenhagen Ø
  Telephone: TRIA 4000
  Telex: 2255
Finska Angfartygs Aktiebolaget
Agent:
  Franck & Tobiesen

Sølvgade 10, 1307 Copenhagen K
Telephone: 15 00 55
Telex: 2352
United Steamship Co.
Agent:
  United Steamship Co.
  Sct. Annæ Plads 30, 1250 Copenhagen K
  Telephone: 15 63 00
  Telex: 9435
Øresund A/S
Agent:
  Dampskibsselskabet Øresund A/S
  Havnegade 49, 1058 Copenhagen K
  Telephone: 14 77 70
CONTAINER REPAIR FACILITIES:
Container Reparationen

Dampfærgevej 17, Frihavnen
2100 Copenhagen Ø
E. Hill-Madsen & Søn A/S
  Gittervej, Frihavnen
  2100 Copenhagen Ø

CONTAINER AND ROLL-ON TRAFFIC:

	No. of Loaded Containers 20 ft equivalents	
Lift-on	*Inwards*	*Outwards*
1970	7,583	6,755
1971 (Estimate)	10,000	8,500
Roll-on:		
1970	2,820	3,131
1971 (Estimate)	3,000	3,500

ESBJERG

Port of Esbjerg Authority,
Esbjerg, Denmark
TELEPHONE: 05 12 41 44 (*General Manager*)
            05 12 92 00 (*Harbour Master*)
PRINCIPAL OFFICIALS:
O. F. Bache (*General Manager*)
C. E. Lyngshøj (*Harbour Master*)

ROLL-ON SERVICES:
United Steamship Company (DFDS) provide
the following services from Esbjerg:
Harwich—5/6 sailings weekly
Hull—twice weekly
Grimsby—twice Weekly
Felixstowe—twice Weekly
Newcastle—twice Weekly

TRAFFIC:
Total roll-on/roll-off traffic both inwards and
outwards in 1968 amounted to approximately
49,000 units, in 1969 the total was 70,000
units (over 500,000 tons) and in 1970 the
total was 70,000 units (520,000 tons).

TERMINAL WORKING HOURS:
24 hours per day

PRINCIPAL CONTAINER FREIGHT FORWARD-
  ING, STORAGE AND STEVEDORING
  COMPANIES:
United Steamship Company, Englandskajen,
Esbjerg
Telephone: 05 12 17 00
Samson Transport Co., D. Lauritzensvej
Esbjerg
Telephone: 05 12 71 00

Esbjerg

Paul Lehmann A/S, Kongensgade 34, Esbjerg
Telephone: 05 12 38 99
Ferrymasters A/S, D. Lauritzensvej
Esbjerg

Telephone: 05.12 91 44
Impex Transport A/S
Cort Adelersgade 1, Esbjerg
Telephone: 05 13 05 10

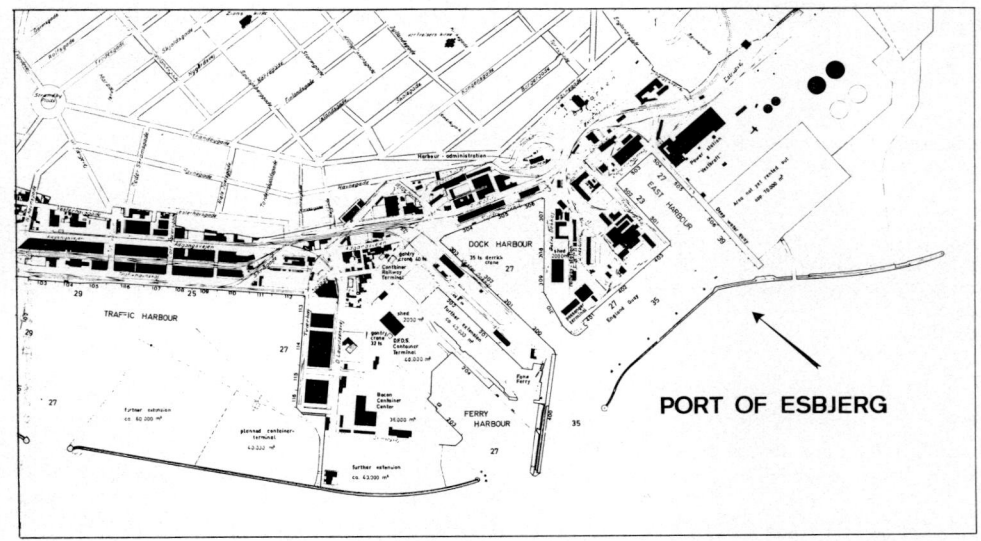

PORT OF ESBJERG

International Container Operators A/S
Cort Adelersgade 2, Esbjerg
Telephone: 05 13 27 00

Inter System Transport A/S
Cort Adelersgade 2, Esbjerg
Telephone: 05 13 14 11

RAIL FACILITIES:
Berths 203 and 206 have rail connections at the back of the berth where a travelling 40 ton container yard gantry crane with a span of 20 m (65·6 ft) operates. Special container trains to Alborg, Arhus, Odense, Glostrup and Copenhagen operate daily.

FUTURE DEVELOPMENTS:

A container berth is planned. The terminal will be equipped with a 38 ton container gantry crane and a link span for roll-on/roll-off operations and is expected to be in operation by the autumn of 1972.

Roll-on/Roll-off Facilities

Berth	Quay Length	Length	Maximum vessel size Beam	Draught	Parking Areas	Ramp Details	Sheds
203	110 m 361 ft	—	19 m 62 ft	6·7 m 22 ft	35,000 m² 8·6 acres	Double deck shore mounted bridge 35·8 m × 5·5 m (118 ft × 18 ft)	—
206	140 m 459 ft	—	22 m 39 ft	6·7 m 22 ft	51,00 m² 12·6 acres	Double deck Shore mounted bridge 40 m × 6 m (131 ft × 20 ft)	2,000 m² (2,392 sq yd)
401	180 m 590 ft	—	22 m 72 ft	6·7 m 22 ft	17,000 m² 4·2 acres	shore mounted bridge 17 m × 5·5 m (56 ft × 18 ft)	2,000 m² (2,392 sq yd)

This berth is equipped with rail access and passenger facilities.

DANISH STATE RAILWAYS

Danish State Railways, Danske Statsbaner (DSB)
40 Solvgade DK-1349
Copenhagen K
GENERAL:
The Danish State Railways provide a door-to-door container service with containers supplied by Team-trailers, Glostrup. During 1970, the number of loaded transcontainers handled was 28,138 expressed as 20 ft units, and it is expected that 35,000 will be dealt with in 1971.

Container traffic is dealt with by Mr. P. Hjelt, Solvgade 40, 1349 Copenhagen K.

CONTAINER TERMINALS:
Copenhagen (Freight Station). Odense, Arhus Alborg
Equipped with 35 ton container yard gantry cranes.
Glostrup, Slagelse, Naestved, Nykobing Fl
Equipped with 30 ton yard gantrys fitted with container spreaders.

Frederica
Equipped with a stationary transfer gantry.
Esbjerg
See crane details under the port entry.
Transcontainers and flats up to a length of 40 ft can be transferred between rail and road vehicles at the following stations:
Copenhagen Freight Terminal
Glostrup (near Copenhagen)
Odense
Fredericia
Esbjerg.

FINLAND

HELSINKI

Port of Helsinki,
PO Box 13026, 10
Eteläranta, Helsinki, Finland
TELEPHONE: 11301
PRINCIPAL OFFICIALS:
S. E. Sjögren (*Chairman of the Harbour Board*)
Keijo Tarnanen (*General Manager*)
S. Järuelä (*Secretary*)
E. Vihko (*Captain of the Port*)
Veikko Mielonen (*Storage Manager*)

Veikko Heinonen (*Crane Engineer*)
CONTAINER FACILITIES:
Situated in the West Harbour the container berth is 200 m (656·2 ft) long with 9·2 m (30·2 ft) of water alongside. There is a total area, including sheds, of 5 hectares (12·36 acres). The berth is equipped with a 40 ton Kone container gantry crane with a lifting capacity of 30 tons on the automatic telescopic spreader and an outreach of 28·04 m (92 ft). Straddle carriers, tug masters, side-

loaders and fork trucks have also been provided.
ROLL-ON FACILITIES:
South Harbour
The passenger and ferry berths are situated in the South Harbour which has a depth alongside of 6·9 m (22·8 ft).
Sörnainen Harbour
Further roll-on freight berths are under construction at the Sompa Pier which used to be used as a timber handling facility.

ROLL-ON SERVICES

Company	Berths used	Service
Oy Finnlines Ltd.	South Harbour and Sompa Quay	Nynäshamn Karlskrona Copenhagen Lübeck 3 times per week
Finland Steamship Co. Ltd.	South Harbour	Copenhagen Lübeck Once every 5 days (winter) 4 days (summer)

CONTAINER SERVICES

Oy Containerships Ltd.	West Harbour	U.K. weekly
Oy AA-Lines Ab.	West Harbour	Lübeck weekly
DFL Container Express	West Harbour	Hamburg Weekly

Helsinki—Loading to rail wagons.

TRAFFIC:
Unit load traffic inwards, including container and flats by roll-on vessels amounted to 19,542 units in 1970. Loaded containers outwards by lift-on vessels amounted to 7,422 units.

TERMINAL WORKING HOURS:
Ship cargo handling and inland transport operations take place between 0800 and 1700 hours.

FREIGHT FORWARDERS:
(Members of the Federation of Forwarding Agents)
Address: Phone:
Oy Beweship Ab, 3, Kruunuvuorenkatu
                                              658 600
Oy Ariel Boman Ab, Hitsaajankatu 3
                                              782 655
Oy Victor Ek Ab, 16, Eteläranta   61 631
Oy H. Elmgren Ab, 7, Kalevankatu 605 445
Eurooppalainen Kuljetus Oy—
   Europeiska Transport Ab,
   3 Kluuvitaku   659 277
Fennohuolinta Oy, 20, Pohjoisranta   13 244
Oy Finnsped Ab, 12, Arkadiankatu 440 161
Axel Holmström Oy-Ab,
   12, Mannerheimintie
Oy Huolintakeskus Ab,

7, Kalevankatu   602 811
Kansainvälinen Huolinta Oy -
   Internationella Speditions Ab,
   3, Kluuvikatu   11 771
Kansainvälinen Kuljetus Oy -
   Internationella Transport Ab,
   3, Kluuvikatu   11 771
Kiitohuolinta,
   3, Köydenpunojankatu   644 404
Konttinen Oy, 1, Keskuskatu   663 425
Oy Lars Krogius Ab,
   4, E. Makasiinikatu   11 500
Maa ja Meri Oy, 29, Sörnäisten
   Rantatie   715 012
Merihuolto Oy, 5, Kruunuvuorenkatu 11 781
Oy Merikiito Ab, 29, Sörnäisten
   Rantatie   716 511
Oy Meriselvitys Ab, 1, Bernhardinkatu 10 651
Henry Nielsen Oy/Ab, 6, Fabianinkatu 61 371
John Nurminen Oy,
   13, Snellmaninkatu   15 155
Oy O. Nyström & Co Ab,
   5, Keskuskatu   11 606
Suomen Huolinta Oy, 5, Keskuskatu   657 597
Hjalmar Suominen Oy,
   5, Kruunuvuorenkatu   666 627
Teollisuushuolinta Oy, 6, Eteläranta 652 855
Uusi Huolintaliike, 6, Kauppiaankatu 634 029
Yleinen Huolinta Oy, 7, Luotsikatu   15 733
STEVEDORES
Oy Edv. Björklund Ab,
   24, Pietarinkatu   656 681
Oy Finnish Stevedores Ab,
   30, Löhnrotinkatu   645 101
Oy Lindgren Stevedores Ab,
   6, Kalevankatu   61 816
Oy Näppärä, 12 Hitsaajankatu   782 611
Päiviö Stevedoring Oy,
   7, Fabianinkatu   11 315
Satama Stevedoring Oy,
   15, Rauhankatu   15 155
Oy Stevedoring Ab, 7, Fabianinkatu   11 315
Oy Sörnäs Stevedoring Ab,
   7, Fabianinkatu   11 315
Oy Akerman Ab, 19, Hietasaarenkatu 641 228

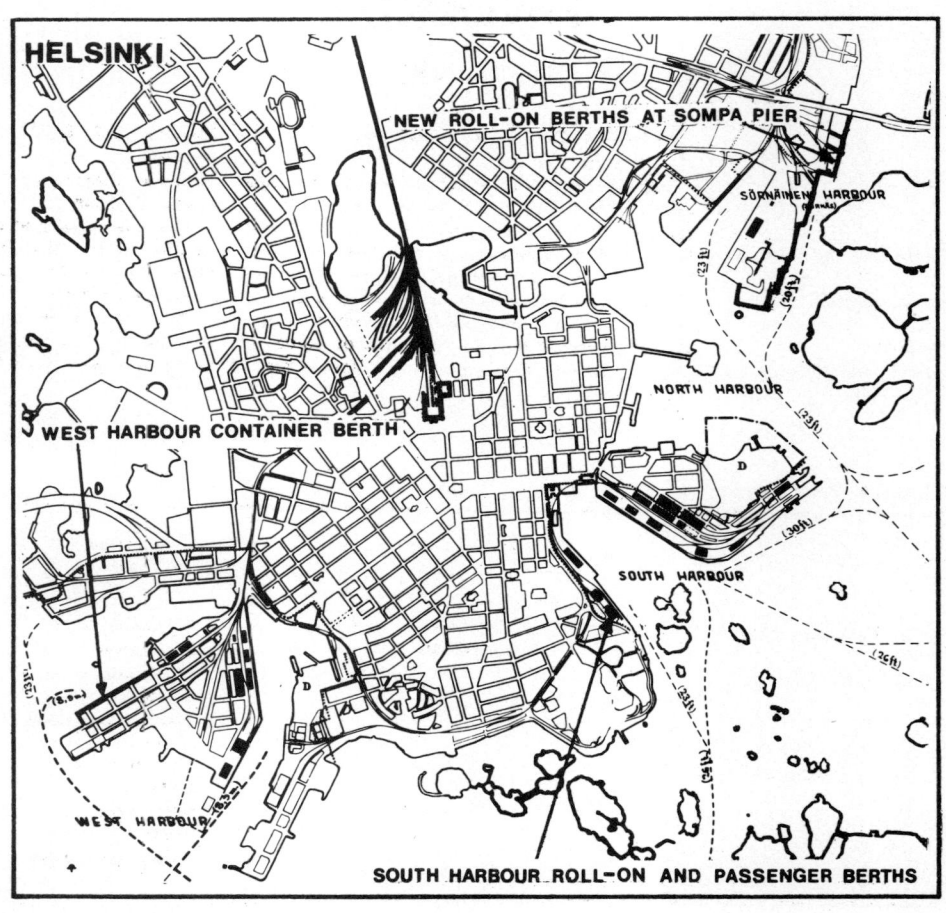

HELSINKI

NEW ROLL-ON BERTHS AT SOMPA PIER

SÖRNÄINEN HARBOUR

NORTH HARBOUR

WEST HARBOUR CONTAINER BERTH

SOUTH HARBOUR

WEST HARBOUR

SOUTH HARBOUR ROLL-ON AND PASSENGER BERTHS

FINNISH STATE RAILWAYS

Valtionrautatiet (V.R.)
Helsinki,
Finland
OFFICIAL IN CHARGE OF CONTAINER
OPERATIONS:
B. L. Pitänen (*Traffic Inspector*)
  Marketing Bureau
  Vilhonkatu 13
  Helsinki 10
CONTAINER FLEET:
  Forty 20 ft ISO type units are owned.
ROLLING STOCK:
  Two hundred flat wagons each capable of carrying two 20 ft units are under construction.
CONTAINER TERMINALS:
  Two terminals are available in Helsinki. Pasila, has been equipped with a Kone 30 ton yard container gantry crane; there is between

1 and 1·5 hectares (2·4-3·7 acres) of container marshalling area. Sompasaari in the Ferry Harbour is equipped with a 25 ton straddle truck.

In addition there are fifteen other rail terminals throughout the country equipped with 30 ton gantry cranes originally designed for the transfer of lumber etc between road and rail but which can equally well be used for container handling operations.

CONTAINER SERVICES:
  Arrangements for door-to-door services are still being made. VR containers are leased to forwarding agents when used for international traffic.

TRAFFIC:
  Some 3,000 loaded containers were handled

Finnish State Railways containers at the Pasila, Helsinki, rail terminal.

in 1970. Estimated traffic for 1971 is 5,000 loaded units.

FRANCE

BORDEAUX

Port Autonome de Bordeaux
2, Place Gabriel,
F.33—Bordeaux
TELEPHONE: (56) 52 60 61
TELEX: 57617
PRINCIPAL OFFICIALS.
A. Pages (*Port Director*)
J. Herman (*Traffic Manager*)
CONTAINER FACILITIES:
Bassens Aval
  This facility has a quay length of about 300 m and comprises a paved area of 10,500 m² (2·48 acres), which can be extended further if required. A shed covering an area of 9,000 m² (97,000 ft²) is available for consolidation of cargo. There are five rail tracks on the quay. Containers are handled by two quay cranes each with a lifting capacity of 24 tons at 23 m (75·5 ft) and capable of being worked by one man electronically, in tandem. Spreaders are available for all lengths of container.
Verdon
  A maritime industrial site is being developed at the month of the River Gironde and the Port Authority plan includes a common user container berth.
CONTAINER SERVICES:
  Ibesca Containerline, the Dart .feeder service, calls at Bordeaux, which as well as providing a service to USA and Canada, offers a service to Belgian, British, German and Scandinavian ports.
  Africatainers, the West African Service offered by Compagnie Maritime de Chargeurs Réunis, calls regularly.

Bordeaux—30 ton fork truck

Bordeaux — The cargo consolidation shed at Bassens-Aval

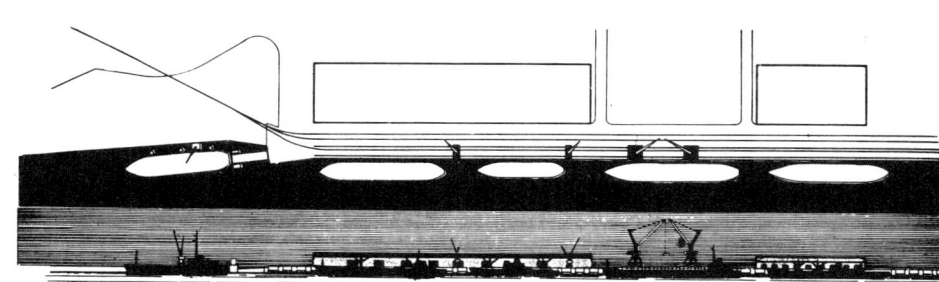

Bordeaux—The Bassens-Aval Development on completion

CALAIS

Chambre de Commerce et d'Industrie,
24 Boulevard des Alliés, 62, Calais, France
TELEPHONE: 34.47.00
TELEX: 81052 Chacom Calais
PRINCIPAL OFFICIALS:
P. Puissesseau (*President*)
P. Cheerbrant (*Directeur des Services*)
ROLL-ON/ROLL-OFF FACILITIES:
  The maximum size of vessel which can use the facilities has a length of 150 m (492 ft)

and a beam of 21 m (68·9 ft).
Carnot Dock:
  This terminal is dual purpose in the sense that general cargo or containers can be handled by 2 × 24 ton and 2 × 12 ton quay cranes. The ramp depends upon the ship for any adjustment required and vessels of up to 7·95 m (26·1 ft) draught can be accepted.
Car Ferry Terminal:
  This berth has two shore based ramps and

can accept vessels of 5·92 m (19·4 ft) draught. There is a covered marshalling area of 4,000 m² (52,743 sq ft).

SHIPPING COMPANIES PROVIDING ROLL-ON
ROLL-OFF SERVICES
Bore Line
Berth: Carnot
Service: Calais–Finland
Three times per month

Townsend Car Ferries
Berth: Car Ferry
Service: Calais–Dover
Daily as required.
SAGA/SNCF
Berth: Car Ferry
Service: Calais–Dover
Daily as required.

ROLL-ON TRAFFIC:

	Tonnage	
	Inwards	*Outwards*
1968	21,039	21,225
1969	83,984	36,143
1970	150,210	106,271

Calais—Roll-on traffic at the Car Ferry terminals

Calais—Bore Line vessels at Carnot Dock

PRINCIPAL CONTAINER FREIGHT FORWARDING
COMPANIES:
Enterprises Maritimes Leon Vincent,
Place de Suede
Telephone: 34.44.00
Telex: 81098
Jokelson & Handstaem,
18, rue du Cdt. Bonningues
Telephone: 34.42.00
Telex: 81090
Sogena (Societe de Gerance et de Naviga-
tion),
Quai de la Loire
Telephone: 34.47.41
Apeness & Cie
55 rue de Londres
Telephone: 34.48.24

Jules Roy,
46 rue de Londres
Telephone: 34.50.21
Societe des Rouleurs de Calais,
2 rue Edison
Telephone: 34.49.12
Ets. J. Derycke
17 Bd Gambetta
Telephone: 34.55.51
Telex–
Ets. Mory S.A.
31 rue Darnel
Telephone: 34.39.19
Telex: 82521
Carpentier, J.,
27 rue de Vic

Telephone: 34.36.14 and 34.57.91
Agence Continentale & Anglaise,
Quai Paul Devot
Telephone: 34.34.34
Comarnord
20 rue du Havre
Telephone: 34.55.03
Telex: 81713

CONTAINER STORAGE AND STEVEDORE
COMPANIES:
(Addresses as above).
E.M.L.V.
Jokelson and Handstaem
SOGENA
Apeness et Cie.

DUNKIRK

Dunkirk—Quay Freycinet XIII.

Port Autonome de Dunkerque
Terre-pleine Guillain,
59, Dunkerque 01, France
TELEPHONE: 66.64.00
TELEX: 82.055
PRINCIPAL OFFICIALS:
Y. Touzet (*Chairman of the Board*)
R. Boeuf (*General Manager*)
CONTAINER FACILITIES:
Quay Freycinet XIII
This facility, situated in Dock No. 6, has
a quay length of 350 m (1,150 ft) with a
depth of water alongside of 13 m (42·7 ft).
It is equipped with two 53 ton container
gantry cranes capable of lifting 45 tons on a
telescopic spreader for 20 to 40 ft units.
They have a useful outreach of 30·48 m
(100 ft) over water and 15·85 m (52 ft)
behind the rear rail. There is a total
container storage area of 8 hectares (19·5
acres) and the berth is served by six rail
tracks four of which run parallel to the
quayside.
ROLL-ON FACILITIES:
Dover Quay
This facility is equipped for handling
passenger/vehicle ferries and rail ferries.
Quay Freycinet XIII
The terminal is provided with a movable
steel ramp 43·28 m (142 ft) long with a
width of 7·31 m (24 ft) which enables two
lines of vehicles to be loaded or discharged
at the same time. The axis of the ramp
runs parallel to the quay 11·58 m (38 ft)
away from it which enables ships with a
beam of up to 23·16 m (76 ft) to be berthed.
PLANNED CONTAINER AND ROLL-ON FACILI-
TIES:
The first tidal basin of the outer harbour,
capable of accepting vessels up to 300,000
dwt is due to come into operation in 1974.
In the first stage some 30 hectares (75 acres)
have been reserved: 18 hectares (45 acres)
for two container berths and 12 hectares
(30 acres) for a combined container/roll-on
facility.

ROAD ACCESS:

The quay Freycinet XIII terminal is directly
linked to the Lille/Dunkirk motorway and

to an important road traffic depot, extending
over some 50 hectares (123·5 acres), at
Lille/Lesquin some 74 kilometres (46 miles)
from Dunkirk. In the future a similar depot
will be provided at Dunkirk.

CONTAINER SERVICES:
European Unit Routes (EUR)
Tilbury—3 sailings weekly

ROLL-ON SERVICES:
French and British Railways
Dover—up to 8 sailings per day
Harwich—up to 2 sailings per day
CONTAINER AND ROLL-ON TRAFFIC:
Traffic moving through the Port in ISO
type containers increased from 84,000 tons
in 1969 to 153,000 tons in 1970. The 1971
figure could be estimated at 240,000 tons.
In 1970 the number of 20 ft equivalent units
was 6,385 loaded and 91 empty inwards, and
4,640 loaded and 1,300 empty outwards.
FREIGHT FORWARDERS:
Sté Angleterre Lorraine Alsace
Gare Maritime
Telephone: 66.08 01
Sté Bourdon & Cie
21, Quai de la Citadelle
Telephone: 66 97 00

Sté Bosteels et Cie
Ghyvelde
Brillet-Telefsen
Rue de la Gare à Gravelines (59)
Telephone: 06 à Grav.
Sté Centrale de Réception de coton
15, Quai de la Citadelle
Telephone: 66 76 22
Collet Taverne & Fils
20, Rue de la Maurienne
Telephone: 66 50 01
Consortium Maritime Franco Americain
8, Place des Nations
Telephone: 66 96 00
Coquelle Gourdin & Fils
5, Bd Ste Barbe
Telephone: 66 78 00
Sté de Courtage & de Consign. Mme
73, Rue Henri Terquem
Telephone: 66 69 14
Sté Daher & Cie
30, Quai des Américains
Telephone: 66 66 06
P. Debruyne
Ghyvelde (59)
Telephone: 02 à Ghyv.
Sté des Anc. Ets Dekeirel & Hardebolle
53, Rue St-Pierre

Telephone: 66 90 22
Agence Mme Ch. Delannoy
10, Quai de la Citadelle
Telephone: 66 92 00
Sté Dewulf Cailleret & Fils
11, Rue des Poilus
Telephone: 66 99 01
Sté Dewulf & Cie
53, Rue de Calais
Telephone: 66 65 05
Docks Industriels S.A.
7, Quay Freycinet
Telephone: 66 48 97
Sté des Ets Ed. Dubois
1, Rue du Rempart
Telephone: 66 68 16
Sté A. T. L. Duforest
Gare Maritime
Telephone: 66 58 05
Entrepots Frigorifiques de L'Union
Quai du Mole III
Telephone: 66 85 10
Sté G. Feron E. de Clebsattel & Cie
5, Bd Ste-Barbe
Telephone: 66 93 00

Sté de Consign. Mme Franco Britannique
9b, Quai de la Citadelle
Telephone: 66 66 00
Agence Mme Freval Sibon & Fils
1, Rue du Rempart
Telephone: 66 31 80
Sté Fse de Transp. Gondrand Fréres
11, Quai du Risban
Telephone: 66 95 00
Sté Goudal & Cie
37 Rue Caumartin
Telephone: 66 60 34
Hernu Peron S.A.
Cour de Gare P.B.
Telephone: 66 86 00
Sté H. Herpin
1, Rue de la Tranquillité
Telephone: 66 88 00
S. A. Jokelson & Handtsaem
8, Place des Nations
Telephone: 66 76 00
Agence Mme Kraemer
6, place de l'Yser
Telephone: 66 56 00
Cie Ch. Le Borgne
1, Rue du Rempart
Telephone: 66 70 06
Sté Leduc & Cie
1, Rue du Rempart
Telephone: 66 72 05
Lemaire Frères & Fils
6, Rue de Beaumont
Telephone: 66 87 00
Cie de Navigation Fruitière/AG. Mmes Lesage
3, Rue Lhermitte
Telephone: 66 89 01
Sté A. & G. Mentre
Rue Belle Vue
Telephone: 66 81 00
Cie des Messageries Maritimes
1, Place de l'Yser
Telephone: 66 91 00
Moor Genestal S.A.
30, Quai des Américains
Telephone: 66 66 10
Sté Mory & Cie
21, Quai de la Citadelle
Telephone: 66 97 00
Agence Mme Nord est
11, Rue des Poilus
Telephone: 66 57 25

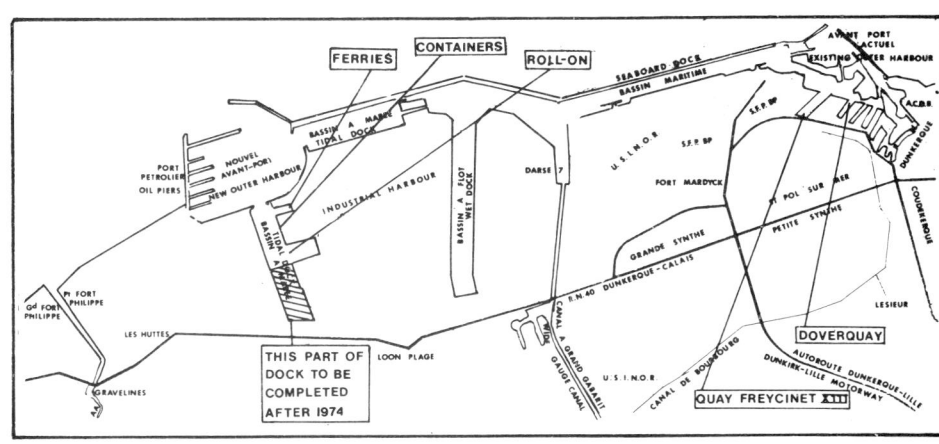

Dunkirk—Plan showing location of existing facilities and those planned for completion by 1974.

Dunkirk — Dover Quay

Sté Nord Transit
B.P. 12 à Petite Synthe (59)
Telephone: 66 95 23

Sté A. Raffin & Cie
36, Rue Carnot
Telephone: 66 63 06

Sté Riss & Cie
5, Bd Sainte Barbe
Telephone: 66 65 15

Robertson & Son
Rue de l'Entrepôt
Telephone: 66 62 14

Agence Mme Rommel
17b, Quai de la Citadelle
Telephone: 66 65 30

Sté J. Roy
6, Place de l'Yser
Telephone: 66 80 10

Samyn Permandt
10, Quai de la Citadelle
Telephone: 66 88 05

S.C.C.T. & S.O.G.E.T.R.A. Réunies
26, Rue du Gouvernement
Telephone: 66 79 03

S.T.I.M.
7, Quai Freycinet
Telephone: 66 54 01

Sté Générale de Surveillance
10, Quai de la Citadelle
Telephone: 66 69 01

Sté Tramar
1, Rue Gaspard Malo

Sté Trancap
3, Rue Lhermitte
Telephone 66 33 15

Cie Générale Transatlantique
19, Quai de la Citadelle
Telephone: 66 69 01

J. & L. Trystram
23, place du Palais de Justice
Telephone 66 84 05

Union Commerciale
1, Place des Nations
Telephone: 66 63 14

Worms C.M.C.
10b, Quai de la Citadelle
Telephone: 66 92 00

Woussen & Cie
23 Rue du Gouvernement
Telephone: 66 56 05

GENNEVILLIERS

Chambre de Commerce et d'Industrie de Paris
Bassin No. 1, PO Box 14
92 Port de Gennevilliers
TELEPHONE: 793-39-30

OFFICIALS:
R. Dufour (*Technical Director*)
GENERAL:
Situated close to Paris, this inland port,

so far as container traffic is concerned, is
used as an international road haulage centre.
It is equipped with a yard gantry crane and
a 25 ton side loader capable of handling

containers up to 40 ft in length.

CONTAINER TRAFFIC:

In 1970 7,270 loaded units moved inwards and 6,650 loaded units moved outwards. In terms of 20 ft equivalents traffic for 1971 is estimated at 11,000 inwards and 10,000 out-wards.

Gennevilliers

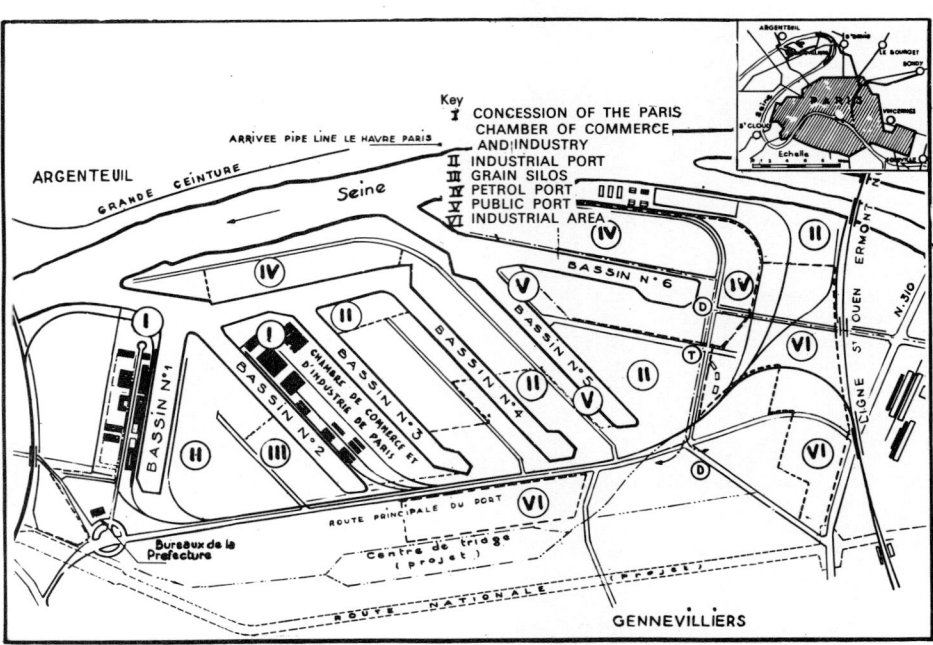

LE HAVRE

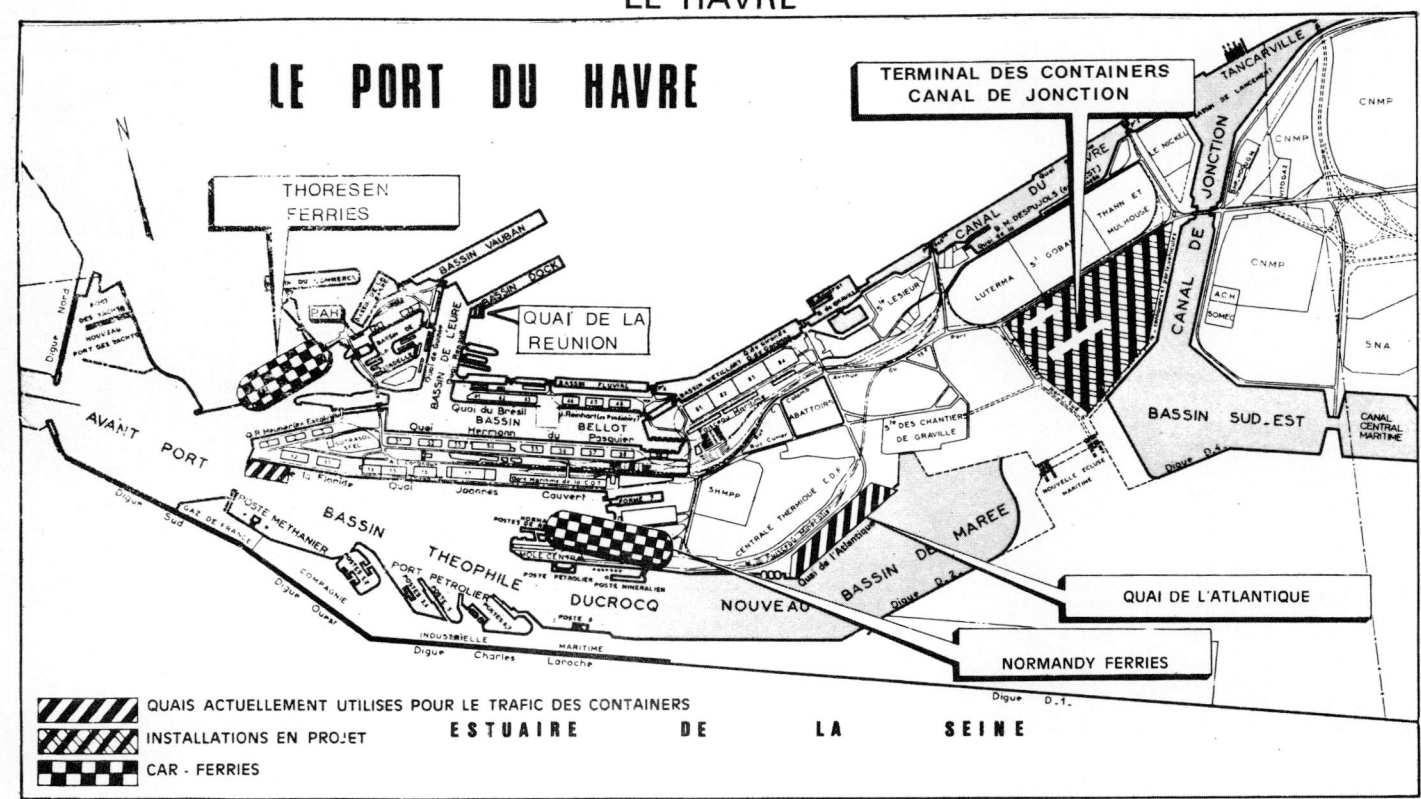

QUAIS ACTUELLEMENT UTILISES POUR LE TRAFIC DES CONTAINERS

INSTALLATIONS EN PROJET

CAR - FERRIES

ESTUAIRE   DE   LA   SEINE

Port Autonome du Havre

Terre-plein de la Barre,
76-Le Havre
TELEPHONE: 42 52 01
TELEX: 79-963 Port Havre
PRINCIPAL OFFICIALS:
M. Thieullent (*President*)
P. Bastard (*General Director*)
R. Genin (*Commercial Director*)
G. Franck (*Technical Director*)
J. C. Ailleret (*Equipment Director*)
J. Dubois (*Works Division Director*)

CONTAINER FACILITIES:

Quai de L'Atlantique:

This terminal has a total length of 800 m (2,625 ft). The depth at lowest tide is sufficient to accept vessels of 11 m (36 ft) draught and, after dredging, will be able to accept deeper draughted ships in the future. The terminal has a stacking area of 16 hectares (40 acres) and is equipped with four 40-ton container gantry cranes. These cranes have an outreach of 35·2 m (115·4 ft) from

the front rail track and 8 m (26·3 ft) behind the rear rail giving 30·4 m (100 ft) outreach over the stacking area; they are capable of 20 cycles per hour. There is also a link-span ramp for roll-on/roll-off operations. No. 1 Berth is equipped with 28 reefer points, and a 60 ton weighbridge. There are two container yard gantry cranes, one of 42 and one of 50 tons, for transfer to rail wagons. These cranes are owned by C.N.C. In addition to the above equipment straddle carriers, side loaders, tractors, slave trailers, road trailers and fork lift trucks are provided by the handling and stevedoring concerns.

Quai de la Reunion:

This area is used by the France Ireland Line for their services to Eire.

Container Terminal du Bassin Sud-est:

Situated on the corner of the Bassin Sud-est and the Canal de Jonction within the enclosed dock system served by the new lock linking the Bassin de Maree with the Bassin Sud-est opening in October 1971, this

terminal will come into service in April and be completed by December 1972. The total quay length is 1,145 m (3,757 ft) providing a principal berth of 900 m (2,953 ft) and a secondary berth of 245 m (804 ft). There will be a depth of water of 15·30 m (50·2 ft) alongside the principal facility and 10·30 m (33·8 ft) alongside the other. The overall area of the facility will be 45 hectares (111·2 acres) and two container freight stations, providing a covered area of 10,000 m² and 6,700 m² (107,640 and 72,120 sq ft) respectively. Handling equipment will consist of four container gantry cranes each with a lift under the spreader of 40tons and out-reaches of 37·70 m (123·7 ft) over the water and 32·30 m (106 ft) on the land side. A roll-on linkspan is also being provided. Quay handling equipment will include 40 ton yard gantry cranes for loading on to rail, straddle carriers, tractors and trailers, etc.

ROLL-ON/ROLL-OFF FACILITIES:

Quai de Southampton:

Situated on the north side of the Port this

facility, used by Thoresen for their Southampton Service, is capable of accepting vessels up to 100 m (328 ft) in length with a draught of 5·18 m (17 ft). It is equipped with a shore based adjustable ramp and has a parking area of 18,900 m² (4·7 acres).

Poste a Manutention Horizontale:

Located on the north side of the Môle Central, this facility can accept vessels up to 140 m (459·3 ft) in length drawing 10 m (33 ft). It is equipped with a shore based adjustable ramp and has a parking area of 24,700 m² (6·2 acres). This is the Normandy Ferries terminal for their Southampton and Eire Services.

ROAD AND RAIL ACCESS

In 1967 the line between Le Havre and Paris was electrified which has made possible the linking of the Port to the Capital with fast and regular services. Some 85 per cent of container traffic through the port is handled by rail. The Paris/Normandy motorway is at present under construction and its completion will improve the hinterland road connections.

Le Havre—Quai de l'Atlantique

TRAFFIC:

Containers:

	1969	1970	ESTIMATE 1971
Number of units handled	31,171	68,070	100,000
Number of units converted in 20′ containers	44,652	108,000	160,000
Gross weight of goods	360,969 mt	858,345mt	1,100,000 mt
Net weight of goods	287,355 mt	—	—

ROLL ON

	Cargo (tonnes)	Cars	Commercial Vehicles
1968	436,100	99,800	27,100
1969	679,800	109,100	33,300
1970	739,837	107,300	32,800

CONTAINER SERVICES

Company	Terminal	Service
Africatainers (C.M. de Chargeurs Réunis)	Quai de l'Atlantique	Abidjan, Libreville, Douala—weekly
Atlantic Container line	Quai de l'Atlantique	Le Havre to New York, Baltimore, Portsmouth, Va and Halifax—weekly
American Export Isbrandtsen Lines	Quai de l'Atlantique	Le Havre to New York, Norfolk and Baltimore—weekly
British & Irish Steam Packet Co.	Quai de l'Atlantique	Ireland—weekly
Dart Containerline	Quai de l'Atlantique	Le Havre to New York, Baltimore, Norfolk and Halifax via Southampton-weekly
France Ireland Line	Quai de la Réunion	Le Havre to full range of American Ports—weekly
Hapag-Lloyd	Quai de l'Atlantique	Le Havre to Belfast, Dublin and Waterford—twice weekly
Sea Land Service Inc.	Quai de l'Atlantique	Le Havre to New York, Philadelphia, Baltimore, Norfolk—weekly
Seatrain Lines	Quai de l'Atlantique	Le Havre to full range of American Ports via Southampton—weekly
United States Lines	Quai de l'Atlantique	Le Havre to full range of American and Far East via New York

ROLL-ON/ROLL-OFF SERVICES

Company	Terminal	Service
Thoresen Car Ferries	Quai de Southampton	Le Havre to Southampton—once to three times daily
Normandy Ferries	Môle Central	Le Havre to Southampton—once or twice daily. Le Havre to Rosslare—once or twice weekly (June to October)

Bore Line and Mountwood shipping Company provide roll-on contract voyages for new cars

TERMINAL WORKING HOURS:

Normally, ship and inland transport operations take place from 0700 to 2300 hours six days per week. Overtime on nights and Sundays 0700 2300 hours, as required.

FUTURE PLANS

In 1975 it is anticipated that container terminals covering an area of 85 hectares (210 acres) will be in operation. It is expected that the container traffic at this time will be 190,000 containers, 2·1 million tons per year. Further roll-on facilities will be built; the forecast for 1975 is 1·185 million tons of roll-on traffic.

CONTAINER REPAIR FACILITIES:
Compagnie Générale d'Entretien et de Réparation (COGER)
Route du Môle Central
Le Havre, BP 1355
TELEPHONE: 48-11-36
TELEX: 79937
GENERAL:

COGER was formed in 1965 to manage the CGT repair facilities for ships, workshops and factories.

A Container Division has recently been set up.

CONTAINER DIVISION:

Captain P. Touquet (*Head of Division*)

Y. Croc (*Technical Manager*)

PLANT AND EQUIPMENT:

Workshops for welding, pressing, sandblasting, painting, washing etc. Mobile units fitted with welding equipment for steel or light alloys.

SPARE PARTS:

Comprehensive stock of spares for all types of containers, chassis, etc, and also for handling equipment.

Le Havre—The Normandy Ferry Terminal

Le Havre—The Thoresen Terminal

MARSEILLES

Port Autonome de Marseille
23 Place de la Joliette, Marseilles
TELEPHONE: (91) 20.69.30 and 20.54.60
TELEX: 42 746
PRINCIPAL OFFICIALS:
Yves Boissereinq (*Director*)
Claude Mandray (*Director of Commerce and Trade*)
GENERAL:

The Port of Marseilles is developing a new industrial port complex some 30 km west of the city and docks of Marseille at Fos. Part of this development is already in service.

CONTAINER TERMINALS—FOS
Fos No. 1 Dock:

This consists of a quay 250 m (820 ft) long with an apron about 100 m (328 ft) in depth for the marshalling of containers. Behind the apron there is a container storage area of 4·5 hectares (11·1 acres). There is a depth of 15 m (50 ft) alongside the quay. The terminal is equipped with a 45 ton gantry crane having an outreach over water of 36 m (118 ft). This crane is capable of handling a 40 ft or two coupled 20 ft containers at 20 cycles per hour and the spreader

allows a 90° rotation of the load. To supplement this crane two 20 ton mineral gantry cranes have been adapted for container handling, using semi-automatic spreaders, at a cycle rate of 10 per hour. Behind the storage area there is a zone of 18 m × 300 m (59 × 984 ft) which has two, eventually three, rail tracks for the handling of railborne container traffic. A 50 ton yard gantry crane, provided by French Railways, is capable of dealing with some 600 containers per day. A consolidation area with a shed of 3,000 m² (32,291 sq ft) and an outside storage area of 7,500 m² (1·85 acres) is capable of a throughput of about 70,000 tons per year. There is ample back-up land in reserve should it be required.

Fos No. 2 Dock:

This facility, which is expected to be completed in 1972 is located on the land between Basins Nos. 2 and 3. There are 200 hectares (494 acres) reserved for container operators. On the western side of Basin 2 there will be five berths each of 250 m (820 ft) in length with a depth alongside of at least 12 m (39·4 ft). The eastern side of Basin 3 has been reserved for roll-on/roll-off and conventional cargo carriers which will allow for the distribution and collection of containers by feeder services throughout the Mediterranean.

Inland Transport Access:

The Lille-Paris-Lyons-Marseilles motorway is connected to Fos and this motorway will be extended eastwards to connect with the Esterel motorway and Italy. A motorway connecting the Rhone valley with Spain is also under construction. Rail connections are completed with the SNCF network and traffic, using the inland waterways will be able to use the Rhone which will be open to 3,000 ton pushed convoys as far as Valence by 1972 and up to Lyons by 1976.

CONTAINER FACILITIES—MARSEILLES
Mourepiane Terminal

There is shed space of 3,500 m² (37,673 sq ft) and a container storage and marshalling area of 1·5 hectares (3·7 acres). An 18 ton quay and a 20 ton floating crane are used to handle containers and a 40 ton gantry crane may be installed. A 30 ton transmitter on pneumatic tyres is used to stack containers two high.

ROLL-ON/ROLL-OFF FACILITIES—MARSEILLES
In service:

Berth 157: Fixed ramp: 12 m—Ro/Ro

Berth 50: inclinable ramp: 6·70 m—car-ferry

Berth 57: inclinable ramp: 7 m—Ro/Ro

Berth 66: inclinable ramp: 7 m—Ro/Ro and car ferry

Berth 81: inclinable ramp: 7 m—car-ferry

Berth 82: inclinable ramp: 7 m—Ro/Ro and car ferry

Berth 84: inclinable ramp: 7·50 m—Ro/Ro and car-ferry

Berth 86: inclinable ramp: 7·30 m—Ro/Ro and car-ferry

Berth 88: inclinable ramp: 7 m—Ro/Ro and car-ferry

Berth 90: inclinable ramp: 7·10 m—Ro/Ro and car-ferry

FORWARDING SERVICE:

Soteco
119 rue de l'Enêché
Marseilles 2 ème
H. M. Elliot (*Président Directeur Général*)
E. Ducani (*Directeur*)

To solve the problems posed by integrated transport and containers 97 Marseilles forwarding agents grouped themselves into an association entitled "Société Technique pour le transport en Containers". The association acts as a container study centre as well as a groupage organisation for containers mainly on the services to the USA. It also deals with degroupage of full containers at Marseilles. It is expected that these services will extend to other services shortly.

CUSTOMS:

The Customs services both on a national and regional scale have the constant concern to foster a rapid development of carriage by con-

Fos—Container Terminal No. I

Marseilles—Roll-on berths, Joliette

Marseilles, Mourepaine Terminal.

tainers. Therefore, the use of the systems already known in recent years, such as house-clearance, internal clearance centres etc., is going to be developed to cut down the normal problems and difficulties of administrative procedure.

DISINFECTION CENTRE:

The disinfection station, consisting of three sterilizers for vegetable products, in Rue Peyssonnel, covers 3,500 sq m (4,184 sq yd). The station is operated by the PAM under the technical supervision of the Service de la Protection des Végétaux (Ministry of Agriculture). In 1970, 9,072 tons of goods, principally fresh and dried fruit, and dried vegetables, were treated here.

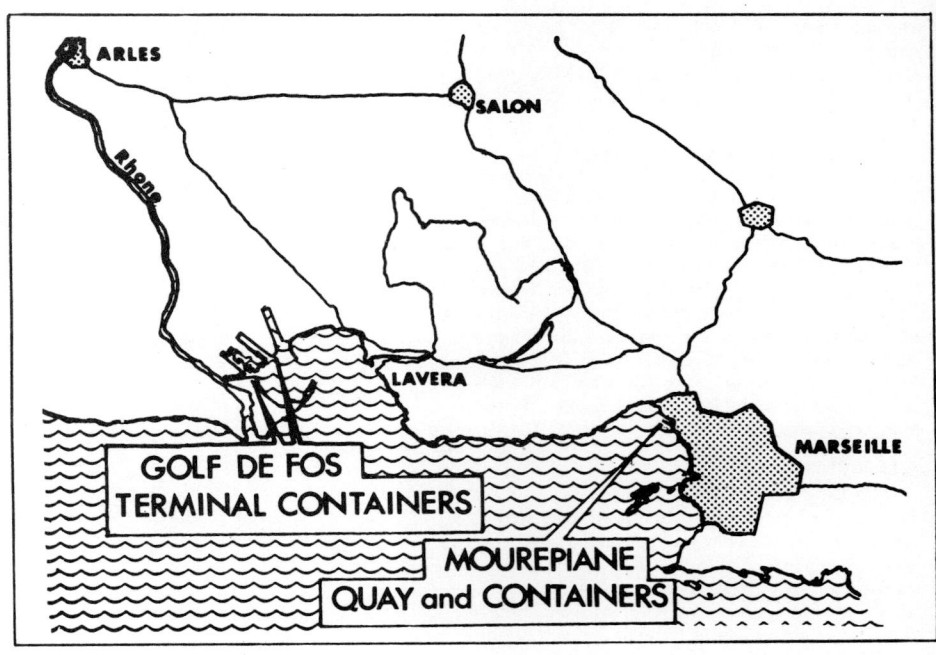

SHIPPING COMPANIES PROVIDING CONTAINER AND ROLL-ON SERVICES:

American Export Isbrandtsen Lines (Full container ships)	New York and Norfolk—Weekly Montreal, Toronto, Detroit, Chicago and Milwaukee
Fabre Line (Full container ships)	Genoa, Leghorn, Barcelona and Lisbon to New York
Hansa Line (Full container ships)	U.S.A.
Ned Lloyd Line (Partial container ships)	Far East
Holland Australia Line (Partial container ships)	Adelaide, Melbourne, Sydney and Brisbane
Promotion Containers (Contships) (Full container ships)	Marseilles, Fos—Casablanca

ROLL ON SERVICES:

Fabre-SGTM 70, rue de la République (2 ème)	Morocco—every 3 days
Grimaldi Agents: Barry-Rogliano 14, rue Beauvau—1 er	Famagousta, Beyrouth, Tripoli, Benghazi,— every 14 days
Malta Cross Line Agents: Barry Rogliano	Malta—every 10 days
Compagnie Generale Transmediterranéenne 61, boulevard des Dames (2°)	Corsica, Balearic Isles, Tunisia, Algeria, Sardinia
Giannoni-Rastit 211, av. Roger Salengro (15°)	Corsica—every 2 days
Ignazio-Messina (Agents: Rodriques-Ely) 15, rue Beauvau (1°)	Israel—every 10 days
J. A. Reinecke (Agents: Subira & Cie) quai de la Joliette (2°)	Morocco

ROUEN

Port Autonome de Rouen
52 Quai Gaston-Boulet, Rouen
TELEPHONE: (35) 71-74-54
GENERAL:

At present the port receives containers from conventional or partially converted ships.

CONTAINER HANDLING FACILITIES:

Containers are handled by quay crane. The Port has, however, in St. Gervais-Basin on the South branch a berth which can accept container ships of 79.25 m (260 ft) in length. There is a marshalling and storage area of about 1 hectare (2.5 acres). A floating crane with a lifting capacity of 30 tons at 20 m outreach is placed between the ship and the shore. If unloading a ship the crane accepts ten 20 ft units on its deck and then places them on the quay where they are taken to storage by a Lancer side loader. Some 10/15 containers per hour can be handled in this manner.

Petit Couronne Quay:

The Port Authority completed a quay of 600 m in length with 10 m of water alongside at Petit Couronne. In 1969 half of this quay was equipped for conventional general cargo handling. The other half is at present being developed as a container and roll-on facility.

CONTAINER SERVICES:

By the end of 1971 services to Portugal, Great Britain (Swansea) and Eire will be operating.

Rouen—Roll-on Berth No. 3 St. Gervais

Rouen, Roll-on Berth No. 2 Molineaux.

STRASBOURG

Port Autonome de Strasbourg

25, Rue de la Nuée Bleue
Strasbourg
TELEPHONE: (8) 32.36-15
GENERAL:

Situated some 700 km (437·5 miles) from the sea this port is equipped with a 300 ton heavy lift gantry crane which has been provided with a second lifting beam fitted with Automatic Container spreader. The crane came into service in 1970. There is a paved area capable of storing 500 containers and a container freight station is planned.

Regular barge services, capable of carrying containers, connect the port with the sea.

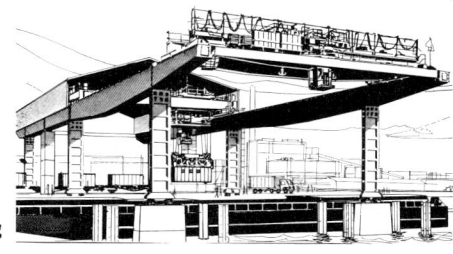

A drawing of the crane at the Strasbourg Terminal.

FRENCH NATIONAL RAILWAYS S.N.C.F.

French National Railways (SNCF)

Société Nationale des Chemins de fer Francais,
88 Rue Saint-Lazare,
Paris (9e), France
REGIONAL OFFICES:
Région de l'Est (Eastern), 13 rue d'Alsace, Paris 10e.
Bounded on the south by the South East Region, on the west by the North Region, and on the east by the Swiss, German, Luxembourg and Belgian frontiers.
Region du Nord (Northern), 18 rue de Dunkerque, Paris 10e.
Bounded by Paris to Dieppe, Paris to Hirson and the Belgian frontier.
Region de l'Ouest (Western), 20 rue de Rome, Paris 8e.
Bounded by Paris to Dieppe, and a line running Paris, Chartres Saumur, Poitiers, Angoulême and Bordeaux.
Region du Sud-Ouest (South western), 1 place Valhubert, Paris 13e.
From the Eastern boundary of the West Region to a line running Paris, Nevers, Clermont-Ferrand, Rodez, and the Spanish border near Font-Romeu.

A typical French rail terminal.

Région du Sud-Est (South-eastern),
20 boulevard Diderot, Paris 12e.
Bounded on the west by the South-west Region, on the south by the Mediterranean Region, on the east by the Italian and Swiss frontiers and on the north by a line running

Belfort, Sens, Melun, and Paris.

Région de la Méditerranée (Mediterranean),
17 avenue de General Leclerc,
Maréchal de France, Marseille (B. du R.).
An area bounded by the coast in the south and
a line running Font-Romeu, near the Spanish
frontier, to Rodez, La Bastide and across to
the Italian frontier near the Modane Pass.

CONTAINERS OWNED AND OPERATED:
All container operations are carried out by
Compagnie Nouvelle de Cadres (CNC), a
subsidiary company of SNCF. French Railways provide rolling stock and handling
equipment for container operations and
schedule any special services which are
required.

CONTAINER TERMINALS:
These are shown under the CNC entry,
it should be noted that the majority of these
terminals can be used for receiving and
delivering foreign containers.

SERVICES:
Internal Container Express:
SNCF runs container trains on the following
routes in both directions:

1. Paris-Bercy to Bordeaux; to Toulouse;to
   Lyon; to Marseille
2. Paris-La Chapelle to Metz; to Strasbourg
3. Marseille to Lyon, to Bordeaux, to Toulouse,
   to Strasbourg
4. Bordeaux to Toulouse

A TIR semi-trailer carrier on a kangaroo wagon.

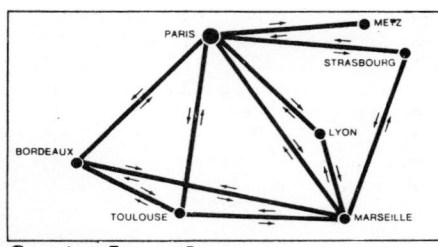

Container Express Routes.

Eleven trains are run nightly on these routes
and the services are expanded as demand
increases.

The tariff is based upon 60 ft of container
length, that is per specially designed wagon,
and includes terminal handling and road
haulage at both ends and the Railway
Company will hire 20 ft units for this purpose.
Later larger units will be made available.
There is a surcharge if containers are very
heavily loaded or the 60 ft length contains a
high proportion of 10 ft units. There are
reduced rates for returning empty units. It is
also possible for private operators to bring
containers to the rail head and ship at rates
negotiated with SNCF.

International
Services are run in conjunction with British
Railways for the carriage of containers
between industrial centres in France and
Britain using terminals in Paris and London.

Kangaroo Services
At Dunkerque a 'kangaroo' piggy-back
terminal is operational which enables semi-
trailers of standard type, but with some
modifications introduced at time of building,
to be carried over long distance by rail.
There is now a through overnight service
between Paris and Milan. These services are
operated by:
Novatrans,
21 rue du Rocher,
Paris 8e
Telephone: 010 331 387.41.79
Telex: 65625

C.N.C.

Compagnie Nouvelle de Cadres C.N.C.

20 Boulevard Diderot—75—, Paris XII
TELEPHONE: 345-32-20
TELEX 22 500
DIRECTORS AND EXECUTIVES:
J. Daudemard-Gregnac (*President Directeur
Général*)
H. Megoeuil (*Directeur de l'Exploitation*)
G. Braud (*Chef du Service du Matérial*)
J. J. Jouve (*Chef du Service Commercial*)

BRANCHES:
CNC has over 50 offices throughout France.
The Company also has offices at Algiers and
Casablanca and is represented by Chemins de
Fer Federaux (DFF) in Genève and Bâsle.
The Compagne Nouvelle de Cadres is a
subsidiary company of SNCF (French Rail-
ways) whose main business is to look after
the transport of containers and trans-
containers.

GENERAL
The company's clients give instructions for
the transport of their own containers or of
containers supplied by the Railways which
the clients have loaded themselves.

To obtain the lowest possible transport
price and to make optimum use of the Railways container rolling stock, C.N.C. endeavour to group several containers together
on the same platform, coming from different
senders and going to different addresses but
travelling on the same section of line.

Using their numerous establishments as
relays they are always able to provide the
Railways with fully utilised wagons and to
obtain for each sector of the line as a whole, a
price which is proportionate to the tonnage
loaded.

C.N.C. are therefore able to offer their
clientele lower prices than they would obtain
if they gave their containers individually to
the Railways.

Furthermore, in order to obtain a complete
service, C.N.C. offer road haulage facilities
in most of the large towns in France where
there is no direct rail access to the customer's
premises.

To develop the technique of transcontainers
in France's inland transport circuit, C.N.C.

C.N.C. containers

French Railways Gantry-crane
have built up a pool of 1,500 transcontainers
which have a length of 20 ft and comply
strictly with all the rules laid down by ISO.
Furthermore, they have, besides the obligatory

end-on door, side doors on either side;
they can thus be handled by special bottom
lifting equipment and packed while standing
on rail cars.

PRINCIPAL CHARACTERISTICS OF TRANSCONTAINERS
Dry Cargo Containers

Serial Nos:	20 014 005 to 20 014 995	20 025 005 to 20 025 995	20 028 005 to 20 028 995	20 029 005 to 20 029 995	20 030 005 to 20 030 995	20 053 005 to 20 057 995	20 091 585 to 20 094 075	20 076 005 to 20 078 495
Gross Weights Tare Net	20,000 kg 2,400 kg 17,600 kg	20,000 kg 2,330 kg 17,670 kg	20,000 kg 2,130 kg 17,870 kg	20,000 kg 2,300 kg 17,700 kg	20,000 kg 2,100 kg 17,900 kg	20,000 kg 2,150 kg 17,850 kg	20,000 kg 2,300 kg 17,700 kg	20,000 kg 2,250 kg 17,750 kg

Common external dimensions for the whole series of transcontainers:

Length: 6,055 m (20 ft); Width 2,435 m (8 ft); Height 2,435 m (8 ft); Gross volume 35,90 m³

Free Internal dimensions: Length mm Width mm Height mm Usable volume Usable surface	5,880 2,315 2,161 29,40 m³ 13,61 m²	5,878 2,315 2,161 29,68 m³ 13,70 m²	5,878 2,315 2,161 29,68 m³ 13,70 m²	5,910 2,337 2,232 30,83 m³ 13,81 m²	5,916 2,336 2,209 30,60 m³ 13,85 m²	5,909 2,337 2,205 30,45 m³ 13,81 m²	5,880 2,310 2,200 29,87 m³ 13,58 m²	5,891 2,337 2,234 30,73 m³ 13,76 m²
End Doors: (One end) Height mm Width mm	2,088 2,265	2,088 2,265	2,088 2,265	2,130 2,280	2,130 2,260	2,130 2,301	2,130 2,300	2,140 2,285
Side Doors: (both sides) Height mm Width mm Floor height mm	2,000 1,500 200	2,000 1,500 200	2,000 1,700 160	2,000 1,700 160	2,000 1,700 160	2,000 1,700 160	2,000 1,700 170	2,059 1,700 163

Tilt Type Containers
These units have external dimensions of 30 × 8 × 8·5 ft with a maximum gross weight of 25,000 kg, a tare of 4,000 kg and a net capacity of cargo of 21,000 kg.
Internal dimensions are as follows:
Length: 8,973 mm, width: 2,290 mm, height: 2,254 mm, volume: 51·6 m³. The rear door opening is 2,290 × 2,176 mm and the maximum lateral opening is 8,145 mm in length with a height of 2,184 mm.
Half Height Containers
These units have external dimensions of 20 × 8 × 4 ft.

Removable Roof and Pivoting Lintle
These units are 20 × 8 × 8. Tare is 2,165 kg and they are designed with a lifting roof with rubber seals and a pivoting lintle to allow fork trucks to be worked easily within the unit and for top loading/discharging by cranes.

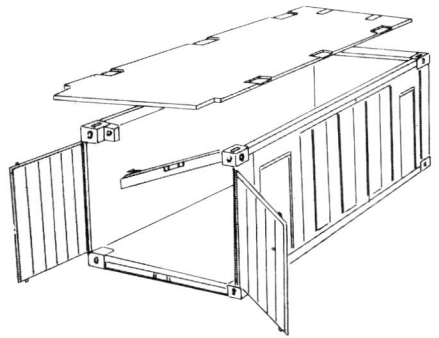

Transcontainer with removable roof and pivoting lintle.

RAIL TERMINAL EQUIPMENT FOR THE HANDLING OF TRANS CONTAINERS AS AT SPRING, 1971

KEY
● TERMINAL EQUIPPED WITH MODERN CONTAINER GANTRY CRANE CAPABLE OF ACCEPTING ALL TYPES OF TRANSCONTAINER
○ TERMINAL WITH LIMITED EQUIPMENT
◉ TERMINAL EQUIPPED WITH OLD HANDLING EQUIPMENT CAPABLE OF ACCEPTING 30 AND 40 ft UNITS

GERMANY
DEMOCRATIC REPUBLIC

Port: Rostock

Railway: Deutsche Reichsbahn,
Voss Strasse 33, 108 Berlin

Ship Operators: VEB Deutsche Seereederei,
Rostock

International Forwarding: VEB Deutrans,
Otto-Grotewohl-strasse 25, DDR-108
Berlin

Telephone: 2201 21

Telex: 101331

GENERAL:

In the summer of 1968 the first Container Rail Link between Dresden-Berlin-Rostock commenced operation. Currently 280 Container trains a week between 16 Container terminals are already operating to a firm timetable. Approximately 1,500 towns and localities are now covered by this Container Rail network. With the development of this Container Rail traffic an extensive container service has been built up.

TYPES OF CONTAINERS:

The containers are the property of the Deutsche Reichsbahn, and are leased to various organisations for internal and international traffic. The internal traffic is operated by Deutsche Reichsbahn, whereas the international traffic is operated by VEB Deutrans, International Forwarding, Berlin. Deutsche Reichsbahn use the following ISO-type containers, all made in the German Democratic Republic:—

Gt   A 20 ft container, covered, access through one end end.

Gft A 20 ft container, covered, with access through one end door and two side doors.

Gft A 20 ft refrigerated container.

Gyr A 20 ft box container with 4 ft high front walls and 5 folding side stanchions.

In addition, for international traffic (where required) 20, 30 and 40 ft containers are rented from foreign container firms and used by VEB Deutrans.

VOLUME OF TRAFFIC:

In 1969 23,100 loaded containers were transported; in 1970 this rose to 119,600. On the basis of figures available for the first months of the year, an estimated 160,000 loaded containers will be transported in 1971.

INLAND TERMINALS:

Inland terminals have been established in the immediate vicinity of industrial centres. Container handling points are situated in the towns of Rostock, Berlin, Dresden, Karl-Marx Stadt, Leipzig, Halle, Erfurt, Gera, Magdeburg, Suhl, Zwickau, Cottbus, Görlitz, Frankfurt/Oder, Wittenberge, Schwerin and Nurebandenburg. The terminals operate within a radius of 40 km. In addition, the West Berlin railway stations of Hamburg-Lehrter and Wilmersdorf connect up with the container network of the Deutsche Reichsbahn. Berlin is the Container Centre of the German Democratic Republic.

RAIL TRANSPORT:

Over the last few years the number of container trains operating has increased considerably. Most travel by night, so that containers loaded in the evening reach the customer by the following morning. The railway network of the German Democratic Republic is also used for moving containers in transit. The time of three days for a journey from Rostock to Hungary or Czechoslovakia is an inducement to choose this route through the German Democratic Republic. This service runs weekly in both directions.

INLAND WATERWAYS:

As the inland waterways are part of the whole container transport system, it is planned to establish various terminals suitable for the trans-shipment of containers from rail to waterway. After initial investigations on the basis of volume of goods to be transported, the following were considered most suitable inland ports for container handling points: Dresden, Riesa, Magdeburg and Eisenhüttenstadt. At present only the inland ports of Riesa and Berliner Osthafen can handle 20 ft containers.

PORTS:

Transit on land to and from Rostock is undertaken by the Deutsche Reichsbahn and Road Hauliers. In September, 1970, a new installation for handling container trains was opened in the port of Rostock. A container train of up to 210 m in length can be handled on the track of this installation by a 30 ton gantry crane with a reach of 12·5 m (41 ft) The container terminal has an area of 16,000 m² (161,459 ft²) for container storage.

Additionally, the port has at its disposal the following technical equipment for container handling and trans-shipment:—

2 general cargo gantry cranes with lifting capacity of 16 tons each.
Spreaders for 20, 20 and 40 ft containers.

3 mobile cranes with lifting capacity of 10·5 tons each.

1 side-loader with lifting capacity of 25 tons.

1 container-loading truck with lifting capacity of 20 tons.

All types of ISO containers can be handled in the port of Rostock.

CONTAINER SERVICES:

In November, 1968, a container service from Rostock to Tilbury was commenced, with the ships *Falke* and *Pinguin*, which had been converted for container transport. In October, 1970, the first purpose-built container ship, *Boltenhagen*, was put into service between Rostock and London/Tilbury. Since then three more ships of the same category have commenced operation: *Dierhagen*, *Trinwillershagen*, and *Nienhagen*. Two of the ships are engaged in the regular full container service operating on the Tilbury-Hamburg-Rostock route providing two sailings weekly and two ships are operating on the Hull-Hamburg-Rostock route also provide two weekly sailings. All ships are owned by VEB Deutsche Seereederei, Rostock.

These vessels can carry up to 39 20 ft containers, or an equivalent number of 30 or 40 ft units. they are also equipped to take up to 12 refrigerated containers.

Boltenhagen

CONTAINER LEASING AND OPERATING:

VEB Deutrans, which operates the container traffic, is the sole container leasing company in the German Democratic Republic, and has at its disposal approximately 3,000 20 ft containers as well as 100 open-top containers. These containers are used for imports and exports of the German Democratic Republic and under a pool system are interchangeable with those of foreign container firms. Within the framework of this pool system, VEB Deutrans have at their disposal a world-wide depot network, 16 of which are in the German Democratic Republic and 8 in Great Britain. This enables them to provide their customers with a choice of all types and sizes of containers, on lease where required, as well as on a through-freight basis.

VEB Deutrans is the sole national representative of the organisation Intercontainer on the territory of Deutsche Reichsbahn, and maintains very extensive container services in co-operation with their foreign partners throughout the sphere of operation of Intercontainer.

VEB Deutrans maintains reciprocal traffic arrangements with transport organisations in socialist countries, especially with the Soviet Union, Czechoslovakia, Hungary and Yugoslavia.

FORWARDING AGENTS:

VEB Deutrans, International Forwarding, Container Leasing and Operating Department,
Otto-Groyewohl Str. 25,
108 Berlin,
German Democratic Republic
Telephone: 220121
Telex: 112331/2

CONTAINER Gt		Length m (ft in)	Width m (ft in)	Height m (ft in)
Ext. Dimensions		6·06 (20 0)	2·44 (8 0)	2·44 (8 0)
Int. Dimensions		5·90 (19 7½)	2·20 (7 7)	2·15 (7 1½)
Door Size		— —	2·16 (7 6)	2·12 (7 0)

Tare Weight 2,050 kg (T 2- 0-1-11)
Cargo Capacity 17,950 kg (T17-13-1- 9)
Internal Cubic Capacity 30 m³ (1,060 cu ft)
  cu ft)

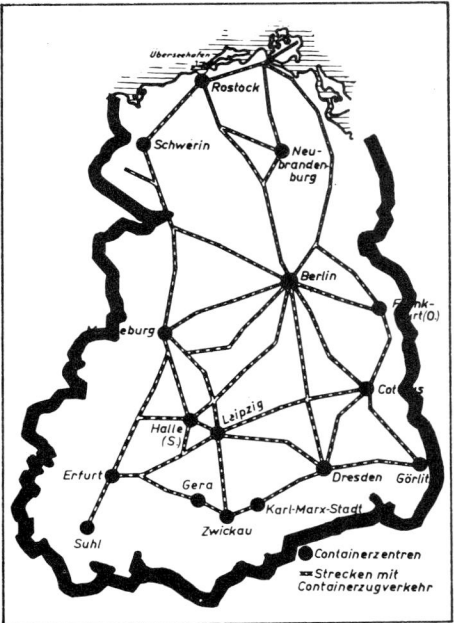

G.D.R. Rail container routes.

Rostock – Rail Terminal

Rostock – Handling operations

AGENTS:
United Kingdom:
Jeppesen Heaton Ltd.
  49 Leadenhall Street,
  London E.C.3
  Telephone: 01-488 4666
  Telex: 22150
Hull:
Oughtred & Harrison Ltd.
  Wellington House, 108 Beverley Road
  Hull, Yorkshire
  Telephone: Hull 27301
  Telex: 52101
Goole:
Oughtred & Harrison Ltd.
  9 East Parade,
  Goole, Yorkshire
  Telephone: Goole 2685
  Telex: 56151
Hamburg
HC Röver GmbH
  2 Hamburg 11, Gr. Burstah 25
  Röver-Haus, Postfach 110609
  Telephone: 361431
  Telex: 02-11601

Helsinki:
  John Nurminen OY,
  Snellmaninkatu 13, Box 10087, Helsinki,
    Finland
  Telephone: 15155
  Telex: 12562
Copenhagen:
  Lehmann Junior,
  Malmögade 3, Copenhagen 0,
  Telephone: Tria 4000
  Telex: 2255

Antwerp:
  SA Kennedy, Hunter & Co. Ltd.,
  2 Quai Ortelius, Antwerp 1.
  Telephone: 325930
  Telex: 03165
Rotterdam:
  Pakhuismeesteren NV,
  v. Oldenbarneveltstr. 12,
    Box 863, Rotterdam 2
  Telephone: 111990
  Telex: 22164

FEDERAL REPUBLIC
BREMEN

Bremen and Bremerhaven
The two ports form a single operational unit under the authority of Senator für Haven, Schiffahrt und Verkehr.
PORT OFFICIALS:
Bremen:
Capt. Hans Loske (*Port Captain*)
Telephone: 385250
Bremerhaven:
H. Ricklefs (*Port Captain*)
Telephone: 4811
CONTAINER TRAFFIC OPERATIONS:
Bremer Lagerhaus—Gesellschaft
  2800 Bremen 1, Postfach 857
  Telephone: 3 89 61
  Telex: 02 44 840
  2850 Bremerhaven, Steubenstrasse
  Telephone: 48 41
  Telex: 2 38 722
GENERAL
  All mobile equipment and other equipment, including gantry cranes if necessary, is interchangeable between the two ports.

Container Terminal—Bremen.

CONTAINER FACILITIES:

Berths 20C, 22C and 24C Basin 11, Neustädter Hafen, Bremen

These three berths provide a total quay length of 800 m (2,625 ft) with a depth of water of 9·75 m (32 ft) alongside. Extension is possible on the east side of Basin 11 if required. At present seagoing vessels of up to 220 m (721·78 ft) can enter the port of Bremen at any time. The depth of water in the River Weser is 9·45 m (31 ft) at normal high tide. Vessels of 220 m in length must not exceed a draught of 8·45 m (28 ft) The total open area amounts to 11·7 hectares (29 acres).

Shed 22C is equipped with two 45 ton Kocks container gantry cranes for 20-40 ft units with outreaches of 28 and 30 m (91·8 and 98·4 ft), respectively. The cranes have a range of 350 m (1,148 ft) along the quay.

Shed 24C is equipped with a 25 ton Paceco type container gantry crane, with an outreach of 29·60 m (97·1 ft) and a back reach of 9 m (29·5 ft), designed for handling 35 ft units. The crane has a range of 150 m (482 ft) along the quay.

In addition there are 12 7·5 ton quay cranes which have a 15 ton capacity when doubled up, and 27 3 ton quay cranes. Mobile handling equipment consists of:

1 Kocks-type van carrier, fully hydraulic, lifting capacity 27 t.

3 Jünkerath-type van carriers } fully hydraulic, lifting capacity 30 t.
6 Peine-type van carriers

1 Magirus truck } with a hydraulic saddle-coupling, for roll-on and container traffic.
8 MAN trucks
1 MAFI truck

8 Service trailers, capacity 30 t for 20 ft— 40 ft containers.

4 Diesel fork lifts, capacity 7 t.
21 Diesel fork lifts, capacity 5 t.
21 Diesel fork lifts, capacity 3·5 t.
202 Diesel fork lifts, capacity 2 t.
86 Fork lifts, capacity 1 t.
26 Trucks for shunting operation.

Sheds 20, 22 and 24 provide a total of about 7,000 m² (75,350 ft²). Floors are at quay level and the width of the total quay apron amounts to 38 m (124·7 ft). The sheds are served by 3 sets of rail tracks in the apron and 2 sets behind the sheds, the container yard behind Shed 24 has 4 sets of rail tracks. Weighbridges are available in the vicinity of the terminal and there are 20 reefer points (220 volt and 50 hertz) at No. 22 and 96 reefer points (380 volts and 50 50 hertz) at No. 24 Shed.

Container Terminal Bremerhaven

Nordhafen East Side has a quay length of 336 m (1,102 ft) and Nordhafen Westside has a quay length of 400 m (1,312 ft) both facilities have depths of 11·6 m (38 ft) alongside. Osthafen quay has a length of 210 m (689 ft). The River Quay has a length of 700 m (2,297 ft) providing two berths which have a depth of water of 14·02 m (46 ft) which can later be deepened to 17·07 m (56 ft). A further 300 m of quay at the riverside facility is planned. Roll-on ramps are available at both the East and West Sides of Nordhafen. Dolphins are available at Osthafen for barge carriers.

Nordhafen East, with Osthafen quay, provides 8·2 hectares (20·3 acres) open storage for containers and cars; Nordhafen West has a total storage area of 12·5 hectares (30·88 acres) and the River Quay will provide on completion 45 hectares (111·2 acres). It will be possible to extend the River Quay marshalling area to 200 hectares (494 acres) should the space be required.

Seven Kochs container gantry cranes (five of 54 tons and two of 45 tons capacity) have been provided. Outreaches vary between 33 to 36 m (108·3-118·1 ft) and a backreach

Container Terminal—Bremerhaven May, 1971.

Container Terminal—Bremerhaven.

of 22 m (72·18 ft) has been provided.

Mobile handling equipment consists of the following:

1 Drott/Mannesmann-type van carrier, lifting capacity 27 t.

16 Peine-type van carriers, } fully hydraulic, lifting capacity 30 t.
5 Jünkerath-type van carrier

19 MAN trucks } with a hydraulic saddle-coupling, for roll-on and container traffic.
1 MAFI truck
2 Tugmaster trucks.

23 Service trailers—capacity 30 t for 20 ft— 40 ft containers.
9 Diesel fork lifts, between 5 and 7 t.
37 Diesel fork lifts, with capacities between 2·5 and 3·5 t.
8 Diesel fork lifts, capacity 2 t.
26 Diesel fork lifts, capacity 1 t.
4 trucks for shunting operation.

All van carriers are suitable for 20 to 40 ft containers. Each container size can be served by simply changing the spreader-frames. The van carriers are able to store containers 2-high.

Service trailers are used for transport between ship's side and storage area, as well as for transport within the port area.

Rail access consists of 2 sets of tracks on the apron and 3 sets in the yard at Nordhafen East with 2 sets in front and 2 sets behind the shed at Nordhafen West. At the River Quay there are two sets of tracks on the apron and six sets at the storage area rail terminal.

There is a rail weighbridge at Kaiserhafen close by and road weighbridge at the entrance to the Terminal.

Over 100 reefer points have been provided of which 78 are at the River Quay.

CONTAINER TRAFFIC:

| | Total number in and out* | | Weight tons |
	Absolute	20ft Equivalents	(1000 kg)
1968	46,873	69,848	464,533
1969	73,334	118,001	822,129
1970	112,191	194,812	1,384,870

*Containers of 20 ft or more only.

CONTAINER SERVICES:

Bremen

Full Container Services

Sea-Land Service Inc.
  Every 5 days
American Export Isbrandtsen Lines
  Weekly sailings
Short Sea Transport AG
  Weekly sailings

Container Services on conventional vessels

Meyer Line
  Weekly Sailings
Combi Line (Hapag Lloyd/Holland America Line) (US-Gulf)
  Weekly sailings
Polish Ocean Lines
  NAWK weekly sailings; Canada/Great Lakes—monthly sailings
Lykes Bros. Steamship Co, Inc
  Weekly sailings
New England Express Line
  Fortnightly sailings
Independent Gulf Line
  (NAOK/US Gulf—3 times a month
Ozean/Stinnes-Linien
  NAOK—fortnightly sailings

Europe Canada Lakes Dienst
    Hapag-Lloyd AG, Poseidon Linien Reederei
    Ernst Russ—weekly sailings
Armement Deppe S.A.
    US-Gulf—sailings once a month
Euro-Pacific Service
    Hapag-Lloyd AG, Compagnie Générale
    Transatlantique, Holland-Amerika Lijn—
    weekly sailings
Bremerhaven:
Full Container Services
Atlantic Container Line
    Weekly sailings
Hapag-Lloyd AG.
    Weekly sailings
Seatrain Lines, Inc.
    Weekly sailings
United States Lines
    Weekly sailings
Australia Europe Container Service
    Sailings every 10 days
Iberhanseatic Transport System (I.T.S.)
    Weekly sailings
IBESCA Container Line
    Sailings every 10 days
Svea Line (SYD) A/B
    Weekly sailings
Container Services on Conventional Vessels
Container Line N.V.
    Sailings twice a month
Hapag Lloyd AG
    Far East-Service—weekly sailings
Koninklijke Nedlloyd NV
    Europe-Far East Service—weekly sailings
Scanservice
    Far East—4 times a month
Scanaustral
    Sailings once a month
Maersk-Kawasaki-Line
    Sailings twice a month
Mitsui-O.S.K.-Line
    Sailings twice a month

Transfer of containers to trucks/railcars by van-carriers at the Container Terminals Bremen/Bremerhaven.

Nippon-Yusen Kaisha Line
    Sailings twice a month
Malaysia International Shipping Corp.
    Sailings once a month
Prinzenlinien
    Sailings every second day
Far East French Service
    Sailings once a month
Hansaetic Vaasa Line
    NAWK—fortnightly sailings

WESERBAHNHOF CONSOLIDATION DEPOTS:
    Some 185,000 tons of consolidated cargo exports are handled annually in Bremen.
    Consolidated cargo is delivered to the Weserbahnhof by rail or road and is then sorted by ports-of-destination, i.e., for delivery to the berths of vessels at the individual loading sheds in the port. Six pairs of rail-tracks inside the Weserbahnhof can handle a goods-train of 45 railcars at the three platforms. The full range of trackage enables a total of 125 wagons to be administered within the Weserbahnhof. At the top

end of this installation is a road-transport yard of more than 5,000 m² (53,820 ft²), There, the lorries deliver their consolidated cargo loads onto a wide ramp. The discharged and palletized consolidated loads are then placed on shelves of a 20,000 square metres storage area for further disposal.
    In accordance with the delivery notes lodged by the authorised forwarding agents, the consolidated cargo lots are then conveyed by wagon or barge to the loading sheds in the freeports. In addition, containers are packed —at the Weserbahnhof—with sorted export consolidated cargo and delivered to the container ships in Bremen and Bremerhaven.
    As the Weserbahnhof is located outside the freeport area the Customs Administration maintains a special customs-office there.
    The Weserbahnhof is on call at all hours of the day Sundays and holidays included. Consolidated cargo trains arrive five times a day at the Weserbahnhof, whilst wagons are despatched to the ships in the freeports from the Weserbahnhof four times a day.

HAMBURG

Hamburg—The Eurokai Terminal at Predohlkai (first stage of development)

Port of Hamburg Authority
2 Hamburg 11,
Alter Steinweg 4,
TELEPHONE: 34 91 21
TELEX: 02 11100
GENERAL:
    The Port of Hamburg has an extensive hinterland in North, Middle, South and South East Europe.
    Hamburg has twelve berths for container vessels, with about 75 hectares (185·3 acres) open air storage space and 90,000 m² (968,752 sq ft) of shed area. There are furthermore possibilities for development to meet future requirements of container services in Hamburg. The port section 'Waltershof' alone with its area of approx 1·8 million m² (420 acres) could be developed into a container terminal with about 17 berths.
    Important centre of freight and particularly container traffic is the 'Uebersee Zentrum'. Here about ½ million tons of consolidated cargo, almost without exception suitable for containerisation, is handled every year. A special container packing station represents the link to container services calling at Hamburg.
    The 'Western By-pass' of the Federal Motorway which is under construction and will be part of European Motorway 3 (Lisbon/Stockholm) will represent a second excellent link with the long distance road network. Equally good connections exist for the railway system with the main lines to the West and South electrified and electric locomotives passing as far as the port railway stations.
    The sea approach of the port, i.e. the mouth of the river Elbe or 'Unterelbe' has a depth of water at mean low tide of 12 m (39·4 ft). 13·5 m (44·3 ft) is planned.

CONTAINER FACILITIES:
Container Terminal 'Burchardkai'
Operator: Hamburger Hafen-und Lagerhaus-AG
    This facility has a total quay length of 1,470 m (4,823 ft), an area of 56 hectares (138·4 acres) of which 56,000 m² (602,779 sq ft) is covered. There is a depth of water alongside of between 10 m and 14 m (33 and 45·9 ft) at low water. There are four berths for fully containerised vessels with four container gantry cranes, two manufactured by Demag and two by Peiner; one of 30·5 tons, one 35 tons and two of 45 tons capacity. Two other berths cater for part container ships and are equipped with two 25-ton cranes and ten 3-ton quay cranes.
    Other equipment in use at this terminal includes one 30 ton container mobile crane, 30 straddle carriers, fork lifts (lifting capacity to 10 tons), trailers, tractors, weigh bridge, container washing plant, repair shop, electric

connections and fittings for refrigerated containers. The facility is rail connected to the quayside and storage area. Behind the berths is a rail transfer terminal equipped with two container yard gantry cranes.
    The seventh berth is under construction; combined with a roll-on/roll-off installation it will be completed at the beginning of 1972. The area then will be enlarged up to 78 hectares (193 acres), three further container cranes will be erected and further straddle carriers will be provided.
    The terminal handles the all-container vessels of the United States Lines, Hapag-Lloyd-Containerlines, Johnson-Line, Australia Europe Container Service, Deutsche Seereederei Rostock, Deutsch-Finnische Line and Ibesca Containerline (Dart containerline feeder service); also the semi-container vessels of the Scanaustral service, Finnlines and ZIM-Israel Navigation Co.

Container Terminal Burchardkai/Hamburg

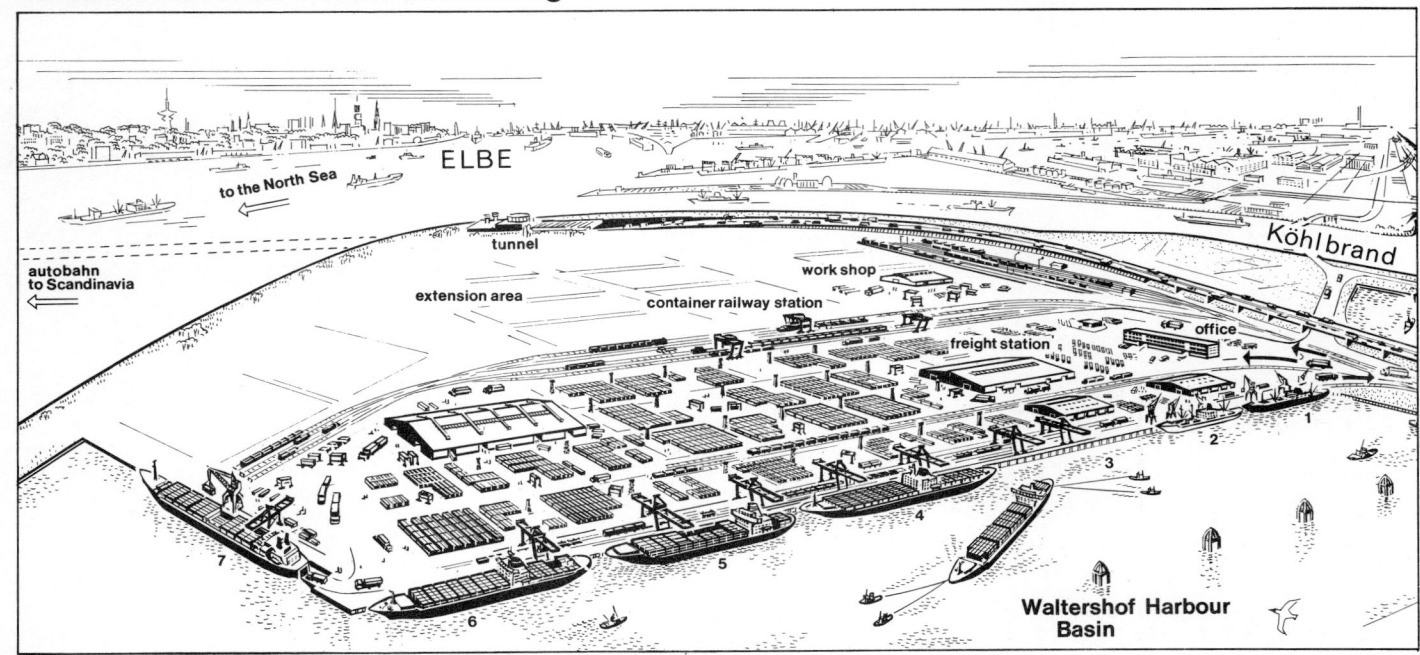

Hamburg—Impression of Burchardkai on completion in 1972

Europakai (*Shed No* 90)

Operator: Lager-und Speditionsges m.b.H

This terminal has a quay length of 650 m (2,132 ft) with an open storage area of 5·2 hectares (12·85 acres) and 18,000 m² (21,528 sq yds) of shedded area. Two of the four berths which the facility provides handle part-container ships. Depth alongside is 10 m (32·8 ft) at mean low water.

Handling equipment consists of two cargo-tainers (25 tons each) with synchronised controls and a fully automatic spreader, two 15-ton cranes with semi-automatic spreader, 12 cranes (5 tons, 3 tons), one 30-ton straddle carrier for 20 and 40 ft containers, fork lifts (lift capacity to 15 tons), trailers, tractors, Mafi trailer and repair shop. There are railway lines to the quayside.

A roll-on/roll-off ramp is under construction.

This section handles semi-container ships of the Meyer line.

By the end of 1972 the length of quay will have been extended by 390 m (1,279·5 ft) with an additional open storage area of 3·4 hectares (8·65 acres) and a shed of 12,000 m² (129,167 sq ft). A container gantry crane will be erected.

Euro-kai -Terminal, Predohlkai

Operator: Euro-Kai KG aA

This is a quay of 580 m (1,903 ft) in length providing four berths with 11 m (36 ft) at mean low water. There are 10 hectares (24·7 acres) of open storage and a 12,600 m² (135,625 sq ft) shed area.

Handling equipment consists of four cargotainers with synchronised controls and fully automatic spreader, fork lifts, trailers, tractors. The berth has a rail connection to the quay side and to the shed.

A roll-on berth is planned; a second container gantry crane will be erected in 1972.

EUR container vessels and semi-container vessels of the New England Express Line are handled.

Uebersee-Zentrum, Moldauhafen:

Operator: Hamburger Hafen-unde Lager-haus-AG

This is a general cargo distribution shed for general cargo export; it has a total area of 14·5 hectares (35·7 acres), of which 1·1 hectares (2·72 acres) is under cover. There is a container loading station of 22,000 m² (26,312 sq yds), a 25-ton crane, two straddle carriers and a van carrier.

Hamburg—Burchardkai

The 20,000 sq m (24,000 sq yd) shed at Burchardkai.

Other facilities:

Further facilities for container handling operations—in conjunction with facilities for conventional handling of general cargo—are available at many other wharves of the free-port area, particularly at quay sheds Nos. 29, 60/61, 73, 75, 55/56, 57/58, 63, 76/77, 83 and 85.

ROLL-ON/ROLL-OFF FACILITIES:

There are two roll-on/roll-off berths of the Hamburger Hafen- und Lagerhaus AG in operation. One at shed No. 10 (Kaiserkai) with an open storage area of 3,500 m² (·86 acres) and one at Dalmannkai with 7,000 m² (1·73 acres) open storage area and a shed of 4,000 m² (43,000 sq ft). Further on there is a roll-on/roll-off berth for ferry-traffic at "Landungsbrücken". Two ferry-services operate here, one to England and one to Norway.

Kaiserkai and Dalmannkai handle the ships of Washbay-Line, bound for Kings-Lynn UK; Argo-Line/Associated Humber Line to Hull UK; Teamline to Stockholm

Sweden; Hanseatic Ipswich Line to Ipswich UK.

There is a roll-on/roll-off berth completed, but not yet in operation at Europakai, one due for completion at Burchardkai in 1972 and at Stoltenkai one berth is planned for Eurokai and one is under construction for Müller.

TERMINAL OPERATING HOURS:

All cargo handling operations take place 24 hours per day, every day.

CONTAINER TRAFFIC:

	Inwards		Outwards	
	Loaded* units	tons	Loaded* units	tons
1969	26,146	160,000	37,605	291,000
1970	36,600	266,000	53,800	436,000
Estimate for 1971	59,000	430,000	86,000	700,000

*20 ft equivalents

RAIL AND ROAD CONNECTIONS:

German Federal Railways have set up an express unit container train service, running between South Germany and port station Hamburg-Waltershof (portions from Hamburg-Harburg to port station Hamburg-Süd).

The Port is well connected by road to most European destinations.

LEASING, FORWARDING, WAREHOUSING:

The following companies are operating as container-leasing container companies, oper-

Hamburg—Dalmannkai Roll-on Terminal.

ators, and warehouse agents:

Gerd Buss (SC1)
    2 Hamburg 11, Cremon 32
Contrans-Gesellschaft für Überseebehälterverkehr (UNIFLEX)
    2 Hamburg 13, Rothenbaumchaussee 38
Integrated Container Service GmbH
    2 Hamburg 11, Katharinenstr. 33
Interpool
    2 Hamburg 11, Bei den Mühren 1
Henry Stahl (Eurocontainer Lines)
    2 Hamburg 11, Alter Fischmarkt 11
Carl Tiedemann (RENTCON/CTI)
    2 Hamburg 11, Rödingsmarkt 20
Max Uhlig & Co (XTRA)
    2 Hamburg 11, Johannisbollwerk 20

Hamburg—Europakai (Shed 90)

CONTAINER REPAIR FACILITIES:

Conrepair, company for container-service 2 Hamburg 95, Rugenberger Damm (also at the Container-Terminal) is engaged in repairs, maintenance, and storage of containers and the provision of spare parts or accessories. Moreover all container handling enterprises are equipped with repair-shops.

DEUTCHE BUNDESBAHN (GERMAN FEDERAL RAILWAY)

**Deutsche Bundesbahn
(German Federal Railway)**
FEDERAL RAILWAY DIRECTOR:
Dr. Schmidt-Sommerfeld
Zentrale Transportleitung
Kaiserstrasse 3
65 Mainz
TELEPHONE: 151/434
TELEX: 04187732
AGENCY FOR INTERNATIONAL CONTAINER TRAFFIC AND FOR NATIONAL INLAND CONTAINER TRAFFIC:
TRANSFRACHT
Deutsche Transportgesellschaft mbH
D 6 Frankfurt (Main) 1
    Gutleutstrasse 160-164
    Telephone 25 12 43, 25 12 26
    Telex: 41 45 45 tfg"
FOREIGN REPRESENTATIVES:
Austria:
    A 1015 Wien, Postfach 290
    Telephone: 65 96 12, 65 83 00
Belgium:
    23 rue du Luxembourg,
    B-1040 Bruxelles
    Telephone: 13 23 54, 12 53 39, 11 24 41
Denmark and Norway:
    Vester Farimagsgade 1/472,
    1606 Kobenhavn V
    Telephone: 140144
France:
    24 rue Condorcet,
    F-75 Paris 9e
    Telephone: 878.50.26
Italy:
    Corso Vittorio Emanuele 15,
    I-20122 Milano
    Telephone: 700 182, 708 670
Luxembourg:
    9, Place de la Gare,
    Luxembourg
    Telephone: 48.89.51
Netherlands:
    Rodezand 34,
    Rotterdam 3001
    Telephone: 12.03.22
North America:
    Suite 446,
    11 West 42nd Street,
    New York, NY 10036
    Telephone: (212)565-7545

Düsseldorf. The Container is being lifted by the ISO type fitting on the spreader.

Ludwigsburg.

Spain and Portugal:
    Agencia de Trafic de los Ferrocarriles federales alemanes
    Mandes 51 (Edificio Minister)
    Madrid 3
Sweden and Finland:
    Barnhusgatan 3/III,

Munich

S-111 23 Stockholm C
    Telephone: 10.12.16

Switzerland:
    CH 4000 Basel 16 (Bad, Bahnhof),
    Schwarzwaldallee 200
    Telephone: 33.37.90

United Kingdom:
  Schenkers Ltd,
  Royal London House,
  13 Finsbury Square,
  London EC2
  Telephone: 606 0610
  Telex: 886 856
Yugoslavia:
  Jugoslovenske Zeleznice Turisticno-
  Transportni Biro,
  Titova 32,
  Ljubljana
  Telephone: 31.18.52

CONTAINER TRAIN SERVICES:

Internal

The freight container express train 'Delphin' operates on weekdays between the German Sea Ports and Frankfurt (Main) East, Mannheim, Ludwigsburg, Nürnburg and Munich.

There are also fast overnight container train services linking all the inland container terminals with each other, and with Amsterdam, Antwerp, Bremen, Bremerhaven, Hamburg and Rotterdam.

International

Great Britain via Zeebrugge/Rotterdam

A daily container train runs from Zeebrugge to Aachen West and beyond there containers are transported by the internal services. On Tuesdays, Thursdays and Saturdays a container train runs from Rotterdam to Kalkenkirchen and then containers are transferred to the internal services.

Benelux Ports

Transport facilities on weekdays by express and fast goods trains to and from all changeover stations. On Wednesdays and Saturdays a freight container train runs between the Benelux Ports, Germany and Italy through Rotterdam/Antwerp, Frankfurt, Basle and Milan Rogoredo.

TRANSCONTAINERS FOR DOMESTIC AND
  EUROPEAN SERVICES:

The following containers and flats which have a height of 2·60 m (8·5 ft), a width of 2·50 m (8·21 ft) are in service:

Type	Length	Number
Closed		
Htt 6/251	20 ft	550
Htt 6/252	20 ft	
Htt 12/501	40 ft	600
Httc 6/311	20 ft	200
Htg 6/271	20 ft	200
Open		
Htto 6/061	20 ft	100
Flats		
Hlv 6/661	20 ft	50

These units are equipped with corner fittings to ISO specification so that they can be handled by standard equipment. The purpose of this design is to utilise the ISO standard and European Railway Pool pallet of 800 × 1,200 mm which has been in use in large numbers for some years. The containers also conform to European road regulations.

As well as being designed for top lifting these units can be bottom lifted with special arms fitted to the crane spreaders.

DOMESTIC DOOR-TO-DOOR OPERATIONS:

The DB owns and operates about 20,000 containers (*pa-Grossbehalter*) of approximately 5·5 tonne load capacity for transporting goods from factories to users. These 'large' containers, i.e. those with a capacity of over 3 m³ (106 cu ft) are called 'pa-Containers' (pa is an abbreviation of *porteur aménagé* or fitted container). The Deutsche Bundesbahn supply their customers with pa containers free of charge outside the freight contract. The organisation of the container service corresponds to a great extent with that of the goods wagon service. Every day the containers are shared out

Type Htt 12/501 40 ft Unit and a Type Htt 6/252 20 ft unit on a 4 axle flat wagon.

CONTAINER TERMINALS AND STATIONS
(January 1971)

Handling station	Lifting capacity	For Containers up to length	Road delivery by DB or by gross weight	For delivery by DB or by tractors	
	tons	feet	tons		
Aachen West	35	40	30	Con	C
Augsburg-Oberhaüsen	35	40	30	DB	C
Basel Bad Bf *	35	40	30	Con	C
Bielefeld Ost Gbf	35	40	30	DB	C
Bochum-Langendreer*	35	40	30	DB	C
Braunschweig Hgbf	30	40	27	Con	P
Bremen Hbf	30	40	30	DB	
Dillingham (Saar)	35	40	30	DB	C
Düsseldorf-Bilk*	35	40	30	DB/Con	C
Duisburg Hbf	35	40	30	Con	C
Ehrang (bei Trier)	35	40	30	DB	C
Ensiedlerhof (bei Kaiserslauten)	35	40	30	DB	C
Fishbach-Weierbach	40	40	30	DB	P
Frankfurt (Main) Ost*	35	40	30	DB	C
Fulda	35	40	30	DB	C
Giessen	32	40	30	DB	M
Göppingen	35	40	30	Con	C
Göttingen Hagen Hbf	35	40	30	Con	C
Hamburg-Wilhelmsburg	35	40	30	DB	C
Hamm (Westf.)	30	40	30	Con	
Hannover-Linden*	35	40	30	DB	C
Ingolstadt Nord	32	40	25	DB	P
Karlsruhe Hbf	35	40	30	DB	C
Kassel Unterstadt	35	40	30	DB	C
Kempton (Allgáu) Ost†	25	40	22	DB	P
Köln-Eifeltor*	35	40	30	DB	C
Kreuztal	35	40	30	Con	C
Kulmbach	35	40	30	DB	C
Landshut (Bay) Hbf	35	40	30	DB	P
Ludwigsburg*	35	40	30	DB	C
Mainz Hbf	30	40	30	DB	
Mannheim Rbf*	35	40	30	DB	C
Marktredwitz	35	40	30	DB	
München Hbf*	35	40	30	DB	C
Münster (Westf.) Hbf	35	40	30	DB	C
Neu Ulm	35	40	30	DB	C
Nürnberg Hgbf*	35	40	30	DB	C
Offenburg	35	40	30	DB	P
Oldenburg (Oldb)	35	40	30	DB	C
Osnabrück	35	40	30	DB	C
Ravensburg	35	40	30	Con	C
Regensburg Hbf	32	40	30	DB	P
Reutlingen Hbf	35	40	30	Con	C
Saarbrücken Hgbf	35	40	30	DB	C
Singen (Hohentwiel)	35	40	30	DB	C
Wetzlar	35	40	30	DB	C
Wuppertal-Langerfeld	35	40	30	DB	C
Würzburg Hbf	35	40	30	DB	C

*Terminal †Private Crane
C=Container Crane
M=Mobile Crane
P=Conventional Port Crane

Using the bottom lifting gear on the crane spreader at Düsseldorf.

Type Ei container

Type EW container.

between the points where they are needed with the reserve pool in Frankfurt (Main).

It is intended that the majority of the DB pa containers will be replaced by the DB transcontainers.

HANDLING POINTS
FOR CONTAINER
TRAFFIC

Lübeck *

*Bremerhaven Seehafen
Hamburg-Wilhelmsburg ●
Hamburg Süd *
Hamburg-Waltershaf *
● Oldenburg (Oldb)
● Bremen Hbf
* Bremen-Grolland
* Bremen-Zollausschluß

● Osnabrück
⊡ HANNOVER-LINDEN
Braunschweig Hgbf

Münster (Westf) Hbf
● Bielefeld Ost
● Hamm (Westf)

Göttingen

Duisburg Hbf ⊡ BOCHUM-LANGENDREER
● Hagen Hbf
⊡ ● Wuppertal-Langerfeld
DÜSSELDORF-BILK
Kassel Unterstadt
● Kreuztal
⊡ KÖLN EIFELTOR
● Aachen West

● Wetzlar
Fulda

Kulmbach

⊡ FRANKFURT (M) OST
Mainz Hbf
Marktredwitz

● Ehrang
● Würzburg Hbf
● Fischbach-Weierbach
● Dillingen (Saar) ⊡ MANNHEIM RBF
⊡ NÜRNBERG HGBF
Einsiedlerhof
● Saarbrücken Hgbf

● Karlsruhe Hbf
● Regensburg Hbf
⊡ LUDWIGSBURG
● Ingolstadt Nord
● Göppingen
● Landshut (Bay) Hbf
Reutlingen Hbf
Neu Ulm
● Augsburg-Oberhausen
● Offenburg
⊡ MÜNCHEN HBF

● Ravensburg
Singen (Hohentwiel) ●
● Kempten (Allgäu) Ost
⊡ BASEL BAD BF

Key

⊡ = CONTAINER TERMINALS
(Binnenland-Terminal)

● = CONTAINER STATIONS

* CONTAINER PORTS

Nürnburg.

Gröppingen

Type Htto 6/061 open top unit.

Discharging European Rail pool pallets from
a D.B. container.

Type Eos container

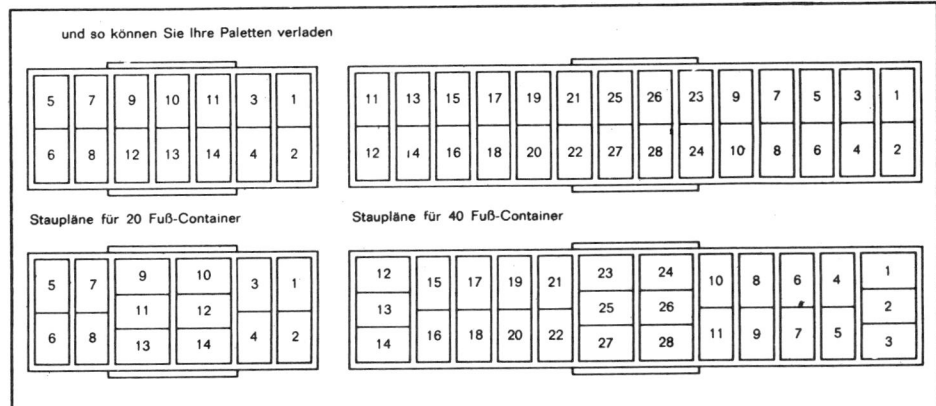

Pallet stowage plan in the 20 and 40 ft D.B. containers of the HC type

GREECE
PATRAS

The Port of Patras Administrative Committee
St. Andrews Street 61.
Patras, Greece
TELEPHONE: 77-093, 77-496, 64-332
TELEGRAMS: Limenikon Tamion-Patras
PRINCIPAL OFFICIALS:
Pan. Bousbouras
John Liourdis
ROLL ON FACILITIES:
Two berths both capable of taking vessels of up to 200 m (656 ft) in length are in operation. One can accept vessels of up to 11 m

(36 ft) draught and has a parking area of 12,000 m² (3 acres) and the other can accept vessels of 9 m (29·5 ft) draught and has a parking area of 8,000 m² (2 ac.es).

A further berth capable of accepting vessels of up to 200 m with a draught of 9 m (29·5 ft) with 18,000 m² (4·4 acres) for parking is proposed. It will be completed in 1973 and will be capable of being used also for container services.
CONTAINER FACILITIES
No facilities exist at present but a berth with

a quay length of 300 m, with a depth of water alongside of at least 12 m (39·4 ft) and 5 hectares (12·3 acres) of back-up land has been proposed for completion in 1976.
ROLL ON SERVICES:

Helmes S.A. Adriatica offer a daily service to Italian ports and Eftimiadis Line offers a twice weekly service also to Italian Adriatic ports.

There are numerous inter-island roll-on/roll-off ferry services.

PIRAEUS

Port of Piraeus Authority
Piraeus.
TELEPHONE: 426-981
PRESIDENT: A. Ikonomau
PRINCIPAL OFFICIALS:
T. G. Savvas (*General Manager*)

CONTAINER DEVELOPMENT:
The Port Authority has provided a quay of 350 m (1,148 ft) in length with a depth alongside sufficient to allow vessels drawing between 10 and 12 m (32·8 and 39·4 ft) to berth. The facility has an area of 8 hectares (20 acres) and a 40 ton container gantry crane capable of handling 20 and 40 ft units has been approved for purchase. A straddle carrier and trailers and tractors will also be available.

ROLL ON FACILITIES:
Coastal shipping lines which own this type of vessel use their usual general cargo berths.

CONTAINER SERVICES:
American Export Lines
Hellenic Lines
ROLL-ON SERVICES:
Inter-island Services
BARGE CARRIER SERVICES:
Prudential Grace Lines—Weekly

TRAFFIC:
1970 container traffic exceeded 10,000 units.

Piraeus—Container handling

Piraeus—Roll-on operations

Piraeus—*Lash Turkiye* alongside

GREEK RAILWAYS

Hellenic State Railways
102 rue Eolou, Athens (TT 131)
TELEPHONE: 315382
TELEX: 215187 CEHA GR

GENERAL:
Some 300 Series 72 U.I.C., type P.A steel containers, with a cargo volume of between 6 and 12 m³ (212-424 cu ft), are in service. These operate between Athens and Thersaloniki.

FUTURE PLANS:
Fruit and vegetables will be brought from Crete to Piraeus by sea and moved to European markets by rail. Twenty foot refrigerated containers to ISO requirements will be used for this sea/rail operation.

Greek Railways containers

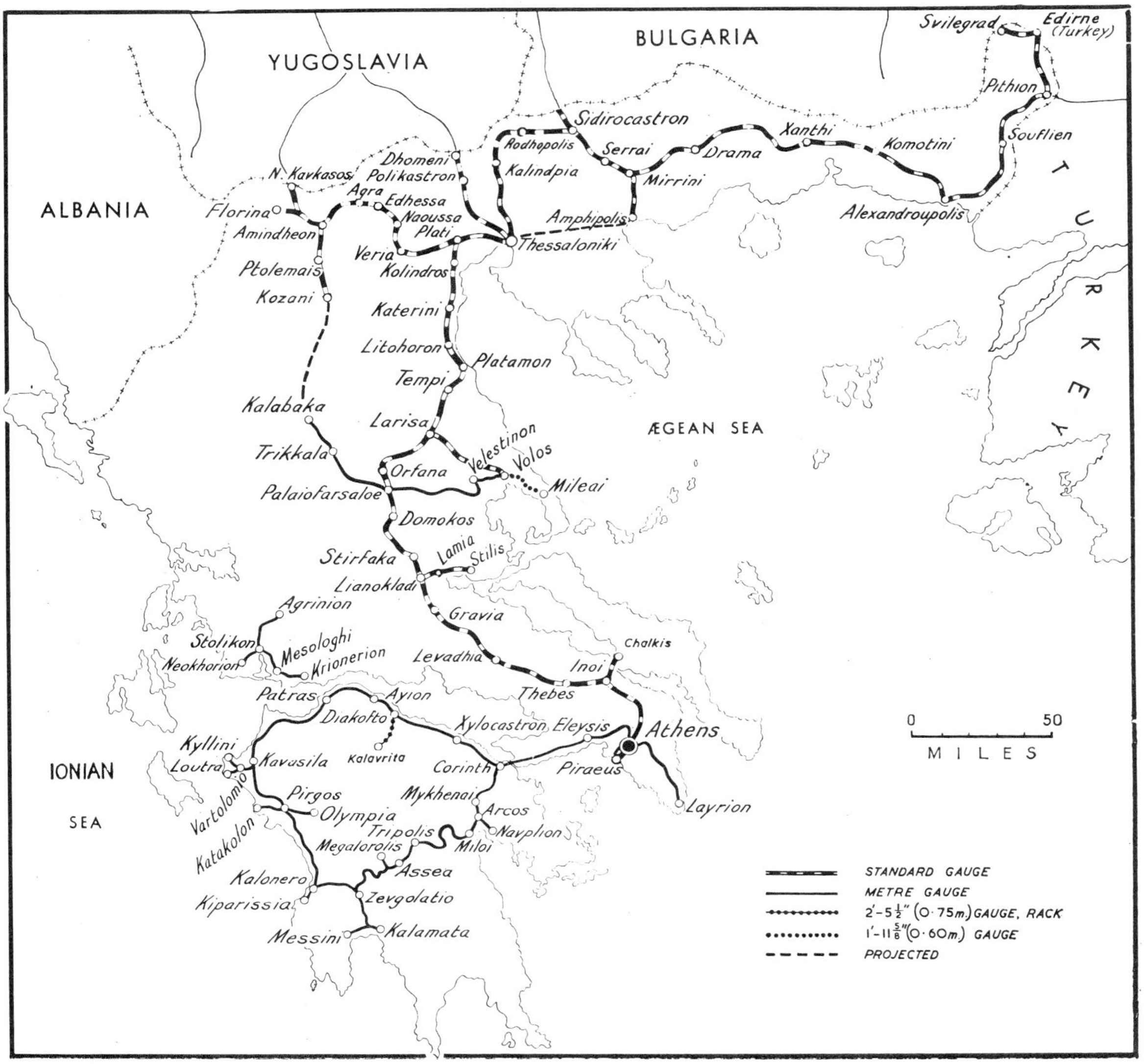

HUNGARY

Rail Transport

ORGANISATION RESPONSIBLE FOR CONTAINER
  POLICY:

**Magyar Allamvasutak Vezérigazgatosaga
MAV (Hungarian State Railways)**

General Directorate, Commercial Management,
Budapest VI, Népköztáraság utja 73/75

TELEPHONE: 228-459
TELEX: 641

ORGANISATION RESPONSIBLE FOR CON-
  TAINER OPERATIONS:

MAV Szallitmanyozasi Iroda (MAVTRANS)

Budapest V Déak Ferenc utja 23

TELEPHONE: 386-187 and 382-324
TELEX: 34-34

GENERAL:

MÁVTRANS is the 'Intercontainer' representative in Hungary, MAV being one of the founder members of the organisation. It is also a member of Interfrigo.

The following stations, included in Transcontainer Tariff No. 9145, have fixed container tariffs to Amsterdam, Rotterdam, Antwerp, Zeebrugge, Bremen, Hamburg, Dunkirk, Trieste, Venice, Koper, Ploce, Rijeka:

  Budafok-Háros
  Budaors
  Budapest-Jozefváros
  Budapest-Kitöto
  Debrecen
  Gyor
  Kecskemét
  Miskole-gömöri pu
  Nagykorös

Hungarian State Railways Container Train.

  Nyiregyháza
  Pecs
  Sopron

East German Ports and conversely MAV-TRANS which is associated with a number of international container owners is able to accept containers and provide a full forwarding service including door-to-door operations

It should be noted that GySEV (Györ-

Budapest—Part of the Csepel Terminal.

Sopron—Eberfurt Railways), which are still privately owned as they operate both in Austria and Hungary, also handle containers.
GySEV General Directorate,
Budapest 1, Szilagyi Dezso ter 1
Telephone: 154.007
GySEV Directorate,
Sopron, Mátyás Király ut 19.
Telephone: 14-10
Telex: Ráberbahn 00-3595

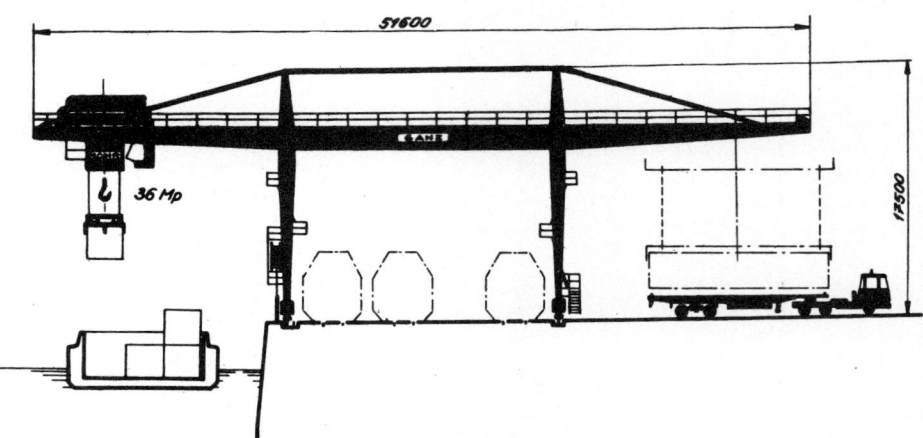

Budapest—Profile drawing of the Csepel Terminal Crane.

MAV–BUDAPEST–JÓZSEFVÁROS CONTAINER TERMINAL:

A rail container terminal in Budapest has been constructed which is capable of handling ISO type containers and also the smaller transcontainers which are in service; two separate parking areas have been provided for these two types. It has been equipped with two 35 ton container cranes and rail/road vehicle transfer equipment.

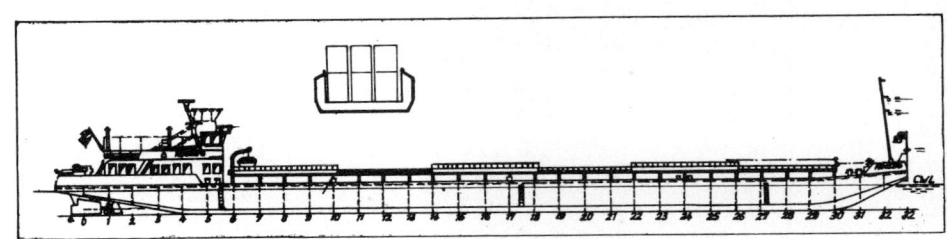

MAHART Barge suitable for container operations

ROAD TRANSPORT:

Road transport is controlled by Autó-közlekedési Tröszt (Road Transport Trust). The following Companies offer Container Services:

Volansped Közuti Szállitmányozási Szolgalat (Volansped Road Transport Service),
Budapest VI, Lenin Krt. 96
Telephone: 124-290, 112-562, 323-764.
Telex: 650, 659, 33-27, 33-84.

Volansped arrange for the loading and unloading of wagons and for collection or delivery of containers without prior notice as follows:

(1) All containers at all Hungarian Railway stations without prior notice provided they do not exceed 5 tons gross weight.
(2) Containers to ISO specifications with a total weight not exceeding 10 tons gross at Budapest, Salgotárjan Miskolc, Eger. Nyiregyháza, Debrecen, Szolnolc, Békéscsaba, Kecskemet, Veszprém, Zalaegerszeg, Szombathely, Tatabánya, Györ.
(3) Containers to ISO specifications up to 30 tons gross weight at Budapest.

Provided prior notice is given all containers can be handled at all stations in Hungary by Volansped at extra charge.

HUNGAROCAMION (International Road Transport Company):

This company, one of the largest in Europe, equipped with a fleet of Mercedes and Volvo trucks and trailers both dry and reefer operates as far afield as the United Kingdom and Afghanistan. The Company equipped itself with vehicles suitable for the carriage of both dry and reefer containers in January, 1969.

INLAND WATER TRANSPORT:

MAHART Magyar Hajozasi Rt.
(Hungarian Shipping Company Ltd.)
Budapest V, Apaczai Cs J.u. 11.
Postal address: PO Box 58, Budapest V
Telephone: 181-880
Telex: Mahart Budapest 616
Fleet: Container Barges of 1,300 tons capacity

OFFICIALS:

Lékai Elek (*General Manager*)
MAHART (Port Management)
Budapest XXI, Szabadkikötö ut.5.
Postal Address: PO Box 95, Budapest Csepel 1
Telephone: 140.660
Telex: Mahart Budapest 616

Budapest — Handling at the Csepel Terminal.

GENERAL:

Budapest has links to the Black Sea at Sulina 1,670 km (1,038 miles) away and will link with the North Sea at Rotterdam 2,155 km (1,339 miles) distant when the Main-Danube transcontinental waterway is completed in 1981. Accordingly a container terminal has been established at Csepel, Budapest Free Port. It was completed in 1971 and all ISO containers up to 40 ft in length are handled by inland waterway, rail and road.

Csepel Container Terminal:

The terminal has a concrete paved parking and marshalling area of 4,500 m² (48,358 sq ft) which is capable of extension when required. It is equipped with a 32 ton container crane, manufactured by Hungarian Ship and Crane Works in co-operation with Mohr and Federhaff of West Germany and is fitted with an automatic spreader. Equipment also includes a 25 ton sideloader and semi-trailer chassis and tractors.

MAHART Fluvial Navigation Management
(Address, telephone, etc as MAHART head office above)
GENERAL:

Towed and pushed barge trains, as well as self propelled barges, are operated along the Danube from Reni up to Regensburg and also on the River Theis. The fleet includes units having holds suitable for the carriage of containers.

MAHART Sea Shipping Management
Budapest XXI, Szabadkikötö ut 5
PO Box 98 Budapest, Csepel 1
Telephone: 478-948
Telex: Detert, Budapest 442

GENERAL:

Seagoing vessels up to 13,600 dwt are operated. These conventional vessels oper-ate scheduled services on Mediterranean, Europe-India, Europe-South America routes; calls include North West European Port. Containers are carried on these vessels as and when required.

Experimental shipments, up to 26 20 ft units at a time, have been made in 1971 with fruit and vegetables to Australia through Hamburg using Hapag Lloyd containers. The rail journey from Budapest to the Federal German Republic took a total of 19 hours.

CONTAINER FREIGHT FORWARDER:
MASPED (Hungarian General Forwarding Enterprise)
Budapest V, Kristóf tér 2
POSTAL ADDRESS: PO Box 123, Budapest V
TELEPHONE: 183-920

TELEX: 984
DIRECTORS:
  Mr. Lendvai
  Dr. Hunkar

MASPED is a nationally owned enterprise which acts as the forwarding agency for all international traffic. Regular container services operate to US, Canada, Australia and UK. MASPED also leases containers and has established a depot for shipping companies and other leasing companies' containers at Budapest. This organisation is responsible for the Hungarian section of the '.Russian Land Bridge' service between Europe and Japan.

The company are agents for Contrans GmbH of Hamburg and Deutrans, Rostock; also sub agents of XTRA of Boston, Mass., USA.

REPUBLIC OF IRELAND

CORK

Cork Harbour Commissioners,
Custom House Street,
Cork
TELEPHONE: Cork 23125 (5 lines)
PRINCIPAL OFFICIALS:
L. A. French, (*General Manager*)
Captain R. P. Tyrrell (*Harbour Master*)
D. J. O'Neill, (*Harbour Engineer*)
J. B. O'Sullivan (*Planning and Development Manager*)
F. C. Cunnane, (*Finance Controller*)
ROLL-ON FACILITIES:
Tivoli

The berth can accept vessels of up to 23 m beam and draught of 5·7 m (18·7 ft). It is equipped with an adjustable ramp and adjoins a compound area of 10 hectares (24·7 acres). The facility also has a modern passenger terminal building.

CONTAINER FACILITIES:
Tivoli

The Tivoli container terminal is 304 m (997·3 ft) in length and with depths alongside varying from 6·0 m to 9·2 m (19·7-30·2 ft). There is an open storage space of up to 15 hectares (37·1 acres) behind the berths. The berths are serviced by a 30 ton Leibherr container crane.

TERMINAL WORKING HOURS:

0800-1800 hours (anytime nights or weekend as necessary for all operations.

SERVICES:
Roll-on:
B + I Line—Swansea
Conventional and Container:
Bugsier—Hamburg and Bremen
Dammers—Rotterdam, Antwerp and Le Havre
Head Line—Antwerp
Kersten and Hunik—Antwerp
Tor Line—Gothenburg
Containers:
Iropa—Rotterdam

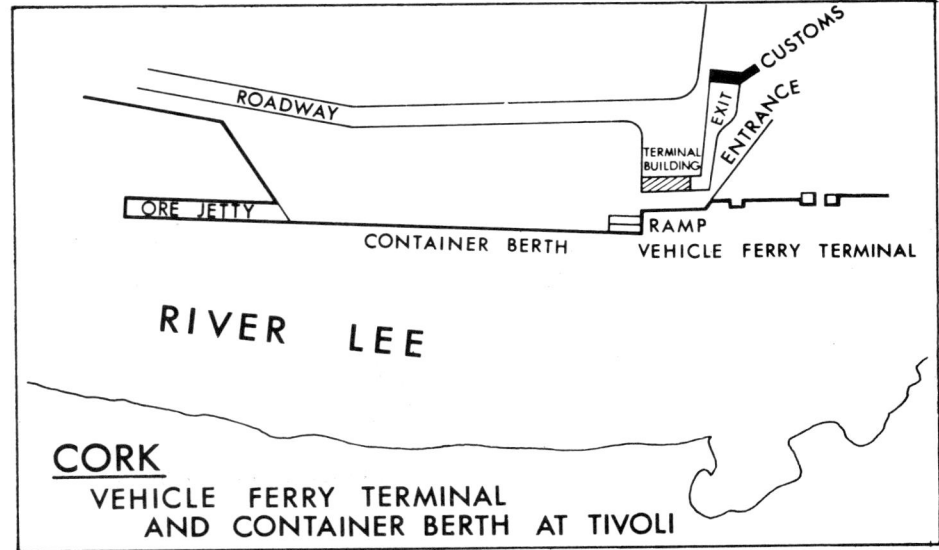

CORK
VEHICLE FERRY TERMINAL
AND CONTAINER BERTH AT TIVOLI

Tivoli Terminal, Cork.

The B + I Line terminal at Cork.

DUBLIN

Dublin Port and Docks Board
19/21 Westmorland Street
Dublin 2 Ireland
TELEPHONE: 778 238
TELEX: 5476
PRINCIPAL OFFICIALS:
D. A. Hegarty (*General Manager*)
J. P. Murphy (*Secretary*)
P. M. O'Sullivan (*Engineer in Chief*)
J Furlong (*Commercial and Warehouse Manager*)
Captain H. J. Walsh (*Harbour Master*)

ROLL-ON/ROLL-OFF FACILITIES
Ferryport
This berth can accept vessels up to 118 m (387 ft) in length, 18·28 m (60 ft) beam with a draught of 5·79 m (19 ft). It is equipped with an adjustable ramp and has 9750 m² (105,000 sq ft) of parking space.

CONTAINER FACILITIES
All berths at present in operation have limited quayside storage and containers are moved to back up areas behind the quay by trailer. All scotch derricks are capable of a loading and unloading cycle of between 10 and 15 units per hour.
B & I North Wall (No 17)
This terminal is capable of accepting two vessels of 78·02 m (256 ft) in length drawing 4·57 m (15 ft). It is equipped with two scotch derrick cranes (28 and 25 tons)
British Railways North Wall
Capable of accepting two vessels of up to 76·2 m (250 ft) in length drawing between 3·96 and 4·57 m (13 and 15 ft), this facility is equipped with one 30 ton scotch derrick, a 4 ton jib derrick and 2 × 7½ ton transporter type cranes.
Bristol Seaway South Bank Quay
This quay has a length of 122 m (400 ft) with a depth alongside of 7·62 m (25 ft) at low water. Equipment consists of one 30 ton container gantry crane and one 30 ton derrick crane. There are 1·62 hectares (4 acres) of parking space for containers.
OCEAN PIER WEST (No. 33)
This terminal, which is equipped with a 35 ton scotch derrick, can accept vessels up to 152·4 m (500 ft) in length with a draught of 9·14 m (30 ft).
OCEAN PIER SOUTH (No. 35)
Equipped with a 32 ton derrick crane, this quay is 142·3 m (467 ft) long with 9·75 m (32 ft) alongside at low water. Used by Palgrave Murphy.
OCEAN PIER EAST (No. 37)
This quay can accept vessels up to 106·7 m (350 ft) in length with a 15·24 m (50 ft) beam. There is one 25 ton derrick crane and 8,000 m² (2 acres) of storage space. Used by Transport Ferry Service.

Dublin—The North Wall facilities can be seen in the background with the Ocean Terminal in the foreground.

Car Ferry Terminal, Dublin.

BRITISH RAILWAYS TERMINAL
This terminal, completed in mid 1970, handles vessels up to 121·9 m (400 ft) in length drawing 5·18 m (17 ft). It is equipped with two container gantry cranes and two Goliath gantry cranes for yard handling and storage. The overall area of the terminal is 3 hectares (7·5 acres).

CONTAINER FACILITIES UNDER CONSTRUCTION
B and I Container Terminal This will be capable of accepting vessels of 5·18 m (17 ft) draught and will be equipped with one container gantry crane. On completion at the end of 1971 it will have 6·07 hectares (15 acres) of parking and marshalling space.

SHIPPING COMPANIES PROVIDING CONTAINER SERVICES:

Company	Berths	Service
Irish Shipping Ltd. (Manchester Liners)	Alexandra Quay/Ocean Pier	Dublin—New York and East Coast USA —every 3 weeks Dublin—Montreal—every 3 to 4 weeks
U.S. Lines	Alexandra Quay/Ocean Pier	Dublin—New York, Baltimore, Norfolk —every 3 weeks.
B. & I. Steam Packet Co. Ltd.	North Wall/Ferry Port	Dublin—Liverpool. Nightly except Saturday
British Railways	North Wall	Dublin—Holyhead
Bristol Seaway	South Bank Quay	Dublin—Bristol. 5 sailings weekly.
Transport Ferry Service	Ocean Pier	Dublin—Preston—daily
Dublin Maritime Ltd.	North Quay Ext./Ocean Pier	Dublin—France/Holland—3 sailings weekly

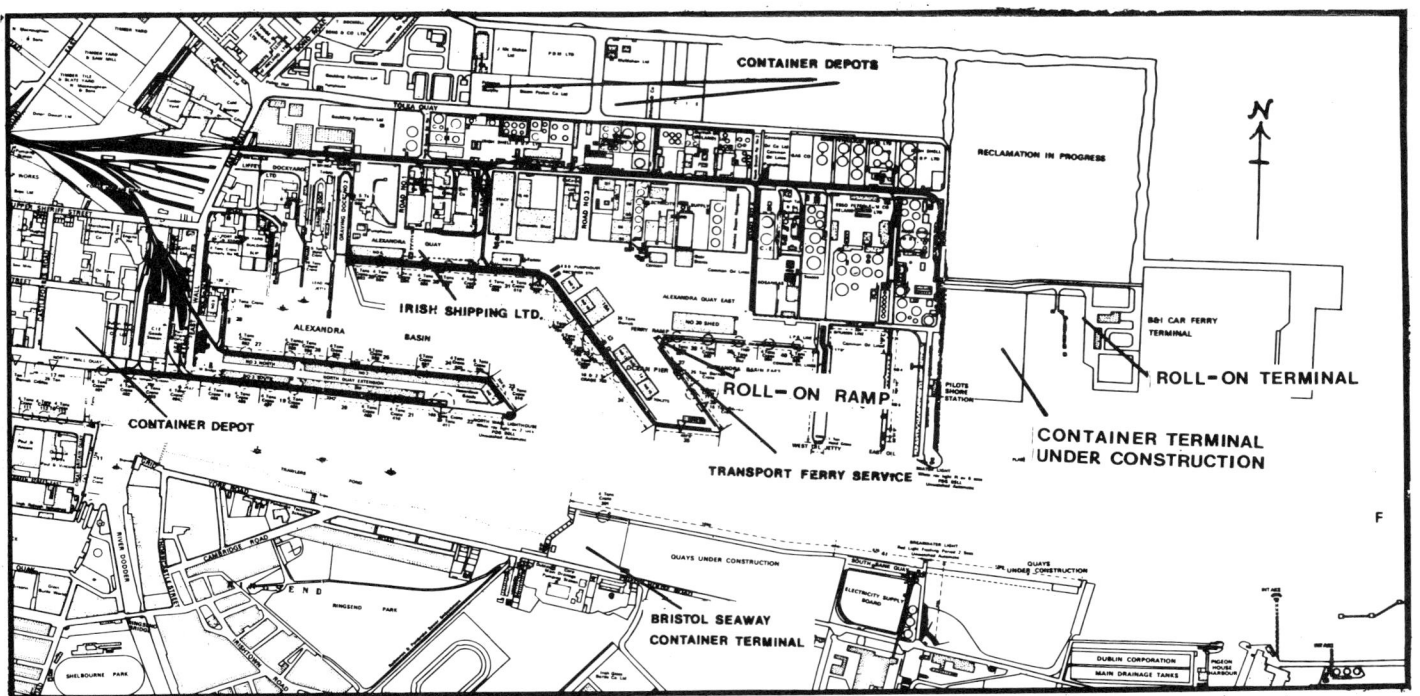

TERMINAL WORKING HOURS
Normal working hours are 0800-1700 hrs. Overtime is worked as and when required.

CONTAINER REPAIR FACILITIES:
Leigh & Son Ltd., 94/99 Francis St., Dublin 8. (Phone 58462)
Owen Butler & Son, East Wall Road, Dublin 3. (Phone 41620).

ROLL-ON SERVICES:
B and I Line operate up to three services daily depending upon the time of year, to Liverpool from the Ferryport. The ramp is designed to take freight (up to 140 ton vehicles) as well as private motor cars and coaches.

A ramp to accommodate vehicle-carrying ferry ships with bow or stern doors is available at the junction of Ocean Pier and Alexandra Quay East.

CUSTOMS REQUIREMENTS:
(a) Groupage type containers cleared immediately on discharge (provided container manifest is available) by landing officer to groupage or inland clearance depot. Container is stripped at such a depot and entries are accepted for each individual consignment, which are then cleared separately.

(b) Ships convenience or L.C.L. containers not carrying own manifest must be stripped into a transit shed and goods are treated as if they had come by conventional stow.

(c) Unit loads are subject to a percentage examination. There is a screening process operating in Dublin and a high percentage of goods are cleared 'without examination' The balance of entries are passed to landing officer who then decides which containers he wishes to examine. This examination may consist only of the opening of a container or probably in the case of high duty goods the actual stripping and checking of the contents. Only a small percentage however are subjected to examination. In general containers are cleared within 24 hours of the lodgement of the entry at the landing station.

UNIT LOAD TRAFFIC—1970

	Cross Channel		Foreign	
	Imports	Exports	Imports	Exports
No. of loaded containers	37,863	32,075	4,764	2,697
No. of loaded flats	23,335	10,494	679	182
	61,198	42,569	5,443	2,879
No. of empty containers	7,315	13,093	346	505
No. of empty flats	50	12,213	13	27
	7,365	25,306	359	532
	Tons	Tons	Tons	Tons
Total weight of above	622,081	459,299	68,700	34,253
Total weight of goods carried	500,120	336,489	55,859	26,432

A B + I Line vessel loading at Dublin

INLAND CONTAINER CLEARANCE DEPOT
    Operated by the Dublin Port and Docks Board.

GROUPAGE:
    Operated by B + I, British Railways and Dublin Port & Docks Board.

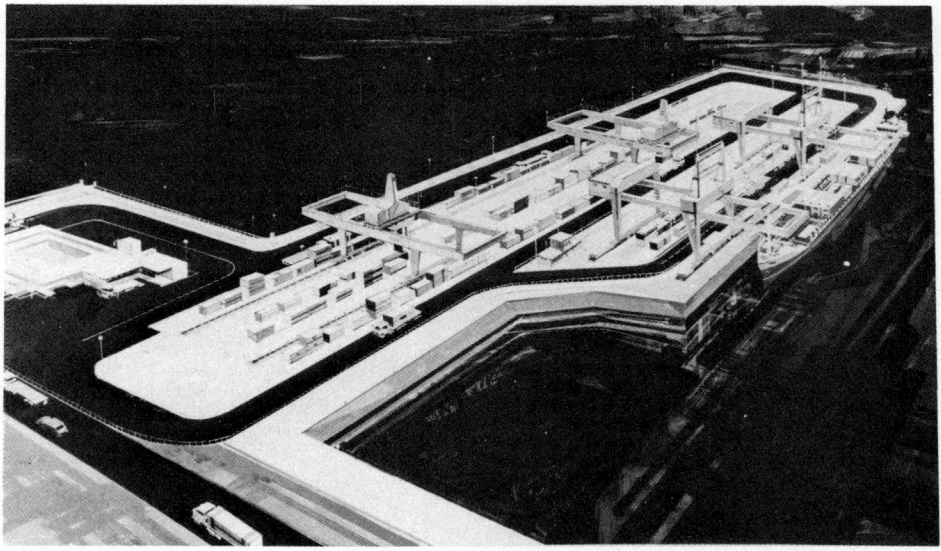

An impression of the British Railways Terminal at Dublin.

New Ross Harbour Board
New Ross
Ireland
TELEPHONE: 21303 (*Harbour Office*)
PRINCIPAL OFFICIALS:
Captain D. M. Carroll (*Secretary and Harbour Master*)

Waterford Harbour Commissioners,
Harbour Office, Ireland
TELEPHONE: 4907/8

PRINCIPAL OFFICIALS:
M. F. McQuillan (*General Manager*)
Capt. R. J. Farrell (*Harbour Master*)
M. J. Curtin (*Collector of Rates*)

CONTAINER TRAFFIC:

Year	Inwards	Outwards
1968	86,772 tons	115,598 tons
1969	117,084 tons	130,485 tons
1970	147,141 tons	185,505 tons

It is estimated that in 1971 the traffic will increase to 162,000 tons (16,900 units) inwards and 212,500 tons (20,000 units) outwards.

NEW ROSS

CONTAINER FACILITY:

The Container jetty, west side, is capable of accepting vessels up to 121·9 m (400 ft) in length, 18·29 m (60 ft) beam on a draught of between 5·79 and 7·0 m (19 and 23 ft). The berth is equipped with a 45 ton derrick crane and there is unlimited space for storing containers.

CONTAINER SERVICE:
British and Irish Steam Packet Co., Ltd. operate a twice weekly service between New Ross and Newport.

WATERFORD

Frank Cassin Wharf, Waterford.

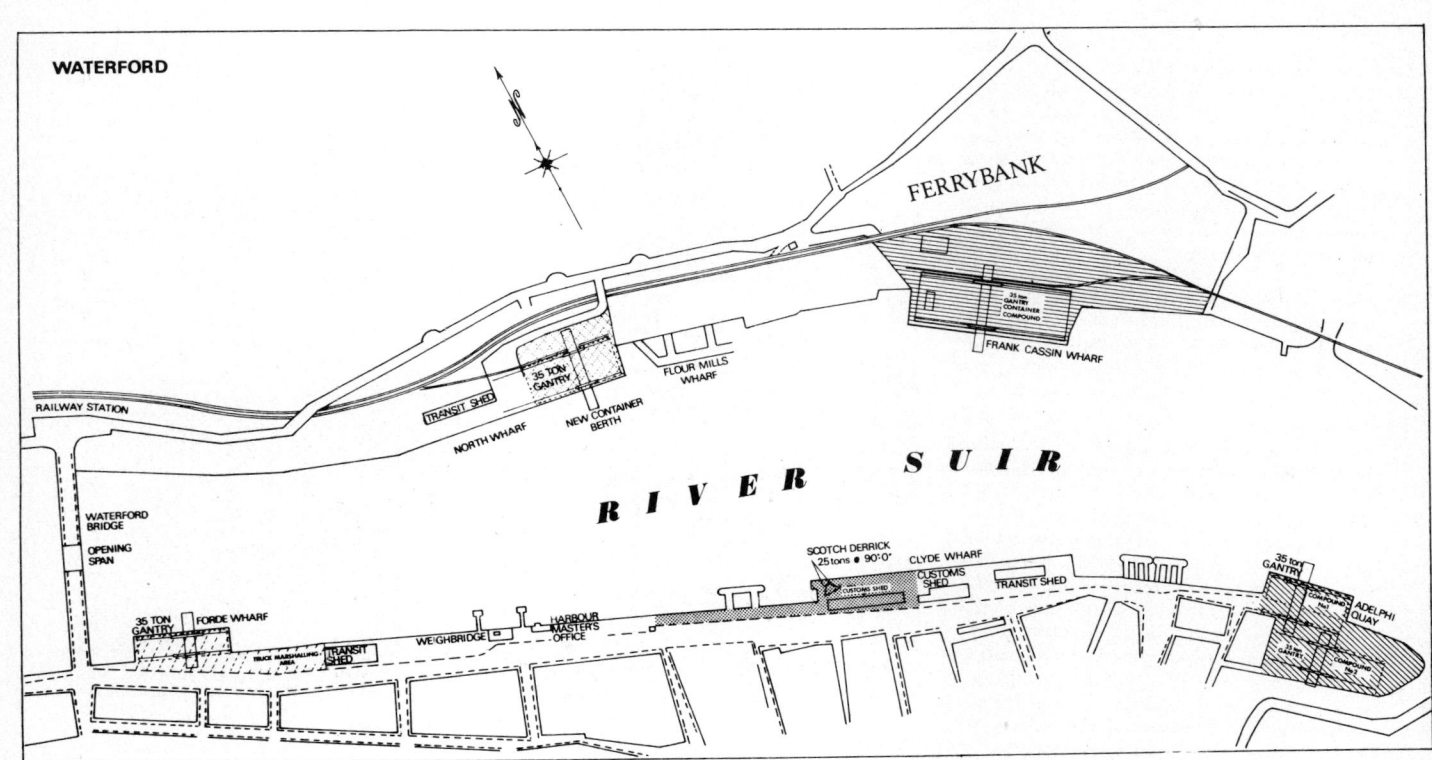

CONTAINER FACILITIES:

Name	Maximum size of vessel accepted due to limits of approaches, lock or berth						Cranage	Parking Areas for containers
	length		beam		draught			
	m	ft	m	ft	m	ft		
Frank Cassin Wharf	144·6	475	16·5	54	6·7	22	1 Gantry	7525 m² (9,000 sq yds)
Adelphi Quay (this wharf to be developed)	91·4	300	15·2	50	4·9	16	1 × 15 ton Scotch Derrick (Gantry to be added)	2257 m² (2,700 sq yds) (to be increased to 6,689 m² (8,000 sq yds)
Clyde Wharf	73·1	240	12·2	40	4·9	16	1 × 25 ton Scotch Derrick	4180 m² (5,000 sq yds) (with use of straddle carrier)
North Wharf	144·6	475	15·2	50	7·6	25	1 Gantry	3679 m² (4,400 sq yds)
Forde Wharf	144·6	475	15·2	50	6·7	22	2 Gantries	2508 m² (3,000 sq yds)

CUSTOMS REQUIREMENTS:
Original invoice, inport licence (if necessary) for clearance. Clearance is given immediately and those containers required for inspection are examined at the berth storage area.

TERMINAL WORKING HOURS:
24 hours per day if necessary.

CONTAINER REPAIR FACILITIES:
None.

SHIPPING COMPANIES PROVIDING CONTAINER SERVICES:

	Name	Berth	Service
1	Bell Line Ferrybank, Waterford Telephone: 5811	Frank Cassin	Waterford to Newport—4 sailings weekly Waterford to Rotterdam—Weekly
2	British Railways Adelphi Quay, Waterford Telephone: 4841	Adelphi	Waterford to Fishguard—3 sailings weekly
3	Waterford Maritime The Quay, Waterford Telephone: 4170	Clyde	Waterford to Rotterdam—Weekly/ to Antwerp Fortnightly

INLAND TRANSPORT

Coras Iompair Eireann (C.I.E.)

Irish Transport Company, Heuston Station, Dublin 8
TELEPHONE: 771871
OFFICIALS:
D. Herlihy (*General Manager*)
J. J. Byrne (*Deputy General Manager*)
E. O'Flaherty (*Asst. Gen Man. Operations*)
L. Collins (*Asst. Gen. Man., Engineering*)
J. P. MacMahon (*Asst. Gen. Man . Marketing*)

Principal Officials concerned with Container Traffic:
E. O'Flaherty (*Assistant General Manager, Operations*)
Heuston Station, Dublin 8

P. J. Darmody (*Transport Control and Planning Officer*)
Connolly Station, Dublin 1
J. P. MacMahon (*Assistant General Manager, Marketing*)
P. G. Byrne (*Commercial Manager*)
35 Lr Abbey Street, Dublin 1

GENERAL:

Scheduled container trains operate between principal cities and towns, including Dublin/Derry & Dublin/Belfast. Mobile gantry cranes of 30-ton capacity for container transfer are located at Claremorris, Cork, Dublin (Heuston), Dublin (North Wall), Dublin (Tolka Quay-Irish Ferryways), Galway, Limerick. Fixed and mobile cranes of lesser lifting capacity are located at principal stations and depots. The company acts as hauliers for companies who own their own containers, such as B. & I. Line, Bellferry Ltd., B.R., B. & L., Guinness, etc. Unit load services are operated by the company's subsidiary, Irish Ferryways, between (Tolka Quay)/Preston, and New Ross/Newport, S. Wales; Drogheda/Preston; and Larne/Ardrossan.

During 1970 40 ft bogie container flat cars were introduced which can take all ISO type units up to 8·5 ft in height. It is proposed to extend container liner train operations in the future.

Cross-channel container traffic

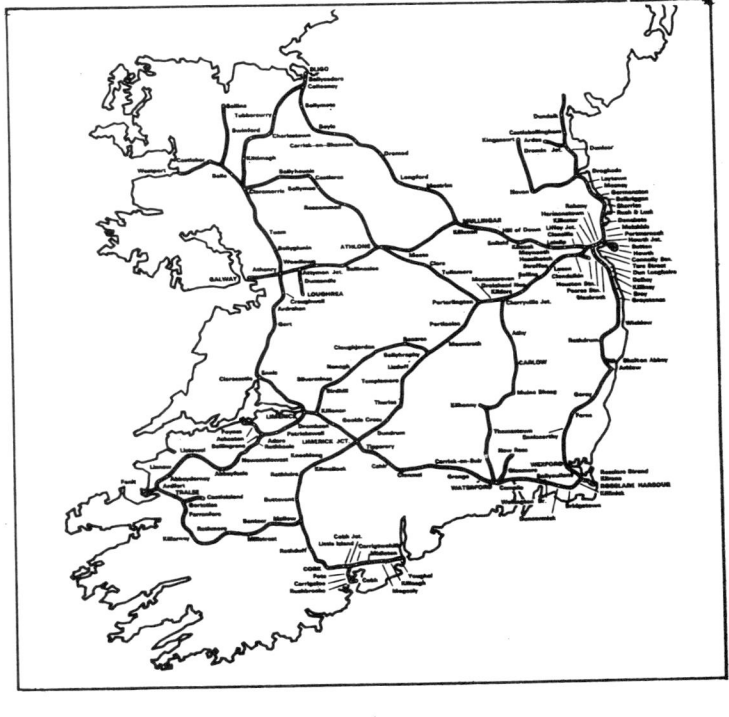

C I E Freight network

CONTAINERS OWNED:
ISO Type:

Dry Cargo	200	20 × 8 × 8
Insulated	100	20 × 8 × 8
Refrigerated	3	20 × 8 × 8
Flats	335	20 × 8

Others:

Dry Cargo	63	18·9 × 7·6 × 7·6
Dry Cargo	30	7·6 × 7·1 × 7·5
Insulated	19	19 × 7·9 × 8·3
Flats	213	20 ·05× 7·3
Glucose Tanks	14	Between 300 and 800 gallons

B + I. Line's Linertrain which operates a daily container rail service between Dublin and Cork.

CIE Hopper Container.

ITALY
BARI

Consorzio del Porto di Bari

Via Marchese di Montrone 11
Bari
TELEPHONE: 21.45.71
CHAIRMAN: On Prof Enrico Alba
CONTAINER FACILITIES:
Provisional Terminal

The Bacino di Levante is at present used for container handling with an area for container stacking of 2 hectares (4·9 acres). The quay has a depth alongside of 9·15 m (30 ft) and is serviced by semi portal quay cranes.

Bacino di Marisabella

This quay is planned with a length of 300 m (984 ft) and a depth alongside of 11 m (36 ft). There will be a total area of 10 hectares (25 acres) and container gantry cranes are planned for installation.

CONTAINER SERVICES:

Refrigerated containers move through Bari en route between Trieste and Catania. It is hoped to introduce services to Greece, Yugoslavia and Eastern Mediterranean Ports.

Bari—Impression of the Terminal at Bacino de Marisabella

RAIL ACCESS:

The Italian State Railways have programmed the construction of a container terminal.

CONTAINER DEVELOPMENT COMPANY:
Sudcontainer S. p-a.
presso Camera di Commercio
Bari

CAGLIARI

Camera di Commercio, Industria Artigianato ed Agricultura di Cagliari
Largo Carlo Felice
TELEPHONE: 666.135

Consorzio per l'area di Sviluppo Industriale di Cagliari
Corso Vittorio Emanuele 1
TELEPHONE: 61.725 665.613

GENERAL:

The Chamber of Commerce are responsible for operating the present port facilities where the Port Captain controls navigational matters. The Industrial Consortium are concerned with the development of a port facility immediately to the west of the Commercial Port.

CONTAINER AND ROLL-ON FACILITIES:
Commercial Port:

Ferry vessels berth stern on to the present quays; these vessels are equipped with their own ramps for these operations.

Cagliari Industrial Area:

The Consortium have plans to develop Cagliari into a Mediterranean transhipment centre for containers. It has been reported that one container berth may be operational in the near future.

CIVITAVECCHIA

Consorzio Autonomo per il Porto Civitavecchia

Largo Cavour 6
Civitavecchia

TELEPHONE: 21 751

CHAIRMAN: Alberto Albicini

CONTAINER FACILITIES:

A small number of containers moves through the Port at present; these are handled by 40 ton quay cranes and on shore by a Belotti mobile crane fitted with container spreader. A quay length of 186 m (610 ft) with 8·8 m (29 ft) depth of water alongside has been reserved in Nuova Darsena No. 1 for container handling in the future.

Civitavecchia—Belotti B69C mobile crane equipped with spreader.

GENOA

Consorzio Autonomo del Porto di Genova,
Palazzo S. Georgio, 16100 Genoa
TELEPHONE: 2090
TELEX: 27112
CHAIRMAN: Dr. F. Manzitti
CONTAINER FACILITIES:

Ponte Libia (West Side)

This terminal has a quay length of 400 m (1,313 ft) with a depth of water alongside of 11 m (36 ft). There is a total container storage area of 4·5 hectares (11·1 acres). (2 hectares in the southern area, 1·8 hectares in the northern area and ·6 hectare to the north of the groupage sheds). The facility is equipped with a 40-ton Paceco-Vickers-Savigliano container gantry crane. The crane has an outreach over water of 28·8 m (94·5 ft). Six 30 ton straddle carriers capable of stacking three high have been provided. There is full rail access with a 14,000 m² rail marshalling yard. A shed with an area of 2,500 m² (26,910 sq ft) has been provided.

Ponte Ronco (East Side)

This terminal will come into service in 1971. The quay length is 400 m (1,312 ft) with a depth alongside of 12 m (39·4 ft) and there will eventually be a total area of between 65,000 m² and 85,000 m² (16 acres and 21 acres). Three 45 ton Paceco-Vickers-Savigliano container gantry cranes with an outreach of 35 m (115 ft) are being provided.

FUTURE DEVELOPMENT:
Plans are being drawn up for a new Port at Voltri Harbour some 7 km from Genoa and the earliest date for the completion of this project, which will include three container facilities and a number of roll-on/roll-off berths, is 1980.

ROLL-ON FACILITIES:
The Shipping Line Grendi-Tarros have a leased berth at Calata Benghasi. Details can be found under this company's entry in the Shipowner's section.

CONTAINER SERVICES
AEIL	US Ports	fortnightly
Fabre Line	US Ports	weekly
Hansa Line	US Ports	fortnightly
Sea Land	US Ports	weekly
Grendi-Tarros	Cagliari	twice weekly

ROLL-ON SERVICES:
Grendi-Tarros	Porto Torres	twice weekly

Genoa—Ponte Libia

Genoa—The Ponte Libia marshalling area.

Ignazio Messina	Tripoli	weekly

TRAFFIC:
Approximately 36,000 containers moved through Genoa in 1969 making a total of about 400,000 tons of cargo handled. In 1970 traffic increased to about 71,000 containers.

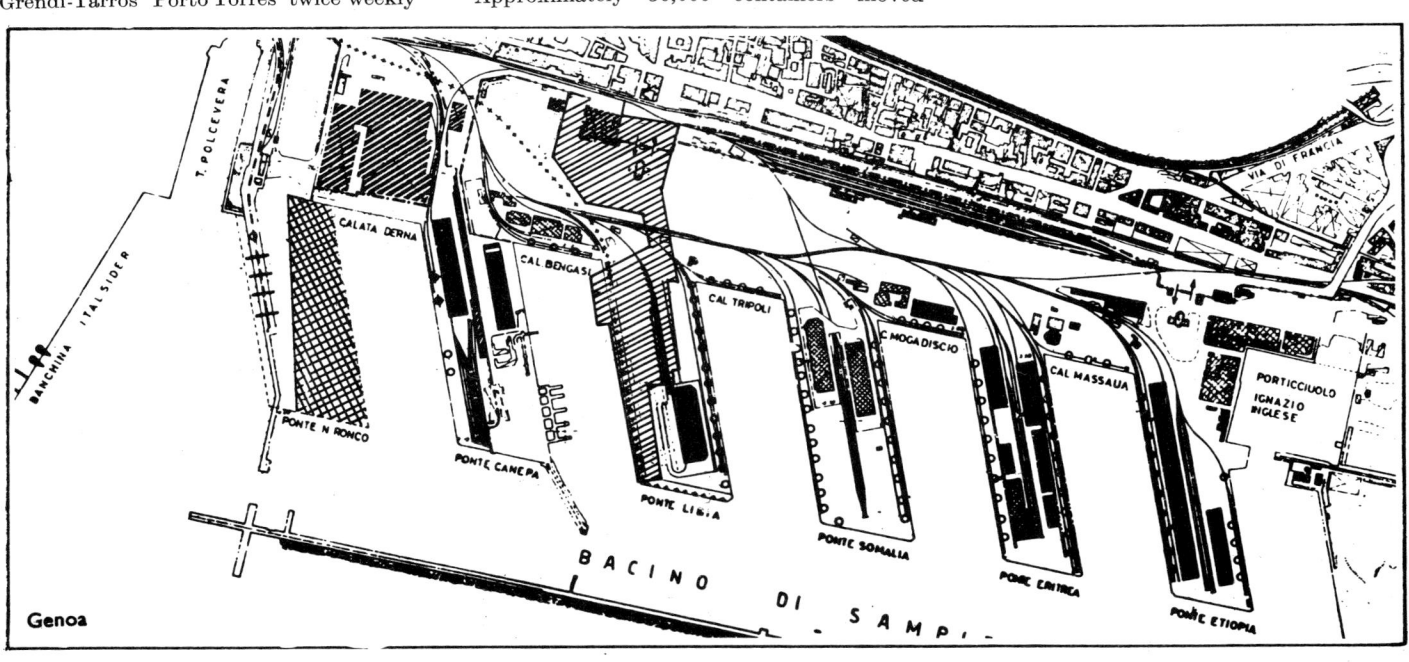

Genoa

LA SPEZIA

Capitaneria di Porto di La Spezia
La Spezia
CONTAINER FACILITIES:

There is a container facility with a quay length of about 100 m (328 ft) equipped with a container gantry crane, the facility came into service in April 1971.

SERVICES:

Ellerman Containership Service to Garston every 7-14 days.

La Spezia—an Ellerman vessel alongside

LEGHORN

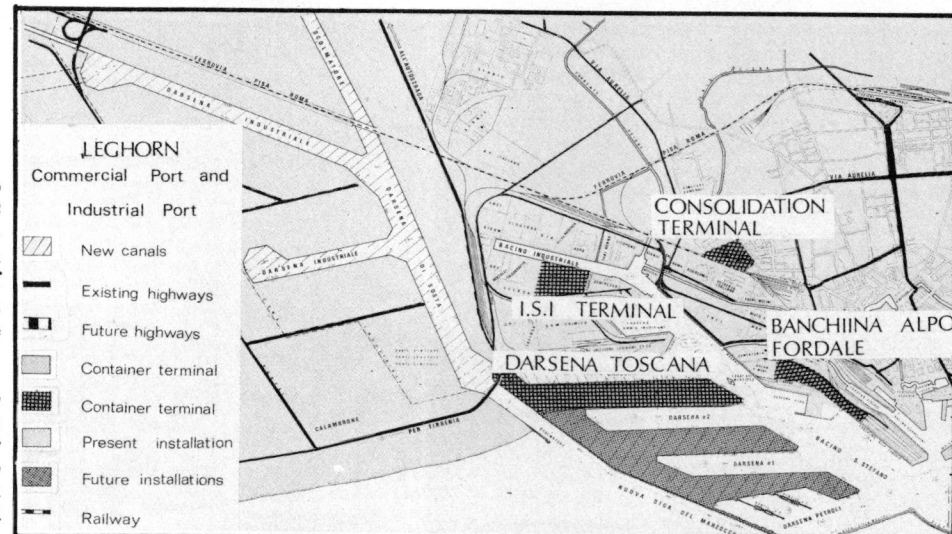

Capitaneria di Porto di Livorno,
Via del Molo Mediceo, 5, Livorno, Italy
Leghorn Chamber of Commerce
Piazza del Municipio 48, Leghorn
TELEPHONE: 23.150
CONTAINER FACILITIES:

AEIL Terminal

Immobiliare Sviluppo Industriale have developed a site covering 11 hectares (27·2 acres) on the Bacino Industriale in conjunction with American Export Isbrandtsen Lines. This facility has a quay length of about 400 m (1,312 ft) with a depth of 10 m (32·8 ft) alongside. It is equipped with a Peiner container gantry crane.

Banchina Alto Fondale

The north east end of the quay of the Banchina and about 10 hectares (25 acres) of land have been reserved for container operations. This facility is planned to come into service in 1971. It will be equipped with two coaling cranes specially adapted for container handling, five straddle carriers, 800 trailers and 70 tractors. The container storage area will cover some 4 hectares (10 acres) and the facility will be operated on a common user basis.

Consolidation Depot

The Leghorn Container Handling Terminal Company have a consolidation and marshalling depot close to St. Marks station in the dock area.

Darsena Toscana

Plans are in hand to develop an area of reclaimed land into a container terminal which will ultimately provide 2,000 m (9,842 ft) of quay length.

CONTAINER SHIPPING SERVICES

American Export Isbrandtsen Lines—USA —fortnightly.

Fabre Line—USA—weekly.

RAIL ACCESS

Italian State Railways have provided a rail served common user terminal equipped with a 40 ton Paceco yard gantry crane. This facility, situated close to the Calata Tripoli, is intended to serve the Railways' container traffic with Sardinia.

Leghorn—The completed AEIL Terminal

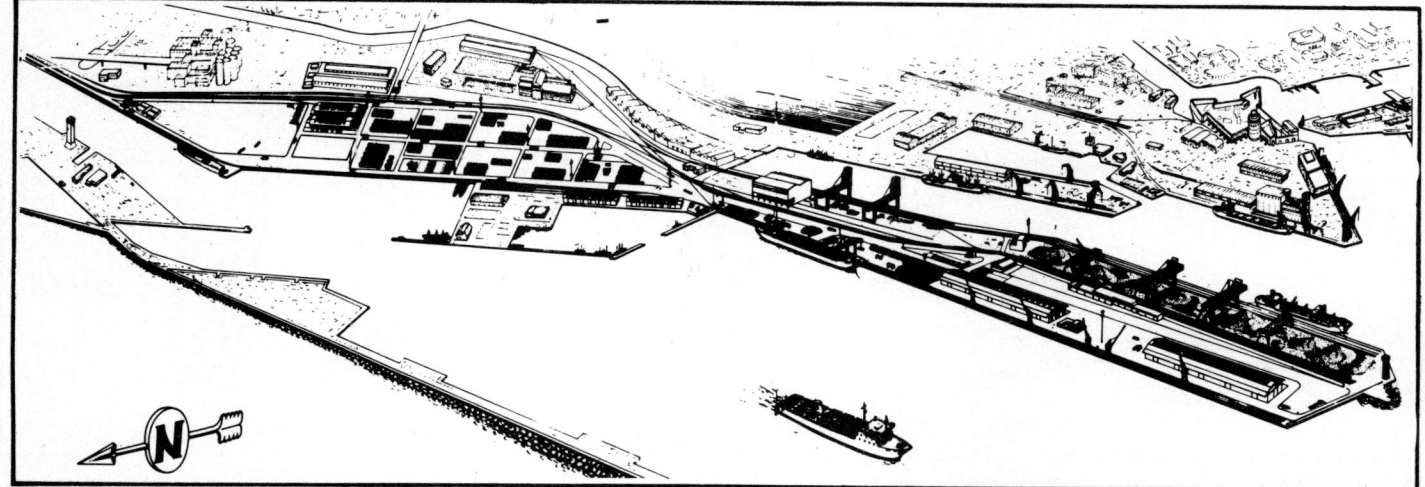

Leghorn—Impression of Alto Fondale Terminal

NAPLES

Ente Autonomo del Porto de Napoli
Molo Pisacane, Naples
TELEPHONE: 32.0954
PRESIDENT: Dott Arch Raimondo Rivieccio
CONTAINER FACILITIES:
Flavia Gioia Quay

Flavia Gioia Quay has been partially equipped for limited container traffic where some 16,000 m² (4 acres) have been cleared. One 40 ton container gantry crane is on order. Additional spaces are being made available for storage in adjacent areas; there are some 5,000 m² (1·2 acres) of space behind Calata Granili which provides a temporary container facility. A further 40,000 m² (10 acres) has been provided at S. Erasmo.

Pontile V E II
OPERATOR:
Magazzini Generale Silos & Frigoriferi S.p.a.
    Piazzale Stazione Marittima Napoli (Porto)
    Casella Postale 347
    Naples
TELEPHONE: 32.18.70

The Pontile V quay has a length of 715 m (2,346 ft) providing four berths. The area for container handling and storage amounts to 3 hectares (7·4 acres). Container handling in the storage area and at the berths is

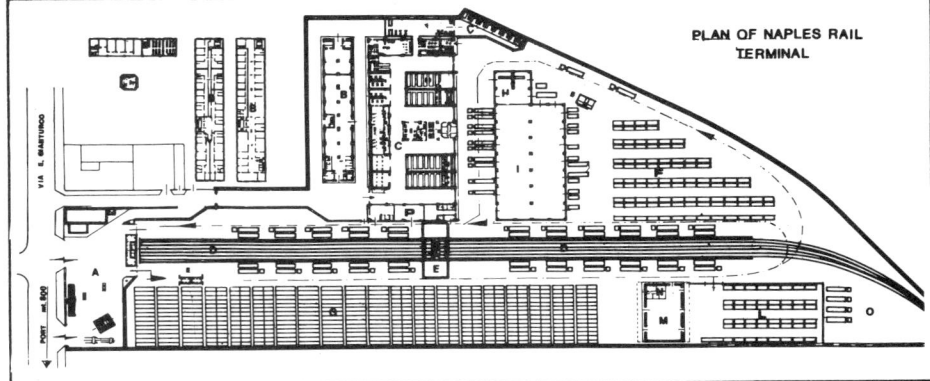

Naples—Plan of the Rail Terminal

undertaken by an 80 ton Ormig mobile crane and empties are stacked using fork lift trucks. The Sea Land and Hansa Line services use the facility.

FUTURE DEVELOPMENT:
A plan to establish a container marshalling, storage and clearance area some 20 km from the Port is under consideration.

RAIL ACCESS:
Italian State Railways have provided a container terminal some 800 m from the port area. It is equipped with a 35 ton 2-3-2 Paceco-Vickers container yard gantry crane.

TRAFFIC:
Some 12,000 containers moved through the port in 1969 and 20,000 units in 1970.

CONTAINER SHIPPING SERVICES:
American Export Isbrandtsen Lines, Hansa Line and Sea Land provide services to the USA.

PALERMO

Ente Autonomo del Porto di Palermo
Palermo
Sicily
DIRECTOR GENERAL: Dott Paolo Cimino
CONTAINER AND ROLL-ON FACILITIES

At present container and roll-on traffic is handled at the Banchina Puntone where a total of 4·5 hectares (11 acres) with a quay frontage with 12 m (39·4 ft) of water alongside is available for these operations.

FUTURE PLANS:
The first phase of development planned is to transform the Pontile S. Lucia into a roll-on quay capable of accepting at least two vessels at the same time. A container crane will be installed if the potential for this form of transport materialises; it has been estimated that some 468,000 tons inwards and 290,000 tons of cargo outwards could be containerised.

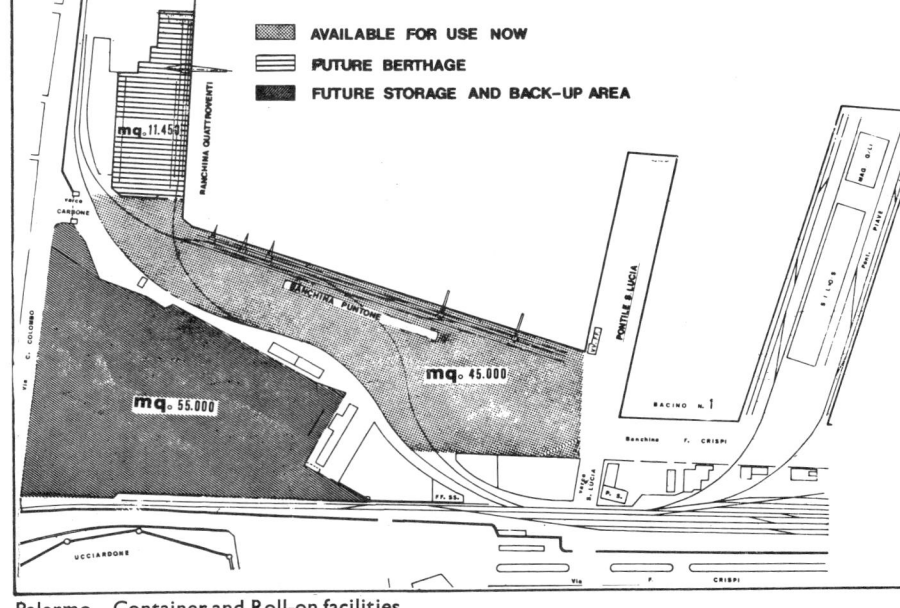

Palermo—Container and Roll-on facilities

Palermo—An impression of the first stage of development.

TRIESTE

Ente Autonomo del Porto di Trieste
Punto Franco Vecchio, Trieste
TELEPHONE: 30.005

CONTAINER FACILITIES

Pier VII, with more than 15 hectares (37 acres) of space, has recently been completed as a facility for container ships but no handling appliances have so far been provided. Pier VII is being used as a starting point for the large trade which is anticipated will develop in the movement of containerised fruit and vegetables which will move from Greece, Israel, Turkey and other Mediterranean and near east ports through the Trieste railhead to Northern Europe. One 45 ton container gantry crane is due for delivery for this facility in 1971.

A model of Pier VII, Trieste.

VENICE

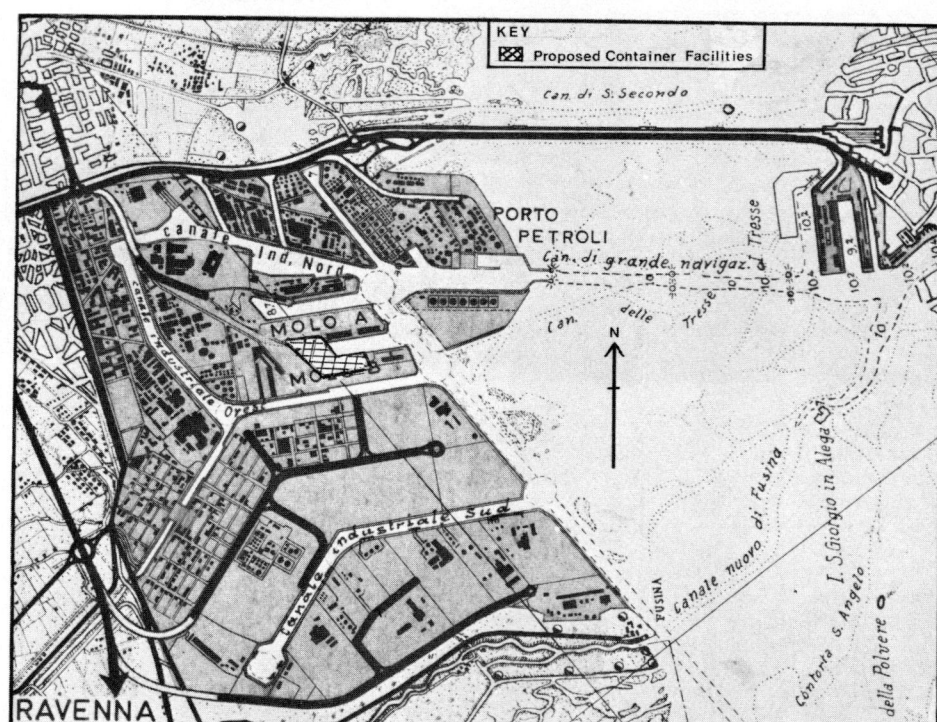

Piovveditorato al Porto di Venezia

Casella Postale N 410,
TELEPHONE: 703.244
CONTAINER FACILITIES:
Pier A, Porto Marghera is at present being developed for container operations. It is equipped for roll-on operations and a fixed 25 ton crane is used for stacking containers. A 35 ton quay crane with spreader is used for ship handling. Some 3·4 hectares (8·5 acres) is available for development.
Pier B, Porto Marghera, is scheduled for development and will provide 7·8 hectares (19·5 acres). A quay length of 250 m (820 ft) is envisaged. A 4ʊ ton container gantry crane and two straddle carriers are planned for installation.

Venice—Location of proposed container facilities

ITALIAN STATE RAILWAYS (FS)

Italian State Railways (FS)
General Management,
Piazza della Croce Rossa, Rome
OPERATIONS DEPARTMENT (Servizio Movimento): for information on operations.
COMMERCIAL AND TRAFFIC DEPARTMENT (Servizio Commerciale e del Traffico): for information on rates, and commercial and legal matters.
GENERAL:
About 4,000 privately-owned ISO containers, 20, 30 and 40 ft in length, are F.S. registered. These are owned by freight forwarding agents, road hauliers and other operators.
INTERNATIONAL SERVICES:
Rotterdam—Milan Rogoredo:
  5 complete trains per week, each way.
Zeebrugge—Milan Rogoredo:
  5 complete trains per week. In addition individual containers are carried in regular fast freight train services.
INTERNAL SERVICES:
A special fast container train operates three times per week between Milan—Monterotondo—Naples. Individual containers are also carried in the regular fast freight services.
CONTAINER TERMINALS:
Milan Rogoredo
This terminal has an overall area of 1·8 hectares (4·45 acres) and is equipped with a 30 ton gantry crane and mobile cranes. Some 14,000 containers moved inwards and 16,500 outwards in 1970 it is estimated that in 1971 the total traffic inwards and outwards will be about 50,000 units.

Milan   Rogoredo Terminal.

Naples Traccia Terminal SOA
OPERATOR:
International Container Terminal S.p.a.
100 E Gianturco Str.
80142 Naples
TELEPHONE: 353880
TELEX: 71347
This common user facility, owned by a subsidiary of the State Railways, has an area of 6·6 hectares (16·3 acres) and is equipped with a 30 ton Paceco Vickers 2-3-2 container yard gantry crane, side-loaders, tractors and trailers and mobile cranes, fork lift trucks, etc. It is situated some 800 m from the port area.

Container Terminals in Service and Proposed

FUTURE DEVELOPMENTS:
Terminals are planned for Castello (Florence), Bari, Pomezia (about 20 km (12·4 miles) South of Rome), Turin, Bologna, Verona, Padua and Ancona.
The need for Maritime terminals at Leghorn, Genoa, Naples and Trieste is also being examined. Moreover, rail terminals to serve the ferry routes from Sicily and Sardinia are also under consideration.

INLAND CLEARANCE DEPOTS

Rivalta Scrivia S.p.a.

HEAD OFFICE:
16121 Genova
Via Ceccardi 1-15
PO Box 670
TELEPHONE: 580865
TELEX: 27367
OPERATIONS CENTRE:
15050 Rivalta Scrivia, Tortona (AL)
PO Box 61
TELEPHONE: 86901
TELEX: 21338
DIRECTOR GENERAL: Avv. Pierluigi Majoli

GENERAL:
The facility acts as a general cargo clearance depot for imports and exports through Ligurian ports and as a container inland clearance depot and consolidation point for both Inland European and Maritime services. Warehousing is also provided.

FACILITIES:
The total area of the terminal is 300 hectares (741 acres). Two single storey warehouses provide 17 hectares (42 acres) of undercover storage and there is an open storage area for containers, timber, vehicles, etc. of 10 hectares (24·7 acres). A 240 room building provides office accommodation for those firms using the terminal and there is a Customs House for clearing operations.

A 27 ton sideloader capable of lifting 40 ft containers is available and maintenance and repair facilities have been installed. Road vehicles are unloaded under cover at bays situated at the ends of the sheds. Rail sidings with three tracks run through the centre of each shed.

ACCESS:
Rivalta Scrivia is located approximately equi-distant from the industrial centres of

Rivalta Scrivia—Containers being handled.

Milan, Turin and Genoa and is served by rail and road; it is a few kilometres from the main Milan/Genoa and Turin/Piacenza autoroutes.

TRAFFIC:
Total container movements were as follows:
1968	1,259	
1969	4,426	
1970	6,127	(January to September)
1970	9,000	Estimate

Centro Operativo di Pioltello-Limito

Via Dante 31
Milan
TELEPHONE: 904.66.77
TELEX: 32516
The centre is operated by the Gondrand group of companies.

GENERAL:
The facility acts as a general cargo consolidation point for industry in the Milan area and is part of the Gondrand transport

network operating throughout Europe.

FACILITIES:
The terminal covers a total area of 21·4 hectares (60 acres) and on completion will have shed space of 7·16 hectares (17·6 acres) of which over a half has been completed. There are 13 hectares (32 acres) of open storage and there are facilities for the handling and storage of containers. The centre is equipped with automated systems for goods handling and an IBM 360 computer has been installed.

Milan—Centro Operativo de Pioltello

NETHERLANDS
AMSTERDAM

Port Management of Amsterdam

Havengebouw, De Ruijterkade 7, Amsterdam
TELEPHONE: 22 12 01
TELEX: 12247
PRINCIPAL OFFICALS:
Ir. J. den Toom
Drs. F. W. Adriaanse
Ir. D. C. P. Stapel

CONTAINER AND ROLL-ON FACILITIES:
The container facility at Amsterdam is operated by N.V. Container Terminal Amsterdam, a separate company:

N.V. CONTAINER TERMINAL AMSTERDAM
Corsicaweg 10,
Amsterdam-16
TELEPHONE: 020-11 31 31
TELEX: 13436
J. van de Flier (*Managing Director*)
The Container Terminal is situated west of the city in the new Westhaven docks, built by the Amsterdam Port Authority and consists of a fenced-in area of 115,000 m² (28 acres), 75,000 m² (18 acres) of which are paved with concrete tiles. The present quay extends over a length of 280 m (920 ft), with a depth of 10·5 m (33 ft) alongside, which will be increased to 12·5 m (40 ft). The quay is equipped with reefer facilities.

A groupage shed of 3,000 m² (33,000 sq ft) has been built for the filling and emptying of containers and the storage of general cargo.

A customs office has been installed in the shed.

EQUIPMENT:
The terminal is equipped with two MAN container gantry cranes with a lifting capa-

Container Terminal—Amsterdam

city of 50 tons (41 tons with a 40 ft spreader) and a 44 m (145 ft) outreach over the water and 36 m (118 ft) over land. The spreaders are designed to lift every size of container as well as two 20 ft 'married' containers. Other handling equipment consists of a 35 ton railway stacker crane, van cranes, transtainers, chassis and tractors.

CONNECTIONS:
(a) Roads. Good roads link the Westhaven area with the Dutch highway network, avoiding crowded city streets.

The Dutch motorways form an integrated part of the European highway network. It takes less than two and a half hours to reach the Ruhr area, the industrial heart of West Germany.

(b) Railway. The container yard and groupage shed are directly connected by dockside railroad tracks with the European railway network which carries goods and containers to all countries on the continent.

(c) Water. The terminal is situated on the west bank of the Westhaven, only 10 sea-miles from the open sea and 8 miles from the sea-locks at Ymuiden via the North Sea Canal.

The present permissible draught is 45 ft. Qualified personnel will pilot the vessels through the Ymuiden locks in about 20 minutes. Owing to the sea-locks the harbour is tideless.

From the Westhaven, it is only a short distance (8 miles) to the entrance of the Amsterdam-Rhine Canal which connects the port of Amsterdam with the river Rhine and the European hinterland. The distance from Amsterdam via this canal to the German frontier is only 126 km (68 miles).

FERRY TERMINAL AMSTERDAM ROLL-ON/ROLL-OFF TERMINAL

Port Management of Amsterdam
    Coenhaven,
    Amsterdam

AGENT:
A.F.A. (Amsterdam Ferry Agenturen N.V.)
TELEPHONE: 62666
TELEX: 11257
TELEGRAMS: Afafer
STEVEDORE: V.C.K. (Verenigd Cargadoors Kantoor = United Shipping Agency)
EQUIPMENT: Ramp with movable link span (twin construction), 12 m (40 ft) wide and 19·5 (63 ft) long, possible height variation 2 m (6 ft 7 in). Parking space 3 ha (7·5 acres) Ample shed space. Quay of 400 m (1,312 ft) depth 10 m (33 ft). The terminal is equipped with a 35 ton mobile container crane, 20 ton side loaders, tug masters, slave trailers, flats containers and fork trucks.

CONTAINER SERVICES:
Holland Container Line
Three times a week to Felixstowe.
MACVAN
Weekly to Leith

ROLL-ON SERVICES:
TOR LINE:
Three times a week to Immingham.
Three times a week to Gothenburg
Fred Olsen:
Three sailings every two weeks to Kristiansand. (May to September).
Bergen Line:
Twice a week to Bergen (May to September).

TRAFFIC:
In 1970 some 14,000 Containers (inclusive of those of less than 20 ft in length) were imported and about 22,000 exported. Total weight of the cargo was 214,000 tons.

TERMINAL WORKING HOURS:
Shiphandling operations are worked, if necessary, around the clock (three shifts) and inland transport handling operations are carried out during the first two shifts (16 hours per day).

CONTAINER REPAIR FACILITIES:
The container terminal has a workshop for maintenance and repairs.

PRINCIPAL FREIGHT FORWARDING COMPANIES
N.V. Amsterdams Havenbedrijf
Vlothavenweg 10
Telephone 63551
Telex: 17136
Amsterdam Ferry Agenturem
Coenhavenweg
Telephone: 62666
Telex: 11257
N.V. Hollandse Stoomboot Maatschappij
Handelskade 3
Telephone: 63430
Telex: 11038
N.V. Wm. H. Müller & Co.,
Havengebouw, Deruyterkade 7
Telephone: 220115
Telex: 12047
N.V. Itramed
Corsicaweg 10
Telephone: 11313¹
Telex: 13298
Vereenigd Cargadoorskantoor
De Ruyterkade 139
Telephone: 64133
Telex: 12071

RHINE-SHIPOWNERS AND AGENTS:
Through connections with cargo motor vessels from Amsterdam to all ports on the river Rhine and to all canal, Main, Neckar and Moselle ports in the German Federal Republic.
Nieuwe Rijnvaart Maatschappij N.V.
  Levantkade 10, Telex Nr. 11155, Telegrammadresse: Wijkdienst
  Telephone 6 34 56
Basler Rheinschiffahrt A.G., Basel
  Herfurth Scheepvaart- en Transport-bedrijf N.V. Binnenkant 30
  Telephone: 22 23 89
Communauté Navigation Française Rhénane, Strassburg
  Segmij, Westerdokdijk 51
  Telephone: 23 98 22
Damco Scheepvaart Mij. N.V., Rotterdam
  Nieuwe Rijnvaart Maatschappji N.V., Levantkade 10
  Telephone: 6 34 56
Fendel A.G., Mannheim
  Cornelder's Scheepvaart Mij. N.V.

Koningsplein 5
  Telephone: 6 48 31
H. M. Milchsack Reederei, Duisburg
  Pakhuismeesteren Amsterdam N.V., Prins Hendrikkade 130
  Telephone: 24 39 69
Wm. H. Müller & Co's Rijnvaart Mij. N.V., Rotterdam
  Wm. H. Müller & Co. (Amsterdam) N.V. De Ruyterkade 7
  Telephone: 22 01 15
Nauta S.A., Basel
  Pakhuismeesteren Amsterdam N.V., Prins Hendrikkade 130
  Telephone: 24 39 69
Navi-fer A.G., Basel
  Gebrs. Scheuer N.V., De Ruyterkade 39-40
  Telephone: 6 32 32
Nederlandsche Rijnvaart Vereeniging N.V. Rotterdam
  Nederlandsche Rijnvaart Vereeniging N.V., De Ruyterkade 125
  Telephone: 6 34 77
Neptun Transport- und Schiffahrts A.G., Basel
  A. M. Lucassen, Binnenkant 22
  Telephone: 24 46 20
Neska Schiffahrt A.G., Dusseldorf
  Ned. Rijnvaartvereeniging N.V., De Ruyterkade 125
  Telephone: 6 34 77
Pakhuismeesteren, Rotterdam
  Pakhuismeesteren Amsterdam N.V., Prins Hendrikkade 130
  Telephone: 24 39 69
Plouvier, Rijn-Schelde, Antwerpen
  A. M. Lucassen
  Telephone: 24 46 20
Raabkarcher Reederei G.m.b.H., Duisburg Ruhrort
  Seam (Scheepvaart- en Agentuur Mij.) N.V. Binnenkaut 47
  Telephone 22 32 93
Reederei Zürich A.G., Basel
  Nederlandsch Bevrachtingskantoor N.V., De Ruyterkade 7
  Telephone: 24 26 66
Rheinunion Transport G.m.b.h. Duisburg
  Gebrs. Scheuer N.V., De Ruyterkade 39-40
  Telephone 6 32 32
Rhenania Allgemeine Speditions A.G., Duisburg
  A. M. Lucassen, Binnenkant 22
  Telephone 24 46 20
Rhenania Schiffahrts- und Speditions G.m.b.H., Mannheim
  A. M. Lucassen, Binnenkant 22
  Telephone: 24 46 20
Rhenus Gesellschaft für Schiffahrt, Spedition Lagerei m.b.H., Mannleim
  Cornelder's Scheepvaart Mij. N.V., Koningsplein 5
  Telephone: 6 48 31

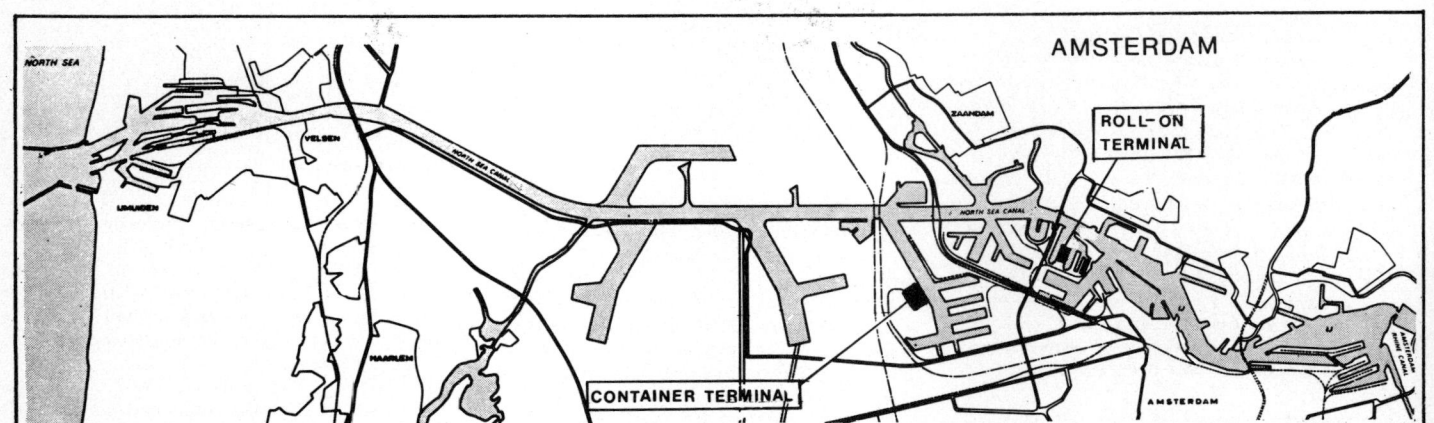

Schweizerische Reederei A. G., Basel
  Ruys & Co., Prins Hendrikkade 86
  Telephone 6 42 02
Seam Scheepvaart-en Agenturen Mij. N.V.
  Rotterdam
  Seam (Scheepvaart- en Agentuur Mij.)
    N.V., Binnenkant 47
  Telephone: 22 32 93
Vola Transport Mij. N.V., Rotterdam
  Gebrs. Scheuer N.V., De Ruyterkade 39-40
  Telephone: 6 32 32
"Vulcaan" N.V., Handels- en Transport Mij.,
  Rotterdam
  "Vulcaan" N.V., Handels- en Transport
    Mij., Stadhouderskade 6
  Telephone: 18 84 53
Westfälische Transport A.G. (WTAG),
  Dortmund
  Nieuwe Rijnvaart Mij. N.V., Levantkade
    10
  Telephone: 6 34 56

Amsterdam—Roll-on Terminal

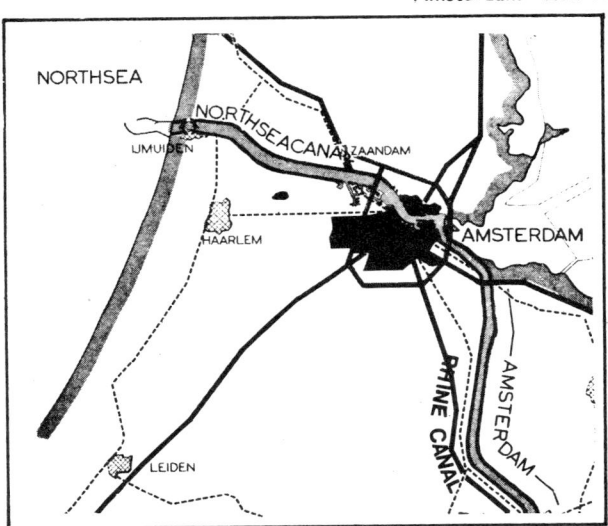

ROTTERDAM

Rotterdam Municipal Port Management,
Stieltjesstraat 27, Rotterdam, Netherlands
TELEPHONE: 010 (Rotterdam)—176960
TELEGRAMS. Eurogate Rotterdam
TELEX: 23077
Ir. F. Posthuma (*Managing Director*)
H. J. Brandenburg (*Harbour Master*)
GENERAL:
  The City of Rotterdam constructs the infrastructure of the port—the waterways, quay walls, wharves, etc—and provides sites for industrial development. It also owns part of the superstructure of the port—sheds, warehouses, cranes, etc. These facilities are leased to private enterprise operators on short or long term contract at rents fixed by the City through the Municipal Port Management. These rents form, together with harbour dues, quayage, pilotage and bridge tolls, the revenue of the Port Management which maintains navigational and other controls over the port area. Private enterprise normally provides its own buildings and installations on the quays and sites rented.

CONTAINER FACILITIES:

*Prinses Margriethaven—Northeast and South
  sides -*
Operator:
Europe Container Terminus Ltd (E.C.T.) -
  Reeweg 25,
  P.O. Box 5143, Rotterdam 22
TELEPHONE: 010 295022
TELEX: 23010
  In 1971 1,079 m (3,542 ft) of quay wall were in service with a back up area of 25 hectares (62 acres). A further 400 m

(1,313 ft) of quay wall is under construction and a further 495 m (1,624 ft) is planned to be added. The maximum draught allowed at low water is 10·06 m (33 ft) fresh water and it is planned to increase this to 10·97 m (36 ft) fresh water. A 60 ton link-span with a net width of 8 m (26·25 ft) has been provided at the eastern end of the terminal. The facility is served by seven container gantry cranes (Demag 37 tons, Peiner 48 tons, Demag 53 tons and four Paceco Vickers of 41 tons).

There are more than 170 special points for storage of refrigerated containers with connections for between 220 V and 380 V.

Two sheds providing 8,200 m² (88,264 sq ft) have been provided for consolidation and general cargo work.

The following mobile equipment is available.

Towing tractors	55
Terminal Chassis	500 various lengths
Fork lift trucks	2·5 tons capacity—12
	10 tons capacity—4
Straddle carriers	32 tons—10
Travel lifts	1 of 32 tons stationary
	1 of 42 tons mobile

The E.C.T. Rail terminal is located on the south side and is equipped with three rail tracks spanned by two 50 ton 2-3-2 container yard gantry cranes. The north-east side of the terminal is equipped with two rail lines between the crane tracks.

A Univac 9,400 computer has been installed to assist administer the movement of containers through the terminal. It is anticipated that in 1975 some 800,000 containers per year will be handled.

Prins Willem Alexanderhaven (North Side)
Operator:
Sea-Land (Nederland) N.V.
  Prins Willem Alexanderhaven
  Striendwaalseweg 30,
  P.O. Box 1560. Rotterdam
TELEPHONE: 010 168000
TELEX: 23308, 23360, 23351

This terminal, part of the Europe Containe Terminus, is leased under a long term contract to Sea Land (Nederland) NV. There is a length of quay of 360 m (1,181 ft) served by two Paceco container gantry cranes, one of 27½ tons and one of 30 tons, and a back up area of 19 hectares (47 acres) The container area will park 830 containers on chassis, including 200 × 40 ft and also 90 × 35 ft in the reefer area (440 v). The terminal also has a cargo consolidation shed of 2,850 m² (30,000 sq ft) which is road and rail served. It is planned eventually to increase the quay length by 980 m (3,220 ft) which will provide marshalling space for 4,200 containers and an overall area of 41·7 hectares (103 acres).

The facility has the use of the E.C.T. Prinses Margriethaven rail terminal.
Brittaniëhaven
Operator:
Bell Lijn N.V.
  Theemsweg 35
  P.O. Box 35, Rozenburg
TELEPHONE: 166700
TELEX: 23491, 23489

The Bell Line NV Terminal consists of a concrete piled jetty 183 m (600 ft) in length with 7 m (23 ft) alongside. The berth is accessible at all states of the tide. The area of the terminal is 2·4 hectares (6 acres) and it is served by a Stothert and Pitt 'Goliath' gantry crane of 25 tons and a Paceco Vickers gantry crane of 32 tons capacity. The effective outreach over water is 19 m (72 ft) and 60 m (197 ft) over the marshalling area and containers are stacked up to six high. The handling operation is controlled by one

Rotterdam ECT Princess Margriet haven.

man who is in touch with the crane driver and the ship by VHF radio.

The terminal handles the daily service to Middlesbrough and the twice weekly services to Waterford and to Bellport (Newport) The terminal is road served at present although there is a rail track adjacent.
Waalhaven
Operator:
Unit Centre
  Waalhaven, Pier 7
  Rotterdam
TELEPHONE: 297988
TELEX: 23657

The temporary terminal at Waalhaven, North side (described in the third edition) will be phased out of service by the end of 1971 when it is anticipated that about 600 m

(1,069 ft) of quay at Pier No. 7 will be operational. On completion in 1972 there will be 800 m (2,624 ft) which will provide two deep sea berths and two berths for feeder vessels with a maximum draught available at low water of 11·3 m (37·2 ft) F.W. Seven former bulk cargo gantry cranes are being converted for use as 45 ton container cranes and three will be in service by the end of 1971; they will have an outreach of 39·8 m (130 ft). Three yard gantry cranes will be in service by the end of 1971 and containers will be stacked 4-5 high under the wharf cranes and 4 high under the yard cranes. There will be a storage and marshalling area of 6 hectares (14·8 acres) which will be expanded to 15 hectares (37 acres). The terminal will be served by rail, road and inland waterway.

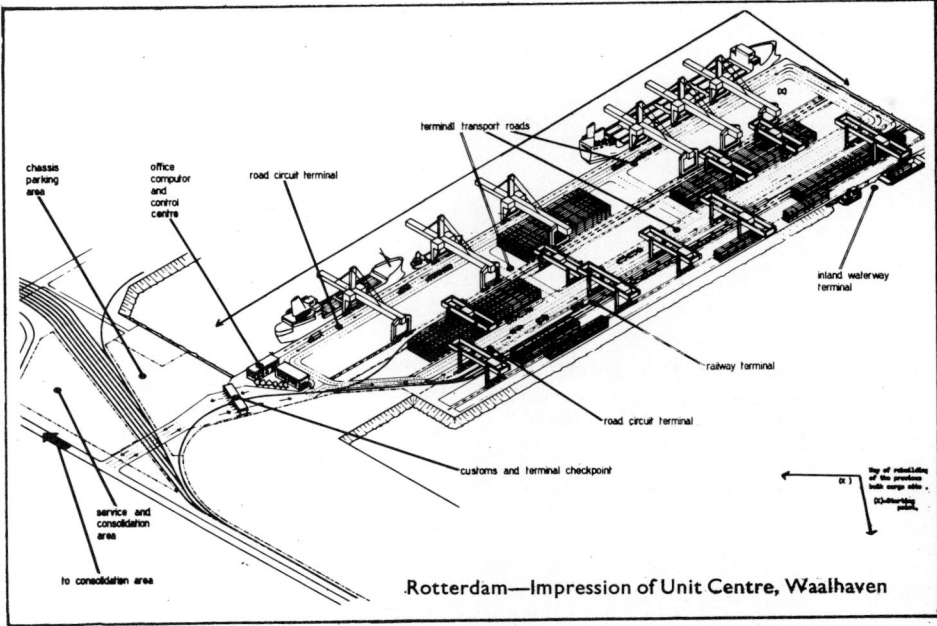

Rotterdam—Impression of Unit Centre, Waalhaven

Beneluxhaven (West side)
Operator:
The Transport Ferry Service (Nederland)
   N.V.
4, Elbeweg-Beneluxhaven,
   West Rozenburg
TELEPHONE: (01888)-2366
TELEX: 22660

A short sea terminal with a quay length of
330 m (1,082 ft) with a depth alongside of 7 m
(23 ft). The terminal has an area of 12 hectares
(30 acres) of which about half is in use. It is
used by Transport Ferry Services and is
equipped with an adjustable ramp and a
32 ton Paceco-Vickers container gantry
crane with an outreach of 20·2 m (70 ft). It
is equipped with a spreader for 20 and 40 ft
containers and those for other sizes will be
provided in due course. In addition there is
one 25 ton fixed crane, one 25 ton mobile
crane and four Tugmaster tractors. The
terminal has both road and rail access.

Beneluxhaven (East Side):
Operator:
Noordzee Veerdiensten/North Sea Ferries
   N.V.
   Scheldeweg, Europoort, Beneluxhaven
TELEPHONE: (01888)-2077
TELEX: 23052

This terminal is used by North Sea Ferries
and has a quay length of 270 m (835 ft) with
a depth alongside of 7 m (23 ft); the total
area amounts to 10 hectares (25 acres). It
has been provided with an adjustable ramp
which extends from a short jetty constructed
about halfway along the berth. Equipment
comprises one 32 ton mobile crane, four
tugmaster tractors, one tractor for towing
caravans and one forklift truck. There is
both road and rail access.

Prins Johan Frisohaven—Southeast Side
Operator:
Havenbedrijf Burger N.V.
   Den Hamweg 55
   P.O. Box 149, Rotterdam
TELEPHONE: 297144
TELEX: 21040

A common user roll-on berth with a 60 ton
bridge ramp with a length of 27 m (89 ft)
a minimum width of 7·5 m (25 ft) and a
distance of 10·8 m (35·5 ft) between the centre
line of the ramp and the front edge of the
quay wall fender. There is a depth of water
of 11 m (36 ft) at low water. The berth is
equipped with two level luffing 17½ ton
quay cranes, a 30 ton fork lift truck and a shed
of 3,500 m² (37,350 sq ft). The total area of
the facility, which is rail and road served, is
2 hectares (4·9 acres).

Users are Fred Olsen Lines; Finland
Steamship Co and Argo Reederei will both
start in 1972.

Hook of Holland (North Side)
Harwich Ferry Argentur N.V.

Rotterdam—Beneluxhaven, West Side

PO Box 4, Hook of Holland
Telephone: 01747-2351
Telex: 31726

This is the ferry terminal for the BR/Zeeland
Services to Harwich. There are three berths,
one of which is fitted with a ramp. A cargo consolidation shed of 1,000 m² (10,760 sq ft) has
been provided and the overall area of the
terminal is 3,300 m² (4/5 acre). It is equipped
with four quay cranes, 2 × 5 tons, 1 × 4·5
tons and 1 × 2 tons capacity and two DAF
tractors.

CONTAINER SERVICES:
*Overseas services excluding short sea and
feeder services:*
Atlantic Container Line
   Weekly to Halifax, New York, Hampton
   Roads and Baltimore (C/RO). ECT Ter-
   minal.
Australia Europe Container Services (AECS)
   Every ten days to Fremantle, Sydney and
   Melbourne (C). ECT Terminal.
C.P. Ships
   Every ten days to Quebec (C). ECT
   Terminal.
O.Y. Finnlines
   Fortnightly to New York (P). Quick
   Despatch Terminal, Pr. Beatrixhaven.
Hapag-Lloyd
   Weekly to New York, Baltimore, Hampton
   Roads and Philadelphia (C). ECT Ter-
   minal.
Lykes Bros. Steamship Co., Inc.
   2 or 3 sailings monthly to US Gulf Ports (P).
   Swarttouws Terminal, Merwehaven.
New England Express Line
   4 sailings monthly to Boston and other
   USEC Ports (P).
Scanaustral
   Fortnightly to Australian Ports (PC/RO
   in 1972-3). Quick Despatch Terminal,
   Pr. Beatrixhaven.

Scanservice
   Far East Ports (C in 1972).
Scanstar
   United States and Canadian West Coast
   Ports (C and P).
Sea Land Service Inc.
   Weekly to United States (C). ECT
   Pr. Wm. Alexanderhaven Terminal.
Seatrain Lines Inc.
   Weekly to United States (C).
   Terminal.
United States Lines Inc.
   Every six days to United States (C).
   ECT Terminal.
(C) = Service maintained by cellular
   containerships.
(P) = Service maintained by ships de-
   signed for a part of their cargo to
   be carried in cellular holds and on
   deck.
(C/RO) = Service maintained by vessels
   designed for cellular and roll-on
   operations.
*Short Sea Container and Container Feeder
Services with full Container Ships:*
Bell Lines
1. Daily to Teesport.
2. Twice weekly to Bellport and Waterford.
   Britanniehaven.
Rotterdam/Harwich Container Service
   (British Railways and Zeeland)
   6 sailings per week to Harwich. ECT
   Terminal.
Cawoods Containers Ltd.,
   Weekly to Belfast and Liverpool. Unit
   Centre, Waalhaven.
Comar Container Lines
   6 sailings weekly to Great Yarmouth.
   ECT Terminal.
Containerships Portugal
   (Ellerman and Papayanni Lines)
   Every 7-10 days to Lisbon and Oporto.

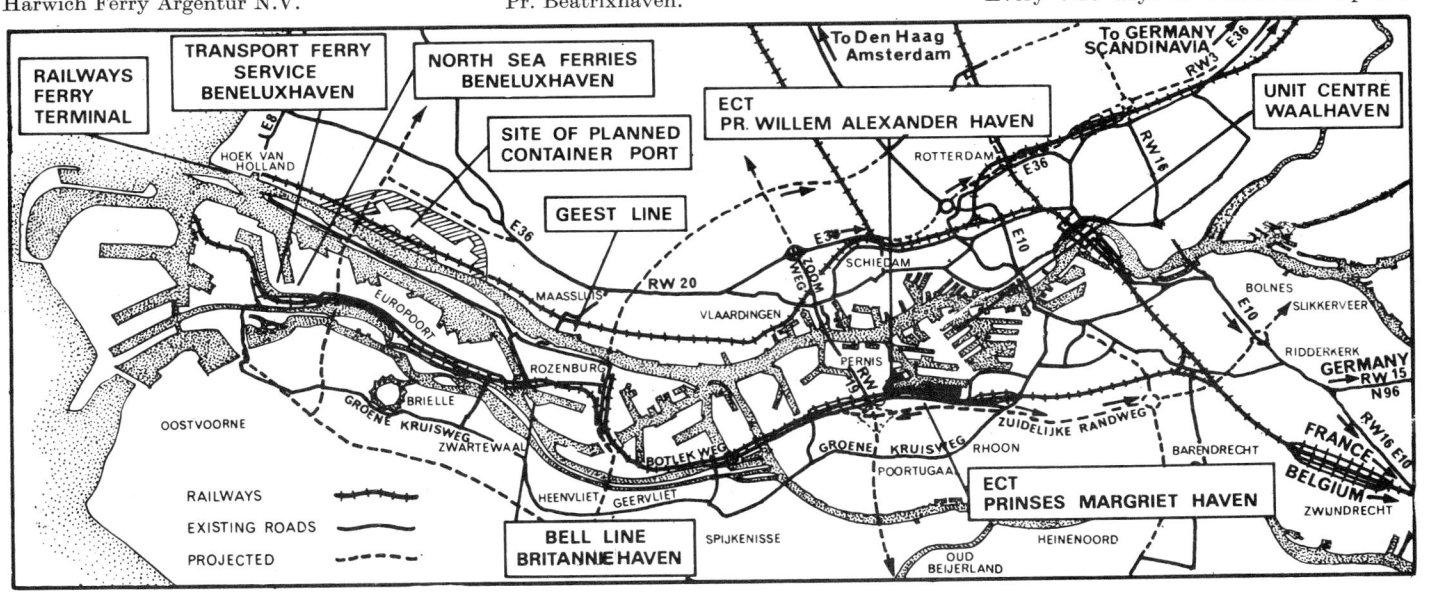

Unit Centre Waalhaven.

Containerships Spain Ltd.
Weekly to Pasajes. Unit Centre, Waalhaven.

European Unit Routes Ltd.
Twice daily to Tilbury. Unit Centre Waalhaven.

Meri Shipping Company
Every 10 days to Maentijluoto. Unit Centre, Waalhaven.

North Sea Ferries
Up to 5 per week to Hull. ECT Terminal.

Sea Land Service Inc.—Feeder Services
3 sailings per week to Felixstowe.
1 sailing per week to Grangemouth.
1 sailing per week to Liverpool.
2 sailings per week to Le Havre.
1 or 2 sailings per week to Gothenburg.

Seatrain Lines Inc.—Feeder Services
Various sailings with two, sometimes three, vessels.

Shortsea Container Services with part Containerships or Unit Load Vessels:
Associated Humber Lines Ltd.

5 sailings weekly to Hull. Müller Terminal, Pr. Beatrixhaven.

Batt Line
2 sailings weekly to Middlesbrough (Tees) Müller Terminal, St. Jobshaven.

Greenore Continental Line
Weekly to Greenore (Ireland). Quick Despatch Terminal, Pr. Beatrixhaven.

MacVan Container Service
Every four days to Leith (Forth). Unit Centre, Waalhaven.

Metric Line
Weekly to Runcorn (Manchester). Vijfvinkel Terminal, Merwehaven.

UNIT TRANSPORT TRAFFIC:
The figures shown below give the gross tonnage—that is the contents plus the weight of the container or flat—which moved through the port in 1970:

INWARDS:

	No. empty	No. loaded	gross tonnage
CONTAINERS:			
Lift-off	8,022	111,218	1,646,129
Roll-off	37	6,994	144,761
FLATS:			
Lift-off	915	9,654	137,070
Roll-off	—	1,550	23,867

ROLLING MATERIAL DRIVEN OFF THE SHIP
| Units | — | 39,084 | 410,700 |

Total lift off and roll-off
traffic   tons gross   2,362,527

OUTWARDS:

	No. empty	No. loaded	gross tonnage
CONTAINERS			
Lift-on	8,170	100,701	1,520,104
Roll-on	76	7,110	149,817
FLATS			
Lift-on	1,514	8,452	125,583
Roll-on	—	1,523	19,424
ROLLING MATERIAL DRIVEN ON BOARD:			
Units	—	26,882	411,529

Total lift-on and roll-off
traffic   tons gross   2,226,457

The table which follows gives the seaborne container traffic and shows the net tonnage of the cargo within the containers.

SEA-BORNE CONTAINER TRAFFIC
ROTTERDAM 1970

		Containers with cargo			Empty containers	
	Total number of containers	number	weight of cargo in tons	average cargo per container in tons	number	In % of Total
Inwards Total						
1968	63,427	52,999	593,864	11·2	10,428	16
1969	103,327	89,766	1,053,878	11·7	13,561	13
1970	126,271	118,212	1,521,176	12·9	8,059	6
EUROPE	62,025	54,883	681,456	12·4	7,142	12
United Kingdom	48,825	43,800	561,649	12·8	5,025	10
of which North Sea Ports	47,163	42,293	541,828	12·8	4,870	10
France	1,218	1,109	14,311	12·9	109	9
W. Germany	2,066	1,986	27,393	13·8	80	4
Ireland	6,664	5,445	51,982	9·5	1,219	18
Sweden	1,801	1,540	16,859	10·9	261	14
Denmark	229	224	812	3·6	5	2
Spain	523	249	3,479	14·0	274	52
NORTH AMERICA	63,031	62,368	831,862	13·3	663	1
United States	54,866	54,551	730,436	13·4	315	1
of which Atlantic ports	51,987	51,703	701,417	13·6	284	1
Pacific ports	1,346	1,343	14,930	11·1	3	0
Canada	5,576	5,366	76,987	14·3	210	4
AUSTRALIA	218	113	986	8·7	105	48
OTHER COUNTRIES	997	848	6,872	8·1	149	15
Outwards Total						
1968	50,586	45,729	544,077	11·9	4,857	10
1969	92,778	80,107	989,253	12·3	12,671	14
1970	116,057	107,811	1,425,355	13·2	8,246	7
EUROPE	76,849	69,800	943,064	13·5	7,049	9
United Kingdom	61,611	56,181	760,071	13·5	5,430	9
of which North Seaports	58,743	53,579	724,528	13·5	5,164	9
France	1,360	1,035	16,335	15·8	325	24
W. Germany	3,501	2,901	36,532	12·6	600	17
Ireland	5,543	5,151	63,298	12·3	392	7
Sweden	3,034	2,940	44,945	15·3	94	3
Denmark	45	27	420	15·6	18	40
Spain	1,312	1,187	16,748	14·1	125	10
NORTH AMERICA	35,609	34,505	448,299	13·0	1,104	3
United States	28,673	27,577	378,075	13·7	1,096	4
of which Atlantic ports	27,940	26,875	368,997	13·7	1,065	4
Pacific ports	580	580	7,554	13·0	—	—
Canada	5,629	5,621	55,785	9·9	8	0
AUSTRALIA	2,460	2,442	23,563	9·6	18	1
OTHER COUNTRIES	1,139	1,064	10,429	9·8	75	7

BARGE CARRIER SERVICES:
Central Gulf Service, which provides two sailings monthly to New Orleans, berths vessels at buoys in Waalhaven near Pier No. 3. Barges are berthed alongside pontoons which provide space for 78 barges. The agents for this service are Ruys & Co N.V.

Lykes Continental Line will commence a monthly service to US Gulf ports at the beginning of 1972. Sailings will be every 10/12 days after July 1972 when three Seebee vessels enter service. The Lykes barge terminal will be in the Caland Canal, Europoort. The agent will be Lykes Lines

Agency and Corns Swarttouw Stevedore Co., Ltd. will load and discharge barge cargoes.

Combi-Line (Holland America and Hapag-Lloyd Lines) will provide a monthly service commencing in early summer 1972 (increasing to two sailings per month later that year)

to US Gulf ports. Rotterdam agents are Holland America Lijn Vrachtbedrijf N.V.

FUTURE DEVELOPMENT

Fifteen container berths, each averaging 300 m (1,000 ft) in length with 13·65 m (45 ft) of water alongside, are planned at Rijnpoort on the Northwest side of the New Waterway, between Hook of Holland and Maasslins. The total land area for this project is 200 hectares (494 acres).

FREIGHT FORWARDERS:

ABRUS CONTAINER & SHIPPING NV
Maasboulevard 557, Schiedam
Telephone: 269461
Telex: 23432 (bruyninckx sdm)
United Kingdom—Continent v.v.

ASSOCIATED FERRY TRANSPORT (HOLLAND) NV
Albert Plesmanweg 105
Telephone: 294666
Telex: 23606
Containers and flats Continent—England v.v.

AUSTRALIA EUROPE CONTAINER SERVICE (AECS)
Agents for the Netherlands:
Ruys & Co. N.V.
Westplain 2, P.O. Box 966
Telephone: 114600
Telex: 21257

BELL LIJN NV
Rozenburg, Brittanniehaven
Telephone: 166700
PO Box 35
Telex: 23489/23491

BRAAMS & VAN VEEN INTERNATIONALE TRANSPORTEN N.V.

Westerstraat 41
Telephone: 128917
Telex: 21645
Containers, trailers and unit loads to and from all destinations UK

COWARD BROSS (EUROPEAN) NV
van Vollenhovenstraat 56
Telephone: 127424
Telex: 23680
Containers and trailers daily Rotterdam-UK.

CORNELDER'S SCHEEPVAART MIJ. NV
Westplein 2
Telephone: 111880
Telex: 21101
Containers and trailers Rotterdam-Felixstowe and Hull, v.v.

DAMMERS & VAN DER HEIDE & Co. (AGENTUREN) VN
Boompjes 57
Telephone: 146011
Telex: 21127
Regular services for containers, pallets and unit loads to Ireland

EUROPEAN UNIT ROUTES LTD.
Heyplaatweg 14
Telephone: 293588
Container forwarding between Rotterdam-Tilbury v.v.

FURNESS' SCHEEPVAART & AGENTUUR MAATSCHAPPIJ NV
Furness Shipping & Agency Co., Calandstraat 11-15
Telephone: 110040

FURNESS TRANSPORT GROUP NV
Van Weerden Poelmanweg 14
Telephone: 010-295000
Telex: 47487

N. DE GROOT CARGADOORS- EN EXPEDITIE-BEDRIJF NV
Veerkade 9
Telephone: 144777
Telex: 23321-24187
Daily transports to all destinations in England with own 10 and 12 meter trailers.

HAKO FERRY SERVICE N.V.
Streuelsweg 700
Rotterdam
Telephone: 172780
Service to UK

NV HARWICH FERRY AGENTUUR
Hoek van Holland
Telephone: 01747-2351
Telex: 31726
Day and night service for roll-on/roll-off Hook of Holland-Harwich.

I. T. HOLLAND NV
Van Graftstraat 49
Telephone: 293144
Container and truck service to Felixstowe, Tilbury, Hull v.v.

HUDIG & PIETERS NV
Calandstraat 49
Telephone: 111500
Telex: 21186
Groupage service to and from all destinations in United Kingdom.

NV AGENTSCHAP HUMBERDIENSTEN
Albert Plesmanweg 135
Telephone: 290144
Telex: 22634
Container forwarding Rotterdam-Hull v.v.

INTERNATIONAAL TRANSPORTBEDRIJF
P. G. KLOOS NV
van Veenendaalweg 18
Telephone: 291066
Containers, trailers and flats to all destinations UK v.v.

LEYS FERRY SERVICES
Parmentier Plein 20
Telephone: 299211
Telex: 22074
Daily container and trailer services to UK v.v.

WM. H. MULLER & Co. (BATAVIER) NV
Westerlaan 1
Telephones: 114300—132680
Telex: 21345/46/48, 23124
Shipping Company
Container pallet and ferry transports Rotterdam-UK v.v.

NOORDZEE VEERDIENSTEN (NORTH SEA FERRIES) NV
Head office: Haringvliet, Rotterdam
Telephone: 142066
Telex: 23152
"Port" Office: Europoort, Beneluxhaven, Scheldeweg, West-Rozenburg
Telephone: 01888-2077
Telex: 23052

RUYS & Co. NV
Albert Plesmanweg 127
Telephone: 291077
Telex: 22313/22699
PO Box: 5226
Container and ferry services, unit load operators, groupage services.

Containers, flats and ferry trailers to all destinations in England v.v.

SLOOTMAKER'S TRANSPORT- EN EXPEDITIEBEDRIJF NV
Scheepmakershaven 34
Telephone: 113475
Telex: 22268
Container, flat and ferry trailers, Rotterdam-Hull v.v., Rotterdam-Felixstowe.

NV SCHEEPVAART MIJ. D. STASSE (FAST FREIGHTS NV)
Eendrachtsweg 65
Telephone: 112855
Telex: 21365
Container and trailer services to all destinations in England v.v.

TRANSLODE UNITS LTD.
Geyssendorfferweg 59
Telephone: 290155
Telex: 23237
Container, flats and ferry trailer services to all destinations in England, Scotland and Ireland v.v.

THE TRANSPORT FERRY SERVICE (NEDERLAND) NV
Beneluxhaven, Elbeweg, West-Rozenburg
Telephone: 01888-2366
Telex: 22660

NV "TRIAS" SCHEEPVAART, AGENTUREN & HANDEL
Wijnhaven 86
Telephone: 137350
Telex: 22009
Container service Rotterdam-Felixstowe, daily v.v.

UNITED CARGO CORPORATION
Atlantic House, Westplein 2
Telephone: 144288
Telex: 23017
Container transports to UK

Container, Flat and Pallet Transport to Scandinavia:

FIRMA D. BURGER & ZOON
Westerstraat 7-11
Telephone: 111220
Telex: 21031
Pallet service to Oslo and East-Norway.

HUDIG & VEDER NV
Willemskade 23
Telephone: 143322
Telex: 22115

Containers, flats, pallets and unit loads. Weekly service to Copenhagen for pallet transport.

Rotterdam—An ACL vessel at ECT Prinses Margriethaven

NV GEBR. VAN UDEN'S SCHEEPVAART &
AGENTUUR MIJ.
Veerhaven 14-15
Telephone: 113300
Telex: 21268
Container and pallet service to Copenhagen
Gothenburg/Malmo and Aarhus
UNIT LOADS LTD.
Schulpplein 15
Telephone: 291455
Telex: 23393
PO Box 5210
Container transports to Scandinavia.
All destinations.

Container Services to USA and Canada:
ATLANTIC CONTAINER LINE (ROTTERDAM) NV
Wilhelminakade 76
Telephone: 172600
Telex: 21607
FURNESS' SCHEEPVAART- & AGENTUUR
MAATSCHAPPIJ NV
Furness' Shipping & Agency Co.,
Calandstraat 11-15
Telephone: 110040
HERFURTH NV
Westerstraat 42
Telephone: 134500
Telex: 22107
Weekly container service to New York and
Norfolk.
HUDIG & VEDER NV
Willemskade 23
Telephone: 143322
Telex: 22115
Regular container service to New York and
Philadelphia v.v.
NV INTERNATIONALE TRANSPORT
AGENTUREN "NEDERLAND" (INTRANED)
Blaak 101
Telephone: 118540
Telex: 22031
Container service to New York and to all
further USA and Canadian destinations.
PHS. VAN OMMEREN (ROTTERDAM) NV
Westerlaan 10
Telephone: 114880
Telex: 21435
Regular container services to USA.
PAKHOED NV
Boompjes 60-86
Telephone: 302911
Telex: 23023
Regular container service Rotterdam-New
York v.v.
RUYS & Co. NV
Veerhaven 7
Telephone: 112800
Telex: 21345/6/7
Weekly container service Rotterdam-New
York v.v. per Seatrain Lines Inc.
SEA-LAND (NEDERLAND) NV
De Ruyterstraat 9
Telephone: 130906
Telex: 23308
SEATRAIN
Bookings Ruys & Co. NV
Veerhaven 7
Telephone: 114800
Telex: 21345/6/7
UNITED CARGO CORP.
Atlantic House, Westplein 2
Telephone: 144288
Telex: 23017
Container transports to USA, Canada.
WAMBERSIE & ZOON C.V.o.A.
Calandstraat 7-11
Telephone: 110400
Telex: 22245
Weekly container service to New York,
Baltimore, Philadelphia and Norfolk.
Italy
FURNESS TRANSPORT GROUP NV
Van Weerden Poelmanweg 14
Telephone: 010-295000
Telex: 47487

Rotterdam—push unit with LASH barges

Hook of Holland. A Roll-on/Roll-off ferry berth.

The "Norwave" at Rotterdam

FURNESS' SCHEEPVAART- & AGENTUUR
MAATSCHAPPIJ NV
Furness' Shipping & Agency Co.
Calandstraat 11-15
Telephone: 110040
See also shipping companies, etc.

Japan
UNITED CARGO CORP.
Atlantic House, Westplein 2
Telephone: 144288
Telex: 23017
Container transports to Japan.

Spain
Incotrans N.V.
P.O. Box 977
Telephone: 111085
Telex: 21265
Weekly to Pasajes

CONTAINER REPAIRING AND CLEANING
DEPOTS:
DAF
Head Office: V.d. Graftstraat 25, Rotterdam
P.O. Box 652
Telephone: 010—290655
Repair of containers and chassis

D. T. S. (DOCKSIDE TRAILER SERVICE)
(NETAM):
Head Office: Van Riemsdijkweg 39, Rotter-
dam
Telephone: 010—295221

CONTAINER & REFRIGERATING ENGINEERING
KOLFF & Co. LTD.
(N.V. Container en Koeltechniek, voorheen
Kolff & Co.)
Head Office: Reeweg 20, Rotterdam
P.O. Box 652
Telephone: 010—294319

VLISSINGEN (FLUSHING)

N.V. Haven van Vlissingen
(Port of Flushing Ltd)
TELEPHONE: 01184-5070
TELEX: 55137
OFFICIALS:
  C. Oreel (*Managing Director*)

CONTAINER TERMINAL:
Operated by the Port Authority this facility has a quay length of 420 m (1,378 ft) with a minimum depth of water alongside of 10·57 m (35 ft). It is equipped with two container gantry cranes, a Peiner and a Paceco, both with an outreach of 35 m (114·83 ft): Van carriers and two mobile cranes have also been provided. The total area of the terminal is 7 hectares (17·3 acres) and there is 2,000 m (21,560 sq ft) of covered space.

SERVICE:
The terminal is used by the Australia Europe Container Service (AECS); vessels call every 10 days.

Vlissingen—Flushing Container Terminal

RAILWAYS

N.V. Nederlandse Spoorwegen
Moreelsepark, Utrecht
TELEX: 47257
TELEPHONE: 1.58.71
CONTAINER TRAIN CONNECTIONS WITH ROTTERDAM AND AMSTERDAM.
TRANS-EUROPE CONTAINER EXPRESS (TECE)
Since February 1971 Rotterdam ECT, Pr. Margriethaven has been linked by a TECE rail service with Antwerp and Paris. The route is through Antwerp "Schijnpoort" to Paris (La Chapelle) where transhipment takes place to connect with Bordeaux, Toulouse, Marseille and Lyon. There are 6 departures and arrivals each week.

A further service is planned to link Rotterdam—Germany (Cologne)—Denmark (Copenhagen) in the near future.

Sea Freightliner:
British Railways direct sea connection linking the European rail network to the British Freightliner system. The vessel arrives Rotterdam ECT at 14.45 hrs daily and departs at 20.15 hrs.

TEZ Line:
Amsterdam — Rotterdam — Antwerp Zeebrugge. Daily for shipowners' containers and private cargo. Connects with Milan service.

Amsterdam	dep	16 44	arr ↑	05 37
Rotterdam	dep	22 40	arr	02 57
Antwerp	arr	01 45	dep	23 05
Zeebrugge	arr ↓	05 20	dep	19 06

Milan Line:
Rotterdam—Basle—Chiasso—Milan. Departs both from Rotterdam and Milan each Monday, Wednesday and Friday. In even months the train is routed through Germany and for the other six months through France.

R'dam dep	23 41	arr ↑	03 56	via
Milan arr	05 12	dep	21 43	Germany
R'dam dep	21 48	arr	06 07	via
Milan arr ↓	05 12	dep	21 43	France

Delta Line:
Rotterdam and Amsterdam to Frankfurt, Manheim and Ludwigsburg. Daily. leaving Mondays, Wednesdays and Fridays.

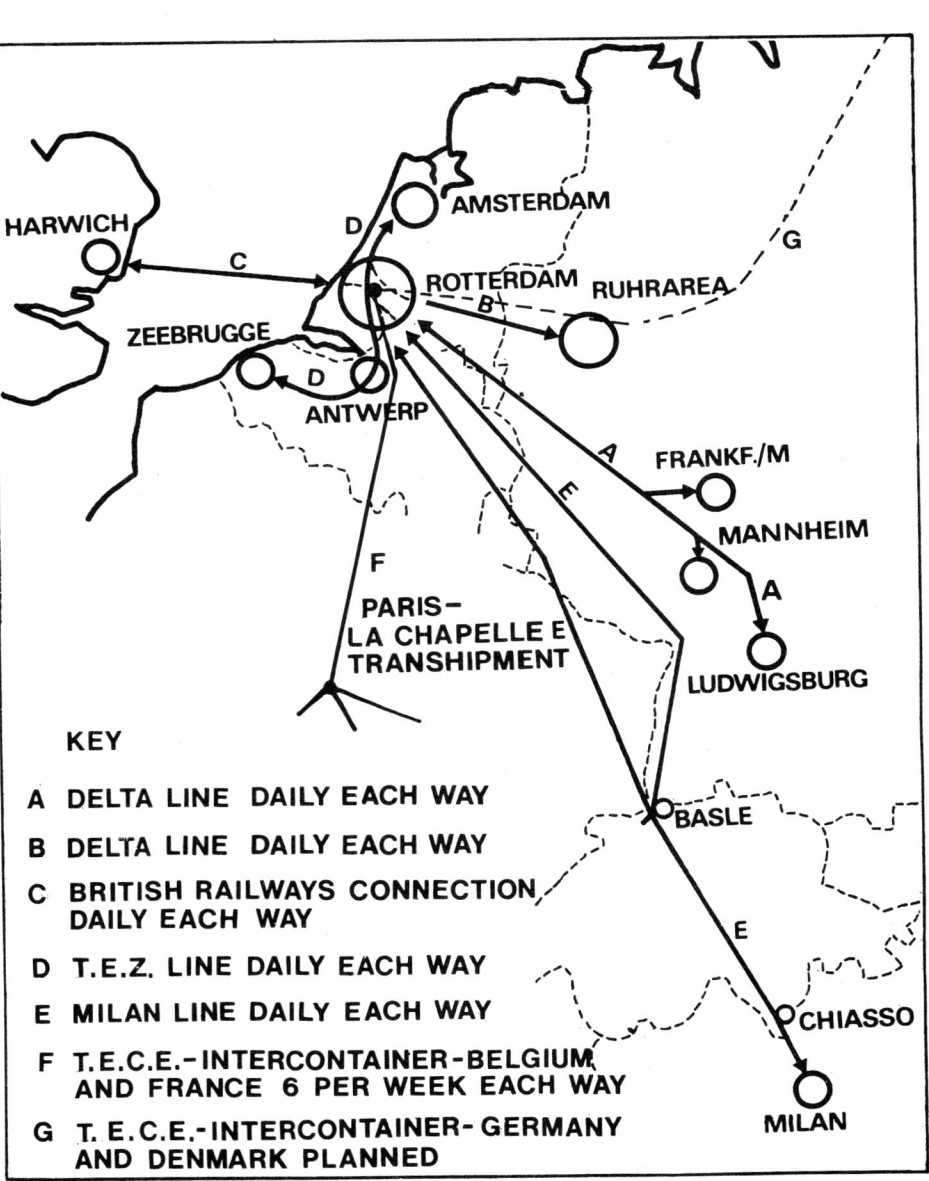

KEY

A DELTA LINE DAILY EACH WAY

B DELTA LINE DAILY EACH WAY

C BRITISH RAILWAYS CONNECTION DAILY EACH WAY

D T.E.Z. LINE DAILY EACH WAY

E MILAN LINE DAILY EACH WAY

F T.E.C.E.-INTERCONTAINER-BELGIUM AND FRANCE 6 PER WEEK EACH WAY

G T.E.C.E.-INTERCONTAINER-GERMANY AND DENMARK PLANNED

WUPPER:

Rotterdam to the Ruhr area and South Germany.

Frequency: 3 times weekly in each direction leaving at 20.52 hrs on Tuesdays, Thursdays and Saturdays (this service connects with TEZ and Sea Freightliner arrivals at Rotterdam) the Wupper service operates from Waalhaven.

Rotterdam—The ECT Rail Terminal

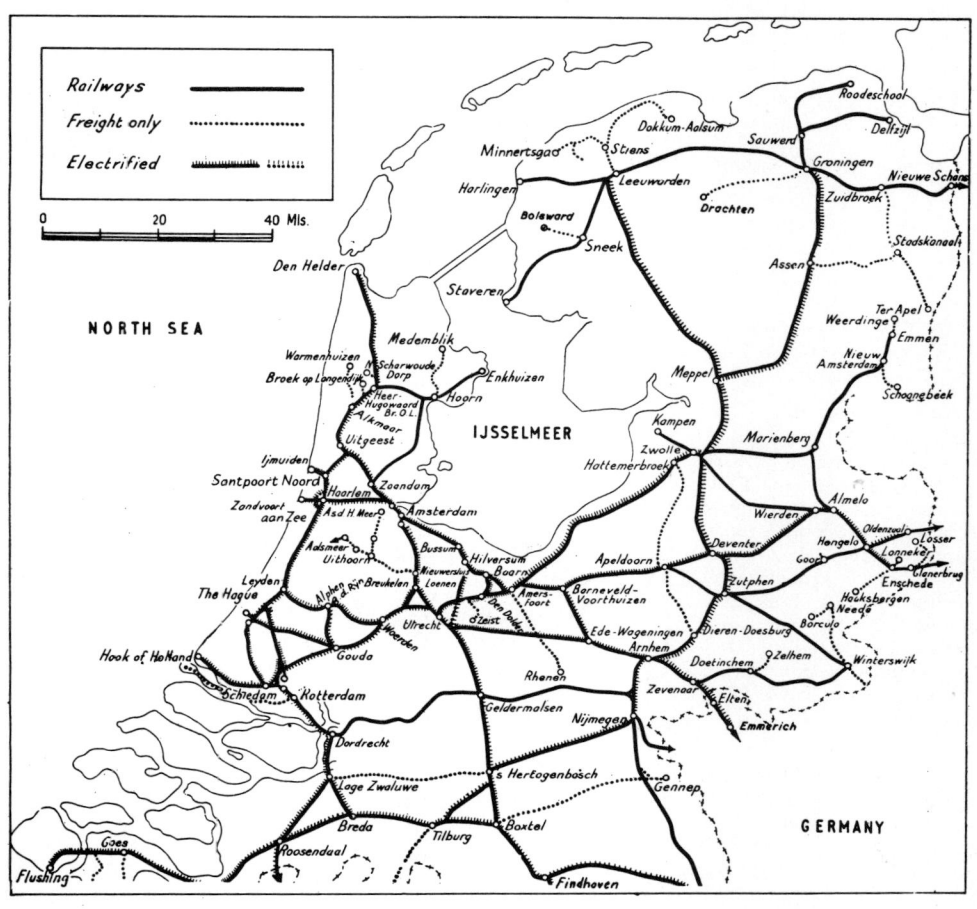

NORWAY
OSLO

Oslo Port Authority

P.O. Box 230,
Oslo 1, Norway
TELEPHONE: 41 68 60
PRINCIPAL OFFICIALS:
J. Hasund (*Acting General Manager*)
GENERAL:

Roll-on facilities are available at various points throughout the port; ramp arrangements depend upon the various types of bow, stern and side port in use.
CONTAINER FACILITIES:

North Sjurøya Pier, one of the roll-on facilities mentioned below, has been equipped with a 30 ton Liebherr container gantry

ROLL-ON SERVICES:

Name of Company:	Routes and Frequency:
Jahre Line,	2 ships, Oslo to Kiel twice weekly.
D.F.D.S. (United Steamship Co., Copenhagen),	2 ships, Oslo to Copenhagen.
	2 ships, Oslo to Frederikshavn.
DA-NO Line,	1 ship, Oslo to Aarhus.
Fred Olsen Line	2 ships, Oslo to Copenhagen
Wilh. Wilhelmsen	1 ship, Oslo to Gothenburg (representing AB Trans-Atlantic)
Erling Mortensen	2 ships, Oslo-Felixstowe
Ellerman's Wilson Line	1 ship, Oslo-Hull

crane which can service vessels of about 18·28 m (60 ft) beam.

Future Development

Further container facilities will be constructed as required.

ROLL-ON AND CONTAINER TRAFFIC:

| | *Inwards* | | *Outwards* | |
	Tons	Loaded Units	Tons	Loaded units
1970	125,000	10,200	56,000	6,000
1971*	160,000	14,000	75,000	8,000

*Estimate

TERMINAL WORKING HOURS:

Regular hours for both ships and Inland transport cargo operations are:

Weekdays 0700—1600 hrs
Saturdays 0700—1300 hrs

CONTAINER SERVICES:

Ellerman's Wilson Line: Oslo Hull—weekly

Oslo – North Sjursoya Pier

ROLL-ON FACILITIES: Name or location of Berth	Maximum size vessels accepted due to limits of approaches, locks or berth						Ship or shore ramp	Parking areas containers	
	length		beam		draught				
	m	feet	m	feet	m	feet		m²	ft²
Hjortnes pier	138·4	454	15·2	50	6·1	20	Shore	5,000	53,820
Filipstad	76·2	250	12·2	40	5·5	18	Ship	3,000	32,292
Pier II West	108·8	357	17·4	57	6·1	20	Shore	2,000	21,528
Pier II East	137·2	450	18·3	60	5·5	18	Ship	2,000	21,528
Palé quay	93·9	308	16·5	54	5·5	18	Ship	2,000	21,528
Kneppeskjær	76·2	250	18·3	60	4·9	16	Ship	10,000	107,640
N. Sjürsøya quay		500	20	66	7·0	23	Shore	5,000	53,820
Sorens Pier		400	15	50	6·4	21	Shore	8,000	86,112

These measurements refer to vessels now calling regularly at the quays mentioned.

Oslo

NORWEGIAN STATE RAILWAYS

Norwegian State Railways, Norges Statsbaner (NSB)

Storgaten 33, Oslo 1

GENERAL:

All containers are carried by regular freight services. Terminals with rail mounted container yard gantry cranes are in service at Oslo West, Andalsnes, Alnabru, Stavanger, Kristiansand, Bergen, and Fauske. Containers owned consist of 28 units of various types including 5 ISO 20 ft containers and 5 20 ft flats; 50 ISO Type 20 ft containers are on order.

Container Terminal—Oslo West Station.

POLAND

Container Transport

INTRODUCTION:

At a symposium organised by the Maritime Institute Gdansk in 1968 it was concluded that work on planning for containerisation, which had been initiated by the Prime Minister in 1964, was completed.

General cargo traffic through Polish ports, suitable for containers, had been estimated to increase to about 6 million tons by the mid 1980s, this excluded containerised domestic traffic. It would seem that ISO recommended sizes have found acceptance.

PORTS:

Container Facilities:

Gdynia will be the first Polish port to be equipped with handling facilities and berths, with large storage yards for containers, equipped with 32 ton container gantry cranes are planned. Gdansk and Szczecin will also be provided with berths in due course.

Roll-on/Roll-off Facilities: The Port of Swinoujscie on the Odra Estuary has been

Szczecinski Urzad Morski
Szczecin, Poland
STEVEDORING AGENCY:
Zarzad Portu Szczecin
CONTAINER FREIGHT FORWARDER:
C. Hartwig S.A.

Kapinat Portu Gdynia
Polska 2
TELEPHONE: 21 65 51
SHIPPING AGENCY:
Morska Agencja w Gdyni
Rotterdamska 3, PO Box 246
Gdynia
TELEPHONE: 21 49 51
TELEX: 051 222
CONTAINER FACILITIES:

A general cargo berth has been converted to container handling by providing a Kone crane able to handle 20-40 ft units, a Lancer

Polskie Kolije Panstwowe (PKP)
Ul. Chalubinskiego 4, Warsaw 67
CONTAINER OPERATING COMPANY:
Przedsiebiorstwo Spedycji Krajowej
(Inland Shipping Company)
Ordona 2, Warsaw
CONTAINER TERMINALS:

Terminals for handling 20 ft units equipped

provided with a ferry terminal suitable for vessels carrying road goods vehicles. Similar facilities will be provided in the future at Gdynia, Gdansk, Kolobrzeg and Szczecin.

HANDLING CHARGES:

Port Tariff handling charges have been reduced by 20 per cent for goods moving in containers.

INLAND TRANSPORT:

Rail: The Railways carry about 90 per cent of all cargoes passing through the ports and it is expected that for some time they will continue to carry the same proportion of containers although they will have to concede traffic to the roads eventually. Fast through container trains running to fixed schedule are planned.

Road: There are relatively few road goods vehicles suited for the carriage of containers and road surfaces will require re-inforcement for this type of traffic. Development programmes are under way and it is estimated that by 1985 some 50 per cent of the container traffic will move by road.

Waterways: A number of barges, shortly to be

put into service, will be adapted for the carriage of containers if the need arises.

SEA TRANSPORT:

Containers have been moving through the ports in small numbers since about 1965 when a refrigerated meat service was opened between Gdynia and London by Polish Ocean Lines and the United Baltic Corporation. In 1967 Gdynia was included as a port of call in the Swedish Rederi A/B Transatlantic service to Australia using Skandia type ships capable of taking 20 and 30 ft containers in their open type hatches. In the same year a container feeder service was opened between Gdynia and Gothenburg by Atlantic Container Lines; this lifts about 10,000 tons of containerised canned meat each year. 1968 saw the introduction of a small container service between Gdynia and Hamburg and also Canadian Pacific Ships' service with .9 m³ containers for textiles transhipped at London.

SZCZECIN

SHIPPING AGENCY:
Morska Agencja w Szczecinie
Plac Batorego 4, P.O. Box 325
Szczecin.
TELEPHONE: 46943, 44745

GDYNIA

Boss sideloader and tractors and semi trailers.

GENERAL:

Container traffic is handled at conventional general cargo berths. There is no tidal range at Szczecin and the maximum draught of vessel accepted is 8·5 m (28 feet) fresh water.

A Jelez 317 tractor and semi-trailer

POLISH STATE RAILWAYS

with mobile cranes, trucks and semi-trailer have been provided at Warsaw, Poznau, Katowice/Sosnowied and Gdynia Port.

CONTAINERS IN SERVICE:

160 general purpose 20 ft ISO type units are in service.

SERVICES:

Containers are moved between Gdynia and

the inland terminals on a fleet of four axle flat cars, they are offloaded at the terminals to semi trailers and Jelcz 317 tractors for final delivery.

It is understood that Container trains operate between Poland and the German Democratic Republic although their frequency of operation has not yet been established.

PORTUGAL
LISBON

Administracao-Geral do Porto de Lisboa
Cais do Sodré,
Lisboa-2
TELEPHONE: 36.23.21

OFFICIALS:

Eng Pedro Nunes (*Presidente do Conselho Administração*)

Dr. H. Darₙes Louro (*Administrador-delegato para os Serviços de Administração*)

Eng Luis Lobo (*Administrador-delegato para os serviços Tecnicos*)

Dr. Antonio J. de Matos (*Secretary General*)

CONTAINER FACILITIES:

Santa Apolonia Terminal

The first stage of this common user facility operated by the Port Authority was completed in October 1970.

The terminal has a quay length of 350 m (1,148·3 ft), a minimum depth of water alongside of 8·5 m (27·9 ft) and a back up area of about 3 hectares (7·5 acres). It is

The Roll-on/Roll-off Terminal at Lisbon.

equipped with two 30 ton container gantry cranes one of which is a Liebherr and the other a Paceco Vickers, two 25 ton and two 30 ton sideloaders and a number of tractors and trailers.

Additional container storage areas totalling 10 hectares (24·7 acres) are being made available at other port authority sites within a 5 kilometre (3·1 mile) radius of the terminal and will have good road and rail connections

Side-loader operations at Lisbon.

to the terminal.

Future Development

The second stage of the Santa Apolonia terminal, a further quay length of 500 m (1,640 ft), with a backup area of about 5 hectares (12·35 acres) is under construction upstream of the present terminal. This will have a minimum depth alongside of 12 m (39·4 ft) and will be designed with a high-span ramp for roll-on traffic.

SERVICES:

Containers:

Anglo Portuguese Container Line to London Weekly.

Ellerman & Papayanni Line to Mersey—Weekly.

Ellerman & Papayanni Lines to Rotterdam—every 10 days.

Roll-on:

Southern Ferries to Southampton—Weekly.

CONTAINER AND ROLL-ON TRAFFIC:

	Inwards		Outwards	
Lift-on	Units	Tons	Units	Tons
1970	6,531	39,323	5,483	40,314
1971	10,400	62,600	8,800	64,700
(Estimate)				

TERMINAL WORKING HOURS:

Ships are worked 24 hours per day if necessary and inland transport handling operations take place between 0800 and 1700 hours.

ROLL-ON FACILITY:

A car ferry ramp at the Alcantara Dock

Lisbon—Santa Apolonia Terminal in May 1971

Passenger Terminal handles commercial traffic. The ramp is a link span capable of accepting 40 tons.

CONTAINER REPAIR FACILITIES:

Eugénio and Severino Lda.

R. Fernão Mendes Pinto, ES, Lisboa-3

SPAIN
BARCELONA

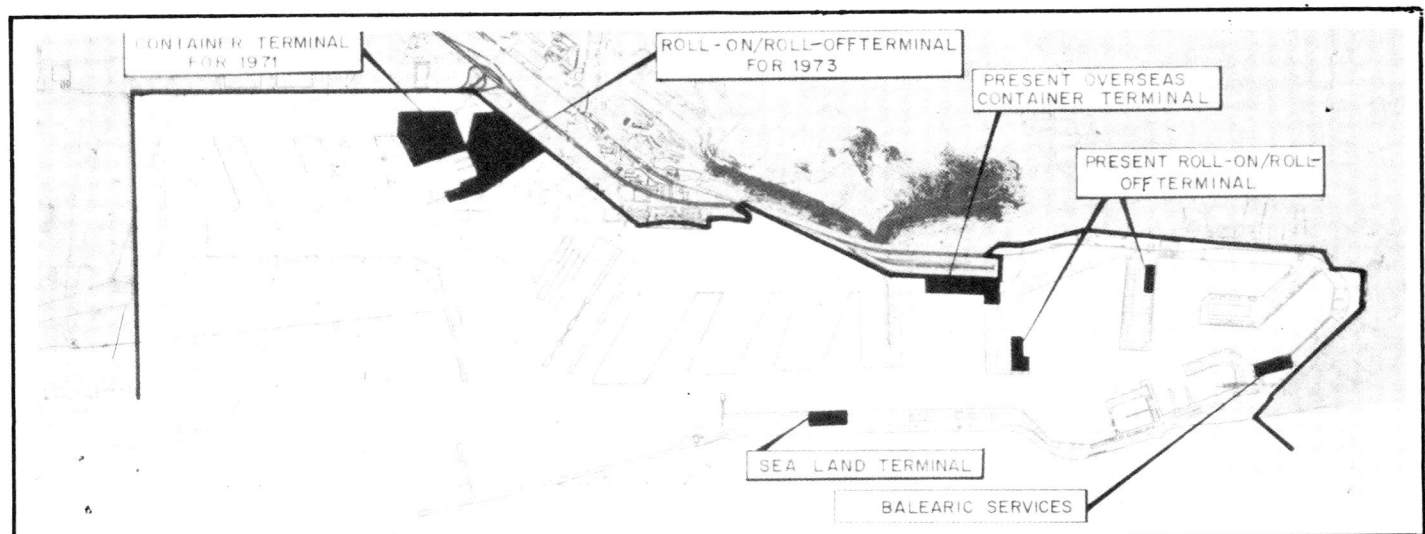

Barcelona.

Junta del Puerto de Barcelona

Puerta de la Paz, 1,

Spain

OFFICIALS:

Aurelio González Isla (*Port Director*)

Joaquim J. Dalac (*Export Manager*)

CONTAINER FACILITIES:

Berth for Majorca and Ibiza Services:

This is used by vessels serving the islands of Majorca and Ibiza. Containers of up to 10 m³ capacity and pallets are used for this trade due to the nature of the cargoes and the inland transport and road limitations in the islands. Quay cranes and forklift trucks are used for handling.

Barcelona—Adosado quay, the Sea-Land Terminal..

Barcelona—Overseas Terminal

Overseas Container Terminal

At the Muelle de Costa, a provisional terminal, containers are handled by three 12 ton quay cranes which are able to deal with 96 per cent of the 20 ft containers handled. The remaining 4 per cent are handled with two cranes working in tandem. The containers are moved into the storage area using four modified Ross straddle carriers capable of handling 20 ft units, a straddle carrier for handling and stacking 40 ft containers is also available. The storage area will accept about 350 units of 20 ft without stacking. Stacking up to 3 high is carried out using side-loaders, fork-lifts, etc. This arrangement has enabled containers to be handled at a rate of up to 10 per hour per crane.

The terminal is controlled by the Port Authority and it is used by four Companies: American Export, Fabre Line, Contenemar Line and Mac-Pack.

Adosado Quay

This terminal is used by Sea Land, with a berth 200 m long.

ROLL-ON/ROLL-OFF FACILITIES:

At present there is one service three times weekly with Genoa and vessels use their own ramps on to the quay.

FUTURE DEVELOPMENTS:

A container berth is under construction. This will have a length of 219 m (718 ft) and a depth of water alongside of 14 m (46 ft). It will have a total area of 6·3 hectares (15·5 acres) which will allow for the storage of 1,300 × 30 ft containers two high. Equipment will consist of a 50 ton container gantry crane and straddle carriers capable of stacking three high if necessary. The terminal will have rail connections and a shed providing an area of 3,750 m² (40,365 sq ft). The facility will be capable of expansion up to 16·7 hectares (41 acres) with a quay length of 430 m (1,410 ft).

A Roll-on/Roll-off facility is also scheduled for development. This will provide a terminal of 9 hectares (22 acres) equipped with end on bridge ramps for two or three ships. There will be two sheds, each of 12,500 m² (134,550 sq ft).

TERMINAL WORKING HOURS:

Ship and inland cargo handling operations take place 24 hours per day, seven days a week, if necessary.

TRAFFIC:

In 1970 some 9,400 loaded 20 ft units moved through the port; this is expected to increase to 13,400 in 1971. Loaded containers of less than 200 ft in length and non-standard box traffic amounted to 66,360 units in 1970 and is expected to increase to 75,000 units in 1971.

CONTAINER REPAIR COMPANIES:
Tecnimecanica Norma SA
C/. Deu y Mata, 152, entro la
TELEPHONE: 2.39.32.29
Talleres Pons
Paseo Nacional, 52

TELEPHONE: 3.19.37.52
Talleres Jimenez
Almogavares 100-104
Barcelona 5
TELEPHONE: 2.25.57.49
Industrial Contemar
Barriada Las Roquetas
San Pedro de Ribas

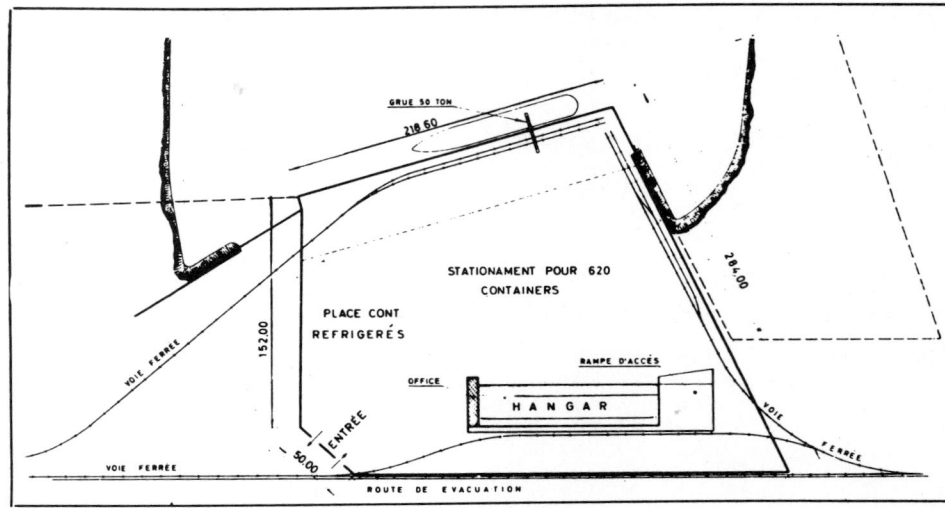

Barcelona—Plan of the Container Terminal under construction

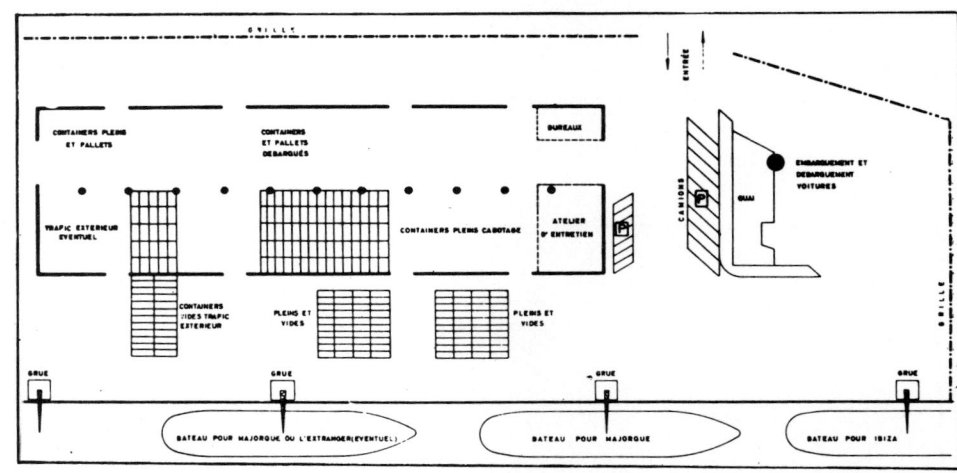

Barcelona—Plan of the berths for the Majorca and Ibiza services

Barcelona—A converted Ross straddle carrier

BILBAO

Junta del Puerto y Ria de Bilbao
Campo Volantin, 41
Bilbao, Espana
OFFICIALS:
D. Fernando Rodriquez Perez (*Director del Puerto*)
D. Luis Molina San Martin (*Jefe de Explotacion*)

CONTAINER AND ROLL-ON FACILITIES:
Muelle de la Reina Victoria Eugenia

With a length of 320 m (1,050 ft) and a depth of water alongside of 10 m (32·8 ft) this facility is equipped with one 30/40 ton and two 12 ton quay cranes. There is storage space for between 1,300 and 1,500 20 ft units. Handling behind the cranes is carried out by two 30 ton Clark straddle carriers, 7 forklifts of between 12 and 25 tons capacity and two 15 ton mobile cranes.

Canal de Duesto

Having a quay length of 300 m (984 ft) and a depth of water alongside of 8 m (26·25 ft) this berth is equipped with two 12 ton quay cranes and a portalift; it has storage for about 600 20 ft units stored one high.

Bilbao—Muelle de la Reina Victoria Eugenia.

Svenska Lloyd Terminal

A roll-on berth served by special tractors and two 30 ton 'U-Wagons', it has storage for about 300 20 ft units.

Terminal de Euronorte

A mixed general cargo and roll-on terminal for Iber Hanseatic Transport system equipped with a 40 ton crane.

FUTURE DEVELOPMENT:

A temporary facility with a quay length of 260 m (853 ft) and 14 m (49·9 ft) of water alongside will come into service in March 1972. It is being equipped with two 45 ton container gantry cranes with an outreach of 38 m (124·6 ft) over water and 37 m (121·4 ft) over the quay. These cranes will be equipped with automatic spreaders for handling 20/40 ft units or 12 ft twin lifts. In 1974 a custom built container terminal will come into service and the container cranes will be transferred to this facility with will be 600 m (1,968·5 ft) in length which a depth of 14 m (45·9 ft) alongside and an area of 13 hectares (32 acres). The temporary facility is operated by a consortium of the users of the Reina Victoria Eugenia facility.

CONTAINER SERVICES:

Muelle de la Reina Victoria Eugenia

Feeder services with Le Havre, Felixstowe and Hamburg linking with AEIL, USA, GCL for Gulf of Mexico, Cast for Canada (Great Lakes), Johnson Line for North American West Coast ports, DFDS for Denmark, Fearnley & Eger for Scandinavian destinations and Europacific Line for US West Coast ports.

Canal de Duesto

Feeder service linking with Dart Line for United States and Canada; services by SBC Container Line linking with Manchester Liners for USA & Canadian destinations; and the Seatrain feeder service.

Other Services

Svenska Lloyd to Southampton and Iber Hanseatic Transport System to Hamburg.

TRAFFIC:

Numbers of containers and their cargo passing though the port is as follows:

1968	3,239 units	31,932 tons
1969	11,519 units	122,347 tons
1970	20,645 units	244,674 tons

In the first 5 months of 1971 112 container vessels entered the port and 11,759 units with 123,006 tons of cargo were handled.

Bilbao—Part of the Svenska Lloyd Terminal.

Bilbao—Part of a storage area adjacent to Muelle de la Reina Victoria Eugenia.

CORUNA

Camera Official de Comercio Industria y Navegacion

La Coruña

OFFICIALS:

Juan Ma Martinex-Barbeito (*President*)
Antonio Tabasda Arceo (*Secretary General*)

GENERAL:

The Muelle de Calvo Sotelo in the southern part of the port is used to handle containers to and from continental vessels. There is a quay length of 200 m (656·2 ft) with a depth of water alongside of 10 m (32·8 ft). A 45 ton quay crane equipped with a spreader for 20 ft units handles directly to rail wagons. There is a stacking area within the crane's radius of 3,000 m² (32,290 ft²)'.

PASAJES

Port of Pasajes

Pasajes, Spain

GENERAL

The port accepts vessels of up to 150 m (492 ft) on a 7·6 m (25 ft) draught in summer and 7·3 m (24 ft) in winter. By Spring 1971 vessels of 180 m (590·5 ft) will be accepted.

CONTAINER FACILITIES

At present containers are handled using two 12-ton cranes in tandem; in the future two 25 ton quay portal cranes fitted with spreaders are to be erected. The facility is located at the Muelle de Molina, where there is an open area of about 3,000 m² (32,292 sq ft) and two sheds each of 1,500 m² (16,146 sq ft) floor area for the packing and unpacking of containers. Containers are handled by a Stephen Conjack and Mobile Cranes.

SERVICES:

Container Ships Spain Ltd—Weekly to the U.K.

OPERATOR:

Gasque y Cruz S.R.C.
Puerto, Pasajes,
TELEPHONE: 99.240

VIGO

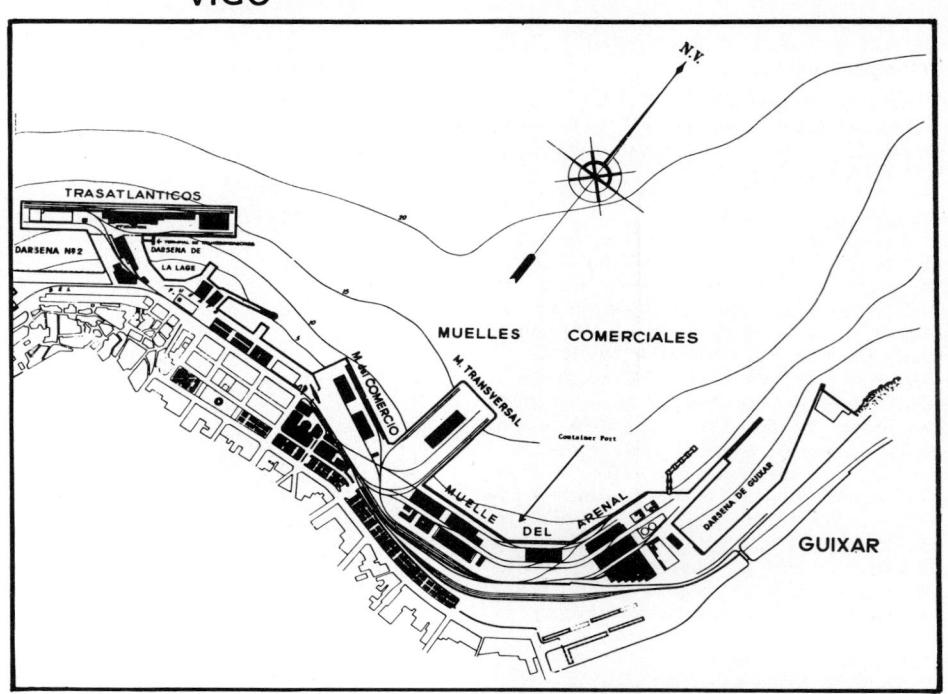

Port of Vigo

Rafael de Aguilary Ojeda (*Captain of the Port*)
GENERAL:
Containers are handled at present at the Muelle del Arenal.
There are plans for a container berth with a quay length of 230 m (754 ft) and a depth alongside of 10 m (33 ft). This will have a shedded area of 8,000 m² (8,600 sq yds) and will be equipped with two quay cranes with capacities of 15 and 20 tons.
FREIGHT FORWARDERS:
Estanislao Duran e Hijos SA
Avda, Canovas Del Castillo 22
Vigo
Telephone: 211245
Telegrams: Duran
Telex: 83057

SPANISH NATIONAL RAILWAYS

Spanish National Railways
Red Nacional de Los Ferrocarriles Españoles (RENFE), Santa Isabel 44, Madrid (12)

CONTAINER TERMINALS:
Terminals equipped with gantry cranes for handling containers are ·under construction for Port-Bou, Barcelona, Zaragoza, Madrid, Córdoba, Sevilla, Cádiz, Valencia, Valladolid. León, Vigo, Irun, Bilbao and Santander.
It is planned to have the programme completed by 1973.
SPECIALISED CONTAINER TRAINS:
Coal:
Spanish Railways (RENFE) and Co-operativa de Mayoristas de Carbon (COMAC) have introduced a container train service for coal between the mines at Ponferrada in North-

west Spain and Madrid, El Salobral terminal. The service, which started in March 1969, uses trains made up of 20 wagons each carrying 3 containers. The RENFE/COMAC agreement calls for 464 wagons which will be operated by the Railways and an unspecified number of containers, which will be provided by COMAC, by 1971. The service will be introduced to other mining areas as the stocks of wagons and containers build up. At present there are 80 wagons and 1,392 containers, sufficient for four unit trains. The new system which is completely mechanised, will centralise Madrid's coal distribution and dispense with some 90 storage and distribution points in the city.
Oranges:
At the end of 1969 ventilated containers

were used for the transport of oranges from Alcira and Villarreal in the Valencia area to the inland terminals in Germany.

CONTAINERS OWNED:
203, 20 ft × 8 ft × 8 ft Dry Freight.

CONTAINER RAILCARS:
At present 60 40 ft flat wagons are in service for the handling of container traffic. 300 60 ft special wagons are under construction.

TRAFFIC:
In 1969 it was estimated that about 25,000 metric tons moved in containers. In 1970 it is expected that some 100,000 tons will be carried by this method.

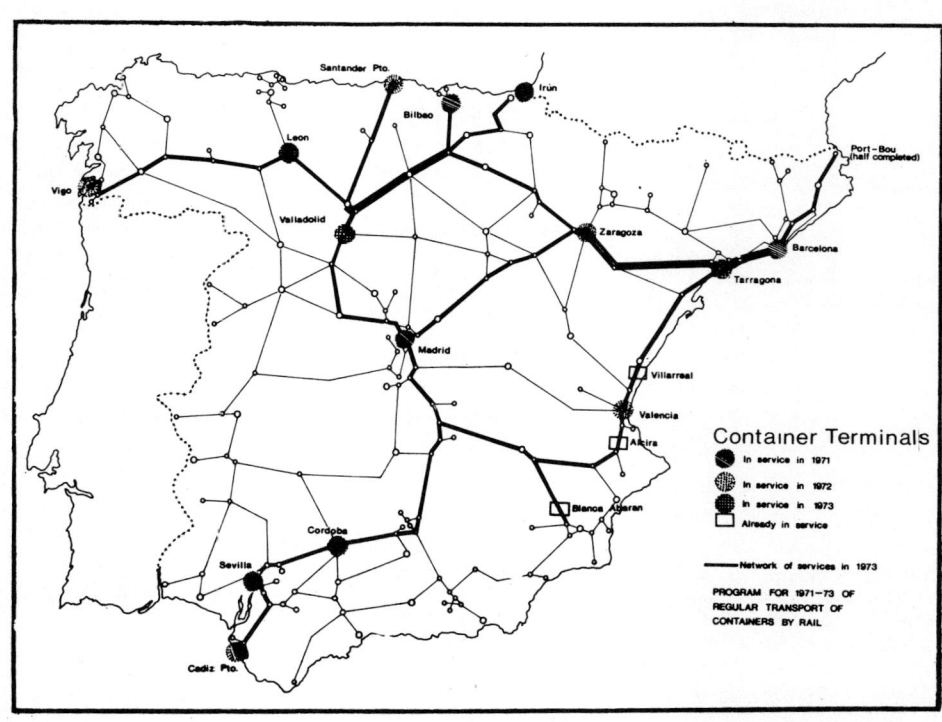

SWEDEN
GOTHENBURG

Port of Gothenburg,
PO Box 2553, S-403 17 Gothenburg 2
TELEPHONE: 17 17 00
TELEX: 20957
PRINCIPAL OFFICIALS:
Sven Ullman (*General Manager*)
Anders Bohlin (*Traffic Manager*)
George Svanteson (*Harbour Master*)
Sture Hernow (*Commercial Manager*)

GENERAL:

The Skandia Harbour at Gothenburg has four fully equipped terminals in use, one of which is for transoceanic container traffic and feeder traffic and three are for European roll-on/roll-off and passenger services. Thirteen berths are completed and in operation. Further extensions are proceeding. The total area of the Skandia Harbour is 1·3 million m² (14 million sq ft). The Skandia Harbour will be completed by the end of 1972.

CONTAINER FACILITIES:

Berths 640-642, 611-615, 601 under the administration of Skandiaterminalen AB. Storage area 30 hectares (74 acres). Three container cranes for 20-40 ft containers: two with a capacity of 40 tons and one with a capacity of 27 tons.

In operation	Length	Water depth
Berth 641-642	260 m (850 ft)	10 m (33 ft)
„ 640	220 m (720 ft)	11 m (36 ft)
„ 615	225 m (740 ft)	9 m (29·5 ft)
„ 614	186 m (610 ft)	10 m (33 ft)
„ 610-611	372 m (1,220 ft)	12 m (39 ft)
„ 612-613	372 m (1,220 ft)	10 m (33 ft)
„ 601	140 m (460 ft)	10 m (33 ft)

TERMINAL WORKING HOURS:

Ships and inland transport operate shifts on ordinary time as follows:

Monday to Friday—0700-1600 and 1600-2359 hours.

Saturdays—0700-1100 hours.

Sundays and other times on weekdays at overtime rates.

UNIT-LOAD TRAFFIC:

Numbers of roll-on units (road vehicles/trailers):

Year	In	Out	Total
1969	34,654	34,397	69,051
1970	39,880	40,658	80,538

Numbers of flats (excl. empty):*

Year	In	Out	Toyal
1969	20,890	22,433	43,323
1970	22,300	25,184	47,484

*Mainly 20 ft

Numbers of containers (excl. empty):

Year	In	Out	Total
1969	23,067	20,605	43,672
1970	34,469	31,046	65,515

NOTE:

i) Converted into 20 ft equivalents the total container traffic in 1969 would have amounted to 53,447 units and in 1970 to 80,786 units.

ii) Unit cargo handling for the four months of 1971 shows a ten per cent increase over 1970.

PRINCIPAL CONTAINER FREIGHT FORWARDING COMPANIES:

Atlantic Container Line,
  PO Box 2158, 403 13 Gothenburg 2
ASG,
  PO Box 219, 401 23 Gothenburg 1
Fallenius & Lefflers AB,
  Fack, 403 10 Gothenburg 2
Ferrymasters AB,
  PO Box 8979, 402 74 Gothenburg 8
AB Godstrafik & Bilspedition,
  Fack, 400 20 Gothenburg
AB Aug. Leffler & Son,
  PO Box 7084, 402 32 Gothenburg 7
Nordisk Transport & Sped. AB,
  PO Box 2532, 403 17 Gothenburg 2

CONTAINER SERVICES:

Transoceanic Traffic	Berth	Services
Atlantic Container Line	Skandia Harbour 641	Halifax, New York, Baltimore, Portsmouth Weekly
Johnson Line	Skandia Harbour 614	USA Westcoast Weekly
Scanstar	Skandia Harbour 670	US West coast 3-4 monthly
Rederi AB Transatlantic	Lundby Harbour 120-121	Australian ports Two per month
Feeder Services:		
Sea Land Service	Skandia Harbour 615	Felixstowe-Rotterdam Weekly
Seatrain Lines	Skandia Harbour 615	Bremerhaven
European Traffic:		
Swedish Lloyd	Skandia Harbour 643	London Four per week
Bore Line	Skandia Harbour 642	Helsinki, Hanko Weekly
Rederi AB Transatlantic	Lundby Harbour 120	Baltic ports, Oslo Weekly
West Norway-Gothenburg Line	Skandia Harbour 615	Norwegian ports Weekly
Veritas Line	Skandia Harbour 613	Norwegian and Danish ports—Weekly
Ellerman-Svea Line	Skandia Harbour 643	Hull Four per week
TOR Line	Skandia Harbour 600	Immingham Five per week
		Amsterdam Three per week
Stena Line	Skandia Harbour 644	Kiel Five per week
Göteborg-Frederikshavn Line	Majnabbe Harbour 53	Frederikshavn Four per day
Stena Line	Stenpiren	Frederikshavn Four per day

Gothenburg – Skandia Harbour, the western side showing two Johnson Line vessels in the foreground and an ACL vessel in the background with Stena Line and Swedish Lloyd vessels at the roll-on terminals.

Nyman & Schultz AB,
  PO Box 7087, 402 32 Gothenburg 7
AB Olson & Wright,
  PO Box 235, 401 23 Gothenburg 1
Scanfreight AB,
  PO Box 8873, 402 72 Gothenburg 8
Sea Land Service,
  PO Box 8978, 402 74 Gothenburg 8
Seatrain Lines,
  Vegagatan 98, 413 11 Gothenburg

Skandiaterminalen AB,
  Stilla Havet, 417 34 Gothenburg
Skandiatransport AB.
  Packhusplatsen 2, 411 13 Gothenburg
Svea Line AB,
  PO Box 99, 401 21 Gothenburg 1
Swedish Lloyd,
  PO Box 2125, 403 13 Gothenburg 2
Stena Lines,

Box 2507, 403 17 Gothenburg 2
TOR Line,
PO Box 8895, 402 73 Gothenburg 8
Wilson & Co.,
PO Box 7091, 402 32 Gothenburg 7
Trailer Express AB,
PO Box 48032. 400 77 Gothenburg 48
PRINCIPAL CONTAINER AND STEVEDORE
COMPANIES:
Skandiaterminalen AB,
Stilla Havet, 417 34 Gothenburg
Telephone: 031/54 01 10
Wilson & Co.,
PO Box 7091, 402 32 Gothenburg 7
Telephone: 031 53 00 90
Trailer Express AB,
PO Box 48032, 400 77 Gothenburg 48
Telephone: 031/54 00 20
ASG,
PO Box 219, 401 23 Gothenburg 1
Telephone: 031/80 09 00

A 25 ton crane mounted on the former ferry
John E. Olsson in the port of Gothenburg.
The ferry is now serving as a floating container
crane.

ROLL-ON/ROLL-OFF BERTHS IN OPERATION:

Berth	Water depth	Parking areas, facilities
Skandia Harbour 600 For TOR Line	8 m (26 ft)	Quay, two ferry ramps for vessels up to 8,000 gr. reg. tons. Fully equipped for roll-on/roll-off handling. Area 80,000 m² (860,000 sq ft), with a container shed.
Skandia Harbour 643 For Hull and London Lines	7 m (23 ft)	Quay, ferry ramp for vessels up to 8,000 gr. reg. tons. Fully equipped for roll-on/roll-off handling. Area 80,000 m² (860,000 sq ft) with a container shed of 9,000 m² (100,000 sq ft).
Skandia Harbour 644 For Stena Line	7 m (23 ft)	Quay, ferry ramp for vessels up to 5,000 gr. reg. tons. Area 30,000 m² (320,000 sq ft).
Majnabbe Harbour 53 For the Frederikshavn Line	7 m (23 ft)	Quay, ferry ramp. Shed and area for vehicles and trailers.
Stenpiren For Stena Line	5·4 m (18 ft)	Quay, ferry ramp, storage area for vehicles and trailers.
Lundby Harbour 119 For Transatlantic Steamship Co.	9 m (29·5 ft)	Accommodation for roll-on/roll-off handling of containers and other units.
Free Port 114 For Seaway Car Transporters		Ferry Ramp, used for motor car imports and container handling

AB Godstrafik & Bilspedition,
Fack, 400 20 Gothenburg
Telephone: 031/20 04 00
Scanfreight AB,
Stora Badhusgatan 30, 411 21 Gothenburg
Telephone 031/17 14 10

CONTAINER REPAIR ORGANISATIONS:

Broströms Tekniska AB
PO Box 8981, 402 74 Gothenburg 8
Telephone: 17.20.20
(Repair facilities at Skandia Harbour)

Gothenburg Unit Transport Berths.

HELSINGBORG

Port of Helsingborg
P.O. Box 260
S-251-04 Helsingborg
TELEPHONE:
042/13 92 10
PRINCIPAL OFFICIALS:
S. Linde (*Port Manager*)
V. Winck (*Harbour Master*)
CONTAINER FACILITIES:
The Skane Terminal:
This facility, which has a quay length of
550 m (1,804·5 ft) with a depth alongside of
8 m (26 ft) at the north end and 11·5 m
(37·73 ft) elsewhere, is equipped with a 45 ton
ASEA container gantry crane with a lift of
30·5 tons on the spreader and an outreach
of 25 m (82·02 ft). The crane operates over
five lanes on the quay apron, three of which

Helsingborg—Skane Terminal

are rail tracks and is equipped with a telescopic spreader for handling 20-40 ft units. The terminal incorporates a container distribution warehouse and packing centre and there are two ramps for roll-on vessels.

The terminal, operated by Skåne Terminalen AB, has a total area of 24 hectares (59·3 acres).

Other Berths:

In the North Harbour there are six ramps for roll-on ferry traffic and three berths equipped with quay cranes capable of handling containers.

TERMINAL WORKING HOURS:
Ships—0600 to 2400 hrs daily.
Inland transport—1000 to 1700 hrs daily.

FORWARDING AGENTS:
Andersson Shipping AB, Hamntorget 5
  Telephone: 042/12 75 60
Carlström & Co, AB, Bollbrogaten 4
  Telephone: 042/12 14 62
Fallenius & Lefflers AB, Sjögatan 4
  Telephone: 042/12 00 50
Hall & Co AB, Stortorget 20
  Telephone: 042/18 04 50
HH-Spedition AB, Kastenholt & Co
  Telephone: 042/13 16 00
Hillerström, AB Otto, Kungsgatan 2
  Telephone: 042/12 09 20
LB-färjorna AB, Järnvägsgatan 9
  Telephone: 042/12 01 80
Nordberg & Johnsson, Kungsgatan 6
  Telephone: 042/11 40 37
Nordisk Transport & Spedition AB, Sydhamnsg
  Telephone: 042/13 92 60
Olson & Wright AB, N Strandgatan 30
  Telephone: 042/13 92 50

Helsingborg Skane Terminal

Pettersson, Johan H., Kungsgatan 8
  Telephone: 042/11 19 80
Skandiatransport AB, Drottninggatan 72 A
  Telephone: 042/12 78 60
Wedlin & Son, AB Morgan, Kungsgatan 4
  Telephone: 042/11 19 89
Wilson & Co AB, Stortorget 20

Telephone: 042/18 04 50
Wistrand, Speditions AB Igor, Hamntorget 5
  Telephone: 042/12 33 94
Witt & Co, Hamntorget 3
  Telephone: 042/12 79 60
Oberg & Horndahl AB Drottinggatan 72 A
  Telephone: 042/12 07 15

TRAFFIC:

	Traffic inwards and outwards	
LIFT OFF	Loaded units	Tonnage
1970	16,000	128,000
Estimate for 1971	21,000	170,000
ROLL-ON:		
1970 Road vehicles	232,000	1,140,000
Rail wagons	205,000	2,115,000

In addition to the above 844,600 private automobiles and 9,400 buses were carried in 1970.

Estimate for 1971		
Road vehicles	260,000	1,250,000
Rail wagons	210,000	2,150,000

CONTAINER SERVICES:

Route	Frequency	Operator
ROLL-ON:		
Helsingborg-Copenhagen	2 daily	LB International Ltd.
Helsingborg-Elsinore	Every 20 mins.	LB International Ltd.
Helsingborg-Elsinore	Every 15 mins.	DSB-SJ Ferry Co.
Helsingborg-Travemünde	3 daily	LB International Ltd.
LIFT-ON:		
Helsingborg-Bremerhaven	1 weekly	Seatrain Lines Inc.
Helsingborg-Copenhagen	3 weekly	Svea Line (Syd) AB
Helsingborg-Copenhagen	1 weekly	b-line container service
Helsingborg-Felixstowe	2 weekly	Svea Line (Syd) AB
Helsingborg-Felixstowe	1 weekly	b-line container service
Helsingborg-Gothenburg	1 weekly	Seatrain Lines Inc.
Helsingborg-Immingham	1 weekly	b-line container service
Helsingborg-Middlesborough	1 weekly	Svea Line (Syd) AB
Helsingborg-New Jersey	1 weekly	Seatrain Lines Inc.
Helsingborg-Oslo	1 weekly	Seatrain Lines Inc.
Helsingborg-Rotterdam	2 weekly	Svea Line (Syd) AB

MALMO

Malmö Hamnförvaltning
Hjämaregatan 1
S-211 20 Malmö,
Sweden
TELEHONE: Malmö 040-71300
PRINCIPAL OFFICIALS:
A. Waldemarson (*Harbour director*), G. Axelsson (*Chief Engineer*), O. Boldt Christmas (*Harbour Master*), A. Carlsson (*Local Manager in the Free Port*)
CONTAINER FACILITIES:
The Free Port Terminal
This berth has a quay length of 200 m (656 ft) and has 1·6 hectares of storage area. It is equipped with a 32 ton Kone portal crane fitted for container handling with an outreach

Malmö—The Ferry Terminals

of 31·5 m (103·3 ft). There is also a 36 ton Lancer Boss sideloader equipped with both forks and top lift spreader.

TERMINAL WORKING HOURS:
Ship cargo handling operations take place round the clock. Inland transport operations are from 0700 to 1600 hours daily.

Gränges, TGOJ,
Port of Oxelösund
S-613 01 Oxelösund
Sweden
TELEPHONE: 0155/31940
TELEX: 640 25
OFFICIALS:
B. Björkman (*Harbour Master*)
N. Janér (*Harbour Inspector*)

CONTAINER TERMINAL:
The facility has a length of 100 m (328 ft) a depth of water alongside of 10 m (32·8 ft); the berth ends in a 25 m (82 ft) traverse which is equipped with a roll-on/roll-off ramp which can accept vessels of up to 22 m (72 ft) beam and a draught of 9·75 m (32·3 ft). Ramp adjustment depends upon both ship and shore; it being possible to raise it to 3·5 m (11·4 ft) or lower to 1·3 m (4·3 ft) above or below mean water level, there being no tidal range. The facility is equipped with a 35 ton ASEA container gantry having an outreach of 12 m (39 ft) and 20 m (65·6 ft) the quay. The storage area of 1·5 hectares (3·7 acres) is equipped with a 35 ton yard container gantry crane with a span of 100 m (328 ft) and a covered area of 2,800 m² (30,140 sq ft).

CONTAINER SERVICES:
Club Line to Rotterdam and Antwerp.

ROAD ACCESS:
Direct connection with European Highway E4.

RAIL ACCESS:
The port is connected by the TGOJ Rail-

ROLL-ON/ROLL-OFF SERVICES:
Schulaner Reederei, Peter Dühle—Lubeck twice monthly.
Lübeck Linie AG—Dagenham, Essex—twice monthly.
Seaway Car Transporters Ltd—Copenhagen and Felixstowe—weekly

Swedish State Railway—Travemünde—twice daily.
Rederi AB Walltank—Harwich—variable sailings.

TERMINAL WORKING HOURS:
24 hours per day.

OXELÖSUND

Oxelösund

way, owned by the Gränges Company, to the central industrial area of Sweden. There is also close co-operation with the Swedish Railways (SJ).

STEVEDORING, FORWARDING, ROAD AND RAIL SERVICES:
All carried out by the Gränges Company.
TERMINAL WORKING HOURS:
Monday-Friday excl Thursday
                 0630-2230 hrs.
Thursday   0630-2300 hrs.

Saturday   0630-1700 hrs
CONTAINER REPAIR FACILITIES:

Oxelösunds Svets & Smith AB
Sundsör
S-613 01 Oxelösund
Telephone: 0155/32046
AB Larssena & Kjellbergs Eftr.
Kaji
S-613 01 Oxelösund
Telephone: 0155/30547

OXELÖSUNDS HAMN

KEY
■ Container and Roll-on/Roll-off Terminal
▨ Container Storage
▤ Covered Storage

SKALA 1:2000

STOCKHOLM

Stockholm Hamn
Sandhamnsgatan 57
S-115 28 Stockholm
Sweden
TELEPHONE: 08/635500
TELEGRAMS: Capitalport
TELEX: 10612
PRINCIPAL OFFICIALS:
Arne Nordström (*General Manager*)
Gunnar Sundberg (*Harbour Master*)
Tore Stålbo (*Superintendent—Free Port*)

CONTAINER FACILITIES:
Container Terminal Stockholm:
A container terminal at Lindarängen in the Free Port came into service in 1969. This gives a quay length of 110 m (364 ft) and a container marshalling area of 4·8 hectares (12 acres). The second stage, to be completed by 1971, will give a further 175 m of quay with an additional 5·2 hectares (13 acres of storage area and a roll-on/roll-off ramp. There is a depth of 10·4 m (34·2 ft) of

water alongside. Two Kone container gantry cranes with a lifting capacity of 20 tons on a 5 ton automatic spreader. The cranes can be linked together for handling 40 ft units. They have an outreach over water of 16·7 m (54·8 ft) and over land of 22·5 m (73·8 ft) giving 9·17 m (30·2 ft) behind the rear rail. Other handling equipment comprises a 34 ton straddle carrier and a 25 ton sideloader both capable of handling 40 ft units. There is also a number of fork trucks with capacities up to 29 tons and a jack wagon for 20 ft units.

Other Berths:

Containers are also handled at other general cargo berths in the port.

CONTAINER SERVICES:

Several shipping companies operate from various berths within the Free Port for their short sea services e.g. Svea Line (Baltic) AB to London, Club line to Benelux ports etc. Other operators in the Free Port with regular container traffic are Rederi AB Transatlantic, Johnson Line and Atlantic Container Line which, however, carry most of their containers by rail or road to Gothenburg etc. Containers are supplied by the above mentioned companies and by e.g. CTI and Contrans. The shipyard Company AB Ekensbergs Varv has a container repair shop within the Free Port.

ROLL-ON SERVICES:

Swedish State Railways with one ferry for 22 railway wagons. Daily sailing to Nadendal from Värtahamnen.

Silja Line with two ferries. Two sailings daily to Abo from Värtahamnen. Teamline with two ships for max 100 containers each. Two sailings weekly to Hamburg/Kiel from Stadsgärdshamnen (The Teamline Terminal at Masthlamnen).

CUSTOMS REQUIREMENTS/FACILITIES:

As the Customs Authority nowadays in Sweden has a very liberal point of view most goods will be customs cleared by documents. The contents of a container must be well specified both in the Bill of Lading as on the container itself. Under these circumstances no difficulties need to occur.

HEALTH REQUIREMENTS/REGULATIONS:

There are no special Health regulations concerning containers in general. Meat, green fruits, vegetables, etc. have to be inspected regularly.

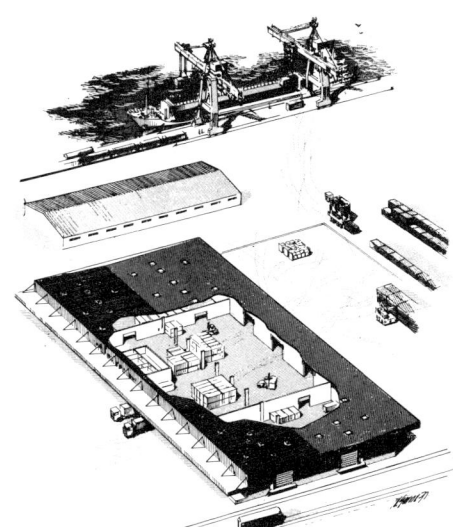

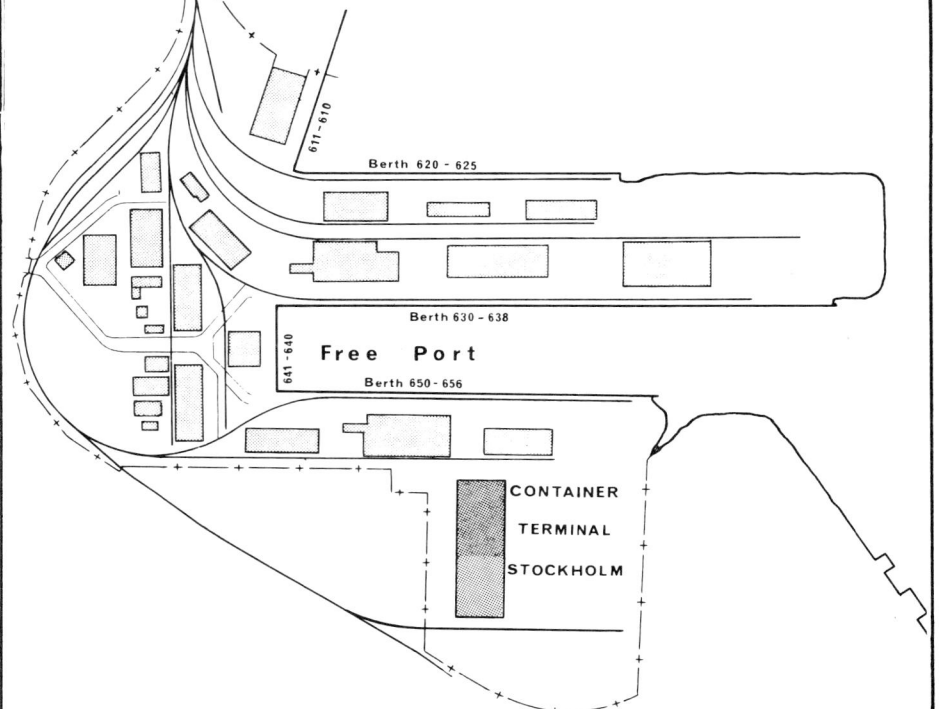

Container Terminal Stockholm.

ROLL-ON FACILITIES

Berth	Depth of water		Parking area for Vehicles		Ramp	
	m	ft	m²	sq. yds.		
Frihamnen 630	9·5	31·3	1,000	1,200	Fixed dual purpose*	
Värtahamnen 514	6·0	19·7	9,000	10,800	Adjustable	
Värtahamnen 507	8·0	26·4	Railway ferry terminal		Adjustable	
S. Hammarbyhamnen 5	6·3	20·7	600	720	Pontoon	dual purpose*
Stadsgärdshamnen 33	9·5	31·3	20,000	23,900	Pontoon	dual purpose*
Stadsgärdshamnen 34	9·5	31·3			Pontoon	dual purpose*

*Dual purpose in this context implies that the berth is used for general cargo handling as well as roll-on/roll-off.

CONTAINER FREIGHT FORWARDING COMPANIES:

Red AB Nordstjernan (Johnson Line)
Stureplan 3, Fack
S-103 80 Stockholm 7
Telephone: 220520 (North Pacific service)

Nordström & Thulin AB (Teamline)
Skeppsbron 34-36
Box 1215
S-111 82 Stockholm 1
Telephone: 231740 (Hamburg-Kiel service)

Svea Line (Baltic)AB
Sandhamnsgatan 57
Box 27014
S-102 51 Stockholm 27
Telephone: 670610

Club Line AB
Sandhamnsgatan 57
Box 27022
S-102 51 Stockholm 27
Telephone: 670610

Nyman & Schultz Transport AB

Södra Hamnvägen 50, Fack
S-102 50 Stockholm 27
Telephone: 225080 (Finland service)

Norrman & Nilsson AB
Skeppsbron 18
Box 2036
S-103 11 Stockholm
Telephone: 233890

Atlantic Container Line Stockholm AB
Jacobsgatan 5
Box 16080

S-103 22 Stockholm 16
Telephone: 237140

Rederi AB Transatlantic
Sandhamnsgatan 79
S-115 28 Stockholm
Telephone: 231785

CONTAINER STORAGE AND STEVEDORE COM-
PANIES:

Container Transport International (Scan-
dinavia) AB
Nybrogatan 38
Box 5206
S-102 45 Stockholm 5

Telephone: 676992

Stockholms Förenade Stuveri AB (The United
Stevedoring Company of Stockholm)
Södermalmstorg 2
Box 15055
S-104 65 Stockholm 15
Telephone: 440940

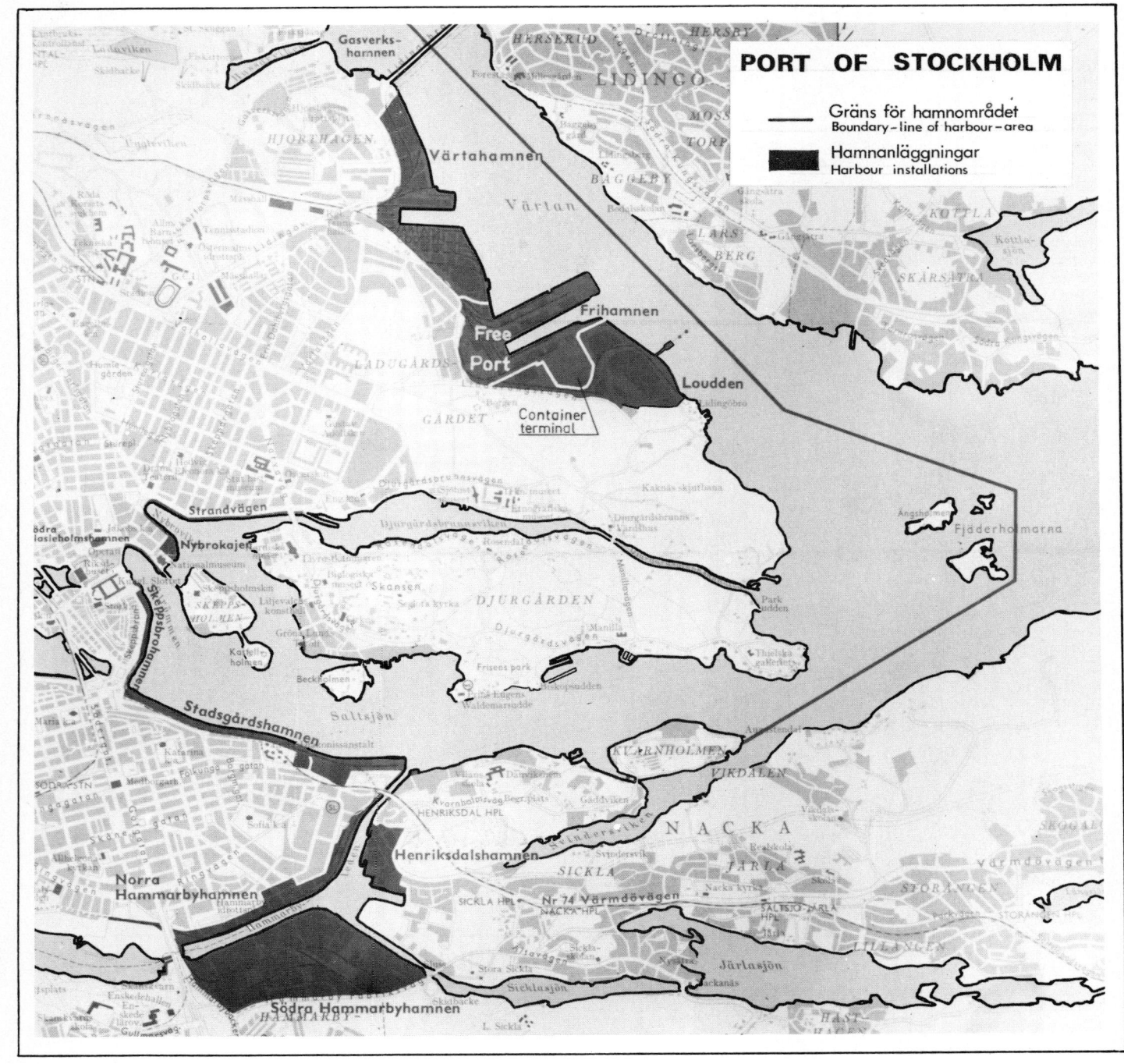

VASTERAS

Vasteras Hamn
Box 256, 72106 Västerås
TELEPHONE: (021) 180100
HARBOUR MASTER: S. Råberg
CONTAINERS AND ROLL-ON TERMINAL:
   A terminal is under construction and will
be completed late in 1971 or early 1972.
The facility will have a quay length of 260 m
(853 ft) with a depth of water alongside of
6·5 m (24·6 ft); the total area available is
20 hectares (49·4 acres) but only the areas
near the quay are surfaced.   There will be

a 30 ton mobile crane for container handling
and a ramp for roll-on traffic and the facility
will be rail served.
STEVEDORING COMPANY:
Västerås Stuveri AB
   Telephone: 13 01 53, 14 26 75
SHIPPING BROKERS, AND AGENTS:
Bergtrans AB
   Telex: 4707
   Telephone: 18 53 60
Norrman & Nilsson AB
   Telephone: 12 04 75

Telex: 40633 NORRCO S
Sten Siöwall AB
   Telephone: 11 02 60
   Telex: 4701 SIOWALL S

SHIPPING AGENTS:
Nordisk Transport & Spedition, AB
   Telephone: 11 73 00, 18 12 20
   Telex: 40639 NTSVS S
AB Skandiatransport
   Telephone: 12 04 60
   Telex: 40655 SKTVTS S

SWEDISH NATIONAL RAILWAYS

Statens Järnvägar (S.J.)
105 50 Stockholm C. Sweden

OFFICIALS IN CHARGE OF CONTAINER
OPERATIONS:
Arne Kock (*Assistant Chief Manager*)
Bertil Karlsson (*Assistant Chief Manager*)

Arnold Andersson (*Executive Officer*)
CONTAINER TERMINALS:
These are located at Gothenburg, Stockholm, Malmö, Orebro and Sundsvall. Gothenburg is equipped with a Travel-lift crane, the other terminals with rail mounted gantry cranes spanning two tracks except at Malmö where a three track crane is in operation.

CONTAINERS OWNED:
Sixty dry freight 20 × 8 × 8 are used on internal container services, and thirty special flat wagons are in service.
TRAFFIC:
In 1969 the total traffic handled amounted to 35,000 containers, in 1970 this is expected to increase to 40,000 units.

SWITZERLAND
BASLE

Port of Basle
Rheinschiffahrtsamt
Ch-4000 Basle 19
Switzerland
TELEPHONE: 32 58 00
PRINCIPAL OFFICIALS:
W. Mangold (*Director*), Dr. K. Waldner, A. Vogel

BERTHS:
No specific container berths or cranes are available. Four heavy-lift cranes distributed over the entire port-area handle containers from ship to rail or road and vice-versa.

SHIPPING SERVICES:
No shipping company of Swiss origin provides regular services but Rhine Container Line operate container services as far as Basle.
CONTAINER FACILITIES:
There is sufficient park-space, cranage and connection facilities for either rail or road and inland waterway to allow for considerably more container traffic to pass through Basle.
CUSTOMS REQUIREMENTS:
Containers are treated as other packaged goods.

TERMINAL WORKING HOURS:
0500-2100 hours Monday to Friday; 0500-1300 hours Saturday. Arrangements

can be made to work 24 hours per day if necessary.
PRINCIPAL CONTAINER FREIGHT FORWARDING COMPANIES:
Reederei Zürich, Basle
Neska, Basle
CONTAINER STORAGE AND STEVEDORE COMPANIES:
Basler Rheinschiffahrt AG, Basle
Schweizerische Reederei AG, Basle
Ultra, Basle
These companies have the necessary heavy-lift equipment to handle loads up to 60 tons and more. The average crane handles between 5 and 10 tons. These four are therefore usually employed to handle containers.

SWISS NATIONAL RAILWAYS

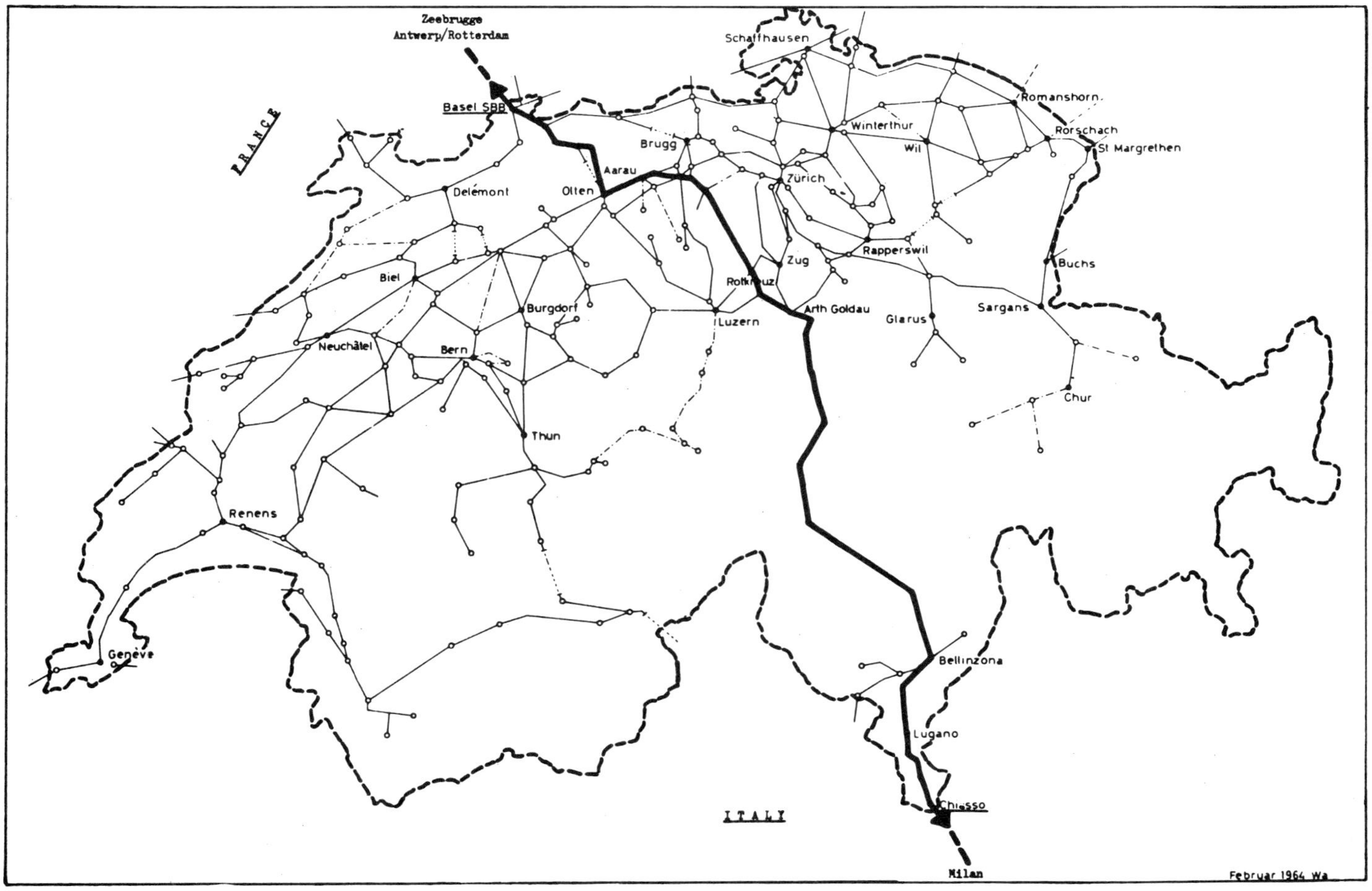

Switzerland. Railway container route.

SCHWEIZERISCHE BUNDESBAHNEN (SBB)
CHEMINS DE FER FÉDÉRAUX SUISSES (CFF)
FERROVIE FEDERALI SVIZZERE (FFS)
Hochschulstrasse 6, CH-3000 BERN

GENERAL:
The only container-trains operated by the SBB are those in transit every week-day between the North Sea ports Zeebrugge/Antwerp/Rotterdam and the Italian terminal

at Milan Rogoredo, crossing Switzerland between Basle in the north and Chiasso in the south. The regular freight trains are used for other destinations.
CONTAINER TERMINALS AND STATIONS
Guterverwaltung SBB, St. Jakobstr. 200, CH-4000 Basle.
One container terminal was opened at Basle in 1969. A second privately operated terminal is operational at Chavornay, near Lausanne, and a third is planned for Stabio, near Chiasso.

Swiss Railways Terminal at Basle.

SERVICES

The services provided are mainly transit traffic with some import and export traffic. The SBB do not own any special rail vehicles for container transport, ordinary flat wagons being used for this purpose. Collection and delivery by road are not carried out by the railway, container movement being confined to rail with transfer being effected either at private sidings or at the nearest station with lifting equipment available.

Since early 1968 the transshipment and storage of containers have been effected with the existing facilities.

A number of stations have equipment capable of handling containers, mobile gantries and gantry cranes, and at the main container-transfer stations special transfer devices are available.

Marmara Bulgesi Limau ve Denizis leri Müdürlügü
Istanbul
TELEPHONE: 44.21.97
GENERAL:
The Galata and Salipazari facilities on the

TURKEY
ISTANBUL

European coast of the Bosphorus are administered by Denizcilik Baukasi TAO (Maritime Bank Inc) and the Hydarpasa facilities on the Asian coast by Turkish State Railways.

CONTAINER FACILITIES:
One container berth is at the planning stage.

TURKISH STATE RAILWAYS

Turkish State Railways TCDD
Genel Müoürlügü
Ankara
GENERAL MANAGER:
Vedit Önsal

GENERAL:
Some 100 small containers of 1 m³ (35 cu ft) and 2 m³ (70 cu ft) are in use. The Railway provides a door-to-door or door-to-storage service.

U.S.S.R.
LENINGRAD

Leningrad
Mezhevoy Kanal 5
Lenningrad L-35 USSR
TELEPHONE: 16.28.01
TELEGRAMS: Lenmortorgport, Leningrad L-35
GENERAL:
A plan has been drawn up for the con-

struction of a container terminal in Leningrad. At present container vessels are handled at a conventional facility equipped with 10 ton quay cranes.
AGENT:
Inflot Agency
Mezhevoy Kanal 5

TELEPHONE: 16.48.12
TELEX: 15.05
SERVICES:
Tilbury, Antwerp, Leningrad Line—every 11 days.
Le Havre—Leningrad Line.

NAKHODKA

Nakhodka
ul. Portovaya, 22 Nakhodka
Primorsky Krai U.S.S.R.
TELEPHONE: 62-98
TELEGRAMS: Torgport Nakhodka

GENERAL:
The port of Nakhodka is situated between the Astafiev and Shefreis Capes in the North West Japan Sea. Navigation is year round but during ice formation assistance of ice breaker tugs is required. Nakhodka is the eastern land terminal of the Trans-Siberian railway landbridge link with Japan.
The port was constructed after 1945 and

consists of a long L shaped quay with 17 berths including 5 for timber and oil. Maximum depth alongside is 11·5 m (37 ft 8 in). Electrical portal cranes of up to 41 tons lifting capacity. Concrete floored transit sheds and single and multi-floor warehouses have also been provided.

It is understood that temporary facilities for handling containers are being made available and should be in service by end 1971 at Nakhodka.
FUTURE DEVELOPMENTS:
Two container berths, each with a length of 350 m (1,148 ft) and a depth of water of

12 m (39·4 ft) are under construction and are due for completion in 1975-76 at Wrangel Some 26 km from the port. The facility will be equipped with two or three container gantry cranes
AGENCIES:
Inflot Agency
Lenınskaya ul., 2
TELEPHONE: 54-05, 56-13
TELEGRAMS: Inflot Nakhodka
Sovfrakht
Nakhodka
OFFICIAL:
Galina Kopylova (Director)

Central Shipping and Container Authorities
Ministry of Merchant Marine
1/3 Zhdanova Str.
Moscow
SHIPPING COMPANIES KNOWN TO HAVE VESSELS IN SERVICE OR PLANNED FOR CONTAINERS:
Latvian Steamship Company,
(See entry in Ship Operator Section).
Far-Eastern Steamship Company
(See entry under Nakhodka-Japan Line in

Ship Operator Section).
Baltic Steamship Company
(See entry under Tilbury-Leningrad Line in Ship Operator Section).
Container Department
Sovfrakht Association
GENERAL:
The Department has been set up very recently by the Ministry of Merchant Marine in the Soviet Sovfrakht Association which handles Seaborne foreign trade.

POLICY:
A stock of about 23,000 10 and 20 ft units will be established for a fleet of 20 container vessels due to enter service during the period 1972-5. The ships will operate between ports in Europe and the Far East and on the trans-ocean routes connecting the USSR with Cuba and the Middle East. The design of these vessels will probably include gas turbine propulsion.

VESSELS ON ORDER OR UNDER CONSTRUCTION:
An unspecified number of container carriers of about 6,000 dwt capable of carrying about 200 20 ft units the first of which will enter service in late 1971 are under construction.

Four 22 knot vessels of about 15,000 dwt capable of carrying 700 20 ft units are reported as having been ordered for delivery in 1973-74.

A total of eight 19° knot general cargo vessels fitted for the carriage of containers are reported on order for delivery in 1972. Four of these vessels will carry 420 20 ft units and the other four, 304 units.

INLAND TRANSPORT

SOVIET RAILWAYS

Soviet Railways
Moscow 107 174, Novo-Basmannaaia 2, Ministry of Communications

Traffic

The Railways in the USSR carry over 65 per cent of the country's total freight traffic. (Water transport accounts for 22 per cent of the traffic, road for about 6 per cent and pipeline the remainder).

In 1970 container traffic reached a total of nearly 27 million tons, and this total is equivalent to between 75 and 80 per cent of the " small sized dispatches ". If 'Wagon load' operations were to be turned over to ISO or similar high capacity type containers, it has been estimated that the traffic potential would be in the region of 110-130 million tons per year by 1975.

Container traffic at present accounts for about 6 per cent of cargo excluding the main bulks such as fuels, grain, ores, forest products, mineral fertilizers and building materials and ferrous metals.

Container Operations—Series 3 Type Units

Containers have been used on the railway system since 1936 and some 900,000 units are in service. There are ten basic types of dry box containers the largest of which is a steel 10.4 m^3 (367·3 cu ft) unit with external dimensions of $2.65 \times 2.10 \times 2.40$ m (8·7 $\times$ 6·9 $\times$ 7·9 ft) and a carrying capacity of 4 tonnes. In addition there are specialised units for the carriage of dry and liquid chemicals, etc.

All containers are provided with four lifting points at the top and transfer operations are carried out by using a four legged sling attached to a single hook on a container yard gantry or other crane.

These electric overhead and gantry cranes have capacities of 5 and 10 tons as do the automatic loaders which are also in service. Jib cranes have capacities of up to 15 tons.

Collection and delivery of containers is undertaken by about 10,000 railway owned road vehicles at the 1,170 container depots situated throughout the country. The Road Delivery Association, acting as agents for the Railways, also undertake collection and delivery operations.

Container Operations—ISO Series 1 Type Units

The Series 1 20 ft units have now been introduced into service, special rolling stock and handling facilities are also in course of being provided. Container trains have been scheduled into service.

These containers are used in international traffic between the USSR and Comecon countries; also between USSR, Yugoslavia, Finland, Italy, Japan and the United Kingdom.

The numbers of large units in service are planned to increase during the period up to 1980 until they account for about half the number in service.

It is planned that terminals coming into service at the major centres will be designed to handle a daily throughput of either 1,500, 2,500 or 4,000 units.

As plans stand at present it is not intended to operate permanently coupled wagons in container trains due to operational and repair difficulties. Flat cars capable of carrying all types of containers are being developed.

Trans-Siberian trains planned for operations from Nakhodka through to Moscow and onwards to either Leningrad or through the Germany/Poland or the Hungary/Austria routes will be composed of 50 flat wagons each carrying two 20 ft units.

Track under Construction:

A 26 km extension of the rail track to link Vrangel, the container port of Nakhodka, to Nakhodka the Trans-Siberian Railhead is due for completion in Summer 1972.

Future Developments:

In 1971-75 five main types of containers will be built with the following specifications:

Type	Tare tons	Lifting Capacity tons	Internal Volume m^3	External Dimension mm
YYK 3	0·56	2·44	5·2	2100 $\times$ 1325 $\times$ 2400
YYK 3 (5)	0·60	4·40	5·2	2100 $\times$ 1325 $\times$ 2400
YYK 5	1·08	3·92	10·6	2650 $\times$ 2100 $\times$ 2400
ID	1·40	8·60	14·6	2989 $\times$ 2436 $\times$ 2435
IC	2·20	17·80	30·3	6055 $\times$ 2436 $\times$ 2435

Leningrad— Rail Container Terminal.

EUROPE—JAPAN VIA TRANS-SIBERIAN RAILWAY:
Jeuro Container Line
Links with Intercontainer train service
Schenker's Trans-Siberian Container Service

Links with European railways or truck service with Moscow.
Trans-Siberian Container Line
Links with Leningrad and sea link.
Unitrans Ltd.

Links with Intercontainer train service or truck service with Moscow.
NOTE:
See non-vessel operating carrier section for details.

Loaded container and roll-on goods traffic by overseas country/trading area, Great Britain, 1965–1970

Source: National Ports Council Container and Roll-on Statistics Great Britain, 1971

Overseas country/trading area	Number of loaded units(1)				Tonnage of goods (thousand tons)							
	1970	1969	1968	1967	1970 Total	1970 Other traffic on roll-on services	1970 Wheeled/container units only	1969(2) Total	1968	1967 Wheeled/container units	1966	1965
Foreign trade												
Near sea												
Irish Republic	223,097	221,419	210,642	158,497	1,535	10	1,525	1,411	1,288	894	754	500
Near Continent												
Western Germany	12,007	9,091			322	152	170	324				
Netherlands	229,013	211,309			2,631	193	2,437	2,378				
Belgium	200,304	171,115			2,256	81	2,175	1,755				
France	142,686	107,015			1,695	144	1,551	1,244				
Unallocated	650	92			4	—	4	—				
Total Near Continent	584,660	498,622	385,895		6,907	570	6,337	5,702	3,518	3,243	2,048	
Total Near sea	807,757	720,041	596,537		8,442	580	7,862	7,112	4,806			
Short sea												
Scandinavia and Baltic												
Denmark	50,598	29,859			711	157	554	390				
Sweden	53,707	45,954			913	291	622	701				
Other	31,350	20,163			381	53	328	219				
Total	135,655	95,976	49,992		2,005	502	1,503	1,309	531			
Iberia and Mediterranean	34,878	19,114			344	2	342	161	531			
Total Short sea	170,533	115,090	49,992		2,349	504	1,845	1,470	531			
Deep sea												
North America												
U.S.A.	104,888	71,393			1,207	—	1,207	791				
Canada	74,842	40,424			885	—	885	455				
Total North America	179,730	111,817			2,091	—	2,091	1,245				
Other	42,931	833			476	—	476	4				
of which: Australasia	40,776				462	—	462					
Total Deep sea	222,661	112,650	72,759		2,568	—	2,568	1,250	709			
Unallocated	—	—	50,009	377,352	—	—	—	—	238	3,243	2,048	1,410
Total Foreign trade	1,200,951	947,781	769,297	535,849	13,359	1,084	12,275	9,832	6,285	4,137	2,803	1,910
Coastwise trade												
Northern Ireland	297,303	291,510	301,074	271,938	2,817	76	2,741	2,572	2,317	1,841	1,721	1,560
Other	92,407	84,331	87,151	13,535	437	—	437	336	288	49	14	10
Total Coastwise trade	389,710	375,841	388,225	285,473	3,254	76	3,178	2,909	2,605	1,891	1,736	1,570
Total Foreign and Coastwise trade	1,590,661	1,323,622	1,157,522	821,322	16,613	1,160	15,453	12,740	8,890	6,027	4,538	3,480
of which:												
Across Irish Sea	520,400	512,929	511,716	430,435	4,351	85	4,266	3,983	3,606	2,735	2,475	2,060
Other	1,070,261	810,693	645,806	390,887	12,262	1,074	11,188	8,757	5,284	3,292	2,063	1,420

(1) Numbers of loaded units are not available for 1966 or 1965.

(2) The tonnage figures for 1969 include 1.1 million tons of import/export vehicles and other goods traffic on roll-on services not on road goods vehicles or in container units which were not previously covered by the returns.

ARDROSSAN

Ardrossan Harbour Co. Ltd.
Ardrossan,
Ayrshire,
Scotland
TELEPHONE: Ardrossan 3972/4
TELEX: 77654
PRINCIPAL OFFICIALS:
J. H. Shields (*General Manager & Secretary*)
W. McCall (*Assistant General Manager & Treasurer*)
Captain T. B. Scott (*Harbour Master*)
Captain W. D. Gillespie (*Traffic Superintendent*)
W. S. Currie (*Engineer*)
CONTAINER FACILITIES
No. 2(a)/3 Eglinton Dock:
No. 4/5 Eglinton Dock:
These berths are capable of accepting vessels of 70·1 m (230 ft) in length 11·58 m (38 ft) beam and 4·72 m (15·5 ft) draught. This limitation is imposed by the container service requirement of being able to arrive and sail at any state of the tide. Both berths are equipped with two Scotch derrick cranes with 25 and 16 ton capacities at No. 2(a)/3 and 32 and 16 ton capacities at No. 4/5 Dock. These four cranes are each capable of a handling cycle of 15 containers on and off per hour. No. 2(a)3 berth has a parking area of 2023m² (½ acre) and No. 4/5 Berth has 4047 m² (1 acre).
ROLL-ON/ROLL-OFF FACILITIES:
No. 10 Berth, Eglinton Basin:
Capable of accepting vessels of 111·2 m (365 ft) in length 17·52 (57·5 ft) and 4·57 m (15 ft) draught, this berth is fitted with an automatically adjusting ramp, it has a parking area of 4047 m² (1 acre).
No. 16 Berth, Old Tidal Basin:
Capable of accepting vessels of 82·3 m (270 ft) in length with a 14·3 m (47 ft) beam and a draught of 3·2 m (10·5 ft), this berth is fitted with an adjustable ramp.
TERMINAL WORKING HOURS:
Services differ, but between 0600 and 2300 hours daily.
PRINCIPAL CONTAINER FREIGHT FORWARDING COMPANIES:
Northern Ireland Trailers (Scotland) Ltd., Dock Road, Ardrossan, Ayrshire
Telephone: 3046
Containerway & Roadferry Ltd., Harbour Street, Ardrossan, Ayrshire
Telephone: 4111
SERVICES:
Containers:
Atlantic Steam Navigation Co. Ltd.
4/5 Eglinton Dock

Ardrossan to Larne—5 sailings per week with two vessels
Roll-on:
Burns and Laird Lines Ltd.
No. 10 Eglinton Basin
Ardrossan to Belfast—6 sailings per week with one vessel.
Burns and Laird Lines Ltd.
No. 10 Eglinton Basin
Ardrossan to Larne—5 sailings per week with one vessel
Caledonian Steam Packet Co. Ltd.
No. 16 Old Tidal Basin
Ardrossan to Brodick (Arran)—18 to 13 sailings per week with one vessel.

Ardrossan—No. 10 Berth

BELFAST

Belfast Harbour Commissioners
Belfast
Northern Ireland
TELEPHONE: Belfast 34422
TELEX: 74204
PRINCIPAL OFFICIALS:
A. Norman Lockhart (*General Manager*)
D. H. McMullen (*Assistant General Manager, Estate Planning*)
Gordon Hutchinson (*Assistant General Manager, Administration*)
Cecil Nimmons (*Assistant General Manager, Finance*)
Kenneth Ross (*Chief Engineer*)
William McKinney (*Port Operations Manager*)
ROLL-ON/ROLL-OFF FACILITIES
Donegall Quay No. 4
Operated by Belfast S.S. Co. this berth has an adjustable ramp and a parking area of 1·34 hectares (3·3 acres).

Donegall Quay No 5
Operated by Burns Laird lines this berth has

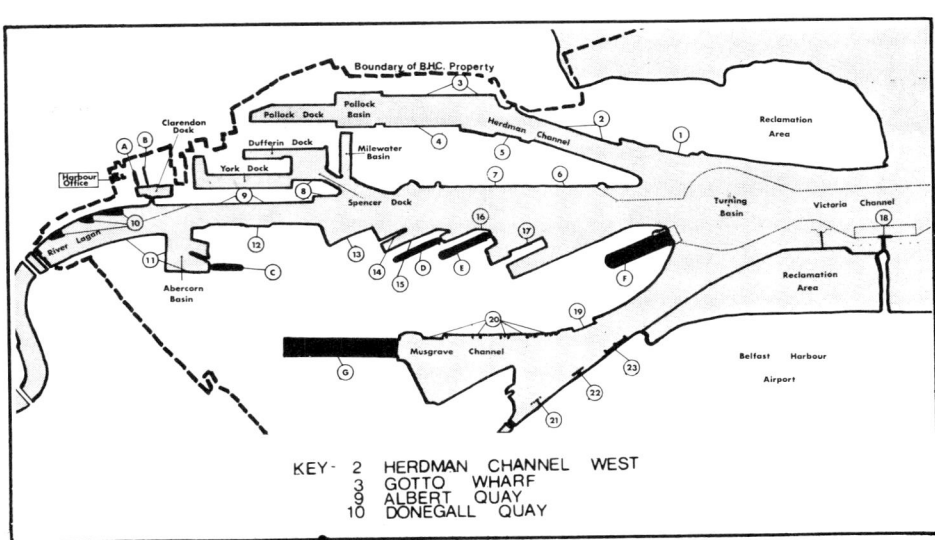

KEY- 2 HERDMAN CHANNEL WEST
3 GOTTO WHARF
9 ALBERT QUAY
10 DONEGALL QUAY

an adjustable ramp and a parking area of 7,107 m² (1·74 acres).
Donegall Quay No. 6
Operated by British Railways Board, this facility has an adjustable ramp and a parking area of 8,361 m² (2·08 acres).

CONTAINER FACILITIES:
Herdman Channel 1
Operated by Atlantic Steam Navigation Co. this berth is equipped with a 30 ton container gantry crane with an outreach of 17·06 m (56 ft) over water and 48·77 m (160 ft) over the quay. It is also equipped with an adjustable ramp for roll-on traffic and it has a parking area of 1·75 hectares (4·32 acres).

Herdman Channel 2
This berth is operated by Cawoods Containers Ltd., and is equipped with a 30 ton gantry crane with an outreach of 13·72 m (45 ft) over water and 15·24 m (50ft) over land. The crane is capable of handling 40 ft units and there is 1·34 hectares (3·31 acres) of parking space.

Ballast Quay and Spencer Dock:
Operated by Belfast Steamship Co it is equipped with three 25 ton scotch derricks. 1 hectare (2·47 acres) of parking and marshalling space is available.

York Dock:
This is a general cargo berth for the side loading, palletised and container services of the Holland-Ireland Line.

Gotto Wharf
Operated by British Railways for their Holyhead service, this facility is equipped with two 30 ton container gantry cranes and two Goliath 2-6-3 yard gantries have been provided to handle the containers to and from the marshalling area. There is a parking area of 2·5 hectares (6·18 acres).

Transport Ferry Service and Cawood's Container Terminals, Herdman Channel

Drive-on/Drive-off berths for Liverpool (Belfast Steamship Company) and Ardrossan (Burns-Laird Line) Passenger and Freight Services.

UNIT LOAD SERVICES:

Company	Service
Belfast Steamship Co., Ltd. 42 Donegall Quay, Belfast	via Liverpool to UK and Europe—daily
Coast Lines, Ltd 42 Donegall Quay Belfast	via Liverpool to UK and Europe—daily
Burns & Laird Lines, Ltd., 42 Donegall Quay, Belfast	via Ardrossan to UK and Europe—daily
British Railways, Donegall Quay, Belfast	via Heysham and Holyhead to UK and Europe—daily
Atlantic Steam Navigation Co., Ltd., (Transport Ferry Service) Herdman Channel West, Belfast	via Preston to UK and Europe—daily
Cawoods Containers Ltd., Herdman Channel West, Belfast	via Garston to UK and Europe—thrice weekly
Containerway & Roadferry Ltd., Cupar Street, Belfast	via Preston to UK and Europe—daily
Belfast Steamship Co. Ltd., Ballast Quay, Belfast	via Liverpool to UK and Europe—daily
Northern Ireland Trailers, Ltd., 171 Limestone Road, Belfast	via Liverpool to UK and Europe—daily
Ulster Ferry Transport, 113 Corporation Street, Belfast	via Liverpool to UK and Europe—daily
Unit Loads (Ireland) Ltd., 61 Gt. Victoria Street, Belfast	via Liverpool, Preston Garston, to UK and Europe—daily
Strangson Shipping Ltd., Dunmurray, Belfast	via Glasson Dock to U.K. and Europe—thrice weekly
G. Heyn & Sons, Ltd., Victoria Street, Belfast	Europe, Canada and USA—weekly
Emerald Line, Ltd., (Corken Howe & Co Ltd) 22 North Street, Belfast	Denmark and Sweden—thrice monthly
Glen & Co. Ltd., (D. Dorman & Co. Ltd.) 25 Corporation Street, Belfast	Sweden and Norway—fortnightly
Dammers Ireland Line, (J. Burke & Co. Ltd.) 83a Corporation Street, Belfast	Holland, Belgium and France—weekly
Holland Ireland Line (G. Heyn & Sons, Ltd.) Victoria Street, Belfast	Holland and France—weekly
Cawood's Containers Ltd., Herdman Channel West, Belfast	Holland—weekly

Belfast Steamship Company's Terminals at Ballast Quay and Spencer Dock

CONTAINER TRAFFIC:
Total Roll-on/Roll-off and Container traffic moving through Belfast was as follows:

1968—Inwards		685,000	tons
Outwards		529,000	tons
1969—Inwards		821,000	tons
Outwards		606,000	tons

1970	*Loaded Units*	*Tons*
Inwards	99,851	943,000
Outwards	69,978	673,000

A ten per cent increase in traffic is anticipated in 1971.

TERMINAL WORKING HOURS:
These are usually 0800 to 1700 hrs daily.

BELLPORT

Bellport

Corporation Road, Newport,
Monmouthshire
TELEPHONE: Newport 73941
TELEX: 49446

GENERAL:
A privately owned and operated facility for the Bell Lines services.

CONTAINER FACILITIES:
This is an impounded graving dock equipped with a Paceco-Vickers container gantry crane which spans the dock and the marshalling yard. The dock has an operating length of 91·4 m (300 ft). A rail spur connects the terminal with the Freightliner network.

Bell Victor at Bellport, Newport.

BRISTOL

Port of Bristol Authority

19 Queen Square, Bristol 1
TELEPHONE: Bristol 25381
TELEGRAMS: Docks Bristol
OFFICIALS
G. Edney (*General Manager*)
R. Woodall (*Chief Docks Manager*)
CONTAINER FACILITIES:
T Berth Avonmouth
This facility has a quay length of 198·1 m (650 ft) and is capable of taking vessels 201·2 m (660 ft) in length, 28·96 m (95 ft) beam with a draught of 10·36 m (34 ft). It is equipped with a 30 ton Strachan and Henshaw container gantry crane capable of 20 cycles per hour which has an outreach over water of 25·9 m (85 ft) and over the quay of 27·12 m (89 ft).
The Storage area is 2·43 hectares (6 acres) and there is an additional supporting area up to 4·04 hectares (10 acres) being constructed partly on reclaimed land to the rear of the berth which ultimately will be linked by two roads with a one-way circulatory traffic system.
N Berth Avonmouth
This facility can accept vessels up to 167·6 m (550 ft) in length, 22.25 m (73 ft) beam and 8·07 m (26.5ft) draught. It is equipped with a 30 Ton Liebherr Container Gantry Crane which feeds a 30 Ton Liebherr Goliath gantry with a span of 35·35 m (116 ft) capable of stacking three high in the yard. The ship/shore gantry is capable of 20 cycles per hour and the total area of the terminal is 1·62 hectares (4 acres).
Inland Clearance Depot
An Inland Clearance Depot, managed by the West of England Freight Terminals Ltd. is at the Avonmouth Docks Estates, Chittening only 2¼ miles away.
TERMINAL WORKING HOURS:
Ship cargo handling and inland transport operations take place between 0800 and 1700 hours and at other times as required.
ACCESS
(1) *Road*
A motorway interchange has been built near

'N' Berth Avonmouth Docks is the Terminal for Bristol Steam Navigation Co. Bristol-Dublin service.

Avonmouth, connecting the M5 with the M4. By 1972 direct motorway access to London, the Midlands and South Wales will be complete.
(2) *Rail*
The transit sheds, quays, and warehouses are rail connected.
(3) *Inland waterways*
The Severn Navigation is available for distribution of cargoes to the Midlands.
CONTAINER SERVICES:
Bristol Steam Navigation Co. (full container ships) from N. Berth Avonmouth to Dublin —twice weekly.
CONTAINER OPERATIONAL GROUPS

Bristol Steam Navigation Co.,
Bathurst Wharf, Bristol
D. Lovell (*Managing Director*)
Telephone: 26321
Telegrams: Besenco
Telex: 44167

'T' Berth Avonmouth Docks, the shed to the left of the picture will be demolished to provide additional space.

CONTAINER TRAFFIC:

Lift on—1970
  Inwards 1,163 units 11,003 tons
  Outwards 2,520 units 22,684 tons

CONTAINER STORAGE & STEVEDORE COMPANIES

Reed Stock & Co. Ltd.,
Avonmouth Docks, Avonmouth
C. Lofthouse (*General Manager*)

INLAND CLEARANCE DEPOT

West of England Freight Terminals Ltd.
Avonmouth Dock Estate
Chittening
G. Osborn-Bartram (*General Manager*)

CONTAINER REPAIR COMPANIES:

E and R Metalcraft
  Unit 14 Severnside Trading Estate,
  Avonmouth, Bristol
  Telephone: Avonmouth 2182

York Trailer Co. Ltd.
  Third Way, Avonmouth, Bristol
  Telephone: Avonmouth 4831

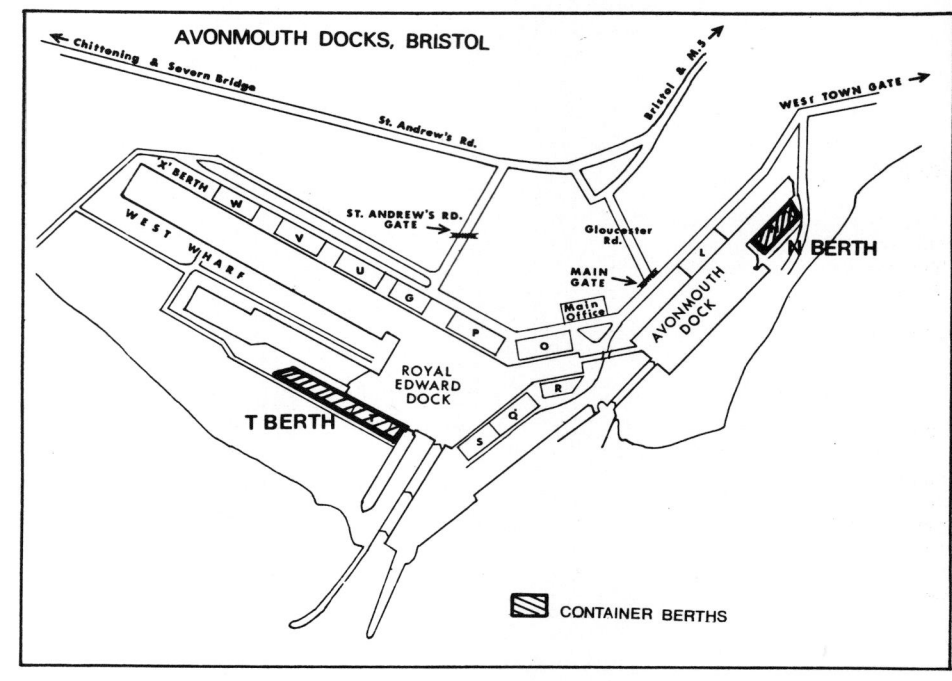

CLYDEPORT

Clydeport Terminal, Greenock.

Clyde Port Authority

16, Robertson Street, Glasgow, C.2
TELEPHONE: 041-221 8733
TELEX: 778446

PRINCIPAL OFFICIALS:

J. P. Davidson (*General Manager*)
J. M. Fletcher (*Assistant General Manager*)
J. B. Maxwell (*Secretary and Solicitor*)
R. B. Braithwaite (*Engineer-in-Chief*)
Captain J. Campbell (*Marine and Operations Manager*)
J. T. McEwen (*Chief Accountant*)

GENERAL:

Clydeport's container terminal is at Greenock where deep water alongside allows access to the riverside terminal at any state of the tide.

From the terminal, trunk roads connect with the national motorway network and from the recently completed railhead adjacent to the terminal, freightliner trains provide a fast rail link with the major industrial centres of Great Britain.

CONTAINER FACILITIES:

The quay has a frontage of 259 m (850 ft) with mooring dolphins at one end and accommodates two vessels with a combined length of 350 m (1,150 ft). Depth alongside is 12·8 m (42 ft) at low water and this can be deepened to 15 m (50 ft) if required. It is situated only 335 m (1,100 ft) from a natural depth of 10 fathoms.

A paved back-up area of 8·9 hectares (22 acres) behind the berth is equipped with straddle carriers and a number of tractor and trailer units on which containers are transported between the terminal and its adjacent railhead.

Two 35 ton Stothert and Pitt container gantry cranes, each with an outreach of 31·9 m (105 ft) over water and 72 ft over land, load and discharge containers at a rate of up to 40 an hour.

FUTURE DEVELOPMENTS:

An additional 102·4 m (336 ft) of quay wall will be completed in Spring 1972, this will provide a total quay length of 361·4 m (1,186 ft). A third container gantry crane is being provided together with additional straddle carriers and the container parking area will be extended by 2·43 hectares (6 acres).

A further 128 m (420 ft) of quay frontage is available for development and the timing of this, and also the provision of a link span for roll-on operations will depend upon the growth of traffic volume and the numbers and frequency of services.

INLAND CLEARANCE DEPOT:

An associated Customs approved Inland Clearance Depot is located at Braehead, Renfrew, five miles from Glasgow and 18 miles from the terminal. Close to the M8 motorway the depot serves importers and exporters of shipments less than a full container load.

Covering an area of six acres, the depot consists of a shed 152 × 30 m (500 × 100 ft) and a paved area for parking and handling containers. The shed is so designed that goods are received and despatched at one side, while

Clydeport—Rail Terminal

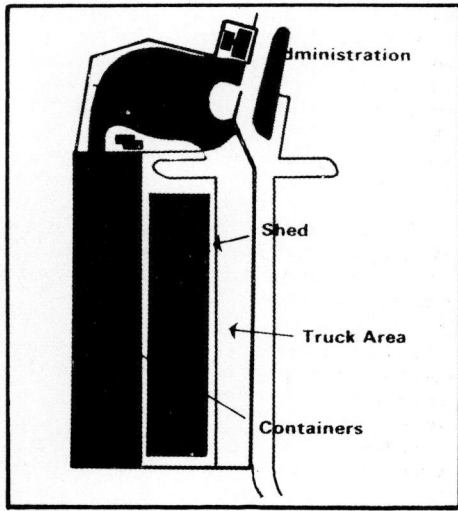

Layout of Braehead Inland Clearance Depot.

containers are packed and unpacked at the other.

The inland clearance depot is operated by Clyde Container Services Limited, a consortium comprising the Clyde Port Authority, and shipping and storage interests.

CUSTOMS FACILITIES FOR CONTAINERS:

H.M. Customs examine (if necessary) and clear house to house containers at the terminal. Examination and clearance of L.C.L. traffic is carried out at Braehead I.C.D. Renfrew.

TRAFFIC:	Inwards Loaded		Outwards Loaded	
	Units	Tons	Units	Tons
1970 Lift on	9,700	95,000	18,150	165,000
1971 Estimate	11,200	110,000	26,500	240,000

CONTAINER SERVICES—CLYDEPORT CONTAINER TERMINAL, GREENOCK

Name of Company	Glasgow Agent	Frequency of service	Area and Ports Served
Atlantic Container Lines	Anchor Line Ltd., 59 Waterloo Street, C.2. 041—221 9809	Weekly	East Canada & USA: Halifax, New York, Portsmouth VA, Baltimore
Hapag-Lloyd Container Line	John G. Boreland & Peat Ltd., 95 Bothwell Street, C.2. 041—248 3651	Weekly	East Coast USA: New York, Baltimore, Norfolk, Philadelphia
Head/Donaldson Lines, C.P. Ships, Manchester Liners	The Donaldson Line Ltd., 14 St. Vincent Place, C.1. 041—221 9161	Weekly	East Canada: Montreal Quebec (Head/ Donaldson, C.P. Ships) Montreal (Manchester Liners)
Gulf Container Line	Currie Line Ltd,. 59, Waterloo Street, 041—221 9809	Fortnightly	USA Gulf Ports: Houston, New Orleans, Mobile Bermuda, Nassau and Miami
United States Lines	W. B. Woolley & Co. 54 West Nile Street, C.1. 041—248 2929	Weekly	East Coast USA: New York, Baltimore, Norfolk
Hapag Lloyd/Holland America/C.G.T. Joint Service	John G. Borland and Peat Ltd., 95 Bothwell Street, Glasgow C2. 041-248-3651	Fortnightly	West Canada and USA: Los Angeles, San Francisco, Oakland, Vancouver, Portland

Note:—All the above services use cellular container vessels.

CONTAINER SERVICES—CONVENTIONAL BERTHS, GLASGOW

Name of Company	Glasgow Agent	Type of Vessel	Frequency of Service	Area and Ports Served
Scanstar	J. S. Nowery & Co. Ltd., 93 Hope Street, C.2. 041—221 3775	Conventional Vessels	10 days	Panama and West Canada and USA: Los Angeles, San Francisco, Seattle, Portland, Vancouver, New Westminster
Head/Donaldson Lines	The Donaldson Line Ltd., 14 St. Vincent Place, C.1. 041—221 3901	Conventional Vessels	Fortnightly	East Canada and USA and Canadian Lakes Ports: Toronto, Toledo, Detroit, Chicago, Milwaukee
Swedish Atlantic— Wilhelmsen Line	Escombe McGrath & Co. Ltd., 89 West Campbell Street, C.2. 041—248 4081	Conventional Vessels	Fortnightly	USA South East & Gulf Ports: Wilmington, Charleston, Savannah, Miami, Mobile, New Orleans, Houston

HEALTH REGULATIONS FOR CONTAINERS:
The requirements/regulations concerning the examination by the Port Health Authority of foodstuffs imported in containers are contained in the Food Drugs—Food Hygiene— The imported Food (Scotland) Regulations 1968.

TERMINAL WORKING HOURS:

Vessels are operated 24 hours per day and inland transport handling operations take place between 0800 and 1700 hours, Monday to Friday. Overtime is worked as and when required.

CONTAINER REPAIR FACILITIES:
Consort (Glasgow)
Burnside Industrial Estate,

Kilsyth,
Glasgow.
Kilsyth-2122
Repcon Ltd.
Containerbase, Gartsherrie Road, Coatbridge
Coatbridge 27260
Archd. Young (Storage) Ltd.
Young's Wharf, Meadowside Road, Renfrew, 041—886 2356

SHIPPING AND FORWARDING AGENTS:
AIRSEA FREIGHT CO. (SCOTLAND) LTD.,
45 West Nile Street, Glasgow, C.1.
041—248 3991

D. C. ANDREWS, BALLANTYNE & CO. LTD.,
136 Buchanan Street, Glasgow, C.1.
041—248 5586

ARBUCKLE, SMITH & CO. LTD.,
91 Mitchell Street, Glasgow, C.1
041—248 5050
R. M. BEVERIDGE & CO. LTD.,
14 St. Vincent Place, Glasgow, C.1
041—221 3615
JOHN G. BORLAND & PEAT LTD.,
95, Rothwell Street, Glasgow, C.2
041—248 3651
BRAES, HALLIDAY (GLASGOW) LTD.,
52, St. Enoch Square, Glasgow, C.1
041—248 3314
J. S. BRAID & CO.,
116 Hope Street, Glasgow, C.2
041—221 0788
CAMERON & CO.,
12 Renfield Street, Glasgow, C.2
041—221 3052

WALDIE & CAMERON LTD.,
5 Catkinview Road, Glasgow, S.2
041—632 9271

CARGO SUPERINTENDENTS LTD.,
50 Wellington Street, Glasgow, C.2
041—248 3129

CONNAL & CO. LTD.,
24 Craigmont Street, Maryhill, Glasgow, NW
041—946 5141

CONTAINERWAY & ROADFERRY LTD.,
17 Tylefield Street, Glasgow, S.E.
041—554 0526

CONVOYS LTD.,
Burnfield Road, Thornliebank, Glasgow
041—632 9165

THOMAS COOK & SON LTD.,
12 Waterloo Street, Glasgow, C.1
041—221 2168

CORY BROS., SHIPPING LTD.,
8 Woodside Terrace, Glasgow, C.3
041—332 2494

CUBE SHIPPING & WAREHOUSING CO. LTD.,
104 West George Street, Glasgow, C.2
041—332 2821

DAVIDSON PARK & SPEED LTD.,
200 St. Vincent Street, Glasgow, C.2
041—221 9591

DAVIES TURNER & CO., LTD.,
14, Mitchell Lane, Glasgow, C.1
041—248 6227

EUROFREIGHT LTD.,
1 Rutherglen Road, Rutherglen, Glasgow
041—647 3833

GELLATLY HANKEY & CO. LTD.,
116 Hope Street, Glasgow, C.2
041—221 7832

GENERAL FREIGHT CO. LTD.,
54 West Nile Street, Glasgow, C.1
041—221 0505

GENERAL STEAM NAVIGATION CO. LTD.,
75 Hope Street, Glasgow, C.2
041—248 7021

GERHARD & HEY LTD.,
93 Hope Street, Glasgow, C.2
041—221 3775

GILLESPIE & NICOL (GLASGOW) LTD.,
142 St. Vincent Street,
Glasgow, C.2
041—221 0623

HENDERSON MACCALL & CO. LTD.,
52, St. Enoch Square, Glasgow, C.2
041—248 3314

LEP TRANSPORT LTD.,
38 Queen Street, Glasgow, C.1
041—248 6484

J. H. LEWIS & PARTNERS LTD.,
67 West Regent Street, Glasgow, C.2
041—332 1341

C. SHAW LOVELL & SONS LTD.,
98 West George Street, Glasgow, C.2
041—332 8892

D. MACKENZIE (TRAVEL) LTD.,
160 St. Vincent Street, Glasgow, C.2
041—248 7781

H. MACLAINE (LONDON) LTD.,
52, St. Enoch Square, Glasgow, C.2
041—248 3314

M. MACLEOD & CO.,
143 West Regent Street, Glasgow, C.2
041—248 4171

WM. MARTIN & CO. (MARINE) LTD.,
24 St. Vincent Place, Glasgow, C.1
041—221 6981

THOMAS MEADOWS & CO. LTD.,
Sandyford Road, Paisley
041—887 1260

J. S. NOWERY & CO. LTD.,
93 Hope Street, Glasgow, C.2
041—221 3775

P.I.E. TRANSPORT INC.
173 St. Vincent Street, Glasgow, C.2
041—221 8955

J. C. PEACOCK & CO. LTD.,
166 Buchanan Street, Glasgow, C.1
041—332 7101

PICKFORD'S SHIPPING AND FORWARDING CO., LTD.,
62, Robertson Street, Glasgow, C.2
041—221 7676

PITT & SCOTT LTD.,
1 Dixon Street, Glasgow, C.1
041—248 5522

PRENTICE, SERVICE & HENDERSON LTD.,
68 Gordon Street, Glasgow, C.2
041—248 4011

JAMES RANKINE & SONS LTD.,
45 West Nile Street, Glasgow, C.1
041—221 9451

ROBERTSON, BUCKLEY & CO. LTD.,
26 West Nile Street, Glasgow, C.1
041—221 5332

ROXBURGH HENDERSON & CO., LTD.,
80, Buchanan Street, Glasgow, C.1
041—221 9891

SCHENKERS LTD.,
38, Queen Street, Glasgow, C.1
041—221 4282

JOHN SCOTT & CO. (SHIPPING) LTD.,
80 Blythswood Street, Glasgow, C.2
041—221 0381

SCOTTISH EXPRESS LTD.,
127 St. Vincent Street, Glasgow, C.2
041—221 2148

JAMES H. SHARPE & CO. (1941) LTD.,
34 West George Street, Glasgow, C.2
041—332 2153

JAMES SPENCER & CO. (STEVEDORES) LTD.,
165 Finnieston Street, Glasgow, C,3
041—221 5224

F. C. STRICK & CO. (GLASGOW) LTD.,
95 Bothwell Street, Glasgow, C.2
041—248 6131

SUTHERLAND INTERNATIONAL DESPATCH LTD.,
82 Mitchell Street, Glasgow, C.1
041—248 6256

THOS. TRAPP & CO.,
Trafalgar House, 75 Hope Street, Glasgow C.2
041—248 7021

WESTERN TRANSPORT SERVICE,
1022 Dumbarton Road, Glasgow, W.4
041—954 6256

W. WINGATE & JOHNSTON LTD.,
98 West George Street, Glasgow, C.2
041—332 5301

W. B. WOOLLEY & CO. LTD.,
54 West Nile Street, Glasgow, C.1
041—248 2929

CONTAINER STORAGE AND STEVEDORING COMPANIES:

STORAGE:
Storage of containers is undertaken by the Clyde Port Authority at Deanside and Braehead Storage Depots, Renfrew and at Laird Street Storage Depot, Greenock.

STEVEDORES:
James Spencer & Co. (Stevedores) Ltd., 165 Finnieston Street, Glasgow, C.3
041—221 5224
Strathclyde Stevedoring Services Ltd., Prince's Dock, Glasgow, S.W.1
041—427 1233

CLYDE PORT AUTHORITY
CONTAINER TERMINAL—GREENOCK
GENERAL LAYOUT PLAN

DOVER

Dover Harbour Board
Harbour House, Dover, Kent.
TELEPHONE: Dover 2381
PRINCIPAL OFFICIAL:
Kenneth Davis, O.B.E.,
(*General Manager and Register*)

ROLL-ON/ROLL-OFF BERTHS:
There are four berths in the Eastern Docks three of which, Nos. 1, 2 and 4 are capable of handling vessels up to 122 m (400 ft) in length with a beam of 21·3 m (70 ft) and a draught of 5·5m (18 ft). The fourth berth 'Camber Berth' takes vessels of 88·4 × 18·3 × 2·7 m (290 × 60 × 9 ft). These four berths have a vehicle marshalling area of 12·14 hectares (30 acres) and are equipped with special ramps which adjust for tide and ships' draught conditions. Container gantries have been provided for handling containers to slave trailers and one acre of shed space has been made available for customs examination of trailers. The Train Ferry Dock in the Western Docks handles vessels up to 115·8 m (380 ft) in length, 18·3 (60 ft) in beam with a draught of 4 m (13 ft). This berth has an adjustable shore ramp and 4·05 hectares (10 acres) of supporting land for marshalling and parking vehicles.

FUTURE DEVELOPMENT::
A further berth with a double deck ramp will be operational in 1973.

TERMINAL WORKING HOURS:
24 hours seven days per week.

DATA PROCESSING EQUIPMENT

On line Argus 400 with 8K storage is available when required.

ROLL-ON ROLL-OFF TRAFFIC:

Number of commercial road haulage vehicles passing through the port:

1968 38,081
1969 54,270
1970 83,277

In addition over 865,000 accompanied motor vehicles and 63,000 import/export cars were handled in 1970.

PRINCIPAL FREIGHT FORWARDERS:

Anglo-Overseas Transport Ltd.,
Eastern Docks,
Dover
British Railways Shipping and International Services Division,
Southern House,
Dover
George Hammond & Co. (Shipping) Ltd.,
134 Snargate Street,
Dover
J. Johnson & Co. Ltd.,
Eastern Docks,
Dover
L.E.P. Transport,
Eastern Docks,
Dover

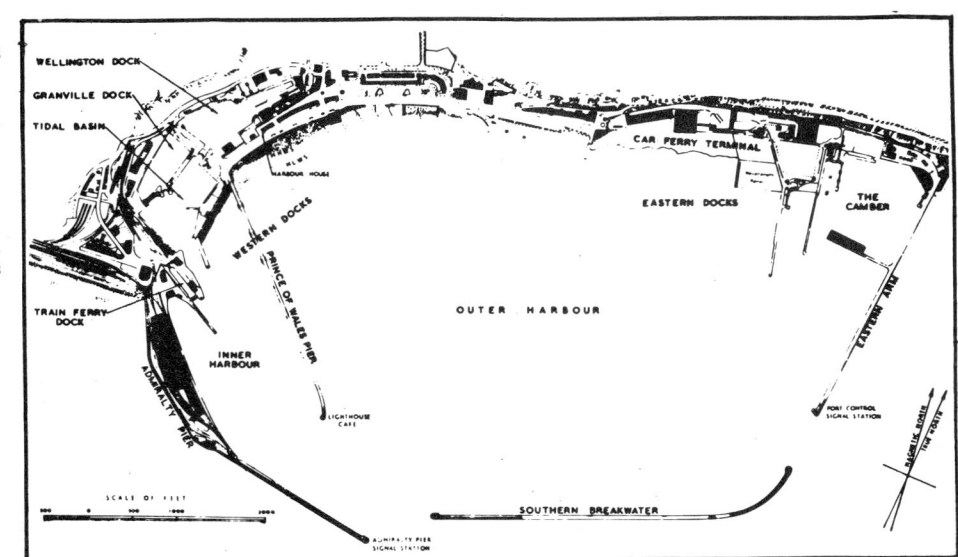

Dover.

M and S Shipping Ltd.,
Eastern Docks,
Dover

Townsend Car Ferries Ltd.,
Eastern Docks,
Dover

ROLL-ON/ROLL-OFF SERVICES:

NAME OF COMPANY	BERTH	NAME OF SHIP	ROUTE AND FREQUENCY
British Railways	No. 2 Berth Eastern Docks	Dover	Dover to: Boulogne up to 4 per day
		Vortigern	Boulogne up to 4 per day
		Lord Warden	Boulogne up to 4 per day
		Maid of Kent	Boulogne up to 4 per day
		Normannia	
French Railways	No. 1 Berth Eastern Docks	Compiegne	Calais up to 4 per day
		Chantilly	Calais up to 4 per day
Belgian Marine Administration		Koningen Fabiola	Ostend up to 2 per day
		Artevelde	Ostend up to 2 per day
		Prinses Astrid	Ostend up to 2 per day
		Prinses Josephine Charlotte	•Ostend up to 1 per day
		Roi Baudouin	Ostend up to 1 per day
Townsend Car Ferries Ltd.	No. 4 Berth Eastern Docks	Free Enterprise I	Calais up to 4 per day
		Free Enterprise II	Calais up to 4 per day
		Free Enterprise III	Zeebrugge up to 2 per day
		Free Enterprise IV	Zeebrugge up to 2 per day
		Free Enterprise V	Zeebrugge up to 2 per day
	Camber Berth Eastern Docks	Autocarrier	Zeebrugge up to 2 per day
British/French Railways	Train Ferry Dock, Western Docks	Vortigern	Dunkirk up to 2 per day
		Twickenham Ferry	Dunkirk up to 2 per day
		St. Germaine	Dunkirk up to 2 per day
		Shepperton Ferry	Dunkirk up to 2 per day
British Rail Hovercraft Ltd.	Hoverport Eastern Docks	Princess Margaret	Boulogne up to 6 per day
		The Princess Anne	Boulogne up to 6 per day

BERTHS ALTERED AS REQUIRED

FELIXSTOWE

The Felixstowe Dock and Railway Company
The Dock, Felixstowe, Suffolk, England
TELEPHONE: Felixstowe 4433
TELEX: 98277
PRINCIPAL OFFICERS:
H. Gordon Parker, M.M., T.E.M. (*Chairman*)
S. Turner (*Managing Director*)
R. W. Kalbraier (*Executive Director, Finance and Admin. and Secretary*)
E. M. Hall (*Operations Manager*)
G. Blackhall M.B.E. (*Manager, General Cargo Division*)
T. L. Simpson (*Manager, Container Division*)
J. H. W. Northfield (*Chief Engineer*)
R. White (*Portmaster*)
J. W. Minns (*Commercial Officer*)
R. W. J. Palmer (*Press Officer*)

Felixstowe

CONTAINER AND ROLL-ON FACILITIES:

Container Terminal:

This facility has a quay length of 405·5 m (1,330 ft) with 10·05 m (33 ft) of water alongside. There is a paved storage area of 32·37 hectares (80 acres) and covered facilities for groupage amounting to 7,246 m² (78,000 ft²) and a transit shed providing an area of 9,858 m² (106,000 ft²). Equipment consists of two 30 ton Paceco Vickers container gantry cranes capable of handling 20-30-35 and 40 ft units on automatic spreaders. There are also ten Clark Vancarriers, ten elevating fifth wheel tractor units with a fleet of 25 ton capacity trailers, two 30 ton mobile cranes, low mast fork trucks for groupage operations and automatic weigh-bridges up to 18·2 m (60 ft) in length with a 60 ton capacity.

The terminal has four sets of rail tracks which enable containers to be loaded direct from freightliner trains under the cranes.

The terminal is being extended at the southern end by a further 182·9 m (600 ft) and an additional 1·2 hectares (3 acres) is being reclaimed to give a total quay frontage of 182·88 m (1,950 ft) all with a depth of water of 10·05 m (33 ft) at low water. A third container gantry crane of 40 tons capacity is planned.

Roll-on Berth

This berth, situated at the northern end of the container quay has a depth alongside of 10 m (33 ft) at low water. It is equipped with a double bridge ramp 29·26 m (95·3 ft) long and unlike the Transport Ferry Terminal where a pontoon was adopted, the bridge is raised and lowered by hydraulic rams. It has two decks, the lower is 6·7 m (22 ft) wide and designed to carry two lanes of lorry traffic and very heavy loads up to 350 tons. Twenty feet above, the upper deck has a 3·65 m (12 ft) wide roadway designed for 30 ton lorries.

This roll-on/roll-off facility accepts all known types and sizes of ferry vessels with bow or stern loading arrangements up to 24·4 m (80 ft) beam and has a least depth of 33 feet at LWOST.

Transport Ferry Terminal

South of the Dock Basin lies the Transport Ferry Terminal, completed early in 1965. Here are provided roll-on/roll-off facilities, available at all states of the tide, for bow and stern loading vessels of up to 450 feet in length in a present least depth of 6·7 m (22 ft) at LWOST. The berth will be dredged to 10 m (33 ft) at LWOST when the demand so requires. The Terminal consists of a floating pontoon 45·7 m (150 ft) in length and 27·4 m (90 ft) wide, with a weight of 2,000 tons, and is connected with the marshalling area by two steel girder bridges each 16 feet wide.

The 64 m (210 ft) long quay is equipped with an electric travelling crane, capable of spanning 20 m (65 ft) wide ships, with a capacity of 32 tons at 33·5 m (110 ft) radius and 24 tons at 38 m (125 ft) radius and is backed by some 13 acres of marshalling area and transit sheds. Labour on the Transport Ferry Terminal is organised in two shifts 08.00 hours–16.00 hours and 16.00–24.00 hours daily.

TERMINAL WORKING HOURS:

Ship cargo handling operations take place between 0800 and 2400 hrs from Monday to Friday. Overtime from 0001 to 0800 hrs as required. Saturdays and Sundays are worked as required.

Inland transport operations take place from Monday to Friday from 0800 to 2400 hrs and on Saturday from 0800 to 1200 hrs.

RAIL ACCESS:

All quays, transit sheds and warehouses within the dock operational area are connected to the Company's marshalling yard which has direct access to British Rail lines.

Felixstowe is linked by 13 miles of railway to Ipswich.

Daily Freightliner trains are in operation for the conveyance of I.S.O. containers between the Port of London, Liverpool, Glasgow, Newcastle, Southampton, Birmingham, Leeds, Manchester and Cardiff.

For the purpose of shunting Freightliner trains the Felixstowe Dock and Railway Co. has obtained a 350 h.p. Diesel Electric 0.6.0 Lister-Blackstone shunting locomotive, fitted with vacuum and compressed air braking systems.

Traditional railway equipment is also playing its part in the advancement of the Port. Trunk rail services leave every evening providing fast services to all parts of the country. Important centres, such as London, Birmingham, Manchester, Liverpool, and Newcastle, are reached early next morning, whilst the more distant destinations such as Glasgow is reached by noon the next day.

In 1970 16 per cent of the Port's container traffic moved by rail and the remainder by road.

ROAD ACCESS:

The approach to the Dock operational area, along the A45 from the Midlands via Ipswich, where it is joined by the A12 from London, is not congested. It will be more efficient when the new Dock Spur Road, by-passing Walton and Felixstowe, is constructed.

In co-operation with the major road haulage contractors operating regular services to and from the Dock, a system of reporting and direction has been evolved which virtualy eliminates waiting. Vehicles arriving at Felixstowe Dock to deliver or collect goods may be assured of very prompt attention and an unusually quick turn round.

The new works, such as the East Quay, the Transport Ferry Service Terminal and the Transatlantic Container Terminal have been designed and constructed specifically to aid handling of vehicular traffic.

Sites with direct access to Dock Road have been allocated for leasing to road haulage contractors for depots, maintenance work-shops and offices.

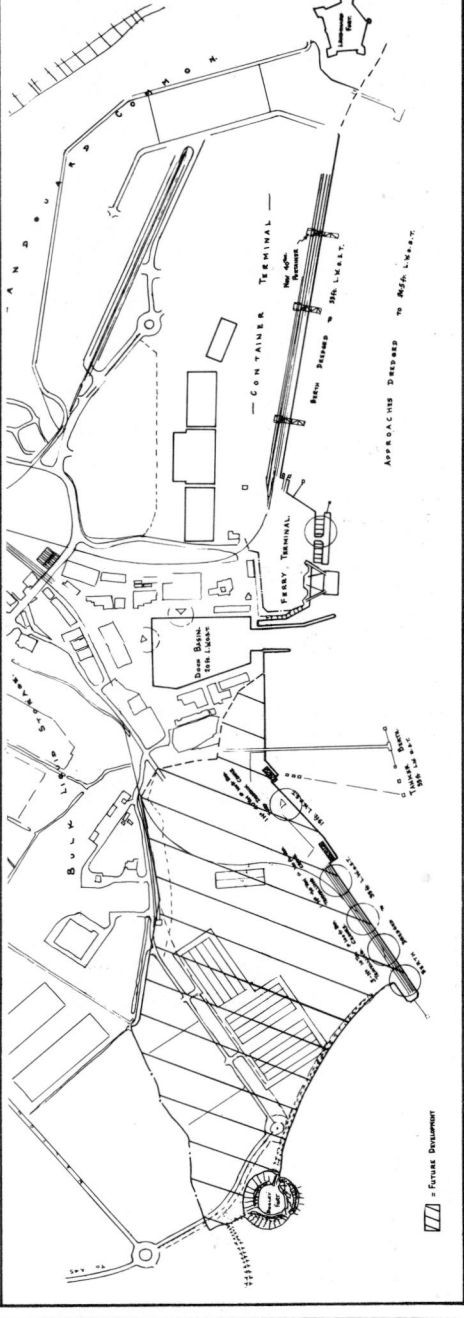

Felixstowe—Transport Ferry Terminal

TRAFFIC:

	Traffic Inwards		Traffic Outwards	
	Tons	No. of Units*	Tons	No. of Units*
Lift-on				
1968	191,122	12,970	128,425	13,108
1969	230,793	20,841	191,771	18,802
1970	303,093	26,017	248,730	23,574
Roll-on				
1968	257,531	—	252,721	—
1969	310,235	—	319,517	—
1970	375,005	—	334,958	—

*Not expressed in terms of 20 ft units.

SERVICES—LIFT-ON:

Deep Sea

Sea-Land Service Inc.
New York—every 5 days.

American Export Isbrandtsen Lines
New York—weekly.

Hapag Lloyd A.G.
New York, Baltimore, Norfolk and Philadelphia—weekly.

United States Lines
New York—weekly.

Seatrain Lines Inc.
New Jersey, Philadelphia, Charleston—fortnightly.

Combi Line
United States South Atlantic and Gulf Ports—weekly.

Gulf Container Line
Houston, New Orleans, Mobile—fortnightly

New England Express Line
Boston—fortnightly

Short Sea

Holland Steamship Co/Phoenix Line
Amsterdam—3 sailings weekly.

Malta Cross-Continent Lines
Malta—fortnightly

SBC Container Lines
Pasajes —weekly

b-Line
Gothenburg, Helsingborg, Århus—weekly.

Short Sea Transport AG
Bilbao—weekly.

Svea Line
Helsingborg, Copenhagen, Rotterdam—2 sailings weekly.

European Unit Routes (EUR)
Rotterdam—5 sailings weekly

Sea-Land Services Inc.
Feeder Services to Gothenburg, Rotterdam, Le Havre—weekly.

SERVICES—ROLL-ON:

Transport Ferry Service
Rotterdam—11 sailings weekly
Antwerp—3 sailings weekly

DFDS (The United Steamship Co. Ltd.)
Ejsberg—2 sailings weekly.

Seaway Car Transporters
Copenhagen, Malmo and Gothenburg—weekly.
Gothenburg—weekly.
Copenhagen—weekly.
Oslo—weekly.

FUTURE DEVELOPMENTS:

In addition to the lengthening of the container terminal reported above further areas of land behind the terminal will be made available for storage and marshalling of containers; the plans allow for the provision of a rail terminal.

To the north of the Dock Basin a quay frontage of 487·7 m (1,600 ft) enclosing an area of 24·3 hectares (60 acres) will provide for future roll-on terminals and general cargo handling facilities as required. Provision for the handling of cargo carrying hovercraft is also being made in this area.

CONTAINER STORAGE AND STEVEDORE COMPANIES:

The Felixstowe Dock & Railway Company supply both facilities.

CONTAINER REPAIR FACILITIES:

Crane Fruehauf Trailers Ltd.

Walton Avenue, Felixstowe
Telephone: 4725

Nu-Con Services Ltd.
The Dock, Felixstowe
Telephone: 6411

Thames Services (Marine) Ltd
Trelawney House, Felixstowe
Telephone: 3962

COMPANIES AND ORGANISATIONS WITH OFFICES AT THE PORT OF FELIXSTOWE:

Thos Allen Ltd.
Tel: 6284. Telex: 98468

Alltransport Ltd.
Tel: 6181. Telex: 98180

American Export Isbrandtsen Lines, Inc.
Tel: 4404. Telex: 98505

Amo-Rovomar Line
Tel: 2831/5330. Telex: 98335

Argo Reederei Richard Adler & Sohne
Tel: 6228. Telex: 98531

Armfields Transport Agency Ltd.
Tel: 3757. Telex: 98352

Atlantic Steam Navigation Co. Ltd.
Tel: 3165. Telex: 98236

Baker Brit Ltd.
Tel: 2746. Telex: 98175

Baxter Hoare & Co. Ltd.
Tel: 4488. Telex: 98217

Brady, Thos & Son Ltd.
Tel: 4601

Brit European Transport Ltd.
Tel: 5616. Telex: 98258

British Road Services Ltd.
Tel: 5532

Brown, Jenkinson & Co. (Shipping) Ltd.
Tel: 5595/8. Telex: 98345

Carlsberg Distributors Ltd.
Tel: 3901

W. Carter (Haulage) Ltd.
Tel: 2623

Channelflow Freight Services Ltd.
Tel: 3757. Telex: 98352

Comprehensive Shipping Ltd.
Tel: 2915. Telex: 98175

Conaught Shipping Agency
Tel: 5646. Telex: 98453

Consolidated Container Services Ltd.
Tel: 6156. Telex: 98256

Containerway & Roadferry Ltd.
Tel: 5612. Telex: 98200

Felixstowe—Impression of proposed northern development

Felixstowe—The roll-on ramp at the north end of the Container Terminal

Cook, Thos. & Son Ltd.
Tel: 5667.   Telex: 98184
Cory Bros. Shipping Ltd.
Tel: 5671.   Telex: 98434
Crane Fruehauf Trailers Ltd.
Tel: 4725
Crowe & Co. (London) Ltd.
Tel: 2203.   Telex: 98206
Davies Turner & Co. Ltd.
Tel: 3370.   Telex: 98430
Ellerman's Wilson Line Ltd.
Tel: 5656.   Telex: 98417
Enso Marketing Co. Ltd.
Tel: 5601.   Telex: 98427
European & General Express Ltd.
Tel: 2202.   Telex: 98206
European Unit Routes Ltd.
Tel: 4177.   Telex: 987119
European Transits & Forwarding Ltd.
Tel: 5217.   Telex: 98186
Felixstowe Dock & Railway Co.
Tel: 4433 P.B.X.   Telex: 98277
Felixstowe International Shipping Ltd.
Tel: 2873.   Telex: 98458
Felixstowe Tank Developments Ltd.
Tel: 6112.   Telex: 98341
Ferry Express (Trailers) Ltd.
Tel: 5425.   Telex: 98356
Ferrymasters Ltd.
Tel: 4422.   Telex: 98122
James Fisher & Son Ltd.
Tel: 3103.   Telex: 98149
General Steam Navigation Co. Ltd.
Tel: 3848/3669.   Telex: 98139
Glover Bros. (London) Ltd.
Tel: 6166/8.   Telex: 98431
Graeechurch Line
Tel: 5595.   Telex: 98345
Hamburg-London Linie A. Kirsten & Co.
Tel: 3848/3669.   Telex: 98139
Harcourt Shipping Agency
Tel: 2915/2746.   Telex: 98175
Hogg-Robinson & Gardiner Mountain Ltd.
Tel: 5681.   Telex: 98247
Holland Container Line
Tel: 6241.   Telex: 98436
Holland Steamship Co. Ltd.
Tel: 6241.   Telex: 98436
International Marine Management Inc.
Tel: 5541.   Telex: 98459
J & H Transport Services (Peckham) Ltd.
Tel: 4682
Ben Jones & Co.
Tel: 5421.   Telex: 98112
K-Line
Tel: 5671.   Telex: 98434
Lambert Bros. (Shipping) Ltd.
Tel: 4471.   Telex: 98247

J. Leete & Son (Cargo Superintendents)
Tel: 6523
Lep Transport Ltd.
Tel: 2202/3.   Telex: 98206
Lewcock & Pemberton Ltd:
Tel: 5671/2.   Telex: 98434
Lloyd, A. C., Ltd.
Tel: 4551/5438
Lloyd Forwarding Ltd.
Tel: 4551/5438
General Cargo Brokers (Mercia) Ltd.
Tel: 6228.   Telex: 98531
Gulf Container Line
Tel: 3103.   Telex: 98149
Lockett Wilson Line Ltd.
Tel: 2813/5330.   Telex: 98335
Manifold Routiers
Tel: 4863/3453
Marine Consultants (Harwich) Ltd.
Tel: 2746/2915.   Telex: 98175
Marriage, E. & Son Ltd.
Tel: 3236/7.   Telex: 98339
M.A.T. Transport Ltd.
Tel: 4471.   Telex: 98529
Mathewson, W. & Co. (London) Ltd.
Tel: 6255/6.   Telex: 98411
Miller, John (Shipping) Ltd.
Tel: 3103.   Telex: 98149
Mountwood Shipping Co. Ltd.
Tel: 2317/3215.   Telex: 98241
Moy & Co. Ltd.
Tel: 2746/2915.   Telex: 98175
Muller, Wm. H. & Co. (Batavier) Ltd.
Tel: 2468/9.   Telex: 98444
Munson, D. R. Ltd.
Tel: 3983
Neale & Wilkinson Ltd.
Tel: 5719/6450.   Telex: 98467
Occident Maritime Agencies
Tel: 2813.   Telex: 98335
Parker Transcontinental Ltd.
Tel: 6329.   Telex: 98371
Pickfords Shipping & Forwarding Co. Ltd.
Tel: 2606.   Telex: 98317
Ports & Terminal Agency Ltd.
Tel: 6236.   Telex: 98109
McGregor, Gow & Howson Ltd.
Tel: 5651.   Telex: 98567
Reece Bros. (Transport) Ltd.
Tél: 4863
Rennie Hogg Ltd.
Tel: 4471.   Telex: 98247
Samson Transport Co.
Tel: 5541.   Telex: 98409
Sea-Land Service Inc.
Tel: 4422.   Telex: 98122
Seaway Car Transporters Ltd.
(Managers—Mountwood Shipping Co.)

Tel: 2317.   Telex: 98241
Seawheel Ltd.
Tel: 3250.   Telex: 98276
C. Shaw Lovell & Sons Ltd.
Tel: 2675.   Telex: 98276
O. J. H. Smith, & Sons Ltd.
Tel: 3423
Stephenson Clarke Shipping Ltd.
Tel: 5671.   Telex: 98434
Henry Summers & Son (Haulage) Ltd.
Tel: 5120
John Sutcliffe & Son (Grimsby) Ltd.
Tel: 6156.   Telex: 98256
Svea Line (Syd) A/B
Tel: 2074.   Telex: 98345
Swedish Lloyd
Tel: 3446.   Telex: 98263
H. G. Taylor, Haulage Ltd.
Tel: 5585.   Telex: 98515
Transport Ferry Service
Tel: 3165.   Telex: 98236
Rankin Kuhn (Freight) Ltd.
Tel: 5691.   Telex: 98407

Trapsko International (U.K.) Ltd.
Tel: 5127.   Telex: 98186
Thos Trapp
Tel: 3848.   Telex: 98139
Turners (Soham) Ltd.
Tel: 2581
United Steamship Co. of Copenhagen
Tel: 3103.   Telex: 98149

T. Ward & Co.
Tel: 6262.   Telex: 98144
Warners Transport
Tel: 2225

J. Watson & Sons (Shipping) Ltd.
Tel: 5686
Watson & Scull Ltd.
Tel: 2517.   Telex: 98137
Wetram (Felixstowe) Ltd.
Tel: 6234.   Telex: 98109

Williams, Samuel & Son
Tel: 6134.   Telex: 98312
W. Wingate & Johnson Ltd.
Tel: 2746.   Telex: 98175
Woodmancy & Co. Ltd.
Tel: 3103.   Telex: 98149
W. B. Woolley & Co. Ltd.
Tel: 6267.   Telex: 98437
World Transport Agency Ltd.
Tel: 2746.   Telex: 98175

Systems Interfreight Ltd.
Tel: 4404.   Telex: 98505
United States Lines
Tel: 5541.   Telex: 98459

FORTH PORTS

Forth Ports Authority
Tower Place, Leith, Edinburgh EH6 7DA
TELEPHONE: 031-554 6473/77
TELEGRAMS: 'Harbour' Leith

CONTAINER FACILITIES:
Grangemouth
A facility at South Quay, Grange Dock has been in operation since May 1966 which can

accept vessels 172 m (565 feet) in length with a beam of 72 feet and a draught of 7·7 m (25½ feet). It is equipped with two 32 ton container gantry cranes. These cranes have

Container Terminal—South Quay, Grange Dock, Grangemouth.

a maximum outreach of 20 m (65 ft 11 in) beyond the quay and 13·2 m (43 ft 4 in) behind the quay; they are capable of completing 20 cycles per hour. The crane tracks have been extended to enable two container vessels to work at the same time. The container parking space has also been increased.

SeaLand Services Inc. use the facility and provide a service to New York every 5 days. Seatrain Lines Inc. provide a weekly service to New York.

Leith

A container berth capable of accepting vessels 90 m (300 ft) in length with a beam of 17·6 m (58 ft) and a draught 7·3 m (24 ft) has been provided on the North Side of Albert Dock. The berth is equipped with one container gantry crane with an outreach of 16·4 m (54 ft) beyond the quay and 135·8 m (118½ ft) behind the quay. The crane is capable of 30 cycles per hour and has a capacity of 30 tons. There is also a scotch derrick with a maximum lift of 20 tons at 60 feet beyond the quay and 120 feet behind the quay. Parking space of 2·02 hectares (4 acres) is provided, the quay apron having been extended by 3,716 m² (40,000 ft²) in 1970;

the crane rails were extended at this time. The facility is used by George Gibson and Co. Ltd. for their MacVan Service to Rotterdam every four days.

Roll-on Berth:

This berth, situated at the corner of No 6 shed, Albert Dock Basin, Leith, has no linkspan; the vessels lower their ramps on the quay apron. There is adjoining open ground for vehicle reception and storage and a shed provides lock-up accommodation, Seaway Car Transporters operate a weekly service to Gothenburg.

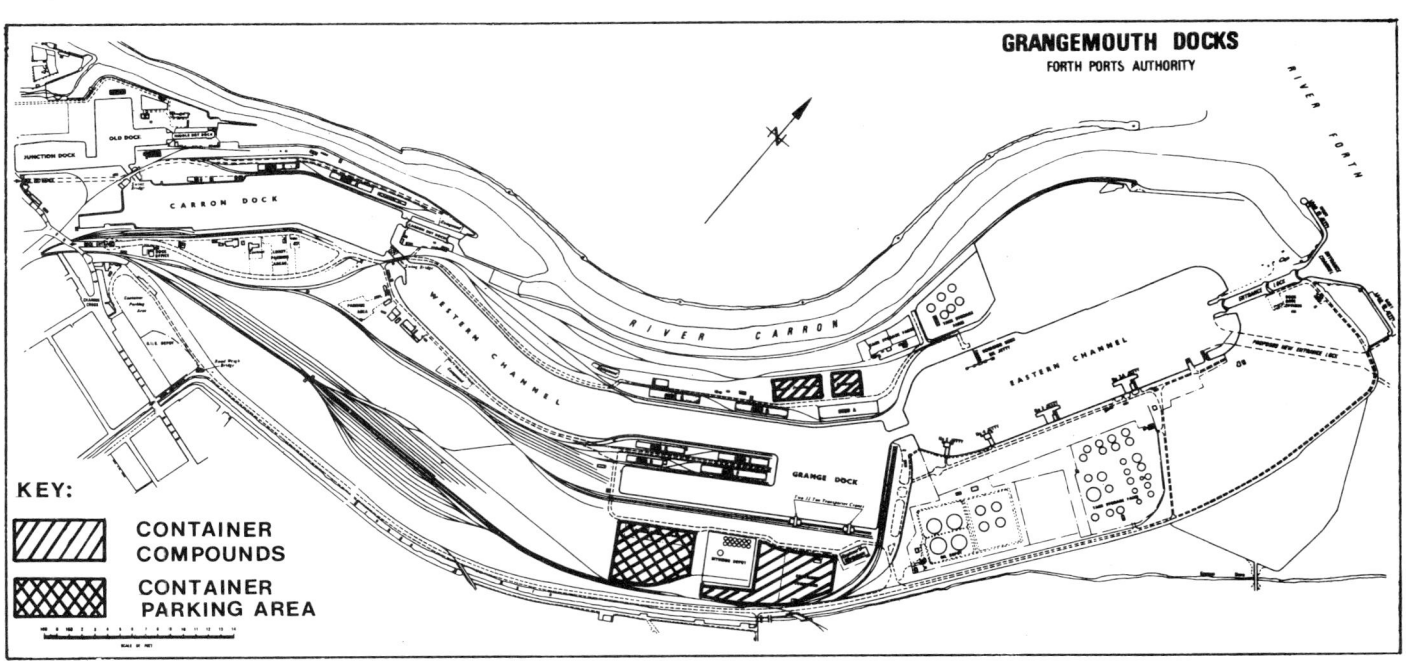

GRANGEMOUTH DOCKS
FORTH PORTS AUTHORITY

KEY:

CONTAINER COMPOUNDS

CONTAINER PARKING AREA

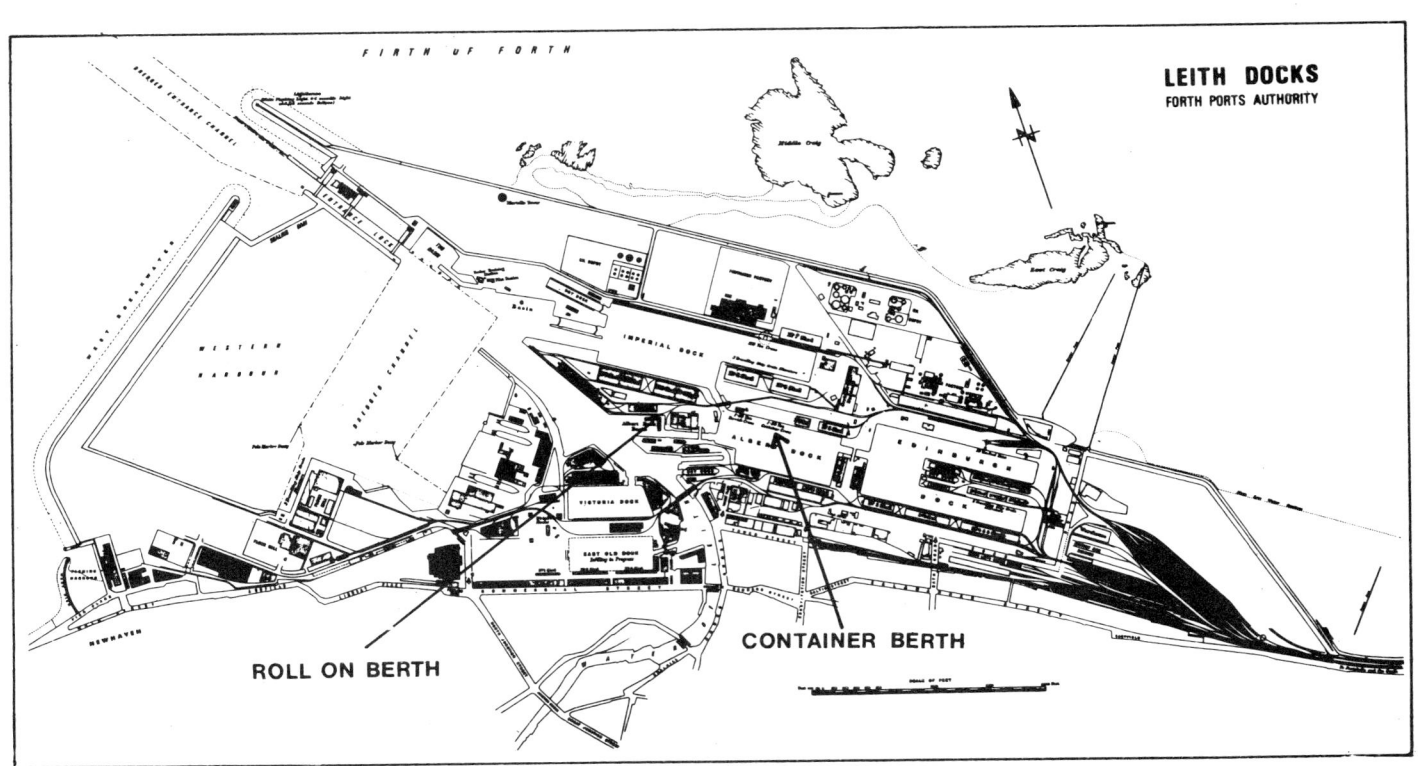

LEITH DOCKS
FORTH PORTS AUTHORITY

ROLL ON BERTH

CONTAINER BERTH

CONTAINER AND ROLL-ON TRAFFIC:
The Port Authority does not publish this information.

TERMINAL WORKING HOURS:
Ships are worked between 0800 and 1200 hours and from 1300 to 1700 hrs Monday to Friday. Overtime can be worked as required. Inland transport operations at Leith are the same as the ships' hours but at Grangemouth they are unrestricted.

STEVEDORING COMPANIES:
George Palmer & Son (Stevedores) Ltd., Station Road, Grangemouth, Stirlingshire
Telephone: Grangemouth 2792
D. Traill & Sons Ltd., Stevedores, Grangeburn Road, Grangemouth
Telephone: Grangemouth 2336
Leslie & Saddler Ltd., Tower Place, Leith, Edinburgh 6
Telephone: 031-554 1126

Seaway Car Transporters *Speedway* at Leith.

Forth Stevedores (Leith) Ltd., Albert Dock, Leith, Edinburgh 6
Telephone: 031 554 7305

CONTAINER REPAIR FACILITIES:
Dundas Engineering Co., The Docks, Grangemouth
Telephone: Grangemouth 2864

Leith Docks.

George Brown & Sons Engineers (Leith) Ltd. Shore, Leith, Edinburgh 6
Telephone: 031-554 5436

GARSTON

British Transport Docks Board,
Garston Docks, Liverpool, L19 2JW.
TELEPHONE: 051-427 5971

PRINCIPAL OFFICIALS:
J. M. Hughes (*Docks Manager*)
B. E. Broadbery (*Assistant Docks Manager*)
B. E. Strangroom (*Docks Engineer*)
Captain J. C. Tharme (*Docks Master*)

CONTAINER FACILITIES:
No. 19 Berth, North Dock. This berth can accept vessels of up to 73 m (240 ft) in length, with a beam of 16 m (53 ft) and a draught of 6 m (20 ft). It is equipped with a 32 ton scotch derrick capable of loading and discharging 15 containers per hour and there are 1·3 acres available for container parking.
No. 9 Berth, Stalbridge Dock. Capable of accepting vessels of up to 152 m (500 ft) in length, 19 m (63 ft) beam and 7·9 m (26 ft) draught. This berth is equipped with a 32 ton container gantry crane with an outreach over water of 27·1 m (89 ft) and over land of 10·4 m (34 ft) capable of 20 cycles per hour. The berth, which has a total area of 2·02 hectares (5 acres) is leased from the British Transport Docks Board by Cawoods Containers who have installed their own handling equipment. The area available for stacking containers is 1·21 hectares (3 acres).

SHIPPING COMPANIES:
Irish Sea Ferries Ltd.,
North Dock, Garston, Liverpool
Telephone: 051-427 5116
Manager: E. Shepherd
Cawoods Containers Ltd.,
Stalbridge Dock, Garston, Liverpool, 19
Telephone: 051-427 6337
English Manager: N. Plevin

CONTAINER SERVICES:
No. 9 Berth:
Cawood's Containers Ltd.—6 sailings weekly

Garston—No. 9 Berth in the foreground.

to Belfast.
Ellerman and Papayanmi Lines—every eight days to Oporto, Leixoes and Lisbon.
Seatrain Lines—weekly to Southampton (Feeder service).
No. 19 Berth:
Irish Sea Ferries Ltd.—daily to Warrenpoint.
ROLL-ON SERVICES:
Grunaldi Lines operate a roll-on new car

Garston—No. 9 Berth.

Garston—No. 19 Berth

service from Italy with Fiat cars inwards and British Exports outwards. Two vessels provide a service every ten days.

TRAFFIC:
It has been estimated that about 25,000 containers could move through the Port in 1971. Roll-on traffic could amount to some 14,000 vehicles inwards in 1971.

GLASSON DOCK

Lancaster Port Commission,
West Quay
Glasson Dock
Nr. Lancaster
DOCK MANAGER:
W. Parry
TELEPHONE: 304

GENERAL:
Container Services to the Isle of Man commenced in September 1967 and to Northern

Ireland in March 1969. There is a quay 121·9 m (400 ft) in length equipped with two 20 ton Caruthers Monobox type travelling gantry cranes with 24·38 m (80 ft) span and cantilever for ship/shore operations. The size of vessel using the port is limited by the depth of water in the lock sill which varies between 3·66 m (12 ft) and 6·09 m (20 ft) depending upon tidal conditions.

SERVICES
Ronagency (Shipping) Ltd.

Glasson Dock to Castledown	5 sailings weekly
Glasson Dock to Northern Ireland	14 sailings per month

STEVEDORES:
Walter Edmundsen (Glasson Dock Ltd.), Glasson Dock
Telephone: Galgate 577

GOOLE

British Transport Docks Board

Dock Office,
Stanhope Street, Goole, Yorkshire
TELEPHONE: 2691
TELEX: 57626
PRINCIPAL OFFICIALS:
E. S. Wilks (*Docks Manager*)
and 17·5 ft).

GENERAL:

The port of Goole is 50 miles from the sea on the River Ouse, eight miles west of the confluence of the Rivers Trent and Ouse, at the head of the Humber estuary. The suggested length and draught of vessels which can use the Port is 91·44 m and 5·33 m (300 ft and 17·5 ft)

The Port has one electric luffing travelling crane of 50 tons capacity which is used for handling unitised cargo and containers; also one crane of 40 tons capacity. A 32 ton scotch derrick crane for containers and unit loads came into service in March 1970.

UNIT LOAD TRAFFIC:
In 1970 35,400 tons moved inwards and 31,600 tons outwards.

TERMINAL WORKING HOURS:
0800 to 1700—overtime worked if required.

CONTAINER REPAIR FACILITIES:
None.

Goole—Stanhope dock.

GREAT YARMOUTH

Great Yarmouth Port and Haven Commissioners
Great Yarmouth, Norfolk.
TELEPHONE: Great Yarmouth 55151

PRINCIPAL OFFICIALS:
Captain L. F. H. Stanton
(*Port Superintendent*)
S. G. Sillis (*Clerk to the Commissioners*)

ROLL-ON/ROLL OFF FACILITIES

The Port has two roll-on/roll-off berths. One, with a shore-based ramp, is used by the Norfolk Line for their daily service to Scheveningen and has a parking area of 1·2 hectares (3 acres). The other, used by Comar Lines for containers, is capable of taking vessels of up to 94 m (309 ft) in length, 18·13 m (59·5 ft) beam with a draught of 5·02 m (16·5 ft); there is 2·83 hectares (7 acres) of land available.

Great Yarmouth—The Comar Line Berth.

GRIMSBY

British Transport Docks Board
Dock Office,
Grimsby, Lincolnshire
England
TELEPHONE: 59181
TELEX: 52250
DOCKS MANAGER: R. Bury
ROLL-ON BERTH:
A Roll-on/Roll-off Berth has been provided on the North East side of the Royal Dock for the containerised bacon services operated by the United Steamship Co. Copenhagen (DFDS) operating between Grimsby and Esbjerg at least twice weekly.

Although the service was introduced originally to revolutionize the traditional methods of handling and transporting Danish Bacon, and later other foodstuffs, from Denmark to the UK, it is now being increasingly used to carry all types of other unit-load traffics in both directions.

The local agents are John Sutcliffe & Son (Grimsby) Ltd., Royal Dock, Grimsby.

Grimsby—Royal Dock Roll-on Terminal.

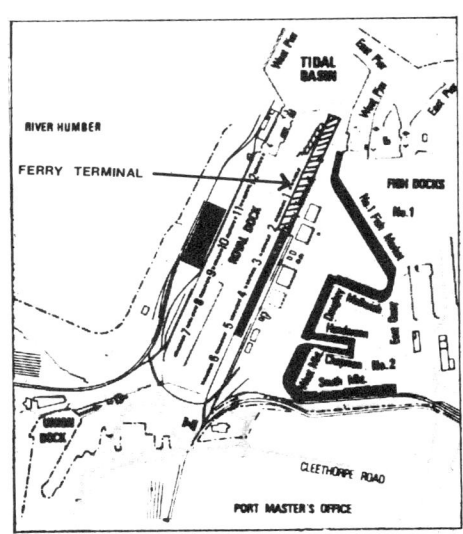

Grimsby.

HARWICH NAVYARD

Harwich Dock Company Limited
Navyard Wharf
Harwich, Essex CO12 3JN.
TELEPHONE: Harwich 2131
TELEX: 18229

DIRECTORS:
P. A. Mann (*Managing Director*)
R. S. Goddard (*Director*)
H. S. Pearson (*Director*)
C. J. M. Van Gelder (*Director*)

PRINCIPAL OFFICIALS:
J. A. Eldridge (*General Manager*)
R. A. Coolen (*Assistant General Manager*)
J. Lord (*Operations Manager*)
GENERAL:
The Harwich Dock Company is a wholly owned Subsidiary Company of Mann & Son (London) Ltd., 19/21 Great Tower Street, London EC.3.

FACILITIES:
Navyard Wharf was designed for the handling of roll-on traffic, together with unit loads and containers. There is a passenger Terminal for handling 800 passengers and 100 passenger cars per hour.

There is a total area of 4 hectares (9·9 acres) of which 3·4 hectares (8·4 acres) can be used for storage of vehicles and containers. In addition, there is a multi-storey car park for 1,100 cars.

A further area is available for storage of vehicles at a compound 5 km (3·1 miles) from Navyard Wharf.

There are four berths in operation, each with adjustable end loading ramps.

	No. 1	No. 2/3	No. 4	No. 5
Length	50 m (164·0 ft)	150 m (492·1 ft)	90 m (259·3 ft)	110 m (360·9 ft)
Minimum Depth	3·0 m (9·8 ft)	8·0 m (26·2 ft)	4·5 m (14·8 ft)	5·5 m (18·0 ft)
Roll-on	Bow only	Bow/Stern	Bow/Stern	Bow/Stern
Loading ramp Capacity	40 tons	90 tons	90 tons	90 tons
Maximum axle Load	18 tons	18 tons	18 tons	18 tons

EQUIPMENT:
Three 24 ton mobile cranes on tracks
One 20 ton gantry crane
Eight Fork trucks (11·5 maximum lift)
Eight Tugmasters
One 40 ton weighbridge

SERVICES:
Wallenius Line
Norway (Drammen). Every Monday.
Denmark (Copenhagen). Each Monday and Friday.
Belgium (Antwerp). Alternate days.
Prins Ferries
W. Germany—Hamburg. Alternate days.
W. Germany—Bremerhaven. Alternate days.
Thereby giving a daily service to West Germany.
Roto Line
Sweden (Wallhamn, near Gothenburg) Each Tuesday and Saturday.
Bore Line
Finland (Turku and Abo). Weekly.

STEVEDORES:
Harwich Dock Company Limited
Service available seven days a week.
Normally 08.00—17.00 Monday to Friday
By prior arrangement
06.00—08.00 and 17.00—22.00 Monday to Friday.
08.00—17.00 Saturdays.
08.00—17.00 Sundays.
Ship Agency, Customs Clearance and Forwarding is also carried out.

CUSTOMS:
Full Customs sufferance (excluding imported tobacco).

CONTAINER REPAIRER:
Winn International
Parkeston Quay, Harwich.

British Railways Board,
Shipping and International Services Division
Parkeston Quay
Harwich, Essex
Telephone: Harwich 2141
Telex: 29284
GENERAL
Parkeston Quay, has a quay length of approximately 1,219 m (4,000 ft) with a back up area of 18·21 hectares (45 acres). The eastern end of the quay is used for container operations and the central section for roll-on services.
ROLL-ON FACILITIES:
There are three roll-on/roll-off ramps, two of which are of portal construction and the third is a pontoon type structure. About one mile to the east of Parkeston Quay there is a train ferry berth.
CONTAINER FACILITIES
The Container terminal is equipped with two 30 ton Stothert and Pitt Container Gantry cranes for ship/shore handling. Two 30 ton Stothert and Pitt Goliath gantry cranes handle containers in the train loading and storage areas where some 250 containers can

Bow loading vessels MS Oberon and MS Porgy loading and discharging on No. 4 and No. 5 berths, Navyard, Harwich.

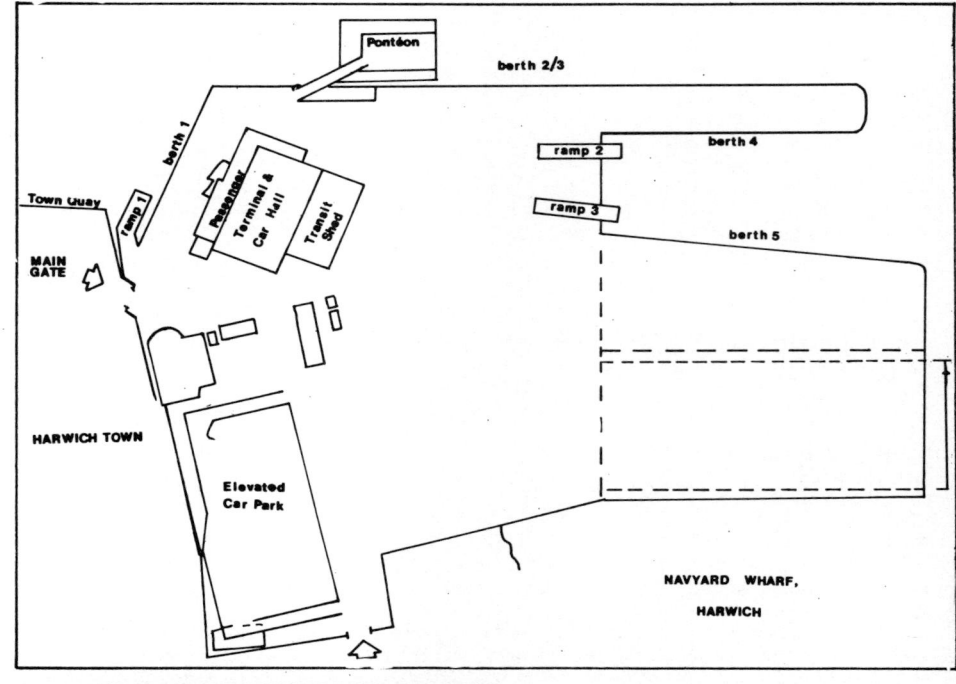

HARWICH-PARKESTON QUAY

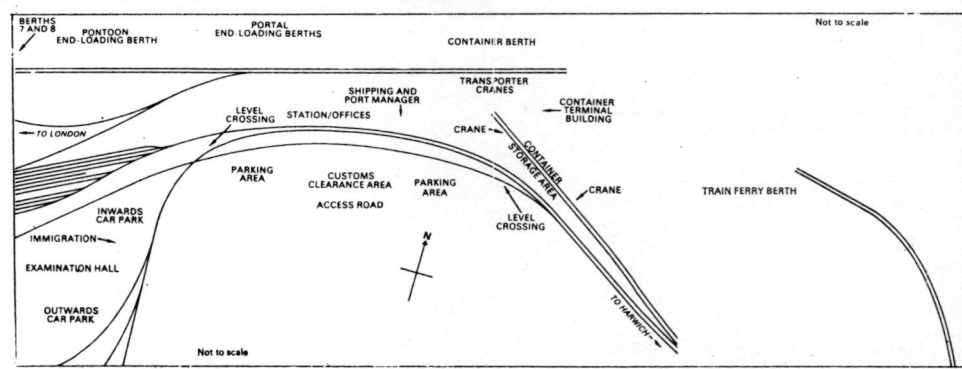

Harwich, Parkeston Quay.

be stored two high if necessary. The system is to link the ship cranes to the yard cranes using trailers with specially designed tractors. Between the two cranes there is a Customs checkpoint where import containers may be examined or sealed before passing through for carriage to an inland depot. Road vehicles are also accepted at the train loading and storage area.

Two further 30 ton gantry cranes, a Liebherr and a Kone, serving a storage area 198·12 m (650 ft) in length are being provided which it is said will increase the capacity of the facility by fifty per cent.
SERVICES
There are daily roll-on/roll-off sailings to Dunkirk, Hook of Holland, Ostend, Esbjerg, Zeebrugge, and to Kristiansand in the

summer months. Daily train ferry sailings connect Harwich with both Zeebrugge and Dunkirk.

The container terminal handles twice daily sailings to Zeebrugge and daily sailings to both Rotterdam and Dunkirk.

ACCESS

Every weekday, Freightliner container trains link the port to the Freightliner and other inland terminals and ports throughout the country. Other Container trains link LIFT and manufacturers premises with the Port. (For details please see under the United Kingdom Railway entry in the book).

Road access to Harwich Parkeston Quay is improving rapidly and the port has been developed to ensure the fast turnround of road vehicles.

Harwich, Parkeston Quay. The Container terminal is in the background and the two portal type roll-on/roll-off ramps can be seen in the foreground.

A container train load of Ford's traffic from Halewood arriving at Parkeston Quay Freightliner Terminal.

Parkeston Quay.

British Railways Shipping & International Services Division

Holyhead,
Anglesey,
North Wales
TELEPHONE: Holyhead 2304
TELEX: 61283
PRINCIPAL OFFICIALS:
W. W. Henderson (*Shipping & Port Manager*)
Captain H. Hughes (*Marine Superintendent*)
D. E. Ing (*Superintendent Marine Engineer*)
B. Arbon (*Assistant Shipping and Port Manager*)

THE PORT

The Port, which is owned by British Railways, consists of an outer and an inner harbour. The inner harbour has a depth of water of 7·9 m (25·7 ft) and has 2,128 m (7,000 ft) of quayage. The sketch map shows how this is utilised at present.

CONTAINER FACILITIES

A Berth capable of accepting vessels up to 121·9 (400 ft) in length, 21·34 m (70 ft) beam and 4·57 m (15 ft) draught came into service in Autumn 1971. It is equipped with two 30 ton Wellman container gantry cranes with an outreach of 21·03 m (69 ft) over water and 30·48 m (100 ft) over the quay, each capable of a handling cycle of 30 per hour. The container storage and marshalling area, capable of holding 700 20 ft units, is served by two Arrol 2-6-3 rail mounted goliath yard gantries, which will span eleven rail tracks, roads or container stacking cranes.

HOLYHEAD

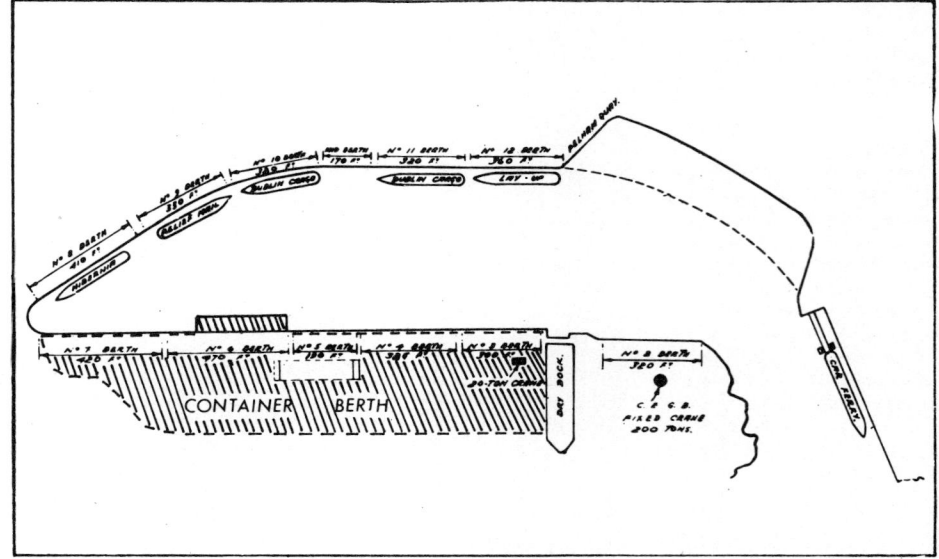

Holyhead

CONTAINER SHIPPING SERVICES

There are daily services to Belfast and Dublin using two vessels each capable of lifting 184 × 20 ft units or a mixture of 20, 30 and 40 ft containers.

INLAND SERVICES:

Holyhead will be served by container trains operated by Freightliners Ltd, and in this way the terminal will be connected to the main industrial centres throughout Britain. The terminal is also road connected.

TRAFFIC:

The service carries both publicly owned and privately owned containers.

PRINCIPAL FREIGHT FORWARDING COMPANIES:

Freightliners Ltd,
British Railways, Shipping and International Services Division.
National Carriers Ltd.

HULL

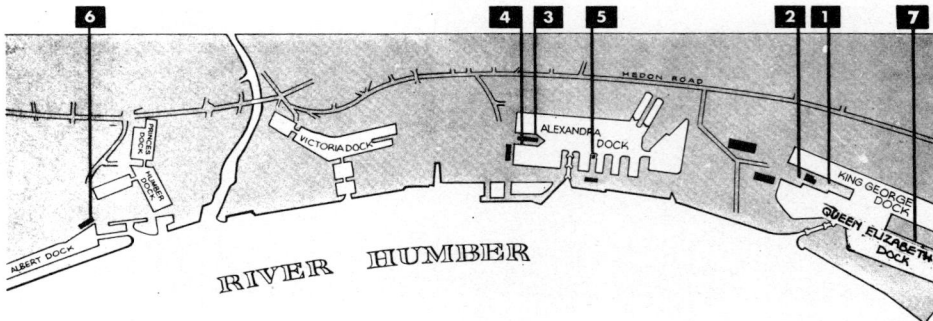

KEY TO FACILITIES:
1 North Sea Ferries—Rotterdam
2 Ellerman's Wilson Line/England Sweden Line—Gothenburg
3 Argo/Associated Humber Lines—Hamburg and Bremen
4 Holland Steamship Co.—Amsterdam
5 Associated Humber Lines—Rotterdam
6 Associated Humber Lines—Antwerp
7 Container Terminal

British Transport Docks Board,

Dock Office, Queen Victoria Square, Hull
PO Box No. 41
TELEPHONE: 0482 27171
TELEX: 52340
PRINCIPAL OFFICIALS:
C. R. Carr (*Docks Manager*)
J. M. Hughes (*Assistant Docks Manager*)
A. Adder (*Commercial Officer*)

GENERAL

Hull is one of nineteen ports for which the British Transport Docks Board is responsible. The port provides four roll-on/roll-off terminals and three lift-on/lift-off berths.

ROLL-ON/ROLL-OFF FACILITIES

King George Dock

The first roll-on/roll-off berth was built at No. 5 Quay, King George Dock and became operational in December 1965. It is laid out for two services and facilities include passenger terminal, two transit sheds for container traffic and a seven acre vehicle park. Customs facilities include offices for the operators of services and traffic agents and under cover Customs inspections lanes. Roll-on/roll-off access to vessels provides a minimum clear height of 5 m (16ft 6in). The two container transit sheds are 219 m (660 ft) × 55 m (180 ft) and 109 m (360 ft) × 45 m (150 ft) respectively.

Alexandra Dock

Developed in 1967, Alexandra Dock provides two specialised berths for stern loading vessels at No. 23 Jetty area at the west end of the dock. The combined area of the terminal is six acres and provides accommodation for shipping companies, offices, assembly area, and a freight vehicle park. The terminal is equipped with a container handling gantry and covered access to the vessels' stern loading ramps via a bridge incorporating a 4·57 m (15 ft) roadway. Containers, flats and unit

Hull—King George Dock Roll-on Terminal

loads are transferred to slave trailers by the gantry-crane and placed on board on the trailers. This method is also available for other traffic.

CONTAINER FACILITIES

Alexandra Dock'

'A' Jetty, on the south side of Alexandra Dock, is used as a lift-on/lift-off berth for which two 32 ton Scotch Derricks are provided. Whilst the emphasis is on unit loads of all kinds, conventional forms of cargo are accepted. Vessels of up to 152·4 m (500 ft) length, 24·38 m (80 ft) beam and 8·23 m (27 ft) draught can be accepted.

Albert Dock

No. 17 Shed berth on the north side of Albert Dock is equipped with a 32 ton Scotch Derrick and provides lift-on/lift-off facilities for unit loads and conventional cargo.

Vessels of up to 137·2 m (450 ft) length, 18·29 m (60 ft) beam and 7·01 m (23 ft) draught can be accepted.

Queen Elizabeth Dock

An extension to the King George Dock was completed in 1969. This added a further mile of quay and was named the Queen Elizabeth Dock.

A container berth has been completed which can accept vessels up to 192 m (630 ft) in length, 24·38 m (80 ft) beam with a 10·67 m (33·5 ft) draught. It is equipped with a 40 ton container gantry crane capable of 25 cycles per hour having an outreach over water of 25·9 m (85 ft) and over the quay of 21·34 m (70 ft). The berth has a back up area of 16·59 hectares (41 acres) and became operational in mid 1971. Five straddle carriers capable of handling 40 ft units have been acquired.

TRAFFIC:

Containers	Tonnage Inwards	Tonnage Outwards
1968	111,000	104,000
1969	142,532	172,960
1970	161,326	185,806

Roll-on/Roll-off	Total Tonnage	
1968	388,000	
1969	426,098	422,046
1970	455,955	433,918

CONTAINER SERVICES:

Company	Berth	Service
Ellerman Wilson Line Ltd.	King George Dock	Two vessels to Oslo, three sailings per week, lift-on/lift-off loading.
Joint service: Ellerman Wilson Line Ltd. and England Sweden Line	King George Dock No. 5 Quay, West	Two vessels to Gothenburg, a minimum of three sailings weekly, freight and passengers. 20 ft containers. Stern, side port and lift-on /lift-off loading.
Associated Humber Lines Ltd.	Alexandra Dock South side. 'A' Jetty, No. 17 Shed	Two vessels to Rotterdam, five sailings weekly. Containers, unit loads, conventional loads. Capacity 65 unit loads. Lift-on/lift-off.
Associated Humber Lines Ltd.	North Side Albert Dock	Two vessels to Antwerp, three sailings weekly. Freight only, containers, unit loads and conventional cargo. Lift-on/lift-off.
D.S.R.	Container Terminal	One sailing to Rostock—weekly.

ROLL-ON/ROLL-OFF SERVICES:

Company	Berth	Service
North Sea Ferries Ltd.	King George Dock No. 5 Quay, East	Two vessels taking up to 40 ft. containers, bow or stern door loading, give 7 sailings per week to Rotterdam
Ellerman's Wilson Line Ltd.	King George Dock No. 5 Quay, West	Weekly to Oslo. 2 sailings per week to Esbjerg.
Joint service: Argo Line and Associated Humber Lines Ltd.	Alexandra Dock No. 23 Jetty, North Quay	Two stern loading vessels provide three sailings weekly to Hamburg and Bremen. Containers, unit loads and conventional loads.
Holland Steamship Company	Alexandra Dock No. 23 Jetty, South Quay	Three sailings weekly to Amsterdam. Unit loads including containers.

Principal container freight forwarding companies

NORTH SEA FERRIES LTD.
King George Dock, Hedon Road, Hull
Telephone: 74106
Telex: 52349

NOORDZEE VEERDIENSTEN
(North Sea Ferries) N.V., Haringvliet 100, P.O. Box 1476, Rotterdam-1
Telephone: (010) 142066
Telex: 23152

ELLERMAN'S WILSON LINE LTD.,
Commercial Road, Hull
Telephone: 26081
Telex: 52277-8

JOHN GOOD & SONS LTD.,
High Street, Hull
Telephone: 25781
Telex: 52271

ASSOCIATED HUMBER LINES LTD.,
Commercial Road, Hull
Telephone: 23197
Telex: 56203

HOLLAND STEAMSHIP COMPANY,
Myton Chambers, Myton Street, Hull
Telephone: 25796
Telex: 52227

HULL-ALEXANDRA DOCK
A JETTY
No23 BERTH NORTH
No24 BERTH SOUTH

IMMINGHAM

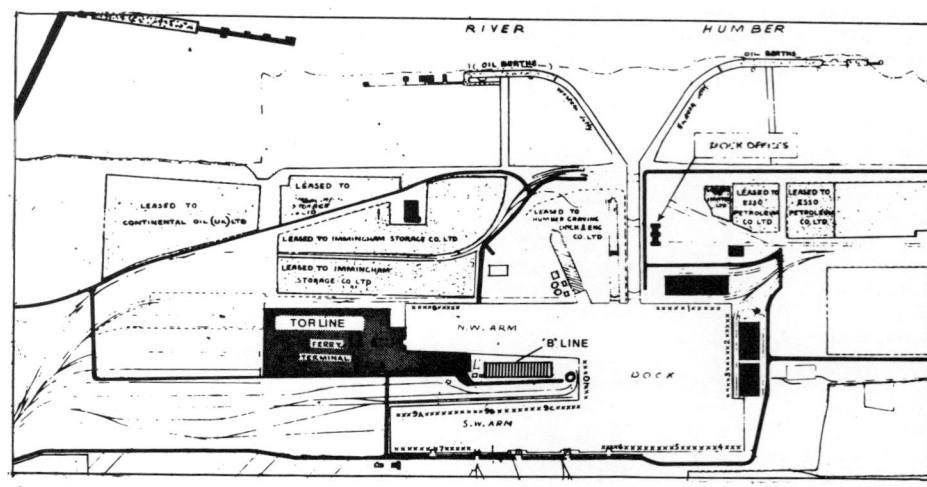

Immingham.

British Transport Docks Board

Dock Office, Immingham, Lincolnshire, England

TELEPHONE: Immingham 3441

TELEX: 52250

DOCK MANAGER: R. Bury

FACILITIES AND SERVICES:

Tor Berth:

A roll-on/roll-off terminal has been provided in the north-west arm of the Dock, for the service operated by Tor Line Ltd. The present schedule of sailings per week is six

Discharge of freight from "Tor Hollandia" at Immingham.

to Gothenburg, three to Amsterdam and one to Oslo—the latter being operated in conjunction with Anglo Norse.

The total area of the terminal is 5·26 hectares (15 acres). The local agents are Tor Lines Ltd., West Gate, King's Dock, Immingham.

'b' Line Berth:

A lift-on/lift-off container service is now in operation from the 300 ft quay situated at the end of Mineral Quay, the containers being discharged/loaded by a 32-ton Scotch Derrick. The service, known as "b" Line is operated by Blaesbjerg & Co. of Aarhus, Denmark, and is weekly to Copenhagen and Aarhus.

The local agents are Thos. E. Kettlewell & Son Ltd., Dock Offices, Immingham.

Ipswich Dock Commission

Old Custom House, Ipswich, IP4 1BY, Suffolk

TELEPHONE: 0473 56011 (6 lines)

PRINCIPAL OFFICIALS:

P. Bamford (*General Manager*)

Captain J. M. Bain (*Harbour Master and Dock Superintendent*)

W. F. Kinsey (*Engineer*)

D. J. Wallace (*Accountant*)

GENERAL:

The Port of Ipswich is situated at the head of the estuary of the River Orwell and is at the junction of the A12 and A45 trunk roads. It provides regular shipping services to and from the near Continent and Scandinavia and is served by rail freight services to all parts of the United Kingdom.

ROLL-ON/ROLL-OFF AND CONTAINER FACILITIES

Orwell Quay

This is a dual purpose berth situated on the eastern side of Ipswich Dock, which can take vessels up to 83·8 m (275 ft) in length, with a beam of 13·7 (45 ft) and a draught of 5·5 m (18 ft). It is equipped with an hydraulic ramp for Roll-on/Roll-off traffic and a scotch derrick with a maximum lift of 32 tons, an outreach of 33·1 m (112 ft), and capable of loading and unloading 12/15 containers per hour. There is a parking area of 1 hectare (2½ acres) with 2 hectares in reserve if required.

The Orwell Quay is used by the Hanseatic Ipswich Line and the Antwerp Ipswich Line.

Cliff Quay

This is a container berth on the riverside quay capable of taking vessels up to 140·2 m (460 ft) in length with a draught of 7·77 m (25 ft 6 in). It is equipped with a scotch derrick with a maximum lift of 32 tons, an outreach of 27·4 m (90 ft) and capable of loading and unloading 12/15 containers per hour. In addition there is one portal 15 ton crane. A Lancer Boss 2,500 side loader is used behind the berth. There is a parking area of 2½ acres for containers. Cliff Quay is used by the Geest Line. United Baltic Corporation, Polish Ocean Lines and Rotterdam Ipswich Line.

IPSWICH

CONTAINER AND ROLL-ON TRAFFIC:

In 1970 a total of 80,986 tons of container and roll-on cargo moved inwards and 78,987 tons outwards.

SHIPPING COMPANIES PROVIDING CONTAINER SERVICES

GEEST INDUSTRIES LIMITED—Ipswich/Maasluis/Emmerich twice daily

Head office:

White House Chambers, Spalding, Lincs.

Port Office:

No. 3 Transit Shed, Cliff Quay, Ipswich

ROTTERDAM/IPSWICH LIJN N.V.—Rotterdam daily

Head Office:

Wijnbrugstraat 22-24 P.O.B. 509, Rotterdam

Port Office (Agents)

General Cargo Brokers (Mercia) Ltd. 82 Fore Street, Ipswich

UNITED BALTIC CORPORATION:

Ipswich/Gdynia weekly

Port Office (Agents):

General Cargo Brokers (Mercia) Ltd, 82 Fore Street, Ipswich

POLISH OCEAN LINES:

Ipswich/Gdynia weekly

Ipswich—Orwell Quay.

Port Office (Agents):

Cory Brothers Shipping Ltd., Powell Duffryn House, Cliff Quay, Ipswich

SHIPPING COMPANIES WITH REGULAR ROLL-ON/ROLL-OFF SERVICES

HANSEATIC IPSWICH LINE—Hamburg every 5 days Bremen fortnightly

Head Office:

Argo Reederei Richard Adler and Sohne, Postfach 82, Argo-Haus Tiefer 12, Bremen 1

Ipswich.

A. Kirsten & Co.
Deichstrabe, 2 Hamburg 11
GENERAL STEAM NAVIGATION Co. LTD.
Three Quays
Tower Hill, London, E.C.3
Port Office (Agents):
General Cargo Brokers (Mercia) Ltd.
82 Fore Street, Ipswich
PRINCIPAL CONTAINER FREIGHT FORWARDING
COMPANIES:
General Cargo Brokers (Mercia) Ltd.
82 Fore Street
Ipswich
Telephone: 58431
Telegrams: OFFA
Telex: 98185 Mr. T. A. Good
Geest Industries Ltd.
No. 3 Transit Shed
Cliff Quay
Ipswich

Telephone- 55032—Mr. J. Kelway
Cory Brothers Shipping Ltd.,
Powell Duffryn House
Cliff Quay
Ipswich
Telephone: 59285
Telex: 98147 Mr. J. R. C. Lloyd

CONTAINER STORAGE AND STEVEDORE COM-
PANIES
Ipswich Dock Commission,
Old Custom House
Ipswich, Suffolk
Telephone: 56011

TERMINAL WORKING HOURS:
0730—1700 (overtime by arrangement).

CONTAINER REPAIR FACILITIES:
None.

The Geest Line operation at Cliff Quay, Ipswich.

KING'S LYNN

British Transport Docks Board,
King's Lynn, Norfolk, UK
TELEPHONE: 2636
TELEGRAMS: BTDB, King's Lynn
TELEX: Docks board KLYN No. 81368
DOCKS MANAGER: B. Pearson

SIZE OF VESSEL:
The Maximum size of vessel which can use
the unit load facilities is 260 feet in length,
46 feet in beam with a draught of 16 feet.

FACILITIES:
Roll-on/Roll-off Berth
No. 6 Berth in Alexandra Dock is used by
the Washbay Line for their service to Cuxhaven
and Hamburg with special connections with
Stockholm and Turku. The ramp is shore
based and there are 5 acres for parking of
vehicles and trailers. A 32 ton scotch derrick
crane has been installed to handle the
increased container traffic.

Lift-on/Lift-off Berth:
There is a lift-on/lift-off berth on the east
side of Bentinck Dock, equipped with one
20 ton portal crane with an outreach of 55
feet capable of handling 12 lifts per hour.
There is one acre available for container
parking.
TRAFFIC:
Over 11,000 tons of roll-on cargo moved
through the port in 1970. It is anticipated
that this figure will have doubled in 1971.

TERMINAL WORKING HOURS:
0800 to 1900 hrs daily for ship and inland
transport handling operations.

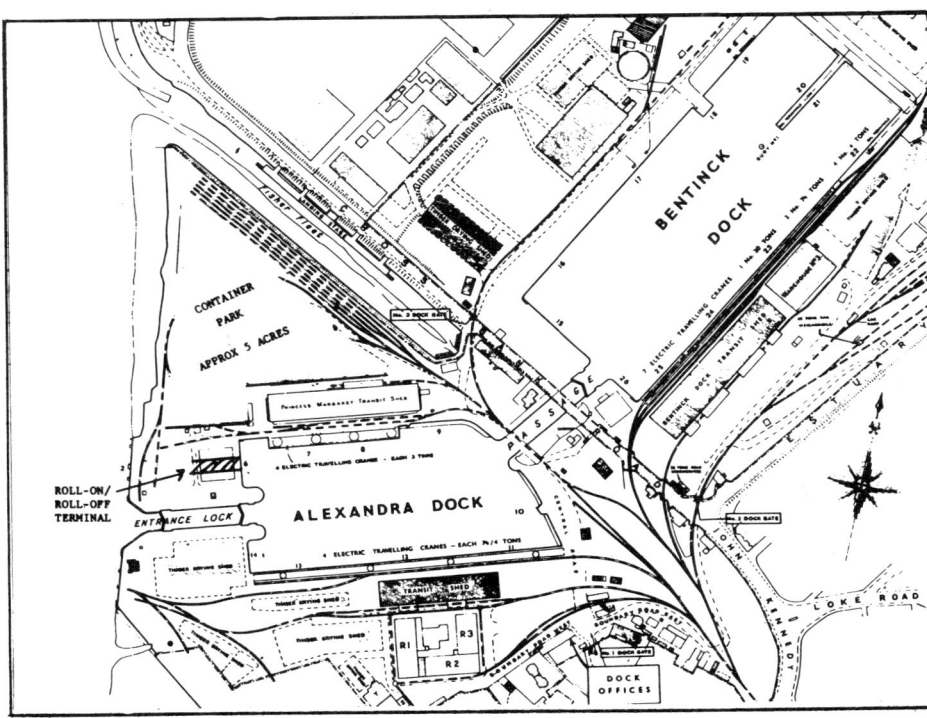

King's Lynn—BTDB Docks

King's Lynn—Roll on berth with part
of adjacent parking area.

LARNE

Larne Harbour Limited
Larne Harbour,
Larne,
Co. Antrim,
N. Ireland, U.K.
TELEPHONE: Larne 2604
Larne 3110
PRINCIPAL OFFICIALS:
R. A. Esler (*Manager and Engineer*)
D. P. Galway (*Assistant Manager and
Engineer*)
N. Magee (*Secretary*)
Captain B. R. Dickinson (*Harbourmaster*)
GENERAL:
Larne Harbour is a privately owned port,
owned and managed by Larne Harbour
Limited. The company also carry out most
of the stevedoring operations.

The port specialises in roll-on and container
traffic with its regular unit load services.
Equipment includes three vehicle ramps
including one of 140 tons capacity, quay
cranes of 35, 32, 25, and 5 ton capacities
and mobile cranes of up to 32 tons. Spacious
unit load storage areas, container and
roll-on/roll-off depots and warehouses are
also available.
UNIT LOAD BERTHS:
Castle Quay. This quay is used for container
handling and can take vessels up to 85·3 m
(280 ft) in length with a draught of 4·5 m
(15 ft). It is equipped with a 32 ton scotch
derrick with a jib of 36·5 m (120 ft) in
length capable of loading and discharging
20 containers per hour. The berth has a
parking area for containers of 2 acres.

Phoenix Quay. A quay, used for container
handling, which can accommodate vessels
up to 76·2 m (250 ft) in length with a draught
of 4·8 m (16 ft). It is equipped with a
32 ton scotch derrick with the same characteristics as Castle Quay and also has 2 acres of
parking space.
Reclamation of 5 acres of additional land
adjacent to the Castle and Phoenix quay
area was completed in 1969.
Curran Quay. This is a dual purpose berth
which can accept vessels up to 121·9 m
(400 ft) in length on a draught of 4·88 m
(16 ft). It is equipped with a 35 ton scotch
derrick with a jib of 45·7 m (150 ft) in length
for handling containers and a 120 ton vehicle
ramp, which can accommodate vessels up to
18· 3m (60 ft) beam. There are 3 acres of

LARNE HARBOUR

CONTINENTAL QUAY IN PROCESS OF RE-DEVELOPMENT

MAILBOAT QUAY

OLDER FLEET QUAY

CONTAINER FREIGHT SHED

CURRAN QUAY

PHOENIX QUAY

CASTLE QUAY

Larne Harbour

parking space.

Olderfleet Quay. A container handling berth capable of accepting vessels up to 115·8 m (380 ft) in length on a 4·88 m (16 ft) draught. It is equipped with a 25 ton scotch derrick with a jib of 36·6 m (120 ft) in length capable of loading and discharging 20 containers per hour. There is a 2 acre parking space.

Continental Quay. This is a dual purpose quay capable of accepting vessels up to 110 m (360 ft) in length with a draught of 4·88 m (16 ft). It is equipped with a 25 ton scotch derrick similar to that at Olderfleet quay and there are three acres of parking space. It is also provided with a 140 ton capacity roll-on ramp capable of being used by vessels with a beam of up to 21·3 m (70 ft).

The area adjacent to the quay was extended in 1971 to provide additional parking and marshalling space, the crane re-sited, flood-lighting installed and a new dolphin built.

Mailboat Quay. This is a roll-on/roll-off facility provided for the Larne/Stranraer passenger, car and vehicle ferry service. It has a parking area of 8,000 m² (2 acres) and a passenger terminal building.

FUTURE DEVELOPMENT

1. Dual carriageway to be extended from Larne to Larne Harbour—completion date 1973. Financed by Larne Borough Council and N. Ireland Government.

2. Fifty-acre area, adjacent to quays, available for development into Depots for Container Freight Forwarding Companies.

FINANCE FOR DEVELOPMENTS:

External road connections—Larne Borough Council

All berths, quay cranes, depots, reclamation of land etc.—Larne Harbour Ltd. Cranes, warehouses and offices inside depots are financed by leaser of depot.

CUSTOMS REQUIREMENTS:

None for containers to and from Great Britain. Necessary arrangements to be made by shipper for containers to or from foreign countries.

HEALTH REQUIREMENTS:

Shippers must ensure that goods are not liable to transmit infectious diseases and Ministry of Agriculture officials carry out inspections.

TERMINAL WORKING HOURS:

Ship handling operations take place 24 hours a day and inland transport operations take place between 0600 and 2200 hours Monday to Saturday and occasionally on Sundays.

CONTAINER REPAIR FACILITIES:

No independent container repairers.

CONTAINER FREIGHT FORWARDING COMPANIES:

Transport Ferry Services, Larne Harbour
Traffic Superintendent—J. I. Duffin
Telephone: Larne 2201
Containerway and Roadferry Ltd.,

Larne Harbour
Manager—R. J. McFetridge
Telephone: Larne 3481
Northern Ireland Trailers Ltd.,
Larne Harbour
Manager—W. Earls
Telephone: Larne 2343/2512
British Transport Ship Management (Scotland) Ltd.
Larne Harbour
Manager—F. Cowan
Telephone: Larne 2171
Ulster Ferry Link Line, Larne Harbour
Manager—D. Brown
Telephone: Larne 2343
Agnew & Lithow, Larne Harbour
Representative—J. McNeill
Telephone: Larne 3194

CONTAINER STORAGE AND STEVEDORE COMPANIES:

Containerway and Roadferry Ltd.
Northern Ireland Trailers Ltd
Ulster Ferry Link Line
Larne Harbour Limited—Port Owners and Stevedores

UNIT TRANSPORT TRAFFIC:

	Inwards		Outwards	
	Tons	Units	Tons	Units
Lift-on				
1968	494,141	57,796	375,631	47,279
1969	479,087	48,847	326,834	37,207
1970	498,166	47,282	311,304	34,634
		(63,042)*		(46,179)*
Roll-on				
1968	100,024		91,136	
1969	165,577		143,766	
1970	200,044		191,949	

NOTES:

1) It is expected that container traffic in 1971 will amount to 865,000 tons and roll-on cargo will be 557,000 tons.

2) Tonnages are net, weights of containers, flats, etc. are not included.

*Units expressed as 20 ft equivalents.

Short Sea Services		Berths used	Vessels	Container Capacity	Cargo	Sailings per Week
British Transport Ship Management (Scotland) Ltd	Larne/ Stranraer	Mail Boat quay	m.v. *Antrim Princess* m.v. *Ailsa Princess*	150	Cars, Caravans,	4 sailings per day Mon/Sat.
	Larne/ Stranraer	Continental	*Stena Trailer*	200	Trailers, Lorries, etc.	all year Suns. from May/Sept.
	Larne/ Stranraer	Continental	*Baltic Ferry*	30	Passengers and Trailers and Mails	4 sailings daily Mon/Sat.
Northern Ireland Trailers Ltd	Larne/ Preston	Castle quay	*Irish Coast Spaniel*	45	Commercial Vehicles	7
	Larne/ Ardrossan	Curran quay	*Lion*	50 50 35	Wheeled Vehicles, and containers, etc. Wheeled Vehicles, and Trailers	5
Transport Ferry Service	Larne/ Preston	Curran and Continental quays	*Bardic Ferry* *Ionic Ferry* *Barbel Bolton*	60 60 80	Wheeled Vehicles, Containers Passengers and General Cargo	6
	Larne/ Preston	Curran and Olderfleet quays	*Orwell Fisher* *Marietta Bolten* *Solway Fisher*	88 80 88	Containers, flats etc.	7
	Larne/ Ardrossan	Phoenix quay	*Moyle* *Curran*	60 60	Containers, flats etc.	5

LIVERPOOL

Mersey Docks & Harbour Company

Dock Office,
Liverpool, LB 1BZ
TELEPHONE: 051-236 6010
TELEX: 627013
PRINCIPAL OFFICIALS:
R. S. F. Edwards, CVO, CBE (*Director General*)
G. W. Brimyard (*Managing Director*)
H. B. Wrigglesworth (*Finance Director*)
J. B. Fitzpatrick (*Personnel and Industrial Relations Director*)

CONTAINER FACILITIES:
Gladstone Terminal
This is a graving dock which has been adapted temporarily for container handling; the facility is operated by the Port Authority on a common user basis.

The dock is 320 m (1,050 ft) long and 36·6 m (120 ft) wide with an available water depth of 13·1 m (43 ft). The adjacent land area to the north is capable of accommodating more than 1,600 containers and the berth has a roll-on ramp. Two 35 ton Stothert and Pitt container gantry cranes equipped with automatic telescopic spreaders have been provided.

Eight series 510 Clark Van Carriers have been supplied. These carriers are capable of moving containers up to 40 ft long and weighing up to 30 tons. They can stack 20 ft containers three high and 40 ft containers two high.

Eight Lancer Boss sideloaders are used for sorting and marshalling containers at any berth where container handling services are required and at Hornby Container Terminal.
Seaforth Container Terminal
The Seaforth project, due to be completed by the end of 1971 will provide facilities for four or five container berths with a total quay length of 3,670 m (12,040 ft) and at least one roll-on/roll-off berth. The Gladstone Dock container cranes will be re-sited and a further three cranes will be provided. The site will have full rail and road access and will have about 24 hectares (60 acres) for container stacking.
Hornby Container Terminal
Designed primarily for handling smaller container vessels this facility is equipped with two 32 derrick cranes and a share of the eight sideloaders mentioned above. It is

Liverpool—The Seaforth project in early 1971. Gladstone Terminal can be seen in the foreground

operated by the Port Authority on a common user basis.
South West Princes Dock
This facility, which is used exclusively by the Belfast Steamship Company, is equipped with two 7½ ton quay portal cranes for the handling of container and flats. There is also a ramp for roll-on traffic.
South East Coburg Dock
This facility, leased to Ireman Stevedoring, is used by the Isle of Man Steam Packet Co

Ltd. It is equipped with a 32 ton derrick crane.
North Carriers Dock
This is a temporary ferry terminal used exclusively by the British and Irish Steam Packet Co Ltd (B & I Line). The line will ultimately be located in the area now taken up by the Trafalgar, Branch, Victoria and West Waterloo Docks which will have facilities for handling the Line's passenger, accompanied car, commercial vehicle, con-

tainer and unit load traffics. This terminal is under construction.

Coast Lines Facilities

Coast Lines lease facilities in Nelson and East Waterloo Docks for container and unit load services to Dublin and Belfast. In all, five derrick cranes have been provided.

TERMINAL WORKING HOURS:
Weekdays 0800-1900 hrs and 2300-0700 hrs
Sundays 0800-1600 hrs
Saturday/Sunday 2300-0700 hrs
Sunday/Monday 2300-0700 hrs

CONTAINER AND ROLL-ON SERVICES:
Irish Sea
Belfast Steamship Co. Ltd.
 Belfast—Daily sailings
British & Irish Steam Packet Co. Ltd.
 Dublin—Daily sailings
Isle of Man Steam Packet Co. Ltd.
 Isle of Man—Daily sailings
Europe
Ellerman and Papayanni Lines Ltd.
 Portugal—Weekly
Mac Pak Container Service
 Spain—Weekly
Contenemar Lines
 Portugal—every ten days
North America
Atlantic Container Line
 USA and Canada—Weekly
Head Line/Canadian Pacific Joint Service
 Canada—Weekly
Sea-Land Service Inc.
 USA—Weekly
United States Lines
 USA—Weekly
SHIPPING COMPANIES AND AGENTS:
United States Lines
 Wellington Buildings,
 The Strand,
 Liverpool, L2 OPS
 Telephone: 051-227 1931
Ellerman & Papayanni Lines Ltd.
 Tower Buildings,
 Liverpool, L69 3BQ
 Telephone: 051-236 9999
A.C.L. Ltd.,
 Cunard Buildings,
 Liverpool, L3 1DY
 Telephone: 051-227 3000
Sea Land Service Inc.,
 (Ferrymasters Ltd),
 Burlington House,
 Crosby Road North,
 Waterloo,
 Liverpool, L22 OLG
 Telephone: 051-928 7151/5
Mac Andrews & Co. Ltd.,
 Royal Liver Buildings,
 Liverpool, L3 1HF
 Telephone: 051-236 3922
Head Line/Canadian Pacific,
 G. Heyn & Sons (G.B.) Ltd.,
 10 Rumford Place,
 Liverpool, L3 9JH
 Telephone: 051-236 9327

Contenemar Lines
 Baxter Hoare & Co. Ltd.,
 Maritime House,
 Derby Road,
 Bootle, 20.
 Telephone: 051-9224071
Scan Star,
 Lamport & Holt Line Ltd.,
 Royal Liver Buildings,
 Liverpool, L3 1JB.
 Telephone: 051-236 5650
J. T. Fletcher (Shpg) Ltd.,
 Yorkshire Insurance House,
 Chapel Street,
 Liverpool, 3.
 Telephone: 051-236 2054
Elder Dempster Lines Ltd.,
 India Buildings,
 Liverpool L2 ORB

CONTAINER AND ROLL-ON TRAFFIC:

| | Traffic Inwards | | Traffic Outwards | |
	Tons	No. of Units	Tons	No. of Units
Lift-on				
1968	335,454	56,541	393,514	47,034
1969	437,933	63,456	513,388	54,678
1970	479,792	63,708	530,889	56,622
Roll-on				
1968	35,548	—	80,673	—
1969	53,564	—	126,691	—
1970	148,018	15,233	258,748	63,132

Note: These figures include all sizes of container moving through the port.

The roll on/roll off ramp at Gladstone Container Terminal, Liverpool.

Liverpool—Model of the B & I Line Terminal now under construction.

 Telephone: 051-236 9421
African Container Express Ltd.,
 3 Noble Street,
 London, E.C.2
Belfast Steamship Company (Coast Lines Ltd)
 Reliance House,
 Water Street,
 Liverpool, L2 8TS
 Telephone: 051-236 5464
British & Irish Steam Packet Co. Ltd.,
 (Coast Lines Ltd.)
 Reliance House, Water Street,
 Liverpool, L2 8TS
 Telephone: 051-236 5464
Irish & Mersey S.S. Co. Ltd.,
 Royal Liver Building,
 Liverpool, L3 1JB
 Telephone: 051-227 3214
Isle of Man Steam Packet Co. Ltd.,
 India Building,
 Liverpool, L2 0PW
 Telephone: 051-236 3214
Holland Steam Ship Co./Metric Line,
 Lamport & Holt Line Ltd.,
 Royal Liver Buildings,
 Liverpool, L3 1JB
 Telephone: 051-236 5650
CONTAINER REPAIRERS:
Repcon Ltd.,

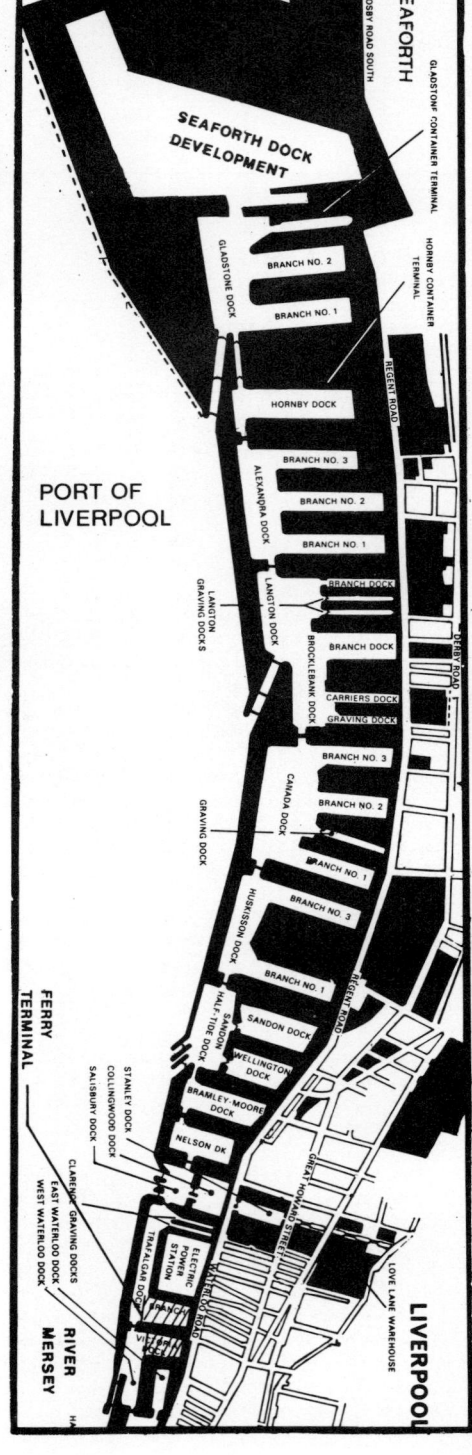

PORT OF LIVERPOOL

6 Firth Street, Liverpool 20
Telephone: 051-922 8561

LONDONDERRY

Londonderry Port and Harbour Commissioners

Harbour Office,
Londonderry, N. Ireland
TELEPHONE: 2553
PRINCIPAL OFFICIALS:
J. S. Watt, MBE (*Manager, Engineer and Secretary*)
Captain D. R. Patterson (*Harbour Master*)
G. S. Wilson (*Accountant*)
CONTAINER FACILITIES:
No. 15 Berth. This berth is capable of taking vessels of up to 76·2 m (250 ft) in length and has a depth of water alongside of 4·88 m (16 ft). There is 3,760 m² (1 acre) of parking space and the berth is equipped with a 32 ton scotch derrick.
SERVICES:
Anglo Irish Transport Ltd operate a four times weekly service to Preston with *Fernfield* (128 containers capacity) and *Terrier* (39 container capacity).
FREIGHT FORWARDERS AND CONTAINER STORAGE COMPANY
Anglo Irish Transport Ltd,
Water Street, Londonderry
Telephone: Londonderry 4204
STEVEDORE:
Scruttons (Cargo Services) Ltd,
Princes Quay, Londonderry
Telephone: Londonderry 4840

Anglo Irish Transport's *Fernfield* at Londonderry.

LONDON-TILBURY (ESSEX)

Port of London Authority

P.O.Box 242,
PLA Building, Trinity Square,
London, EC3P 3BX
TELEPHONE: 01-481 2000
TELEX: 264176
PRINCIPAL OFFICIALS:
Rt Hon. Lord Aldington, PC, KCMG, CBE, DSO, TD (*Chairman*)
Sir Andrew Crichton (*Vice-Chairman*)
John Lunch (*Director General*)
William Bowey (*Deputy Director General*)
R. H. Butler (*Director of Tilbury*)
P. Padget (*Docks Manager, Tilbury Docks*)
CONTAINER FACILITIES:
No. 40 Berth:
This berth has a quay length of 213 m (700 ft) with a depth of 13 m (42·5 ft) alongside. The total berth area is 4·8 hectares (12 acres). Equipment comprises two 30 ton Paceco Vickers container gantry cranes, a 50 ton weigh bridge, 60 power points for reefer units and one drive through vehicle washer. Straddle carriers are used to move containers from under the crane to the storage area; delivery and receipt to and from road vehicles is by the same method. Buildings include an office block, a customs' examination shed, a maintenance shed with attached workshop and a messroom and amenity block.
The facility is used by Anglo-Portuguese Container Line, United Baltic Corporation and Contenemar Lines.
No. 39 Berth:
This berth as a quay length of 259 m (850 ft) with a depth of 13 m (42·5 ft) alongside. The total terminal area is 7·7 hectares (19 acres); the main terminal area being 5·2 hectares (13 acres) and the annex 2·5 hectares (6 acres). Equipment comprises one ASEA twin lift 45 ton container gantry crane, two 45 ton twin lift ASEA stack gantry cranes. Four straddle carriers (2 Peiner and 2 Demag), a 14,000 lb fork lift truck, and nine tractors and 13 m (43 ft) trailers.
The container stack area 259 m × 52 m (850 × 170 ft) has aluminium cladding on all

London—Tilbury Dock.

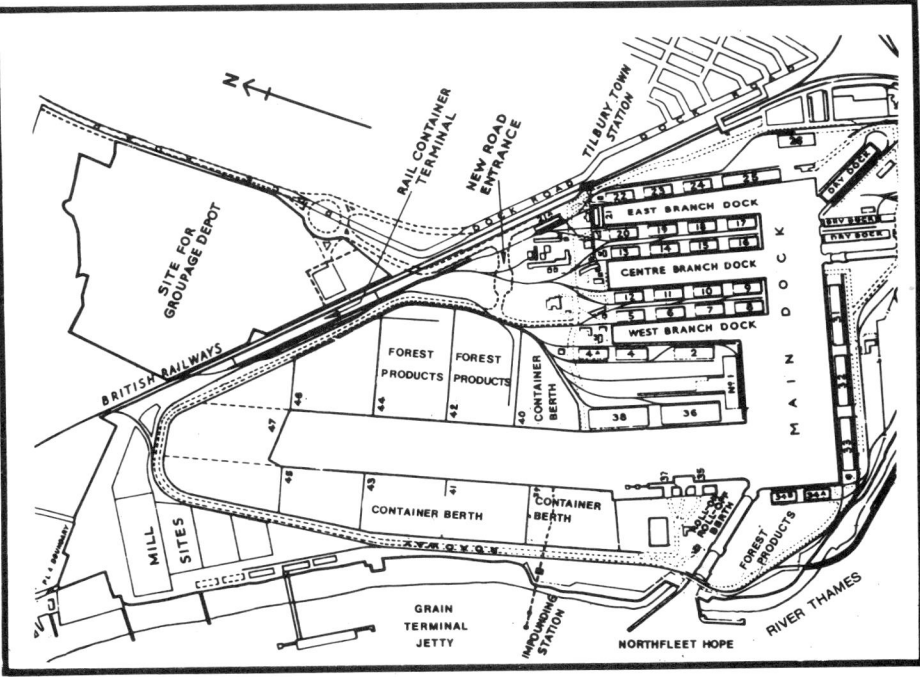

sides to afford protection to the 5 high stack spanned by the two ASEA gantry cranes. One end of the stack is used for handling refrigerated units and this has been covered to protect the units and equipment from inclement weather and solar radiation.

The facility is on lease to OCL and is used as the UK port of call for the Australian Europe Container Service.

No. 41/43 Berth:

The berth has a quay length of 520 m (1,700 ft) with a depth of water alongside of 13 m (42·5 ft). The total berth area is 10·5 hectares (26 acres). Equipment comprises two 30 ton Paceco-Vickers container gantry cranes and straddle carriers are used to move containers from under the cranes and to road transport vehicles from the stack.

The facility is used by EUR, CP Ships, VEB Deutsche Seereederei and Joint Lines (Finland Steamship Co. Ltd., OY Finnlines and United Baltic Corporation) and Anglo-Soviet Shipping Co. It is operated by the Authority on a common user basis.

No. 4 Shed:

This is a general cargo berth used by Johnson Line for their container and general cargo services to American Pacific coast ports and Honolulu. (The Line operate cellular container vessels fitted with their own handling gear). The shed dimensions are 125 m × 36·8 m (410 × 121 ft); equipment comprises Stothert and Pitt 5 ton at 30·5 m (100 ft) radius, fork lift trucks for internal shed working and tractors and trailers and straddle carriers are used for moving containers.

The facility is used, under an annual Quay and Shed space agreement, by Johnson Line (London) Ltd.

Rail Container Terminal

Equipped with two 30 ton Herbert Morris 060 type container yard gantry cranes which span two rail tracks and four roadways, the terminal can handle 15 wagon unit trains capable of carrying the equivalent of 45 20 ft units. Up to 5 trains per day can be turned round and services are in operation between Tilbury and Birmingham, Leeds, Manchester and Glasgow.

ROLL-ON FACILITIES:

Nos. 35 and 37 Berths:

No. 35 Berth is 152·4 m (500 ft) in length and No. 57 Berth is 182·8 m (600 ft) in length with a depth of water alongside of 6·6 m (21·5 ft) and there is a total area of 4 hectares (10 acres). Each berth is equipped with a scotch derrick crane (No 35-20 tons capacity at 36 m (118 ft) radius and 32 tons at 27·3 m (90 ft) radius and No. 37-18 tons at 38 m (125 ft) and 25 tons at 32·6 m (107 ft) radius).

On the main area and serving both berths is an aluminium clad transit shed 98·8 m × 57·6 m (324 × 189 ft) and with a clear internal height of 9·6 m (31·5 ft) necessary for the operation of mobile cranes. The primary purpose of the shed is for cargo and vehicle examination by H.M. Customs and it can accommodate a minimum of 90 vehicles at any one time. There are also open storage and parking areas for 200 road vehicles and a rail link to a loading ramp.

No. 26 Berth:

The facility, used by Swedish Lloyd Line, has a quay length of 143·3 m (470 ft) with a depth of water of 11·6 m (38 ft) alongside. There is a total berth area of 3·8 hectares (9·4 acres) and the equipment consists of three 20 ton hydraulic lift platform trucks, nineteen fork trucks varying in capacity from 1½ to 30 tons and one trailer prime mover.

A large aluminium clad shed 103·6 m × 33·5 m (340 × 110 ft) with a 9·14 m (30 ft) wide canopy on one side is used for con-solidating cargo. Delivery and receipt of containers and flats to and from road vehicles is carried out by large fork lift trucks. The

London, Tilbury—No. 26 Berth.

containers and flats stored on the berth are placed on small concrete blocks one to each corner to enable the lift platform trucks to be positioned beneath the units.

CONTAINER SERVICES:

Australia Europe Container Service
    Australia—Every 5 days
Johnson Line
    Los Angeles, Seattle, San Francisco, Oakland, Portland, Vancouver—Weekly
    Honolulu—Monthly
C.P. Ships
    Quebec—Weekly
Joint Lines
    Helsinki—Every 5/6 days
European Unit Routes
    Rotterdam—6 sailings per week
    Antwerp—6 sailings per week
    Dunkirk—3 sailings per week
    Hamburg—Weekly
V.E.B. Deutsche Seereederei
    Hamburg and Rostock—Weekly
    Antwerp—3 sailings per week
Anglo-Soviet Shipping Co. Ltd.
    USSR—Weekly
Anglo-Portuguese Container Line
    Lisbon—Weekly
Contenemar—Madrid
    Bilbao—Weekly

London, Tilbury—Rail Terminal

ROLL-ON SERVICE:
Swedish Lloyd Line
    Gothenburg—6 sailings per week
TERMINAL WORKING HOURS:
24 hours per day seven days per week.

TRAFFIC IN FREIGHT CONTAINERS* 1970

	Inwards		Outwards	
Container Lengths (ft)	No. of loaded Units	Weight of contents (long tons)	No. of loaded Units	Weight of contents (long tons)
LIFT-ON/LIFT-OFF SERVICES:				
8	582		11,354	
20	42,115		55,034	
30	4,673		5,299	
40	6,288		5,739	
	53,658	646,754	77,426	663,879
ROLL-ON/ROLL-OFF SERVICES:				
8	—		8	
20	4,078		4,468	
30	10		38	
40	4		8	
Others	15		91	
	4,107	28,489	4,613	33,656
Total	57,765	675,243	82,039	697,535

*British Standard 3951

All bulk liquid containers have been excluded, though some may have complied with this standard.

N.B. In addition to the loaded units 28,382 empty units were handled in 1970, 23,438 inwards and 4,944 outwards. Of the total number of empty units handled 25,178 were freight containers.

LONDON—VICTORIA DEEP WATER TERMINAL

Victoria Deep Water Terminal Ltd.
231 Tunnel Avenue
London SE10
TELEPHONE: 01-858 8161
TELEX: 897379
OFFICIALS:
R. G. Wilson (*Managing Director*)
A. B. Reid (*Operational Director*)
W. V. Tweedy (*Terminal Manager*)
E. J. Herivel (*Operational Manager*)
H. O'Brien (*Operational Manager*)
D. E. Rushbrooke (*Senior Supervisor*)
W. C. Reaston (*Terminal Engineer*)
UNIT LOAD AND CONTAINER FACILITIES:

The facility has a quay length of 144·8 m (475 ft), with a depth of water alongside of 6·7 m (22 ft) MLWS, equipped with one 32 ton travelling quay crane capable of handling heavy lifts, containers and flats, two 12 ton and two 5 ton quay cranes. Cranes are equipped with semi-automatic spreaders for handling all sizes of container. Other quay handling equipment includes side loaders and fork trucks with a capacity of up to 20,000 lbs. There is a 4,645 m² (50,000 sq ft) transit shed and a 4,645 m² warehouse.

The quay length is being extended by a further 221 m (725 ft) which will provide a total of 365·8 m (1,200 ft) and the total area of the terminal will be about 7·3 hectares (18 acres). The extension will be a purpose built container terminal equipped with two gantry cranes and storage for some 2,000 units is being provided.

CONTAINER SERVICES:
Associated Antwerp Lines
    Antwerp—Twice weekly
Müller
    Rotterdam—Twice weekly
Svea Line
    S. Swedish Ports—Weekly
Lusitainer Container Service
    Lisbon and Leixos—Every 8 days
Containerships Portugal
    London/Rotterdam/Opporto/Lisbon/
        London—Every 8 days
Westcott and Lawrence Line and Ellermans
    Oslo—Weekly
UK/Israel Joint Container Service
    Ashdod—Every 12 days
TERMINAL OPERATING HOURS:

The terminal operates from 0700 to 2100 hours on a two shift system; a third shift from 2300 to 0700 hours can also be worked. There are optional facilities for overtime working between 2100 and 2300 hours and also on Saturdays and Sundays with two shifts 0700 to 1400 and 1400 to 2100 hours.
CONTAINER REPAIR FACILITIES:

These are being provided on the terminal extension under construction.

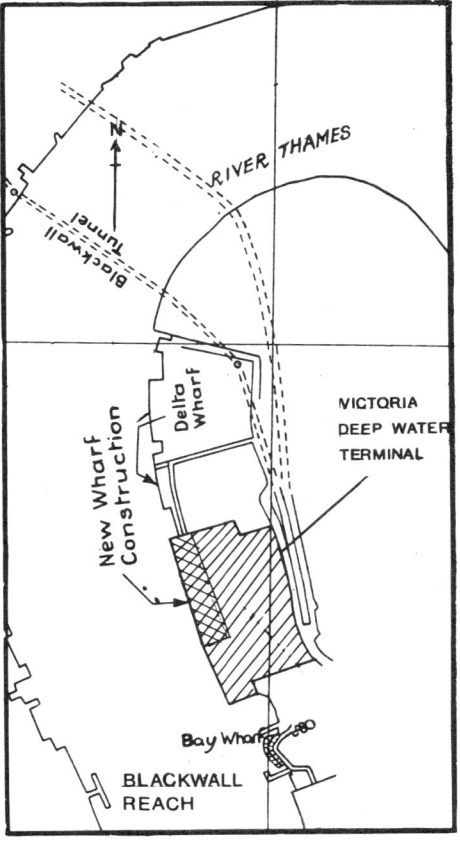

MANCHESTER

Port of Manchester,
Manchester Ship Canal Company
Ship Canal House,
King Street,
Manchester, England
M2 4WX
TELEPHONE: 061-832 2244
TELEX: 669025
PRINCIPAL OFFICIALS:
D. K. Redford (*Managing Director*)
A. Ferguson (*Manager*)
R. A. H. Collinge (*Secretary*)
F. W. N. Cowgill (*Commercial Manager*)
J. Snell (*Marketing Manager*)
R. A. Hansell (*Senior Assistant Manager*)
G. R. A. Harris (*Personnel Manager*)
P. Lawson (*Assistant Manager*)
B. Lee (*Assistant Manager*)
A. E. Blyth (*Chief Engineer*)
A. S. J. Campbell (*Mechanical and Electrical Engineer*)
J. Field (*Docks Manager*)
G. W. Cranmer (*Harbour Master*)
GENERAL

The Port of Manchester consists of numerous facilities along a 36 mile ship canal connecting a dock system in the centre of Manchester with the River Mersey only a few miles from the Liverpool Docks. Ships of 12,500 tons deadweight regularly navigate the canal to Manchester Docks; maximum beam acceptable through the whole lock system is about 19·3 m (63·5 ft).
CONTAINER FACILITIES:
No. 9 Dock, Manchester:

This terminal, used by Manchester Liners has a quay length of 259 m (850 ft). It is equipped with two Stothert and Pitt container gantry cranes (one of 25 tons and one of 35 tons capacity). Clarke, series 512, straddle carriers are used for handling to and from the 4·05 hectare (10 acre) storage area. At the rear of the terminal there are consolidation sheds providing facilities for

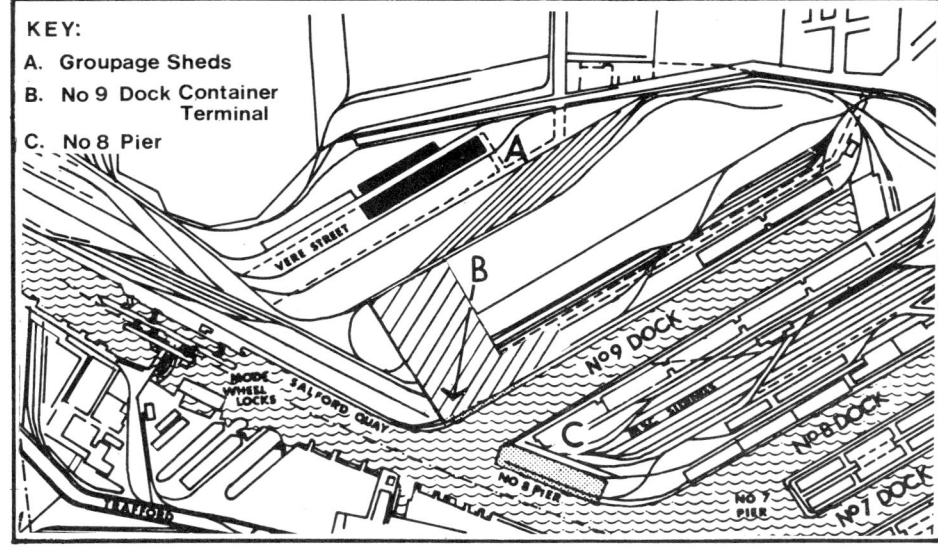

KEY:
A. Groupage Sheds
B. No 9 Dock Container
    Terminal
C. No 8 Pier

packing, unpacking and clearing less than container loads. Other public consolidation sheds with full customs facilities are available close by.

No. 8 Pier, Manchester:

This berth is used by vessels carrying part container loads. It is equipped with a 32 ton derrick crane.

Francis Wharf, Runcorn:

This berth, used by the Metric Line for their fully containerized service, is equipped with a 32 ton derrick crane served by a fleet of internal dock trailers. There is a container yard and groupage shed at the rear of the facility.

CONTAINER SERVICES:
Manchester Liners Ltd.
1. Canada (Montreal) twice weekly with cellular vessels

2. Eastern Mediterranean Ports—fortnightly with cellular vessels
3. Canadian, Great Lakes and US East Coast ports with conventional vessels modified for the carriage of containers.
Metric Line
    Antwerp and Rotterdam—Weekly
TERMINAL WORKING HOURS:

Both ships and inland facilities work as follows:
Monday to Friday   0800-1900 hours
                    2200-0800 hours
Saturday   2200-0800 hours
Sunday   0800-1700 hours
                    2200-0800 hours
CONTAINER REPAIR FACILITIES:
    Morrell Mills & Co. Ltd, Trafford Wharf, Manchester 17.
    Telephone: 061-872 1094

Manchester—Container Terminal

Du Pont Company (UK) Ltd

Acton Grange Distribution Centre
Birchwood Lane, Moore,
Near Warrington, Lancs.
MANAGER: B. Dennington
GENERAL

A privately owned and operated facility
situated in the Manchester Ship Canal. It is
equipped with a 30 ton Liebherr container
gantry crane. The berth has a length of
106·7 m (350 ft) and is backed by a shed
with an area of about 13,580 m² (140,600
sq ft). The facility covers a total area of
7·5 hectares (17·5 acres).
SERVICE

The company's products are carried
between Acton Grange and Londonderry by
two chartered vessels *Marwit* and *Klaus
Block* each capable of lifting about 70 20 ft
units.

Du Pont Company's Terminal on Manchester Ship Canal at Acton Grange

NEWHAVEN

British Railways Board

Shipping and International Services Division
Newhaven Harbour, Sussex
TELEPHONE: 4131
TELEX: 87151
SHIPPING AND PORT MANAGER:
M. B. Sellers

ROLL-ON/ROLL-OFF FACILITIES:

There is one roll-on/roll-off berth on the
East quay capable of accepting vessels of
112·78 m (370 ft) length, 17·68 m (58 ft)
beam and 3·66 m (13 ft) draught equipped
with a shore adjusted ramp. Parking space

is available for trailers.
SERVICES:

British and French Railways operate a
daily service to Dieppe increasing to six
sailings per day in each direction during the
peak months.

NEWPORT (MONMOUTHSHIRE)

British Transport Docks Board

Alexandra Dock,
Newport, NPT 2UW
Monmouthshire
NPT 2UW
TELEPHONE: 0633-65411
TELEX: 49585
PRINCIPAL OFFICIAL:
J. V. Snow (*Docks Manager*)

GENERAL:

The entrance lock to the Port is 304·8 m
(1,000 ft) long and 30·48 m (100 ft) wide.

CONTAINER FACILITIES:

East Lock. This facility is used by the
British and Irish Steam Packet Co. Ltd. for
their twice weekly service to New Ross, Eire
using a vessel with a capacity of 45 × 20
feet units. The berth, equipped with a
32 ton Scotch Derrick, is road served and has
an adjacent parking area.

Newport Container Terminal:
Operator:
Newport Container Terminals Ltd.
Barclays Bank Chambers,

Newport, Mon.
Telephone: 62221
Telex: 49213

The terminal has a quay length of 304·8 m
(1,000 ft) with a depth alongside of 10·66 m
(35 ft). There is a container marshalling
area of 1·82 hectares (4½ acres) and a further
5·66 hectares (14 acres) available for development. There is a 45 ton Paceco-Vickers
container gantry crane with an outreach of
37·7 m (115 ft) over water and 34·14 m (112
ft) over land. Sideloaders, forklift trucks

and mobile cranes are also available.

RAIL ACCESS:
The terminal is served with twin railway lines and rail wagons can be integrated with the national freightliner network.

TERMINAL WORKING HOURS:
Vessels with cargo from 0600 to 2200 hrs; inland transport operations take place between 0730 and 1700 hrs. Arrangements can be made to receive or deliver cargo outside these hours if necessary.

Newport Container Terminal, the East Lock facility can be seen in the background

NEWRY

Newry Port and Harbour Trust
Harbour Office
Newry,
C. Down, N. Ireland
TELEPHONE: 2042

Kathleen Lavery (*Secretary*)

CONTAINER SERVICE

Anglo Irish Transport Ltd operates a container service to Preston three times a week. The Port Authority own the berth at which the Company's ships berth; but crane and parking facilities are both provided by the Operator.
OPERATOR:
Anglo Irish Transport Ltd
Albert Basin
Newry.

PRESTON

Port of Preston Authority
Dock Offices
Watery Lane
Preston PR2 2XE Lancashire
TELEPHONE: Preston 726711
PRINCIPAL OFFICIALS:
W. B. Acheson (*General Manager and Engineer*)
B. H. Smith (*Dock Manager*)
F. Fisher (*Traffic Manager*)
W. E. E. Lockley (*Secretary and Solicitor*)

ROLL-ON FACILITIES
Nos. 1 and 3 Berths. These berths can accept vessels of up to 109·7 m (360 ft) in length 18·23 m (60 ft) beam and 6·01 (20 ft) draught. They are equipped with adjustable ramps and each has a parking space for vehicles of 1·7 hectares (4·2 acres). Both these berths are dual purpose as they are equipped with 32 ton scotch derricks.

CONTAINER FACILITIES:
Basin Berth and Nos. 2, 4, 5, 6 and 7 Berths. These berths are capable of handling vessels of a length of between 64 m (210 ft) at Basin Berth, and 91·4 m (300 ft) at No 4 Berth. All the facilities are limited to handling vessels of 18·23 m (60 ft) beam and 6·01 m (20 ft) draught. Each berth is equipped with a 32 ton Scotch Derrick crane with an outreach of 29 m (95 ft) over water and 27·4 m (90 ft) over land. The cranes are each capable of loading and discharging 17 containers per hour. Each berth has a storage and marshalling area of 1·7 hectares (4·2 acres)
The port is equipped with 5 Customs examination sheds.

Port of Preston.

TERMINAL WORKING HOURS:
The Port is open 24 hours a day.

CONTAINER REPAIR FACILITIES:
Preston Container Repair Service.

Repair Service

North Shipping Office,
Preston Dock,
Telephone: 726706
North Western Trailer Co. Ltd,
    Sandhurst Avenue, St. Annes
    Telephone: St. Annes 26717
Stan Foster Ltd.
    Fylde Road, Preston
    Telephone: 26776
Cravens Homalloy (Preston) Ltd.
    Joe Lane, Catterall, Garstang, Lancs.
    Telephone: Garstang 2031
TRAFFIC:
The total Roll-on/Roll-off and Container
traffic through the Port was as follows:

1968—	643,472	Tons Inwards
—	794,087	Tons Outwards
1969—	487,771	Tons Inwards
—	694,432	Tons Outwards
1970—	627,805	Tons Inwards
—	874,977	Tons Outwards

The number of containers on the lift-on/
lift-off services was as follows:

1968—	57,197	Units Inwards
—	76,643	Units Outwards
1969—	39,484	Units Inwards
—	55,495	Units Outwards
1970—	63,091	Units Inwards
—	78,464	Units Outwards

It is important to note that the Port was
closed for 10½ weeks in the Autumn of 1969
due to an industrial dispute and for this
reason the traffic figures are down on those
for 1968.

SERVICES:	Berth	Route and frequency
Roll-on/Roll-off		
Transport Ferry Service	Nos. 1 and 3	Preston to Larne—Daily
		Preston to Belfast—3 sailings per week
Container Services:		
Transport Ferry Service	Nos. 1, 2, 3 and 4 also Basin	Preston to Belfast—6 sailings per week
		Preston to Larne—8 sailings per week
Transport Ferry Service/Coast Lines		Preston to Drogheda—3 sailings per week
Transport Ferry Service		Preston to Dublin—6 sailings per week
Greenore Ferry Service Ltd	No. 6	Preston to Greenore—3 sailings per week
Anglo Irish Transport Ltd	No. 5	Preston to Newry—3 sailings per week
Northern Ireland		Preston to Londonderry—4 sailings per week
Trailers Ltd	No. 7	Preston to Larne—Daily

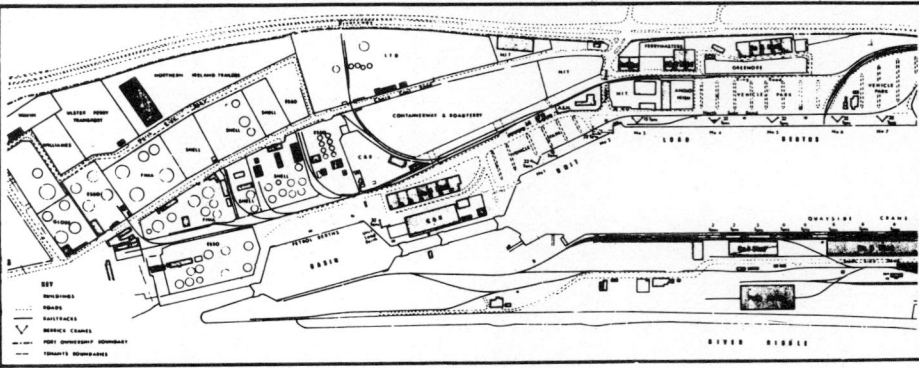

Plan showing unit load berths at Preston.

ST HELIER

States of Jersey Harbours and Airport Committee
Harbours and Airport Committee
Harbour Office,
St. Helier, Jersey, C.I.
TELEPHONE: Central 34451
PRINCIPAL OFFICIALS:
Captain R. S. Taylor (*Harbourmaster*)
D. H. Tavernor (*Chief Civil Engineer*)
CONTAINER FACILITIES:
Containers are handled at Berths No. 2, 6
and 7 using four 7 ton level luffing cranes.
These berths can accept vessels of 76·2 m
(250 ft) length, 18·29 m (60 ft) beam with a
draught of 3·68 m (12 ft).
CONTAINER SERVICES:
British Railways operate a daily service to

Weymouth and Southampton and Commodore Shipping Line sail daily to Portsmouth. Channel Island Services (J. W.
Huelin) operate daily to Portsmouth.
FUTURE DEVELOPMENTS:
A 32 ton scotch derrick crane is to be installed
at No. 2 Berth and a 35 ton scotch derrick
crane at No. 7 Berth.

PRINCIPAL FREIGHT FORWARDING COM-
PANIES:
British Railways, Bond Street, St. Helier.
Telephone: Central 23412
Commodore Shipping Services,

Albert Quay,
St. Helier.
Telephone: Central 34561
J. W. Huelin,
Victoria Quay, St. Helier.
Telephone: Central 30383
J. G. Renouf,
New North Quay, St. Helier.
Telephone: Central 23352

STEVEDORES:
J. W. Huelin (address above)
George Troy & Sons,
New North Quay, St. Helier.
Telephone: Central 24401

SOUTHAMPTON

British Transport Docks Board
Southampton Docks
TELEPHONE: 0703 23844
TELEX: 47334
OFFICIALS
D. A. Stringer (*Port Director*)
W. D. Noddings (*Docks Manager*)
B. Bostock (*Development Manager*)
I. A. Reid (*Commercial Manager*)
Charles A. Hare (*Operations Manager*)
C. N. Phelan (*Container Terminal Manager*)
F. Pinckney (*Superintendent—Container Depot*)
D. J. Doughty, (*Chief Docks Engineer*)
Captain E. J. Kirton, (*Dock and Harbour Master*)

CONTAINER FACILITIES:
Western Docks Container Terminal
    No. 201 Berth. This facility has a quay
length of 305 m (1,000 ft) and is capable of
accepting the largest container vessels in
service. It is equipped with two 30 ton Paceco
Vickers container gantry cranes. A link span
has been provided for roll-on/roll-off traffic.
Other handling equipment includes straddle
carriers, side loaders and towing units. The
facility, operated on a common user basis,
has a total area of 8·09 hectares (20 acres)
and is connected by road to the existing

Southampton—Princess Alexandra Dock

dock system and the Container Clearance Depot. The Southampton Freightliner Terminal operated by British Railways is close by. *No. 202 Berth.* At present under construction and scheduled to come into service in 1972 with completion at the end of the year, this 274·3 m (900 ft) long facility, adjacent to No. 201 Berth, will be operated on a common user basis and will be equipped with a container gantry crane of up to 45 tons capacity. The berth will have an area of 6·68 hectares (16·5 acres).

Nos. 204 and 205 Berths. These berths, with a total quay length of 640·1 m (2,100 ft) and a back up area of 20·23 hectares (50 acres) are due to be part operational in 1972 and will be used by OCL/ACT for their Far East Container Service. Three container gantry cranes of up to 45 tons capacity are being provided.

Road and Rail Access. A dual carriageway road bridge is being built across the London/Bournemouth rail line to give direct access to the terminal from the main trunk roads. Freight Liner Ltd plan to provide a rail terminal adjacent to the container complex.

ROLL-ON ROLL-OFF FACILITIES:

In addition to the link span at the Western Docks Terminal there are four specially designed terminals in the Eastern Docks. There are three link spans in the Princess Alexandra Dock with widths of 5 m (16·5 ft) and 6·2 m (20·5 ft) and one at Berth 49 of 7·2 m (23·6 ft).

FUTURE DEVELOPMENTS:

After the completion of the present development in 1972 there is space for a further quay length of 1,829 m (6,000 ft) for deepwater quays with a total area of 91·1 hectares (225 acres) available for container operations.

Southampton—Cargo awaiting shipment at No. 201 Berth

TERMINAL WORKING HOURS:

The Container Terminal operates from 0800 to 0600 except on Saturday when the hours of work are 0800 to 1300 hours and 2000 to 0600 hours.

CONTAINER REPAIR FACILITIES:

Containercare Ltd.
 Ryde Terrace, Southampton SO1 1FY
 Telephone: 24186
Crane Fruehauf Trailers
 West Bay Road, Western Docks, Southampton
 Telephone: 20462

STEVEDORES:

The licensed employer of port labour at Southampton is:
Southampton Cargo Handling Co.,
1, Orchard Place,
Southampton SO1 1BR
Telephone: 22632

CUSTOMS REQUIREMENTS/FACILITIES

Customs and Excise, H.M. Customs House, Orchard Place SO9 12D
Telephone: Southampton 20323

BONDED CONTAINER CLEARANCE DEPOT
To speed the clearance and handling of the ever-increasing number of containers and

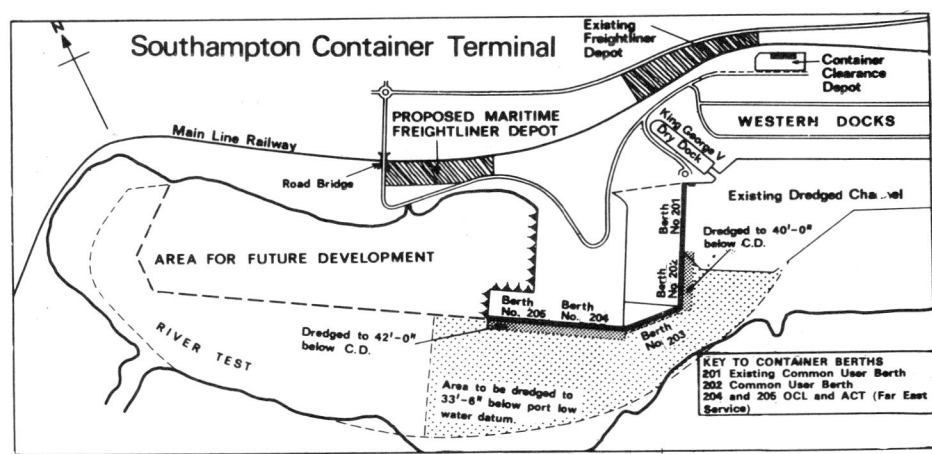

Southampton Container Terminal

CONTAINER SERVICES

Company	Berth	Service
Atlantic Container Line	No. 201	Southampton to Halifax, New York, Baltimore and Portsmouth Va.—Weekly.
Dart Containerline	No. 201	Southampton to Halifax, New York and Norfolk Va.—Weekly.
Seatrain Lines	No. 201	Southampton to New York, Baltimore, Charleston, Norfolk Va. and Philadelphia—Weekly.

ROLL-ON ROLL-OFF SERVICES

Company	Berth	Service
MacPac Container Services (MacAndrews & Co. Ltd. in conjunction with Swedish Lloyd).	Pr. Alexandra Dock No. 3	Southampton to Bilbao— 3 sailings each fortnight
Normandy Ferries	Pr. Alexandra Dock No. 2S	Southampton to Le Havre— daily
Southern Ferries	Pr. Alexandra Dock No. 2S	Southampton to Lisbon—Weekly calling Tangier also each fortnight
Thoresen Car Ferries Ltd.	Pr. Alexandra Dock Nos. 6, 7 and 2N	Southampton to Le Havre— up to three per day Southampton to Cherbourg— up to five per day

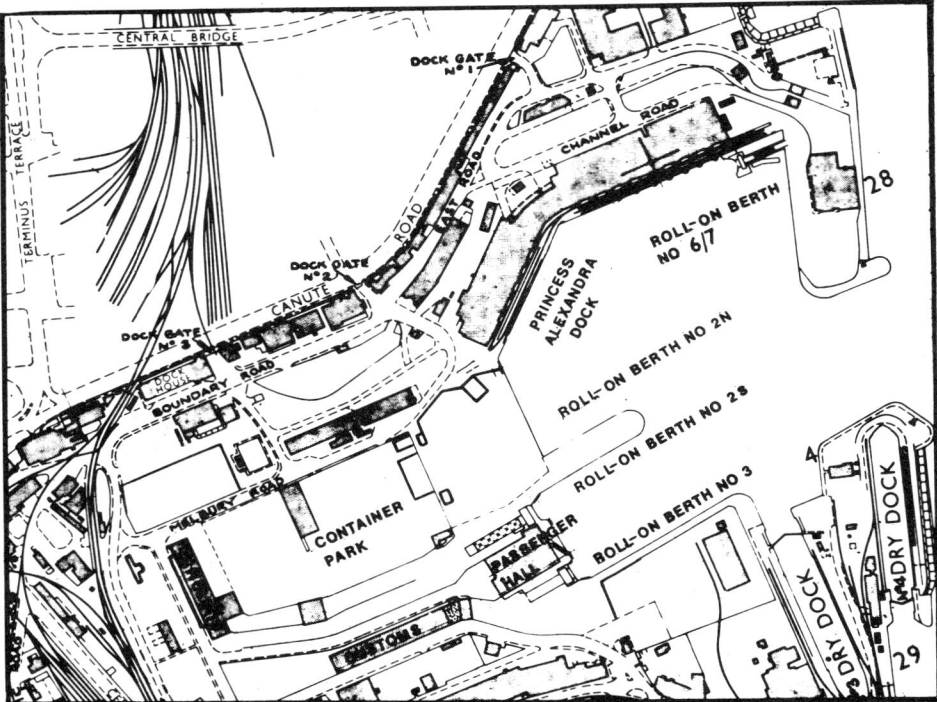

Southampton—Princess Alexandra Dock. Nos. 6/7 and 2N Berths are used by Thoresen Ferries No. 2S Berth is used by Normandy and Southern Ferries and No. 3 Berth by Swedish Lloyd

other unit loads imported and exported via Southampton Docks, a Bonded Depot has been built.

The depot is situated at the Western Docks, and extends over 3¾ acres, with space for expansion to 20 acres should the demand arise. There is a Customs examination shed

124 m (407 ft) × 24 m (78 ft), an H.M. Customs and administration office, and a concreted stacking and parking area for containers and trailers.

The British Transport Docks Board operate the depot on a common user basis, and provide the following services:

Atlantic Container Line's *Atlantic Causeway* at Southampton.

CONTAINER AND ROLL-ON TRAFFIC

		No. of loaded Units		Tonnage of Goods carried	
		Inwards	Outwards	Inwards	Outwards
Lift-on	1968	3,562	7,696	36,836	22,638
	1969	9,387	15,579	87,386	83,459
	1970	18,272	29,176	198,556	206,631
Roll-on	1968	11,404	11,400	137,670	106,664
	1969	13,279	13,618	154,095	152,576
	1970	13,624	14,206	183,523	166,129

(*a*) Storage of full or empty containers and trailers received from ship or awaiting shipment.

(*b*) Production of containers and contents from H.M. Customs examination and clearance.

(*c*) Emptying mixed consignments from containers for individual delivery.

(*d*) Receiving export consignments and consolidating into container or unit loads.

The transit shed can accommodate 1,200 tons of freight, depending on the type of goods. On the concrete area there is accommodation for 230 containers (stacked one high) or 230 trailers. Containers can also be stacked two high to increase overall floor

Seatrain Lines' *Euroliner* at Southampton.

space capacity.

Mechanical equipment includes a straddle carrier of 22½ ton gross lifting capacity, and

Dart Containerline's *Dart Europe* at Southampton.

fork lift trucks of varying working loads from 1½ tons to 20 tons, together with pallet trucks and gravity rollers.

STRANRAER

Shipping and International Services Division of British Railways Board

British Transport Ship Management (Scotland) Ltd.
Stranraer Harbour,
Wigtownshire
TELEPHONE: 2262 Stranraer
TELEX: 778125
HEAD OFFICE:
87 Union Street, Glasgow, C.1.
TELEPHONE: 041 248 2911
SHIPPING AND PORT MANAGER:
Captain L. J. Unsworth

ROLL-ON/ROLL-OFF FACILITY:
The East Pier can accept vessels of 112·5 m (369 ft) length 17·4 m (57 ft) beam and 3·35 m (12 ft) draught. There are 1·8 hectares (4·5 acres) of parking and marshalling space for vehicles.

ROLL-ON SERVICES:
Stranraer—Larne—Four services daily by the Passenger/vehicle ferries *Antrim Princess* and *Caledonian Princess* and one sailing per day by *Stena Trailer* for freight vehicles only.

Antrim Princess at Stranraer

SWANSEA

British Transport Docks Board

Adelaide Street, Swansea, S. Wales
TELEPHONE: Swansea 50855
TELEX: 48150
PRINCIPAL OFFICIALS:
W. G. King (*Docks Manager, Swansea and Port Talbot*)
T. Phillips (*Operations Manager*)
K. J. Langden (*Docks Engineer*)
Captain E. J. N. White (*Dockmaster*)
ROLL-ON/ROLL-OFF FACILITY
Swansea Ferry Terminal, completed in May 1969, is used by vessels of 118 m (387·7 ft) in length, 17·7 m (58·5 ft) beam with a draught of 4·4 m (14·5 ft). The terminal is equipped with an automatically controlled link span bridge which is self adjusting under tidal conditions. There are 1940 m² (2,320 sq yds) available for marshalling and parking vehicles. An area has been set aside in a nearby transit shed for customs clearance of containers and part of the terminal building has been set aside for the checking of vehicles and trailers.

Swansea—B & I Line's Car Ferry and Roll-on Terminal

The Terminal is used by the British and Irish Steam Packet Co. Ltd. for their daily service to Cork in the summer and thrice weekly service in winter.

TEES AND HARTLEPOOL

Tees & Hartlepool Port Authority
Queen's Square
Middlesborough,
Teesside,
T52 1AH
TELEPHONE: 0642 48321
TELEX: 58675
PRINCIPAL OFFICIALS:
A. G. Robinson (*Managing Director*)
P. Collin (*Deputy Managing Director*)
R. L. Harper (*Secretary & Treasurer*)
Captain T. Hand (*Harbourmaster*)
E. Bicknell (*Commercial Manager*)
S. Wright (*Operating Manager—Tees Dock*)

CONTAINER FACILITIES:
Tees Dock:
   This common user facility, equipped with two 35 ton Butters scotch derrick cranes has about 1·6 hectares (four acres) of paved storage and marshalling area. Three 23 ton and one 35 ton sideloaders are operated.
Bell Terminal:
   This terminal with a quay length of 134 m (440 ft) owned by the Port Authority and leased to Bell Line Limited, is equipped with a 32 ton Paceco-Vickers goliath container crane which spans both the ship and the yard.
   The container yard will shortly be doubled in size and a Paceco Vickers Goliath container gantry crane added.

TERMINAL OPERATING HOURS:
   Ships and inland transport cargo handling operations take place between 0600 and 2200 hours daily.

CONTAINER SERVICES:
   Finland s.s. Co. and United Baltic Corporation—to Helsinki every 5 days.
   Batt Line—to Rotterdam twice weekly.
   Bell Line—to Rotterdam daily.
   Meri Shipping OY—to Mantyluoto fortnightly.
   Svea Line—to Copenhagen and Helsingborg weekly.
   Leffler Line—to Gothenburg weekly.

TRAFFIC:
   Traffic over the Tees Dock Terminal in 1969 amounted to 169,699 tons (83,646 tons—7,107 loaded units inwards and 86,053 tons and 7,812 loaded units outwards). Container traffic is estimated at about 125,000 tons for 1971. (It should be noted that these figures do not include the Bell Terminal).

PRINCIPAL CONTAINER FREIGHT FORWARDING COMPANIES:
Clarkson Bros. & Casper
   34 Marton Road, Middlesbrough
   Telephone: 43662. Telex: 58500
Tarmac Shipping:
   Teesport, Grangetown, Middlesbrough
   Telephone: 2691. Telex: 58584
Svea Line
   J. G. Peckston, Dundas House, Dundas Street, Middlesbrough
   Telephone: 45141. Telex: 58534
Bell Line
   Bell Terminal, Teesport, Middlesborough
   Telephone: 4188. Telex: 58651 and 2

SHIPPING COMPANY AGENTS:
Batt Line Ltd.
   Batt Line Ltd., PO Box 46, Zetland House, Middlesbrough, Teesside
   Telephone: M'bro 47484
UBC/Finska
   Clarkson Bros. & Casper Ltd.,
   34 Marton Road, Middlesbrough, Teesside
   Telephone: M'bro 43662

Bell Line Ltd.
   Bell Line Ltd, Teesport, Grangetown, Middlesbrough, Teesside
   Telephone: Eston Grange 4188
Meri Shipping O/Y
   Tarmac Shipping, Teesport, Middlesbrough, Teesside
   Telephone: Eston Grange 2691
Svea Line
   J. G. Peckston Ltd., Dundas House, Dundas Street- Middlesbrough, Teesside
   Telephone: M'bro 45141
A/B August Leffler & Son
   Metcalfe, Son & Co., Lloyds Bank Chambers, Church Square Hartlepool, Co. Durham
   Telephone: Hartlepool 3241

STEVEDORES:
All stevedoring is undertaken by the Port Authority

STORAGE:
Container storage is arranged by the Port Authority

Tees Dock Terminal

Bell Terminal, Teesport.

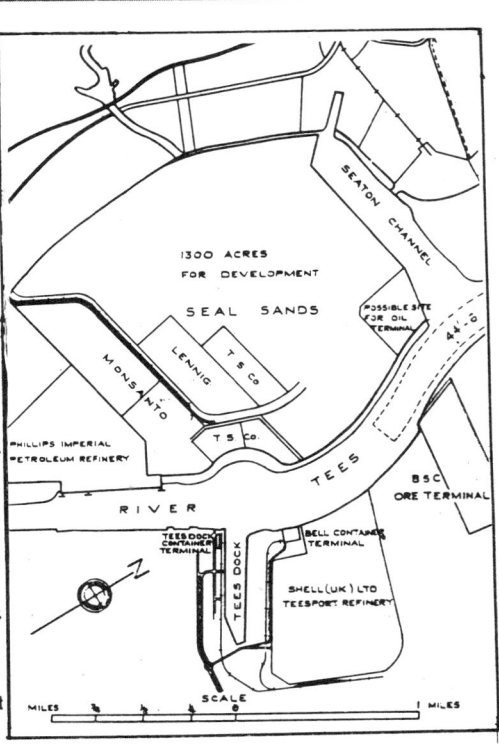

WARREN POINT

Warrenpoint Harbour Authority
Warrenpoint Northern Ireland
TELEPHONE: 3601/3
TELEX: 74660
OFFICIALS:
W. Devlin (*Managing Director*)
CONTAINER FACILITY:
Victoria Berth is capable of accepting vessels
of up to 67 m (220 feet) in length, 10·7 m

(35 feet) in beam with a draught of 4·3 m
(14 feet). It is equipped with a 25 ton scotch
derrick capable of loading and discharging
twelve containers per hour. There are 2
acres of parking space for containers.

CONTAINER SERVICE:
Victoria Berth is used by Irish Sea Ferries
Ltd. for their daily service to Garston.

CONTAINER TRAFFIC:
Some 6,400 loaded units were handled in
1970; this is expected to increase to 7,000
in 1971.
FUTURE DEVELOPMENT:
The authority acquired all the harbour
facilities in May 1971. A development
programme, costing £2 million is underway
to provide new container berths and other
cargo handling facilities.

WESTON POINT DOCKS

British Waterways Board
Weston Point Docks
Near Runcorn, Cheshire
TELEPHONE: Runcorn 2218
Manager: H. Holland
CONTAINER FACILITIES
No. 2 Wharf which is capable of taking

vessels 67·5 m (220 ft) in length, 11·0 m (36 ft)
in beam with a draught of 4·57 m (15 ft) is
a dual purpose berth in that ship's ramps
can be placed directly on to quay. It is equipped with a 32 ton Scotch derrick which can
load and discharge containers at a rate of
about 10/15 per hour. There is a parking area

of 6000 m² (1·5 acres) behind the quay.

SERVICES
British and Irish Steam Packet Co. of Dublin
operate a thrice weekly service to Dublin
with various vessels carrying up to 40 containers each.

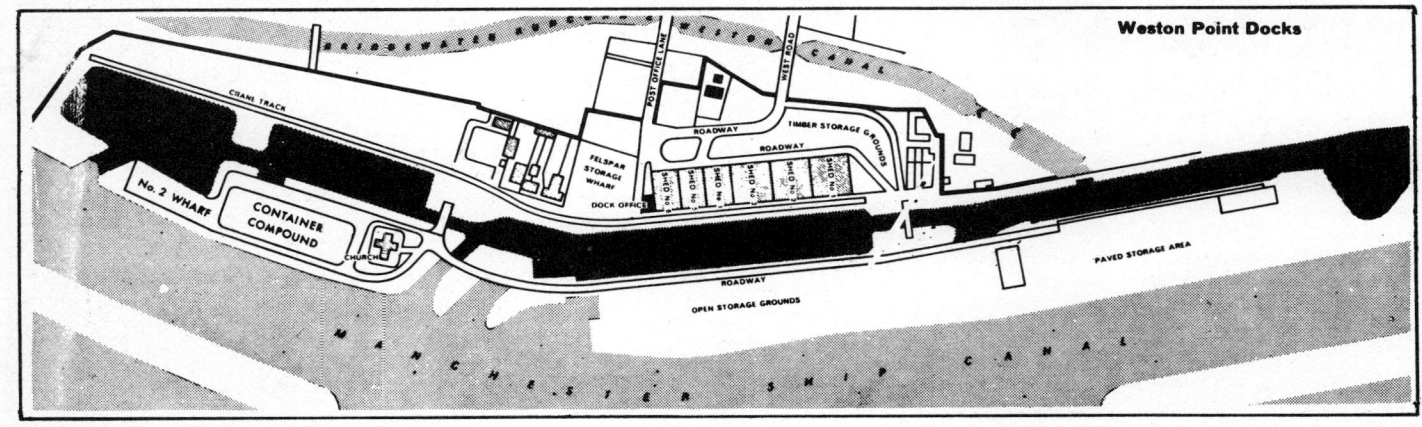

Weston Point Docks

U.K. INLAND TRANSPORT

United Kingdom Publicly Owned Freight Organisations
The 1968 Transport Act re-organised the

structure of nationalised transport and the
position, so far as container and shipping
services are concerned, is as follows:

British Railways Board
222 Marylebone Road,
London, N.W.1.
TELEPHONE: 01 262-3232

The Board, through their Regions, are re-
ponsible for providing rail wagons and motive
power for the transport of containers between
terminals on the Freightliner network, rail-
connected premises (whether railway-owned
or privately-owned), inland customs depots
(Containerbases) and the ports. They also run
container trains to link with European
railways via container shipping services to
Continental ports and container vessels
serving other parts of the world.
BRITISH RAILWAYS SHIPPING AND
INTERNATIONAL SERVICES DIVISION.
Liverpool Street,
London, EC2.

TELEPHONE: 01-283 7535.
OFFICIALS:
D. McKenna (*Chairman*)
J. L. Harrington (*Deputy Chairman*)
J. Posner (*General Manager*)
S. A. Claydon (*Deputy General Manager*)
J. H. Bustard (*Chief Operations Manager*)
R. L. P. Cobb (*Chief Commercial Manager
Irish & Estuarial*)
D. D. Kirby (*Chief Commercial Manager
(Continental and Channel Islands)*)
J. W. Read (*Controller of Finance*)
This Division is responsible for the manage-
ment and operation of railway-owned ports
and for providing lift-on/lift-off and roll-on/
roll-off container shipping services based at
Harwich, Dover, Newhaven, Fishguard,
Holyhead, Heysham and Stranraer.
The Division also operates the London
International Freight Terminal (LIFT).

Entries for the ports and for the fleet will
be found under the relevant sections in the
Book; LIFT is described at the end of this
section.
FREIGHTLINERS LTD:
This is a private limited company, 51 per cent
of whose shares are owned by the NFC and
49 per cent by the BRB. Its task is to provide
a nationwide service for the movement of
containers. It is a full door-to-door service,
including collection and delivery, or movement from factory to port or between
terminal and terminal. These terminals may
be owned and operated by the Company or,
in the case of ports and inland customs depots
(Containerbases), by other bodies. Freightliners Ltd carry their own or privately-
operated containers, the former remaining
within the UK. (Please see the full section
on Freightliners Ltd. below.)

National Freight Corporation
Argosy House,
215 Great Portland Street,
London, W1N 6BD

TELEPHONE: 01-636 8688
This body controls the nationalised sector of
road transport and all the shipping and freight
companies previously owned by the Transport

Holding Company. It has also a 51 per cent
interest in Freightliners Ltd and controls the
former British Rail Sundries Division under
the title of National Carriers Ltd.

Tartan Arrow Service Ltd
Tartan Arrow Centre
353, Kentish Town Road, London NW5.
TELEPHONE: 01-485 5699
TELEX: 23938

GENERAL:
In August 1966 the company became
associated with the road haulage interests of

the Transport Holding Company and in
February 1967 control of the company
was shared equally between the Transport
Holding Company and British Railways
Board. Under the Transport Act 1968
Tartan Arrow became part of the National
Freight Corporation on 1st January 1969.

SERVICES:
General
A daily road/rail integrated service
between England and Scotland accepting
packages weighing between 21 lb (9·52
kilos) and 2,240 lb (1,016 kilos). Freight
is consolidated into container loads. In

May 1969 Tartan Arrow introduced a London Parcels service which guarantees next day delivery.

Rail

Tartan Arrow operate five container trains per week in each direction (Mondays to Fridays) between London and Glasgow using their own terminals.

Road:

Tartan Arrow road collection and delivery areas cover the whole Scottish mainland and South East England. The Company continues to handle bulk haulage and furniture by road between London, Liverpool and the North of England.

CONTAINER FLEET:

Dry Box	10 × 8 × 8	
Dry Box	20 × 8 × 8	
Dry Box	30 × 8 × 8	
Flats	20 × 8	
Flats	30 × 8	

Tartan Arrow's London Terminal.

The 20 ton container yard gantry crane at Tartan Arrow's London Terminal.

VEHICLE FLEET:
250 Road Vehicles, 125 of which are

capable of carrying containers up to 40 ft in length.

National Carriers Limited

NCL House, 21A John Street, London WC1N 2BX
TELEPHONE: 01-242-9050
OFFICIALS:
H. Kinsey (*Managing Director*)
R. H. Teager (*Assistant Managing Director*)
National Carriers Limited is divided into 7 areas: Eastern, London, Midland, North Eastern, Scottish, Southern and Western;

with a headquarters at John Street, London.

NCL gives a complete door-to-door service —collection, trunk haul and delivery—for consignments in the small and medium-weight freight range. Its Yellow Diamond service guarantees next day delivery on more than 200 routes between important centres.

The company owns a fleet of 3,000 small wheeled containers, with a capacity of 70

cu. ft. and a maximum payload of 1 ton. These containers can be sent anywhere in Great Britain, and to addresses in Northern Ireland, Dublin and the Isle of Man. They do not operate internationally.

The NCL road vehicle fleet of 8,500 motive units and 21,000 trailers collects and delivers from a network of 160 depots covering the whole country.

Channel Islands Unit Load Service

British Rail Shipping and International Services Division
50 Liverpool Street,
London EC2M 72H
TELEPHONE: 01-283 7535
TELEX: 886821

GENERAL:

In 1972 the British Railways Board will introduce a unit load system into the Channel Islands shipping services. It is planned to operate from Portsmouth to Jersey and Guernsey daily with two conventional non cellular ships each able to lift the equivalent

of 80 20 ft units.

The Channel Islands Unit Load Service will provide insulated, covered and flats, etc in 20 ft and 10 ft lengths.
SERVICE:
Portsmouth to St Helier, Jersey and St. Peter Port, Guernsey—daily.

Freightliners Limited

43, Cardington Street,
London, N.W.1
TELEPHONE: 01 387 9400
Freightliners Limited, formerly the Freightliner Division of British Railways, was set up as a Limited Liability Company by the Transport Act of 1968.
DIRECTORS:
T. G. Gibb (*Chairman*)
L. S. Payne

E. G. Marsden, O.B.E.
C. W. Reeves
W. O. Reynolds
S. C. Robbins
A. W. Tait
CHIEF EXECUTIVES:
T. G. Gibb (*Managing Director*)
T. R. V. Bolland (*Assistant Managing Director*)
D. J. Cobbett (*Assistant Managing Director*)

AREA MANAGERS:
London and Home Counties Area

J. R. Burnham
167/9, Westbourne Terrace,
London, W.2
Telephone: 01 262 5466
North Western and West Midlands Area
R. W. Hall,
Quay House,
Quay Street,

Drott Travelift 0 - 4 - 0

Lancer Boss Side-Loader

Morris Crane 0 - 4 - 0

Allen Crane 0 - 4 - 0

Arrol Crane 2 - 6 - 2

Manchester, 3.
Telephone: 061 834 3642
North Eastern and East Midlands Area
I. J. James
St. Pauls House,
20, St. Pauls Street,
Leeds, 1
Telephone Leeds 31711
South Western Area
G. Body
Tower House, Fairfax Street,
Bristol, 1
Telephone: Bristol 21382

Scotland
J. H. Young,
Ingram House,
227, Ingram Street,
Glasgow, C.1
Telephone: 041 332 9876 extn. 2480
OPERATING PROCEDURE
The service is fully bookable and advance
notice is essential. In the first instance the
Area Manager should be contacted.

The Terminal Manager allocates space on
the train and informs customers of the latest
time of acceptance at the terminal. Confir-
mation of the booking ensures that consignments travel by the booked service. Charges
are on a container basis.
GENERAL
The first Freightliner train ran in November,
1965. By the end of 1970, 150 daily services
were in operation between twenty-eight
terminals (including ports) and the number
of loaded containers carried was in excess of
half a million per year.

The Company's business continues to
expand. Additional capacity is expected to
be provided at Tilbury (PLA) and Felixstowe
(Felixstowe Dock and Railway Co) during
1971. Expansion of services with Ireland
through Holyhead which was delayed through
damage to the bridge carrying the line over
the Menai Straits, dividing the mainland
from the Isle of Anglesey on which Holyhead
is situated will take place in the latter part
of 1971.

FREIGHTLINER TERMINALS WITH SERVICES
IN OPERATION AND PLANNED
Aberdeen
120 Market Street
Aberdeen AB9 2EZ
Tel: Aberdeen 54817/8
Telex: 73163
  Glasgow
  London, King's Cross
Belfast
Manager
Northern Ireland
20 Donegall Quay
Belfast
Tel: Belfast 28061
Ext 14
Telex: 74456
  Birmingham
  London, York Way
  Leeds*
  Manchester*
  Nottingham*
  Sheffield*
Birmingham
Dudley Terminal
Castle Hill, Dudley
Tel: Dudley 53754
Telex: 338539
  Glasgow
  Newcastle
  Stockton
Landor Street Terminal
Landor Street
Birmingham 4
Tel: 021-359 1985
Telex: 338044
  Belfast
  Dublin
  Felixstowe Docks
  Harwich†

Birmingham Freightliner Terminal

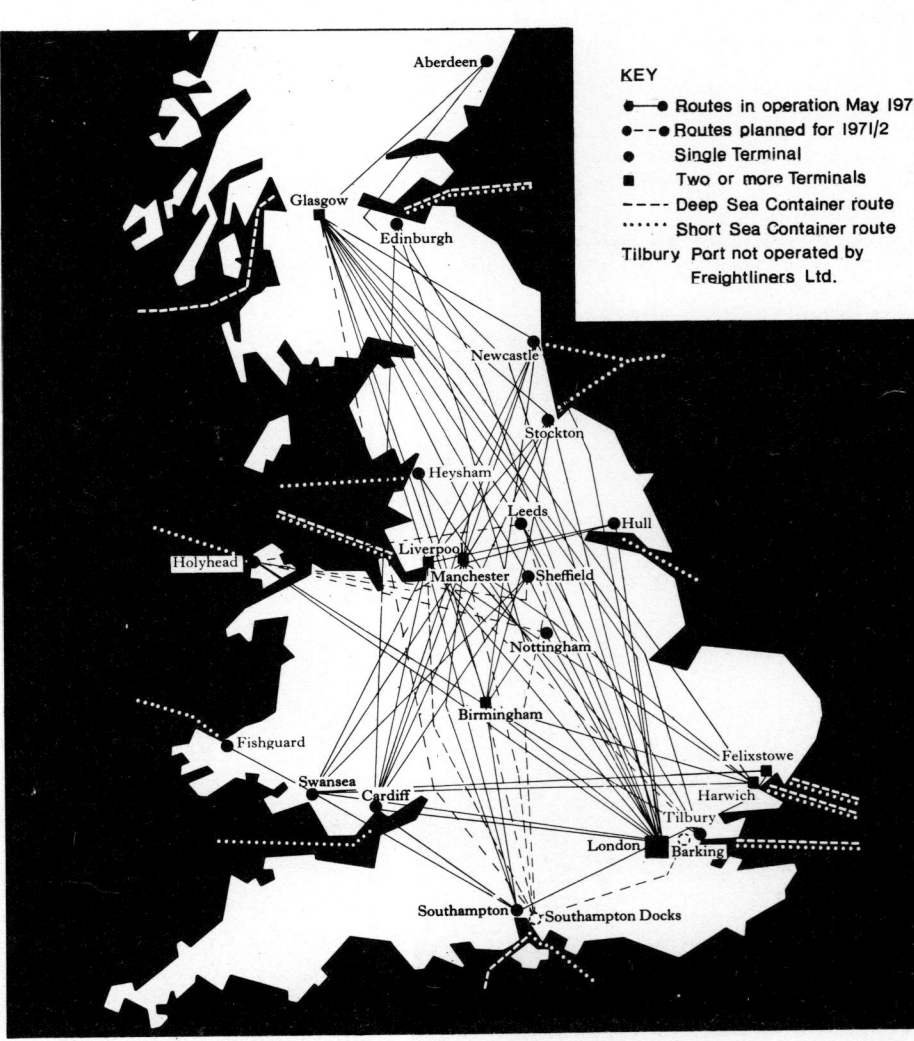

KEY
●━━● Routes in operation May 1971
●--● Routes planned for 1971/2
● Single Terminal
■ Two or more Terminals
---- Deep Sea Container route
······ Short Sea Container route
Tilbury Port not operated by
   Freightliners Ltd.

  London, Willesden
  Southampton
  Tilbury Docks
Cardiff
Rover Way, Pengam
Cardiff CF2 2YG
Tel: Cardiff 397314
Telex: 49333
  Edinburgh
  Liverpool
  London, Stratford
  London, Willesden
  Manchester
  Newcastle
  Sheffield
  Southampton
  Stockton

Dublin
North Wall, Dublin
Tel: Dublin 42931 Ext: 49
Telex: Dublin 5354
  Birmingham
  London, Willesden
  Leeds*
  Manchester*
  Nottingham*
  Sheffield*
Edinburgh
St. Marks Place
Portobello
Edinburgh EH15 2QA
Tel: 031-669-6211
Telex: 72215
  Birmingham

Freightliner train. southbound from Scotland.

Cardiff
London, Stratford
London, Willesden

Felixstowe Docks
Trelawney House
Felixstowe Docks
Tel: Felixstowe 6532
Telex: 98522
  Birmingham
  Glasgow
  London, Stratford
  Manchester

Glasgow
Gushetfaulds Terminal
100 Cathcart Road
Glasgow S2
Tel: 041-332 9876
Ext 2018
Telex: 778148
  Aberdeen
  Birmingham
  Leeds
  Liverpool
  London, Stratford
  London, Willesden
  London, York Way
  Manchester
  Newcastle
  Sheffield
  Stockton
Coatbridge
Containerbase
Gartsherrie Road
Coatbridge
Tel: 0236 24331
Telex: 778576
  Felixstowe Docks
  Harwich†
  Tilbury Docks

Harwich
(from the Continent)
Parkeston Quay, Essex
Tel: Harwich 2141
Ext 500
Telex: 98413
  Birmingham
  Glasgow
  Liverpool
  London, Stratford
  Manchester
  Swansea
  Waterford

Hull
Clyde Terrace
Brighton Street
Hessle Road, Hull
Tel: Hull 37691/2
Telex: 52239
  Liverpool
  London, King's Cross
  Manchester

Leeds
Wakefield Road
Stourton, Leeds LS10 1SD
Tel: Leeds 72921/2
Telex: 55370
  Glasgow

London, Stratford
London, Willesden
Tilbury Docks
Belfast*
Dublin*

Liverpool
Garston Terminal
Dock Road, Garston
Liverpool
Tel: 051-427 7941
Telex: 627017
  Cardiff
  Glasgow
  Harwich†
  Hull
  London, Stratford
  London, Willesden
  Newcastle
  Southampton
  Stockton
  Swansea
  Tilbury Docks
  Waterford

London
King's Cross Terminal
Goods Way, N1
Tel: 01-278 5378
Telex: 262963
  Aberdeen
  Edinburgh
  Hull
  Stockton
Stratford Terminal
Temple Mills Lane, E15
Tel: 01-534 6205
Telex: 896012
  Cardiff
  Edinburgh
  Felixstowe Docks
  Glasgow
  Harwich†
  Leeds
  Liverpool
  Manchester
  Newcastle
  Southampton
  Swansea
  Waterford

Willesden Terminal
Stephenson St, NW10
Tel: 01-965 8971
Telex: 264000
  Birmingham
  Cardiff
  Dublin
  Glasgow
  Leeds
  Liverpool
  Manchester
  Newcastle
  Swansea
  Waterford
York Way Terminal
York Way, N7
Tel: 01-485 1486
Telex: 262474
  Belfast
  Glasgow
  Nottingham
  Sheffield

Manchester
Longsight Terminal
New Bank Street
Manchester 12
Tel: 061-273 2631
Telex: 668793
  London, Stratford
  London, Willesden
Barton Dock Road
Containerbase
Barton Dock Estate
(West) Urmston
Lancs N31 2LP
Tel: 061-748 9511
Telex: 668421
  Harwich†
  Tilbury Docks
Trafford Park Terminal
Westinghouse Road
Trafford Park
Manchester 17
Tel: 061-228 2141
Ext 2992
Telex: 668489
  Cardiff
  Felixstowe Docks

Parkeston Quay Freightliner Terminal, Harwich.

Glasgow
Hull
Newcastle
Southampton
Stockton
Swansea
Waterford
Belfast*
Dublin*

Newcastle
Follingsby Lane
Wardley, Gateshead NE10 8YA
Tel: Newcastle 693741
Telex: 53170
Birmingham
Cardiff
Glasgow
Liverpool
London, Stratford
London, Willesden
Manchester

Nottingham
Beacon Road
Beeston, Notts
Tel: Nottingham 48531
Ext 2400
Telex: 37663
London, York Way
Belfast*
Dublin*

Sheffield
The Ickles
Sheffield Road
Rotherham
Tel: Rotherham 3294
Telex: 54413
Cardiff
Glasgow
London, York Way
Swansea
Waterford
Belfast*
Dublin*

Southampton
Millbrook Road
Southampton
Tel: Southampton
30223 Ext 2487
Telex: 47596
Birmingham
Cardiff
Liverpool
London, Stratford
Manchester
Swansea
Waterford

Stockton
Haverton Hill Road
Stockton-on-Tees
Co. Durham LTS18 2NX
Tel: Stockton 66219
Telex: 58478
Birmingham
Cardiff
Glasgow
Liverpool
London, King's Cross
Manchester

Swansea
Crymlyn Burrows, Swansea
Tel: Swansea 42821
Telex: 48257
Harwich†
Liverpool
London, Stratford
London, Willesden
Manchester
Sheffield
Southampton

Tilbury Docks

Tilbury Docks, Essex
Tel: Tilbury 3165/2918
Telex: 897151
Birmingham
Glasgow
Leeds

Stratford Freightliner terminal

Manchester
Liverpool
Waterford
Adelphi Wharf
Waterford
Tel· Waterford 4841
Harwich†
Liverpool
London, Stratford
London, Willesden
Manchester
Sheffield
Southampton

†for Continent

Other Freightliner Services
There are additional Freightliner routes which involve container transfer between trains at intermediate terminals.
Information about these can be obtained from the local Area Manager or Terminal Manager.

OTHER TERMINALS SERVED BY FREIGHTLINER SERVICES:
B.R.B. TERMINALS
London (Park Royal)
Telephone: 01-965 7031
Harwich (Shipping Division)
Telephone: Harwich 2141
Supt. J. B. Taylor
Heysham (Shipping Division)
Telephone: Heysham 52373. Shipping Port Capt. C. Blackmore (*Manager*)
Holyhead (Shipping Division)
Telephone: Holyhead 2304. Shipping Port Capt. R. A. H. Lord (*Manager*)

FELIXSTOWE DOCKS AND RAILWAY CO.
Felixstowe
Agent: R. W. Meredith
Telephone: 039-42 6532

CONTAINERBASE FEDERATION LTD.
Manchester (Barton Dock Road Containerbase Ltd.)
Telephone: 061-748 9511
Coatbridge Containerbase Ltd.
Telephone: 041-20 24331
Liverpool (Aintree) Containerbase Ltd.
Telephone: 051-525 7461

PORT OF LONDON AUTHORITY
Tilbury Rail Container Terminal
Telephone: Tilbury 2918
Tilbury 3165

SPECIAL CONTAINER TYPES
Customers are encouraged to use privately owned custom built units, if their needs are specialised, provided they conform to Freightliner/ISO requirements. Terminal Managers can give further details.

CRANES AND HANDLING EQUIPMENT

Terminal	Cranes
Aberdeen	2 × 48′ Drott Travelifts
Birmingham (Landor St.)	2 × 2-6-3 Arrol Class III
Cardiff	2 × 0-4-0 Morris Class III
	1 × 0-4-0 Allen Class II*
	1 × S & D Freightlifter†
Dudley	2 × 0-4-0 Morris Class III
Edinburgh	1 × 0-4-0 Morris Class III
	1 × 0-4-0 Allen Class II
Glasgow	2 × 2-6-2 Arrol Class III
	1 × 36′ Drott Travelifts†
Hull	1 × 0-4-0 Morris Class III
	1 × 0-4-0 Allen Class II
Leeds	2 × 0-4-0 Morris Class III
Liverpool	2 × 2-6-2 Arrol Class III
	2 × 48′ Drott Travelifts†
London (Kings Cross)	2 × 0-3-0 Allen Class II
London (Stratford)	2 × 0-4-0 Morris Class III
	2 × 2-6-2 Stothert & Pitt Class III
	1 Lancer Boss Sideloader (on hire)†
London (Willesden)	2 × 0-4-0 Morris Class III
	3 × 2-6-3 Arrol Class III
London (York Way)	4 × 48′ Drott Travelifts
	1 Rapida Static Crane†
Manchester (Longsight)	3 × 48′ Drott Travelifts
Manchester (Trafford Park)	2 × 2-6-3 Arrol Class III
Newcastle	2 × 0-4-0 Morris Class III
	1 × 0-4-0 Allen Class II
Nottingham	2 × 0-4-0 Morris class III
Sheffield	2 × 0-4-0 Morris Class III
Southampton	2 × 0-4-0 Morris Class III
Stockton	2 × 0-4-0 Morris Class III
Swansea	2 × 0-4-0 Morris Class III

*Limited use pending transfer
†In use in container storage areas

CONTAINERS PLANNED TO BE IN SERVICE—
DECEMBER 1971:

Type	Description	Number
A & G	10 ft Covered	535
B L & S	20 ft Covered	2,120
P	20 ft Insulated	291
D & N	30 ft Covered	1,326
M	30 ft Curtain sided	377
H & W	20 ft Open	562
K & Y	30 ft Open	1,261
V	30 ft Open top	50

Notes:
(i) All containers are 2,435 mm in width, except types W and Y Mk. IV which are 2,500 mm.
(ii) All covered containers are 2,435 mm in height.
(iii) In addition special insulated 20 ft containers have been developed for the carriage of meat either stacked or on the hook. Capacities are 25·4 m³ (900 cu. ft.), 16,500 kgs stacked or 7,000 kgs on the hook.

CONTROL OF CONTAINER MOVEMENT
The immediate control and allocation of containers is exercised at the terminals. The overall balancing of containers throughout the system is directed from Headquarters in the light of the position established at 10.00 and 14.00 hours each day.

LIFT (London International Freight Terminal)

British Railways Board
Shipping and International Service Division
Liverpool Street, London EC2M 7QH
Telephone: 01-283 7535
Telex: 886821

Alongside the Stratford Freightliner Terminal in London, British Rail have developed a 35 acre inland Customs Terminal at a total cost of £1½ million. It links TIR trailers with the Freightliner network and has direct line connections to the Port of London Authority Docks. By road the Terminal will connect with the M11 Motorway and a new flyover has been constructed to ease the road traffic flow from central London. Three rail sidings are available for making-up trains and three for Customs clearance. Each participating agent has been allocated its own Customs officer and is responsible for its own documentation and handling etc.

The following agents operate independently in LIFT:

Alltransport Ltd.
Anglo Overseas Transport Co. Ltd.

Conemar Ltd.
Crowe & Co.

Davies Turner & Co. Ltd
Gentransco Services Ltd.
Lep Transport Ltd.
M.A.T. Transport Ltd.
Panalpina Ltd.
Schenkers Ltd.
Van Oppen & Co. (1935) Ltd.

INLAND WATERWAYS

British Waterways Board

Sharpness Docks
Gloucestershire
England
TELEPHONE: 228

GENERAL:
Both Sharpness and Gloucester are closely linked also with the surrounding areas by road, rail and waterway services. The size of vessel is governed by the entrance lock to the 16 mile canal which provides a depth of water on the outer sill of 8·8 m (29 ft). Depth of water on the inner sill is 6·7 m (22 ft) and the minimum width is 17·3 m (57 ft) with a length of 274·5 m (900 ft).

WAREHOUSE ACCOMMODATION
Transit sheds provide accommodation for the handling and storage of all types of goods.

CRANES
The Waterways Board have installed a 32-ton Henderson Scotch Derrick Crane and provided a new storage compound, a warehouse and office block. Other modern appliances include a Mafi Portalift of 25-tons capacity

CONTAINER SERVICES:
Greenore Ferry Services Ltd. to Ireland.

The 32-ton Henderson Scotch Derrick Crane installed by the British Waterways Board at their Sharpness Docks to handle unit loads for Greenore Ferry Services Ltd.

CONTAINERBASE FEDERATION

Containerbase Federation Limited,

22-25 Finsbury Square,
London E.C.2.
TELEPHONE: 01-638 8301
John Reid (Chief Executive)
MEMBERS OF THE FEDERATION:
Containerbase (Birmingham) Ltd
Containerbase (Scotland) Ltd
Containerbase (Leeds) Ltd
Containerbase (Liverpool) Ltd
Containerbase (Manchester) Ltd

Addresses and Executives for these organisations are shown in the Inland Clearance Depot List.

GENERAL:
The five containerbases are separate companies offering services to container and TIR vehicle operators. A number of major transport organisations are partners in each containerbase. They include both nationalised and private concerns.

Their aim in forming Containerbase companies has been to serve the transport industry, and through that industry, the transport user, by providing all the terminal services needed for container operations. The movement of containers to or from containerbases is left to the operator, but at the base all the consolidation, inspection, distribution and documentation services necessary at the start or at the end of a container transit are available.

To ensure co-ordination of policy at National level and to provide centralised services for each containerbase all the partners involved are represented in Containerbase Federation Limited. In this way the operating responsibilities of each containerbase are firmly localised, but certain aspects of overall commercial policy are decided centrally.

Plans have been made to expand the areas occupied by the Containerbases.

INLAND CLEARANCE DEPOTS APPROVED BY H.M. CUSTOMS
FOR CLEARANCE OF GOODS IMPORTED
OR EXPORTED IN CONTAINERS

London (Stratford) International Freight Terminal
Temple Mill Lane,
Stratford, London, E15
Operator:
British Railways Board, Eastern Region
Shed Operators:
Alltransport Ltd, Depot No 3, LIFT
Anglo Overseas Transport Ltd,
29 Mincing Lane, London, EC3
Panalpina International Transport Ltd.
Cap House, Long Lane, London, EC1
Constantine Terminals
2 Shed, Stratford International Terminal E15
Davies Turner & Co Ltd,
4, Lower Belgrave Street, London, SW1
General Transport Co Ltd,
PO Box 166, Central House,
32 Stratford High Street, London, E15
LEP Transport Ltd,
Sunlight Wharf,
Upper Thames Street, London, EC4
MAT Transport Ltd,
36 Holywell Lane, London, EC2
Van Oppen & Co (1935) Ltd,
90 Fenchurch Street,
London, EC3

Inland Customs Clearance Depot,
Perry Barr
Birmingham.
Operator:
Containerbase (Birmingham North) Ltd,
College Road, Perry Barr,
Birmingham 22B
Telephone: 021-356 7421
Telex: 338085
E. Sharrock (*Manager*)

Hull Euroscan Ltd.
Dairycoates, Brighton Street
Hull, Yorks, HU3 4XL
Operator:
Hull Euroscan Ltd.

Inland Customs Clearance Depot
Liverpool
Operator:
Containerbase (Liverpool) Ltd.,
Orrell Lane,
Bootle L20 6NR Lancs.
Telephone: 051 525 7461
Telex: 62649
L. Carlile (*Manager*)

Inland Customs Clearance Depot,
Stourton, Leeds
Operator:
Containerbase (Leeds) Ltd,
Wakefield Road, Stourton,
Leeds 10
Telephone: 0532-73681/7
Telex: 557429
D. J. M. Durbin (*Manager*)

Inland Customs Clearance Depot,
Urmston,
Manchester
Operator:
Containerbase (Manchester) Ltd.,
Barton Dock Road,
Manchester M31 2LP
Urmston,
Telephone: 061-748 9511/7
Telex: 668421
J. Thompson (*Manager*)

Sheepy Park, Renfrew
Operator:
Clyde Container Services Ltd,
Braehead, Renfrew, Scotland
Telephone: 041-886 3755

Inland Customs Clearance Depot,
Coatbridge

Operator:
Containerbase (Scotland) Ltd.
Gartsherrie Road, Coatbridge,
Lanarkshire.
Telephone: 0236-24331/7
Telex: 778576
J. L. Cameron (*Manager*)

West of England Freight Terminal (WEFT)
Bristol
Owner:
West of England Freight Terminal Ltd,
Chittening Estate,
Avonmouth.
G. D. Osborne-Bartram (*Manager*)

London (East) ICD Ltd.
Chobham Farm, Leyton Road, London E15
Orsett Depot,
Brentwood Road, Orsett, Grays,
Essex, RM16 3PB
South London Inland Clearance Depot,
Bugsby's Way, Charlton, London SE7

Wharves and Airports approved by Customs for examination and clearance of goods *imported* and removed by rail/road from any port.

Emerson Wharf,
London, SE1
Operator:
Knight & Morris Ltd,
(Service Wharves Ltd.)
80 Bankside,
London SE1

Express Wharf,
London, E14
Operator:
Freight Express Ltd,
38 West Ferry Foad,
London, E14

Hermitage Wharf,
London, E1
Operator:
1 Wapping High Street,
London, E1

Lovells Wharf,
London, SE10
Operator:
C. Shaw Lovell & Sons, Ltd,
Lovell House, Pelton Road,
London, SE10

Ratcliff Cross Wharf,
386 The Highway,
London, E1
Operator:
Spedex Shipping Ltd.,
392 The Highway,
London E1

South-Eastern Wharf,
London, SE1
Operator:
Baxter, Hoare & Co Ltd,
145 Borough High Street,
London, SE1

Standard Wharf,
London E1
Operator:
Standard Wharves Ltd,
48/60 Wapping High Street,
London, E1

Sunlight Wharf,
London, EC4
Operator:
Lep Transport Ltd.,
37 Upper Thames Street,
London, EC4

East Midlands Airport
Operator:
East Midlands Airport Joint Committee
Castle Donington, Derbyshire

Ashford Airport, Kent,
Operator:
Skyways Coach and Air Ltd.,
Ashford Airport,
Nr. Hythe, Kent

Corporation Quay, Sunderland,
Operator:
River Wear Commissioners
St Thomas Street,
Sunderland

Tower Wharf, Northfleet
Operator:
Baxter Fell & Co Ltd
Tower Wharf, Northfleet
Kent

Albert Edward Dock, Northshields
Operator:
Port of Tyne Authority

Alexandra & Bentinck Docks, Kings Lynn
Operator:
British Transport Docks Board

Butler's Wharf
Shad Thames, London S.E.1
Operator:
Butler's & Colonial Wharves Ltd

Columbia Wharf
261 Rotherhithe, London S.E.16
Operators:
Red Lion and Three Cranes Wharf Ltd

Dagenham Dock, Essex
Operators:
Samuel Williams Thanes Terminal Ltd

Dufferin Dock No. 3 Belfast
Operator:
Belfast Harbour Commissioners

Free Trade Wharf
The Highway, London E.1.
Owners:
Free Trade Wharf Ltd

Gladstone Container Terminal
Bootle, Lancs.
Operators:
Mersey Docks and Harbour Company

Manston Airport
Ramsgate, Kent
Operator:
Invicta International Airlines

Regent Quay, Aberdeen
Operator:
Aberdeen Harbour Board

Victoria Deep Water Terminal
231, Turmel Avenue, London S.E.10
Operator:
Victoria Deep Water Terminal Ltd

Woolwich Wharf
Warspite Road, London S.E.18
Operator:
Convoys (London Wharves) Ltd

CUSTOMS REQUIREMENTS

PROCEDURES:

The procedures are laid down in *Goods in Containers* (including transport under TIR carnet)—*Customs Requirements Procedures and facilities.* April, 1969 Customs and Excise Notice No. 464, as well as in the following Customs Notices:—

No. 309 —Containers and Packing: Customs Duties and Procedures.

No. 309A—Use of temporarily imported foreign-owned freight containers for domestic freight.

No. 309B—"No documentation" procedure for re-imported and temporarily-imported freight containers.

No. 310 —Filled Carrier—controlled Transport Containers—Revised Procedures.

It should be noted that Notices 309, 309A 309B and 310 are in course of being re-issued; they should be available by the end of 1971.

GENERAL:

(Numbers refer to Customs Note No. 464).

Definition of "container"

8 In Parts I and II of this Notice the term "container" is used to cover not only containers as such (i.e. articles of transport equipment suitable for repeated use and designed to facilitate carriage of goods by any mode of transport without intermediate re-loading) but also portable tanks, road vehicles, trailers and semi-trailers, rail wagons and road and rail tank wagons. It includes containers which have been approved under the provisions of the Customs Convention on Containers, 1956, and road vehicles and containers approved under the TIR Convention, 1959.

9 "Containers" as defined above which are used for inland transport of goods under Customs control must comply with certain requirements regarding size, security, etc.

Where containers may be imported and exported:

10 Goods in containers may be imported or exported at any place which is approved by Customs for the importation or exportation of the goods concerned and which has adequate facilities for the custody, handling and examination of the containers and the goods carried in them.

Access to containers:

11 At all places where goods in containers are imported, exported or examined, safe and easy means of access must be provided in order that Customs officials may, without risk of injury, inspect the containers and any locks or seals on them, apply or remove official locks or seals and, where necessary, examine and take account of the goods.

12 When goods are imported in containers, particulars of each container and its contents must be shown in the "report" which is made by the Master of the importing ship (or his agent). The required particulars may be given, if desired, in container manifests incorporated in the ship's report.

13 Shipping companies should therefore arrange as necessary to obtain from container operators or foreign shippers the following information:—

identifying mark and/or number of each container; and, in respect of each consignment of goods in it:—

marks and numbers of packages or pieces;
number and description of packages or pieces;
description of goods; and
name of consignee of goods.

The description of the goods must sufficiently identify them. General descriptions such as "machinery" should not be used.

Customs entry of goods in containers:

14 Goods imported in containers, like other imported goods, must be entered with the Customs before they can be cleared. With certain exceptions, Customs will accept an entry at any time within four days before the date of expected arrival of the goods in the United Kingdom. This arrangement provides an opportunity for importers and agents to complete their documentation before the goods arrive, and is an aid to early clearance. Traders are therefore advised to take steps to obtain the necessary commercial documents in good time, and to lodge entries with the Customs as early as possible within the permitted period.

Importance of accurate documentation:

15 The importance of complete and accurate documentation of goods imported in containers cannot be overstated. Inadequate or incorrect information in ships' reports and Customs entries is liable to cause delay in clearance. Importers and container operators are therefore advised, in their own interest, to take whatever action is necessary to ensure that the various commercial documents which form the basis of ship's reports and Customs entries give a full and correct description of all the goods being imported in containers.

Custody of uncleared containers and goods:

16 Containers awaiting Customs clearance must be kept in secure custody in the Customs-approved area: the conditions of custody in particular cases depend on local circumstances and the nature of the goods and type of container concerned.

17 Any goods which, before being cleared out of Customs charge, are unloaded from containers into an approved transit shed will be subject to the normal regulations and conditions governing the operation of transit sheds.

Facilities for Customs examination:

18 Port authorities, dock companies, wharfingers, etc., must, where required, provide at the port of importation the equipment necessary to enable containers to be brought into, or alongside, an approved transit shed for Customs examination. Satisfactory facilities for examination must also be provided, and these must include sufficient space for goods to be unloaded from containers to the extent necessary for Customs to examine selected packages and to check (if necessary by complete turn-out of the contents) that all the goods in the container have been fully declared.

19 When goods are regularly imported in specialised (e.g. refrigerated) containers, the facilities provided should include any special equipment needed to enable the goods to be examined—e.g., in appropriate cases, a fixed or portable "cold-chamber" into which refrigerated goods can be unloaded.

Customs examination:

20 When goods imported in containers are unloaded into transit sheds for trade purposes, consignments are selected for examination, and examination is carried out, as if the goods had been imported otherwise than in containers.

21 Any goods are not so unloaded, examination may present certain difficulties. Before giving clearance, Customs must be satisfied that all the goods in the containers have been properly entered, but at the same time they understand trade concern to avoid delay in clearance and major disturbances to goods which in many cases have been expertly packed in the containers for through transport to the premises of the consignee.

22 The difficulties can be minimised if:—

(a) container operators, importers, etc., ensure that complete and correct information is made available to the ship's Master or the shipping company to enable the legal requirements of "reporting" goods to be complied with (see paragraphs 12-13);

(b) the dock company, wharfinger, etc., notifies the Customs Officer in writing before any of the goods in the container are cleared, that it is not intended to unload the goods at the port of importation for trade purposes; and

(c) in cases where a container contains more than one consignment of goods, or a consignment consists of goods of different descriptions, the importer or container operator provides the Customs Officer with stowage-plans for the container or ensures by other means (e.g. segregation or distinctive marking or labelling) that the different consignments or descriptions can be readily identified.

GOODS EXPORTED IN CONTAINERS:

Export control of goods exported in containers:

23 All goods exported from the United Kingdom are subject to Customs control at the port of shipment, and must be made available there for examination, if required. This control applies equally to goods which are exported in containers.

24 Goods of certain types, in which there is a substantial revenue interest, are required to be produced to the Officer of the port.

25 For the majority of goods, however, formal production for examination at the port is not required and Customs control is therefore exercised without difficulty and does not normally involve unloading of containers or delay or disturbance to goods.

Facilitation of export control:

26 Export control at the port of shipment is facilitated, and delay and disturbance minimised:—

(a) If containers containing goods which have to be produced (see paragraph 24), and the relevant shipping documents, are prominently marked "Produce to Customs", and the goods concerned are loaded in an accessible position in the containers.

(b) If the container operators, or exporters who pack their goods into containers for shipment, arrange to show on their shipping documents details of the contents of each container, including the marks and numbers of the internal packages, the quantity and description of the goods, the consignor of the goods and the reference numbers of any related shipping bills.

(c) If the shipping bills for goods which have to be entered before shipment are endorsed "Goods packed in container No. ...."

Facilities for Customs examination:

27 Satisfactory facilities must be provided for any necessary examination of goods or identification and examination of containers to be done under cover, for the unloading of goods from containers as required for official examination, and for any necessary re-loading.

Custody of containers:

28 Containers of export goods which have been passed by Customs and are awaiting shipment must be kept in secure custody in the Customs-approved area (see paragraph 16).

Particulars of containers and goods to be shown in manifest of exporting ship:

29 When goods are exported in containers, particulars of each container and its contents must be shown in the manifest of the exporting ship, which has to be lodged by the shipping company within six days of the date of clearance of the ship. These particulars may be given, if desired, in container manifests incorporated in the ship's manifest.

30 Container operators, or traders who export goods in containers, should therefore arrange for the following information to be available to the shipping company:—

Identifying mark and/or number of each container; and, in respect of each consignment of goods in it:

marks and numbers of packages or pieces;

number and description of packages or pieces;

description of goods; and

name and address of consignor.

NOTE:

The following Customs Notices are also available from HM Customs and Excise:

No. 461 General Information for Importers

No. 463 Outline of Customs Import Entry Procedure

No. 198 Transit and Transhipment Procedures

No. 466 Export Documents and Trade

Statistics

No. 217 Import Duty Drawbacks.

Copies may be obtained from:

HM Customs and Excise

Kings Beam House, Mark Lane, London EC3

or from the office of any Collector of Customs and Excise.

YUGOSLAVIA
RIJEKA

Poduzece Luka-Rijeka

Poduzece Luka-Rijeka Pretinoc 146, Rijeka

TELEPHONE: 31-555

TELEX: 24-165-YU-ZLP-R1

OFFICIALS:

Kazimir Jelovica (*General Manager*)

CONTAINER FACILITIES:

Temporary Terminal at Trscanska Obala

This facility came into service in March 1971. It is 208 m (682 ft) in length and has a depth of water between 5 and 7 m (16·4 and 19·7 ft) alongside. Storage on this berth and at adjacent sites provide space for between 300 and 400 20 ft units. Handling is undertaken by two floating cranes as required; these cranes also transport the containers within the port as required and up to 20 units can be moved at one time. Handling in the quay is at present undertaken by mobile crane but a Belotti straddle carrier, due in service in early 1972, will enable containers to be stacked two or three high at the temporary facility.

Future Development:

Two sites are under consideration for development into the port's container terminal and consultants will report in the Autumn of 1971; a decision will than be taken as to the area most suitable for construction.

Rijeka – Temporary Container facility

CONTAINER SERVICE:

Jugolinija part Container service to East Coast, North American Ports and to Italy.

CONTAINER REPAIR FACILITIES:

Zanatsko poduzece "IVAN DUJMIC" Bakar

Bakar

Telephone: 24945

Poduzece Luka Rijeka

Obala Jug. mornarice 1, Rijeka

Telephone: 31555

AFRICA

ALGERIA

Societe Nationale des Chemin de fer Algériens (SNCFA)

21-23 Boulevard Mohamed V, Algiers

OFFICIALS:

C. J. Benmehdjouba (*Director General*)

GENERAL:

The SNCFA owns and operates a pool of 730 containers of various types, and also transports containers belonging to private concerns. No container-trains are operated, the movement being by ordinary freight train. Container traffic by rail averages about 200 tonnes per month, and is confined entirely to internal movement.

Developments in this mode of transport are being studied with a view to future action as necessary.

CONGO

Compagnie des Chemins de fer Kinshasa— Dilolo—Lubumbashi (KDL)

Boite Postale 297

Lubumbashi

Republique Democratique du Conge

OFFICIALS:

G. Davain (*Secretary General*)

R. de Zwaef (*Public Relations*)

GENERAL:

KDL do not possess any containers and semi trailer operations do not exist. However, a certain number of rail users possess 3,175 small general cargo containers, between 1·85 and 8 m³ (65·3 and 282·5 ft³), none of which is refrigerated or insulated.

No terminals, as such exist, and containers are handled by mobile cranes. Tare of containers is excluded from rail charges.

DAHOMEY

Organisation Commune Dahomey—Niger des Chemins de fer et des Transportes (OCDN)

Boite Postale 16

Cotonou

Republique du Dahomey

GENERAL

OCDN operate a very small number of 3 and 8·8 m³ containers on the internal rail services. Société de Transit SOCOPAO of Cotonou own eight of 35 × 8 × 8·5 units which are operated by road, rail and sea to France.

EAST AFRICA

East African Harbours Corporation
GENERAL:

The Corporation is the authority for Ports in Kenya and mainland Tanzania. Tentative plans for the provision of container facilities have been reported. Container traffic at present is carried in conventional vessels. mainly using 10 ft units.

MALAGASY

Réseau Nationale des chemins de fer Malagasy
Gare de Soarano
Tananarive
GENERAL:

A fleet of small 5 tonne containers is operated.

A small number of 20 ft units has been acquired for the carriage of frozen meat. The containers are carried on standard flat wagons.

Malagasy Container and Chartering Company (SMCA)

Set up in late 1968 this organisation is 51 per cent owned by the Railway Company, the National Investment Company and the Maritime Transport Company. The remaining 49 per cent of the shares are owned by the private sector. The purpose of the Company is to make all the arrangements for hiring, transport, groupage operations, and the fixing of container tariffs.

CNC Containers at Tananarive Station

MALAWI

Malawi Railways Ltd.
PO Box 5144
Limbe, Malawi

GENERAL:

The question of the increased use of containers on rail, road and lake is under investigation.

SIERRA LEONE

Sierra Leone Ports Authority
Queen Elizabeth II Quay
Cline Town, Freetown
Sierra Leone
TELEPHONE: 3389
TELEX: Freetown 262
PRINCIPAL OFFICIALS:

Captain A. R. N. Macauley (*General Manager*)
J. Mears (*Acting Operation Manager*)
CONTAINER FACILITIES:

Queen Elizabeth II quay extension has No. 6 berth, with 9·90 m (32·5 ft) of water alongside, suitable for container traffic; it is equipped with a thirty-five ton mobile crane.

TERMINAL WORKING HOURS:

0800-1200 and 1300-1700 hrs on Monday to Friday. Saturday 0800-1200. Overtime may be worked on weekdays between 1200 and 1300 and between 1700 and 0800 hrs. Saturdays from 1200 to 2400 and Sundays 0001-2400 hrs.

SOUTH AFRICA

SAR Mobile Container

SAR Portable Container

Introduction

It has been reported that large sums of money are being invested in container terminals at ports and inland sites and also in containers themselves and wagons by South African Railways and Harbours in order to meet the demands of industry for containerisation. It has been estimated that South Africa will spend about R250 million on containerisation, including specialised ships, during the next few years.

South African Railways and Harbours Administration
Paul Kruger Building
Wolmarans Street
Johannesbourg
OFFICIALS:

J. G. H. Loubser (*General Manager*)

Railways
OFFICIALS IN CHARGE OF CONTAINER OPERATIONS:

J. H. F. Grobler (*Assistant General Manager, Commercial*)

CONTAINERS IN SERVICE:

936 'Mobile' units (trailers with a 25 m³ (883 ft³) capacity. 330 'Portable' units with external dimensions of 2·99 × 2·13 × 2·13 m (9·8 × 7 × 7 ft). 719 ISO type units 10 × 8 × 8.

CONTAINER TRAFFIC:

In 1970 44,694 loaded containers were handled. In 1971 it is estimated that this will increase to 55,000 loaded units.

CONTAINER TERMINALS:

At present no terminals are in operation.

It has been reported that these will be set up at Johannesburg, Capetown and Durban.

ROLLING STOCK:

At present no special wagons are in service. It has been reported that 400 special wagons are being acquired with the object of operating container trains between the ports and inland centres; probably Johannesburg to start with where two sideloaders will be supplied for the terminal

Ports
GENERAL:

The Working Group appointed by the Minister of Economic affairs to investigate the whole question of unitisation of cargo as it affects South Africa, has completed its terms of reference, its main finding being that containerisation is the obvious mode of unitisation for sea-borne cargo between South Africa and other countries and that, as South Africa is dependent on the overseas trade, the revolutionary transformation of cargo unitisation would be forced onto the country, all interested parties, e.g. the shipping companies and the S.A. Railways, having to adopt flexible attitudes towards it and seek flexible solutions to the problems it poses. These views are on par with those of the S.A. Railways and Harbours Administration.

Although the S.A. Railways and Harbours Administration is in the course of preparing itself for the advent of containerisation, advice from the shipping lines in regard to the type of container vessel that will be used on the South African run, is still awaited.

PROPOSED PORT FACILITIES:

It is proposed that the ports of Durban and Cape Town be fully equipped to handle not only container ships but also roll-on traffic and other multi-purpose ships. Port Elizabeth will be developed to a lesser degree and East London for coaster containers only.

Particulars of the facilities considered are as follows:—

At Durban:

Provision of six fully equipped container berths for ocean-going vessels and one container berth for coasters.

At Cape Town:

Provision of two fully equipped container berths for ocean-going vessels and one container berth for coasters.

At Port Elizabeth:

Berths 1 and 2 at the Charl Malan Quay will be used for ocean-going vessels whilst Berth No 12 will be adapted for coasters and roll-on traffiic.

At East London:

Container-handling facilities of international standards will not be provided This port will be served by a feeder service from Port Elizabeth and Durban.

In the initial stages of containerisation, e.g. until 1975/1976, containers arriving at all harbours will be handled with existing facilities.

HARBOUR CHARGES:

In so far as harbour charges are concerned, it is the policy to exempt the containers themselves from the payment of inwards/ outwards wharfage charges, but full tariff charges are payable on the contents when landed. Containerised and palletised goods shipped overseas are afforded a rebate of 5 % of the shipping charges normally applicable to such goods. When landed or shipped empty, inwards or outwards wharfage is exempted, but landing and shipping charges are levied, calculated on two cubic metres to the ton.

Containers not exceeding 4,000 kg must be handled by wharf cranes. Where the gross loaded weight exceeds 4,000 kg, units may be discharged or loaded by ships' gear without payment of crane charges, whether or not departmental equipment of sufficient lifting capacity is available. However, if a request is made for such units to be handled by wharf cranes, crane charges in terms of the tariff are payable.

The packing or unpacking of containers is not permitted in the harbour area. Containers must be consigned direct from one consignor to one consignee, and no liability is accepted for damage to containers. The tare and maximum gross mass must be shown on the outside of the container.

The only handling equipment reported on order to August 1971 was six sideloaders, including the two mentioned above, believed to be for Johannesburg.

ASIA
CEYLON
COLOMBO

Colombo Port Commission,
Colombo, Ceylon
OFFICIALS:
Port Commissioner A. N. S. Kulasinghe
Chief Engineer: L. S. de Silva
Chairman and Chief Executive,
Port (Cargo) Corporation H. A. de Silva

DEVELOPMENT PLANS:

The northern end of the Queen Elizabeth quay is being filled to provide a fifth berth which will be operated by the Port (Cargo) Corporation as a container facility for imports and exports and also as a transhipment point.

The berth will be 305 m (1,000 feet) in length with a depth alongside of 12·8 m (42 feet). The backup area will be 4·05 hectares (10 acres) and crane facilities will be provided. It is expected that the facility will be completed in 1973.

HONG KONG
HONG KONG

Marine Department, Government of Hong Kong
102, Connaught Road, Central
Hong Kong
TELEPHONE:
TELEX:
OFFICIALS:

CONTAINER FACILITIES:

Kwai Chung Terminal—No. 1

Operator:

Modern Terminals Ltd.

A company owned by OCL, ACT and Butterfield and Swire (Hong Kong) Ltd.

Having a quay length of 304·8 m (1,000 ft) and a depth of water alongside of 12·8 m (42 ft) and a total area of 10·12 hectares (25 acres) this facility, due to come into service in mid 1972, will be equipped with two 35 ton container gantry cranes each with an outreach of 33·53 m (110 ft) and a covered area of 16,722 m² (180,000 ft²). Twelve straddle carriers capable of stacking 40 ft units three high will be provided. The facility will handle the vessels of the operators in the Trio container service.

Kwai Chung Terminal—No. 2

Operator:

Kowloon Container Warehouse Company Ltd.

A company owned by Oyama, NYK, K Line and Japan Line.

This facility has a quay length of 304·8 m (1,000 ft) a depth of water of 12·8 m (42 ft) and a total area of 10·12 hectares (25 acres). It will be equipped with two container gantry cranes and should be in service by mid 1972.

Kwai Chung Terminal—No. 3

Operator:

Sea-Land Orient Ltd.

This facility has a quay length of 304·8 m

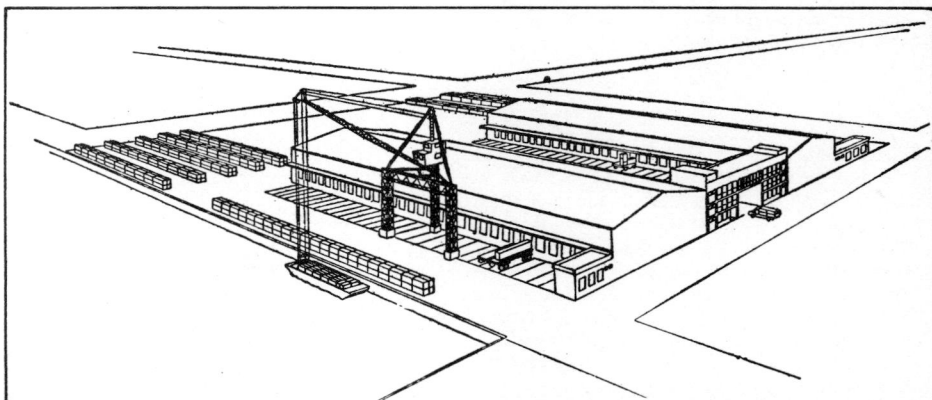

Hong Kong—Impression of the North Point Terminal

(1,000 ft), a depth of water of 12·8 m (42 ft) and a total area of 14·57 hectares (36 acres). It will be equipped with two container gantry cranes and will be used by Sea-Land Services Inc.

Common User Terminal—Tsim Sha Tsui

Operator:

Hong Kong and Kowloon Wharf and Godown Company Ltd.

This facility, with a quay length of 457·2 m (1,500 ft) and a depth of water alongside of 9·75 m (32 ft), has a total area of 6·07 hectares (15 acres). It is equipped with three sheds having a total area of 11,150 m² (120,000 ft²). A 25 ton container gantry crane with a lifting capacity of 25 tons on the spreader is being provided; it will have an outreach of 31·7 m (104 ft). Future plans include the lengthening of the quay by a further 76·2 m

(250 ft) which will add 1·21 hectares (3 acres) and the provision of a second container gantry crane with a capacity of 30 tons on the spreader and an outreach of 34·75 m (114 ft). Covered space will be increased by a further 5,574 m² (60,000 ft²).

The terminal is used by Sea-Land, American President Lines, American Mail Lines, Barber, Knutsen, PFEL, and American States Lines.

North Point Terminal, Kwun Tong

Operator:

North Point Wharves Ltd, a subsidiary of China Provident Co. Ltd.

343 Des Voeux Road West, Hong Kong
Telephone: H 460201

This common user facility has a quay length of 150·88 m (495 ft) with a depth of water alongside of 9·14 m (30 ft). It is equipped with two 35 ton Butters Derrick cranes fitted with spreaders. A further crane of the same capacity is planned. Total open storage area amounts to 8,094 m² (2 acres) and there is a total of 40,469 m² (10 acres) of undercover storage available. The facility is linked to a container freight station in the Kowloon area by using six specially designed barges each of which can carry 18 20 ft or 6 40 ft units. The CFS

is equipped with one of the Butters cranes and a Lancer side-loader for yard handling.
Hong Kong and Whampoa Dock Co. Terminal
Operator:
Hong Kong & Whampoa Dock Company
This facility handles AEIL and Orient Overseas Line part container vessels.
Pacific Container and Godown Co. Ltd Terminal
Operator:
Pacific Container and Godown Co. Ltd.

This company handles part container vessels having a storage area for about 180 20 ft units and a container repair service.
New Tech Services Terminal
Operator:
New Tech Services Inc. (Hong Kong) Ltd.
This facility located in the Yantong Bay area has a quay length of 76·2 m (250 ft) and a total area of 2,787 m² (30,000 ft²). It is equipped with a container gantry crane.

INDIA
BOMBAY

Bombay Port Trust
Bombay
GENERAL:
There are at present proposals to develop Berths at Alexandra Dock and at Sheva Basin to accept container traffic.

Alexandra Dock would provide a quay length of 180 m (590·5 ft) with a depth of water of 10·36 m (34 ft) and a total area of 4·04 hectares (10 acres).

Sheva Basin would provide a quay length of 300 m (984·2 ft) with a depth of water alongside of 13 m (42·65 ft) and a total area of 6·07 hectares (15 acres).

CALCUTTA (HALDIA)

Commissioners for the Port of Calcutta
15, Strand Road, Calcutta 1
GENERAL
As the existing facilities at Calcutta are limited by draught in the river channel to 8 m (26 ft) and, by length of lock, to vessels of 175 m (575 ft) in overall length, it was decided to construct a modern facility at Haldia some 90 km (56 miles) below Calcutta.
HALDIA DOCK
The first phase of development provides for a riverside oil berth and an impounded dock system with a lock entrance of 307·8 m (1,010 ft) and a width of 39·6 m (130 ft) and constant depth of water in the dock of 14 m (45 ft). The dock will have six berths, one of which will be equipped for heavy lifts and container operations.
Container Facility:
The terminal will have a quay length of 219·4 m (720 ft) and will be equipped with a 30 ton container gantry crane with an outreach of 35·05 m (115 ft) and a backreach of 10·67 m (35 ft). The marshalling area will be capable of accommodating over 1,500 containers stacked three high and will be

Indian Railways—FCLI Type Containers on a metric gauge wagon

equipped with a 30 ton yard container gantry crane.
The dock is scheduled for completion at the end of 1971.
Future Development
There are plans, when the dock is extended,

to provide a further 658·4 m (2,160 ft) of quay equipped with container gantry cranes.
ROAD AND RAIL ACCESS:
Some 80 km (50 miles) of both roads and rail track are being provided to link Haldia with the existing systems.

INDIAN RAILWAYS

Ministry of Railways,
(Railway Board)
Rail Bhavan,
New Delhi 1, India
CONTAINER SERVICES:
The Railway provides container services on the following routes:
Bombay—New Delhi
Bombay—Ahmedabad
Bombay—Madras
Bombay—Secunderabad
Bombay—Bangalore
Calcutta—New Delhi
Madras—Bangalore
There are nine transfer terminals each equipped with a general service crane for container handling operations.
A "Freight Forwarders" scheme operates between New Delhi and Bombay, under which the freight forwarder offers traffic in container loads for movement by rail at lump sum container rates. He has his own machinery to provide terminal collection/delivery and road transport services to his customers.
CONTAINER TRAFFIC:

Year	Loaded Containers	Tonnage Carried
1968	8,400	26,803
1969	17,433	52,858
1970*	24,900	76,500

*Estimate

FCL type Containers with 4·5 tons effective load on a standard gauge wagon.

CONTAINERS IN SERVICE:
FCL—These are general cargo boxes with a capacity of 8·3 m³ (293 ft³) or 4·5 tonnes and a tare of 1·55 tonnes; dimensions are 3·16 × 1·77 × 2·35 m (10·4 × 5·8 × 7·35 ft). They are suitable for use on broad gauge only and about 180 units are in service.

FCLI—These are general cargo boxes with a capacity of 9 m³ (318 ft³) or 5 tonnes and a tare of 1·3 tonnes; dimensions are 2·7 × 1·93 × 2·3 m (8·8 × 6·35 × 7·5 ft). They are suitable for use on both gauges and about 950 units are in service.

FUTURE DEVELOPMENTS:

The Railway has a three point container development plan:

1. Containers will be introduced on all major internal trunk routes using broad and narrow gauges with suitable transfer points as required.
2. ISO type containers are planned to be handled and new terminal facilities at Bombay and Calcutta will include provision for handling these units.
3. The domestic services will be inter-linked with the proposed trans-Asia rail link under consideration at present.

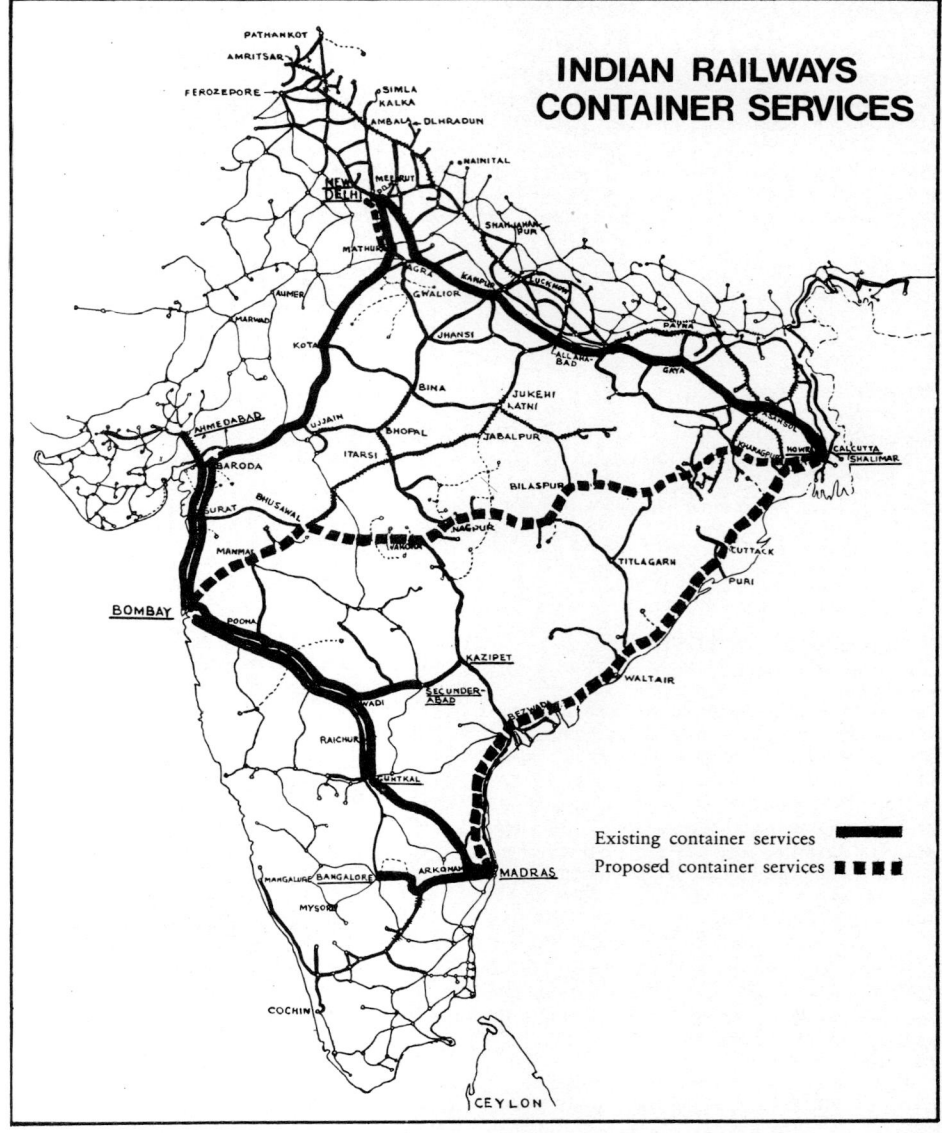

INDIAN RAILWAYS CONTAINER SERVICES

Existing container services ▬▬▬▬
Proposed container services ▰▰▰▰

ISRAEL

Israel Ports Authority

P.O.B. 20121
Tel-Aviv Israel
TELEPHONE: 38911
TELEGRAMS: Rashutnam Tel-Aviv
DIRECTOR GENERAL:
Aharon Remez

GENERAL:

The Israel Ports Authority, formed in July 1961 as a statutory body, has the task of planning, developing, managing and maintaining the Ports of Haifa, Ashdod and Eilat. It is required to manage each port as a separate self-sustaining enterprise.

CONTAINER DEVELOPMENT:

During 1970/71 49,891 tons import and 52,132 tons export of containerized goods were handled by Israel Ports. It is estimated that about 250,000 tons of various imported and exported goods will be containerized during 1971/72—out of which 145,000 tons will be imported and 105,000 tons exported.

Forecasts for 1975/76 are: 565,000 tons import and 535,000 tons export. The imbalance in trade could be rectified by containerization of citrus fruit.

ISRAEL LAND-BRIDGE:

• During 1970/71 35,000 tons of various goods passed through the land-bridge serving traffic between Europe, the Far East, Australia and East Africa, using the ports of Ashdod and Eilat. It is assumed that by 1971/72, 45,000 tons of various goods will pass through the land-bridge.

CONTAINER FACILITIES:

Container traffic is handled by quay

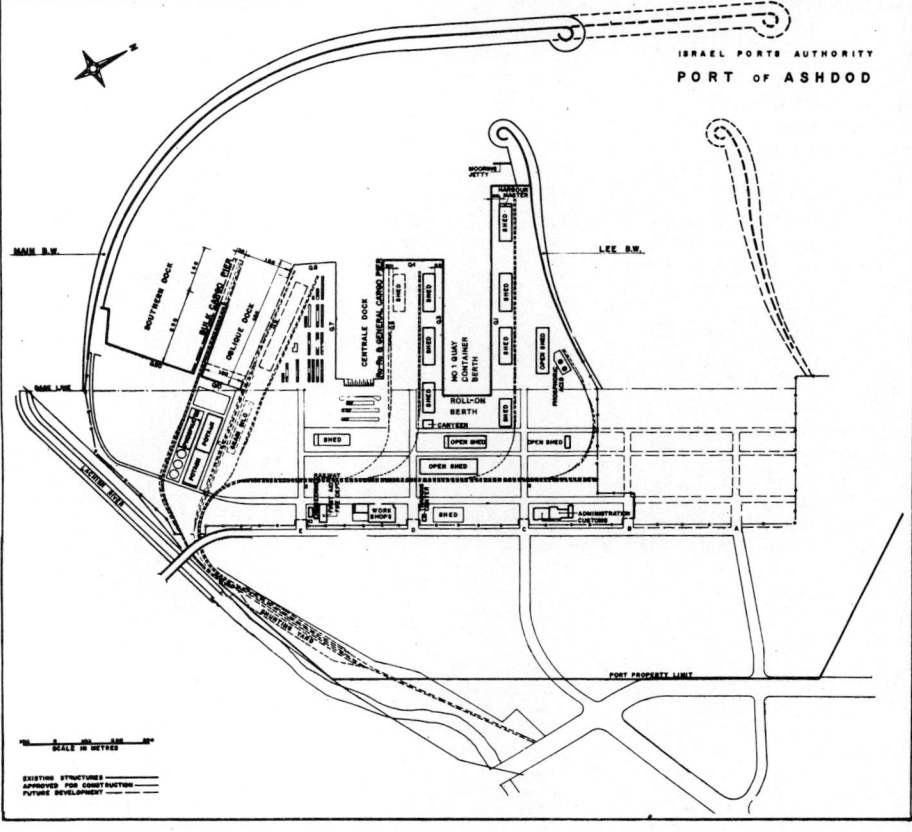

ISRAEL PORTS AUTHORITY
PORT OF ASHDOD

Ashdod—The container storage area

TRAFFIC:	Inwards		Outwards	
		No. of		No. of
	Tons	Loaded Units	Tons	loaded Unit
Lift-on/Lift off 1970	32,750	5,590	34,130	4,850
Estimate for 1971	116,000	11,600	110,000	11,000
Roll-on/Roll-off 1970**	1,025	76	1,154	74
Cars-Roll-on/Roll-off 1970	9,116	—	—	—
Estimate for 1971				
Roll-on/Roll-off**	2,000	120	2,000	120
Cars—Ro/Ro	13,000	—	—	—
**Not including trucks.				

cranes from conventional ships. Specialized container berths have been planned at Ashdod and Haifa for 1973.

ROLL-ON FACILITIES:

One special berth is at present available at Ashdod. Two additional berths are planned for Ashdod and Haifa ports for 1973.

CONTAINER SERVICES

American Export Isbrandtsen—Mediterranean Marine Lines Service to USA.

Zim/Prince/Ellerman/Moss Hutchinson service to London every 12 days (weekly in 1972)

Zim/Prince/Ellerman/Moss Hutchinson service to Liverpool—every 12 days (weekly in 1972)

Manchester Liners service to UK—weekly

CONTAINER SERVICES USING CONVENTIONAL VESSELS:

Zim Lines

Israel to US Ports

Zim Lines—Israel to Mediterranean and N.W. European Ports

Manchester Liners

ROLL-ON SERVICES:

Ferrytrans provide a weekly service between Ashdod and Trieste using the Dyvi Anglia for the transport of new cars only.

Zim Lines operates M.V. Arktos weekly between Ashdod and Trieste with 40 ft. refrigerated containers.

Ashdod—Zim's Trieste Roll-on service

TERMINAL WORKING HOURS:

Ship cargo operations take place between 0630-1430 and 1500-2300 hrs. (Night shift available on request).

Inland transport operations take place between 0630 and 1800 hrs.

ROLL-ON/ROLL-OFF AND CONTAINER SERVICES:

Ferrytrans provide a weekly service between Ashdod and Trieste using the Dyvi Anglia for the transport of new cars only.

M.V. Arktos operates between Ashdod and Trieste with 40 ft refrigerated containers.

ASHDOD

Israel Ports Authority—Port of Ashdod,

P.O.B. 16, Ashdod

TELEPHONE: 32121

TELEX: 69622

TELEGRAMS: Ashnam

OFFICIALS:

Mordechai Berger (*Port Manager*)

Isaac Binovitch (*Head of Operations*)

Moshe Navot (*Head of Administration*)

Zvy Raana.1 (*Head of Finance Department*)

Capt. Eliahu Seemann (*Head of Traffic Department*)

Dan Halber (*Head of Engineering*)

GENERAL:

The port of Ashdod lies 38 km (23 miles) to the South of Tel-Aviv. There is a quay length of 1,400 m (4,480 ft) with 10·3 m (33·8 ft) depth of water alongside for handling conventional vessels carrying containers By the end of 1971 a further 400 m of quay will be completed. The port has adequate provision for handling containers with shoreside equipment and there is a roll-on ramp.

Ashdod—Container operations

This facility has sufficient depth of water to handle vessels of 12 m (39 ft) draught and a parking area of 10 hectares (24·7 acres). By July 1972 a further 600 m (1,968 ft) of quay will have been completed this will have an additional roll-on berth.

JAPAN
KITAKYUSHU

Kitakyushu Port Authority

Fukuoka Prefecture

Japan

GENERAL:

Kitakyushu is the Authority for the ports of Moji, Kokura, Tobata, Yajata and Wakamatsu.

CONTAINER FACILITIES:

Tanoura Terminal

This facility has a quay length of 300 m (984 ft) with a depth alongside of 12 m (39 ft)

and a total area of 7 hectares (17 acres). It is equipped with a 27·5 ton container gantry crane.

FUTURE DEVELOPMENT:

It is planned to build four further container berths during the period 1972/75.

Kitakyushu—Plan of Tanoura Container Terminal

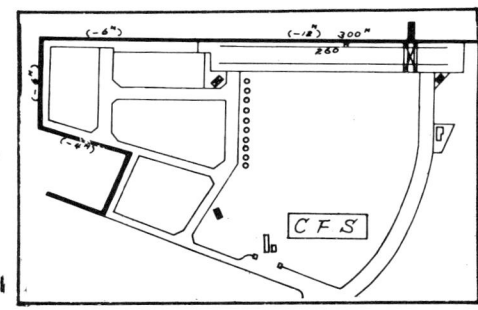

KOBE

Kobe—Maya Terminal

Port and Harbour Bureau,
Kobe City Hall, Ikuta-Ku, Kobe
TELEPHONE: 33-8181
PRINCIPAL OFFICIALS:
Yaswhiko Nagatu (*Director*)
T. Taguchi (*Harbour Master*)
DEVELOPMENT AUTHORITY:
Hanshin Port Development Authority,
27, Naniwa-cho, Ikuta-ku, Kobe
Telephone: Kobe (078) 32-2701
Principal Officials:
T. Hori (*President*)
Y. Yomota (*Vice-President*)
Y. Orabe
R. Katayama
J. Hanoh   } *Managing Directors*
Y. Watanabe
Y. Iwani (*Director—Kobe Construction Office*)
CONTAINER FACILITIES:
No. 4 Maya Pier:

This is a temporary public container terminal with a quay length of 600 m (1,968·5 ft) which is divided into two separate berths one of which is managed by Japan Line and three other major shipping companies who also use an adjacent transit shed as a consolidation centre. This operating company is known as Kobe Container Terminal k.k. (KCT). Two container gantry cranes serve the berths one is a 25·4 ton Paceco-Mitsui which handles 20 and 24 ft containers on a cycle of 20 per hour. The other, manufactured by Kawasaki Dockyard has a lifting capacity of 30·5 tons and handles containers of up to 40 ft. There is a total container storage area behind the cranes of 8 hectares (19·8 acres) and a further storage area of 1·8 hectares (4·4 acres) at Pier No. 1.

Port Island Terminal:

This facility consists of nine container berths each with a depth alongside of 12 m (39·4 ft). No 1 Berth has a quay length of 300 m (984 ft) the others each have 250 m (820 ft). No 1 Berth has a total area of 10·5 hectares (26 acres), the others have, on average, slightly less than 10 hectares (24·5 acres) each.

No. 1 Berth:

Leased to Sea Land Services Inc., this berth came into service in May 1970. It is equipped with two 38·5 ton container gantry cranes, with an outreach of 31·5 m (103·3 ft) and covered cargo space of 6,672 m² (71,800 ft²).

No. 2 Berth:

This has been made available for the co-operative use of Japan and Yamashita-Shinnihon Lines. It has a 44 ton container gantry crane with an outreach of 33·0 m (108·2 ft); a further crane is planned.

Kobe—Maya Terminal

Nos. 3 & 4 Berths:

To be used by NYK Line it is understood that this facility is due to come into service at the end of 1971 with two 44 ton container gantry cranes.

No. 5 Berth:

This facility is believed to be due for completion in 1972 and will be used by American President Lines and American Mail Lines.

No. 6 Berth:

This facility has been reserved for United States Lines who are at present sharing No 1 Berth.

Nos. 7 & 8 Berths:

This facility has been reserved for Mitsui/OSK Lines.

No. 9 Berth:

Not yet allocated—it is believed that this will be completed by 1975.

FUTURE DEVELOPMENT—ROKKO ISLAND:

A further port island has been planned for development. The time scale has not yet been decided upon but the island, which will cover a 6 km² (2·32 sq miles) area, will include facilities for general cargoes by sea and air with particular emphasis on distribution, urban housing and recreational

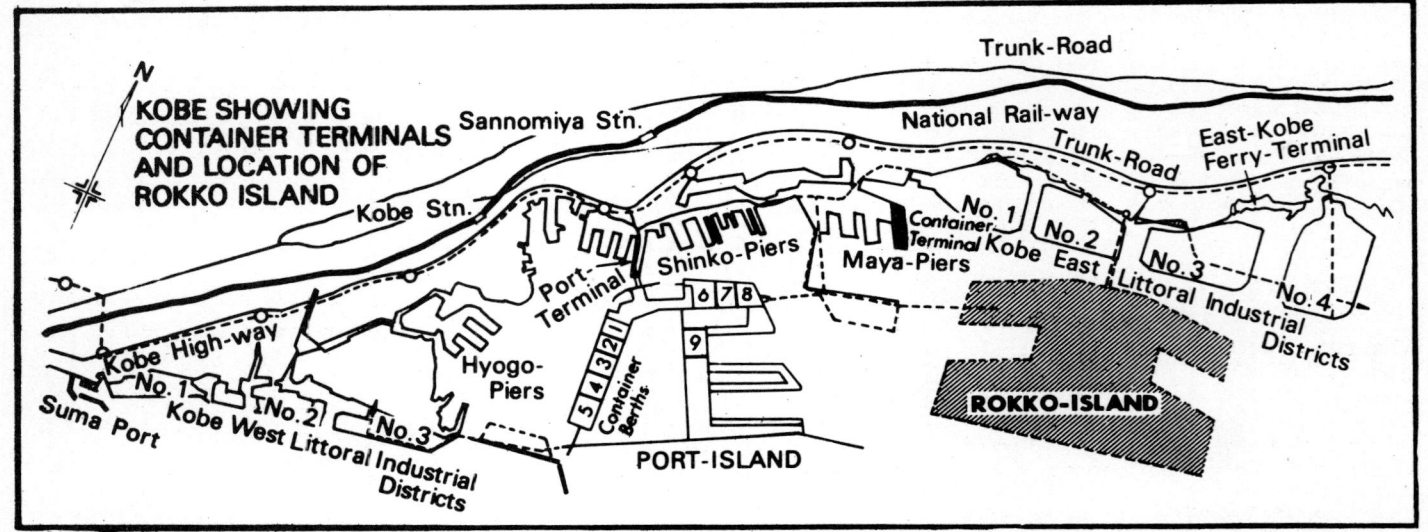

KOBE SHOWING CONTAINER TERMINALS AND LOCATION OF ROKKO ISLAND

facilities.

CONTAINER SERVICES:

Japanese Lines—Kobe to California—weekly.

Japanese Lines—Kobe to Pacific North West American Ports—every 10 days.

Sea-Land Services—US West Coast Ports—Weekly.

CONTAINER SHIPPING COMPANY AGENTS:

Japan Line Ltd., Kobe Branch.

Denden Building. Naniwa-cho, Ikuta-ku Kobe

Telephone: 39-6601

Butterfield and Swire (Japan) Ltd.,
Edo-machi Ikuta-ku, Kobe

Telephone: 39-6721

CONTAINER TRAFFIC:

1970	Freight	Units	
	tons	loaded	empty
Inwards	523,663	45,109	16,820
Outwards	834,620	44,924	7,542
1971 (Estimate)			
Inwards	970,000	77,000	29.000
Outwards	1,480,000	84,000	12,000

CONTAINER REPAIR ORGANISATION:

Mitsubishi Heavy Industry Co. Ltd.

1 Wadasaki-cho, 3-chome, Hyogo-ku, Kobe 652

TELEPHONE: 671-5061

Kawasaki Heavy Industry Co. Ltd.

16-1 Nakamachi-dori, 2-chome, Ikuta-ku, Kobe 650

TELEPHONE: 341-7731

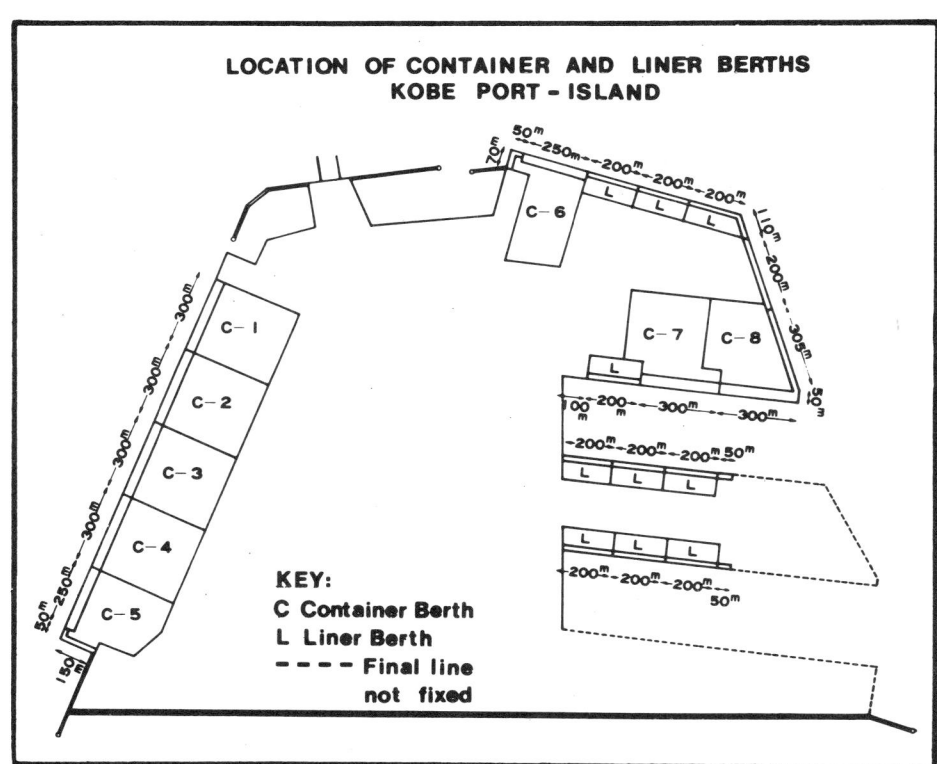

LOCATION OF CONTAINER AND LINER BERTHS
KOBE PORT - ISLAND

KEY:
C Container Berth
L Liner Berth
- - - - Final line
not fixed

Kobe—No. 2 Berth Port Island

Kobe—No. I Berth Port Island

NAGOYA

Nagoya Port Authorty,

7, 6-chome, Minato Honmachi, Minato-ku, Nagoya City

CONTAINER FACILITIES:

Kinjo Pier

This common user facility operated by the Port Authority, with a quay length of 470 m (1,542 ft) and a depth of water alongside of 10·5 m (34·4 ft), provides two berths each equipped with a 37·5 ton Sumitomo container gantry crane with an outreach of 35 m (114·83 ft). The total area available for storage and marshalling of containers is 10·3 hectares (25·4 acres) including the two consolidation sheds. There are 78 points for refrigerated units and the yard handling equipment consists of six straddle carriers, two for 40 ft units one of which can also lift 20 ft units and 4 for 20 ft units, and a 30 ton fork lift.

West 4 Section

This section of the port, on the opposite side to the Kinjo Pier, will be developed into a container terminal providing 1,650 m (6,413 ft) of quay which will give a total

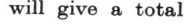
Nagoya—Kinjo Pier.

terminal area of 56·6 hectares (139·8 acres) for six berths.

West 5 Section

An area of land approximately 82·5 hectares (215 acres) has been reserved for container development.

The facility will be equipped with twelve 37·5 ton container gantry cranes.

CONTAINER SERVICES:

OSK, YS, Japan and K Lines to US Pacific Ports—four sailings monthly

NYK and Showa Lines to US Pacific Ports—two sailings monthly.

NYK, Showa, OSK, YS, K and Japan Lines—to US and Canadian North West Ports—three sailings monthly.

E.S.S. (K, ANL and Flinders) to Australian Ports—3 sailings monthly.

AJCL with NYK, MOSK and YS Joint Service.

to Australian Ports—five sailings monthly.

TRAFFIC:

In 1970 214,031 freight tons (10,799 units) moved inwards and 504,792 freight tons (25,529 units) moved outwards; the size of containers varied from 10 to 40 feet in length.

CONTAINER REPAIR FACILITIES:

Daiichi Kogyo Co., Ltd.
1, 4-chome, Masago-cho, Minato-ku, Nagoya
Telephone: 651-9151

Chubu Shizai Co., Ltd.
1, 5-chome, Hama-cho, Minato-ku, Nagoya
Telephone: 661-7231

Taisho Kogyo Co., Ltd.
Tsukimori-cho, Minato-ku, Nagoya
Telephone: 651-5451

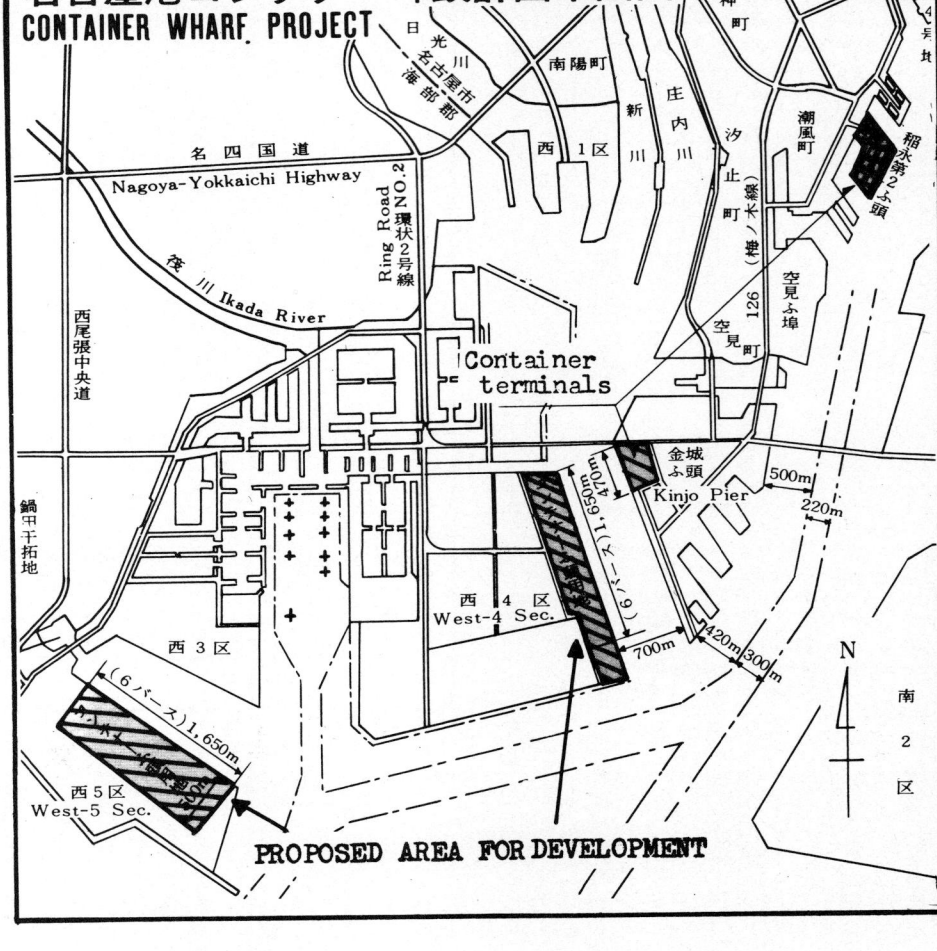

Nagoya—Container Facilities.

NIIGATA

Niigata Port Authority
Port and Harbour Section
1-5290 Gakko-machi-dori
Niigata City

TELEPHONE: (23) 5511
Port Management Office
4963-1 Nuttari-Ryugashima
Niigata

GENERAL:

The Port is situated on the Shinano River

It is understood that a container berth is planned at the East Port development now under construction.

OSAKA

Port and Harbor Bureau, City of Osaka
8 Chikko 2-chome, Minato-ku, Osaka
TELEPHONE: (06) 572-5121
PRINCIPAL OFFICIALS
Kiyoshi Kano (*General Manager*)
Masaya Nishio (*Director of Administration Division*)
Osamu Takamura (*Director of Engineering Division*)
Hideo Onishi (*Director of South Port Development Division*)

Hanshin (Osaka Bay) Port Development Authority
2 Mamabe-dori 5-chome Fukiai-ku, Kobe
TELEPHONE: Kobe 078 (23)-4641
PRINCIPAL OFFICIALS:
T. Hori (*President of the Board*)
K. Fujihara (*Vice-President*)
Y. Otabe
R. Katayama
J. Kanoh   } (*Joint Managing Directors*)
Y. Watanabe

CONTAINER FACILITIES:

South Port No. 1 Wharf

This facility has a quay length of 273 m (896 ft) with a depth of water 12 m (39 ft). The container marshalling area has an area of 5·98 hectares (14·8 acres) and the berth is equipped with a roll-on ramp and a 37·5 ton container gantry crane with an outreach of 34 m (100 ft).

The wharf is leased to E.S.S. for their service three times monthly to Australian Ports.

South Port No. 2 Wharf

A quay length of 250 m (820 ft) with a

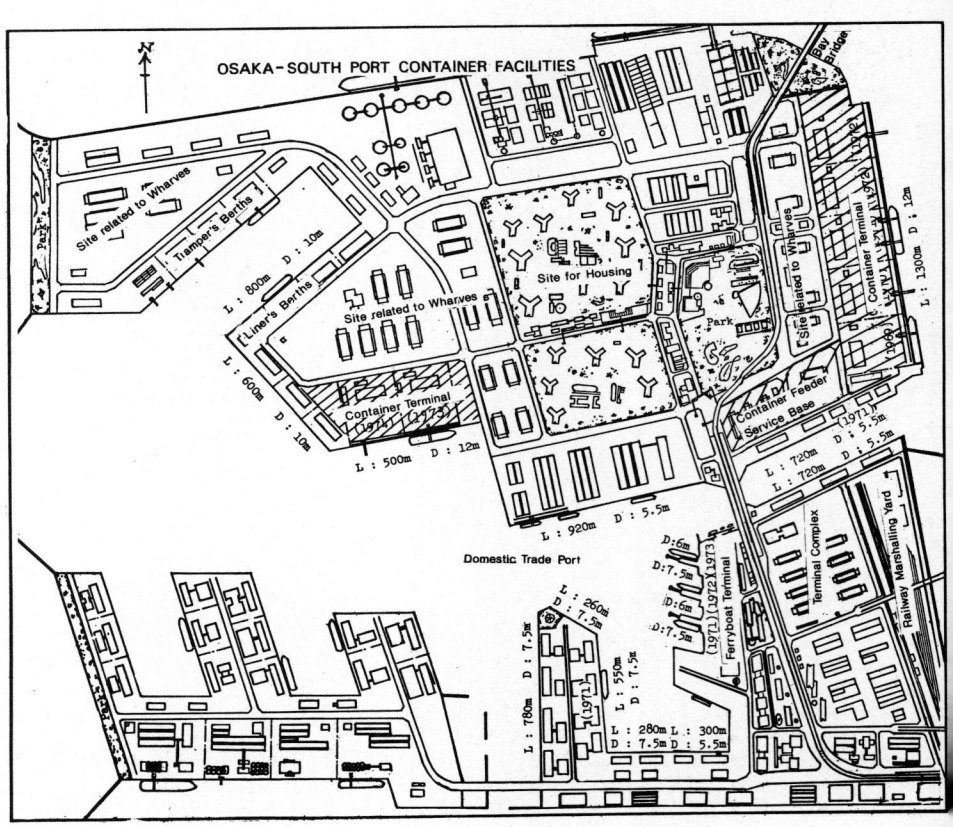

depth of 12 m (38 ft) and a marshalling area of 6·13 hectares (15·1 acres) comprises this berth which is equipped with a 37·5 ton container gantry crane with an outreach of 34 m (100 ft). The facility is leased to the AJCL and Mitsui/OSK, NYK, and YS Lines for their 5 times monthly service to Australian Ports.

Nos. 3, 4 and 5 Wharves

These berths, similar to No. 2 Wharf are due for completion in late 1971 and 1972 it is understood that these facilities will be at least 300 m in length.

Container Feeder Service Base

This facility, scheduled for completion in late 1971 will have a total length of 720 m (2,362 ft) and a depth alongside of 5·5 m (18 ft).

Nos. 6 and 7 Wharves

Situated in the Foreign Port Zone this facility, scheduled to come into service in 1973 and 1974, will have a total quay length of 580 m (1,640 ft) with a depth of 12 m (39 ft) alongside. The facility will be equipped with two container gantry cranes. and have a total area of about 15 hectares

Osaka South Port—Wharves Nos. 1 and 2.

(37 acres).

CONTAINER TRAFFIC:
1970
Inwards   10,157 Units   145,846 tons

Outwards 20,071 Units   327,396 tons

It is not made clear if the units are loaded or the tonnage is expressed in freight, long or metric tons.

SHIMIZU

Shimizu Port Administration
2-9 Hinide-cho
Shimizu City, Shizouka Prefecture,
Japan
TELEPHONE: (0543) 53-2201
CONTAINER FACILITIES:

Okitsu Terminal:

Operated by Marine Terminals Corporation, this facility came into service late in 1970 with a quay length of 225 m (738 ft), a depth of water alongside of 12·19 m (40 ft) and an area of 3 hectares (7·4 acres). It is equipped

with a 30 ton container gantry crane. A further 225 m (738 ft) of quay equipped with a similar container gantry crane is due to come into service in 1972. A further 600 m (1,968 ft) of quay equipped with two container gantry cranes is planned.

TOKYO

PORT AUTHORITY:
The Bureau of Port and Harbour
Tokyo Metropolitan Government
8-1 Marunouchi, 3 Chiyoda-ku, Tokyo
TELEPHONE: Tokyo 212-5111
TELEGRAMS: Tochiji ,Tokyo
PORT DEVELOPMENT AUTHORITY:
Keihin (Tokyo Bay) Port Development Authority
Kotohira Kaikan Building,
No. 1 Shiba Kotohira-cho,
Minatu-ku, Tokyo.
TELEPHONE: (03) 503-4351
OFFICIALS:
Y. Minami (*President*)
S. Hibino (*Vice-President*)
K. Sonoda   ⎫
T. Tsunai   ⎪
N. Tsuchihashi ⎬ (*Managing Directors*)
K. Teranishi   ⎭
T: Ishii (*Director-Tokyo Construction Office*)
CONTAINER FACILITIES:
Shinagawa Wharf:

A quay 539 m (1,768 ft) in length with 10-10·5 m (32·8-34·5 ft) of water alongside. Shinagawa is a temporary facility until such time as the construction work at present being undertaken at the Ohi complex is completed. It is laid out as two berths and has been provided with one 30 ton and one 37·5 ton container gantry crane. There is a total open storage area of 5·80 hectares (14·3 acres) of which 2·05 hectares (5·04 acres) is available for general use, the remainder being reserved. There are two freight stations covering 2·32 hectares (5·7 acres) of which 4,325 m² (46,000 sq ft) is covered. There are 170 points for reefer containers.

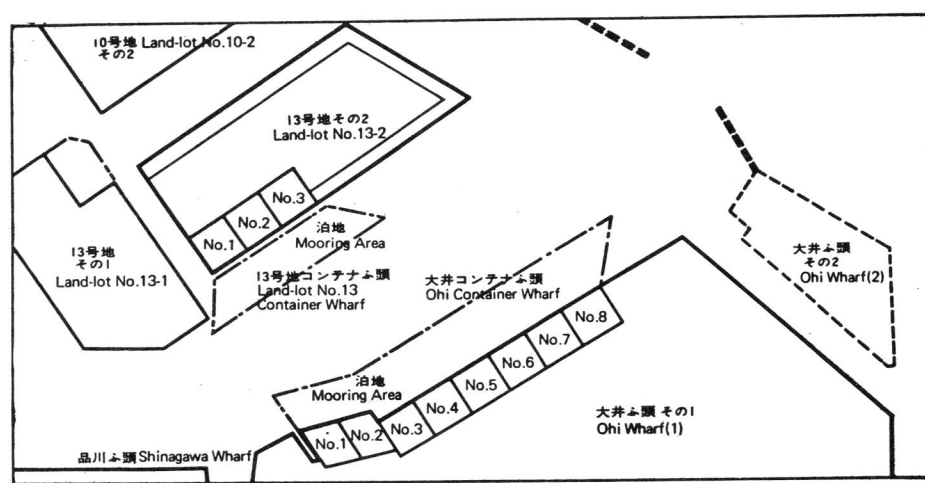
Tokyo—Plan showing Shinagawa, Ohi and Land Lot 13 Terminals

Shinagawa wharf, Tokyo.

Ohi Terminal

This facility consists of eight berths each of which is being equipped with two 37·5 ton container gantry cranes. All berths at the terminal have a depth of water alongside of 12 m (39·4 ft). Berths, or groups of berths have been allocated to operators on an exclusive user basis.

Nos. 1 and 2 Berths: Allocated to 'K' Line, this facility has a total quay length of 500 m (1,640 ft) and a total area of 15 hectares (37 acres). It is due to come into service in April 1973.

Nos. 3, 4 and 5 Berths: Allocated to Mitsui/OSK Lines this facility has a total quay length of 850 m (2,789 ft) and a total area of 27 hectares (109 acres). It is due to come into service over the period January to April 1972.

Nos. 6 and 7 Berths: Allocated to NYK Line this facility has a total quay length of 600 m (1,968·5 ft) and a total area of 18 hectares (44·5 acres). It is due to come into service in April 1972.

No. 8 Berth: Allocated to Japan Line and Y.S. Lines on a joint user basis, this facility has a total quay length of 250 m (820 ft) and a total area of 7·5 hectares (18·5 acres). It is planned to open in 1973.

Land Lot 13-2 Terminal

Situated on a reclaimed site opposite Ohi Terminal this terminal will have three berths each of which will have a quay length of 300 m (984 ft) and a total area of 10·5 hectares (26 acres). Each berth will be equipped with two 37·5 ton container gantry cranes. Berths Nos 1 and 2 will become operational in mid 1973 and No. 3 in mid 1974.

TRAFFIC:

In 1969 the amount of container cargo, excluding the weight of the containers was 250,024 tonnes inwards and 169,961 tonnes outwards.

SHIPPING COMPANIES PROVIDING REGULAR CONTAINER SERVICES FROM SHINAGAWA TERMINAL:

NYK Line—Showa Shipping Co.—
Tokyo to North American Pacific Ports—2 sailings monthly.

Japan Line—Kawasaki Kisen Kaisha Ltd.—
Mitsui/OSK Lines—Yamashita Shinnahon & Co. Ltd.
Tokyo to North American Pacific Ports—4 sailings monthly

CONTAINER STORAGE AND STEVEDORING COMPANIES:

Nippon Container Terminal Ltd.,
20-1 Maranouchi 2, Chiyoda-ku, Tokyo.
Telephone: 212-1779

Tokyo International Transportation Co. Ltd.,
8-8 Higashishinagawa 5, Shinagawa-ku,
Tokyo
Telephone: 471 0341

CONTAINER FREIGHT FORWARDING COMPANIES:

Nippon Container Yuso Co. Ltd.,
20-1 Maranouchi 2, Chiyoda-Ku, Tokyo, Japan.
Telephone: 212-4211, Ext. 682

International Container Transport Co. Ltd.,
3-3 Akasakas, Minato-Ku, Tokyo, Japan.
Telephone: 581-8421, 8424

Japan Express Transportation Co. Ltd.,
3, Kabutocho 2, Nihonbashi, Chuo-Ku, Tokyo, Japan.
Telephone: 699-2271

Nippon Express Co. Ltd., Tokyo Shipping Branch, Shinagawa Wharf Office,
7-28 Higashishinagawa 5, Shinagawaku, Tokyo, Japan
Telephone: 471-5331

Tokyo Izumi Unso Co. Ltd.,
28 Echizenbori 2, Chuo-Ku, Tokyo, Japan
Telephone: 551-7291

Yamato Transport Co. Ltd.,
12-16 Ginza 2, Chu-Ku, Tokyo, Japan
Telephone: 541-3411

Suzue Lines Co. Ltd., Shinagawa Container Office.,
3-32 Konan 5, Minato-Ku, Tokyo, Japan.
Telephone: 471-4372

YOKKAICHI

Yokkaichi Port Authority
9 Chitose-cho, Yokkaichi City
Mie Prefecture
TELEPHONE: (53) 5541/6
TELEX:
OFFICIALS:
Satoru Tanaka (*President and Governor of Mie Prefecture*)
GENERAL:

The Port Authority was established under the Harbour Law on 1st April 1966 and is a special local government body with a board of nine members drawn from the Prefecture and the City. The Port is situated on the northern section of Ise Bay which is located midway along Japan's Pacific Coast.

CONTAINER FACILITIES:

The berth at Pier No 3 is 245 m (804 ft) in length with a container marshalling area of 3·14 hectares (7·77 acres) behind the quay apron and a Freight Station of 3,000 m² (·75 acres). The facility is equipped with a 37·5 ton capacity Hitachi container gantry crane and an adjustable ramp at the western end for roll-on traffic which feeds on to a separate area of 8,460 m² (2·1 acres) laid out for this type of traffic. The ramp has a bridge 17 m (55·8 ft) long with a levelling flap of 5 m (16·4 ft) and a maximum roadway width of 8·2 m (29·6 ft). The centre line of the ramp is approximately 14 m (42·6 ft) from the quay face. Mobile handling equipment consists of two 20 ton straddle carriers and heavy capacity fork trucks.

SERVICES:

Japan Trans-Pacific Service—Weekly.
Eastern Searoad Service to Australia—3 sailings monthly.

TRAFFIC:

In 1970 10,915 loaded units moved inwards with 258,319 freight tons and 1,429 loaded units with 17,373 freight tons moved outwards. In 1971 imports will probably be 14,000 units and exports 1,750 units.

FUTURE DEVELOPMENTS:

By 1975 some 200 hectares (494 acres) will have been reclaimed in the Kasumigaura area of the Port some 4 km (2½ miles) to the northeast of the present container facility. The South Wharf of this development will provide six container berths by

Yokkaichi—Pier 3

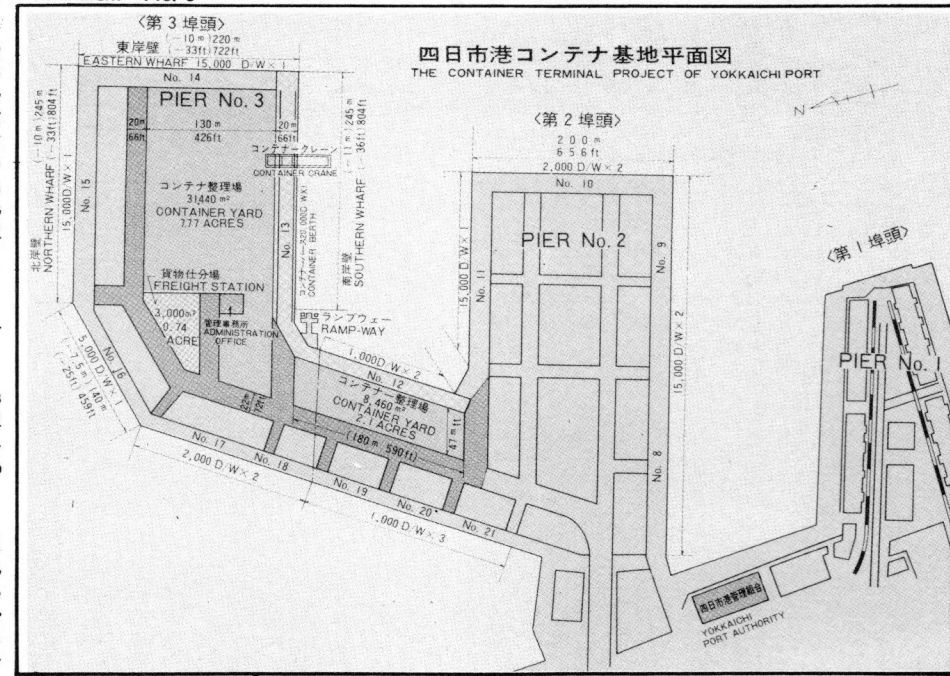

1980. Each berth will be 250 m (820 ft) in length with a depth of water alongside of 12 m (39·4 ft) and an area of 8·25 hectares (20·5 acres). Each will be equipped with a 37·5 ton container gantry crane. The first berth to be completed will also be equipped with a roll-on link span ramp. The next berth is scheduled for 1975 completion.

YOKOHAMA

Honmoko Terminal, Yokohama

Bureau of Ports and Harbours,
1, Minatu-Machi, Naka-ku, Yokahama City.
Keihin (Tokyo Bay) Port Development Authority,
Kotohira Kaikau Bldg., No. 1 Shiba Kotohira-cho, Minatu-ku, Tokyo
OFFICIALS: See entry under Tokyo for full list.
T. Noguchi (*Director Yokohama Construction Office*)
GENERAL:

The port is operated by the Municipal port authority but container development, berth leasing, etc. is under the control of the Keihin PDA.

CONTAINER FACILITIES:
Honmoko Container Terminal:

This facility has three berths each 250 m (820 ft) in length with a depth of water alongside of 12 m (39·4 ft). Crane tracks run the whole length of the quay and each berth is equipped with one 30·5 ton container gantry crane, a single storey shed providing an area of 5,120 m² and power sources for reefer containers. The quay aprons are 40 m (131 ft) wide behind which is a container storage and marshalling area of between 6·4 and 6·6 hectares (16 acres) depending upon the berth.

No. 1 berth is equipped with roll-on/roll-off facilities for the E.S.S. service to Australia and No. 2 is used by NYK, Mitsui-OSK, Japan Line and Y.S. for their service to West Coast N. American Ports.

The fourth berth, which will be 300 m (984 ft) in length will be completed in 1973.

PIER D:
The North side of Pier D will be used by American President Lines as a container terminal.

Daikokucho Container Terminal:
This facility will provide two 250 m (820 ft) berths with 12 m (39·4 ft) of water alongside; they will be completed in 1974 and 1975.

ACCESS
The road access to Yokohama is poor and the Government is planning five highways into the port, some of which are already under construction.

PRINCIPAL ROAD OPERATORS:
Sagami Transportation Co. Ltd.,
23, 4-chome, Kaigan-dori, Naka-Ku, Yokohama.
Nissin Transportation & Warehousing Co.,
Keihin Building, 6-28 Ohoe-cho, Naka-Ku, Yokohama.
WAREHOUSING COMPANIES
Tsurumi Warehouse Co.,
1-1, 2-chome, Namamugi, Tsurumi-Ku, Yokohama.
Yokohama Boeki Soko Co. Ltd.,
40-13, 1-Chome, Hiranuma, Nishi-Ku, Yokohama.

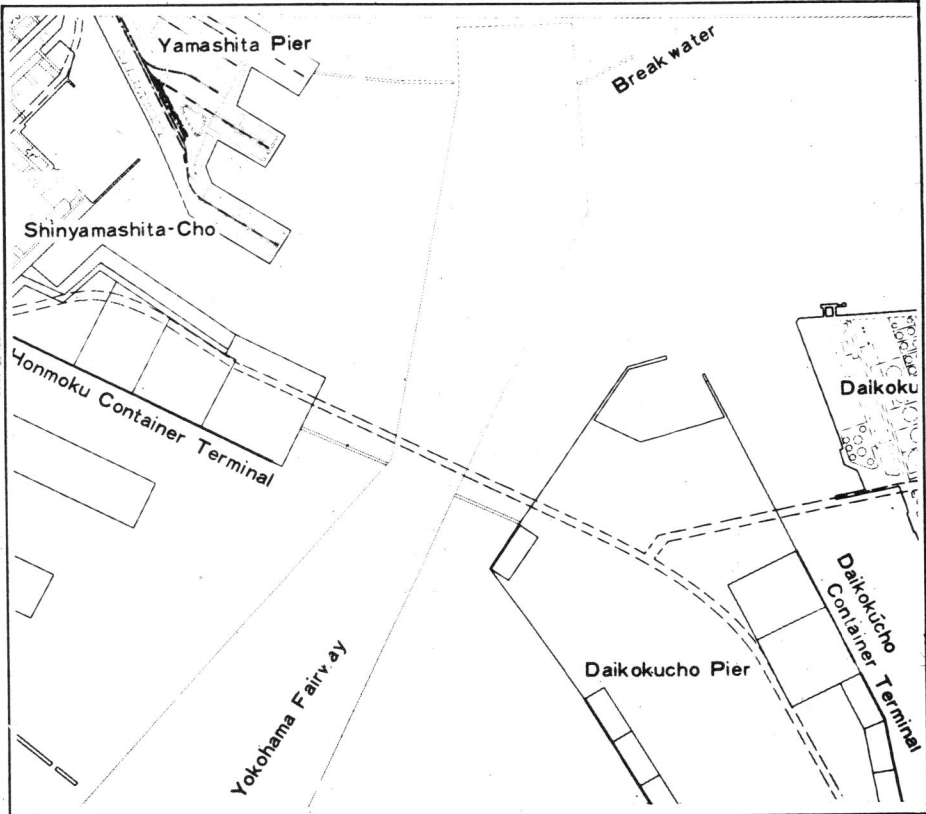

Yokohama

Nissin Transportation & Warehousing Co.,
Keihin Building, 6-28 Ohoe-cho, Naka-Ku, Yokohama.
FREIGHT FORWARDERS
Z. Horikoshi & Co. Ltd.,
28 Yamashita-Cho, Naka-Ku, Yokohama.
Sagami Uhyu Fabuskihi Kaisha,
No 23, 4-chome, Kaigan-dori, Naka-Ku,

Yokohama.
CONTAINER REPAIR FACILITIES:
Daito Unyu Ltd.
7-32 Yamashita-cho, Naka-ku, Yokohama
Telephone: 045 6212921
Kanto Unyu Ltd.
Yamashita-cho, Yokohama
Telephone: 045 622-9901

JAPANESE NATIONAL RAILWAYS

Japanese National Railways (JNR)
6-5-1 chome, Marunouchi, Chiyoda-ku, Tokyo
TELEPHONE:
Head Office: 212-6311
International Department: 212 3591
OVERSEAS OFFICES:
New York
45 Rockefeller Plaza
New York, NY 10020, USA
Telephone: PL 9070-7
Paris
104 Rue de Richelieu, Paris 2e
Telephone: 742 5757

DIRECTORS:
Board
Satoshi Isozaki (*President*)
Akihoshi Yamada (*Vice President*)
Tatsuo Iwabuchi, Shokichi, Funayama, Kin-ich Aoki (*Part Time Members*)
Kenjiro Miyaji (*Chief Engineer*)
Members of the Board:
Shigeo Yamaguchi, Kokichi Haraoka, Masao Nagahama, Masatomo Kobayashi, Hirosho Manabe, Kin-ichi Yamaguchi (*Head Office*)
Atsushi Doi (*Hokkaido Region*)
Hidekatsu Kitazawa (*Sendai*)
Takeo Seki (*Tokyo*)

JNR—"KOKI 1000" type wagons

Koichi Hatagawa (*Nagoya*)
Yukio Ichijyo (*Osaka*)
Seiji Shibusawa (*Kyushu*)
Shigeo Yamaguchi (*New Tokaido Line*)
DIRECTORS OF DEPARTMENTS:
Yoshio Jyojyu (*Public Relations*)
Nobuo Yanai (*International Department*)
Ken Kambayashi (*Computerization*)
Tsuneo Morigaki (*Corporate Planning*)
Yoshiro Tomii, Takashige Uchida (*High-speed Network Planning*)
Hiroshi Manabe (*Staff Relations*)
Shinichi Hayami (*Welfare*)
Tatsujiro Ishikawa (*Finance and Accounting*)
Tokuji Kagaya (*Purchasing and Stores*)
Tomoo Ie, Takeo Seki (*Passenger*)
Yukio Izumi (*Freight*)
Hiroshi Suzuki (*Train Operation*)
Takashige Uchida, Minoru Ishikawa (*Construction*)
Katsuo Takahashi (*High Speed Railway Construction*)
Kantaro Kitaoka (*Track and Structures*)
Kin-ichi Yamaguchi (*Electrical Engineering*)
Shin Otokozawa (*Rolling Stock and Mechanical Engineering*)
Jun Ikegami (*Motor Transportation*)
Noboru Sasao (*Ferry Service*)
Tetsundo Kaji (*Railway Police*)
Ukon Matsuda (*Inspection and Audit*)
INTERNAL CONTAINER TRANSPORT:
The containers owned and operated by the Japanese National Railways are mostly 5-ton containers, and their volume is 14 cubic metres. The size of the containers was determined by the unit of transaction and the road conditions in Japan. Door to door through transport is carried out as the responsibility of the Japanese National Railways. Lorries are used to carry containers between the consignor's and consignee's door and the railway station, and exclusive flat wagons capable of carrying five containers are used for transport between stations. Fork lift trucks are the principal means for transfer between lorry and wagon at the station.

The number of containers possessed by the Japanese National Railways has been increasing year after year since 1959 when they were put into service for the first time. On April 1st, 1971 the Japanese National Railways owned about 29,000 containers and about 3,700 wagons exclusively for containers, carrying about 8·7 million tons of goods annually, or 4·4 per cent of the total freight tonnage of the Japanese National Railways. At present containers are handled at 149 stations. Collection and delivery is made within a range of 20 km (12 miles) of those stations, but in the case of freightliners, the range is 30 km (18 miles). The total number of freight stations is about 2,600.

TOKAIDO FREIGHTLINER:
JNR started Tokaido Freightliner service as a modernised method of freight transportation. On 1st April 1971 the number of freightliner trains was extended to 9 sections, 29 round trips per day.

The freight cars used in this service are KOKI 10000 and 5500 types.

JNR is planning to extend this service countrywide in the future.

JNR—Yokohama terminal

JNR—40 ft units on KOKI 1000 wagons at Tokyo terminal

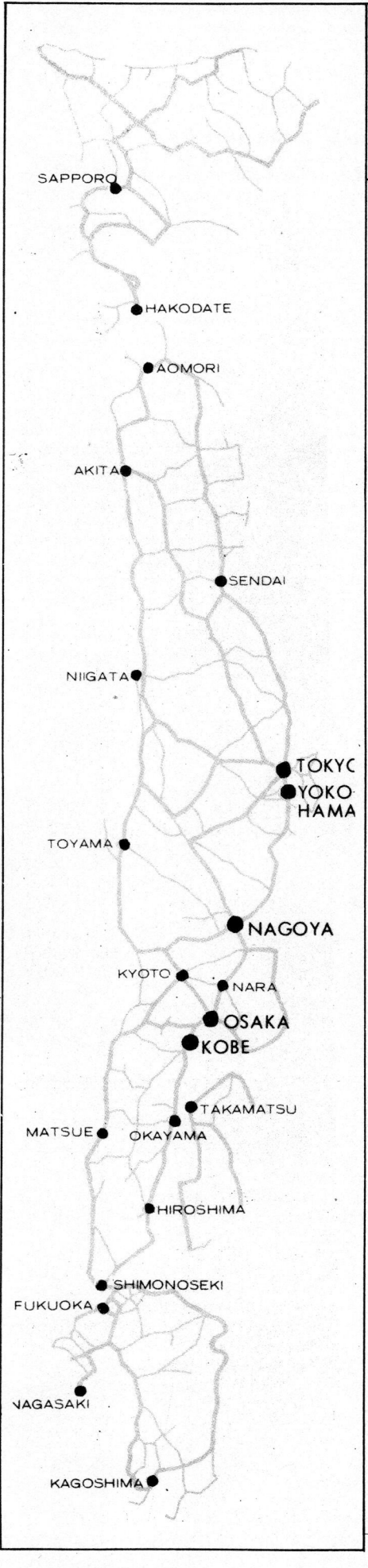

JNR Container Network

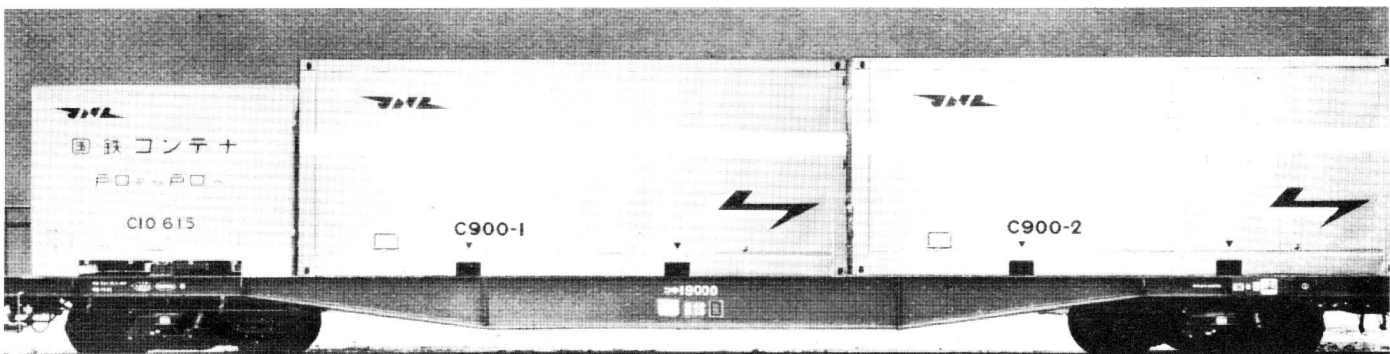

JNR—Tokaido Freightliner wagon

CONTAINER TRANSPORT OPERATION

JNR Container Transport note the incidence of damage to goods has decreased sharply, being 0·7% in the case of container freight as against 4·9% for wagon-load freight.

The timetable schedule of container trains is separate from the general freight train schedules, and concentrates on certainty of arrival time. JNR fixes 2,100 sections among the 149 container handling stations and, assigning a certain number of containers to each section for daily transit, operates the flat wagons loaded with those containers by coupling them, with priority, to the previously designated fastest freight train which makes a through run on the section. Any such train is a limited express, express or yard-passing train. The typical ones are the 16 high speed limited express freight trains linking Northern Kyushu, Osaka, Nagoya, Tokyo and Hokkaido at a maximum speed of 100 km (62 mph) per hour.

For wagon-load freight in general JNR fix rates according to the weight and kind of goods. For containerised freight there is a uniform rate regardless of the commodities, based on the cost-of-service principle.

As regards the feeder service of the international ocean-going containers, 20% will go to wagon-load and 80% to LCL, or part-load, according to an estimate being made in Japan. But, the proportion may eventually become fifty-fifty when transport to the inland depots is included. The same thing can be said about part-load shipment.

The container of the Japanese National

JNR—Kobe rail terminal

Railways is about half the cubic capacity standard 20 ft container, so it is particularly convenient for part-load shipment. JNR expects to have a greater share of wagon-load freight traffic against road transport than the railways in Europe. For Japan's roads are too congested to allow the traffic of large-sized vehicles, except for some toll roads. JNR operates its network all over the country, and provides industrial sidings at any ports, warehouses and factories or other plants which are concerned with exported or imported goods, so is in a favourable position to render door-to-door service for internationally transported containers.

INTERNATIONAL CONTAINER SERVICE

The containers carried by ocean-going liners to Tokyo or Shinagawa wharf are reshipped on container cars at the Shinagawa Terminal. Those arriving at Kobe and Maya wharves are transported by train from Kobe-Ko Station.

The Honmoku Terminal in Yokohama plays a significant role in transshipment of containers carried by vessels from and to Yokohama Port. In addition, new terminals for container service are to be constructed in other major ports to meet the growing demand for container service.

International containers are transported

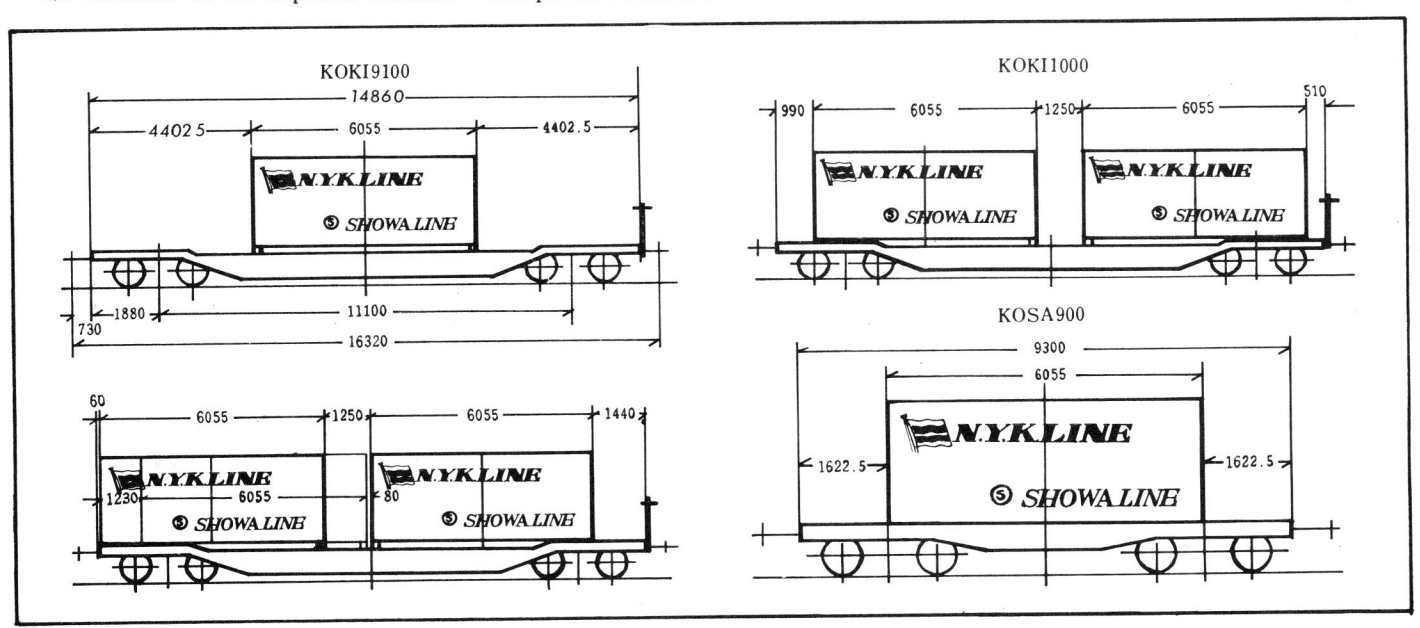

SPECIFICATIONS

Type of Car		Loading Capacity (tons)	Tare Weight (tons)	Dimensions				Loading Capacity			
				Distance Between Bogie Center mm	Car Length mm	Width mm	Floor Height mm	ISO 1A Type	ISO 1B Type	ISO 1C Type	ISO 1D Type
Exclusive Use	KOKI 1000	41	19	11,100 (36'5")	16,320 (53'7")	2,600 (8'6")	1,020 (3'4")	1	1	2	
	KOKI 9000	41	19	11,100 (36'5")	16,320 (53'7")	2,600 (8'6")	1,020 (3'4")	1	1	2	
	KOSA 900	15	15	6,000 (19'8")	10,760 (35'4")	1,669 (5'6")	1,030 (3'5")				

by JNR express container trains, since some 200 inter-block express trains are being operated daily throughout the country. In addition, exclusive container trains, can be provided if necessary.

Terminals for this traffic are situated at Kobe-ko station, Shinagawa Wharf Tokyo, Honmoku Wharf, Yokohama and Nishi Nagoya station. The Kobe terminal is equipped with a 37·5 ton container gantry crane and that at Tokyo with a 20 ton gantry type crane and a 37 ton truck crane The terminals at Yokohama and Nagoya have 22·7 and 37 ton cranes, respectively.

TYPES OF CONTAINER

All JNR containers are of steel, painted light-green. Besides ordinary covered containers, there are refrigerator containers, tank containers, ventilated containers and hopper containers. Among the ordinary covered containers some have openings on both sides, some at front and both sides, and some can be opened at the top.

Box type for general merchandise
Most of the recently manufactured containers use corrugated steel plates for outside panels, combining functions of structural members. The inside is lined with plywood, except the floor. Metal fittings secure the container to the wagon. Volume/load ratio is comparatively high.

Refrigerated container
Uses anti-atmosphere corrosion steel plate for outside and inside panels, and glass fibre (100 to 150 mm [3⅞–5⅞ in] thick) for insulation. One type is equipped with a 2-3-step detachable rack, and another with a rack to store dry ice. A new type of refrigerator container with an insulation layer composed of hard polyurethane foam in place has been test-manufactured.

An instance of performance: 5 tons of meat of standard quality in 37 hours over 900 km (559 miles) using 57 kg (125 lb) of dry ice maintained the inside temperature at 6°C and the temperature of the commodity at 12°C.

Ventilated container
The number of this type in use is small, it is used for commodities in need of the circulation of fresh air.

Tank container
Used to carry door-to-door animal or vegetable oil, insulation oil, etc. Since these oils are regarded as dangerous goods stipulated as category 4 (a flash point 130°C or more) in the Fire Brigade Law, they are subject to certain restrictions concerning road transport. Therefore, the tank container is required to have a special shape and equipment. In the case of hardened vegetable oil, the law provides that it shall take 24 hours or more for the temperature of the liquid oil to lower from 70°C to 50°C when the atmospheric tempera-

JNR—Type R12 refrigerated container

JNR—Type C10 one side openable dry cargo unit

JNR—Type C12 top openable containers

JNR—Type T12 tank container

JNR—Type H10 hoppercontainer

ture is 50°C. In this connection, the tank container is equipped with a heating pipe with which to heat the oil by steam when necessary.

Hopper Container
Used to carry crude synthetic resin from silo

to silo. Since this particular commodity rejects moisture, the outlet is strictly airtight.

Open top container
For such heavy loads as motors, pumps, and

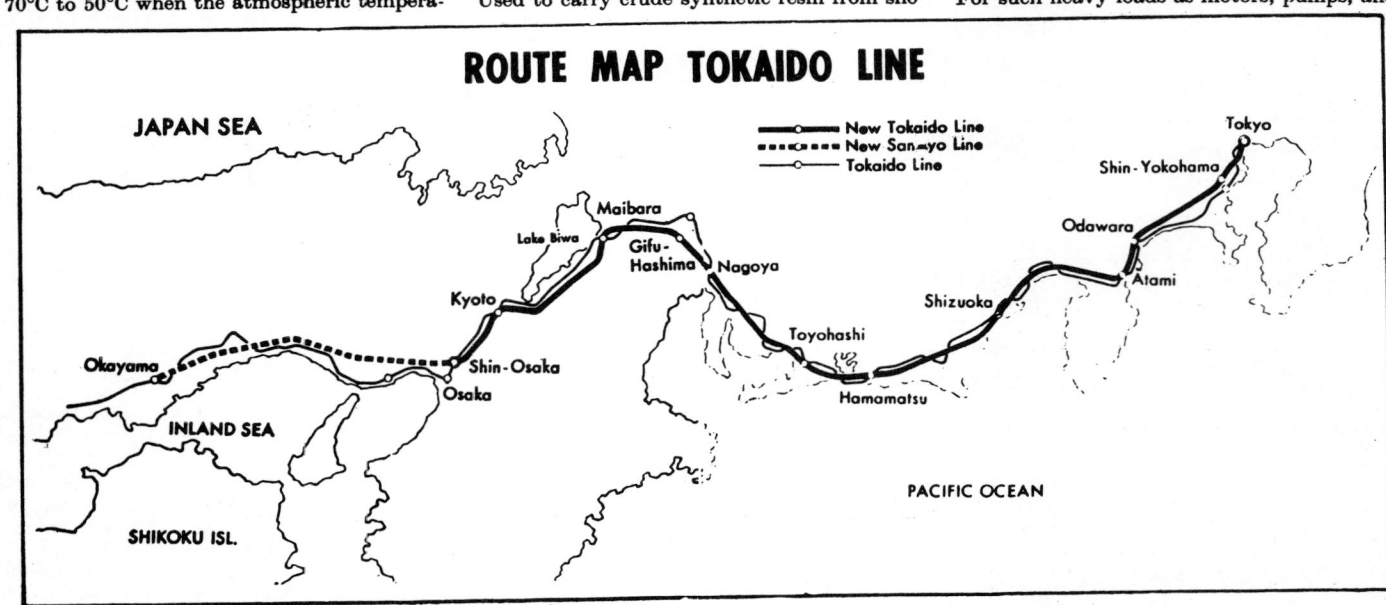
ROUTE MAP TOKAIDO LINE

safes handled by crane. The top is divided into two parts and each of them slides out to the end. One end has a two-leaf door to facilitate the handling of pallets by fork-lift truck.

Formerly, JNR's containers were, as a rule, manufactured for fork-lift trucks. But at present, designs which permit handling by crane are being adopted because of the increase in the number to be handled and in terminal facilities.

TERMINAL LAYOUT:

For the base station facilities, JNR has provided each platform with roofing and lowered floor for easy handling, and for major base stations, the following points are taken into consideration:

(i) The effective length of the loading side track and platform should accommodate a whole train, but for the time being is required to accommodate half a train.

(ii) The width of an island platform should be 38 m (124 ft), so that there will be room enough for the manoeuvring of fork-lift trucks, for container parking and for truck parking. The width of a side platform is to be 24 m (78 ft).

(iii) To raise the turnover efficiency of the loading side track, there is to be a supplementary side track.

HANDLING EQUIPMENT:

For container handling, fork-lift trucks are

JNR—Type C11 two-side openable unit

exclusively used, except at some major stations, where gantry cranes are installed to facilitate loading containers from one train to another and also to make some saving in the platform length.

INSPECTION AND MAINTENANCE:
Container inspection, washing and cleaning, and minor repairs facilities are set up in the Inspection and Repair Shed of main container base stations.

MALAYSIA
PENANG

Penang Port Commission
Penang, Malaysia.
TELEPHONE: Penang 63571
TELEGRAMS: Wharves Penang.
PRINCIPAL OFFICIALS:
Tan Sri Abdul Jamil bin Rais PMN, PJK (*Chairman*)
Ismail bin Ngah Marzuki (*General Manager*)
A. Nallusamy (*Assistant General Manager*)
Mohd Idris bin Kamaruddin (*Secretary*)
Lim Teik Chuan (*Traffic Manager*)
Foo Fatt Kong (*Chief Accountant*)
Mohamed Azuddin bin Haji Zainal Abidin (*Chief Engineer*)
J. W. Anchant (*Dockyard Manager and Chief Marine Engineer*)
Loke Soon Chuan (*Civil Engineer and Maintenance Engineer*)
Teh Eng Kim (*Personnel Manager*)
C. Natkunesingam (*Management Services Manager*)
GENERAL:
There are no container handling facilities in operation at present, but the expansion plans of the port have provided for the development of these facilities as and when required. Two of the new deep water berths at Butterworth opposite Penang Island, completed in July 1969, are capable of accommodating these ships and have been built for this purpose

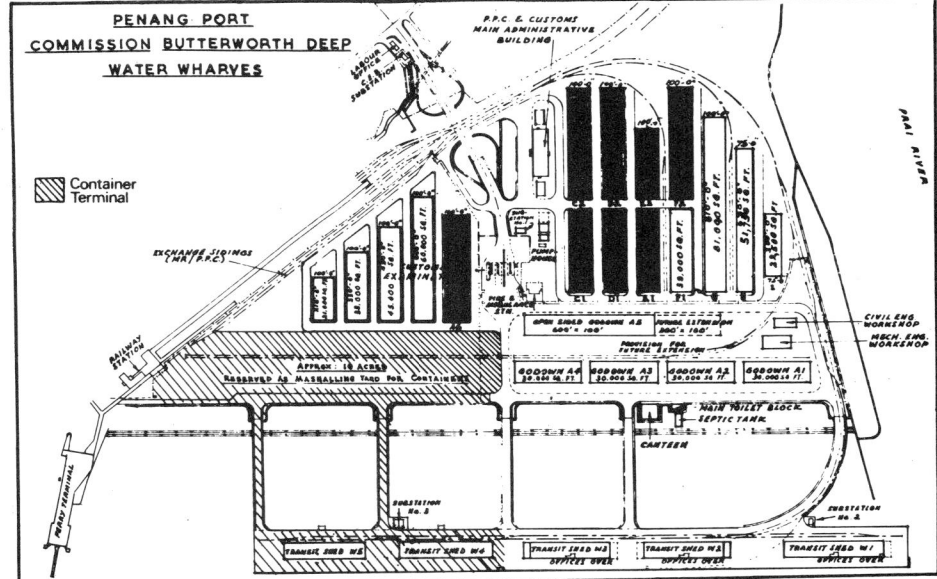

having been specially strengthened to take gantry cranes. The berths have a supporting

parking and marshalling area of about 10 acres.

PORT SWETTENHAM

Port Swettenham Authority
Port Swettenham, Malaysia
CONTAINER FACILITIES:

Two berths, each with a quay length of 320 m (1,050 ft) are under construction; they will have a depth alongside of 12·8 m (42 ft)

and a total area of about 10 hectares (25 acres). It is planned to equip the facility with two container gantry cranes.

SINGAPORE

The Port of Singapore Authority,
P.O. Box 300, Singapore.
TELEPHONE: 76021
TELEGRAMS: ' Tanjong Singapore '.
OFFICIALS:
Howe Yoon Chong (*Chairman/General Manager*)
Loh Heng Kee (*Director-Operations*)
Wee Keng Chi (*Director Administration*)

A. Vijiaratnam (*Director, Engineering Services*)
Chas. W. Meyer (*Secretary-Sp. Duties*)
Billie Cheng Shao Chi (*Deputy Director-Finance*)
R. B. Milne (*Deputy Director-Staff and Training*)
GENERAL:
The Authority has completed plans to provide wharf and shore facilities for the handling

of container ships and containerised cargo.

In 1972 full container ships will be operating in the Pacific and South East Asia from Europe, America, Japan and Australia. Singapore, in the centre of this region, is now preparing for this traffic.
CONTAINER TERMINAL:
The PSA is constructing two container berths with a total length of 636 m (2,250 ft)

having 13·41 m (44 ft) alongside at low water and also a 213 m (700 ft) cross berth for feeder services with 10·36 m (34 ft) alongside at low water. The cross berth was completed in October 1970 and the first container berth will be operational by November 1971 and the whole project should be completed by the end of 1972.

A sheet piled breakwater will also be installed to ensure protection during the monsoon period.

There will be a total back-up area of approximately 40·47 hectares (100 acres), the container complex occupying 24·28 hectares (60 acres) of the land.

Initially three single lift 35 ton container gantry cranes will operate along the main container berths. The first will be erected in November 1971 the second in mid 1972 and the third by the end of that year. One 30 ton straddle carrier capable of stacking 20 ft units three high and 40 ft units two high is in service. Orders for a further 7 carriers have been placed. Two weigh-bridges of 60 ton capacity and one weigh-bridge of 40 tons capacity have been installed. The ancillary services include two freight stations at the container berths 164·59 × 45·72 m (540 × 150 ft), an additional transit shed 128·02 × 45·72 m (420 × 150 ft) to serve the cross berth for containerised transhipment cargo, a marshalling yard of 10·52 hectares (26 acres), a workshop, an administrative block and a control tower.

The terminal will cater for about six thousand 20 ft units stacked 2 high and 106 20 ft refrigerated containers. The deck will also be capable of supporting 40 ft containers.

Future Development

Plans are in hand to extend the container berths by a further 304 m (1,000 ft).

ROLL-ON FACILITIES:

Berth G19. This berth will take vessels up to approximately 140·2 m (460 ft) in length 19·8 m (65 ft) in beam with a draught of 8·2 m (27 ft). It was constructed of as a berth for L.S.L. vessels.

Berth G21/2. This berth will accept vessels of approximately 106·7 (350 ft) length 16·8 m (55 ft) beam and 8·2 (27 ft) draught. It was constructed as a berth for L.S.T. vessels.

Both berths are equipped with fixed ramp structures designed for accepting both bow and stern loaders.

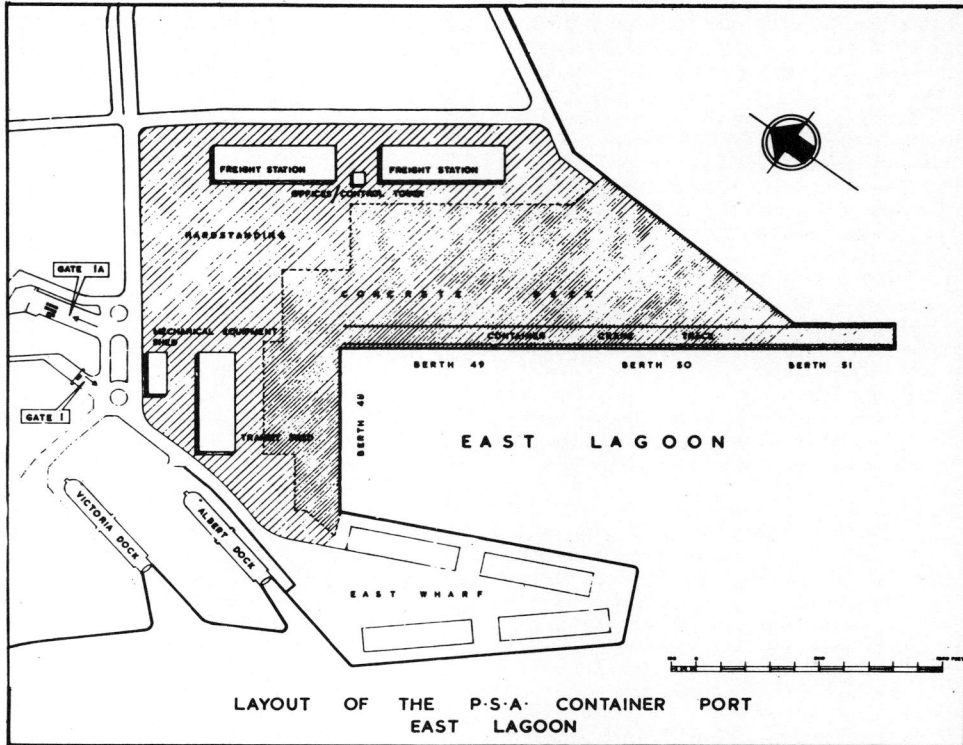

LAYOUT OF THE P·S·A· CONTAINER PORT EAST LAGOON

TERMINAL WORKING HOURS:

Ships are worked in three shifts round the clock. Inland transport operations are handled by private transport companies who work round the clock if required.

TRAFFIC:

In 1970 some 3,000 ISO type 20 ft units together with nearly 6,000 containers of various dimensions were handled in conventional vessels. The 1971 20 ft ISO type total handled is estimated at about 4,700.

INLAND CONTAINER DEPOT:

To secure adequate space for packing, unpacking storage of containers etc the Authority is acquiring 52·61 hectares (130 acres) of land lying between the PSA wharves and Jurong Port. It is linked to the port areas by rail and by highways which eventually lead to West Malaysia.

Singapore Roll-on Berth No. 21 G, Empire Dock

TAIWAN

KEELUNG

Keelung Harbour Bureau
Keelung, Taiwan
TELEPHONE: 24111

TELEGRAMS: 0321
PRINCIPAL OFFICIALS:
K. C. Tsao (*Director*)

C. S. Lin (*Deputy Director*)
T. C. Wang (*Harbour Master*)
T. Y. Chung (*Chief of Traffic Dept.*)

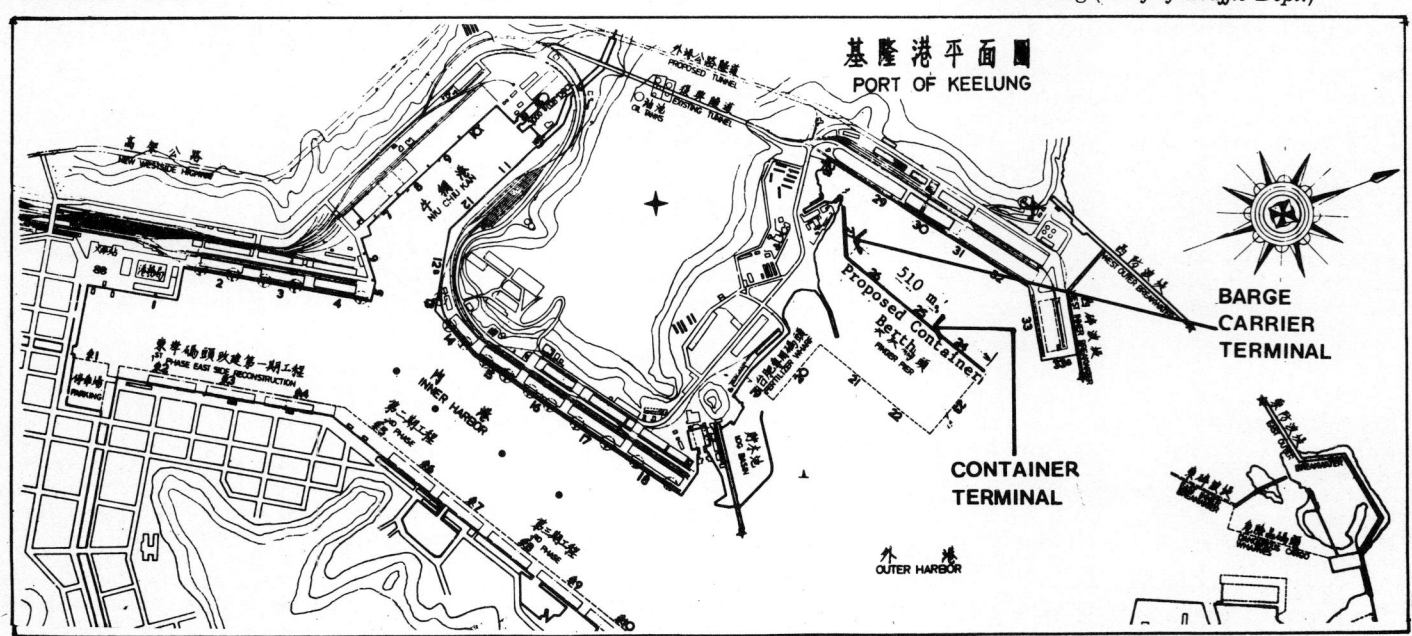

基隆港平面圖
PORT OF KEELUNG

BARGE CARRIER TERMINAL

CONTAINER TERMINAL

外木
OUTER HARBOR

CONTAINER FACILITIES:

At present containers are handled at Pier 32 which has a yard of 1·4 hectares (3·46 acres) and at other general cargo facilities using ships' gear.

A terminal with a total quay length of 910 m (2,985·5 ft) is at present under construction. One half of the pier, providing a quay length of 450 m (1,476·4 ft), with a depth of water of between 11 and 12 m (36 and 39 ft), is scheduled for completion at the end of 1971. Some 8 hectares (20 acres) of marshalling area will be available and the facility is being equipped with a 37·5 ton container gantry crane and straddle carriers.

BARGE CARRIER FACILITIES:
No. 27 Berth

This berth, which became operational in August 1971, is shown in an artist's impression as having been equipped with a covered berth for loading and discharging LASH barges.

CONTAINER TRAFFIC:
Traffic Inwards

	Tons*	No. of Loaded Units
1968	32,724	1,818
1969	139,600	4,249
1970	239,320	5,983
1971†	340,000	8,500

Traffic Outwards

	Tons	No. of Units
1968	17,298	961
1969	113,341	3,467
1970	380,480	9,512
1971†	480,000	12,000

*Freight Tons
†Estimates

KAOHSIUNG

Kaohsiung Harbour Bureau
Kaoshsiung
Taiwan
CONTAINER FACILITIES:

Containers are at present discharged at Piers 40, 41 and 42 which provide an area of 4·25 hectares (15·4 acres) for storage. Ships use their own gear.

Piers 63/66

Four berths, each with a quay length of 250 m (820 ft) and a depth of water alongside of 12 m (39·4 ft) are under construction. They will have a total area of 45·4 hectares (112 acres) and each will be equipped with a 45 ton container gantry crane with an outreach of 30·78 m (101 ft) and a backreach of 13·11 m (43 ft).

Piers 68/70

Three further 300 m (984 ft) berths with a depth alongside of 13 m (42·7 ft) are planned.

AUSTRALASIA

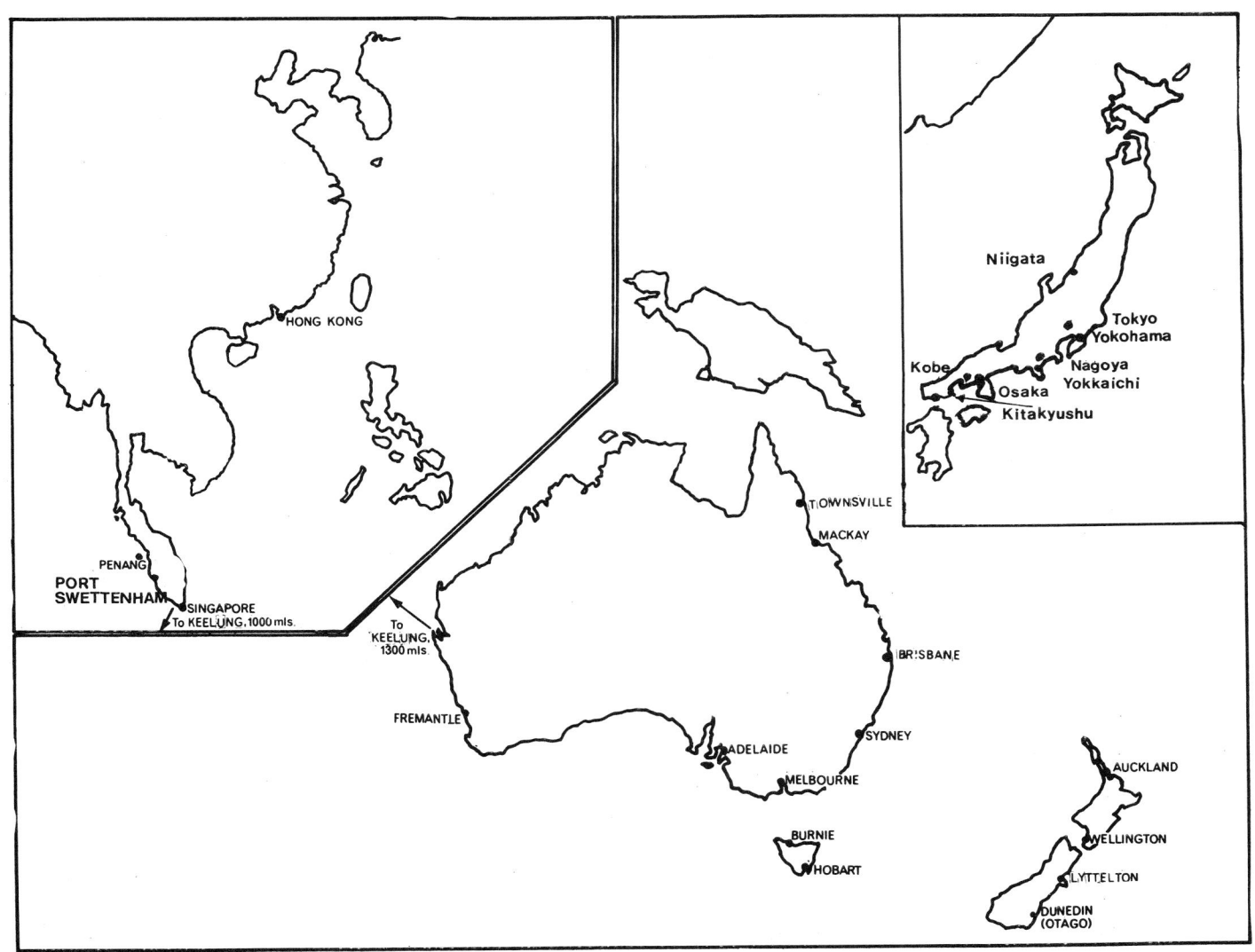

AUSTRALIA
ADELAIDE

The Department of Marine and Harbors
Box 679E, GPO, Adelaide, S. Australia 5001
TELEPHONE: 51-1471
TELEGRAMS: Harbors Adelaide
OFFICIALS:
J. R. Sainsbury (*Director of Marine and Harbors*)
Captain W. H. Hilder (*Ports and Traffic Manager*)
R. J. Wight (*Secretary*)
H. W. Taylor (*Port Superintendent*)
Captain F. H. Olson (*Harbourmaster*)

GENERAL:

Port Adelaide, for the next few years, will only handle direct shipments of overseas containers in the combination or unit load type of ship, equipped with stern ramps.

Other overseas containers will travel

between Port Adelaide and a terminal port in the eastern states by rail (OCL and ACT consortia traffic) and by roll-on/roll-off ship (Aust National Line). For the latter the Department has constructed a roll-on/roll-off berth (No. 25) in No. 3 Dock. The berth, which has about 4 acres of supporting area for marshalling vehicles will be capable of taking vessels up to 137 m (450 ft) in length 21·3 m (70 ft) beam and 8·5 m (28 ft) draught. It has a shore based adjustable ramp and the wharf is equipped with a 25 ton fixed crane of 33·5 m (110 ft) radius.

OCL and ACT each have established a container packing and sorting depot on land made available by the Department and within half a mile of the riverfront berths.

A wool dumping centre has been established alongside the container depots on land made available by the Department. Wool is to be dumped to high density and packed in containers and other unit loads.

CONTAINER SERVICES:

Certain shipping companies handle containers at general cargo berths.

Associated Steamships Pty Ltd use No. 5 Inner Harbour for their weekly service to Eastern and Western States.

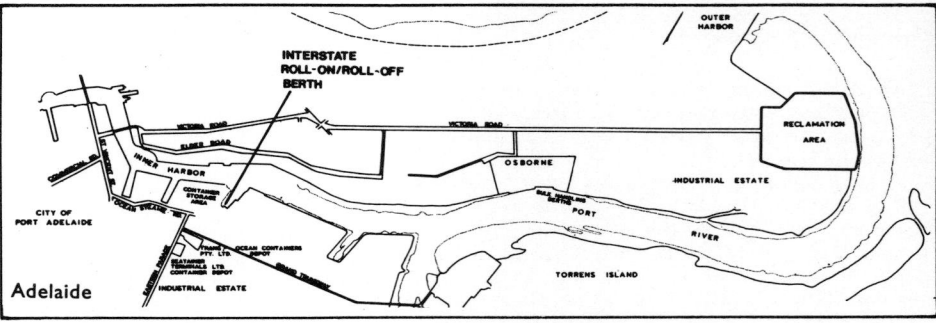

Adelaide

ROLL-ON/ROLL-OFF SERVICES:

Australian National Line operate weekly between Port Adelaide and East States.

FREIGHT FORWARDING COMPANIES:

Brambles Transport
285 St Vincent Street, Port Adelaide, S. Aust, 5015
Tel: 4-2173

Mayne Nickless Ltd
20 Divett Street, Port Adelaide, S. Aust, 5105
Tel: 47-4343

Port Carriers Pty Ltd
29 Divett Street, Port Adelaide, S. Aust, 5015

Tel: 4-1886

CONTAINER STORAGE AND STEVEDORE COMPANIES:

South Australian Stevedoring Co Pty Ltd
124 Lipson Street, Port Adelaide, S. Aust, 5015
Tel: 4-1468

The Adelaide Stevedoring Co Pty Ltd
12 Todd Street, Port Adelaide, S. Aust, 5015
Tel: 4-1184

James Patrick & Co Pty Ltd
15 Divett Street, Port Adelaide, S. Aust, 5015
Tel: 4-3801

BURNIE

The Marine Board of Burnie
Marine Terrace, Burnie, Tasmania 7320
TELEPHONE: 31-3444
TELEGRAMS: Marine Board Burnie
OFFICIALS:
L. Turnidge (*General Manager*)
Capt F. H. Whitley (*Harbour Master*)
H. Miller (*Secretary*)

GENERAL:

Roll-on/Roll-off and lift-on/lift-off (including ISO Containers) Services are operated by the Australian National Line to Melbourne twice weekly and Sydney weekly.

The berth is equipped with a 40 ton portal crane with 10 ton auxiliary hoist. There is 1,783 m² (19,000 sq ft) of covered storage and 2·0 hectares (5 acres) of open storage serving the berth, plus 0·8 hectares (2 acres) of storage area.

The wharf is 85 m (278·9 ft) in length and will berth vessels up to 198 m (649·6 ft) long and 8·84 m (29 ft) draught. The stern ramp is 8 m (26·25 ft) wide with an axle loading of 50 tons.

A new general cargo berth will be commissioned in 1972 capable of handling ISO Containers ex ships gear also roll-on/roll-off quarter ramps. Axle loading will be 50 tons and the berth will be provided with extensive covered and open storage.

CONTAINER AND ROLL-ON TRAFFIC:

	Inwards	Outwards
1969/70	195,934 units	238,107 tons
	16,300 units	19,800 units
1970/71	169,000 tons	239,083 tons
(Estimate)	14,000 units	19,800 units

NOTES:

i) The year is from 1st July to 30th June.
ii) Numbers of units are approximate.

TERMINAL OPERATING HOURS:

Both ship and inland transport cargo handling operations take place 24 hours per day if required.

FREIGHT FORWARDING COMPANIES:
F. H. Stephens (Burnie) Pty. Ltd.
80 Marine Terrace, Burnie 7320

STEVEDORING COMPANIES:

All interstate ferry cargo is stevedored by the Australian National Line, Ocean Wharf, Burnie 7320.

CONTAINER REPAIRERS:
Emu Bay Railway Co. Ltd.
Wilson Street
Burnie, 7320
Telephone: 31 2822

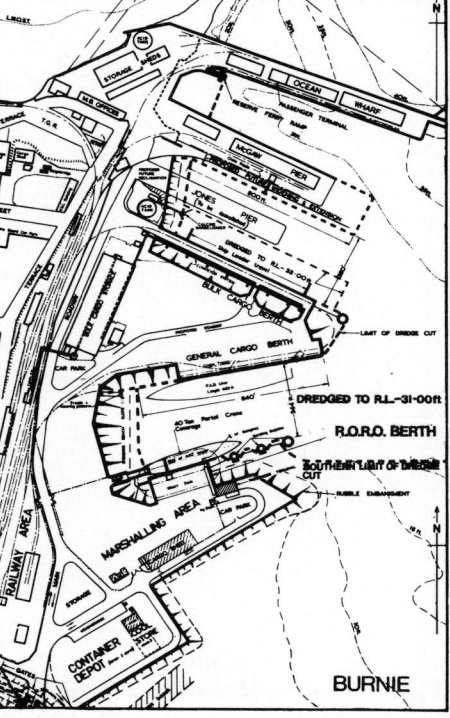

BURNIE

Burnie—Roll-on Berth

FREMANTLE

Fremantle Port Authority
1 Cliff Street
Fremantle, Western Australia 6160
TELEPHONE: 35-3981
PRINCIPAL OFFICIALS:
COMMISSIONERS
  J. McConnell (*Chairman*)
  M. N. B. Grace
  J. G. Manford
  W. J. Hughes
  L. R. Forrester
EXECUTIVE OFFICERS:
  H. C. Rudderham (*General Manager*)
  Captain B. L. Noble (*Divisional Manager Operations*)
  C. A. Faulds, (*Divisional Manager Administration*)

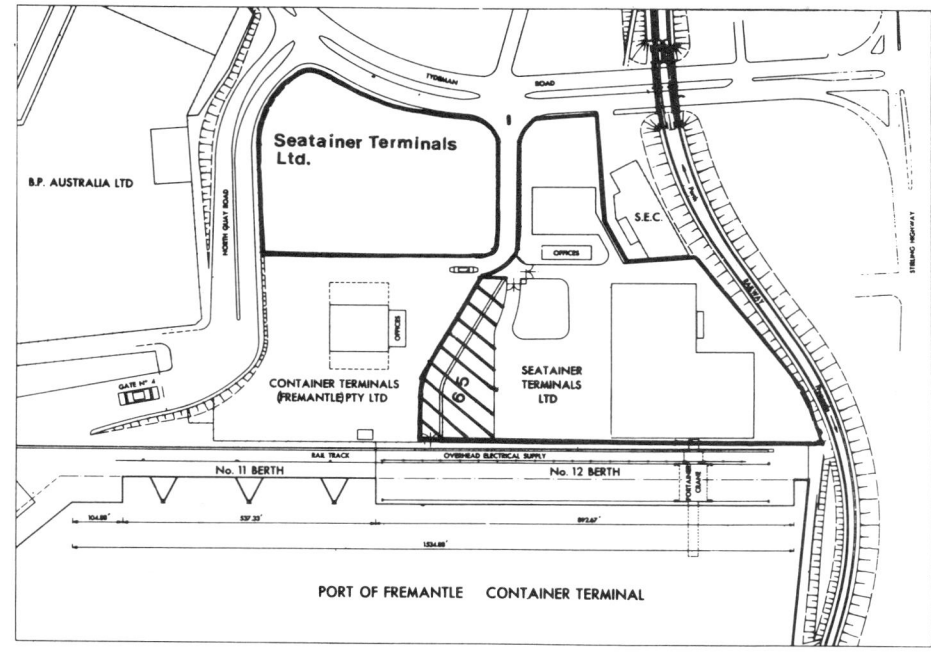

PORT OF FREMANTLE   CONTAINER TERMINAL

CONTAINER FACILITIES:

No. 12 Berth, North Quay:

This Berth, which is 272 m (893 ft) in length with 11 m (36 ft) alongside at low water, was completed early in 1969 and is controlled and operated by the Port Authority on a common user basis. It is equipped with a Paceco type container gantry crane, with an outreach over water of 31 m (102 ft), which has a maximum lifting capacity of 65 tons, and, with spreader attached, can handle two 20 ft or .one 40 ft container up to a maximum of 45 tons. The crane is also equipped as a heavy lift crane with a maximum capacity of 65 tons. Approximately 7·28 hectares (18 acres) of land to the rear of the berth have been leased to container operating companies which provide and operate the buildings, internal cranes, side loaders, prime movers and trailers, and other equipment required for container handling within their own leased areas. They are also responsible for transporting the containers to and from the container gantry crane.

A six lane road system serving the terminal is connected to the State's main highway system at controlled traffic points. The berth is also connected to the 1·075 m (3·5 ft)

gauge State railway system and provision has been made for standard rail gauge connections in due course.

Future Development

In the course of construction of No. 12 Berth provision was made for a second container berth (No. 11) of 196 m (640 ft) length to meet the possible demands of the future.

Berths 6 and 7 North Quay are being reconstructed and will provide 335·3 m (1,100 ft) of heavy duty quay suitable for roll-on, unit cargo, conventional cargo and container cargo operations. These two berths will be equipped with a modern clear span transit shed, and the new installation of

berth and shed will be fully operational by October 1971.

CONTAINER SERVICES:

Seatainer Terminals Ltd

Australia Europe Container Service provides one north bound and one south bound sailing through the port every 5 or 6 days. Associated Steamships Pty Ltd operate a weekly inter-state service.

TERMINAL WORKING HOURS:

24 hours a day if required for both ship and inland transport cargo operations.

CONTAINER REPAIR FACILITIES:

Seatainer Terminals Ltd,
  Brack Street, North Fremantle
  Telephone: 35.6611

The Inner Harbour of the Port of Fremantle showing No. 12 Berth North Quay in the foreground.

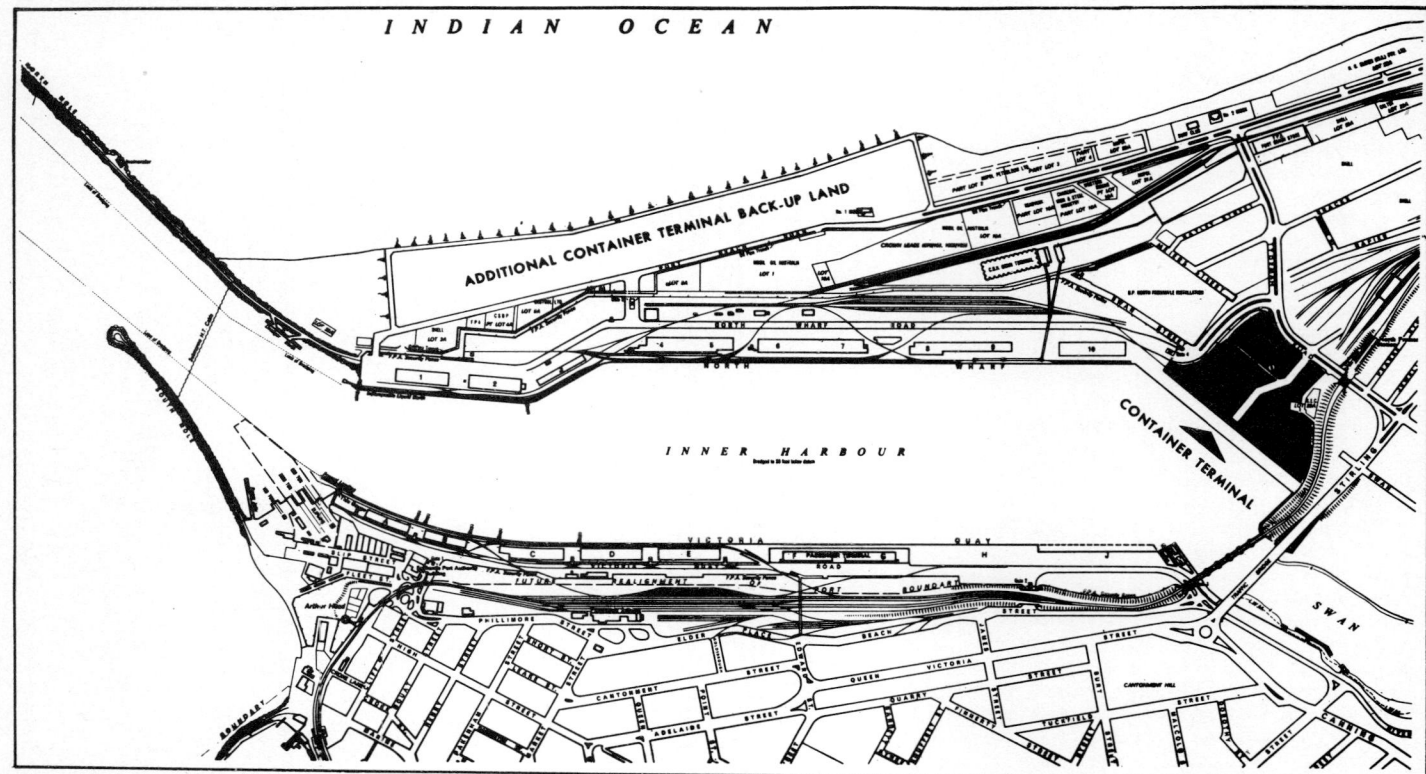

Inner Harbour—Port of Fremantle.

HOBART

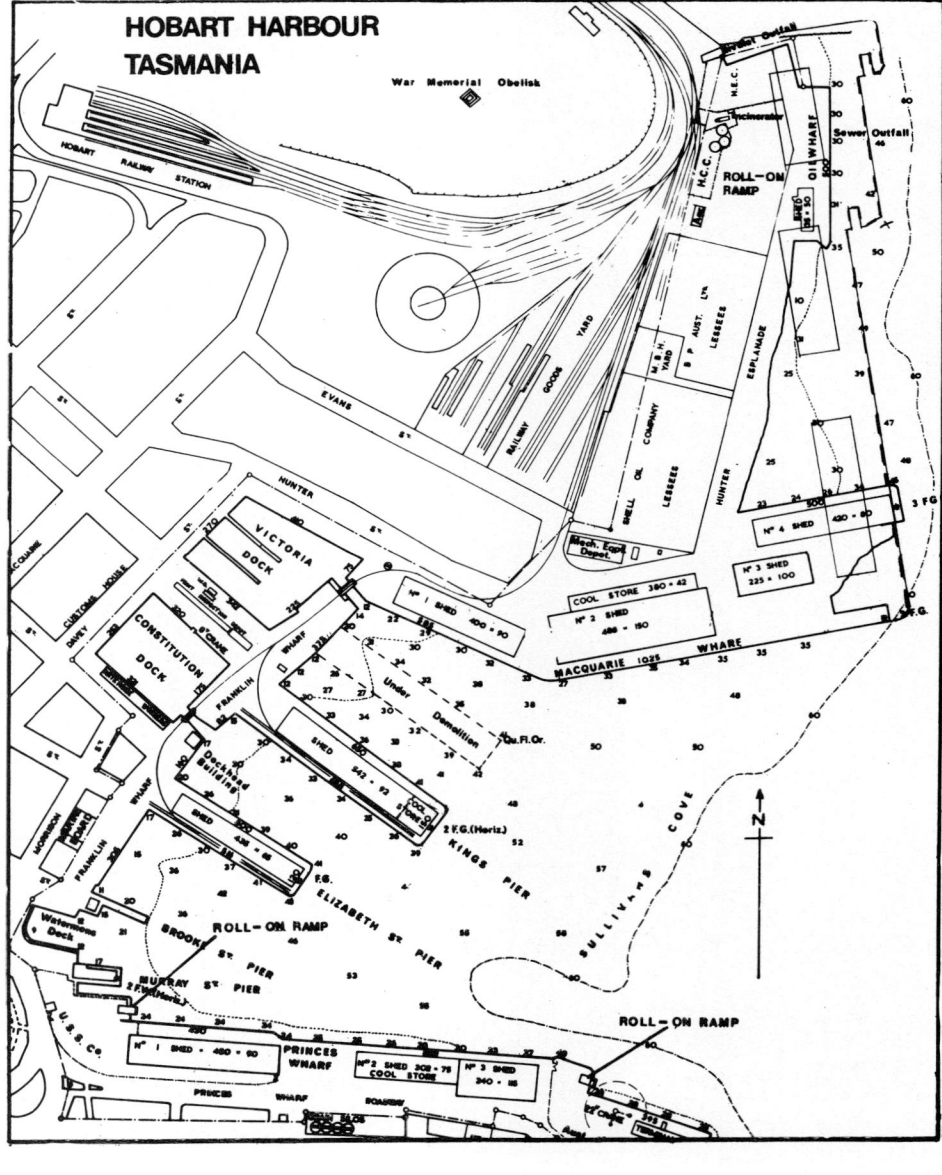

Marine Board of Hobart

GPO Box 202B, Hobart, Tasmania 7001

TELEPHONE: 27371

OFFICIALS:

D. Brown (*Acting General Manager*)

J. Macquarie (*Secretary General*)

Captain C. A. Woods (*Harbour Master*)

GENERAL:

There are no regular container services to Hobart, but a limited number of containers are handled at the roll-on berths.

ROLL-ON FACILITIES:

Princes No. 1 Wharf: This facility is used by the Union Steamship Company of New Zealand for their weekly services to Sydney and Melbourne using MVs *Seaway King* and *Seaway Queen*. The berth has a length of 131 m (430 ft) and a depth alongside of 7·3 m (24 ft). The quay apron is 12·2 m (40 ft) wide and there is a transit shed 137·2 × 27·4 m (450 × 90 ft).

Princes No. 4 Wharf: Used by the Australian National Line for their fortnightly services to Sydney (MV *Empress of Australia*, 150 pallets or containers) and to Brisbane with transhipment Melbourne (MV *Sydney Trader* 160 units) this facility has a length of 122 m (400 ft) and has a depth alongside of 7·62 m (25 ft). There is a transit shed 33·5 × 30·5 m (110 × 100 ft).

TERMINAL OPERATING HOURS:

0700 to 2300 hrs for ship operations. Inland transport operations can take place 24 hours per day if required.

FUTURE DEVELOPMENT:

Work has now commenced on Stage I of the re-alignment of berths at Macquarie Point to provide 648 m (2,125 ft) of quay wall with two roll-on ramps and a depth of water alongside of 12·8 m (42 ft). There will be a 25 ton travelling quay crane and the total area will be 8·09 hectares (20 acres) of which 13,378 m² (144,000 sq ft) will be covered.

FREIGHT FORWARDING COMPANIES:

F. H. Stephens Pty Ltd

   57 Lampton Avenue, Derwent Park

   Tel: 72-6653

TNT Tasmania Pty Ltd

   29 Federal Street, North Hobart

Tel: 34-3584
Wm Holyman & Sons Pty Ltd
  8 Montpelier Retreat, Battery Point
  Tel: 2-3013
Frank Hammond Pty Ltd
  66 Burnett Street, North Hobart
  Tel: 34-2111
Rigby Bros Ltd
  39 Campbell Street, Hobart
  Tel: 2-5333
All the above firms have container storage
facilities.
STEVEDORING COMPANIES:
Tasmanian Stevedoring Co
  16 Montpelier Retreat, Battery Point
  Tel: 2-7738
Wm Holyman & Sons Pty Ltd
  8 Montpelier Retreat, Battery Point
  Tel: 2-3013
Union Steam Ship Co of New Zealand
  2 Elizabeth Street, Hobart
  Tel: 2-2651
CONTAINER AND ROLL-ON TRAFFIC:
  The Marine Board do not publish this
information.

MV 'Seaway Queen' berthed at Princes No. I
Wharf, Hobart, showing stern loading ramp
and cargo assembly area

LAUNCESTON

Port of Launceston Authority
Box 257C, Launceston, Tasmania 7250
TELEPHONE: 2 5901
TELEGRAMS: Portlaun
PRINCIPAL OFFICIALS:
  R. A. Ferrall (*Master Warden*)
  K. N. Tainsh (*Secretary*)
  J. K. Edwards (*Port Manager*)
  W. G. Skinner (*Harbour Master*)
ROLL-ON/ROLL-OFF FACILITIES:
  Ferry Terminal: This facility can accept
vessels of up to 198 m (650 ft) in length and
it has a depth of water of 8·53 m (28 ft) at
low water and 10·06 m (34 ft) at high water.
There is a 25-ton capacity wharf crane for the
handling of containers and unit loads and
1·2 hectares (3 acres) of parking space for
vehicles adjoining. The facility is used by
Australian National Line on their weekly
services between Bell Bay and Sydney and
Bell Bay and Melbourne.
FREIGHT FORWARDING COMPANIES:
Australian National Line
  GPO Box 2238T, Melbourne 3001
Holyman's
54 Brisbane Street, Launceston 7250
TERMINAL WORKING HOURS:
  Ship cargo handling takes place as required
to ensure fast turnround. Inland transport
operation takes place between 0800 and 1700
hours.
ROLL-ON TRAFFIC:
  1968/69 156,201 tons inwards
             134,253 tons outwards
  1969/70 196,081 tons inwards
             178,188 tons outwards
  1971/70 245,000 tons inwards
(Estimate) 198,000 tons outwards
Note:
  Records date from 1st July to 30th June.

Ferry Terminal, Launceston.

MACKAY

The Mackay Harbour Board
PO Box 96, Mackay, Queensland, Australia,
4740
TELEPHONE: 94106
TELEGRAMS: Mackay Harbour Board
PRINCIPAL OFFICIALS:
E. J. Cliffe (*Chairman*)
G. F. Bell (*Deputy Chairman*)
PRINCIPAL OFFICERS:
E. N. Lever (*Secretary*)

P. D. Coghlan (*Engineer*)
EXECUTIVE IN CHARGE OF CONTAINER
OPERATIONS
Captain C. Gillanders (*Pier Master*)
GENERAL:
  The Mackay container terminal is such
that containers, pallets, pre-slung and unit
loads will be most efficiently handled by the
25 ton fixed crane located on the wharf
with a 33·5 m (110 ft) radius to plumb the

container deck of the ship. It will be capable
of taking vessels 137 m (450 ft) in length with
a 21·3 (70 ft) beam and a 9·14 m (30 ft)
draught.
  The wharf is so located as to enable a
roll-on/roll-off ramp to be constructed should
the trade develop in this direction.
  The whole terminal area covers 4·4 acres
while there is some 20 acres of reserve area
nearby, bordering the access road shown in

Mackay.

the port plan.

The coastal container feeder shipping service which came into operation in September, 1969, is operated by the Australian National Line using new ships with operating speeds of 17 knots. Fortnightly services are operated from Melbourne and Sydney and these will be increased in frequency as trade develops.

TRAFFIC:

8,000 tons in 700 units 16·67 ft long moved inwards and 950 tons in 90 units moved outwards in 1970. The same order of traffic is anticipated in 1971.

CONTAINER OPERATORS:

Australian National Line
Berths used: Container berth; 25 ton shore crane
Coastal interstate shipping service commenced September, 1969, to take 20 ton containers and unitized cargo
Services: Melbourne, Sydney, Port Alma, Mackay, Townsville, Cairns, fortnightly

FREIGHT FORWARDING COMPANIES:

J. Michelmore & Co Pty Ltd
Telephone 2111

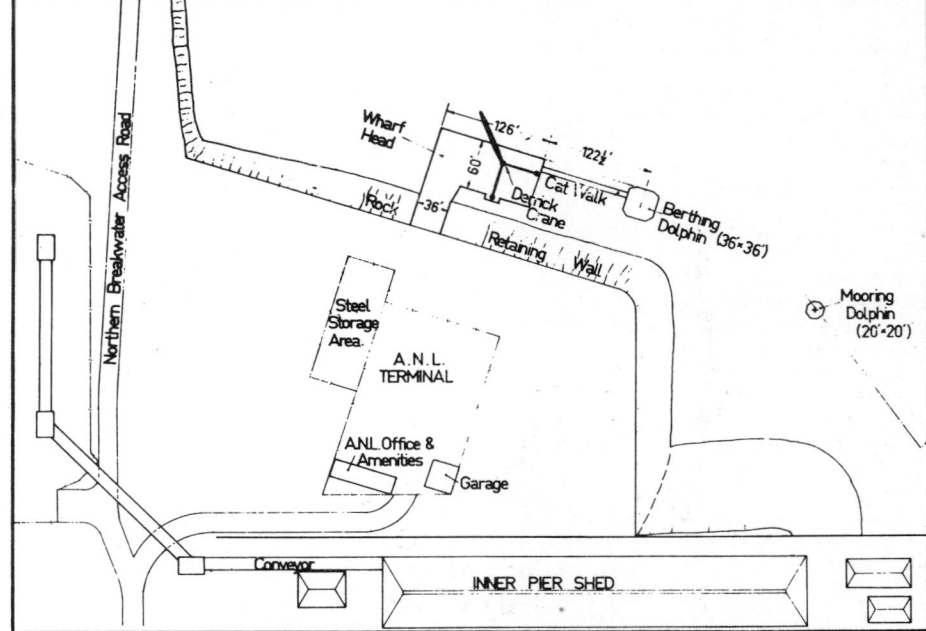

Mackay.

A. W. Rasmussen Pty Ltd,
54 Gregory Street, Mackay
McAleese & Co,
33 Victoria Street, Mackay
CONTAINERS, STEVEDORE AND STORAGE COMPANIES:
A. W. Rasmussen Pty Ltd,

54 Gregory Street, Mackay
McAleese & Co,
33 Victoria Street, Mackay
J. Michelmore & Co Pty Ltd (Stevedoring),
Overseas & General Stevedoring Co Pty Ltd (Stevedoring),
Telephone 94432

MELBOURNE

GENERAL:

The first stage of the Swanson Dock container complex was completed in April, 1970 comprising 1,050 ft of wharf apron at Berths No. 1 and 2 West and terminal facilities at the rear of the berth. These terminal facilities have been provided by Seatainer Terminals Ltd. on land leased from the Commissioners.

The construction of two common-user container berths at No. 1 and 2 East Swanson Dock is also proceeding. 800 ft of wharf apron was completed in November 1970 including the provision of a 45 ton twin-lift container crane. No. 2 East, extending over 850 ft. will be completed by November 1971. Terminal and depot operators have developed facilities on land leased from the Commissioners in the area between Swanson Dock and Appleton Dock at the rear of the common-user berths and a new road system in the area is under construction. A wool dumping depot has been developed in this area. An area of approximately 10 acres in

Melbourne—A general view with Swanson Dock in the foreground

Melbourne—Nos. 1 and 2 West Swanson Dock

ROLL-ON FACILITIES:		Maximum Size of Vessels accepted						
		Length		Beam		Draught		*Parking areas for vehicles*
Facility		*ft*	*m*	*ft*	*m*	*ft*	*m*	*trailers, containers and unit loads*
Berth No. 1 North Wharf		371	113·08	52	15·85	24	7·31	Approx 2·4 hectares (6 acres) operated by
Berth No. 2 North Wharf		430	131·06	63	19·20	24	7·31	Union Steamship Co. of N.Z. Ltd.
Berth No. 1 Webb Dock		444	135·33	70	21·33	23	7·0	Approx. 8·09 hectares (20 acres) operated by
Berth No. 2 Webb Dock		323	98·45	57	17·37	23	7·0	the Australian National Line.
Berth No. 3 Webb Dock		594	181·05	82	24·99	31	9·45	
Berth No. 3 Footscray		141	42·98	26½	8·07	10	3·05	Cargo shed 22·86 m × 12·19 m (75 ft × 40 ft) operated by R. H. Houfe & Co. Pty. Ltd

Note: Berths have been designed for vessels of dimensions shown above.

the vicinity of the berths has been reserved for common-user operations. This area could be served with rail if the necessity arises.

The ultimate development for Swanson Dock is for four berths totalling 3,200 feet on the west side and four berths totalling 3,000 ft on the east side. The additional berths will be constructed as the trade demands. About 121 hectares (300 acres) around and adjacent to the Swanson/Appleton Dock container terminal have been leased.

CONTAINER FACILITIES

No. 19 South Wharf. Operated by William Holyman & Sons P/L this berth can accept vessels of 182·9 m (600 ft) in length, 24·4 m (80 ft) beam with a draught of 8·53 m (28 ft). There is no craneage and approximately 9,000 m² (2·25 acres) of parking space for containers.

Nos. 1 and 2 West Swanson Dock: Operated by Seatainer Terminals Ltd. No. 1 Berth can accept vessels up to 228·6 m (750 ft) in length and No. 2 berth can accept vessels up to 182·9 m (600 ft). Both berths are dredged to accommodate vessels of 9·6 m (31·5 ft) draught and this will be increased to 10·05 m (33 ft) in 1972. Each berth is provided with a Paceco 45 ton twin lift container gantry crane with an outreach over water of 31·08 m (102 ft) and over land of 39·62 m (130 ft). Containers can be stacked 5 high under overhead travelling cranes. There is a storage capacity of 3,000 × 20 ft containers. The area behind the berths has a rail connection.

No. 1 East Swanson Dock. This is a common user berth capable of accepting vessels up to 228·6 m (750 ft) in length with the same draught conditions described above. It is equipped with one 45 ton Paceco twin lift gantry crane with the same outreach as the two described above. 11·3 hectares (28 acres) of parking area is operated by Liner Services P/L; 8·1 hectares (20 acres) is leased to ACTA; 8·1 hectares (20 acres) to Freightbases; and 4·05 hectares (10 acres) to Wooldumpers (Victoria) P/L.

ROLL-ON/ROLL-OFF FACILITIES:

Note: All existing roll-on/roll-off berths in the Port of Melbourne are provided with stern loading ramps.

At Berths No. 1 and 2 Webb Dock, and No. 3 Footscray ramps are dependent on shore for raising to parked position and lowering onto ship and also for adjustment with change of tide and draught.

At Berths No. 3 Webb Dock and 1 and 2 North Wharf ramps are dependent on shore for raising and lowering but are freely supported on stern of vessels during operations requiring no adjustments for change in tide and draught.

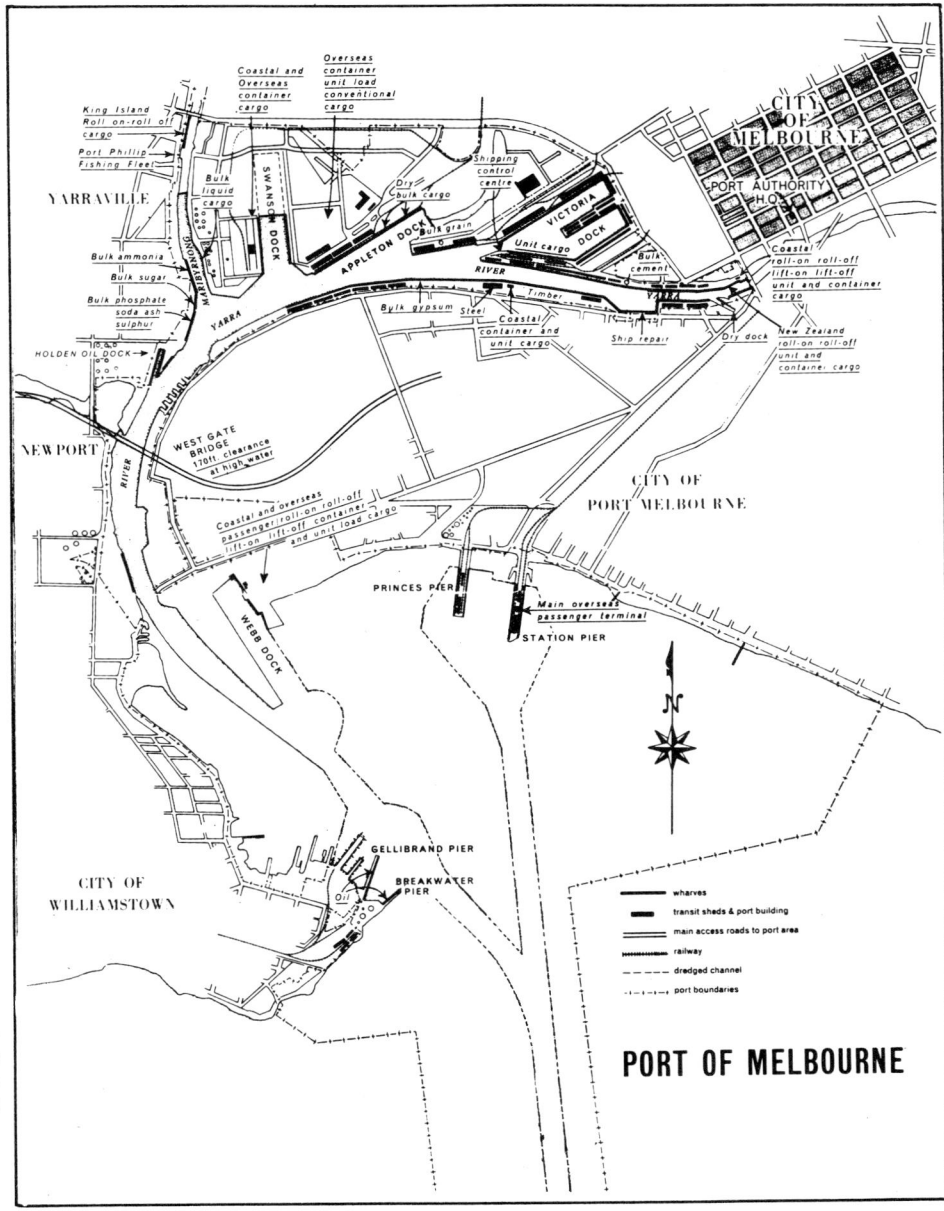

PORT OF MELBOURNE

Shore cranes are provided at Berths No. 1, 2 and 3 Webb Dock for the purpose of loading deck containers and unit loads. They are a 25 ton stiffleg derrick crane at No. 1, a 15 ton of similar type at No. 2 and a 25 ton level lifting 360° slewing portal crane at No. 3 which may also be used for loading cellular container ships.

A passenger terminal is provided at Berth No. 1 Webb Dock.

Webb Dock No. 3

TERMINAL WORKING HOURS:

Three 8 hour shifts are worked on ship cargo handling. Road and rail operate 7 days per week 24 hours per day except for one hour between 0630 and 0730 hours.

CONTAINER REPAIR FACILITIES:

Seatainer Terminal P/L
    Sudholz Street,
    West Melbourne
    Telephone: 329-7588
Freightbases P/L
    Appleton Dock Road,
    Footscray, Melbourne
    Telephone: 68-7371
Liner Services P/L
    Appleton Dock Road,
    Footscray, Melbourne
    Telephone: 62-6246

TRAFFIC:

Total unitised traffic in 1970 amounted to 1,241,079 tons inwards and 1,510,488 tons outwards.

Lift-on and roll-on traffic in containers amounted to 1,000,944 tons inwards and 1,245,523 tons outwards.

Melbourne—Nos. 1 and 2 East Swanson Dock—February 1971

Melbourne—Webb Dock Terminal

SERVICES:

Transocean Lift-on

Australia Europe Container Line—Swanson Dock—Europe Weekly.

NYK/Mitsui, OSK/Yamashita
and
Australia Japan Container Line—Swanson Dock—Japan Weekly

Columbus Line—Swanson Dock No. 1 East —East Coast North America every three weeks

Union Steamship of N.Z. Ltd.—No. 2 North Wharf—New Zealand, Fortnightly

Transocean—Roll-on
Pacific America Direct (PAD) Line— Appleton Dock—West Coast North America

Eastern Searoad Services—No. 3 Webb Dock—Japan Fortnightly

Short Sea or Coastal—Lift-on:

Assoc. Steamships Pty. Ltd.—Swanson Dock —Sydney and Brisbane, Weekly. Fremantle, Fortnightly

Wm. Holman—No. 19 South Wharf— Launceston, 3 times every 14 days.

Short Sea or Coastal—Roll-on:
See separate table

SHORT SEA AND COASTAL ROLL-ON SERVICE

Name of Company	Name of Location of Berths Used	Name of Ships with Container Capacity	
Australian National Line	No. 1 Webb Dock	"Princess of Tasmania" 30 containers (14 ft 5 in) 36 semi-trailers 100 automobiles in in addition to 90 passengers' cars	Three round trips per week between Melbourne and Northern Tasmania
Australian National Line	No. 1 Webb Dock	"Australian Trader" 110 containers (14 ft 5 in) 22 semi-trailers 15 automobiles in addition to 60 passengers' cars	Three round trips per week between Melbourne and Northern Tasmania
Australian National Line	No. 2 Webb Dock	"Bass Trader" 60 containers (14 ft 5 in) 30 semi-trailers 19 automobiles	Voyages per fortnight. Four round trips to Northern Tasmania and one to Southern Tasmania
Australian National Line	No. 3 Webb Dock	"Brisbane Trader" 216 containers (16 ft 8 in) or alternate unit loads	Melbourne-Brisbane Weekly turnround
Australian National Line	No. 3 Webb Dock	"Townsville Trader" 216 containers 16 ft 8 in or alternate unit loads	Melbourne-Sydney North Queensland Fortnightly turnround.
Australian National Line	No. 3 Webb Dock	"Sydney Trader" 216 containers (16 ft 8 in or alternate unit loads	Melbourne, Adelaide, Hobart Fortnightly turnround
		"Darwin Trader" 10,850 tons ore 240 × 20 ft containers 40 × 10 ft containers flats and heavy lift cargoes.	East Coast to Darwin, Groote Is. and Bell Bay 28 day turnround
Union Steamship of New Zealand Ltd	No. 1 North Wharf	"Seaway King" and "Seaway Queen" Each ship 273,939 cubic feet of space for containers, unit loads, vehicles or or combination	Each ship per fortnight provides one round trip Melbourne-Hobart Melbourne and one round trip Melbourne-Hobart Sydney-Hobart-Melbourne
Union Steamship of New Zealand Ltd.	No. 2 North Wharf	*Marama* 370 units including 20 × 8 × 8 units and all types of vehicle	Melbourne-Auckland Wellington Fortnightly
R. H. Houfe and Co. Pty. Ltd	No. 3 Footscray	"King Islander" 120/4 ft × 6 ft × 6 ft containers or combination of units loads—six vehicles	Three round trips per week Melbourne-King Island

SYDNEY

Maritime Services Board of New South Wales
Box 32, GPO, Sydney, NSW 2001
TELEPHONE: 2 0545
TELEGRAMS: Marboard
OFFICIALS:
W. H. Brotherson (*President*)
G. P. Hill (*Vice-President*)
Captain H. J. Harvey (*Harbour Master*)
H. B. Cadell (*Secretary*)

CONTAINER FACILITIES:
White Bay Terminal, Balmain

This Terminal has a quay length of 664·5 m (2,180 ft) which provides two berths with a total area of 9 hectares (22 acres). The berth at the eastern end, 396 m (1,300 ft) in length with a stacking area of about 5·1 hectares (12·5 acres), has been leased to Seatainer Terminals Ltd. to handle the Australia Europe Container Service. It is equipped with two twin lift 45 ton Paceco-Hoskins gantry cranes with an outreach of 30·48 m (100 ft). Containers are stacked five high in the storage area by two electric overhead gantry cranes which span the full width of the terminal area. These cranes are also used for loading on to road vehicles or rail wagons. Other equipment consists of straddle carriers, side-loaders and forklifts. The western end of the terminal is operated by the Maritime Services Board on a common user basis. It is equipped with a 45 ton twin lift container gantry crane with an outreach of 30·48 m (100 ft).

The ANL Tasmanian Service at Mort Bay Terminal.

Glebe Island Terminal

This facility, due to come into service in mid 1972 and to be completed by the end of the year, will have a quay length of 457·2 m (1,500 ft) and an area of 8·9 hectares (22 acres). There will be a depth of water of 12·19 m (40 ft). Two 35 ton container gantry cranes with an outreach of 33·53 m (110 ft) are being provided.

INLAND DEPOTS:

Seatainer Terminals Pty. Ltd. have an inland depot at Chullora which is road and rail served and provided with a shed 91 m (300 ft) long by 117 m (388 ft) wide. Trans-Ocean Containers Pty. Ltd. have similar facilities under construction at Villa Wood.

RAIL CONNECTIONS:

The NSWGR provide shuttle service trains of 17 flat wagons, each wagon capable of carrying two 20 ft units, between the Container Terminal and the Inland Depots.

SHIPPING COMPANIES PROVIDING CONTAINER SERVICES:

The Australia Europe Container Service provides a five day service between Australia and European Ports and Associated Steamships Pty Ltd provide a coastal container feeder service from White Bay.

ROLL-ON SERVICES:

Australian National Line operate between Sydney and Tasmania from their own terminal at Mort Bay where a special berth has been provided for their joint service to Japanese ports in conjunction with 'K' Line.

The Union S.S. Co. Ltd., of New Zealand operate roll-on services between Sydney and Hobart and also between Sydney and New Zealand from Berth No. 7 Darling Harbour which has been leased from the Maritime Services Board.

TERMINAL OPERATING HOURS:

Ship cargo handling and inland transport operations are continuous except for five special holidays.

Sydney—White Bay Terminal, Balmain

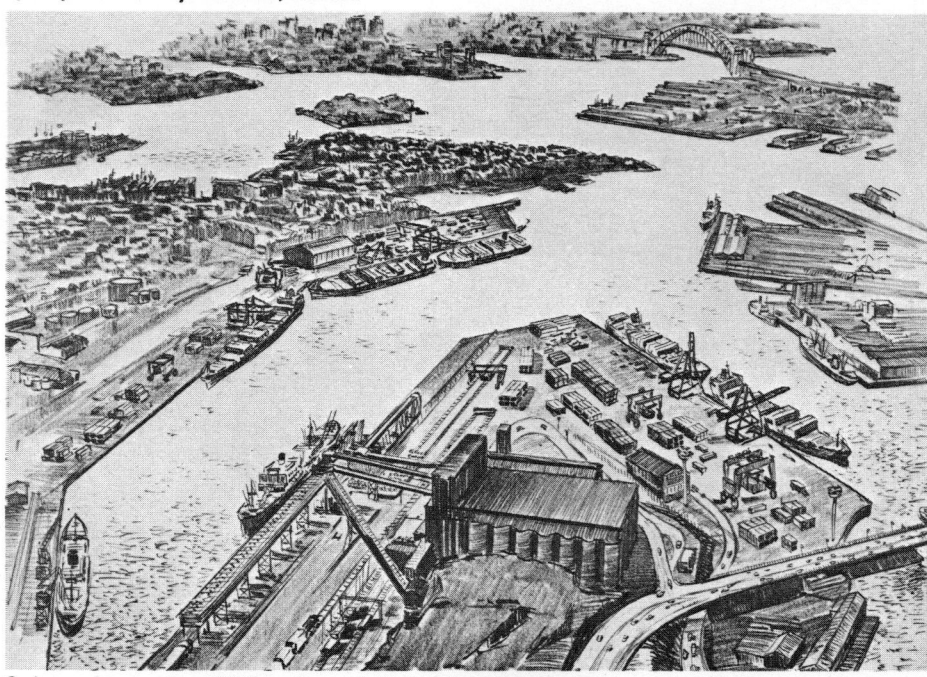

Sydney—Impression of White Bay and Glebe Island Terminals

The ANL Mort Bay Terminal for their joint Eastern Sea Road Service with "K" Line.

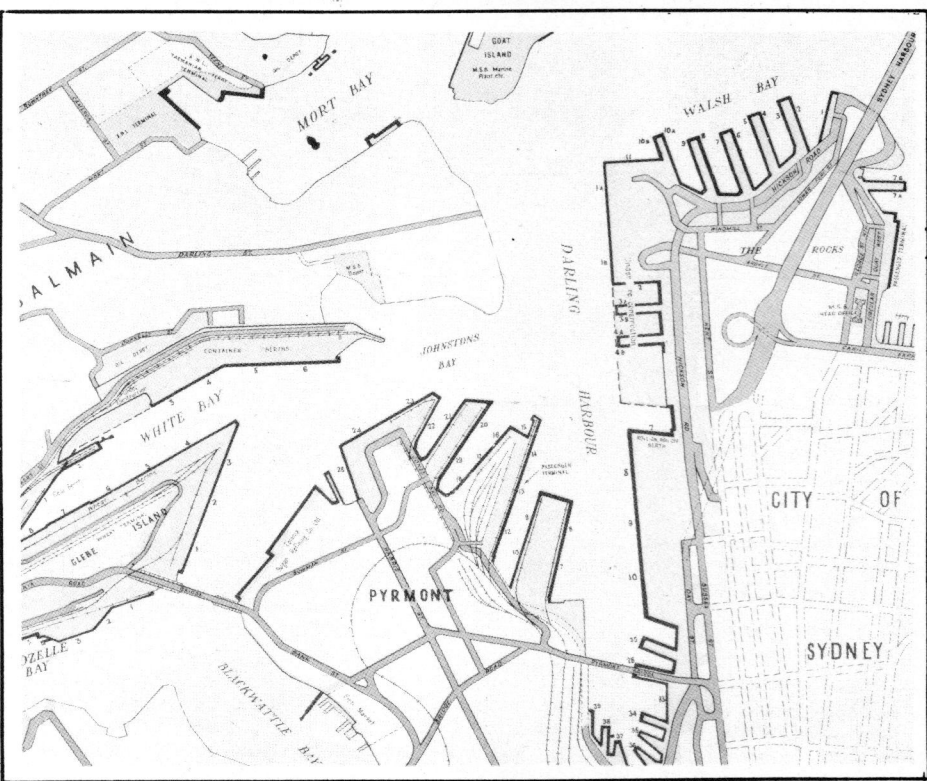

Botany Bay:

It is planned that reclamation work of Stage One of the Board's Botany Bay Port development will commence early in 1971. The initial planning for the Stage One area does not include the provisions of a container terminal but the need for such a facility will be considered as the stage progresses against the background of the need for a further facility beyond the ones located or likely to be located in the port of Sydney.

CONTAINER REPAIR FACILITIES:

Repairs to containers are carried out by numerous ship building and ship repairing organisations in the vicinity.

Sydney—The Union S.S. of N.Z. Roll-on Berth, No. 7 Darling Harbour

TOWNSVILLE

Townsville Harbour Board
The Strand, Townsville, Queensland
TELEPHONE: 721011
TELEX:
CONTAINER FACILITIES:
Australian National Line Searoad Berth

This facility has a quay length of 68·9 m (226 ft), a depth alongside of 8·5 m (28 ft) and is designed for the stern loading ANL vessels. There is a total area of 2·02 hectares

(5 acres) and the facility is equipped with a 25 ton quay crane.
No. 3 Berth

This facility, at present under construction, will have a quay length of 256 m (840 ft) a depth alongside of 12·19 m (40 ft) and a total area of 2·02 hectares (5 acres). It will be operated as a common user facility by the Harbour Board. Equipment planned is

reported as a 40 ton derrick crane.
Columbus Line Terminal

This facility, at present under construction will have a quay length of 213·4 m (700 ft), a depth alongside of 9·75 m (32 ft) and a total area of about 5,000 m², just over 1 acre. It will be operated by Columbus overseas Services Pty Ltd. for the Columbus Line service to East Coast North American ports.

CUSTOMS PROCEDURES

Customs procedures and arrangements related to goods carried in containers are at present under review.

Information concerning Australian Customs requirements for the carriage of goods in containers can be obtained from the offices listed below:
In Europe:
The Australian Customs Representative, Canberra House, Maltravers Street, off Arundel Street, Strand, London, W.C.2, UK
In America:
The Australian Customs Representative, 636 Fifth Avenue, New York, N.Y. 10020, USA

In Asia:
The Australian Customs Representative, Sankaido Building, 9-13 Akasaka, 1-Chome, Minato-ku, Tokyo, Japan

In New Zealand:
The Australian Customs Representative, C/- Australian Government Trade Commission, A.N.Z. House, 203 Queen Street, Auckland, N.Z.
In Australia:
The Comptroller-General, Department of Customs and Excise, Canberra, A.C.T.

The Collector of Customs, Sydney, N.S.W.

The Collector of Customs, Melbourne, Vic.

The Collector of Customs, Adelaide, S.A.

The Collector of Customs, Brisbane, Qld.

The Collector of Customs, Perth, W.A.

The Collector of Customs, Darwin, N.T.

AUSTRALIAN RAILWAYS

INTRODUCTION:
There are seven major railway systems in Australia; each state has its own Government owned railway and the Commonwealth

Government owns and operates several lines essential to the country as a whole on standard gauge.

The Eastern States have been linked with

Western Australia by standard gauge on the Trans-Australia railway line from Brisbane to Fremantle via New South Wales and South Australia.

COMMONWEALTH RAILWAYS

Commonwealth Railways
325 Collins Street
Melbourne Victoria 3000
TELEPHONE: (03) 62 5911
TELEX: 31109
OFFICIALS:
K. A. Smith, OBE (*Commissioner*)
N. F. Brealey (*Chief Traffic Manager*)
H. N. Turner (*Secretary*)
DUAL PURPOSE CONTAINERS:

The Railway has recently called for tenders to construct open type containers designed to carry cars on two levels and with sufficient strength on the lower deck for concentrates in either bagged or palletised form. There will be two sizes: a single unit of 16·2 ft in length with a total gross weight of 14 tons and a double unit 32·6 ft in length, 26 tons.

Commonwealth Railways – Transfer operations at Alice Springs. Where containers are distributed throughout the Northern Territory by road. The lorry is pulling three loaded trailers.

The use of these containers will enable the Railway to utilise flat or general purpose wagons for a traffic which now requires specialised vehicles.

CO-ORDINATED CONTAINER SERVICE:
Regular container services operate between Adelaide (Mile End) and Alice Springs, Mount Isa, Tennant Creek and Darwin.

PIGGYBACK SERVICE:
C.R. operates a piggyback service from South Australia to Western Australia.

CONTAINER TYPES IN SERVICE:

Class	Type	External Dimensions Length	Width	Height	Internal Capacity Cu. Ft.
ICS	Ice cooled	16′ 0″	7′ 3″	7′ 9″	447
MRA	Mech. refrigerated	20′ 0″	8′ 0″	8′ 0″	770
MRB	,, ,,	19′ 10½″	8′ 0″	8′ 0″	770
MRC	,, ,,	19′ 10½″	8′ 0″	8′ 0″	760
MRD	,, ,,	40′ 0″	8′ 0″	9′ 5″	1,550
MRS	,, ,,	16′ 0″	8′ 0″	8′ 0″	408
ZA	Dry goods	20′ 0″	8′ 0″	8′ 0″	1,090
ZB	,, ,,	19′ 10½″	8′ 0″	8′ 0″	1,090
ZS	,, ,,	16′ 8″	7′ 11″	8′ 6″	790
NVB	,, ,,	40′ 0″	8′ 0″	8′ 0″	1,960
CR	Multi purpose tray	37′ 0″	8′ 2½″	8′ 0″	2,070
CT	,, ,, ,,	37′ 0″	8′ 2½″	8′ 0″	2,070
CCS	Motor vehicle frame	16′ 2½″	8′ 2½″	5′ 9½″	625

NEW SOUTH WALES RAILWAYS

Department of Railways
Railway House
19 York Street
Sydney, NSW

GENERAL
NSW Railways do not own any 8 ft × 8 ft cross section containers nor do they operate any terminals. Private containers are carried on a fleet of 70 rail cars.

The following container terminals are rail served:
(1) Balmain Container Terminal (Eastern Berth), Sydney, operated by Seatainer Terminals Pty. Ltd.,
(2) Balmain Container Terminal (Western Berth), Sydney, operated by Maritime Services Board of New South Wales.
(3) Newcastle Container Terminal

Rail served Container Consolidation Depots are established at Chullora and Leightonfield, Sydney. These are operated by Seatainer Pty. Ltd., and Trans-Ocean Containers Ltd., respectively.

SOUTH AUSTRALIAN RAILWAYS

South Australian Railways
Adelaide, South Australia 5000

EXECUTIVES IN CHARGE OF CONTAINER OPERATIONS:
M. L. Stockley (*General Traffic Manager*)
T. A. Snigg (*Commercial Manager, Adelaide*)

GENERAL
Containers owned by the Railway vary in internal cubic capacity between about 7 cu ft and 700 cu ft depending upon their designed purpose. No ISO type units are owned. Railway and privately-owned containers whose dimensions go up to 35 × 8 × 8·5 ft, are carried on a fleet of general purpose flat or open type wagons.

During 1969 nine polastream liquid nitrogen refrigerated containers were introduced to service.

Steadman type equipment is being used by private operators for open containers on special flat wagons for increasing traffic from the South East of South Australia to Eastern States.

Privately owned containers are used extensively for traffic to Alice Springs and Darwin in the Northern Territory.

Insulated Containers for meat traffic—S.A. Railways.

Steel container jointly owned by NSW and S.A. Railways used for general cargo.

Six 75 ft wagons built to carry two 37 ft or three 20 ft containers are now in service.

OVERSEAS CONTAINERS:
To June 1971 36 63 ft special flat wagons each designed to carry three 20 ft units came into service. These 20 ft containers move between the container depots at Port Adelaide and the Overseas Shipping Terminal at Swanson Dock, Melbourne, and other points as required.

TASMANIAN GOVERNMENT RAILWAYS

Tasmanian Government Railways,
1 Collins Street
Hobart Tasmania

EXECUTIVES IN CHARGE OF CONTAINER OPERATIONS:
C. G. Collins (*General Manager of Railways*)
R. C. Brazier (*Chief Traffic Manager*)

CONTAINER TERMINALS AND HANDLING EQUIPMENT:
Terminals are located at Hobart, Launceston, Devonport and Burnie and the handling

CONTAINERS IN SERVICE:

Type	No. of Units	Designation	Overall Dimensions Height	Width	Length	Interior Dimensions Height	Width	Length
FICC	2	Insulated	7 ft 4 in	8 ft 0 in	14 ft 5 in	6 ft 2 in	7 ft 3¼ in	13 ft 9 in
FIC	2	Insulated	7 ft 4 in	7 ft 0 in	8 ft 0 in	6 ft 3 in	6 ft 2½ in	6 ft 11 in
FRCC	2	Refrigerated – Frozen Goods	7 ft 4¼ in	8 ft 0 in	14 ft 5 in	6 ft 2 in	7 ft 3 in	13 ft 5 in
RCC	16	Refrigerated – Frozen Goods	7 ft 4¼ in	8 ft 0 in	14 ft 5 in	6 ft 2 in	7 ft 3 in	13 ft 5 in
C2R	86	Refrigerated – Peas, beans etc	8 ft 0 in	8 ft 0 in	16 ft 8 in	7 ft 2 in	7 ft 3 in	15 ft 8 in
RCM	2	Refrigerated – Hanging Meat	7 ft 4¼ in	8 ft 0 in	14 ft 5 in	6 ft 2 in	7 ft 3 in	13 ft 5 in
RRO	639	Open pallet units – Gen. Cargo	4 ft 9 in	8 ft 0 in	14 ft 5 in	4 ft 9 in	7 ft 8 in	13 ft 1 in
GC	6	Open container – Sand, gravel	5 ft 3 in	5 ft 3 in	3 ft 9 in	3 ft 9 in	5 ft 0 in	5 ft 0 in
OC	106	Open container – bricks, pipes				2 ft 8¼ in	6 ft 3 in	6 ft 9 in
WOC	26	Closed container – hides, skins	7 ft 6 in	7 ft 0 in	6 ft 0 in	6 ft 9 in	6 ft 11 in	5 ft 11 in
FCC	10	Closed container – bulk barley, malt and cement	6 ft 10 in	8 ft 0 in	14 ft 5 in	6 ft 3 in	7 ft 8 in	13 ft 8 in
CID	60	Bulk container – superphosphate	6 ft 10⅛ in	5 ft 6 in dia.	—	6 ft 3½ in	5 ft 0 in dia.	
CIH	4	Bulk containers – tallow	8 ft 2 in	7 ft 0 in	9 ft 5½ in	Capacity 1300 gallons.		

equipment consists of fork lift trucks up to 8 tons capacity, gantries up to 30 tons capacity, and tractors and four wheeled trailers.

SERVICES:

Door to Door or Terminal to Terminal or a combination of either are offered.

TRAFFIC:

In 1968/69 a total of 11,619 containers were moved in and out of Tasmania

TGR – C2RT Type refrigerated vegetable container.

VICTORIAN RAILWAYS

Victorian Railways,

Railway Buildings
67, Spencer Street
Melbourne, Victoria, 3000

EXECUTIVE IN CHARGE OF CONTAINER OPERATIONS:

J. S. Bell (*Manager Freight Operations*)

CONTAINERS AND WAGONS:

The railway own 330 containers all with a length of 8 ft by 7 ft wide and varying in height between 8·2 ft and 7·8 ft. The fleet consists of 62 bulk tallow tank, 140 bulk malt, 65 insulated and 63 general purpose units.

A fleet of 40 flat top wagons each capable of carrying two or three 20 ft units has been provided. These are fitted with equipment to lock into the container corner fittings. There are also 73 flat top wagons 75 ft in length each of which can carry two 37 ft long by 8·2 ft wide tray type containers.

TERMINALS AND HANDLING EQUIPMENT:

Containers are handled at Dynon and Melbourne goods yards using yard gantry cranes.

SERVICES:

Door to Door, Terminal to Terminal or a combination of either using owned or private containers. Shipping ocmpanies' containers are transported between Swanson Dock and Freight Bases Container Terminals at Melbourne and privately owned sidings.

WESTERN AUSTRALIAN GOVERNMENT RAILWAYS

Western Australian Government Railways
Bank of New South Wales Building
Corner Murray and William Streets
Perth, Western Australia 6000
TELEPHONE: 28 7777
OFFICIALS:
J. B. Horrigan (*Commissioner of Railways*)
R. J. Pascoe (*Assistant Commissioner*)
K. D. Reeves (*Secretary for Railways*)
I. J. Kinshela (*Chief Traffic Manager*)
B. W. E. Copley (*Commercial Manager*)

GENERAL:

In October 1970, narrow gauge (3 ft 6 in) freight operations on the Eastern Railway. between Northam and Kalgoorlie were transferred to the standard gauge (4 ft 8½ in) railway between these points. This railway is the western link of the interstate service. Additional containers have been provided to accommodate the various traffic conveyed to and from this railway and connecting narrow gauge lines.

All containers in service and on order may be transported on wagons of both gauges.

25 ton capacity gantry cranes in addition to mobile freight handling equipment have been provided at Kewdale, Forrestfield, Avon Yard, Merredin and West Kalgoorlie. A new complex including a Freight Terminal will be completed at Robb Jetty (near Fremantle) and brought into operation early in 1972.

The main Freight Terminal is at Kewdale 6 miles south east of Perth where complete facilities to integrate road and rail transport have been provided. In addition to the above, these include side and end loading ramps and platforms. container storage accommodation and elevated loading ramps.

Port container terminals are operating at North Fremantle where narrow gauge rail connections have been provided and standard gauge are proposed.

Facilities for the handling of containers also are available at various other points throughout the rail system.

IRON ORE HANDLING:

Western Australia's Charcoal Iron and Steel Industry at Wundowie has depended on

WAGR – Refrigerated containers on standard gauge wagons.

WAGR – General purpose open containers.

WAGR – Dry freight containers.

CONTAINERS IN SERVICE:

Numbers	Description	Dimensions ft
32	Refrigerated Freight	20 × 8 × 8
6	Refrigerated	16 × 8 × 7·9
2	Refrigerated	16·7 × 8 × 7·9
103	Dry Freight	20 × 8 × 8
4	General Purpose	16·7 × 8 × 8·5
6	Goods Freight	7 × 8 × 7·9
239	General Purpose Open (a number of these containers have been specially adapted and treated for the carriage of salt and superphosphate)	20 × 8 × 8
2	Collapsible	8 × 8 × 6
4	Collapsible	8 × 8·3 × 6·9
1	Tray Type	3·2 × 2·7 × 3
52	Iron Ore	17·2 × 8 × 5·5
2	Iron Ore	17·2 × 7·5 × 5·5
10	Louvred Fruit	20 × 8 × 8
140	Sheep	20 × 8 × 8
35	Cattle	20 × 8 × 8
19	Bulk Cement	8 × 7·5 × 4
130	Open Bulk Superphosphate	13 ft for 10 ton consignments)

Unloading iron ore at Wundowie.

An ISO lifting frame loading empty iron ore containers from Wundowie at Avon Yard.

WAGR – A sheep container and a cattle container mounted on a narrow gauge container wagon.

iron ore from Koolyanobbing since 1946.

Wundowie is located in the Darling Ranges, between Northam and Midland, and was served by the old narrow gauge railway to Kalgoorlie.

The new standard gauge line from Perth to the Eastern States, bypasses Wundowie and the steep grades of the Darling Ranges on a new route through the Avon Valley.

Following the transfer of all narrow gauge operations between Northam and Kalgoorlie to standard gauge, the WAGR introduced special containers to carry iron ore to Wundowie.

The iron ore is road hauled in tip trucks from the nearby deposits to elevated loading ramps at Koolyanobbing. Here it is tipped direct into specially designed containers, three of which are mounted on each WAGR standard gauge flat top wagon.

On arrival at Avon Yard near Northam, the containers are transferred by a 25-ton capacity gantry crane, fitted with an ISO top lifting frame, onto narrow gauge wagons.

The containers are securely locked to the wagons by means of the corner locating brackets and locking bars.

One track of the old narrow gauge main line between Northam and Wundowie has been retained for the iron ore traffic. The WAGR have arranged for the empty containers from Wundowie to be exchanged simultaneously with loaded containers at the Avon Yard.

At Wundowie, the container still mounted on its narrow gauge wagon is end tipped, and the ore is discharged through the flap doors at the end of the container.

The iron ore is railed a distance of 239 miles from Koolyanobbing and is reaching Wundowie at the rate of 100,000 tons per annum.

PORT TERMINAL AND ISO OPERATORS FREIGHT PTY. LTD.

Freightbases Pty Ltd
HEAD OFFICE:
Pangas House, 15/17 Hunter Street
Sydney NSW 2000
TELEPHONE: 28-2121
TELEX: 21369
OFFICIALS:
W. S. Bengtsson (*Chairman*)
H. B. Dean
R. D. Eabry
H. J. O'Regan
Sir J. P. Williams
R. D. Robin (*Directors*)
P. G. Morgan (*General Manager*)
SERVICES:
Container handling, storage, cleaning, repairs, packing, unpacking, leasing, cargo consolidation, distribution, transport.

All depots have HM Customs Staff and facilities:
BRANCHES:
Miller Road, Villawood, Sydney, NSW 2162
    Telephone: 728-1922
Appleton Dock Rd , Footscray, Melbourne, Victoria 3011
    Telephone: 68-6071
Cnr. Grand Trunkway and Eastern Parade, Port Adelaide, S A 5015
    Telephone: 4-1104
North Quay, Fremantle, WA 6160

The Melbourne Depot of Freightbases Pty. Ltd.

    Telephone: 5-4469
Kingsford Smith Drive, Hamilton, Brisbane,

QLD 4007
Telephone: 68-2511

OVERSEAS CONTAINERS AUSTRALIA PTY. LTD.

Overseas Containers Australia Pty., Limited,
38 Bridge Street, Sydney, NSW 2000
TELEPHONE: 2 0575
TELEX: 21258
BRANCHES:
Victoria:
446/452 Collins Street, Melbourne
South Australia:
C/- Elder Smith Goldsbrough Mort Limited,

Santo Parade, Port Adelaide
Queensland:
    C/- P & O Lines of Australia Pty. Ltd.,
    113 Eagle Street, Brisbane
Western Australia:
    C/- P & O Lines of Australia Pty. Ltd.
    21 Phillimore Street, Fremantle
Tasmania:
    C/- H. Jones & Co. Pty. Ltd.

23 Old Wharf, Hobart 3000
DIRECTORS:
R. W. Eaton (*Chairman and Managing Director*)
M. N. Speyer (*Deputy Chairman*)
A. S. Mayne, J. C. Jenkins, N. S. Heron (*Executive Directors*)

EXECUTIVES IN CHARGE OF CONTAINER OPERATIONS:

A. K. Wrench (*General Manager, Operations*)
J. W. Webster (*Operational Planning Manager*)

SERVICE:

A through, door-to-door transport service between Australia and the UK and between Australia and Japan. The Company controls the sea-leg of the journey and also land transport, by road or rail.

DEPOTS:

Collection and delivery can be made direct to exporters' or importers' premises. Depots are available where cargoes can be received and distributed. The Company provides for shippers who wish to use a full container and pack it themselves (FCL) plus a consolidation service at the receiving end and distribution service at the consignees' end for cargo which cannot fill a container (less than container loads/LCL's).

SEATAINER TERMINALS LTD.

Seatainer Terminals Ltd..
459 Little Collins Street, Melbourne 3000
TELEPHONE: 67 6294
TELEX: 30078
DIRECTORS:

A. C. Boehme (*Managing*)

BRANCHES:

Sydney, Melbourne, Adelaide, Fremantle

CONTAINER SERVICES:

Australia/United Kingdom
Australia/Interstate Trade
Australia/Japan

CONTAINER TERMINALS:

(1) White Bay, Sydney
   Telephone: 8271955
(2) Swanson Dock, Melbourne
   Telephone: 6891611

(3) North Wharf, Fremantle
   Telephone: 51091

CONTAINER PARK FACILITIES:

Terminals equipped with Portainer and Overhead cranes, to handle cellular container vessels in the Interstate and Overseas Trade. There are depots for break-bulk cargo and for packing containers for export.

SEATRANS PTY. LTD.

Seatrans Pty. Ltd
A consortium of:
George Wills & Co., Adelaide
John Sanderson & Co (Shipping) Pty Ltd,

Melbourne
Gilchrist Watt and Sanderson Pty Ltd, Sydney
Interocean Australia Services Pty Ltd

The company handles the cargoes of Messageries Maritimes, Hapag Lloyd, Lloyd Triestino and Holland Australia Lines at Australian Ports.

NEW ZEALAND
AUCKLAND

Auckland Harbour Board
P.O. Box 1259, Auckland, 1, New Zealand
TELEPHONE: 74610
TELEGRAMS: Haboard
OFFICIALS:

R. T. Lorimer (*General Manager*)
Captain R. Carter (*Harbour Master*)
V. A. C. Christiansen (*Secretary*)

CONTAINER AND ROLL-ON FACILITIES:

Fergusson Wharf Terminal

The Terminal provides 457·2 m (1,500 ft) of berthage with a water depth alongside of 12·19 m (40 ft) M.L.W.S.T.

Some 3·64 hectares (9 acres) of reclaimed land has been developed as the Terminal which is fully equipped with a 45-ton twinlift PACECO container crane, straddle carriers, large fork lifts, trailers and tractors for container handling.

A further 4·04 hectares (10 acres) of reclaimed land adjoining the berth and terminal is available for future expansion as container services develop.

A Container Base (break bulk depot) is operated in conjunction with the Terminal. Ample additional land is available.

Adequate access is provided to the Terminal from the mainline railway system and internal motorways.

The Terminal is operated on a common user basis and services to North America are provided by Farrell Lines, Columbus Lines and PACE Line.

Seacargo Roll-on Terminal

This facility is situated at Fergusson Wharf. It is capable of taking vessels 121·9 m (400 ft) in length, 20 m (65 ft) beam with a draught of 6·70 m (22 ft) and is equipped with an adjustable ramp.

An area of 1·6 hectares (4 acres) backing the berth is used for the assembly and handling of unitised cargo. Terminal operations are at present operated under licence by the Union Steamship Co. Ltd. who operate the following services:

Auckland/Lyttelton/Dunedin—weekly
Auckland/Lyttelton and return—weekly
Auckland/Wellington/Sydney—fortnightly

TERMINAL WORKING HOURS:

Ship cargo operations take place from 0730 to 1730 hours subject to extensions as required.

Inland transport operations take place from 0730 to 1700 hours.

STEVEDORING COMPANIES

Waitemata Stevedoring Co
PO Box 1291, Auckland
Auckland Stevedoring Co

Aukland—Fergusson Wharf with *Columbus New Zealand* alongside

PO Box 2962, Auckland
Leonard & Dingley Ltd
PO Box 1145, Auckland
Seatrans Consolidated N.Z. Ltd.
PO Box 3900, Auckland

PRINCIPAL FREIGHT FORWARDING COMPANIES

Union Steamship Co Ltd
PO Box 12, Auckland
Mogal Transportation
PO Box 1665, Auckland
Rudders Customs & Shipping N.Z. Ltd.,
PO Box 1742, Auckland
Service Haulage Ltd
PO Box 1549, Auckland
Freightways N.Z. Ltd
PO Box 12199, Auckland
Container Freights Ltd
PO Box 2057 Auckland
Service Haulage Ltd
PO Box 1549, Auckland
N.Z. Express Ltd
PO Box 15, Auckland
Service Haulage Ltd.
PO Box 1549, Auckland
Freight Ways N.Z. Ltd.
PO Box 12199, Penrose

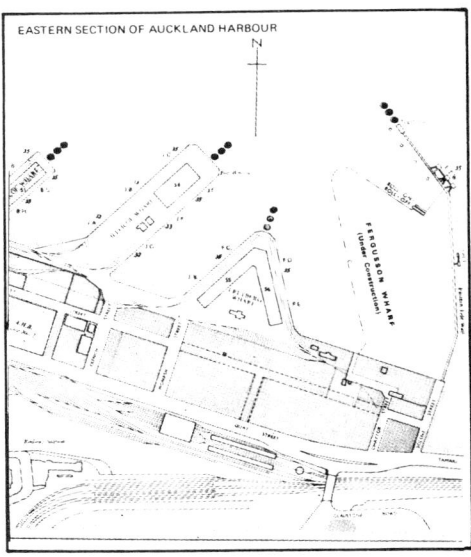

EASTERN SECTION OF AUCKLAND HARBOUR

N.Z. Express Co. (Auckland): Ltd.
PO Box 15, Auckland

Container Freights Ltd.
PO Box 2057, Auckland

CONTAINER REPAIR FACILITIES:
Facilities will be offered where required.

TERMINAL OPERATING HOURS:
At the roll-on/roll-off berth shiphandling operations take place between 0730 and 1830 hrs. These times can be extended as required.
Inland transport operations take place between 0730 and 1700 hrs.

TRAFFIC:

	Inwards (tons)	Outwards (tons)
1969	115,109	121,498
1970	178,630	167,135
1971 (Estimate)	233,000	194,000

The container terminal became operational in June 1971 and it was estimated that some 1,500 20 ft units would be handled in the remainder of the year.

LYTTELTON

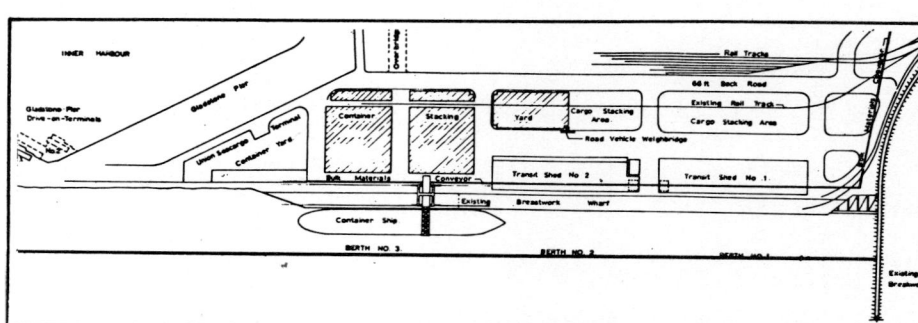

Lyttelton Harbour Board
PO Box 2108
Christchurch, NZ
TELEPHONE: 60079
PRINCIPAL OFFICIALS:
A. J. Sowden (*General Manager*)
J. B. Bushell (*Chief Engineer*)
D, Holden (*Harbour Master*)
ROLL-ON/ROLL-OFF FACILITIES:
There are two roll-on/roll-off facilities situated in the Inner Harbour. One of these is used for the steamer Express Inter-Island Service and the other for the coastal and Trans-Tasman Service; a third berth is under construction.
CONTAINER FACILITIES:
Cashin Quay Terminal
This facility, at present under construction, will adjoin two modern general cargo berths and will have a quay length of 282 m (925 ft). It will be equipped with a dual purpose bulk and container transporter crane and will have an area of 16·2 hectares (40 acres) available for storage.
TRAFFIC:
In 1970, roll-on traffic amounted to 349,473 tons inwards and 296,182 tons outwards. Estimates for 1971 are 350,000 tons inwards and 300,000 tons outwards.
TERMINAL WORKING HOURS:
Roll-on Terminals (Special Agreements)
0500-1700 plus supplementary hours to 2300 hrs. Seven day week as required. Inter-Island steamer Express Passenger/ cargo as and when required.
Inland Transport Operations
Normally 0700 to 1800 hrs but special services as required for roll-on operations.
CONTAINER REPAIRERS:
None.

Lyttelton

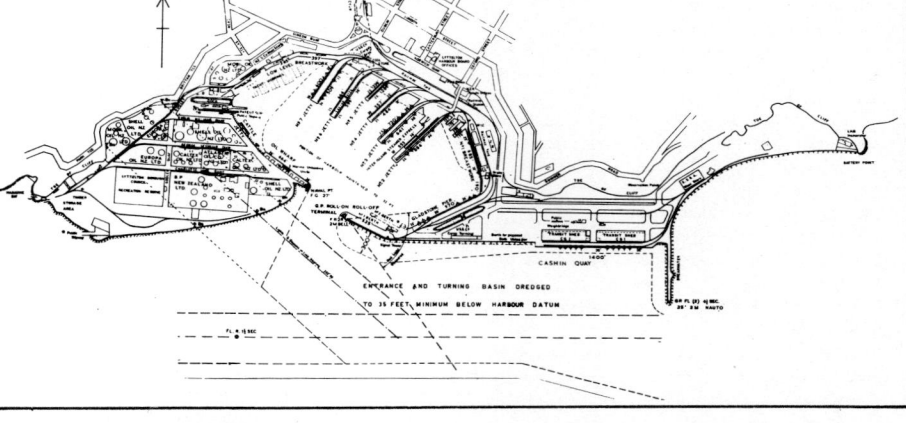

DUNEDIN

Otago Harbour Board,
PO Box 1, Dunedin
TELEPHONE: 77-881
TELEGRAMS: Koputai
OFFICIALS:
R. F. de Lautour (*General Manager*)
R. M. Davis (*Chief Engineer*)
P. M. Church (*Harbour Master*)
G. T. Gray (*Secretary*)
ROLL-ON/ROLL-OFF FACILITY:
Dunedin Ferry Terminal can accept vessels 146·3 m (480 ft) in length 20·73 m (68 ft) beam with a draught of 6·40 m (21 ft).

It is equipped with an automatically adjusting ramp and there are 2·83 hectares (7 acres) of parking space. An adjacent area with a potential for larger berths will provide a draught maximum of 7·92 m (26 ft) and 5·66 hectares (14 acres) of additional storage when required.
The facility is used by Union Steamship Co. which maintains a weekly service to Wellington and Auckland linked with fortnightly Trans-Tasman Services to Melbourne and Sydney and with frequent Lyttelton, Wellington and Auckland services. A further

service, possibly to Melbourne, Sydney and Lyttelton is under study. The vessels cater primarily for 'Sea Freighter' collapsible pallet units of about 13 tons weight and for all forms of vehicles and trailers. 20 ft containers can be lifted in limited numbers.
CONTAINER FACILITIES:
Beach Street Wharf:
The Authority have recently completed a wharf at Port Chalmers. The maximum draught of vessel which can be accepted at present is 10·06 m (33 ft) due to the depth of channel which is still being dredged.

The facility is used temporarily by Columbus Lines for their service to East Coast North American Ports. On completion of the George Street facility described below it will be used for the handling of forest products.

Future Plans:

The authority is progressing the development of a new container complex at George Street Wharf with two berths each 304·8 m (1,000 ft) in length with a back up area of 10·92 hectares (27 acres)

Land has been cleared for the storage of containers and reclamation for Phase 1 development started in 1970. This will provide a quay length of 304 m (1,000 ft) with a depth alongside of 12·19 m (40 ft). A container gantry crane is to be provided.

TERMINAL WORKING HOURS:

Ships working and inland cargo operations take place between 0700 and 2300 hrs.

TRAFFIC:

Roll-on:

In 1970 87,000 tons in 7,500 'seafreighter' units of 15 tons maximum gross weight moved inwards and 46,000 tons in 4,000 units moved outwards. In 1971 inwards cargo is expected to decrease by some 2,000 tons and outwards to increase to 75,000 tons.

Lift on:

This traffic is estimated at about 450 20 ft units inwards and 750 units outwards for the latter part of 1971.

PRINCIPAL CONTAINER FREIGHT FORWARDING COMPANIES:

Container Freights Ltd.
Private Bag, Dunedin
Telephone: 79-582

Mogal Transportation Ltd.
P.O. Box 45, Dunedin
Telephone: 79-582

Holymans Transport Pty. Ltd.
P.O. Box 46, Green Island, Otago
Telephone: 32-454

Cooltainer Services Ltd.
P.O. Box 950, Dunedin
Telephone: 79-856

Swiftrail N.Z. Ltd.
P.O. Box 706, Dunedin
Telephone: 79-001

Freightways N.Z. Ltd.
P.O. Box 582, Dunedin
Telephone: 76-130

Maritime Container Terminals (South Island) Ltd.
P.O. Box 1019, Dunedin
Telephone: Port Chalmers 8134

Alltrans Freight Ltd.
P.O. Box 1292, Dunedin
Telephone: 55189

CONTAINER REPAIR ORGANISATIONS:

Maritime Container Terminal (South Island) Ltd.
P.O. Box 1019 Dunedin

Otago Harbour—Dunedin Roll-on Terminal

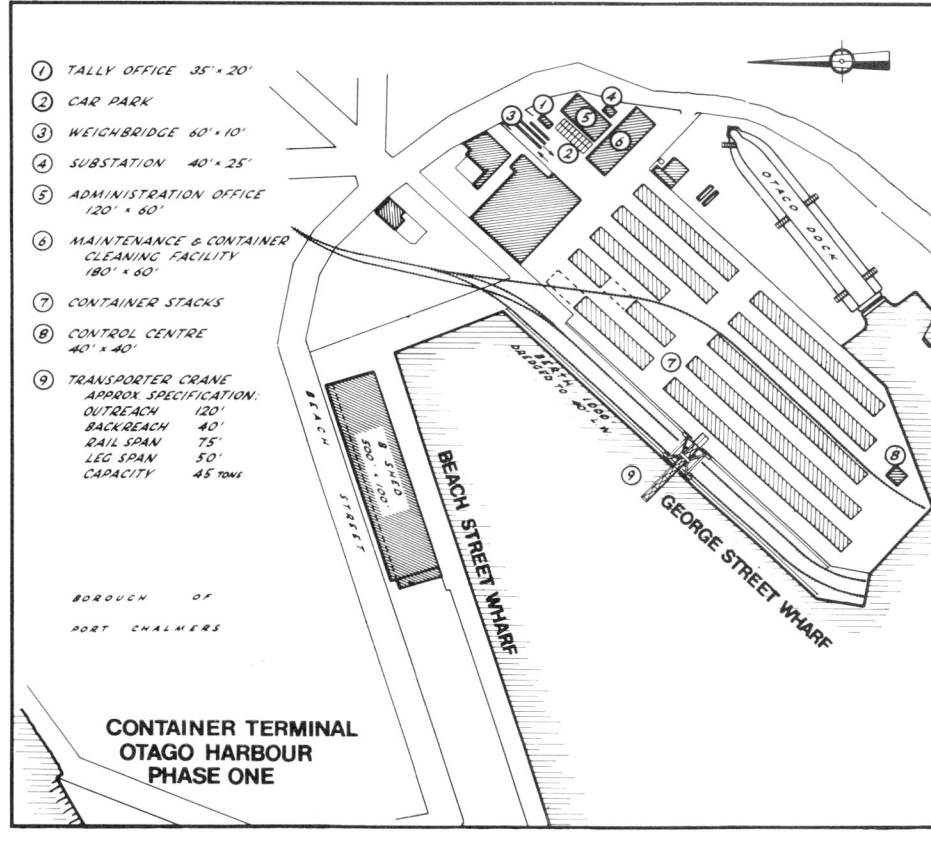

① TALLY OFFICE 35' × 20'
② CAR PARK
③ WEIGHBRIDGE 60' × 10'
④ SUBSTATION 40' × 25'
⑤ ADMINISTRATION OFFICE 120' × 60'
⑥ MAINTENANCE & CONTAINER CLEANING FACILITY 180' × 60'
⑦ CONTAINER STACKS
⑧ CONTROL CENTRE 40' × 40'
⑨ TRANSPORTER CRANE
  APPROX. SPECIFICATION:
  OUTREACH   120'
  BACKREACH   40'
  RAIL SPAN   75'
  LEG SPAN   50'
  CAPACITY   45 TONS

CONTAINER TERMINAL OTAGO HARBOUR PHASE ONE

Telephone: 77-515
USS Co. of N.Z. Ltd.

P.O. Box 650, Dunedin
Telephone: 77-201

WELLINGTON

Wellington Harbour Board

PO Box 893, Wellington, New Zealand

TELEPHONE: 59-820

CABLES: Harbord, Wellington

OFFICIALS:

R. R. Reeves (*General Manager*)

G. E. Fisher (*Secretary*)

J. F. Stewart (*Assistant General Manager*)

C. R. Thompson (*Assistant to General Manager, Traffic*)

R. G. Powell (*Treasurer*)

K. L. Woolston (*Chief Accountant*)

K. S. Renner (*Chief Engineer*)

N. K. Sanders (*Traffic Manager and Chief Wharfinger*)

Captain D. W. Galloway (*Harbour Master and Chief Pilot*)

Wellington—Rail Road Terminal

CONTAINER FACILITIES:

Thorndon Terminal:

This facility has a quay length of 579·2 m (1,900 ft) and a width of 25·6 m (84 ft) with a depth of water alongside of 12·2 m (40 ft). It has been provided with a 45 ton Stothert & Pitt container gantry crane with an outreach of 35·05 m (115 ft) over water and 10·67 m (35 ft) on the landside. The crane will be operated by the Harbour Board and will serve the two 289·6 m (950 ft) Berths.

No. 1 Berth. This is due for completion in 1973 and has a total area of 9·71 hectares (24 acres).

No. 2 Berth. Operational since June 1971 this facility will be completed in 1972. There is a total area of 3·64 hectares (9 acres) and there is a container freight station with an area of 3,066 m² (33,000 ft²) adjacent. The berth is used by Columbus Line and Farrell Lines for their services to East Coast USA and it is operated on their behalf by:

Maritime Container Terminals Ltd.

P.O. Box 478, Wellington

Rail Terminal

New Zealand Railways are providing a rail terminal equipped with a 35 ton container yard gantry crane.

ROLL-ON FACILITIES:

General:

All roll-on berths are provided with stern loading ramps.

Taranaki St. Terminal: Capable of accepting vessels up to 152·4 m (500 ft) in length with a draught of 7·9 m (26 ft) this berth has 1·82 hectares (4½ acres) of parking space. There is a transit shed 36·5 × 91·4 m (120 × 300 ft) in size and a further 1·6 hectares (4 acres) of parking space is available adjacent to the berth. The berth is equipped with a stern loading link span ramp a special feature of which is a series of independently hinged sections enabling the road way width to be varied up to 6·09 m (20 ft). The ramp is 25·3 m (83 ft) long including the link span 7·01 m (23 ft).

Inter-Island Terminal: Designed for vessels up to 121·9 m (400 ft) in length with a draught of 7·9 m (26 ft) this berth has a stern bridge ramp with a 3·65 m (12 ft) carriageway and a length of 17·37 m (57 ft). There is a parking area of 4,735 m² (1·17 acres).

Rail/Road Ferry Terminal: Vessels of 103·6 m (340 ft) length 18·6 m (61 ft) beam use this specialised terminal which has 1 hectare (2½ acres) of space which includes a rail marshalling area.

Under construction is an additional Rail/Road Ferry Berth which will come into service in January 1972. It will be capable of accepting vessels 109·7 m (360 ft) in length 18·6 m (61 ft) in beam and drawing 9·14 m (30 ft). An adjacent marshalling area which will include 2·4 hectares (6 acres) for marshalling rail wagons.

The terminal is owned and operated by New Zealand Railways.

CONTAINER FREIGHT FORWARDING COMPANIES

Allied Freightways Ltd.,
 PO Box 3026, Wellington
 Telephone: 41-771

Associated Container Transportation (N.Z.) Ltd.,
 PO Box 192, Wellington
 Telex: NZ3468

Container Freights Ltd.,
 PO Box 1309, Wellington
 Telex: 3598

Associated Container Transportation (NZ) Ltd.
 P.O. Box 192, Wellington
 Telex: N.Z. 3468

Cooltainer Services Ltd.,
 C/- R. Underwoods Ltd.,
 PO Box 161, Wellington

Wellington—Thorndon Container Terminal in June 1971, The Rail Road Terminal can be seen at the top right of the picture

Wellington—Taranaki Street Terminal

Wellington—Inter-Island Terminal

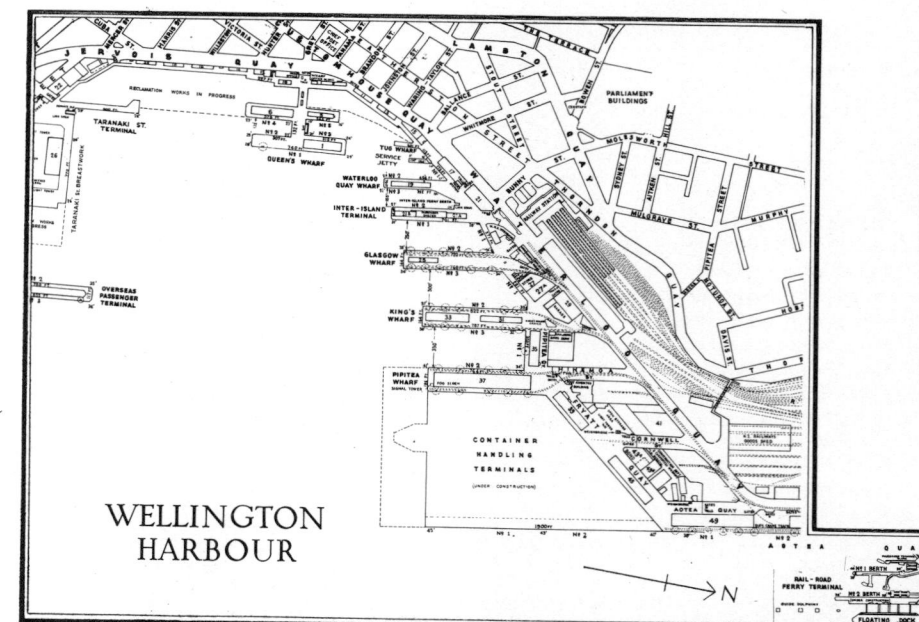

WELLINGTON HARBOUR

Telephone: 40-196/7
Freight Ways (N.Z.) Ltd.,
PO Box 3613, Wellington
Telephone: 42-611
Mogal Transportation Ltd.,
PO Box 89, Wellington
Telephone: 552-097/98
Swiftrail (N.Z.) Limited,
PO Box 3596, Wellington
Telex: 3581
CONTAINER SERVICING FACILITIES:
Fruehauf International Ltd.—Agent in New
Zealand,
Donnett Truck & Trailer Co. Ltd.,
PO Box 86, Fielding
CONTAINER STEVEDORE COMPANIES:
Gannaway & Co. Ltd.,
PO Box 245, Wellington
Telephone: 41-285
New Zealand Stevedoring and Wharfing Co.
Ltd.,
PO Box 1817, Wellington
Telephone: 51-114
Seatrans Consolidated (N.Z.) Ltd.,
PO Box 3596, Wellington
Telephone: 44-054
Union Steamship Co. of N.Z. Ltd.
PO Box 1799, Wellington
Telephone: 59-876
Wellington Stevedoring Co. Ltd.
PO Box 2861, Wellington
Telephone: 70-244
Geo. H. Scales (Pacific) Ltd.,
PO Box 1392, Wellington
Telephone: 50-035

ROLL-ON SERVICES:

Company	Berth	Ships	Service
N.Z. Railways	Rail/Road Ferry	Two with two being built	Wellington/Picton, 21 sailings per week
Union Steamship Co. of N.Z. Ltd.	Inter-Island Terminal	One with a second being built	Wellington/Lyttelton, 5 sailings per week
Holm & Co. Ltd.	Inter-Island Terminal	One	Wellington/Lyttelton 3 sailings per week
Union Steamship Co. of N.Z. Ltd.	Taranaki Street Terminal	One	Wellington/Sydney fortnightly
Union Steamship Co. of N.Z. Ltd.	Taranaki Street Terminal	One	Wellington/Melbourne fortnightly
Union Steamship Co. of N.Z. Ltd.	Taranaki Street Terminal	One*	Auckland/Wellington/ Lyttelton, weekly
Union Steamship Co. of N.Z. Ltd.	Taranaki Street Terminal	One*	Auckland/Wellington Dunedin/Wellington twice weekly (Wellington)

*(A third roll-on ship for the N.Z. East Coast service is planned for the Union Steam Ship Co. of N.Z. Ltd.)

ROLL-ON/ROLL-OFF TRAFFIC

	Traffic Inwards	Traffic Outwards
1969	738,733 tons	828, 438 tons
1970	815,372 tons	898,912 tons
1971*	870,000 tons	960,000 tons

*Estimate

CUSTOMS REQUIREMENTS

Proposed Customs procedures for containerised cargo at New Zealand ports—Issued by H.M. Customs, Head Office, Wellington, New Zealand in 1968

1. Introduction

1. The procedures set out are those which Customs feel will best meet all situations likely to arise in the container field and, at the same time, ensure:

(a) That the Department is geared to give an effective and efficient service should there be any substantial increase in the volume of container cargo entering and leaving New Zealand.

(b) That the Department's responsibility to observe and administer the laws of the country is not compromised.

PROCEDURES APPLY TO CARGOES TRANSPORTED BY SEA AND BY AIR

2. Emphasis throughout is on cargo transported by sea; but the proposals will apply in principle to air cargo also. However, we envisage that Customs Containerbases for such cargo would be located at airports.

PROCEDURES ARE SUBJECT TO THE REQUIREMENTS OF OTHER AGENCIES

3. The procedures oulined will be subject to the requirements of other Government agencies relating to the removal of goods from ship or wharf.

PROCEDURES ARE IN DRAFT FORM ONLY

4. The procedures are in draft form only at this stage. They may be varied or amended in the light of comments and suggestions received from interested parties.

CHANGED PROCEDURES DESCRIBED IN DETAIL

5. Proposals which differ in any marked degree from present procedures are described in detail. We have not felt it necessary to give similar treatment to those procedures which remain substantially unchanged.

CHANGES IN LEGISLATION

6. Last year, legislative changes were made to permit the free movement of containers into and out of the country with a minimum of Customs formalities.

7. Further changes in legislation will have to be made before some of the procedures proposed here can be implemented. The necessary amendments have been drafted; but no further action will be taken until all comments received have been studied.

CO-OPERATION BETWEEN AGENCIES

8. In individual approaches, we have had the fullest co-operation from interested parties. We feel, however, that there is room for a greater degree of consultation and co-operation between the various Government agencies, public bodies, and public and private interests who will be affected by the movement and facilitations of maritime traffic in the container field.

9. To this end, Customs have already advocated the establishment in New Zealand of a permanent Maritime Facilitation Committee to deal with the continuing implications of containerisation and administrative matters related to maritime traffic and procedures. Our views on this subject have been made known to the Transport Commission.

2. Terms and Abbreviations

12. The explanations given of terms and abbreviations used are intended only for the reader's guidance. They do not purport to be strict definitions in the legal sense.

DEFINITION OF 'CONTAINER'

13. The definition of 'container' set out below conforms to that contained in Article I of the Customs Convention of Containers of 18 May 1956.

14. The term 'Container' means an article of transport equipment (lift van, moveable tank or other structure):

(a) Of a permanent character and accordingly strong enough for repeated use;

(b) Specially designed to facilitate the carriage of goods by one or more modes of transport, without immediate reloading;

(c) Fitted with devices permitting its ready handling, particularly its transfer from one mode of transport to another;

(d) So designed as to be easy to fill and empty;

(e) Having an internal volume of one cubic metre (35·3 cu. ft) or more.

15. The normal accessories and equipment of the container, when imported with the container, are included under the definition; vehicles and conventional packing are NOT.

'G' OR GROUPAGE CONTAINERS:

16. 'G' or Groupage Containers are those which contain more than one consignment belonging to more than one shipper, having been consolidated and packed at a depot. They are sometimes known as 'mixed' containers or a 'multiple consignment'.

'F' OR FULL CONTAINERS

17. 'F' or Full Containers are those which contain only one consignment from one shipper. They are usually packed at private premises and may be delivered to the consignee on a door-to-door basis. They are often referred to as a 'Single Consignment'.

BILL OF LADING

18. A Bill of Lading is a negotiable transport document of title to the goods, made out to a named person, to order, or to bearer, signed by the carrier and handed to the sender after acceptance of the goods.

HOUSE BILL OF LADING

19. A House Bill of Lading is a document issued by a forwarding agent to the shippers of the various consignments consolidated in a

'G' container.

SHIP'S MANIFEST

20. A Ship's Manifest is a descriptive list of the goods making up a vessel's cargo and including, in particular, the details needed for Customs purposes.

EXAMINING PLACE

21. An Examining Place is a place appointed by the Customs for the examination of goods under Customs control.

CUSTOMS CONTAINERBASE

22. A Customs Containerbase is a common-user complex for storing, breaking-down and/or consolidating containerised cargoes. It includes accommodation for Customs officers and facilities and equipment for examining, weighing, fumigating, disinfecting, and destroying goods.

23. Requirements for containerbases are dealt with more fully in Section 4.

C.C.C.

24. 'C.C.C.' is an abbreviation for Customs Co-operation Council, an international body whose membership comprises various Customs administrations throughout the world.

25. The Secretariat of the C.C.C. is made up of Customs experts drawn from the membership.

26. New Zealand is a member country of C.C.C.

3. Containers

27. This section is concerned ONLY with containers. It does not deal in any way with the goods carried in them.

DEFINITION OF 'CONTAINER'

28. For the definition of 'Container' refer to paragraphs 13-17.

TYPE APPROVAL

29. It is unlikely that Customs will require containers to be of approved types. We would however, suggest that containers manufactured in New Zealand for international use be made to such a standard that they provide adequate security against pillage or the insertion of unmanifested goods.

REGISTRATION AND MARKING

30. Containers will not need to be registered with the Department. However, for control and accounting purposes, owners will be required to:

(a) Allocate permanent identification numbers to them.

(b) Mark each container with: its identification number; the name or mark of its owner; its nationality.

(c) Keep and maintain records of the containers to the satisfaction of the Collector of Customs.

31. The C.C.C. will be recommending a standard place for marks to be shown by containers.

32. Customs will not require details of size, weight or type to be shown on containers; but these details may be required by other Authorities.

NATIONALITY

33. The nationality of containers will have to be established and will be a determining factor in the granting of facilities for use and free circulation.

34. So far as nationality is concerned, containers will fall into one or other categories:

(a) New Zealand.

(b) Foreign.

CONTAINERS OF N.Z. NATIONALITY

35. To qualify for New Zealand nationality a container must either:

(a) Have been manufactured in New Zealand for use internationally by a New Zealand based operator; or

(b) Have been imported from overseas for use by a New Zealand based operator in internal trade and have paid all duty and taxes at the time of the original importation.

36. Containers of N.Z. nationality may be imported without documentation, and there

will be no restriction on their free circulation in New Zealand.

CONTAINERS OF FOREIGN NATIONALITY

37. Foreign containers are those which do not qualify for New Zealand nationality.

Temporary Importation of Foreign Containers

38. Provision has already been made for the temporary importation of foreign containers into New Zealand:

(a) Without the need for an import licence.

(b) Free of duty: under Tariff item 86.08.01 for containers; under 87.14.13 for wagons, trolleys, etc.

39. Certain conditions must be complied with before the above provisions can apply. These are set out below.

Covenant required

40. New Zealand owners or operators of foreign containers will be required to enter into a covenant with the Collector of Customs.

41. The covenant will be a permanent or standing one—i.e. a separate covenant will not be required of each shipment.

42. Under the covenant, the owner or operator will undertake to keep a record of his containers and to pay duty and taxes if:

(a) A container is not exported within three months of the date of its importation.

(b) A container is used in the domestic carriage of goods in New Zealand OTHER-WISE THAN:

(i) In the case of journeys which are extensions of the journey or importation or exportation—i.e. on importation: from the importing vessel to the consignee; on exportation: from consignor to exporting vessel.

(ii) *Once* in internal traffic in circumstances where it would otherwise move empty—e.g., in a 'positioning' journey from a point where it was unloaded to the point where it is to be packed for export.

(c) A container is sold or otherwise disposed of in New Zealand.

(d) A container is not accounted for to the satisfaction of the Collector of Customs following inspection of the container record.

Container Record

43. Under the covenant, the owner or operator of the containers will be required to keep a container record. (He will probably have to do this for his own purposes anyway.)

44. We do not propose to prescribe any particular form of record as we appreciate that systems used by operators will vary. However, the form of record kept must meet with the approval of the Collector and show this information for each container:

Container number:

Imported: Date; vessel; port

Exported: Date; vessel; port

Disposal otherwise than by export

Details of any inland journey or use other than the journey of importation or exportation.

45. The container record must be available at all times for inspection by the Collector.

No Entry Form Required

46. No form of entry will be required for the temporary importation of foreign containers.

'IN TRANSIT' CONTAINERS

47. International agreement has not yet been reached on a standard form of treatment for containers entering one country in the course of transhipment to another country. It is possible that a form of carnet will be adopted by most countries. If it is, New Zealand will do the same.

48. In the meantime, normal transhipment procedures will apply to containers landed in New Zealand for removal to other vessels for export.

EXPORT OF CONTAINERS

49. No form of export entry will be required for containers exported. Customs will maintain control through the container records

kept by the owner or operator.

SEALING OF CONTAINERS

50. It is the practice in some countries for containers to be sealed by the Customs prior to export. We don't propose to adopt this practice unless special circumstances arise.

51. The Department will not require containers coming into New Zealand to be 'Customs' sealed in the country of export. Nor, unless unusual circumstances arise, will it require sealing of containers moving internally under bond.

ACCESSORIES AND SPARE PARTS FOR CONTAINERS

52. Accessories permanently mounted on the container are regarded as part of the container and will be treated as such.

53. Parts and accessories imported with the container, not permanently attached, but to be used exclusively with the container and exported with it, will also receive the same treatment as the container.

54. Various methods for dealing with spare parts used in the repair of containers in New Zealand have been considered. The following has been adopted:

(a) Spare parts imported specifically for the repair of foreign containers must be warehoused.

(b) The incorporation of any such spares into a foreign container will be regarded as evidence of export and the goods may be cleared from warehouses, free of duty, on an export ex warehouse entry.

55. If a container is repaired with duty paid materials (i.e., other than those held in warehouse), no drawback of duty will be allowable. However, refund of any sales tax paid will be allowed under the provisions of Regulation 26 of the Sales Tax Regulations 1933.

4. Customs containerbases

56. This section deals in general terms with the establishment and operation of what we propose to call 'Customs Containerbases'.

DEFINITION OF 'CUSTOMS CONTAINERBASE'

57. The definition of 'Customs Containerbase' is set out in paragraph 22. In brief, it is a common-user complex for storing, breaking-down, and/or consolidating containers.

THE NEED FOR CONTAINERBASES

58. In many countries, normal wharf facilities have proved inadequate where any volume of containerised cargo has to be handled. The same position could well apply in New Zealand; and the position as we see it can be illustrated by:

(a) Outlining the essential elements of the process for dealing with conventional cargo; and then

(b) Considering the physical nature of containerised cargo.

PROCEDURE FOR CONVENTIONAL CARGO

59. The procedure followed in the processing of conventional cargo is, briefly, this:

(a) The importing ship, acting in accordance with Customs authority, discharges its cargo on to the wharf for storage in transit sheds pending delivery to the importer.

(b) Delivery is given to the importer only after Customs are satisfied that the requirements of the law have been met—i.e., that duty has been paid, import licences have been presented, and the goods are not otherwise subject to prohibition or restriction.

(c) Most cargo is contained in individual packages consigned to one importer and of a size and weight which enables them to be handled manually; each package has an individual marking which enables it to be identified with the ship's manifest, the Customs entry, and the supplier's invoice and other documents; the goods in each package are usually of a like kind.

(d) Each ship's cargo is systematically stored in wharf sheds where it can be readily located by the various people who might require access to it—e.g., Customs, Agriculture and Forestry officers; Harbour Board employees; Customs Agents; carriers; importers.

PHYSICAL NATURE OF CONTAINERISED CARGO

60. Because of its physical nature, a different set of circumstances has to be met in the case of containerised cargo. Such factors as the following must be taken into account:

(a) The standard sized container measuring 20 ft × 8 ft × 8 ft is itself the equivalent of a small ship. It can't be manhandled or stored in confined areas in any numbers.

(b) Some containers may hold may packages of goods of different kinds, consigned to various importers in scattered locations.

(c) The packages within a container can be identified only after the container has been opened.

(d) Part only of the packages in a container may qualify for immediate release from Customs control; the balance may have to be held for one or more of a variety of reasons. Provision must, therefore, be made to allow delivery of goods which qualify for immediate release without weakening Customs control over those which must be held.

(e) Each container is itself a valuable article. It would not normally be owned by the importer, and could be required urgently to receive goods for export.

61. The above factors and the problems they present demand that the traditional methods of dealing with cargo be modified to meet the needs of containerised cargo.

62. We believe that the solution to the problem lies in the establishment of Customs Containerbases. Indeed, we think they are an essential requirement for dealing with any volume of containerised cargo.

PROPOSALS FOR ESTABLISHMENT OF CUSTOMS CONTAINERBASES:

63. We will be recommending an amendment to the legislation

(a) Providing for the appointment of Customs Containerbases subject to such *conditions* as may be prescribed and to such *security* as may be required.

(b) Prescribing the duties and responsibilities of the owners and operators of such bases.

64. Because of the capital outlay which could be involved, we envisage that containerbase would be operated by public bodies or by consortiums. In the public interest, it appears desirable that they should be accessible to all who require such facilities and who are prepared to meet the proper charges imposed by the owner or operator.

65. In our view, it is essential for reasons of efficiency, economy, control and administration that the number of containerbases in any port be kept to a minimum. This will be the Department's policy in approving the establishment of bases. It is in line with the practice followed in other countries—for example, we understand that there are only seven containerbases in the whole of the United Kingdom to cope with a substantial volume of containerised cargo.

66. We also see advantages in the bases being sited as near as possible to the point of discharge of the container, whether received direct from overseas or on transhipment from the original port of entry. In the case of air cargo, the bases would be located at the airports.

USE OF CONTAINERBASES

67. When a containerbase has been duly appointed under the Customs Act, the Customs procedures set out below will apply to its use and operation.

Removal of Containers from Ship to Containerbase

68. The owner or operator of the containerbase will receive from Customs a formal authority to uplift containers (and their contents) from ship or wharf and transport them to the approved containerbase.

69. This authority will be in the form of a 'Collector's Permit'. It will be a standing or continuing authority—i.e. no form of Customs entry and no specific Customs release in respect of individual containers will be required.

Goods Remain Subject to Customs Control

70. The contents of the container will be stored under Customs control in the containerbase and may be removed therefrom only with specific Customs authority (normally in the form of the usual Customs delivery order given after entry formalities have been completed).

71. The owner or operator will be responsible for the custody and security of all goods in his containerbase and will be required to account for all goods he receives.

'G' and 'F' Containers

72. For the definitions of 'G' and 'F' Containers refer to paragraphs 16 and 17.

73. While it will be necessary for all 'G' containers (multiple consignments) to be dealt with in Customs containerbases, we envisage that few 'F' containers (single consignment) will need to enter such bases.

74. Provision will be made for 'F' containers to be uplifted by the consignee direct from the ship's side—provided Customs clearance has been obtained. (The Collector's Permit will operate ONLY to allow removal of containers to Customs containerbases.)

Transhipment of Goods from Customs Containerbase

75. The Department will be proposing amendments to the Customs Act to provide for under bond transhipment of goods from Customs containerbases.

Repacking of Goods in Customs Containerbase

76. Amendments to the legislation will also be proposed to enable goods to be repacked from one container to another in a Customs containerbase for under bond transhipment.

INTERIM ARRANGEMENTS UNTIL CONTAINERBASES ARE ESTABLISHED

77. The establishment of Customs containerbases represents a major undertaking and, until they are constructed, it will be necessary for interim arrangements to be made for handling containerised cargo already arriving at our ports.

78. The Department's policy is that, in the interests of economy and efficiency, existing Customs examining places and wharf transit sheds should be used where they are available and suitable. In the main, they already have the basic facilities and equipment to cope with the present volume of containerised cargo.

79. Where existing examining places or wharf transit sheds are not available or are unsuitable—but only in such circumstances—the Department will consider the appointment of other examining places. However, any such appointments will be on a temporary basis only and will be revoked if Customs containerbases are established.

80. Because of the temporary nature of such appointments, the Department will consider application only in respect of already existing buildings or premises.

81. Collectors of Customs have been advised of the Department's policy in this regard. Applications for the appointment of examining places should be made to the Collector of Customs at the appropriate port.

5. Imports

82. It will be clear from Section 4 which deals with Customs Containerbases that amendments to existing procedures must occur if full advantage is to be taken of this new concept in transport. A careful study of procedures has revealed the encouraging fact that the necessary changes:

(a) Are neither extensive nor complex.

(b) Should not involve increased administrative costs of any substance either to importer or Department.

CHANGES PROPOSED

83. The changes proposed are listed below under appropriate headings. A basic and fundamental change from present procedures will speed the removal of containers and their contents from ship's side or wharf—because:

(a) Import entries will not be required for the containers themselves (paragraph 46)

(b) Provision is being made for containers to be uplifted from ship's side or wharf for removal to a Customs containerbase without, in effect, any formalities at all so far are concerned (paragraphs 69-68).

DOCUMENTATION

84. There will be no essential change in the documents required to clear goods through the Customs. The main documents are:

(a) Manifests.

(b) Invoices and related documents.

(c) Customs entries.

Manifests

85. For the definition of 'Ship's Manifest' refer to paragraph 20.

86. Ships' inwards manifests must continue to list all the cargo carried—i.e., each individual package, whether carried in a container or otherwise, must be listed.

87. The form in which the packages are listed may, however, be varied from that used at present. Provided container contents lists or manifests are attached to the ship's manifest, the latter need show only:

(a) Ports of destination.

(b) Identification marks and numbers of each container carried.

(c) The consignee's name in each case.

88. The following provisions will apply to container lists or manifests:

(a) They must show the marks and numbers of the packages in the container and a description of the goods in each package.

(b) A copy of the container manifest must be attached to the ship's manifest.

(c) A second copy of the container manifest should be attached to the container concerned. (This would enable quicker location of goods requiring Customs or other examination and be of assistance to all parties having a legitimate interest in the contents of particular containers.)

Invoices and Associated Documents

89. Marks and numbers of packages and containers must be shown on invoices and associated documents in accordance with these rules:

(a) *All* invoices, etc, must show the identifying marks and numbers of the individual packages to which they relate.

(b) The container number and identifying mark must also be shown on invoices in the case of single consignment shipments ('F' containers).

(c) The container number need not be shown on invoices in the case of multiple consignment shipments ('G' containers)—because the supplier of the goods will rarely know it when he prepares his invoice.

Customs Entries

90. Container numbers must be shown on Customs entries in *all* cases before delivery of goods from Customs control. Space for this will be provided on entry forms.

91. This should present no problems in the case of 'F' containers (single consignment). In these cases, the container number will usually be shown on the invoice from which the entry is compiled.

92. In the case of 'G' containers (multiple consignment), the importer may not know the container number at the time he prepares his entry. However, he should know it by the time duty is paid—i.e. when the entry is passed in the Long Room. He may then give

the information to the cashier for endorsement on the entry before the delivery order is uplifted.

EARLY LODGMENT OF ENTRIES

93. It cannot be emphasised too strongly that importers will gain the full benefits and advantages of containerisation only if documents are available in advance of the ship's arrival. This applies particularly to importers at the first port of call.

94. There is generally no reason why the Customs invoice can't be prepared and sent in advance of the despatch of the goods. All importers should seek the co-operation of their suppliers in this regard.

95. If this document alone were despatched early it would enable importers to prepare and, in most cases, lodge their entries with the Customs well in advance of the importing vessel's arrival—and thereby help both themselves and the Department.

96. A recent survey conducted by the Department showed that:
(a) 40% of entries were lodged with Customs five days or more before the arrival of the vessel at the port concerned.
(b) 20% were lodged less than 5 days before the vessel's arrival.
(c) 40% were lodged *after* the arrival of the vessel.

97. This situation must be improved if delays in clearing goods are to be avoided. The remedy lies in importers' hands—they should make maximum use of the Department's pre-check service.

PRE-PAYMENT OF DUTY

98. We have considered a proposition to allow duty to be paid before the importing ship arrives in New Zealand. (At present the ship must be in New Zealand waters before duty may be paid.)

99. There appears to be little interest in this proposition and we have decided not to proceed further with it in the meantime.

EXAMINATION OF GOODS

100. Where examination of goods is required this may be done, at Customs discretion, in a Customs Containerbase, an approved Examining place, or at the importer's premises.

101. In exercising this discretion, Collectors of Customs will take into account such considerations as: the type of shipment ('G' or 'F' container); the nature of the goods; the reputation of the importer; the convenience of the examination locale; and the availability of examination staff.

6. Exports

102. In the export field, changes in Customs procedures required to cope with containerised cargo will be neither extensive nor expensive.

PACKING FOR EXPORT

103. We envisage that much of the packing for export of 'G' containers (multiple consignments) will be done in Customs Containerbases.

104. Customs will NOT, however, require goods for export in containers to be packed in Customs Containerbases and stored there

while awaiting shipment.

105. In short, containers for export may be packed anywhere so far as Customs are concerned.

PROCEDURES FOR EXPORT:

106. The procedures which we propose for goods exported in containers vary according to whether the container is a 'G' type (multiple consignment) or 'F' type (single consignment)

Multiple Consignment Procedure ('G' Containers):

107. The procedure for the export of multiple consignments in 'G' containers will be:
(a) The EXPORTER will:—
Send his goods to the container consolidator.
Receive from the consolidator his 'house bill of lading' (see Chapter 2, paragraph 19 for definition).
Present export entry and house bill of lading to Customs.
Receive back from Customs stamped export entry and stamped house bill if export is approved by Customs.
Hand stamped export entry and house bill to consolidator.
(b) The CONSOLIDATOR will then:—
Pack goods into container.
Prepare ship's bill of lading.
Enter ship's name on export entry.
Present ship's bill of lading, relevant export entries and house bills to Customs.
Receive back from Customs stamped ship's bill of lading and house bills (Customs will retain the export entry) Present both sets of bills to shipping company.
(c) The SHIPPING COMPANY will accept only bills of lading which have been stamped by Customs.

108. This departure from current practice is designed to:—
(a) Ensure that the Customs approval is obtained before the goods are packed in container for export.
(b) Permit the ship's bill of lading to show a minimum of information—simply, details of the container.
(c) Ensure that the name of the exporting vessel appears on the export entry.

Single Consignment Procedure ('F' Containers)

109. Present export procedures will apply to the export of single consignments in 'F' containers. The exporter will present his shipping company bill of lading and export entry to Customs in the normal way.

110. The contents of each container will need to be described on the ship's documents—either on the ship's bill of lading or on an attached container manifest. Shipping company requirements will dictate where and how these details are to be shown.

Container Numbers on Export Entries:

111. Container numbers will not have to be shown on export entries EXCEPT in the case of:—

(a) Goods exported under Drawback.
(b) Goods exported ex Warehouse.

APPROVAL FOR EXPORT

112. For both classes of shipment ('G' and 'F'), the onus for obtaining Customs approval for the export of the goods remains with the exporter. The consolidator and the shipping company have responsibilities too:
(a) The consolidator must not pack goods until he has evidence that Customs approval has been given. He is also responsible for making the final presentation of shipping documents and export entries to the Customs.
(b) The shipping company must check that export has been approved by Customs.

EXPORT MANIFESTS

113. The provisions which apply to import manifests apply in all respects to export manifests. For details refer to paragraphs 84-87.

DRAWBACK PROCEDURE

114. The foregoing rules will apply to exports under drawback.

Examination for Drawback

115. Where drawback is involved, the goods are examined by Customs. As at present, the exporter will be responsible for arranging with Customs for all such examinations.

116. 'F' class shipments will normally be examined at the exporter's premises; 'G' class at the consolidator's depot. However, provision will also be made for examination of 'G' class shipments at the exporter's premises where this is necessary.

Documentation for Drawback

117. The normal documentation will apply to drawbacks except in the case of 'G' class shipments. Here the position will be:—
(a) One copy only of the new combined export/drawback entry form will be returned by Customs to the exporter for presentation to the consolidator with the stamped 'house bill of lading'.
(b) The consolidator will give the certificate of shipment on this entry when the goods have been packed into the container and the container is secured. This certified copy of the entry will be presented to Customs at the time the ship's bill of lading is presented.

Payment of Drawback

118. At present, payment of drawback may be allowed when the Collector is satisfied that the goods have been shipped for export.

119. This provision will still apply; but we are going to propose an amendment to the legislation to allow payment of drawback when the goods have been secured in the exporting container *in a Customs Containerbase.*

120. It must be noted that the proposed new provision will apply only to drawback goods packed in a Customs Containerbase. For containers packed elsewhere, drawback will be allowed only when the goods have been shipped for export.

NEW ZEALAND RAILWAYS

New Zealand Railways
Bunny Street, Wellington
POSTAL ADDRESS: Private Bag, Wellington 1
TELEGRAMS: Railhead
GENERAL MANAGER: I. Thomas

GENERAL:
The New Zealand Railways Department operates a container and cargo system in conjunction with its air link between the North and South Island rail systems. (The

actual aircraft operation is undertaken by a private firm, Safe Air Ltd, under contract to the Department). A stock of 175 containers 7 ft 4 in long by 6 ft 4 in wide by 6 ft high and with a capacity of 230 cubic feet is available for use on this service. These containers are also used for other purposes, e.g. Household removals either inter-island or within the one island. The Department also owns two British Rail type 20 ft × 8 ft × 8 ft containers and two British Rail type tilt containers of similar measurements. These four containers are being used for experimental purposes. Rail facilities are being geared to handle all containers within I.S.O. specifications including refrigerated and insulated containers.

These containers, when loaded on normal flat deck wagons, can travel throughout the New Zealand railway system except on the short Johnsonville line (a line in the Wellington Suburban Area, North Island) and through the Manawatu Gorge (between Ashhurst and Woodville, North Island). Special bogie well-wagons have been constructed to permit ISO containers to be transported over these restricted lines. A number of wagons equipped with small diameter wheels are to be built to enable 20 ft × 8 ft × 8·5 ft containers to be carried.

In addition to operating an air link between

New Zealand Two ISO 20 ft containers on "UR" class wagon.

the two islands the Department also operates two roll-on roll-off ferry vessels between Wellington in the North Island and Picton in the South Island. A third vessel for this service is at present building. This sea service facilitates the movement of containers between the two islands.

TRAFFIC:

During the year ended 31 March 1970 the

Department transported over 31,600 10 ft × 8 ft × 8 ft containers forwarded internally by freight consolidators. These containers are loaded four to a wagon.

Some 4,085 loaded movements were made during the year with the Department's rail/air containers whilst a considerable number of all types of containers were conveyed to and from overseas vessels.

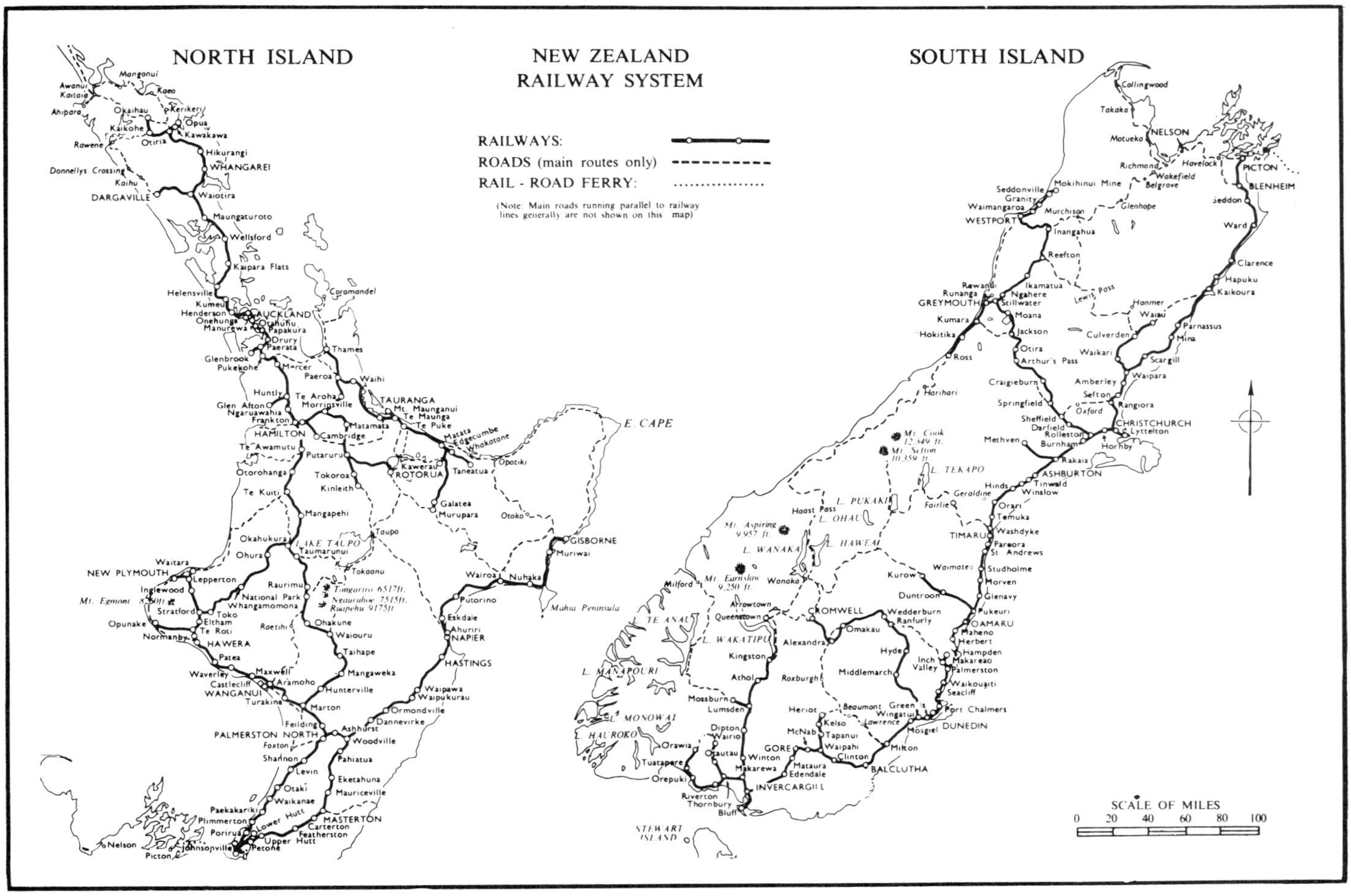

NEW ZEALAND RAILWAY SYSTEM

NORTH ISLAND   SOUTH ISLAND

RAILWAYS:
ROADS (main routes only)
RAIL - ROAD FERRY:

(Note: Main roads running parallel to railway lines generally are not shown on this map)

SCALE OF MILES
0   20   40   60   80   100

PACIFIC ISLANDS

HONOLULU

State of Hawaii, Department of Transportation
Harbor Division
Honolulu, Hawaii 96809

OFFICIALS:
Melvin E. Lepine (*Chief, Harbor Division*)
Captain D. J. O'Connell (*Harbor Master*)

CONTAINER FACILITIES:
Fort Armstrong Container Terminal
This terminal, operated by Matson Lines

has a quay length of 579 m (1,900 ft) with an allowable vessel draught of 10·06 m (33 ft) alongside. It is equipped with two 25 ton Paceco container gantry cranes, with an outreach of 28·96 m (95 ft), a 33 ton Hitachi container gantry crane with an outreach of 33·53 m (110 ft) approximately and a 45 ton portal crane fitted with container spreader. The total stacking area is 17·6 hectares (43·5 acres) and there is a cargo consolidation area of 43,664 m² (470,000 sq ft) in two sheds. Containers are handled by a fleet of about 12 van carriers.

Sand Island Container Terminal

This terminal, operated by Seatrain Terminals of California Inc., has a quay length of 207 m (680 ft) and an allowable vessel draught of 9·75 m (32 ft) alongside. It is equipped with two 45 ton Aston container gantry cranes with an outreach of 30·5 m (100 ft).

Pier 39

U.S. Lines is using this facility as a temporary measure.

SERVICES:

Matson—Hawaii to Seattle, Portland, Oakland, Los Angeles—every 3 days.

Seatrain—Oakland, Hawaii, Guam—every 5 days.

U.S. Lines—Europe, East Coast North America, Los Angeles, Oakland, Hawaii, Far East—every 6 days.

TRAFFIC:

	Inwards	
Lift-on 1970	*Tons*	*Loaded Units*
	1,500,000	119,000
	Outwards	
	Tons	*Loaded Units*
	600,000	48,000

Note: Tonnage estimated and Number of units handled given in 20 ft equivalents.

TERMINAL OPERATORS:

Matson Navigation Company

PO Box 899, Honolulu, Hawaii 96808

Seatrain Lines, Inc.
Sand Island Access Road, Area 1, Honolulu, Hawaii 96819

Theo H. Davies & Company, Inc.
Agents: United States Lines
PO Box 3020, Honolulu, Hawaii 96802

CONTAINER REPAIR ORGANISATIONS:
See Terminal Operators list above.

Honolulu—Fort Armstrong Terminal

Honolulu—Sand Island Terminal

GUAM, MARIANAS ISLANDS

Guam container Terminal

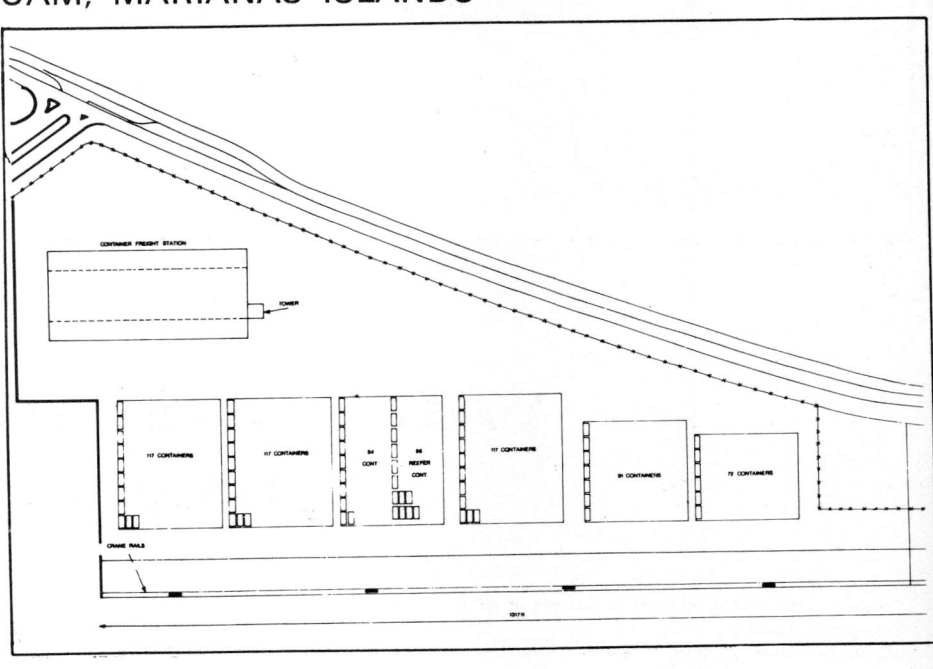

Commercial Port, Government of Guam
PO Box 1445,
Agana, Guam, 96910

GENERAL:

The commercial port of Guam, situated at the western end of Cabras Island, has two general cargo berths and a container terminal which came into service in July 1969.

CONTAINER TERMINAL:

The facility, which is 401·6 m (1,317 ft) in length with a depth of 10·97 m (36 ft) alongside, has a total area of 4·86 hectares (12 acres). It is equipped with a 30 ton Paceco container gantry crane and is laid out to accommodate 624 containers including 56 reefer units. There is also a container freight station providing a total of 3,066 m² (33,000 sq ft) of covered space; the freight station has a terminal control tower attached.

It should be noted that the crane rails serve both the terminal and the adjoining general cargo berth giving a total length of rail of 600 m (1,975 ft).

CONTAINER SERVICES:

Pacific Far East Line operates a service to Guam from US Pacific coast ports.

THE AMERICAS

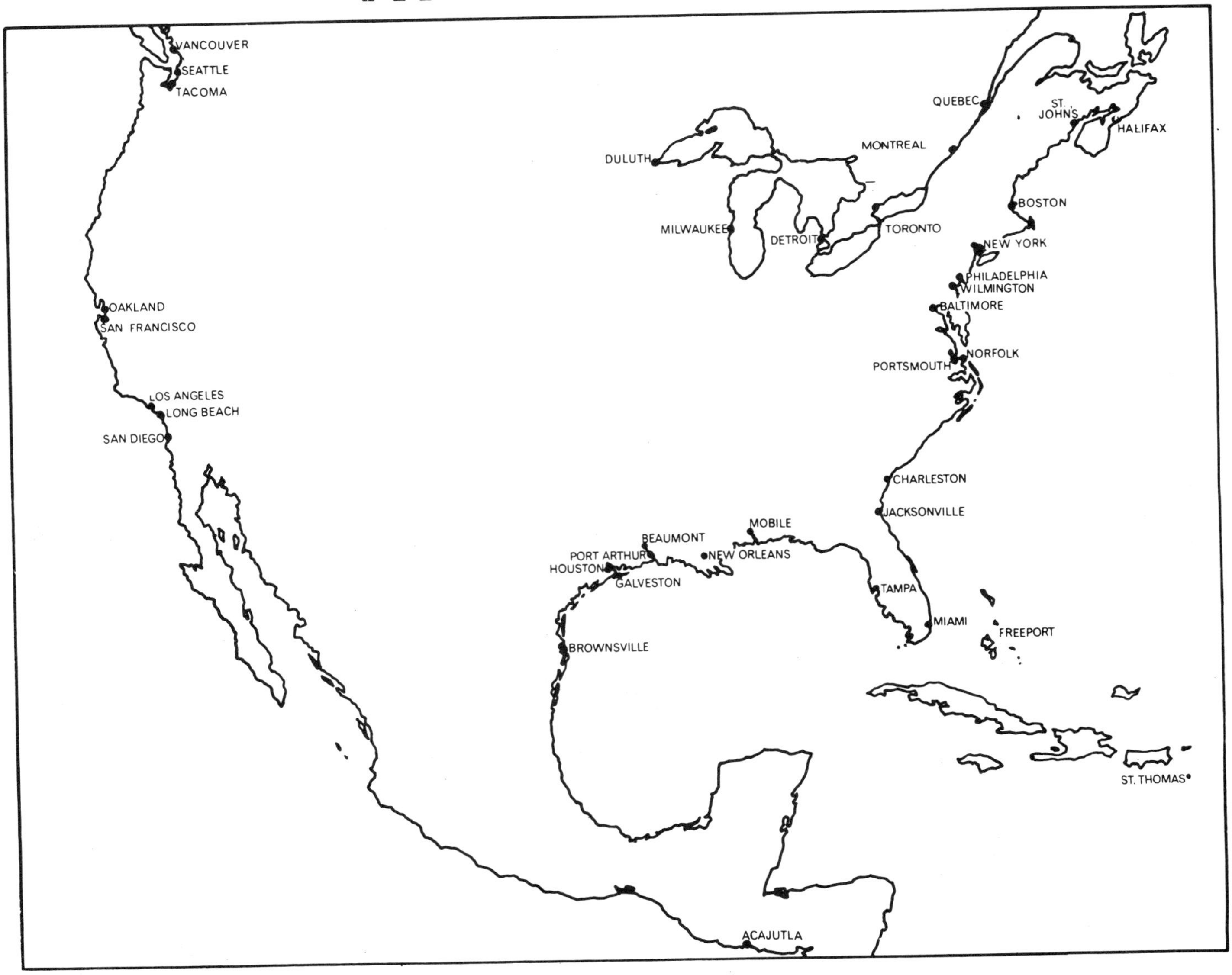

VANCOUVER
SEATTLE
TACOMA
QUEBEC
ST. JOHN'S
HALIFAX
DULUTH
MONTREAL
BOSTON
MILWAUKEE
DETROIT
TORONTO
NEW YORK
PHILADELPHIA
WILMINGTON
BALTIMORE
OAKLAND
SAN FRANCISCO
NORFOLK
PORTSMOUTH
LOS ANGELES
LONG BEACH
SAN DIEGO
CHARLESTON
JACKSONVILLE
MOBILE
BEAUMONT
PORT ARTHUR
HOUSTON
NEW ORLEANS
GALVESTON
TAMPA
MIAMI
FREEPORT
BROWNSVILLE
ST. THOMAS
ACAJUTLA

CANADA
HALIFAX

Port of Halifax,
National Harbours Board
Halifax, Nova Scotia
TELEPHONE: 426 3643
TELEX: 014622643
OFFICIALS:

J. E. Lloyd (*Port Manager*)
R. V. Beck (*Deputy Port Manager*)
W. E. Johnston (*Engineer*)
G. D. Merrigan (*Administrative Assistant*)
C. Fiander (*Harbour Master*)

GENERAL:

This harbour, unaffected by ice, is North America's easternmost port and nearest to European shipping points for all vessels using the North Atlantic sea lanes. It is linked to central Canada and the Eastern United States by rail services and highways.

Halifax is a deepwater port, averaging 13·7 m (45 ft) at all major wharves.

Halifax—Berth 41 and the Roll-on ramp in operation—November 1970

CONTAINER TERMINAL
Operator:
Halterm Limited
PO Box 1057
Main Port Office, Halifax N.S.
Telephone: (902) 423-8361
Telex: 014 422885
B. A. Dokerty (*Terminal Manager*)
E. Hare (*Marketing Manager*)

Berths 41 and 42, Pier C became operational in Autumn 1970. The quay is 518 m (1,700 ft) in length and is equipped with two 45 ton Star container gantry cranes. The total area of the facility is 22·23 hectares (55 acres) of which 10·1 hectares (25 acres) is used for parking and marshalling. Behind the parking and marshalling area is a container train terminal equipped with two gantry cranes for transferring units to and from rail cars. The rail terminal is operated by Canadian National Railways and the sea terminal, leased to Halterm Ltd., is operated on a common user basis. A roll-on ramp has been provided.

CONTAINER SERVICES:
The Dart Containerline provide a weekly service between Antwerp and Southampton and Halifax and New York.
Atlantic Container Line provide a weekly service between Halifax and European Ports
Amerind Line provide a service to U.S. East Coast ports and the West Indies.
Columbus Line use the facility for their service to Australia and New Zealand.

CONTAINER AND ROLL-ON TRAFFIC:
In 1970 traffic, including roll-on, amounted to 108,875 tons inwards and 265,826 tons outwards. Lift-on amounted to 9,352 loaded 20 ft equivalent units inwards and 10,991 20 ft units outwards. Estimate for 1971 is a total of 60,000 units or 78,000 20 ft equivalents through the port.

TERMINAL OPERATING HOURS:
A 24 hour day is worked both on ship

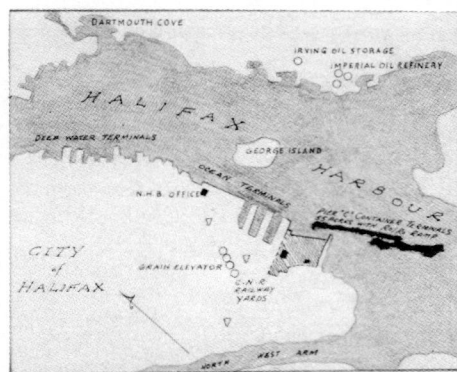

cargo and inland cargo operations.

CONTAINER REPAIR FACILITIES:
Trailco Limited
P.O. Box 434
Dartmouth, Nova Scotia

MONTREAL

Port of Montreal
National Harbours Board
Cité du Havre,
Montreal, Quebec
TELEPHONE: 849-3781
TELEX: (05) 26-76-99
Guy Beaudet (*Port Manager*)

CONTAINER FACILITIES:
Berth 68-70. Operated by Furness Withy for Manchester Liners the terminal covers 7·28 hectares (18 acres) with a quay frontage of 152·4 m (500 ft). The facility is equipped with a 25-ton Clyde Crane and Booth container gantry crane and a 35 ton container gantry crane. Four Clark 512 van carriers, which are capable of stacking three high with 20 ft units, have been provided. Containers are stored in a shed 320 × 280 ft, with open ends, which provides protection from snow; the shed can accommodate 750 containers stacked two high. A Drott travelift loads to rail wagons and the facility is designed to handle sixty-six 40 ft rail wagons at any one time.

Loaded export containers are weighed on a Fairbanks Morse weighbridge which has a capacity of 140,000 lb—capable of weighing van carrier and container.

Cargo of less than container load (LCL) quantity is loaded and discharged from containers and inland transport at a specially designed warehouse-type shed which is fitted out with pallet racks 12 ft high and served by eight electric Clark lift trucks. Cargo is handled on "take-it-or-leave-it" pallets. The shed has 12 truck doors and 20 container doors.

Large volume container load lots are handled direct to containers over a 300 ft long 16 ft wide platform.

Berth 43—Operated by Cast Containers Ltd. and Task Terminals Ltd., this terminal maintains a weekly service between Montreal and Antwerp with four unitized ships each carrying 300 20 ft containers plus other cargo. Comprising an area of 2·43 hectares (6 acres), it is equipped with a mobile crane, a sidelift and front loaders of 100—25 and 30 tons respectively.

Berth 73—This terminal is operated for public use by SABB (Société d'Arrimage des Battures de Beauport). The facility is equipped with a 30-ton crane and van carriers with a consolidation shed for stuffing and unstuffing containers.

TERMINAL OPERATING HOURS:
0800 to 1200 and 1300 to 1700 hours. Overtime for ship handling can be worked in the evenings and at weekends if required. Inland transport overtime can be worked evenings only.

Montreal—Berths 68-70

CONTAINER TRAFFIC:

| | *Inwards* | | *Outwards* | |
Lift-on	Tons	Loaded Units	Tons	Loaded Units
1970	339,327	31,114	563,392	33,511
1971	435,000	40,000	820,000	50,000
(Estimate)				

CONTAINER REPAIR COMPANIES:
J. & R. Weir Ltd.
33 Nazareth Road, Montreal, P.Q.
Fruehof Trailer Co. of Canada Ltd.
1515 Montée de Liesse,
Montreal 384, P.Q.
Canadian Car Trailer Sales, Division of
Hawker Siddeley Canada Ltd.
7214 Newman Street, Montreal P.Q.
Automotive Sales and Service Ltd.
300 Montée de Liesse, Montreal, 377

STEVEDORES:
Brown & Ryan Limited
360 St. James St. W.
Montreal 126 PQ

Ceres Stevedoring Co. Ltd.
300 St. Sacrament St.,
Montreal 125 PQ

Cullen Stevedoring Co. Ltd.
360 St. James W.,
Room 1420, Montreal 126 PQ
Eastern Canada Stevedoring Ltd.
282 Notre Dame W.
Montreal 126 PQ

Empire Stevedoring Co. Ltd.
440 St. Nicholas,
Montreal 125 PQ

Wolfe Stevedores Ltd.
300 St. Sacrament St.,
Montreal 125 PQ

Federal Stevedoring Co. Ltd.
3800 Place Victoria,
Montreal 115 PQ

Economic Stevedoring Corp. of Montreal Ltd.
315 St. Sacrament St.
Montreal 125 PQ

Montreal St. John Stevedoring Co.
410 St. Nicholas St.
Montreal 125 PQ

St. Lawrence Stevedoring Co. Ltd.
5250 de Maisonneuve W.,
Montreal 260 PQ

QUEBEC

Port of Quebec

National Harbours Board,
PO 'ox 2268, Quebec 2, PQ Canada
TELEPHONE: 694-3588
OFFICIALS:
Paul Bousquet (*Port Manager*)
J. Robert Tanguay (*Supervisor of Operations*)
Capt. H. Allard (*Harbour Master*)
CONTAINER FACILITIES:
Terminal Operat.
Société d'Arrimage des Battures de Beauport
Inc. (SABB)
109, Dalhousie Street, Quebec 2 PQ
Telephone: 418 (692-1180)

Late in 1967 SABB, Inc (Societe d'Arrimage des Battures de Beauport, Inc.) was formed for the express purpose of providing container handling facilities at Quebec. It was a joint venture of the St. Lawrence Stevedoring Co., Ltd, and Albert G. Baker Ltd.

Beauport Flats Terminal:

This facility is open to all containership operators and consists of a quay frontage of 640 m (2,100 ft) with a depth alongside of 12·2 m (40 ft). The quay can be extended by a further 427 m (1,400 ft). At present there are 6·9 hectares (17 acres) of parking and marshalling space for container and a 36 ton container gantry crane with a maximum outreach of 30·5 m (100 ft) has been provided.

There are two lift trucks, one of 30 tons capacity fitted with a spreader and one of 23 tons capacity fitted with forks. Three straddle carriers are also in service and further carriers may be provided.

Quebec—Wolfe's Cove with *CP Voyageur* alongside

The container gantry crane at Beauport Flats Terminal, Quebec.

Quebec—Wolfe's Cove rail terminal at the back of the facility

Wolfe's Cove Terminal:

This facility was designed for the CP Ships Service from Europe. The quay is 365·76 m (1,200 ft) in length, and is equipped with a 35 ton Paceco-Vickers container gantry crane having an outreach of 35·05 m (115 ft) and a backreach of 9·14 m (30 ft). The total area of the terminal is 7·28 hectares (18 acres) and straddle carriers stack 3 high. A rail terminal half a mile in length with four tracks is spanned by a 35 ton container yard gantry crane. Plans are under way to acquire a second crane.

PART CONTAINER FACILITY:

Ships carrying part container cargoes can be accommodated at Pier 27 which is 329 m (1,084 ft) in length and 90·8 m (298 ft) wide and the large storage area together with the shed located on this pier makes it suitable for combined carriers.

TERMINAL OPERATING HOURS:

Ship and inland transport cargo operations take place round the clock.

CONTAINER SERVICES:

CP Ships London and Rotterdam—every six days.

CP Ships/Head Donaldson, Liverpool and Clyde—every ten days.

TRAFFIC:

In 1970 128,131 tons in 10,256 loaded units

moved inwards and 172,455 tons in 10,827 loaded units outwards. In 1971 it is expected that 360,000 tons (30,000 units) will move inwards and 565,000 tons (35,000 units) outwards.

CONTAINER STORAGE AND STEVEDORE COMPANIES:

Canadian Pacific Steamship Co.
Wolfe's Cove, Quebec City, PQ,

Telephone: 522-2081

SABB,
109 rue Dalhousie, Quebec 2.
Telephone: 692-1180.

SAINT JOHN (NEW BRUNSWICK)

Port of Saint John

National Harbours Board
PO Box 429,
Saint John., New Brunswick, Canada
TELEPHONE: 506-693 3503
TELEX: 014-47281
PRINCIPAL OFFICIALS:
G. C. Mouland (*Port Manager*)
R. P. Fudge (*Administrative Officer*)
G. M. MacNeil (*Harbour Master*)

GENERAL:

Operating all year, Saint John has 27 berths at 35-40 feet owned by the National Harbours Board as well as 5 private berths including a new deep water oil facility.

The port is served by CN and CP rail with 64 miles of track serving all berths, and by all major North American truck lines.

CRANEAGE:

Two floating cranes capacity 65 tons,

numerous 5 ton rail cranes and mobile cranes of up to 200 tons are available. Containers have been loaded onto conventional ships in a three minute cycle with mobile cranes.

ROLL-ON/ROLL-OFF

Modifications have been carried out to Pier 3 and several vessels of this type have been accommodated.

A C.P. Rail roll-on ferry vessel provides two sailings daily to Digby. Nova Scotia

PIER 1
CONTAINER TERMINAL

LONG WHARF PROPOSED
CONTAINER FACILITY

ROLL ON BERTH PIER 3

Saint John, New Brunswick

from the Ferry Terminal.

CONTAINER TERMINAL DEVELOPMENT

Pier 1 Container Terminal:

OPERATOR:

Brunterm Limited

OFFICE:

133 Prince William Street
Saint John, N.B.

MAIL ADDRESS:

P.O. Box 492, Place D'Armes,
Montreal 126, PQ
Telephone: (514) 849-6111
Telex: 05-25-197

Brunterm Limited is owned by CP Rail
and McLean Kennedy Ltd.

Pier 1 has a total length of 376·5 m (1,235
ft) which can be increased by a further 117·65
m (386 ft) if required. The container
terminal is 248·41 m (815 ft) in length and
can accept vessels of up to 274·32 m (900 ft);
there is a depth of 10·97 m (36 ft) alongside
(LWOST). The total area of Pier 1 is 11
hectares (27 acres); at present the storage
area paved amounts to 4·05 hectares (10
acres) and this can be doubled easily if
necessary. The facility is equipped with a
45 ton Paceco Vickers container gantry crane
with a capacity of 40 tons under the spreader,
an outreach of 35·05 m (115 ft) and a backreach of 18·29 m (60 ft). There are also 3 lift
trucks with top lifting spreader for 20 and
40 ft units, 5 tractors and chassis. This
equipment will be supplemented with straddle
carriers or side loaders, if traffic warrants.

The Berth is served by a rail terminal
having two 335·3 m (1,100 ft) lengths of
track. Regular CP Rail services link with
the national network.

Long Wharf. This site is developed to the
extent that the installation of a crane could
be completed very quickly. Fenced, paved and
served by rail this facility has an area of 5·6
hectares (14 acres) which could be extended
to 20 acres. There is 12·2 m (40 ft) alongside
at low water.

CONTAINER SERVICES:

ACT (Canada) Ltd—Australia and New

Saint John, New Brunswick—Pier I

Zealand Service. CP Ships use the facility
in the winter months.

TRAFFIC:

Lift-on traffic amounted to 41,881 tons
(3,457 loaded units) inwards and 47,930 tons
(3,800 loaded units) outwards; the 1971
estimate is 6,400 units inwards and 6,800
outwards.

TORONTO

The Toronto Harbour Commissioners,
60, Harbour Street,
Toronto 1 Canada
TELEPHONE: (416) 863-2000
TELEX: 06-219 666
PRINCIPAL OFFICIALS:
E. B. Griffith (*General Manager*)
W. M. H. Colvin (*Secretary*)
Captain W. S. Culbertson (*Director Terminal Operations*)
AREA OFFICES:
PO Box 1379 Genoa Italy
Telephone: 205-751
3, Lower Regent Street, London, SW1
Telephone: 01-930 4565
PO Box 2071, The Hague, Netherlands
Telephone: (070) 836 196
1-1 Uchisai waicho 2-chome Chiyodaku
Tokyo, Japan
Telephone: 501-2210
GENERAL:
At present containers are handled at the various general cargo terminals. A 200 ton mobile crane has been provided to handle containers.
CONTAINER FACILITIES:
Marine Terminal 51, completed as a general cargo facility in 1966, has been provided with 11,705 m² (126,000 sq ft) container warehouse (Warehouse 52) for packing and unpacking operations. The shed has been designed so that it will be possible to increase the size to 27,871 m² (300,000 sq ft) as traffic builds up, and it has also been located in such a way that it will be able to serve more than one berth. The warehouse is road and rail

Toronto—Container Warehouse 52

served. Additional areas of Terminal 51 will be paved and it will be available for the part-container ships which operate between European and Great Lakes Ports.
TERMINAL WORKING HOURS:
Five days per week 0800 to 1200, 1300 to 1700 hours with extensive overtime as required.
CONTAINER SERVICES:
Services using part-container ships, are being provided by Europe Canada Lakes Line; Fjell/Olsen Line; Zim-Israel Line; Atlanttrafik Express Service; Arctic Steamship Lines; Black Sea Steamships; Black Star Lines; Netumar Lines; Shipping Corp. of India; Head/Donaldson Lines; Polish Ocean Line; Christensen Canadian African Lines; K lines; Scanlake Line; Odfjell Lines; Hycar

Toronto—Mobile Container Crane

Line; Europe Canada Lakes Line; Mitsui O.S.K. Line; Scindia Line; Medlakes Line; Federal Atlantic Lakes Line; Federal Pacific Lakes Line; Federal South East Asia Line; Volta Line; N.Y.K. Line.
TRAFFIC:
Lift-on traffic amounted to 33,319 tons (3,320 loaded units) inwards and 11,280 (1,128 loaded units) outwards.

VANCOUVER

National Harbours Board
Port of Vancouver, B.C., Canada
TELEPHONE: 604-255-3565
TELEGRAMS: Port of Vancouver, B.C.
TELEX: 0450111

OFFICIALS:
W. Duncan (*Acting Port Manager*)
W. E. Pickering (*Chief of Administration*)
L. W. Marks (*Manager, Real Estate*)

CONTAINER FACILITIES:
No. 6 Centennial Pier
This facility, which has a depth alongside of 12·2 m (40 ft) has a length of 209·4 m (687 ft) and is equipped with a Star Starporter 40 ton container gantry crane with an outreach of 35 m (113·5 ft). The back-up area is 6 hectares (15 acres) and a portion of Shed 5 is used as a container freight station. Four rail tracks accommodate over sixty container flat cars. Four straddle carriers and two lift trucks have been provided and future plans call for the purchase of handling equipment for the rail yard.
The terminal is leased from the National Harbours Board by Empire Stevedoring Co. Ltd. 395 Railway Street Vancouver B.C.

Vancouver—No. 6 Pier

CONTAINER SERVICES:
A service every 10 days is proivded by Japanese Lines serving the port.
Scanstar container service to Europe—every two weeks from December 1971.

TRAFFIC:
Traffic through the port for 1970 amounted

to 33,421 tons (5,079 loaded units) inwards and 97,856 tons (6,116 loaded units) outwards. Estimate for 1971 is 84,000 tons (14,000 loaded units) inwards and 240,000 tons (16,000 units) outwards.

RAILWAYS:
Through interchange facilities the port is served by the Canadian National, Canadian Pacific, Burlington Northern and Pacific, Great Eastren Railways.

RAIL
CANADIAN NATIONAL RAILWAYS

Canadian National Railways
935 de la Gauchetiere Street West,
P.O. Box 8100, Montreal 101, Quebec
Canada
OFFICERS:
EXECUTIVE:
N. J. MacMillan, QC, LLD (*Chairman of the Board and President*)
W. Toulmin (*Executive Assistant*)
W. C. Bowra (*System Vice-President*)
A. H. Hart, QC, LLD (*Vice-President, Marketing*)
M. Archer (*Senior Vice-President*)
G. R. Johnson (*Vice-President, Freight Marketing*)
E. T. Hurley (*Vice-President, Purchases and Stores*)
W. T. Wilson (*Vice-President, Personnel and Labour Relations*)
R. H. Tarr (*Vice-President, Hotels and Telecommunications*)
J. L. Toole (*Chairman, CN Investment Division (Vice-President CN)*)
A. V. Johnston (*General Manager CN International Consulting Division*)
L. Côté, QC (*Vice-President and General Counsel*)
E. J. Cooke (*Vice-President. Express and Highway Services*)
R. T. Vaughan, QC, LLD (*Vice-President and Secretary*)
W. R. Corner (*Vice-President and Comptroller*)
E. J. Denyar (*Treasurer*)
C. A. Harris (*Director of Public Relations*)

PASSENGER SALES AND SERVICE:
A. Olynyk (*General Manager, Passenger Sales and Services*)
H. F. Murray (*System Manager, Services*)
W. G. Edge (*Coordinator, Financial Control*)
J. G. Leduc (*System Customer Relations Officer*)
C. C. Bright (*Manager, Customer and Catering Services*)
L. F. McCarthy (*Manager, Station and Sales Services*)
G. E. Crooker (*Manager, Equipment Development*)
R. E. Rose (*Manager, Passenger Sales and Promotion*)
EXPRESS AND HIGHWAY SERVICES:
E. J. Cooke (*Vice-President*)
SYSTEM:
R. E. Lawless (*General Manager, Express and Intermodal Services*)
L. K. Ash (*General Manager, CN Transport Ltd.*)
I. W. Shepherd (*Manager, Automotive Equipment*)
L. A. Hewitt (*Comptroller*)
G. A. Duthie, Sr. (*Administration Officer, Express Services*)
J. H. Matthews (*Manager, Air Express*)
A. F. Hebert (*Manager, Foreign Express*)
J. M. Beaupre (*Manager, Piggyback Services*)
GENERAL:
Canadian National, principally a railway, but owning hotels, ships, telecommunication and active in trucking and in Air Canada, is owned by the Canadian Government.

Directors and the President are Government appointed. The system of 24,714 route miles (39,766 kms) extends across Canada from Newfoundland to British Columbia.

Through its wholly owned subsidiary, The Grand Trunk Western Railroad Company, it serves Chicago and Detroit and thus the United States Mid West.

FINANCIAL:
1970 Railway operating revenue was Can.$1·042 million (Can.$1,014 million in 1969) and operating expense was Can.$1,028 million (Can. $996 million in 1969).

Net railway operating income was lower at Can. $14·7 ($18·4) million.

Consolidated result, after interest on debt was Can. $30 million deficit.

TRAFFIC:
Revenue ton miles of freight increased 8% to 56,049 millions.

Piggyback traffic decreased slightly measured by both trailers handled and by piggyback flat car miles.

PIGGYBACK:
E. J. Cooke (*Vice-President, Express and Highway Services*)
J. M. Beaupre (*Manager, Piggyback Services*)
Plans: 1, 2, 2½, 3, 4.
Revenue: piggyback trailers handled

1970	1969
66,819	79,353

Piggyback flat car miles

69·0 million	79·2 million

Containers handled—import/export
Container flat car miles

Canadian National Toronto Railtainer yard.

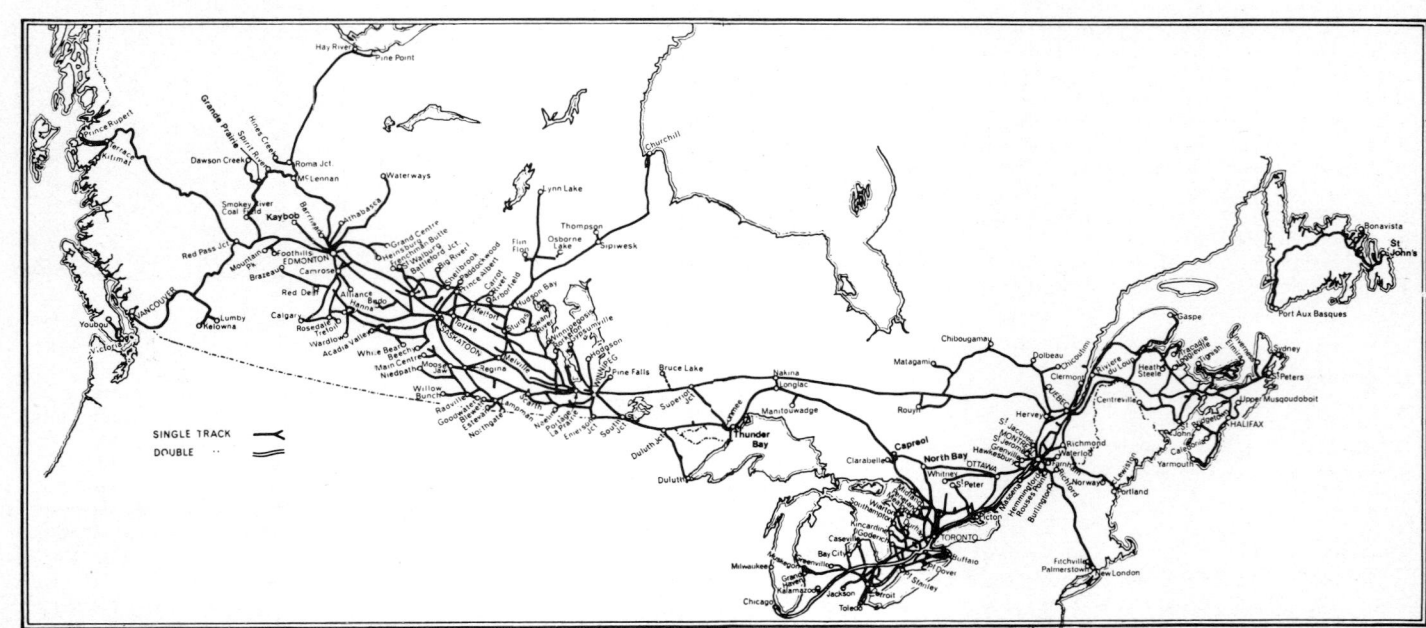

51,950   19,630
—domestic
18·4 million   17·1 million
—import/export
16·9 million   6·9 million

PIGGYBACK:

The significant growth of Piggyback traffic on CN, which started in 1968 with the introduction of an all-Piggyback train between Vancouver and Toronto-Montreal, exhibited same reduction in 1970. A direct result of this growth was the opening of a modern terminal in West Toronto to assure efficient handling of additional trailers. In Eastern Canada Piggyback was expanded with the inauguration of Plan II service in Prince Edward Island.

RAMP LOCATIONS:

At 84 cities.
11 in Atlantic Region
18 in St. Lawrence Region
16 in Great Lakes Region
27 in Prairie Region
12 in Montana & Pacific Region

CONTAINER AND TRAILER FLEET:

CN owns or leases 499 trailers and 1,115 20 ft containers, and 923 container flat cars

CONTAINER SYSTEMS:

Canadian National has its own fleets of pick-up and delivery vehicles and its subsidiary highway trucking companies. In CN's import-export container systems at the present time, shipping lines do not supply chassis for the inland movements. Containers destined for inland distribution are moved between ports and CN's inland container terminals on container rail cars without chassis. At the inland terminals, CN can provide the pick-up and delivery with their own vehicles.

Gantry cranes, bridge cranes or van lifters equipped with twist locks on spreaders are used at CN's major inland container terminals for the fast and efficient transferring of import-export containers, as is the case in Europe and most of the United States. In addition to this type of container handling equipment, widespread use is made of the side-transfer system incorporated into the vehicle itself, which simply slides the containers to or from the rail cars. The operation requires no heavy lifting equipment and the container transfer can be effected by the drivers in as little as five minutes. The same vehicle can then deliver the container to a consignee's door and place it on legs for unloading, after which it is picked up and returned to the nearest rail head. Thus, any point in Canada where this type of equipment is available is, in effect, a small or intermediate-sized inland container terminal and, of course, more or heavier equipment is acquired and assigned as container volumes demand.

The side-transfer system was originally developed and used for the handling of containers in domestic express services. Canadian National began using containers in these services over fifteen years ago. These 20 × 8 × 8 containers were designed for a closed system and consequently, are not identical to ISO containers being generally of lighter construction and having side doors (as well as end doors).

IMPORT-EXPORT CONTAINERS:

Canadian National became part of the import-export container network in November, 1968, when the Manchester Liners' purpose-built cellular container ship docked at Montreal. Since then CN have become line hauliers at Halifax for Containers from the services of Dart Containerline, Atlantic Container Line, Caribbean Container Line and at Montreal for CAST (Canadian Air and Sea Transport) Containers. In spring 1970 the Japan Pacific North West service of NYK, Showa, K, Japan, MOSK and Y-S

Silent Hoist Front Loader placing container on adaptor at a major terminal to enable side-transfer at an intermediate terminal.

Paceco Transtainer Crane removing containers from rail car at CN's inland container terminal at Toronto.

Lines commenced calling at Vancouver and CN provide the line haul on some of the containers on this service destined for inland destinations.

TRAFFIC:

In the relatively short time since Canadian National entered import-export container operations, volumes have grown at a rapid rate and services have been steadily expanding. In their first full year of involvement with these systems, CN handled some 2,000 twenty-foot import-export containers per month in rail services and through their inland container terminals. These containers were destined to Montreal, Toronto, Southwestern Ontario, Winnipeg, Edmonton, Vancouver, and US midwest points through Chicago and Detroit. By mid-summer of 1970, CN was handling some 3,500 containers per month in their import-export services.

Neither the volumes handled nor the distribution is fully significant as a trend indicator, since the main influencing factor is

the number of systems of which CN becomes a part. During the first year, only two systems were operational, one for the full year and the other for six months. Since that time, CN has become part of several new systems whose volumes are expected to increase when they have passed through their build-up stages.

INLAND CONTAINER TERMINALS AND EQUIPMENT:

Canadian National realized at the outset that, to become part of import-export container systems, their responsibility could not be restricted solely to the overland haul. They were convinced that, to derive the full benefits that containerization had to offer, services previously performed only at the Port of Entry would have to be provided at inland terminals. This meant that, in addition to transfer equipment and a fleet of pick-up and delivery vehicles, planning would have to include facilities for customs clearance, unpacking of contents where multi-deliveries are involved, consolidation of outward

Silent Hoist Front Loader placing container on one of CN's 4-container rail cars at CN's inland container terminal at Montreal.

movements, plug-in facilities for heated or reefer containers and storage areas for containers and/or their contents. It should be noted that, in addition to the specialized equipment listed below, which does not include the side-transfer vehicles which are part of every major terminal to complement the regular operation, Canadian National had provided equipment handling 40 foot containers as well as 20-footers by the end of 1970.

Major Inland Container Terminals
Montreal:

Equipped with a Front Loader Container Handlier (Silent Hoist—FK 30), which top-lifts containers by means of twist locks on a spreader and is capable of stacking containers 3-high, this terminal has storage space for over 300 containers stacked 2-high. The Front Loader can transfer containers directly between rail cars and motor vehicles or place them in the storage area adjacent to the tracks

Toronto:

This terminal is equipped with a 74-foot, mobile, rubber-tired, container gantry yard crane (Paceco Transtainer) which straddles two rail tracks, a storage area and two roadways. The transtainer has an 80,000 lb lifting capacity and is designed to transfer 20-foot and 40-foot containers and piggyback trailers.

Two Front Loader Container Handlers (Silent Hoist—FK 30), which top-lifts containers by means of twist locks on spreaders and a Side Loader Container Handler (Lancer Boss), which top-lifts containers by means of twist locks on a spreader, have also been installed.

All the equipment is capable of stacking containers 3-high.

There is storage space for over 1,000

containers stacked 2-high. The container crane, the front loaders and the side loader can transfer containers directly between rail cars and motor vehicles or place them in the storage area adjacent to the tracks.

Chicago:

A mobile, rubber-tired, container gantry yard crane (Drott) which straddles one track, one roadway and a rail-side storage area has been provided. It has an 80,000 lb lifting capacity and is designed to transfer 20-foot and 40-foot containers and piggyback trailers. It is capable of stacking containers 2-high.

There is storage space for over 70 containers stacked 2-high. The crane can transfer containers directly between rail cars and motor vehicles or place them in the storage area adjacent to the tracks.

Detroit

A crawler-type crane, equipped with a spreader for top-lifting 20-foot containers, having a 40,000 lb lifting capacity has been provided. There is storage space for 80 containers stacked 2-high adjacent to the tracks.

The expansion and improvement of the handling facilities is under consideration.

Edmonton

A mobile, rubber-tired, container gantry yard crane (Drott), with an 80,000 lb lifting capacity, which can transfer 20-foot and 40-foot containers as well as piggyback trailers has been provided.

The terminal is capable of storing over 50 containers stacked 2-high.

Other Inland Container Terminals

In addition to the foregoing major inland container terminals, side-transfer units are assigned to the following locations, which could be considered as small or intermediate-size inland container terminals.

Belleville, Ont.	Quebec City, Que.
Calgary, Alta.	Regina, Sask.
Campbellton, N.B.	Saskatoon, Sask.
Hamilton, Ont.	Saint John, N.B.
London, Ont.	Vancouver, B.C.
North Sydney, N.S.	Windsor, Ont.
Ottawa, Ont.	Winnipeg, Man.

CONTAINER EQUIPMENT—RAIL CARS

Apart from the cars used in express container services, CN had close to 700 container cars assigned exclusively to the hauling of import-export containers by the end of 1970, the majority of which can handle either 20-foot or 40-foot containers. Fifty of these cars are 4-container cars capable of handling any combination of 20-foot or 40-foot containers.

DOMESTIC SERVICES:

The widespread acceptance of containers as a new form of transportation in the world's import-export operations has created a vastly increased demand for their use within Canada's domestic market. Canadian shippers and receivers are anxious to derive the full benefits that containerization has to offer. To respond to this demand, Canadian National is working towards the development of a domestic container system which will be completely compatible with their import-export container systems so that all specialized handling equipment, rolling stock, terminals and other facilities will be completely interchangeable.

CANADIAN PACIFIC RAILWAY COMPANY

Canadian Pacific
Windsor Station, Montreal 101, Quebec
OFFICIALS:

N. R. Crump (*Chairman*)

I. D. Sinclair (*President and Chief Executive Officer*)

F. S. Burbidge (*Vice-President*)

T. F. Turner (*Secretary*)

K. Campbell (*Vice-President, Administration*)

J. A. Wright, QC (*Vice-Presdient, Law*)

F. A. Rutherford (*Vice-President and Comptroller*)

C. A. Colpitts (*Chief Engineer*)

G. J. van den Berg (*Vice-President, Finance*)

J. C. Machan (*Chief of Investigation*)

D. B. Wallace (*General Manager, Public Relations*)

H. M. Romoff (*Manager, Research*)

CP AIR:

J. C. Gilmer (*President*)

CP EXPRESS:

W. J. Bowers (*President*)

CP HOTELS:

H. M. Pickard (*President*)

CP RAIL:

F. S. Burbidge (*Senior Executive Officer*)

D. M. Dunlop (*Vice-President, Operation and Maintenance*)

J. C. Anderson (*Vice-President, Industrial Relations*)

J. M. Bentham (*Vice-President, Purchases and Stores*)

A. F. Joplin (*Vice-President, Marketing and Sales*)

P. A. Nepveu (*Vice-President, Accounts and Data Systems*)

J. N. Fraine (*Senior Regional Vice-President, Pacific Region*)

R. S. Allison (*Vice-President, Prairie Region*)

G. E. Benoit (*Vice-President, Atlantic Region*)

L. R. Smith (*Vice-President, Eastern Region*)

H. W. Hayward (*Chief of Motive Power and Rolling Stock*)

A. E. Jenner (*System Manager, Piggyback Services*)

CP SHIPS:

W. J. Stenason (*Vice-President, Transport and Ships*)

CP rail freight train at Middleton Bridge, Ont.

Rail/Road transfer operations.

Truck Trailer on Flatcar

R. Y. Pritchard (*General Manager*)

S. Byars (*Manager, North Atlantic Freight Services*)

FINANCIAL:

Net railway earnings for 1970 amounted to $38·4 million, an increase of $3·8 million compared with 1969. The ratio of net earnings to railway revenues was 6·2 per cent, an increase from the 6·0 per cent of the previous year, and the rate of return on the net investment in railway property was approximately 3%.

Railway revenues, at $616 million, were $36 million higher than in 1969.

Railway expenses for 1970 amounted to $578 million, $32 million higher than 1969. Freight revenue was at an all-time high of $540 million).

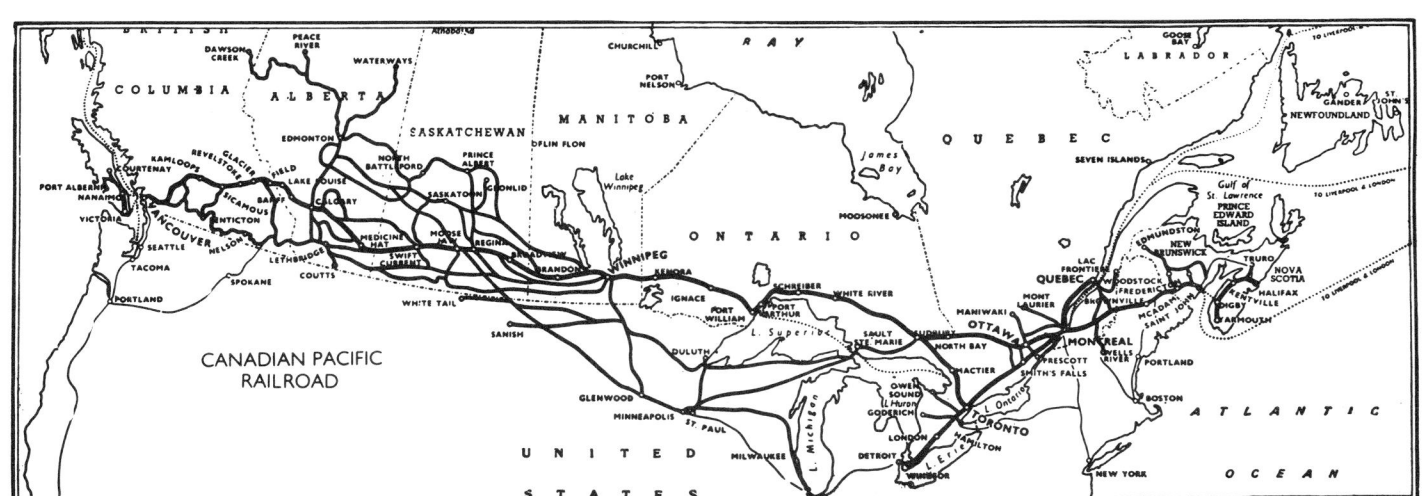

CANADIAN PACIFIC RAILROAD

TRAFFIC RESULTS:		
Freight Traffic:	1970	1969
Tons of revenue freight (*millions*)	77·4	67·2
Agricultural products	+43%	—2%
Mine products	+21%	+9%
Manufacturers	+4%	+4%
Ton-miles of revenue freight (*millions*)	41,994	36,200
Average revenue per ton	$7·04	$7·50
Average revenue per ton mile (*cents*)	1·30	1·39
Tons per train	1,755	1,597
Average miles hauled	543	538
Gross ton miles per train hour	78,368	72,375
Train speed m.p.h.	22·8	22·4
Gross ton miles (*millions*)	83,824	74,585
Passenger Traffic		
Revenue passengers carried (*millions*)	5·3	5·1
Revenue passenger miles (*millions*)	428	485
Average revenue per passenger	$2·33	$2·21
Revenue per passenger mile	2·9 cents	2·8 cents
Total passenger car miles (*millions*)	40·1	42·4
Train miles freight (millions)	24·4	23·1
Train miles passenger (millions)	5·0	5·7
Diesel locomotive unit miles (millions)		
Freight	62·9	61·1
Passenger	7·0	7·1
Switching	11·0	11·0

DEVELOPMENTS:

The New National Transportation Act presented substantial opportunities for Canadian Pacific development, including new pricing techniques, and the management organization has been restructured to stimulate the search for new areas of service and sales.

Unit Trains:

CP Rail continued transcontinental shipments of liquified petroleum gas. A new unit train will ship sulphur from Alberta to Pacific ports.

In April 1970, CP operated the first of its unit trains to commence an annual movement of 5·7 million tons of coking coal from the mines of Kaiser Resources Limited, at Sparwood, B.C. to the new Roberts Bank super port, 20 miles south of Vancouver, on the Pacific, over a 700 mile CP rail route.

6 trains, each carrying 9,240 tons of coal will be moving on a 72 hour cycle, employing $24m of new equipment in Canada's most expensive application of the unit train principle.

A similar train operation will develop from the Fording River through a coal sale negotiated in 1969 with Japanese interests, for 45m tons of coking coal over 15 years, commencing April 1972.

Slurry Pipeline:

Shelpac, a joint Shell-CP company, continued research on a project to build a 419 mile pipeline to carry coal in slurry form from the Kootenay area of British Columbia to the coast.

Road Services:

Trucking operations showed continued growth and orders were placed for further tractors, city trucks, and highway trailers.

Air Services:

CP Air expanded existing domestic and overseas services and the fleet became all jet, consisting of 7 standard DC8's, 4 DC-8-63 (Spacemasters), and 7 Boeing 737's.

Recently delivered, are 4 Boeing 727 tri-jets.

Shipping Services:

The CP Ships' container vessels, *CP Voyageur, CP Trader and CP Discoverer* entered service in 1971.

In December the container terminal at Wolfe's Cove at Quebec was opened. As a rail and truck terminal operations. As a result of the new integrated operation, transit times between the United Kingdom and eastern Canada will shortly be reduced to 10-12 days as compared with about 42 days a year ago.

The first of the cellular container ships linking Canada, Australia and New Zealand is expected to arrive at Saint John, N.B., about mid-May. The container terminal there, which is served by CP Rail, commenced operation on an interim basis in November, 1970.

PIGGYBACK AND CONTAINER SERVICES:

Piggyback services are available in and between 62 points in all provinces in Canada except Prince Edward Island and Newfoundland. International and overhead (international) piggyback traffic is handled through established interchange points with US rail carriers.

In general, services run daily except Sunday from points of origin, using piggyback trains between Toronto-Montreal, and fast freight trains on routes. Semi-trailers owned and leased by CP Rail number 276 built to specifications which will meet piggyback handling and over-the-road service. They range in length from 35 ft to 45 ft and include both dry and insulated vans, and stake and racks. There is no specialized equipment. "Circus type" loading is performed by road tractors using end ramps.

Terminal-to-terminal service is provided for motor common carrier and private industry semi-trailers. Door-to-door service is provided by railway-owned semi-trailers. The latter are used in international service. This is limited to the number of vehicles in the inventory and the demands of domestic market. Trailers are returned loaded or empty to the owning line in accordance with A.A.R. rules. Users are the "for-hire" motor common carriers, new trailer manufacturers and industry owning its own highway trailer equipment.

TOFC COFC

CP Express is the land agent in Eastern Canada for CP Rail, CP Ships, the Head Line and Associated Container Transportation (Canada), providing both door-to-door and terminal services.

The express company performs mounting and demounting of containers from rail to road; highway line haul services to perimeter towns from main rail terminals, and operates from main rail terminals, and operates groupage terminals for consolidation and deconsolidation of less than container lot traffic. CP Transport performs the same functions in Western Canada. New container facilities at CP Express terminals in Montreal and Toronto are geared to handle unit train loads of containers. The facilities are designed around a mechanized rack storage system. Special fork lift trucks fit inside containers and stack traffic 20 ft high. Paceco transtainers have 74 ft lift spans, lift 75,000 pounds and handle 20 ft and 40 ft containers. Each terminal building has more than 30,000 square feet of handling and storage space. Each yard can accommodate 700 containers.

CP Ships two container services provide weekly door-to-door service between Canada, the UK and Western Europe.

BRUNTERM, the new CP Rail—McLean Kennedy Ltd container terminal at Saint John, N.B., began operations during the summer of 1971, handling containers for ACT (Canada).

Inland movement of containers from Quebec City and other ports is by CP Rail CP Express and Smith Transport.

CP Rail Landbridge Operations

In September 1970 the first Japanese containers via Vancouver was received in Montreal. The total time taken Japan-Montreal was 15 days.

CP Rail also provides inland links with the port of Saint John where it is a partner in the operation of Brunterm, the new portainer equipped container terminal. CP Rail has overnight service to Montreal from this terminal which is equipped to permit direct on and off-loading from ship to rail car.

From Quebec City, CP Rail moves container trainloads to Montreal in four hours or to Toronto overnight. Handling at these terminals is effected by CP express with 35-ton, four-track yard gantry cranes and other equipment.

CP Rail has developed a lightweight container flatcar with cushioned couplers which carries four 20-foot or two 40-foot containers, all loaded to maximum weight.

There are nearly 550 container flatcars in the fleet, of which 350 have a load limit design of 202,000 lb. Two hundred were added in 1970 and delivery of a further 200 is expected in 1972.

The trucking companies have acquired a variety of container handling equipment including side transfer and overhead lift units. CP Express has installed automated cargo sorting equipment at both its Montreal and Toronto terminals.

CONTAINERS IN SERVICE:

Deliveries will be completed in 1971 on additions to CP Ships' original orders for 3,000 containers of 12 different standard varieties. New orders expand the fleet total to over 4,000 containers.

WHITE PASS AND YUKON ROUTE

British Yukon Ocean Service Ltd,
(White Pass & Yukon Route),
510 Hastings Street, Standard Building,
Vancouver 2, BC, Canada
OFFICERS:
EXECUTIVE DEPARTMENT:
F. H. Brown, CBE (*Chairman*)
A. P. Friesen (*President*)
F. D. Smith (*Vice-President, Finance, Treasurer and Comptroller*)
M. P .Taylor (*Vice-President, Operations*)
J. S. Butterfield (*Secretary*)
R. S. Minter (*Vice-President*)
SALES AND SERVICE DEPARTMENT:
F. G. Downey (*Passenger Sales Manager Seattle*)
J. H. Wood (*Manager, Freight Sales and Service Department*)
R. C. Beaumont (*District Sales Representative*)
J. Jogan (*Agent, Dawson*)
I. Butterworth (*Agent, Watson Lake*)
ACCOUNTING DEPARTMENT:
J. A. Sinclair (*Manager of Systems*)
R. W. Unsworth (*Assistant Comptroller*)
OPERATING DEPARTMENT:
M. P. Taylor (*Manager, Northern Operations*)
D. W. Pepper (*Superintendent Rail Division, Skagway*)
D. H. Sladden (*Manager, Ocean Division*)
D. W. Stinson (*Manager, Highway Division*)
P. Loiselle (*Manager, Loiselle Transport*)
P. G. Delaney (*Manager, Petroleum Services*)
G. L. Budd (*Superintendent, Pipeline Division*)
E. C. Hanousek (*Manager, Skagway Bulk Terminal*)
M. M. Knapp (*Master Mechanic Rail Division*)
F. G. Downey (*Purchasing Agent, US Operations, Seattle*)
G. E. Harrison (*Purchasing Agent, Canadian Operations*)
GENERAL:
The Company operates a through container service using a container module of 25 × 8 × 8 feet from Vancouver to Skagway by sea using two vessels each capable of lifting 260 units equipped with their own 40 ton Munck container gantry cranes. From Skagway containers are transported to Whitehorse, a distance of 110 miles over a narrow gauge railway where they are transferred to road transport for oncarriage to the dispersed mining communities in the area. Clark straddle carriers capable of lifting a 30 ton

container to a height of 22 ft are used at all transfer points.

In addition to normal and industrial freight, the Company transports lead and zinc concentrates from the rich fields of Anvil in the centre of the Yukon to a storage terminal at Skagway for oncarriage to Japan and Germany in bulk cargo tonnage. A special 'tear drop' design 36-ton hopper container, 19 ft × 8 ft × 8 ft, suitable for both road and rail vehicles has been designed for this purpose.

Two hundred and eighty concentrate containers are employed—one hundred and eighty of them constructed of aluminium and one hundred of steel. In addition to handling concentrates the steel containers carry quick lime and coal.

Lead and zinc concentrates are hauled south to railhead at Whitehorse by a fleet of heavy duty White Pass tractor-trailer units. Each tractor hauls one container loaded with thirty tons of metal concentrate giving the unit an all up weight of 42·4 long tons.

At Skagway, trains pull into the concentrate shed siding where a gantry lifts each container from its flat car; transports it horizontally to the closest shed opening; projects it into the shed; removes the lid; lowers and rotates the container—dumping the concentrate. By reversing the cycle the container is returned to the flat car.

The concentrate shed 219·5 m (720 ft) long, 45·7 m (150 ft) wide, and 50 ft high, its floor area is some 10,000 m² (2·5 acres) providing storage space for 100,000 tons of concentrates. The bulk concentrates are transferred from the shed to a ship loader by a series of vibrating belt feeders.

TRAFFIC:
A great proportion of traffic is handled by containers. Freight handled exceeds 250,000 tons and the number of passengers approximates 30,000.

FLEET:
(Please see Shipowner section under British Yukon Navigation Co. Ltd, for details of ships).

White Pass "Teardrop" container for carrying lead and zinc concentrates

White Pass Skagway Terminal with
Frank H. Brown alongside

CANADIAN FREIGHT FORWARDERS

The Canadian International Freight Forwarders Association Inc.
P.O. Box 156, Place d'Armes, Montreal 126
Quebec

Able Customs Brokers Ltd.,
159 Bay St., Toronto 1, Ont.

Adanac International Forwarders Ltd.,
1690 West 2nd Ave.,
Vancouver, B.C.   732-8611

Affiliated Customs Brokers
(Montreal) Limited,
450 St. Helen Street, Montreal, P.Q.
                                   845-1211

Allports Customs Brokers Ltd.,
407 McGill St., Montreal 125, P.Q.
                                   288-3225

Beacon International Despatch Ltd.,
P.O. Box 1582, Brantford, Ontario 756-6463

Bechard McMahon & Co.,
410 St. Nicholas St., Montreal, Que.
                                   842-5411

Bensol Customs Brokers Ltd.,
410 St. Nicholas St., Montreal, Que.
                                   842-8036

Blaiklock Bros. Ltd.,
300 St. Sacrament St., Montreal, Quebec
                                   842-5231

Border Brokers Limited,
Suite 52E, Place Bonaventure,
Montreal, P.Q.   849,3751

Cargo Expediters Ltd.,
300 St. Sacrament St., Montreal, P.Q.
                                   844-8486

Cargotainers Reg'd.,
1608 The Queensway, Toronto 18, Ont.
                                   252-2663

G. W. Clark & Co. Ltd.,
43 Green St., Lambert, P.Q.   671-5555

P. F. Collins,
8-12 King's Rd., St. John's, Newfoundland
                                   726-7596

Davidson & Sons,
1023 West Pender Street, Vancouver, B.C.
                                   681-5132

Dawson Customs Brokerage Co.,
77 York St., Toronto 1, Ont.

Delmar Customs Brokers Ltd.,
353 St. Nicholas St., Montreal, P.Q.
                                   849-2127

Denning Freight Forwarders Ltd.,
407 McGill Street, Montreal, P.Q. 845-2211

Yvon Dolbeg Engr.,
124 Rue St. Pierre, Quebec 2, P.Q. 692-0450

Dubois International Despatch,
68 Broadview Avenue, Toronto 8, Ont.
                                   465-7511

Edgar Doucet Ltee.,
417 St. Peter Street, Montreal, P.Q.
                                   849-2463

Russell A. Farrow Limited,
747 Huron Line, Windsor, Ontario   242-4415

Gillespie-Munro (1969) Limited,
465 St. John Street, Montreal, P.Q.
                                   288-2291

Guy Tombs Limited,
1085 Beaver Hall Hill, Montreal, P.Q.
                                   866-2071

Harte & Lyne Limited,
20 Hunter St., East, Hamilton, Ontario
                                   522-9244

J. Rene Herbert Ltee.,
300 St. Sacrement St., Montreal, P.Q.
                                   845-5191

Import Customs Brokers Ltd.,
186 Bay St., Toronto, Ont.

International Customs Brokers Ltd.,
P.O. Box 524, Place Bonaventure,
Montreal, P.Q.   866-9751

Johnson & Dever Limited,
300 St. Sacrament St., Montreal, P.Q.
                                   845-8212

Kerrin, Egan, Freeman Co.,
637 Craig St. West, Montreal, P.Q. 866-3044

David Kirsch Ltd.,
751 Victoria Square, Montreal, P.Q.
                                   288-2106

Kuehne & Nagel (Canada) Limited,
485 McGill Street, Montreal, P.Q.   866-9521

The A. W. W. Kyle Co. Ltd.,
353 St. Nicholas Street, Montreal, P.Q.
                                   849-2161

Lee Agencies,
3971 St. Antoine St., Montreal, P.Q.
                                   931-5269

Leith & Dyke Limited,
505 Burrard St., Rm. 260   685-3555
Vancouver, B.C.

LEP Transport (Canada) Ltd.,
407 McGill Street, Montreal, P.Q.   849-9321

W. H. Martin (Canada) Ltd.,
53 Yonge St., Toronto 1, Ont.   368-8484

Thomas Meadows & Co (Canada) Ltd.,
759 Victoria Square, Montreal, P.Q.
                                   849-1243

Mendelssohn Bros. (Canada) Limited,
300 St. Sacrament St., Montreal, P.Q.
                                   849-3651

Merchant Customs Brokers Limited,
353 St. Nicholas Street, Montreal, P.Q.
                                   844-3421

Milgram & Co. Limited,
407 McGill Street, Montreal, P.Q.   288-2161

J. O. Moquin Engr.,
353 St. Nicholas St., Montreal, P.Q.
                                   288-8915

Murray & Robinson Limited,
110 Yonge St., Toronto, Ontario   364-7141

Nelson & Harvey Limited,
1043 West Pender Street, Vancouver, B.C.

Panalpina World Transport Limited,
410 St. Nicholas St., Montreal, P.Q.
                                   849-4235

P.I.E. Transport (Canada) Ltd.,
410 St. Nicholas, Montreal, Que.   849-9291

G. M. Patry Ltd.,
Air Cargo Bldg. Rm. 109, Montreal Airport,
Dorval. P.Q.   636-3450

Peacebridge Brokerage Ltd.,
P.O. Box 218, AMF International Airport.
Dorval, Quebec   631-4521

C. E. Racine & Cie. Ltee.,
300 St. Sacrament St., Montreal, P.Q.
                                   849-5291

Reynalds & Christie Ltd.,
95 Hollis St., Halifax, Nova Scotia 422-8501

Wm. J. Ross Ltd.,
300 St. Sacrament St., Montreal, P.Q.
                                   849-2565

Ross & Ker Ltd.,
980 West Pender St., Vancouver, B.C.
                                   681-7321

St. Arnaud & Bergevin Ltd.,
410 St. Nicholas St., Montreal 125, P.Q.
                                   845-4161

J. P. St. Arnaud & Cie Ltee.,
407 McGill Street, Montreal, P.Q.   844-3341

Paul E. Samson,
219 St. George St., Bathurst, New Brunswick
                                   546-9841

Samuels & Co. Limited,
410 St. Nicholas Street, Montreal, P.Q.
                                   842-5027

Schenker of Canada Limited,
353 St. Nicholas Street, Montreal, P.Q.
                                   849-3676

J. Macd. Thomson Ltd.,
160 Bay Street, Toronto, Ontario   363-3707

A. Trepanier & Fils Ltee.,
17 St. James Street, Quebec, City, P.Q.
                                   692-1040

Trans Europe Freight Forwarders
P.O. Box 1297, Terminal "A",
Toronto 1, Ont.   429-2999

Universal Customs Brokers Limited,
36-38 Front Street West, Toronto 1, Ont.

United Customs Brokers Ltd.,
407 McGill Street, Montreal, P.Q.   845-3172

Vancouver Weighmark Co. Ltd.,
502-355 Burrard St., Vancouver, B.C.
                                   683-4301

H. L. Weiss Forwarding Ltd.,
159 Bay St., Toronto, Ontario   363-6286

J. A. Leveillé,
250, St. Urbain St., Granby, P.Q.
                                   514-378-8474

McAvoy & Levy Limited,
485 McGill Street, Montreal, P.Q.
                                   878-3641

CANADIAN WAREHOUSING AND TRUCKING ORGANISATIONS

Denning Freight Forwarders Ltd.
407 McGill Street, Montreal 125 P.Q.
SERVICES:
Warehousing, Forwarding, De-consolidation,
Trucking

Hendrie & Co.
3 Peter Street, Toronto, Ontario
SERVICES:
Warehousing, Trucking

Howell Warehouses Ltd.
156 Front Street West, Toronto 1, Ontario
SERVICES:
Warehousing, Trucking.

Johnson Terminals Ltd.
2020 Yukon Street, Vancouver 10, B.C.
SERVICES:
Warehousing, Trucking, Forwarding.

Kuehne & Nagel (Canada) Ltd.
159 Bay Street, Toronto

SERVICES:
Warehousing, Trucking, Forwarding.

Mint Warehousing Ltd.
500 Keele Street, Toronto 167, Ontario
SERVICES:
Warehousing, Trucking.

J. D. O'Hearn Container Service
159 Bay Street, Toronto
SERVICES:
Warehousing, Trucking, Forwarding.

P.I.E. Transport (Canada) Ltd.
34 King Street, Toronto 1, Ontario
SERVICES:
Warehousing, Trucking, Forwarding.
Smith Transport (US) Ltd.
20 Toronto Street, Toronto 1, Ontario

SERVICES:
Warehousing, Trucking.
Toronto Harbour Commissioners
60 Harbour Street, Toronto 1, Ontario
SERVICES:
Warehousing, Trucking, Forwarding.

Universal Container Services Ltd.
10755 Côte de Liesse Rd., Dorval 760, P.Q.
69 Yonge Street, Suite 606, Toronto, Ontario

SERVICES:
Warehousing, Trucking, Forwarding.

UNITED STATES OF AMERICA

ANCHORAGE

Port of Anchorage
2,000, Anchorage Port Road
Anchorage, Alaska 99501
TELEPHONE: 272-1531
OFFICIAL:
E. E. Davis (*Port Director*)

CONTAINER FACILITIES:
Terminal 1 (Sea-Land) and Terminal 2
These terminals have a total quay length of 368·8 m (1,120 ft) in length with 10·76 m (35 ft) of water alongside. There is a total area of 14·2 hectares (35·5 acres) and the

facility, which is served by rail, is equipped with two 27½ ton Paceco container gantry cranes with an outreach of 23·16 m (76 ft). The Sea Land terminal takes up 8·5 hectares (21·5 acres) and the remainder is used as a common user berth.

BALTIMORE

The Maryland Port Administration
Pier 2, Pratt Street, Baltimore, Maryland, 21202
TELEPHONE: 383 5700
OFFICIALS:
Joseph L. Stanton (*Maryland Port Administrator*)
W. Gregory Halpin (*Deputy Maryland Port Administrator*)

Dr. Walter C. Boyer (*Deputy Maryland Port Administrator for Engineering and Planning*)
Charles W. Meyers (*Director of Terminal Operations*)
Philip G. Kraemer (*Director of Transportation*)

OVERSEAS TRADE DEVELOPMENT OFFICES:
Brussels, London, Tokyo

CONTAINER FACILITIES:
Dundalk Marine Terminal
The Terminal is owned and operated by the Maryland Port Administration. The six container berths and backup area are offered on a public basis, assigned on a guaranteed day schedule. The guaranteed day schedule is coordinated with the Authority's present berthing commitments and the sailing

Baltimore—Dundalk Marine Terminal

Baltimore—Canton Seagirt Terminal

schedule of the individual lines. The open storage area and consolidation shed space are leased to individual operators on a time basis agreeable to the Dundalk Marine Terminal and the operators. Normally, leases for these areas are on a yearly basis. Container cranes and straddle carriers are leased to the individual operators on an as-required basis. Containers are placed on both the ground and on chassis, depending on individual preference of the operator.

The south side of the Terminal provides two berths (Nos. 7 and 8) of 182·88 m (600 ft) and two berths (Nos. 9 and 10) of 217·93 m (715 ft) which provides a total quay length of 807·72 m (2,650 ft). A roll-on platform is situated between Berths 8 and 9.

Two berths (Nos. 11 and 12) providing a total quay length of 457·2 m (1,500 ft) on the south side of the facility will be completed in 1972.

The depth at low water alongside all the facilities is 10·97 m (36 ft).

Backup area is provided directly behind each berth for staging, loading and unloading of containers. A minimum of 1·62 hectares (4 acres) is provided for each backup area.

Over 48·56 hectares (120 acres) of paved, heavy-duty open storage area is provided adjacent or near the container berths. Adequate area will be leased to each operator on a first-come, first-serve basis.

Three 40 ton Paceco container gantry cranes with an outreach of 32 m (105 ft) over water; and two with an inboard reach of 30·48 m (100 ft) and one with 9·14 m (30 ft) are in operation. Four 40 ton IHI container cranes with the same outboard and inboard reaches as the larger Pacecos above have also been provided. All are equipped with spreaders for 20 ft and 40 ft units.

All seven cranes will be operational by 1972.

Also available are two 50 ton and two 60 ton electric portal quay cranes equipped with 30 and 40 ft self-levelling spreaders.

The Port Administration leases and maintains 5 straddle carriers capable of stacking 20 ft units 3 high and 40 ft units 2 high.

The Terminal has three container consolidation sheds to serve the six container berths. One 65,000 sq ft shed is adjacent to Berths 7, 8, 9 and 10 with dimensions 650 ft by 100 ft. One 65,000 sq ft shed and one 62,500 sq ft shed are adjacent to Berths 11 and 12 with dimensions 650 ft by 100 ft and 625 ft by 100 ft.

Locust Point Marine Terminal:

Quay cranes which will eventually be

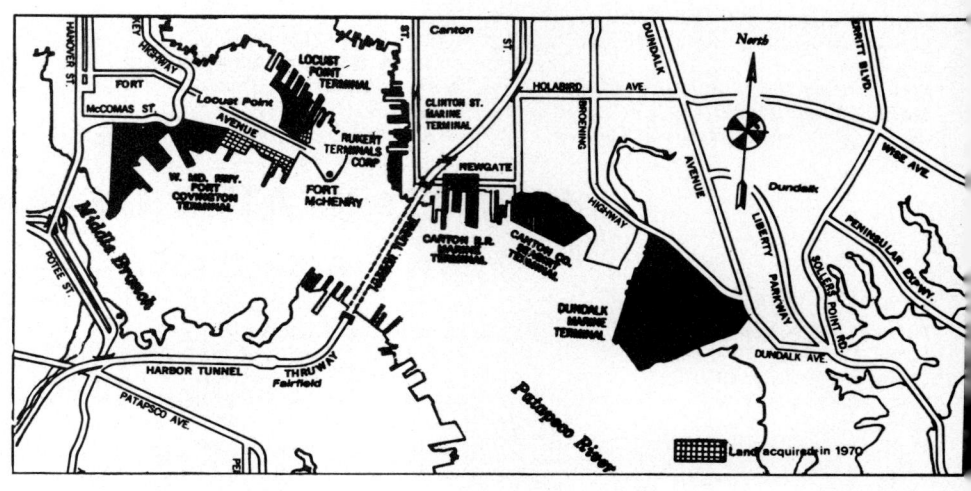

Baltimore

equipped with container spreaders have been installed at the Pier 4-5 Complex which provides a facility for container/break bulk operations. The Terminal is 366 m (1,200 ft) in length, 114 m (375 ft) wide with covered storage of over 18,000 m² (190,000 sq ft).

Future Development:

The port Authority acquired a further 20·23 hectares (50 acres) in August 1970. It is expected that construction will start at the end of 1971 on a new terminal in this area which will include three marginal quay berths in addition to the two existing freight piers. It is probable that container handling facilities, including a container gantry crane, will be provided.

Canton Seagirt Terminal

This facility, which has an area of 7 hectares (17·5 acres) with a marshalling area capable of taking 480 35 ft units on trailers is leased to Sea Land Services Inc. A 27·5 ton Paceco container gantry crane and 4,645 m² (50,000 sq ft) of covered space have been provided. It is served by a two-track rail siding.

TERMINAL OPERATING HOURS:

Ship cargo handling operations normally take place between 0800-1200 and 1300-1700 hrs. Overtime from 1900 to 2400 hrs as required.

Container Services:

Atlantic Container Line

Fabre Line

Hapag-Lloyd Container Line

Mediterranean Marine Lines (American Export)

Norfolk, Baltimore and Carolina Line

Prudential—Grace Lines

Sea Land Services Inc.

Seatrain Lines

United States Lines

TRAFFIC:

Lift-on and Roll-on

	Inwards		Outwards	
	Tons	Units	Tons	Units
1970	558,463	—	539,941	—
1971*	506,000	39,843†	594,000	46,772†

*Estimate for Dundalk Terminal Only

†20 ft units

CONTAINER REPAIR ORGANISATIONS:

Dundalk Container Services Inc.
Dundalk Marine Terminal
2700 Broening Highway
Baltimore, Maryland 21222

Patapsco Trailer Service & Sales Inc.
3510 Marmenco Court
Baltimore, Maryland 21230
Telephone: 636-2000

Warner Fruehauf Trailer Company Inc.
Bush & Hamburg Streets
Baltimore, Maryland 21230
Telephone: 727-1111

Chesapeake Trailer & Equipment Co. Inc.
1111 Frankfurst Avenue
Baltimore, Maryland 21225
Telephone: 355-1170

Most of the container companies around the Port of Baltimore do their own repair work.

BOSTON

Massachusetts Port Authority
470 Atlantic Avenue
Boston, Massachusetts 02210
Telephone: (617) 482-2930
OFFICIALS:
Edward J. King, (*Executive Director*)
Thomas T. Soules, (*Port Director*)
Joseph J. Connolly, (*Superintendent of Marine Terminals*)
A. R. Ollerherd (*Director of Trade Development*)
Chester H. Gourley (*Traffic Manager*)
Jim McDonald (*Trade Representative*)
James A. Hickey (*Trade Representative*)
CONTAINER FACILITIES:
Castle Island Terminal:
Sea Land Services, Inc. has leased a berth and 4.05 hectares (10 acres). A Paceco crane has been installed and the terminal is ready to go into service.

Boston-Mystic Terminal:

This facility, the first phase of which came into service in Spring 1971 has 274 m (900 ft) of quay frontage equipped with a 70 ton Hitachi container gantry crane and a 50 ton Le Tourneau container yard gantry crane.

There will be 18·2 hectares (45 acres) available for storage, road and rail handling warehouse and office space. There is a further 335·3 m (1,100 ft) of quay length with back up space available for further development.

ACCESS:

Superhighways from Boston proper connect with throughways which extend to virtually all points in the United States and Canada, affording fast motor truck service to and from the Port.

Excellent service is also available from shipside on three railroads.

Boston-Mystic Public Container Terminal—early Spring 1971

SHIPPING SERVICES:

The Port is served by more than 90 steamship lines offering regular and frequent sailings to and from 315 world ports.

The New England Express Line has provided a fortnightly container service to Hamburg, Bremen, Antwerp and the Havre since July 1969.

TERMINAL WORKING HOURS:

Ships are worked from 0800 to 0300 hours Inland transport operations take place from 0730 to 1700 hours.

CONTAINER REPAIR FACILITIES:

Fruehauf Trailer Div.
Fruehauf Corp.,
550 Winter St., Waltham, Mass.
849-7000
Brown Trailer Div.
Clark Equipment Co.,
69 Norman St., Everett, Mass.
389-8000
Trucktor Equipment Co.
26 S. Eden St., Charlestown, Mass.
242-2426

The New England Express Line operation at Boston.

Model of Boston-Mystic Public Container Terminal

BROWNSVILLE

Brownsville Navigation District
PO Box 231, Brownsville, Texas
TELEPHONE: 542-4351
OFFICIALS:
Ygnacio Garza, Jr (*Chairman*)
James R. Batsell (*Secretary*)
Al Cisneros (*General Manager and Port Director*)
Maurice Tipton, Jr. (*Commissioner*)
George Metzenthin (*Comptroller and Director of Finance*)
Ersel G. Lantz (*Director of Engineering and Port Development*)
GENERAL

Port Brownsville is the southernmost port in Texas and the southern terminus of the Intercoastal Waterway System.

CONTAINER FACILITIES:

Containers are mainly handled at No. 11 Dock on the south side of the Turning Basin. This facility is 183 m (600 ft) in length with a width of 85·3 m (280 ft). It has two rail tracks on the apron.

There are two mobile 50-ton and one 250 ton cranes available in the port area, but no container cranes at present. There is a 6·1 hectare (15 acres) storage yard adjacent to Terminal 11.

STEAMSHIP AGENTS AND LINES:

Dix Shipping Company
P.O. Box 2046
Telephone: TE 1-4228

Europe: Deppe, Finnlines, Combi Line, Independent Gulf Line, Ozean/Stinnes, Polish Ocean, Swedish Atlantic Wilhelmsen. *Mediterranean:* Fabre, Hellenic, Jugolinija, Jugooceanija, Saguaro Sidarma. *Africa:* Belgian African, Hellenic, Nopal West Africa, Safmarine. *Middle East-India:* Bar-

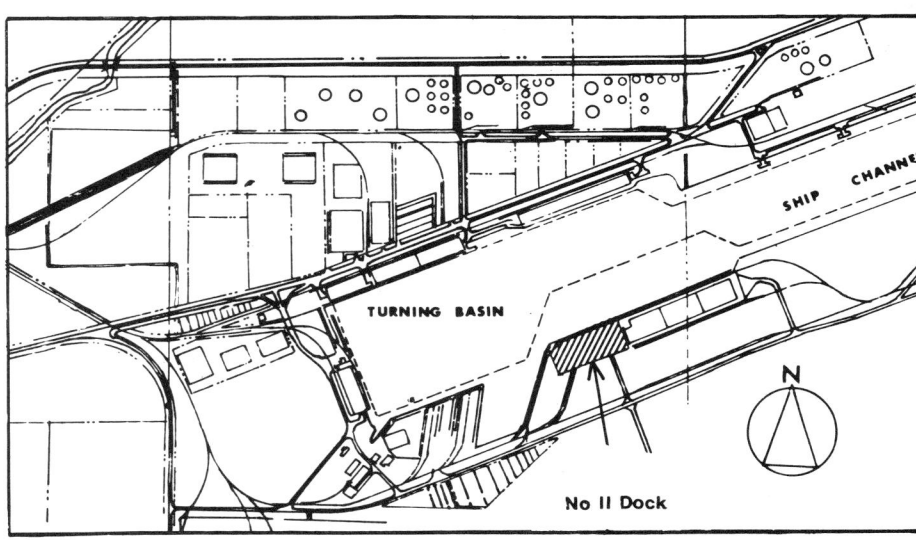

Brownsville.

ber Middle East, Concordia, Hellenic, Nedlloyd, Scindia Steam Navigation Co., Shipping Corp. of India, Ltd. *Far East-Australia:* Bank Line, China Merchants, China Union, Farrell Line, Fern Lines, Mitsui-OSK, NYK Line, Orient Overseas. *Caribbean-Central America:* Azta, Coldemar, Flomerca, Guatamalan, Gulf-Caribbean Mamenic, Marine Express, Royal Netherlands Steamship, Mini Line, United Fruit Co. *South America:* Argentine Lines, Chilean Line, Coldemar, Nopal, Peruvian State Line.

Philen Shipping Company,
P.O. Box 271

Telephone: LI 2-3591
Europe: Gulf Container Line, Mexican Line, Waterman. *Mediterranean:* Deep Sea Med. Line, Nervion, Nordana, States Marine Lines. Zim Israel. *Africa:* Black Star, Westwind Africa Line. *Middle East-India:* Central Gulf, Djakarta Lloyd Line, Isthmian Lines, Ocean Wide Shipping. *Far East:* Blue Sea, "K" Line, Maritime Company of the Philippines, States Marine Lines, Yamashita-Shinnihon Line. *Caribbean-Central America:* Booth Line, Gallen Lines, Grancolombiana, Venezuelan Line. *South America:* Navem Line, Bolivian Grancolombiana, West Coast.

FREIGHT FORWARDERS
Bartz Forwarding Co (FMB-145)
  PO Box 1992
  Tel: LI 2-7457
Brito Forwarding Co (FMB-294)
  PO Box 450
  Tel: LI 6-1701

Carlos A. Cisneros
  1207 E. Washington Street
  Tel: LI 2-3240
Corrigan Dispatch Co
  PO Box 2315
  Tel: LI 2-3556
Ernesto Perez & Co
  408 E. 13th Street
  Tel: LI 2-5635
Oscar Perez Forwarding Co
  PO Box 1107
  Tel: LI 2-3881
Jovita Perez (FMB-1131)
  PO Box 328
  Tel: LI 2-5659
Soto Forwarding Agency
  PO Box 1091
  Tel: LI 2-7203

Tom J. Watts (FMB-906)
  PO Box 1673
  Tel: LI 2-8943
STEVEDORES:
Border Stevedoring
  PO Box 271
  Tel: LI 2-3591
Dix Shipping Company,
  PO Box 2046
  Tel: TE 1-4228
Plitt & Company
  PO Box 1331
  Tel: TE 1-4053
Port Brownsville Stevedoring Co
  PO Box 31
  Tel: LI 2-3762
RAILROAD
  Port Brownsville has over 16 miles of railroad trackage, with rail sidings service warehouses, industries and all docks in the port area. General cargo facilities, with the exception of Docks 7 and 8, have two shipside tracks, and all general cargo facilities have double depressed tracks at the rear of the transit sheds. Storage and classification tracks are capable of holding 300 cars.

Switching within the port area is performed by the Missouri Pacific Railroad Co under contract, and reciprocal switching connections are maintained between the following trunk line railroads:
Missouri Pacific Railroad Company
  600 E. Fronton St. Brownsville, Texas
  Tel: LI 6-2226
Southern Pacific Lines
  921 E. 7th St, Brownsville, Texas
  Tel: LI 2-3549
National Railways of Mexico
  Calle Hidalgo entre 9 y 10, Matrimoros, Mexico
  Tel: 2-02-55
CUSTOMS FACILITIES:
  Containers bound for Mexico can pass through Brownsville "in-bond" thereby not requiring any US customs inspection. If containers move by road on flat-bed Mexican trucks they are inspected at Matamorus Border Inspection Building. Containers moving on flat-bed rail cars into Mexico by National Railways of Mexico are not inspected until container is discharged at ultimate destination.

CHARLESTON

The South Carolina State Ports Authority
PO Box 817
Charleston, South Carolina
TELEPHONE: 723-8651
TELETYPE: 810-881-1860
OFFICIALS:
Capers G. Barr, Jr (*General Manager*)
James M. Tobias (*Assistant for Development*)
Coyte W. White (*Assistant for Communications*)
J. J. Scott (*Chief Engineer*)
G. Luther Rosebrock (*Controller*)
Marion S. Moore, Jr. (*General Traffic Manager*)
Wade H. Brinson (*General Operations Manager*)
Charles McSwain (*Sales Manager*)
Greenville:
P.O. Box 9033
Francis M. Curtis (*District Sales Manager*)
New York:
17 Battery Place
New York, N.Y. 10004
Telephone: 425-3693
Andrew J. Corbett (*District Sales Manager*)
Andrew J. Corbett, Jr. (*Assistant District Sales Manager*)

CONTAINER FACILITIES:
State Pier 8, Columbus Street Terminal
  This facility, operated by Sea Land Services Inc. is equipped with one 50 ton and one

Charleston—State Pier 8, Columbus Street Terminal

75 ton quay crane.
North Charleston Terminal:
  This is a public container facility equipped with a 40 long ton container gantry crane and two 50 ton quay cranes capable of

handling containers. Berth backup space amounts to 10 hectares (25 acres).
CONTAINER SERVICES:
Sea Land Service Inc.
Seatrain Lines

CLEVELAND

Cleveland-Cuyahoga County Port Authority
(Port of Cleveland)
101 Erieside Avenue
Cleveland, Ohio 44114
TELEPHONE: 241-8004
OFFICIALS:
Richard L. Schultz (*Executive Director*)
Robert E. Deveney (*Trade Representative*)
Paul R. Lynham (*Public Relations Representative*)

GENERAL:
  The port is able to accommodate the largest ships capable of passing through the St. Lawrence Seaway and it is usually the first United States port of call into the Great Lakes, and similarly, the last U.S. port of call on the way out of the lakes.
  Navigation of the St. Lawrence Seaway is annually of about eight months' duration

Cleveland—Container operations

from the first or second week in April until the first week in December.

Containers are currently handled satisfactorily at conventional berths and studies have indicated that no additional or specialized facilities will be required until after 1972.

Detroit-Wayne County Port Commission,
Veterans Memorial Building,
151 W. Jefferson Avenue,
Detroit, Michigan, 48226
TELEPHONE: 224-5656
OFFICIALS:
F. C. Lind (*Port Director*)

SHIPPING COMPANIES PROVIDING CONTAINER SERVICES:

American-Export Isbrandtsen to Europe
Europe Canada Lakes Line ECL) to Europe
Head Line to UK and Ireland
'K' Line to the Far East

DETROIT

D. E. Clark (*Traffic and Rate Analyst*)
CRANEAGE:
Quay cranes and mobile cranes are used for container handling.
TERMINAL WORKING HOURS:
Ship and inland transport cargo operations are carried out 24 hours per day.

Manchester Liners to Europe via Manchester
Mediterranean Lake Services to the Mediterranean
Mitsui-O.S.K. to the Far East
Fred Olsen Line to Europe
Yugoslav Great Lakes Line to Mediterranean
NYK Line to the Far East

TRAFFIC:

	Inwards		Outwards	
Lift-on	Tons	Units	Tons	Units
1970	15,702	1,241	10,498	875
1971 Estimate	20,000	1,500	14,000	1,200

CONTAINER FACILITIES:

Containers can be handled at all general cargo terminals which are as follows:	Length		Covered Storage and Transit Sheds		Container Storage
	m	ft	m²	sq. ft	acres
Harbour Terminal	708	2,325	74,000	800,000	20
Marine Terminal	433	1,420	7,400	80,000	45
Nicolson Terminal	932	3,055	3,000	33,000	30
Detroit Processing Terminal	631	2,069	20,400	220,000	10
Federal Marine Terminal	158	520	4,360	47,000	5

DULUTH

Port of Duluth,
Seaway Port Authority of Duluth,
PO Box 310, Duluth, Minnesota 55801
TELEPHONE: 727-8525
TELEGRAMS: SPAD
TELEX: FBN
OFFICIALS:
C. Thomas Burke (*Port Director*)

Robert H. Smith (*Director of Traffic*)
GENERAL:
Duluth Public Marine Terminal, 1200 Garfield Avenue, operates the container berths. Facilities include two electric portal cranes with a maximum lift of 10 tons at 110 ft and 90 tons at 30 ft. 12·2 hectares (30 acres) of parking area are available.

TERMINAL OPERATING HOURS:
Ship and inland transport cargo operations are carried out from 0800 to 1200 hours and 1300 to 1700 hours; overtime on request.

SHIPPING LINES OPERATING REGULAR CONTAINER SERVICES WITH CONVENTIONAL TONNAGE:
Cast Line
Agent: Svensson Shipping Company
500 Board of Trade Building
Federal & Atlantic Lakes Line
Agent: Alastair Guthrie, Inc.
600 Board of Trade Building,

Duluth—Berths used for containers shown in the foreground

Hamburg-Chicago Line.
Agent: Alastair Guthrie, Inc.,
600 Board of Trade Building,
Manchester Liners, Ltd.
Agent: Alastair Guthrie, Inc.
600 Board of Trade Building
Moore-McCormack Lines, Inc.
Agent: General Steamship Agencies, Inc.
Board of Trade Building

RAILROADS

The Port of Duluth is serviced by the following railroad lines: Burlington Northern Inc. Soo Line Railroad, Chicago, Milwaukee, St. Paul & Pacific Railroad, Chicago & North Western Railway Co., Northern Pacific Railway, Canadian National Railways, Duluth, Missabe & Iron Range Railroad.

GALVESTON

Galveston Wharves (The Port of Galveston)
PO Box 238, Galveston, Texas 77550
TELEGRAMS: Galtex
OFFICIALS:
C. S. Devoy (*Port Director and General Manager*)
O. L. Selig, (*Director of Administration and Finance*)
Carl S. Parker Jr., (*Traffic Manager*)
Jack Collier (*Director of Operations and Sales*)
GENERAL:
Galveston is the world's leading cotton exporting center, handling at the present time about 50 per cent of all American exports of cotton. The citizens of Galveston in March, 1970, voted $7·7 million in tax obligations bonds to which will be added $10 million in port revenues over a 10-year period to build on the Galveston waterfront a $9·2 million container terminal, a barge consolidation terminal, berths for LASH and SEABEE ships, and a 15-acre barge fleeting station.

FACILITIES:
Barge Carrier Terminal:
Piers 34 and 35 will be developed into a

Galveston

barge carrier terminal, a consolidation and covered loading terminal and a break bulk dock.

Seabee Ship Base—Pelican Island:

This terminal for Lykes Bros. Steamship Co. will be operational by the end of 1971. All barges loaded in the West Gulf of Mexico from Brownsville to Lake Charles will be brought to Galveston for consolidation.

Container Terminal Piers 10-14:

This terminal will have a quay length of 518·16 m (1,700 ft) and an area of 26·71 hectares (66 acres). This area is at present under development.

Drawing of the Container Terminal to be built at Piers 10-14.

RAILROADS
Atchison, Topeka & Santa Fe Railway Co
  Rosenberg and Strand, SO 5-6709
Burlington Lines
  33rd and Market, SO 5-7717
Chicago, Rock Island & Pacific Railroad Co
  33rd and Market SO 5-7717
Fort Worth & Denver Railway Co
  33rd and Market, SO 5-7717
Galveston, Houston & Henderson Railroad Co
  33rd and Market, SO 2-3212
Galveston Wharves Terminal Railway
  33rd and Wharves Road, SO 5-9321

Missouri-Kansas-Texas Railroad Company
  2705 Palmer Highway, Texas City, EN 3474
Missouri Pacific Railroad and Texas & Pacific Railway
  323 Thirty-Third, SO 5-5514
Southern Pacific Company
  5102 Strand, SH 4-5252
Western Weighing & Inspection Bureau
  Santa Fe Building, SO 5-5477
STEVEDORES:
Atlantic & Gulf Stevedores, Inc
  2411 Strand, SO 2-4200
Bulk Packaging Corporation
  Pier 38, SO 5-5414
Dixie Stevedores
  US National Bank Bldg, SO 5-9463
Gulf Stevedore Corporation
  Cotton Exchange Bldg, SO 2-9633
Liberty Stevedore, Inc
  Cotton Exchange Bldg, SO 3-6466
National Stevedore Co
  Cotton Exchange Bldg, SO 5-5085
Southern Stevedoring & Contracting Co
  101 Rosenberg, SO 2-0230
Stevedore Equipment Corporation
  Pier 39, SO 2-1166
Strachan Shipping Co
  US National Bank Bldg, SO 3-2351
Suderman Stevedores, Inc
  US National Bank Bldg, SO 3-4334
Texas Contracting Co
  Cotton Exchange Bldg, SO 5-6357
Texas Forwarding Co, Inc
  Pier 20, SO 2-8019
Texas Star Stevedoring Co
  Pier 34, SO 5-7364
Texas Stevedores Corp
  Pier 39, SO 2-7323
Texas Transport & Terminal Co
  Pier 16, SO 3-8680
Texla Stevedores
  101 Rosenberg, SO 2-0230

Texports Stevedore Co
  US National Bank Bldg, SO 5-6345
United Stevedoring Div, of States Marine Lines Inc
  Pier 33, SO 3-8945
Young & Company
  Cotton Exchange Bldg, SO 5-5085

FREIGHT FORWARDERS:
Acme Fast Freight, Inc
  3001 Postoffice, SO 3-8801
Herbelin, F. J. Forwarding Co, Inc
  509-37th St, SO 3-6441
Michels, J. R. Inc
  Cotton Exchange Bldg, SO 3-4694
R E A Express
  2520 Santa Fe Place, SO 3-8891
Schurig, H. E. & Co, Inc
  Cotton Exchange Bldg, SO 2-9685
Darrell J. Sekin
  PO Box 1333, SO 2-6277
Stone Forwarding Co, Inc
  US National Bank Bldg, SO 3-1674
Zanelli, Hugo & Co
  405 National Hotel Bldg, SO 3-4469
Zanes, W. R. & Co
  US National Bank Bldg, SO 3-2305
Zeigler, H. L. Inc
  US National Bank Bldg, SO 2-4632

Impression of piers 34 and 35

HAMPTON ROADS

Virginia Port Authority
1600 Maritime Tower
Norfolk Virginia 23510
TELEPHONE: 622-1671
OFFICIALS:
Ephraim P. Holmes, Adm. USN, Ret.
  (Executive Director)
GENERAL:
The Port of Hampton Roads, at the confluence of the James, Nansemond and Elizabeth Rivers, consists of the port cities of Norfolk, Portsmouth, Chesapeake and Newport News. Containers are handled at four terminals within the port area—Norfolk International Terminals, Newport News Terminal, Portsmouth Marine Terminal, and Lamberts Point Terminal.
TRAFFIC:
Virginia port terminals handled 101,300 containers during the twelve months ending April 1971. There was a near balance between inbound and outbound containers. Traffic for 1971 may be estimated at about 130,000 units.

Estimated traffic figures for 1970 and 1971 are as follows for both lift-on and roll-on traffic.
1970
  Inwards   323,400 tons   24,500 units
  Outwards 534,600 tons   40,500 units
1971
  Inwards   488,000 tons   37,000 units
  Outwards 799,000 tons   60,500 units

TERMINAL WORKING HOURS:
0800 to 1700 hrs Monday to Friday. Overtime for other hours can be arranged.

FREIGHT FORWARDING AND STEVEDORING COMPANIES:
The Freight Forwarding and Stevedoring companies listed below serve the whole area of Hampton Roads.

Freight Forwarders:

Alltransport Incorporated
  147 Granby St.,
  Norfolk, VA
Anders Williams and Co., Inc.
  1 Commercial Place
  Norfolk, VA
Black & Geddes Inc.
  Byed International Airport
  Richmond, VA
Browing, W. J. Co., Inc.
  Royster Building,
  Norfolk, VA
Cavalier Shipping Co., Inc.
  Law Building,
  Norfolk, VA
Martin E. Day
  147 Granby St.,
  Norfolk, VA
Gaskell, Fred P., Co., Inc.
  301 E. Plume Street,
  Norfolk, VA
General Freight Forwarders Inc.
  304 E. Plume St.
  Norfolk, VA
Harper, Robinson, and Co. Inc.
  606 First and Merchants National Bank Bldg.
  Norfolk, VA
Hasler & Co.
  1428 Maritime Tower,
  Norfolk, VA
Hipage Co., Inc.
  The Citizens Bank Building,
  Norfolk, VA
Intermodal Freight-Forwarding, Inc.
  PO Box 3223,
  Norfolk, VA

Norton & Ellis, Inc.
  120 Atlantic Street,
  Norfolk, VA

REA Express,
  2202 Redgate Ave.,
  and 1401 Peachtree St., N.E.
  Atlanta, GA 30309
Schade, Wilfred, & Co., Inc.
  C/O Bldg. N. News 23607
Schenkers International Forwarders, Inc.
  2600 Washington Avenue,
  Newport News, Virginia 23607
Smith, W. O. & Co., Inc.
  523-527 Law Building,
  Norfolk, VA
Southern Overseas, Corp
  Board of Trade Bldg., RM 616
  Norfolk, VA
Stone, Wm., & Co., Inc.
  212 E. Plume Street,
  Norfolk, VA
Universal Van Lines, Inc.,
  (Overseas Division)
  117 W. Va., Beach Blvd.,
  Norfolk, VA
Vanderberry, E. L., Co.,
  PO Box 3411
  Norfolk, VA
Virginia Shipping, Inc.
  109 E. Main St.
  Norfolk, VA
Stevedores:
Atlantic & Gulf Grain Stevedoring Associates
  115 Atlantic Street
Atlantic & Gulf Stevedores, Inc.,
  115 Atlantic Street
Dore, Inc.
  715 Orapax Street,
Hampton Road, Stevedoring Corp.
  1 Commercial Place
Lavino Shipping Company, Stevedoring Division
  C. & O. Building,
  and Law Building
  Newport News, Va. 23607

Marine Stevedoring Corp.
  PO Box 10085
Maritime Ship Watch Service Corp.
  237 W. 24th Street
Nacirema Operating Co., Inc.
  1 Commercial Place
Old Dominion Stevedoring Corp.
  301 E. Plume Street
Rogers Terminal & Shipping Corp.
  Barnes Rd., Chesapeake, Va. 23515
Southern Stevedoring Corp.
  13 Selden Arcade
Tidewater Dunnage & Supply Co., Inc.
  231 Sir Oliver Road,

Tidewater Stevedoring Corp.
  C. & O. Building, Newport News, Va 23607

RAILWAYS:

Chesapeake & Ohio Railroad Company, affiliated with the Baltimore & Ohio Railroad, is the principal railway serving Newport News.

Piggy-back services are operated by the Chesapeake & Ohio, the Norfolk & Western, the Southern Railway System and Seaboard Coast Line, all of whom have designated Norfolk International Terminals and Portsmouth Marine Terminal as Ramp Points. C+O/B+O also designate Pier 6, Newport

News as a Ramp Point.

ROAD ACCESS:

A modern network of interstate and local highways permits fast and direct transport. Interstate 64 passes within one mile of the entrance to Norfolk International Terminal. Hampton Roads Tunnel provides access to Interstate 95, and the Chesapeake Bay Bridge-Tunnel connects Tidewater Virginia with the eastern shore and a direct route to New York.

TRUCK SERVICE:

Over 130 motor carriers serve the port on a regular basis.

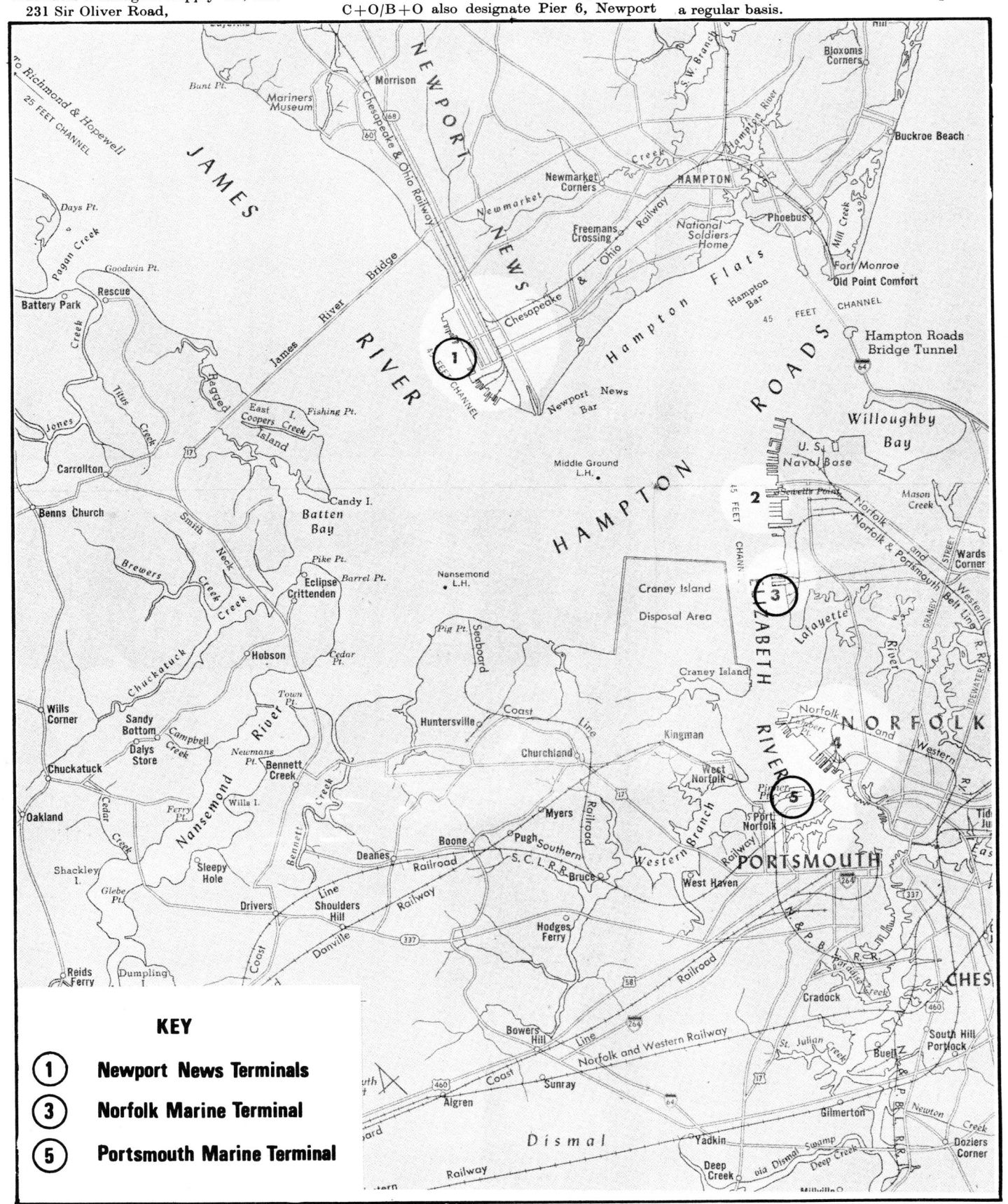

KEY

1. **Newport News Terminals**
3. **Norfolk Marine Terminal**
5. **Portsmouth Marine Terminal**

Ports of Hampton Road

Newport News Terminal

PO Box 338, Newport News
Virginia 23607
TELEPHONE: 244-8471
OWNERS OF THE GENERAL CARGO FACILITY:
Peninsula Ports Authority

OFFICIALS:
King Meehan (*Executive Director, PPA*)
Marvin V. Craft, Jr., (*Deputy Director, PPA*)

GENERAL:
Located on the North side of Hampton Roads,
just east of the mouth of the James River,
Newport News Terminals is operated by the
Chesapeake & Ohio Railway for Peninsula
Ports Authority of Virginia. Pier B is equipped
with a special 50-ton mobile leTourneau crane
and a straddle carrier capable of handling 20
and 40-foot containers. The pier also has an
assembly area to accommodate about 800
containers. Pier B is a 3 berth, fireproof pier
183 m (600 ft) by 183 m, built in 1967.
LANDSIDE CONNECTIONS:
Railroad: Chesapeake & Ohio Railway
Highway: Thru streets to US 1, Interstate 64,
US 60 and all local routes.

Norfolk International Terminals

Maritime Tower, Norfolk, Virginia 23510
Telephone: 625-8291

OFFICIALS:
James N. Crumbley (*General Manager,
PIA*)
Richard D. O'Leary (*Assistant General
Manager*)
Raymond Brewer (*Terminal Manager,
NTC*)
OWNERS:
City of Norfolk
OPERATOR:
Norfolk Port and Industrial Authority
OPERATING AGENTS:
Norfolk Terminal Corporation
GENERAL:
The Norfolk International Terminal served as
an army port from 1918 until 1965. Already
it is an important container handling terminal
and has large scale projects to provide the
most modern facilities available. There is a
quay length of 484·5 m (1,587 ft) on a marginal wharf which provides two containership
berths. Three Paceco container gantry cranes
(with lifting capacities of 34 and 50 tons)
together with three rubber tyred and four
rail mounted 40 ton yard transfer gantry
cranes have been provided. In addition
there are four 'Tainer trains (coupled trailers
drawn by a tractor and specially designed
for the terminal).

A paved area adjacent to the container
berth provides marshalling space for some
5,400 20 ft units, a further area of 12·14
hectares (30 acres) is being paved.

There are two covered concrete piers,
combined berthing space for 8 to 12 vessels,
five brick and concrete warehouses, gantry
cranes and other modern equipment for
general cargo.
TERMINAL WORKING HOURS:
Ship cargo handling operation takes place
24 hours daily.
Inland transport during normal working
hours; a 24 hour sevice can be arranged.
FUTURE DEVELOPMENT:
Up to six berths equipped with container
gantry cranes are envisaged.
TRAFFIC:
In 1970 56,000 containers were handled.
In 1971 it is estimated that 70,000 will
move through the terminal.
CONTAINER SERVICES:
American Export Isbrandtsen Line
(N.W. Europe and Mediterranean services)
Dart Containerline
Hapag Lloyd Container Line
Seatrain Lines
United States Lines

Impression of Pier C. Newport, News

FUTURE DEVELOPMENT:
Pier C, when completed late in 1972 will
berth three ships at one time enabling
containerships, combination vessels and break
bulk freighters to be handled.

Norfolk International Terminal. A third container gantry crane was installed in July 1971

A Tainer train at Norfolk, Virginia.

CONTAINER REPAIR ORGANIZATIONS
Atlantic and Gulf Container Repair
7737 Hampton Boulevard
Norfolk, Virginia 23505
Telephone: (703) 423-5419
Container Repair Corporation
P.O.B. 3384
Norfolk, Virginia 23514
Telephone: (703) 625-6008)
Foley Warehousing, Inc.
24th Street and Morton Avenue
Norfolk, Virginia 23517
Telephone: (703) 627-8769, (703) 622-5418
Seaboard Avenue,
Portsmouth, Virginia 23707
Telephone: (703) 622-5418
Marine Stevedoring Corporation
P.O.B. 10085
Norfolk, Virginia 23513
Telephone: (703) 423-6863

Maritime Services, Inc.
237 W. 24th Street
Norfolk, Virginia 23517
Telephone: (703) 627-1764
Maritime Ship Watch Service Corporation
237 West 24th Street
Norfolk, Virginia 23517
Telephone: (703) 627-1764
Ship Tank Container Corporation
419 West 22nd Street
Norfolk, Virginia 23517
Telephone: (703) 622-2520
Fruehauf Division, Fruehauf Corporation
500 Newtown Road
Virginia Beach, Virginia 23462
Seaway Container Corporation of America
1516 E. Princess Anne Road
Norfolk, Virginia 23516
Trailer Service and Refrigeration Company
516 S. Military Highway
Norfolk, Virginia 23502

CONTAINER LEASING OPERATIONS:
Container Transport International Inc.
  Law Building
  Plume and Granby Streets
  Norfolk, Virginia 23510

Container Carrier Corporation
7737 Hampton Boulevard
Norfolk, Virginia 23505
Foley Leasing Company
24th and Morton Streets

Norfolk, Virginia 23517
Marine Trailers of Norfolk, Inc.
  237 W. 24th Street
  Norfolk, Virginia 23517

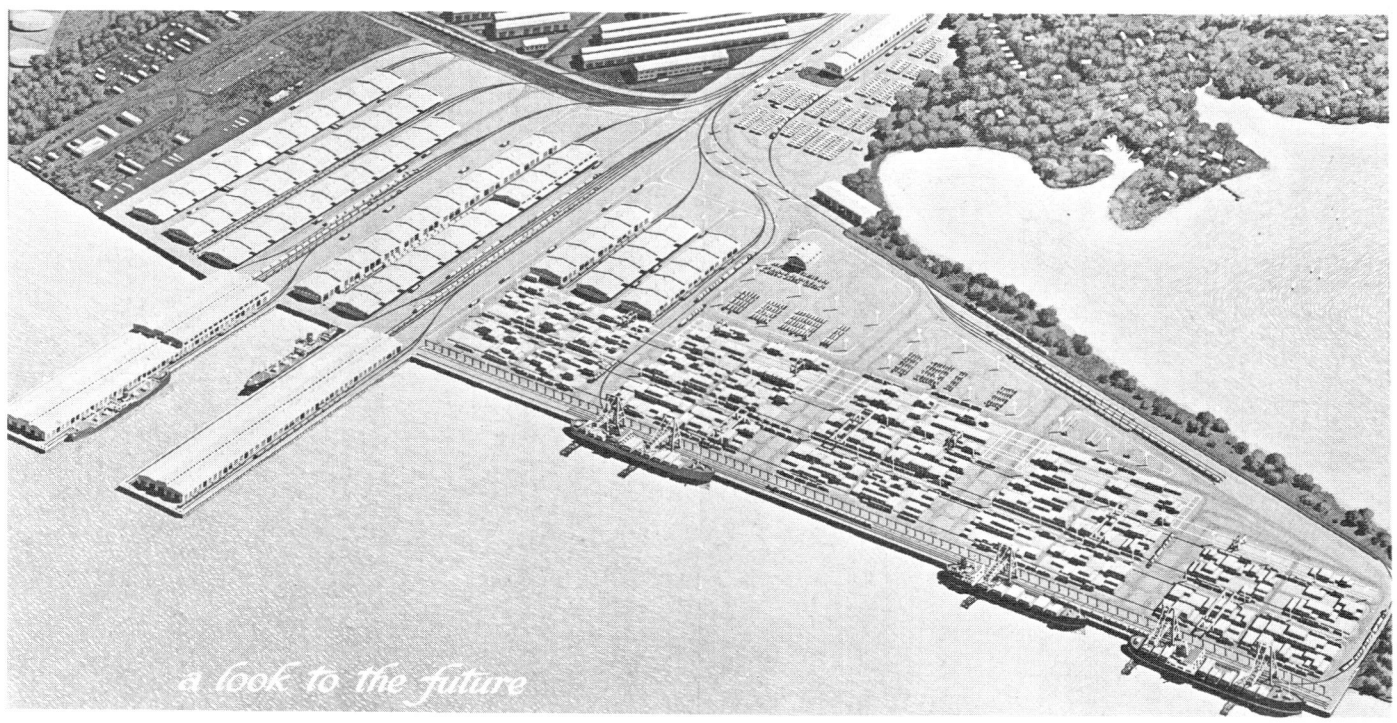

An artist's drawing of Norfolk International Terminals with facilities completed

Portsmouth Marine Terminal

PO Box 1057
2000 Seaboard Avenue, Portsmouth,
  Va. 23707
Telephone: 399-3091
OFFICIALS:
G. H. Stroud, Jr. (*Assistant Director of Port
  Operations*)
OWNERS:
  Virginia Port Authority
OPERATOR:
  Portsmouth Terminals, Inc.

GENERAL:
Located at Pinners Point, on the Elizabeth
River, about 4 miles from the Hampton Roads
roadstead, the Portsmouth Marine Terminal
was built to accommodate container and
general cargo vessels. There is a 426·7 m
(1,400 ft) marginal wharf which provides for

one containership berth and one break bulk
berth or two container berths as required.

One container berth has a link span and
a ramp for handling roll-on/roll-off vessels.
Open and covered storage is available in the
terminal area. There are two 34 short ton
Paceco container gantry cranes with an
outreach of 32·00 m (105 ft) and a 110 ton
quay crane on the wharf. A rail crane
handles containers on and off rail cars. There
is a 10 hectare (25 acre) paved container
marshalling area available with unlimited
additional storage if required. Meat inspection and fumigation facilities are available.

FUTURE DEVELOPMENT:
Berths: at least 3 container berths; 3 or 4
general cargo and/or bulk cargo berths; barge
berthing with at least 3 container gantry
cranes and 4 or 5 quay cranes will ultimately
be provided.

Portsmouth Marine Terminal—Master Plan

The plan envisages a terminal of approximately 203 hectares (500 acres) with a rail
yard to accommodate about 2,000 cars and
about 55,700 m² (600,000 sq ft) of covered
storage area.

Portsmouth Marine Terminal

HOUSTON

Port of Houston

The Harris County Houston Ship Channel
Navigation District
PO Box 2562 (1519 Capitol Avenue)
Houston, Texas 77001
TELEPHONE: CA5-0671
OFFICIALS:
G. W. Altvater (*Executive Director*)
C. E. Bullock (*Deputy Director of Port
Operations*)
Milton Eckert (*Counsel*)
Henry M. Broadnax (*Director of Trade
Development*)
Richard P. Leach (*Deputy Director of Engin-
eering & Planning*)
J. R. Curtis (*Terminal Manager*)
CONTAINER FACILITIES:
Wharf No. 16. The Sea-Land terminal, with
approximately 7·1 hectares (17·5 acres) of
storage and marshalling space, has a 27½ ton
Paceco container gantry crane. An electric
portal quay crane of 35 tons capacity is also
available.
Wharves 23, 26, 29. These wharves in
addition to handling all kinds of general cargo
are being used for container operations. The
facility has been equipped with a Paceco
container gantry crane to handle containers
at the ship/shore interface from No. 23 to
No. 31 wharf. These wharves have been
provided with a container marshalling area
of 8 hectares (20 acres) behind the sheds.
TERMINAL WORKING HOURS:
Ship and inland cargo handling operations
take place between 0800 and 1700 hrs;
overtime can be worked as required.
SERVICES:
Sea-Land Services Inc provide a weekly
world-wide service with transshipment at
Elizabeth N.J.
Gulf Container Line provide a direct
container service between Houston and
UK/Continent.
Combi Line, Lykes Line, Holland America,
Delta provide container services using part
container vessels. Containers are also carried
in the conventional vessel services provided
by the majority of companies calling at the
Port.
TRAFFIC:
Traffic in 1971 is expected to be about
30,000 units in the foreign trades. In
addition, Sea Land handle about 10,000
containers annually through the Port on
their coastwise services.
CONTAINER TERMINALS:
Terminal Services, Houston, Inc.
John Nicholson (*Manager*)
Telephone: 675/7571
Container Trailer Marrying Company
P.O. Box 1171, Houston, Texas
A. G. Adams (*President*)
Telephone: 675/7571
Sea-Land Services, Inc.
8402 Clinton Drive, P.O. Box 447
Galena Park, Texas
W. R. Gibson (*Southwestern Sales Manager*)
North Atlantic Division 8402
Telephone: 672-6651
Port Container Industries, Inc.
8400 Clinton Drive, Houston,
Texas 77029
William Walker (*Manager*)
Telephone: 672-0521
CONTAINER AND CHASSIS LEASING:
ATC Leasing Corporation
Agent: Missouri Pacific Intermodal
Transport, Inc.
6800 Kirkpatrick Blvd., 77028
Telephone: 227-3151
Container Transport International
Agent: Gulf Ports Crating Co.
1600 North 75th St.
Telephone: 923-5551
or Common Market Forwarders
309 Houston World Trade Center

Houston.

Houston—Wharf 16, the Sea-Land Terminal.

Telephone: 225-3521
Integrated Container Service
Agent: Auto Terminal & Stevedoring Co.
421 Cotton Exchange Bldg, 77002
Telephone: 227-0215
Interpool
Sea-Container
Uni-Flex Container Corp.
XTRA, Inc.
Agent: Port Container Industries, Inc.
4800 Clinton Drive, 77029
Telephone: 672-0521
Rail Trailer
Agent: Auto Terminal & Stevedoring Co.
421 Cotton Exchange Bldg., 7702
Telephone: 673-4993
RenTco, Div. Fruehauf Corp.,
7402 Eastex Freeway
Telephone: 697-2709
Transport Pool Inc.
2100 N. Wayside
Telephone: 672-8373
NON VESSEL OPERATING CARRIERS:
Thrutainer Division of Universal Carloading
Company
Mr. Joe Blalock (*Manager*)
201 McFadden Building
Houston, Texas 77002
Telephone: 223-4109
Southern Pacific Marine Transport Corpora-

tion
San Francisco, California
Missouri Pacific Intermodal Co.
St. Louis, Missouri
STEAMSHIP SERVICES:
Amerind Shipping Corp.
906 Petroleum Bldg.
Independent Gulf Line
Telephone: 227-5355
Biehl & Company
6th Floor World Trade Bldg.
Telephone: 222-9961
Barber Line (Far East Service)
Barber Line (Middle East Service)
Combi Line
E. S. Binnings, Inc.
711 Fannin
Telephone: 225-0531
French Line
Hansa Line
Lone Star Shipping Inc.
1505 Texas Avenue
Telephone: 224-7531
Seven Seas (African Line)
Zim Israel Navigation Company Ltd.,
Flomerca Line
Dalton Steamship Corp,
7th Floor World Trade Building
Telephone: 228-8661
Alcoa Line

Concordia Line
Finnlines
Jugolinija Line
N.Y.K. Line
Polish Ocean Lines
Delta Steamship Lines, Inc.
1315 Cotton Exchange Bldg.
Telephone: 227-5101
Furness, Withy & Co., Ltd.
814 World Trade Building
Telephone: 227-1521
Gulf Container Line
Gulf Motorships, Inc.
421 Cotton Exchange Bldg,
Telephone 227-0215
Hansen & Tideman, Inc.
16th Floor, Cotton Exchange Bldg.
Telephone: 223-4181
d' Amico Line
Deppe Line

Hellenic Lines, Ltd.
303 Petroleum Bldg.
Telephone: 224-8607
Kerr Steamship Company, Inc.
506 Caroline
Telephone: 227-0165
Kawasaki Kisen Kaisha, Ltd.
Le Blanc-Parr, Inc.
Cotton Exchange Bldg.
Telephone: 224-1893
Harrison Line
Lykes Bros. Steamship Co., Inc.
Cotton Exchange Bldg, 3rd Floor
Telephone: 227-7211
Sea-Land Service, Inc.
8402 Clinton Drive
Telephone: 672-6651
Strachan Shipping Co,
Cotton Exchange Bldg.

Telephone: 228-1431
Argentine Lines
Bank Line
Chilean Line
Mitsui-OSK Lines, Ltd.
Royal Netherlands Line
Texas Transport & Terminal Co., Inc.
11th Floor, 711 Fannin
Telephone: 225-5461
Yamashita-Shinnihon Line
C. A. Venezolana de Navegacion
Thrutainer Division-Universal Carloading &
Distributing, Inc.
1717 Prairie, Room 201
Telephone: 223-4109
Wilkens Shipping Co.
Cotton Exchange Building
Telephone: 227-4395
Waterman Steamship Corp.

JACKSONVILLE

Jacksonville—Sealand Terminal

Jacksonville Port Authority
PO Box 3005
Jacksonville, Florida 32206
TELEPHONE: 356-1971
TELEX: 353-2456
OFFICIALS:
R. C. Peace (Managing Director)
CONTAINER FACILITIES:
Sealand Terminal:
A two berth container terminal at Talleyrand Docks, leased to Sea Land, has been operational since 1965. It consists of a 366 m (1,200 ft) marginal wharf and a 27½ ton Paceco container gantry crane, as well as 5·3 hectares (13 acres) of paved container marshalling area. The SCL Railroad and the SRS Railroad provide connections.
Blount Island Terminal:
This facility was completed in August 1971. It comprises a 426·7 m (1,400 ft) marginal wharf, a 45 ton Alliance container gantry crane with an outreach of 34·6 m (113·5 ft), 15 acres (6 hectares) of paved storage area, a 120,000 sq ft transit shed. It is a public facility designed for the handling of all sizes of containers. The SCL Railroad provides connections. Blount Island with its eight miles of deep water frontage is located ten miles nearer to the open sea than Talleyrand Docks and Terminals.
TERMINAL WORKING HOURS:
Terminals are open on a 24 hours per day basis for both ship and inland transport cargo handling.
CONTAINER SERVICES.
Sea Land's weekly services to Puerto Rico, West Coast USA and Alaska, the Far East

and Europe.
Moore McCormack Lines, with ships carrying up to 260 containers, sail weekly to the West Coast of South America and the Canal Zone.
Sea Land's weekly US coastline services
Various conventional cargo services, lifting containers two or three times each month, to the East Coast, South America, East and South America.
ROLL-ON/ROLL-OFF SERVICES:
Norwegian Caribbean Lines operate a weekly service between Florida and The

Bahamas with the M.V. Trailer Express having a capacity of 60 trailers.
TMT Trailerferry Inc. operate tugs and barges to Puerto Rico every four days. The barges have a capacity of about 60 trailers each.
Wallenius-Caribbean Line have two vessels which carry about 45 trailers per week to the Republic of Panama.

ROAD ACCESS:
All terminals are within a short distance of Jacksonville Expressway System providing

Jacksonville—Blount Island Terminal

limited access, four lane connections with all Interstate Highway routes converging on the city

CONTAINER REPAIR FACILITIES:
Jacksonville Shipyards, Inc.
  P.O. Box 2347
  Jacksonville, Florida 32203
  Telephone: 398-3081

TRAFFIC:

	Inwards		Outwards	
Lift-on	Tons	Units	Tons	Units
1970	101,400	6,760	507,000	33,800
1971 Estimate				
	110,000	7,200	600,000	37,000
Roll-on				
1970	10,380	680	43,680	3,120
1971 Estimate				
	11,400	740	48,000	3,700

LAKE CHARLES

Lake Charles Harbour and Terminal District
P.O. Box AAA, Lake Charles, Louisiana 70601
TELEPHONE: (318) 439-3661
OFFICIALS:
  H. M. Neely (Director of the Port)

CONTAINER FACILITIES:
The Public Open Dock has been reserved for container operations; it has a quay length of 182·9 m (600 ft) with a depth of water of 10·67 m (35 ft) alongside. One 50 ton container crane is being provided and the total open area available is 5,800 m² (62,500 ft²) with undercover storage of 1,850 m² (20,000 ft²).

LONG BEACH

Port of Long Beach
The Board of Harbor Commissioners
925 Harbor Plaza,
Long Beach, California 90802
TELEPHONE: 437-0041
TELEGRAPH: PORTOBEACH
OFFICIALS:
Llewellyn Bixby, Jr. (President, Board of Harbour Commissioners)
Thomas J. Thorley (General Manager)
L. T. Cornish (Director of Port Administration)
Lee Sellers (Director of Port Operations)
James H. McJunkin (Assistant General Manager)
Dean J. Petersen (Director of Trade Department)
Elmar Baxter (Director of Public Relations)

CONTAINER FACILITIES:
Pier J.232 and 233
Operated by Sea Land, this terminal has two berths served by two Paceco container gantry cranes with 7·8 hectares (17·5 acres) of parking space which will accommodate 426 35 ft units.

Pier J. 245, 246 and 247
Operated by Transocean Gateway Corporation (subsidiary of American Export Industries) this terminal has three berths served by two 50 ton Peiner container gantry cranes. There are 13 hectares (32 acres) of parking space acpable of accommodating 4,538 20 ft units. The facility is served by three trans-continental railroads and modern dual highways.

Pier J. 243 and 244
Unassigned 16·2 hectares (40 acres) container terminal was completed in 1971.
Under Construction

Pier J. 232, 233 and 234
This 28·3 hectare (70 acres) container terminal is assigned to the 'K' Line. It will be equipped with four container gantry cranes and is to be completed in 1972.

Pier G 226, 227, 228, 229, 230
This 32·4 hectare (80 acre) container terminal is assigned to Sea-Land Service, Inc. and will be equipped with eight container gantry cranes. The terminal is to be in operation by 1973. This terminal is supplemented by an adjacent 6·6 hectare (16·3 acre) container freight station.

Pier J 234, 235, 236
The south-east corner is being expanded by 16·2 hectares (40 acres) which will provide a 22·25 hectare (55 acre) combination container and automobile terminal.

Pier J Rail Facility:
To support the container complex on Piers G and J a 30 acre railroad container ramping facility is to be constructed on the southeast

Artist's concept of aerial view of the Port in 1973, at which time the construction of planned container terminals will be completed.

Long Beach—Mid-1971 Transocean Gateway Terminal is in the foreground; to the right is the unallocated terminal (Berths 243 and 244); in the middle distance is the K Line terminal; and to the left the reclamation work in progress for the Sea Land terminal

Projection of Sea-Land Services, Inc. 100 acre Container Terminal on Berths 227 to 230 Pier "G" due for completion 1973.

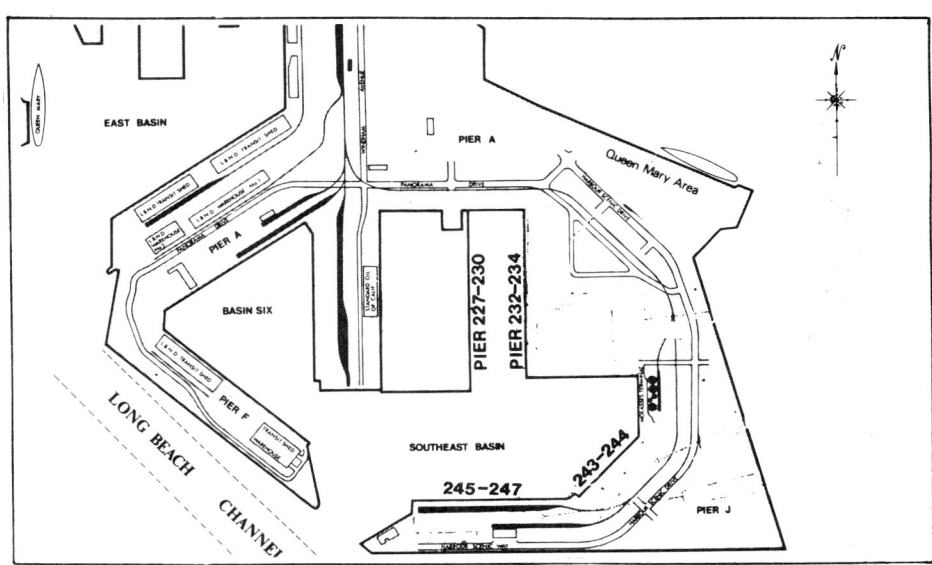

corner of Pier J. This facility will have 6 loading tracks 3,000 ft long spanned by two bridge cranes. Completion is scheduled for 1972.

TERMINAL WORKING HOURS:

Ships cargo handling operations take place between 0800 and 0300 hrs daily.

Inland transport operations take place between 0800 and 1700 hrs daily.

CONTAINER SERVICES:

Sea-Land operates a weekly transpacific, intercoastal service.

Orient Overseas Container Line operates a weekly transpacific service with its only port of call in North America at the Port of Long Beach.

US Lines calls every six days in each direction as part of the tri-continent service linking Europe. US East Coast, US West Coast, Hawaii and the Far East.

States Steamship Co. and Hapag Lloyd are among those lines providing part container services.

TRAFFIC:

Lift-on	Inwards		Outwards	
	Tons	Units	Tons	Units
1970	525,395	25,019	350,264	16,679
1971 Estimate				
	754,500	35,900	503,000	24,000

WAREHOUSING AND CONSOLIDATORS:

Crescent Terminals Inc.
Pierpoint Warehouse Co.
Transoceanic Warehouse Agency
Westcoast Warehouse Corp.

STEVEDORE COMPANIES:

Crescent Wharf and Warehouse Co.
Marine Terminals Corp.
Matson Terminals Inc.
Metropolitan Stevedore Co.

CONTAINER REPAIR ORGANISATIONS:

Pacific-Gulf Marine Services Inc.
2350 W. 17th Street, Long Beach, Calif.
Telephone: 437-6101

RAILROADS:

Atchison, Topeka and Santa Fe Railway Co.

Projection of 21 acre Sea-Land Service, Inc. Container Freight Station adjacent to their Container Terminal.

Southern Pacific Transportation Co.
Union Pacific Railroad Co.

All three transcontinental railroads have direct access to the Port.

MOTOR CARRIERS:

Over 1,100 local and transcontinental truck lines serve the Port of Long Beach. The freeway extension into the harbour area has been completed providing expressway access to Southern California and the U.S. Interstate Highway System.

Projection of Terminal on Berths 232, 233 and 234 Pier "J" due for completion 1972.

Projection of 40 acre Container Terminal on Berths 243 and 244 Pier "J" completed summer 1971

Transocean Gateway Corporation Container Terminal.

PORT OF LONGVIEW

Port of Longview
PO Box 1258, Longview, Washington 98632
TELEPHONE: (206) 42 3305
TELEX: (910) 473 8615

CONTAINER FACILITIES:

A berth with a quay length of 365·76 m (1,200 ft) and an area of 8·5 hectares (21 acres) has been made available for container operations. The facility is at present equipped with a quay crane and there are plans to install a container gantry crane.

LOS ANGELES

Port of Los Angeles,
PO Box 151,
San Pedro, California 90733
TELEPHONE: 832-7241
OFFICIALS:
Bernard J. Caughlin (*General Manager*)
John F. Parkinson (*Assistant General Manager*)
Fred B. Crawford (*Assistant General Manager*)
Kermit R. Sadler (*Director of Trade
  Promotion*)

CONTAINER FACILITIES:

East West Container Terminal (Berth 131)

The Los Angeles Container Terminal Co, Berth 131, Port of Los Angeles lease the facility which is used by OSK, Y-S, K and Japan Lines' weekly service. It has a total quay length of 792·5 m (2,600 ft) with a depth alongside of 10·67 m (35 ft) and a total storage area of 10·12 hectares (25 acres) of which 5,574 m² (60,000 ft²) is covered. Handling equipment consists of a 45 short ton Paceco twin-lift container gantry crane with an outreach of 32·46 m (106·5 ft) and a backreach from the dock rail of 27·74 m (91 ft), a Paceco transtainer, and chassis.

Overseas Terminal (Berths 228 D&E and 229)

Operated on a preferential use basis by the Overseas Shipping Company, 615 S. Flower Street, Los Angeles this facility has a quay length of 548·6 m (1,800 ft) with a depth alongside of 10·67 m (35 ft). It is equipped with a 33 ton Houben Industries container gantry crane having an outreach of 33·53 m (110 ft). There is space for 3,000 containers and the facility is used by a number of European container operators. A further Houben Crane is planned for the facility.

Matson Terminal (Berths 207-209)

Operated on an exclusive lease by Matson Navigation Company, 523 W 6th Street, Los Angeles, this terminal has a quay length of 457·2 m (1,500 ft) with 10·67 m (35 ft) of water alongside. There are 20·23 hectares (50 acres) of container storage with 6,503 m² (70,000 ft²) of shed space. The terminal is equipped with two 28 short ton capacity Paceco container gantry cranes, with an outreach of 31·09 m (102 ft) and a back reach from the dock rail of 22·71 m (71·5 ft). Two further 28 short ton cranes are planned. Containers are handled by straddle carriers.

Johnson Line Berth, Berth 142

Operated on a preferential use basis by Ocean Terminals Ltd this facility has a quay length of 207 m (679 ft) with 10·67 m (35 ft) depth of water alongside and a total area of 4·73 hectares (11·7 acres). There are no handling facilities as Johnson Line vessels are equipped with shipboard gantry cranes.

Consolidated Marine Terminal (Berths 87-93 A B C)

This facility operated by Consolidated Marine Ltd, has a quay length of 320·04 m (1,050 ft) with a depth of water alongside of 10·67 m (35 ft). A further 243·8 m (800 ft) of quay is under construction. A 30 ton container gantry crane is planned.

PFEL Barge Carrier Terminal (Berth 232-235)

This terminal is planned with a quay length of 307·4 m (1,008 ft) and a back up area of 12·14 hectares (30 acres) shedded space of 5,574 m² (60,000 ft²) is being provided and a container gantry crane may be installed but initially PFEL LASH vessels will be equipped with shipboard gantry cranes for container handling.

CONTAINER TRAFFIC:

In 1970 91,351 containers, both loaded and empty moved inwards. Total gross weight i.e. including tare amounted to 1,210,383 short tons. 74,034 containers moved outwards with a gross weight of 915,774 short tons. A breakdown of this traffic can be given as follows:

Los Angeles—Matson Terminal.

Los Angeles—East-West Terminal

Inwards Loaded:		
length	No.	gross short tons
Less than 20 ft	3,129	16,930
20 and 24 ft	63,573	971,754
40 ft	6,368	198,536
Inwards Empty:		
Less than 20 ft	180	160
20 and 24 ft	17,945	22,531
40 ft	156	472
Outwards Loaded:		
Less than 20 ft	1,664	9,055
20 and 24 ft	57,054	814,288
40 ft	2,808	68,815
Outwards Empty:		
Less than 20 ft	365	407
20 and 24 ft	9,858	16,108
40 ft	2,285	7,101

The estimate for 1971 is that a total of 107,000 loaded and empty containers with a gross weight of 1,425,000 short tons will move inwards and a total of 97,000 units, 1,075,000 short tons will move outwards.

TERMINAL WORKING HOURS:

Ships

East West	0800-1700, 1800-0300 hrs.
Matson	0800-1700, 0300-0800 hrs.

Inland Transport

East West & Matson	0800-1700 hrs.
	0800-0300 hrs.

CONTAINER REPAIR FACILITIES:

Matson, East-West and Sea Land have their own facilities on their terminals.

Fruehauf Corporation
144 S. Alameda, Los Angeles
Telephone: (213) 747-6181

Trailmobile
1765 E. 46th St. Los Angeles
Telephone: (213) 231-9283

Pacific Gulf Marine Inc.
Long Beach

GENERAL CARGO AND CONTAINER LINES AND OPERATORS WITH BERTHS USED:

American Export-Isbrandtsen S.S. Co.
Berth 146
American Mail Line
Berths 90-93A & B
American President Lines
Berths 90-93A & B
Argonaut Terminal Co.
Berths 153-158
Bakke S.S. Corp.
Berths 195-199
Balfour, Guthrie & Co., Ltd.

Berths 153-158
Barber S.S. Line
Berths 228D & E
China Union Lines
Berths 142-145
Columbus Line
Berth 54
Consolidated Marine, Inc.
Berths 90-93A & B
Crusader Line
Berths 136-139
d'Amico Line
Berth 189
East-West Container Terminal
Berths 130-132
Edgington Oil Co.
Berths 163-164
Fellows & Stewart, Inc.
Berths 207-108, 213-214
Fern Line
Berths 228D & E
Fern-Ville Caribbean Line
Berths 228D & E
Furness, Withy & Co., Ltd.
Berths 136-138
General S.S. Corp., Ltd.
Berths 142-145
Grace Line
Berths 52-60
Grancolombiana Line
Berths 154-155
Great Eastern Line
Berths 142-144
Hamburg-American Line
Berths 153-158
Hanseatic Vaasa Line
Berths 174-178
Holland-America Line

Berths 136-139
Indies Terminals
Berths 219-225
Italian Line
Berths 142-144
Japan Lines
Berths 219-225
Jayanti Shipping Co.
Berths 195-199
Johnson Line
Berths 142-143
Klaveness Line
Berths 228D & E
Knutsen Line
Berths 195-199
Maersk Line
Berths 174-178
Marine Terminals Corp.
Berths 188-191
Maritime Company of Philippines, Inc.
Berth 137
Matson Navigation Co.
Berth 207
Meridian S.S. Corp
Berth 199
Metropolitan Terminal
Berths 136-139
Mitsui O.S.K. Line
Berths 174-178
Monitor S.S. Agency
Berth 189
Nedlloyd Lines
Berths 219-225
North Pacific Coast Line
Berths 136-139
Ocean Terminals
Berths 142-145
Oceanic S.S. Co.

Berth 207
Olympic S.S. Co.
Berth 189
Orient Overseas Line
Berth 158
Overseas Shipping Co.
Berths 228D & E 229
P. & O. Lines
Berths 90-93A & B
Pacific Australia Direct
Berths 142-145
Pacific Far East Line, Inc.
Berths 90-93A & B
Pacific Islands Transport Line
Berths 142-145
Scanstar Line
Berths 228D & E 229
Showa Line 189
Transpacific Transportation Co.
Berths 219-225
Union S.S. Co. of New Zealand
Berths 174-178
United Fruit Co.
Berth 147
United Philippine Lines
Berths 142-145
United Yugoslav Lines
Berth 189
Wallenius Line
Berths 232A & B
Waterman S.S. Corp.
Berth 178
Westfal-Larsen Lines Co. (So. America Service)
Berths 142-145
Williams, Diamond-Rountree Agencies
Zim Israel Navigation Co.
Berths 174-178

MIAMI

Port of Miami

(A Department of Metropolitan Dade County Government)
1015 Port Boulevard
Miami, Florida 33132
TELEPHONE: 377-5841
OFFICIALS:
I. J. Stephens, Rear Admiral USCG (Ret) (*Port Director*)

Robert Waldron (*Assistant Port Director*)
Douglas Gillett (*Business Development*)

GENERAL:
Miami is a new, uncongested port still building for future needs. It has multiple facilities and services for international trade: finance, forwarding, shipping, insurance and international cruise travel.

The Port of Miami is situated on 121 hectares (300 acres), with a 2·8 km (1¾ miles) berthing area, turning at berthsite on the 274 m (900 ft) wide approach channel. The inside turning basis is 503 m (1,650 ft) × 518 m (1,700 ft).

The port has a water depth of 9·14 m (30 ft) with 21·3 m (70 ft) dock aprons. There is over half a million square feet in transit cargo buildings.

The port is served by the FEC. and SCL. Railways

ROLL-ON FACILITIES:
There are ten roll-on/roll-off berths for trailer operations. Six are in the cargo area and four adjacent to the passenger terminal to serve those vessels which also carry vehicles. The berths have a total of about 40 hectares (100 acres) of parking area.

Services include daily sailing to the Bahamas; weekly or more frequent sailings to the Caribbean, Central and South America, most of Europe and the Far East.

A shed with an area of 9,290 m (100,000 sq ft) for trailer and container packing and unpacking was added in 1970.

Miami.

ROLL-ON/ROLL-OFF SERVICES:
Norwegian Caribbean Lines
Agents: Transcaribbean Maritime Service, Inc
501 N.E. 1st Ave.
Telephone: 358-1790
Twice weekly to Bahamas; weekly to Jamaica, Dominican Republic, Haiti and Virgin Islands.
Windward Shipping Co.
Agents: Shaw Company, a Division of Luckenbach S.S. Co.
501 N.E. First Ave.
Telephone: 371-4581

Every 3 weeks to Bahamas; every 2 weeks to Grand Canyon.
Universal Alco, Ltd.
Agents: Alco Transport, Inc.
1001 Port Boulevard
Telephone: 3/9-0855
3 a week to the Bahamas
Pan American Mail Line
Agents: Chester, Blackburn & Roder, Inc.
1040 Biscayne Blvd.
Telephone: 377-3781
1 a week to Jamaica, Lesser Antilles, Panama, Costa Rica; every 2 weeks to

Aruba, Curacao, Bonaire.
Jamaica Fruit & Shipping Co.
Agents: Canadian Gulf Line of Florida, Inc.
P.O. Box 4301 Miami 33101
Telephone: 374-2681
1 a week to Jamaica
Atlantic Lines, Ltd.
Agents: Chester, Blackburn & Roder, Inc.
1040 Biscayne Blvd.
Telephone: 377-3781
1 a week to Virgin Islands, Lesser Antilles, Trinidad.
Coordinated Caribbean Transport
Agents: Coordinated Caribbean Transport Inc
1001 Port Blvd.
Telephone: 358-1551
1 a week to the 5 countries of Central America—every 2 weeks to Pto. Cortes, Honduras.

TERMINAL OPERATING HOURS:
0800 to 1700 hours daily. It is possible to work 24 hours per day if necessary.

TRAFFIC:
Lift-on traffic in 1970 was 20,000 loaded units and roll-on traffic amounted to 10,690 loaded units (100,000 tons) inwards and 11,741 loaded units (120,700 tons) outwards.

Maimi—One of the roll-on operations

MILWAUKEE

The Board of Harbour Commissioners
City of Milwaukee, Room 606 City Hall, Milwaukee, Wisconsin, 53202
TELEPHONE: 276-3711
TELEGRAMS: Milharco, Milwaukee
OFFICIALS:
J. S. Seefeldt (*Municipal Port Director*)
J. L. Haskell (*Deputy Municipal Port Director*)
J. J. Kuchnowski (*Dock Superintendent*)
R. K. Jorgensen (*Port Traffic Manager*)

GENERAL:
Although there are as yet no specially built container ships operating in the Great Lakes-St Lawrence Seaway trade containers are regularly carried on this route and there are facilities in regular use for the handling of containers at the Port of Milwaukee. There are adequate storage areas and nine cranes with capacities ranging from 20 tons to 200 tons. Containers are available from shipping companies serving UK and Scandinavia. Some lines serving the Far East also make containers available. Good road and rail facilities exist with connections to main lines and main roads. The City of Milwaukee under the management and control of the Board of Harbour Commissioners, owns, operates, builds and leases the facilities at the Port of Milwaukee.

PRINCIPAL CONTAINER FREIGHT FORWARDING COMPANIES:
D. C. Andrews International Ltd.
1225 South Carferry Drive
Telephone: 482 3360
M. E. Dey & Co
759 N. Milwaukee St
Tel: 271-7461

Ray C. Fischer Co, Inc
312 E. Wisconsin Ave
Tel: 271-4960
Foreign Forwarding of Milwaukee
PO Box 2991, Hampton Station
Tel: 461-6230
C. S. Greene & Co
647 W. Virginia St
Tel: 271-8307
Salentine & Co
734 N. Jefferson St
Tel: 271-8404

STORAGE AND STEVEDORE COMPANY:
Board of Harbour Commissioners
Room 606, City Hall
Tel: 276-3711
Hanson Seaway Service Ltd
126, N. Jefferson
Tel: 276-5770
1500 S. Lincoln Memorial Drive
Tel: 481-7000
Pier, Inc
1200 S. Lincoln Memorial Drive
Tel: 482-1720
Stearns Milwaukee Marine Terminal, Inc
1304 S. Lincoln Memorial Drive
Tel: 481-1300

PRINCIPAL CONTAINER POOL OPERATORS:
S.S.I. Container Corp.
1500 S. Lincoln Memorial Drive
Tel: 481-7000
Integrated Container Service
1500 S. Lincoln Memorial Drive
Tel: 481-7000
Interpool Inc.
4001 West Green Tree Road
Tel: 352-3514

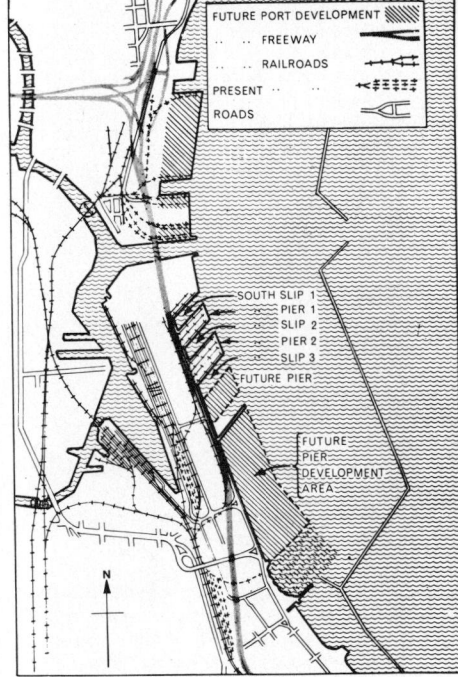

Milwaukee

Container Transport International
300 E. Ward Street
Tel: 384-7680

Port of Mobile
Alabama State Docks Dept.
PO Box 1588, Mobile, Alabama 36601
TELEPHONE: 438-2481
OFFICIALS:
Reuben E. Wheelis (*Director*)
R. M. Hope (*Operations Manager*)
Julian W. Smith (*General Sales Manager*)

CONTAINER FACILITIES:
General cargo handling berths with open areas have been adapted for container handling. These are Berths Nos. 1, 2, and 5; also the ends of Piers A, B and C and Pier D.
A Le Tourneau mobile crane serves Berths 1 and 2 and there are cranes capable of

MOBILE

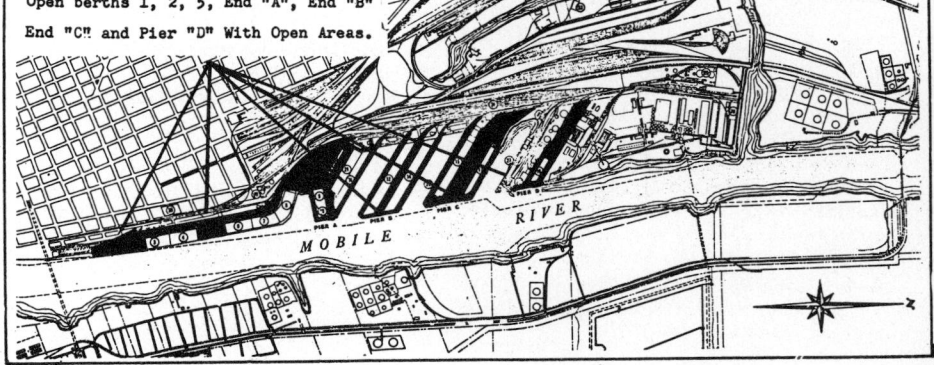

Open berths 1, 2, 5, End "A", End "B" End "C" and Pier "D" With Open Areas.

handling containers available at the other locations.

PLANNED FACILITIES:

Planning and design studies are continuing in order to ascertain the most suitable location for a specialised container terminal.

Board of Commissioners of the Port of New Orleans

Port of New Orleans
P.O. Box 60046, New Orleans, Louisiana, 70160
TELEPHONE: 522-2551
OFFICIALS:
Edward S. Reed (*Executive Port Director and General Manager*)
Henry G. Joffrey (*Associate Port Director*)
Henry R. Rauber (*Deputy Port Director*)
James W. Martin (*Deputy Port Director*)
CONTAINER FACILITIES:
France Road Terminal:

Located at the Mississippi River-Gulf outlet this terminal will eventually consist of nine ship berths equipped with container gantry cranes, marshalling areas and specialised shore handling equipment. The total area of the facility will be 1,133 hectares (280 acres).

The first phase of development, to be completed in early 1972, will consist of one berth with a quay length of 252·98 m (830 ft) with facilities for roll-on operations.

The France Road Terminal is part of the Centroport industrial and port complex being developed by the Port Authority.

Henry Clay—Nashville Avenue Wharf

Large marshalling areas are situated at each end of the quay which is 1,066 m (3,500 ft) in length. The facility is used by the following operators using part container ships:

Farrell Lines—every 3 weeks to Australia.
Combi Line—weekly to Europe.
Lykes Lines (containers on existing conventional services, to N.W. European, Mediterranean, African, and Far Eastern Ports).
Gulf Container Line—Fortnightly to Europe

Napoleon Avenue Wharf:

This facility is 944,9 m (3,100 ft) in length has a wharf apron of 32·9 m (108 ft) and is supported by an open section of berth and adjoining marshalling yards for containers. It is used by Cartainer Line for their Service with European ports and by States Marine Isthmian ships.

Governor Nicholls Street Wharf:

This wharf is used by Lykes and Nopal Lines for their regular sailings using part container ships.

Bienville Street Wharf:

This wharf is used by Delta Lines for their frequent services to E. Coast South American and West African ports.

TERMINAL WORKING HOURS:

0700 to 1700 hours daily. Overtime for inland transport operations by arrangement.
ROAD AND RAIL TRANSPORT:

Thirty motor carriers serve the port. Alabama State Docks operates its own truck control centre. Alabama State Docks operates

NEW ORLEANS

Galvez Street Wharf:

This wharf is used by Swedish American Lines' weekly services to Europe using part container ships.
Perry Street Wharf:

This facility is used by Central Gulf Steamship Co. as a barge loading point for their European Service.
Morrison Road Wharf:

Situated on the Industrial Canal, this facility is used by Gulf-Puerto Rico Lines for their weekly roll-on and container service.

There is a warehouse and marshalling area for 360 containers nearby used by Sea Land.
TRAFFIC:

In 1970 a total of 16,681 containers moved through the port.

It is reported that in 1971 containers are passing through the port at a rate of some 25,000 per year. It is estimated that export containers account for some 60 per cent of this traffic.

its own Terminal Railway that connects with the four major railroads through a joint interchange yard.
CONTAINER REPAIR ORGANISATIONS:
Betbeze Body & Truck Equipment
1224 South Beltline Highway
Mobile Alabama

New Orleans—Morrison Road Wharf

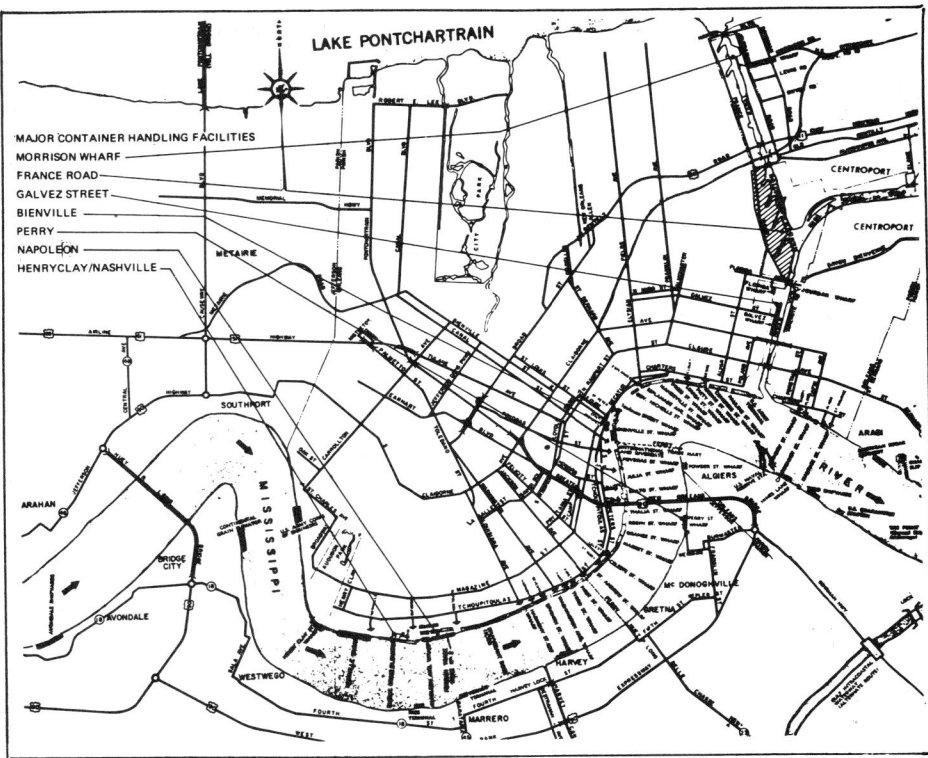

New Orleans —Impression of the completed France Road Terminal at Centroport

CONTAINER LEASING COMPANIES:
CTI Container Transport International, Inc.
1608 International Trade Mart
New Orleans, La. 70130
Telephone: 532-1178
4 to 40-foot containers
Container pool depot
Grainger Leasing Corp.
315 Julia Street
New Orleans, La. 70013
Telephone: 525-5168
20 and 40 ft chassis
Container pool depot
Integrated Container Service (ICS)
315 Julia St.
New Orleans, La. 70013
Telephone: 522-9968
20 and 40-foot containers
Container pool depot
Interpool, Inc.
P.O. Box 53324
New Orleans, La. 70150
Telephone: 524-0644
20 and 40-foot containers
Container pool depot
Norbel Container & Drayage Service Inc.
7020 Franklin Ave.
New Orleans, La. 70122
Telephone: 282-3476
20 and 40-foot containers
Container pool depot
XTRA, Inc.
1801 International Trade Mart
New Orleans, La. 70130

The Port of New York Authority
111 Eighth Avenue,
New York,
NY 10011
TELEPHONE: (212) 620-7000
OFFICIALS:
Austin J. Tobin (*Executive Director*)
Matthias E. Lukens (*Deputy Executive Director*)
Roger H. Gilman (*Director of Planning and Development*)
A. Lyle King (*Director of Marine Terminals*)
TRADE DEVELOPMENT OFFICES:
Eastern US
170 Broadway, New York, NY 10038
(212) 267-5805
Cleveland
Terminal Tower Building, Cleveland, Ohio 44113
(216) 621-3188
Chicago
Prudential Plaza, Chicago, Illinois 60601
(312) 236-0075
Washington D.C.
1001 Connecticut Avenue, N.W., Washington D.C. 20036
(202) 783-5450
Pittsburgh
3 Gateway Center, Pittsburgh, Pennsylvania 15222
(412) 261-2513
Latin America
Eastern Airlines Bldg., Room 919, Santurce, San Juan, Puerto Rico 00911
(809) 722-2635
Far East and Pacific Area
Kokusai Building, 1-1, 3-chome, Marunouchi Chiyoda-ku. Tokyo, Japan
213-2856
London
130 Fenchurch Street, London EC3M 5ED
England
01-623 9131
Continental Europe
Talstrasse 66, 8001 Zurich, Switzerland
27-06-15
General
The Port of New York Authority is the self-supporting agency of the States of New Jersey and New York. Operating without burden to the taxpayer, it was created in 1921 by treaty between the two States to

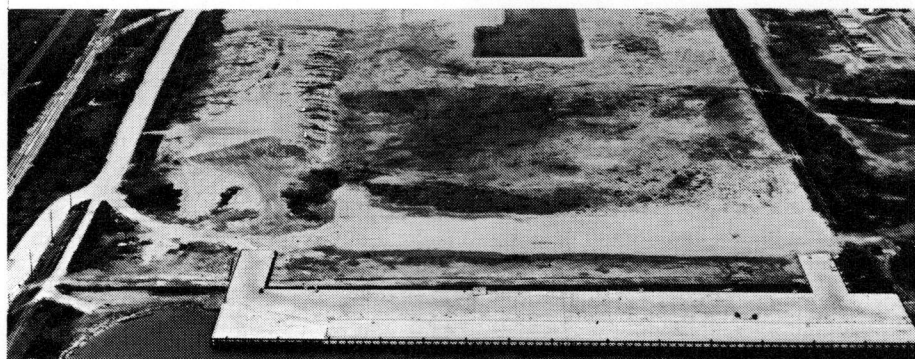

New Orleans—No. 1 Berth, France Road Terminal—Mid 1971

Téléphone: 525-4016
20 and 40 foot containers
Container pool depot
Marine Container Corp.
1800 Engineers Road
Belle Chasse, La. 70037
Telephone: 367-7156
Norbel Container and Drayage Service Inc.
7020 Franklin Ave.
New Orleans, La. 70122
Telephone: 282-3476
Olympia Co. Inc.
2930 Frenchmen, New Orleans, La 70122
Telephone: 895-7786
Waterfront Repair Service
315 Julia Street, New Orleans, La. 70013
Telephone: 525-5168

New Orleans—Napoleon Avenue Wharf

NEW YORK

deal with the planning and development of terminal and transportation facilities, and to improve and protect the commerce of the Port District.

Department of Ports and Terminals, New York City, Economic Development Division
Battery-Maritime Bldg.,
New York, N.Y. 10004
Patrick F. Crossman (*Commissioner*)
TELEPHONE: 566-7700
General

The Department of Ports and Terminals is the City of New York agency responsible for carrying out varied functions connected with the New York City waterfront.

The department is concerned with development of waterfront and terminal properties and with the management of certain market facilities. To this end the Department can assemble land parcels for the tenants, construct facilities to suit, offer expertise in the fields of architecture, design, engineering and planning and through the use of municipal bonds offer low cost financing. The Department manages approximately 110 City owned pier and waterfront properties 372 hectares (919 acres) it will have 25 berths for deep sea vessels supported by 321 hectares (793 acres) of open storage area and 418,000 m² (4½ million sq ft) of shed space. It is anticipated that the annual traffic throughput will shortly reach 9 million tons. The Elizabeth Channel has been dredged to 10·67 m (35 ft) and has been accepted by the Army Corps of Engineers as a Federal Channel. The berths vary in length between 190·2 m and 248·4 m (625 and 815 ft) with apron widths varying between 52 m and 251·2 m (172 and 825 ft). The facility is rail served and linked to interstate and super highways. There are at present three terminal operators on the south side of the channel.

Fifteen berths have been completed and a further ten are under construction.
CONTAINER FACILITIES:
ELIZABETH PORT AUTHORITY MARINE TERMINAL:
Sea-Land Services Inc.
Corbin and Fleet Streets P.O. Box 1050
Elizabeth, New Jersey 07207
Telephone: 289 6000 (NJ)
This comprises five berths served by four 25 ton Paceco container gantry cranes. The

facility has a total paved area of 45 hectares (111 acres) and the park is capable of accepting over 2,000 trailers.
International Terminal Operating Co.
2 Broadway, New York
NY 10004
Telephone: (212) BO9-2200
This facility has three berths served by four Paceco container gantry cranes and a total land area of 34·4 hectares (85 acres). There is also a cargo consolidation shed with an area of 14,493 m² (156,000 sq ft). The facility is used by United States Lines, Dart Containerline and Hapag-Lloyd Line for their Atlantic services. Straddle carriers are used for quay handling operations which can involve three high stacking of containers.

Container Terminals N.Y. Inc.
Bldg 217, No. Fleet Street,
Port Newark, N.J.
Telephone: (201) 289-3000
Having a total area of 37·6 hectares (93 acres) this terminal has facilities for handling two vessels at the same time. It is served by two Paceco container gantry cranes. There are also two linkspan ramps for roll-on/roll-off operations. It is used by Atlantic Container Line. At present there are 52·5 acres developed. This consists of a 20 acre container park between a 42,000 sq ft export shed and 83,000 sq ft export shed behind which is a 20 acre park for up to 3,500 cars for import and export.

Maher Terminal—Berths 80-82
Operator:
Maher Terminals Inc.
80 Broad Street New York, NY 10004
TELEPHONE: HA5-5030
OFFICIALS:
Michael Maher (*President*)
This facility, to be leased to Maher Stevedoring Company from mid 1972, will have a quay length of 487·7 m (1,600 ft) and a total area of 35·2 hectares (87 acres). It will be equipped with four 40 ton low profile Mach 9 Heavy Lift Paceco container gantry cranes with an outreach of 35·05 m (115 ft) and a backreach of 26·82 m (88 ft). The cranes will also be capable of handling heavy lifts of up to 65 tons with some adjustment of reach and speed. The facility will be

equipped with consolidation buildings, weigh-bridge, etc and will be provided with rail access.

PORT NEWARK

This facility, developed by the Port of New York Authority, comprises 34 vessel berths. Five new berths are under construction, two of which will be full containership berths. The total area available is about 286 hectares (707 acres). The Grace Line, American President Lines, 'K' Line and Pacific Star Line use berths at Newark for their part container services. A rail container transfer yard to speed the movement of containers between railcars and ships will be completed by the end of the year. It will be operated by the Penn Central Transportation Company and will initially be able to handle 60-car train loads.

Universal Terminal

Universal Terminal and Stevedoring Corporation
1 Broadway, New York, N.Y. 10004
Telephone: (212) 269-5121

This facility, operational at the beginning of 1971, will ultimately have a quay length of 1,165 m (3,822 ft) and a total area of 16·2 hectares (40 acres). The terminal is designed for container/truck bulk operations with a total covered area of about 46,451 m² (½ million sq ft). Two 50 ton container gantry cranes are also planned for the facility which is used by Meyer Line.

BROOKLYN

North East Marine Terminal

North East Marine Terminal Co. Inc.
17, Battery Place, New York, N.Y. 10004
Telephone: (212) HA5 8850

North East Marine Terminals, in conjunction with the City of New York is re-developing the area between 33rd Street and 39th Street to provide a container terminal which will provide two container ship berths. The total area of the facility is 34·4 hectares (85 acres) and it will be operational in June 1972 when the installation of a Star Container gantry crane capable of handling 20 and 40 ft units will have been completed.

Bush Terminal

Universal Terminal and Stevedoring Corporation
1 Broadway, New York, N.Y. 10004
Telephone: (212) 269-5121

Arrangements are being made between Bush Universal and the City of New York to develop a container and break bulk facility which will be leased back to Universal Terminal and Stevedoring Corporation who are a subsidiary of Bush. The facility will have a total area of 40·47 hectares (100 acres.)

STAPLETON TERMINAL:

Trans-Ocean Gateway Corporation
26 Broadway, New York 10004
Telephone: (212) 797-3000

Situated on Staten Island, north of the Verrazano Narrows Bridge, this terminal is being developed by the American Export Industries subsidiary, Transocean Gateway Corporation, in conjunction with the City of New York which owns the land. The plan was to reclaim 14·2 hectares (35 acres) of additional land adding it to the existing 11·3 hectares (28 acres) round Pier 13. All AEI container ships use the terminal which is backed by a COFC/TOFC rail centre.

The terminal is served by two 50 ton Peiner container gantry cranes. It is also equipped with ramps to serve the roll-on/roll-off vessels of Trans-American Trailer Transport Inc.

It is not clear if this is a temporary facility or not. At present the American Export Organisation uses Pier 13 only and, now that Howland Hook has been developed, the Company may transfer all operations there.

HOWLAND HOOK:

This terminal, on the north east side of Staten Island, is being constructed by American Export Industries. Three container berths with a total quay frontage of about 610 m (2,500 ft) are planned. The first 487·7 m (1,600 ft) of quay has been completed and is expected to be operational by mid summer 1971 with four 50 ton container gantry cranes in service. The final plan envisages eight 50 ton cranes. A covered area of 11,148 m² (120,000 sq ft) was completed in January 1971. The terminal will be operated 24 hours per day to service vessels of companies not possessing shoreside facilities.

PORT SEATRAIN, WEEHAWKEN, N.J.

Seatrain Lines Inc.

Port Seatrain, Weehawken, New Jersey

The former Erie Railroad yard at Weehawken has been reconstructed. It has been designed with a 36·58 m (120 ft) wide fringe pier about 274·3 m (900 ft) long equipped with three sliding boom 45 ton container gantry cranes capable of spanning both sides of the pier. The area of the facility is 34·2 hectares (80 acres) and it serves the company's European operations.

PORT JERSEY CONTAINER TERMINAL

Global Container Services Inc.

An organisation set up by Columbus Line, Dart Containerline and Fabre Line to operate the Port Jersey Container Terminal. The 25 hectare (62 acre) terminal, which is situated on the New Jersey and Bayonne municipal boundary is under construction. It will be operational in early 1972 and equipped with two 45 ton Starporter container Gantry Cranes.

CONTAINER AND ROLL-ON SERVICES:

§Full cellular service

*Containers and General Cargo with, so far as is known, specially adapted vessels.

‖Combination roll-on and cellular container service.

†Roll-on only.

‡Barge Carriers.

American Export Industries
  Container Marine Lines—Europe weekly from Pier 13, Stapleton
  †Container Mediterranean Lines—Mediteranean weekly from Container Terminal New York (Elizabeth)
  *AEIL—Far East—every two weeks from Pier 6 Bush Terminal
American President Lines
  *Far East—Weekly from Shed 152 Port Newark
Amerind Container Services—Bermuda Service
  §Caribbean—weekly
Atlantic Container Line
  ‖Europe—three sailings weekly from container Terminal, New York (Elizabeth)
Atlantic Lines
  *Carribbean—weekly from shed 291, Port Newark
Barber Line
  *Far East—three sailings monthly from 9A Brooklyn, P.A. Terminal
  *Middle East—two sailings monthly from 9A Brooklyn, P.A. Terminal
Caribbean Trailer Express
  †Jamaica and Dominican Republic—weekly from Pier 12, Brooklyn, P.A. Terminal
Columbus Line
  §Australia and New Zealand—every 3 weeks from 60th Pier, Brooklyn Army Terminal
Dart Containerline
  §Europe—weekly from ITO Terminal

(Elizabeth)

Dominican Container Line
  §Dominican Republic—weekly from Pier 13, Stapleton
Fabre Line
  §Mediterranean—weekly from 60th Street Pier, Brooklyn Army Terminal
Farrell Lines
  §Australia New Zealand—every three weeks from Pier 4-5 Brooklyn Port Authority Terminal
  *West Africa—every 15 days from Pier 4-5 Brooklyn P.A. Terminal
Finn Lines
  N.W. Europe including Scandinavia—weekly from Shed 137 Port Newark

Flota Mercanti Dominicana C. for A.
  §Bahamas—weekly from Pier 13 Stapleton
Grancolombiana
  *South America up to 2 sailings weekly from Pier 3 Brooklyn P.A. Terminal
Hansa Line
  §Mediterranean—every 2 weeks from ITO Terminal (Elizabeth)
Hapag Lloyd
  §Europe—weekly from ITO Terminal (Elizabeth)
  *Europe Weekly
Jamaican Container Line
  §Jamaica—weekly from Pier 13 Stapleton
Japan Line
  *Japan—every 2 weeks from Pier 8 Brooklyn P.A. Marine Terminal
K Line
  *Japan—every 10 days from Pier 9B Brooklyn P.A. Marine Terminal
Maersk Line

  *Far East—weekly from Pier 11 Brooklyn P.A. Marine Terminal

Meyer Line
 *Europe—weekly from Universal Terminal, Newark
Mitsui OSK Lines
 *Japan—weekly from Foot of 39th Street, Brooklyn
Moore McCormack Line
 *E. Coast S. America—weekly from Foot of 23rd St. Brooklyn
 *South Africa—every 2 weeks from Foot of 22nd St. Brooklyn
NYK Line
 *Japan—every 10 days from Pier 7, Brooklyn P.A. Terminal
Orient Overseas Line
 *Far East—2 sailings weekly from Pier 1 Brooklyn P.A. Terminal
PACE (Pacific America Container Express)
 §Australia and New Zealand every 12 days from ITO Terminal (Elizabeth)
Pacific Star Line
 *Far East—Monthly from Shed 145 Newark
Peruvian State Line
 *W. Coast S. America—fortnightly from Pier Foot of 31st Street, Brooklyn
Polish Ocean Line
 *Europe—weekly from Pier 3 Erie Basin, P.A. Terminal
Prudential Grace Lines
 *Caribbean—weekly from Pier 40 North River
 ‡Mediterranean—every 10 days from 4 Bush Terminal, Brooklyn
 *West Coast South America—weekly from Shed 138, Newark
Royal Netherlands Steamship Lines
 *Caribbean—weekly from foot of 39th St. Brooklyn
Sea Land Service Inc.
 §Caribbean—3 sailings weekly
 §Coastwise via Panama Ports—weekly
 §Mediterranean—weekly
 §N.W. Europe—2 sailings weekly
 §Puerto Rico—4 sailings weekly
 All sailings from Sea Land Terminal (Elizabeth)
Seatrain Lines Inc.
 §Puerto Rico—2 sailings weekly from Weehawken Terminal
 §Europe—weekly from Weehawken Terminal
Transamerican Trailer Transport Inc.
 †Puerto Rico—twice weekly from Pier 13, Stapleton
United Philippine Lines
 *Far East—every two weeks from Pier 12 Brooklyn P.A. Terminal
United States Lines
 §Far East—weekly from ITO Terminal (Elizabeth)
 §U.S. West Coast Ports—weekly from ITO Terminal (Elizabeth)
 §Europe—weekly from ITO Terminal (Elizabeth)
Yamashita-Shinnihon Line
 *Far East—every 10 days from Pier 6, Brooklyn P.A. Terminal
Zim Israel Navigation Co. Ltd.
 *Israel & Greece—every three weeks from Shed 145 Newark
§Full cellular service
*Containers and General Cargo with, so far as is known, specially adapted vessels.
‖Combination roll-on and cellular container service.
†Roll-on only.
‡Barge Carriers.

TRAFFIC:

The Port of New York Authority state that in 1970 a total of 425,475 units, 6,017,504 tons was handled through Elizabeth Port Authority Marine Terminal.

It should be noted that this does not include the traffic moving through the many other terminals which cater for both full and part containerships; also the lines which carry up to sixty or so containers on their conventional cargo vessels. The Port Authority estimates that by 1975 some 11·3 million long tons of foreign commerce will move through the port in containers; this figure represents about 67 per cent of the total general cargo projected for that date.

NON VESSEL CONTAINER OPERATORS
 ABC Overseas Transport

 Container Transport International (CTI)
 Greene Seatrailer Inc.
 Helm's Express
 Intermodal Freight Forwarding Inc.
 Mid-Pacific Freight Forwarders
 North American International
 Penn Central
 Transconex Inc.
 Transconex Jamaica Inc.
 United Cargo Corporation (UCC)

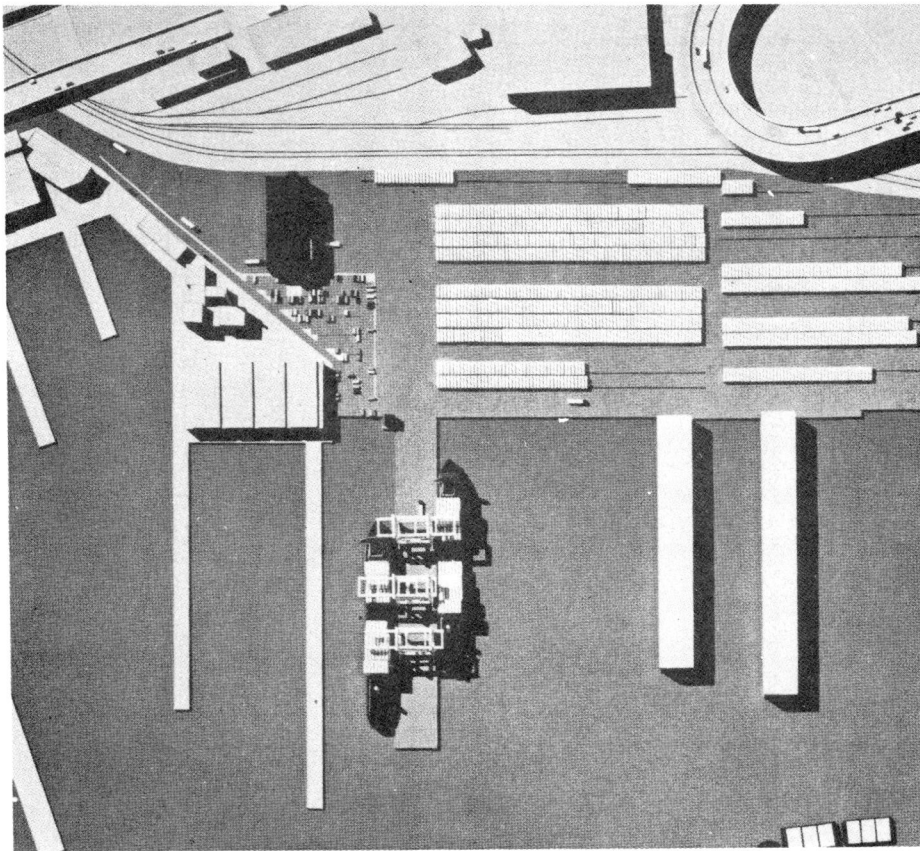
Model of Port Seatrain, Weehawken, N.J.

Pier 13, Stapleton

 Universal Car Loading & Distributing

RAILWAYS
General

Fourteen railroads serve the Port of New York—eight trunk line railroads with interline connections spanning the entire country and reaching into Mexico and Canada—and six short line railroads connecting the trunk lines within the Port District by transferring and shifting cars from one terminal to another.

Some of the piers in New York have railroad sidings; however, every pier in New York can be served by the railroads via carfloat or lighter.

Carfloats are long steel barges equipped, usually, with a double set of tracks on to which freight cars are rolled by means of a link-span ramp.

RAILWAYS—TRUNK LINE

THE BALTIMORE & OHIO RAILROAD COMPANY
General Offices, Foreign Freight Department amd Lighterage Department:
233 Broadway, N.Y., N.Y. 10004
Digby 4-1600
Telephone:

THE ERIE-LACKAWANNA RAILROAD COMPANY
General Offices, Foreign Freight Traffic Department:
140 Cedar St., New York, N.Y. 10006
Telephone: 227-2500

THE LEHIGH VALLEY RAILROAD COMPANY
Foreign Freight Traffic Department and Lighterage Department:
140 Cedar St., N.Y., N.Y. 10006
TELEPHONE: 227-5400

THE NEW YORK SUSQUEHANNA & WESTERN RAILROAD COMPANY
General Offices and Traffic Department:
Tri-Terminal Building, 309 River Rd., Edgewater, N.J. 07020

THE CENTRAL RAILROAD COMPANY OF NEW JERSEY
General Office, Freight Traffic Department and Foreign Freight Office:
1100 Raymond Boulevard, Newark, N.J. 07102
Telephone: (201) 643-6800

THE READING RAILROAD SYSTEM
Local Offices:
233 Broadway, N.Y., N.Y. 10007
Telephone: Digby 9-2175

THE LONG ISLAND RAIL ROAD
General Offices and Freight Department:
Jamaica Station, Jamaica, N.Y. 11435
Telephone: JAmaica 9-0600

PENN CENTRAL
Local Offices:
Freight Sales Department, International Sales and International Container Sales, located at 466 Lexington Avenue, New York, N.Y. 10017.
Manager International Sales—340-3523

RAILWAYS—SHORT LINE

BROOKLYN EASTERN DISTRICT TERMINAL (BEDT)
General Offices:
86 Kent Ave., Brooklyn, N.Y. 11211
EVergreen 8-8300

BUSH TERMINAL RAILROAD COMPANY (BT)
General and Sales Offices:
107-48th Street, Brooklyn, N.Y. 11232
STerling 8-1000

NEW YORK DOCK RAILWAY (NYD)
General Offices and Foreign Freight Department:
Joralemon and Furman Sts., Brooklyn, N.Y. 11201
MAin 4-3400 and DElaware 3-8154

EAST JERSEY RAILROAD AND TERMINAL COMPANY (EJR&T)
General Offices:
E. 22nd St., Bayonne, N.J. 07002
HEmlock 7-2626

HOBOKEN SHORE RAILROAD (HSR)
General Offices:
1419 Bloomfield St., Hoboken, N.J.
OLdfield 9-2468-9

STATEN ISLAND RAPID TRANSIT RAILWAY COMPANY (SIRT) (BALTIMORE AND OHIO RAILROAD COMPANY)
General Offices:
Baltimore & Ohio Building, 2 North Charles Street, Baltimore
Md 21201, Area Code 301-237-2000
Local Offices:
General Manager-Superintendent, Pier 6, St George, Staten Island, N.Y. 10301
Sales Office:
St. George Ferry Terminal, Staten Island, N.Y. 01301
TELEPHONE: Area Code 212-Gibraltar 7-1220

A model of Port Seatrain N.J.

ROAD TRANSPORT:
Some 10,000 trucks are registered to operate within the New York Port District.
Two Union Motor Truck Terminals are operated by The Port of New York Authority, one in Manhattan and the other in Newark, N.J. Cargo for export is delivered directly to the piers.
Common carrier rates on interstate and foreign traffic are regulated by the Interstate Commerce Commission; contract motor freight rates are not. Truckers are exempted from rate regulation when they transport agricultural, horticultural or fishery products. Within the Commercial Zone, in the Port District, local traffic is free from rate regulation. Interstate traffic in New York is regulated by the Public Service Commission of the State of New York; in New Jersey it is not regulated.
Importers receiving cargo via Port of New York can effect savings in the cost of trucking less-carload-lots from steamship and waterfront warehouses within the lighterage limits of the Port to the rail carriers lighterage loading points by taking advantage of the carload consolidation provision of the rail tariff.

CONTAINER MAINTENANCE AND REPAIR
Ace Container Repair Co.
151 Howell Street, Jersey City N.J.
(201) 653-5538
A.G. Ship Maintenance Corp.
Alert Service Inc.
161 Marsh Street, Port Newark, N.J.
(201) 624-9299

Atlantic Coast Industries Corp. (Container M/R Division)
68 Summit Street, Brooklyn, N.Y.
UL 8-8910
Bay Refractory Co., Inc. (Container M/R Division)
164 Wolcott Street, Brooklyn, N.Y.
MA 5-3750
Castelo & Sons Container Repair Corp.
38 First Street, Hoboken, N.J.
(201) 656-0021
Charlton Marine, Inc
46-50 Arlington Ave., Jersey City, N.J.
(201) 434-2121
Flexi-Van Service Center, Inc.
1 Gilbert Drive Secaucus, N.J.
(201) 866-0500
Great Eastern Maintenance & Service Corp.
Hammond Marine Contracting Corp. (Container M/R Division)
340 Hamilton Avenue, Brooklyn, N.Y.
UL 2-4777
Integrated Container Service Inc.

230 Park Avenue, New York, N.Y.
685-5132
Intermodel Industries Inc.
International Container Repair Inc.
P.O. Box 462, Metuchen, N.J.
(201) 494-1666
Interstate Maintenance Corp. (Container M/R Division)
17 Battery Place, New York, N.Y.
WH 3-7676
Iron Works Container Repair Corp.
133 Dwight Street, Brooklyn, N.Y.
UL 5-5220
Marine Trailers
358 St. Marks Place, Staten Island, N.Y.
447-7708
Nat's Trailer Repair
Box 2058, Route 9, Lakewood, N.J.
(201) 363-2750
Oceanic Container Service Inc.
Realco
219 East 42 St., New York, N.Y.
557-8863
Ship Tank Containers Corp.
Foot of Grace St., Secaucus, N.J.
(201) 864-0550
Strick Corporation
2480 Secaucus Road, North Bergen, N.J.
(201) 864-1215
Arthur Tickle Engineering Works Inc. (Container M/R Division)

Trans-World Equipment Corp.
624 Patterson Plank Road
227-3750
East Rutherford, N.J.
(201) 935-1290

Trans-World International, Inc.
56 Oak Street, Bayonne, N.J.
(201) 437-9250
Uncas Maintenance & Repair Co., Inc.
308 Front Street, Staten Island, N.Y.
981-1195
Van-Dorn Equipment Co., Inc.
316 19 St., Carlstadt, N.J.
(201) 939-3800

An artist's impression of one of the three Herbert Morris container-handling cranes.

OAKLAND

Port of Oakland,
66 Jack London Square,
Oakland, California 94607
TELEPHONE: 444-3188
OFFICIALS:

Ben E. Nutter (*Executive Director*)

Robert W. Crandall (*Manager Marine Terminal Department and Traffic Manager*)

GENERAL:

The Port of Oakland is on the mainland side of San Francisco Bay.

CONTAINER FACILITIES:
Sea Land Terminal

This facility, operated by Sea-Land Services Inc., has a quay length of 413 m (1,355 ft) equipped with three 27½ short ton Paceco container gantry cranes with an outreach of 34·14 m (112 ft). There are 24·28 hectares (60 acres) of marshalling area including a 3 hectare (7·4 acre) truck and rail terminal. There is also a terminal building and a maintenance depot. Over 2,000 containers including 250 refrigerated units can be stored and handled at the terminal.

7th Street Terminal

This terminal, completed May 1971, has 56·66 hectares (140 acres) of active facilities. It includes Berths D and E, Berth G, a three berth Public Container facility (Berths H, I & J), and Berth O, also a public facility.

Berths D and E

This facility, operated by Matson Terminals has a quay length of 411·5 m (1,350 ft). It is served by two container cranes. with an

outreach of 23 m (105 ft); one a 27½-short-ton Paceco gantry crane and one 25-short-ton Star container gantry crane. The 18·21 hectare (45 acre) facility includes 13·76 hectares (34 acres) of container marshalling and storage yard, and a 4·45 hectare (11 acre) container freight station. Matson Navigation Company uses this terminal for their Hawaiian services while N.Y.K. and Showa use the terminal for their services to Japan. The container yard is a straddle carrier operation with containers stacked two high.

Berth G

This facility, with a quay length of 191·4 m (628 ft) has 3·15 hectares (7·8 acres) of container storage area and a 2,972 m² (32,000 ft²) covered container freight station. It is equipped with one 33-short-ton Paceco sliding boom type crane with an outreach of 31·09 m (102 ft). An additional sliding boom container crane with a 40-long-ton capacity and an outreach of 32·15 m (115·5 ft) may be employed from adjoining Berth H. The facility is used by Japan Line. "K" Line, Mitsui-O.S.K. and Yamashita-Shinnihon for their weekly service to Japan.

Berths H, I and J. (Public Container Terminal)

This facility, operated by Marine Terminals Corporatoin, consists of two container berths (Berth H and I) and one berth designed for a combination of containers and break bulk cargo (Berth J).

Berth H has a quay length of 233·47 m (765 ft), has 2·52 hectares (6·3 acres) container storage area and a 4,645 m² (50,000 ft²)

covered container freight station. It is served by one Paceco 40-long-ton sliding boom crane that has an outreach of 32·15 m (115·5 ft). Additional cranes may be employed from adjoining Berths G or I.

Berth I has a quay length of 234·7 m (770 ft), and has 2·32 hectares (5·68 acres) of container storage area. It is served by one 40-long-ton Paceco sliding boom container crane with an outreach of 32·15 m (115·5 ft). An addtiional crane from adjoining Berth H may be employed.

Berth J has a quay length of 244·45 m (802 ft) has 1·05 hectares (2·6 acres) of container storage area and a 5,704 m² (61,440 ft²) combination container freight station/ transit shed. Crane rails have been installed should future operations require a shore-side container crane. The public facility is utilised by Johnson Line for its European service. United States Lines for its tricontinent service, ScanStar for its European service and Berth J is utilised by Pacific Australia Direct for its roll-on service.

Berth O

This public facility is also operated by Marine Terminals Corporation as a combination break-bulk/container berth. It has a quay length of 185·3 m (608 ft) and offers 1·39 hectares (3·45 acres) of storage area. Crane rails have been installed should future operations require shore-side container cranes. The storage yard is constructed for a straddle carrier type operation with containers two high.

PORT OF OAKLAND CONTAINER FACILITIES

1 Sea–Land Terminal
5 Seventh Street — Matson Terminal
6 ″ ″ ″ — Oakland Terminal
7,8,9 Seventh Street — Public Container Terminal
10 ″ ″ ″ 'O' Berth
11 Middle Harbour Terminal
12 Sea–Train Lines

Port of Oakland.

Seatrain Terminal

This facility has one 213·36 m (700 ft) long berth with a 152·4 m (500 ft) extension planned. The 12·95 hectare (32 acre) terminal has storage area for 1,000 containers and chassis, an office and a maintenance building. It is served by two 45-ton Alliance sliding boom container cranes that have an outreach of 27·43 m (90 ft). The facility is used for Seatrain's Guam and Hawaii services.

Middle Harbor Terminal (under construction)

The Port is developing a 21·04 hectare 52 (acre) area adjacent to the Seatrain Terminal as another major container base. It will be a quay wall terminal; one end of the wall will join Seatrain's extended wharf and the other will abut Western Pacific Railroads piggy-back yard. The quay wall length will be approximately 509 m (1,670 ft) A 20 hectare (50 acre) container storage area will be included and a container freight station will also be available.

CONTAINER TRAFFIC:

1970

Inwards	1,135,997 tons	109,962 units*
Outwards	2,514,702 tons	226,402 units*
Total	3,650,699 tons	336,364 units*

1971 (Estimate 4,000,000 to 4,500,000 tons)

Inwards	1,240,000 tons	120,038 units*
Outwards	2,760,000 tons	248,648 units*
Total	4,000,000 tons	368,686 units*

*The number of units in 20 ft equivalents.

TERMINAL OPERATING HOURS:

Ship cargo handling operations take place between 0800 to 1700 hours and 1700 to 0200 hours. These are the normal shifts but a third shift could be worked to give 24 hour availability.

Inland cargo handling operations take place 24 hours per day.

CONTAINER REPAIR FACILITIES:

Basically, the container operators repair their own equipment; however, Matson Terminals, in addition to doing their own work will undertake outside work on a contract basis. Additionally, Pacific Coast Container Corporation maintains facilities for repairing containers.

Matson Terminals, Inc.
3050—7th Street, Oakland, 94607
Telephone: (415) 893-2456

Pacific Coast Container Corporation.
1776 Neptune Street, San Leandro, 94577
Telephone: (415) 357-8226

RAILROADS:

Atchison, Topeka and Santa Fe Railway Co
235 West MacArthur Boulevard
Oakland, 94611
Telephone: (415) 658-4226

Oakland Terminal Railway
1925 Sherman Street, Alameda 94502
Telephone: (415) 655-3900

Southern Pacific Co.
1707 Wood Street, Oakland 94612
Telephone: (415) 832-2121

Western Pacific Railroad Co.
8201 Edgewater Drive, Oakland 94621
Telephone: (415) 832-2604

COFC operations take place at piggyback ramps located at nearby marshalling yards.

IMPORT/EXPORT DISTRIBUTION CENTRES

Containerfreight Corporation.
1285—5th Street, Oakland, 94607
Telephone: (415) 465-1725

Mid-Pacific Freight Forwarders
755 Ferry Street, Oakland, 94607
Telephone: (415) 465-4850

Montgomery Ward Import Depot
2695—14th Street, Oakland, 94607
Telephone: (415) 451-2070

Oakland Distribution Centre
7th & Terminal Streets, Oakland, 94607
Telephone: (415) 839-2800

Regal Apparel, Ltd.
2694—14th Street, Oakland, 94607
Telephone: (415) 465-3771

UC Express
801 Maritime Street

Oakland – Seventh Street Terminal.

Oakland – Sea-Land Terminal.

Oakland, 94607
Telephone: (415) 654-1730

TERMINALS AND TERMINAL OPERATORS:

General American Transportation Corp.
735 Terminal Street, Oakland, 94607
Telephone: (415) 834-5140

Howard Terminal
95 Market Street, Oakland, 94607
Telephone: (415) 451-4722

Marine Terminals Corporation.
Main Office:
260 Embarcadero, San Francisco, 94105
Telephone: (415) 986-6576

9th Avenue Terminal, Oakland, 94606
Telephone: (415) 452-3742
Public Container Terminal

5160—7th Street, Oakland, 94607
Telephone: (415) 836-0386

Matson Terminals, Inc.
100 Mission Street, San Francisco, 94105
Telephone: (415) 982-7700

Oakland Container Terminal

5100—7th Street, Oakland, 94607
Telephone: (415) 834-5822

Sea-Land Service, Inc.
1425 Maritime Street, Oakland, 94607
Telephone: (415) 835-8340

Seatrain Lines
1395 Middle Harbor Road,
Oakland, 94607
Telephone: (415) 465-1800

STEAMSHIP LINES AND AGENTS:

American Mail Line
   601 California Street,
   San Francisco 94108
   Telephone: (415) 981-5543
American President Lines
   601 California Street,
   San Fransisco 94108
   Telephone: (415) 981-6000
Bakke Steamship Corporation
   650 California Street,
   San Francisco 94108
   Telephone: (415) 433-4200
Balfour, Guthrie & Co. Ltd.
   One Maritime Plaza
   San Francisco 94111
   Telephone: (415) 433-1550
Barber Lines
   (Agent: Overseas Shipping Co.)
Brasileiro, C. N. Lloyd
   (Agent: Kerr Steamship Co. Inc.)
Columbus Line
   (Agent: Bakke Steamship Corp.)
Crusader Shipping Co. Ltd.
   (Agent: Monitor Steamship Agency)
d'Amico Mediterranean Pacific Line
   (Agent: J. H. Winchester & Co. Inc.)
East Asiatic Co. Inc., The
   650 California Street,
   San Francisco 94108
   Telephone: (415) 391-5000
Euro-Pacific
   (Agent: Balfour, Guthrie & Co. Ltd.)
Fesco Pacific Line
   (Far Eastern Steamship Co.)
   (Agent: Interocean Steamship Corp.)
Flota Mercante Grancolombiana
   (Agent: Balfour, Guthrie & Co. Ltd.)
Fritz Maritime Agencies
   615 Battery Street,
   San Francisco 94126
   Telephone: (415) 433-6590
General Steamship Corp., Ltd.
   400 California Street,
   San Francisco 94104
   Telephone: (415) 392-4100
Great Eastern Line
   (Agent: General Steamship Corp., Ltd.)
Hanseatic-Vaasa
   (Agent: Williams, Dimond & Co.)
Interocean Steamship Corporation
   680 Beach Street,
   San Francisco 94109
   Telephone: (415) 771-6400
Italian Line
   (Agent: General Steamship Corp., Ltd.)
Ital-Pacific Line
   (Agent: Transmarine Navigation Corp.)
Japan Line
   (Agent: Japan Line (USA) Ltd)
Japan Line (USA) Ltd.
   One California Street,
   Room 3125
   San Francisco 94111
   Telephone: (415) 781-6226
"K" Line (Kawasaki Kisen Kaisha, Ltd.)
   (Agent: Kerr Steamship Co., Inc.)
Kerr Steamship Co., Inc.
   One California Street,
   San Francisco 94111
   Telephone: (415) 391-3800
Johnson Line
   (Agent: General Steamship Corp., Ltd.)
Knutsen Line
   (Agent: Bakke Steamship Corp.)
Learner Co., The
   2200 Jerrold Avenue
   San Francisco 94124
   Telephone: (415) 648-6687
Lilly Shipping Agencies
   One California Street,
   San Francisco 94111
   Telephone: (415) 781-3600
Maersk Line
   One Maritime Plaza,
   San Francisco 94111

Oakland – Middle Harbour Terminal under construction with adjacent Seatrain Terminal and rail facilities.

Telephone: (415) 398-1515
Maritime Co. of the Philippines
   (Agent: North American Maritime Agencies)
Matson Navigation Company
   100 Mission Street,
   San Francisco 94105
   Telephone: (415) 982-7700
Mitsui O.S.K. Lines, Ltd.
   (Agent: Williams, Dimond & Co.)
Monitor Steamship Agency, Inc.
   2, Pine Street,
   San Francisco 94111
   Telephone: (415) 986-6584
Nedlloyd Line
   (Agent: Transpacific Transportation Co.)
Nedlloyd and Hoegh Lines
   (Agent: Transpacific Transportation Co.)
N.Y.K. Line (Nippon Yusen Kaisha)
   (Agent: Transmarine Navigation Corp.)
North American Maritime Agencies
   214 Front Street,
   San Francisco 94111
   Telephone: (415) 981-0343
Olympic Steamship Co., Inc.
   425 California Street,
   San Francisco 94104
   Telephone: (415) 434-0120
Orient Maritime Agencies
   311 California Street,
   San Francisco 94104
   Telephone: (415) 981-7340
Orient Overseas Line
   (Agent: Orient Maritime Agencies)
Overseas shipping Company
   One California Street,
   San Francisco 94111
   Telephone: (415) 986-2114

Pacific Australia Direct Line
   (Agent: General Steamship Corp. Ltd.)
Pacific Far East Line, Inc.

One Embarcadero Center,
San Francisco 94111
Telephone: (415) 576-4000
Pacific Islands Transport Line
   (Agent: General Steamship Corp., Ltd.)
Prudential-Grace Lines, Inc.
   One California Street,
   Suite 1201,
   San Francisco 94111
   Telephone: (415) 781-3800
ScanStar
   (Agent: East Asiatic Co., Inc., The)
Scindia Steam Navigation Co., Ltd.
   (Agent: Transmarine Navigation Corp.)
Sea-Land Service Inc.
   1425 Maritime Street,
   Oakland 94607
   Telephone: (415) 835-8340
Seatrain Lines, California
   1395 Middle Habor Road,
   Oakland 94607
   Telephone: (415) 465-1800
Shipping Corp. of India, Ltd., The
   (Agent: Olympic Steamship Co.)
Showa Shipping Company
   (Agent: Transmarine Navigation Corp.)
States Marine International
   (Agent: States Marine-Isthmian Agency, Inc.)
States Marine-Isthmian Agency Inc.
   100 Bush Street,
   San Francisco 94104
   Telephone: (415) 986-3800
States Steamship Company
   320 California Street,
   San Francisco 94104
   Telephone: (415) 982-6221
Suan Shipping Company
   (Agent: The Learner Company)
Taiwan Navigation, Ltd.
   (Agent: World Tradeways Shipping, Ltd.)
Transmarine Navigation Corporation

555 California Street,
Suite 2175
San Francisco 94104
Telephone: (415) 989-4550
Transpacific Transportation Co.
650 California Street,
San Francisco 94108
Telephone: (414) 986-0786
Toko Line
(Agent: Fritz Maritime Agencies)
United Philippine Lines
(Agent: General Steamship Corp., Ltd.)

United States Lines, Inc.
One California Street,
San Francisco 94111
Telephone: (415) 397-5011
United Yugoslav Lines
(Agent: Monitor Steamship Agency, Inc.)
Westfal-Larsen Line
(Agent: General Steamship Corp., Ltd.)
Williams, Dimond & Company
215 Market Street,
San Francisco 94105
Telephone: (415) 982-8350

Winchester, J. H. & Co., Inc.
351 California Street,
San Francisco 94104
Telephone: (415) 781-0918
World Tradeways Shipping Ltd.
One California Street,
San Francisco 94111
Telephone: (415) 982-8364
Yamashita-Shinnihon Steamship Co.
(Agent: Lilly Shipping Agencies)
Zim Israel Navigation Co., Ltd.
(Williams, Dimond & Company)

PHILADELPHIA

Port of Philadelphia
Delaware River Port Authority
Public Ledger Building
Philadelphia Pa 19106
TELEPHONE: 215 WA3-1840
OFFICIALS:
T. H. Lipscomb (*Executive Director*)
C. H. McWilliams (*Secretary and Deputy Executive Director*)
T. J. Auchter (*Treasurer and Director of Finance*)
OVERSEAS REGIONAL OFFICES
London
128 Mount Street, London W1Y 5HA
Telephone: 01-499 5853
Brussels
536 Avenue Louise, Brussels 5
Telephone: 48.80.64
Tokyo
Suite 1214, World Trade Center Bldg.,
5, 3-chome, Hamamatsu-cho, Minatu-ku,
Tokyo
Telephone: 436-5581

CONTAINER FACILITIES:
Tioga Marine Terminal
This facility, at present operational, is still under construction. On completion it will have a straight quay length of 981 m (3,220 ft) with a right angled berth of 198·1 m (650 ft) at one end, there is a depth of water alongside of 10·67 m (35 ft) and the total area will be 30·3 hectares (75 acres) of which 21·45 hectares (53 acres) will be paved open storage. A transit shed of 27,871 m² (300,000 sq ft) will also be provided. A 45 ton Kocks container gantry crane with an outreach of 34·59 m (113·5 ft) and an inboard reach of 56·08 m (184 ft) has been provided.
Packer Avenue Marine Terminal
Operated by the Lavino Shipping Company this facility with 10·67 m (35 ft) water alongside is a 18·2 hectare (45 acre) extension of the existing break bulk and unitised cargo terminal. This will give a total of 23·07 hectares (57 acres) of paved open storage, a quay length of 365·76 m (1,200 ft) equipped with a 45 ton Kocks container gantry crane with an outreach of 34·59 m (113·5 ft) and an inboard reach of 56·08 m (184 ft). There will also be a roll-on berth 251·46 m (825 ft) in length at right angles to the container berth and handling equipment includes a 75 ton mobile crane.
TERMINAL OPERATING HOURS:
Ship cargo handling operations take place between 8 and 16 hours per day depending on requirements.
Inland transport handling operations take place 24 hours per day.
TRAFFIC:
Lift-on traffic was 112,000 tons in 1970, the figure for 1971 is estimated at 300,000 tons.

Philadelphia—Tioga Marine Terminal—April 1971

Philadelphia—Packer Avenue Marine Terminal

PORTLAND

The Port of Portland
P.O. Box 3529
Portland, Oregon 97208
TELEPHONE: 233-8331
CONTAINER REPAIR ORGANISATIONS:
Coastal Marine Service
  1051 Houston Avenue
  Port Arthur, Texas 77640
  Telephone: A/C 713 983-1616
Twx: 910-464-6151
CONTAINER FACILITIES:
Terminal 4

This terminal, used by Matson on a preferential berthing arrangement and available to other operators, has sufficient length to berth two vessels simultaneously. There is a container parking area of 2·43 hectares (6 acres) which can be doubled if necessary. Handling equipment consists of a 33 ton Hitachi container gantry crane with an outreach of 31·39 m (103 ft) capable of handling 40 ft units and equipped with hook, magnet and grab for other cargoes as necessary. There is a shed of 10,405 m² (1,121,000 sq ft).

Terminal 2

This includes a 10·5 hectare (26 acres) yard, a container freight station, a 40-ton Hitachi container gantry crane and two 65-ton whirleys. The reinforced concrete pier is 408 m (1,340 ft) long and 20·7 m (68 ft) wide. There is a shed of 8,360 m² (90,000 ft.) and four straddle carriers carry out handling operations in the yard.

TERMINAL OPERATING HOURS:
24 hours per day on ship and inland transport cargo operations.

FUTURE DEVELOPMENT:
Clearing has begun on additional container facilities adjacent to Terminal 4 downriver from Terminal 2.

To be developed as business warrants, this area will have a quay length of 442 m (1,450 ft), two container gantry cranes and 20 acres of paved open storage. It has easy access to highway and rail facilities.

Portland—Terminal 2.

The Commission plans eventually to develop Pier B, between Berths 1, 2 and 3 and also Berths 5, 6 and 7 at Terminal 1 as a storage area for 225 containers. The 2½ acre storage area will be paved and have flush rail tracks.

Containers will be shuttled about by straddle carriers and fork lift truck, with a top handling spreader.

Portland—Terminal 4.

Port of Port Arthur
PO Box 1428, Port Arthur, Texas 77640
TELEPHONE: 983-2011
OFFICIALS:
  Dow Wynn (*General Manager*)
  Ben Goldstein (*Assistant General Manager*)
  John Ragland (*Traffic Manager*)
GENERAL

The Public Ocean Terminal, a general cargo facility, is equipped with a 75 ton level luffing portal jib crane which is fitted with spreader for container handling as required. The facility with quay length of 365 ·8m (1,200 ft) and an apron of 91·4 m (300 ft) occupies some 10 hectares (25 acres) and has ample storage space for containers. Straddle carriers are available.

TERMINAL OPERATING HOURS:
Ship operations take place 24 hours a day. Inland transport facilities operate between 0800° to 1200 hrs and 1300 to 1700 hrs; overtime is worked if authorised.

Richmond Port Commission
Richmond, California
GENERAL:
Situated in the northeast corner of San Francisco Bay the port is linked by a channel

PORT ARTHUR

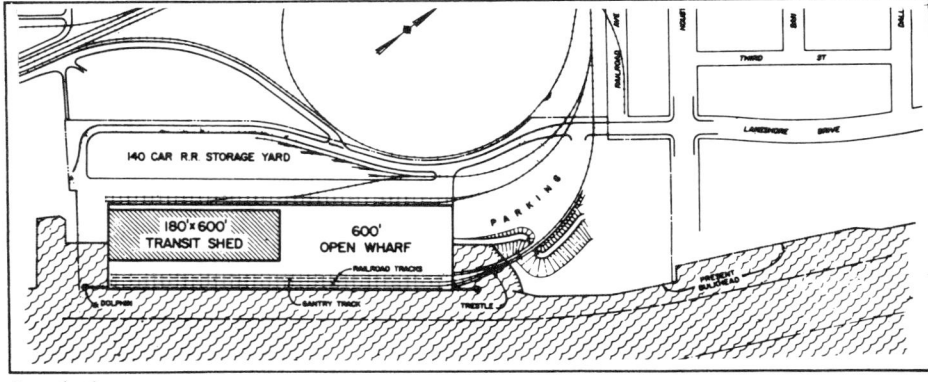

Port Arthur.

CONTAINER REPAIR ORGANIZATIONS:
  Coastal Marine Service
  1051 Houston Avenue

Port Arthur, Texas 77640
TELEPHONE: A/C 713 983-1616

RICHMOND, CALIFORNIA

with a depth of 10·67 m (35 ft) to the deep water in the Bay.
CONTAINER FACILITIES:
The Port Commission have announced that they intend converting Terminal No. 3, presently leased to the Port Terminal Company, into a container terminal.

SAN FRANCISCO

The San Francisco Port Commission

Port of San Francisco,
Ferry Building, San Francisco, California 94111
TELEPHONE: 391-8000
OFFICIALS:
Miriam E. Wolff (*Port Director*)
Edward L. David (*Port Facilities Manager*)
Don E. DeLone (*Trade Promotion Manager*)
Eugene L. Sembler (*Chief Harbor Engineer*)
John D. Yeomans (*Port Controller*)
Donald Taggart (*Public Relations Director*)

CONTAINER FACILITIES:

Army Street Terminal:

The total area of the terminal is 27·5 hectares (68 acres). It has a continuous 808 m (2,657 ft) wharf equipped with a 30 ton quay crane capable of lifting 20 and 40 ft units.

A central storage area with a capacity for 8,000 standard 20 ft containers is accessible to the terminal's three working sides.

Piers 27 and 50:

The two-berth Pier 27, which features 43,700 m² (470,000 sq ft) of concrete deck, and the 11·7 hectares (29 acres) Pier 50, which contains large storage and marshalling areas, both have facilities for handling containerised cargoes.

India Basin Terminal

Now scheduled for completion in early 1972 this 19·4 hectare (48 acre) facility, part of a large development covering 93 hectares (230 acres) is situated directly across the Islais Creek Channel from the Army Street Terminal. The terminal, to be used by Pacific Far East Line barge carriers and containers ships, will be designed to include two berths with concrete decks and a large back-up area for container storage, a long cargo transit shed and adjacent lighter loading berths, and an anchorage basin for the lighters. The facility will be equipped with a container gantry crane. Good road and rail access has been planned.

CONTAINER STORAGE YARD:

Container storage yards have been installed at various locations along the San Francisco waterfront.

VERTICAL CONTAINER STORAGE:

The Port Commission are reported as evaluating two proposals for vertical container storage systems.

RAILROADS:

San Francisco is a major terminal for three trans-continental railroads—Santa Fe, Southern Pacific and Western Pacific. They offer fast, frequent and direct service between the Port of San Francisco and destinations in all sections of the United States, Canada and Mexico.

All three railroads have a marshalling yard in San Francisco near the waterfront. Rail car switching services between these yards and each pier is performed by the Port's State Belt Railroad, which places the rail cars on the docks in the early morning hours before the work day begins.

Southern Pacific Company:

65 Market Street,
Telephone: 362-1212

This railroad serves the 12 states in the West and Southwest. Southern Pacific has one of the largest fleets of piggy back equipment in the United States serving hundreds of communities through more than 60 strategically located ramps.

Western Pacific Company:

526 Mission Street
Telephone: 982-2100

Western Pacific concentrates on specialized freight with more than 50 per cent of its fleet equipped for special cargoes. Each type

San Francisco—Impression of India Basin Barge Carrier Terminal.

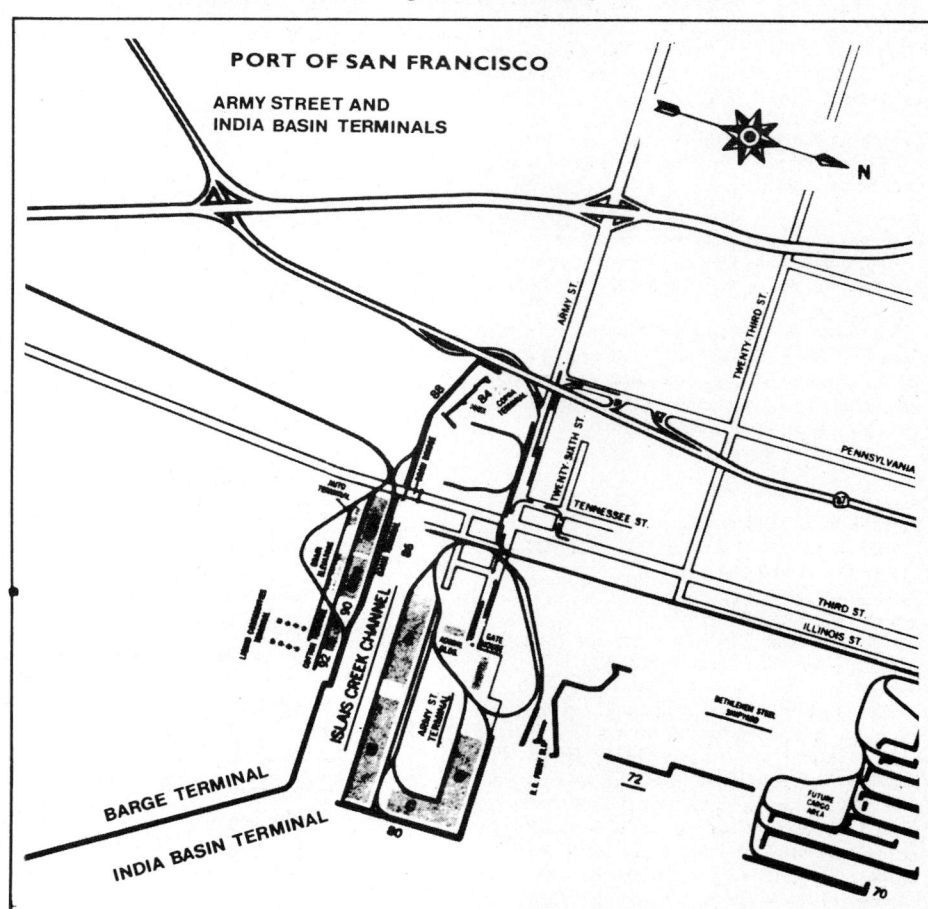

PORT OF SAN FRANCISCO
ARMY STREET AND INDIA BASIN TERMINALS

is designed to fit a particular shipper requirement and keyed to reduction of shipper handling and transportation costs.

WP's marshalling yard and connection with the State Belt Railroad is on the North side of Islais Creek Channel, adjoining the Army Street Terminal.

Atchison, Topeka & Santa Fe Railway Company, 114 Sansome Street, 781-7600.

The Santa Fe is a 13,000-mile long railroad spanning the continent from the West Coast to the Great Lakes area and the Gulf Coast.

The Port of San Francisco has a direct and convenient ferry link from a centrally located landing to the Santa Fe overland train. Ferries leave the port at 7-30 pm and

9-30 pm for the 1 am departure of the eastbound train.

TRUCKING AND MOTOR FREIGHT ROUTES

About 75 per cent of the port's inbound and outbound cargo moves to and from piers by truck. More than 200 western and transcontinental trucking firms form a steady stream of motor traffic along the waterfront. and Harrison, or via The Embarcadero to Third and Berry and thence south on Third Street to James Lick Freeway.

The Embarcadero, a four-lane thoroughfare, provides access to most of the piers. It links to a network of highways, expressways and main streets that serve the city.

New freeway arteries provide additional approaches to the James Lick Freeway at Sixth Street, and at Army Street, within a block of the port's new Army Street Terminal. Plans call for an additional link direct to The Embarcadero.

East bound traffic may use Highway 101 for access to the San Francisco-Oakland Bay Bridge. The bridge connects to three major highways: Interstate 80 northeast-bound, Interstate 580 eastbound, and State Route 17 southbound.

CONTAINER LEASING COMPANIES

Advance Distribution Co
351 California St, 981-5770
California Cargo Containers
801 Maritime St (Oakland) 835-4484
Compass Container Co
311 California St, 232-4264
Container Transport International
105 Market St, 391-2346
Fruehauf Trailer Corp
850 92nd Ave (Oakland), Enterprise 1-0957
General American Transportation Corp
Russ Bldg, 362-8222
North American Van Lines
3600 3rd St, 826-2700
Smyth Van & Storage of California, Inc
3600 Third St, 826-2700
Xtra, Inc
311 California St, 98/-1-7065

TERMINAL COMPANIES

California Maritime Terminals
Army Street Terminal
Tel: 285-5600
California Stevedore & Ballast Co
Army Street Terminal
Tel: 285-6500
Jones Stevedoring Co
465 California Street
Tel: 391-4590
Marine Terminals Corp
260 Embarcadero
Tel: 986-6576
Matson Terminals
100 Mission St
Tel: 982-7700
Pacific-Oriental Terminal Co.
Piers 19-23
Tel: 781-4891
Star Terminal Co, Inc.
Pier 46-A
Tel: 981-6622

SHIPPING LINES AND AGENTS:

Atlas Steamship Agency
141 Battery Street, 94111
Tel: 981-7313
U.S. Lines
Bakke Steamship Corporation
650 California Street, 94108
Tel: 433-4200
Columbus Lines
Knutsen Line
Balfour, Guthrie & Co, Ltd
One Maritime Plaza, 94111
Tel: 433-1550
Flota Mercante Grancolombiana
Hamburg-American Line
North German Lloyd
Blue Star Line
417 Montgomery Street
Tel: 986-3975
Crusader Shipping Company
East Asiatic Company
650 California Street, 94108
Tel: 392-7324
EAC Lines
Maersk Line
Möller Steamship Co Inc
General Steamship Corp, Ltd
400 California Street, 94111
Tel: 392-4100
Great Eastern Shipping Co, Ltd
Italian Line
Johnson Line
Pacific Australia Direct Line
Pacific Islands Transport Line

San Francisco—Army Street Terminal

United Philippine Lines
Venezuelan Line
Westfal-Larsen Line
Holland-America Line
350 Sansome Street, 94104
Tel: 362-7510
Furness Lines
North Pacific Line
Royal Mail Lines, Ltd
Interocean Steamship Corporation
680 Beach Street, 94109
Tel: 771-6400
New Zealand Pacific Line, Ltd
Pacific European Line, Ltd
Parcel Tankers, Inc
Polynesia Line, Ltd
Interolsen Agencies, Inc
160 Sansome Street, 94104
Tel: 433-4900
Fred. Olsen Interocean Line
French Line
Scindia S. N. Co Ltd
Kerr Steamship Company, Inc
One California Street, 94111
Tel: 391-3800
P. N. Djakarta Lloyd
Kawasaki Kisen Kaisha, Ltd
C. N. Lloyd Brasileiro S. S. Co
Lilly Shipping Agencies
One California Street, 94111
Tel: 781-3600
Yamashita-Shinnihon Line
Matson Navigation Company
100 Mission Street, 94105
Tel: 982-7700
Oceanic Steamship Co
Monitor Steamship Agency, Inc
2 Pine Street, 94111
Tel: 986-6584
Korea Shipping Corp
United Yugoslav Lines
Fred F. Noonan Company, Inc
465 California Street, 94104
Tel: 981-6204
Wallenius Line
North American Maritime Agencies
214 Front Street, 94111
Tel: 981-0343
Maritime Co of the Philippines
Olympic Steamship Co, Inc
425 California Street, 94111

Tel: 434-0120
S.C.I. Line
Showa Shipping Co
Orient Maritime Agencies
311 California Street, 94111
Tel: 981-7340
Orient Overseas Container Line
Overseas Shipping Company
One California Street, 94111
Tel: 986-2114
Barber Line
Prudential Grace Lines Inc
One California Street, 94111
Tel: 781-3800
Prudential Grace Lines
Star Terminal Inc
Pier 46-A, 94107
Tel: 981-6622
Canadian Gulf Line, Ltd
Canadian Transport Company
States Marine-Isthmian Agency
100 Bush Street, 94104
Tel: 986-3800
States Marine Lines
Isthmian Lines Inc
Transmarine Navigation Corp
351 California Street, 94108
Tel: 982-3887
Ital-Pacific Line
NYK Line (Nippon Yusen Kaisha
Transpacific Transportation Co
351 California Street, 94108
Tel: 986-0786
Japan Line
Nedlloyd Lines
Nedlloyd and Hoegh Lines
Williams, Dimond and Company Inc
215 Market Street, 94105
Tel: 982-8350
Hanseatic-Vaasa Line
Mitsui-OSK Lines, Ltd
P & O Lines
Zim Israel Navigation Co
J. H. Winchester and Company
351 California Street, 94104
Tel: 781-0981
D'Amico Mediterranean Pacific Line
Magsaysag Line
World Tradeways Shipping Ltd.
One California Street, 94111
Tel: 982-8364
Taiwan Navigation Co

Georgia Ports Authority
PO Box 2406
Savannah, Georgia 31402
TELEPHONE: (912) 236-1561
TELEX: TWX 810-784 5634
OFFICIALS:
CONTAINER FACILITY:
Garden City Container Facility

Port of Seattle,
PO Box 1209
Seattle, Washington 98111
TELEPHONE: MA2-8124
TELEX: Portsea Sea
OFFICIAL:
J. Eldon Opheim (*General Manager*)

CONTAINER FACILITIES:

Terminal 5

Sea-Land Service, Inc, set up a base at Terminal 5 for its container ship service in 1964, since when it has expanded and its working areas now cover 12·9 hectares (32 acres) handling trade to Alaska and Military traffic to Okinawa, the Philippines and Vietnam. In late 1968, Sea Land Service began an eastbound container operation from Tokyo to Seattle.

Its two berths are served by three 27·5 short ton capacity container gantry cranes. The storage yard has a capacity of 750 containers. There is a 151 m × 24·4 m (496 ft × 80 ft) freight station for consolidation of cargo.

Terminal 18

Located on the northeast corner of Harbour Island, Terminal 18 has three 219·5 m (720 ft) berths with a waterside depth of 15·2 m (50 ft)

There is a total area of 43·7 hectares (108 acres).

Another berth, 259·1 m (850 ft) in length, may be built on the north side.

Two 30 ton Hitachi container gantry cranes equipped with their own diesel generators have been installed.

The facility is used by the Japan Six Lines' Pacific North West Service and Matson Line.

Terminal 20

A facility for part containership services. The transit sheds provide 29,170 m² (314,000 sq ft) of space, and three back-up warehouses have 13,471 m² (145,000 sq ft).

Development of 4 hectares (10 acres) of container storage provides accommodation for mixed break bulk and container operations.

Five ships can be berthed at one time along the 814 m (3,000 ft) pier.

Four quay cranes—three of 40-ton capacity and one of 50 tons—which can travel the entire length of the pier, plus a large fleet of straddle and forklift trucks, have been provided.

Pier 46

Three berths having a total length of 653·5 m (2,144 ft) are served by two 50-ton travelling quay cranes. There is a total of 8·5 hectares (21 acres) with nearly 4 hectares (10 acres) of storage and handling area.

Alaska Steamship Co, a major carrier in the Alaska service, leases the pier, which has among its facilities a 7,710 m² (83,000 sq ft) transit shed. American Mail Line and Johnson Line use the facility.

Pier 39

A general cargo facility used by 'K' Line for their service to the Far East using converted cellular vessels equipped with their own handling gear.

SAVANNAH

A common user berth with a quay length of 306·9 m (1,007 ft) and a total area of 8·09 hectares (20 acres) has been provided. It is equipped with a 45 ton container gantry crane with an outreach of 34 m (113·5 ft).

BARGE CARRIER FACILITY:

A dolphin berth has been provided by the Port Authority at the mouth of the Savannah River some eighteen miles from the port. The River is navigable for LASH barges for over 220 miles. Prudential Grace LASH vessels use the facility.

FUTURE DEVELOPMENT:

Two additional container berths of the same size as the Garden City facility can be provided as required.

SEATTLE

Seattle—Terminal 18 'K' Lines *Golden Arrow* and a Matson vessel are alongside. Barges are being loaded for Prudhoe Bay, Alaska and this terminal is being used temporarily for this operation. Terminal 5 can be seen in the background.

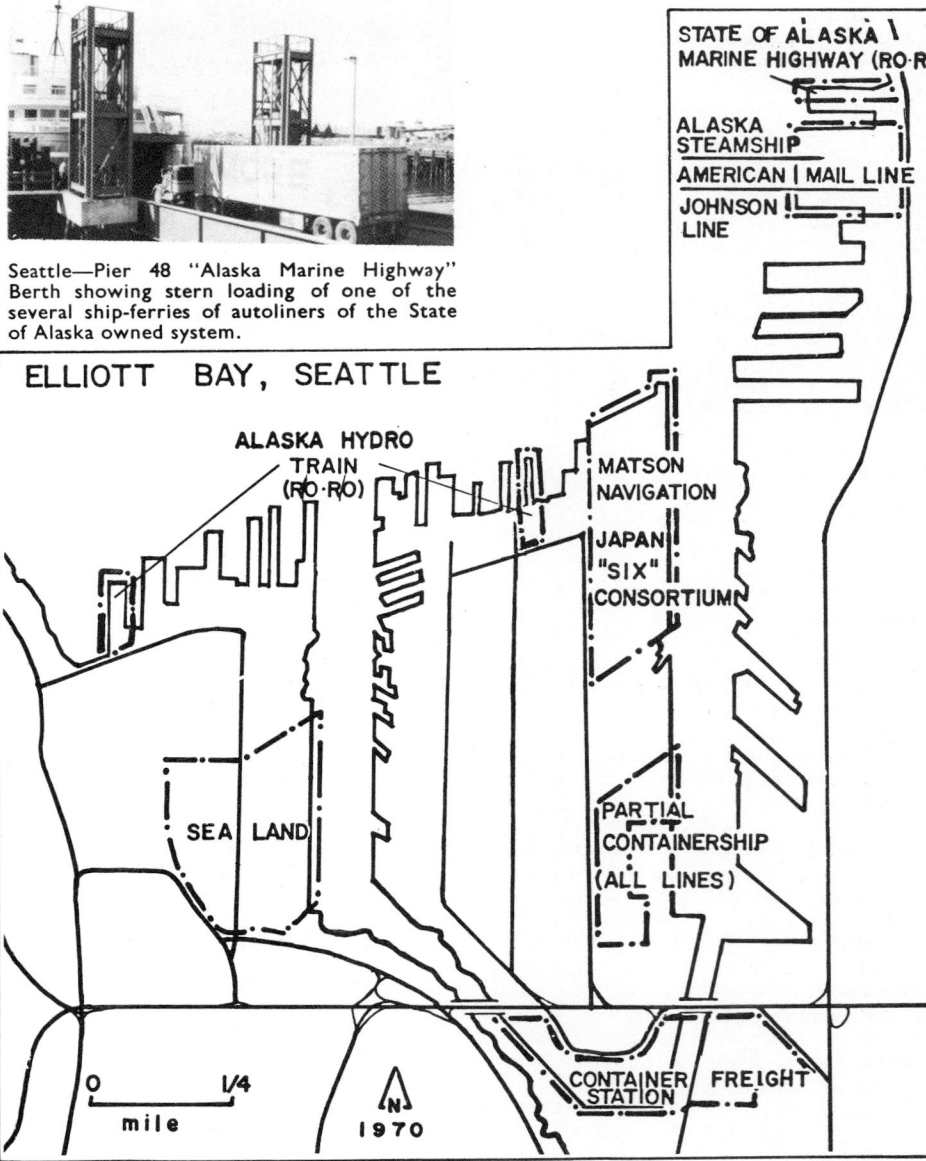

Seattle—Pier 48 "Alaska Marine Highway" Berth showing stern loading of one of the several ship-ferries of autoliners of the State of Alaska owned system.

Foss Alaska Line Terminal

Situated on the Duwamish Waterway just north of First Avenue Bridge the terminal has a total area of 4·04 hectares (10 acres), a quay length of 176·8 m (580 ft) and a container freight station. Barge loading is carried out by two 21·5 ton fork lifts fitted with spreaders.

CONTAINER SERVICES:

Alaska Steamship Co.—Weekly barge service to S.E. Alaska and a steamship service to the remaining Alaskan Ports every two weeks from Pier 46.

American Mail Line—Trans-pacific services about every ten days. Piers 28 (Home base) and 46.

Johnson Line—European service about every two weeks. Piers 28 and 46.

Sea Land Services—Alaskan Service—two sailings per week. Transpacific service—weekly. USA East Coast about every four days. Terminal 5.

Japanese Six Lines Container Service—Transpacific service about every ten days. Terminal 18.

Matson Line—Bi-monthly service to Hawaii. Terminal 18.

'K' Line—Formosa, Hong Kong, Korea every 15 days. Pier 39.

ROLL-ON/ROLL-OFF SERVICES:

Alaska Hydro-trains—Alaska two or three times per week. Piers 2 and 17 .

State of Alaska Marine. Alaska every three or four days. Pier 48.

Foss Alaska Lines—'Van liner' service to Alaska—weekly.

STEVEDORING COMPANIES:
Albin Stevedore Co,
1860 11th Ave SW,
Seattle, Wash 98134
Telephone: MA 2-7551
American Mail Line,
Pier 28
Seattle, Wash 98134
Telephone: MA 4-4400
Matson Terminals Inc,
Terminal 18
Seattle, Wash 98134
Telephone: MU 2-5887
Rothschild-International Stevedoring Co,
2247 E Marginal Way S,
Seattle, Wash 98134
Telephone: MA 3-7966
Seattle Bulk Loading, Inc,
Pier 48
Seattle, Wash 98104
Telephone: MA 2-3707
Seattle Stevedore Co,
3415-11th Ave SW
Seattle, Wash 98134
Telephone: MA 3-0304

Port of Stockton
P.O. Box 2089
Stockton, California 95201
TELEPHONE: 466-6011
OFFICIALS:
George T. Hench (*Port Director*)
Clem W. Phelps (*Assistant Director of the Port*)
Robert J. Strange (*General Sales Manager*)
Ralph W. Clay (*Operations Manager*)
GENERAL

The Port of Stockton is 75 nautical miles east of the entrance to San Francisco Bay. The approach to the port is through San Francisco Bay, San Pablo Bay, Carquinez Strait, Suisun Bay, and Stockton Channel.

Facilities at present comprise eight general cargo berths equipped with transit sheds and one open berth. Containers are at present handled using the Port's two quay cranes or ships' gear.

BARGE CARRIER TERMINAL:

Docks 10 and 11 have been filled in to provide a temporary terminal with a quay frontage of 256 m (840 ft), equipped with

The Sea-Land container freight station for consolidation of cargo at Seattle showing the 80 bays where incoming (and outgoing) containers are backed awaiting consolidation of cargo for one basic destination and eventual delivery across the street to the container cranes and shipberths (upper part of photo shows a small portion of the shoreside of Sea-Land's operation). The 14-railcar freight station is at the right of the truck station building. The dark building lower right is the covered space for special cargo handling and for utility and maintenance.

Terminal 5 Seattle, showing berths 4 and 5 where Sea-Land Services maintain their principal operation.

STOCKTON

container gantry crane rails although a container gantry crane is not included in the first phase of the plan. Between two and four 7½ ton mobile cranes will be provided for handling cargo to and from the barges.

The final location of the permanent Barge Carrier terminal has not yet been decided.

TACOMA

Port of Tacoma,
PO Box 1837
Tacoma, Washington 98401
TELEPHONE: FU3-5841
TWX: 910-441-2646
OFFICIALS:
E. L. Perry (*General Manager*)
Marcus E. Anderson (*Manager, Industrial Division*)
Ray Heinke (*Terminal Manager*)
Reed Jones (*Sales Manager*)
CONTAINER TERMINAL:
The terminal at Pier 4 has a quay length of 378·6 m (1,242 ft) with 50 ft alongside at low water. There is hard standing for containers of 8·09 hectares (20 acres). There is a transit warehouse of 13,935 m² (150,000 sq ft). The facility is equipped with a 50 ton Peiner container gantry crane with an outreach of 35·05 m (115 ft).
TERMINAL WORKING HOURS:
Open at all times except five public holidays.
CONTAINER SERVICES:
American Mail Line and States Line services to Japan and Korea.
STEVEDORE COMPANIES:
Rothschild International Stevedoring Co
615 Port of Tacoma Road, Tacoma, Washington
Seattle Stevedore Co.
801 Port of Tacoma Road, Tacoma, Washington

Tacoma Container Terminal.

Crescent Wharf & Warehouse Co.
c/o Port of Tacoma, PO Box 1837, Tacoma, Washington 98401

CONTAINER REPAIR FACILITIES:
The Port undertakes repairs as requested.

TOLEDO

Toledo-Lucas County Port Authority,
241 Superior Street, Toledo, Ohio 43604
TELEPHONE: 243-8251
TELEGRAMS: Portol
OFFICIALS:
Louis C. Purdey (*Executive Director*)
Edwin F. Avery (*Manager of Commerce and Traffic*)
John A. McWilliam (*General Manager*)
Russell B. Voegtien (*Director of Development and Operations*)
GENERAL:
The Port's overseas cargo complex consists of a quay nearly a mile long with a back up area of 125 acres which includes space for general cargo and container handling. The whole length of quay is served by two heavy lift rail mounted portal quay cranes capable of lifting 72·5 and 110 tons (they are also capable of lifting 150 tons if used in tandem). The position of the cranes can be switched if necessary by using a special rail spur. The Great Lakes only operating foreign trade zone is situated a few hundred feet behind the dockside.
Containers up to 40 ft have been handled for a number of years from conventional cargo vessels calling at the port.
The Port Authority has provided 20 ft container chassis, and converter dollies to enable tandem loads to be transported. These units are leased to shippers on a first come first served basis to assist in the movement of containers between the port and its hinterland.
Container Transport International Inc. (CTI) and the Jones Transfer Co. have jointly established a container 'pool' in Toledo and CTI 20 ft vans are now available within 24 hours to industry in the Ports' hinterland.
CONTAINER SERVICES:
Head Donaldson Line—UK Ports
Manchester Liners—Europe every 10 days

Toledo—Overseas cargo complex.

Europe Canada Lakes Line (ECL) a joint service by Hapag Lloyd, Ernst Russ and Poseidon Lines to Europe weekly.
RAILROADS
The Port of Toledo is the hub of a vast network of railroads that connect it with the major industrial and agricultural areas of the East Coast and the Midwest, with branch lines to many other points. Served by nine trunk lines and two switching carriers, all connected by a belt line circling the city, Toledo is one of the nation's largest rail centres. Huge marshalling yards have a capacity of nearly 60,000 cars. All port facilities are served by one or more railroads.
MOTOR CARRIERS:
Overnight service to and from any place in Ohio and many cities of Indiana, Illinois, Kentucky, and Michigan is provided by 101 inter- and intra-state motor freight lines serving the Port of Toledo. Trailer interchange service is available in Toledo eliminating, in many cases, the physical transfer of freight. Trucking companies maintain warehouses and terminals with many thousands of square feet of storage space. More than 2,600 trucks, trailers, semis, and tractors are available daily. Extensive local and short haul service is also obtainable.

HIGHWAYS:
Toledo is served by United States Routes 20, 23, 24, 25, and 223; Ohio State Routes 2, 51, 65, 120, 199 and 246; and Interstate Routes 80 and 90 (the Ohio Turnpike), 280 (the Detroit-Toledo Expressway) and 75 and 475, currently being completed. Port Installations are on or within minutes of these arteries. A modern network of urban expressways is also under construction in Toledo.

CUSTOMS REQUIREMENTS:

GENERAL:

Under General Headnote 6, Tariff Schedules of the United States (TSUS), containers imported into the United States are subject to duty unless imported under a provision specifically exempting them from duty. Item 808.00, TSUS, provides that containers, if products of the United States, or if of foreign production and previously imported and duty (if any) thereon paid, or if of a class specified by the Secretary of the Treasury as instruments of international traffic; and repair components for a particular container of foreign production which is an instrument of international traffic, may be admitted free of duty.

Containers of United States or foreign origin or ownership arriving in the United States loaded or empty, in use or to be used in the shipment of merchandise in international traffic, may be released without entry or payment of duty under the provisions of section 10.41a, Customs Regulations, but are subject to the restrictions on use in United States domestic traffic found in section 10.41 a(f).

Loaded containers admitted as instruments of international traffic may not be used in point-to-point local traffic within the United States except to pick up and deliver loads at intervening points en route between the port of arrival and the point of destination of their imported cargo. During their return from such point of destination to an exterior port of departure (not necessarily the port of entry), they may not engage in point-to-point local traffic unless such traffic is incidental to their efficient and economical use in international traffic. Empty containers admitted as instruments of international traffic may proceed to a point of lading or export cargo but may not engage in point-to-point local traffic en route to or from that point.

A notice of proposed rule making published in the Federal Register on June 24, 1969 (34 F.R. 9754), proposes to amend section 10.41 a(f) to liberalize the existing restrictions by implementing Resolution No. 24 adopted 23rd May, 1968, by the Working Party on Customs Questions affecting Transport of the United Nations Economic Commission for Europe, of which the United States is a participating member.

The regulation if amended would permit the use of containers loaded with merchandise admitted as instruments of international traffic in point-to-point local traffic on a route which would bring the container by a reasonably direct route to, or nearer to, the place where export cargo is to be loaded or where the container is to be exported empty. It would not relax the prohibition against empty containers so admitted engaging in local traffic. Final action, however, has not as yet been taken on the proposal.

No special documentation is required for movement of containers admitted as instruments of international traffic into or through the United States, but such containers must be listed on appropriate customs manifests. The container owner is required by section 10.4a(c) of the regulations to file a surety bond with the customs in the amount of $10,000, or in such larger amount as customs may deem necessary, to ensure that the containers will not be diverted from international traffic into local traffic in the United States.

Containers of foreign manufacture holding merchandise and suitable for re-use for that purpose also may be admitted free of duty under the provisions of Item 864.45, TSUS, and section 10.31, Customs Regulations, but entry is required. Under this procedure, which is rarely used, the importer must furnish, on each importation, a separate bond in an amount equal to double the duties payable had the container been entered for consumption. The bond is valid for one year and may be extended up to two additional years at yearly intervals. Containers so admitted may be used in local traffic in the United States without restriction but must be exported, either loaded or empty, before the bond expires.

Serially numbered containers which are the product of the United States and which have been exported may on later importations be released without entry or payment of duty under the provisions of section 10.41b(b), Customs Regulations, and used in domestic traffic without restriction. Serially numbered duty paid containers of foreign manufacture may be used in domestic traffic without limitation and if exported from the United States may be released on later importations without entry or payment of duty under the provisions of section 10.7 or 10.41b(c), Customs Regulations, for use in domestic traffic without restriction.

Except as provided in the last proviso to section 27 of the Merchant Marine Act, 1920, as amended (46 USC 883), as implemented by section 4.93, Customs Regulations, foreign flag vessels may not carry containers, regardless of build or ownership, between points in the United States embraced within the coastwise laws. This restriction does not apply to vessels of the United States prohibited from engaging in the coastwise trade.

CUSTOMS CONVENTION ON CONTAINERS:

The United States on 3rd December, 1968, deposited instruments of accession to the Customs Convention on Containers and the Customs Convention on the International Transport of Goods under Cover of TIR Carnets (TIR Convention). These Conventions went into force on 3rd March, 1969.

The Customs Convention on Containers, among other things, provides for the temporary entry of containers, whether loaded or empty, their normal accessories and equipment, and component repair parts for the repair of a particular container already temporarily imported, free of import duties and import taxes and free of import prohibitions and restrictions, subject to re-exportation within three months of the date of importation.

The Convention provides that the procedure for the temporary admission of containers and component parts free of import duties and import taxes shall be governed by the regulations in force in the territory of each country involved. Amendments to the Customs Regulations necessary to implement the Convention on behalf of the United States accordingly were published on 9th July, 1969, as Treasury Decision 69-146. The amended regulations do not require containers and component parts admitted without entry and the payment of duty to be re-exported within the three months' period mentioned in the Convention and place no time limitation on their use in the United States, subject to the restrictions on their use in local traffic previously mentioned.

TIR CONVENTION:

The TIR Convention is designed to facilitate the international movement of goods by providing favourable customs treatment for the passage of containers or road vehicles across national frontiers without customs inspection at intermediate points and with a minimum of other formalities. Amendments to the Customs Regulations necessary to implement the TIR Convention are in process.

CLEARANCE OF CONTAINERS:

Containers and the merchandise therein may be cleared by customs at any port of entry whether that port is a seaport, an airport of entry, a border port, or an inland port of entry. Section 1.2 of Customs Regulations lists all ports of entry.

LOCATIONS OF CONTAINER STATIONS.

The designation of such stations is left to the appropriate district director of customs. These stations are usually established only when the volume of containerized cargo makes it desirable to have a special location for unpacking containers and delivering cargo. Therefore, most ports of entry do not have such stations and clearance of containers is effected in the same way as break bulk cargo.

DUTIABILITY AND USE OF CONTAINERS:

General Headnote 6 and Item 808.00, TSUS; sections 4.93, 10.1 through 10.7, 10.31, 10.41, 10.41a, and 10.41b, Customs Regulations, deal with the dutiability and use of containers; TD 69-146, amends the regulations to implement the Customs Convention on Containers.

Piggyback and container services on North American Railroads

1970 piggyback and container services on North American Railroads must be reviewed against the general levels of the national economy and total railroad traffic of all types—and 1970 was a bad year.

Revenue freight ton miles on all US railroads (762,431 million) fell less than 1%, compared with 1969, but freight car loadings fell 3·8%, due to the continuing trend towards heavier loading in larger cars.

Due to two increases in freight rates operating revenue rose to $12 billion (billion as used in the American section is equal to a thousand millions), the highest ever, but expenses—especially labour costs—rose even more (to $9·8 billion), so that net railway operating income fell 37 to $411 million.

Important economic factors during the year were, record bad weather in the East; the Penn Central bankruptcy; the slowdown of the national economy; a truckers' strike in the Chicago area; the GM strike of ten weeks; and a short duration railroad strike. Against this background, piggyback and container traffic fell. Flatcars handled at 1·264 million were 6% lower. This compares with 1·034 million in 1965, and 0·55 million in 1960.

Trailers and containers handled numbered 3.061 million of which 2·07 million were in revenue service, 7% less than in 1969. 1971 traffic seems to show a continued slight fall of, perhaps, 4%. Some operators believe piggyback and container traffic in USA has reached a plateau, and that it is a time for major review, in view of the possibility that there may now exist excess capacity in facilities and equipment. Reviews of profitability of various types of traffic are being re-examined.

There are two principal forms of unitised door-to-door freight transport by rail: "Piggyback" or Trailer-on-Flat-Car (TOFC) or Container-on-Flat-Car (COFC).

In TOFC the highway trailer complete with its wheels is carried on a rail flat car with special locking devices, and loading and unloading is accomplished either "circus-style" at ramps or by being lifted bodily by a crane, usually either a straddle crane or a side lifter.

There are two forms of COFC.

In the first, the highway trailers have removable wheels (such as the original Flexivan) and the trailer is backed up to a special flatcar with a turntable. The road wheels are hitched and the trailer body is rotated on the turntable and locked into position, the wheels being left behind.

In the second, maritime or similar standard containers are used. Transfer between ship and train, and road vehicle and train, is by means of cranes, often straddle cranes. Flat top trailers or special container chassis are provided for collection and delivery.

In USA and Canada, piggyback TOFC was introduced in a substantial way before equal interest in containers COFC developed. Because of the heavy commitment to, and investment in, piggyback this has seen most of the traffic, and the use of containers, though growing more rapidly, has perhaps been restrained.

In 1970, when total trailers and containers handled exceeded three million, the number of containers handled approximated 300,000.

International traffic accounts for only 5% of the total North American railway traffic, and the railways accordingly have been reluctant to alter their car fleets to comply with international standards. But there has been a tendency toward the introduction of railway flatcars having hold-down devices which can accomodate either trailers with wheels or containers without wheels on a mixed basis. Such cars are operated by individual railways and also by Trailer Train, the railway owned company, which operates a pool of flatcars for the major lines.

TOFC

There are five basic plans under which rail piggyback (TOFC) movements are carried out.

Plan 1. The railroad carries truckers' trailers under contract ramp-to-ramp, including loading and unloading, under rates in motor carrier tariffs, with billing done by the railroad.

Originally important, this plan is now less used, perhaps 10% of total traffic.

Plan 2. The railroad carries its own trailers or containers and includes pickup and delivery under regular tariffs, with billing by the railroad.

This plan is directly competitive with the truckers, is a widely used plan, though its use is decreasing slightly. It currently represents perhaps 40% of all traffic.

Plan 2¼. This corresponds with plan 2, except that the railroad either picks up or delivers, but not both.

This plan is the only one to show major increase and, together with plan 2½ below, represents perhaps 40% of all traffic.

Plan 2½. This is another variation of plan 2 in which the railroad owns the trailer or container, which they move only, however, ramp-to-ramp, with the shipper and receiver performing their own pickup and delivery from, and to, ramp sites.

Plan 3. The railroad carries shipper-or forwarder-owned or leased trailers or containers under ramp-to-ramp rates, with no pickup and delivery service.

This plan was never popular, and is scarcely used today.

Plan 4. This corresponds with plan 3, but the shipper or forwarder owns, or provides, the trailer or container and also the railway flatcar, and the railroad makes a flat charge for empty or loaded movements This plan is growing in popularity and, currently may represent some 7% of total traffic.

Plan 5. Railroad and trucker are partners, each performing part of the service under joint, or combination, rates in railroad or motor carrier tariffs.

This plan has never been very popular and may, today, represent 3% of total traffic.

In addition to the above plans, there has been increased use of TOFC and COFC for handling US mail, especially since the railways have ceased to operate passenger trains. This plan is referred to as plan 8.

The pattern of growth in TOFC/COFC

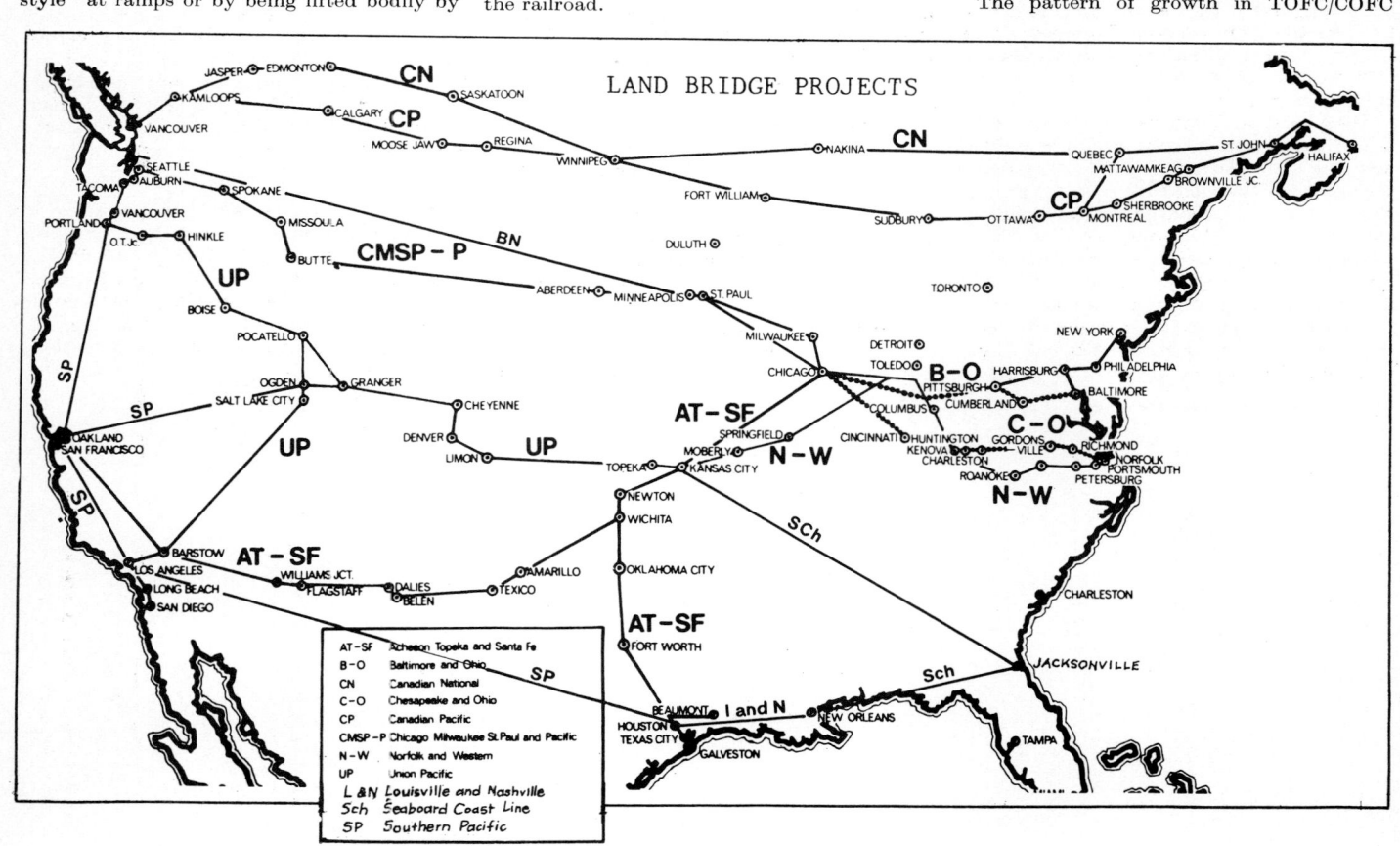

LAND BRIDGE PROJECTS

AT-SF Atchison Topeka and Santa Fe
B-O Baltimore and Ohio
CN Canadian National
C-O Chesapeake and Ohio
CP Canadian Pacific
CMSP-P Chicago Milwaukee St. Paul and Pacific
N-W Norfolk and Western
UP Union Pacific
L & N Louisville and Nashville
Sch Seaboard Coast Line
SP Southern Pacific

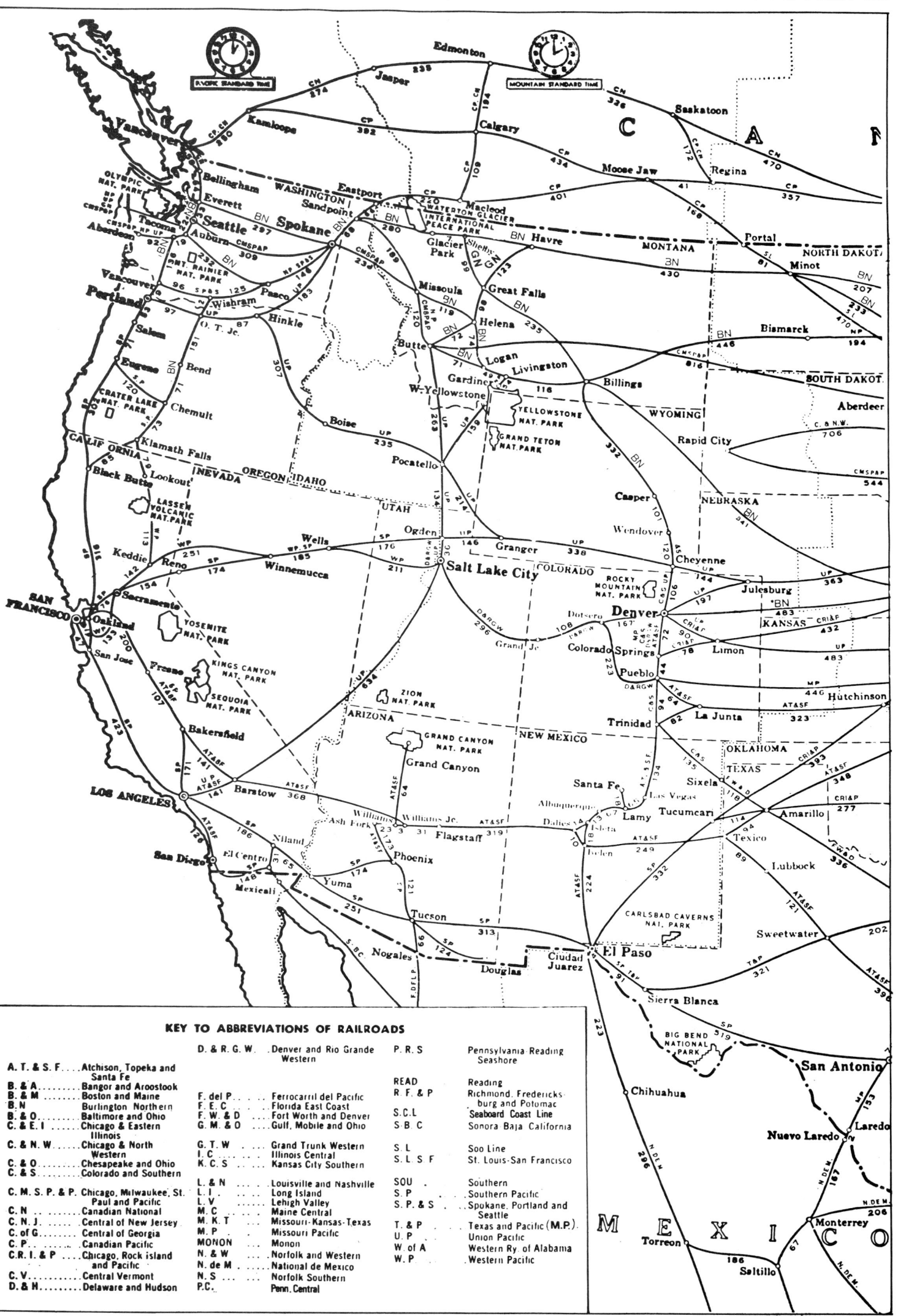

KEY TO ABBREVIATIONS OF RAILROADS

Abbreviation	Railroad
A. T. & S. F.	Atchison, Topeka and Santa Fe
B. & A.	Bangor and Aroostook
B. & M.	Boston and Maine
B. N.	Burlington Northern
B. & O.	Baltimore and Ohio
C. & E. I	Chicago & Eastern Illinois
C. & N. W.	Chicago & North Western
C. & O.	Chesapeake and Ohio
C. & S.	Colorado and Southern
C. M. S. P. & P.	Chicago, Milwaukee, St. Paul and Pacific
C. N.	Canadian National
C. N. J.	Central of New Jersey
C. of G.	Central of Georgia
C. P.	Canadian Pacific
C. R. I. & P.	Chicago, Rock Island and Pacific
C. V.	Central Vermont
D. & H.	Delaware and Hudson
D. & R. G. W.	Denver and Rio Grande Western
F. del P.	Ferrocarril del Pacífico
F. E. C.	Florida East Coast
F. W. & D.	Fort Worth and Denver
G. M. & O.	Gulf, Mobile and Ohio
G. T. W.	Grand Trunk Western
I. C.	Illinois Central
K. C. S.	Kansas City Southern
L. & N.	Louisville and Nashville
L. I.	Long Island
L. V.	Lehigh Valley
M. C.	Maine Central
M. K. T.	Missouri-Kansas-Texas
M. P.	Missouri Pacific
MONON	Monon
N. & W.	Norfolk and Western
N. de M.	National de Mexico
N. S.	Norfolk Southern
P. C.	Penn Central
P. R. S	Pennsylvania-Reading Seashore
READ	Reading
R. F. & P.	Richmond, Fredericksburg and Potomac
S. C. L	Seaboard Coast Line
S. B. C	Sonora Baja California
S. L	Soo Line
S. L. S. F	St. Louis-San Francisco
SOU	Southern
S. P.	Southern Pacific
S. P. & S.	Spokane, Portland and Seattle
T. & P.	Texas and Pacific (M.P.)
U. P.	Union Pacific
W. of A	Western Ry. of Alabama
W. P.	Western Pacific

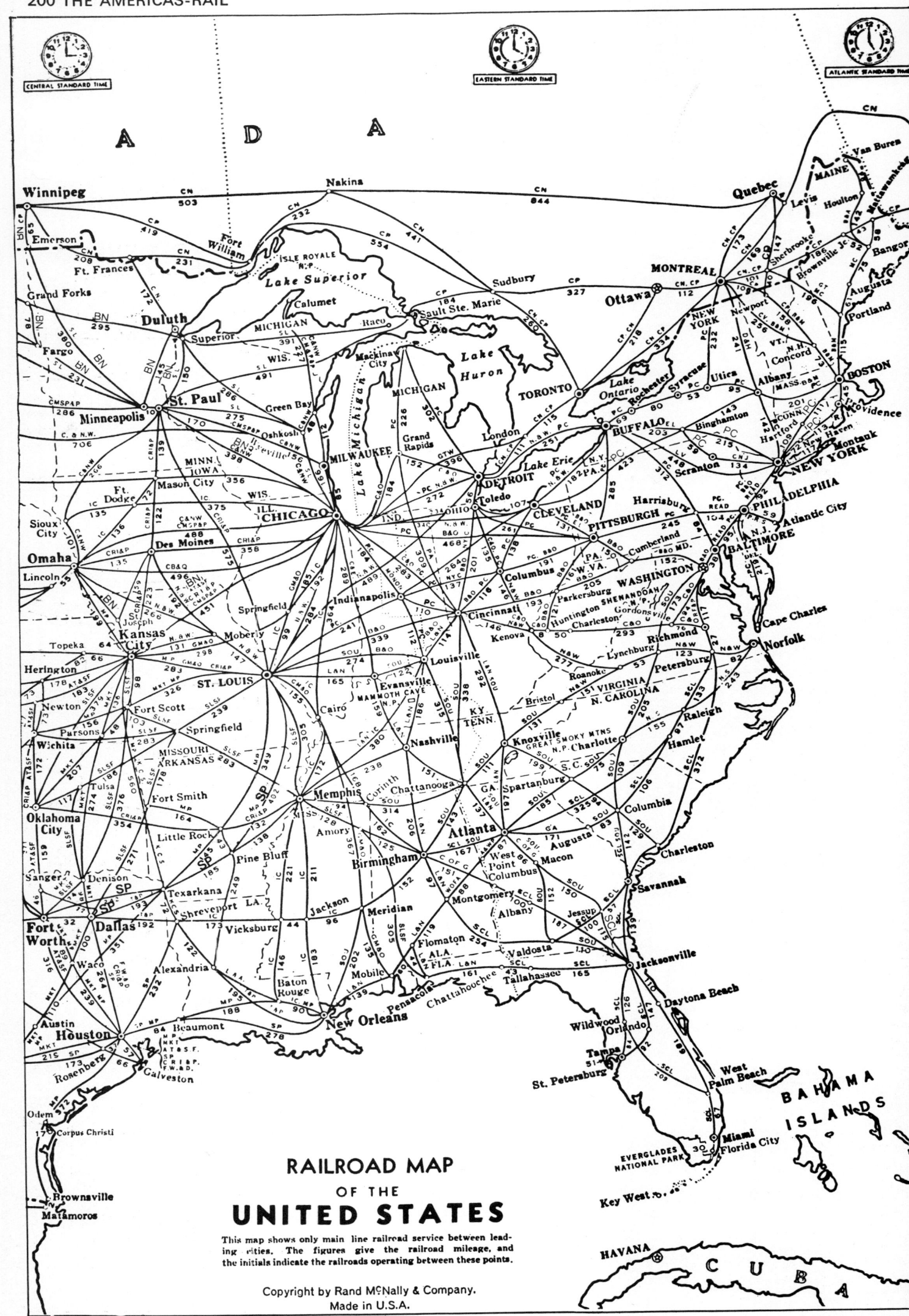

RAILROAD MAP
OF THE
UNITED STATES

This map shows only main line railroad service between leading cities. The figures give the railroad mileage, and the initials indicate the railroads operating between these points.

Copyright by Rand McNally & Company.
Made in U.S.A.

traffic is not uniform on individual Canadian and US railroads. In 1970, the railroads showing greatest increase in piggyback traffic were the Santa Fe, Illinois Central, L & N, Milwaukee, Frisco, N & W, as well as the Canadian roads.

Some 1,400 terminals are spread across the continent, all equipped with ramps and with many major terminals with lifting facilities and substantial storage areas. Recent installations appear to tend towards wider use of side loader type lifting equipment

Land Bridge Projects

Principal Canadian and US railroads have shown interest in the so-called land bridge concept, under which containers moving between Europe and the Orient would travel across the North American Continent instead of through the Panama Canal or around the Cape of Good Hope.

Various alternative routes have been discussed, and some of these are indicated on the map.

Incentive rates have been offered, but despite new container ships, advanced port handling equipment and unit trains, it does not, so far, appear that traffic volume available is sufficient to make land bridge operation economical, and interest in the project seems to have cooled. Reasons cited are the large number of authorities involved in a complete shipment; imbalance of traffic eastbound and westbound; in-sufficient difference and saving in transit time to justify substantial investments; and the possibility of unpredictable delays due to labour disputes in transit.

Diminished wartime traffic, as operations in Vietnam decrease, may show very substantial reductions of total traffic across the Pacific.

But Canadian National and Canadian Pacific both exhibit great interest in Intermodal movements, introducing new ships, port facilities and special unit trains. Import-export containers, handled by CN in 1970, more than doubled over the previous year and this rate of growth was expected to accelerate in 1971.

THE ALASKA RAILROAD

The Alaska Railroad,
US Department of Transportation,
Federal Railroad Administration,
PO Box 7-2111 Anchorage, Alaska 99501,
USA
OFFICERS:
EXECUTIVE DEPARTMENT:
John A. Volpe (*Secretary, Department of Transportation, Wash., DC*)
R. N. Whitman (*Administrator, Federal Railroad Administration Wash., DC*)
J. E. Manley (*General Manager*)
R. H. Bruce (*Assistant General Manager*)
E. E. Callihan (*Comptroller*)
J. M. Karterman (*Supply Officer*)
J. Glen Cassity (*Chief Counsel*)
William E. Fravel (*Assistant to the General Manager, Wash., DC*)
Russell R. Mack (*Personnel Officer*)
Merle Akers (*Real Estate Officer*)
OPERATING DEPARTMENT:
W. C. Davidson (*Superintendent of Transportation*)
Irvin P. Cook (*Chief Engineer*)
G. V. Randall (*Chief Mechanical Officer*)
Andrew J. Clark, Jr. (*Chief Communications Officer*)
TRAFFIC DIVISION:
D. L. Allen (*General Traffic Manager, Seattle*)
F. W. Hoefler (*Assistant General Traffic Manager*)
J. P. Triber (*Traffic Manager, Rates, Rate Research and Passenger Service*)
E. G. Loudon (*General Agent, Fairbanks*)
R. W. Clegg (*General Agent, Seattle*)

GENERAL:
The Alaska Railroad runs from Seward on the Gulf of Alaska, northward through the McKinley National Park to Fairbanks, a distance of 470 miles (756·7 km) and eastward to Eielson 498 miles (801·8 km). With branches the total route length is 541·2 miles (871·3 km).

FINANCIAL:
Revenue for 1970 was $18·89 million (+11%) and expenses $18·68 million (+12%).

TRAFFIC:
1,404,423 tons of freight was carried an average distance of 191 miles.
79,965 passengers travelled an average 156 miles.

PIGGYBACK:
Alaska RR has 343 flatcars and 136 trailers; 328 containers, and 91 shipping platforms.

HANDLING EQUIPMENT:
Terminal handling equipment used by the Alaska Railroad includes quay cranes at Seward and Fairbanks for train to ship movement, and an American yard gantry crane at Anchorage for train to road trans-

An Alaska Railroad container being transferred from rail to road vehicle at anchorage.

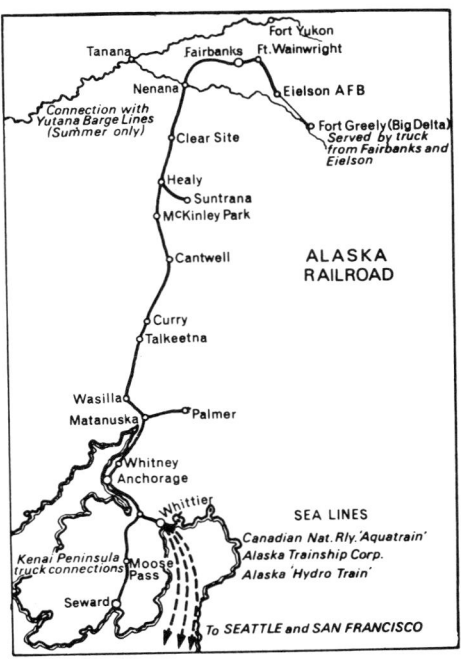

ALASKA RAILROAD

SEA LINES
Canadian Nat. Rly. 'Aquatrain'
Alaska Trainship Corp.
Alaska 'Hydro Train'

To SEATTLE and SAN FRANCISCO

port movement.
FUTURE DEVELOPMENT:
Development of the oil fields on the north slope in Alaska should bring additional

Crane used at Fairbanks for unloading containers, Alaska Railroad.

traffic, including piggyback and containers; the railroad plans to build, in 1971, a new railway extension to Fairbanks airport and to develop air freight traffic.

ATCHISON, TOPEKA AND SANTA FE RAILWAY SYSTEM

Atchison, Topeka and Santa Fe Railway System

80 Easy Jackson Boulevard,
Chicago, Illinois 60604
TELEPHONE: (312) 427-4900

OFFICIALS:

Ernest S. Marsh (*Chairman, Chicago*)

John S. Reed (*President and Chief Executive Officer, Chicago*)

John C. Davis (*Vice President, Executive Department, Chicago*)

L. Cena (*Vice President, Operations, Chicago*)

L. C. Hudson (*Vice-President, Traffic, Chicago*)

Starr Thomas (*Vice-President, Law, Chicago*)

O. H. Osborn (*Vice-President, Personnel, Chicago*)

W. E. Willingham (*Vice-President and General Auditor, Chicago*)

R. W. Harper (*Vice-President, Finance, Chicago*)

J. R. Scott (*Vice-President, Real Estate and Industrial Development, Chicago*)

R. M. Champion, Jr. (*Vice-President, Information Systems, Chicago*)

R. M. Clark (*Vice-President, Washington*)

R. W. Walker (*Vice-President, Executive Representative, San Francisco*)

C. J. Nassimbene (*Executive Assistant, Highway Motor Transport, Chicago*)

W. S. Autrey (*Chief Engineer System*),

J. E. Eisemann (*Director of Purchases and Materials, Topeka*)

J. A. Grygiel (*General Manager, Freight Traffic, Chicago*)

E. L. Petersen (*General Manager, Passenger Traffic, Chicago*)

THE SANTA FE TRAIL TRANSPORTATION COMPANY:

C. J. Nassimbene (*President, Chicago*)

R. W. Dills (*Vice-President, Chicago*)

LINES AND TERRITORIES:

Santa Fe operates 12,908 miles (20,771 km) of route between Chicago and the Pacific Coast and south to the Gulf of Mexico generally through southwest states.

FINANCIAL:

1970 operating revenue was $755·2 million (5% more than 1969); and expenses $603·2 millions, an increase of 4·7%.

Consolidated income was $49·2 million—down from $61 million.

Santa Fe TOFC operations

TRAFFIC:

Revenue freight ton miles in 1970 rose to 48,328 million from 47,363 million in 1969. Carloadings decreased 3%.

Piggyback and container traffic registered a gain of 10%.

Containers moving through the Railway increased from 5,386 units in 1969 to 8,352 in 1970.

PIGGYBACK:

B. J. Nash (*Manager, TOFC-COFC*)

Plans: 1, 2, 2¼, 2½, 3, 4, 5.

Santa Fe's motor carrier trucking subsidiary Santa Fe Trail Transportation Company, handled a 3% traffic increase to 114·3 million ton miles yielding record revenue of $27·8 million. The motor carrier subsidiary owns 243 trucks, 685 truck tracks

CONTAINERS MOVING ACROSS THE SANTA FE

8352
5386
1626
year....... 1968 1969 1970

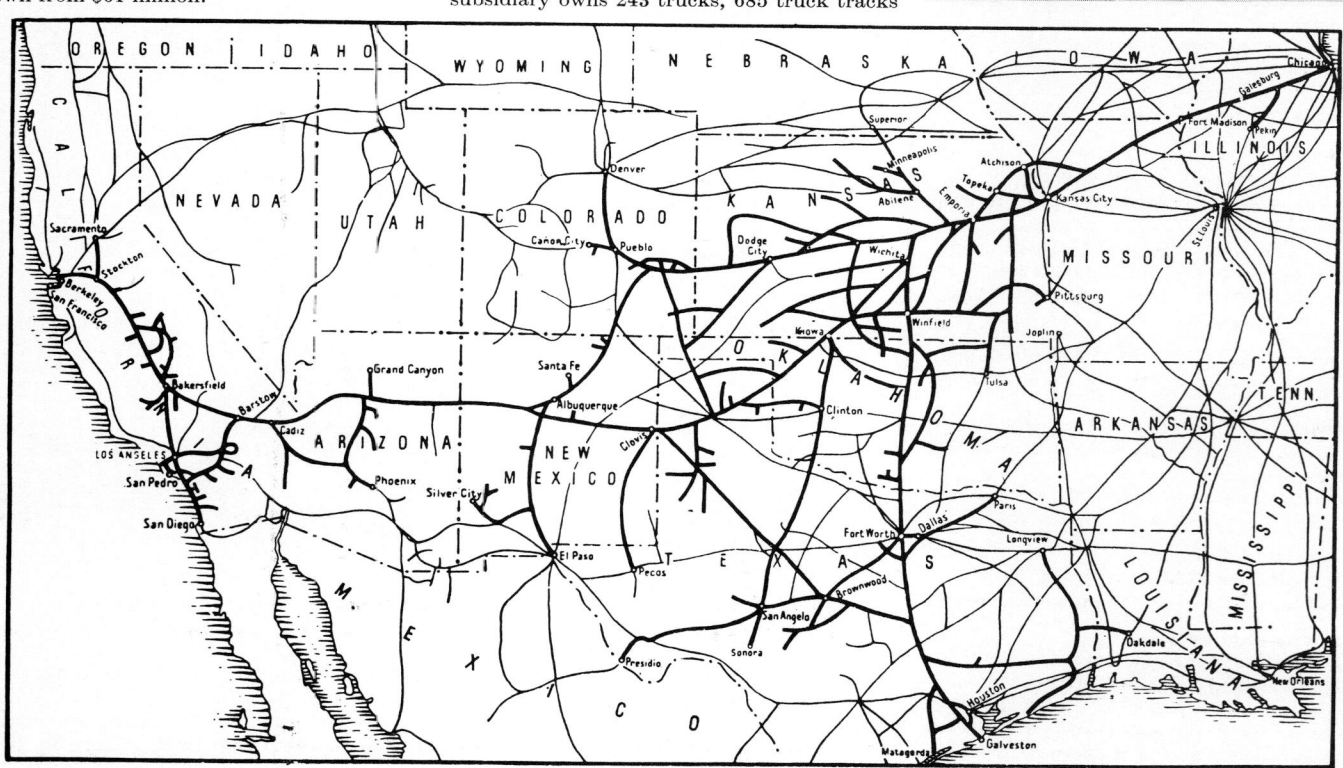

and 4,728 highway trailers and 773 containers. 1971 plans include purchase of 146 tractors and 40 trailers.

TRAILERS:

Ramp loading facilities exist at 109 locations in the states of Arizona, California, Colorado, Illinois, Iowa, Kansas, Missouri, New Mexico, Oklahoma, and Texas.

Arizona: Aguila, Flagstaff, Phoenix, Parker Holbrook, Prescott, Kingman, Winslow.

California: Richmond, San Bernardino, Bakersfield, Los Angeles, Barstow, Fresno, Merced, Stockton, Exeter, San Diego, Needles, Cucaman GA, Del Ray, Long Beach, Oceanside, Pico Rivera, Pond, San Francisco,

Colorado: Denver, Pueblo, Colorado Springs La Junta.

Illinois: Chicago, Galesburg, Joliet, Morton.

Iowa: Fort Madison.

Kansas: Hutchison, Salina, Emporia, Wichita, Garden City, Great Bend, Argentine, St. Jo. Mo., Kansas City, Dodge City, Chanute, Coffeyville, Topeka, McPherson, Temple, Arkansas City, Pratt, Newton,

Pittsburg, Abilene, Lawrence, Ottawa, Winfield.

Missouri: Kansas City, Carolltown, St. Joseph, Henrietta, Waconda.

New Mexico: Alberquerque, Belen, Carlsbad, Clovis, Sallup, Las Cruces, Las Vegas, Riswell, Santa Fe.

Oklahoma: Tulsa, Altus, Ardmore, Bartlesville, Ponca City, Clinton, Wichita, Oklahoma City, Enid, Perry, Woodward.

Texas: Lubbock, Houston, Dallas, Fort Worth, Galveston, Amerillo, El Paso, Sweetwater, Beaumont, San Angelo, Brownwood, Braby, Bovina, Brenham, Canadian, Duma, Hereford, Pampa, Paris, Firana, Temple.

Crane facilities exist at Chicago, Kansas City, Richmond California, Los Angeles, Houston and Dallas (with ocean rail and truck facilities).

CONTAINERS:

THE RAILWAY OPERATES THE FOLLOWING CONTAINER TERMINALS:

Chicago,

Richmond, California (S. Francisco and Oakland)

Los Angeles (Long Beach and LA Harbour), Houston, Texas, Dallas, Texas, and Kansas City, Kansas.

All except Chicago have ocean, rail and truck connections. Chicago connects with many eastern railroads and trucks.

The railway provides daily service to connect at Santa Fe-served ports and connection railroads for international service.

Claimed as the worlds fastest freight train, the "Super C" operates daily between Chicago, Kansas City and Southern California handling Piggyback and Container freight on a 40 hour schedule for the 2,250 miles with 99% on time performance. This cuts 20 hours from the fastest previous service and matches the speed of the best passenger trains.

Revenue from mail handled by Super C, was up 18·5% in 1970.

BURLINGTON NORTHERN INC.

Burlington Northern Inc
176 East Fifth Street St. Paul
Minnesota 55101

OFFICERS:

Louis W. Monk (*Chairman and Chief Executive Officer*)

Robert W. Downing (*President and Chief Operating Officer*)

John M. Budd (*Director and Chairman of Finance Committee*)

Norman M. Lorentzsen (*Executive Vice-President*)

Frank H. Coyne (*Vice President, Finance*)

Anthony Kane (*Vice-President, Law*)

C. Robert Binger, (*Vice President, Resources Development*)

Ivan C. Ethington (*Vice-President, Operations*)

M. M. Scanlan (*Vice-President, Marketing*)

Fred E. Deines (*Vice-President, Sales and Service*)

Worthington L. Smith (*Vice-President, Marketing Planning*)

James D. Nankivell (*Vice-President, Intermodal Sales*)

Clarence E. Larsen (*Vice-President, Pricing*)

Thomas J. Lamphier (*Vice-President, Management Services and Planning*)

William N. Ernzen (*Vice-President and Controller*)

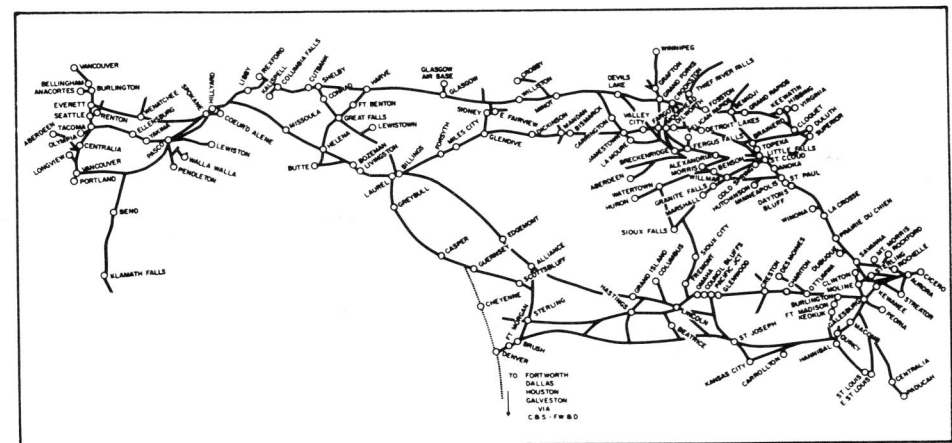

Frank S. Farrell (*Vice-President and General Counsel*)

Lloyd L. Duxbury (*Vice-President, Eastern Counsel*)

John C. Ashton (*Vice-President, Washington, D.C.*)

Wilbur K. Bush (*Vice-President, Executive Department, St. Paul*)

Clark A. Eckart (*Vice-President, Executive Department, Seattle*)

Robert J. Crosby (*Vice-President and Regional Counsel, Portland*)

George F. Defiel (*Vice-President, Industrial and Economic Development*)

Thomas C. DeButts (*Vice-President, Labor Relations*)

Albert M. Rung (*Vice-President, Public Relations and Advertising*)

Harold H. Holmquist (*Vice-President, Personnel*)

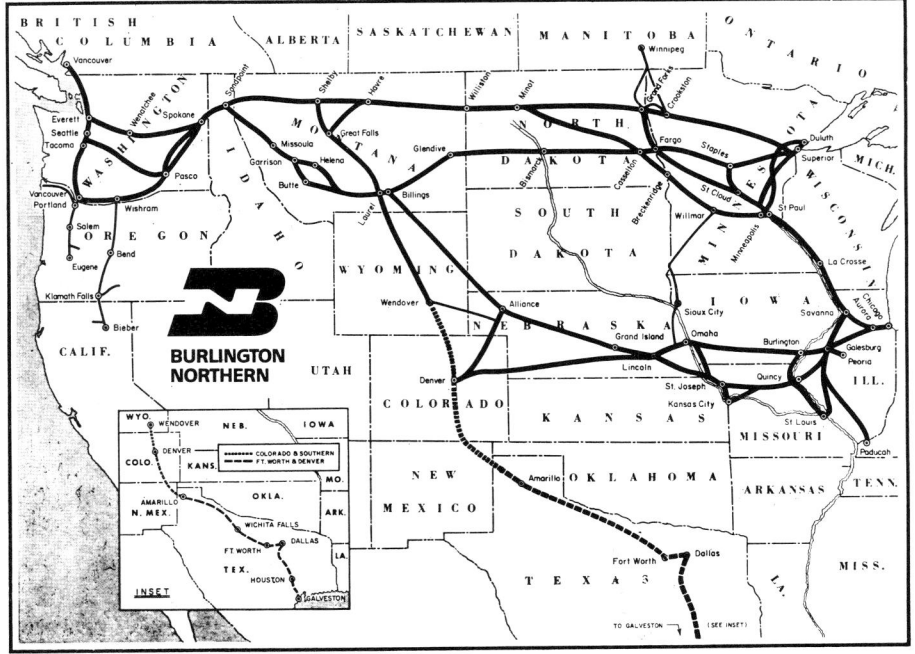

Guy deLambert (*Vice-President, Purchasing and Material*)

Donald H. King (*Regional Vice-President, Chicago*)

Wilburn R. Allen (*Regional Vice-President, Minneapolis*)

Richard A. Beulke (*Regional Vice-President Omaha*)

John O. Davies (*Regional Vice-President, Billings*)

Ralph L. Merklin (*Regional Vice-President, Seattle*)

Harry J. Surles (*Regional Vice-President, Portland*)

Richard M. O'Kelly (*Secretary*)

Leo N. Assell (*Treasurer*)

GENERAL:

Effective March 1969, nine years after the application was first filed, Burlington Northern came into operation merging the Chicago, Burlington and Quincy railroad, the Great

Northern and the Northern Pacific Railways, and their subsidiaries.

BN lines comprise 23,609 miles (38,014 km) of route between Chicago to the Pacific North West, principally in the States of Illinois, Wisconsin, Iowa, Minnesota, North Dakota, Nebraska, Colorado, Wyoming, Montana, Idaho and Washington.

FINANCIAL:

1970 operating revenues were $953 million (up from $907 million) and expenses $913 million ($851 million). Net transportation income was $40 million.

TRAFFIC:

Revenue net ton miles in 1970 were 56,857 millions (60,727 million).

1970 TOFC/COFC traffic increased 9% over 1969.

PIGGYBACK:

L. J. King (*General Manager, Terminals and TOFC/COFC*)

BN—Piggyback operations

M. H. Steele (*Director, TOFC/COFC*)
W. J. Niemiec (*Assistant Director, TOFC/COFC*)

Plans: 1, 2, 2¼, 2½, 3, 4, 5.

BNs fleet includes 2,810 trailers, 200 containers and 205 chassis and bogies. Most trailers and containers are 40 ft long.

Loading ramps are located in 173 cities.

CHICAGO AND NORTH WESTERN RAILROAD COMPANY

Chicago and North Western Railway Company
400 West Madison Street,
Chicago, Illinois 60606
EXECUTIVE AND STAFF OFFICERS:
Ben W. Heineman (*Chairman*)
Larry S. Provo (*President*)
H. L. Gastler (*Vice-President, Operations*)
W. E. Braun (*Vice-President, Sales and Marketing*)
Richard M. Freeman (*Vice-President, Law*)
J. M. Butler (*Vice-President, Finance*)
R. D. Leach (*Vice-President, Systems and Information Services*)
I. Robert Ballin (*Vice-President, Materials and Real Estate*)
Robert W. Russell (*Vice-President, Personnel*)
James R. Wolfe (*Vice-President, Labour Relations*)
J. R. Brennan (*Vice-President*)
Carl R. Hussey (*Assistant to the President, Special Projects*)
G. R. Carr (*Comptroller*)
W. Krucks (*Treasurer*)
W. P. Allman (*Assistant Vice-President, Staff Services*)
H. A. Lenske (*Director Commuter and Passenger Services*)
R. J. Hill (*Secretary*)
GENERAL:

The Chicago and North Western Railway ($300 million a year revenue) is part of Northwest Industries, (about $700 million a year), who, in 1969, planned to sell the railway to a company formed by the employees, NETCO (North Western Employees Transportation Corporation).

The Chicago and North Western operates an average of 11,043 miles (17,773 km).

On 1st July, 1968, the Chicago Great Western Railway was merged into the North Western Railway. On 29th July, 1968, North Western Railway purchased the Des Moines and Central Iowa Railway Company, which then owned over 89 per cent of the stock of the Ft. Dodge Des Moines and Southern Railway Company. On 1st August 1968, North Western Railway and Missouri-Pacific Railroad, acting through a jointly-owned company; together purchased the physical assets of Alton and Southern Railway, a connecting and switching carrier in the East St. Louis-St. Louis terminal area.

FINANCIAL RESULTS:

In 1970 revenue was $314 million (+$28m) and expenses $255 million (+$7m). After taxes, rentals and interest results show a profit of $5 million, against a loss of $8·7 million in 1969.

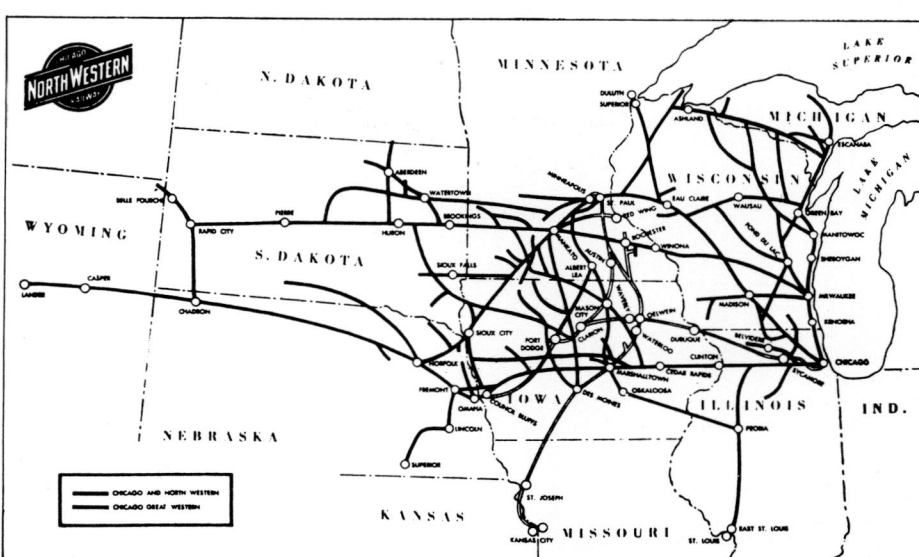

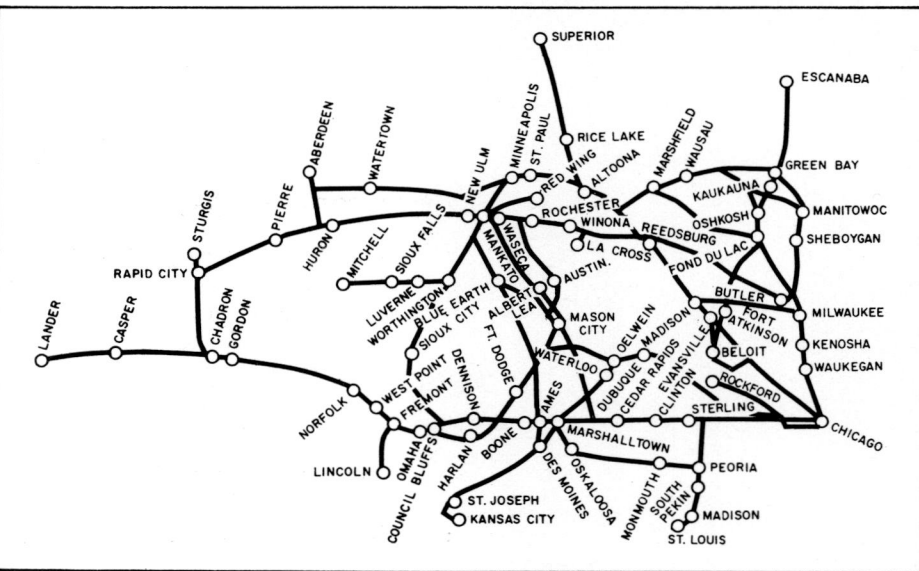

PIGGYBACK:
J. M. Tierney (*General Manager, Intermodel Sales*)
TOFC Plans: 1, 2, 2¼, 3, 4 and 5.
TRAILER FLEET:

400 Closed vans	40 ft
123 Open vans	40 ft
463 Insulated vans	40 ft
1,898 Refrigerated vans	40 ft
15 Flat bed vans	40 ft
4 Drop frame vans	14 ft
Total 2,903	

TOFC RAMP FACILITIES:
Illinois: Chicago (Proviso), Chicago (Wood

St.), Madison (St. Louis), Monmouth, Peoria, Sterling, Waukegan.

Iowa: Ames, Boone, Cedar Rapids, Clinton-Council Bluffs, Deniston, Des Moines, Ft. Dodge, Harian, Marshalltown, Mason City, Sioux City, Waterloo.

Michigan: Escanaba.

Minnesota: Albert Lea, Austin, Blue Earth,

Luverne, Mankato, Minneapolis, New Ulm, Red Wing, Rochester, St. Paul, Waseca, Winona, Worthington.

Missouri: Kansas City, St. Joseph, St. Louis (Madison).

Nebraska: Chadron, Fremont, Gordon, Lincoln, Norfolk, Omaha, West Point,

South Dakota: Aberdeen, Huron, Mitchell,

Pierre, Rapid City, Sioux Falls, Sturgis, Watertown.

Wisconsin: So. Janesville, Altoona (Eau Claire), Butler, Fond du Lac, Green Bay, Kaukauna, Kenosha, La Crosse, Madison, Manitowoc, Marshfield, Milwaukee, Oshkosh, Reedsburg, Rice-Lake, Sheboygan Superior, Wausau.

Wyoming: Casper.

CHICAGO, MILWAUKEE, ST PAUL AND PACIFIC RAILROAD COMPANY

Chicago, Milwaukee, St. Paul and Pacific Railroad Company (The Milwaukee Road), 516 West Jackson Boulevard, Chicago, Illinois 60606

OFFICERS:

William J. Quinn (*Chairman of the Board*)
Curtiss E. Crippen (*President*)
Francis G. McGinn (*Vice-President, Operations*)
Raymond K. Merrill (*Vice-President, Law*)
Richard F. Kratochwill (*Vice-President, Finance and Accounting*)
George H. Kronberg (*Vice-President, Traffic*)
Burton J. Worley (*Vice-President, Chief Engineer*)
Byron E. Lutterman (*Vice-President and Western Counsel*)
Edward J. Stoll (*Vice-President, Real Estate, Economic and Resource Development*)
Lawrence W. Harrington (*Vice-President, Labor Relations*)
Gaylord A. Kellow (*Vice-President, Management Services*)

GENERAL:

The Milwaukee Road operates 10,448 route miles (16,812 km) of railroad, the line extending from Chicago to the Pacific North Coast port cities of Seattle, Tacoma, Longview, Wash., and Portland, Ore. The line also extends west and southwest from Chicago to Omaha, Neb., and Kansas City, Mo.

The railroad's wholly owned subsidiary companies are Milwaukee Land Company; The Milwaukee Motor Transportation Company and Bremerton Freight Car Ferry, Inc.

FINANCIAL:

Railroad operations in 1970 produced a net loss of $8,891,108, after a write-off of more than $700,000 in accounts receivable from other railroads which are undergoing reorganization. Operating revenues reached $277,540,108 and operating expenses were $237,411,328. A net loss of $12,888,151 from railroad operations was experienced during 1969, based on operating revenues of $269,108,190 and operating expenses of $230,631,170.

Consolidated operations showed a net loss of $10,992,173 for the full year 1970, despite consolidated operating revenues of $283,197,199. Operating expenses were $244,470,485. Consolidated net results for the year 1969 showed a loss of $5,641,369 on operating revenues of $275,572,653 and operating expenses of $238,583,993. The 1969 results had the benefit of more land sales than was the case in 1970.

TRAFFIC:

Net ton miles of revenue freight in 1970 amounted to 17,510,170,000.

FOREIGN FREIGHT, TOFC/COFC:

Foreign Freight Sales:
G. F. Flynn (*Manager, Chicago*)
Rail-Highway Sales:
W. A. Zimmerman (*Manager, Chicago*)
Piggyback Plans: 1, 2, 2½, 3, 4, 5.

The Milwaukee has 2,116 trailers and Flexi-van containers.

The expansion of piggyback/container facilities at Seattle, the Twin Cities and Chicago (Bensenville), plus the acquisition of container handling equipment by the Milwaukee Motor Transportation Company, the motor carrier subsidiary of the railroad, enabled the railroad to continue its leadership in the movement of traffic to and from the Pacific North Coast ports.

RAMP LOCATIONS:

Aberdeen, S.D.; Austin, Minn.; Billings, Mont.; Bozeman, Mont.; Butte, Mont.; Chamberlain, S.D.; Chehalis, Wash.; Chicago, (Bensenville), Ill.; Cloquet, Minn.; Council Bluffs, Ia.; Davenport, Ia.; Deer Lodge, Mont.; Des Moines, Ia.; Dubuque, Ia.; Duluth, Minn.; Everett, Wash.; Fargo, N.D.; Great Falls, Mont.; Green Bay, Wis.; Harlowtown, Mont.; Iron Mountain, Mich.; Kansas City, Mo.; LaCrosse, Wis.; Lewistown, Mont.; Longview, Wash.; Madison, Wis.; Mankato, Minn.; Marion, Ia.; Mason City, Ia.; Menasha, Wis.; Metaline Falls, Wash.; Miles City, Mont.; Milwaukee, Wis.; Missoula, Mont.; Mitchell, S.D.; Mobridge, S.D.; Moses Lake, Wash.; Oshkosh, Wis.; Othello, Wash.; Ottumwa, Ia.; Portage, Wis.; Portland, Ore.; Postville, Ia.; Rapid City, SD; St. Paul, Minn.; Seattle, Wash.; Sioux City, Ia.; Sioux Falls, S.D.; Spencer, Ia.; Spokane, Wash.; Tacoma, Wash.; Warden, Wash.; Wausau, Wis.; Winona, Minn.; Wisconsin Rapids. Wis.

In 1970, system piggyback and container traffic showed an overall decrease of 10 per cent. This was due principally to the motor carrier strike and threatened rail strikes during the year and the general overall economic condition as experienced by the transportation industry. One bright spot was the increasing balance of import container and trailer traffic moving via the railroad's Pacific North Coast ports.

The Milwaukee Road has maintained a freight sales office in Tokyo, Japan since March 1, 1968. The railroad has experienced a steadily rising volume of traffic en route to and from the Pacific North Coast ports and the Orient, particularly Japan. In 1970, Japanese shipping companies started their container ship service to Pacific North Coast ports, and the railroad anticipates further increases in export container traffic over its long haul route serving Midwest points.

Most of the American and Japanese line container vessels now calling at Pacific North Coast ports discharge containers for Milwaukee Road handling to the Midwest and points beyond via connecting carriers.

PIGGYBACK/CONTAINER FACILITIES:

Expansion of Milwaukee Road piggyback/container facilities at Seattle, Wash.; St. Paul, Minn., and Bensenville, Ill., near Chicago, plus the acquisition of container handling equipment by the Milwaukee Motor Transportation Company, the motor carrier subsidiary, enabled the railroad to continue its development of traffic to and from Pacific North Coast ports.

Work began on the further expansion of Piggyback Park, the piggyback/container facility adjoining the freight classification yard at Bensenville. Two straddle cranes and two Piggy Packers are used for the loading and unloading of trailers and containers. Storage tracks are being extended and other trackage relocated for faster operation and additional storage space. Some 700 40 foot piggyback trailers, or larger number of contaniers will be stored, if necessary.

The piggyback/container facility at Stacy Street Yard in Seattle is located within a five-minute drive of all waterfront container terminals, freight forwarders and express companies. The terminal was expanded in 1970 to accommodate up to 154 piggyback trailers or a larger number of container.

Two tracks, each 1,800 feet in length, were constructed for loading and unloading, while another of equal length is being constructed for storage in 1970.

COMMUNICATIONS:

In 1970, another refinement was added to Carscope, the Milwaukee Road's freight car information centre in Chicago, with the introduction of "Direct Customer Inquiry" service as an added capability of that computer-based system.

Direct Customer Inquiry enables shippers with access to Telex facilities to dial directly into the Milwaukee's Carscope computer for tracing information on shipments, and receive replies in the same fast and direct manner. Shippers without Telex units can utilise the same basic information system as before, by making inquiry through the nearest Milwaukee Road traffic office.

THE C & O/B & O RAILROADS

C&O/B&O Railroads
Terminal Tower, Cleveland,
Ohio 44101

OFFICERS:

Hayes T. Watkins Jr. (*President and Chief*)

Gregory S. DeVine (*President and Chief Executive Officer, C & O/B & O*)

Cyrus S. Eaton (*Chairman, C & O , Director, B & O*)

John E. Kusik (*Vice-Chairman, C & O, Senior Vice-President, B & O*)

C. Vernon Cowan (*Senior Vice-President*)

C. A. Sandmann (*Vice-President, Coal Traffic*)

Kenneth H. Ekin (*Vice-President, Law*)

Owen Clarke (*Vice-President, Labor Relations and Personnel*)

Robert C. McGowan (*Vice-President, Planning Group*)

K. T. Reed (*Vice-President, Operating*)

J. T. Ford (*Vice-President, Finance*)

C. R. Zarfoss (*Vice-President, Merchandise Freight Group*)

Charles W. Campbell (*Vice-President, Freight Sales, C & O*)

Thomas A. Keefe (*Vice-President, Merchandise Freight Sales, B & O*)

William J. Eck (*Vice-President, Purchasers and Materials*)

William L. Ollerhead (*Vice-President, Industrial Development*)

John P. Ganley (*Vice-President, Taxes*)

Howard Skidmore (*Vice-President. Public Relations and Advertising*)

Charles J. Henry, Jr. (*Vice-President, Commercial Development*)

E. W. Wright (*Vice-President, Trailer Service*)

M. C. Mulligan (*Asst. Vice-President, Real Estate Development*)

R. G. Rayburn (*Asst. Vice-President, Transportation*)

Kenneth T. Reed (*Asst. Vice-President, Maintenance*)

W. F. Howes Jr. (*Director of Passenger Services*)

E. T. Wright (*Vice-President and General Manager, The Greenbrier*)

L. C. Roig, Jr. (*Treasurer*)

William R. Althans (*General Counsel*)

Ross Conlin (*Asst Vice-President, Coal Freight Sales (B&O)*)

H. Preston Henshaw, Jr. (*Asst. Vice-President, Coal Freight Sales (B&O)*)

GENERAL:

The Chesapeake and Ohio Railway Company owns 93 per cent stock of the Baltimore and Ohio Railroad and a controlling interest in Western Maryland Railway and publishes a consolidated financial statement. Of its total revenues 30% comes from handling coal and 50% from general merchandise.

LINES AND TERRITORY:

The C and O operates 5,067 miles (8,163 km) of route, and is a major coal handling road from the bituminous fields in West Virginia and Kentucky, to outlets on the Atlantic coast at Newport News, and on the Great Lakes at Toledo, Ohio.

Heavy merchandise traffic is handled from production centres in Michigan and agriculture in Ohio and Southern Canada.

On May 1 1971 C and O/B and O passenger operation was taken over by Auctrak—the National Railroad Passenger Corporation. Service consisted of a daily train, Washington DC (with connections to Newport News) to Cincinnati.

The B and O operates 5,687 miles (9,152 km) of route from the Atlantic to the Midwest, serving the industrial and agricultural areas of Ohio and Pennsylvania and the Coalfields of W. Virginia.

Western Maryland Railway operates freight trains only, with substantial coal traffic from Western Pennsylvania and West Virginia to Baltimore.

TRAFFIC:

122 million tons of coal was hauled in 1970, up 10 million from 1969, and future growth seems certain. Forty-six mines (capacity 11 million tons per annum) will open on the C and O/B and O system in 1971.

Merchandise freight, at 110,000 million tons (2·4 million carloads) was slightly less than 1969. The GM strike and the general slow pace of business were causes. Piggyback traffic was about the same as 1969.

PIGGYBACK:

S. Christovich, 2 N. Charles Street, Baltimore, Md 21201 (*Director of Trailer Service*)

C & O TRAILER SERVICE—RAMP LOCATIONS:

Benton Harbour, Mich., Buffalo, N.Y., Charleston, W.Va., Chicago, Ill., Cincinatti, Ohio, Columbus Ohio, Detroit, Mich., Flint, Mich, Grand Rapids, Mich., Huntington, W. V., Lansing, Mich., Lynchburg, Va, Midland, Mich., Milwaukee, Wis., Newport News, Va., Norfolk, Va., Portsmouth, Va., Richmond, Ind., Richmond, Va., Saginaw, Mich., Staunton, Va., Toledo, Ohio, Washington, DC.

B & O TRAILER SERVICE—RAMP LOCATIONS:

Akron, Ohio; Baltimore, Md.; Chicago, Ill.; Chillicothe, Ohio; Cincinnati, Ohio; Cleveland Ohio; Columbus, Ohio; Connersville, Ind.; Dayton, Ohio; East St. Louis, Ill.; Elizabethport, N.J.; Indianapolis, Ind.; Jeffersonville, Ind.; Lima, Ohio; Newark, Ohio; New York (Jersey City, N.J.); Parkersburg, W.Va.; Philadelphia, Pa.; Pittsburgh, Pa.; Toledo, Ohio; Washington, D.C.; Wheeling, W.Va.; Wilmington, Del.; Youngstown, Ohio.

FINANCIAL:

1970 consolidated revenue, including $370 million coal and $570 million merchandise totalled $1,047 million.

Expenses included tax interest and rentals totalled $992 million and of this payroll amounted to $449 million.

Earnings were practically unchanged at $52·9 million ($52·5 million in 1969).

WESTERN MARYLAND RAMP LOCATIONS:
Baltimore, Md.; Cumberland, Md.; Hagerstown, Md.; Hanover, Pa.; York, Pa.
TOFC Plans: 1, 2, 2½, 3, 5.
TRAFFIC:
In 1970 piggyback shipments increased by 7·1% over 1969 to 284,000 trailer loads.
TRAILER FLEET:
C & O/B & O and WM together own 4,500 trailers, mostly 40 ft vans; some 280 refrigerator vans; 400 new trailers were bought in 1970.

Fast direct trailer trains operate daily. C & O/B & O transports containers in Trailer Service at domestic piggyback rates. There are daily fast schedules to and from the eastern seaports which assure connection with container ship services.

Interchange agreements with all major steamship lines and operators provide unlimited availability of equipment.

Intermodal containers move in daily Services over the entire system.

In early 1970 C & O/B & O added 1,000 trailers and installed a crane at South Charleston, W. Virginia.

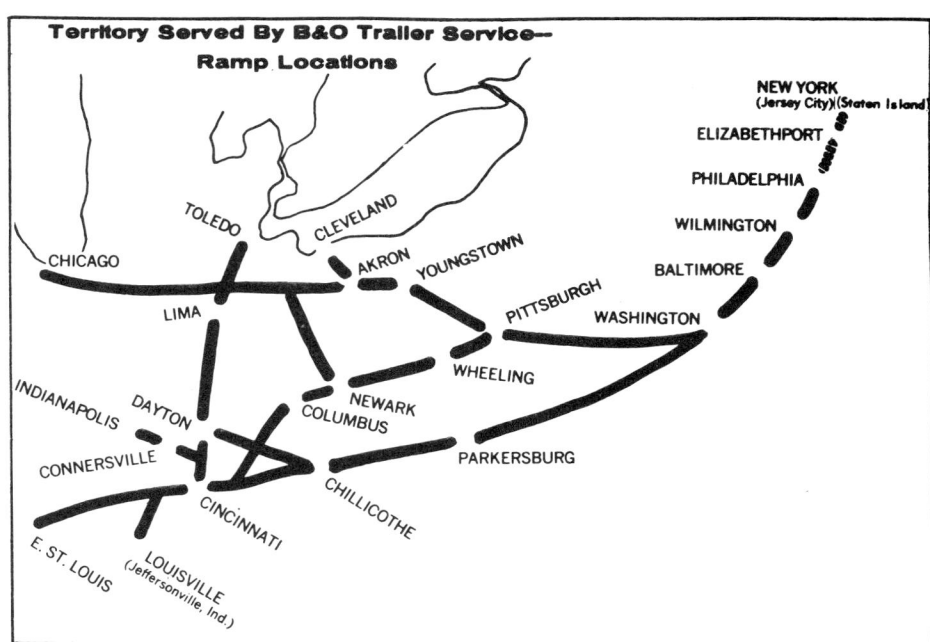

A highway trailer is lifted on a flatcar at C&O/B&O's piggyback terminal at Chicago.

C & O TOFC Service

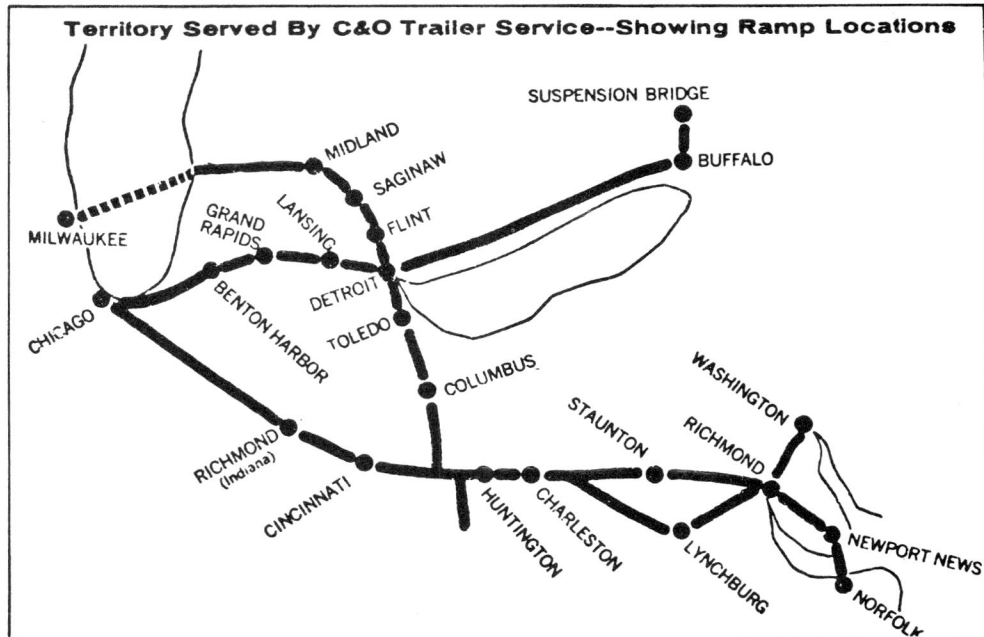

CHICAGO, ROCK ISLAND AND PACIFIC RAILROAD COMPANY

Chicago, Rock Island and Pacific Railroad Company
La Salle Street Station, Chicago, Illinois 60605
OFFICERS:
Peter Kiewit (*Acting Chairman*)
T. H. Desch (*Vice-Chairman and Chief Executive Officer*)
William J. Dixon (*President*)
John B. Buffalo (*Vice-President, Operations and Maintenance*)
Albert F. Hatcher (*Vice-President, Traffic*)
Guy E. Mallery (*Vice-President, Labor Relations*)
John M. Spann (*Resident Vice-President, Fort Worth*)
John A. Burnett (*Director of Purchases and Stores*)
Ben W. Crume (*Treasurer*)

E. F. Wilkinson (*Secretary*)
C. James Taylor (*Comptroller*)
James G. Pate (*Director of Public Relations*)
Charles E. Weller (*Chief Engineer*)
Frank B. Findling (*Chief Mechanical Engineer*)
Howard S. Ownley (*General Manager TOFC*)
Paul F. Kluding (*Rock Island Motor Transit Co., President*)
R. P. Leonetti (*Director of Terminals*)

GENERAL:

The Rock Island operates in the middle west States with a total route mileage of 7,336 miles (11,800 km) and has important traffic both west from Chicago and north and south, but has severe competition since its lines parallel other railroads.

The Rock Island Railroad hopes to complete negotiations for a merger with Union Pacific to make it part of a strong transcontinental system.

FINANCIAL:

1970 operating revenue was $287 million (+$15 million) and operating expenses $234 million. But after taxes, rents and fixed charges there was a net loss of $16 million.

TRAFFIC:

Net ton miles of freight in 1970 was 20,557 million—up from 19,600 million.

In 1970, the three-month trucking strike cut sharply into piggyback loadings.

Much of the new equipment acquired is under investment credit leases.

PIGGYBACK:

H. S. Ownley (General Manager, TOFC)
Plans offered: 1, 2, 2¼, 2½, 3, 4, 5.

CRI owns 4,267 trailers; over 1,200 are refrigerated.

Acquisitions in 1970 include 50 high-side open-top trailers.

Ramps are provided at Chicago, Peoria, Davenport, Des Moines, Minneapolis, Sioux Falls, Omaha, Denver, Colorado Springs, Topeka, Kansas City, St. Louis, Wichita, Amarillo, Tucumcari, Little Rock, Memphis, Galveston, Iowa Falls, Ottawa, Mankato, Belle, Houston, Ft. Worth, Liberal and Mason City. In 1970 two new ramps were added at Shawnee, Okla., and Boneville, Ark.

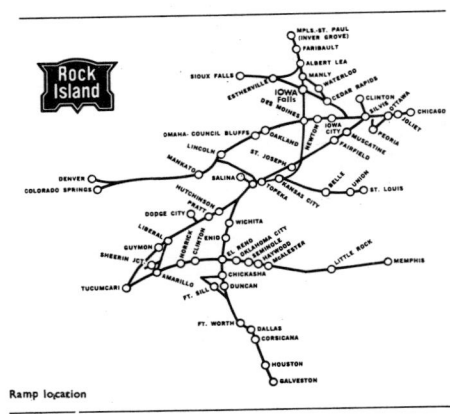

Ramp location

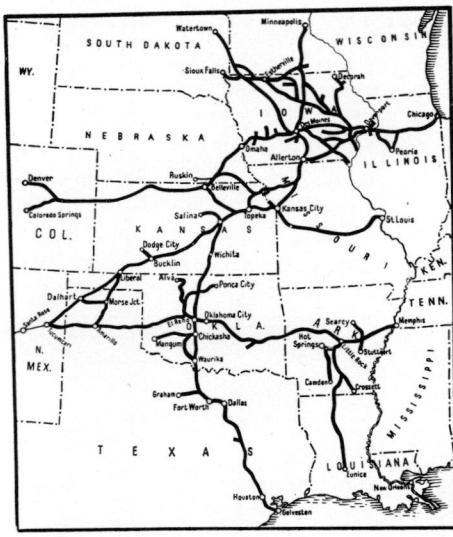

GULF MOBILE AND OHIO RAILROAD

Gulf, Mobile and Ohio Railroad Company
104 St. Francis Street
Mobile, ALA 36601

OFFICERS:

G. P. Brock (President, Mobile)
B. V. Bodie (Executive Vice-President and General Manager, Mobile)
R. E. Stevenson (Senior Vice-President, Mobile)
E. B. deVilliers (Vice-President, Traffic, Mobile)
Y. D. Lott (Vice-President and Comptroller, Mobile)
J. N. Ogden (Vice-President and General Counsel, Mobile)
T. T. Martin (Vice-President, Industrial Development, Mobile)
F. C. Clark (Manager, Purchases and Stores, Mobile)
F. J. Lott (Assistant Vice-President, Mobile)
C. B. Whitlow (Assistant to President, Jackson, Tenn.)
W. J. Wall (Treasurer, Mobile)
Kenneth D. Horton (Secretary, Mobile)
B. M. Sheridan (Assistant Vice-President, Public Relations, Mobile)

LINES AND TERRITORY:

G. M. & O operates 2,704 miles (4,307 km) of mainly local lines between Mobile on the Gulf, north to St. Louis and Chicago, with connecting lines to Kansas City, New Orleans, and Montgomery, Ala.

A merger with Illinois Central is likely.

TRAFFIC:

In 1970, tons handled at 28·5 millions, and revenue ton-miles at 8,285 millions, showed a slight increase.

1970 TOFC traffic increased 23% over 1969.

FINANCIAL:

Revenue rose to $104 million, but higher expenses $79·5 million resulted in lower income of $6·5 million ($7·9 in 1969).

TOFC/COFC:

J. E. Billingsley (Manager, TOFC)
Plans: 1, 2, 2¼, 2½, 3, 4, 5.

RAMPS:

Ramp locations shown on map.

All TOFC terminals operated by circus type loading or unloading.

EQUIPMENT:

All equipment is leased.

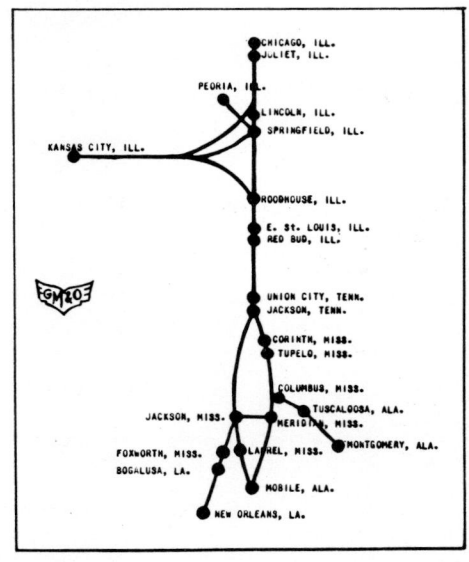

ILLINOIS CENTRAL RAILROADS

Illinois Central Industries Inc,
Illinois Central Railroad,
135 East Eleventh Place,
Chicago, Illinois 60605
TELEPHONE: 922-4811
OFFICERS:
William B. Johnson (*Chairman and Chief Executive Officer*)
Alan S. Boyd (*President*)
Otto H. Zimmermann (*Senior Vice-President, Operations*)
Jack C. Humbert (*Vice-President, Operations*)
Paul H. Reistrup (*Vice-President, Traffic*)
John W. Ingram (*Vice-President, Marketing*)
Allen L. Sams (*Vice-President and Chief Engineer*)
B. A. Logan (*Director, Piggyback Sales*)
W. F. Geserick (*Director TOFC/COFC Operations*)

FINANCIAL:
1970 Revenue was up 5% to $340 million. Expenses, at $268 million were $13 million higher. Operating income was $14.4 million.
TRAFFIC:
Freight traffic increased 2% to 83 million tons but ton miles increased 3% to 23,800 million.
PIGGYBACK:
1970 TOFC/COFC traffic increased 16% from 90,000 loads.
TOFC Plans: 1, 2, 2½, 3, 4, 5.
A new rail/road Intermodal terminal has been built in Chicago.
GENERAL:
Designed to handle 250 loaded trailers per day the terminal has parking space for 475 trailers. It is equipped with two 40 ton Drott Travelifts. Train services from the terminal will include I.C.S. all piggyback 'Fastback' trains which run daily between Chicago and Memphis; further services will be introduced in the future.

IC fleet comprises 3,000 trailers including 800 refrigerated trailers.
Containers are used fairly extensively on shipments through Gulf ports. IC owns 81 containers "Flexivans" and 82 bogies.
PIGGYBACK RAMP LOCATIONS:
Anna, Ill.; Ashland City, Tenn.; Baton Rouge, La.; Birmingham, Ala.; Bloomington, Ill.; Bloomington, Ind.; Cairo, Ill.; Carbondale, Ill.; Cedar Rapids, Ia.; Central City, Ky.; Centralia, Ill.; Champaign, Ill.; Cherokee, Ia.; Chicago, Ill.; Clarksville, Tenn.; Cleveland, Miss.; Clinton, Ill.; Council Bluffs, Ia.; Covington Tenn.; Decatur, Ill.; Denison, Ia.; Dubuque, Ia.; Dyersburg, Tenn.; East St. Louis, Ill.; Evansville, Ind.; Ft. Dodge, Ia.; Fulton, Ky.; Gibson City, Ill.; Gramercy, La.; Greenville, Miss.; Greenwood, Miss.; Gulfport, Miss.; Haleyville, Ala.; Hattiesburg, Miss.; Herrin, Ill.; Hopkinsville, Ky.; Indianapolis, Ind.; Iowa Falls, Ia.; Jackson, Miss.; Jackson, Tenn.; Kankakee, Ill.; Kosciusko, Miss.; Laurel, Miss.; Le Mars, Ia.; Louisville, Ky.; Mattoon, Ill.; Memphis, Tenn.; Meridian, Miss.; Monroe, La.; Muldraugh, Ky.; (Ft. Knox); Nashville, Tenn.; Natchez, Miss.; New Orleans, La.; Olney, Ill.; Ownesboro, Ky.; Paducah, Ky.; Peoria, Ill.; Princeton, Ky.; Reserve, La.; Robinson, Ill.; Rockford, Ill.; St. Francisville, La.; Shreveport, La.; Sioux City, Ia.; Sioux Falls, S.D.; Springfield, Ill.; Storm Lake, Ia.; Tallulah, La.; Vicksburg, Miss.; Waterloo, Ia.; Wildwood (Chicago) Ill.

A merger with the Gulf Mobile and Ohio Railroad is planned and this would expand ramp facilities at 25 cities in 7 states.

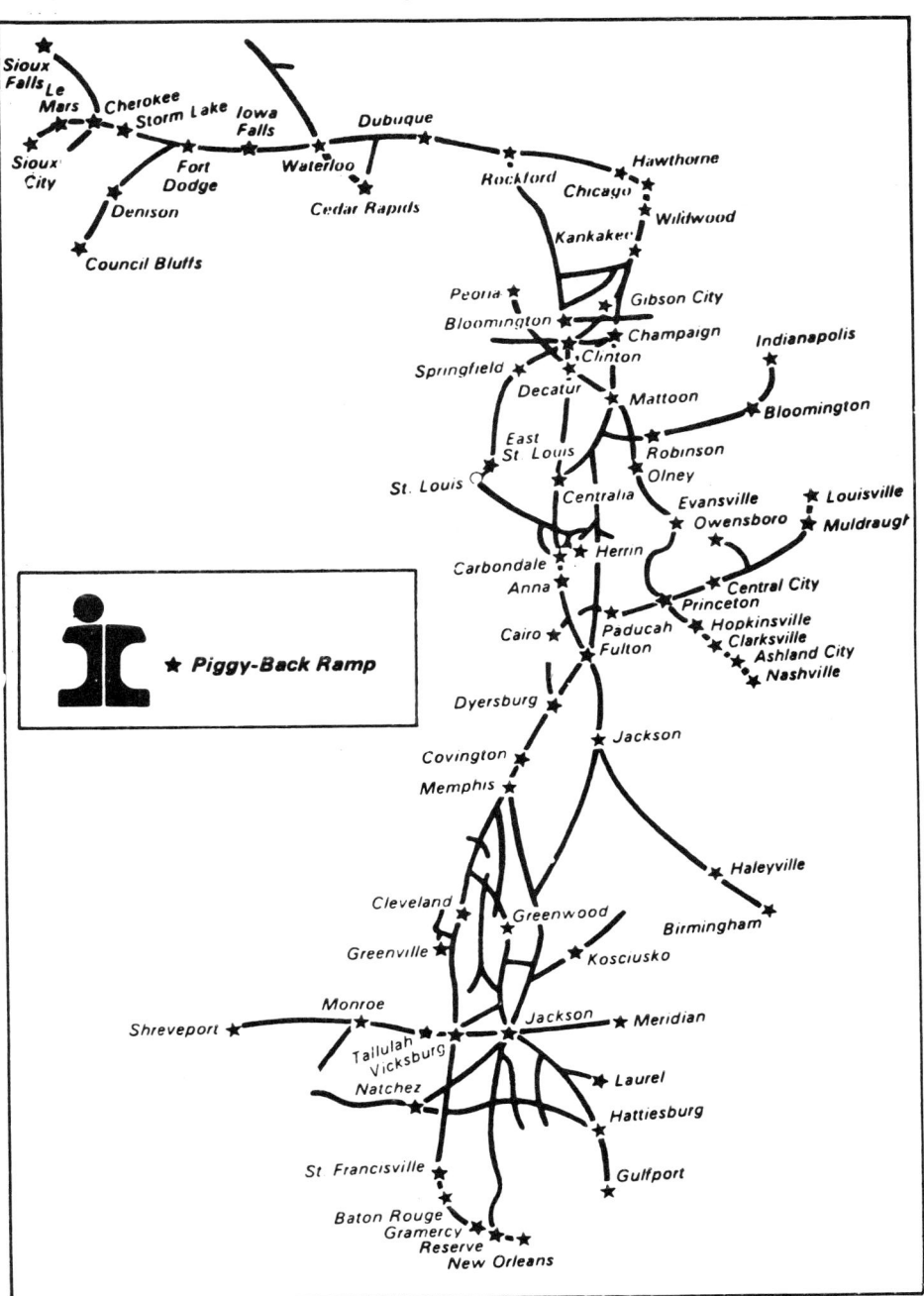

★ Piggy-Back Ramp

An Illinois Central Trailer Terminal.

KANSAS CITY SOUTHERN RAILWAY CO.

Kansas City Southern Railway Company
114 W. 11th Street, Kansas City,
Mo. 64105
OFFICERS:
W. N. Deramus III (*President*)
L. O. Frith (*Executive Vice-President*)
M. F. McClain (*Vice-President, Traffic*)
R. J. Blair (*Vice-President and General Manager*)
D. F. Nicola (*Superintendent of Transportation*

GENERAL:
Kansas City Southern Railway is a subsidiary of Kansas City Southern Industries, which also owns other smaller railways, three trucking companies and industrial businesses.

KCS Railway operates 1,650 route miles (2,657 km) from Kansas City in the north to New Orleans and Port Arthur in the south, and Dallas, Texas in the west.

Woodpulp, paper, and petroleum products are important to KCS.

TRAFFIC:
Gross tons of revenue freight handled rose from 24·8 million in 1969 to 26·2 million in 1970. Net ton miles handled per freight-train-hour (a measure of operating efficiency) increased to 54·186 (against 52·563 in 1969).

Overall TOFC/COFC traffic in 1970 showed a decrease from 1969. Containers handled rose substantially to 1,000.

FINANCIAL:
1970 Revenue was $119·8 millions (up $12m) and expenses $104·2 million leaving income $6·2 million.
PIGGYBACK:
A. C. Stockinger (*Manager, Truck and*

TOFC Sales)
Plans: 1, 2, 2½, 3, 4, 5.
Trailers 300 (mostly vans)

Ramps: 17 points:
Alexandrea, La.; Baton Rouge, La.; Dallas, Tex.; Fort Smith, Ark.; Gramercy, La.; Greenville, Tex. (crane); Joplin, Mo.; Kansas City, Mo.; Lake Charles. La,.; Minden, La.; Neosho, Mo.; New Orleans, La.; Pittsburg, Kan.; Port Arthur, Tex.; Sheveport, La.; Siloam Springs, Ark.; Texarkana, Tex.

MAINE CENTRAL RAILROAD

Maine Central Railroad Company
242 St. John Street,
Portland, Maine 04102
OFFICERS:
EXECUTIVE DEPARTMENT:
E. Spencer Miller (*President*)
Archibald M. Knowles (*Vice-President*)
Arnold J. Travis (*Assistant to President*)
John F. Gerity (*Clerk of Corporation*)
Bradley L. Peters (*Director of Public Relations*)
ACCOUNTING AND FINANCE DEPARTMENTS:
Horace N. Foster (*Vice-President, Accounting and Finance*)
John F. Gerity (*Comptroller*)
Eric P. Smith (*Director, Statistical Studies and Cost Research*)

LAW DEPARTMENT:
Archibald M. Knowles (*Vice-President, General Counsel*)

MARKETING DEPARTMENT:
George H. Ellis (*Vice-President, Traffic and Marketing*)

OPERATING, ENGINEERING AND MECHANICAL DEPARTMENTS:
James W. Wiggins (*Vice-President, Operations*)
Willard E. Pierce (*General Manager*)
Ansel N. Tupper (*General Superintendent*)
James O. Born (*Chief Engineer*)
S. P. Park Jr. (*Chief Mechanical Officer*)
PURCHASING AND STORES DEPARTMENT:
Arnold J. Travis (*Assistant to President*)

LINES AND TERRITORIES:
Maine Central Railroad operates 921 miles (1,480 km) of route, mainly in Maine, but also in New Hampshire and Vermont. It joins the Canadian Pacific route to Montreal and the Boston and Maine at Portland. The pulp and paper industry is important (50% of all traffic).

TRAFFIC:
Revenue freight tons in 1970 was slightly down to 8·35 million and ton miles were 950 million net and 2,087 million gross. Average cars per train was 43.
FINANCIAL:
1970 operating revenue of $25·8 million was up $0·6 million and operating expenses

$22·3 million up $0·6 million on 1969. The 1969 loss of $1·1 million was reduced to a loss of $0·45 million.

PIGGYBACK:

M. C. Olsen (*Sales Manager, TOFC*)

Maine Central has nine ramp facilities in Maine.

Plans: 2, 2¼, 2½, 3 and 5.

Trailers handled in 1970 increased 7 % on 1969. Trailer fleet (leased) increased from 300 to 325.

Maine Central does not offer COFC.

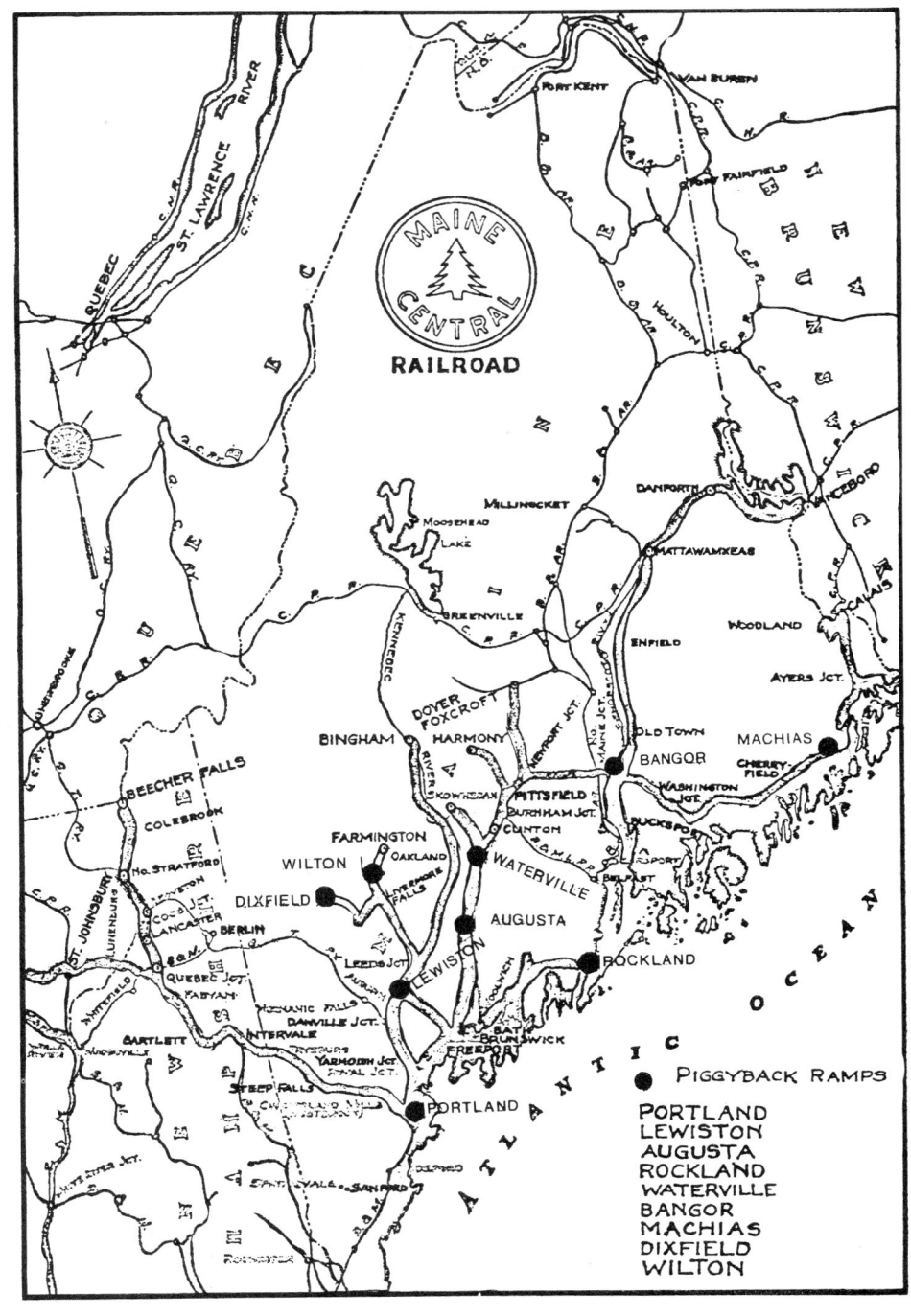

MISSOURI-KANSAS-TEXAS RAILROAD CO.
(MKT-KATY RAILROAD)

Missouri-Kansas-Texas Railroad

Katy Building, Dallas,
Texas 75202

OFFICERS, EXECUTIVE DEPARTMENT:

Reginald N. Whitman (*President and Chairman*)

George R. Herzog (*Vice-President, Finance Cleveland*)

Frank J. Heiling (*Vice-President, Sales and Services*)

Billy R. Bishop (*Vice-President, Operations*)

William A. Thie (*General Counsel*)

Kenneth R. Langford (*Comptroller*)

Karl O. Jansson (*Secretary and Treasurer*)

Fred R. Carroll (*Manager of Personnel*)

John H. Hughes (*Chief Engineer*)

Lawrence I. Nearmyer (*Communications Engineer*)

Harry A. Steel (*Signal Engineer*)

Martin F. Rister (*Chief Mechanical Officer*)

Charles E. Reasoner (*Director of Purchases and Stores*)

Hollis E. Dunivant (*General Storekeeper*)

LINES AND TERRITORY:

MKT Railroad operates 2,772 miles of route (4,486 km) from Kansas City and St. Louis in the north, to Keyes in western Oklahoma, and south to San Antonio and Galveston in Texas.

FINANCIAL:

1970 operating revenue was $67 million and operating expense over $50 million. After rent, taxes, and interest Katy RR made a loss.

TRAFFIC:

Revenue ton miles remained about 5,000 million.

PIGGYBACK:

W. H. Wiley (*Vice-President and General Manager*)

MKT Transportation Company
P.O. Drawer 38385
Dallas, Texas 75235
Plans: 2, 2¼, 2½, 3, 4, 5.

Trailers 217 mostly closed van.
Ramps at 20 locations shown on map.

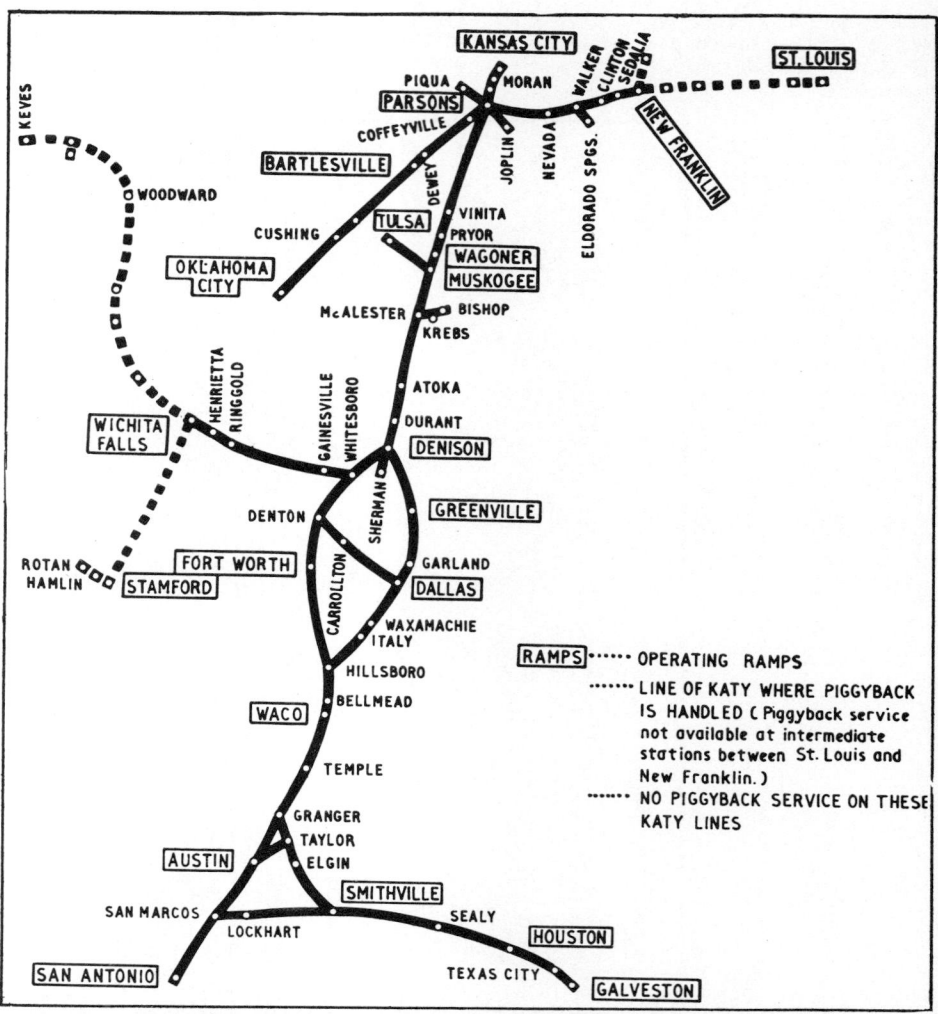

MKT—Piggyback and container terminal at Dallas, Garland.

DENVER AND RIO GRANDE WESTERN RAILROAD

Denver and Rio Grande Western Railroad
Rio Grande Building, PO Box 5482,
Denver, Colorado 80217

OFFICERS:

G. B. Aydelott (*Chairman of the Board and President*)
W. J. Holtman (*Executive Vice-President and General Manager*)
Clarence R. Lennig (*Vice-President, Traffic*)
John Ayer, Jr. (*Vice-President, Technical Services*)
H. W. Bushacher (*Vice-President, Finance and Comptroller*)
Ernest Porter (*Vice-President and General Counsel*)
W. G. Prescott (*Secretary*)
D. L. Clavel (*Assistant Secretary*)
M. E. Masterson (*Treasurer*)
E. L. Main (*Assistant Secretary*)

Jack D. Key (*General Traffic Manager*)
R. C. Cavness (*Director, Industrial Development*)
F. E. Long (*Passenger Traffic Manager*)
Alexis McKinney (*Director, Public Relations*)
C. D. Brainard (*Director of Marketing*)
M. F. Black (*Superintendent of Communications*)

D. J. Butters (*Chief Transportation Officer*)
P. D. Starr (*Chief Mechanical Officer*)
E. H. Waring (*Chief Engineer*)
B. C. Eaton (*Signal Engineer*)
R. L. Jacobsen (*Director, Transportation Research*)
R. S. Eno (*Director, Safety and Rules*)
R. O. Williams (*Purchasing Agent*)

LINES AND TERRITORY:

D & RGW runs across the Rocky Mountains at high altitude from Denver Colorado 600 miles (960 km) west to Salt Lake City.

TRAFFIC:

Freight revenue ton miles in 1970 were

substantially unchanged at 7,800 million. Average gross train load was 3,554 tons; D & RGW operates short fast freight trains.

FINANCIAL:

1970 Net income after tax and fixed charges was $11·8 million ($11·4 million in 1969).

TOFC/COFC:

R. L. Taylor (*Director of TOFC/COFC*)
    Plans: 1, 2, 3, 4 and 5.

RAMP LOCATIONS:

Alamosa, Colo.; Clearfield, Utah; Colorado Springs, Colo.; Craig, Colo.; Denver, Colo.; Glenwood Springs, Colo.; Grand Junction, Colo.; Ogden, Utah, Provo, Utah, Pueblo, Colo.; Sabida, Colo.; Saeida, Colo.; and Salt Lake City, Utah.

D & RG owns 153 trailers and 50 Containers type R6CU for dry cargo.

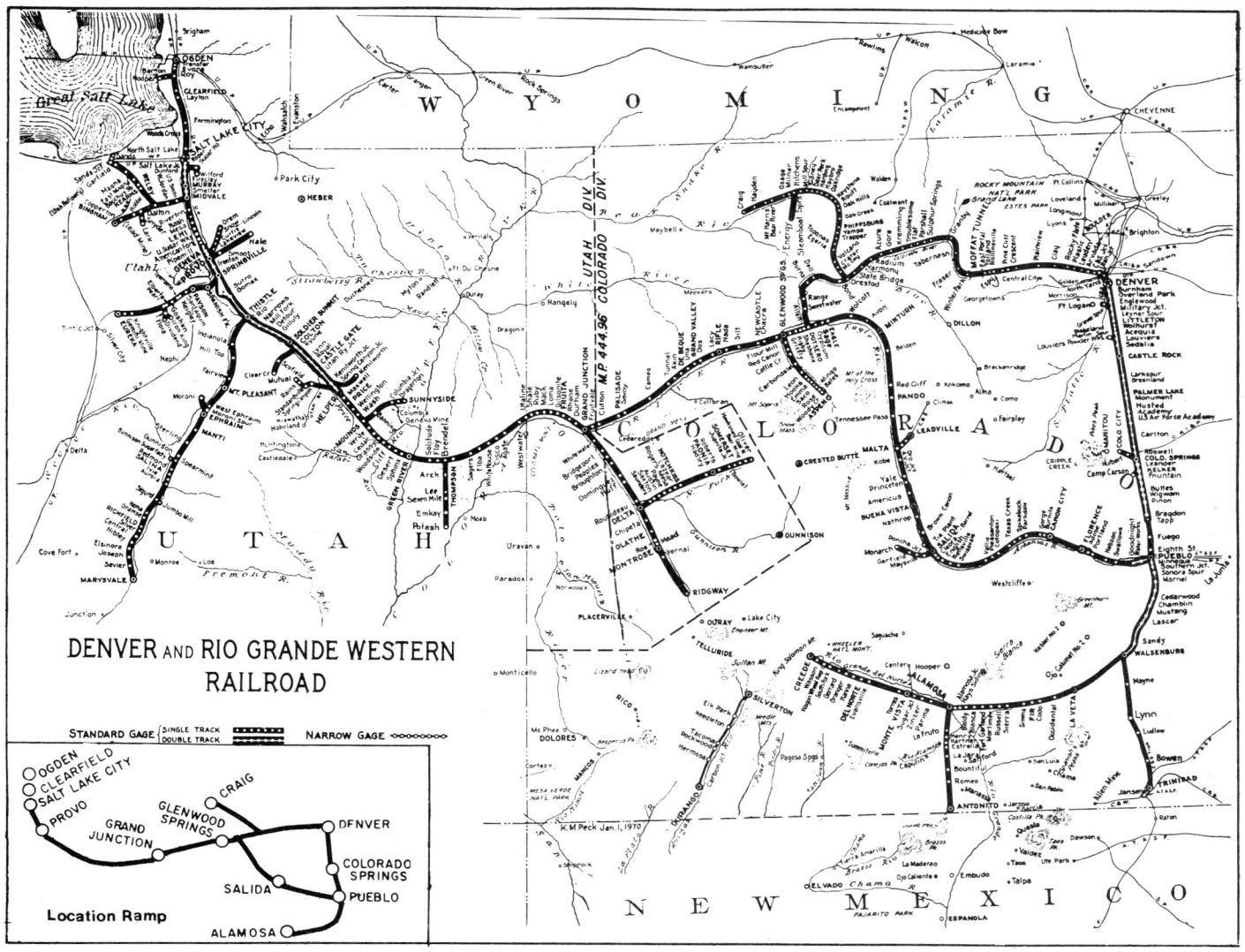

DENVER AND RIO GRANDE WESTERN RAILROAD

LOUISVILLE AND NASHVILLE RAILROAD

Louisville and Nashville Railroad
908 West Broadway,
Louisville, Kentucky 40201

LINES:

Operates from Chicago south and southeast to the Gulf.

OFFICERS:

W. H. Kendall (*President*)
R. E. Bisha (*Vice-President, Executive Department*)

J. W. Hoeland (*Vice-President, Marketing*)
D. McKeliar (*Vice-President, Sales*)
P. M. Lanier (*Vice-President, Law*)
C. R. Yates (*Vice-President, Finance*)
L. W. Adkins (*Vice-President, Accounting and Taxation*)
D. D. Strench (*Vice-President, Operations*)
F. D. Brooke (*Resident Vice-President*)
D. L. Morris (*Comptroller*)
C. H. Edwards (*Secretary and Treasurer*)
J. B. Clark (*Assistant Vice-President, Personnel and Public Relations*)
J. C. Pickett (*Assistant Vice-President Industrial and Real Estate*)
S. A. Alward (*Director, Management Information Services*)

W. Knight (*Director of Public Relations*)
N. F. Hurt (*Director of Special Studies*)

OPERATING DEPARTMENT:

D. D. Strench (*Vice-President, Operations*)
C. N. Wiggins (*Assistant Vice-President, Mechanical*)
C. D. Leddon (*Director of Industrial Engineering*)
J. I. Adams (*Chief Engineer*)
C. A. Love (*Chief Mechanical Officer, Equipment*)
Gordon H. Kendall (*Chief Mechanical Officer, Motive Power*)
D. A. Reavis (*General Superintendent, Equipment*)
W. S. Scholl (*Director of Personnel*)
S. P. Strickland (*Chief Transportation Officer*)
A. James, Jr. (*General Manager, Northern Region*)
K. S. Dufford (*General Manager, Southern Region*)

PUBLIC RELATIONS DEPARTMENT:

W. Knight (*Director of Public Relations*)
E. L. Koester (*Manager, Public Communications*)

C. N. Beasley (*Advertising Manager*)
E. H. Thomas (*News Bureau Manager*)
M. J. Robards (*Editor L & N Magazine*)

TRAFFIC DEPARTMENT:

J. W. Hoeland (*Vice-President, Marketing*)
T. Leslie Smith (*Director of Marketing Research*)

SALES:

Douglas McKellar (*Vice-President, Sales*)
J. E. Nall (*Director, Sales*)

INDUSTRIAL DEVELOPMENT:

J. C. Pickett (*Assistant Vice-President*)
N. C. Keiffer, Jr. (*Director*)

INTERMODAL (PIGGYBACK) TRAFFIC:

D. F. Jones (*Assistant Vice-President*)
C. E. Thomas (*Director, Sales*)
J. L. Blair (*Assistant Director, Sales*)
R. F. Summerville (*Manager, Service and Equipment*)
F. R. Whitman (*Manager, Traffic*)
L. R. Worey (*Assistant Manager, Traffic*)

FINANCIAL:

1970 operating revenue was $381 millions (up $41 millions) and expenses $301 millions (up $30 millions) net income was $27 millions.

TRAFFIC:

Freight tons rose 6% to 118 millions, and ton miles rose 4%.

INTERMODAL:

D. F. Jones (*Director of Intermodal Traffic*)

Intermodal (piggyback) traffic increased 8·9% during 1970, to 103,500 trailer loads.

Plans: 1, 2, 2½, 3, 4, 5.

L and N trailer fleet consists of over 2,300 leased units, predominantly dry van and flat bed.

TOFC RAMP LOCATIONS:

Alcoa, Tenn.; Anniston, Ala.; Athens, Tenn.; Atlanta, Ga.; Bardstown, Ky.; Birmingham, Ala.; Bowling Green, Ky.; Bruceton, Tenn.; Calhoun, Tenn.; Cartersville, Ga.; Chattanooga, Tenn.; Chicago, Ill.; Chipley, Fla.; Cincinnati, O.; Clarksville, Tenn.; Columbia, Tenn.; Cookeville, Tenn.; Crossville, Tenn.; Dalton, Ga.; Decatur, Ala.; Dolton, Ill.; Evansville, Ind.; E. St. Louis, Ill.; Fayetteville, Tenn.; Florence, Ala.; Frankfort, Ky.; Franklin, Ky.; Gadsden, Ala.; Glasgow, Ky.; Gulfport, Miss.; Hopkinsville, Ky.; Humboldt, Tenn.; Huntsville, Ala.; Jackson, Tenn.; Knoxville, Tenn.; Lawrenceburg, Tenn.;

Lebanon, Tenn.; Lewisburg, Tenn.; Lexington, Ky.; Lexington, Tenn.; Louisville, Ky.; Memphis, Tenn.; Mobile, Ala.; Montgomery, Ala.; Morrison, Tenn.; Murfreesboro, Tenn.; Nashville, Tenn.; New Johnsonville, Tenn.; New Orleans, La.; Oak Ridge, Tenn.; Old Hickory, Tenn.; Owensville, Ky.; Paris, Tenn.; Pascagoula, Miss.; Pensacola, Fla.; Pulaski, Tenn.; Richmond, Ky.; Ringgold, Ga.; Sparta, Tenn.; Springfield, Tenn; Sylacauga, Ala.; Tate, Ga.; Terre Haute, Ind; Tuscaloosa, Ala.; Williamsburg, Ky.

*Handles watermelons only.

L & N Bulk Intermodal Distributions

A Side-Porter handling L & N Trailers.

Service—"DIBS"—provide truck delivery service which results in economy. Terminals in: Atlanta, Chicago, Cincinnati, Dalton, Knoxville, Louisville, Memphis, Mobile, Nashville, New Orleans, Pensacola and St. Louis; and planned ones at Birmingham, Chattanooga, Evansville and Montgomery. Almost any liquid or dry bulk product can be transferred from railroad cars to highway trailers for short-haul delivery.

In 1970 new ramps were opened at Danville, Illinois and Tullahoma, Tennessee.

L & N Bulk Intermodal Distributions Service—"BIDS"—provide truck delivery service which results in economy. Terminals in: Atlanta, Birmingham, Chattanooga, Chicago, Cincinnati, Dalton, Knoxville, Louisville, Memphis, Mobile, Nashville, New Orleans, Pensacola and St. Louis; and planned at Evansville. Almost any liquid or dry bulk product can be transferred from railroad cars to highway trailers for short-haul delivery.

MISSOURI PACIFIC RAILROAD SYSTEM

Missouri Pacific Railroad Company and Texas and Pacific Railway Company

Missouri Pacific Building,
210 North 13th Street,
St. Louis Missouri 63103

GENERAL:

The Missouri Pacific Railroad System totals 12,000 miles (17,703 km) and operates in 12 states in the Mid-west and Southwest United States. Territories served by the Missouri Pacific System extend from Chicago, Illinois (through Chicago and Eastern Illinois Railroad, which is controlled by Missouri Pacific Railroad System) on the Great Lakes, south to the Gulf of Mexico and Mexico, and west to the Colorado Rocky Mountains and New Mexico.

The Missouri Pacific Railroad System is supplemented by the Missouri Pacific Truck Lines, Inc., and Texas and Pacific Motor Transport, Inc. These two wholly owned and operated motor carrier subsidiaries are under joint management and have 17,000 miles (27,360 km) of highway operating rights closely paralleling the railroad. The motor carrier subsidiaries perform all terminal and TOFC-COFC loading and unloading for the Missouri Pacific Railroad System. They also perform substitute motor carrier service on the highway on railroad billed freight in

Containers at Dallas, Texas en route, by Missouri Pacific container service, for Japan via Oakland.

lieu of rail service. Also, routing concurrences are maintained with over 400 motor carriers at 51 junction points in the 12 state area served by the Missouri Pacific System.

FINANCIAL:

1970 consolidated operating revenue was $534 million (up $40 million) and operating expenses $417 million.

Net income was $21 million.

TRAFFIC:

Revenue ton miles at 35,800 million were up from 34,371 million.

CONTAINERS:

C. T. Groton Jr. (*President, Missouri Pacific Truck Lines Inc.*)

Trains

All trains handle containers and the system has five daily TOFC-COFC trains between Chicago, Ill., St. Louis, Missouri, and Dallas-Ft. Worth and Houston, Texas.

Fleet

Fifty (50) containers are owned by the system. System owns 50 container chassis, which handle both ISO 20 ft. containers and 24 ft. Matson Navigation containers.

Terminals

Container Terminals with gantry cranes capable of handling all containers up to 40 ft. are located at St. Louis, Missouri; Kansas City, Missouri; Wichita, Kansas; Memphis, Tennessee; Little Rock, Arkansas; Chicago, Illinois; Monroe, Louisiana; New Orleans, Louisiana; Abilene, Texas; Fort Worth, Texas; Dallas, Texas; Longview, Texas; San Antonio, Texas; Houston, Texas; Corpus Christi, Texas; Harlingen, Texas.

Traffic

Traffic at 15,000 loads was small but was treble the 1968 traffic.

Containerpak Service

I Flatcar all the way.

Container is placed on a flat car at ship side or container yard and moves by rail to customers' sidings where it remains on flatcar during packing or unpacking operation.

II Wheels at both ends.

Container is delivered on wheels, removed from the chassis and placed on flatcar for rail movement at destination, container is placed on chassis and delivered to customers premises. Railroad performs all handling operations.

III Wheels all the way (Piggyback).

PIGGYBACK:

Plans: 1, 2, 2½, 3, 4, 5.

Ramps

TOFC ramps are located at the container terminals listed above and at the following cities:

Arkansas: Crossett, El Dorado, McGehee, Nashville, Newport, Texarkana, Van Buren, Wynne.

Colorado: Pueblo.

Kansas: Arkansas City, Coffeyville, Concordia, Hoisington, Salina, Topeka. Winfield.

Louisiana: Addis, Alexandria, Anchorage, Lake Charles, Shreveport.

Missouri: Carthage, Jefferson City, Joplin, Poplar Bluff, Sedalia, St. Joseph, Springfield.

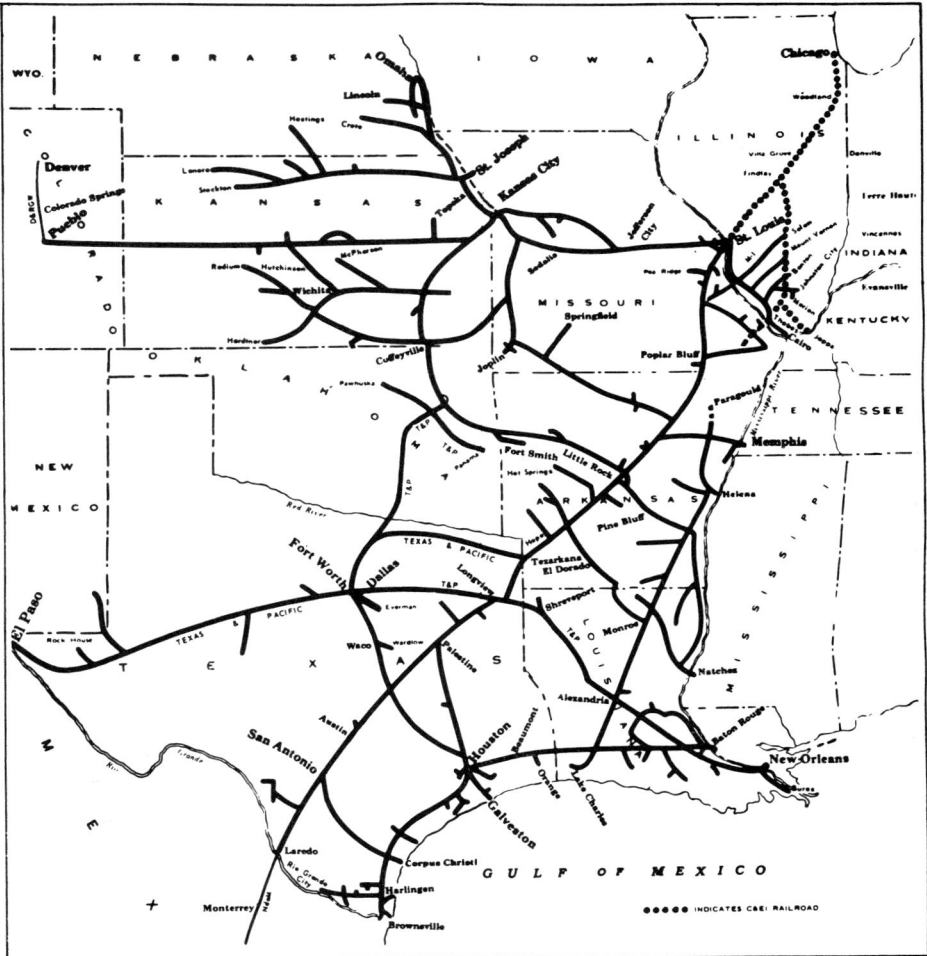

Nebraska: Lincoln, Omaha.

Oklahoma: Henryetta, Muskogee, Tulsa.

Texas: Arlington, Austin, Beaumont, Big Springs, Bloomington, Bonham, Brownsville, Crystal City, El Paso, Galveston, Laredo, Odessa, Palestine, Taylor, Waco.

Connections are made with steamship lines at New Orleans, Lake Charles and Baton Rouge, Louisiana; Beaumont, Orange, Houston, Texas City, Galveston, Freeport, Corpus Christi, Port Isabel and Brownsville, Texas.

Through other rail connections all United States ports are served, Storage is in regular TOFC-COFC yards and is adequate.

LCL SERVICE:

Less-than-carload (LCL) service is available at all points on the Missouri Pacific Railroad and Texas and Pacific Railway in the 11 states served by the system.

NORFOLK AND WESTERN RAILWAY

Norfolk and Western Railway Company,
8 North Jefferson Street,
Roanoke, Virginia 24011

OFFICIALS:

J. P. Fishwick (*President and Chief Executive Officer*)

R. B. Claytor (*Executive Vice-President*)

H. M. Redman (*Vice-President, Finance*)

J. A. Barrett (*Vice-President, Merchandise Traffic*)

R. F. Dunlap (*Vice-President, Operations*)

L. T. Forbes (*Vice-President, Coal and Ore Traffic*)

J. E. Carr (*Vice-President, Industrial Development, Real Estate and Taxation*)

J. S. Shannon (*Vice-President, Law*)

E. A. Manetta (*Vice-President, Personnel*)

I. H. Soldwish (*Vice-President, Budget and Planning*)

E. J. Gentsch (*Vice-President, Material Management*)

H. J. Brinner (*Comptroller*)

F. R. McCartney (*Treasurer*)

W. H. Ogden (*Secretary*)

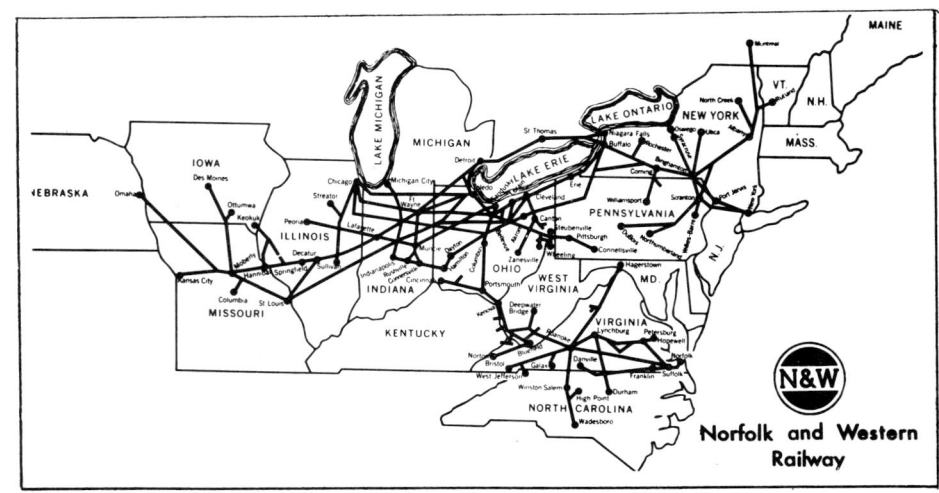

GENERAL:

Norfolk and Western is an amalgamation of the previous Norfolk and Western, Nickle Plate, Virginia and Wabash Railways, and now the Erie-Lackawanna and Delaware and Hudson Railways, and operates a total route of 7,595 miles (12,224 km) from Omaha, Nebraska, in the west, through the industrial centres of Chicago, Detroit and Cleveland and Pennsylvania to New York, and north to Montreal and southeast through its base city of Roanoke to Norfolk on the Atlantic Coast. A merger which was under consideration with the C and O/B and O, has now been abandoned.

FINANCIAL:

Consolidated 1970 operating revenue was $1,077 million ($62 million up) and operating expenses were $1,010 million. Earnings after depreciation, taxes, interest etc., were $65 million ($22 million less than 1969).

Gross revenue from TOFC and COFC fell 9·7% due to lower business activity and a truckers' strike.

TRAFFIC:

Freight revenue tons was down to 164 million (169 million) and ton miles 52,800 million.

PIGGYBACK (TOFC/COFC):

Plans: 1, 2, 2¼, 2½, 3, 4, 5, 8 (mail), 9 (express).

R. B. Short (Director, TOFC/COFC)
L. P. Keoughan (Manager, TOFC/COFC Operations)
W. E. Leight, Jr. (GTM, TOFC/COFC Pricing)
J. H. Pfaffenber (General Manager TOFC Terminal and Intermodal Equipment)

TRAFFIC:

Fell to 221,347 trailers and containers from 245,000 in 1969, but export/import handling of containers through east coast ports increased 91%.

Trailers:

N & W fleet totals 2,378 units, with permanent wheel assemblies, 40 ft long 8 ft wide 12 ft 6 in high, tare weight 12,000 lb, capacity 55,000 lb with identification marks NWKZ, NWVZ, NWWZ, NWZ, PWV, RNWZ, WABZ.

RAMPS:

These are located as follows:

Illinois: Chicago, Danville, Decatur, East St. Louis, Madison, Peoria, Quincy, Streator.

Indiana: Fort Wayne, Kokomo, Lafayette, Marion, Muncie, South Bend (NJI & I).

Iowa: Council Bluffs, Des Moines.

Michigan: Adrian, Detroit.

Missouri: Columbia, Kansas City, St. Louis.

Ohio: Bellvue, Brewster, Cincinnati, Cleveland, Columbus, Conneaut, Ironton, Lima, Montpeller, Napoleon, Portsmouth, Toledo.

Pennsylvania: Erie, Pittsburg.

Norfolk and Western Railway Co. trailer on flat car.

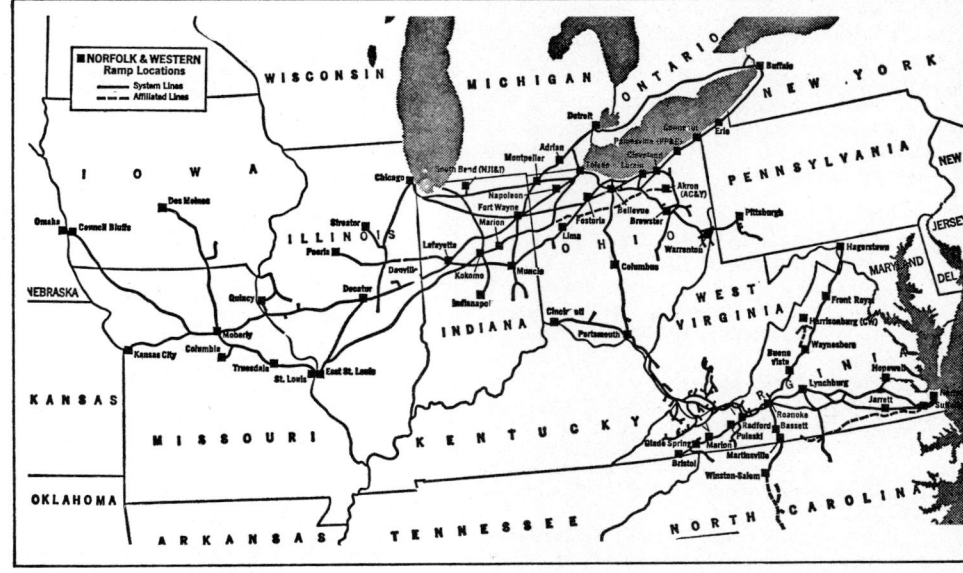

Virginia: Bassett, Bristol, Churchland (N F & D), Glade Spring, Harrisonburg (GW), Lynchburg, Marion, Martinsville, Norfolk, Radford, Roanoke, Waynesboro.

CONTAINERS:

N and W does not own any containers or any container handling cars.

Containers are handled at Norfolk International Terminal, at Portsmouth, Va. Marine Terminal (see entry for Hampton Roads) and at Calumet, Chicago with one Le Tourneau Side Porter SP70.

PENN CENTRAL COMPANY

Penn Central Company
Six Penn Center Plaza,
Philadelphia Pa. 19104

GENERAL:

Penn Central Company is the holding company that owns all of the outstanding stock of Penn Central Transportation Company, the railroad operating company.

Penn Central Transportation Co. filed a petition for reorganisation under bankruptcy proceedings in June 1970.

Penn Central Transportation Co

Penn Central, now the largest railway in USA for traffic, operates almost 22,000 miles (35,400 km) serving 16 states, 2 provinces of Canada, and the District of Columbia. It covers the major industrial and population centres of New York, Philadelphia, Boston, Washington DC, Detroit, Pittsburg, Cincinnati, Chicago and St. Louis.

FINANCIAL:

Preliminary 1970 railway operating revenues are $1,691 million and railway operating expenses $1,635 million. But after adding other income and deducting costs, taxes, interest etc., Penn Central showed a loss of $431 million including special retirement and

write-down expenses (net) of over $84 million.

Penn Central Company is being operated by trustees under Section 77 of the Bankruptcy Act.

Piggyback service decreased 8% and produced $123 million revenue.

TRAFFIC:

1970 freight revenue tons were 282 million and ton miles 84,228 million.

Piggyback loads at 422,000 units was more than 20% of the national total.

PIGGYBACK:

Plans: 1, 2, 2½, 3, 5.

Penn Central is the nation's largest container and piggyback operator.

80 new trailers were delivered in 1970 with mechanical refrigeration. Total fleet now exceeds 11,000 units.

Daily operations include 34 trains in piggyback and also 14 trains handling US mail in containers. There are 41 Trail-Van terminals—6 equipped with mechanical loaders.

The company's new trade name—Trail-Van—replaces the former Pennsylvania Truc-Train and the former New York Central Flexi-Van.

A New York Central trailvan in the old livery.

In the development of intermodal container traffic, PC has equipment interchange agreements with 42 steamship companies, and has opened a new international container terminal at Port Newark-Elizabeth, N.J. for the purpose of handling export and import container traffic. This rapidly growing service increased 46 % in 1970 and now exceeds 24,000 units per year.

Flexi-Flo intermodal bulk shipments expanded over 15 % during 1970 to include a wide number of food grade products. Transfer from rail cars to containers for export and import commodities was a significant innovation during this year. Penn Central has twelve Flexi-Flo terminals located throughout its territory.

TRAILVAN TERMINALS.

Albany, NY; Altoona, Pa.; Baltimore, Md.; Boston, Mass.; Buffalo, NY.; Canton, Ohio; Chicago, Ill.; Cincinnati, Ohio; Cleveland, Ohio; Columbus, Ohio; Detroit, Mich.; Elkhart, Ind.; Ft. Wayne, Ind.; Grand Rapids, Mich.; Harrisburg, Pa.; Indianapolis, Ind.; Johnstown, Pa.; Kalamazoo, Mich.; Lancaster, Pa.; Louisville, Ky.; (Jefferson-ville, Ind.); New Haven, Ct.; New York, NY (Bronx and Highbridge, NY; North Bergen, NJ; Kearney and Weekawken, NJ); Philadelphia, Pa.; Pittsburg, Pa.; Providence, R.I.; Rochester NY.; Springfield, Mass.; St. Louis, Mo.; (E. St. Louis, Ill.); Syracuse, NY.; Toledo, Ohio; Trenton, NJ; Worcester, Mass.; York, Pa.

The New England Transportation Company is the highway transport subsidiary of the former New Haven. With the rapid development of piggyback and containerised shipments, this company's trucking routes will figure prominently in the Penn Central's restructuring programme.

Terminal expansions were completed at Boston, Chicago, North Bergen, Philadelphia and Springfield. A new terminal was opened at Weehawken, for the exclusive handling of meat for the New York area.

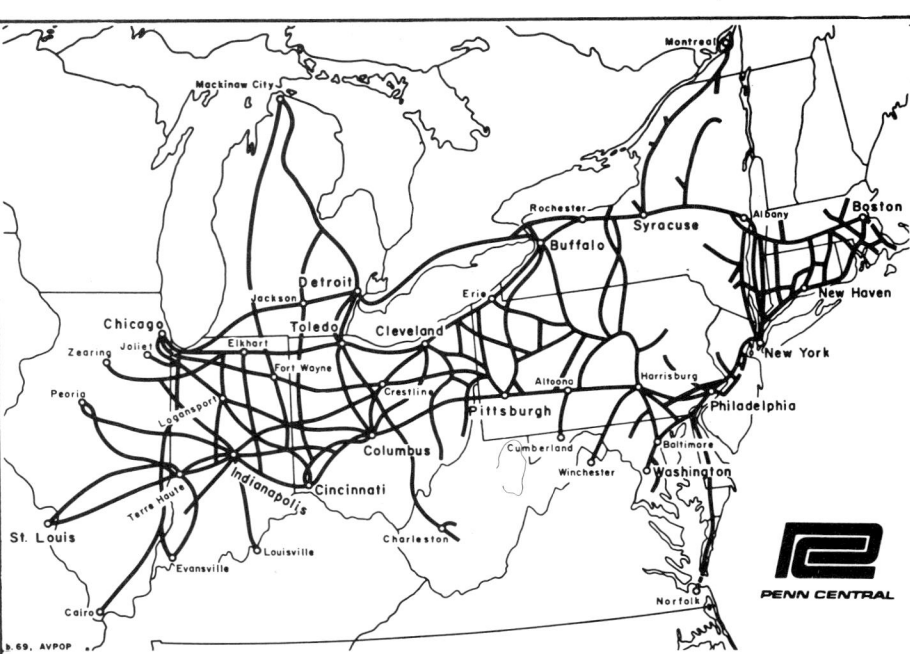

Penn Central—Handling at a Trailvan Centre with a Piggypacker

READING COMPANY

Reading Company
Reading Terminal
12th and Market Streets,
Philadelphia, Pa. 19107
TELEPHONE: WA 2-6100

OFFICERS:
William R. Daley (*Chairman of the Board*)
Charles E. Bertrand (*President and Chief Executive Officer*)
Alfred W. Hesse, Jr. (*Vice-President and General Counsel*)
Julian R. Greene (*Vice-President, Finance*)
Franklin G. Fisher (*Vice-President, Operations and Maintenance*)
Oscar P. Benjamin (*Vice-President, Traffic*)

GENERAL AND FINANCIAL:
The year was a disappointment with a net loss of $5,617,000 on a total operating revenue of $118,720,000. This was due in most part to a decrease in carloads of 6·7 % and the impact of inflation reflected in increased costs of $6·2 million in wages and materials.

PIGGYBACK:
J. I. Smith (*Assistant Vice-President, TOFC*)
1970 TOFC traffic was down 1·1 % compared to 1969, with 23,472 On Line Loads being handled.
TOFC Plans: 1, 2, 2¼, 2½, 3 and 5 are available.
A new TOFC Terminal is being constructed at 2nd and Erie Avenue, Philadelphia, to replace present facility at Wayne Junction. This terminal is expected to be completed in October, 1971, and will consist of two tracks capable of handling 24 cars, a Drott Overhead Crane, and parking facilities for 210 trailers. Room is available for expansion of track facilities and parking area.

Reading Company Fleet consists of 600 trailers.

Port Reading, N.J., was included in the New York City Commercial Zone in November, 1970, by order of the Interstate Commerce Commission. This action placed Reading Company in a more competitive position with other TOFC ramps in the North Jersey area.

PIGGYBACK RAMP LOCATIONS:
Allentown, Pa.; Harrisburg, Pa.; Hershey, Pa.; Lancaster, Pa.; Port Reading, N.J.; Reading, Pa.; Swedeland, Pa.; and Wayne Junction (Philadelphia), Pa.

RICHMOND, FREDERICKSBURG AND POTOMAC RAILROAD

Richmond, Fredericksburg & Potomac Railroad Company
Broad Street Station
Richmond, Va.
TELEPHONE: (703) 257-3304
OFFICIALS:
J. J. Newbaner Jr. (*Assistant to President*)

R . Beadler (*Executive Assistant Staff*)
W. W. Young Sr. (*Special Representative*)
TOFC/COFC:
William E. Turner (*Vice-President, Traffic and Industrial development*)
TOFC Plans: 2, 2½, 3, 5.

The Railroad's Potomac yard piggyback facility was completed in early 1970 and equipped with a piggy packer loader. Further rail-highway facilities will be provided. Services are operated in conjunction with Penn Central and Seaboard Coast Line.

ST. LOUIS-SAN FRANCISCO RAILROAD

St. Louis-San Francisco Railroad,
906, Olive Street, St. Louis, Missouri 63101
OFFICIALS:
J. E. Gilliland (*Chairman of the Board*)
R. C. Grayson (*President and Chief Executive Officer*)
E. D. Grinnell, Jr. (*Vice-President, Traffic—Industrial Development*)
J. H. Brown (*Vice-President, Operations*)
H. B. Parker (*Vice-President—Controller*)
J. K. Beshears (*Vice-President, Personnel*)
J. E. McCullough (*Vice-President and General Counsel*)
G. M. Rayburn (*Vice-President—Secretary-Treasurer*)
P. E. Odom (*Vice-President—Management Services*)
J. W. Tipton (*Vice-President, Intermodal Services*)

New refrigerated trailer (also capable of heating).

GENERAL:
The "Frisco" operates 7,860 km (4,967 miles) of route in the mid-western and southern states from Kansas City and St. Louis in the north, to Dallas, Texas; Mobile, Alabama; and Pensacola, Florida, in the south.
Its central, in-between location makes it an important link in transcontinental and north-south routing.

FINANCIAL:
1970 operating revenue was $197·8 million ($187 million in 1969) and operating expenses $148 million ($136 million in 1969). Net income after fixed charges and tax was $13·1 million.

TRAFFIC:
Net ton miles (revenue) were 13,400 million (unchanged) and gross ton miles 30,390 million (31,059 million).

PIGGYBACK:
J. W. Tipton (*Vice-President, Intermodal Services*)
W. R. Eilers (*Manager TOFC Sales*)
Plans: 1, 2, 2¼, 2½, 3, 4, 5, 8 (mail) (express).
Piggyback traffic revenue in 1970 was $12·3 million, down some 4% from 1969.

In conjunction with Union Pacific and Seaboard Coast Line, "Frisco" operates, at reduced schedule time, through trains between Jacksonville, Florida and the Pacific Northwest.

Direct connection with the Atchison Topeka and Santa Fe at Floydada, Texas, also produces a competitive service between the Southeast, as well as the East and California points.

Ramp Locations:
Aberdeen, Miss.; Ada, Okla.; Altus, Okla.; Birmingham, Ala.; Blytheville, Ark.; Carthage Mo.; Chickasha Okla.; Clinton. Okla.; Crystal City, Mo.; Dallas (Irving), Tex.; Durant, Okla.; Enid, Okla.; Fayetteville,

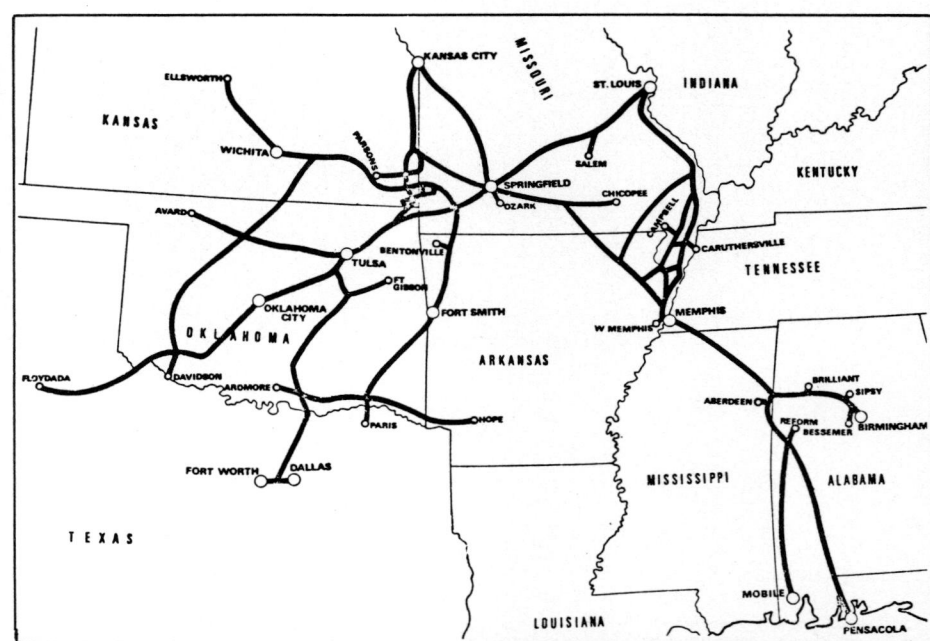

Ark.; Ft. Smith, Ark.; Ft. Worth, Tex.; Frisco City, Ala.; Henryetta, Okla.; Jonesboro, Ark.; Joplin, Mo.; Kansas City, Mo.; Lawton, Okla.; Memphis, Tenn.; Miami, Okla.; Mobile Ala.; Monett, Mo.; Muskogee Okla.; Neosho, Mo.; Oklahoma City, Okla.; Okmulgee, Okla.; Osceola, Ark.; Oswego, Kan.; Paris, Tex.; Parsons, Kan.; Pensacola, Fla.; Rogers, Ark.; St. Louis, Mo.; Sherman, Tex.; Sikeston, Mo.; Springdale, Ark.; Springfield, Mo.; Tulsa, Okla.; Tupelo, Miss.; Vinita, Okla.; West Plains, Mo.; Wichita, Kan.; Lamas, Mo.; Trumann, Ark.

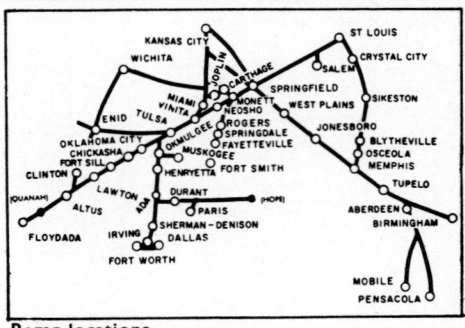

Ramp locations

SEABOARD COAST LINE RAILROAD COMPANY

Seaboard Coast Line Railroad Company,
500 Water Street,
Jacksonville, Fla. 32202

OFFICERS:
EXECUTIVE:
W. Thomas Rice (*Chairman of the Board, and Executive Officer*)
Prime F. Osborne, III (*President*)
J. R. Thorne (*Vice-President, Executive Department*)
J. A. Stanley, Jr. (*Vice-President and Comptroller*)
D. C. Hastings (*Vice-President, Operations*)
H. M. Emerson (*Vice-President, Freight Traffic*)
J. R. Getty (*Vice-President, Passenger Traffic*)
Erle J. Zoll, Jr. (*Vice-President and General Counsel*)
C. R. Yates (*Vice-President*)
L. G. Anderson (*Treasurer*)
F. J. Primosch (*Secretary, Assistant Vice-President and Assistant Treasurer*)
L. T. Oliver (*Administrative Assistant to President*)
Thomas Fuller (*Assistant to President*)
H. W. Martens (*Assistant to President*)
P. J. Lee (*Assistant to President*)
D. T. Martin (*Assistant Vice-President, Public Relations and Advertising*)
Dr. Adney K. Sutphin (*Chief Medical Director*)
C. E. Mervine, Jr. (*Vice-President, Personnel and Labour Relations*)
L. H. Scott, Jr. (*Assistant Vice-President, Systems and Information Services*)
OPERATING DEPARTMENT:
D. C. Hastings (*Vice-President, Operations*)
L. T. Andrews (*General Manager, Transportation*)
T. B. Hutcheson (*Assistant Vice-President, Engineering and M of W*)
M. W. Clark (*Chief Engineer*)
J. R. DePriest (*Superintendent Communications and Signals*)
R. D. Liggett (*Chief Engineer Communications and Signals*)
F. D. Sineath (*Chief of Motive Power*)
A. Keigs, Jr. (*Assistant Vice-President, Purchasing and Stores*)
J. W. Hawthorne (*Assistant Vice-President, Equipment*)

FREIGHT TRAFFIC DEPARTMENT:
H. M. Emerson (*Vice-President*)
Trailer Train Service:
J. W. Plant (*Assistant Vice-President*)
E. W. Thomas (*Director Trailer Train Service*)
Automobile Traffic:
R. L. Mott (*Assistant Vice-President*)

LINES AND TERROTORIES:
SLC was formed in 1968 by merging Seaboard Air Line and Atlantic Coast Railways. With 9,260 miles (14,902 kms) of route SLC constitutes the major railway systems of Florida and the states to the north.

FINANCIAL:
1970 operating revenue was $506 million ($21 million more than 1969) and 1970 operating expense was $384 millions ($18 million more than 1969). Net income after taxes, rents etc. was $37 million.

PIGGYBACK:
J. W. Plant (*Assistant Vice-President*)
Plans: 2, 2½, 3, 5, 4

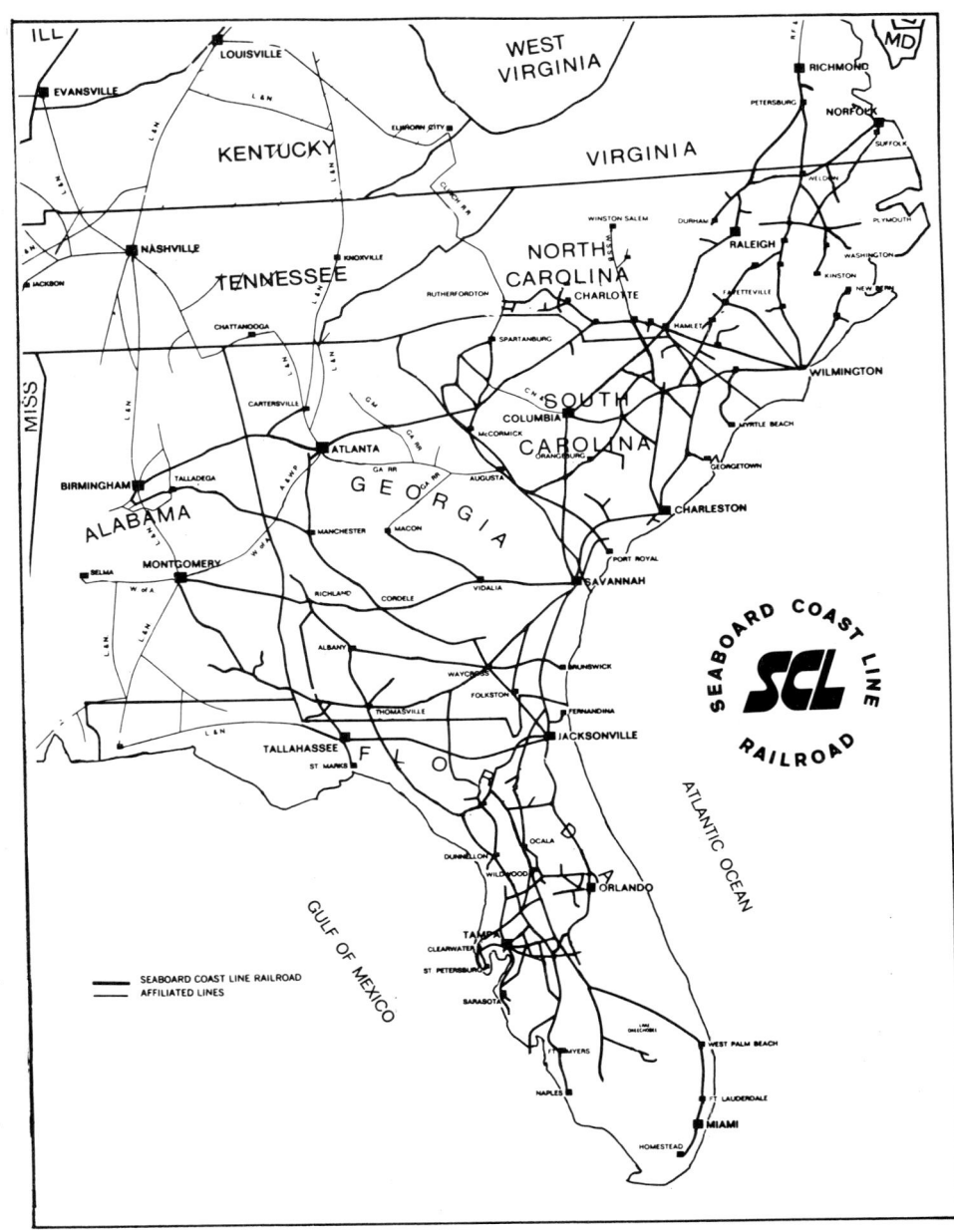

1970 Piggyback trailer traffic increased slightly with revenue 5·7% up to $35·4 million. Included is a substantial movement of containers through ports served by the railroad. Trailers owned exceeded 3,000.

RAMP LOCATIONS:
Alabama:
Birmingham, Dothan, Elba, Enterprise, Montgomery.

Florida:
Arcadia, Avon Park, Bartow, Bell, Bradenton, Brooksville, Clearwater, Clewiston, Dade City, Duda Ft. Lauderdale, Forest City, Fort Myers, Gainesville, Groveland, High Springs, Homestead, Immokalee, Jacksonville, Jasper, Lakeland, Lake Wales, Leesburg, Live Oak, Miami, Ocala, Orlando, Palatka, Plymouth, Pompano Beach, St. Petersburg, Sanford, Sarasota, Tallahassee, Tampa, Trenton, Umatilla, West Palm Beach, Winter Garden.

Georgia:
Albany, Americus Athens, Atlanta,
Augusta, Bainbridge, Brunswick, Cedartown, Columbus, Cordele, Dublin, Fitzgerald, Gainsville, Jesup, LaGrange, Macon, Manchester, Moultrie, Oglethorpe, Savannah, Thomasville, Tifton, Tucker, Valdosta, Vidalia, Waycross, Woodbine.

No. Carolina:
Aberdeen, Ahoskie, Charlotte, Durham, Fayetteville, Gastonia, Goldsboro, Greenville, Hamlet, Henderson, Jacksonville, Lowe, Maxton, Raleigh, Rocky Mount, Roanoke Rapids, Smithfield, Wilmington, Wilson.

So. Carolina:
Anderson, Barnwell, Camden, Charleston, Chester, Columbia, Denmark, Estill, Florence, Georgetown, Greenville, Greenwood, Hampton, Inness, Lobeco, Orangeburg, Port Royal, Spartanburg, Stono, Sumter.

Virginia:
Franklin, Jarratt, Portsmouth (Norfolk), Petersburg, Richmond, Suffolk.

SOO LINE RAILROAD

Soo Line Railroad Company
Soo Line Building
Minneapolis, Minnesota 55440
TELEPHONE: (612) 332-1261
OFFICERS:
Leonard H. Murray (*President*)
Joseph D. Bond (*Executive Vice-President*)
Thomas R. Klingel (*Executive Vice-President*)
Kenneth J. Sherwood (*Vice-President, Traffic*)
Fordyce W. Crouch (*Vice-President, Law*)
Thomas M. Beckley (*Vice-President, Staff*)
Robert L. Murlowski (*Vice-President, Accounting*)

GENERAL:

The Soo Line serves seven Upper Midwestern States: Minnesota, Wisconsin, North and South Dakota, Illinois, Michigan (Upper Peninsula) and Montana. Piggyback and Container traffic is handled through all major on-line points. On-line trailer or container location information is immediately available through Sales Offices or by direct telex inquiry to the Company's computer centre in Minneapolis.

FINANCIAL:

1970 revenues were up 7% over 1969 to a record high of $113 million. Net income posted a 9·5% gain to $6·1 million.

TRAFFIC:

Freight traffic throughout the year remained somewhat stable with a light increase in freight ton-miles. During 1970, the Soo Line handled 23,100,404 tons of revenue freight.

Container traffic on the Soo Line increased 300% over the previous year. Piggyback traffic was up 2%.

A. T. Johnson (*Manager of TOFC/COFC Sales*)

TOFC Plans: 1, 2, 2¼, 2½, 3, 4, 5, Mixture.

A new piggyback/container terminal facility is being constructed at Schiller Park, Illinois to serve the Chicago area.

The Soo Line offers connections for eastern and Pacific ports for both piggyback and container shipments, through direct interchange with all eastern roads at Chicago and western roads at Minneapolis; as well as

Soo Line Container Train.

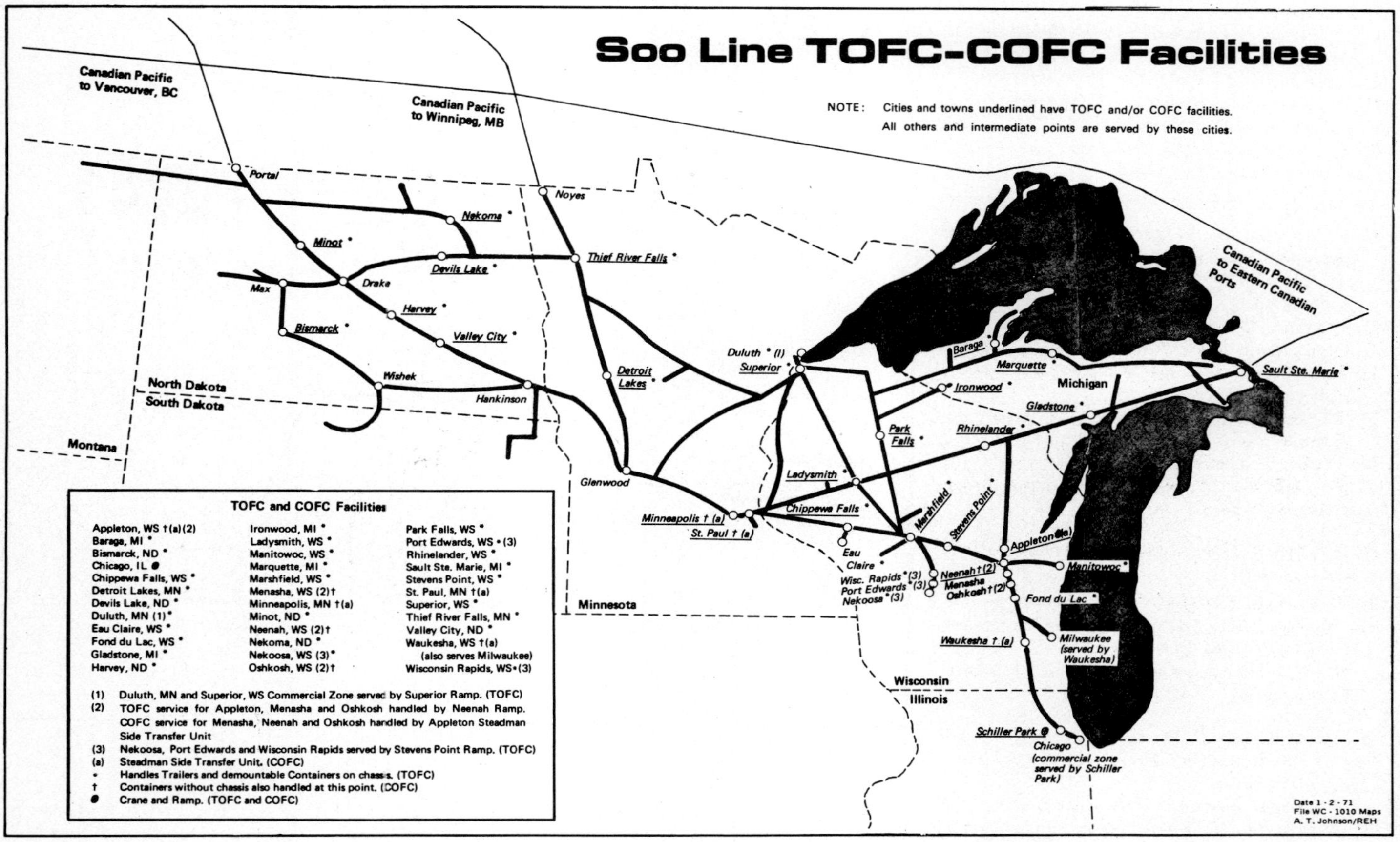

serving the Canadian ports in connection with the Canadian Pacific Railway Company. Container agreements are in effect with all major steamship companies.

Soo Line offers ramp facilities for trailers at 26 locations, container handling facilities utilising the Steadman Side Transfer System at 4 locations, and a combination crane/ramp facility to service Chicago.

Soo Line TOFC-COFC Facilities

NOTE: Cities and towns underlined have TOFC and/or COFC facilities.
All others and intermediate points are served by these cities.

Canadian Pacific to Vancouver, BC

Canadian Pacific to Winnipeg, MB

Canadian Pacific to Eastern Canadian Ports

Portal
Noyes
Nekoma
Minot
Thief River Falls
Devils Lake
Drake
Max
Harvey
Bismarck
Valley City
Wishek
North Dakota
South Dakota
Hankinson
Montana
Detroit Lakes
Duluth (1) Superior
Baraga
Marquette
Sault Ste. Marie
Ironwood
Michigan
Gladstone
Park Falls
Rhinelander
Glenwood
Ladysmith
Minneapolis † (a)
St. Paul † (a)
Chippewa Falls
Marshfield
Stevens Point
Appleton †(a)
Eau Claire
Wisc. Rapids (3)
Port Edwards (3)
Nekoosa (3)
Neenah †(2)
Menasha
Oshkosh †(2)
Manitowoc
Fond du Lac
Minnesota
Waukesha † (a)
Milwaukee (served by Waukesha)
Wisconsin
Illinois
Schiller Park
Chicago (commercial zone served by Schiller Park)

Date 1 - 2 - 71
File WC - 1010 Maps
A. T. Johnson/REH

TOFC and COFC Facilities

Appleton, WS †(a)(2)	Ironwood, MI *	Park Falls, WS *
Baraga, MI *	Ladysmith, WS *	Port Edwards, WS * (3)
Bismarck, ND *	Manitowoc, WS *	Rhinelander, WS *
Chicago, IL ⊘	Marquette, MI *	Sault Ste. Marie, MI *
Chippewa Falls, WS *	Marshfield, WS *	Stevens Point, WS *
Detroit Lakes, MN *	Menasha, WS (2)†	St. Paul, MN †(a)
Devils Lake, ND *	Minneapolis, MN †(a)	Superior, WS *
Duluth, MN (1) *	Minot, ND *	Thief River Falls, MN *
Eau Claire, WS *	Neenah, WS (2)†	Valley City, ND *
Fond du Lac, WS *	Nekoma, ND *	Waukesha, WS †(a)
Gladstone, MI *	Nekoosa, WS (3) *	(also serves Milwaukee)
Harvey, ND *	Oshkosh, WS (2)†	Wisconsin Rapids, WS*(3)

(1) Duluth, MN and Superior, WS Commercial Zone served by Superior Ramp. (TOFC)
(2) TOFC service for Appleton, Menasha and Oshkosh handled by Neenah Ramp. COFC service for Menasha, Neenah and Oshkosh handled by Appleton Steadman Side Transfer Unit
(3) Nekoosa, Port Edwards and Wisconsin Rapids served by Stevens Point Ramp. (TOFC)
(a) Steadman Side Transfer Unit. (COFC)
* Handles Trailers and demountable Containers on chassis. (TOFC)
† Containers without chassis also handled at this point. (COFC)
⊘ Crane and Ramp. (TOFC and COFC)

SOUTHERN RAILWAY SYSTEM

Southern Railway Company
PO Box 1808, Washington DC 20013
OFFICERS:
W. G. Clayton, Jr. (*President*)

L. S. Crane (*Executive Vice-President, Operations*)

R. S. Hamilton (*Executive Vice-President, Marketing and Planning*)

W. V. Burke (*Executive Vice-President, Sales and Public Affairs*)

J. H. McGlothlin (*Executive Vice-President, Law and Finance*)

G. S. Paul (*Executive Vice-President Administration*)

OPERATIONS:
L. S. Crane (*Executive Vice-President, Operations*)
H. R. Moore (*General Manager, Eastern Lines*)
E. B. Burwell (*General Manager, Western Lines*)
D. Eyler (*General Manager, Rail-Highway*)
R. A. Wharton (*Assistant Vice-President, Operations Planning*)
P. C. Shu (*Assistant Vice-President Security and Special Services*)
F. M. Kaylor (*Assistant Vice-President, Safety and Freight Claim Prevention*)
W. W. Simpson (*Vice-President, Engineering*)

C. E. Webb (*Assistant Vice-President, Engineering and Research*)

J. G. Moore (*Assistant Vice-President, Mechanical*)
R. A. Kelso (*Chief Engineer*)
N. C. Pace (*Assistant to Vice-President, Communications*)
J. T. Mattison Jr (*Assistant to Vice-President, Signal and Electrical*)
J. R. Tipton (*Assistant Vice-President, Stations and Terminals*)
MARKETING AND PLANNING:
R. S. Hamilton (*Executive Vice-President, Marketing and Planning*)

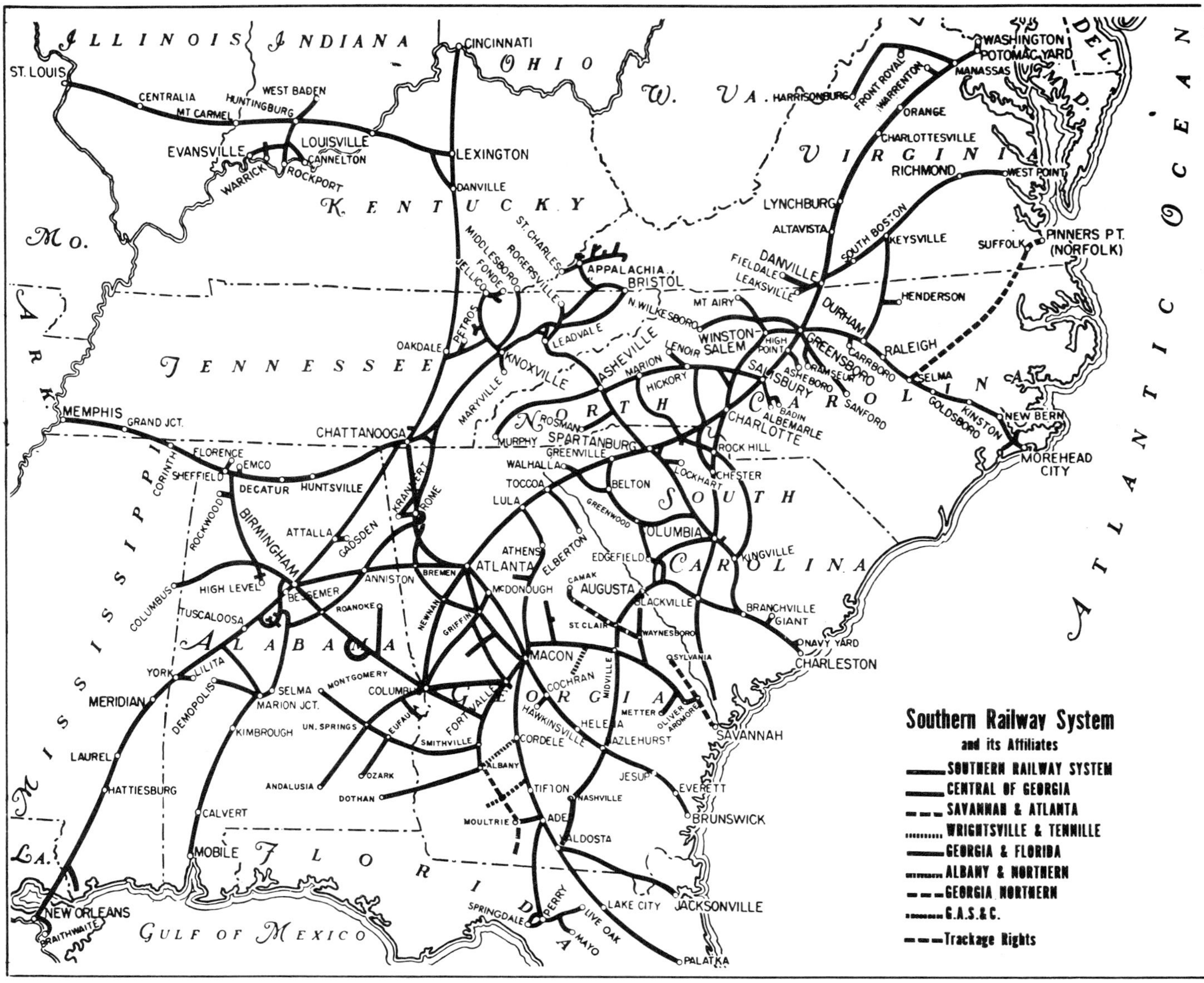

Southern Railway System
and its Affiliates

— SOUTHERN RAILWAY SYSTEM
— CENTRAL OF GEORGIA
–– SAVANNAH & ATLANTA
········· WRIGHTSVILLE & TENNILLE
— GEORGIA & FLORIDA
—·—·— ALBANY & NORTHERN
– – – GEORGIA NORTHERN
—··— G.A.S.&C.
– – –Trackage Rights

L. O. Tessier (*Assistant Vice-President, Marketing*)

P. H. Banner (*Assistant Vice-President, Market Research*)

E. A. Eyers (*Assistant Vice-President, Markets Management*)

J. P Duncan Jr. (*Director, Agri-Business Service*)

J. L. Townshend (*General Manager, Industrial Development*)

P. A. Dieffenbach (*Director, Corporate Planning*)

SALES AND PUBLIC AFFAIRS:
W. V. Burke (*Executive Vice-President, Sales and Public Affairs*)

S. S. Wilbanks (*Vice-President*)

E. L. Dearhart (*Assistant Vice-President Sales*)

W. F. Geeslin (*Assistant Vice-President Public Relations*)

H. C. Mauney (*Resident Vice-President New Orleans*)

G. E. Taylor (*Resident Vice-President, Birmingham*)

A. H. Douglas (*Resident Vice-President, Atlanta*)

LAW AND FINANCE:
J. H. McGlothlin (*Executive Vice-President, Law and Finance*)

K. A. Stoecker (*Vice-President, Finance*)

W. D. McLean (*Vice-President, Purchasing and Real Estate*)

J. A. Bistline (*Assistant Vice-President and General Counsel*)

A. B. McKinnon (*Vice-President, Law*)
Total route miles are 10,125 (16,304 km).

W. G. Handfield (*Assistant Vice-President, Taxation*)

ADMINISTRATION:
G. S. Paul (*Executive Vice-President, Administration*)
J. L. Jones (*Vice-President, Management Information Services*)
R. E. Loomis (*Assistant Vice-President, Labor Relations*)
R. D. Hedberg (*Assistant Vice-President, Personnel Administration*)

GENERAL:
Main lines of the Southern Company are in the States of Alabama, Georgia, North Carolina and South Carolina, with connections into Florida; New Orleans, Memphis, St. Louis, Cincinnati, and Washington DC.
Total route miles are 10,125 (16,304 km).

FINANCIAL:
1970 operating revenue $603 million ($569 million in 1969) operating expenses $436 million ($408 million in 1969).

Net income (after taxes) $56 million ($46 million in 1969).

TRAFFIC:
1970 revenue ton miles were 40,700 million, an increase of 1% from 40,200 million in 1969.

PIGGYBACK:
D. Eyler (*Director Rail-Highway Service*)
Plans: 2, 2½, 3, 5.

Fleet:
Fleet containers 756 trailers, 2,395 containers, 2,195 chassis and 58 bogies. 1969 purchases included 490 trailers, 600 containers (40 ft) and 50 drop frame vans.

SR rail-highway traffic continued to expand, by 8% in revenue, at a time when national figures were decreasing. To meet increased demand, rail-highway facilities were enlarged at Alexandria, Virginia, Charlotte, North Carolina, and Jacksonville, Florida. Enlargement of other existing facilities is under active study.

A new facility was opened at Calhoun, Tenn.

There is an ever-increasing volume of mail and express traffic but the largest single element of increase is in traffic formerly moved in private motor carrier service.
Location of facilities for handling trailers and ocntainers:
Albany, Ga.*; Alexandria, Va.; Anniston,

Containerized freight moving on the Southern Railway System.

Ala.; Asheville, N.C.; Athens, Tenn.; Atlanta, Ga.; Augusta, Ga.*; Birmingham, Ala.; Calhoun, Tenn.*; Charleston, C.S.*; Charlotte, N.C.; Chattanooga. Tenn.; Cincinnati, Ohio; Columbus, Ga.; Dalton, Ga.; Danville, Ky.; Danville, Va.*; E. St. Louis, Ill.; Greenville, Tenn.; Greensboro, N.C.; Greenville, C.S.; Hickory, N.C.; Holston, Tenn.; Jacksonville, Fla.; Knoxville, Tenn.; Lexington, Ky.*; Louisville, Ky.; Macon, Ga.;

Memphis, Tenn.; Meridian, Miss.; Mobile, Ala.; Morristown, Tenn.; New Orleans, La.; Norfolk, Va.*; Portsmouth, Va.; Savannah, Ga.; Spartanburg, S.C.; Spencer, N.C.; Tuscaloosa, Ala.*

Handles Trailers Only.

At the 31 locations handling containers in addition to trailers there are gantry cranes available, having capacities from 80,000 lb to 100,000 lb (36.288 kg to 45,360 kg).

SOUTHERN PACIFIC RAILROAD

Southern Pacific Company
One Market Street, San Francisco, Cal. 94105
TELEPHONE: DO2-1212
Southern Pacific Company is a holding company, whose principal asset is the Southern Pacific Transportation Co.

OFFICERS:
D. J. Russell (*Chairman*)
B. F. Biaggini (*President and Chief Executive Officer*)
John B. Reid (*Senior Vice-President*)
L. E. Hoyt (*Vice-President*)
D. K. McNear (*Vice-President*)
A. D. DeMoss (*Vice-President, Purchasing*)
Alan C. Furth (*Vice-President and General Counsel*)
W. M. Jaekle (*Vice-President, Engineering and Research*)
F. E. Kriebel (*Vice-President, Traffic*)

E. J. Larson (*Vice-President, Rates and Divisions*)
Robert J. McLean (*Vice-President and Treasurer*)
H. A. Nelson (*Vice-President and Controller*)
R. D. Spence (*Vice-President, Operations*)
A. E. Hill (*Secretary*)
C. A. Ball (*Assistant Vice-President, Labor Relations*)
P. V. Garin (*Assistant Vice-President, Research*)
M. A. McIntyre (*Assistant Vice-President, Personnel*)
C. E. Ward (*Assistant Vice-President, Traffic*)
GENERAL:
SP operates 13,718 miles (22,077 km) of railway route in the US west and southwest.

Western lines run from San Francisco, north to Portland, east to Ogden and south

to Los Angeles and thence east, parallel to the Mexican border, to Phoenix and El Paso.

SP also operates 27,209 miles (43,615 km) of highway truck routes, roughly following the routes of the railway lines; the Pacific Motor Trucking Company west of El Paso, Southern Pacific Transport in Texas and Louisiana, and Southwestern Transportation Company along Cotton Belt Lines from St. Louis, through Arkansas to the Gulf. B. R. Johnson is President of these subsidiaries.

FINANCIAL:
1970 operating revenue was $1,055 million (down from $1,073 million in 1969) and operating expenses were $828 million (up from $804 million).

Net income was $78 million ($14 million down).

TRAFFIC:

Revenue tons of freight was down to 136. million (from 140 million) and ton miles 74,115 million from 75,500 million.

Main increases were in farm products, food, paper and pulp, chemicals and ores and fuels.

PIGGYBACK:

T. A. Fante (*General Manager, TCF Service*)

Plans: 1, 2, 2½, 3, 4, 5.

The SP trucking subsidiaries operated over 27,093 miles (43,515 km) of route: had gross 1970 revenues of $92·8 million a decline of $3·2 million on 1969.

Income before tax decreased to $2·2 million from $3·3 million.

Capital expenditures of $8 million in 1971 include 600 new units of trucking and automotive equipment. At the end of 1970 the trucking companies owned 8,141 units of highway equipment.

Total *trailers* 4,394, including 242 refrigerated vans, over 1,000 PFC mechanical refrigeration and many dry vans.

Loading Ramps:

Loading ramps are located at more than 80 cities.

Albany, Ore.; Austin, Tex.; Avondale, La.; Bakersfield, Calif.; Beaumont, Tex.; Brooklyn, Ore.; Brownsville, Tex.; Chico, Calif.; Colton, Calif.; Coos Bay, Ore.; Corpus Christi, Tex.; Crowley, La.; Dallas. Tex.; Del Rio, Tex.; East Bernard, Tex.; Edinburg, Tex.; El Campo, Tex.; El Centro, Calif.; El Paso, Tex.; Ennis, Tex.; Eugene, Ore.; Eunice, La.; Flatonia, Tex.; Fr. Worth, Tex.; Fresno, Calif.; Galveston, Tex.; Gregory, Tex.; Guadalupe, Calif.; Harlingen, Tex.; Hearne, Tex.; Houston, Tex.; Indio, Calif.; Jennings, La.; Klamath Falls, Ore.; Lafayette, La.; Lake Charles. La.; Livingston, Tex.; Los Angeles, Calif.; Lufkin, Tex.; McAllen, Tex.; Mathis, Tex.; Miller, Tex.; New Orleans, La.; Nogales, Ariz.; Nome, Tex.; Oakland, Calif.; Ogden, Utah.; Opelousas, La.; Oxnard, Calif.; Paris, Tex.; Phoenix, Ariz.; Plano, Tex.; Port Arthur, Tex.; Portland, Ore.; Port Lavaca, Tex.; Raymer, Calif.; Rayne, La.; Redding, Calif.; Reno, Nev.; Roseburg, Ore.; Roseville, Calif.; Sacarmento, Calif.; Salem, Ore.; Salinas, Calif.; San Antonio, Tex.; San Diego, Calif.; San Francisco, Calif.; San Jose, Calif.; San Luis Obispo, Calif.; Santa Barbara, Calif.; Shreveport, La.; Sparks, Nev.; Stockton, Calif.; Tucson, Ariz.; Victoria, Tex.; Waco. Tex.; Welsh, La.; Wharton, Tex.; Yuma, Ariz.;

New rail-truck terminals were added at Benicia, Calif. and Dallas, Tex.

Lifting equipment consists of Piggypackers at Los Angeles, Oakland, St. Louis and Houston and gantry types at other locations.

CONTAINERS:

Services and Destinations:

Containers move daily in expedited Piggyback trains and trans-continental manifest trains, on 85 ft and 89 ft cars as well as sets of 2 articulated 52 ft 6 in cars.

One prototype, 319-foot-long articulated container car with a payload capacity of 1·1 million pounds was developed and placed in service between San Francisco and Los Angeles. Tie-down systems are adjustable to accommodate loadings of 20, 24, 27, 30, 35 and 40 foot containers.

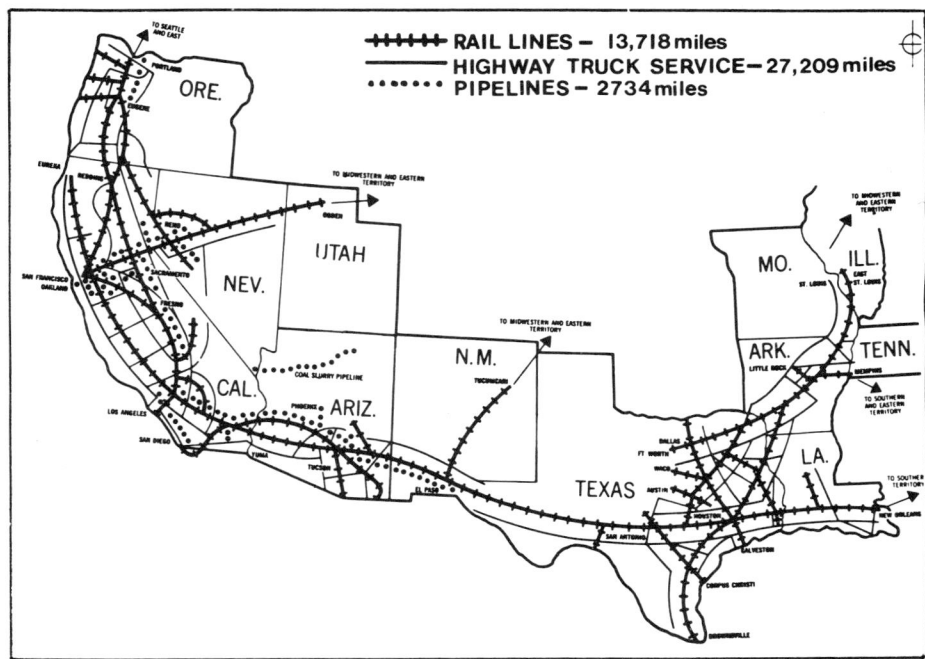

RAIL LINES – 13,718 miles
HIGHWAY TRUCK SERVICE – 27,209 miles
PIPELINES – 2734 miles

Piggy Packers helped move over a quarter million trailers and containers in 1970. They move a 45-ton trailer on or off a flat car in just 90 seconds.

CONTAINERS OWNED:

Dry 20 40 × 8 × 8·5 'PMT'

Dry 75 24 × 8 × 8·5 'SPUU'

The great majority of containers in rail-water carrier intermodal service to and from points in the United States are furnished by water carriers or container leasing companies on a per diem charge basis.

Container Terminals:

Portland, Oregon; San Francisco, California; Oakland, California; Wilmington Terminal Island, Los Angeles Harbour, California; Long Beach, California; Houston, Texas; New Orleans, La; San Diego, California.

These connect with all US and foreign flag ocean carriers calling at Pacific Coast and Gulf ports. They participate in routes with all trans-continental rail carriers.

Scheduled National Services:

Between United States and Hawaii through Pacific Coast ports.

Scheduled International Services:

Between United States and Japan, Hong Kong, Australia, Singapore and other Far Eastern ports, as well as Europe.

Planned International Services:

Land-Bridge movement—From Far East ports to Pacific Coast thence rail to Atlantic Coast and by ship to Europe.

Serial numbers allocated: 263,000 through 263,074.

Serial numbers reserved but not yet allocated: 263,075 through 263,999.

UNION PACIFIC RAILROAD COMPANY

Union Pacific Corporation

EXECUTIVE OFFICES:
345 Park Avenue, New York,
New York 10002

GENERAL OFFICERS:
E. R. Harriman (*Honorary Chairman, Board of Directors*)

F. E. Barnett (*Chairman, Board of Directors and Chief Executive Officer*)

J. H. Evans (*President*)

TRANSPORTATION DIVISION:
1416 Dodge Street
Omaha, Nebraska 68102

E. H. Bailey (*President*)

J. C. Kenefick (*Chief Executive Officer*)

R. F. Pettigrew (*Vice-President, Traffic*)

G. L. Farr (*Vice-President, Labour Relations*)

R. M. Brown (*Chief Engineer*)

GENERAL:

The Union Pacific operates an average of 9,473 miles (15,247 km) of route. The system extends from Council Bluffs, Iowa and Kansas City, Missouri in the east, to the Pacific Coast ports including Portland, Oregon, Seattle, Washington and Los Angeles areas.

Railway operations of the Union Pacific come under the control of the company's transportation division; this is the major division, the other two being the natural resources division (oil and gas operations) and the land division (real estate and indus-

Piggyback handling at Seattle, Washington.

Ocean-going containers used in Thrutainer service of Universal Carloading and Distributing Co., Inc. are packed at Chicago terminal for shipment through New York.

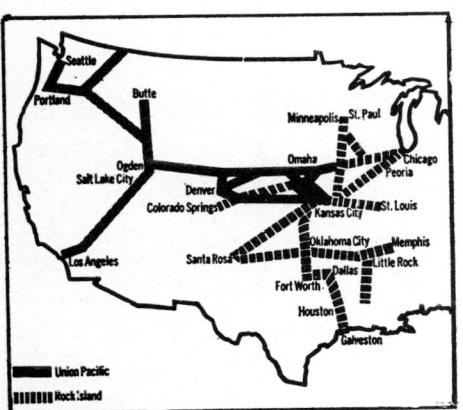

Ramp locations

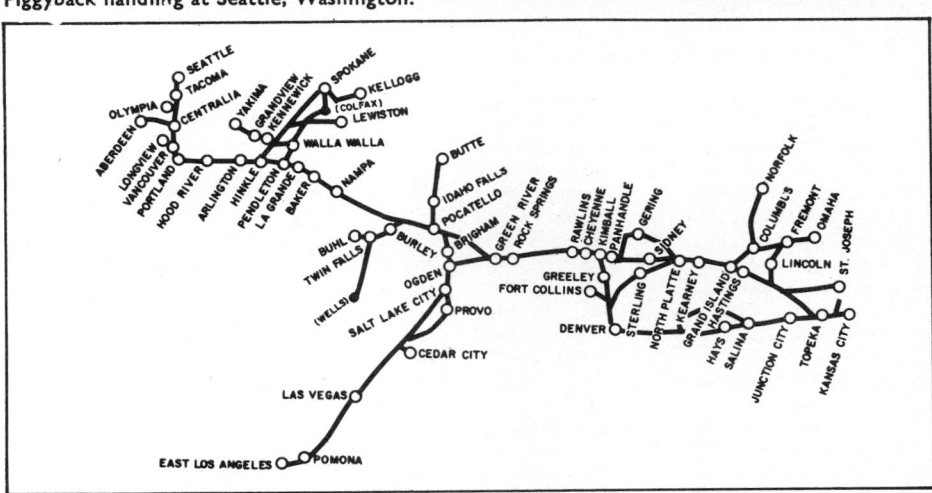

trial development).

The Union Pacific has a reciprocal arrangement with other railroads to avoid breaking up trains and switching at intermediate points.

Pacific Fruit Express Company, a partially owned subsidiary of Union Pacific, has a fleet of 3,100 mechanically refrigerated 12·2 m (40 ft) highway trailers to meet the demands of growing piggyback business. Additionally, Union Pacific owns 1,800 dry trailers of various types plus several hundred of various types under lease. Flat cars of 27·1 m (89 ft) are used for transportation of these vehicles.

FINANCIAL:

Union Pacific freight revenues for 1970 were $630 million, an increase of $43 million over the 1969 figures. Net income for 1970 was $75 million ($78 million in 1969).

TRAFFIC:

Freight traffic: 71 million tons revenue freight and 47,574 million ton miles, both about the same as 1969.

Trailer/container traffic increased about 10%.

PIGGYBACK AND CONTAINERS:

C. C. Larkin (*Manager, Trailer Container Operations*)

Container Handling Equipment:

Gantry cranes equipped with spreaders to handle 20 ft and 24 ft marine containers are located at Kansas City, Denver and Salt Lake City. At East Los Angeles, the yard is equipped with two 40 ton straddle cranes. At Seattle, the trailer/container yard is equipped with a 45 ton sideloader (piggypacker). The straddle cranes and piggypacker are capable of top or bottom lifting trailers or containers of lengths of 20 to 40 ft.

To handle the growing volume of import-export traffic, as well as domestic piggyback traffic, major trailer/container facilities are being constructed at Denver, Salt Lake City and Seattle.

Piggypacker units of 45-ton capacity were acquired for both Seattle and Denver. They are capable of top lifting containers 20 feet to 40 feet in length, and bottom lifting trailers up to 45 feet in length.

Additional trailers with load restraining devices, both DF and Aeroquip were obtained.

The Seattle TOFC/COFC Yard was enlarged and modernised. A new TOFC/COFC Centre at Denver is expected to be completed and in operation by July, 1971.

Traffic—Trailers and Containers:

In 1970 UP carried 100,000 trailer/containers.

Fleet—Trailers and Containers:

UP owns 75 containers, 940 refrigerated flexivans and 1,840 trailers.

The new container handling concept, developed by Union Pacific, of positioning two containers aboard a flat car with ample space in the centre for either manual or fork lift loading has enabled the railroad to extend container service to cities where lifting apparatus is not available.

Union Pacific trainload of containers passes over the Rockies en route to the Mid-West from Los Angeles.

UNITED STATES OF AMERICA
STATE SIZE AND WEIGHT LIMITS

STATE		SIZE RESTRICTIONS Width (Inches)	Height (Feet)	LENGTH (feet) Single Unit	Trailer	Tractor Semi-Trailer	Other Combinations	Number of Trailers (Semi-Trailer—½)	Minimum tandem Axle Spacing	Pounds Per Inch of Tire Width	Per Axle (1000 lb.)	Tandem Axles 4 feet apart (1000 lb.)	GROSS WEIGHT LIMITS (In thousands of pounds) pneumatic tires only 2-Axle Single Unit	3-Axle Single Unit	2-Axle Tractor 1-Axle Semi-Tr.	2-Axle Tractor 2-Axle Semi-Tr.	3-Axle Tractor 2-Axle Semi-Tr.	Maximum allowable gross weight
ALABAMA	A	96	13½	40	HI NR	55	NP	½	40	NS	18	36	36	54	54	72	73.2	73.2
ALASKA	C	96	13½	40	40	60	65	2	42	500	20	34	40	54	60	74	85	100
ARIZONA	A	96	13½	40	H 40	65	65	1½	40	NS	18	32	36	50	54	68	76.8	76.8
ARKANSAS	C	96	13½	40	NR	55	65	NR	40	NS	18	32	30	44	48	62	73.2	73.2
CALIFORNIA	A	96	14	40	D 40	60	65	NR	NS	NS	18	32	36	50	54	68	76.8	76.8
COLORADO	B	F 96	N 13½	D 35	NR	N 65	N 65	2	40	NR	18	36	30	46	54	66	73.6	73.6
CONNECTICUT	C	102	13½	55	HI 40	55	NP	½	NS	600	22.4	36	32	53.8	53.8	67.4	73	73
DELAWARE	A	96	13½	40	D 40	J 55	65	1½	48	700	20	36	30	65	48	66	73.2	73.2
DIST. OF COLUMBIA	A	96	12½	40	NR	50	50	1 or ½	40	NS	22	38	44	60	66	70	70	70
FLORIDA	A	96	13½	G 40	H 35	55	55	1 or ½	40	NS	20	40	40	60	60	66.6	66.6	66.6
GEORGIA	C	96	13½	55	NR	55	55	NR	40	NR	20.3	40.6	40.6	61	61	73.2	73.2	73.2
HAWAII	B	108	13	40	NR	55	65	1½	42	—	24	32	48	54	54	65	73.2	73.2
IDAHO	A	96	14	35	NR	J 60	65	1½	NS	800	18	32	36	50	54	68	76.8	76.8
ILLINOIS	C	96	13½	42	42	J 55	N 65	1½	40	NS	18	32	36	50	50	64	73.2	73.2
INDIANA	C	96	13½	D 36	NR	J 55	65	2	40	800	18	32	36	50	54	68	72	72
IOWA	A	96	13½	D 35	H 35	J 55	J 60	1½	40	NR	18	32	36	50	54	68	72.6	72.6
KANSAS	A	96	13½	42½	42½	J 55	65	NR	40	NR	18	32	36	50	54	68	73.2	73.2
KENTUCKY	C	96	N 13½	N 35	I NR	N 55	PN 65	½	42	600	18	N 32	N 36	N 50	N 54	N 68	N 73.2	N 73.2
LOUISIANA	C	96	13½	D 35	NR	60	65	1 or ½	40	450	18	32	E 18	E 32	E 36	E 50	E 64	E 68
MAINE	A	96L 102	13½	55	NR	55	55	1 or ½	48	600	22	32L 36	32	51.8	51.8	66.3	73.2	73.2
MARYLAND	A	F 96	13½	55	NR	55	N 65	NR	NS	NS	22.4	40	44.8	55	55	65	73.2	73.2
MASSACHUSETTS	A	96	13½	35	HI 33	55	I NP	½	NS	800	22.4	36	44.8	58.4	60	73	73	73
MICHIGAN	C	96	13½	D 35	NR	J 55	N 65	1½	42	—	18	N 32	36	N 50	54	N 68	N 73.2	M
MINNESOTA	A	96	13½	40	40	55	55	1 or ½	40	NR	18	32	36	54	54	64	73.2	73.2
MISSISSIPPI	A	96	13½	D 35	NR	55	55	1 or ½	40	Table	18	N 32	N 36	N 50	N 46	N 60	N 73.2	N 73.2
MISSOURI	A	96	13½	40	NR	J 55	N 65	NR	40	NR	18	32	36	50	54	68	73.2	73.2
MONTANA	A	96	13½	D 35	NR	60	P 65	1 or ½	40	NS	18	32	36	50	54	68	76.8	76.8
NEBRASKA	A	96	13½	40	H 40	60	65	2	40	NR	18	32	36	50	54	68	71.1	71.1
NEVADA	A	96	NR	40	NR	70	70	NR	42	NS	18	32	36	50	54	68	76.8	76.8
NEW HAMPSHIRE	A	96	D 13½	35	NR	55	55	NR	NS	600	22.4	36	33.4	47.5L 55	52.8	66.4	73.2	73.2

| STATE | | SIZE RESTRICTIONS | | | | | | Number of Trailers (Semi-Trailer—½) | Minimum Tandem Axle Spacing | Pounds Per Inch of Tire Width | Per Axle (1000 lb.) | Tandem Axles 4 feet apart (1000 lb.) | GROSS WEIGHT LIMITS (In thousands of pounds) pneumatic tires only | | | | | |
| | | Width (Inches) | Height (Feet) | LENGTH (feet) | | | | | | | | | 2-Axle Single Unit | 3-Axle Single Unit | 2-Axle Tractor 1-Axle Semi-Tr. | 2-Axle Tractor 2-Axle Semi-Tr. | 3-Axle Tractor 2-Axle Semi-Tr. | Maximum allowable gross weight |
				Single Unit	Trailer	Tractor Semi-Trailer	Other Combinations											
NEW JERSEY	C	96	13½	35	35 H	55	55	2	40	800	22.4	32	22.4 E	32 E	44.8 E	73.2	73.2	73.2
NEW MEXICO	A	96	13½	40	NR	65	65	1½	40	600	21.6	34.3	43.2	55.9	64.8	77.5	86.4	86.4
NEW YORK	B	96	13½	35 D	35 H	55	55	1 or ½	46	800	22.4	36	44.8	58.4	67.2	71	71	71
NORTH CAROLINA	C	96	13½	35 D	NR	55	55	1 or ½	48	600	18	36	30	47.5	47.5	64	70	73.2
NORTH DAKOTA	B	96	13½	40 G	NR	60	65 N	1½	40	550	18	32	36	50	54	64	64	64
OHIO	B	96	13½	40	40 H	55	65	NR	NS	650	19	32	38	51	57	70	75.8	78
OKLAHOMA	A	96	13½	40 D	NR	55	65	1½	40	650	18	32	18 E	32 E	36 E	50 E	73.2	73.2
OREGON	A	96	13½	35	35	50	65 N	1 or ½	40	550	20 / 18L	34 / 32L	36	50	36 E	50 E	76 N	76 N
PENNSYLVANIA	C	96	13½	35 D	40	55	55	1 or ½	36	800	22.4	36	33	47	50	60	71.1	71.1
RHODE ISLAND	C	102	13½	40	40 H	55	55	1 or ½	40	NS	22.4	NS	36	44	53.8	67.4	73.2	73.2
SOUTH CAROLINA	C	96	13½	40 G	NR	55 J	55	1 or ½	40	NR	20	32L / 36	35	46	50	65	73.2	73.2
SOUTH DAKOTA	A	96	13½	35 D	NR	65 O	65 O	1 or ½	40	600	18	32	36	50	54	68	73.2	73.2
TENNESSEE	C	96	13½	40	NR I	55	55	½	40	NS	18	32	36	50	48	62	73.2	73.2
TEXAS	A	96	13½	40	40	55	65	NR	40	650	18	32	36	50	54	68	72	72
UTAH	A	96	14	45	45	60	60	NR	40	NS	18	33	36	51	54	69	79.9	79.9
VERMONT	A	96	13½	55	NR	55	55	1 or ½	48	600	22.4	36	30L / 44.8	40L / 55	50L / 67.2	60L / 73.2	60L / 73.2	60L / 73.2
VIRGINIA	A	96	13½	35 D	NR	55	55	1 or ½	40	650	18	32	36	50	54	68	70	70
WASHINGTON	A	96	13½ K	35	40	60 O	65	1½	42	550	18	32	28	36	46	60	68	72
WEST VIRGINIA	A	96	13½ NK	40 G	NR	55 N	55 N	1 or ½	40	NR	18	32	36	50	54	70 N	70 N	70 N
WISCONSIN	A	96 F	13½	35 D	35	55	55	1 or ½	42	NS	18	32	36	50	54	68	73	73
WYOMING	A	96	13½	50	NR	65 J	65	2	40	NS	18	32	36	50	54	68	73.9	73.9

Key to Symbols—Footnotes

A. Gross weight determined by table of axle spacing and/or sum of axle weight limits

B. Gross weight determined by bridge formula.

C. Weight limits fixed by state law

D. Buses permitted length of 40 ft in Colorado, Indiana, Iowa, Michigan, Montana, New Hampshire, Pennsylvania, South Dakota, Virginia, Wisconsin, Louisiana, Mississippi, North Carolina, New York; buses permitted 45 ft in Oklahoma, 42 ft in Delaware, 60 ft for articulated buses in California.

E. Plus weight on front axle.

F. Bus width 102 in Colorado, 104 in Wisconsin.

G. Vehicles over 35 ft in length, except buses, must have 3 axles in Florida, South Carolina; vehicles over 35 ft including buses, must have 3 axles in North Dakota and West Virginia.

H. Semi-trailer length not restricted; 3 axle trailers allowed 40 ft in Florida.

I. Full trailers not permitted in Alabama, Connecticut, Kentucky; restricted to 3,000 lbs and 33 ft length in Massachusetts, 3,500 lbs in Tennessee.

J. Auto transporter length 60 ft in Delaware, Illinois (65 ft on 4-lane highways), Indiana, Iowa (also double bottoms), Kansas, Montana, Michigan, South Carolina; 70 ft in Wyoming; 65 ft in Idaho on designated highways; Double bottoms 65 ft in Michigan on designated highways.

K. Auto transporter height 13·5 ft in West Virginia; 14 ft in Washington.

L. Limit on Interstate System only.

M. Subject only to axle limits.

N. On designated highways.

O. 65 ft with load

NP—Not Permitted.

NR—Not Restricted.

NS—Not Specified

CARIBBEAN
BAHAMAS
FREEPORT

Grand Bahama Port Authority Ltd
Harbour Division, PO Box F 2465, Freeport
Bahamas
TELEPHONE: 4-1333
TELEGRAMS: Portauth Harbour
OFFICIALS:
Keith S. Gonsalues (*Chairman*)
John T. Kimball (*President*)
Capt. R. Nalecx-Tyminski, OBE, DSC, VM,
KW, SQA, PN (*Port Director*)
A. R. Hawkins (*Assistant Port Director*)
M. C. Horsfall (*Assistant Port Director Adm*)
ROLL-ON/ROLL-OFF FACILITIES:
Basin No. 2. This berth is capable of accepting
vessels of 107·6 m (353 ft) length, 18 m (59 ft)
beam and 4·42 m (14·5 ft) draught. The shore
ramp is not adjustable and there is adequate
parking space for vehicles. It is used by the
Tropical Shipping Co. Ltd.

Basin No. 1 (N.E.) This berth can accept
vessels up to 137 m (450 ft) in length, 18·9 m
(62 ft) beam and 7·92 m (26 ft) draught. The
shore ramp is not adjustable and there is
adequate parking space.

Basin No. 1 (S.W.). This berth can accept
the same size vessels as the NE Berth and is
fitted with an adjustable ramp. It is used
exclusively by Universal Alco Ltd.
ROLL-ON/ROLL-OFF SERVICES:

Tropical Shipping Company provide five
sailings weekly to West Palm Beach, Florida
with various vessels with capacities of up to
16 40 ft trailers. Universal Alco Ltd.
provide three sailings weekly to Miami with
one vessel having a capacity of 33 40 ft
trailers.
GENERAL

Container traffic other than those carried
on the roll-on/roll-off services is occasional
but there are indications that this may increase in the future. The Main Wharf is
capable of berthing vessels up to 204·2 m
(670 ft) in length with a draught of 8·23 m
(27 ft). A Hyster Fork Truck of 62,000 lbs
lifting capacity with an attachment for 20
ft container handling is available.
CUSTOMS FACILITIES:

Vans and trailers with goods for one
consignee are cleared and released for
delivery. If goods are carried for several

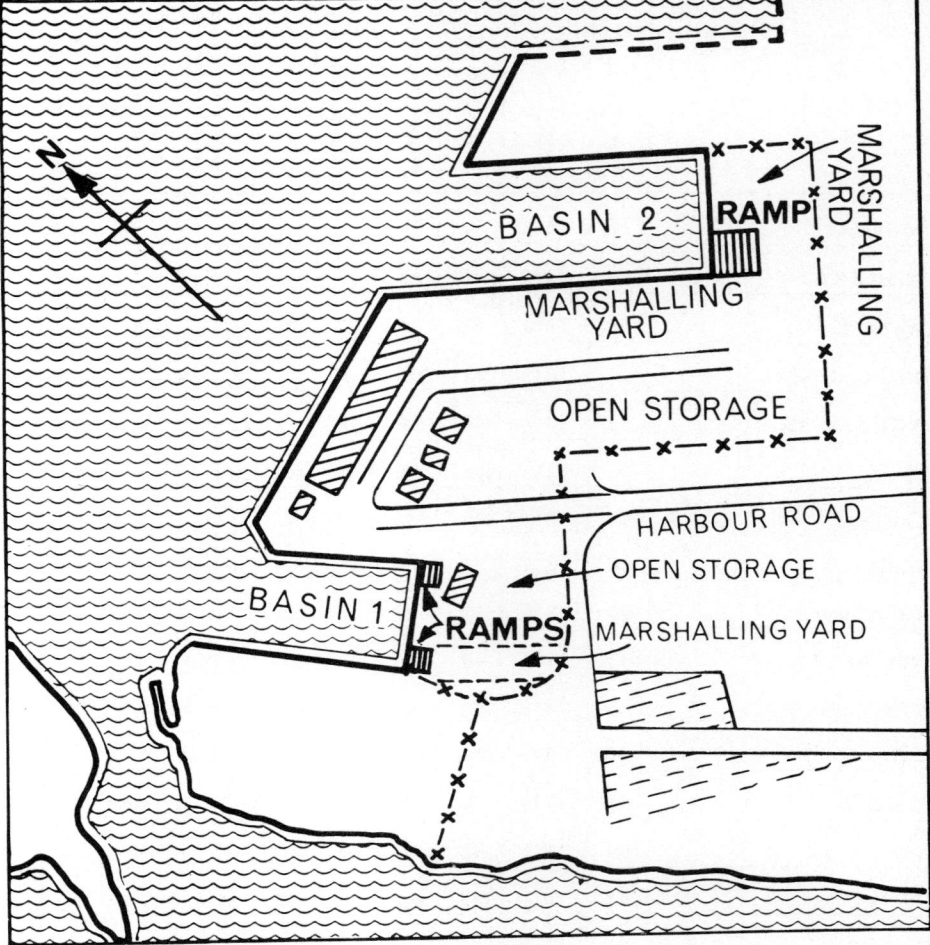

consignees trailers must be discharged into
the transit shed before delivery.
PRINCIPAL FORWARDING COMPANIES:
E. H. Mundy & Co (*Bahamas*) Ltd
PO Box F 2492, Freeport, Bahamas
Tel: 4-1111
Darvikson Bahamas Ltd
(Customs Brokers)

PO Box F 553, Freeport, Bahamas
Tel: 2-5195
United Shipping Co Ltd
PO Box F 2552
Freeport, Bahamas
Tel: 4-1010
STORAGE AND STEVEDORE COMPANY:
Grand Bahama Port Authority Ltd

JAMAICA
KINGSTON

Port of Kingston
CONTAINER FACILITIES:
Newport West Terminal:
Operator:
Kingston Wharves Ltd.

Newport West, Kingston, Jamaica
This facility consists of an open quay
with a total length of 914 m (3,000 ft) with
a depth alongside of 10·67 m (35 ft) and a
total back up area of 16·2 hectares (40 acres).

Equipment consists of a mobile crane with a
capacity of 21·5 tons at 15·24 m (50 ft). A
container gantry crane is planned for installation in the future; this will serve a 274·3 m
(900 ft) section of the quay.

PUERTO RICO
SAN JUAN

Puerto Rico Ports Authority
GPO Box 2829
San Juàn, Puerto Rico 00936
TELEPHONE:
723-2260, 724-3262 (Operating Division)
OFFICIALS:
César S. Canals (*Executive Director*)
Francisco Jiménez-Mercado (*Assistant Execu-
tive Director*)

América Lameiro de Irizarry (*Secretary and
Counsel*)
José Ysern de la Cruz (*Chief, Maritime Dept.*)
José A. Reinés (*Special Assistant for Maritime
Affairs*)
CONTAINER FACILITIES:
Puerto Nuevo Berths, C, D, E, F
This facility, operated by Sea-Land Ser-
vices Inc, has a length of 731·5 m (2,400 ft).

Four 25 ton Paceco container gantry cranes
operate on a quay length of 366 m (1,200 ft)
with 9·14 m (30 ft) of water alongside.
There is ample space for container marshalling
and storage.
Isla Grande-San Antonio Channel
This is the Seatrain Line facility; it has a
quay length of 182·9 m (600 ft) and is
equipped with container gantry crane and a

125 t 1 crane originally designed for rail car handling. There is a wide apron and considerable space for both container and railcar marshalling.

CONTAINER SERVICES:
Sea-Land of Puerto Rico Inc.
   P.O. Box 2648, San Juan PR 00903
   Telephone: 783-1414
Seatrain Lines Inc.
   P.O. Box 4552, San Juan PR 00905
   Telephone: 722-5200
ROLL-ON SERVICES:
Transamerican Trailer Transport Inc.
   P.O. Box 3928, San Juan, PR 00936
   Telephone: 783-8686
Roll-on Services—Tug and Barge
Berwind Lines Inc.
   P.O. Box 4975, San Juan, PR 00903
   Telephone: 724-6500
TMT Trailer Ferry Inc
   P.O. Box 3921, San Juan, PR 00904
   Telephone: 725-5600

San Juan – Isla Grande Terminal.

San Juan – Puerto Nuevo Terminal.

TRINIDAD
PORT OF SPAIN

Port of Spain, Trinidad
CONTAINER FACILITIES:
Operator:
Trinidad & Tobago Port Contractors Ltd.

A 182·9 m (600 ft) length of general cargo berth with a back up area of 3·64 hectares (9 acres) is used for container handling; there is a depth of water of 9·75 m (32 ft). A 60 ton floating crane is used for handling.

It is proposed to increase the depth alongside to 10·67 m (35 ft) and to increase the back up area by 1·21 hectares (3 acres).

VIRGIN ISLANDS
ST. THOMAS

Department of Commerce, St. Thomas
Marine Division, Box 36
St. Thomas, Virgin Islands, W.I. 008u-
TELEPHONE: 774-2333 and 774-2250

GENERAL:
No special facilities exist to handle containers
but there are roll-on/roll-off facilities used by

Brewin Lines and SACAL, Inc. Both Lines
ship to the USA, Puerto Rico and the Islands.
Both Companies route cargo through Puerto
Rico where it is trans-shipped to St. Thomas
by barge in the case of Brewin Lines and ship
in the case of SACAL.

OPERATORS:

Brewin Lines, Inc.
PO Box 3158,
St. Thomas, V.I.
Capt. John Wimmers (*Terminal Manager*)
SACAL, Inc.
PO Box 2218,
St. Thomas, V.I.
George N. Noland (*General Manager*)

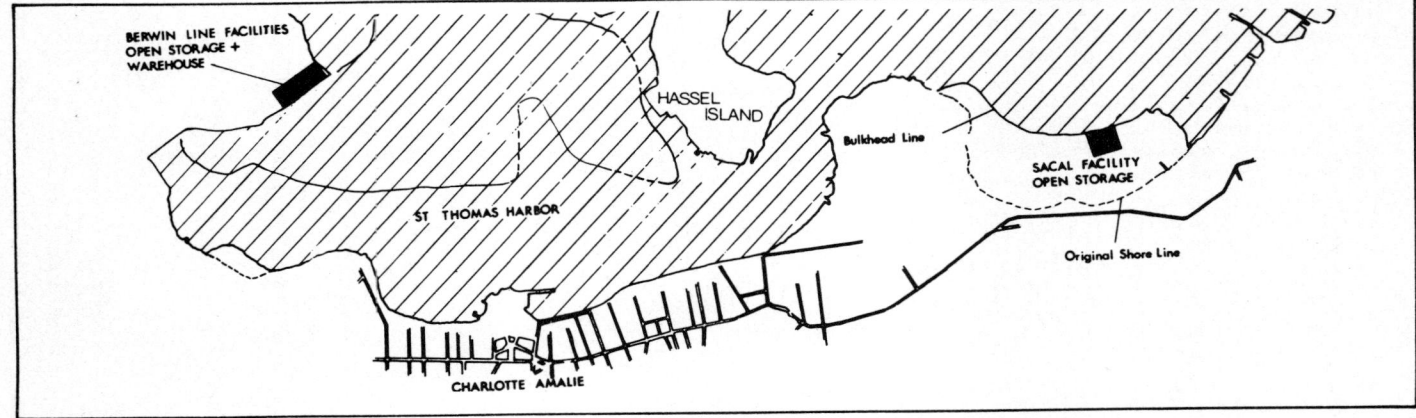

CENTRAL AND SOUTH AMERICA

ARGENTINE

Bahia Blanca
Situated about 550 miles south of Buenos
Aires, the port district of Bahia Blanca is
the outlet for the majority of the grain grown
in the southern parts of the provinces of
Buenos Aires and La Pampa. The major port
in the district is Ingeniero White.

CONTAINER DEVELOPMENT:

A plan has been drawn up to develop two
berths on a length of marginal wharf. The
facility will be equipped with two 30 ton
container gantry cranes with an adequate

back up area which will include covered space
for consolidation and warehousing activities
and a container park and marshalling area
equipped with reefer points. Further handling
equipment will be provided as the traffic
builds up.
There will be road and rail access.

BRAZIL
SANTOS

Companhia Docas de Santos (SDC)
São Paulo, Brazil
GENERAL
The port of Santos serves the whole of the
country but is of greatest use to the States of
São Paulo and Mato Grosso, the North of
Paraná, the South East of Minas Berais and
a large part of Goiás.
There are no regular fully cellular container
services at present and containers are carried
in conventional vessels.

CONTAINER TRAFFIC:
1969 Inwards 1,290 units
Outwards 1,315 units
Containers varied in size but the majority
were of the ISO 20 ft type.

TERMINAL WORKING HOURS:
0700 to 1100 hrs
1300 to 1700 hrs
1900 to 2300 hrs
2400 to 0400 hrs

Additional working on holidays and
Sundays can be arranged.
ROAD AND RAIL ACCESS:
The main communications are the fine
Via Achieta, a dual carriageway road 65
kilometres long with each track 7 metres
wide, and two railways. The first a 1·60 m
gauge line 130 kilometres long from Santos
to Jundiái and the other a one metre gauge,
the Sorocabana covering 77 kilometres in
the Serro do Mar.

CONTAINER DEVELOPMENTS
CONTAINER PLANNING UNIT
D.N.P.V.N.
10, Praca Maná
Rio de Janiero G.B.
Brazil
GENERAL:
It has been decided to adapt a bulk liquid
berth at Santos for container handling. This
berth will be equipped with two Paceco
Vickers gantry cranes and six straddle carriers
and will serve as a central major container
terminal for a number of operators. Feeder
services will connect with other ports in the
area, the first of which will be Rio de Janeiro
which will be equipped with a Liebherr
container gantry crane and sideloaders.

BRAZIL STATE RAILWAYS

Rede Ferroviaria Federal (State Railways)
OFFICIALS:
Francisco Rubens Vieira, Engineer
(*General Superintendent of Transport*)
Agostinho Pignataro, Engineer

(*Head of Operations Department*)
Alberto Hazan, Engineer
(*Head of Transport Coordination Department*)
GENERAL
The Rede Ferroviaria Federal Sociedade

Anôminá owns 31 20 ft containers which are
controlled from:
General Superintendent's Office,
Praça Duque de Caxias No. 86,
Rio de Janeiro, Brazil

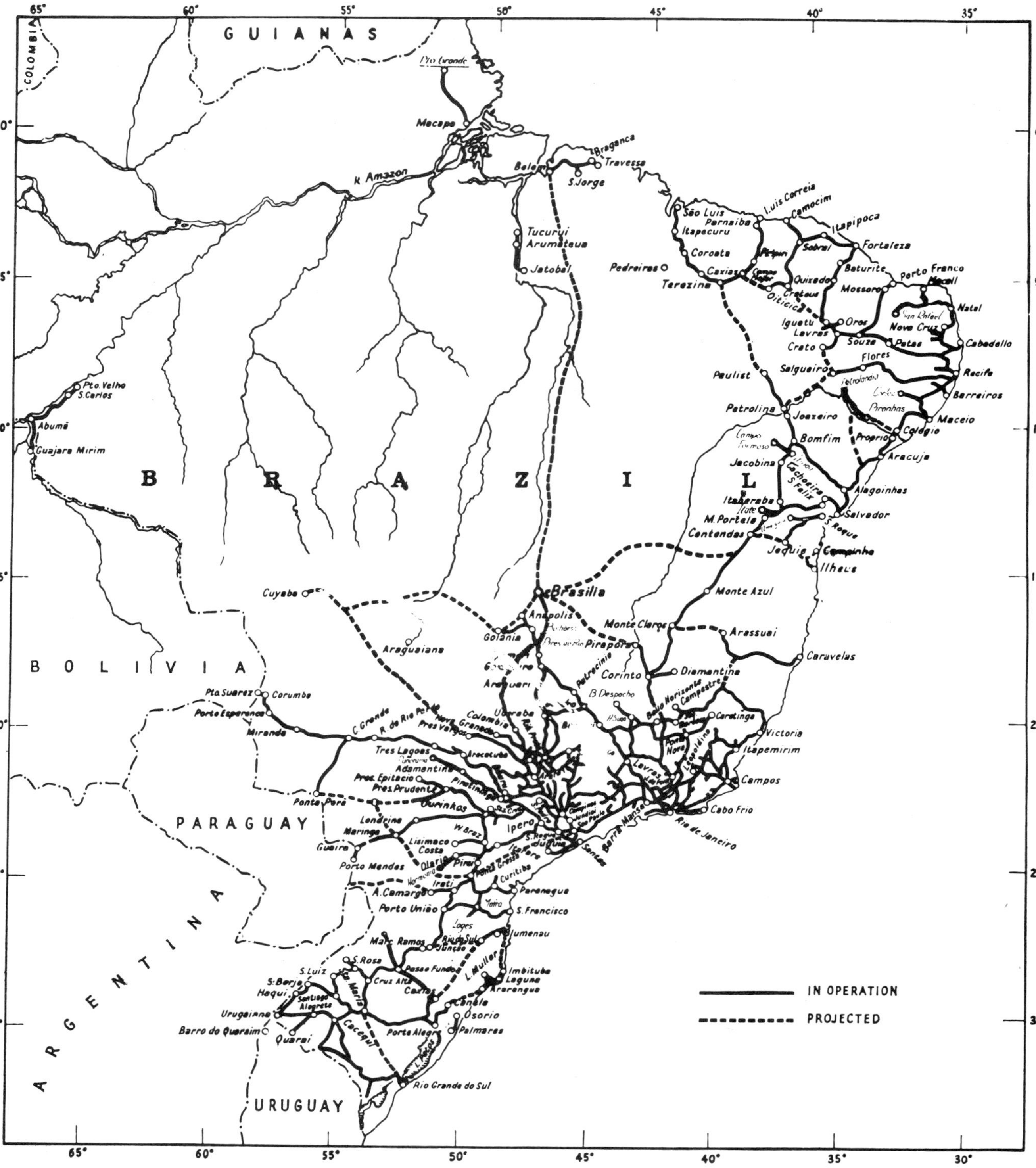

[Map of Brazil and surrounding countries showing rail routes, with legend: IN OPERATION (solid line), PROJECTED (dashed line)]

CONTAINER TRANSPORT:

Combined road and rail transport of containers between Rio de Janeiro and São Paulo through the Brazil Central and Transrodo-National Container Co. showed the following increase in the two-year period 1968-69 in units transported in both directions:

1968   7,691
1969   9,147
Increase   20%

At the moment there are in service 150 containers size 20 × 8 × 8 ft., 16 of them isothermal, as well as 120 2-wheel trucks, 120 flat trucks and 34 mechanical horses which are located at the two terminals to handle transport.

The Brazil Central has in service 24 54-ton flat wagons fitted with securing tackle (TIRE-DONE) for 2 containers size 20 × 8 × 8 feet each, and 11 60-ton flat wagons, which take 3 containers of the same type.

2 trains are made up daily, except Sundays, one in each direction, leaving each terminal

Interlocked 20 ft containers on the Central route of RFFSA for the Rio-Sao Paulo line

at 1900 hrs and reaching destination the following morning.

Combined sea and land transport by containers is carried out by road from the ports of Santos and Rio de Janeiro, where terminals specifically for containers are being constructed; these are expected to be com-

'Transrodo' containers handled by a 20 ton bridge crane on the Rio-Sao Paulo route.

pleted in 1971.

The port of Paranaguá also is being modified for the same purpose.

On the Paraná Santa Catarina Transit System, conteiners of the following type are transported:

	Width	Length	Height
External dimensions	2·10 m (6 ft 11 in)	2·40 m (7 ft 10 in)	2·30 m (7 ft 7 in)
Internal dimensions	2·00 m (6 ft 7 in)	2·27 m (7 ft 5 in)	1·94 m (6 ft 4 in)
Capacity	8·8 m² (311 cu ft)		
Tare weight	400 kg (880 lb) to 1 ton (depending on the material used in construction)		
Total loaded weight	5·5 to 6·0 tons		
Material used	Steel or aluminium		

These containers are only used in the districts served by the railway (State of Paraná and Santa Catarina) and normally for the transport of cereals in bulk or in sacks.

These two terminals are fully operational and at the moment plans are afoot to extend both to take about 1,000 to 1,500 containers of 20 × 8 × 8 ft.

SUMMARY

1. The final cost for this type of transport is still being studied.
2. RFFSA has no intention at the moment of studying rates for the transport of containers in international traffic.
3. At the moment there are no plans for the transport of containers into the interior of the country, and viability studies only exist for the coordination of road-rail-sea traffic.
4. For international traffic, the construction of a container terminal in the port of Rio de Janeiro is planned.
5. Containers owned by the Federal Railways are not and will not be used in international transport.

COLOMBIA
BUENAVENTURA

Empresa Puertos de Colombia,
Buenaventura
Colombia.
OFFICIALS:
Oscar Zamerano (*General Manager*)
Heriberto Posse Villabón (*Port Captain*)
CONTAINER FACILITIES:·

Containers are handled at the general cargo berths, which have a depth of water at low tide of 9·14 m (30 ft), with quay cranes which have a capacity of up to 20 tons. There are also mobile diesel cranes of between 25 and 40 tons capacity available. Containers are handled on the quay by a 25 ton fork lift truck and tractors with skeletal trailers. All the handling equipment except the trailers is owned by the Port Authority.

CONTAINER SERVICES:
Grace Line provide a weekly service between New York, the Caribbean, and ports in Colombia Ecuador and Peru.

BARRANQUILLA

Empresa Puertos de Colombia,
Barranquilla,
Colombia.
OFFICIALS:
Enrique López (*General Manager*)
Ernesto Nieto (*Port Captain*)

CONTAINER FACILITIES:
There is a quay 770 m (2,526 ft) in length which provides five berths for vessels up to 10 m (33 ft) draught. Quay cranes up to 20 tons capacity are available and containers are handled on the quay by a 25 ton fork lift truck and tractors with skeletal dock trailers owned by the Port Authority.

CONTAINER SERVICES:
Grace Line provide a weekly service between New York, the Caribbean and ports in Colombia, Ecuador and Peru.

CARTAGENA

Empresa Puertos de Colombia,
Cartagena
Colombia.
OFFICIALS:
Alfonso Villera (*General Manager*)
Captain Enrique Baquero (*Port Captain*)
CONTAINER FACILITIES:
Containers are handled at general cargo berths which have a depth of water alongside of 10 m (33 ft). Handling equipment for containers consists of tractors and trailers. Grace Line have a 25 ton fork lift truck for container transfers.
CONTAINER SERVICES:
Grace Line provide a weekly service between New York and ports in the Caribbean, Colombia, Ecuador and Peru.

ECUADOR
GUAYAQUIL

Autoridad Portuaria de Guayaquil
Puerto Maritimo,
Casilla 5739
Guayaquil
TELEPHONE: 342 120
TELEGRAMS: Aportuaria
OFFICIALS:
Lic. Armando Espinel Elizalde (*President*)
DIRECTORS:
Sr. Carlos Espinoza Pereira
Ing. Rubén Chalela Costa
CP.CB Pedro Larco Díaz
Sr. John Gomez Ycaza
Lic. Pedro Hidalgo Gonzalez (*Acting General Manager*)
Abog. Juan Trujillo Bustamante (*Secretary*)
CONTAINER FACILITIES:
Containers are handled at a 900 m (2952 ft) quay which is believed to have 10 m (33 ft) of water alongside. The port is accessible to vessels drawing 7·6 m (25 ft) at all states of the tide and there is a tidal range of about 2·5 m (8 ft). Containers are handled on the quay using a 25 ton fork lift truck and tractors with skeletal trailers owned by the Port Authority.
CONTAINER SERVICES:
Grace Line operate a weekly service between New York and ports in the Caribbean, Colombia, Ecuador and Peru.
A number of shipping companies use containers on general cargo services.
TRAFFIC:
In 1970 74,082 tons moved inwards and 66,369 tons outwards in containers. The 1971 estimates are for 80,000 tons inwards and 70,000 tons outwards.
FUTURE DEVELOPMENT
There are plans to increase the channel depth and to provide three further berths, two for banana handling and one for general cargo although the design of this latter berth has not yet been fixed.

SHIPPING AGENTS:
Anglo-Ecuatoriana (Agencias) C. Ltda.
Junin 105 y Malecón
Telephone: 511640
Agents for: The Pacific Steam Navigation; Westfal Larsen Line; The Bank Line.
Compañia Frutera Chileno- Ecuatoriana S.A.
9 de Octubre 424,
Telephone: 516089-518757
Agents for: Linea Mexicana del Pacifico.
Compañia de Intercambio y Credito
Junin y Malecón, 1er. piso alto
Telephone: 512310-514087
Agents for: Compañia Real Holandesa de Vapores; Royal Interocean Lines (R.I.L.); "K" Line—Ballenar-Inca; Lineas Maritimas Argentinas
Francis V. Coleman (Com) S.A.
Malecón 2306
Telephone: 513380
Agents for: Belgian Fruit Lines; J. Lauritzen Lines

Europacifico S.A.
9 de Octubre 424, 11o. piso, Of. 1103
Telephones: 525721-525727
Agents for: F. Laeisz-Hamburgo; Compañia Peruana de Vapores S.A. (Corporation Peruana de Vapores); Daei Maritime Co. Ltda.; Singi Navigation Corporation.
Flota Mercante Grancolombiana
Aguirre 104
Telephone: 512793
Agents for: Flota Mercante Grancolombiana.
Grace & Compañia (Ecuador) S.A.C.
P. Icaza y Córdova, esq., 3er. piso
Telephone: 511240
Agents for: Prudential Grace Lines Inc., Gulf & South American Steamship; Johnson Line.
Interoceanica Cia. Ltda.
P. Icaza 452
Telephone: 513601
Agents for: Italian Line; "Italia, Societa per Azioni di Navigazione-Genova.

Guayaquil

Investamar S.A.
Pichincha 334
Telephone: 526710
Agents for: W. Bruns & Co.; Slomans.
Representaciones Internacionales Cia. Ltda.
Panamá 511
Telephone: 527273
Agents for: Polish Ocean Line; Marasia S.A.
Sociedad General
P. Icaza 110
Telephone: 511150
Agents for: Cia. Sudamericana de Vapores (Chilean Line).

Transoceanica Cia. Ltda.
Malecón 1400
Telephone: 511290
Agents for: Hapag-Lloyd AG.—Flotta Lauro; Nippon Yusen Kaisha (N.Y.K. Line); Rudolf A. Oetker; Salen Shipping Companies; Bohannan S.A.
Luis Vernaza, Rep. Maritimas & Comerciales C. Ltda.
9 de Octubre 416
Telephones: 515922-513997
Agents for: French Line (CGT); Consorcio Naviero Peruano.

EL SALVADOR
ACAJUTLA

Comision Ejecutiva Portauria Autonoma,
Avenida Cuscatlán 317
San Salvador, El Salvador C.A.
TELEPHONE: San Salvador 23-4122, Acajutla 52-3000
TELEGRAMS: CEPA
TELEX: CEPA
PRINCIPAL OFFICIALS:
Ing. Mauricio Borgouovo (*President*)
Lic. Atilio Viéytez (*General Manager*)
Ing. Baltasar Parada Sandoval (*Gerente General*)

Ing. Herberto Reyes Ventura (*Planning Manager*)
Ing. Guido Armando Lucha (*Port Manager*)
GENERAL:
The port serves the western and central regions of the country and also parts of neighbouring Guatemala and Honduras.
CONTAINER FACILITIES:
A pier with a length of 360 m (1,181 ft) and a width of 28 m (92 ft) has recently been constructed. It is capable of accepting vessels with a draught of 11·43 m (37·5 tt), and is

equipped with a travelling 25 ton gantry crane with an outreach of 20·0 m (65·6 ft). The facility has also been designed for the handling of bulk materials which are fed to storage by conveyor belt. A container storage area of 12 hectares (30 acres) is in course of construction.
TERMINAL OPERATING HOURS:
24 hours per day.

CUSTOMS REQUIREMENTS:
If arrangements are made in advance with

customs, containers can be sent direct to consignees's warehouse and a Customs Officer will attend to break the seals and examine contents.

ROAD AND RAIL CONNECTIONS:

Roads. The Panamericana and the Litoral (coast road) connects the port with the chief cities and the industrial zones, besides providing a route to the Republic of Guatemala.

Rail. The Port is served by a railway belonging to the State and administered by the Port Authority. This railway links up with the main railway that crosses the width of El Salvador and connects with Guatemala.

FUTURE DEVELOPMENTS:

An extension of the breakwater will be started in 1972.

International Railways of Central America

Guatemala City, Guatemala,
Central America.
TEL: 83031
TELEGRAMS: GUARAILCO
TELEX: None

Acajutla

Acajutla – Dual purpose berth

GUATEMALA

DIRECTORS AND PRINCIPAL OFFICIALS
Louis Yaeger (*Chairman of the Board and President*)
15 Exchange Place, Jersey City, N.J., U.S.A.
M. D. Cure (*Vice President and General Manager*)
Guatemala City, Guatemala, Central America.

BRANCHES
San Salvador

CONTAINER ROUTES SERVED
Puerto Barrios to Guatemala City
Puerto Barrios to San Salvador

PANAMA
PUERTO BAHIA LAS MINAS

Puerto Bahia Las Minas
Marine Department,
Refineria Panama S.A.
Puerto Bahia Las Minas
Republic of Panama
GENERAL:

Operated by Refineria Panama SA, the port has a small general cargo pier principally used by roll-on services which also carry containers on trailers. Close by the pier is

an open fenced bonded area operated by Muelles SA. Covered storage will be provided by the end of 1971.
LOCAL AGENTS:
Inter-American Lines
PO Box 5072
Cristobal, Canal Zone
Telex: Tropical 9257
All American 3482089

Florida Panama Lines
P.O. Box 4658
Panama 5 R.P.
Panama Bulk Lines Inc.
c/o PO Box 5072
Cristobal, Canal Zone
Telex: Tropical 9257

PANAMA CANAL ZONE
PORT OF CRISTOBAL

Port of Cristobal
GENERAL:

The port handles containers through existing general cargo facilities. The following equipment is available for quay handling:
One—20 ton fork truck
One—30 ton fork truck
Six —30 ton flat bed trailers
One—15 ton mobile crane

LOCAL SHIPPING AGENTS:
Panama Bulk Lines Inc.
c/o PO Box 5072
Cristobal, Canal Zone
Telex: Tropical 9257

PERU
CALLAO

Empresa Nacionale de Puertos
Terminal Maritimo
Callao, Peru.
TELEGRAMS: Enapu Peru
OFFICIALS:
Meliton Carvajal Pareja (*Chairman and Managing Director*)
Ricardo Zeuallos Newton (*Terminal Administrator*)
Jorge Telaya Hidalgo (*Assistant Terminal Administrator*)

CONTAINER FACILITIES:
Containers are handled at general cargo facilities which enable vessels of 9·75 m (32 ft) draught to berth. Mobile cranes up to 20 tons capacity together with a 45 ton heavy lift crane and travelling quay cranes of 27 tons are available. Quay handling is carried out by a 25 ton fork lift truck with tractors and trailers.

CONTAINER SERVICES:
Grace Line operate a weekly service from New York via Caribbean, Colombia and Ecuador ports to Callao.

Flota Mercante Gran Colombiana, Compañia Peruana de Vapores and Johnson Line handle containers through the port.

MATARANI

Port Terminal Matarani,
Port Terminal,
Matarani.
OFFICIALS:
G. Prentice (*Port Captain*)
S. D. Tafur (*Terminal Administrator*)
CONTAINER FACILITIES:
Containers are handled at the general cargo facilities which consist of a quay 366 m (1200 ft) long.
Quay handling is by 25 ton fork lift truck with tractors and trailers. Equipment is owned by the Terminal's Port Services.
CONTAINER SERVICES:
Grace Line operate a weekly service to Matarani from New York via Caribbean, Colombia and Ecuador ports using Container vessels.
RAIL SERVICES:
Matarani serves part of the Bolivian hinterland by means of the Railway operated by Ferrocarriles del sur del Peru (Peruvian Corporation Ltd, Apartado 194, Arequipa, Peru). This Railway Company own 70 light alloy Containers 2·08 m (5·88 ft) long 2·39 m (7·88 ft) wide and 2·08 m (6·88 ft) high. These are operated on the route from Matarani to Puno where they are transferred to ship on Lake Titicaca and transported to Guaqui in Bolivia for on carriage by rail to La Paz, Oruro and Cochabamba.

SHIP OPERATORS

SHIP OPERATORS
ADRIATICA

'Adriatica' S.p.A.N.

30123 Venice
Zattere, 1411 (CP 495)

TELEPHONE: 704/322
TELEX: 41045
Passenger and freight from Italy to the Eastern Mediterranean.

FLEET:
Roll-on and conventional vessels.
CONTAINERS IN SERVICE:
Dry 50 10 × 8 × 8

AFRICATAINER

Africatainer Line
Société Navale Delmas-Vieljeux (SNDV)
29 Rue Galilee, Paris 16e
Cie Maritime des Chargeurs Réunis
3 Boulevard Malesherbes, Paris
SERVICE:
North West European Ports to Western African Ports—weekly.
FLEET:
A fleet of modern 18 knot, 16,000 dwt conventional cargo carriers, specially designed for the carriage of general cargo, vehicles, containers and logs.

Africatainer's *Bellatrix* at Bordeaux

A.E.I.L.

AEIL's *Sea Witch*

American Export Industries Inc.
26 Broadway,
New York, New York 10004
PRINCIPAL SUBSIDIARY COMPANIES CONCERNED WITH GENERAL CARGO AND CONTAINER OPERATIONS:
United States:
American Export Freight Inc.
American Export International Inc.
American Export Isbrandtsen Lines Inc.
Amexi Leasing Corporation
Eastern Express Ltd.
National Car Loading Corporation with—
Inter-Freight International —a Division of the Corporation
National Transport Corporation
R-C Motor Lines Inc.
Transocean Gateway Corporation
Europe:
Global Leasing Company, Glarus Immobiliare Sviluppo Industriale S.p.A., Leghorn.
Inter-Freight Continental SA, Brussels
Inter-Freight Benelux, Antwerp
Inter-Freight Detjen, Hamburg
Inter-Freight Espana, Madrid
Inter Freight Italia, Florence
Inter-Freight Nederland, Amsterdam
Inter-Freight SA, Paris
Systems Inter-Freight, London
Tesco N.V. Rotterdam and Leghorn
Transport Containers Agency SA, Liechtenstein.
DIRECTORS:
Peter L. Keane (*Chairman*)
R. Canon Clements (*Vice-Chairman*)
Harold L. Fates (*Vice-President*)
A. R. Gale (*Senior Vice-President*)
Jakob Isbrandtsen (*President*)

AEIL's *Export Challenger*

Albert E. Rising, Jr
John M. Will (*Chairman of the Board and President AEIL Inc.*)
OFFICERS:
Jakob Isbrandtsen (*President*)
Manuel Diaz (*Senior Vice-President*)
A. R. Gale (*Senior Vice-President*)
Frederick J. Mayo (*Senior Vice-President*)
Alfred F. Tweed (*Senior Vice-President*)
David A. Hamond (*Vice-President, Finance*)
Walter H. Elliott, Jr (*Treasurer*)
Richard M. McCostis (*General Counsel and Secretary*).

GENERAL:
The Inter-Freight Organisation is understood to be responsible for the co-ordination and movement of freight on both internal United States routes and throughout the world using the services and facilities provided by American Export Companies.

MARITIME OPERATIONS:
The Company operate the following services and are believed to be concerned with Amerind, whose activities are described under a separate entry:
Break Bulk using Container or Conventional Vessels as required:
New York, Philadelphia, Baltimore, Norfolk to South Mediterranean and Near East ports.
New York, Philidelphia, Baltimore, Norfolk to India, Pakistan and Ceylon.
Combination Break Bulk and Container Services:
New York, Philadelphia, Baltimore, Norfolk, Savannah to Inchon, Hong Kong, Kaohsiung, Keeling, Kobe/Osaha, Nagoya, Pusan, Yokohama.
Cellular Container Service:
New York, Baltimore, Norfolk to Amsterdam, Antwerp, Århus, Bordeaux, Bremen, Copenhagen, Felixstowe, Hamburg, LeHavre, Odense, Rotterdam.
Cellular Container and Roll-on Service:
New York, Baltimore, Norfolk to Alicante, Ashdod, Barcelona, Bilbao, Cadiz, Catania, Genoa, Haifa, Leghorn, Marseilles, Naples, Piraeus, Seville, Valencia.

FLEET:
C/V Sea Witch, C/V Lightning, C/V Staghound
These vessels, operating on the North West European service, have a capacity of 928 20 ft equivalents (316 × 20: 306 × 40), a length of 185·9 m (610 ft) a beam of 23·8 m (78·2 ft) and a loaded draught of 9·60 m (31·6 ft).
Container Forwarder, Container Dispatcher
With a capacity of 738 20 ft equivalents (638 × 20: 50 × 40) these vessels have a length of 177·4 m (582 ft), a beam of 23·8 m (78·2 ft) and a draught of 9·75 m (32·0 ft).
Defiance, Great Republic, Red Jacket, Young America
These vessels (together together with *Export Commerce*) maintain the Mediterranean container service; they were purchased in 1970 from Moore McCormack Lines. With a speed of 24·5 knots they have a length of 183·5 m (602 ft) a beam of 27·4 m (90 ft), a draught of 9·4 m (31 ft) and are capable of lifting the equivalent of 824 20 ft units with an additional 3,150 m² (34,000 sq ft) available for roll-on traffic on the second deck, the whole of which can be used for this traffic. Vessels are fitted with side ports at No. 7 hatch measuring 4·57 m high and 4·42 m wide (15 ft × 14·5 ft) and a stern door with the same dimensions but able to accept heavy equipment etc.
Export Challenger, Export Champion, Export Commerce, Export Courier
These vessels, with the exception of *Export Commerce*, are understood to be in service on the Far East route. They have a container capacity of between 440 and 468 20 ft units, a length of 105·3 m (493 ft), a beam of 22·3 m (73 ft) and a draught of 9·14 m (29·9 ft).

AEIL's *Container Despatcher*

AMERICAN MAIL LINE LTD.

American Mail Line Ltd.
1010 Washington Building
Seattle, Washington 98101
TELEPHONE: MAin 4-4400
TELEX: 032583
TWX: 910-444-1355
DIRECTORS:
Anson Brooks, W. B. Fowler, Charles F. Frankland, G. H. Gallaway, Thos. F. Gleed, G. E. Karlen, A. R. Lintner, Harold A. Miller, Arthur B. Poole, E. C. Sammons, Fred C. Shanaman, Lawson P. Turcotte
EXECUTIVE IN CHARGE OF CONTAINER OPERATIONS
W. O. Schiffner (*Vice-President*)
CARGO SUPERINTENDENTS:
Captain J. M. Jorgensen, James Aschbrenner, Captain Joseph Cormier, J. F. Nicholson, Harold Emerson
BRANCHES:
Portland, Oregon, 97204
San Francisco, California, 94108
Chicago, Illinois, 60606
New York HX10004
SERVICES:
U.S. Pacific North West to Japan—RPI—Hong Kong Twice per month.
FLEET:
Five partial container ships, *Alaskan Mail, Indian Mail, Korean Mail, Hong Kong Mail*

American Mail Line's *Alaskan Mail*

and *American Mail* each carry 409 20 foot containers. The vessels are 184·4 m (605 ft) in overall length with a beam of 25 m (82 ft) and a draught of 10·36 m (34 ft). They have an n.r.t. of 10,002 tons.
Washington Mail   *Japan Mail*

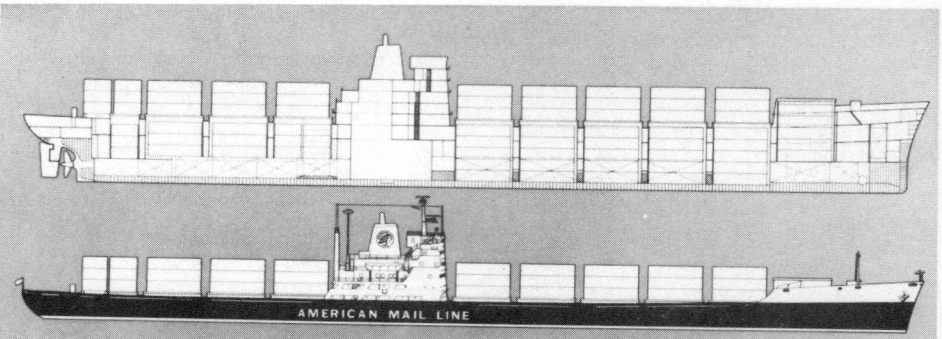

Profile drawing of AML's C6 conversion.

American Mail Line's *Alaskan Mail*

Philippine Mail   Oregon Mail

These C6 type vessels are having a cellular mid section added to enable them to carry the equivalent of 894 20 ft units, about one quarter of which could be refrigerated. The first of these vessels, *Washington Mail*, re-entered service in September 1971, *Japan*

Mail is scheduled to be completed by December 1971 and the others follow in February and April 1972. This 22 knot class of vessel is 203·85 m (668·7 ft) in length with a beam of 23·16 m (76 ft) and a draught of 9·60 m (31·5 ft).

CONTAINERS IN SERVICE:

Dry	1,480	20 × 8 × 8
Dry	500	20 × 8 × 8·5
Dry	401	40 × 8 × 9
Refrigerated	103	20 × 8 × 8·5
Posted Flatracks	300	20 × 8 × 8·5

PRINCIPAL OVERSEAS AGENTS:
Everett Steamship Corporation S/A throughout the Far East.

YOKOHAMA HEAD OFFICE: Yokohama Port P.O. Box 300 Japan.
TELEPHONE: (201) 4171-8
TELEGRAMS: Everett
TELEX: YH 7722-YH7744

AMERICAN PRESIDENT LINES

American President Lines
601, California Street,
San Francisco, California 94108, USA
TELEPHONE: 415 981 6000
TELEGRAMS: Preslines San Francisco
TELEX: *WUI* 67656 *RCA* 27205 *ITT* 470174
BRANCHES:
Los Angeles, California
San Diego, California
Dallas-Texas
New York, New York
Boston, Massachusetts
Baltimore, Maryland
Charleston, Carolina
Norfolk, Virginia
Philadelphia, Pennsylvania
Washington, D.C.
Chicago, Illinois
Honolulu, Hawaii
Tokyo, Japan
Yokohama, Japan
Kobe, Japan
Osaka, Japan
Manila, Philippines
Hong Kong, BCC
Singapore, Singapore
Medan, Sumatra (Indonesia)
DIRECTORS:
William J. Biehl
Arnold B. Chace
Norman Scott
Forrest M. Chumway
C. Neil Ash
Robt. E. Benedict

Peter T. Albert
Ralph K. Davies
Worth B. Fowler
George Killion
Chandler Ide
Howard F..Lucas
EXECUTIVES IN CHARGE OF CONTAINER OPERATIONS:
R. F. Fay (*General Manager, Container Division*)
J. T. Lindstrom (*Manager, Container Operations*)
CARGO SUPERINTENDENTS:
C. D. Doan, (*Acting Manager, Terminal and Cargo Operations*)
N. Olov Sundstedt (*Superintendent, Container Operations*)
SERVICES:
(i) *Trans-Pacific* California to Japan, Okinawa, Korea, Taiwan, Hong Kong, Philippines —approximately every 10 days.
(ii) *Atlantic-Straits* US Atlantic and Pacific Coast ports to Manila, Saigon, Djarkarta, Malaysia, Singapore, Hong Kong, Japan— about two sailings per month.
(iii) *Round the World* US Atlantic and Pacific Coast ports to Japan, Korea, Okinawa, Taiwan, Hong Kong, Singapore, Bombay, Karachi, New York, two sailings per month.

CONTAINERS IN SERVICE:

Dry	3,300	20 × 8 × 8
Refrigerated	150	20 × 8 × 8
Flat Racks	25	20 × 8 × 8

FUTURE PLANS:
Four container vessels of 20,200 tons deadweight, each able to lift 1,204 containers, are on order for delivery in 1972. They will be capable of a speed of 23 knots.
PRINCIPAL OVERSEAS AGENTS:
Castle & Cooke, Inc.
PO Box 2990
Honolulu, Hawaii 96802
Telephone: (808) 531 6921
Nippon Express Co., Ltd.
No. 16, 1-chome, Hinode-cho
Shimizu, Japan
Cable Address: NEXCO
Toyo Shipping Agency, Inc.
1-2, Kakomachi, 2-chome
Nakamura-ku, Nagoya, Japan
Cable Address: TOYOSHIP
Nippon Express Co., Ltd.
No. 1-3, Sakae-Machi, Moji-ku

A model of one of the planned APL vessels.

FLEET:

Name	20 ft Container capacity	Net Reg. Tons	Length ft in m	Beam ft in m	Loaded draught ft in m
President Lincoln	472	8,037	563 0 171·6	76 0 23·2	31 6 9·6
President Tyler	472	8,037	563 0 171·6	76 0 23·2	31 6 9·6
President *Van Buren	227 (884)	9,663	573 11 175	82 0 25	30 7 9·32
President *Fillmore	227 (884)	9,605	573 11 175	82 0 25	30 7 9·32
President *McKinley	227 (884)	9,605	573 11 175	82 0 25	30 7 9·32
President *Grant	227 (884)	9,588	573 11 175	82 0 25	30 7 9·32
President *Taft	227 (884)	9,605	573 11 175	82 0 25	30 7 9·32

Presidents *Polk, Monroe* and *Harrison* to be in service by August 1972 (capacity 685 20 ft units or the equivalent).

*To be in service as full containerships with a capacity of the equivalent of 884 20 ft units by August 1972.

American President Lines' *President Lincoln*

Kitakyushu City
Fukuoka Pref., Japan
Cable Address: NEXCO
Connell Bros. Co., Ltd.
CPO Box 57
Naha, Okinawa
Cable Address: CONNELL
FEMTCO Shipping Co., Ltd.
Intl. PO Box 1334
Seoul, Korea
Cable Address: FEMTCO
Telephone: 22-5181-5
Getz Bros. & Co., Inc.
PO Box 354
Taipei, Taiwan
Cable Address: PRESLINES

Telephone: 515131
Sime Darby Malaysia Ltd.
PO Box 393
Penang, Malaysia
Cable Address: SIMESHIP
Telephone: 3791
Alkis Petropoulos
P.O. Box 2945
Kebon Sirih, 16
Djakarta, Indonesia
Forbes, Forbes Campbell & Co. Ltd.,
Forbes Building, Home Street, P.O. Box 79
Bombay 1, India
Binny Ltd., P.O. Box 6 Cochin 1, India
Forbes Forbes Campbell & Company Ltd.

PO Box 4659
Karachi, Pakistan
Cable Address: KARACHI
Telephone: 222616
Adriatic Shipping Co. SRL
18, Via Cairoli
16124, Genoa, Italy
Cable Address: ADRIASHIP
Telephone: 201-581
Reed and Mackay Ltd.
107 Leadenhall Street
London, E.C.3, England
Getz Bros. & Co.
P.O. Box 43, 26, 28 Dai-Lo Ham Nghi
Saigon, South Vietnam

AMERIND

Amerind's *Gwendolen Isle*

Amerind Shipping Corporation
17 Battery Place, New York
NY 10004
TELEPHONE: (212) 943-0500
CONTAINER SERVICES:
Dominican Container Line
Jamaican Container Line
Bahamas Service
Halifax and New York to Santo Domingo,
Kingston and Nassau—weekly.
MAIN AGENTS:
Flota Mercant Dominicana C. por A.
1 La Catolica 70, Santo Domingo
Dominican Republic
Telephone: 689-6171
International Shipping, Ltd
71½ Harbour Street, Kingston,
Jamaica
Telephone: 13861
R. R. Farrington & Sons
P.O. Box 93, Nassau,
Bahamas
Telephone: 22203, 23127
F. K. Warren Ltd
P.O. Box 1117, 1695 Hollis Street,
Halifax, N.S., Canada
FLEET:
Weser Isle, Ida Isle, Gretchen Isle
These 14/15 knot vessels are each capable
of lifting between 152 and 160 containers.
Virgin Island Container Line
New York to Virgin Islands—Weekly
MAIN AGENTS:
Abrahams Shipping Co. Inc.
P.O. Box 1098, Christiansted,
St. Croix, V.I.
Telephone: 773-0707
FLEET:
Gwendolen Isle, Christine Isle
These 14 knot vessels are each capable of
carrying 86 20 ft units.
Amerind Bermuda Line
New York to Hamilton—weekly.
Jacksonville to Hamilton—fortnightly.
MAIN AGENTS:
John H. Darrell & Co. Ltd.
Front Street, Hamilton, Bermuda
Telephone: 13861
FLEET:
Jasmine
This 15 knot vessel is capable of carrying
81 20 ft units (on the New York run).

Hibiscus
This 18 knot vessel is reported as capable
of carrying 250 20 ft units.
Amerind Bahamas Service
Jacksonville to Nassau—fortnightly (in con-
junction with part of the Amerind Bermuda
service reported above.
MAIN AGENTS:
McGiffin & Co. Inc.
1510 Tallyrand Avenue,
Jacksonville, Florida
Telephone: 904-353-1741
R. R. Farrington & Sons
P.O. Box 93, Nassau, Bahamas
Telephone: 22203, 23127
FLEET:
Hibiscus

Amerind's *Jasmine*

CONTAINER EQUIPMENT:
All lines use 20 × 8 × 8 dry cargo, refrig-
erated, insulated and open top containers.
Units of 40 × 8 × 8·5 are in service on all
routes except Jacksonville to Bermuda and
Bahamas.

ANGLO-IRISH TRANSPORT LTD

Anglo Irish Transport Limited (Coast Lines Group)
Water Street, Londonderry
TELEPHONE: 4204/5
TELEX: 74565
BRANCHES:
The Docks, Preston, Lancs
TELEPHONE: 728131. TELEX: 67579
Albert Basin, Newry, Co- Down
TELEPHONE: 3416 TELEX 74324
DIRECTORS:
R. W. Berkeley, CBE, JP (Chairman)
G. A. Ashley
R. G. Clarke
H. O. McMurray
Cdr. P. C. D. Campbell, MVO, RN(Rtd)
W. Sanders
T. Atkins
CARGO SUPERINTENDENT:
W. J. Woods
SERVICES:
Londonderry/Preston, 4 times weekly
Newry/Preston, 3 times weekly
PRINCIPAL AGENTS:
Coast Lines Limited
Reliance House, Water Street, Liverpool 2
FLEET:
Fernfield

Container capacity 28
Net reg tons 265·52
Length 60·96 m (200 ft)
Beam 9·14 m (30 ft)
Draught 2·44 m (8 ft)
Terrier
Container Capacity 36
Net reg tons 616·28
Length 60·96 m (200 ft)
Beam 10·67 m (35 ft)
Draught 1·68 m (5·5 ft)
Wirral Coast
Container capacity 28
Net reg tons 384·25
Length 60·96 m (200 ft)
Beam 9·14 m (30 ft)
Draught 2·44 m (8 ft)
CONTAINERS IN SERVICE:

Dry	14	18·5 × 7 × 8
Dry	42	20 × 8 × 8
Dry	6	30 × 8 × 8
Insulated	8	9 × 6·5 × 6·5
Flats	205	20 × 7
Flats	160	24 × 7·75
Flats	24	30 × 8

GROUPAGE SERVICE:
There is a daily collection service in the Lancashire and West Yorkshire areas for small consignments and part lots through an associate company, Road Services (Caledonian) Ltd. This service is also available at the following depots:
Liverpool
Lodwick Street
Bootle, 20
Telephone: Central 0201
Dumfries
Glasgow Road
Telephone 3171 Telex: 77301
London
Eley Estate
Angel Road, Edmonton, N.19
Telephone: Edmonton 8681/6 Telex: 23837
Bristol
Flowershill
Brislington
Telephone: 79408/9 Telex: 44764
Glasgow
97a, Hawthorn Street, N.1
Telephone: Possill Park 8284 Telex 77335
Newcastle
Stoneygate Lane
Felling
Telephone: Felling 693241/2, 692490

ANGLO PORTUGUESE CONTAINER LINE

Anglo Portuguese Container Line
(UK & Portugal Lines Conference)

MEMBERS:
Currie Line—Leith
C.N.C.A.—Lisbon
MacAndrews & Co. Ltd.—London

SERVICE:
London to Lisbon—weekly
FLEET:
Chartered cellular container vessel capable of lifting 120 20 ft units in service.
LONDON OFFICES:
Currie Line Ltd.,
Bankside House, Leadenhall Street, EC3
MacAndrews & Co. Ltd.
Plantation House, Mincing Lane, EC3
Brown Jenkinson & Co. Ltd.,
Dunster House, Mark Lane, EC3
Agents for C.N.C.A. Lisbon.

ASSOCIATED CONTAINER TRANSPORTATION (AUSTRALIA) LTD.

Associated Container Transportation (Australia) Ltd.
136 Fenchurch Street, London E.C.3
TELEPHONE: 01-481 2567
TELEX: 886361
BRANCHES:
London Region
Associated Container Transportation (Australia) Ltd.,
Brentwood Road, Orsett, Essex.
Telephone: 0375 5181
Telex: 27602
Midland Region
Associated Container Transportation (Australia) Ltd., College Road, Perry Barr, Birmingham B44 8DR
Telephone: 021-356 8531
Telex: 338094
North Western Region
Associated Container Transportation (Australia) Ltd., Barton Dock Road, Barton Dock Estate (West), Urmston, Manchester M31 2LP
Telephone: 061-748 9121

ACT Australia Ltd's *ACT I*

Telex: 668423
North Eastern Region
Associated Container Transportation
(Australia) Ltd., Wakefield Road,
Stourton, Leeds 10.
Telephone: 0532 72211
Telex: 557336
Scottish Region
Associated Container Transportation
(Australia) Ltd., Gartsherrie Road,
Gartsherrie, Coatbridge, Lanarkshire.
Telephone: 0236 22414
Telex: 778582
DIRECTORS:
Sir Basil Smallpiece, KCVO (*Chairman*)
E. H. Vestey (*Deputy Chairman*)
J. D. M. Hearth
D. G. Hollebone
D. A. Lloyd
R. A. Lloyd
D. F. Martin-Jenkins
J. G. Payne
N. S. Thompson
B. R. Hazlitt

EXECUTIVES IN CHARGE OF CONTAINER
  OPERATIONS:
  A. J. Macintosh (*General Manager*)
  I. R. Weatherston (*Financial Controller*):
  R. L. Davis (*Marketing Manager*)
  L. B. Fiddock (*Commercial Manager*)
SERVICES:
  Australia—UK/Continent—Weekly.
  An integrated service with Overseas
Containers Ltd and Australian National Line.
See also PACE Line and PAD Line.
FLEET:
  Two ships, *ACT* 1 and *ACT* 2 with the
following characteristics:
  20 ft Container capacity: 1223
  Net registered tonnage: 14,471
  Length: 214·5 m (715 ft)
  Beam: 29 m (95·2 ft)
  Loaded draught: 9·75 m (32 ft)
  Dilkara. See PAD Line entry.
  ACT 3, *ACT* 4, *ACT* 5. See PACE Line
entry.
CONTAINERS IN SERVICE:
  Dry   6,228   20 × 8 × 8

Dry	250	40 × 8 × 8
Open top	143	20 × 8 × 8
Insulated	1,850	20 × 8 × 8
Liquid Bulk, Non-hazardous, non heated 19,093 litres	8	20 × 8 × 8
Posted Flats	5	20 × 8 × 8

PRINCIPAL OVERSEAS AGENTS:
Associated Container Transportation
Australia Pty Ltd.
  Royal Exchange Building, 56 Pitt Street,
  Sydney
  Telephone: 27-7911
  Telex: AA 21369
ACT (USA),
  90 West Street, New York, 10006
  Telephone: (212) 732-4803
  Telex: RCA 222618
ACT (NZ),
  P.O. Box 396, I.B.M. Building,
  157, The Terrace, Wellington 1
  Telephone: 59919
  Telex: 74 3468

ASSOCIATED HUMBER LINES

Associated Humber Lines Ltd.
Commercial Road, Hull
TELEPHONE: 23197
TELEX: 56203
BRANCHES:
London—44/6 Leadenhall St EC3
Telephone 01-481 1445/6
Ellerman's Wilson Line Ltd
Birmingham—St. Martins House, Bull Ring
Telephone: 021-643 5760, 7700
Bradford—25 Sunbridge Road
Telephone: 0274-31418
Leeds—Yorkshire House, Greek Street
Telephone: 0532 34081/2
Manchester—11a Albert Square
Telephone: 061-834 5237/9
Sheffield—Yorkshire Insurance House,
  Market Place
Telephone: 0742 27429
DIRECTORS:
F. B. Bolton, MC (*Chairman*)
Colonel G. W. Bayley, OBE
J. Gillespie,
H. E. Osborn, CBE
SERVICES:
  Hull-Rotterdam, 5 sailings per week
  Hull-Antwerp, 3 sailings per week

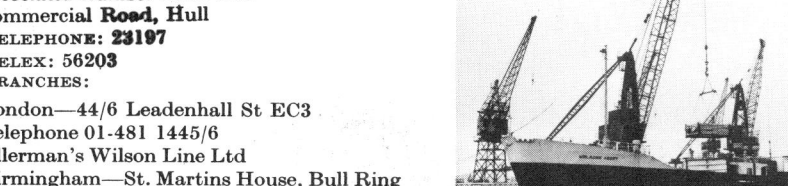

Associated Humber Line's *Melrose Abbey*

CARGO SUPERINTENDENTS:
  Ellerman's Wilson Line Limited
  Commercial Road, Hull
PRINCIPAL OVERSEAS AGENTS:
N. V. Agentschap Humberdiensten, Albert
  Plesmanweg 135, Rotterdam
  Tel: 290144. Telex: 22634
Westcott Limited SA, Brouwersvliet, 21,
  Antwerp
  Tel: 312920. Telex: 31343
FLEET:
Bolton Abbey and *Melrose Abbey*
  Container capacity: 65

Associated Humber Line's *Leeds*

Net reg tons: 1,706
Length: 107·9 m (354 ft)
Beam: 13·72 m (45 ft)
Draught: 4·27 m (14 ft)
Leeds and Wakefield
  Container capacity: 35
  Net reg tons: 480
  Length: 74·37 m (244 ft)
  Beam: 11·89 m (39 ft)
  Draught: 4·01 m (13 ft 2 in)
CONTAINERS IN SERVICE:
  Dry   70 20 × 8 × 8
  Flats 180 20 ft

ASSOCIATED STEAMSHIPS PTY LTD

Associated Steamships Pty. Ltd.
Scottish House, 94 William Street,
Melbourne,
Victoria 3001
TELEPHONE: 67 9972
TELEX: 30078
DIRECTORS:
Sir Ian Potter (*Chairman*)
T. L. Webb
C. J. Waugh
J. G. Felgate
H. H. Lloyd
K. W. Russell
K. W. Thomas
E. H. P. Abeles
J. R. Cribb
J. H. H. Paterson (*Managing*)
ACTING CHIEF MANAGER:
P. W. Naughton
BRANCHES:
SYDNEY
10-14 Underwood Street, Sydney,
N.S.W. 2001
Telephone: 27 5985
Telex: 20774
PORT KEMBLA
Five Islands Road, Port Kembla,
N.S.W. 2505
Telephone: 4 0375
Telex: 29005

Associated Steamships' *Kanimbla*

MELBOURNE
Sudholz Street, West Melbourne,
Victoria 3003
Telephone: 30 4971
Telex: 30098
PORT ADELAIDE
1 McLaren Parade, Port Adelaide, S.A. 5015
Telephone: 4 1631
Telex: 82099
FREMANTLE
10 Phillimore Street, Fremantle, W.A. 6160
Telephone: 5 1091
Telex: 92136
BRISBANE
99, Eagle Street,
Brisbane, Q'ld 4000
Telephone: 2 2606
Telex: 49584

Kingsgrove Service Centre
32, Commercial Road,
Kingsgrove NSW 2208
Telephone: 50 0261
Telex: 20815

OPERATIONS:
These are Australia-wide. They include:—
1. Door-to-Door shipping services between Brisbane and Fremantle.
2. General cargo services from Sydney, Newcastle and Port Kembla to Melbourne, Port Adelaide, Whyalla and Fremantle.
3. Management of Australian coastal tankers on behalf of British Petroleum, Mobil, Esso and Shell Oil companies.
4. Operation of bulk carriers for carriage of bulk ironstone etc. around Australian Coast.

UNIT LOAD SERVICES:
Kanimbla, *Manoora* and *Kooringa* operate a weekly service: Brisbane—Sydney—Melbourne—Fremantle—Melbourne—Sydney—Brisbane.

CONTAINERS IN SERVICE:
'K' Dry	589	20 × 8 × 8·5
'L' Dry	445	20 × 8 × 6·32
'M' Dry	165	20 × 8 × 4·25
Cartainers	72	20 × 17·32 × 5·0

CONTAINERS USED:
The containers used by Associated Steamships Pty. Ltd. are universally known as Seatainers; these are of four principal types.

"*K*"—*Fully Enclosed Dry Cargo Container*
Measurement	Internal		External	
	ft	in.	ft	in
Length	19	4	19	10½
Width	7	7	8	0
Height	7	10	8	6
Gross Deadweight			22·50 tons	
Cargo Capacity	1140 cub ft		20·00 tons	
Door Opening	7 ft 5 in high, 7 ft 5 in wide			

"*L*"—*Open Top Container*
Measurement	Internal		External	
	ft	in	ft	in
Length	19	4	19	10½
Width	7	7	8	0
Height	3	9	4	3
Gross Deadweight			22·50 tons	
Cargo Capacity	540 cub ft		21·00 tons	
Door Opening	7 ft 0 ins wide			

"*M*"—*Fixed Ends Open Top With Portable Side Gates*
(*Each unit equipped with a tailor-made vinyl cover*)
Measurement	Internal		External	
	ft	in	ft	in
Length	19	2	19	10½
Width	7	5	8	0
Height	5	7½	6	4
Gross Deadweight			22·50 tons	
Cargo Capacity	800 cub ft		19·00 tons	

"*D*"—*Fully Enclosed Dry Cargo Container*
(*The Seatainer*)
Measurement	Internal		External	
	ft	in	ft	in
Length	5	8	6	0
Width	3	11	4	2
Height	5	4	6	0
Gross Deadweight			3 tons	

Associated Steamships' *Manoora*

CONTAINERSHIP FLEET:
Vessel	20 ft Container Capacity	n.r.t.	Length m	Length ft	Beam m	Beam ft	Loaded Draught m	Loaded Draught ft
Kooringa	276	2965	126·2	414	19·12	62·75	7·6	25
*Kanimbla**	528	8261	156·7	514	21·94	72	9·14	30
*Manoora**	528	8261	156·7	514	21·94	72	9·14	30

*These vessels are owned by Bulkships Ltd and operated by the Company.

Kooringa after conversion

'D' Type Seatainer

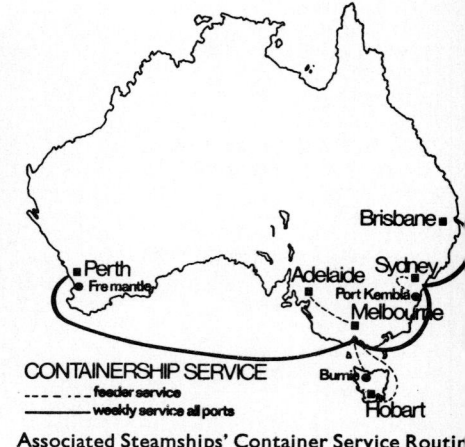

CONTAINERSHIP SERVICE
- - - - feeder service
——— weekly service all ports

Associated Steamships' Container Service Routir

Cargo Capacity 120 cub ft 2·60 tons
Door Opening 5 ft 4 in high, 5 ft 8 in wide

The 'D' type Seatainer, readily handled by fork lift trucks of suitable capacity, is carried in all Associated Steamships' vessels, excluding 'Kooringa'.

ASP Cartainer

Each container, which has a base 20 ft × 17·4 ft wide with sides of 5 ft, holds three cars. Two containers, one stacked and locked on the other comprise an intermediate lift. However, as twin lift cranes are available, two intermediate lifts can be handled at one time lifting 26 tons (12 cars). Containers are stacked nine high in the ships holds. ASP containers are designed with special wheel wells and equipped with rubber chocks.

'M' Type Pallet

Yet another cargo container used by Associated Steamships Pty. Ltd., is the Sea pallet (designated 'M' pallet). This consists of a metal base equipped with removable gate sides and is ideal for handling packages up to nineteen feet long. Because the unit's sides can be removed, cargo can be loaded and off-loaded with fork lift trucks from the sides of the unit.

'K' Type Container

'L' Type Container

Cartainer

'M' Type Container

ATLANTICA LINE

Atlantica s.p.A.
A joint service operated by:
Deutsche Dampschiffahrt Gesellschaft Hansa
Schlacte 6, Postfach 4,
28 Bremen 1
TELEPHONE: 0421-36651
TELEX: 02-44 581
DIRECTORS:
Georg Heinemen
H. C. Helms
Villain *and* Fassio e Compagnia Internazionale di Genova Societa Riunite de Navigazione S.p.A. (Fassio Line)

Via E de Amicis, PO Box 1287 Genoa

TELEX: 27211
SERVICE:
Genoa, Leghorn, Naples and Marseilles to East Coast United States and Canadian Ports—weekly.
FLEET:
Goldenfels, Gutenfels
These 20 knot vessels, originally designed as conventional carriers, have a capacity for 475 20 ft equivalents. They are equipped with their own handling gear but since all

ports of call are now equipped with container gantry cranes, the ships' gear is no longer used for container handling.
Geyerfels, Gruenfels
These 20 knot vessels, also designed originally as conventional carriers, are equipped with four cellular holds and have a capacity of 700 20 ft equivalents.

CONTAINERS IN SERVICE:
Hansa Line have been reported as having some 3,000 20 and 40 ft units in service and Fassio could be estimated to have about 500 20 ft units.

ATLANTIC CONTAINER LINE

Atlantic Container Line Limited
Hamilton, Bermuda
AN AFFILIATE OF:
Compagnie Générale Transatlantique, Paris
The Cunard Steam-Ship Co Ltd, London
Holland America Line, Rotterdam
Swedish American Line, Gothenburg
The Transatlantic Steamship Company Ltd.
  Gothenburg
Wallenius Line, Stockholm
OFFICIALS:
P. G. Carlsson (*Chairman*)
Jacques M. Ribiere (*Deputy Chairman*)
Philip E. Bates
David Graham
John D. M. Hearth
Leif Janson
A. M. Lels
James E. Pearman
J. Kleberg
C. Vail Zuill

General Consultants for operation of the consortium's vessels, co-ordination of Agents' marketing and sales activities in USA and Europe:

Atlantic Container Line Services Limited.
Overline House, Central Station,
Southampton SO9 1HA
TELEPHONE: Southampton 21351
TELEGRAMS: Atconline
TELEX: 47231
OFFICIALS:
Philip E. Bates (*Chairman*)
A. G. M. Koch (*Managing Director*)
P. R. Auriacombe (*Operations Director*)

Atlantic Span

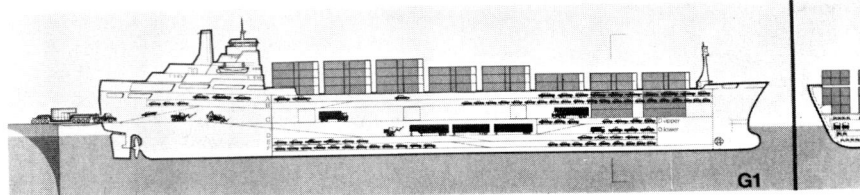

A profile of the ACL 'S' Class vessels

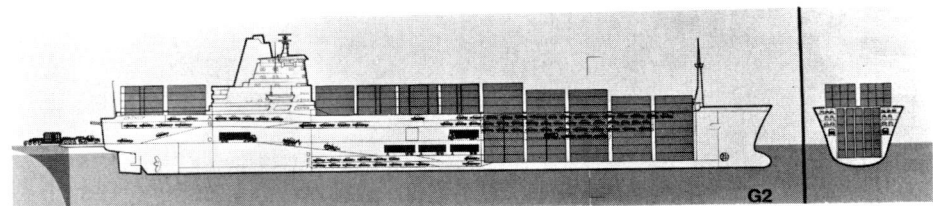

A profile of the ACL 'C' Class vessels

M. S. V. Turner (*Finance Director*)
O. I. M. Porton (*Director, North America*)

SERVICES:

Service A—Weekly
Gothenburg—Halifax, Nova Scotia—
New York—Portsmouth Va.—Baltimore,
Maryland—Gothenburg.

Service B—Weekly
Southampton — Rotterdam — Le Havre—
New York — Baltimore, Maryland —
Portsmouth, Va. —Southampton.

Service C—Weekly
Antwerp — Bremerhaven — Liverpool —
New York — Baltimore, Maryland —
Portsmouth, Va. — Liverpool.

CONTAINERS IN SERVICE

The total fleet of 10,000 units comprises
the following main types:

Dry	20 × 8 × 8
Dry	40 × 8 × 8
Dry	40 × 8 × 8·5
Refrigerated	40 × 8 × 8·5
Insulated	40 × 8 × 8·5
Open Top	40 × 8 × 8
Open Top	40 × 8 × 8·5
Open Top	40 × 8 × 4·25
Open Top	20 × 8 × 8
Bulk liquid	40 × 8 × 4·25
twin tanks	(4,400 Imp gallons, 5,250 US Gallons)

ROLL-ON CAPABILITY:

The company offer facilities for cargo
unsuitable for containers. Low loaders
with capacities of 20, 30, 40 and 55 tons are
available on a pier-to-pier basis. All descriptions of tracked and wheeled vehicles
can be loaded over the rear ramp into
the trailer deck. Heavy lifts, up to 250 tons
can be rolled on in this manner.

General Agents:

Atlantic Container Line (Rotterdam) NV,
P.O. Box 977, Wilhelminakade 76,
Rotterdam 20,
Telephone: 010.172600
Telex: 21607

Atlantic Container Line, AB
P.O. Box 2158, S-40313
Gothenburg 2, Sweden
Telephone: 172020 (long distance 031 175100)
Telex: 20841

Atlantic Container Line Ltd.
80 Pine Street,
New York, N.Y. 10005
USA
Telephone: 212 248200
Telex: 421900

Atlantic Container Line (Canada) Ltd,
465 St. John Street,
Montreal 1,
P.Q. Canada
Telephone: (514) 845-5101
Telex: 01-26156

Cunard-Brocklebank Ltd.
Cunard Building,
Liverpool L3 1DY
England
Telephone: 051-227 3000
Telex: 62343

Compagnie Generale Transatlantique,
Cedex 6,
92 Paris—La Defense,
France
Telephone: 7751411
Telex: Putau 61669

Motor Cars:

Scandinavian Motorships AB,
Osthammargat 70,
P.O. Box 27052 S/10251
Stockholm 27,
Sweden
Telephone: 631290
Telex: 10040

TERMINALS:

Skandiaterminalen A.B. Skandiahammen,
Gothenburg

FLEET:

First Generation Ships
Atlantic Saga, Atlantic Song, Atlantic Span,
Atlantic Star

Total loaded container capacity including trailer deck	527 × 20 ft equivalents 1,190 vehicles
Car carrying capacity	197 m (647 ft)
Length	26 m (86 ft)
Beam	8·9 m (29 ft)
Draught	16,005 metric tons
Deadweight tonnage	15,755 long tons
Service speed	20·5 knots

Second Generation Ships
Atlantic Causeway, Atlantic Champagne,
Atlantic Cinderella, Atlantic Cognac, Atlantic
Conveyor, Atlantic Crown

Total loaded container capacity including trailer deck	804 × 20 ft equivalents 990 vehicles
Car carrying capacity	212 m (695 ft)
Length	28 m (91 ft)
Beam	9·3 m (30 ft 7 in)
Draught	18,511 metric tons
Deadweight tonnage	18,219 long tons
Service speed	24 knots

Atlantic Saga at Dundalk Marine Terminal, Baltimore

Representative: Atlantic Container Line
Telephone: 542820
Autoumschlaganlage Bremerhaven — Nord-
hafen
Representative: Karl Geuther & Co.
Bremen
Telephone: 42738
Container Terminal Prinses Margriethaven,
Margriethaven, Rotterdam
Representative: Atlantic Container Line

NV, Rotterdam
Telephone: 293481
Hessenatie Container Terminal, Churchilldok,
Antwerp
Representative: Sasse & Co.
Telephone: 313670
Dundalk Marine Terminal, Baltimore
Representative: Ramsay Scarlett & Co. Inc.
Telephone: 539-5061
Portsmouth Marine Terminal, Portsmouth,

Virginia
   Representative: Ramsay Scarlett Co. Inc.
   Telephone: 622-4354
Container Terminals N.Y. Inc., Port Newark, New Jersey
   Representative: Atlantic Container Line Ltd.
Halifax Container Terminal, Halifax, Nova Scotia
   Representative: Atlantic Container (Canada) Ltd.,
   Telephone: 425-3711
Quai de l'Atlantique, Nouveau Bassin de Marée, Le Havre
   Representative: Cie. Generale Transatlantique
Greenock Container Terminal, Glasgow
   Representative: Cunard-Brocklebank Limited
Gladstone Container Terminal, Liverpool
   Representative: Cunard-Brocklebank Limited
Southampton Container Terminal,
   Representative: Cunard-Brocklebank Limited

Atlantic Crown at Le Havre

ATLANTIC STEAM NAVIGATION CO. LTD

Atlantic Steam Navigation Co. Ltd.,
(The Transport Ferry Service)
Craig's Court House, 25 Whitehall, London, SW1
Telephone: 01-930 2363
Telex: 23482
Branches:
   Tilbury, Felixstowe, Preston, Larne,

Belfast and Ardrossan (UK).
   Roche (Shipping) Limited (Dublin.)
   Agence Maritime Anversoise SA (Antwerp).
   The Transport Ferry Service (Nederland) NV (Europoort).
Directors:
F. B. Bolton, M.C. (*Chairman*)
Michael K. Bustard (*General Manager*)

G. A. Ashley (*Deputy General Manager*)
H. W. Elliott, C.B.E.
J. Gillespie
M. T. Turnbull

Executive in Charge of Container Operations
Captain W. N. Johnson, O.B.E.

Fleet:

Roll-on/Roll-off Vessels:	20ft Container Capacity	Net Reg. Tons	Length		Beam		Loaded Draught	
			m	ft	m	ft	m	ft
Celtic Ferry	VD 52 at 26 ft + UD 41 at 20 ft	2,225·21	140·74	461·75	22·3	73·2	5·05	16·6
Bardic Ferry	VD 37 at 26 ft + UD 22 at 20 ft	1,150·32	102·43	339·3	16·79	55·1	3·87	12·7
Ionic Ferry	VD 37 at 26 ft + UD 15 at 20 ft	1,132·33	102·43	339·3	16·79	55·1	3·87	12·7
Cerdic Ferry	VD 45 at 26 ft + UD 24 at 20 ft	1,072·38	110·16	361·4	16·79	55·1	3·88	12·8
Doric Ferry	VD 45 at 26 ft + UD 24 at 20 ft	887·61	110·16	361·4	16·79	55·1	3·88	12·8
Gaelic Ferry	VD 47 at 26 ft + UD 36 at 20 ft	779·74	111·56	366	17·09	56·1	4·12	13·5
Europic Ferry	VD 75 at 26 ft + UD 61 at 20 ft (Single Tier)	1,499·17	148·25	453·6	21·06	69·1	4·57	15

VD — Vehicle Deck.
UD — Upper Deck.

Container Vessels:

	20ft Container Capacity	Net Reg. Tons	Length		Beam		Loaded Draught	
			m	ft	m	ft	m	ft
Barbel Bolten	88	669·21	86	284·6	15·12	49·6	3·82	12·5
Marietta Bolten	88	669·20	86	284·6	15·12	49·6	3·82	12·5
Coria	52	295·52	60	197·0	11·02	36·2	4·05	13·25
Linda	52	312·76	60	197·0	10·72	35·2	3·91	12·8
Curran	53	873·54	63·75	229·2	10·97	36·0	4·05	13·25
Moyle	53	873·54	63·75	229·2	10·97	36·0	4·05	13·25
Goodwill Merchant	45	261·71	59·9	196·7	10·24	33·6	3·86	12·7
Goodwill Trader	42	277·44	59·9	196·7	10·18	33·4	3·82	12·5
Goodwill Traveller	54	285·88	66·37	217·7	10·69	35·1	3·78	12·4
Orwell Fisher	85	627·13	90·1	295·7	15·29	50·2	3·78	12·4
Solway Fisher	85	627·13	90·1	295·7	15·29	50·2	3·78	12·4

SERVICES:
Continental:
Felixstowe/Europort—11 sailings per week.
Felixstowe/Antwerp—3 sailings per week.

Irish-Ferry:
Preston/Larne—6 sailings per week.
Preston/Belfast—3 sailings per week.

Irish-Container:
Preston/Larne—7 sailings per week.
Preston/Belfast—6 sailings per week.
Preston/Dublin—5 sailings per week.
Preston/Drogheda—3 sailings per week.
Ardrossan/Larne—5 sailings per week.

M.V. *Bardic Ferry.*

M.V. *Europic Ferry.*

M.V. *Gaelic Ferry.*

M.V. *Doric Ferry.*

M.V. *Ionic Ferry.*

M.V. *Cerdic Ferry.*

AUSTRALIA EUROPE CONTAINER SERVICE

Australia Europe Container Service (AECS)
78/79 Leadenhall Street,
London EC3A 3DN
TELEPHONE: 01-283-5971
TELEX: 885713
COORDINATING DIRECTOR:
Rear Admiral J. C. Bartosik, CB, DSC
GENERAL:
On the 1st September 1970 the various services provided by the following companies operating between Europe and Australia came under the control of AECS:
Overseas Containers Ltd.
Hapag Lloyd A.G.
Koninklijke Nedlloyd n.v.
Cie des Messageries Maritimes S.A.

Lloyd Triestino S.p.a.N.

AECS schedules the vessels and allocates space to the various Marketing Zones. Each national line is responsible for marketing operations and inland movement of containers in their zones on behalf of all constituent members.
SERVICES:
There are two services:—
Tilbury-Rotterdam-Fremantle-Sydney-Melbourne-Fremantle-Flushing-Tilbury
Tilbury-Hamburg-Fremantle-Sydney-Melbourne-Fremantle-Zeebrugge-Bremerhaven-Tilbury
a weekly service should be provided when

all vessels are in service.

FLEET:
This consists of:

OCL—Six *Bay* Class vessels with a capacity of 1,522 20 ft containers.

Hapag Lloyd AG—Two vessels *Melbourne Express* 1,526 containers, *Sydney Express* 1,589 containers.
Cie Messageries Maritimes—One vessel *Kangourou* 1,492 containers.
Nedlloyd—One vessel *Abel Tasman* 1,589 containers.
Lloyd Triestino—One vessel under construction about 1,500 containers.

AUSTRALIA JAPAN CONTAINER LINE (A.J.C.L.)

Australia Japan Container Line

MANAGING AGENTS:
Overseas Containers Ltd.,
St. Mary Axe House, St. Mary Axe, London,
EC3
TELEPHONE: 01-283 5991
TELEX: 883947

DIRECTORS:
Sir Andrew Crichton   K. St. Johnston
N. P. F. Hillerstrom   A. C. Swire
C. O. M. Hillerstrom   L. G. Hudson
J. G. Payne   P. J. Fuller

GENERAL

The Australia Japan Container Line replaces the conventional services operated for nearly 100 years by the Australian West Pacific Line, the China Navigation Company Limited, and the Eastern and Australian Steamship Company Limited. The new line was formed by these three companies together with Overseas Containers Limited and Associated Container Transportation Limited.

Since January 1971 AJCL has operated an integrated service with NYK, Mitsui/OSK Lines and YS steamship Co each of whom have one container ship on the berth and so a regular weekly service is provided. Although the service is integrated operationally with each line carrying a share of other lines' containers on a space charter system, cargo is marketed and booked independently through the lines' present agents.

Arafura.

AGENTS:
Overseas Containers Australia Pty. Ltd.,
   38 Bridge Street, Sydney, New South
      Wales 2000
   Telephone: 27-9851
   Telex: 21258
Swire MacKinnon
   C.P.O. Box 703, Tokyo, 100-91, Japan
   Telephone: 213-3611
   Telex: TK 2248
FLEET:
Arafura, Ariake
20 ft container capacity: 1,100 of which
190 refrigerated.
19,000 kt dwt

Length: 212 m (695·5 ft)
Beam: 30 m (98·4 ft)
Draught: 9·5 m (31·1 ft)
Speed: 23 knots
CONTAINERS OWNED/OPERATED:
   Dry   2,780   20 × 8 × 8
   Refrigerated 460   20 × 8 × 8
   Wet Hide   80   20 × 8 × 8
   Flatracks   300   20 × 8 × 8
   Bulk   100   20 × 8 × 8
SERVICE:
Brisbane, Sydney and Melbourne to Yokkaichi, Nagoya, Yokohama and Osaka—weekly.
Commenced Autumn 1970.

AUSTRALIAN NATIONAL LINE

Australian National Line

65-79 Riverside Avenue,
   South Melbourne, Victoria, 3205, Australia
TELEPHONE: 62-0681 (Melbourne)
TELEX: AA30584
BRANCHES:
   Sydney, Brisbane, Adelaide, Newcastle,
   Port Kembla, Whyalla, Devonport,
   Townsville, Darwin.
COMMISSIONERS:
   Capt. Sir John Williams, CMG, OBE
      (Chairman)
   H. P. Weymouth, C.B.E. (Vice-Chairman)
   N. G. Jenner
   A. G. Thomson, O.B.E.
   D. D. Bibra, O.B.E.
GENERAL MANAGER:
   R. D. Robin
REPRESENTATIVES:
   In London and Tokyo.
CONTAINERS IN SERVICE:

Dry cargo	906	20 × 8 × 8
Dry cargo	120	10 × 8 × 8
Refrigerated	72	20 × 8 × 8
Refrigerated	185	20 × 8 × 8·5
Bulk	64	20 × 8 × 8
Ventilated Hide	48	20 × 8 × 8
Open Top	22	20 × 8 × 8
Flats (overseas)	860	20 × 8 × 8
Flats (coastal)	685	16·7 × 8·2 × 5·5
Flats (coastal)	488	16·7 × 8·2 × 8
Flats (coastal)	138	14·4 × 8·2 × 5·5
Flats (newsprint)	325	14·4 × 6·2 × 8

Australian Endeavour.

Brisbane Trader.

Bass Trader.

Fleet	Capacity	Nett Tonnage	LOA		Beam		Draught		Speed
			m	ft	m	ft	m	ft	knots
Australian Enterprise	642 20 × 8 × 8 120 cars	9,666	181·66	596	25·00	82	8·99	29·5	21
Australian Endeavour	1,263 20 × 8 × 8	14,403	217·32	713	28·96	95	10·52	34·5	22
Searoad Ships Coastal Service									
Empress of Australia	160 30 cars	6,657	135·63	445	21·34	70	6·10	20·0	20
Princess of Tasmania	30 containers or 600 linear ft of trailers 110 cars	1,781	113·08	371	17·68	58			17
Australian Trader	126 containers 6-20 ft 2-16·7 ft 118-14·4 ft or 516 linear ft of trailers		135·63	445	21·34	70			17·5
Bass Trader	78-14·4 ft containers 30 trailers 30 cars	1,994	98·15	322	17·37	57	4·69	15·4	14
'Searoader Class' *Brisbane, Sydney* *& Townsville Traders*	148-16·7 ft containers 42 20 ft containers 240 motor cars		136·55	448	21·34	70	6·10	20·0	17
Darwin Trader	Northbound: containers 226-20 × 8 × 8 46 10 × 8 × 8 Up to 1,000 tons-unitised cargo, steel etc. Southbound: Bulk ore		139·60	458	21·34	70	9·14	30·0	15·5

OVERSEAS CONTAINER AND ROLL-ON/
ROLL-OFF OPERATIONS:
Eastern Searoad Service:

Australian Enterprise 9666 NT vehicle deck container ship. With her two sister ships *Australian Searoader* of the Japanese "K" Line and *Matthew Flinders* of the Flinders Shipping Co Pty Ltd. This ship maintains a 28 day service between the Eastern Seaboard of Australia and Japan.

Australian Enterprise has a capacity for 642 20 × 8 × 8 units including 111 reefer containers. General cargo semi-trailers and 120 motor vehicles are also carried. Designed for front loader fork lift operations in stowing containers, 378 are carried in the vehicle decks and 264 containers are loaded by crane on the upper deck.

Europe, Australia Container Service:

Australian Endeavour maintains a regular service between Australia and the UK/Continent in conjunction with British and other European ship operators. Capacity is 1,263 20 ft containers; 326 are refrigerated.

OVERSEAS CARGO FEEDER SERVICE

Echula, capable of carrying 148 20 ft units, entered service in mid 1971.

COASTAL OPERATIONS (SEAROAD SERVICE)
Northern Tasmanian Service:

Princess of Tasmania maintains three sailings per week from Melbourne to Devonport with 324 passengers and roll-on freight.
Australian

Australian Trader and *Bass Trader* each maintain 3 sailings per week from Melbourne to Tasmanian Ports of Burnie, Bell Bay and Devonport. Both ships carry roll-on/roll-off freight and containers and in addition

Empress of Australia.

Australian Trader carries 190 passengers.
Sydney Tasmanian Service:

Empress of Australia maintains three sailings per fortnight with 250 passengers and roll-on/roll-off freight one to Hobart and two to Tasmanian ports of Burnie and Bell Bay.

S.E. Coast/Tasmania Trade

Sydney Trader maintains a fortnightly sailing out of Sydney to Melbourne and Adelaide thence Tasmania, Melbourne, Hobart, Melbourne and Sydney with roll-on roll-off freight and containers
Queensland Service:

Brisbane Trader maintains a weekly service between Melbourne and Brisbane with containers and roll-on/roll-off freight.
North Queensland Service:

Townsville Trader maintains a fortnightly sailing between Melbourne, Sydney and North Queensland ports with containers and roll-on/roll-off freight.

Crane deck of *Searoader* class ship being loaded

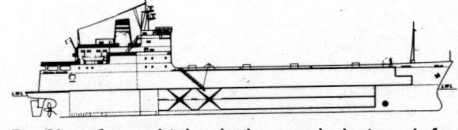

Profile of a vehicle deck vessel designed for the carriage of unitised steel

Northern Trade:

Darwin Trader maintains a monthly schedule from Melbourne, Sydney and Brisbane to Darwin with containers, heavy steel and general cargo returning via Groote Eylandt with ore for Tasmania thence Melbourne.
NSW—Victoria Service:

Two vehicle deck vessels, specially designed for the carriage of up to 6,000 tons unitised steel products are due in service in 1972.

In addition, ANL owns a fleet of 21 conventional, bulk and ore carriers engaged in the Australian Coastal Trades.

Ь-LINE CONTAINER SERVICE

Ь-Line Container Service
Gotlandsgade 2
8100 Aarhus C
Denmark
A wholly owned subsidiary company of
Blaesbjerg & Co, Aarhus, Denmark
TELEPHONE: 06-134733

TELEX: 4695/4497
DIRECTORS:
Ib. Hansen (*Managing*)
Niels Blaesbjerg (*Chairman*)
FLEET:

Baltic Unit
A 13·5 knot vessel capable of carrying 148 20 ft units (16 refrigerated).
Unit Scan I, Unit Scan II
Each 13·5 knot vessel is 499 nrt; it can lift 80 20 ft units and is equipped with its own gear.

CONTAINER FLEET:

Dry	600	20 × 8 × 8
Dry	100	40 × 8 × 8·5
Refrigerated	20	20 × 8 × 8
Insulated	60	20 × 8 × 8
Curtain sided	60	20 × 8 × 8
Flats	90	20 × 8

FUTURE DEVELOPMENTS:
Services may be extended to include Gothenburg and a Scottish port by 1972.
BRANCHES:
Copenhagen:
b-Line Container Service

Barber Lines A/S
A joint venture of:
Wilh. Wilhemsen
Fearnley & Egers
A. F. Klaveness
AGENTS:
Barber Steamship Lines Inc.
17 Battery Place, New York 10004 N.Y.
TELEPHONE: (212)944 1300
TELEX: 222 373/420067

OFFICIALS:
E. J. Barber (*President*)
W. J. Shields (*Executive Vice-President*)

Faergehavn Nord, 2100 Copenhagen
Telephone: 01-293355
Telex: 7247
Immingham:
Brit-Den Unit Service Inc.
Immingham Dock, Immingham, Lincs.
Telephone: 3721
Telex: 527045
Felixstowe:
International Marine Management Inc.
Trelawney House, Felixstowe, Suffolk
Telephone: 5541
Telex: 98459

(Also general UK agents)
Helsingborg:
AB Olson and Wright
Flygandsgaten, Nox 110 44
250 11 Helsingborg
Telephone: 042-139250
Telex: 72237/72356
(Also general agents in Sweden)
SERVICES:
Immingham, Copenhagen, Helsingborg, Århus—Two sailings weekly.
Felixstowe, Copenhagen, Helsingborg, Århus —Two sailings weekly.

BARBER LINES

Profile drawing of a lengthened Barber Lines vessel

FLEET:
Nine conventional cargo carriers are being lengthened to carry a total of 195 20 ft containers, 42 of which will be on deck. The vessels are also equipped with sideports for unitised cargo.

SERVICE:
United States East Coast Ports to the Far East.
CONTAINERS OWNED/OPERATED:

Dry	1,300	20 × 8 × 8
Dry	200	8 × 8 × 8

BATT LINE

See Wm. H. Muller & Co (Batavier) NV for details.

BELL LINES

Bell Lines
Glen House, Stag Place,
London SW1
TELEPHONE: 01-828 4343
TELEX: 919055
OFFICIALS:
G. W. Hollwey (*Chairman & Managing Director*)
E. Kaspers (*Head of Operations*)
J. E. Larkin (*Head of Engineering*)
R. N. Ellis (*Accounts*)
N. A. Jenkinson (*In charge of Commercial Activities—Ireland*)
E. W. Davies (*In charge of Commercial Activities—UK*)
R. Ottenhoff (*In charge of Commercial Activities—Continent*)
COMMERCIAL OFFICES:
London, Manchester, Glasgow, Birmingham, Dublin, Cork, Belfast, Dusseldorf, Milan.
GENERAL:
The Container Services of The George Bell Group have been renamed Bell Lines incorporating Bellferry Ltd., Bell Line Ltd. and Bell Lijn N.V. All the services now come under the same management team.
SERVICES:
The company operates fully integrated door to door container services between the U.K., Ireland and the Continent, using its own land transport, container trains and ships.

Line 1
Bellport (Newport Mon.) to Waterford— 4 times weekly.
Line 2
Teesport to Rotterdam—5/6 times weekly.
Line 3
Waterford to Rotterdam—Twice weekly.
Line 4
Bellport to Rotterdam—Twice weekly.
FLEET:
All vessels are on long term charter and are capable of at least 12·5 knots.
Bell Vigilant
Bell Vigour
Capable of carrying 88 20 ft units these vessels are 80·77 m (265 ft) in length with a beam of 12·43 m (40·8 ft) and a draught of 3·72 m (12·2 ft).
Bell Venture
Bell Valiant
Bell Victor
Bell Vanguard
Bell Volunteer
Capable of carrying 80 20 ft units these vessels are 74·5 m (244·4 ft) in length, with a beam of 13 m (42·7 ft) and a draught of 3·7 m (12 ft).
TERMINALS:
(Please also see entries for Rotterdam, Tees, Bellport and Waterford).
Rozenburg
Bell Terminal
Postbox 35, Rozenburg (Europoort)

Rotterdam
Telephone: Rotterdam 166 700
Telex: 12021, 23489
A 183 m (600 ft) quay equipped with two container gantry cranes and its own two-spur rail terminal with daily departures to Switzerland, Italy and other destinations.
Teesport:
Bell Terminal
Teesport, Middlesbrough, Teesside
Telephone: Eston Grange 4188
Telex: 58651
A 134 m (440) ft quay equipped with one container gantry crane.
Bellport:
Bellport
Corporation Road, Newport, Monmouthshire
Telephone: Newport 73941
Telex: 49446
A 91·4 m (300 ft) quay equipped with one container crane and with a direct rail link to the freightliner network.
Waterford:
Bell Terminal
The Quay, Waterford, Republic of Ireland
Telephone: Waterford 5811
Telex: 6708
A 152·4 m (500 ft) quay equipped with one container gantry crane and with its own rail terminal with services to Dublin, Cork and Belfast.

BEN LINES

Ben Line Containers Ltd.
Incorporating Ellerman Lines
In conjunction with Associated Container Transportation Ltd.
10 North St. David Street
P.O. Box 65
Edinburgh EH2 1YD
TELEPHONE: 031-225 2622
TELEX: 72611
DIRECTORS:
M. F. Strachan   D. F. Martin-Jenkins
H. R. MacLeod   J. P. Lloyd (*Alternate*)

W. R. E. Thomson D. A. Lloyd
F. D. D. Thomson
SERVICE:
Ben Line Containers Ltd's service between Europe and the Far East will commence in January 1972 and by mid 1972 a fortnightly service will be offered in conjunction with other lines. (See TRIO service).
FLEET:
Three 26·5-knot vessels with a length of 289·56 m (950 ft), a beam of 32·31 m (106 ft) and a maximum draught of 13 m (42·65 ft)

Impression of a Ben Line container vessel with one of the present general cargo liners in the foreground.

are on order. Two vessels will enter service in 1972 and the third in 1973. The ships are designed to carry the equivalent of 2,000 20 ft units underdeck.

CONTAINERS IN SERVICE:

By late 1972 it is planned to have about 5,700 20 × 8 × 8 units and 1,500 ISO 40 ft units in service. In addition a limited number of insulated and other special containers will be used.

PRINCIPAL AGENTS:

Germany:

Messrs Menzell & Co.
 Alterwall 67/69, 2 Hamburg 11
 Telephone: 361081
 Telex: 211557

Netherlands:

Messrs D. Burger & Zoon
 Westerstraat 7-11, P.O. Box 149,
 Rotterdam
 Telephone: (010) 111220
 Telex: 21031

United Kingdom:

Killick Martin and Company Ltd

Dunster House, 20 Mark Lane
London EC3
Telephone: 01-623 2100

Malaysia:

Ben Line Containers (Malaysia)
 Sdn. Berhad, 16th Floor,
 Lee Yan Lian Building, P.O. Box 994
 Jalan Mountbatten, Kuala Lumpur
 Telephone: 26576-8 and 22132
 Telex: KLTX 225

Singapore:

Ben Line Containers Singapore (Pte) Ltd.
 Maritime Building, P.O. Box 580
 Singapore
 Telephone: 93421
 Telex: 258

Hong Kong:

Ben Line Containers (Hong Kong) Ltd.
 The Chartered Bank Building,
 4-4a Des Voeux Road Central,
 P.O. Box 319, Hong Kong
 Telephone: H-231021
 Telex: BEN HX 3227

A Ben Line Container in service

Japan:

The Ben Line Steamers Ltd.
 C.P.O. Box 1908, Tokyo
Location Address:
 Kyodo Building (Tokyo Ekimae),
 8th Floor, No. 3, 2-Chome, Yaesu,
 Chuo-ku, Tokyo

BERWIND LINES

Berwind Lines Inc.
Isla Grande Terminal
P.O. Box 4975
Old San Juan, Puerto Rico 00905
TELEPHONE: 724 6500

OFFICIALS:
 V. R. Bericochea (*Vice-President*)

ROLL-ON SERVICE:
 Puerto Rico to US Virgin Islands.

TERMINALS:
 P.O. Box 3158, St. Thomas, V.I.
  TELEPHONE: 774 4325
 P.O. Box 397, Christiansted, St. Croix, V.I.
  TELEPHONE: 773-3119

BLUE STAR LINE

The Line is part of the ACT Consortium and a partner in Scanstar Ltd.

BORE LINE

Bore Steamship Co. Ltd.
Slottsgaten 36
Abo/Turku
Finland
TELEPHONE: 20 300

TELEX: 62 230
MANAGING DIRECTOR: G. Von Rettig
SERVICES:
Roll-on/Roll-off Finland—Harwich (Mann's Navyard) Dunkirk and Rouen.

UK AGENTS:
Mann & Son (London) Ltd
Riverside House,
High Street, Woolwich,
London, S.E.18

BRISTOL STEAM NAVIGATION CO. LTD

Bristol Steam Navigation Co. Ltd.
P.O. Box 8, St. Brendans Way,
Avonmouth, Bristol BS11 9EZ
TELEPHONE: Avonmouth 4581
TELEX: 44796

BRANCHES:
 Birmingham, London, Dublin.
ASSOCIATED COMPANIES:
Seawheel Ltd.
Lovells Groupage Ltd.

DIRECTORS:
D. D. Lovell
G. E. Lovell
H. W. Gale
E. R. Jordan

Bristol Steam Navigation Co's *Apollo* alongside the Company's berth at Bristol

A. J. Martin
F. L. Fewell
M. M. Melsom
IRISH SERVICE GENERAL MANAGER IN CHARGE
SHIP AND TERMINAL OPERATION:
M. M. Melsom
SERVICE:
Bristol to Dublin—4 sailings per week.
CONTAINERS IN SERVICE:

All containers, other than 150 small dry cargo units (7 ft 9 in × 6 ft 10 in × 6 ft 7 in) are owned and operated by associated companies or other unit load operators.
PRINCIPAL OVERSEAS AGENTS:
Bristol Seaway Ltd., Georges Quay, Dublin

Telephone: Dublin 774351
Telegrams: Besenco Dublin
Telex: 5114

FLEET DETAILS:			Length		Beam		Loaded Draught	
Name	20 ft Container Capacity	n.r.t.	ft.	m	ft	m	ft	m
Apollo	75	522	278	85	39	12	13·2	4·01
Echo	75	504	278	85	39	12	13·2	4·01

B & I LINE

British & Irish Steampacket Company Ltd.
North Wall House, 12 North Wall, Dublin
TELEPHONE: Dublin 41821
TELEGRAMS: Ladyships, Dublin
TELEX: Dublin 5356
Also see entry under Iropa Transport.
BRANCHES:
B + I Line, Penrose Quay, Cork
 Tel: 51321. Telex: 6137
B + I Line, Merchant's Quay, Drogheda, Co. Lough
 Tel: Drogheda 8794
B + I Line, Regent House 89/97 Kingsway, London WC2 2B6RH
B + I Line, First Floor, Cunard Building, Liverpool 8
 Tel: Central 20479. Telex: 62293
DIRECTORS:
 Liam St J. Devlin (*Chairman*)
 Kevin Briscoe
 Dr Juan Greene
 P. H. Greer
 Paul Alexander
 M. J. O'Keeffe
 Brian Daly
EXECUTIVES IN CHARGE OF CONTAINER OPERATIONS:
 Don Palmer (*Dublin*)
 A. Danahar (*Liverpool*)
 J. Ferns (*Birmingham*)
 P. J. Wright (*London*)
SERVICES:
Dublin–Liverpool—Daily, roll-on/roll-off and container ships.
Dublin–Weston Point—Three times per week, container ships.
Swansea–Cork—Daily in summer, three times per week in winter, roll-on/roll-off ships.
(See entry under Iropa Transport for services between Ireland and Holland and France in conjunction with Holland America Line).
CONTAINERS IN SERVICE:

Dry	530	20 × 8 × 8
Dry	25	30 × 8 × 8·5
Insulated	5	30 × 8 × ·8·5
Insulated	100	20 × 8 × 8
Insulated	50	20 × 8 × 8·5
Open Top	30	20 × 8 × 8

B & I Lines' *Kildare*

Open Top	25	20 × 8 × 8·25
Tiltainers	30	20 × 8 × 8
Flats	80	30 × 8
Flats	650	24 × 8
Flats	100	20 × 8

FUTURE DEVELOPMENTS:

A cellular 180 ft × 20 unit ship was launched in June 1971 for the high density Liverpool/Dublin route which commences in November. A second similar ship may follow and in the interim m.v. '*Kildare*' is being cellularised. A £2½ million terminal complex is under construction by M.D. & H.C. in Liverpool; the freight section of which opens in November 1971; car and passenger ferryport section is to open in April 1972. This facility is situated on a 6·88 hectare (17 acres) site and will include sophisticated groupage facilities. In Dublin, the Dublin Container Terminal Company will operate modern terminal facilities for B+I Line and British Railways Board. There will be separate facilities within the same general area adjacent to existing B+I Ferryport; and new groupage facilities will be provided.
Coast Lines Ltd (Agents), Reliance House Water Street, Liverpool 2
 Tel: Central 5464. Telex: 62293
B + I BRANCH DEPOTS:
Limerick:
B+I Line, c/o C.I.E.
 Careys Road Transit Shed, Limerick
 Telephone: 48777. Ext: 65
Birmingham:
·B + I Line
 Groupage Depot, Sampson Road, North, Birmingham 11
 Telephone: 021 772 2791

B & I Line's *Tipperary*

Part of the B & I Line terminal at Dublin

Office Telephone: 021 643 7788
 Telex: 338024
Bradford:
Transflash Units Ltd.
 Mount St., Bradford
 Telephone: 33871
 Telex: 51360
Glasgow:
B + I Line Groupage Depot
 Lloyd St., Farmelone Rd., Rutherglen, Glasgow
 Telephone: 041 647 8507
 Telex: 77179
Liverpool:
B + I Line
 South East Princes Dock, Liverpool 2
 Telephone: 051 236 5464
 Telex: 627673
London:
B + I Line, Groupage Depot
 Abbey Rd., Stratford, London E.15

FLEET:
Container Vessels:

Name	20ft Container capacity	Net. Reg. Tons	Length		Beam		Loaded draught	
			ft	m	ft	m	ft	m
Kildare	74	415	256·7	78·2	43·5	13·26	11·8	3·58
Tipperary	74	415	256·7	78·2	43·5	13·26	11·8	3·58
Siegerland	45	326	222·8	67·86	34·5	10·49	12·9	3·93
Rolf	47	327	222·9	67·86	34·5	10·49	12·9	3·93
Kora	47	327	222·9	67·86	34·5	10·49	12·9	3·93

(Also *Mayo* and *Embdena* with Iropa Transport)
Roll-on Vessels:

Name	20ft Container capacity	Net. Reg. Tons	Length		Beam		Loaded draught	
			ft	m	ft	m	ft	m
Munster	35	1751	361·7	110·2	58·6	17·83	14·7	4·44
Leinster	38	2419	387·7	118·13	58·6	17·83	15·8	4·77
Innisfallen	38	2419	387·7	118·13	58·6	17·83	15·8	4·77

Telephone: 01 555 0204
Telex: 896484
Office Telephone: 01 405 7774
Telex: 22741

Manchester:
B + I Line, Groupage Depot
Seaway House, Hope St., Salford M5 HWL
Telephone: 061 736 4511

Nottingham:
B + I Line Groupage Depot
A. R. Marshall & Sons (Bulwell) Ltd.
Hucknall Lane, Bulwell, Nottingham
NG6 8AN
Telephone: 271283

Swansea:
B + I Line, Groupage Depot
'K' Shed, Kings Dock, Swansea
Telephone: 0792 50406 52012
Telex: 48259

LONDON:
Gentransco (Overseas) Ltd.
PO Box 200
Abbey Road, Stratford E.16,

SWANSEA:
Coast Lines Ltd., Exchange Buildings,
Swansea
Tel: 0792-52016

WESTON POINT:
Coast Lines Ltd., Weston Point Dock,
Runcorn, Cheshire
Tel: 0928 and 2821   Telex: 627 023

A model of the B + I Line Dublin terminal showing the completed layout.

The B+I roll-on/roll-off and car ferry Termina
at Dublin with the M.V. *Munster.*

BRITISH RAILWAYS

British Railways Board
Shipping and International Services Division
Liverpool Street, London, EC2M 7QH
TELEPHONE: 01-283 7535
TELEX: 886821
SERVICES:
British Railways operates the following
services.

Roll-on/Roll-off:
Stranraer to Larne
Newhaven to Dieppe (in conjunction with
French Railways)
Dover to Calais/Dunkirk/Boulogne
Harwich to Hook of Holland (in conjunction
with Zeeland Shipping Co.).
Harwich to Ostend and Dover to Ostend
(in conjunction with B.M.A.)

Train Ferries:
Harwich to Zeebrugge/Dunkirk
Dover to Dunkirk

Containers:
Holyhead to Dublin—6 sailings weekly
Holyhead to Belfast—6 sailings weekly
Fishguard to Waterford—Daily
Harwich to Dunkirk—Daily (in conjunction
with French Railways)
Harwich to Zeebrugge—2 sailings daily
Harwich to Rotterdam—Daily (in conjunc-
tion with Zeeland Shipping Co.)

Brian Boroime

Colchester

Sea Freightliner II.

FLEET:

ROLL-ON/ROLL-OFF VESSELS:

A fleet of passenger/car ferries also carry commercial vehicles and trailers.

TRAIN FERRIES:

Eight specially equipped train ferry vessels are operated.

CONTAINER SHIPS:

A substantial fleet of vessels is engaged on the Board's Container Services. The following have been specially built or converted for the carriage of 20 ft ISO units.

Sea Freightliners I and II: These 13½ knot cellular vessels are 118·4 m (388·5 ft) in length, 16·79 m (55·1 ft) beam with a draught of 4·42 m (14·5 ft) and are capable of lifting between 108 × 40 ft, 148 × 30 ft, or 218 × 20 ft containers or a mixture of lengths as required.

Brian Boroime
Rhodri Mawr

Two 14 knot cellular vessels with a length of 107·1 m (351·4 ft), a beam of 16·8 m (55·1 ft) and a draught of 4·1 m (13·5 ft) came into service in 1970. These ships, having a capacity of 184 20 ft units or their equivalent, are employed on the Holyhead/

Dublin and the Holyhead/Belfast services.

Isle of Ely:

A 13½ knot vessel, operating on the North Sea Services, with a length of 73·61 m (241·5 ft), a beam of 11·43 m (37·5 ft) a draught of 4·36 m (14·3 ft) and a capacity of 44 20 ft equivalents.

Colchester:

Operating on the North Sea Services this 13½ knot vessel has a length of 90·21 m (295·8 ft), a beam of 11·43 m (37·5 ft), a draught of 4·42 m (14·5 ft) and a capacity of 86 20 ft equivalents.

BRITISH YUKON NAVIGATION (WHITE PASS AND YUKON ROUTE)

British Yukon Navigation Co. Ltd.
510 West Hastings Street,
Vancouver 2, BC, Canada
TELEPHONE: 683-7221
TELEX: 045-613
PRINCIPAL OFFICIALS:
F. H. Brown (*Chairman of the Board*)
A. P. Friesen (*President*)
F. D. Smith (*Vice President, Finance, Treasurer and Comptroller*)
M. P. Taylor (*Vice President, Operations*)
R. S. Minter (*Vice President, Corporate Communications*)
S. Kollbaer (*Manager—Ocean Division*)
CONTAINER SERVICES:
Vancouver to Skagway—Weekly
(White Pass & Yukon Route)
FLEET:

Two cellular container vessels, the *Frank H. Brown* and the *Klondike*. These 13½ knot ships are 120 m (394 ft) in length, 21·3 m (70 ft) beam with a draught of 6·09 m (20 ft). They are capable of lifting 200 25·25 × 8 × 8 containers underdeck and also a load of general freight and containers on deck. Each vessel is equipped with a 40 ton Munck container gantry crane.

Frank H. Brown at Skagway

CONTAINERS IN SERVICE:

Dry	355	25·25 × 8 × 8	Open tray	170	25·25 × 8 × 4
Insulated	105	25·25 × 8 × 8	Racks	30	25·25 × 8 × 4
Refrigerated	15	25·25 × 8 × 8	Posted high racks	20	25·25 × 8 × 8

INLAND TRANSPORT LINKS:
See entry under White Pass & Yukon Route in the Canadian Rail Section.

BURNS AND LAIRD

Burns & Laird Lines, Limited
(Coast Lines Group)
Argos House, Oswald Street
Glasgow C.1.
TELEPHONE: Glasgow 041-221 6301
TELEX: 778115
PORT OFFICE AND COMMERCIAL DEPARTMENT:
Winton Pier, Ardrossan
Telephone: 0294 61621
Telex: 778310
AGENTS:
Coast Lines Offices as Agents
DIRECTORS:
R. W. Berkeley
J. N. Burrell
R. T. Robinson
N. C. B. Wright (*Director & General Manager*)
SERVICES:
Ardrossan/Belfast Vehicle Ferry (m.v. *Lion*)
Daily Round Trip except Sundays.

Ardrossan/Larne Vehicle ferry—5 times weekly in each direction.
FLEET:
m.v. *Lion*
Passenger and Vehicle Ferry.
Gross tons: 3,333
Net reg. tons: 1,024
Length: 103·63 m (340 ft) b.p.
Beam: 17·07 m (56 ft)
Draught: 4·30 m (14·1 ft).
Vehicle deck area: 1,174·3 m² (12,640 sq ft).
Vehicle deck height: 4·42 m (14·5 ft).
Maximum load per axle: 12 tons.
Container or vehicle capacity—approx: 40 × 20 ft.
CONTAINERS:
None owned or operated.
PRINCIPAL AGENTS:
Belfast Steamship Co. Ltd.
42 Donegall Quay, Belfast

M.V. Lion.

Telephone: 0232 20211
Telex: 74546
Anglo Irish Transport Ltd.
Water Street, Londonderry
Telephone: 0504 4204/5
Telex: 74565

C P SHIPS

Canadian Pacific Steamships Ltd.
62 Trafalgar Square, London, WC2
TELEPHONE: 01-930 5100
TELEGRAMS: Paccanos, London
TELEX: 22151/2
OFFICIALS DEALING WITH CONTAINERS:
S. Byars (*Manager, North Atlantic Freight Services—CP Ships*)
D. R. Newberry (*Deputy Manager, North Atlantic Freight Services—CP Ships*)
L. N. J. Smet (*Regional Manager, Europe,*

Freight Services—CP Ships)
R. L. Purdy (*Regional Manager, North America, Freight Services—CP Ships*)
J. A. Davies (*Regional Manager UK Freight Services—CP Ships*)
G. H. Creighton (*System Manager, Foreign Freight—CP Rail*)
GENERAL:
Canadian Pacific, utilising certain of its subsidiaries, operates an integrated transportation system.

CONTAINER OPERATIONS:
CP Ships, CP Rail, CP Transport, CP Express and Smith Transport and affiliates have cooperated to develop port terminal and inland distribution services for overseas cargo. CP Ships and CP Rail have their own or agency representation in all major European cities and at strategic North American centres.
SERVICES:
London and Rotterdam to Quebec—

weekly.

Liverpool and Clyde to Quebec—weekly in conjunction with Donaldson/Head Line.

CONTAINERS IN SERVICE:

Dry	2,150	20 × 8 × 8
Dry	250	20 × 8 × 8·5
Dry	375	40 × 8 × 8
Dry	100	40 × 8 × 8·5
Insulated	120	20 × 8 × 8
Refrigerated	100	40 × 8 × 8·5
Open top	40	20 × 8 × 8
Open top	65	20 × 8 × 8·5
Dry bulk	40	20 × 8 × 8·5
Half height	360	20 × 8 × 8

TRUCKING OPERATIONS:

The trucking companies have acquired a variety of special container handling equipment including side transfer and overhead lifting units. CP Express has installed automated cargo sorting equipment at its Montreal and Toronto terminals.

CP Voyageur in the St. Lawrence River

FLEET:

	20 ft Container capacity	Speed Knots	n.r.t.	Length m	Length ft	Beam m	Beam ft	Draught Loaded m	Draught Loaded ft
C.P. Voyageur	707	20	7,804						
C.P. Trader	707	20	7,246	165·8	544	25·6	84	9·14	30
C. P. Discoverer	707	20	7,246						
Beavermondo	140	—	1,045	99·06	325	14·48	47·5	6·22	20·4
Beaverrando	140	—	1,045	99·06	325	14·48	47·5	6·22	20·4
C.P. Ambassador	322	—	3,756	131·8	432	17·37	57·0	8·08	26·5
Eemstroom	150	—	2,197	118·2	338	15·56	51·0	6·01	20·0
Hope Isle	150	—	564	95·7	314	16	52·5	4·20	13·8
Hother Isle	316	—	4,055	137·6	451	19·07	62·5	6·53	21·4
Weser Isle	150	—	561	95·7	314	16	52·5	4·20	13·8

Note: Draughts for *Beavermondo* and *Beaverrando* shown as closed shelter deckers. *C.P. Ambassador* previously known as *Beaveroak*.

CARIBBEAN TRAILER

Caribbean Trailer Express Ltd.
Bank of Bermuda Building
Hamilton, Bermuda
GENERAL AGENTS: Shipcraft (Agency), Inc.
Suite 2101, 42 Broadway, New York
TELEPHONE: 943-8160
TELEGRAMS: Friendline New York
TELEX: (W.O.) 126941
        (R.C.A.) 222413
        (I.T.T.) 422238
HEAD OFFICE:
Bank of Bermuda Building
Hamilton, Bermuda
BRANCHES:
Shipcraft Agency (Miami) Inc.
Pier 3, Dade Country Seaport
Miami, Florida
Telephone: 377-9328
Telegrams: Friendline Miami
Telex: (W.U.) 51-9441

DIRECTORS:

G. A. Common	J. W. Common
W. T. Wilson	J. A. Larson
R. H. Chapman	C. T. Collis

EXECUTIVE IN CHARGE OF CONTAINER OPERATIONS:
Ralph Maldonado
SERVICES:
Roll-on/Roll-off services operated on the following routes:
Miami-Venezuela—This service has been withdrawn temporarily pending the delivery of further time chartered tonnage.

Co-ordinated Caribbean Transport Inc.
1001 Port Boulevard, Miami, Florida
CHIEF EXECUTIVE:
H. Calderon

Cast Containers Ltd.
1, Westmount Square
Montreal 216, P.Q. Canada
SERVICE:
Canada-Europe
The *Blue Box* service for full loads and

New York to Jamaica and the Dominican Republic—weekly
OVERSEAS AGENTS:
Common Brothers Ltd.
Exchange Buildings
Quayside, Newcastle-upon-Tyne
Telephone: Newcastle 25011
Telegrams: Common Newcastle
Telex: Newcastle 53267
FLEET:
Caribbean Venture and Caribbean Enterprise
CAPACITY:
50 × 40 ft Refrigerated or Dry Cargo Trailers 593·63 n.r.t.
Length 94·38 m (309 ft 8 in)
Beam 16·81 m (55 ft 2 in)
Draught 4·80 m (15 ft 9 in)
Speed 16 knots
Vehicles are loaded through stern doors giving an opening 13·7 m (45 ft.) by 4·2 m (14 ft) high; the stern door forms the loading ramp. Vehicles are raised to the weather deck by a 33 ton capacity elevator. The vessels are also equipped with deep tanks giving a total capacity of 360 tons for bulk liquid cargoes.
TRAILER FLEET:
About 235 leased trailers dry and refrigerated 40 × 8 × 8·5 and flatbed 40 × 8 are employed in the service.
FUTURE DEVELOPMENTS:
Two trailer ships, each capable of lifting 92 × 40 ft trailers, are under construction for delivery at the end of 1971.

CARIBBEAN TRANSPORT

SERVICE.
Roll-on service—weekly from Miami to Puerto Cortes, Honduras and St. Thomas de Castilla.

CAST

groupage operates between Montreal and Antwerp. Weekly during the navigation season and every two weeks in winter.
CONTAINERS IN SERVICE:
Over 2,000 20 ft units are in service.
FLEET:

Caribbean Trailer Express' *Caribbean Venture* showing the stern ramp.

Caribbean Venture.

FLEET:
Mar Caribe: A 15 knot vessel capable of carrying 112 trailers.

Four vessels, *Alida Gorthon, Atlantic Skou, Ragnild* and *Himmeland* believed to be partly fitted for the carriage of containers, have been taken on long term charter by Cast Transportation Ltd., Shed 42, Berth 43, Montreal, P.Q.

CAWOODS CONTAINERS

Craigavad alongside Cawoods Berth, Belfast

Cawoods Containers Ltd.,
Herdman Channel West, Belfast, BT3 9AL
TELEPHONE: 0232 747334
TELEX: 74406
DIRECTOR AND GENERAL MANAGER:
W. N. K. McClelland
BRANCHES:
Stalbridge Dock, Garston, Liverpool 19.
Telephone: 051-427 6337
Telex: 627258
63/65 Crutched Friars, London, EC3
Telephone: 01-488 3717
Telex: 887130
GENERAL:

The company operates a door-to-door service between Belfast, Northern Ireland and Liverpool (Garston) using their own road vehicles, ships, containers, Demag straddle-carriers and Strachan & Henshaw container gantry cranes. Other 20 ft, 30 ft and 40 ft containers also accepted. Operations have been extended to include a service between Belfast and Rotterdam.
SERVICES:
Belfast/Garston—Daily.
Belfast/Rotterdam—Weekly.
FLEET:

Two cellular vessels *Craigavad* and *Craigantlet*, with a capacity of 84 and 107 20 ft units respectively, maintain the Belfast/Garston service and one vessel, capable of carrying 64 20 ft units, operates on the Belfast/Rotterdam service. Two cellular vessels, each with a capacity of 134 20 ft units are scheduled to enter service in March 1972.

CONTAINERS IN SERVICE:

Dry cargo	280	20 × 8 × 8
Dry cargo	220	20 × 8 × 8·5
Dry cargo	36	40 × 8 × 8
Dry cargo	100	40 × 8 × 8·5
Halftainers	50	20 × 8 × 4
Tiltainers	25	20 × 8 × 8·5
Open tops	16	40 × 8 × 8

Craigantlet

CENTRAL GULF LINES

Central Gulf Lines
2700 International Trade Mart
New Orleans, USA
OFFICERS:
Niels F. Johnsen (*Chairman*)
Niels W. Johnsen (*Vice-Chairman*)
Erik F. Johnsen (*President*)
VICE-PRESIDENTS:
Harold S. Grehan, Jr.
William T. Toomey (*Operations*)
Charles F. Monninger (*Traffic*)
Dr. Joseph C. Morris
US OFFICES:
1 Whitehall Street, New York, NY 10004
711 Fannin Street, Houston, Texas
PRINCIPAL OVERSEAS OFFICES:
PO Box 487, Wittet Road,
Ballard Estates, Bombay
Yurakucho Bldg., Room 1614
No. 5, 1-Chome, Yuraku-cho
Chiyoda-ku, Tokyo
SERVICES:

US East and Gulf Ports to the Mediterranean, Red Sea, Persian Gulf, Pakistan, India, South East Asia and the Far East. The Barge carriers provide a fortnightly service between the US Gulf and United Kingdom and Continental European ports. The vessels carry the products of the International Paper Company, USA, eastbound.
FLEET:

11 Conventional cargo vessels. Two Barge Carriers, *Acadia Forest* and *Atlantic Forest* on charter from Norwegian owners.

These vessels are 262·13 m (860 ft) overall length, 32·6 m (107 ft) beam with a deadweight of 43,500 tons and a speed of 19·5 knots on a draught of 8·53 m (28 ft); 18 knots at 11·43 m (37 ft) draught. 73 Barges can be carried capable of lifting about 27,000 tons of cargo.
Barges:
Overall length—18·74 m (61·5 ft)
Overall breadth—9·5 m (31·2 ft)
Draught-saltwater—2·53 m (8·3 ft)
Inside height at the side amidships—
3·96 m (13 ft)
Bale Capacity—563·57 m³ (19,900 cu ft)
Grain Capacity—583·39 m³ (20,600 cu ft)
Some 500 lighters are being provided to maintain the service.

Stern view of *Acadia Forest* showing the loading of a barge whilst another is being placed in position for loading

Handling: Barges are loaded and discharged by a travelling gantry crane which when in the lifting position is extended over the vessel's stern on cantilevers. The crane is capable of lifting 510 tons and will complete a handling cycle in 20 minutes. It is powered by four independent gantry drives any two of which are capable of maintaining the full lift capacity. In order to handle lighters in choppy seas the crane, manufactured by Morgan Engineering Company, Alliance, Ohio, is equipped with constant tension devices to accommodate as much as four feet of vertical movement between the lighter and the ship.

Barges are stored in 5 holds containing 14 loading bays and also on deck.

UK AGENTS FOR BARGE CARRIERS:
Lambert Bros. (Shipping) Ltd
Cunard House,
88 Leadenhall Street
London, EC3

Acadia Forest

Comar Shipping and Trading Ltd.

A joint venture of Erlebach & Co. and the Great Yarmouth Warehousing Co.

Clarke Traffic Services Limited
PO Box 730, Station 'B'
Montreal 102, PQ—Canada
TELEPHONE: 861-1651
TELEX: 01-2508
GENERAL:
A member of the Dart Containerline consortium.
BRANCHES:
St. Johns, Nfld; Corner Brook, Nfld; Sept

COMAR LINE

UK AGENTS:
G-Y-Lines (Agency) Ltd.

East Quay,
Great Yarmouth
GENERAL MANAGER:
H. Walford

CLARKE TRAFFIC SERVICES

Iles, PQ; Quebec, Que; Toronto, Ont, etc.

DIRECTORS:
S. D. Clarke (*President*)
J. Hutcheson (*Vice-President–operations*)

EXECUTIVE IN CHARGE OF CONTAINER OPERATIONS:
A. Marchand (*Manager, Newfoundland Services*)

COLUMBUS LINE

See entry under Hamburg Sudamerikanische Dampschiffahrts Gesellschaft Eggert and Amsinck.

COMBI LINE

TELEPHONE: 010-1725 60

TELEX: 21172

SERVICE:
North Continental Europe—United States-Gulf Ports.

Hamburg, Bremen, Rotterdam, Antwerp, Grangemouth, Felixstowe to New Orleans and Houston (weekly); Wilmington and Savannah (fortnightly); and Tampa, Mobile

FLEET:
Isar. A chartered vessel capable of carrying 65 × 20 ft containers.
SERVICES:
London and Felixstowe
Rotterdam

FLEET:
2 partial container ships, the *Cabot* and the *Chimo* each able to lift 45 × 20 ft containers and equipped with 20 ton slewing deck cranes.
CONTAINERS IN SERVICE:
Dry   1   20 × 8 × 8
Refrigerated 20 20 × 8 × 8
SERVICES:
Montreal to St. John's and Cornerbrook, Newfoundland—2 sailings per week.

and Charleston (monthly).
FLEET:
The service is maintained by a fleet of conventional cargo vessels. In 1972 two barge carriers will enter service. The 20 knot barge carriers will be 262 m (859·6 ft) in length with a beam of 32·5 m (106·6 ft). There will be a fleet of 30 barges, each weighing 80 tons and measuring 18·74 × 9·50 × 3·96 m (61·4 × 31·2 × 13 ft).

Combi Line
A joint venture of:
Hapag Lloyd Aktiengesellschaft
2 Hamburg 1, Ballindaum 25
TELEPHONE: (0411) 32.10.81
TELEX: 02 161 988
and
Nederlandsch-Amerikaansche Stoomvaart-Maatschappij Holland Amerika Lijn
Wilhelmskade 86, Rotterdam

Compagnie Générale Transatlantique
Tour Atlantique
92-Puteaux, Cedex 6, Paris, La Défense
Paris 9e France
TELEPHONE: 775.14.11
TELEX: 124 1445
BRANCHES:
London: 20, Cockspur Street, SW1
New York: 17, Battery Place, NY10004
Nice, Dunkirk, Fort de France, Le Havre
Bordeaux, Marseilles, Nantes.
DIRECTORS:
E. Lanier (*Chairman*)

CGT (FRENCH LINE)

P. Panard (*Managing*)
J. Ribiere (*Deputy Managing*)

SERVICES:
The company operates on the North Atlantic as one of the partners in Atlantic Container Line. Two ships, the Atlantic Champagne and the Atlantic Cognac are owned by the company.

CGT also run services from North Europe to Canada, West Coast USA, Central and West Coast South America and the French

West Indies with vessels capable of carrying 104 × 20 ft containers.
FLEET:
Pointe Allegre
Pointe Marin
Pointe Des Colibris
These vessels are fitted for the carriage of up to 104 20 ft units.

CONTAINERS IN SERVICE:
Dry   530 20 × 8 × 8
Dry   10 40 × 8 × 8

C.G.T.B.

Compagnie Générale Transbaltique
Cedex 6-92, Paris La Defénse
TELEPHONE: 775-1411
TELEX: 61669

The company is part of the C.G.T. Group.

SERVICE:
France—Netherlands—Sweden—U.S.S.R.
Le Havre—Leningrad.
FLEET:
Borodine
A specially designed 16 knot roll-on

vessel, with a strengthened hull for navigation in ice fields, entered the Le Havre-Leningrad service in summer 1971. The vessel is 106 m (347·8 ft) in length with a beam of 17·5 m (75·4 ft) and a deadweight capacity of 5,350 tons.

COSTA ARMATORI S.p.A.

Costa Armatori S.p.A.
Via G. D'Annunzio, 2/20—16121 Genova
TELEPHONE: 5483
TELEGRAMS: Costeria
TELEX: 27.068 Costeria
DIRECTOR:
Giacomo Costa Fu Federico
BRANCHES:
20121 Milano: Linea 'C'—Costa Armatori
S.P.A.—Foro Buonaparte 71
Telephone: 866.033—866.064
Telex: 32631
FLEET:

The fleet consists of four conventional cargo vessels capable of carrying containers.

Maria Costa and *Pia Costa* both of which have been specially adapted for the carriage of 100 20 ft units in two holds and on deck are 167·64 m (550·3 ft) in length with a draught of 9·45 m (31 ft) . The *Paola Costa* can carry 35 containers and is 145·95 m (478 ft 10 in) in length with a draught of 8·23 m (27 ft 8 in).

The *Etha* with a capacity of 135 20 ft units has been taken on long term charter. This vessel is 166·35 m (545·75 ft) in length with a draught of 8·85 m (29·9 ft).

SERVICES:
Costa Line, fortnightly service between USA (New York—Norfolk) and western Mediterranean.

PRINCIPAL OVERSEAS AGENTS:
Overseas Consolidated Co
26, Broadway, NY, 10004
Telephone: HA 5.1600
Telegrams: Skysail
Telex: RCA 222.689, Western Union 62.836

CONTAINERS IN SERVICE:
Dry 500 20 × 8 × 8

CUNARD BROCKLEBANK

Cunard-Brocklebank Ltd.
Cunard Building
Liverpool L3 1DY
TELEPHONE: 051-227 3000
TELEX: 62343
DIRECTORS:
N. S. Thompson (*Chairman*)
T. H. Telford (*Managing Director*)
W. B. Slater (*Deputy Managing Director*)
F. K. Crawford
K. R. Edmondson

G. Mearns
B. C. G. Place
OFFICIALS:
R. F. Orman (*ACL Divisional Manager*)
J. D. Hoskin (*ACL Divisional Manager, Sales*)
T. H. Davies (*UK Traffic Manager*)
Captain M. Forster (*Port Operations Manager*)
BRANCHES:
London
Southampton
Birmingham

Bradford
Bristol
FLEET AND SERVICES:
The Cunard Steam-ship Company is a member of Atlantic Container Line Ltd (ACL). Cunard-Brocklebank acts as general agents in the United Kingdom and Republic of Ireland for ACL, and also manages the *Atlantic Causeway* and *Atlantic Conveyor*, which operate within the ACL fleet of ten vessels.

DART CONTAINERLINE

Dart Containerline Company Ltd.
Hamilton, Bermuda
U.K. Head Office:
DART CONTAINERLINE LIMITED:
Dart House, Canute Road, Southampton,
S01 1AA
TELEPHONE: 29124
TELEX: 47239
London Office:
12-20 Camomile Street, London, E.C.3
TELEPHONE: 01-623 6611
TELEX: 884445
A Joint Venture of:
Compagnie Maritime Belge
(The Belgian Line)
61 St. Katelijnevest, Antwerp 1, Belgium
Telephone: 33,88.90, 32.18.90, 32.19.10
Telex: 31366, 31367, 31335
Bristol City Line Limited,
  129 Cumberland Road, Bristol 1, England
  Telephone: Bristol 24101
  Telex: 44150
Clarke Traffic Services
  1155 Dorchester West, P.O. Box 730,
  Station 'B', Montreal 2, Canada
  Telephone: 861-1651
  Telex: 12508
U.K. EXECUTIVES:
D. B. Hall (*Managing Director*) Southampton
Capt. P. W. Doble (*Operations Manager*) Southampton
M. J. Jordan (*Sales/Marketing Manager*) London.
SERVICES:
United Kingdom and Continent to Canada and USA through Antwerp, Southampton, Halifax, New York, Norfolk and Baltimore weekly.

This service is augmented by a feeder service operated by Ibesca Containerline using chartered tonnage and calling at ports in Europe in the range Scandinavia-Spain.

Dart America

Dart Containers

This service will also lift containers between European destinations.
FLEET:
Dart America
Dart Europe
Dart Atlantic

Three fully cellular container vessels with a capacity of the equivalent of 1,556 20 ft units. These 23 knot ships are 231·8 m (760 ft) in length with a beam of 30·5 m (100 ft) and a draught of 9·14 m (30 ft).
CONTAINERS IN SERVICE:
Excluding leased equipment, approximately 11,000 20 ft equivalent units comprised of 40 ft open top, dry cargo, and insulated

Dart Europe at Southampton

containers and 20 ft dry cargo, open hard top, canvas top, and other specialised units are in service.

DELTA LINE

Delta Steamship Lines, Inc.
International Trade Mart
P.O. Box 50250,
New Orleans, Louisiana 70150
TELEPHONE: (504) 522-3492
TELEX: 058-297

BRANCHES:
New York, Washington, Chicago, Houston, Mobile.
SERVICES:
U.S. Gulf—East Coast South America.
U.S Gulf—West Africa.

U.S. Gulf—Caribbean Ports.
Mexico—East Coast South America, Caribbean Ports.
FLEET:
Twelve conventional cargo vessels all of which are capable of handling containers.

On May 19, 1971 a contract was signed with Avondale Shipyards for construction of three Delta LASH-type vessels; delivery is for 1973 and they will be employed on the Caribbean and East Coast South American Service.

Principal characteristics of these 22 knot vessels are: length over-all 845 ft; beam moulded 100 ft; and total displacement of 38,000 tons at 28 ft 0 in design draught. Each vessel will be capable of carrying a maximum of 74 barges or, alternatively a maximum of 1,740 containers, or a combination of the barges and containers in varying numbers as required. Initially Delta plans to carry approximately 288 containers, including refrigerated units. The design provides for a

Impression of a Delta Line containership

highly flexible arrangement for bulk liquids, dry bulk cargoes, refrigerated cargoes, heavy lifts, etc.

CONTAINERS IN SERVICE:

Dry Cargo (closed)	350	20 × 8 × 8
Dry Cargo (closed)	4	40 × 8 × 8

DEUTSCHE SEEREEDEREI

Deutsche Seereederei

See entry under East Germany in Ports and Inland Transport Section.

DFL CONTAINER EXPRESS

DFL Container Express

A joint venture of Finska Angfartygs AB and United Owners Company (H. M. Gehrckens and Ernst Russ).

GENERAL OFFICE:

H. M. Gehrckens
2 Hamburg 11
Bei dem Neuen Krah
TELEPHONE: 361141
TELEX: 02-11117

SERVICE:
Hamburg—Helsinki, Weekly.
FLEET:
Cranz II. A 13 knot vessel with a capacity of 74 20 ft equivalents.

DFDS

DFDS A/S
Sankt Annae Plads 30,
1295 Copenhagen K, Denmark
Telephone: 01-15.63.00
Telex:Cph 9435 forenede
BRANCH OFFICES:
Aalborg, DFDS Ekspedition
Telephone: (08) 12 51 00
Telex: 9722
Aarhus, DFDS Ekspedition
Telephone: (06) 12 83 00
Telex: 4234
Esbjerg, DFDS Ekspedition
Telephone: (051) 2 17 00
Telex: 3251
Frederikshavn, DFDS Ekspedition
Telephone: (084) 2 03 33
Telex: 9784
Odense, DFDS Ekspedition
Telephone: (09) 13 00 32
Telex: 9853
MAIN OFFICE FOR GREAT BRITAIN:
(Freight)
DFDS (UK) Ltd.
Mariner House, Pepys Street,
London, E.C.3

DFDS Surrey

Telephone: 01-488 3886
Telex: 26 2175
MAIN OFFICE FOR BELGIUM:
Agence Maritime Belgo-Danoise SA,
20 Ankerrui, Antwerp
Telephone: 33.58.77
Telex: 31 217
DIRECTORS:
Knud Lauritzen (*Chairman*)
Henry Jensen (*Vice-Chairman*)
G. Andersen
T. Kristensen
O. Lippmann

Baron Ebbe Wedell-Wedellsborg
GENERAL MANAGERS:
Helge Jensen
R. Beir
EXECUTIVES IN CHARGE OF CONTAINER
OPERATIONS:
UK/Denmark services:
C. J. Olsen (*Esbjerg and Copenhagen services*)
B. Leth (*Container Control and combined container transports*)
FLEET-ROLL-ON VESSELS:
Suffolk, Sussex
These 14 knot vessels are capable of

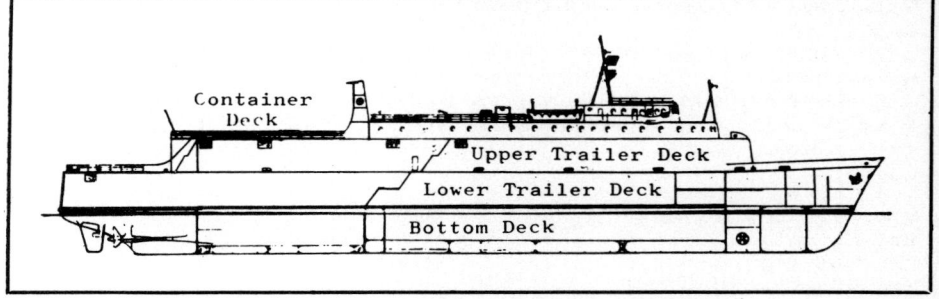

Elevation and cross section of the new DFDS Roll-on/Roll-off container ship.

carrying 70 20 ft units.

Somerset, Stafford

These 18 knot vessels carry up to 148 20 ft units.

Surrey

This 18 knot vessel carries up to 215 20 ft units.

Winston Churchill

A combined passenger/cargo liner this 22 knot vessel is capable of carrying 35 20 ft units.

SERVICES:

UK/Denmark Roll-on/Roll-off:

Felixstowe/Copenhagen, with transhipment via Esbjerg, (non-wheeled units only)—twice a week

Harwich/Esbjerg—5 sailings a week

Harwich/Copenhagen, with transhipment via Esbjerg, (ISO containers and flats only)—5 sailings a week

Grimsby/Esbjerg—twice a week

Grimsby/Copenhagen, with transhipment via Esbjerg, (non-wheeled units only)—twice a week

Newcastle/Esbjerg, twice a week.

Newcastle/Copenhagen, with transhipment via Esbjerg, (non-wheeled units only)—twice a week

Hull/Copenhagen with transhipment via Esbjerg (non wheeled units only)—Twice weekly.

Hull-Esbjerg—Twice weekly (a service operated jointly with Ellerman's Wilson Line).

FUTURE PLANS:

A new roll-on/roll-off service Hull/Esbjerg was inaugurated in May 1971 with sailings twice a week in either direction. German roll-on ship *Nordic Marc* chartered for initial operations, but a sistership to the *Surrey* is presently being built with Robb Caledon in Scotland for this service which is operated in co-operation with Ellerman's Wilson Line of Hull. The ship ordered with Robb Caledon is being built for joint account.

PRINICPAL OVERSEAS AGENTS:

UK:

DFDS (UK) Ltd.

Mariner House,

Pepys Street,

London, E.C.3

Telephone: (01) 480 7801

Telex: 262175

Detail of the lifting gear in *Surrey*.

CONTAINER FLEET:

Dry Cargo	1,128	20 × 8 × 8
Dry Cargo	146	10 × 8 × 8
Insulated	25	20 × 7·9 × 7·9
Refrigerated	80	20 × 8 × 8
Flats	100	20 × 8

DOMINICAN CONTAINER LINE

Dominican Container Line

See entry under Amerind Shipping Corporation.

DU PONT COMPANY

Du Pont Company (UK) Ltd.

See under Manchester Ship Canal in the Ports section. The company operate two chartered vessels, *Marwit* and *Klaus Block* each capable of carrying about 70 20 ft units, to transport their products between their premises near Manchester and those in Londonderry, Northern Ireland.

EAST ASIATIC COMPANY

East Asiatic Company Ltd.

A partner in ScanAustral, ScanService and ScanStar.

EASTERN SEAROAD SERVICE

Eastern Searoad Service

An Association of:

AUSTRALIAN NATIONAL LINE

73-79 Riverside Avenue, South Melbourne, Victoria 3205, Australia

KAWASAKI KISEN KAISHA LTD. (K LINE)

Ilno Building, 1-1, 2 chome

Uchisawai-cho, Chiyoda-ku, Tokyo

FLINDERS SHIPPING CO. PTY. LTD.

160 Queen Street, Melbourne, Victoria 3000 Australia

SERVICE:

Australia—Japan—every ten days.

FLEET:

Australian Searoader, Australian Enterprise, Matthew Flinders

These 21 knot multi-purpose vessels are capable of lifting 600 20 ft containers or unit loads and 120 cars. The ships are 181·7 m (596 ft) long with a beam of 25·0 m (82 ft) and a draught of 9·0 m (29·5 ft)

FUTURE DEVELOPMENTS:

A fourth vessel will ultimately be built which will provide a weekly service.

Australian National Lines' "Australian Enterprise"

The upper vehicle deck of a vessel on the ESS route.

ELLERMAN CONTAINERSHIP SERVICES

Ellerman Containership Services

Tower Building, Water Street, Liverpool, L69 3BQ

TELEPHONE: 051-236 9999

TELEX: 62214, 627373

OFFICIALS:

Geoffrey Holmes (*Chief Executive, Ellerman Short Sea Services*)

E. Roocroft (*Israel Trade Manager*)

N. F. Sheldon (*Director of Marketing—Containerships Portugal*)

F. Whitehurst (*Containerships Italy*)

SERVICES:

Liverpool to Lisbon, Setubal, Leixos, Oporto—every 5/7 days. M.Vs *Tagus* and *Tronto*.

Liverpool to Ashdod and Haifa—every 12 days in a joint service with Moss Hutchison Line Ltd and Zim Israel Navigation Co. Ltd. M.Vs *Tua* and *Tiber*.

Garston to La Spezia—every 7/14 days.

M.V. *Tormes*.

FLEET:

Minho	*Tiber*	*Tronto*
Tagus	*Tormes*	*Tua*
Tamega		

These 15 knot vessels have a capacity of 123 20 ft equivalents; they have a length of 85·8 m (281·5 ft), a beam of 13·87 m (45·5 ft) and an operating draught of 4·72 m (15·5 ft).

CONTAINERS IN SERVICE:

Dry Cargo	243	40	× 8	×	8·5
Dry Cargo	1,476	20	× 8	×	8·5
Dry Cargo	112	20	× 8	×	8
Dry Cargo	43	8	× 6·6	×	7·4
Open Top	100	20	× 8	×	5·66
Flats	50	20	× 8	×	4

BRANCHES AND MAIN AGENTS:

United Kingdom:

Ellerman & Papayanni Lines Ltd.
11 Albert Square,
Manchester, M2 54D
Telephone : 061-843 5913/3589

Ellerman & Papayanni Lines Ltd.
12-20 Camomile Street,
London, EC3A 7 EX
Telephone : 01-283 4311
Telex : 884771

Morison, Pollexfen & Blair, Ltd.
Waterloo House, 20 Waterloo Street,
Birmingham
Telephone : 021-643 4077/9
Telex : 33236

Ellermans' Wilson Line Ltd.
26 Sunbridge Road,
Bradford
Telephone : 0274-31418

Mark Whitwill & Sons Ltd.
17 Queen Street, Bristol, 1
Telephone : 0272-25211
Telex : 44127

Frank C. Strick & Co. (S. Wales) Ltd.
Seaway House, Bute Street,
Cardiff
Telephone : 0222-31321
Telex : 49236

John Bruce & Co. (Shipping) Ltd.
75 Bothwell Street, Glasgow
Telephone : 041-248 3581
Telex : 77151

G. A. Woodcock Ltd.
Park Farm Industrial Estate,
Westland Road, Leeds, 11
Telephone : 0532-73497/8

Loading marble in a special open top container for shipment on the Ellerman service through La Spezia.

The Morison Group
Coventry Road, Narborough,
Leicester
Telephone : 053-728 4314

T. A. Bulmer & Co. Ltd.
Erimus Chambers, Queens Square,
Middlèsbrough
Telephone : 0642-47891
Telex : 58594

C. Hassell & Son Ltd.
3 Queen Street, Quayside,
Newcastle-on-Tyne
Telephone : 0632-26257

Jones, Heard & Co. Ltd.
107 Dock Street, Newport,
Mon.
Telephone : 0633-64011
Telex : 49301

Morison, Pollexfen & Blair, Ltd.
4c Christchurch Road,
Northampton, NN1 5LL
Telephone : 0604-37666
Telex : 31355

Morison, Pollexfen & Blair Ltd.
14 Winckley Square,
Preston
Telephone : 0772-84150

Morison, Pollexfen & Blair Ltd.
15 Station Road,
Reading
Telephone : 0734-57186

Morison, Pollexfen & Blair, Ltd.
The White Building,
Fitzalan Square,
Sheffield
Telephone : 0742-23966

Morison, Pollexfen & Blair, Ltd.
Federation House,
Station Road,
Stoke-on-Trent
Telephone : 0782-45641

Burgess & Co. Ltd.
Queens Buildings, Swansea
Telephone : 0792-50021/8
Telex : 4833

Israel:

Associated Maritime Agencies (AMA) Ltd.
Shalom Towers,
9 Ahad Haam Street,
Tel Aviv
Telephone : 59446/8
Telex : 033249

Associated Maritime Agencies (AMA) Ltd.
Pavilion No. 10, Port Rear Area,
P.O. 4036, Ashdod
Telephone : 23111/3

Associated Maritime Agencies (AMA) Ltd.
Haifa Levant Building,
Palmer Gate, P.O. Box No. 782,
Haifa
Telephone : 520471/3

Italy:

Container Service Agency S.R.L.
Piazza San Stefano 6,
Milan

Ellerman's *Minho* at Liverpool

Telephone: 860188/879757
Telex: 32080 (Temporary)
Eugenio Lardon & Co.
Via F. Crispi 39-A,
19100 La Spezia
Telephone: 32040/1
Telex: 27482
Portugal:
A. J. Goncalves de Moraes Lda.
Rua de S. Paulo 20/26, Lisbon
Telephone: 34943
Telex: 1296/1297/1298
Wall & Co. Ltd.
55 Rua da Reboleira, Oporto
Telephone: 37841
Telex: 2767

Ellerman's *Tormes* at La Spezia

ELLERMAN'S WILSON LINE LTD.

Ellerman's Wilson Line, Limited,
Commercial Road, Hull, Yorkshire
TELEPHONE: 0482 26081
TELEX: 52277-8-9
DIRECTORS:
D. F. Martin-Jenkins, T.D. (*Chairman*)
Col. G. W. Bayley O.B.E., E.R.D. (*Managing*)
J. W. B. Fewlass
R. H. Dales
BRANCHES:
Birmingham:
St. Martin's House, Bull Ring,
Birmingham, B5 5HH
Telephone: 021-643 1929, 5760, 7700

Bradford:
25 Sunbridge Road, Bradford BD1 2BQ
Felixstowe:
Trelawny House, The Dock, Felixstowe,
IP11 8RS
TELEPHONE: 5656/9
TELEX: 98417
Goole:
3 St. John's Street, Goole
Telephone: 0405-2654
Telex: 57943
Grangemouth:
PO Box 44, 2, Lumley Street, Grangemouth
Telephone: 3677
Telex: 778585
Grimsby:
Wilson Line House, 163 Cleethorpe Road,
Grimsby
Telephone: 0472 57314
Telex: 52194
Immingham:
Immingham Dock, Immingham
Telephone: 0469-2 2383/4
Leeds:
Yorkshire House, Greek Street, Leeds
LS1 5SH
Telephone: 0532 34081/2
London:
12-20 Camomile Street, London EC3A 7EX
Telephone: 01-283 4311
Telex: 884771/2

Manchester:
11a Albert Square, Manchester M2 5HH
Telephone: 061-834 5237/9
Telex: 66 167
Newcastle:
C. Hassell & Son Ltd,

Euro-Pacific Service
A joint service provided by Hapag Lloyd
AG, Compagnie Generale Transatlantique
and Holland America Line.

3 Queen Street, Quayside, Newcastle-upon-
Tyne 1
Telephone: 0632-2 6257
Sheffield:
Yorkshire Insurance House, Market Place,
Sheffield S1 1RX
Telephone: 0742 27429 (2 lines)
ROLL-ON SERVICES:
Hull to Gothenburg—3 sailings weekly.
Hull to Oslo, Drammen—weekly.
Hull to Esbjerg—2 sailings weekly.
ROLL-ON FLEET:
Spero: Capable of carrying 100 20 ft units
this 3,403 nvt vessel has a length of 138·4 m
(454·3 ft), a beam of 20·7 m (68 ft) and a
draught of 5·33 m (17·5 ft).
Destro:
Nordicmark:
Domino: These 590 n.r.t. vessels, capable
of carrying 185 20 ft units, have a length of
109·8 m (360 ft) a beam of 19·2 m (63 ft) and
a draught of 4·95 m (16·3 ft).
CONTAINERS IN SERVICE:

Dry	36	10 × 8 × 8
Dry	360	20 × 8 × 8
Refrigerated	4	20 × 8 × 8
Flats	792	20 × 8·2

PRINCIPAL OVERSEAS AGENTS:
Svea Line (Göteborg) AB,
Box 99 Gothenburg
Telephone: 031/17.85.70
(Terminal) 031/53.00.80
H. Heitmann & Son A/S,
Prinsensgt 3A, Oslo 1
Telephone: 33.41.80
Telex: 11572
B. H. Bamberg
P.O. Box 652,
Drammen,
Telephone: 83 14 90
Telex: 16306
DFDS A/S
Sankt Annae Plads 30
Copenhagen K,
Telephone: (01) 15 63 00
Telex: 9435
DFDS A/S
Englandskajn,
Esbjerg
Telephone: (05) 12 17 00
Telex: 3251

EURO-PACIFIC SERVICE

SERVICE:
General cargo and containers from North
West European Ports to West Coast North
American Ports—weekly.

Ellerman's Wilson Line *Spero*

Destro—Container Deck

Ellerman's Wilson Line *Destro*

FLEET:
Conventional carriers adapted for the
carriage of part container cargoes.

EUROPEAN UNIT ROUTES

European Unit Routes Limited

15 St. Helen's Place, London, E.C.3

TELEPHONE: 01-588 1344

TELEX: 885844

A member of the P & O group.

DIRECTORS:

D. L. J. Mortelman, OBE (*Chairman*)

W. M. Lang (*Managing Director*)

D. E. Grover

MARKETING MANAGER:

S. D. Sussex

SERVICES:

Tilbury/Rotterdam—Five sailings weekly.

Tilbury/Antwerp—Three sailings weekly

Tilbury/Dunkirk—Three sailings weekly

Tilbury/Hamburg—Two sailings weekly

GENERAL:

European Unit Routes Ltd. is a result of considerable study by its parent company, General Steam Navigation Co. Ltd., a member of the P & O Group. GSN has nearly 150 years' experience of operating the short sea trades between the U.K. and the Continent. It has been experimenting with containers for over 10 years. The results of these experiments have been backed up by feasibility studies and market research surveys.

The service offers a port to port vehicle for the Freight Forwarder with his own ISO units or with units hired from EUR. The sole function of EUR is to convey containers to and from its sea terminals. EUR does not undertake door to door movements. All such enquiries from merchants and manufacturers are passed to Freight Forwarders specialising in container movements to the areas concerned.

FLEET:

Chartered tonnage is being used at present and there are plans to operate with owned specialised tonnage.

LEASING:

The Company leases containers and details are given under the leasing section.

FUTURE PLANS:

Other short sea services are under consideration.

EUR's *Impala*

EUR's *Caribou*—capacity 106 20 ft units

Two EUR vessels alongside at Tilbury No. 43 Berth.

EUROPE CANADA LINES

Europe Canada Lines

GENERAL:

A joint service provided by Hapag Lloyd AG, Poseidon Lines and Reederei Ernst Russ.

SERVICE:

Container and general cargo from North West European Ports to Canadian and Great Lakes Ports—weekly.

FLEET:

Conventional carriers adapted for the carriage of part container cargoes.

FABRE LINE

Compagnie FABRE Société Générale de Transports Maritimes

70-72, rue de la Republique

13-Marseille 2e

TELEPHONE: 20.55.30 A34

TELEX: 41905

DIRECTORS:

R. Courau (*President*)

J. P. Gautier (*General Manager*)

EXECUTIVES IN CHARGE OF CONTAINER OPERATIONS:

J. Ph. Huchet (*Mediterranée/USA Dept.*)

M. Salinas (*Sud France/Maroc Dept.*)

L. Garin (*Mediterranée/Antilles françaises Dept.*)

SERVICES:

Containers:

Lisbon, Barcelona, Marseilles, Genoa and Leghorn to New York and Baltimore—weekly.

Part Containers:

Sète, Marseilles to Pointe à Pitre and Fort de France—fortnightly.

Roll-on

Marseilles to Casablanca and Port Vendres—three or four times per week.

CONTAINER FLEET:

Dry	2,715	20 × 8 × 8
	130	40 × 8 × 8·5
Refrigerated	100	20 × 8 × 8
Open Top	300	20 × 8 × 8
Open Top	50	40 × 8 × 8·5

FUTURE DEVELOPMENTS:

Four cellular container vessels with a capacity of 704 20 ft units are scheduled to enter service at the end of 1972 and beginning of 1973 on the Mediterranean/USA service. These vessels will have a gross registered tonnage of 13,000, a length of 163·90 m

(534·7 ft), a beam of 23 m (75·4 ft) and a loaded draught of 7·80 m (25·8 ft).

PRINCIPAL OVERSEAS AGENTS:

NEW YORK:
Columbus Line Inc.
26, Broadway, New York 10.004
Telephone: HA.5.6700
Telex: 710-581 2716

GENOA:
Lertora Brothers & Courtman
Via Cairoli 18 (I-16.100) Genova
Telephone: 205.751
Telex: 27.234

LEGHORN:
Agenzia Marittima Gabriel
Via Montegrappa 6, Int B-1st Floor,
B.P. 382 (I.57.100)
Telephone: (I.28.368/9
Telex: 50.149

BARCELONA:
Agencia Maritima Delgado
Via Layetana No. 5 7 Barcelona 3
Telephone: 219.63.50, 210.20.94
Telex: 54.751

LISBON
Sociedade Commercial Orey Antunes & Ca,
Lta, 4 Praca Duque da Terceira
B.P. 2233 Lisbonne (2)
Telephone: 32.22.71, 33.254, 33.255
Telex: 1181 A & B

FLEET:
Container Ships Managed:

Name	20ft Container capacity	Net Reg. Tons	Length m (ft)	Beam m (ft)	Loaded draft m (ft)
Meta Reith	260	3,929	123·83 m (406·1 ft)	17·60 m (57·66 ft)	7·58 m (24·9 ft)
Ede Sottorf	258	3,771	124·50 m (408 ft 6 in)	17·60 m (57 ft 7 in)	7·58 m (24·9 ft)
Helene Roth	245	3,770	124·50 m (408 ft 6 in)	18·00 m (59 ft 0 in)	7·58 m (24·9 ft)
Willi Reith	124	3,927	123.83 m (406 ft 2 in)	17·60 m (57 ft 6 in)	7·58 m (24 ft 9 in)
Juno	122	3,455	125 m (410 ft)	17·70 m (57 ft)	7·65 m (25·1 ft)

CASABLANCA (Maroc)
Compagnie de Navigation Paquet
65, avenue de l'Armée Royale B.P. 60
Telephone: 638.21/22/23
Telex: 21.025

POINTE A PITRE (GUADALOUPE):
M. R. Pétrelluzzi
2 rue Henri IV BP61
Telephone: 82 03 41

FORT DE FRANCE (MARTINIQUE):
Plissoneau et Cie

34 rue Eneste Deprage BP519
Telephone: 64.94
Telex: 634

Roll-on/Roll-off Vessels:
Cab~ies, Carnoules, Cogolin, Cotignac
Each of these vessels has a capacity for 31 semi-trailers.
Net. reg. tons: 272
Length: 76·40 m (250·7 ft)
Beam: 13·22 m (44 ft)
Draught: 4·17 m (13·7 ft)

FARRELL

Farrell Lines Incorporated
One Whitehall Street, New York, NY 10004
TELEPHONE: Whitehall 4-7460

TELEX: RCA International: 222396 Farship; ITT World Communications: 420187 Farship; Western Union Intl: 62529; French Cable Co.: Farship 82683.

BRANCHES:
Baltimore, Boston, Chicago, Cleveland, Detroit, Philadelphia, Washington—USA. Accra, Ghana; Harbel, Liberia; Johannesburg, South Africa; Monrovia, Liberia; Nairobi, Kenya; Sydney, Australia; Wellington, New Zealand.

DIRECTORS:
James A. Farrell, Jr.
Frank B. Cavanagh

Mrs. John J. Farrell
Robert P. MacFadden
Ira O. Lewis
George F. Lowman
Thomas J. Smith
Carl W. Swenson
George Wauchope
John M. Wilson, Jr.

EXECUTIVES IN CHARGE OF CONTAINER OPERATIONS:
David B. Letteney (Manager, Container Development Programme)
Richard H. Ford (Terminal Manager)

SERVICES:
From US East Coast and Gulf Ports to:
West Africa every 10 days

South Africa every 14 days
Australia and New Zealand every 21 days
FLEET:
The Company is at present operating ships on the Australia and New Zealand service capable of lifting the equivalent of 232 × 20 ft containers or 180 × 20 ft and 20 × 40 ft. They will be replaced by four full container ships which will provide a fortnightly service to Australia and New Zealand. They will lift 872 × 20 ft containers, and will be 203·6 m (668 ft) in length, with a beam of 27·4 m (90 ft) having a service speed of 23 knots. Additional containers on deck will increase the ship's capacity to 978 containers. Vessels are being named Austral Envoy, Austral Ensign, Austral Endurance and Austral Entente.

Profile drawing of a Farrell Lines new building

Fassio Line
See entry under Atlantica Line.

FASSIO LINE

FINLAND STEAMSHIP CO. LTD

Suomen Höyrylaiva Osakeyhtiö—(Finland Steamship Company, Ltd) Finska Angfartygs Aktiebolaget

HEAD OFFICE:
Eteläranta 8, Helsinki 13
TELEPHONE: 10901
TELEGRAMS: Finska
TELEX: 12-1410
DIRECTORS:
Göran Ehrnooth (Chairman)
Lars Langenskiöld (Managing Director)

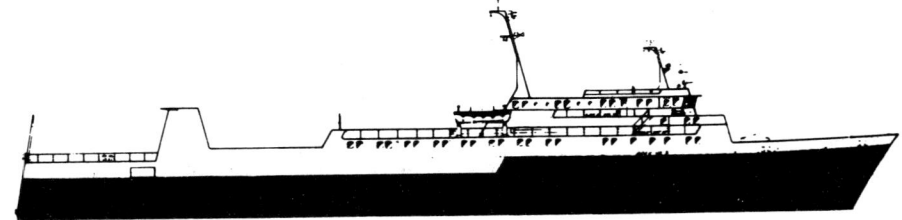

Profile of roll-on/roll-off new buildings for Finland Steamship Co Ltd,

SERVICES:
Containers:
Helsinki/Tilbury/Middlesbrough—
Fortnightly in conjunction with United Baltic Corporation Ltd, which gives a weekly service.

Helsinki to Hamburg—
Weekly (DFL Express in conjunction with United Owners Co Gehrckens and Russ)

FLEET:

Roll-on/Roll-off
Helsinki/Copenhagen/Lübeck/Trauemünde
PRINCIPAL OVERSEAS AGENTS:
Charles Gee and Co, 48 Fenchurch Street, London, EC3
Freight Forwarding—See entry for Oy AA Lines under Freight Forwarders—Finland.

Artist's impression of the Finland steamship's dual purpose vessels due to come into service in 1972.

Name	20ft Container Capacity	Length		Beam		Draught	
		m	ft	m	ft	m	ft
Container Vessels:							
Osternburg	42	71·9	235·9	11·1·	36·4	5·57	18·3
Iris	72	76·3	250·3	11·9	39	—	—
Roll-on/Roll-off Vessels:							
Finlandia	90 + 36 Semi-trailers and 320 cars	153	502	20	65·6	5·6	18·4
New Building delivery September, 1971	—	106	347·8	16	52·5	5·8	19
New Building delivery March, 1972	—	106	347·8	16	52·5	5·8	19
Dual Purpose Vessels: 3 New Building for delivery in June, September and November, 1972		118·5	388·7	22·0	72·2	6·0	19·7

FINLAND/UNITED KINGDOM CONTAINER SERVICE

Finland/United Kingdom Container Service

A joint venture operated by:
Finland Steamship Co.
O.Y. Finnlines
United Baltic Corporation

SERVICE:
Helsinki - Tilbury - Middlesbrough - Helsinki,

weekly using chartered cellular tonnage.

FLEET
Baltic Concord, on charter from Johann Kahrs, Stade, Germany, has a capacity of 63 × 20 ft containers.
Iris, on charter from Karl Heinz, Danz, Germany, has a capacity of 72 × 20 ft units.

Iris at Tilbury.

FINNLINES

Oy Finnlines Ltd.

Korkeavuorenkatu 32
PO Box 13218, Helsinki 13, Finland
TELEPHONE: 649811
TELEGRAMS: 'Finnlines', Helsinki, Finland
TELEX: 12-642
DIRECTORS:
H. Holma (*Managing Director*)
R. Sundstrom (*Technical Director*)
T. Falenius (*Liner Services*)
SERVICES:
Weekly liner service Finland-Hamburg-USEC - Rotterdam - Hamburg - Finland monthly to Gulf Ports. Also Finland–UK, Finland–Mediterranean. Passenger ferries in Baltic and special vessels.
PRINCIPAL OVERSEAS AGENTS:
Boise-Griffin Steamship Co, Inc,
90 Broad Street, New York, New York
'Boigrif',
944-8000

FLEET:
The Company have a total fleet of 35 vessels.
Eight vessels of the *Finnclipper* class are capable of lifting 168 × 20 ft units. Three special purpose 20 knot vessels fitted with a stern port and side ports for handling roll-on and palletised cargoes entered service in 1971. These vessels are also designed for the carriage of containers with two cellular holds and are capable of carrying up to 220 × 40 ft units. These ships have a length of 173·75 m (570 ft) a beam of 25·40 m (83·3 ft) and a

Finnclipper

'draught of 9·15 m (30 ft).

Designed specifically for the Baltic and Scandinavian waters the *Finnclipper* came into service on the Helsinki/Lübeck and Copenhagen routes in late 1969; two further vessels are on order for delivery in 1972 and 1973. This class of vessel has a length of 137·33 m (418·6 ft), a beam of 24·56 m (75·3 ft), a draught of 6·10 m (18·6 ft) and an operating speed of 18 knots. The five deck cargo layout consists of an open top deck for cars, two vehicle decks each divided into seven lanes for wheeled traffic and two cargo decks for unit loads and containers. Double stern doors aft and side ports forward are used for cargo operations. The Finnflow cargo handling system is utilised; pallets and containers are brought aboard by straddle carriers or tractors towing trailers on rollers. From the lower vehicle deck they are lowered by one of seven 20-ton capacity lifts to three holds. When the lift reaches the selected deck level, a trolley on rails laid athwartships is winched underneath the pallet or container. Pneumatic pads lift the load and the trolley is winched along the rails to the required

Impression of a Finn Lines special purpose unitised cargo vessel

position. The pads are deflated, the load secured, and the trolley is free for the subsequent load.

All the cargo and vehicles below decks are separated and protected by heavy duty air cushions suspended from the deckheads. Primarily, they are provided to prevent cargo from shifting on the rare occasions when *Finncarrier* needs to roll through heavy ice.

FLOTA MERCANTE DOMINICANA C. POR A.

Flota Mercante Dominicana C. Por A.
See Amerind Shipping Corporation.

GRANCOLOMBIANA

Flota Mercante Grancolombiana SA
Carrera 13, 27-75 Apartado Aereo No. 4482
Bogota, Colombia
Telephone: 415-952
Telex: 044 853
General Manager: Dr Alvaro-Diaz
Services:
Colombia-Ecuador—United States—weekly.
Trident service with CAVN and KNSM to Europe weekly.

Fleet:
Seven part container ships each with a capacity for 88 20 ft units. These vessels have a length of 166 m (544·5 ft), a beam of 21·18 m (69·5 ft) and a draught of 9·14 m (30 ft). Two part container vessels for the "Trident" service each capable of carrying 80 20 ft units were delivered in 1971. Three

One of the Flota Mercanti Grancolombiana fleet equipped for the carriage of 88 20 ft units

further part container ships, each capable of carrying 120 20 ft units are on order for delivery in late 1971, 1972 and 1973.

Agency:
Grancolombiana (NY) Inc,
79 Pine Street, New York, NY10005
Telephone: (212) WH3-7200

FOSS ALASKA

Foss Alaska Lines
Foss Launch and Tug Co.
660 West Ewing Street
Seattle 99, Washington 98119
Telephone: (206) 2850150
Telex: 32-0132

Officials:
S. D. Campbell (*President*)
Drew Foss (*Vice-President Alaskan Operations*)
Container Services:

'Vanliner' service weekly to southeast Alaskan ports.
Fleet:
Tugs and specially designed barges for containers including refrigerated units.

FRANCE-IRELAND LINE

NV Maatschappij Zeevaart
France-Ireland Line
Holland-Ireland Line
Willemskade 23, Rotterdam, Holland
Telephone: 010-14 33 22
Telex: 22115
Branches:
Dublin Maritime Ltd, Dublin, Ireland
Waterford Maritime, Waterford, Ireland
Directors:
W. Veder

G. A. Fontein
Cargo Superintendent:
L. Lucking
Services:
Rotterdam–Dublin—twice weekly
Rotterdam–Belfast—weekly
Amsterdam–Dublin–Belfast—weekly
Dublin–Le Havre—twice weekly
Fleet:
Tyro
Container capacity 25

Net reg. tons 619·14
Length 84·24 m (276 ft 4 in)
Beam 14·0 m (46 ft)
Draft 4·5 m (14 ft 9 in)

Hagno
Container capacity 37
Net reg. tons 217·36
Length 79·07 m (259 ft 5 in)
Beam 11·25 m (37 ft)
Draft 3·68 m (12 ft)

FRENCH LINE

French Line
See Compagnie Générale Transatlantique.

GEEST LINE

Waling van Geest & Zonen, N.V.
Monsterseweg 117, 's-Gravenzande, Holland
TELEPHONE: 's-Gravenzande 3841
TELEX: 2021 31103
BRANCHES:
Waling van Geest & Zonen NV
Burgemeester de Jongkade 33, Maassluis, Holland
DIRECTORS:
J. van Geest, C.B.E.
L. van Geest
L. van Straalen
EXECUTIVE IN CHARGE OF CONTAINER OPERATIONS:
J. B. H. Delfgaauw
CONTAINER SERVICES:
Ipswich to Maassluis—daily except Sunday.
Ipswich to Emmerich (West Germany)— twice weekly.
FLEET:
Geest-sluis, Geest-diep, Geest-duin
The first two vessels are capable of lifting

40 8 × 8 × 8 ft containers. They have a length of 51·81 m (170 ft), a beam of 7·31 m (24 ft) and a draught of 3·12 m (10·25 ft) with a net registered tonnage of 270 to 290 tons. and a deadweight of approximately 400 tons. The *Geest-duin* is capable of lifting 113 8 × 8 × 8 units and has a length of 70·61 m (232 ft) a beam of 10·27 m (34 ft) and a draught of 3·52 m (12 ft); nvt is 300 tons dwt approximately 1,000 tons.

A further vessel of the *Geestduin* class, capable of carrying 113 8 ft long containers is under construction.

CONTAINERS IN SERVICE:

Dry	780	8 × 8 × 8
Insulated	516	8 × 8 × 8
Refrigerated	22	8 × 8 × 8
Dry (on hire)	150	20 × 8 × 8

Loading a Geest vessel at Ipswich.

M.V. *Geestduin.*

GEO GIBSON

Geo. Gibson & Co. Ltd.,
64 Commercial Street,
Leith, Edinburgh 6
See Macvan Container Services

REDERIAKTIEBOLAGET GOTEBORG -FREDERICKSHAVEN-LINJEN

Rederiaktiebolaget Goteborg-Frederikshavn- Linjen
Majnabbe, Postbox 120 65,
402 41 Gothenburg 12, Sweden
TELEPHONE: 12 49 00
TELEX: 208 86
BRANCHES:
Rederi A/S Göteborg-Frederikshavn-Linjen, Vesterbro 48, Aalborg, Denmark
DIRECTOR:
Captain Ulf Trapp (*General Manager*)
CARGO SUPERINTENDENT:
Captain Arne Karlsson

SERVICES:
Gothenburg—Frederikshavn:
8 sailings per day
FLEET:
Two ferry vessels, *Princessan Christina* and *Princessan Desiree* each capable of lifting passengers and 39 trailers. These ships have a length of 132·9 m (436 ft) a beam of 19·2 m (63 ft) and a draught of 5 m (16·5 ft).

Prinsessan Christina—showing layout of accommodation

GREAT EASTERN

The Great Eastern Shipping Company Limited
Mercantile Bank Building, 60 Mahatma Gandhi Road, Bombay 1

TELEPHONE: 258961
TELEX: 217
SERVICE:

India to Pacific Coast of USA and Canada.
FLEET:
Two vessels capable of lifting 264 20 ft units.

GREENORE FERRY SERVICES

Greenore Ferry Service Limited
34 Upper Fitzwilliam Street, Dublin 2
TELEPHONE: 65467
TELEX: 5182
BRANCHES:
Greenore, Dundalk, Co. Louth
Telephone: 3/10/33
Telex: 6541
The Docks, Preston, Lancs
Telephone: 26081
Telex: 67595
The Docks, Sharpness, Gloucester
Telephone: 378
Telex: 43114
Seagoe Industrial Estate, Craigavon, Porta- down, Co. Armagh
DIRECTORS:
A. O'Rahilly (*Chairman*)
D. Morley

M. O'Rahilly
W. F. Southern (*Managing*)
B. Price
W. J. McEnery
SERVICES:
Greenore/Preston—Three sailings weekly.
Greenore/Sharpness—2 sailings weekly.
FLEET:
Owenro 50 20 ft units
Owenbawn 50 20 ft units
Owenglas 70 20 ft units

CONTAINER FLEET:
Number of containers operated not dis- closed, but all containers are 8 × 8 cross section. Dry boxes in 20 and 30 ft lengths, insulated in 12 and 24 ft lengths, flats in 20 and 26 ft lengths and tanks and tiltainers in 20 ft lengths are operated.

Greenore Continental Unitload Ltd.
Address, telephone and telex are the same as Greenore above.
BRANCHES:
Kersten Hunik's Scheepvaartmig N.V.
Westplein 2, PO Box 623, Rotterdam
Telephone: 114720
Telex: 22184
DIRECTORS:
W. F. Southern (*Chairman*)
J. D. Dikken
H. F. Kersten
A. O'Rahilly
J. J. Palmer
A. A. Teenwisse
SERVICE:
Greenore—Rotterdam—Weekly
FLEET:
Owen Kersten 63 20 ft units

GRENDI-TARROS SpA

**GRENDI-TARROS
(M. A. Grendi & F. 10 S.p.A.—T.A.R.R.O.S. S.p.A.)**
Genoa-Italy, Piazza De Marini, 1
TELEPHONE: 291.441
TELEX: 27295
BRANCHES AND CONTAINER TERMINALS:
Genoa:
Elicoidale Via di Francia
   Telephone: 685947-67206
   Telex: 27654
Milan:
Via Ripamonti 286
   Telephone: 531561-530841
Turin:
Via Valprato 78
   Telephone: 273004
Bologna:
Via Emilia Ponente 252
   Telephone: 389534
   Telex: 51070
Ravenna:
c/o International Docks
   via Magazzini Anteriori 27
   Telephone: 34748
Anzio:
Zona portuale
Cagliari:
V. le Elmas km. 1,2
   Telephone: 24231
   Telex: 79041
Porto Torres:
s.s. 131 km. 2
   Telephone: 54322
   Telex: 79126
SENIOR EXECUTIVES:
Capitain Sergio Podestà (*Line's Director*)
Rag. Franco Compagnino (*Cargo Superintendent*)

SERVICES:
Genoa-Sardinia—daily.
Anzio (Rome)-Sardinia—twice weekly.
Italy-Greece—weekly
Ravenna-Turkey—weekly.

The Grendi City Terminal at Genoa

FLEET Name	Container Capacity 20 ft Equivalent)	Net Reg. Ton	Speed Knots	Length m	ft	Beam m	ft	Draught ft	m
Vento del Golfo	30	377·73	—	72·30	237	9·19	30	3·97	13
Vento di Levante	50	451·64	—	88·85	292	10·52	34·5	3·30	10·8
Vento di Tramontana	160	1,434·00	—	96	318	14	46	6	19·7
Vento di Scirocco Vento di Maestrale	111	880·89	15	86·8	284·7	13·70	44·9	4·70	15·4

Vento del Golfo

Vento di Scirocco

Part of the Grendi Terminal at Genoa with the *Vento di Levanti* at the berth, 120 containers can be accommodated.

NOTE:

Vento del Golfo has a bow ramp and the *Vento di Levante* has a stern loading ramp thus allowing the vessels to accept containers on slave trailers. The *Vento di Tramontana*, *Vento di Scirocco* and *Vento di Maestrale* are fitted with 30 ton Liebherr container cranes which are used for loading containers from the deck and the underdeck on to road vehicles or slave trailers which are then rolled through the stern ramp. Reefer points for 33 20 ft units or 20 40 ft units have been fitted in the latter two vessels.

CONTAINER FLEET:

Dry	2,395	20 × 8 × 8
Insulated	30	20 × 8 × 8
Refrigerated	31	20 × 8 × 8
Open	72	20 × 8 × 8
Tilt-bulk	15	20 × 8 × 4

The fleet includes these units owned by:

Gulf Container Line
19 Leadenhall Street, London EC3
TELEPHONE: 01-283 4321
TELEX: 883496
OFFICIALS:
D. G. Franks (*Line Manager*)
E. Pilcher (*Sales Manager*)
R. E. Skinner (*Assistant Sales Manager*)
G. K. Burnham (*Assistant Sales Manager*)

Vento di Tramontana

Tarros S.p.A.—Traghetti Autotrasporti Rapidi Regione Organizzazione—Sarda

Piazze De Marini 1
16123 Genoa

GULF CONTAINER LINE

GENERAL:

The Line is a wholly owned subsidiary of Furness Withy & Co. Ltd.
SERVICE:
Felixstowe and Greenock—Bermuda, Miami, Nassau, Houston, New Orleans and Mobile —every 14 days.
FLEET:
Three chartered vessels each with a capacity of approximately 200 20 ft equivalents.
CONTAINERS IN SERVICE:
At present 20 and 40 ft units are in service; all are leased.
FUTURE PLANS::
It is hoped to introduce vessels with a capacity of about 400 20 ft equivalents into the service shortly.

HAMBURG-AMERICA LINE

Hamburg Sudamerikanische Dampschiffahrts Gessellschaft Eggert and Amsinck
2000 Hamburg 11, Ost-West-Str 59.
Postfach 111540
TELEPHONE: 30051
TELEX: 02 14991
SERVICES:

The company operates services with conventional tonnage from Europe to East Coast South America, New Zealand, New Caledonia and the Mediterranean. The Columbus Line Services are operated from Canadian and US West Coast ports and from Canadian and US East Coast ports to Australia and New Zealand. This latter service is operated by fully cellular container vessels. They are equipped with their own handling gear.
Columbus Line Container Service:

Hampton Roads, Philadelphia New York and Halifax to Melbourne, Sydney, Brisbane, Port Alma, Townsville, Auckland, Wellington and Port Chalmers—every three weeks.
FLEET:
Columbus New Zealand

Columbus – New Zealand

Columbus Australia
Columbus America
These 22 knot vessels have a capacity of 1,178 20 ft units including 454 insulated containers. They have a length of 194 m (636·5 ft), a beam of 29·30 m (96·1 ft) and a draught of 10·75 m (35·27 ft).
CONTAINERS IN SERVICE:

Dry	3,000	20 × 8 × 8·5
Insulated	2,500	20 × 8 × 8

HANSA LINE

Hansa Deutsche Dampfschiffahrts Gesellschaft

See entry under Atlantic Sp.A.

FLEET:
Four 20 knot vessels all capable of carrying 675 20 ft units. They are 153·25 m (502·75 ft) in length, 23 m (75·4 ft) in beam with a draught of 9 m (29·5 ft).

HAPAG-LLOYD

Hapag-Lloyd Aktiengesellchaft
2 Hamburg 1, Ballindamm 25
TELEPHONE: (0411) 32.10.81
TELEX: 02 161 988
and
28 Bremen, Gustav-Deetjen-Allee 2/6
TELEPHONE: (0421) 3 50 01
TELEX: 02 44 241
SERVICES:
Europe to USA—Fully cellular service Weekly

Hapag-Lloyd North Atantic Service vessel

Europe to Australia (AECS service) Hapag Lloyd are responsible for the marketing of the AECS service in Germany, Austria, Scandinavia and Eastern European countries.

Europe to the Far East TRIO Service.

FLEET:
Alster Express, Elbe Express,
Mosel Express, Weser Express,
These 20 knot vessels operate on the North Atlantic service; they have a length of 170·77 m (560·2 ft) a beam of 24·50 m (80·4 ft) and a draught of 7·89 m (25·9 ft). Carrying capacity is 736 20 ft units, 40 ft containers can also be accepted.
Sydney Express, Melbourne Express:
These 22 knot, 1,526 20' ft unit capacity vessels have a length of 217·9 m (715 ft) a beam of 29·0 m (95 ft) and a draught of 11·5 m (37·7 ft). They operate on the AECS service.

An extensive fleet of part container ships capable of lifting between about 120 and 140 20 ft units are also in service.

Far East Vessels
Four 26 knot, 2,300 20 ft units capacity vessels are under construction for delivery in 1972. These ships will be 276·5 m (907 ft) in length with a beam of 32·2 m (106 ft) and a draught of 12 m (39·4 ft) and will be used on the TRIO Service.
CONTAINERS IN SERVICE:
In April 1971 the company owned over

Model of a Hapag-Lloyd Far East Service vessel

Hapag-Lloyd Australian Service vessel

Hapag-Lloyd part-container vessel

10,000 containers of all types as well as 1,800 chassis. A considerable number of rented containers and chassis are used in addition to the hired ones.

HEAD DONALDSON LINE

Head Donaldson Line
See entry under Ulster Steamship Co. Ltd.

Nederlandsch-Amerikaansche Stoomvaart-Maatschappij Holland Amerika Lijn
Wilhelminakade 86
Rotterdam
TELEPHONE: 010-17 25 60
TELEX: 21172
EXECUTIVE BOARD:
Jhr. H. Reuchlin
N. van der Vorm
A. M. Lels (*in charge of LASH and container vessels*)

HOLLAND AMERICA LIJN

GENERAL:
A partner in Atlantic Container Line, the company ordered in August 1969 two barge carriers of the LASH type, each of which will have a capacity of 75 400 ton barges, for their service between the US 'Gulf and Rotterdam.

The ships which will come into service at the end of 1971 and in mid-1972 will be 262 m (859·6 ft) in length with a beam of 32·5 m (106·6 ft) and will have a speed of 20 knots.

The barges measure 18·74 × 9·50 × 3·96 m (61·4 = 31·2 = 13 ft) and will weigh 80 tons, 300 have been ordered.

A barge terminal and fleeting area will be laid out in Waalhaven, Rotterdam and the barges will operate on the European waterway system. Plans are also in hand to design "Kangaroo" vessels to lift up to five barges for short and near sea feeder services to Scandinavian and British ports.

HOLLAND CONTAINER LINE

NV Hollandsche Stoomboot Mij—Phoenix Line Joint Service
O. Handelskade, 3 Amsterdam C PO Box 506
TELEPHONE: 020-113333
TELEX: 11038
United Kingdom
Holland Container Line Agency
The Dock, Trelawney House
Felixstowe
Telephone: 394-2-6241
Telex: 98436
BRANCHES:
London, Birmingham, Manchester, Liverpool, Hull, Shoreham
DIRECTOR:
G. L. Medendorp
ROLL-ON SERVICES:
m.v. *Zaanstroom*
Amsterdam to Felixstowe—3 sailings weekly.

Amstelstroom loading containers in Amsterdam.

m.v. *Amstelstroom*
Amsterdam to Hull—3 sailings weekly.
m.v. *Spaarnestroom*

Rotterdam to Leith—weekly.
m.v. *Rijnstroom*
Amsterdam to Shoreham—2 sailings weekly

PRINCIPAL OVERSEAS AGENTS:
Agents in all major cities in Germany, Switzerland, Italy, Austria, and at all Rhine ports.

IBER HANSEATIC TRANSPORT SYSTEM (ITS)

Iber Hanseatic Transport System (ITS)
A roll-on and container service operated jointly by:
Deutsche Dampfschiffahrt Gesellschaft, Hansa,
Schachte 6, Postfach 4, Bremen
Koninklijke Nederlandsche Stoomboot Mij,

N.V. (KNSM),
Scheepvaarthuis,
Prins Hendrikkade 108,
Amsterdam 1001.
Compania Maritima del Norte and Euromar, Madrid.
SERVICE:

Bremen/Bremerhaven, Amsterdam, Le Havre, Bilbao—weekly.
FLEET:
Meteoor   Cometa
These vessels are specially designed for the carriage of containers on deck and trailers are loaded underdeck through a stern ramp.

IBESCA CONTAINERLINE

Ibesca Containerline
Part of the Dart Containerline.

INDEPENDENT GULF LINES

Independent Gulf Lines
a division of NV Stoomvaart-Maatschappij "Oostzee", managers Vinke & Co Amsterdam
107, de Ruyterkade, P.O. Box 485
TELEPHONE: 64133
TELEX: 11444 3 lines
DIRECTORS:
E. P. Dumas
G. Warnderink Vinke
Container Operations: G. F. Renooy

PRINCIPAL OVERSEAS AGENTS:
Amerind Shipping Corporation
17 Battery Place, New York, N.Y. 10004
Telephone: 212 Whitehall 3-0500
Telex: RCA 222873
        ITT 420862
        Western Union 62857
Teletype: 212-571-0356
FLEET:
In addition to the fleet of general cargo vessels carrying limited numbers of contain-

ers, two vessels of about 14,600 tons deadweight came into service during 1971.
These two vessels have special features including sideports for unitized cargo and a 35 ton derrick to permit handling of 20 ft and 40 ft containers. The maximum container capacity of the vessels is 278 20 ft units (200 with a height of 8·5 ft), of which 184 under deck and 94 on deck. In addition 32 gondolas of 20 ft can be carried under deck.

IRISH SEA FERRIES

Irish Sea Ferries Limited
The Docks, Warrenpoint, Northern Ireland
TELEPHONE: Warrenpoint 3222/3
TELEX: 64697
BRANCH:
North Dock, Garston, Liverpool 19

TELEPHONE: Garston 5116 and 5117
TELEX: 62638
J. Coulthard (*Managing Director*)

SERVICE:
Three sailings per week between Warren-

point and Garston.

FLEET:
Irishgate
Container capacity 33
Net. reg. tons 900

IROPA TRANSPORT

Iropa Transport
GENERAL:
A service operated jointly by British and Irish Steam Packet Company Ltd and Holland America Line. Please see the individual entries for B&I and Holland America for details of agents etc.
SERVICES:

Dublin/Rotterdam/Le Havre/Cork—weekly.
Dublin/Rotterdam/Le Havre—weekly.
FLEET:
Mayo—Capacity: 74 20 ft units.
Embdena—Capacity: 65 20 ft units.
CONTAINERS IN SERVICE:
Dry   200   20 × 8 × 8·5
Refrigerated   50   40 × 8 × 8·5

Iropa Transport's *Mayo*

ISLAND NAVIGATION CORPORATION

Island Navigation Corporation
See Orient Overseas Line

JAMACIAN CONTAINER LINE

Jamaican Container Line
See Amerind Shipping Corporation.

JAPAN LINE

Japan Ace

Japan Line Ltd.
Kokusai Building, 1-1 Marunouchi 3,
Chiyoda-ku, Tokuo
TELEPHONE: 212-8211
BRANCHES:
Tokyo (head office) Osaka, Kobe, Yokohama, Nagoya, Kitakyushu, Sapporo.
SERVICES:
Joint service, every five days, from Tokyo, Nagoya and Kobe to Oakland and Los Angeles.

Joint weekly trans-pacific service with other Japanese owners from Yokohama, Nagoya and Kobe to Seattle, Portland and Vancouver.
FLEET:
Japan Ace. This 26 knot vessel is 202·7 m (616·6 ft) in length with a bean of 27·2 m (82·8 ft) and a draught of 10·43 m (31·8 ft). There is a capacity for 728 20 ft units.
Golden Arrow. Owned jointly with "K" Line.
A new vessel, capable of lifting 1,070 20 ft units and owned jointly with 'K' Line comes into service in early 1972 on the Japan-California service.
CONTAINERS IN SERVICE:

Dry Cargo	2,700	20 × 8 × 8
Dry Cargo	480	40 × 8 × 8·5
Refrigerated	120	20 × 8 × 8
Refrigerated	30	40 × 8 × 8·5
Open Top	100	20 × 8 × 8
Flat Rack	100	20 × 8 × 8
Tank	6	20 × 8 × 8

FUTURE PLANS:
A vessel capable of carrying 1,500 20 ft units is on order for the Japan-New York service commencing in Autumn 1972.
STEVEDORES AND FORWARDERS:
KOBE:
Kamigumi Co. Ltd.
1-5-4, Hamabe-dori, Fukiai-ku, Kobe
Telephone: 22-4151
NAGOYA:
Fujiki Kaiun Kaisha, Ltd.
2-3-5, Minato-honmachi, Minato-ku, Nagoya
Telephone: 651-6151
Sanshin Unyu Kaisha, Ltd.
2-5, Minato-honmachi, Minato-ku, Nagoya
Telephone: 651-3181
SHIMIZU:
Amano Kaisoten Ltd.
74-3, Minato-cho, Shimizu
Telephone: 53-2151

YOKOHAMA:
Keihin Warehouse Co Ltd.
Room 301, Silk Center 1
Yamashita-cho, Naka-ku, Yokohama
Telephone: 651-1641
TRUCKING:
Kobe:
Kamigumi & Co., Ltd.
Maya Pier Business Center, Nada-ku Kobe
Telephone: 88-2835
Kobe Yamato Transport Co., Ltd.
26-2 Youyahama-cho, Hyogo-ku, Kobe
Telephone: 67-4834
Nagoya:
Fujiki Kaiun Kaisha, Ltd.
2-3-5 Minato-honmachi, Minato-ku, Nagoya
Telephone: 651-6151
Shimizu:
Minato Trucking Co., Ltd.
13-27 Umeda-cho, Shimizu
Telephone: 52-0141
Suzuyo Trucking Co., Ltd.
5-3, Irifune-cho, Shimizu
Telephone: 53-3111
Tokyo & Yokohama:
Suzue Lines, Co., Ltd.
3-9 Kaigan-dori, Naka-ku, Yokohama
Telephone: 201-4961
Yamato Transport Co., Ltd.
12-16-2 Ginza, Chuo-ku, Tokyo
Telephone: 541-3411
Tokyo:
Suzuegumi Warehouse Co., Ltd.

1-14-2 Shiba Kaigan-dori, Minato-ku, Tokyo
Telephone: 434-8621
AGENTS:
Los Angeles:
Japan Line (U.S.A.) Ltd.
One Wilshire Bldg., Los Angeles, Calif. 90017
Telephone: 213-629-2551
San Francisco:
Japan Line (U.S.A.) Ltd.
One California St., San Francisco, Calif. 94111
Telephone: 415-781-6226
Portland:
Japan Line (U.S.A.) Ltd.
421 S.W. Sixth Ave., Portland, Oregon 97204
Telephone: 503-227-1621

Seattle:
Japan Line (U.S.A.) Ltd.
2220 Pacific Bldg., 720 Third Avenue, Seattle, Washington 98104
Telephone: 206-682-2671
New York:
A. L. Burbank & Co., Ltd.
120 Wall St., New York, N.Y. 10005
Telephone: 212-944-9300
Vancouver:
Westward Shipping Ltd.
1250-1055 W. Hastings St., Vancouver 1, B.C.
Telephone: 683-7585

JEURO CONTAINER LINE

Jeuro Container Line
A joint venture of:
All Soviet External Transport Public Corporation
CTI (Japan) Ltd.

MAT Transport
See entry under NVOC as major transport link is by rail.
SERVICE:
Europe to Japan by Trans-Siberian Rail-

way to Nakhodka, thence by sea with three sailings per month.
FLEET:
One vessel capable of carrying 60 20 ft units.

JOHNSON LINE

Johnson Line (Rederi AB Nordstjernan)
Stureplan 3, Stockholm, Sweden
Postal address: Fack, S-103 80 Stockholm 7, Sweden
TELEPHONE:
Long distance (08) 22 05 20
Local 22 05 00
TELEX: 17100
DIRECTORS:
Axel Ax:son Johnson (*President*)
Allan Björklund (*Executive Vice-President*)
Gunnar Westerberg (*Director*)
Swen Lagerberg (*General Traffic Manager*)
Carl-Eric Carlson (*Technical Director*)
CARGO SUPERINTENDENT:
Captain Einar Arvidsson

Axel Johnson

SERVICES:

Sweden, Denmark, Northern Continent and U.K. to the West Coast of the U.S. and Canada, and Hawaii—weekly (Hawaii monthly).

FLEET:

Full Container Ships:

Axel Johnson   Annie Johnson
Margaret Johnson   San Francisco

The Line is at present phasing into service five 23 knot cellular container ships, four of which came into service in 1969-70. These vessels, which are equipped with two (one 20 ton and one 30 ton) gantry cranes, are capable of carrying the equivalent of 744 20 ft units in 20 ft or 40 ft lengths. There is also one 25 ton ship crane for handling 20 ft units. These ships have also 170,000 cu ft of non-containerised general cargo space and 250,000 cu ft of refrigerated space. The vessels have a length of 174 m (571 ft) a beam of 25·8 m (84·5 ft) and a loaded draught of 10 m (33 ft).

Partial Container Ships:

Rio de Janeiro   Buenos Aires
Montevideo   Santos
Rosario   Brasilia
Bahia Blanca

Seven "Rio" Class vessels have been lengthened to provide a cellular section amidships capable of carrying 126×20 ft units. Additional containers can be carried in the general cargo spaces if required.

CONTAINERS IN SERVICE:

The Line provides standard ISO dry cargo containers in 20 and 40 ft lengths. In the 20 ft length, open top, half open top, bulk liquid and flats are available. The Line also has containers with inside capacity of 3·5 m³ (126 cu ft) 8 m³ (283 cu ft) and 9·7 m³ (345 cu ft) for use on its other services.

Dry	1,800	3·5 to 10 m³
Dry	5,100	$20 \times 8 \times 8$
Dry	150	$20 \times 8 \times 8·5$
Dry	360	$40 \times 8 \times 8$
Open top	350	$40 \times 8 \times 8·5$
Open top	1,985	$20 \times 8 \times 4$
Fruit Flat	520	$20 \times 8 \times 8$
Tank	9	18,000 litre
Tank	8	23,000 litre

PRINCIPAL AGENTS IN EUROPE AND USA —CONTAINER SERVICE:

Axel Johnson Corporation (General Agents USA)
   400 California Street
   San Francisco, Calif 94104
   Telephone: (415) 421-7771
   Telex: RCA 27705, ITT 470031
            WU INTL 034 236

General Steamship Corporation Ltd., (US West coast Agents)
   400 California Street,
   San Francisco, Calif. 94104
   Telephone: (415) 392-4100
   Telex: RCA 27705

General Steamship Corporation, Ltd.
   550 South Flower Street
   Los Angeles, Calif. 90017
   Telephone: (213) 624-7412
   Telex: (Use San Francisco telex)

A lengthened "Rio Class" Johnson Line vessel.

   425 S.W. Washington Street
   Portland, Oregon 97204
   Telephone: (503) CA 8-7214
   Telex: (Use San Francisco telex)

General Steamship Corporation, Ltd.
   3131 Seattle First National Bldg.
   1001 Fourth Avenue
   Seattle, Washington 98104
   Telephone: (206) MA 2-4701
   Telex: (Use San Francisco telex)

Axel Johnson Corporation
   110 East 59th Street, New York,
   N.Y. 10022
   Telephone: (212) 758-3200
   Telex: RCA 224013-jolpac
         ITT 421881-jolpac
   TWX: 710-581-3381-jolpac

C. Gardner Johnson Ltd.
   One Bentall Centre, 505 Burrard Street
   Vancouver, 1 B.C., Canada
   Telephone: 684-4221
   Telex: 610 922-5015

A. Johnson & Co. (London) Ltd.
   Fountain House, 130 Fenchurch Street
   London E.C.3, England
   Telephone: 01-623 5831
   Telex: 885 141

A. Johnson & Co. G.m.b.H.
   Glockengiesserwall 17, Hamburg 1,
   Germany
   Telephone: 32991
   Telex: 021-61877

A. Johnson & Cie SA
   105 Rue du Faubourg Saint-Honoré
   PO Box 494-08, Paris 8e, France

A Johnson Line Fruit Flat

   Telephone: 256-0727, 359-2915
   Telex: 28976-ajandco

Johnson Line (Belgium) SA
   31 Rue Montoyer B-1040 Brussels, Belgium
   Telephone: 130030
   Telex- 24131

A. Durot SA
   Tavernierbuilding, Tavernierkaai 2
   Antwerp, Belgium

   Telephone: 327850
   Telex: 31155-trouda

Holm & Wonsild
   Amaliegade 36, Copenhagen K. Denmark
   Telephone: 01-140069
   Telex: 2574, 5269

Wambersie & Zoon C.V.o.A.
   7 Calandstraat, PO Box 1182
   Rotterdam, Holland
   Telephone: 010-110400-130600
   Telex: 22245

JUGOSLAVENSKA LINES

Jugoslavenska Linijska Plovibda
Rijeka (P.O. Box 379) Jugoslavia
TELEPHONE: 22-651
TELEGRAMS: Jugolinija Rijeka
TELEX: 24-218
CONTAINERS OWNED:
   Dry 328 $20 \times 8 \times 8$
   Dry 100 $8 \times 8 \times 8$
FLEET:
Containers transported (own and others) on existing ships
SERVICES:
   Adriatic and Mediterranean Ports to:

1. North Europe—every 10 days
2. North America—every 10 days
3. U.S. Gulf—Two sailings monthly
4. Iran and Iraq—monthly
5. India, Pakistan and Burma—Two sailings monthly
6. Levant—4/5 sailings monthly
7. South America—2/3 sailings monthly
8. Far East—monthly
9. Peoples Republic of China—monthly

PRINCIPAL OVERSEAS AGENTS:
Jadranska Pomorska Agencija, Rijeka

Handling Jugolinija Containers.

Anglo Yugoslav Shipping Co. Ltd., London
Crossocean Shipping Co., Inc., New York

Nanyo Bussan Co. Ltd., Tokyo
FUTURE PLANS:

The construction of container ships is under consideration

"K" LINE

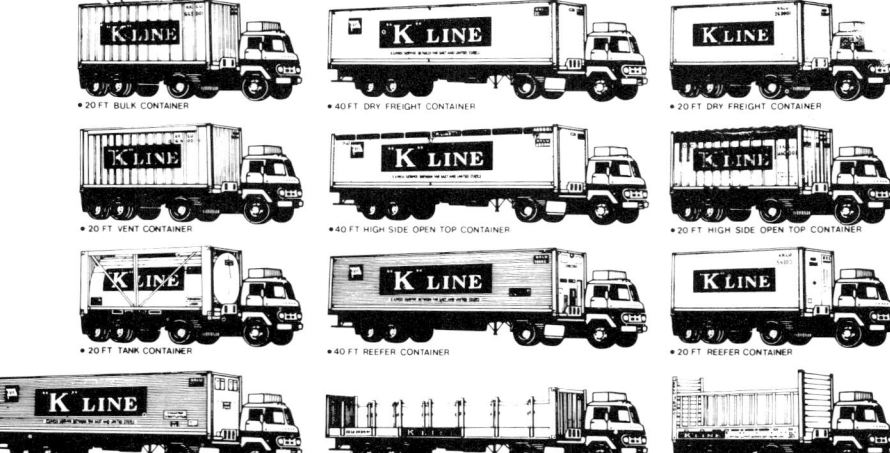

'K' Line Container Types

Kawasaki Kisen Kaisha Ltd.,
Iino Building, 1-1, 2-chome, Uchisaiwai-cho, Chiyoda-ku, Tokyo
TELEPHONE: Tokyo 03-506 2000
TELEX: TK 2361, 2461, 4516, 4348
'K' Line Agency Ltd.—Tokyo (Head Office) Kobe, Yokohama, Nagoya and Osaka.
DIRECTORS:
Motozo Hattori (*Chairman of the Board of Directors*)
Mamoru Adachi (*President*)
EXECUTIVES IN CHARGE OF CONTAINER OPERATIONS:
Masashi Fujitani (*Executive Director*)
Hiroshige Matsumari (*General Manager, Container Division*)
GENERAL:
"K" Line inaugurated their container service in October 1968, with *Golden Gate Bridge*, between Japan and California, and, at the same time, commenced a weekly container service on the same route using three other containerships owned by different Japanese shipping companies, all of which use the "space-charter system".

The company use six container terminals in Japan, four container terminals under similar conditions in U.S.A. and Canada and 3 container terminals in Australia, each of which has one or two gantry cranes capable of lifting 40 ft containers and a container freight station, as well as other facilities necessary for handling imports and exports..

The Eastern Searoad Service (ESS), a joint venture with the Australian National Line and the Flinders Shipping Co. Pty, Ltd. commenced in August 1969. Each of the companies has built one vehicle deck containership roll-on/roll-off type, *Australian Enterprise*, *Australian Searoader* and *Matthew Flinders*, which can accommodate every commodity suitable for liner vessels, and each of these 21 knot vessels has a capacity

of about 500 20 ft containers plus 100 cars.

A service between Japan and the Pacific North West Coast of the U.S.A. and Canada with the 22 knot *Golden Arrow*, capable of carrying 736 20 ft containers, started in 1970.

A fortnightly container service linking southeast Asia with Canada, and the United States started in October 1971.
CONTAINER SERVICES:
Japan/California Container Service—weekly
Japan/N.W. Coast of USA and Canada—every ten days.
Japan/Australia (Eastern Searoad Service)—every ten days.
Hong Kong, Kaoshung, Keelung and Pusan/Canadian and U.S. Ports—fortnightly.
CONTAINER SERVICES USING CONVENTIONAL SHIPS (Main routes only):
Far East/New York

Far East/Europe via Cape and Panama.
ROLL-ON SERVICE:
Japan/Australia (Eastern Searoad Service)—every ten days.

Two 26 knot vessels capable of carrying 1,800 20 ft units are reported to have been ordered jointly with Maersk for the Japan Europe service in 1973-74.

CONTAINER FLEET:
Dry	1,550+20 × 8 × 8
Dry	2,950+40 × 8 × 8.5
Insulated	50+40 × 8 × 8.5
Refrigerated	250+20 × 8 × 8.5
Refrigerated	200+40 × 8 × 8.5
Others	1,700 includes low side flat rack containers

Name	20 ft Container Capacity	Speed Knots	Net Reg. Ton	Length m	Length ft	Beam m	Beam ft	Draught m	Draught ft
Cellular:									
Golden Gate Bridge	800	21	8,770	175	574	25	82	9.7	31.9
*Golden Arrow	830	21	8,639	175	574	25	82	10.7	35.1
*"A Vessel"	1,070	23	—	211	692	36.6	100	10	32.8
†Colorado Maru									
†Oregon Maru	600	17	—	168.8	552	20.5	67.25	9.77	32.0
†Montana Maru									
Roll-on/Roll-off:									
Australian Searoader	600	21	3,465	168	551	25	82	8.23	27

*Owned jointly with Japan Line
†Equipped with two 35 ton Paceco container gantry cranes.

'K' Line's *Golden Gate Bridge*

PRINCIPAL OVERSEAS OFFICES:
"K" Line New York, Inc.
29 Broadway, New York, NY 10006, USA
Telephone: 212-344-4800
c/o Kerr Steamship Co. Inc.
Suite 2925, 1, California Street, San Francisco, Calif. 94111
Telephone: 415-982-2600
Kawasaki Kisen Kaisha Ltd. (Los Angeles)
Room No. 1322-1323 Douglas Oil Bldg., 530 West 6th Street, Los Angeles Calif. 90014, USA
Telephone: 213-622-2601
Kawasaki Kisen Kaisha, Ltd. (Chicago)
Chicago Representative Office:
208 South La Salle Street (Suite 679), Chicago Illinois, 60604, USA
Telephone: 312 CE6-4592
Kawasaki Kisen Kaisha, Ltd. (Seattle)

c/o Kerr Steamshsip Co., Inc.
Suite 3801, Seattle First National Bank Bldg., 1001 4th Avenue, Seattle, Washington 98104, USA
Telephone: 260-622-5160
Kawasaki (London) Ltd.
17 St. Helen's Place, London, E.C.3, England
Telephone: London Wall 4246
Kawasaki (Bangkok) Co., Ltd.
326/12-15 Suriwongse Road, Bangkok, Thailand
Telephone: 33901/9
Kawasaki (Hong Kong) Ltd.
6th Floor, Bank of Canton Bldg., No.6 Des Voeux Road, Central, Hong Kong
Telephone: Hong Kong 234051-6
c/o The McArthur Shipping & Agency Co. Pty. Ltd.

"Kyle House" 27-31 Macquarie Place, Sydney, N.S.W. 2000, Australia
Telephone: 27-4461/9
Kawasaki Kisen Kaisha, Ltd. (Melbourne)
c/o the Australian National Line
73-79 Riverside Avenue (Box 2238T GPO Melbourne, Victoria, 3001) Australia
P.O. Box 653, Fremantle WA 6160 Australia

Kawasaki Kisen Kaisha, Ltd. (Perth)
c/o Wigmores Ltd.
149 St. George's Terrace, Perth, W.A. 6,000 Australia

Telephone: 35-4211
Other representative offices:
Singapore, Johannesburg, Lagos, Dusseldorf, Mexico City, Caracas, Lima and Santiago.

Knut Knutsen OAS
Haugesund
Norway
CONTAINER SERVICE:
Australia-Far East-US West Coast.

KNUTSON LINE

FLEET:
Five general cargo vessels have had a cellular section added amidships which enables them to carry about 215 20 ft units.

Koninklijke Nedlloyd N.V.
PO Box 240 Rotterdam
TELEPHONE: 010-366600
TELEX: 24690

GENERAL:
Containers are at present used in the Company's conventional general cargo carriers.

KONINKLIJKE NEDLLOYD

CONTAINERS OWNED/OPERATED:

Dry	2,456	20 × 8 × 8
Dry	180	40 × 8 × 8 ·5
Insulated	30	20 × 8 × 8
Refrigerated	5	20 × 8 × 8
Open top	50	20 × 8 × 8

FLEET:
Abel Tasman, a 21·5 knot vessel capable

of lifting 1,590 20 ft units, operating in the Australia/Europe Container Service. Two 26 knot container vessels, capable of lifting 2,100 20 ft units and scheduled for delivery in December 1972 and July 1973, will operate in the Europe/Far East trade in conjunction with ScanService.

Latvian Steamship Company
2, Soviet Boulevard,
Riga
SERVICE:
Riga — Ventspils — Rostock — Rotter-

LATVIAN LINES

dam — Antwerp — Liverpool — joint services with other companies every 14 days.
FLEET:
Containers are at present carried on conventional vessels; the first specialised

container vessel built in the German Democratic Republic will enter service in late 1971.
CONTAINERS IN SERVICE:
Some 250 'heavy duty' containers are at present in service.

Lion Ferry A/B
P.O. Box 199
S-30104 Halmstadt 1, Sweden
TELEPHONE: 035/1191 90
TELEX: 38654
BRANCHES:
Varberg, Sweden
Telephone: 0340/161 35
Telex: 3462
Grenå, Denmark

FLEET:

LION FERRY AB

Telephone: 06/32 03 00
Telex: 4430
London, England
Telephone: 01-629 7961
Telex: 264311
Portland, Maine USA
Telephone: (207) 775-5616
Telex: 94-4446
DIRECTORS:
H. Meijer

ROLL-ON SERVICES:
Varberg to Grenå—Daily.
Hamburg to Harwich—every two days.
Hamburg and Bremerhaven to Harwich—every two days
Portland, Maine to Yarmouth, Nova Scotia—6 sailings per week.
AGENTS:
Karl Geuther & Co, Martinstrasse 58, 28 Bremen

	n.r.t.	Length		Beam		Draught		Trailer capacity
		ft	m	ft	m	ft	m	40 ft units
Europafergen I	789	485	86·9	50	15·5	14·5	4·40	17
Europafergen II	1,222	306	93·2	53·1	16·2	13·1	4·00	20
*Gustav Vasa**	1,482	361	110·2	57·7	17·6	14·3	4·35	24
*Kronprins Carl Gustav**	1,666	361	110·2	57·7	17·6	14·3	4·35	24
Prins Oberon	4,321	440	134·0	67·9	20·8	16·1	4·90	50
Prince of Fundy	2,907	387	118·0	57·7	17·8	15·6	4·75	30

New building—train-ferry—under construction

*On charter to Swedish Railways.

Societe per Azioni di Navigazione Lloyd Triestino
Palazzo del Lloyd, Piazza Unita 1, Trieste
TELEPHONE: 35341
TELEX: 46013
OFFICIALS:
Dott. Ing. G. Bartoli (*Chairman*)

LLOYD TRIESTINO

Dott. Ing. S. Cirriucione (*Managing Director and General Manager*)

GENERAL:
The company are part of the Soc. Finanziaria Marittima Group

FLEET:
The company have one 1,600 container capacity vessel on order with a length of 227 m (744·75 ft) a beam of 30·5 m (100 ft) and a draught of 10·7 m (35 ft) for service in mid 1972 with the Australia/Europe container service (AECS).

LUSITAINER CONTAINER SERVICE

Sociedade Geral de Commercio Industria e Transportes
11, Rua dos Douradores, Lisbon
TELEPHONE: 37051
TELEX: 543

Lykes Bros. Steamship Co., Inc.
PO Box 53068
New Orleans, La 70150
U.S.A.
TELEPHONE: 504-522-6661
TELEGRAMS: Lykes
TELEX: 504-822-5261
DIRECTORS:
J. T. Lykes, Jr.
Solon B. Turman,
Frank A. Nemec
Chester Ferguson
Lloyd G. Fitzpatrick
J. M. Lykes, Jr.
W. J. Amoss Jr.
R. T. Reckling
J. J. Creevy
Edward E. Lynn
BRANCHES:
U.S.A.: Houston, Galveston, Beaumont, Corpus Christi, New York, Chicago, Dallas, Kansas City, Lake Charles, Memphis, Mobile, Washington D.C.
Overseas: Durban, Genoa, Tokyo, Hong Kong, San Juan, London, Bremen, Antwerp.
FLEET:
The Company operates a fleet of forty-eight general cargo liner vessels, including nine part-container ships of the *Gulf Pacer* class. These nine vessels, formerly of the *Gulf Pride* class built in 1960/62, are being lengthened from 150·9 m (495 ft) to 180·4 m (592 ft). A number of these vessels have already rejoined the fleet after conversion and all nine will be in service by mid-1972. The conversion provides sufficient space to enable 60 containers to be stored under deck and 98 above deck. Sideports are fitted for unit load handling using fork lift trucks.
Three barge carriers, at present scheduled for delivery during the latter part of 1971 and early 1972 will have the following characteristics:
BARGE FLEET:
A total of 265 barges with a length of 29·71 m (97·5 ft), 10·67 m (35 ft) beam with a capacity of 1,133 m³ (40,000 cu ft) and 850 tons deadweight of cargo are under construction. Some 37 barges are scheduled to be completed monthly from November 1971.
CONTAINER FLEET:
Dry   487 20 × 8 × 8
Dry   16 20 × 8 × 8·5

SERVICE:
Lisbon and Leixos to London (Victoria Deepwater Terminal)—every ten days.
FLEET:
Actuaria.

LYKES LINES.

Impression of the *Seabee* class of barge-carriers   at present under construction for Lykes Lines

An artist's conception of the profile of the new Seabee class barge and intermodal carriers to be built for Lykes Bros. Steamship Co., Inc.

Length Overall	266·7 m (875 ft 0 in)
Load Waterline Length	225·6 m (740 ft 0 in)
Beam, Max.	32·6 m (107 ft 0 in)
Operating Draught	9·45 m (31 ft 0 in)
Maximum Draught	11·9 m (39 ft 0 in)
Deadweight @ 31 ft	25,625 tons
Deadweight @ 39 ft	40,000 tons
Deadweight excluding weight of Barges	20,000 tons
Service Speed	21 knots
Barge Capacity No.	38
Cargo Cubic (less tanks)	39,600 m³ (1,900,000 cu ft)
Deep Tank Cubic (usable)	22,600 m³ (800,000 cu ft)
Total Cargo Capacity	62,300 m³ (2,200,000 cu ft)
Container capacity	1,800 20 ft units

Artists conception of one of the lengthened Lykes vessels due to be phased into service in 1971.

MACPAK CONTAINER SERVICE

Macpak Container Service

MANAGERS:
Mac Andrews & Co. Ltd.,
Plantation House, Mincing Lane, London,

EC3M 3LP
TELEPHONE: 01-626 1543
TELEX: 888352
BRANCHES:
Royal Liver Building, Liverpool L3 1HF

Telephone: CENtral 3922
Telex: 62324
DIRECTORS:
Hon. A. C. R. Weir (*Chairman*)
Hon. J. V. Weir

A. L. Billington
P. B. Larsen
K. G. Reid
Mogens Steincke (Danish)
SERVICES:
Southampton to Bilbao—3 sailings per fortnight in winter and every four days in summer. (*Patricia*).
Liverpool to Bilbao—weekly (*Velazquez*)
Liverpool to Cartagena, Barcelona, and Valencia—weekly (*Churruca* and *Cervantes*).
CONTAINERS IN SERVICE:

Dry	182	20 × 8 × 8
Dry	150	20 × 8 × 8·5
Tilt units	475	20 × 8 × 8·5
Mesh	40	20 × 8 × 8
Flats (open sided)	100	20 × 8 × 8

PRINCIPAL OVERSEAS AGENTS:
Hurtado de Amèzaga 4, 1 Centro, (Apartado

FLEET:

Vessel	20 ft Container Capacity	Net Reg. Ton	Length m	Length ft	Beam m	Beam ft	Draught m	Draught ft
*Patricia**	25	4,071	141·2	463	20·7	68	5·5	18·1
Velazquez†	102	295	77·25	253	12·8	42	—	
Churruca†	100	728	98·70	323	13·4	44	4·8	16·0
Cervantes †	100	728	98·70	323	13·4	44	4·8	16·0

*Roll-on vessel owned by Swedish Lloyd.
†Container vessel on charter.

357) Bilbao-8 Vizcaya
Tel: 21-59-08.   Telex: 33730
Calle de Marques de Casa Riera 4 (Casa del Suecia), (Apartado 959) Madrid-14

Tel: 221-64-13.   Telex: 27643
Central Office for Spain, Plaza del Duque de Medinaceli 5, (Apartado 441), Barcelona-2
Tel: 231-37-07.   Telex: 54752

MACVAN CONTAINER SERVICE

Macvan Container Service
Operated by
George Gibson & Co. Ltd.
64 Commercial Street, Leith, Edinburgh, 6
TELEPHONE: 031 554 1621
TELEX: 72227
S.S.M. Transport N.V.
Veerkade 5, Rotterdam
TELEPHONE: 11 23 20
TELEX: 23047
and
Hollandsche Stoomboot Maatschappij,
Oostelijke Handelskade 3, Amsterdam
TELEPHONE: 11 33 33
TELEX: 13623
DIRECTORS:
P. C. Somerville

C. A. Somerville
T. Macgill

SERVICES:
Leith-Rotterdam   } 4 opportunities
Leith-Amsterdam   } per week
Leith-Antwerp—3 sailings per fortnight

FLEET:
Nieuwland   81 Units
Tweed   72 Units
Ronan   88 Units

PRINCIPAL OVERSEAS AGENTS:
S.S.M. Transport N.V.
  Veerkade 5, Rotterdam
  Telephone: 132320

Telex: 23047
Hollandsche Stoomboot Maatschappij,
  Oostelijke Handelskade 3, Amsterdam
  Telephone: 11 33 33
  Telex: 13623
D. Burger & Zoon
  7 Westerstraat, Rotterdam
  Telephone: 11 12 20
  Telex: 21031
Vereenigd Cargadoorskantoor
  139 de Ruyterkade, Amsterdam
  Telephone: 62216
  Telex: 12071
Hefurth & Boutmy N.V.
  Cassiersstraat 15/19, Antwerp
  Telephone: 315890
  Telex: 31333

Managing owners for Maersk Line:
A. P. Moller
Kongerns Nytory 8, DK-1098-Copenhagen
TELEPHONE:
TELEX:

MAESK LINE

GENERAL:
The company are believed to be building one or more 1,800 container vessels in conjunction with 'K' Line for introduction into the Europe/Far East Service in 1973.

MALTA CROSS CONTAINER SERVICES

Malta Cross Continent Containers Ltd.
202 Old Bakery Street
Valletta, Malta
TELEPHONE: 26987-21758
TELEX: MW321
EXECUTIVES IN CHARGE OF CONTAINER OPERATIONS:
D. A. H. Howell (*Director*)
W. Aquilina (*Malta*)
J. Taylor (*London*)
SERVICES:
Malta to Marseilles, Livorno, Naples, Malta every ten days with on carriage to numerous European destinations using own through transport arrangements. Also to U.S.A. and Canada.
Malta to UK—Two direct sailings per month.
FLEET:
Malta Cross
Used on the Mediterranean round service, this 11 knot vessel with a length of 67·9 m (222·7 ft), a beam of 13 m (42·6 ft) and a draught of 3 m (9·84 ft) is capable of carrying 66 20 ft units. Equipment comprises roll-on ramps on both bow and stern and side ports for pallet handling if required. A 5 ton deck crane is used for handling hatch covers and general cargo which can be carried in addition to the containers or roll-on traffic. Two chartered vessels maintain the direct service with the United Kingdom.
CONTAINERS IN SERVICE:
ISO Type 10 and 20 ft dry cargo units and

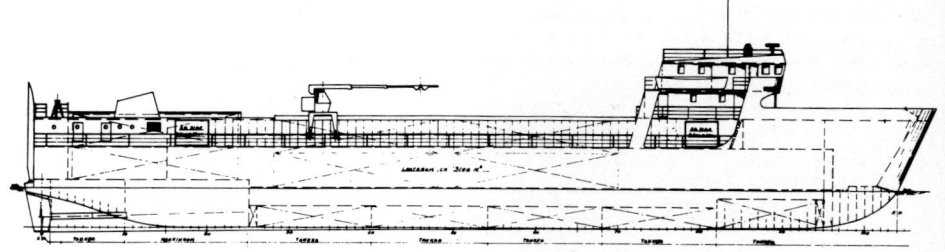

20 ft refrigerated containers are in service.
PRINCIPAL AGENTS:
United Kingdom:
Malta Cross-Continent Container Agencies Ltd.
  Peek House, 20 Eastcheap, London EC3
  Telephone: 01-626 1457
  Telex: 887039
France:
Barry Rogliano et Cie
  14 Rue Beauvan, Marseille 1
  Telephone: 33 67 40
  Telex: 41715
Belgium, Germany, Holland
Rhenus Antverpia
  Rue de Ankverten
  Antwerp
  Telephone: 41 68 90
  Telex: 31346

Malta Cross

MANCHESTER LINERS

Manchester Liners Ltd.
P.O. Box 189
Port of Manchester, Manchester M5 2XA
TELEPHONE: 061-872 4466
TELEX: 667001
DIRECTORS:
R. B. Stoker
Sir Leslie Roberts, CBE
J. A. MacConochie, MBE
P. V. O. Evans
W. A. L. Roberts
C. A. Skelton
M. Pattinson

EXECUTIVE IN CHARGE OF CONTAINER
OPERATIONS:
Captain G. M. Evans

CARGO SUPERINTENDENT:
Captain G. R. Clayton

CONTAINER SERVICES:
North Atlantic:
Manchester—Montreal, Toronto and Hamilton, weekly.
Clyde—Montreal, Toronto and Hamilton—weekly (joint service with Head-Donaldson and Canadian Pacific).
Mediterranean:
Manchester—Malta, Cyprus and Israel. Twice monthly.
Great Lakes:
Montreal—Great Lakes Ports Feeder Service.
Flying Fish Service—This service accepts cargo from Europe, Africa and the Middle East by air into Manchester Airport. It is then containerised for the voyage to Montreal and flown from Montreal Airport to final destination. It is claimed that a transit time of eight or nine days between a variety of points in the eastern and western hemisphere can be achieved and cost savings, compared with all-air rates can be as much as 75 per cent.

Manchester Merit, purchased in October 1970, has a total capacity of 168 units, 130 of which are carried under deck. A further vessel of this class is under construction.

Manchester Rapido and *Manchester Mercurio* each capable of carrying 54 20 ft plus 12 40 ft units under deck and 28 20 ft units on deck, have been chartered for the Montreal—Great Lakes Service.

Two cellular vessels, each capable of carrying 600 20 ft units, have been ordered for delivery in 1975.

CONTAINERS OWNED:

Dry	4,133	20 × 8 × 8
Dry	272	40 × 8 × 8·5
Top loading	573	20 × 8 × 8
Open Top	806	20 × 8 × 4
Insulated	712	20 × 8 × 8
Bulk	403	20 × 8 × 8

A *Challange* class vessel.

Manchester Concorde alongside Manchester Container Terminal.

Manchester Challenge alongside Montreal Container Terminal.

FLEET:

	Net Reg. Tons	Length m	Length ft	Beam m	Beam ft	Draught m	Draught ft	Container capacity Under deck only
Manchester Renown	5,017	153	502	18·9	62	8·53	28	68
Manchester City	4,688	153	502	18·9	62	8·53	28	68
Manchester Port	5,284	153	502	18·9	62	8·83	29	146
Manchester Progress	5,229	153	502	18·9	62	8·83	29	146
*Manchester Challenge**	7,234	156·06	512	19·53	63·5	8·23	27	500
*Manchester Courage**	7,269	156·06	512	19·35	63·5	8·23	27	500
*Manchester Concorde**	7,269	156·06	512	19·35	63·5	8·23	27	500
*Manchester Quest**	5,625		448	18·9	62	8·53	28	312
*Manchester Crusade**	7,364	161·5	530	19·35	63·5	8·23	27	500
*Manchester Merit**	2,499	94·49	310	15·24	50	5·49	18	130
Merit class vessel under construction	2,499	94·49	310	15·24	50	5·49	18	130

*Cellular vessels

PRINCIPAL OVERSEAS AGENTS:
Furness Withy & Company Ltd
Furness House
315 Sacrament Street
Montreal 125
Telephone: 849-1223
Telegrams: Furness Montreal
Telex: 01-2420
AGENTS:
Malta:

John Ripard & Son Ltd.
  Telex: 252
Cyprus:
Francoudi & Stephanon Ltd.
  Telex: 2243
Israel:
Ardo Shipping Ltd.
  Telex: 600

Manchester Merit loading at Manchester

MATSON NAVIGATION COMPANY

Matson Navigation Company
100 Mission Street, San Francisco,
California 94105
Subsidiary Companies:
Matson Terminals, Inc.
Matson Research Corp.
The Oceanic Steamship Company
Matson Services Company
SERVICES:
US West Coast ports to Hawaii.
BRANCHES:
Honolulu, Hilo, Kahului, Lihue, Hawaii;
Wilmington, California; Portland, Oregon;
Seattle, Washington; Chicago, Illinois; Washington D.C.

Foreign offices
Tokyo and Kobe, Japan; Vancouver, British
Columbia; Melbourne and Sydney, Australia;
Auckland, New Zealand
GENERAL:
  Matson Navigation Company announced
its withdrawal from Pacific/Far East
container operations in July 1970. At
the time of going to press it had been
reported that the Company's Far Eastern
and Australian services had been taken
over by Pacific Far East Line.

Matson Navigation Company's *Hawaiian Progress*

Matson Navigation Company's *Hawaiian Enterprise.*

CONTAINERS IN SERVICE:

Dry	9,250	24 × 8 × 8·5
Insulated	300	24 × 8 × 8·5
Refrigerated	1,470	24 × 8 × 8·5
Bulk	125	24 × 8 × 8·5
Flat rack	600	24 × 8 × 8·5
Auto Frame	216	24 × 8 × 8·5
Low Profile	35	40 × 8 × 4·25

FLEET:

Name of Ship	n.r.t.	Length m	Length ft	Beam m	Beam ft	Draught m	Draught ft	Container Capacity in units 24 × 8 × 8·5 ft
Container Vessels:								
Californian	9,408	185·9	610·5	21·4	71·5	10·0	33·0	527 containers
Hawaiian	9,938	185·9	610·5	21·4	71·5	10·0	33·0	527 containers
Hawaiian Monarch	13,859	184·7	606·2	21·4	71·5	10·0	33·0	193 vehicles and 701 containers
Hawaiian Queen	13,569	184·7	606·2	21·4	71·5	10·0	33·0	192 vehicles and 701 containers
Hawaiian Motorist	4,572	142·7	468·5	21·2	69·5	8·9	29·5	517 vehicles and 220 containers
Hawaiian Legislator	7,142	151·4	497·0	21·8	71·5	9·9	32·7	457 vehicles and 242 containers
Hawaiian Citizen	8,522	142·7	468·5	21·2	69·5	8·9	29·5	488 containers
Hawaiian Princess	3,110	97·0	315·7	15·8	52·0	5·6	18·5	187 containers
Islander (Barge)	3,340	95·0	312·0	15·2	50·0	5·3	17·7	190 containers
Hawaiian Enterprise	16,472	219·0	719·0	28·9	95·0	10·4	34·0	1016 containers
Hawaiian Progress	16,483	219·0	719·0	28·9	95·0	10·4	34·0	1016 containers
Other Vessels:								
Pacific Trader	10,113	158·8	521·0	21·2	69·5	9·6	31·5	505 containers
Pacific Banker	10,028	158·8	521·0	21·2	69·5	9·6	31·5	505 containers

S.S. *Hawaiian Queen* at Matson Line's container yard, Oakland, California.

MESSAGERIES MARITIMES

Compagnie des Messageries Maritimes.
12, Bd de la Madeleine
75, Paris 9e

AFFILIATED CONTAINER COMPANY:
Societé Commerciale Transoceanique des
Conteneurs (SCTC)

See the entry under SCTC.

METRIC LINE

Metric Line Ltd.

Victoria Buildings, High Street,
Runcorn, Cheshire
TELEPHONE: 092-857 2259
TELEX: 627325

SERVICES:
Manchester and Liverpool to Rotterdam—
weekly.
FLEET:
Decimal
CONTAINERS IN SERVICE:
Containers and flats—20 ft.

MEYER LINE

P. Meyer
Kronprinsesse Marthais Pl.1,
Oslo, Norway
TELEPHONE: 427120
TELEX: 11161
DIRECTORS:
Hans Otto Meyer
Per Fermann Meyer
Peter Meyer
SERVICE:
US east coast ports—Europe—Weekly.
FLEET:
Six part container vessels.
NEW YORK AGENCY:
Boyd, Weir and Sewell Inc, 17 Battery Place,
New York, NY 10004
Telephone: (212) 425-6800

Meyer Line container operations at Bremen.

MITSUI OSK LINES LIMITED

Mitsui OSK Lines, Ltd
MAIN OFFICE:
3-3, 5-Chome, Akasaka, Minatoku, Tokyo,
Japan (PO Box No. 6, Akasaka, Tokyo)
TELEPHONE: Tokyo 584-5111
TELEGRAMS: Themoline Tokyo
TELEX:
TK2266, TK2383, TK2431, TK2463
BRANCHES:
Interior:
Sapporo, Tokyo, Yokohama, Nagoya, Osaka,
Kobe, Moji
Foreign:
New York, London, Hong Kong.
Representatives:
Montreal, Chicago, Caracas, Paris, Dusseldorf,
Hamburg, Rotterdam, Lagos, Beirut,
Sydney, Melbourne, Wellington, San Fran-
cisco, Los Angeles, Seattle, Sao Paolo,
Rio de Janeiro, Buenos Aires, Lima,
Nairobi, Johannesburg, Durban, Tehran,
Bombay, Calcutta, Singapore, Bangkok,
Hong Kong, Taipei.
DIRECTORS:
Koji Shindo (*Chairman*)
Hisao Fukuda (*President*)
J. Gonda
S. Kumano
Y. Shinoda
S. Shimada
T. Yamada
S. Okada
T. Mishima
I. Maeda
N. Nagai
M. Tajiri
H. Mori
H. Ibuki

Mitsui OSK Lines' *America Maru*

Mitsui OSK Lines' *Australia Maru*

K. Tsukamoto
H. Yamamoto
R. Tamaki
Y. Hirai

SERVICES:
Japan—California—Weekly.
Japan—American North West Pacific Ports—
Weekly.

Japan—Australia.

Future Services:

Japan—US East Coast Ports—Weekly.
Japan—Europe—Weekly.

FLEET:

America Maru

Capable of carrying 716 20 ft units, this vessel has a length of 175 m (574 ft) a beam of 25 m (82 ft) and a draught of 9·5 m (31·2 ft).

Australia Maru

Capable of carrying 1,016 20 ft units this vessel is operating on the Australia Japan

Container Service.

Tohgo Maru

Owned jointly with NYK and Yamashita Shinnihon. Capable of a speed of 23 knots this vessel has a carrying capacity of 1,150 20 ft units.

Beishu Maru

Owned jointly with Yamashita-Shinnihon this vessel has a carrying capacity of 1,010 20 ft units. The vessel, completed in October 1970, has a length of 200 m (656 ft) a beam of 30 m (98·4 ft) and a draught of 10·5 m (34·4 ft).

Tonnage on Order:

New York Maru, New Jersey Maru.

Two 25 knot vessels capable of carrying 1,830 20 ft units are due for delivery in 1972 for the Japan-U.S. East Coast Service.

Rhine Maru, Elbe Maru:

Two 26 knot vessels are on order for the Japan-Europe service. These vessels are likely to be able to carry about 2,000 20 ft units and are scheduled for delivery in January 1972.

MONARCH LINE

Monarch Line

MANAGERS:

Hellenic Shipping and Trading Co. Ltd.
Dublin

SERVICE:

Roll-on: Dublin-Runcorn-Antwerp-Hamburg
—weekly

FLEET:

Two vessels each capable of carrying 140 20 ft units or 50 trailers and 40 containers.

MOORE McCORMACK LINES

Moore-McCormack Lines, Inc.

2, Broadway, New York, N.Y. 10004

TELEPHONE: (212) 363-6600

DIRECTORS:

James R. Barker (*Chairman and President*)
Lawrence F. Fiske (*Vice-Chairman*)
Laurence J. Buser
Robert E. O'Brien
B. J. Fennick
P. R. Tregurtha

EXECUTIVE IN CHARGE OF OPERATIONS:

Captain B. J. Fennick

BRANCHES:

Baltimore, Chicago, Cleveland, Detroit,

Norfolk, Philadelphia, Rochester, Savannah, San Francisco, Washington.

Montreal, Toronto, also East Coast, South America and South and East Africa.

FLEET:

Fourteen conventional cargo vessels (8 Robin Line and 6 American Republic's Line).

CONTAINER SERVICES:

Containers are carried on the following conventional cargo services:

Robin Line

Cargo, mail, deep tank, refrigerated and

passenger service, between East Coast United States, Great Lakes, Canada and South Africa, Mozambique, Tanzania, Kenya, East Africa, Malagasy, Mauritius and Reunion—weekly.

American Republics Line

Cargo, mail, deep tank, refrigerated and passenger service, between East Coast United States, Canada, the Great Lakes and Trinidad, Brazil, Uruguay, Argentina—weekly.

CONTAINERS IN SERVICE:

It has been reported that some 1,850 20 and 40 ft dry general cargo units are in service.

MÜLLER (BATAVIER)

Wm. H. Muller & Co. (Batavier) n.v.

St. Jobsweg 20, PO Box 795,
Rotterdam, Netherlands

TELEPHONE: Rotterdam 235480

TELEX: 24065

DIRECTORS:

R. J. Linde
F. Sinha

BRANCHES:

Wm. H. Müller & Co. (Batavier) Ltd.,
Custom House and Wool Quays,
Lower Thames Street,
London EC3
Wm. H. Müller & Co. (Batavier) Ltd.,
Zetland House, PO Box 46
Middlesbrough
Telephone: 47484
Telex: 58332

SERVICES:

Rotterdam—Middlesbrough. Twice weekly

FLEET:

Brittenburgh capable of carrying 18 20 ft units.

CONTAINERS OWNED:

Dry	7	10 × 8 × 8
Dry	14	20 × 8 × 8
Dry	20	8 × 6·6 × 7·4
Stackable Flats	52	20 × 8 × 8

NAKHODKA-JAPAN LINE

Nakhodka—Japan Line

A joint venture believed to be between:
Far-Eastern Shipping Company,
Vladivostock, 15, 25 Oktiabria St. and
Yamashita Shinnihon Line,
1-1 Hitosubashi, 1-chome, Chiyoda-ku,
Tokyo

SERVICE:

Yokohama, Kobe, Nagoya, and Niigata to

Nakhodka—up to six sailings per month.

FLEET:

Kavalerovo Grodekovo

These vessels, operated by FESCO, are reported to be of recent construction and to have been fitted for container transport, they are believed to have a capacity of

60 20 ft units. A third vessel, a timber carrier of 5,100 tons, has been converted to carry 100 20 ft units, is also in service.

It has been reported that three Japanese owners, one of whom is believed to be Y.S. Line, will place two fully cellular vessels in the service by early 1972.

NEW ENGLAND EXPRESS LINE

New England Express Line

c/o Ruys & Co. S.A.
Britselei 23-35
Antwerp

SERVICE:
North West European Ports to Boston Mass—
fortnightly.
FLEET:
Four chartered vessels capable of carrying

between 150 and 180 20 ft equivalents.

AGENTS:
Patterson Wylde & Co. Inc.
Boston, Mass.

NIPPON YUSEN KAISHA

N.Y.K. Line,
3-2 Marunouchi, 2 chome,
Chiyoda-ku, Tokyo, Japan
TELEPHONE: Tokyo (212) 4211
TELEX: TK 2236, 2465, 2466, 4473, 4479

DIRECTORS:
Yoshiya Ariyoshi (*Chairman of the Board of Directors*)
Shojiro Kikuchi (*President*)
Isamu Kannauchi (*Executive Vice-President*)
Toshiaki Niitsu (*Managing Director*)
Kazumasa Suga (*Managing Director*)
Taro Izumi (*Managing Director*)
Yasuyuki Mizuno (*Managing Director*)
Takushi Maruo (*Managing Director*)
Mitsuru Sharina (*Managing Director*)
Tsuneo Taki (*Managing Director*)
Masanori Kurokawa (*Managing Director*)
Susumu Ono (*Managing Director*)
Tadashi Suhara (*Director*)
Susumu Kobaysahi (*Director*)
Yoshito Yamanaka (*Director*)
Shuhei Shoda (*Director*)
Masanosuke Takeda (*Director*)
Toshihiko Yamada (*Director*)
Yasushi Hibino (*Director*)
Teru Yagi (*Director*)
Mitsuo Ogasawara (*Director*)
Ataru Kobayashi (*Director*)
Kenjiro Imaida (*Auditor*)
Toshiro Kurashige (*Auditor*)
Masaaki Yonesato (*Auditor*)
Shinsuke Asao (*Board Counsellor*)
Tadayasu Kodama (*Board Counsellor*)
EXECUTIVES IN CHARGE OF CONTAINER OPERATIONS:
Yasuyuki Mizuno (*Managing Director in charge of container planning*)
Susumu Ono (*Managing Director in charge of container operation and planning*)
BRANCHES:
New York, San Francisco, Los Angeles, Seattle, Vancouver, Chicago, Montreal, London, Hamburg, Dusseldorf, Paris, Milan, Beirut, Rotterdam, Sydney, Melbourne, Tokyo, Otaru, Sapporo, Yokohama, Nagoya, Osaka, Kobe, Moji.

NYK's *Hakozaki Maru*

NYK's *Haruna Maru* owned jointly with the Showa Line

NYK's *Hakone Maru*

FLEET:	Container Capacity 20 ft	Net Reg. Tons	Length		Beam		Draught		Speed in knots
Name			ft	m	ft	m	ft	m	
IN SERVICE:									
Hakone Maru	859	8,367	613·5	187	85·3	26·0	34·6	10·52	22·6
Haruna Maru	859	8,373	613·5	187	85·3	26·0	34·6	10·52	22·6
Hakozaki Maru	1,178	12,791	697·2	212·5	98·3	30·0	31·1	9·50	23·1
Tohgo Maru	1,012	13,980	689	210	101·6	31·0	31·1	9·50	23·0
Hotaka Maru	783	11,547	643	196	90·5	27·6	31·1	9·50	22·4

UNDER CONSTRUCTION FOR THE JAPAN/ EUROPE SERVICE:	Container Capacity 20 ft	Net Reg. Tons	Length		Beam		Draught		Speed in knots
Name			ft	m	ft	m	ft	m	
Kamakura Maru	1,838	abt. 31,700	856·03	261	105·08	32·2	39·04	12·00	26·15
Kurama Maru	1,838	abt. 31,700	856·03	261	105·08	32·2	39·04	12·00	26·15
Kitano Maru	1,838	abt. 31,700	856·03	261	105·08	32·2	39·04	12·00	26·15
UNDER CONSTRUCTION FOR THE JAPAN/ CALIFORNIA SERVICE:									
Hiei Maru	1,010	12,900	697·02	212·5	98·05	30·0	34·6	10·5	22·4
PLANNED FOR THE JAPAN/NEW YORK SERVICE:									
Kurobe Maru	1,827	abt. 24,000	793·12	242·0	105·08	32·2	34·05	11·50	25·3
Kiso Maru	1,827	abt. 24,000	793·12	242·0	105·08	32·2	34·05	11·50	25·3

SERVICES:

(i) *Japan/California Container Service:*
(Tokyo, Nagoya and Kobe to Oakland and Los Angeles), 2 Sailings per month. (*Hakone Maru, Haruna Maru and Hiei Maru* (April 1972)).

(ii) *Japan/Australia Container Service:*
(Yokkaichi, Nagoya, Yokohama and Osaka) to Sydney, Melbourne and Brisbane), 3 sailings per month, jointly operated with MOSK and YS. (*Hakosaki Maru and Tohgo Maru*).

(iii) *Japan/PNW Container Service:*
(Kobe, Nagoya, Yokohama to Seattle, Vancouver and Portland), 3 sailings per month jointly operated with MOSK, K, YS, JPN and Showa. (*Hotaka Maru*) and three further vessels will be assigned to the route by 1974.

(iv) *Europe/Far East Container Service:*
Opening at the end of 1971 this service will ultimately provide two sailings weekly in conjunction with other Japanese and European operators on a space charter system. NYK will operate *Kamakura Maru, Kurama Maru* and *Kitano Maru* on this service.

(v) *Japan/New York Container Service:*
To be inaugurated in Summer 1972 in conjunction with other Japanese Lines this service will provide weekly sailings and *Kurobe Maru* and *Kiso Maru* will be assigned to this route.

CONTAINERS IN SERVICE:
The company owns 20 ft × 8 ft × 8 ft, 40 ft × 8 ft × 8·5 ft dry freight containers, 20 ft × 8 ft × 8 ft ventilated, refrigerated, flat rack, open top, pen, tank, bulk and platform units. It is not their policy to divulge the number in service.

NORFOLK, BALTIMORE AND CAROLINA LINE

Norfolk, Baltimore and Carolina Line (NBC)
This company is a feeder service for Dart Containerline.
OFFICIALS:
H. G. Williams (*President*)

SERVICE:
The service varies according to the requirements of the Dart Containerline calls but covers ports on the East Coast North American Coast.

NORFOLK LINE

Norfolk Line Ltd.

Atlas House, Southgates Road,
Great Yarmouth, Norfolk
TELEPHONE: 4971
TELEX: 97449

OFFICIALS:
L. Remeeus (*Chairman*)
F. J. N. Walker (*General Manager*)
SERVICE:
Holland to United Kingdom. An integrated haulier service using own ships and terminals—Scheveningen to Great Yarmouth—up to 14 sailings per week.

FLEET:
Duke of Norfolk
Duke of Holland
These Roll-on vessels accept about 20/25 vehicles; a further vessel is planned.

NORTH SEA FERRIES LTD

North Sea Ferries Limited
Noordzee Veerdiensten (North Sea Ferries), NV,
Haringvliet 100, Rotterdam 1, (PO Box 1476)
TELEPHONE: (010) 142066
TELEX: 23152
BRANCHES:
Port Office: Noordzee Veerdientsten (North Sea Ferries NV, Beneluxhaven, Scheldeweg, Europoort, Rotterdam.

TELEPHONE: 01888-2077
TELEX: 23052
North Sea Ferries Ltd,
King George Dock, Hedon Road, Hull
Telephone: (0482) 74106
Telex: 52349

DIRECTORS:
D. L. J. Mortelman, OBE
J. N. Burrell
H. Kirsten
G. L. Medendorp
I. M. Churcher (*General Manager*)

PRINCIPAL OFFICIALS:
I. M. Churcher, (*General Manager*)
C. S. Paterson (*Manager for UK and Eire*)
E. D. Davidson (*Freight Manager*)
W. H. Walker, MBE (*Quay Superintendent UK*)

ROLL-ON SERVICES:
Hull to Rotterdam (Europoort), ten sailings per week each way including drive-on, drive off passenger vessels daily sailing at 1800 hours.

HULL, QUEEN ELIZABETH DOCK TO ROTTERDAM ECT CONTAINER SERVICE:
Commencing in October 1971 there will be 3 sailings per week each way; this will be increased to 5 sailings when a further vessel of the *Norbank* class enters service in early 1972.

North Sea Ferries' *Norcape*

FLEET:
ROLL-ON VESSELS:
Norwave:
Container capacity 100 × 20 ft + 65 cars
Net reg tons 1,544·49
Length 108·80 m (357 ft)
Beam 18·80 m (61 ft 8 in)
Draught 5·00 m (16 ft 5 in)

Norwind:
Container capacity 100 × 20 ft + 65 cars
Net reg. tons 1,660·51
Length 108·80 m (357 ft)
Beam 18·80 m (61 ft 8 in)
Draught 5·00 m (16 ft 5 in)

Norcape:
Container capacity 100 × 20 ft + 60 cars
Net reg. tons 780
Length 103·85 m (340·7 ft)
Beam 18·50 m (60·7 ft)
Draught 5·0 m (16·4 ft)

CELLULAR CONTAINER VESSEL:
Norbank:
Container capacity 91 × 20 ft
Net reg. tons about 750
Length 78·63 m (258 ft)
Beam 12·95 m (42·6 ft)
Draught 4·72 m (15·5 ft)

CONTAINERS OWNED/OPERATED:
None.

NORTHERN IRELAND TRAILERS

**Northern Ireland Trailers Ltd
(Coast Lines Group)**

The Docks, Preston, Lancs. PR2 2XT.
TELEPHONE: Preston 728222
TELEGRAMS: Trailers, Preston
TELEX: 67532 and 67644
BRANCHES:
Stephenson Street, Canning Town, London
   E16
Scala House, Holloway Circus, Birmingham 1
Pucklechurch Trading Estate, Pucklechurch,
   Bristol
Errington Street, Derby Road Liverpool, 5
Imperial Crossroads Garage, Hanchurch,
   Stoke-on-Trent
171 Limestone Road, Belfast
The Harbour, Larne

DIRECTORS:
  L. J. Donkin   J. B. Griffiths
  R. T. Robinson   H. O. McMurray
  J. R. Turner

SERVICES:
  Preston-Larne-Preston—daily
  Ardrossan-Larne-Ardrossan—6 sailings per
week

FLEET:
Spaniel:
  This vessel, with a container capacity of
50 20 ft units, is 68·18 m (233·75 ft) in length
with a beam of 11·4 m (37·4 ft) and a draught
of 4·57 m (15·01 ft).

Irish Coast:
  This vessel is capable of carrying 71 20 ft
units; she has a length of 78·42 m (257·4 ft)
a beam of 11·61 m (38·1 ft) and a draught of
4·02 m (13·2 ft).

CONTAINERS IN SERVICE:
ISO

Dry cargo	97	20 × 8 × 8
Insulated	15	20 × 8 × 8
Refrigerated	5	20 × 8 × 8
Refrigerated	4	30 × 8 × 8

Others

Dry cargo	46	16·5 × 7·5 × 6·5
Dry cargo	51	30 × 7·5 × 6·9
Insulated	62	18 × 7·3 × 6·5
Insulated	5	10 × 7·5 × 6·5

NOPAL

**Nopal Lines (The Northern Pan-American
Line A/S, Oivind Lorentzen)**

Oslo
TELEPHONE: 55 91 90
TELEGRAMS: Sobral
TELEX: 11227 Olao N 16886 Quick N
BRANCHES:
  General Agents: Oivind Lorentzen, Inc,
  New York

MANAGING DIRECTOR:
  Olav. G. Henriksen

CARGO SUPERINTENDENTS:
  Captain Lars Riise
  Captain Peder Sydnes

SERVICES:
  US Gulf/Mexico-Brazil/Argentina/Uruguay

and vice versa, fortnightly sailings
each direction
US Gulf/Mexico-West Africa and vice
versa, one sailing every 3 weeks each
direction.

FLEET:
  A fleet of nine liner vessels, each of which
is capable of carrying between 60 and 80
20 ft units is operated.

NORWEGIAN CARIBBEAN LINES

Norwegian Caribbean Lines
Transcaribbean Maritime Service Inc.
501 N.E. First Avenue, Miami, Florida 33132
TELEPHONE: 305 (358) 1790
TELEX: 519413
TWX: 810-848-9231
SERVICES:
Roll-on between Miami, Jacksonville, Nassau,
  Freeport-Bahamas, arriving Freeport every
  Sunday and Nassau every Monday, Wed-
  nesday and Friday.
FLEET:
  Trailer Express—A roll-on vessel designed
with a stern ramp.
AGENTS:
Nassau:
Commonwealth Shipping Co. Ltd.
  P.O. Box 4252, Nassau
  Telephone: 28056/7

Norwegian Caribbean Lines' *Trailer Express.*

Freeport:

Darvikson Ltd.
  PO Box 553, Freeport
  Telephone: 25195/6

Jacksonville:
Transcaribbean Maritime Service Ind.
  PO Box 515, 2701 Tallyrand Avenue,
  Jacksonville, Fla. 32201
  Telephone: (804) 356-3013

ORIENT OVERSEAS LINE

Orient Overseas Line
GENERAL MANAGERS:
Island Navigation Corporation
20 Exchange Place, New York, N.Y. 10005
401 Nikkatsu International Building, Hibiya,
Chiyoda-ku, Tokyo
Affiliated companies in Hong Kong and
  London.

GENERAL:
Orient Overseas Line is part of the Chinese
Maritime Trust Ltd. founded in 1940 by
Mr. C. Y. Tung. It is also known as the
C. Y. Tung Group and the Island Navigation
Corporation acts as operator and manager of
the group's large fleet of vessels of all types,
some of which operate container services.

SERVICES:
Far East—Europe.
Far East, eastbound round the World.
Far East—W. Coast North America.

Oriental Comet.

Orient Overseas Container Services Ltd.
operate weekly between Hong Kong and
West Coast North American ports via

Formosa and Japan. Further container
services are understood to be under consideration.

FLEET:
  Partial container ships capable of carrying
up to 140 20 ft units.

Oriental Arrow, Oriental Comet, Oriental Despatcher, Oriental Express

These part container vessels have each had cellular compartments added to provide a capacity of about 300 30 ft units.

Oriental Leader, Oriental Chevalier

These two 22 knot vessels, together with a further two under construction and due for delivery by 1972, have a reported capacity of between 907 and 1,200 20 ft units (including 100 refrigerated at No. 5 hold). They have a length of 205 m (672·6 ft) a beam of 26 m (85·3 ft) and a mean draught of 9·25 m (30·3 ft). It is possible that the Company may also have chartered two vessels from Bahamas Ocean Development.

Partial container ships capable of carrying up to 140 20ft units.

Further vessels are being converted to partial container carriers for the trans-pacific trade.

OVERSEAS CONTAINERS LTD

Overseas Containers Limited
St Mary Axe House,
St Mary Axe, London, EC3A 8BE
TELEPHONE: 01-283 5991
TELEX: 883947

(The Company are also Managing Agents for the Australian Japan Container Line which entry please see for details).

U. K. MARKETING HEADQUARTERS (AND HANDLING AND PACKING ADVISORY BUREAU):
17a/18 Bevis Marks, London, EC3A 7JB
TELEPHONE: 01-283 4242
TELEX: 883947/8
EUROPEAN OFFICE:
P.O. Box 362, Karklaan, Rotterdam
TELEPHONE: 360266
TELEX: 21481

DIRECTORS:
Sir Andrew Crichton (*Chairman*)
R. O. C. Swayne (*Deputy Chairman*)
H. R. Hildyard (*Joint Managing Director*)
K. St. Johnston (*Joint Managing Director*)
P. A. Tobin (*Joint Managing Director*)
A. J. Butterwick (*Director of Marketing*)
J. M. Corbet-Singleton (*Australian Trade Director*)
R. F. Cornwell (*Finance Director*)
R. B. Monteath (*Technical Director*)
K. Reynolds (*Far East Trade Director*)
R. P. M. Wormal (*Director of Operations*)

SERVICES:
UK/Australia:
The Company have six vessels operating on the Australia Europe Container Service which provides through transport services every 5 days between the United Kingdom and Australia.

Europe/Far East
The Company have five vessels under construction for delivery starting in early 1972 all scheduled to enter service in 1972 together with vesesls belonging to other countries, which will provide a weekly or more frequent service by the end of the year.

The OCL service will operate between Hamburg or Bremerhaven, Rotterdam and Southampton and Japan (early 1972) Hong Kong and Singapore (mid 1972), South Korea and Taiwan (probably a feeder service mid 1972), West Malaysia (early 1973) and the Philippines at a date to be announced.

FLEET:
Australian/Europe Container Service:

Encounter Bay	*Flinders Bay*
Moreton Bay	*Discovery Bay*
Botany Bay	*Jervis Bay*

These vessels have been modified to carry 774 20 ft units below deck and 736 20 ft equivalents above deck giving a total of 1,510 20 ft equivalents to include 304 insulated units.
Gross tonnage: 27,000
Length overall: 227·3 m (745 ft 9 in)
Beam: 30·5 m (100 ft)
Loaded Draught; 10·67 m (35 ft)
Speed: 22 knots
Europe/Far East Container Service:

Tokyo Bay	*Cardigan Bay*

OCL's *Encounter Bay* after modification with a deckload of 766 containers

Osaka Bay	*Liverpool Bay*
Kowloon Bay	

20 ft Container Capacity below deck —1,948 units.
20 ft Container Capacity above deck—352 units stacked 1 high.
Length overall: 289·55 m (950 ft)
Beam: 32·26 m (105·8 ft)
Design draught: 10·97 m (36 ft)
Speed: 26 knots
Gross tonnage: 58,000 (estimated)
CONTAINERS IN SERVICE:
The number of units in service in the Australian service has not been made available by the company.

For the Far East Service erders for 14,215 20 and 40 ft containers and 1,500 flats have so far been placed.

INLAND CONTAINER BASES
Collection and delivery can be made direct to exporters' or importers' premises. Inland containerbases are available where cargoes can be received and distributed. The company provides for shippers who wish to use a full container and pack it themselves (FCL) plus a consolidation service at the receiving end and a distribution service at the consignees' end for cargo which cannot fill a container (LCL).
Location:
Manchester (Urmston)
Leeds (Stourton)
Birmingham North (Perry Barr)
Liverpool (Aintree)
Glasgow (Coatbridge)
REGIONAL OFFICES:
South Region:
Overseas Containers Limited
  78 Broadway, Stratford,
  London, E15 1NG
  Tel: 01-555 0911. Telex: 897388
Overseas Containers Limited
39/40 Queen Square,

Bristol, BS1 4QR
  Tel: 0272-26225. Telex: 449193
Midland Region:
Overseas Containers Limited
  College Road, Perry Barr,
  Birmingham, B44 8DR
  Tel: 021-356 7344. Telex: 338082
North East Region:
Overseas Containers Limited
  Wakefield Road, Stourton, Leeds, 10
  Tel: 0532-76801. Telex: 557332
Overseas Containers Limited
  16 Portland Terrace
  Newcastle-upon-Tyne, 2
  Tel: 0632 810261
North West Region:
Overseas Containers Limited,
  Orrell Lane, Bootle, Lancs, L20 6NT
  Tel: 051 525 2275/8321. Telex: 627006
Overseas Containers Limited
  Barton Dock Road,
  Barton Dock Estate (West),
  Urmston, Manchester, M31 2LP
Scottish Region:
Overseas Containers Limited
  Gartsherrie Road, Coatbridge,
  Lanarkshire, ML5 2DY, Scotland
  Tel: 0236-24922. Telex: 778577
AGENTS IN IRELAND:
W. E. Williames & Co. Ltd.
  82/86 High Street, Belfast BT1 2BD
  Tel: Belfast 29281. Telex: 74619
W. E. Williams & Co. (I) Ltd.
  42/44 Lower Mayor Street, Dublin 1
  Tel: Dublin 45186. Telex: 5466
AGENTS—AUSTRALIAN TRADE:
Netherlands and for exports only in Belgium and Luxemburg:
Ruys & Co.
Box 966, Westplein 2, Rotterdam
  Tel:.114600. Telex: 21257
France and for imports only in Belgium and Luxemburg:
Soc. Com. Transoceanique Des Conteneurs

12, Boulevard de la Madeleine, 75-Paris 9
Tel: 0730760.   Telex: 21043
Germany:
Hapag-Lloyd AG
Ballindamm 25, 2 Hamburg 1
Tel: 32 10 81.   Telex: 021-61 988
Italy:
Lloyd Triestino, S.P.A.N.
Palazzo Del Lloyd Triestino,
Piazza Dell'Unita d'Italia 1, Trieste, Italy
Tel: 35341.   Telex: 46072
MARKETING OFFICES—AUSTRALIA:
Overseas Containers Australia Pty. Ltd.
17 Phillimore Street, Fremantle, W.A.
Tel: 35 5122.   Telex: 92244
Overseas Containers Australia Pty. Ltd.
3 Santo Parade, Port Adelaide, S.A. 5015
Tel: 4 3366.   Telex: 82726
Overseas Containers Australia Pty. Ltd.
446-452 Collins Street, Melbourne, Vic.
Tel: 67 9901.   Telex: 31449
Overseas Containers Australia Pty. Ltd.
38 Bridge Street, Sydney, N.S.W.
Tel: 2 0575.   Telex: 21258
Overseas Containers Australia Pty. Ltd.
113 Eagle Street, Brisbane, Q'ld.
Tel: 31 0471.   Telex: 41026
AGENTS—FAR EAST TRADE:
Germany:
M & O Container Transport GmbH
Postfach 1046, Ansgaritrankpforte 1,
D-2800 Bremen 1
Tel: 31731.   Telex: 245927
Holland:
M.G.S. Container Transport N.V.
P.O. Box 451, Rotterdam
Tel: 114900.   Telex: 21188

Belgium:
M.G.S. Container Transport (Belgium) N.V.
23 St. Paulustraat, Antwerp
Tel: 327946.   Telex: 31365
Switzerland:
Jacky, Maeder & Co.
Wallstrasse 8, CH-4002, Basle
Tel: 248820.   Telex: 62191 and 62131
France:
Hernu Peron
15 Rue de Nancy, 75-Paris 10
Tel: 205-95-67.   Telex: 21-722
Austria:
Enrico Sperco & Sohn A.G.
Postfach 1, 1015 Vienna
Tel: 52-42-11/55-54-42
Telex: 11834
Finland:
Axel Holmstrom A/B
P.O. Box 10327, Mannerheimintie 12 B,
Mannerheimvagen, Helsinki, Heisingfors10
Tel: 64-85-11.   Telex: 12-423
Sweden:
Emil R. Boman A/B
Box 2054, 103, 12 Stockholm 2, Sweden
Tel: 08-249500.   Telex: 1348 Bomans 6
Frostenson & Larsson A/B
Postbox 101, 13 B Skeppsbron,
Malmo, Sweden
Tel: 727 40.   Telex: 3338
C. A. Lagerwall A/B
Box 7007, Gothenburg, Sweden
Tel: 128295.   Telex: 20627

Norway:
Lingeagenturer AS
Fred Olsensgt 11, Oslo 1

Tel: 42-07-80.   Telex: 11112
Denmark:
Heckscher & Son Succesrs.
63 Bredgade, DK 1260 Copenhagen K
Tel: 11-38-30.   Telex: 9026
Tokyo:
Swire MacKinnon
C.P.O. Box 703, Tokyo 100-91, Japan
Tel: 213-3611.   Telex: 2248
Hong Kong:
Butterfield & Swire (Hong Kong) Ltd.
P.O. Box 1, Hongkong
Tel: H-246191.   Telex: 3206
Singapore:
Mansfield & Co. (Pte) Ltd.
P.O. Box 398, Singapore
Tel: 76051.   Telex: 301
West Malaysia:
Container Agencies Sendirian Berhad
P.O. Box 1011
Kuala Lumpur, West Malaysia
Tel: 51594/5.   Telex: 433
Philippines:
Soriamont Steamship Agencies
P.O. Box 2039, Manila D-406
Philippines
Tel: 50-20-11.   Telex: RCA 7227694
Bangkok:
The Borneo Co. (Thailand) Ltd.
1041 Silom Road, Bangkok, Thailand
Tel: 31090.   Telex: 316

Taiwan:
Jardine Matheson & Co. Ltd.
P.O. Box 81, Taipei
Taiwan, Republic of China
Tel: 571281.   Telex: 391

PACIFIC AMERICA CONTAINER EXPRESS (PACE LINE)

Pacific America Container Express
A joint venture of:
Blue Star, Ellerman and Port Lines through
Associated Container Transportation (Australia) Ltd.
New Zealand Shipping Co. Ltd and Shaw
Savill and Albion Ltd.   Through Overseas
Containers Ltd.
Australian National Line
SERVICE:
Australia and New Zealand to East Coast
North America.
FLEET:
Five vessels, three of which, *ACT 3*, *ACT 4*
and *ACT 5*, are provided by ACT(A) and
one each by OCL and ANL.   These vessels
have a length of 217·24 m (712·7 ft), a beam
of 28·95 m (95 ft) and a service draught of
9·91 m (32·5 ft).
Four vessels are designed to carry 1,138
20 ft units plus 20 40 ft units giving a total
20 ft equivalent capacity of 1,178.   In

Profile of a PACE Line vessel

addition, these ships have a non cellular
hold for the carriage of heavy and awkward
loads with a capacity of 168,000 ft³ or 30
general cargo containers.   The fifth vessel
carries 1,200 20 ft units plus 20 40 ft units
giving a total 20 ft equivalent capacity of
1,240.   All five vessels are designed to carry
556 refrigerated units under deck.
PRINCIPAL OPERATING AGENTS:
ACT(A) Pty Ltd.
Royal Exchange Building,
25, Pitt Street, Sydney

Telephone: 27-7911
Telex: AA21369

ACT (NZ)
P.O. Box 396, IBM Building,
157 The Terrace, Wellington 1
Telephone: 59919
Telex: 743468

ACT (USA)
90 West Street, New York 10006
Telephone: (212) 732-4803
Telex: RCA 222618

PACIFIC FAR EAST LINE

Pacific Far East Line Inc.

One Embarcadero Center
San Francisco 94111
California
TELEX: SF-514

BRANCHES:
Prudential Plaza, Chicago 1 Ill,
612, South Flower Street, Los Angeles
1, Broadway, New York, NY 10004
Room 302, World Center Building, 918
Sixteenth Street, Washington DC

DIRECTORS:
Leo C. Ross (*President*)
Howard C. Adams (*Executive Vice-President*)
Kenderton S. Lynch (*Vice-President, Finance
and Secretary*)
Peter A. Smith (*Vice-President, Sales*)
Sam N. Mercer (*Vice-President, Passenger
Division*)

PFEL'S *Guam Bear*

SERVICES:
(i) US West Coast to Hongkong, Philippines,
and Japan—every 12 days.
(ii) US West Coast to Japan, Korea, Okinawa,
Taiwan, Hongkong, Thailand, Vietnam
—every 12 days.
(iii) US West Coast to Guam—every 12 days.

(iv) U.S. West Coast to South Pacific—every
three weeks.

FLEET:
9 Mariner vessels
2 C-3 vessels
2 Passenger Liners

Container Vessels:
Guam Bear, Hawaii Bear. These vessels are capable of carrying 800 20 ft units.

Two 23 knot container vessels, each capable of carrying 956 20 ft units, are on order for delivery at the end of 1972.

Barge Carriers:
The first of six LASH barge carriers is due for delivery in December 1971. These 23 knot vessels, capable of carrying 61 barges or 1,200 20 ft units will be phased into Pacific services in 1972.

PACIFIC AUSTRALIA DIRECT LINE (PAD LINE)

Pacific Australia Direct Line
A joint venture of:
Rederiaktiebolaget Transatlantic
Fack S-403 10
Gothenburg 2, Sweden
Telex: 2300
Australian National Line
73-79 Riverside Avenue,
South Melbourne
Victoria 3205
Telephone: 624671
Telex: AA30584
Associated Container Transportation
(Australia) Ltd. (ACTA)
136 Fenchurch Street,
London EC.3
Telephone: 01-481 2567
Telex: 886 361
SERVICE:
Between Australian Ports in the Adelaide/ Brisbane range, Honolulu, and ports on the West Coast of USA and Canada. The Service commenced at the beginning of March 1971 when m.v. *Paralla* entered service. There is a sailing every three weeks.

FLEET:
Three 20,300 dwt roll-on vessels. m.v. *Paralla* is operated by Swedish Transatlantic, m.v. *Dilkara* by ACT(A) Ltd and m.v. *Allunga* (owned by PAD Shipping (Australia) Ltd, a company formed by Australian National Line, Elder Smith & Co and Trans-Austral Shipping Pty. Ltd.) is operated by A.N.L. They have a service speed of 22·5 knots on a draught of 8·25 m (27 ft). Dimensions are: length 199·01 m (652·9 ft); beam 28·65 m (94 ft); loaded draught 9·59 m (31·5 ft). There are two doors situated at the stern, the starboard door 10·5 × 5·6 m (34·4 × 18·4 ft) is equipped with an hydraulic angled ramp whose dimensions are 32 × 7·0 m (105 × 23 ft) the maximum load of which is a vehicle of 65 tons. The port side stern door is 7 × 5·6 m (23 × 18·4 ft).

VESSEL LAYOUT:
There are four continuous steel decks below the weather deck which extends almost from stem to stern. Each deck, also the weather deck, is reached by fixed ramps with a breadth of 7 m (23 ft) and an incline of 1 : 10. There are four hatches. Nos 1 and 2 holds are served by two 18 ton ASEA tandem cranes and No 1 hold is laid out for handling bulk cargoes.

PAD Lines' *Paralla*

VESSEL EQUIPMENT:
Each vessel is equipped with two 25 ton straddle carriers designed for the handling of steel and lumber. These are equipped with 18 ton capacity magnet lift gear as additional equipment. Two 13·5 ton straddle carriers, two 20 ton fork lifts, one 'C' Van for handling and stacking 40 ft containers two high, four 8 ton fork lift trucks, also three three-wheeled motor cycles (to which a sweeping machine can be attached) for distribution of lashings and inspection of cargo.

CONTAINERS IN SERVICE:
Dry freight containers are leased. The Line operates a total of 315 20 × 8 × 8 refrigerated and insulated units.

PRINCIPAL AGENTS:
Sydney:
Trans-Austral Shipping Pty. Ltd.
19 Pitt Street,
Box 5339 GPO
Sydney NSW 2001
Telephone: 27 2441
Telex: 21204

San Francisco
General Steamship Corporation Ltd.
400 California Street,
PO Box 3450
San Francisco,
Calif 94119
Telephone: 415-392-4100
Telex: 14-27705
230-34236
13-470031

POLISH OCEAN LINES

Polish Ocean Lines
ul.10 Lutego 24
Gdynia, Poland
TELEPHONE: Central 21-29-01
TELEX: 051-231
BRANCH OFFICE:
ul Aleje Jerozolimskie 44
Warsaw, Poland
Telephone: 27-3488
Telex: 52424
GENERAL:
Containers are carried on three part-container vessels on the North Atlantic service to United States East Coast Ports; on one part-container ship to Great Lakes Ports (80 20 ft equivalents on each); and on board the Company's general cargo vessels on on the North Atlantic service, United Kingdom Liner Service and Gdansk/Helsinki Line. Two ferry vessels maintaining the Service Swinoujscie/Ystad are also carrying containers and trailers.

CONTAINER FLEET:

Dry	205	20 × 8 × 8
Dry	223	40 × 8 × 8
Refrigerated	11	20 × 8 × 8
Refrigerated	48	40 × 8 × 8

FUTURE PLANS:

Three part-container vessels of about 12,500 dwt, carrying about 300 containers have been planned for the North Atlantic service. Delivery should take place in 1973. The construction of cellular container vessels of about 15,000 dwt, carrying approximately 800 20 ft equivalents has been postponed until after 1975.

One cellular container vessel of about 2,000 dwt, carrying about 100 20 ft containers will be put into the Poland/UK Service in 1973.

POSEIDON LINES

Poseidon Schiffahrt Gesellschaft mit Beschraenkter Haftung
Jungfernstieg 30, 2000 Hamburg 26
TELEPHONE: 341013
TELEX: 021 3081

GENERAL:
A partner in Europe Canada Line (ECL) which entry please see.

PRUDENTIAL GRACE LINES

Prudential Grace Line Inc.
1, White Hall Street,
New York, NY 10004, USA
TELEPHONE:
TELEX:
OFFICIALS:
Spyros S. Skouras (*Chief Operating Officer*)
Arthur C. Novacek (*President, Combined Operations*)

SERVICES:
New York to the Caribbean, Central and West Coast South America—Weekly.

U.S. East Coast to the Mediterranean—every 10 days.

It has been reported that one barge carrier may be employed experimentally on the South American service.

FLEET:
Part Container Vessels:
Santa Magdalena, Santa Mariana, Santa Maria, Santa Mercedes

Part container vessels each capable of lifting the equivalent of 263 20 ft units with space for 44 40 ft units. These 20 knot vessels have a length of 166·7 m (547 ft) a beam of 24·1 m (79 ft) and a draught of 8·23 m (27 ft); they are fitted with container gantry cranes fore and aft.

Barge Carriers:
Lash Italia, Lash Turkiye, Lash Espania, Lash Hellas, Lash Portugal

Five 23 knot barge carriers (LASH) type with a length of 235·4 m (772·5 ft), a beam of 30·5 m (100 ft) and a draught of 8·5 m (27·9 ft). These vessels have a carrying capacity of 61 barges or a combination of bulk cargoes, barges and containers. In addition deep tanks provide a storage capacity of 1,040 tons.

Barge Specifications:		
Length overall:	18·7 m	(61·5 ft)
Beam:	9·5 m	(31·2 ft)
Draught:	2·5 m	(8·3 ft)
Maximum height under deck:	4·42 m	(14·5 ft)
Minimum height under deck:	3·96 m	(13·0 ft)
Hatch openings:	12·8 × 6·4 m	(42 ft × 21 ft)
Capacity bale:	563·5 m³	(20,000 cu. ft)
grain:	583·4 m³	(20,600 cu. ft)

A *Santa Magdalena* class vessel on the Prudential Grace service to the Pacific Coast of South America

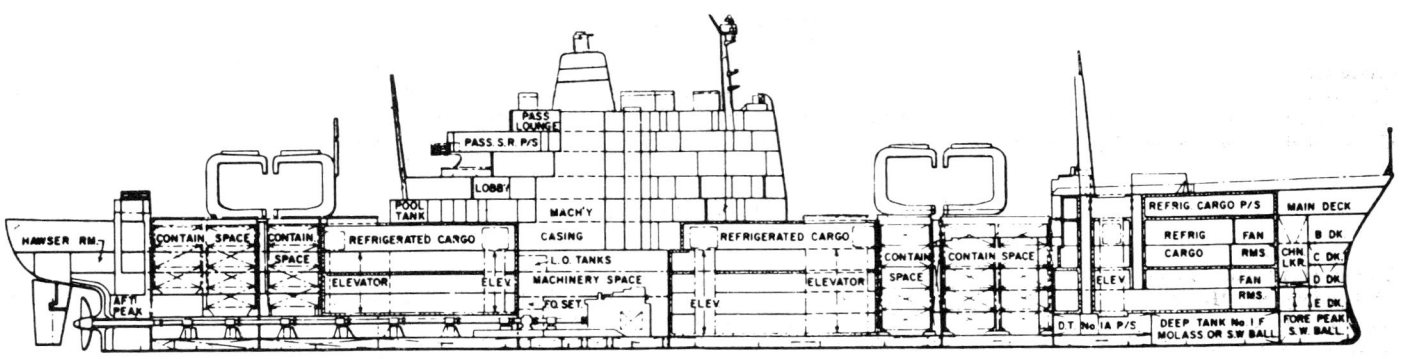

Sectional drawing of the Prudential Grace Line Santa Magdalena class.

RHEINTAINER LINE

Rneintainer Line

MANAGERS:
A. Kirsten
Postfach 1110, Deichstrasse 29
2 Hamburg II

TELEPHONE: 362 361
TELEX: 021 3252
SERVICE:
Emmerich—Tilbury—weekly.
FLEET:
Donau This vessel is capable of carrying

63 20 ft equivalents.

U.K. AGENTS:
Cutting & Co. Ltd.
Room 14, Amenity Block,
Grain Terminal, Tilbury, Essex

RONAGENCY

Ronagency (Shipping) Ltd.
The Quay, Castletown, Isle of Man
TELEPHONE: Castletown 2313, 2314
TELEX: 627054
DIRECTORS:
J. A. Bird   J. Counsell
K. E. Costain   J. W. Edmundson
G. E. Duke. O.B.E.   C. A. Welding
T. S. Wilkinson
CARGO SUPERINTENDENT:
Walter Edmundson Limited,

Glasson Dock,
Lancaster

Telephone: Galgate 577
Telex: 6573
AGENTS:
Walter Edmundson Limited
Lodge Street, Preston
Telephone: 54593

SERVICES:
Glasson Dock to Castletown—Five sailings weekly

Glasson Dock to Belfast N.I.—Three sailings weekly.

FLEET:
  M.V. *Northgate*. Container capacity: up

to 25 containers depending upon size.
Net reg. tons: 283·81 tons. Length: 60·29 m (165 ft); Beam: 8·6 m (28 ft 6 in); Draught: 8 ft (loaded with containers).
  M.V. *Tower Duchess*. Container capacity: 25 20 ft units; 161 nrt.

CONTAINER FLEET:

Dry	15	10 × 8 × 8
Dry	105	20 × 8 × 8
Insulated	20	19 × 7·5 × 7·5
Flats	70	25 × 8
Flats	20	20 × 7·5

SBC CONTAINER LINES

S.B.C. Container Lines Ltd.
AGENTS:
Wetram (U.K.) Ltd.
Sub-Station Road, The Dock,
Felixstowe

TELEPHONE: 6234
TELEX: 98109

SERVICE:
Felixstowe, Rotterdam, Pasajes—weekly.

FLEET:
Tamega
  A 16 knot fully cellular vessel capable of carrying 120 20 ft units 30 of which can be refrigerated.

SCANAUSTRAL

Scandinavian Australia Carriers Ltd (Scanaustral A.S.)
Maries vei 20, PO Box 210,
13222 Høvik, Norway
TELEPHONE: 11 1200
TELEX: 11208
A joint service by:
The East Asiatic Co. Ltd.
  Copenhagen
The Transatlantic S.S. Co. Ltd.
  Gothenburg
Wilh. Wilhelmsen
  Oslo
DIRECTORS:
L. T. Løddesøl
B. Ostberg
EXECUTIVE IN CHARGE OF CONTAINER OPERATIONS:
K. Raaum
SERVICE:
Europe-Australia, 48 sailings per year on three services:
  (i) Oslo or Gothenburg, Bremen, Hamburg, Antwerp and Rotterdam to Australian ports via the Cape and alternatively by Panama—fortnightly.

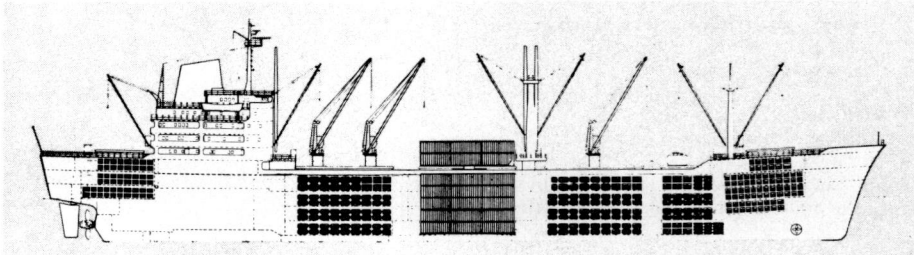

Profile of a *Scandia* class vessel jumboised in 1970-71 for the carriage of containers in one cellular hold

  (ii) Baltic and Scandinavian ports to Australian ports returning via the N.W. Europe ports as inducement offers— 16 sailings per year.
  (iii) Mediterranean-Australian ports—6 sailings per year.

FLEET:
  Six general cargo 'Scandia' vessels each capable of carrying between 173 and 222 20 ft units including a small number on deck.

Five roll-on/roll-off vessels, with a container capacity of 1,330 20 ft units, are on order and are due in service in 1972 and 1973. These 22 knot ships will be 208 m (682·4 ft) in length, 29·6 m (97·1 ft) in beam with a draught of 9·5 m (31·2 ft)

CONTAINER FLEET:

Dry	1,250	20 × 8 × 8
Flats	450	15 × 8 × 7

These units are leased.

SCAN DUTCH

Scandutch
OFFICIALS:
Börge Rathje (*Managing Director*)
H. Rootlieb (*Deputy Managing Director*)

GENERAL:
  ScanDutch is an amalgamation of the Scan Service Consortium and Kolikje Nedlloyd. The new company will operate 55 convent-

ional vessels between Europe and the Far East. Six container vessels (4 Scan Service and 2 Nedlloyd) will enter service in 1972/73 on this route.

SCANSERVICE

Scandinavian Joint Shipping Service I/S
35 Amaliegade, DK 1256,
Copenhagen K
TELEPHONE: (01) 11 23 11
A joint venture of:

The East Asiatic Company Ltd., Copenhagen
The Swedish East Asia Co Ltd, Gothenburg
Wilh. Wilhelmsen, Oslo
OFFICIALS:
B. Rathje (*Managing Director*)

GENERAL:
  Scanservice was formed in April 1969 to provide a container and general cargo service between Europe and the Far East.
  It has been announced that the two

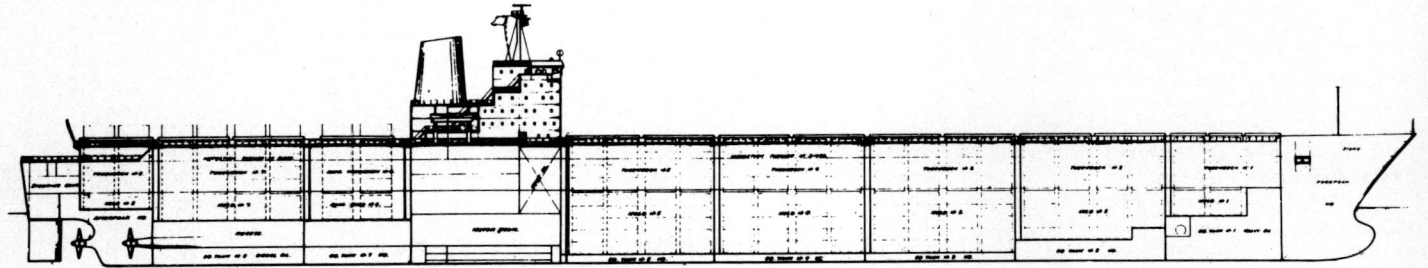

Profile of a Scanservice containership

vessels to be operated by Koninklijke Nedlloyd NV will be included in the service.

SERVICE:
Europe—Far East—Europe. Eight sailings per month with conventional vessels. By the end of 1972 containerships will provide a fortnightly service together with a number of conventional sailings per month.

FLEET:
Conventional vessels capable of carrying a limited number of containers.

Four 26 knot triple screw container vessels are on order, they will have a length of 274 m (900 ft), a beam of 32·20 m (106 ft) and a draught of 11·28 m (37 ft) with a carrying capacity of 2,000 20 ft units. The East Asiatic Company will own two of the vessels and the other members of the group one each.

CONTAINER FLEET:
About 10,000 20 × 8 × 8 and 40 × 8 × 8·5 units will be operated.

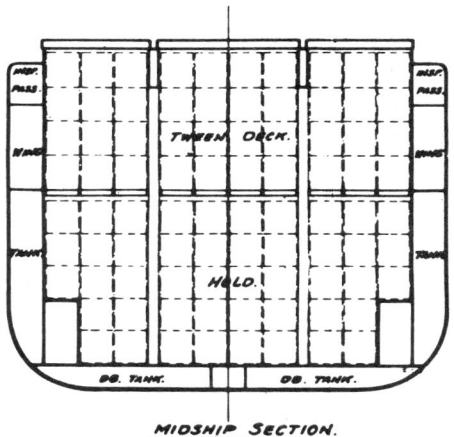

Cross-section of a Scanservice containership

SCANSTAR

Scanstar Limited
Albion House,
34, Leadenhall Street,
London, EC3A 1BB
TELEPHONE: 01 709 0481
TELEX: 888217

GENERAL:
A joint venture of Blue Star Line Ltd, London and East Asiatic Company Ltd, Copenhagen.

DIRECTORS:
S. Storm-Jorgensen (*Danish*)
E. H. Vestey
H. H. Sparsø (*Danish*)
D. J. Wortley

OFFICIALS:
P. M. Mace (*Manager*)
K. C. Larsen (*Deputy Manager*)

SERVICES:
Scandinavia, North Continent, United Kingdom and Ireland to West Coast U.S.A. and Canada fortnightly from April 1972 and three weekly until then.

The first fully cellular containership was introduced in May 1971, the second and third followed in September 1971; the fourth enters service in April 1972.

BRANCH OFFICE:
ScanStar
650 California Street, San Francisco
California 94108
Telephone: 391 5000
Telex: 470025

PRINCIPAL AGENTS:
The Blue Star Line Inc.
615 Flower Street,
Los Angeles,
California 90017
The East Asiatic Co. Inc.,
650 California Street,
San Francisco,
California 94108

California Star at Clydeport

Johnson, Walton Steamships Ltd.,
1201, West Pender Street,
Vancouver 1, B.C. Canada
Dovar Shipping Agency Inc.
19th Floor, 21 West Street,
New York, N.Y. 10006

FLEET:
California Star	*Falstria*
Columbia Star	*A Vessel*

These vessels with a service speed of 2·15 knots are capable of lifting some 900 20 ft units. The *Star* class vessels are 203·1 m (619·13 ft) in length with a beam of 25·82 m (84·75 ft) and a draught of 8·92 m (29·25 ft).

The *Falstria* class are reported as being 201·9 m (615·5 ft) in length with a beam of 26 m (85·3 ft) and a draught of 8·8 m (28·87 ft).

All vessels are capable of lifting up to 125 insulated containers.

CONTAINERS IN SERVICE:
Dry Cargo	20 × 8 × 8
Dry Cargo	40 × 8 × 8·5
Bin Containers	20 × 8 × 4
Tank Containers	20 × 8 × 8
Insulated for	
Cargoes down to —23°C	20 × 8 × 8

It has been reported that, in all, some 5,000 units will be required.

SEA-LAND

Sea-Land Service, Inc.
Corbin and Fleet Streets P.O. Box 1050
Elizabeth, New Jersey 07207
TELEPHONE: 289-6000 (N.J.)
TELEX: 12-5734
New York WH3-6060

OFFICIALS:
Michael R. McEvoy (*Chairman*)
Paul F. Richardson (*President*)
Kenneth G. Younger (*Executive Vice President and General Manager*)

BRANCHES:
Sea Land has offices throughout the United States, and offices in the Dominican Republic, Puerto Rico, Virgin Islands, Curacao, Haiti, Trinidad, Panama and

throughout Europe. In the **Far East** it has offices in Japan, the Philippines, the Ryukyu Islands, South Vietnam, Hong Kong and Taiwan.

SERVICES:

Between Europe and East Coast, USA— Two sailings per week

Between. Mediterranean and East Coast, USA—One sailing per week

Between Puerto Rico and East Coast, USA —Four sailings per week

Between Jamaica, Dominican Republic and East Coast, USA—One sailing per week

Between Seattle and Alaska—Two sailings per week

Between Hong Kong, Keelung, Kobe, Yokohama and Oakland, Long Beach, Seattle—One sailing per week

Containers move from any point to any point within the area of the Company's operations.

CONTAINER SIZE:

The company operates containers of 35 ft and 40 ft in length, 8 ft wide with a height of 8·5 ft or 4·25 ft on tank containers.

FLEET

225 Container Carriers: *Afaundria, Arizpa, Wacosta, Warrior*

226 Container Carriers: *Azealea City, Beauregard, Bienville, Fairland, Gateway City, Raphael Semmes, Summit*

274 Container Carriers: *Mayaguez, Ponce*

290 Container Carriers: *Mostangen, Mosbay, Mosangen, Mosgulf*

325 Container Carrier: *Charleston*

332 Container Carriers: *Houston, Jacksonville, Tampa*

354 Container Carriers: *Anchorage, Seattle*

360 Container Carriers: *Baltimore, Boston, Brooklyn, Galveston, Mobile, Newark, New Orleans, Philadelphia, Portland*

476 Container Carriers: *Elizabethport, Los Angeles, San Francisco, San Juan*

602 Container Carriers: *Pittsburg, Rose City, San Pedro*

609 Container Carriers: *Long Beach, Oakland, Panama, Trenton*

622 Container Carriers: *Chicago, St. Louis*

733 Container Carriers: *SL·180, SL·181*

In addition the *Rio Haina* (26 containers and the *Detroit*, a car carrier, are in service. The company charters for feeder services in Europe as required and the following vessels are understood to be currently in service: *Black Swan* (120 × 35 ft units), *Greyhound* (211 × 35 and 40 ft units), and *Ragna, Stadt Aachendorf* and *Plainsman* (62 × 35 ft units).

NEW BUILDINGS:

Eight 33 knot vessels each capable of lifting 1,085 containers are on order for delivery starting in 1972. These ships will have a length of 287·7 m (944 ft), a beam of 32·2 m (105·5 ft) and a draught of 9·1 m (30 ft).

CONTAINER FLEET:

Dry	36,220	35 × 8 × 8·5
Dry	1,757	40 × 8 × 8·5
Insulated	1,280	35 × 8 × 8·5
Refrigerated	5,410	35 × 8 × 8·5
Tank	537	35 × 8 × 4·25
Open top	1,560	35 × 8 × 8·5
Flat bed	450	35 × 8 × 8·5
Cartainer	127	35 × 8 × 5·1
Cartainer	101	35 × 8 × 6·7
Cattlecar	1	35 × 8 × 10·2

SEA-LAND OFFICES:

BELGIUM

Antwerp

Sea-Land (Belgium) S.A.
Churchilldok Hoek Muisbroeklaan-Noorderlaan, Antwerp 3
Telephone: Sales 03/413261
                    Operations 03/413337
Telex: 32350

FRANCE:

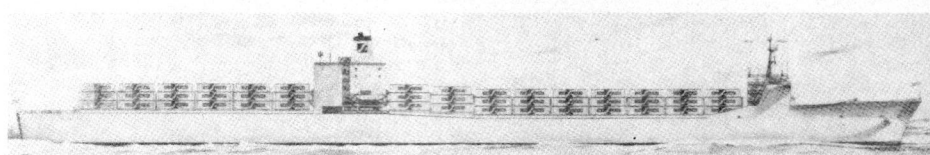
Artist's impression of the 33 knot 1,100 35 ft carriers being built for Sea-Land Service Inc.

Le Havre

Sea-Land Service, Inc.
136 Rue Victor Hugo, P.O. Box No. 1195
76 Le Havre
Telephone: (35) 42 00 96
Telex: 79969

Marseille

Sea-Land Service, Inc.
c/o Agena S.A.
31 Rue de Mazenod, 13-Marseille, 2
Telephone: 20-0748
Telex: MAR SOV 41860

Paris

Sea-Land Service, Inc.
c/o Agena S.A.
37 Rue Des Acacias, Paris 17
Telephone: 380-7909
Telex: 65740

WEST GERMANY:

Bremen (Sales)

Sea-Land (Germany) Transport GmbH
Knochenhauerstrasse 18, P.O. Box 1745
28 Bremen
Telephone: 315066
Telex: 245479

Bremen (Operations)

Sea-Land (Germany) Transport GmbH
Neustaedter Hafen, Schuppen 24C
P.O. Box 40221, 28 Bremen
Telephone: 540072
Telex: 244914

Frankfurt

Sea-Land (Germany) Transport GmbH
Ziel 65-69, Frankfurt 6
Telephone: 294180/294420
Telex: 414444

ITALY:

Genoa

Mediterranean Container Service, Italia
S.p.A.
Ponte Libia, Porto di Genova
Telephone: 41 64 51/2/3

Leghorn

Mediterranean Container Service, Italia
S.p.A.
C-P 736
57100

Milan

Mediterranean Container Service, Italia
S.p.A.
c/o. Paolo Scerni
Via Napo Torriani 31
Telephone: 635-761

Rome

Mediterranean Container Service, Italia
S.p.A.
Grattacielo Italia
Piazza Guglielmo Marconi, 25 (Eur)
Rome 00144
Telephone: 593-492, 594-089

THE NETHERLANDS:

Rotterdam

Sea-Land (Nederland) N.V.

Striendwaalseweg 30
P.O. Box 1560
Telephone: 16 80 00
Telex: 233 08

SPAIN:

Barcelona

Sea-Land Iberica, S.A.
Muelle Adosado, Port of Barcelona
Telephone: 319 4944/3521/4010

Madrid

Sea-Land Iberica, S.A.
Comandante Zorita 49.5°, Madrid 20
Telephone: 2330334

SWEDEN:

Gothenburg

Sea-Land Service
Vasaplatsen 7, S-411-26
Telephone: 17 68 30
Telex: 20676

Stockholm

Sea-Land Service
Birger Jarlsgatan 33B
Telephone: 141440
Telex: 17683

UNITED KINGDOM:

Felixstowe

Sea-Land Containerships Ltd.
Pier House, Dock Road
Felixstowe-Suffolk
Telephone: 6196
Telex: 98122

Grangemouth

Sea-Land Containerships Ltd.
South Quay, Grange Docks, P.O. Box 24
Grangemouth, Stirlingshire
Telephone: 3244-3786/89
Telex: 778362

Liverpool

Sea-Land Containerships Ltd.
Old Custom House
Gladstone Container Terminal, Bootle
Lancashire
Telephone: (051) 922-7701

London

Sea-Land Containerships Ltd.
16, New Street, London, E.C.2
Telephone: (01) 626-2461
Telex: 262991

SEA-LAND AGENTS IN COUNTRIES WITHOUT
    SEA-LAND OFFICES:
AUSTRIA:
Vienna
    Paul Gunther
    Schwedenplatz 2
    Telephone: 63 8847
    Telex: 75638

DENMARK
Copenhagen
    Henrik Strandvold A.T.
    Toldbadgade 33, 1253 Copenhagen
    Telephone: (01) 15 46 74
    Telex: 2944
EIRE:
Dublin
    B & I Lines Ltd.
    North Wall House, 12, North Wall
    Dublin 1
    Telephone: 41821
    Telex: 5356
FINLAND:
Helsinki
    Polar Express A.B.
    Fredrikinkatu 37, P.O. Box 10659
    Telephone: 13566
    Telex: 12856

MILITARY CARGOES:
    It was reported at the end of June 1971,
that the Company has been awarded a
$112·4 million contract for the carriage of
military cargo from the US West Coast to
Vietnam for the next two years. It is
projected by the US Defense Department
that 1·3 million measurement tons will be
carried annually. The Company are reported
to have moved 720,000 measurement tons
annually on the initial $72 million contract
won for the 1967/69 period.

Sea-Land feeder operational at Fos, Marseilles.

Greyhound

Sea-land container types

SEATRAIN

Seatrain Lines Inc.
Container Division
    Port Seatrain, Weehawken, NJ 07087
    TELEPHONE: (201) 866 5300
    TELEX: 12499, 125065

OFFICIALS:
    Joseph Kahn (*Chairman*)
    Howard M. Pack (*President*)
    Arthur C. Novacek (*President, Container
        Division*)
    Frank D. Troxel (*President, Seatrain Lines
        of California*)
    William O. Gohlke (*Senior Vice-President
        Corporate Planning*)
    John J. Haggerty (*Vice-President, Market-
        ing USA*)
    Neal Nunnelly (*Vice-President and General
        Manager for Europe*)

SERVICES:
    US East Coast Ports—Puerto Rico—twice
        weekly.
    US East Coast Ports—North West Europe—
        Weekly.
    US West Coast Ports—Hawaii—Weekly.
    US West Coast Ports—Far East
    US West and East Coast Ports—Far East
        (Military Transport Service)
        UK Coastal Feeder Service to Southampton
        Scandinavian Feeder Service to Bremen-
        haven.
        Europe to US Pacific Coast (Los Angeles)
    and Oakland).

Euroliner

Seatrain's *Eurofreighter*

FLEET:

Container Vessels:

Seatrain Maine, Seatrain Maryland, Seatrain New Jersey, Seatrain Texas, Seatrain Georgia, Seatrain Louisiana

These 15 knot vessels carry containers on special dollies below deck and containers on deck.

Seatrain Carolina, Seatrain Delaware, Seatrain Florida, Seatrain New York, Seatrain Ohio, Seatrain Puerto Rico, Seatrain San Juan, Seatrain Washington

These 15 knot vessels have a capacity of the equivalent of about 700 20 ft units.

Transchamplain, Transoneida, Transontario,

These vessels are capable of carrying 606 containers.

Transindiana, Transoregon, Transhawaii, Transidaho

These vessels are capable of carrying the equivalent of 964 20 ft units.

Transcolorado, Transcolumbia

These vessels are on charter to MSTS.

Euroliner, Eurofreighter

2 Vessels:

Four 28 knot gas turbine driven container vessels entered service in 1971. They have a length of 242 m (749 ft) a beam of 30·5 m (100 ft) and a draught of 10·7 m (35·1 ft) with a carrying capacity of the equivalent of 1,900 20 ft units.

Taeping

On charter from Bahamas Ocean Development.

Two further vessels are reported to be at the planning stage.

Three 22 knot chartered vessels *Spindrift Isle, Fiery Cross Isle* and *Lord of the Isle* provide the service between Europe and the US Pacific Coast.

CONTAINER FLEET:

40 *ft Units*

Dry	8,609
Insulated	107
Refrigerated	301
Open top	650
Auto Racks	130
Tank	4

27 *ft Units*

Dry	3,290
Insulated	11
Refrigerated	300
Flatracks	225

The total 40 ft chassis in service in 6,119 and there are 2,350 27 ft chassis in service.

OFFICES IN UNITED STATES:

New York, N.Y. 10004
25 Broadway
Telephone: (212) 425-8990
Telex: 128196

Atlanta, Ga. 30341
Room 122,
1 Dunwoody Park
Telephone: (404) 458-9626

Baltimore, Md. 21222
Dundalk Marine Terminal,
2700 Broening Highway
Telephone: (301) 282-6200
Telex: 87668

Boston, Mass. 02110
140 Federal Street,
Room 1317
Telephone: (617) 426-8967-(8)-(9)
Telex: 940215

Charleston, S.C. 29411
P.O. Box 10205
Charleston Heights

Taeping

Seatrain San Juan

Telephone: (803) 744-5362
Telex: 576414

Chicago
Arlington Heights, Ill. 60004
120 W. Eastman Street
Telephone: (312) 394-3600
Telex: 282443

Cleveland, Ohio 44122
Shaker Building
3645 Warrensville,
Center Road,
Room 307
Telephone: (216) 283-1020-(1)
Telex: 980327

Guam 96910
Agaña, M.I.
Apra Harbor
Commercial Port of Guam
Telex: 721170

Honolulu, Hawaii 96813
Sand Island Access Road,
Area 1
Telephone: (808) 531-8141

Norfolk, Va. 23505
Norfolk International Terminusl,:
7737 Hampton Boulevard
Telephone: (703) 489-3900
Telex: 823436

Oakland, California 94607
1395 Middle Harbor Road,
Telephone: (415) 465-1800
Telex: 336372

Philadelphia
Bala-Cynwyd, Pa. 19004
1 Belmont Avenue
Telephone: (215) 667-1490
Telex: 845148

Rochester, N.Y. 14614
1 Main Street, West
Telephone: (716) 454-1950
Telex: 978254

Seattle, Wash. 98169
12855 48th Street South
Telephone: (206) 246-5200
Telex: 320201

Vernon, California 90023
3600 East Washington Street.
Telephone: (213) 264-2031
Telex: 677330

Washington, D.C. 20036
1000 Connecticut Avenue,
Room 200
Telephone: (202) 659-4485
Telex: 892359

OFFICES IN PUERTO RICO:

San Juan 00905
Puerto Rico
Isla Grande Airport
Mail: P.O. Box 4552
Telephone: (809) 722-5200
Telex: RCA 102-3252480
ITT 103-3450255
WU 101-385283

Ponce, P.R. 00732
P.O. 151, Playa Station
Telephone: (809) 842-8274
WU 101-385346

Arecibo, P.R. 00612
P.O. 1626
Telephone: (809) 878-4020
WU 101-385610

Mayaguez, P.R. 00709
P.O. 3518, Marina Station
Telephone: (809) 832-8830
WU 101-385415

Caguas, P.R. 00625
P.O. 518
Telephone: (809) 743-9473

OFFICES IN GREAT BRITIAN:

London: H.Q. Office,
Seatrain U.K. Ltd,
26-28 Mark Lane,

London EC.3
Telephone: 01-623 0061
Telex: 887794

Birmingham
Seatrain U.K. Ltd.
Vehicle & General House
Hurst Street, Birmingham 5
Telephone: 021-622 2651
Telex: 339183

Glasgow
Seatrain U.K. Ltd,
95 Bothwell Street,
Glasgow C2
Telephone: 041-248 6711
Telex: 778736

Liverpool
Seatrain U.K. Ltd.
Harley Building,
11 Old Hall Street,
Liverpool L2 1BB
Telephone: 051-236-6844/5/6
Telex: 627674

Southampton
Seatrain U.K. Ltd.,
Container Terminal,
Western Road,
Southampton Docks
Telephone: 72421
Telex: 47115

OFFICES AND AGENTS IN CONTINENTAL
EUROPE:
Rotterdam: HQ Office Europe,
Seatrain Europa N.V.,
18 Wijnbrugstraat,
Rotterdam
Telephone: 010-147144
Telex: 22588

Amsterdam:
Ruys & Co. N.V.
Seatrain Dept.
Kabelweg 53-55, Amsterdam
Telephone: 164944
Telex: 11250

Antwerp:
Ruys & Co. N.V.
Seatrain Dept.
Britselei 23-25
2000 Antwerpen
Telephone: 321880
Telex: 31245

Basle:
"Neska" Schiffahrts A.G.
Seatrain Dept.
Südquaistrasse 55,
4000 Basel 19
Telephone: 326060
Telex: 62171

Berlin:

Berliner Seefrachten-Kontor
Erich Heckmann
1 Berlin 33 Dahlem
Am Hirschsprung 3
Telephone: 766723
Telex: 185778

Bremen:
Seatrain G.m.b.H.
28 Bremen, Löningstrasse 35
Telephone: 320361
Telex: 245726

Copenhagen:
Seatrain Danmark
Filialkontor Nordiska Havstag AB
Borgergade 32,
1300 Köbenhavn
Telephone: 124514
Telex: 7239

Düsseldorf:
Seatrain G.m.b.H.
4 Düsseldorf
Bismarkstrasse 66
Telephone: 360697
Telex: 8587119

Frankfurt a.M.
Seatrain G.m.b.H.
6 Frankfurt a.M.
Niddastrasse 42-44
Telephone: 231352
Telex: 411766

Gothenburg:
Nordiska Havstag A/B
Filialkontor Göteborg
Vegagatan 48
S-413 11 Göteborg
Telephone: 031-124890
Telex: 21177

Hamburg:
Seatrain G.m.b.H.
2000 Hamburg 1,
Grosse Allee 9
Telephone: 242756
Telex: 2162758

Hannover:
Seatrain G.m.b.H.
2 Hannover
Georgstrasse 40
Telephone: 26831
Telex: 922552

Hälsingborg:
Nordiska Havstag A/B
Stortorget 13
S-252 20 Hälsingborg
Telephone: 042-144095
Telex: 72457

Helsinki:
AB Lars Kogius OY
Södra Magasinsgatan 4
Helsinki 13
Telephone: 11500
Telex: 12509

Le Havre:

Jokelson & Handtsaem S.A.
Seatrain Dept.
Containers Terminal
Quai de L'Atlantique
76 Le Havre
Telephone: 480085/6
Telex: 19381

Munich:
Seatrain G.m.b.H.
8 München,
Elektrastrasse 11
Telephone: 911866
Telex: 522313

Nürnberg:
Seatrain G.m.b.H.
85 Nürnberg,
Hauptmarkt 2
Telephone: 203066
Telex: 622175

Oslo:
Skandinaviske Godscentraler A/S
Seatrain Dept.
Bispegaten 13, Oslo 1
Telephone: 203052
Telex: 18380

Paris:
Jokelson & Handtsaem S.A.
Seatrain Dept.
Tour Atlantic
92 Putaux, Paris/La Défense
Telephone: 7751511
Telex: 62558

Rotterdam:
Ruys & Co. N.V.
Seatrain Dept.
Veerhaven 4-7 Rotterdam
Telephone: 365800
Telex: 23737

Stockholm:
Nordiska Havstag AB
Danviksgatan 10
116 41 Stockholm
Telephone: 08-443998
Telex: 17560

Stuttgart:
Seatrain G.m.b.H.
7 Stuttgart,
Hausmannstrasse 181
Telephone: 464486
Telex: 723021

Vienna:
Seatrain G.m.b.H.
A1010 Wien
Kramergasse 3/7/22
Telephone: 222/639869
Telex: 75870

SHORT SEA TRANSPORT AG

Short Sea Transport AG
Glarus, Switzerland
SERVICE:
Felixstowe—Bilbao—weekly.
FLEET:
Two chartered 15 knot vessels. *Ellen Isle*
capable of carrying about 150 20 ft units

and *Kormoran Isle* capable of carrying about
100 20 ft equivalents.
CONTAINERS IN SERVICE:
Dry Cargo   200   40 × 8 × 8·5
Tilt   76   20 × 8 × 8
AGENTS:
Glover Brothers (London) Ltd.

Ibex House, Minories, London EC3
Telephone: 01-709 0722.   Telex: 886907
Trelawney House, The Dock, Felixstowe
Telephone: 6166.   Telex: 98431
George A. Morrison & Co. Ltd.
Leith

SHOWA

Showa Shipping Co. Ltd.,
Muromachi Bldg., 1, Nihonbashi-Muromachi,
4-chome, Chuo-ku, Tokyo, Japan
TELEPHONE: (270) 7211
TELEX: TK 2310 TK 2630

BRANCHES:
Yokohama, Osaka and Kobe.

DIRECTORS:
Toshiharu Matsue (*President*)
Haruo Oda (*Vice-President*)

Kuniaki Satoh (*Senior Managing Director*)
Zentaro Satoh (*Senior Managing Director*)
Sadamu Kitaka (*Senior Managing Director*)
SERVICES:
Japan to Pacific South West Coast of USA
(PSW)—every 10 days from March 1972.
Japan to Pacific North West Coast of USA
and Canada (PNW)—every 10 days.
PSW:
This service commenced in August, 1968
under a business tie-up with NYK Line

putting two same-type full container ships
Haruna Maru and *Hakone Maru* into service.
A container vessel, capable of carrying
about 1,000 twenty foot containers, will enter
this service in March 1972.
PNW:
Full container service on this route
started in May 1970 under a space charter
agreement.
Showa Line/NYK Line jointly own and
operate *Hotaka Maru*, Japan Line/K Line,

Golden Arrow and MOSK/Y-S Line, *Beishu Maru*.

Under the agreement each line has its own space on the above three vessels.

Showa has space of 122 containers both on *Golden Arrow* and *Beishu Maru* and on the *Hotaka Maru* space of around 220 containers is available.

FLEET:

Haruna Maru:

Container Capacity	752
Length (O.A.)	187·00 m (613 ·5ft)
Breadth	26·00 m (85·3 ft)
Draught	10·52 m (34·5 ft)
Gross Tonnage	16,214
Dead weight	19,620
Service Speed	22·6 knots

Hotaka Maru:

Container Capacity	783
Length (O.A.)	196·00 m (643·05 ft)
Breadth	27·60 m (90·55 ft)
Draught	10·52 m (34·5 ft)
Gross Tonnage	21,057·01
Dead weight	20,077·00
Service Speed	22·15 knots

A vessel of 23,000 dwt capable of carrying about 1,000 20 ft units is due to enter service in March 1972 and a further vessel is on order for delivery in March 1973.

CONTAINERS IN SERVICE:

Dry	200	40 × 8 × 8·5
Dry	1,400	20 × 8 × 8
Open Top	65	20 × 8 × 8
Bulk	250	20 × 8 × 8
Side Open	200	20 × 8 × 8
Flat Rack	250	20 × 8 × 8
Refrigerated	150	20 × 8 × 8
Tank	2	20 × 8 × 8

PRINCIPAL OVERSEAS AGENTS:

Olympic Steamship Co, Inc.
1000 Second Avenue, Seattle,
Washington 98104, U.S.A.

Olympic Steamship Co, Inc.
812 World Trade Building,

Showa's *Haruna Maru* owned jointly with NYK Line

333 SW Oak Street, Portland,
Oregon 97204, U.S.A.

Olympic Steamship Co, Inc.
230 North Michigan Avenue, Suite 1805,
Chicago, Illinois 60601, U.S.A.

Transmarine Navigation Corp.
555 California Street, San Francisco,
California 94104, U.S.A.

Transmarine Navigation Corp.
824 Wilshire Boulevard, Los Angeles,
California 90017, U.S.A.

Norton Lilly & Co, Inc.
90 West Street, New York N.Y. 10006,
U.S.A.

Clarke Traffic Services Ltd.
1155 Dorchester Boulevard West,
P.O. Box 730, Station Bldg.,
Montreal 102, Canada

Clarke Traffic Services Ltd.
199 Bay Street, Toronto 116,
Ontario, Canada

Kingsley Navigation Co, Ltd.
744 West Hastings Street,
Vancouver 1, B.C., Canada

Tatham Bromage & Co, Ltd.
46 St. Mary Axe,
London EC 3A 8EY, England

Showa's *Hotaka Maru* at Honmoku Terminal, Yokohama.

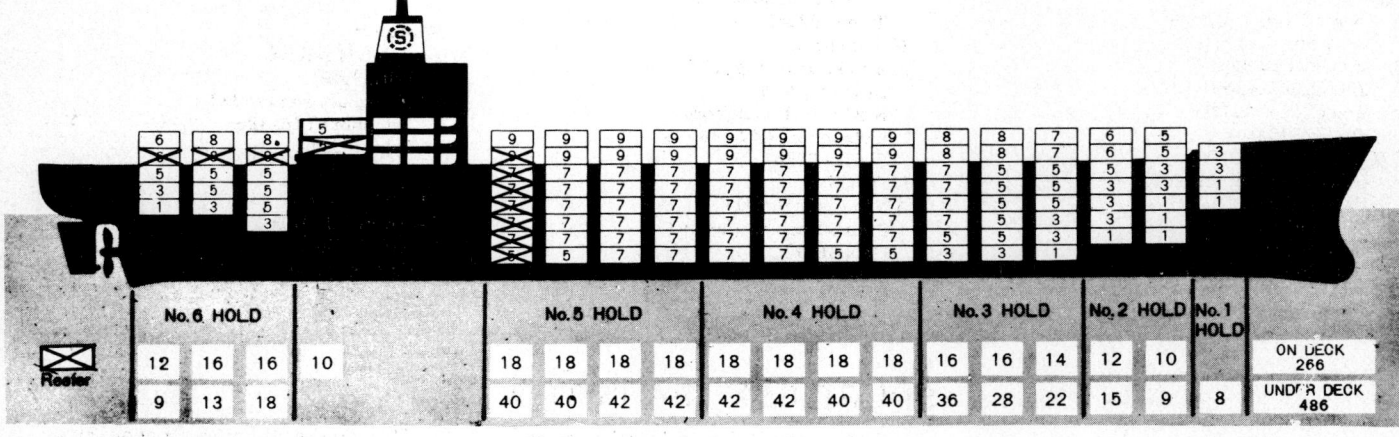

Haruna Maru—Container stowage plan.

	No. 6 HOLD			No. 5 HOLD				No. 4 HOLD				No. 3 HOLD			No. 2 HOLD	No. 1 HOLD	
Reefer 12	16	16	10	18	18	18	18	18	18	18	18	16	16	14	12 10		ON DECK 266
9	13	18		40	40	42	42	42	42	40	40	36	28	22	15 9	8	UNDER DECK 486

SCTC

Société Commercial Transocéanique des Conteneurs (SCTC)
12 Boulevard de la Madeleine, Paris, 9e
TELEPHONE: 073 07 60
TELEX: MESEHS 21043
BRANCHES:
Europe, Africa, Madagascar, Australia, Pacific Islands and South America.

OFFICIALS:
Roger Carour (*Chairman*)
Robert Gueguen (*Deputy Chairman*)
André Daneau (*Managing Director*)
Louis Cochet (*Manager, Marketing*)
Guy Adam (*Manager, Operations*)
Jacques Maupoix (*Head of Australian Service*)

GENERAL:
The subsidiary company of Compagnie des Messageries Maritimes responsible for container operations.

CONTAINER SERVICES:
Australia:
SCTC is a participant in the Australia/Europe Container Service (AECS) and is the AECS agent in France, Belgium and Luxemburg, (Northbound), Spain and Portugal. The company also controls the AECS terminal at Zeebrugge and will also control the terminal at Fos, Marseilles.

New Zealand:
Details of this service have not yet been

announced at the time of going to press; three general/container/reefer vessels each able to carry 302 20 ft units will be in service by the end of 1971 or early 1972.

Far East:
One container vessel is under construction for this trade for delivery at the end of 1972, a further vessel with the same specifications is on order for delivery in late 1974.

FLEET:
In Service:
Kangourou
A 22 knot vessel capable of carrying 1,492 20 ft units of which 302 can be refrigerated length 228 m (748 ft) beam 30·5 m (100 ft),

draught 10·66 m (35 ft).

Under construction or on order:
Zambeze
Zanzibar
Zeebrugge

Three 21 knot part container vessels capable of carrying 302 20 ft units All hatches are fitted with electric deck cranes capable of lifting loaded containers.

Far East Service Container Ship:

This 26·5 knot vessel will have a capacity of 2,900 20 ft units of which 120 can be refrigerated. Scheduled for delivery in December 1972 the vessel will have a length of 289 m (1,276·25 ft) a beam of 32·3 m (105·9 ft) and a deadweight tonnage of 35,000.

A further vessel is on order for delivery in September 1974.

Kangourou

CONTAINERS IN SERVICE:

Dry	1,300	20	× 8	× 8	
Dry	100	40	× 8	× 8·5	
Refrigerated	12	20	× 8	× 8	
Open top	30	20	× 8	× 8	
Tanks	15	20	× 8	× 8	

SCTC BASES:

Base Gennevilliers
SCTC
c/o France Container Services
Route du Bassin No. 1
Telephone: (1) 793 4802
Telex: 62391

Base Lille
SCTC
c/o DIP
Port Fluvial de Lille—Bât F—Pl. Lerouxde Faukemont
59 Lille
Telephone: (20) 54 60 64

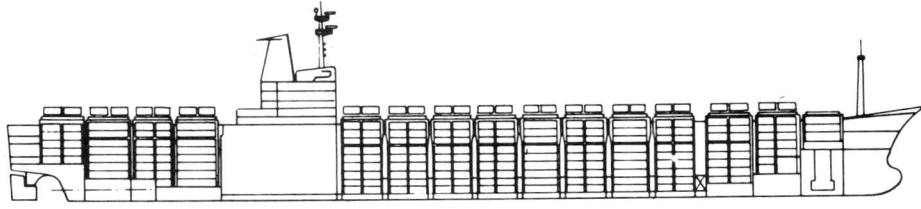
Profile drawing of SCTC Far East Vessels

Base Cognac
SCTC
c/o Danzas SA
15 Avenue du Général-Leclerc-BP2-10
Cognac
Telephone: (45) 82 01 71
Telex: 58834

Base Bordeaux
SCTC
c/o SUDOC
Rue de la Faïencerie-33 Bordeaux
Telephone: (56) 44 12 42
Telex: 56051

Zambeze

S.N.C.F.

Service de l'Armement Naval de la Soc. Nationale des Chemins de Fer Francais
51 rue de Londres, Paris 8, France.
TELEPHONE: 387 04 30
TELEGRAMS: Sonaferarm, Paris
TELEX: 28 549
OFFICIALS:
P. Graff (*Shipping Manager*)
Commandant P. Soulez (*Assistant Shipping Manager*)
HEAD OFFICE:
SNCF, Direction Générale,
88 rue St-Lazare, Paris
BRANCHES:
Dunkerque:
Société ALA
Gare Maritime Dunkerque (59)
Telephone: 66.80.01
Telex: 82.047
London Branch:

Représentation Générale de la SNCF en Grande-Bretagne,
179 Piccadilly, London, W1
Telephone: 01-493 9731
Telegrams: Sonafer London
Telex: 24 651
Paris:
Direction Commerciale de la SNCF
54 Bd Haussmann, Paris 9éme
Telephone: 874.76.00-744.74.10

CONTAINER SERVICES:
Dunkerque-Harwich—Three times weekly

ROLL-ON/ROLL-OFF SERVICES:
Calais-Dover—up to 8 sailings per day.
Dunkerque-Dover—up to 8 sailings per day (in conjunction with British Railways)
Dieppe-Newhaven— (in conjunction with British Railways).

SNCF's *Transcontainer*

FLEET—ROLL-ON/ROLL-OFF:	Container	nrt	length		beam		loaded draught	
Name	Capacity		m	ft	m	ft	m	ft
Transcontainer 1*	194	759	104	342·5	18·7	61·05	4·68	15·4
Villandry	25	982	105	344·5	17	55·10	3·95	12·9
Valencay	25	977	105	344·5	17	55·10	3·95	12·9
Compiegne	29	691	114·8	377·3	17·78	57·16	4·00	13·0
Chantilly	28	872	109·9	360·8	17·78	57·16	4·01	13·2
St. Germain	58	845	115·7	380	18·44	60·06	4·11	13·4

*This vessel is a dual purpose ship. She is fitted with a stern ramp for loading containers by means of slave trailers or carrying roll-on/roll-off traffic. Alternatively, the ship can be loaded by gantry cranes through openings in the deck.

STATES LINE

States Steamship Co. (States Line)
320 California Street, San Francisco, California, 94104
TELEPHONE: 982-6221
PRESIDENT:
J. R. Dant

CONTAINER DIVISION:
F. P. Zinn (*Manager*)
N. E. Whitbeck (*Asst. Manager*)
ROUTES:
Pacific Coast (Vancouver, B.C. to San Diego) to Honolulu to Japan, Korea, Naha, Formosa,

Hong Kong, Manila, Vietnam, Bangkok; approximately six sailings monthly both Eastbound and Westbound with a fleet of 14 part-container ships.
FLEET
Six vessels are capable of lifting 167 20 ft

units, two vessels 110 units and the latest Colardo Class 23 knot vessels can lift 214 20 ft containers.

SERVICES AND FLEET:
i. Pacific North West Ports to Japan, Korea and Taiwan—monthly with two 20 knot vessels capable of lifting 60 containers each on deck.
ii. California and Pacific North West Ports to Manila, Saigon, Bangkok returning via Hong Kong and Taiwan—monthly and to Japan, Korea amd Taiwan returning via Japan—monthly
These services are carried out by six 20 knot vessels each capable of lifting 114 containers on deck.
iii. California to Honolulu, Japan, Korea, Okinawa, Manila Hong Kong, returning via Hong Kong Taiwan Japan and Honolulu—twice monthly with five 23 knot vessels each capable of lifting 96 containers on deck.

SUID AFRIKAANSE SKEEPIAART LYNE

Suid Afrikaanse Skeepvaart Lyne
This coastal shipping company operating between Durban and Walvis Bay have announced plans to operate container vessels by 1974.

SVEA LINE

Stockholms Rederi AB Svea,
Skeppsbron 28, PO Box 2065
103 12 Stockholm 2
TELEPHONE: 08-229060
TELEX: 1147/8/9
MANAGING DIRECTOR:
C. W. Högberg
BRANCHES:
Svea Line (Göteborg) AB
Telephone: 031-178570
Svea Line (SYD) AB,
Halsingborg
Telephone: 042-144490

SERVICES:
Gothenburg to Hull—3 sailings weekly.
Tees-Copenhagen-Helsingborg—weekly.
Helsingborg to Felixstowe/Rotterdam—2 sailings weekly.
Stockholm/Gefle to London/Felixstowe—1 sailing weekly.

PRINCIPAL OVERSEAS AGENTS:
Amsterdam, Vereenigd Cargadoorskantoor
Antwerpen, Agence Maritime E, Sasse SA
Bordeaux, Henri Ferriere
Bremen, Gottfr. Steinmeyer & Co.
Bryssel, Sasse & Co. SA
Calais, Gérard R. Dumont
Delfzijl, Vereenigd Cargadoorskantoor
Felixstowe, Svea Line (Syd) A.B.
c/o Brown Jenkinson & Co. Ltd.
Trelawny House, The Dock, Felixstowe
Telephone: 5595
Telex: 98345

FLEET:

Vessel	20ft Container Capacity	Net Reg. Tons	Length m	Length ft	Beam m	Beam ft	Draught m	Draught ft
Servus*	124	—	109	357·6	16·7	54·8	—	—
Freja	63	338	74	242·8	10·8	35·4	3·96	13·0
Birka	130	738	75	246·1	14·2	46·6	4·95	16·2
Brage	130	738	75	246·1	14·2	46·6	4·95	16·2
Bele	72	373	76·3	250·3	11·9	39·0	4·01	13·1
Destel	63	338	74	242·8	10·8	35·4	5·06	16·6
P518	130	738	75	246·1	14·2	46·6	4·95	16·2
P519	130	738	75	246·1	14·2	46·6	4·95	16·2

*This vessel can also be used for roll-on/roll-off operations.

Felixstowe (Swedish East Coast Service)
Ellerman's Wilson Line
Trelawny House, The Dock, Felixstowe
Telephone: 5656
Telex: 98417
Gent, Reyniers Freres
Glasgow, Glen & Co Ltd
Grangemouth, J. T. Salvesen & Co Ltd.
Helsingfors, Finska Ångfartygs AB (Stockholmstrafiken)
Hull, Ellerman's Wilson Line Ltd.
Kiel Canal, Sartori & Berger
Köpenhamn, Frank & Tobiesen
La Rochelle-Pallice, Comptoir Général Maritime
Le Havre, Claude Colin-Olivier
Leith, Chr. Salvesen & Co.
Liverpool, A. Coker & Co. Ltd.
London, The United Shipping Co. Ltd.

Lübeck, Armin v. Hoerschelmann
Manchester, Ellerman's Wilson Line Ltd.
Herbert Watson & Ltd.,
Mariehamn, AB Samseglingsagenturen
Middlesbrough, Clarkson Bros & Casper Ltd.
Paris, La Franco—Nordique
Rotterdam, D. Burger & Zoon
Rouen, Jules Roy SA
Tees, J. G. Peckston
Vasa, Lennart Backman
Åbo, OY Wikenström & Krogius AB.

CONTAINER FLEET:
Dry   465 20 × 8 × 8
Dry   31 10 × 8 × 8
Insulated   60 20 × 8 × 8
Refrigerated   4 20 × 8 × 8
Flats   802 20 × 8 × 8
Flats   250 20 × 8
Flats   10 10 × 8 × 4

Rederi AB Svenska Lloyd,
S-403 13 Gothenburg, 2, PO Box 2125, Sweden
TELEPHONE: 031/174300
TELEX: 2208/20653
BRANCHES:
Rederi AB Svenska Lloyd,
PO Box 16275, S-103 25 Stockholm 16, Sweden
Telephone: 08/234545
Telegrams: "Svenskalloyd"
Telex: 1138
Swedish Lloyd (UK) Ltd.,
Marlow House, Lloyd's Avenue, London, EC3, England
Telegrams: "Lloydferry"
Telephone: 01-709 0416/9
Telex: 886509
DIRECTORS:
Torgeir Christoffersen (Managing Director)
Leif Graaf (Technical Director)
Uno Widesjö (Financial Director)
EXECUTIVES IN CHARGE OF CONTAINER OPERATIONS:
Hans Pihlo (Cargo Traffic Manager)
Herbert Olson (Manager, GB Traffic)
Gösta Ternmalm (Manager, Mediterranean Traffic)

SVENSKA LLOYD

SERVICES:
Gothenburg/London/Gothenburg—3 sailings weekly
Halmstad/London—2 sailings monthly
Southampton/Bilbao/Southampton—(MACPAK)—3 sailings weekly

FLEET:
No cellular container ships being built yet, but all cargo vessels carry containers.
ROLL-ON/ROLL-OFF VESSELS:
Saga, Hispania and Patricia are sister vessels carrying passenger accompanied motor cars and also containers with capacities (20 ft containers/cars as follows):

Saga   112/100 Cars
Hispania   100/90 Cars
Patricia   25/205 Cars

Gothia, on charter carries 94 containers and two new buildings, due to come into service in January and May 1972, respectively, will carry 160 20 ft units each.
CONTAINERS IN SERVICE:
Dry   400 20 × 8 × 8
Flats   600 20 × 8
PRINCIPAL OVERSEAS AGENTS:
Gothenburg/London service:
Swedish Lloyd (U.K.) Ltd.

Discharging "Saga"

The British and Northern Shipping Agency Ltd.
Marlow House, Lloyds Avenue, London, EC3
Telephone: 01-488 3161
Telex: 28512/3
Southampton/Bilbao Service:

ENGLAND:
MacAndrews & Co. Ltd.,
Plantation House, Mincing Lane, London,
    EC3
Telephone: Mansion House 1543
Telex: 24227
SPAIN:
MacAndrew Line,
Amezaga 4, Bilbao
Telephone: 24.58.63
Also in Barcelona, Madrid, Valencia

The Svenska Lloyd terminal at Gothenburg with *Saga* alongside

TEAMLINE

Teamline (In cooperation with Reederei HM Gehrckens and Mathies Reederei KG)

HAMBURG:
    H. M. Gehrckens,
    2 Hamburg 11, Beim Neuen Krahn 2
    TELEPHONE: 36 11 41
    TELEX: 02/11 117
    Mathies-Reederei KG
    · 2 Hamburg 11, Baumwall 3
    TELEPHONE: 35 16 77
    TELEX: 02/11 153
KIEL:
    Kieler Lagerhaus GmbH
    23 Kiel-Wik, Postfach 887
    TELEPHONE: 3 09 32
    TELEX: 02/99 839
    Sartori & Berger
    23 Kiel 1, Postfach 227
    TELEPHONE: 4 51 01-04
    TELEX: 02/92 832
STOCKHOLM:
    Nordström & Thulin AB
    Stockholm C, Skeppsbron 34
    TELEPHONE: 23 17 40
    TELEX: 13 54

Teamline's *Hansa*

ROLL-ON/ROLL-OFF SERVICES:
Stockholm-Kiel-Hamburg and vice versa,
    twice weekly
FLEET:
Hansa:
Container capacity about 100 20 × 8 × 8 ft
    Net reg tons 528
    Length overall 78·1 m (256 ft)
    Beam 13·8 m (45 ft 4 in)
    Draft 4·3 m (14 ft)
Wasa:
    Container capacity about 100 20 × 8 × 8 ft
    Net reg tons 528
    Length overall 78·1 m (256 ft)
    Beam 13·9 m (45 ft 4 in)
    Draft 4·3 m (14 ft)

THORESEN

Thoresen
See Townsend Thoresen Car Ferries.

TIRRENIA

ROLL-ON/ROLL-OFF SERVICES:
Mediterranean ports and inter-island (Sicily and Sardinia) ferry routes:
Genova to Porto Torres—daily.
Porto Torres to Civitavecchia—daily.
Civitavecchia to Cagliari—daily.
Naples to Palermo—daily.
Naples to Cagliari—twice weekly.
Palermo to Cagliari—twice weekly.
Naples and Palermo to Tunis—Weelky.
Syracusa to Malta—3 times weekly.
La Maddalena and Palau and S. Teresa Gallura to Bonifacio, Corsica—daily, exc. Sundays.
Carloforte to Calasetta, Sardinia—Frequent sailings daily.

Tirrenia's *Sicilia*

Tirrenia's *Boccaccio*

Carloforte to Portovesme, Sardinia—Frequent sailings daily.
La Maddalena to Palau, Sardinia—Frequent sailings daily.

FLEET—ROLL-ON/ROLL-OFF:

Calabria	Sardegna
Lazio	Sicilia

These vessels are 4,808 grt.

Boccaccio	Pascoli
Carducci	Manzoni
Leopardi	Retrarca

These 20/22 knot vessels are 131 m (430 ft) in length, with a beam of 20 m (65·6 ft) and a draught of 5·56 m (18·3 ft). They are capable of carrying 110 cars and 42 trailers.

La Valletta
This vessel entered service in summer 1971. Designed with a speed of 18 knots it is 89·5 m (293·8 ft) in length, 14 m (46 ft) beam with a draught of 4·25 m (14 ft).
FUTURE PLANS:
Three multi-purpose vessels for the Italy/North Europe service, at present using conventional tonnage, are planned.
CONTAINERS IN SERVICE:
At present a few 20 ft dry cargo and open side units are owned in order to experiment on two of the company's services using containers on special trailers. It is planned to increase the number of containers owned very shortly.

TMT TRAILER FERRY INC.

ROLL-ON SERVICE:
Frequent sailings between Jacksonville and San Juan and Miami and San Juan.
FLEET:
TMT Biscayne, TMT Carolina, TMT Florida, TMT Puerto Rico, TMT San Juan
These vessels, former US Navy LSTs, have been converted to roll-on barges by the removal of former superstructure, machinery and quarters, the replacement of bow sections and doors with new ones of special design, the strengthening of upper decks and structural reinforcement of the hulls to permit high speed towing and extended hull life. Each barge carries 55 40 ft standard highway trailers, 100 cars and other miscellaneous cargo such as tractors, trucks, construction equipment, heavy and large indivisible loads, etc.

TMT Florida loading at Jacksonville

Trailers are loaded on the weather deck using side ramps installed at each terminal; other cargoes are loaded through the bow doors.

Specially designed heavy duty tractors capable of pulling a 100 ton load up a 10 degree incline are used to tow trailers on to barges.

Barges are towed by chartered tugs.

TRAILERS IN SERVICE AND OPERATIONS:
Several hundred company owned trailers of all types are operated; these are supplemented by leased equipment as required. TMT is a member of the National Railroad Trailer Pool and thus can offer shippers trailers at the point of shipment; the company are also members of American Trucking Association and Trailer Interchange As-

sociation thus allowing free exchange of equipment with all member lines.

TERMINALS:

The Jacksonville terminal is located on the St. John's River within the Jacksonville port area. Like all of the terminal facilities, it is developed for TMT use and has an area of 4 hectares (10 acres). Included in this facility are administration building, warehouse, dock, maintenance shop, and marshalling yard for trailers. The terminal is served by private rail tracks with switching from both Seaboard Coastline and Southern Railways. Twenty motor truck lines operating from midwest and southern points also serve this terminal.

TMT's Miami terminal is located on Biscayne Bay adjacent to port area and is similar to Jacksonville terminal except that it is not as large in area.

In San Juan the terminal is located in Isla Grande on land designated for their use by Puerto Rico Ports Authority. Docking facility, warehouse and marshalling yard occupy approximately 4 hectares (10 acres). This terminal is now inadequate and a new, larger terminal will soon be constructed. In Puerto Rico, TMT owns Trans Caribbean Motor Transport, which distributes cargo throughout the island under authority granted by the Puerto Rico Department of Public Works.

Underdeck car storage in a T.M.T. barge.

TOR LINE

Tor Line AB, with affiliated companies

HEAD OFFICE:
Tor Line AB, PO Box 8895, S 402 73, Gothenburg 8, Sweden
TELEPHONE: Gothenburg 540 300
TELEGRAMS: Torline
TELEX: 527104
BRANCHES:
Tor Line Ltd, West Gate, Immingham Dock, Grimsby, Lincs
Telephone: Immingham 3161
Telex: 52362
DIRECTORS:
Hans Laurin (*Managing Director*)
Magnus Bergelin (*Vice Managing Director*)

CARGO SUPERINTENDENT:
Captain Gosta Jakobsson
SERVICES:
Gothenburg-Amsterdam—3 sailings weekly
Gothenburg-Immingham—5 sailings weekly
Amsterdam-Immingham—2 sailings weekly

PRINCIPAL OVERSEAS AGENTS:
Vereenigd Cargadoors Kantoor,
De Ruyterkade 139, Amsterdam

Telephone: 6 22 16
Telex: 12071

FLEET (Passenger and cargo ferries):
Tor Anglia
Capacity 80 containers
Net reg. tons 3,077
Tor Hollandia
Container capacity 80 containers
Net reg. tons 3,361
Tor Mercia and *Tor Scandia* (Charter)
Capacity 115 containers (20 ft)
2,750 tons deadweight
Two new buildings for delivery 1971-2 (Charter)
Capacity 232 containers (20 ft)
5,500 tons deadweight

CONTAINERS IN SERVICE:
67 20 × 8 × 8 dry containers (plus 215 leased)
982 20 × 8 flats
15 30 × 8 × 8 open top containers (8 leased)

Tor Mercia

Profile of one of the Tor Line chartered vessels now building.

TORM LINES

Torm D/S
42, Holmens Kanal
Copenhagen 1060
TELEPHONE: 122437
TELEX: 2515
GENERAL AGENTS:
Peralta Shipping Corporation
85, Broad Street
New York, N.Y. 10004
TELEPHONE: 212-943-4466
TWX: 710-581-2835

BRANCHES:
Jacksonville, Savannah, Charleston, Baltimore, Norfolk, Philadelphia, Boston, Chicago, Detroit, Cleveland, Milwaukee, New Orleans.

DIRECTORS:
Armando de Peralta (*President*)
Oscar Birkholz (*Vice-President*)
Frank J. Lipari Jr. (*Director of Sales*)
Hector de Peralta (*General Traffic Manager*)

FLEET:
Alice Torm and *Thyra Torm*, partially converted conventional cargo carriers with a container capacity of 75 and 100 20 ft units, respectively.
SERVICE:
U.S. North Atlantic, South Atlantic and Gulf Ports to the Mediterranean—every three weeks. A fleet of 20 ft containers is operated between the USA and the Canary Islands, Spain, Portugal Alexandria and Beirut.

TOWNSEND, THORESEN

Townsend Thoresen Car Ferries
1 Camden Crescent, Dover, Kent
TELEPHONE: Dover 2721/2724
TELEX: 96254 (Speartown Dover)
and
Car Ferry House, Canute Road, Southampton, SO9 5GP
TELEPHONE: 26721/31221
TELEX: 47619

DIRECTORS:
Townsend Car Ferries:
R. B. Wickenden (*Managing Director*)
D. J. Bradford
J. J. Briggs
K. Dybwad
C. H. Fenn
G. Nott
G. Parker
K. Siddle
Thoresen Car Ferries:
L. Usterud-Svendsen (*Chairman, Norway*)
R. B. Wickenden (*Managing Director*)

T. Byrne (*Deputy Managing Director*)
R. P. Aukner (*Norway*)
K. Dybwad (*Norway*)
J. D. Green
R. N. Kirton
A. F. Klaveness Jr. (*Norway*)
T. Lund (*Norway*)
R. F. Pugh
Townsend Thoresen Car Ferries:
R. B. Wickenden
B. H. Thompson

EXECUTIVES IN CHARGE OF OPERATIONS:
J. J. Briggs (*Dover*)
R. M. Kirton (*Southampton*)
SERVICES:
Dover/Zeebrugge—Up to 5 daily.
Dover/Calais—Up to 12 daily.
Southampton/Le Havre—Up to 3 daily.
Southampton/Cherbourg—Up to 4 daily.

FLEET:
Ten vehicle carrying vessels of which two,

Autocarrier and *Viking IV* are specialised freight ships. *Autocarrier* carries 24 lorries or 12 lorries and 30 20 ft containers and *Viking IV* has a capacity of 45 lorries or 80 20 ft containers and 150 export cars. *Free Enterprise I-V* and *Viking I-III* carry between 10 and 40 trailers in addition to passenger vehicles. The company also has on order five passenger/vehicle ferries due for delivery between 1972 and 1974. Two of these vessels follow the design of *Free Enterprise V* and the other three are Danish designed and will carry up to 260 cars.

PRINCIPAL OVERSEAS ADDRESSES:
Calais:
Port Office, Gare de Transit
Telephone: 34.38.36
Zeebrugge:
Car Ferry Terminal, Zeebrugge
Telephone: 54874/75/76
Telex: 19160

Cherbourg:
    Worms C.M.C.
    P.O. Box Cherbourg B.P.4.1
    Telephone: Gar Maritime 29.98
    Telex: 77765 Agmacherb
Le Havre:
    Worms C.M.C.
    Quai de Southampton, Le Havre
    Telephone: 42-72-81

Amsterdam:
    Hemonylaan 4
    Telephone: 715040
    Telex: 14601

Antwerp:
    Travel Furness Ltd.
    Gramayestraat 4, Antwerp 1
    Telephone: 33.87.50

Paris:
    Worms C.M.C.
    45 Boulevard Haussman, 75-Paris 9e
    Telephone: 073 62.50
    Telex: 21679 (Ferycar Paris)
Dusseldorf:
    General Steam Navigation Co. M.B.H.
    4 Dusseldorf 1, Bismarckstrasse 89
    Telephone: (0211) 35 90 41/42
    Telex: 8582 327

TTT

Transamerican Trailer Transport Inc.
358 St Marks Place
Staten Island,
NY 10301
TELEPHONE: 212-447-2600
TELEX: Twx 710-584-3004
BRANCHES:
Puerto Neuvo, San Juan PR
DIRECTORS:

Frank H. Wyman   Michael Pschorr
Peter Holzer   Richard D. Carter
Houston H. Wasson   John S. Huntington

Ralph Murray   Roberto Lugo
William Acton   George Liacouvis
EXECUTIVES IN CHARGE OF CONTAINER
OPERATIONS:
Captain B. Szolkowski (*Vice-President
                                operations*)
R. Homan (*Terminal Manager*)
SERVICES:
Pier 13, Staten Island NY to San Juan,
Puerto Rico—twice weekly.
FLEET:
    The Company operate the 26 knot Roll-

on/Roll-off vessels *Ponce de Leon* and the *Eric K. Holzer* of 15,134 n.r.t. whose length is 213·36 m (700 ft) with a beam of 28·04 m (92 ft) and a loaded draught of 8·20 m (26 ft 11 ins). The vessels are capable of carrying 240 40 ft trailers and 500 cars and any size vehicles. Any standard trailer and/or container can be carried and there is also a bulk liquid storage capacity of 16,000 gallons. Vehicles are driven on through three side ramps.

M.V. *Ponce de Leon.*

TRANSPORT FERRY SERVICE

The Transport Ferry Service.
See Atlantic Steam Navigation Co. Ltd.

TRIDENT SERVICE

Trident Service
A joint venture by:
KNSM—Royal Netherlands Steamship Company
    Pr. Hendrikkade 108-114
    P.O. Box 209, Amsterdam
    Telephone: 020-64411
    Telex: 12202
Flota Mercante Grancolombiana SA
    Carrera 13, 27-75 Apartado Aereo No. 4482
    Bogota, Columbia
    Telephone: 415-952
    Telex: 044 853
C. A. Venezolana de Navegación
GENERAL:
    Each of the three companies acts as general agent for the service in their own country with the understanding that KNSM remains general agent for all Europe.
SERVICE:
    Western European Ports to the main Ports of Atlantic Colombia and Venezuela—weekly.
FLEET:
    Six 20 knot multi-purpose general cargo vessels of the *Trident* class with one cellular

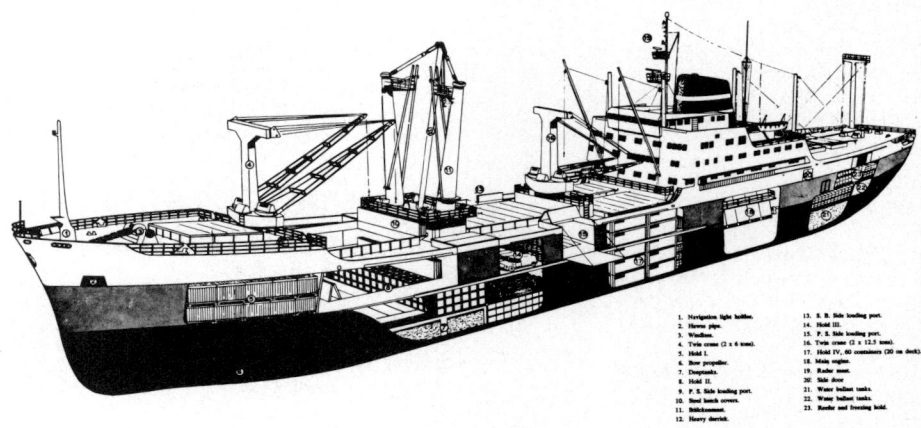

Drawing of a Trident Service Vessel.

hold—No. 4—fitted for the carriage of 60 20 ft units with a further 20 on deck. Side-

ports for handling vehicles, etc, are also fitted at No. 3 'tween deck.

TRIO CONTAINER SERVICE

Trio Container Service
A joint British, German and Japanese service with the following companies providing tonnage and operating a space charter system in which each is responsible for their

own marketing:
Ben Line Containers Ltd.
Hapag-Lloyd AG
Mitsui O.S.K. Lines
N.Y.K. Line

Overseas Containers Ltd.
SERVICE:
    Europe to the Far East—every 4 or 5 days either via the Cape of Good Hope or the Panama Canal by 1973 when all vessels are

scheduled into service.

The first vessels will enter service at the beginning of January 1972 and initially it will operate between Tokyo, Kobe, Bremerhaven, Rotterdam and Southampton. By mid 1972 a weekly service will include Hong Kong and Singapore and this will be extended to include Taiwan and Korea and the Philippines probably with transhipment.
FLEET:
Ben Line—3 vessels.
Hapag-Lloyd—4 vessels

Mitsui OSK.—2 vessels.
N.Y.K.—3 vessels.
O.C.L.—5 vessels.
Capacities and dimensions of these vessels will be found under the Companies' entries in this section.

ULSTER STEAMSHIP CO. LTD

The Ulster Steamship Company Limited (Head Line & Donaldson Line)
Head Line Buildings, Belfast, BT1 3GP
TELEPHONE: 0232 30581
TELEX: 74.534
ASSOCIATED COMPANIES:
G. Heyn & Sons (G.B.) Limited
Royal Liver Buildings, Liverpool, L3 1LE
Telephone: 051 236 9327
Telex: 627479
110, Fenchurch Street, London E.C.3
Telephone: 01 481 1712
The Donaldson Line Limited
14, St. Vincent Place, Glasgow, C.1.
Telephone: 041 221 9161
Telex: 778071
DIRECTORS:
J. M. Stewart OBE (*General Manager*)
R. A. R. Vartan (*Deputy General Manager*)
Sir Cecil J. Bateman, KBE (*Financial Controller*)
I. H. Eakin, OBE
W. R. Eakin
R. G. McBoyle
H. McWilliams
A. Turnbull (The Donaldson Line)
EXECUTIVE IN CHARGE OF CONTAINER OPERATIONS:
G. W. Gilliland, Belfast
Telephone: 0232 30581
FLEET:
Inishowen Head. Capacity 350 20 ft Containers. (40 ft units also accepted). Five partially converted vessels with capacities of between 30 and 80 20 ft containers.
SERVICES:
Joint cellular container service with CP Ships.
Clyde and Liverpool to Quebec.
Conventional breakbulk service using partially converted ships.

Inishowen Head at Liverpool

Belfast, Dublin, Clyde, Liverpool—Montreal and Great Lakes ports.

CARGO SUPERINTENDENTS:
Captain Porteous, The Donaldson Line Ltd.
York Hill, Glasgow
Telephone: 041-339 2318
R. Cleaver, Head Line
Gladstone Container Terminal, Liverpool
Telephone: 051-922 8284
T. Templeton, Head Line, York Dock, Belfast
Telephone: OBE 2 744236
Mr. Newman, Dublin Maritime Ltd.
20 Eden Quay, Dublin
Telephone: Dublin 41231

PRINCIPAL OVERSEAS AGENTS
Montreal, Toronto and St. John N.B.
McLean Kennedy Ltd.
410 St. Nicholas Street, Montreal
Telephone: 514-849-6111
Telex: 01-2185
Hamilton:
The Hamilton Shipping Co. Ltd.,
Main PO Box 889
Telephone: JA 8-0271
Telex: 021679

Chicago, Cleveland, Detroit, Milawukee and Toledo:
International Great Lakes Shipping Co.
111 East Wacher Drive, Chicago
Telephone: (312) 644-6730
Telex: 02-53314

Unicorn Shipping Lines Ltd.
Standard House
275, Smith Street
Durban, Natal
TELEPHONE: 311411
TELEX: 6-7267
OFFICIALS:
W. M. Grindrod (*Managing Director*)

UNICORN LINE

GENERAL:

This company operates a number of coastal services on the African Coast, and with the Islands in the Indian Ocean.

It was reported early in 1971 that the company had purchased or leased land at

four ports for container operations and that a terminal with a 25 ton container gantry crane was planned.

The company have one vessel, *Voorloper*, capable of carrying 111 20 ft units.

The company is also agent for Sea Containers Inc.

Unimar Container Line
MANAGERS:
Glover Brothers (London) Ltd,
Ibex House, Minories, London EC.3
TELEPHONE: 01-623 1311
SERVICES:
Felixstowe and Tilbury to Lisbon, Leixos/

UNIMAR CONTAINER LINE

Oporto—every 8/9 days.
Liverpool to Lisbon, Leixos/Oporto—every 10 days.
FLEET:
Ruth Gertrud Bos
These 12·5 knot vessels have a capacity of 72 20 ft equivalents.

AGENTS:
Liverpool:
Baxter, Hoare & Co, Ltd.
Maritime House, Derby Road, Bootle, 20
TELEPHONE: 051-992-4071
TELEX: 62496

Union Steam Ship Company of New Zealand Limited

P.O. Box 1799,
36 Customhouse Quay,
Wellington, 1,
New Zealand
TELEPHONE: Wellington 59-876

UNION S.S. N.Z. LTD

TELEX: N.Z. 3693
DIRECTORS:
F. K. Macfarlane *Chairman and Managing Director* H. H. Dobie, P. B. Marshall, A. T. Waugh, I. T. Cook, B. S. Cole.
OFFICIALS:
A. T. Waugh (*General Manager*)

B. S. Cole (*Assistant General Manager*)
T. D. McNee (*General Traffic Manager*)
FLEET:

All vessels in the fleet have been designed for roll-on/roll-off using "Seafreighter" collapsible containers 14 ft 5 in in length, 8 ft in width with a load height of 5 ft which can

Felixstowe, Bremerhaven, Hamburg, New York—weekly.

Ports in Spain, Italy, Denmark, Sweden, Finland, Norway, Poland and Portugal are served with transhipment.

The routing provides a twice weekly service to all destinations as both services are scheduled to be in Rotterdam at the same time and cargo is transhipped from vessel to vessel.

US East Coast to Far East:

New York, Baltimore, Norfolk, Long Beach, Oakland, Honolulu, Hong Kong, Yokohama, Kobe—weekly.

Ports in Taiwan, Korea and the Philippines are served with transhipment.

BRANCHES AND AGENTS:
*Denotes United States Lines Office.
UNITED STATES:
*Baltimore, Md.—P.O. Box 1775 (301) 285-5200, Dundalk Marine Terminal
*Boston, Mass.—40 Broad St. (617) 426-4406
*Chicago, Ill.—600 Enterprise Drive, Oakbrook, Ill. (312) 986-1170
*Cleveland, Ohio—1 Erie View Plaza (216) 522-1585
*Dallas, Texas—405 Cotton Exchange Bldg. (214) 741-3128
*Detroit, Mich.—1249 Washington Blvd. (313) 961-5057
*Linden, N.J.—1051 Edward St. (201) 862-0440
*Long Beach, Cal.—Pier J, Berth 246 (213) 435-3761
Louisville, Ky.—(502) 583-3638
Milwaukee, Wis.—Enterprise 8890
*Norfolk, Va.—200 E. Main St. (703) 625-8129
*New York, N.Y.—1 Broadway (212) 344-5800
*Oakland, Cal.—5160 7th St. (415) 465-4010
*Philadelphia, Pa.—1310 Mall Bldg. (215) 627-8000
Pittsburgh, Pa.—Zenith 2929
*Rochester, N.Y.—Temple Bldg. (716) 546-7676
*San Francisco, Cal.—One California St. (415) 397-5011
*Washington, D.C.—3930 Walnut St., Fairfax Va. (703) 273-8222
*West Hartford, Conn.—125 La Salle Rd. (203) 232-4809
*Winston Salem, N.C.—First Union Natl. Bank Bldg. (919) 725-3402
St. Louis, Mo (314) 231-9240 (415) 362-8680
Savannah, Ga.—Strachan Shipping Co., ADams 4-6671
*Savannah, Ga.—1409 Savannah Bank Trust Co. Bldg., (912) 234-6671
*Washington, D.C.—1825 'K' Street, N.W. (202) 223-4361
CANADA:
Montreal—Universal Container Services, Ltd. 10755 Cote de Liesse Rd. Montreal, Quebec, Canada (514) 631-9083
Toronto—Universal Container Services, Ltd. 69 Yonge Street, Toronto 1, Ontario (416) 863-0706
EUROPE:
*Liverpool, England—7 ,The Strand
*London, England—58 St. James St. S.W.1
Manchester, England—B. Ackerley & Son Ltd., 62 Bridge Street
Southampton, England—B. Ackerley & Son Ltd., Canute Chambers, Canute Rd.
Antwerp, Belgium—Agence Maritime de Keyser Thornton S.A. 14 Lange Gasthuisstraat
Brussels, Belgium—Voyages de Keyser, Thornton S.A., 63 rue de la Madeleine
Amsterdam, Holland—Royal Holland Lloyd, Oostelijke Handelskade 12

American Legacy—A US Lines' Leader Class Vessel

American Astronaut—A US Lines' Lancer Class Vessel

*Rotterdam, Holland—40 Westerstraat
Madrid, Spain—Contenemar S.A., Juan Hartado de Mendoza 9
Santander, Spain—Contenemar S.A. Juan de Herrera 2
Dublin, Eire—George Bell & Co., Ltd., 15 Hawkins St.
Glasgow, Scotland—W. B. Woolley & Co. Ltd., 54 West Nile Street
Belfast, No. Ireland—Cawoods Containers Ltd Herdman Channel West
Felixstowe, England—International Marine Management, Trelawney House, The Dock
Lisbon, Portugal—Unimar, Praca de D. Luis 9-4DTO
Milan, Italy—Societa General Transporti, S.r.l., Via Valtellina 20
Oslo, Norway—E. Angell Bordewick, Karl Johansgate 7
Bordeaux, France—Société Navale Delmas—Vieljeux, 15 quai Louis xviii
Le Havre, France—Consortium Maritime Franco American, 34 rue Pierre Brossolette
La Pallice, France—Societe Navale Delmas-Vieljeux Boulevard, Emile-Delmas
Paris, France—Consortium Maritime Franco American, 25 Place du Marché St. Honore
St. Nazaire, France—Soc. Nouvelle de Consignation et de Gerance, Quai Pereire
*Bremen, Germany—28 Bremen 1, Bahnofsplatz
*Bremerhaven, Germany—Nordhaven, gatehouse
Dusseldorf, Germany—Hans Wagner, Worringerstrasse 70
Frankfurt, Germany—Axel von Wietersheim Untermainkai 82
*Hamburg, Germany—1 Ballindamn
Hannover, Germany—H. H. Baecker, Morgenstwenweg 3
Munich, Germany—Frachtkontor H.Ihle Schoenfeldstrasse 19
Nuernberg, Germany—H. Ihle, 3, Hallplatz
Stuttgart, Germany—H. Ihle, Rosenbergstrasse 18

Vienna, Austria—Enrico Sperco & Sohn GmbH, 33 Kaerntnerstraase
Basle, Switzerland—Gondrand Freres, PO Box 267 and Jacky Maeder & Co., Wallstrasse 8/10
Honolulu, Hawaii—Theo. H. Davies & Co. Ltd., 800 Fort Street

FAR EAST:
*Manila, Philippines—Lands Bldg, 1515 Roxas Blvd.
*Hong Kong, B.C.C.—616 Union House, Charter Rd.
Saigon, Sud Vietnam—Denis Freres, P.O. Box Central 6
*Kobe, Japan—New Jarvis Building 75, Kyo-Machi, Ikuta-ku
Moji, Japan—Showa Marine Agency, 4-23 Minato-machi, Moji-ku, Kitakyshu
Nagoya, Japan—Nagoya Shipping Agency, Ltd., 2-24 Hanaguruma-cho, Nakamura-ku
*Osaka, Japan—No. 25, 4-chome, Doshomachi, Higashi -ku
Shimizu, Japan—Suzuyo & Co., Ltd., 12, 3-chome, Irifune-Cho, Shizouka Pref
Tokyo, Japan—2-6 Akasaka 3 Chome, Minato-ku
*Yokohama, Japan—No. 71 Yamashita-cho, Naka-ku
Keelung, Taiwan (Formosa)—Jardine Matheson & Co. Ltd., P.O. Box 81, Taipei
Taipei, Taiwan—Jardine Matheson & Co. Ltd., P.O. Box 81, Taipei
Kaohslung, Taiwan—Jardine Matheson & Co. Ltd., P.O. Box 81, Taipei
Inchon, Korea—Far Eastern Marine Transport Co. Ltd., Shin Seng Bldg, P.O. Box 55
Pusan, Korea—Far Eastern Marine Transport Ltd., No. 85, 4-Ka. Chung Ang Dong
Seoul, Korea—Far Eastern Marine Transport Co. Ltd., Bando Building 204-212
LATIN AMERICA:
Cristobal, Canal Zone—Panama Agencies Company, P.O. Box 5097
*Denotes United States Lines' Office.

be increased. The maximum deadweight load of a "Seafreighter" is 13½ tons with a tare of 1½ tons. Cargo is moved in and out of the ships either by using heavy duty fork lift trucks or special cargo trailers. All vessels are capable of carrying ISO containers.

VESSELS UNDER CONSTRUCTION:

Rangatira is a roll-on/roll-off passenger cargo vessel of 9,000 gross tons with a length BP of 137·16 m (450 ft), a beam of 22·1 m (72·5 ft) and a draught of 5·61 m (18·4 ft). This vessel, which will have cabin accommodation for passengers, will enter the Wellington/Lyttleton Steamer Express Service late in 1971. *Rangatira* will have capacity for more than 200 passengers' motor cars or a combination of Seafreighter cargo units on trailers and passengers' motor cars.

An unnamed roll-on/roll-off cargo vessel of 3,800 tons deadweight with a length BP of 121·92 m (400 ft), a beam of 19·66 m (64·5 ft) and a draught of 5·60 m (18·5 ft). This vessel will be engaged in the Hobart/Sydney Seaway Express Cargo Service and is due for completion in 1972.

Wanaka

BRANCHES

NEW ZEALAND BRANCHES	*Address*	*P.O. Box*
Auckland	36-38 Quay Street	12
Blenheim	63 High Street	24
Christchurch	Cnr Armagh and Colombo Street	2090
Dunedin	38 Water Street, C.1.	650
Gisborne	Chr. Peel St. & Gladstone Rd.	57
Greymouth	58-60 Mackay Street	380
Invercargill	The Crescent	3
Napier	Hawkes Bay Motor Co. Ltd. Bldg., Dickens Street	717
New Plymouth	9 Devon Street	545
Oamaru	Thames Street	41
Picton	9 High Street	14
Tauranga (Mt. Maunganui)	Cnr Tasman Quay and Hull Road	4,120
Timaru	33 Strathallan Street	185
Wellington	38-48 Customhouse Quay	1799
Westport	Cnr Wakefield and Palmerston Streets	246
Whangarei	2 Clyde Street	749
SOUTH SEA ISLAND BRANCHES		
Suva, Fiji	Thomson Street	43
Lautoka, Fiji	Vitogo Parade	49
Apia, Western Samoa	Main Beach Road	50
Rarotonga, Cook Islands	Avarua	54
Nukualofa, Tonga	Tungi Arcade	4
AUSTRALIAN BRANCHES		
Burnie, Tasmania	9 Marine Terrace	300
Devonport, Tasmania	Rooke & King Streets	20
Hobart, Tasmania	2 Elizabeth Street	1023K
Launceston, Tasmania	T & G Building, cnr. Charles and Paterson Streets	292
Melbourne, Victoria	59 William Street, Dominion Chambers	754F
Newcastle, N.S.W.	31 Watt Street	F490
Port Kembla, N.S.W.	66 Wentworth Street	42
Sydney, N.S.W.	339 George Street	534

FLEET:

Name	*Type*	*Net Reg. Tons*	*Length (B.P.)*		*Beam*		*Loaded Draught*	
			ft	m	ft	m	ft	m
Maori	Roll-on/roll-off Passenger	3010	425	129·3	63	19·2	17·1	5·18
Hawea	Roll-on/roll-off Cargo	801	338	102·9	56	17·1	16·4	5·00
Wanaka	Roll-on/roll-off Cargo	744	338	102·9	56	17·1	16·4	5·00
Seaway Queen	Roll-on/roll-off Cargo	1,112	340	103·6	52	15·8	18·8	5·74
Seaway King	Roll-on/roll-off Cargo	1,112	340	103·6	52	15·8	18·8	5·74
Maheno	Roll-on/roll-off Cargo	1,660	399	121·6	63	19·2	19·5	5·94
Marama	Roll-on/roll-off Cargo	1,660	399	121·6	63	19·2	19·0	5·94

SERVICES:

Wellington/Lyttelton—daily from each port
Sydney/Hobart/Sydney—weekly
Melbourne/Hobart/Melbourne—twice weekly
Auckland/Wellington/Dunedin/Wellington/
Auckland—weekly
Auckland/Lyttleton/Auckland—weekly

PRINCIPAL OVERSEAS AGENTS:
Union Steam Ship Company of New Zealand
Limited
Three Quays, Tower Hill, London, E.C.3
Telex: 834598

CONTAINERS IN SERVICE:
Seafreighter‡ 2,714 14·4 × 8 × 5·75
"W" Type 427 6·2 × 4·1 × 6·05
"MW"
(Sundry small) 499 Various
‡These are collapsible units with a maximum
height of 1·75 m (5·75 ft)

Maheno

UNITED BALTIC

United Baltic Corporation Ltd
21 Mincing Lane, London, EC3
TELEPHONE: 01-626 3311
TELEX: 28130
DIRECTORS:
The Lord Inverforth (*Chairman*)
Mogens Pagh (*Deputy Chairman-Danish*)
Hon A. C. R. Weir

Hon J. V. Weir
K. G. Lommer (*Danish*)
P. B. Larsen
Mogens Steineke (*Danish*)
CARGO SUPERINTENDENT:
Captain A. Morgan
SERVICES:
Tilbury/Middlesbrough/Helsinki every fort-

night in conjunction with the Finland Steam-
ship Co Ltd, giving a weekly service. (See
Finland United Kingdom Container Service)
PRINCIPAL OVERSEAS AGENT:
Finland Steamship Co.Ltd.
Etelaranta 8, Helsinki 13
Telephone: Helsinki 10901
Telex: 12-1410

U.K. TO ISRAEL CONTAINER SERVICE

UK to Israel Container Service.
A joint service operated from Liverpool by:
Zim Israel Navigation Co., Haifa
Ellerman and Papayanni Lines, Liverpool
Moss Hutchison Lines, Liverpool

From London by:
Zin Israel Navigation Co, Haifa
Westcott and Lawrence Line Ltd, London
Prince Line

Ellerman's Wilson Line
SERVICES:
Liverpool—Ashdod—weekly
London—Ashdod—weekly

UNITED STATES LINES

United States Lines
INTERNATIONAL HEADQUARTERS:
1, Broadway,
New York, NY 10004
TELEPHONE: (212) 344-5800
TELEX: 212-571-1136
EXECUTIVES IN CHARGE OF CONTAINER
OPERATIONS:
R. B. Murphy (*Vice-President—Container
Division*)
V. Barba (*General Manager, Container
Operations*)
WEST COAST (USA) HEADQUARTERS:
One California St.
San Francisco, Cal. 94111
EUROPEAN HEADQUARTERS:
58 St. James's Street, London, S.W.1
Telephone: 01-499 0081
Telex: 22367
FAR EAST HEADQUARTERS:
Akasaka-Chuo Bldg., 2-6, 3-Chome
Minato-Ku, Tokyo, Japan
FLEET:
Lancer-Class—Fully Containerised.
American Lark American Lynx
American Liberty American Legion
American Lancer American Apollo
American Astronaut American Aquarius

These vessels have a length of 312·4 m
(700·5 ft) with a beam of 27·4 m (90 ft),
and a draught of 9·75 m (32 ft). They have
a service speed of 23 knots. The *Lancer* and
Legion have a carrying capacity of 1,178
20 ft equivalents. *Apollo* and *Aquarius*
have a carrying capacity of 1,240 20 ft
equivalents. The four remaining vessels are
capable of carrying 1,210 20 ft equivalents.
Leader Class—Full Container Conversion.
American Leader American Legend
American Ace American Alliance
American Argosy American Archer
American Accord American Legacy

American Legion.

Eight *Mariner* Class vessels have been
converted into full containerships. They
have a carrying capacity of 929 twenty foot
equivalents and a 20 knot service speed.

Challenger 1 Class (Partially Containerised)
American Chieftain 72 20 ft equivalents
American Champion 72 20 ft equivalents
American Courier 128 20 ft equivalents
Pioneer Moon 128 20 ft equivalents
Pioneer Contender 128 20 ft equivalents
Pioneer Contractor 128 20 ft equivalents
Pioneer Crusader 128 20 ft equivalents
Pioneer Commander 128 20 ft equivalents
American Challenger 72 20 ft equivalents
American Charger 128 20 ft equivalents
American Corsair 36 20 ft equivalents
Challenger 2 Class (Partially Containerised)
American Racer 70 20 ft equivalents
American Ranger 70 20 ft equivalents

American Reliance 70 20 ft equivalents
The Challenger vessels are partial container
vessels in that they can carry 70 to 128
twenty foot equivalents with a system
stowage.
CONTAINER FLEET:
Dry 4,600 20 ft length
Dry 11,215 40 ft length
Refrigerated 970
Open top 356 40 × 8 × 8·5
Open top 45 40 × 8 × 4·25
Tank 100 40 ft length
capacity 6,100 galls.

SERVICES:
North Atlantic:
New York, Baltimore, Norfolk, Rotterdam,
Le Havre, Liverpool, Clyde, New York—
weekly.
New York, Baltimore, Norfolk, Rotterdam,

VIRGIN ISLAND CONTAINER LINE

Virgin Island Container Line
See entry under Amerind Shipping Corporation.

WALLENIUS LINES

Wallenius Lines
Soya Rederi A/B
Svedenborgsgaten
PO Box 17086, S-10462, Stockholm 17,
Sweden
TELEPHONE: 680 285
TELEX: 19010
PRINCIPAL OFFICIALS:
John G. Kleberg (*Managing Director*)
GENERAL:
The company is one of the partners in
Atlantic Container Line.
ROLL-ON/ROLL-OFF SERVICES:
Harwich-Antwerp
Harwich-Copenhagen-Drammen
Jacksonville Fla.-Miami-Panama
Miami-Caribbean Ports
Soderfalje-Lübeck

ROLL-ON/ROLL-OFF FLEET

Wallenius Line Undine

	Trailers and Cars	or	Cars only
Aniara (bow loader)	20	+ 100	250
Oberon (bow loader)	20	+ 100	250
Elektra (bow loader)	20	+ 100	250
Don Juan (bow loader)	26	+ 120	300
Don Carlos (bow loader)	26	+ 120	300
Bess (bow loader)	20	+ 100	200
Undine (stern loader)	50 or 30	+ 150	410
Salome (stern loader)	50 or 30	+ 150	410
Aida (stern loader)	50 or 30	+ 150	410
Otello (stern loader)	50 or 30	+ 150	410
Mignon (stern loader)	58 or 38	+ 250	400

All stern loading vessels are also equipped for the carriage of containers. There are further stern loaders due to come into service from late 1971 until 1972. These vessels, two of which will be on long term time charter to the Company, will have a deadweight tonnage of about 5,000 and a capacity of 500 cars.

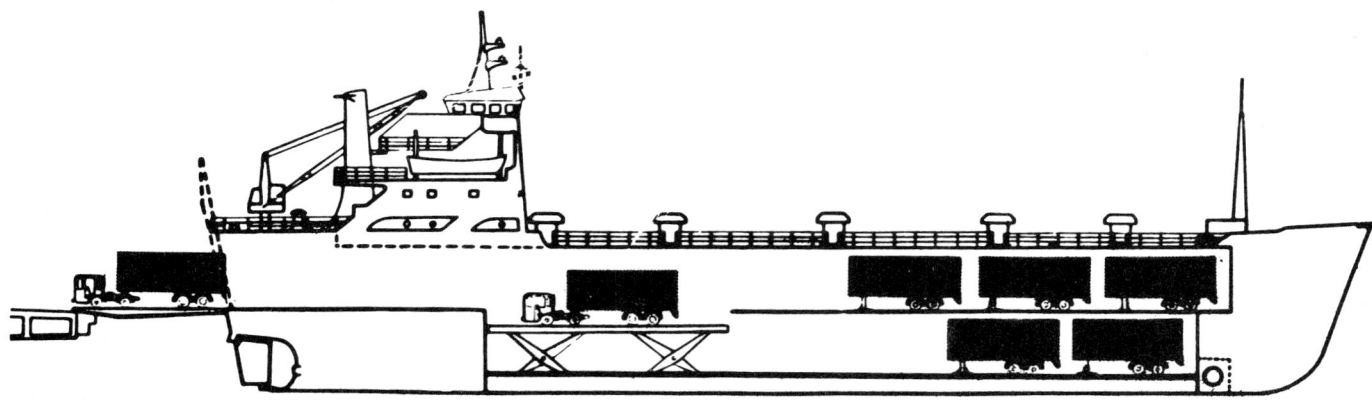

Wallenius Stern loader with hydraulic lift.

WASHBAY LINIE

Washbay-Linie G.m.b.H.
2 Hamburg 11, Alter Fischmarkt 11,
Postfach 110444, West Germany
AGENT:
Henry Stahl, Shipbroker, 2 Hamburg 11,
Alter Fischmarkt 11, Postfach 110444,
West Germany
TELEPHONE: 321 321
TELEX: 0216 1331
BRANCHES:
UK-agents:—
Lynn Ferries Ltd, Kings Lynn (Norfolk),
130 Norfolk Street
Tel: 63231. Telex: 81217
DIRECTORS:
Peter Stahl
H. H. Schulte

Washbay-Linie's *Lynn* at Kings Lynn

Dr. J. Wagner
CARGO SUPERINTENDENT:
Captain K. O. Poll

SERVICES:
Regular roll-on and container service between Hamburg and King's Lynn calling also at Cuxhaven, Emden, Boston (Lincs), Great Yarmouth and Lowestoft.

FLEET:
R.o.m.v. *Alster*
  Container capacity 65 20 ft
  Net reg tons 269
  Length 67 m (220 ft)
  Beam 12 m (39 ft 6 in)
  Draught 3·80 m (12 ft 6 in)
R.o.m.v. *Lynn*
  Container capacity 71 20 ft
  Net reg tons 269
  Length 67 m (220 ft)
  Beam 12 m (38 ft 6 in)
  Draught 3·80 m (12 ft 6 in)
m.v. *Alster II*
  Container capacity 22 20 ft
  Net reg tons 263
  Length 52 m (170 ft)
  Beam 9 m (30 ft)
  Draught 3·42 m (11 ft 6 in)
FUTURE DEVELOPMENTS:
An additional vessel with a capacity of about 100 20 ft units is planned for the Hamburg/King's Lynn service and will commence operations by the end of 1971 or early 1972.

WATERMAN STEAMSHIP CORP.

Waterman Steamship Corporation
140 Broadway, New York, NY 10005
TELEPHONE: (212) 344-2460
TELEX: 01-26118
OFFICIALS:
C. S. Walsh (*Chairman*)
E. P. Walsh (*President*)
SERVICE:
  US East Coast to N.W. Europe—Part

Container vessels.
  The Company also operate a service with conventional carriers from U.S. East Coast and Gulf ports to the Persian Gulf, Pakistan and India. It has been announced that three LASH vessels have been ordered for this service.
FLEET:
  Conventional cargo vessels, two or three of which have been partly converted for the carriage of containers.
  Three LASH vessels on order with further barge carriers reported to be at the planning stage.

CONTAINERS IN SERVICE:
  Some 200 20 and 40 ft dry cargo units are reported in service.

Y-S LINE

Yamashita-Shinnihon Steamship Co., Ltd.
1-1, Hitotsubashi 1-Chome, Chiyoda-ku, Tokyo, Japan
TELEPHONE: Tokyo (03) 216-2111
TELEX: TK 2345
DIRECTORS:
  K. Yamagata (*Chairman*)
  S. Yamashita (*President*)
  Y. Tanigawa ⎱ (*Senior Managing*
  M. Tomita ⎰ *Directors*)
  K. Hayashi
  N. Dan
  F. Ishibashi
  Y. Yamakoshi ⎱ (*Managing Directors*)
  T. Tani
  Y. Goko
  T. Kobayashi
  K. Tatsuuma
  T. Murakami
  K. Tsuji ⎱ (*Directors*)
  S. Imamura
  K. Ogawa
BRANCHES IN JAPAN:
Kobe:
  83, Kyomachi, Ikuta-ku, Kobe
  Telephone: Kobe (078) 39-7271
Yokohama:
  Miyoshi Bldg., 31, Yamashita-cho, Naka-ku, Yokohama
  Telephone: Yokohama (045) 681-5291

YSL'S *Kashu Maru*

Osaka:
  Junkei-Sanwa Bldg., 25, 4-chome, Junkei Machi-dori, Minami-ku, Osaka
  Telephone: Osaka (06) 271-5971
Moji:
  6-9, 1-chome, Nishikaigan-dori, Moji-ku, Kitakyushu
  Telephone: Kitakyushu (093) 33-2181

Sapporo:
  Mitsui Bldg., 1, Nishi 4-chome, Kitanijo, Sapporo

  Telephone: Sapporo (011) 261-5641
OVERSEAS REPRESENTATIVES OFFICES:
  New York, Seattle, San Francisco, Chicago, Los Angeles, Toronto, Oslo, London, Bombay, Sydney, Melbourne.
SERVICES:
  Japan/California—Weekly
  Japan/Pacific North West—10 days
  Japan/Australia—6 days
  Trans Siberian Container Service—10 days
  *Japan/New York —weekly.
  *This service will be maintained by conventional vessels until such time as the vessels

planned are in service.

FLEET:

Vessels	20 ft container capacity	Beam		Loaded draught		n.r.t.	Speed	Length	
		m	ft	m	ft			m	ft
Japan/California trade:									
Kashu Maru	800	25·7	84·3	9·72	31·9	9,282	22·5	188	616·8
New Building (Launch Nov. 1971)	1,100	30·0	98·4	9·50	31·2	12,610	23·0	212	695·5
Japan Australia Trade:									
Tohgo Maru	1,100	60·0	98·4	9·50	32·1	12,610	23·0	122	965·5
Japan/Pacific North West trade:									
Beishu Maru	1,100	30·0	98·4	10·50	34·4	12,600	23·0	212	695·5
Japan/New York trade:									
New Building (Launch Aug. 1972)	1,800	32·0	105·0	9·5	31·2	—	25·2	230	784·6

CONTAINERS IN SERVICE:

Dry cargo, ventilated, refrigerated. flat rack, open top, livestock and bulk units of 20 × 8 × 8 and 40 × 8 × 8·5 are in service. Numbers in service were reported in the last edition but the company now state that figures are not available.

OVERSEAS AGENTS:

U.S.A. and Canada:

San Francisco:
Lilly Shipping Agencies
1, California Street, Suite 2300
San Francisco, Calif. 94111, USA
Telephone: 415-781-3600

Los Angeles:
Lilly Shipping Agencies
210 West 7th Street, Los Angeles,
California 90014, USA
Telephone: 213-627-3651

Portland:
International Shipping Co., Inc.
200, World Trade Building,
Portland, Oregon 97204, USA
Telephone: 503-226-7681

Seattle:
International Shipping Co., Inc.
916 Norton Building, Seattle,
Washington 98104, USA
Telephone: Main 3-5511/7

Vancouver, B.C.
North Pacific Shipping Co., Ltd.
One Bentall Building, 505 Burrard Street,
Vancouver 1, B.C., USA
Telephone: 682-2811

New York:
Texas Transport and Terminal Co., Inc.
21 West Street, New York, N.Y. 10006,

USA
Telephone: 797-2200

Chicago:
Texas Transport & Terminal Co., Inc.
39 South La Salle Street, Chicago,
Illinois 60603, USA
Telephone: 312-782-0475

New Orleans:
Texas Transport & Terminal Co., Inc.
International Trade Mart, New Orleans,
La. 70130, USA
Telephone: 504-529-2241

Houston:
Texas Transport & Terminal Co., Inc.
711 Fannin Street,
Houston, Texas 77002, USA
Telephone: 713-225-5461

Australia:

Sydney:
SHIPTRACO Sea Transport Services Pty.,
Ltd.
"Scottish House", 17-19 Bridge St.,
G.P.O. Box 49, Sydney, N.S.W. 2001
Australia
Telephone: 22-4147, 27-3861

Melbourne:
SHIPTRACO Sea Transport Services Pty.,
Ltd.
c/o Howard Smith Industries Pty., Ltd.
522 Collins Street, Melbourne, Victoria
3000
Telephone: 62-3711

Brisbane:
Howard Smith Industries Pty., Ltd.
78 Eagle Street, G.P.O. Box 20A,
Brisbane, Queensland, 4001 Australia
Telephone: 31-3161

Adelaide:
Howard Smith Industries Pty., Ltd.
3 Todo Street, P.O. Box 163,
Port Adelaide, S.A. 5015, Australia
Telephone: 4-3921

EUROPEAN AGENTS FOR TRANS SIBERIAN CONTAINER SERVICE:

West Germany:
Danzas & Cie, GmbH
D-6000 Frankfurt/M8
Telephone: 691116

Switzerland:
Danzas Ltd.
CH-4002 Basle P.O.B.
Telephone: 220400

France:
Danzas & Cie
SA 15, Rue de Nancy,Paris
Telephone: 208-81-50

Netherlands:
Van Gend & Loos
Catharijnesingel, 47 Utrecht
Telephone: 030-28311

Italy:
Ditta Ed Canali Fu Camillo
20124 Milano
Telephone: 691645

Finland:
O. Y. Rajahuolinta AB,
Hameentie 10 Helsinki
Telephone: 716549

London:
Simpson Spence & Young
28 St. Mary Axe.,
London, E.C.3
Telephone: 01-283-5200

ZEELAND

Stoomvaart Maatschappij Zeeland

PO Box 2, Stationsweg 10,
Hook of Holland
TELEPHONE: 01747-2441
TELEX: 31272

FLEET:
Domburgh capable of lifting 77 20 ft units or their equivalent in 30 and 40 ft units.

CONTAINERS IN SERVICE:
None.

ZIM ISRAEL

Zim Israel Navigation Co. Ltd.
209 Hameg In Im Avenue, PO Box 1723,
Haifa, Israel
TELEPHONE: 40711
DIRECTORS:
M. Tzur (*Chairman*)
M. Kashti (*Managing Director*)

OFFICIALS:
Captain I. Adelstein (*Container Project Division*)
SERVICES:
Israel—United Kingdom:
In partnership with the Moss Hutchinson Line (P & O group) and the Companies in

Ellerman's Containership Services, the Company provides a 12 day service Liverpool-Ashdod with two vessels and a 12 day service London-Ashdod with two vessels. It is planned to provide weekly services by adding an additional vessel to each of the services. Chartered tonnage is employed with a capacity of 175 20 ft units in each vessel.

Mediterranean—US East Coast and Great Lake Service:

Four conventional carriers have been jumboised to carry 180 20 ft units and two sailings per month are made.

Mediterranean Services:

A roll-on service between Ashdod and Trieste is operated weekly. Four roll-on vessels are due to come into service in late 1971 and in 1972.

USA and Far East Service:

Six 22/23 knot, 1,300 20 ft unit, vessels are under construction in Europe and will enter service in 1972.

CONTAINERS IN SERVICE:

Some 3,000 dry cargo containers are in service; the majority have a length of 20 ft but some of 8 ft and 40 ft length are also used. The refrigerated fleet consists of 2 40 ft and 8 20 ft units.

BRANCHES:

Tel Aviv:
9, Ahad Haam St.
Migdal Shalom,
P.O.B. 20144

Ashdod:
P.O.B. 4001

Eilat:
P.O.B. 11

Jerusalem:
25 Jaffo Road, Generali Bldg.,
P.O.B. 1151

Antwerp:
22/24 Huidevetter Straat

Genoa:
4 Via Edilio Raggio,
P.O.B. 3141

London:
310, Regent Street, W.1
194/200, Bishopsgate E.C.2

New York:
American-Israeli Shipping Co. Inc.
42, Broadway, N.Y. 10004

Tokyo:
Central P.O.B. 2042

Accra:
Bungalow 8, Lartebiokorshie Estate,
P.O.B. 4303

NON VESSEL
OPERATING CARRIERS

NON VESSEL OPERATING CARRIERS
NVOC
OY AA LINES AB

Oy AA Lines Ab,
Eteläranta 8,
Helsinki 13, Finland
TELEPHONE: 10758
TELEX: 121071
PRINCIPAL OFFICIAL:
Nils von Troil (*Managing Director*)
BRANCHES:
Germany:
AA Lines GmbH,
24 Lübeck, Trauemünder Allee 16
Denmark:
AA Lines,
Kronprincessgade 54, Copenhagen K
France:
SATCO (as agents)
20-22 Boulevard des Belges, Rouen
SATCO (as agents)
14 rue Clapeyron, Paris 8

SERVICES:
Helsinki — Lübeck — Copenhagen — Rouen
—Twice weekly.

GENERAL:
The service is operated using 300 own
and 100 leased 20 ft flats and containers.
The Company specialises in the bulk liquid
transport with tank containers.

TERMINALS:
Oy A-A Lines Ab
Helsinki Western Harbour
TELEPHONE: 10758
AA Lines GmbH
Lübeck, Nordlandkai
TELEPHONE: 41824
SATCO Terminal
Rouen
TELEPHONE: 711200

An AA Lines 20 ft dry cargo unit

ABC OVERSEAS TRANSPORT

ABC Overseas Transport,
201 Eleventh Avenue, New York,
New York 10001

OFFICIALS:
D. D. Jordan (*General Traffic Manager*)

TRADING SCOPE:
1 From: ports in Maryland, New Jersey,
New York, Pennsylvania.
To: Antwerp, Belgium; Bremen, Bremerhaven, and Hamburg, Germany; Amsterdam
and Rotterdam, Holland.
2 From: Antwerp, Rotterdam and Amster-

dam.
To: New York, Boston, Philadelphia, Baltimore, Norfolk and/or Newport New Jersey.

3 From: Ports in Maryland, New Jersey, New
York, Pennsylvania.
To: London on cargo destined to points UK.

AFRICAN CONTAINER EXPRESS

African Container Express Ltd.
Salisbury Square House,
8, Salisbury Square, London, EC4P 4HA
TELEPHONE: 01-353 5362
TELEX: 22542
OFFICIALS:
G. W. Howe (*Chairman*)
OPERATIONS OFFICE:
African Container Express Ltd,
605, Liver Building, Liverpool L3 1HB,
TELEPHONE:
TELEX:
Manager: F. R. Drury
SERVICE:
Regular shipments by UK/West African
Lines Express Service vessels from London
and Liverpool to main West African ports.

Handling an African Container Express 10ft unit

ALLTRANSPORT LTD.

Alltransport Ltd.,
Kestral House,
Stratford High Street,
London E15 2UA
TELEPHONE: 01-534 5500
TELEX: 897451

DIRECTORS:
B. Kelleher (*Managing*)
K. M. Gunthardt
E. Battershall
R. W. Grassley

BRANCHES:
Birmingham, Bradford, Dublin, Felixstowe,
Hull, Liverpool Manchester, Southampton,
Stoke, London International Freight Term-
inal.

CONTAINER SERVICES WITH OWN OR LEASED
CONTAINERS:
Norway, Sweden, Finland, Denmark, Bel-

gium, Holland, W. Germany, Switzerland,
Italy, France, Portugal, Spain, Austria,
Australia, Canada and USA.

INLAND TERMINALS USED:
(1) Alltransport Ltd.,
Containerbase,
Barton Dock Road,
Urmston,
Lancs.
Telephone: 061-748 9211
Telex: 668358
Representative: Mr. B. Haindl
(2) Alltransport Ltd.,
Containerbase,
Scala House,
Holloway Circus,
Birmingham 1
Telephone: 021-643 5172/3
Telex: 338199
Representative: Mr. D. P. I. Sergeant
(3) Alltransport Ltd.,

Containerbase,
10 Duke Street,
Bradford 1.
Telephone: 32803/4
Telex: 51514

Representative: Mr. W. J. Mace

(4) London International Freight Terminal
No 3 Shed,
Temple Mill Lane,
Stratford E.15
Telephone: 01-534 4244
Telex: 896014

CONTAINER PARK, PACKING AND UNPACKING
FACILITIES:
Felixstowe, London, Birmingham, Bradford
and Manchester

AMERICAN FREIGHT FORWARDING

American Freight Forwarding Corp,
PO Box 12184
Oakland, California 94604
OFFICIALS:
M. M. Bedacht (*Director of Traffic*)

D. C. Andrews Ballantyne & Co, Ltd.
Lynton House, 255/259 High Road,
Ilford, Essex
TELEPHONE: 01-553 3991
TELEX: 897176

DIRECTORS:
P. T. Ballantyne (*Chairman*)
E. J. Furze (*Managing Director*)

BRANCHES:
Northampton, Leicester, Nottingham,
Sheffield, Newcastle, Glasgow, Liverpool,

TRADING SCOPE:
1 From: North Atlantic Ports.
To: Ports of Amsterdam, Rotterdam, Holland; Antwerp, Belgium; Bren, Bremerhaven and Hamburg.

ANDREWS, BALLANTYNE

Whitstable, Hull and London-Manchester-Prestwick-Glasgow Airports.

CONTAINER SERVICES WITH OWN OR
LEASED CONTAINERS:
USA—New York—weekly
Canada—Montreal and Toronto—weekly
Australia—Fremantle, Adelaide, Melbourne and Sydney—weekly
Eire—Dublin—daily
CONTAINER TERMINALS USED:
Western Boulevard, Leicester (own)
Telephone: 0533 23127
Shepcoté Lane, Sheffield (own)

2 From: Amsterdam, Rotterdam, Antwerp, Bren, Bremerhaven, Hamburg and via these ports from points in Western Europe.
To: North Atlantic Ports in the Hampton Roads/Eastport, Maine Range.

Telephone: 0742 42424
Bugsby Way, Charlton, London (shared)
Leicester Air Freight Terminal.
Freeman's Common, Leicester.
Telephone:

Telephone: 01 858 2649
Grant Street, Nottingham
Telephone: 0602 71462
Representative: R. G. Roberts
Telephone: 021-359 3296
AVC Depot, Cotton Street, Liverpool
Telephone: 051-236 5156
Representative: S. J. McAndrew

ANGLO-OVERSEAS TRANSPORT

Anglo Overseas Transport Company Ltd.,
16 New Street, London EC2M 4TY
TELEPHONE: 01 283 7121
TELEX: 883188, 887034
DIRECTORS AND EXECUTIVES IN CHARGE OF
CONTAINER OPERATIONS:
J. Wilden (*Managing Director*)
R. A. Crane (*Development Manager*)
V. D'Bras (*Container Marketing Manager*)
D. A. Mordy (*Container Controller*)
BRANCHES:
London International Freight Terminal, Hither Green, Covent Garden, Birmingham, Harwich, Hull, Dublin, Leeds, Leicester, Liverpool, Manchester, Southampton, Stoke-on-Trent, Swansea, Glasgow, London Airport, Ringway Airport, Southend Airport, Prestwick Airport.

CONTAINER SERVICES WITH OWN OR LEASED
CONTAINERS
London, Manchester, Liverpool, Birmingham, Glasgow and Leicester to Koln, Brussels, Milan, Amsterdam, Rotterdam, Bochum, Basle, Chiasso and to any Western European Destination—Service upon negotiation. Full and Part Loads accepted—Daily despatches.

CONTAINER TERMINALS USED:
(1) 9 Shed, London International Freight Terminal (Own Depot)
Representative: J. E. Thorn
Telephone: 01-534 0111
(2) Birmingham, Lawley Street, (BR)
Representative: J. Burnham
Telephone: 021-236 5253
(3) Leicester, H. W. Coates

Main Street, Cosby, Leics.
Representative: G. Wills
Telephone: 053 729 4321
(4) Manchester, Liverpool Road (own depot).
Representative: G. Maddock
Telephone: 061-236 3661
CONTAINER PARK FACILITIES AND BREAK
BULK PACKING AND STORAGE:
Break bulk and receiving facilities at 9 L.I.F.T. Manchester (Liverpool Road), Birmingham (Lawley Street), Leicester. Export storage facilities in London, Birmingham, Leicester, Liverpool, Glasgow, Manchester, Stoke-on-Trent.

Container Parks at 9 L.I.F.T., Birmingham, Glasgow, Leicester, Stoke-on-Trent, and Warrington.

ARBUCKLE SMITH

Arbuckle Smith & Co. Ltd.,
91, Mitchell Street,
Glasgow.
TELEPHONE: 041-248 5050
TELEX: 778212

EXECUTIVES IN CHARGE OF CONTAINER
OPERATIONS
G. E. F. Johnston (*Director*)
I. McDougall (*Container Manager*)

BRANCHES:
London, Liverpool, Manchester, Southampon, Bradford, Stoke-on-Trent, and subsidiary companies in Dublin, Cork, Montreal, Toronto and Winnipeg

SERVICES WITH OWN OR LEASED CONTAINERS:
Scotland to Montreal, New York, Toronto, Winnipeg, Gothenburg, Dublin.
Manchester to Montreal Toronto, Winnipeg, Dublin.

TERMINALS USED:
Carfin Container Depot,
Telephone: 606-4191
Representative: I. McDougall
(Bonded goods can be received at Carfin which is owned by the Company)
Victoria Warehouse, Hollingwood,
Manchester
Telephone: 061-681 2314
Representative: A. Gray
Other depots throughout the country are used for groupage operations.

ARMFIELDS INTERNATIONAL

Armfields International Ltd.,
35/39 Marshgate Lane, Stratford, London E15
TELEPHONE: 01-534 6622
TELEX: 887126

DIRECTORS:
C. H. Armfield (*Chairman and Managing Director*)
N. L. Liddiard
D. G. Liddiard
C. S. Brunt

BRANCHES:
Hull, Liverpool, Manchester, Felixstowe, Leicester, and London, Manchester and Southend airports.
SERVICES WITH OWN OR LEASED CONTAINERS:
London to: Rotterdam, Amsterdam, Vienna, Basle, Zurich, Gothenburg, Oslo, Halsingborg, Malmo and Toronto.
Hull to: Rotterdam, Vienna, Gothenburg. Basle and Zurich.
Manchester to: Toronto and Vancouver
London—Stockholm groupage service.

TERMINALS USED:
(1) Armfield House, Marshgate Lane, London, E.15 (own).
Representative: A. McCouat
Telephone: 01-534 6622
(2) Armfield House, Smith Street, Manchester, 16 (own).
Representative: C. S. Brunt
Telephone: 061-872 5135
(3) Trans-European Pallets Ltd.,
Freightliner Terminal, Brighton Street, Hull
Telephone: Hull 227714

ASCANIA UNIT LOADERS

Ascania Unit Loaders Ltd (AUL Ltd.)
Three Quays, Tower Hill, London, E.C.3
TELEPHONE: 01-623 3000

Astron Forwarding Company,
PO Box 161, 75 Market Street,
Oakland, California 94604
TELEPHONE: (415) 834-1730

TELEX: London 28234
DIRECTORS AND PRINCIPAL OFFICIALS
D. L. J. Mortleman (*Chairman*)
D. W. Neighbour (*Director*)

ASTRON FORWARDING

OFFICIALS:
Lester A. Dent (*President*)
Frank Consul (*Vice-President*)
Ken S. Ross (*Sales Manager*)

R. A. Forster (*General Manager*)
SERVICES:
Tilbury—Rotterdam, Antwerp, Hamburg and Dunkirk daily.

TRADING SCOPE:
Between: United States ports and ports in. Central and South America, Canada and the West Indies. Also with Africa, Asia and Europe.

ATLAS VAN SERVICE

Atlas Van Service, Inc,
2506 West 6th Street, Los Angeles,
California
OFFICIALS:

Les. T. Mullette (*General Manager*)
TRADING SCOPE:
Between: Los Angeles and San Francisco
and Yokohama, Japan and Naha, Okinawa.

AUSTRALIAN FORWARDING AGENCY GROUP

Australian Forwarding Agency Pty Ltd.
46-48 Pyrmont Bridge Road, Pyrmont,
NSW 2009
GPO Box 5313, Sydney, NSW 2001
TELEPHONE: 6603822
TELEX: AA 21438
OFFICIALS:
C. A. Timson (*Sales Director*)
J. A. Kildea (*Sales Manager*)
I. D. Wheeler (*Operations Manager*)

GROUP COMPANIES:
Australian Forwarding Agency (Vic) Pty
Ltd.,
99 King Street, Melbourne, Victoria 3000
PO Box 4752, Spencer Street, Melbourne,
Victoria 3001
TELEPHONE: 625582
TELEX: 30512
OFFICIALS:
R. P. Connolly (*Regional Manager*)
W. R. Pickering (*Commercial Manager*)

Australian Forwarding Agency (Qld) Pty
Ltd,
503-505 Queen Street, Brisbane, Qld. 4000.
PO Box 568, Brisbane, Qld. 4001.
TELEPHONE: 28960
TELEX: 41240
OFFICIALS:
G. V. Cole (*Director*)
R. Watkins (*Manager*)
J. G. Dalton (*Sales Manager*)
Australian Forwarding Agency (WA) Pty
Ltd,
4 High Street, Fremantle WA 6160,
PO Box 484, Fremantle WA 6160.
TELEPHONE: 351377
TELEX: 92456
OFFICIALS:
A Weeks (*Manager*)
Hargrave (Tasmabia) Pty Ltd,
4 Patrick Street, Hobart, Tas. 7000,
GPO Box 322D Hobart, Tas., 7001.
TELEPHONE: 342244
TELEX:

OFFICIALS:
R. E. Shepherd (*Manager*)
Butler, McHugh & Co Pty Ltd,
306 St, Vincent Street, Port Adelaide,
SA 5015.
PO Box 198 Port Adelaide, SA 5015.
TELEPHONE: 41181
TELEX: AA 82627
OFFICIALS:
F. Cottle (*Managing Director*)
R. Gosling (*Sales Manager*)
BRANCHES:
Sydney, Melbourne, Hobart, Brisbane,
Newcastle, Canberra, London, Hong Kong,
Auckland NZ.

SERVICES WITH OWN OR LEASED CONTAINERS:
Australia—Europe.
Australia—New Zealand.
Australia—South Africa.
FUTURE DEVELOPMENT:
Container Base for Sea/Air transport
in Sydney, Melbourne and Brisbane.

BAHR BEHREND

Bahr Behrend & Co. Ltd., (Direkttransport)
P.O. Box No. 28,
India Buildings,
Water Street,
Liverpool L69 2BW.
TELEPHONE: 051-236 4871

TELEX: 62235

DIRECTOR AND MANAGER IN CHARGE OF
CONTAINER SERVICE:
J. E. Behrend (*Director*)
R. Jones (*Manager*)

SERVICES WITH OWN OR LEASED EQUIPMENT
UK to Sweden—Full unit daily
—Groupage weekly ex Manchester
UK to North Continent—Full unit daily
A member of the Direkttransport Routes
Network.

BAXTER HOARE

Baxter, Hoare & Co. Ltd.,
17/19 Redcross Way, London S.E.1.
TELEPHONE: 01-407-4455
TELEX: 887 559
DIRECTORS AND EXECUTIVES IN CHARGE
OF CONTAINER OPERATIONS:
R. Stanley (*Director*)

D. Amos (*General Manager*)

BRANCHES:
Liverpool, Manchester, Hull, Felixstowe,
Harwich, Birmingham, Newcastle-on-Tyne,
Southampton, Immingham, Avonmouth.

SERVICES WITH OWN OR LEASED CONTAINERS:
Groupage, full and part load service twice
weekly to and from Netherlands, Belgium,
France, Switzerland, W. Germany, Austria,
Italy, Denmark, Finland, Norway, Sweden,
Republic of Ireland and Persia.

BELL LINES

Bell Lines Ltd.
Hawkins House, Hawkins Street, Dublin 2
TELEPHONE: 777117
TELEX: Dublin 5164
DIRECTORS AND EXECUTIVES IN CHARGE OF
CONTAINER SERVICES:
G. W. Hollwey (*Managing Director*)
N. A. Jenkinson (*Commercial Manager*)

V. C. Ellis (*Operations Manager*)
BRANCHES:
Belfast, Birmingham, Cadenazzo, Cork,
Dublin, Dusseldorf, Glasgow, London,
Manchester, Middlesbrough, Milan, Newport,
Rotterdam, Waterford.
SERVICES WITH OWN CONTAINERS:
Bellport—Waterford
Rotterdam—Waterford

CONTAINER TERMINALS USED:
Name of terminal: Bellport, Monmouthshire.
Representative: Paul Dunn
Telephone: Newport 73941
Name of terminal: Waterford
Representative: F. R. Kelly
Telephone: Waterford 5811
The Company uses its own ships, trains and
road transport.

BEVERLEY HILLS TRANSPORT AND STORAGE

Beverley Hills Transfer & Storage Co,
221 South Beverly Drive,
Beverly Hills, California
OFFICIALS:

Wesley McKay (*Traffic Manager*)
TRADING SCOPE:
Between: United States ports including
Alaskan and Hawaiian and world ports.

BOYD, BOYD

T. Boyd Boyd & Co. Ltd.,
74/5 Watling Street,
London, E.C.4.
Telephone: 01-248 4433
Telex: 883548
DIRECTORS:
R. Boyd (*Chairman*)
L. T. Knights (*Vice-Chairman*)
S. J. Roche (*Managing Director*)

L. A. Faul
D. H. Marsland
B. B. Cooper
G. Muggleton
BRANCHES:
15 Bloom Street,
Manchester
Tower Buildings,

Water Street, Liverpool
Proctor House,
Side,
Newcastle-upon-Tyne, NE1 3JJ
SERVICES WITH OWN OR LEASED CONTAINERS:
UK to USA, Canada and Australia.
TERMINALS USED:
Express Container Depots at London SE7

BRITISH COMMERCIAL TRANSPORT

British Commercial Transport Co. Ltd.,
233/4 Blackfriars Road, London, SE1 8NP
TELEPHONE: 01-928 4966
TELEX: 28406
DIRECTORS AND EXECUTIVES IN CHARGE OF
CONTAINER SERVICES:
E. F. Keat (*Director*)
T. Beels (*Director*)

Brown, Jenkinson & Co. Limited,
Dunster House, 17/19 Mark Lane,
London, E.C.3.
TELEPHONE: 01-623 7555
TELEX: 262872/3
DIRECTORS:
A. F. Bedford
R. H. Poulter,
A. M. Marfleet,
R. F. G. Smith
R. G. Tarry
BRANCHES:
Brown, Jenkinson & Co. (Shipping) Ltd.,
75, Harborne Road,
Birmingham
Telephone: 021 EDG 5751
Telex: 3381185
Brown Jenkinson & Co. (Liverpool) Ltd.
565 Sefton House,
Exchange Building,
Liverpool
Telephone: 051-236 3742
Telex: 62219
Brown, Jenkinson & Co, (Shipping) Ltd.,

Canuk Container Service
A joint venture of:
Davies Turner and Company,
326 Queenstown Road,
London, S.W.8.

Channelflow Freight Services Ltd.,
CFS Freight Terminal,
River Road,
Barking, Essex.
TELEPHONE: 01-594 5566
TELEX: 896386
King George Dock, Hull, Yorkshire
Telephone: 0482-71893
Telex: 52414
DIRECTORS AND EXECUTIVES IN CHARGE OF
CONTAINER SERVICES:
S. S. Simpson (*Managing Director, South*)
A. E. Cooper (*Managing Director, North*)
J. T. Hughes (*General Manager, London*)
J. Kirby (*General Manager, Hull*)
J. G. Ronald (*General Manager, Scotland*)
BRANCHES:
No. 2 Pier Road, Felixstowe, Suffolk
24a Bernard Street, Leith
Dodge Works, Kew, Surrey
Elstree Way, Borehamwood, Herts.
Thorpe Road, Howden, E. Yorks.
8, Lad Lane, Liverpool 3

Club Line AB
Box 27022
S-102 51 Stockholm 27
GENERAL:
Club Line is a joint enterprise of:
N. V. Scheepvaartbedrijf Kroonburgh

"CS" Comprehensive Shipping Limited
Metropolitan Wharf,
Wapping Wall,
London E1 9SS
TELEPHONE: 01-480-5656

F. Cox (*Assistant Director*)
J. F. Palmer (*Assistant Director*)

BRANCHES:
Harwich, London Airport, Liverpool, Birmingham, Hull, Manchester, Newcastle, Grangemouth, Leith, Glasgow and Southampton.

BROWN JENKINSON
Trelawney House,
The Dock,
Felixstowe
Telephone: 03942 3878
Telex: 98345
SERVICES WITH OWN CONTAINERS:
United Kingdom to US East Coast, Canada
Great Lakes, US Gulf, Scandinavia, Portugal,
and Australia.
TERMINALS USED:
(1) No. 10 Shed L.I.F.T.
Stratford
London, E16
Representative: T. Crane
Telephone: 01-623 7555
(2) Concord Terminal
No. 2 Shed L.I.F.T.
Stratford,
London, E16
Representatives: G. A. Hall, R. J. Nicola
Telephone: 01-623 7555
(3) Container Terminal,
No. 40 Berth.
Tilbury.

CANUK
(For full details see separate entry), and
Border Brokers Ltd,
Box 4040 Terminal A, Toronto 1.
TELEPHONE: EM6-8482
TELEX: 022881

CHANNELFLOW
11 Brook Gate, South Liberty Lane,
Ashton Vale Trading Estate, Bristol 3
SERVICES WITH OWN OR LEASED CONTAINERS:
London to Gothenburg, Stockholm, Malmo,
Halsingborg and Boras—3 times weekly.
Hull to Gothenburg, Stockholm, Malmo,
Halsingborg and Boras—daily.
London, Goole and Leith to Copenhagen—
twice weekly.
London to Djulfa—weekly
London to Continent via Rotterdam and
Antwerp—Daily
Hull to Continent via Rotterdam and
Antwerp —Daily
Leith to Continent via Rotterdam and
Antwerp—twice weekly
London, Liverpool, Glasgow, Grangemouth,
Felixstowe to USA, Canada, etc—regular
services
TERMINALS USED:
(1) C.F.S. Freight Terminal,
Barking
Telephone: 01-594 5566

CLUB LINE
(KNSM Group), Rotterdam.
Ahlers Line NV, Antwerp.
Svea Line, Stockholm.
Unit loads and containers between Rotterdam—Amsterdam—Antwerp and Stockholm—Norrkoping—Oxelosund—Vasteras—Gefle.

SERVICES OFFERED WITH OWN OR LEASED
CONTAINERS:
USA, Canada, Sweden, Germany, Austria,
Italy, Australia.

CONTAINER TERMINALS USED:
No. 10 Shed, L.I.F.T., Temple Mills Lane,
Stratford, London, E15 (participate)
Telephone: 01-534 7680

CONTAINER SERVICES:
Leasing:
Extensive facilities for long or short periods
Lease-purchase facilities
EQUIPMENT:
Used equipment is purchased or for sale
VALETING SERVICE:
Full facilities for the maintenance and
cleaning of equipment can be arranged at
United Kingdom, Continental and USA ports,
elsewhere by arrangement.

The Company have over 60 branches
throughout Canada.
SERVICE:
United Kingdom—Canada with full or
part container loads.

Representative: D. J. Bourne
(2) C.F.S. Freight Terminal,
Howden
Telephone: Howden 594
Representative: P. Everingham
(3) C.F.S. Freight Terminal,
Bonnybridge
Telephone: 031-554 2574
Representative: P. Stewart
(4) C.F.S. Freight Terminal,
Kew
Telephone: 01-876 7751
Representative: D. O'Neill
(5) C. F. S. Freight Terminal,
Borehamwood
Telephone: 01-953 1661
Representative: G. Webster
C.F.S. Freight Terminal
Harrowbrook Industrial Estate,
Hinckley, Leicestershire.
Telephone: 04553 5281
Representative: J. A. W. Wilbur
CFS Freight Terminal, Bristol 3

CONTAINERS IN SERVICE:
Some 20 20 × 8 × 8 dry cargo containers
and 10 20 × 8 × 4 flats. The service has
only just been introduced and it is expected
to increase the number of units in service
shortly.

C. S. COMPREHENSIVE SHIPPING
TELEX: 883256
DIRECTORS AND EXECUTIVES:
D. J. Harrington (*Managing Director*)
W. J. Dmochowski (*Administrative*

Director)
J. K. Struwe (*Financial Director*)
W. H. Pitcher (*Operations Director*)
M. E. Barnes (*Secretary*)
R. A. J. Stewart (*General Sales Manager*)

BRANCHES:
Harwich, Liverpool, Bedfont, Middx.

SERVICES USING OWN ON LEASED EQUIPMENT
Austria
Groupage Services
Container: Daily to Vienna
        Once Weekly to Linz
        Once weekly to Graz
Trailer: Three times weekly to:
        Dornbirn

Consolidated Container Services Ltd.,
110 Bishopsgate
London, EC2
(Subsidiary Company of John Sutcliffe & Son
(Grimsby) Ltd)
TELEPHONE: 01-588 6881
TELEX: 888040
DIRECTORS AND EXECUTIVES IN CHARGE OF
CONTAINER SERVICES
R. G. Pilgrim (*Managing Director*)
J. H. James (*Director*)
M. J. Bonnington (*Director*)
M. Schoon (*Traffic Controller—Leeds*)
A. D. King (*Traffic Controller—London*)
BRANCHES:
Birmingham, Manchester, Leeds, Grimsby,

Consolidated Express Inc.,
629 W. 54th Street,
New York, N.Y.
TELEPHONE: (212) LT-1- 7210
OFFICIALS IN CHARGE OF CONTAINER
SERVICES:
R. A. Catinchi (*President*)

Constantine Forwarding Ltd.
1/7 Rangoon Street,
London E.C.3
TELEPHONE: 01-488 4525
TELEX: 887360
DIRECTORS:
T. A. Sheriden (*Manager*)

Bregenz serving adjacent Swiss
and Southern German Border,
Tyrol, Innsbruck and Vorarlberg
areas. Full container or trailer
loads throughout Austria
Switzerland
Full Trailer loads throughout by "CS"
TIR fleet Groupage Services to Eastern
Switzerland.
Belgium:
Weekly container groupage services to

CONSOLIDATED CONTAINER SERVICES

Felixstowe, Nottingham and Hull.

SERVICES:
London, Leeds, Manchester, Birmingham
and Nottingham to Esbjerg, Copenhagen,
Herning, Odense, Århus, Mälmo and Helsingborg—Daily from Leeds and twice weekly
from other depots. Also London to Rotterdam.

TERMINALS USED:
(1) London (East) ICD
    Chobham Farm, Leyton Road,
    London E.15
    Telephone: 01555 0418
(2) Containerbase Leeds

    Telephone: 0532 700431

CONSOLIDATED EXPRESS

R. M. Jacobs (*Vice President*)
John Beer (*Operations*)

BRANCH:
GPO Box 2080 San Juan, Puerto Rico 00809
SERVICES:
New York—Puerto Rico, Bi-weekly (LTL

CONSTANTINE FORWARDING

J. R. Dougall
E. A. Woodford
G. J. Hillyear
BRANCHES:
    Birmingham, Manchester, Hull, Harwich,
    Liverpool, Southampton, Felixstowe.

Antwerp and Brussels serving Northern
Germany and Northern France. Full
Trailer loads throughout by "CS" TIR fleet.
Germany.
Weekly service to Frankfurt and Haiger.
Central Europe:
Served by TIR fleet.
TERMINALS USED FOR CONTINENTAL UNIT
LOADS:
Through offices at Harwich/Zeebrügge/
Europort and Rotterdam.

(3) CCSL
    60 Anne Road, Smethwick,
    Warley Works,
    Telephone: 021-558 3011
(4) Manchester Ship Canal Co
    Container Depot
    56 Water Street, Manchester 3
    Telephone: 061-237 1133
(5) CCSL
    The Mill house, Ilkeston Rd.,
    Nottingham,
    Telephone: 0532 700431

STORAGE, PACKING AND UNPACKING
FACILITIES
All available at the above terminals.

shipments only)
TERMINALS:
Head office above:
Consolidated Express Inc.,
Building C, Mercado Central,
Pueblo Nuevo, San Juan P.R.
Telephone: (809) 783-9292

SERVICES:
Container, road and train ferry weekly
groupage services to Austria, Belgium,
Denmark, France, Germany, Iran, Italy,
Sweden, and Switzerland.
For full load service see the entry under
Eurocontainer Line.

CONTAINER TRANSPORT INTERNATIONAL

Container Transport International Inc,
Thomas G. Newman (*President*)
17 Battery Place, New York, New York 10004

TRADING SCOPE:
Between: US Ports and foreign ports in the
continents of Africa, Asia, Europe, Australia,
Central and South America.

CONTAINERWAY AND ROAD FERRY

Containerway and Roadferry Ltd.
GROUP HEADQUARTERS:
Tower Bridge House,
    198-204 Tower Bridge Road, London S.E.1
    TELEPHONE: 01-592 7344
Containerway and Road Ferry Ltd,
16-20 North Howard Street, Belfast,
BT13 AT
and at Cupar Street, Belfast, BT13 2LT
TELEPHONE: 20244
TELEX: 74498
BRANCHES:
Ardrossan, Barking, Belfast, Glasgow,
Larne, Leicester, Manchester, Newcastle,
Preston.
SERVICE:
Belfast—Preston
Larne—Preston

Larne—Ardrossan
At least 32 sailings per week for full and
part container loads.
Ferry Trailer Ltd.
    The Docks, Preston, Lancs, PR2 2XY
    TELEPHONE: 26255
    TELEX: 67408
GENERAL:
    The Company trades as Irish Ferryways.
BRANCHES:
    Dublin, Newport, New Ross.
SERVICES:
    Dublin—Preston
    New Ross—Newport (Wales(
    Larne—Ardrossan
Containerway Europe Limited
Containerway House,
    Ripple Road, Barking, Essex

TELEPHONE: 01592 7344
TELEX: 261043
BRANCHES:
    Felixstowe, Harwich, Hull, Immingham,
Tilbury.
SERVICES:
    Daily services for full and part container
loads between United Kingdom and Con-
tinental Europe through Southampton and
Harwich to Le Havre and Dunkirk; through
Felixstowe, Harwich and Hull to Rotterdam,
Antwerp, Zeebrugge, Hamburg, Bremen and
Bremerhaven.
Belgian Branch:
N.V. Containerway Belgium SA,
    Kaai 326, 6 Havendok, Antwerp
    TELEPHONE: 010-323 4160
    TELEX: 2026 33128

CONTRACTAVAN

Contractavan (Leyton) Ltd,
28 Eatington Road,
London E.10
TELEPHONE: 556-6841

DIRECTORS:
L. J. Foulkes
M. J. Foulkes

SERVICES:
UK—Europe—weekly.

Cory Cargo Services
130-138 Minories, London, EC3N 1NS
TELEPHONE: 01-481 1245
TELEX: 888381

Cosmos Shipping Co. Ltd.,
222 West Adams Street,
Chicago, Illinois 60606
TELEPHONE: 236-7554
TELEX: 910-221-5129
DIRECTOR IN CHARGE OF CONTAINER
OPERATION:
Norman G. Jensen (*Vice-President*)

T. H. Couch Ltd.,
6, Wind Street,
Swansea, S. Wales
Telephone: 53921
Telex: 48230

DIRECTORS AND EXECUTIVES IN CHARGE OF
CONTAINER OPERATIONS:
G. P. Welchman (*Director*)
J. M. Sampson
L. T. Benyon

BRANCHES:
Swansea, Cardiff, Newport.

DAT Nederlan-Engeland Transport NV
Meent 93c
Telephone: 133466/141837

Davies Turner and Company Ltd.,
4, Lower Belgrave Street,
London, SW1.
Telephone: 01-730 3455
Telex: 28471
SHIPPING OFFICE:
326-340 Queenstown Road,
London S.W.8.
Telephone: 01-622-9361
Telex: 28471
DIRECTORS AND EXECUTIVES IN CHARGE OF
CONTAINER OPERATIONS:
H. S. Waterhouse (*Vice-President-Exports*)
M. Chapman (*Vice-President-Imports*)
W. Behr (*European Traffic Manager*)

Denning & Wohlstetter,
Allen P. Wohlstetter,
1 Farragut Square South,
Washington, DC, 20006

VEB Deutrans
See Entry under German Democratic Republic.

Direkttransport Holdings SA
Luxembourg
TELEPHONE:
TELEX:
OFFICIALS:
GENERAL:
The Direkttransport Container network has partnership agreements for USA with Thrutainer and for the Far East with Nippon International Containers (NIC).
CONTAINER ROUTES NETWORK:
Belgium:

CORY CARGO SERVICES

OFFICIALS:
J. H. Arbuthnott (*Director*)
J. F. A. Osborne (*Traffic Manager*)
BRANCHES:
London International Freight Terminal,

COSMOS SHIPPING

BRANCHES:
17, Battery Place, New York, NY 10004
504, Cigali Bldg., New Orleans, La 70130
404, Realty Bldg., Savannah, Ga 31204
SERVICES:
'Shipcosmos Thrucontainer'—weekly services from (i) USA to Europe via US North Atlantic Ports in the Hampton Roads/ Eastport Maine Range and Antwerp, Ham-

COUCH

SERVICES WITH OWN OR LEASED CONTAINERS:
South Wales to Austria, Germany, Netherlands and Ireland.

One of the T. H. Couch Units.

DAT

Telex: 23418
International forwarding agents, ferry transport from and to Europe, England and Sweden.

DAVIES TURNER

P. J. Fowler (*Shipping Manager, Export*)
T. Key (*Continental Manager*)
W. Steele (*Scandinavian Manager*)
BRANCHES:
Southampton, Birmingham, Manchester, Glasgow, Liverpool, Felixstowe, Harwich, London Airport, Bristol and Hull.
SERVICES WITH OWN OR LEASED CONTAINERS:
Complete loads daily to Holland, Belgium, Germany, Austria, Switzerland, Italy and France. Weekly groupage to Sweden, Denmark, Norway, Rotterdam, Dusseldorf, Salzburg, Vienna—Twice weekly groupage to Milan and Turin. Daily groupage to Basle. 'Canuk' Service with full or groupage

DENNING AND WOHLSTETTER

TRADING SCOPE:
Between United States ports and ports in the continents of Africa, Asia, Australia, Europe, North America, South America.

DEUTRANS

DIREKTTRANSPORT

Direkttransport SA,
Churchilldok-Noorderlaan,
PO Box 464, B-2000 Antwerp
Tel: 41 70 80   Telex: 31893
Representative: Mr. Wijnants
17-21 rue Vanden Boogaerde,
B-1020, Brussels 2
Tel: 02282020   Telex: 21727
Representative: F. Halbert
Denmark:
Direkttransport Containerservice (Danmark) A/S,

Stratford E 15; Liverpool; Yeadon; Manchester; Halesowen; Newcastle.
SERVICES:
London—Basle, twice weekly.
London—Zurich, twice weekly.

burg, Bremen, Rotterdam, UK Ports, Mediterranean Ports. (ii) USA via US North Atlantic Ports to the Far East and (iii) USA via US North Atlantic Ports to Puerto Rico.

TERMINALS:
Murphy Terminals Co.,
932 S Clark Street,
Chicago, Illinois

Container transport all over the world. Hire of containers. Speciality: joint cargo transport to England. Warehousing and superintending.

Containers to Canada in conjunction with Border Brokers Limited, Box 4040. Terminal A Toronto 1, Ontario.
TERMINALS USED:
London International Freight Terminal.
Telephone: 01-534 0045
Representative: Mr. Deefholts,
    Battersea Wharf
Telephone: 01-622 9342
Representative: Mr. Merryweather
STORAGE, PACKING AND UNPACKING FACILITIES
These are available at Battersea Wharf, Battersea Warehouses and Battersea packing station.

Nørre Voldgade 6,
DK-1358, Copenhagen K.
Tel: 01 123022   Telex: 7476
Representative: F. Hollesen
Osteraa 17,
DK-9000, Aalborg
Representative: P. Bohndsen
Tel: 08-16 11 99   Telex: 30329
Representative: P. Bohnsen
Ireland:
Direkttransport Ireland Ltd,
    45 Lower Gardiner Street,

Dublin 1
Tel: 44250   Telex: 4120
Representative: P. C. Knight
Finland:
Direkttransport Oy.
S Magasinsgatan 4,
Helsinki 13
Tel: 115 00   Telex: 12506/12509
Representative: Lars Krogius
France:
Direckttransport SA
24 rue Caumartin,
Paris IX
Tel: 742-87-87   Telex: 21034
Representative: Frédéric Boutin
22 quai du Lazaret
F-13 Marseille 2
Tel: 21 08 60   Telex: 41702
Representative: J. F. Eymard
Germany:
Direkttransport Internationaler Container-
dienst GmbH,
Schillerstrasse 26,
D-2, Hamburg 50
Tel: 38 13 91   Telex: 212429
Representative: Willi Dous
Great Britain:
Direkttransport Containers (UK) Ltd.
8th Floor, Post and Mail House,
26, Colmore Circus,
Birmingham 4
Tel: 236 5505   Telex: 339101
Representative: Bill Middleton
Trelawny House, Room 214,
The Dock,
Felixstowe
Tel. 6228   Telex :98531
Representative: Mr. Stefford
47 Kings Head Street,
Harwich
Tel: 4337   Telex: 98540
Representative: D. King
71 High Street,
Hull, HU1 1QT
Tel: 25781   Telex: 52271
Representative: Andrew Good
318 High Road,
Ilford, Essex
Tel: 01.553 3225   Telex: 897173
Representative: W. Barker
82 Fore Street,
Ipswich
Tel: 58431   Telex: 98185
Representative: Anthony Good
Direkttransport,
India Buildings, Water Street,
PO Box 28,
Liverpool L69 2BW

Tel: 051-236-4871   Telex: 62235
Representative: John E. Behrend
196 Deansgate,
Manchester M3 3NJ
Tel: 061-834 2512   Telex: 668337
Representative: D. Mead
Greece:
Direkttransport SA Greece,
Gounari 15,
Piraeus
Tel: 427909   Telex: 212460
Representative: Phaeton Devletoglou
Italy:
Direkttransport Italia,
Via Anzalone 7,
I-951 31 Catania
Tel: 21 29 62   Telex: 97029
Representative: Oreste Geraci
Via Meravigli 16,
I-201 23 Milan
Tel: 87 66 19/87 66 90
Telex: 32250 pp mi (public telex)
Representative: Angelo Giorgi
Palazzo Centrale,
PO Box 722,
I-571 00 Livorno
Tel: 34051/2   Telex: 50109
Representative: Melchior Bournique
Via Medina 24,
I-801 33 Naples
Tel: 32 09 78/32 14 61
Telex: 71023
Representative: Ivar Klingenberg
Via della Borsa 3,
PO Box 1394,
I-341 00 Trietse
Tel: 24941/4   Telex: 46135
Representative: Livio Pesle

The Netherlands:
Direkttransport (International) NV,
Stationsweg 56
PO Box 810,
The Hague
Tel: 00931-70 18 32 40
Telex: 33120
Representative: Jan Oosterhuis
Spain:
Direkttransport SA,
Plaza Medinaceli 4, 1°
Barcelona (2)
Tel: 2223145   Telex: 54518 barca e
Representative: Fredrik Dahl
Calle Marques de basa Riera 4,
Madrid 14
Sweden:
AB Direkttransport
Packhusgatan 2 B,

PO Box 44
S-401 20 Göteborg 1
Tel: 031/17 14 10
Telex: 20875 directz s
Representative: Rolf Lundberg

Drottninggatan 56
PO Box 347
S-801 05 Gavle 1
Tel: 026/12 23 28
Telex: 81044 haegers s
Representative: Björn Ericsson

Hans Michelsensgatan 2
PO Box 264
S-201 22 Malmo 1
Representative: Torsten Gustafson
Tel: 040/384 10
Telex: 32325   32542 almship s
Representative Torsten Gustafson

Gyllenstiernsgatan 4,
PO Box 27020
S-102 51 Stockholm 27
Tel: 08/63 51 45
Telex: 17525 directz s
Representative: Tommy Junker

Switzerland:
Direkttransport AG,
Untere Rebgasse 7,
CH-4000, Basel 5
Tel: 061-33 7850
Telex: 62328 abal ch
Representative: Claudio Plüss

South Africa:
Direkttransport (SA) (Pty) Ltd,
Power House,
Fraser Street,
Johannesburg
Representative: Bob Robertson
PO Box 31763
Braamfontein, Transvaal
Tel: 834-2226   Telex: 43-8352 SA

Canada:
Direkttransport Containers Canada Ltd,
300 St. Sacrement Street,
Montreal
Tel: 845 5228/5229
Telex: 05 24371 dirco mtl
Representative: Hamm or Metzen
Iran:
Direkttransport Middle East Ltd,
Ave Saadi,
Toghinia Building,
Teheran
Tel: 302223-6   Telex: 2315

DUFOREST,

Louis Duforest Ltd.,
Duforest House, 19 Ropemaker Street,
Moorgate, London, E.C.2.
TELEPHONE: 01-638 6232
TELEX: 22495
DIRECTORS AND EXECUTIVES IN CHARGE OF
CONTAINER SERVICES:
E. Button (*Director*)
W. H. Hart (*London Traffic Manager*)
B. Paniale (*Bradford Traffic Manager*)
T. Fawcett (*Manager, Leeds*)

BRANCHES:
Central House,
Forster Square,
Bradford, 1
Telephone: Bradford 26451
Telex: 5149.
Room 21
Leeds Container Base
Wakefield Rd.,
Stourton, Leeds 10
Telephone: Leeds 74048
Telex: 557 340

CONTAINER SERVICES WITH OWN OR LEASED
CONTAINERS:
Weekly groupage and full load services to:
France, Switzerland, Italy, Austria, Germany
and Scandinavia
CONTAINER TERMINALS USED:
Leeds Container Base
Storage, packing and unpacking facilities:
Louis Duforest Unit Load Terminal
Shipley Station,
Shipley, Nr. Bradford, Yorks.
Telephone: Bradford 28261

EAST AFRICAN CONTAINERS

East African Containers Ltd.
PO Box 7793, Nairobi, Kenya
TELEPHONE: 20330
TELEX: 22274
A subsidiary company of Express Trans-
port Co. Ltd., Nairobi with an affiliate
company, East African Containers (GB) Ltd.,
in the United Kingdom.

BRANCHES:
Express Transport Co. (MGS) Ltd.,
PO Box 884, Dar-es-Salaam

Telephone: 22401
Express Transport (U) Ltd.,
PO Box 7194, Kampala
Telephone: 57493

East African Container (GB) Ltd.,
46 Dorset Street, London W1H 3FH
Telephone 01—935 9690
DIRECTORS AND EXECUTIVES IN CHARGE OF
CONTAINER SERVICES:
J. L. Ruben (*Managing Director*)—Nairobi
J. F. Soper—Mombasa
J. T. Jenner—Dar-es-Salaam

W. T. James—Kampala
A. N. Johnson—London
SERVICES:
Worldwide from and to East Africa.
LEASING SERVICE:
Containers are leased on a single journey
or contract basis.
TERMINALS USED:
Company's premises at Nairobi, Mombasa,
Dar-es-Salaam and Kampala where facilities
exist for clearing, forwarding, packing
unpacking and onward transportation.

EUROCONTAINER

Eurocontainer Lines (ECL)
Constantine Forwarding Ltd.
Constantine House, London International
Freight Terminal, London E.15
TELEPHONE: 01 534 5522
TELEX: 896415

OFFICIALS:
R. D. Smith (*Director*)
T. B. Paul (*Container Manager*)

European Trucking Services Ltd. (ETS)
Boompjes 102
Telephone: 126217/113617

BRANCHES:
Birmingham, Manchester, Liverpool,
Southampton, Woburn Sands, Haverhill,
Heathrow, Bristol.

SERVICES:
Full loads in 20, 30 and 40 ft units to
Germany, France, Italy, Switzerland, Austria, Belgium, Netherlands and Norway.
Tank and bulk traffic in containers are
handled on a contract basis—for groupage

services see the entry under Constantine
Forwarding Ltd.
EQUIPMENT IN SERVICE:
General cargo rigid box, Full Tilt, Open
Top, Side Door, Bulk Grain, Half Height
and Liquid Tank units in 20, 30 and 40 ft
lengths.
FUTURE DEVELOPMENTS:
The bulk liquids and solids traffic in
tanks, open tops and powder carriers,
is being expanded.

EUROPEAN TRUCKING SERVICE

Telex: 23409
Trucking of containers and ferry-trailers;
Roll-on/roll-off traffic to England and
Sweden.

EXPRESS CONTAINER TRANSPORT

Express Container Transport Ltd.
110 Powis Street, London S.E.18.

TELEPHONE: 01 855 5491-7
TELEX: 897858

GENERAL MANAGER:
H. J. Hooper

CONTAINER ROUTES SERVED:
UK/USA   UK/Europe

UK/Canada   UK/Scandinavia
UK/Australia
CONTAINER TERMINALS USED:
1 Express Container Transport Depot,
Bugsby's Way, London, SE7

FERNANDO ROQUE

Fernando Roqué Transportes Internacionales SA
Av. Valladolid 65
Madrid

TELEPHONE: 241.50.08
TELEX: 7524

BRANCHES:
Barcelona, Bilbao, Valencia, Zaragoza, Port
Bou, Irun and Cerbere (France)
SERVICES:
Fernando Roque Transportes Internacionales SA, in collaboration with their British
Agents LEP Transport operates regular

train ferry groupage services Madrid and
Barcelona to London.
OVERSEAS AGENTS:
LEP Transport (Spanish Department)
Sunlight Wharf,
Upper Thames Street,
London EC4

FNS

**F.N.S. Container & Eurotransport Division of
F.N.S. Corporation**
1 Park Row, New York, NY 10038
TELEPHONE: 212-964 4541
TELEX: 62423

OFFICIALS:
Fred N. Sucher (*President*)
Martin N. Schneer (*Secretary & Treasurer*)
F. J. Feig (*Vice-President & Import
Manager*)

CONTAINER ROUTES SERVED:
USA – Europe (weekly)
TERMINALS:
FICO, Terminal Building No. 265, Port
Newark, NJ

FREYMAN & VAN LOO

Agence Maritime A. Freyman & Van Loo,
9/33 Cadixstraat, Antwerp
TELEPHONE: (03) 32.38.20
TELEX: 31433

EXECUTIVE IN CHARGE OF CONTAINER
SERVICES:
N. Gosselin (*Managing Director*)
A. De Laet (*Export Manager*)
R. Libot
L. De Proost
BRANCHES:
Brussels, Kortrijk, Ostend, Zeebrugge,
Zaventem
CONTAINER SERVICES:
Belgium to:
USA and Canada
Scandinavia
United Kingdom
Japan
Australia
Portugal and Spain
TERMINALS USED:
(1) Freyloo I,

AG. MAR. A Freyman and Van Loo terminal, Antwerp

Corner of Hamburg & Bremenstraat,
Antwerp.
Telephone: 41 06 98
(2) Freyloo II,

Kustlaan, Zeebrugge.
Telephone: 050-551-01
CONTAINER PARK:
Zeebrugge.

GEEST LINE

The Geest Line
White House Chambers, Spalding, Lincs
PE11 2AL
TELEPHONE: Spalding 3901
TELEX: 32235
EXECUTIVE IN CHARGE OF CONTAINER
SERVICES:
A. T. Day (*Manager, Container Services*)
BRANCHES:
No. 3 Shed, Cliff Quay, Ipswich.
Langthwaite Grange Industrial Estate, South
Kirby, Yorkshire
'A' Shed, 2 Dock, Barry, Glamorgan.

CONTAINER SERVICES:
Ipswich—Maassluis—Daily excluding Sundays.
Ipswich—Emmerich—Weekly.
TERMINALS USED:
(1) Geest Industries Limited, Ipswich, Suffolk.
Telephone: Ipswich 55032
Telex: 98173
(2) Waling Van Geest & Zonen
Maassluis, Holland.
Telephone: Maassluis 3516
Telex: 23466

(3) Van Geest and Sohn' Emmerich,
W. Germany
Telephone: Emmerich 3413
Telex: 8125126
GROUPAGE CENTRES:
Geest Line
Barry, Glamorgan
Telephone: 044 62 4121
Telex: 49428
Kiilick Martin (Birmingham) Ltd.,
St. Martin's House, Bull Ring,
Birmingham 5
Telephone: 021-643 9051

Telex: 338807
Geest Line
Langthwaite Estate, South Kirkby,
Yorkshire
Telephone: South Elmsall 3333
Telex: 557
Geest Line
   No. 3 Transit Shed, Cliff Quay,

Ipswich, Suffolk
Telephone: Ipswich 55032
Telex: 98173
Geest Line
   Byng Street, Bootle, Lancs.
   Telephone: 051-922 3516
   Telex: 627001

Killick Martin (Southampton) Ltd.

100 Canute Road,
Southampton SO1 1AG
Telephone: Southampton 32711
Telex: 47444
Killick Martin & Co. Ltd.,
   Crown House, Linton Road,
   Barking, Essex
   Telephone: 01-594-7191
   Telex: 897886

GENERAL SHIPPING AND FORWARDING

General Shipping & Forwarding Company,
Prince Rupert House, 64 Queen Street,
London, EC4.
TELEPHONE: 01-248 1761
TELEX: 887101
DIRECTORS:
E. A. Newson
J. M. Newson

BRANCHES:
   Building 521, Office 30G, Heathrow Airport,
Hounslow, Middlesex.
GSF Liverpool Ltd.
16-18 Hackins Hey
Liverpool 2
Telephone 051 236 9334
Telex: 627110 (Prefix messages 'For GSF')

SERVICES WITH OWN OR LEASED CONTAINERS
   United Kingdom, Europe, North America,
Canada and Australia.
CONTAINER TERMINALS USED:
   Express Container Transport Limited,
Charlton, London, SE7
Telephone: 01-858 6624

GENTRANSCO

Gentransco Services Ltd.,
PO Box 166, Central House,
Stratford, London, E15.
TELEPHONE: 01-534 6655
TELEX: 897153/4
DIRECTORS AND EXECUTIVES IN CHARGE OF
   CONTAINER SERVICES:
F. Rose (*Deputy Chairman*)
G. Wells (*Container Manager, Operations*)
H. Bultmann (*Container Manager, Rates*)
N. Smith (*Container Manager, Commercial*)
BRANCHES:
   Atherstone, Birmingham, Bradford, Cardiff,
Hull, Liverpool, Manchester, Bristol and
Belfast.

SERVICES WITH OWN OR LEASED CONTAINERS:
   Full loads: Austria, Belgium, Denmark,
France, Germany, Italy, Netherlands, Spain
and Switzerland.
   Groupage: The Company operates about
50 services to and from Europe. A considerable and ever increasing number of these
services use containers but train ferries and
TIR Trailers are used when a better service

Loading groupage cargo at a Gentransco Terminal.

can be obtained.
TERMINALS USED:
(1) Gentransco No. 5 Shed,
   London International Freight Terminal
(2) Gentransco Warehouse,

Liverpool Road, Manchester
STORAGE, PACKING AND UNPACKING FACILI-
TIES:
   Gentransco House, Abbey Road, London,
E15.

GONDRAND

Societe Francaise de Transports Gondrand Freres
Paris
GENERAL:
   The Company operate container services,
using owned and leased containers, through-
out Europe.
COMPANIES WITHIN THE GROUP:

Societé Francaise de Transports Gondrand
Frères in Belgium, France, Germany, Luxem-
burg, United Kingdom.
   Societé Anonyme de Transports Mitjaville-
Gondrand in France.
Societé de Transports Internationaux TRAN-
SEST in France, Germany.
   Allgemeine Transportgesellschaft vorm Gon-

rand Maugili in Germany.
   Transport Maatschappij Traffic N.V. in the
Netherlands.
SNT Fratelli Gondrand in Italy and Ethiopia.
   Gondrand Española S.A. in Spain.
   Societé Anonyme Internationale de Trans-
ports Gondrand Frères in Switzerland.

GOOD

John Good & Sons Ltd.,
71 High Street,
Hull, HU1 1QT
TELEPHONE: 0482-25781

TELEX: 52271
DIRECTORS:
   J. Good, T. G. Good, E. S. Good, T. A.
Good

BRANCHES:
   Birmingham, Felixstowe, Goole, Grimsby,
Harwich, Immingham, Ipswich, London.
ASSOCIATED COMPANY:
   Direkttransport Containers (UK) Ltd.

HAESAERTS

R. Haesaerts

Astridlaan 29
2659 Breendonk, Belgium

TELEPHONE: (03) 78.71.65
TELEX: 32579
OFFICIALS:
R. Haesaerts (*General Director*)

Ch. Van den Heuvel (*Commercial Director*)
SERVICES WITH OWN CONTAINERS:
   Europe, America and Africa.

HARTRODT, LOCK

Hartrodt Lock Ltd.,
52/6 Osnaburgh Street
London, NW1
Telephone: 01-387 5633

Telex: 20875
DIRECTORS AND EXECUTIVES IN CHARGE OF
CONTAINER SERVICES:
H. M. J. C. Somerset

D. M. Hamilton
P. M. Low
A. J. K. Wenzel

BRANCHES:
Liverpool, Manchester, Walsall.

SERVICE WITH OWN OR LEASED CONTAINERS:
Groupage: Melbourne to Sydney.

P. Hauser Ltd.,
35/37 Whitworth Street West,
Manchester, M60 1NS
Telephone: 061-236 9761
Telex: 669325
DIRECTOR IN CHARGE OF CONTAINER SERVICE:
P. M. Hauser

TERMINALS USED:
(1) Barking,
Essex
Telephone: 01-387 5633
(2) Chasetown

HAUSER

BRANCH:
Harwich.
SERVICES WITH OWN OR LEASED CONTAINERS:
Regular services from Manchester to Chiasso and Aachen
TERMINALS USED:
Leased premises at

Nr. Walsall
Staffs.
Telephone: Burntwood 2345/6
Packing and Unpacking facilities exist at Chasetown and Gidea Park.

Ardwick East Goods Depot
Manchester
Telephone: 061-236 9761
STORAGE, PACKING AND UNPACKING FACILITIES:
Packing operations carried out on a leased site at Ardwick East Goods Depot.

HERNU, PERON & STOCKWELL

Hernu Peron and Stockwell Ltd.,
(Thos. Cook and Son Ltd.,)
70/77 Cowcross Street, London, EC1
TELEPHONE: 01-253 3011
TELEX: 21940
DIRECTORS AND EXECUTIVES IN CHARGE OF CONTAINER SERVICES:
M. Bannister
H. J. Rutishauser
F. J. Everett

BRANCHES:
Birmingham, Manchester, Liverpool, Glasgow, Bristol, Harwich, Felixstowe, Hull, Newcastle, Belfast, Cardiff, Dublin, Dover, Edinburgh, Immingham, Liverpool, Leeds, Leicester, London Airport, Manchester, Newhaven, Tilbury, Southampton.

SERVICES WITH OWN OR LEASED CONTAINERS:
Denmark (Copenhagen, Århus, Odense, Esbjerg) via Felixstowe and Harwich—twice weekly.
Finland (Helsinki) from London, Manchester, Birmingham, Hull and Leeds—weekly.
France (Paris) via Harwich, Zeebrugge and Dunkirk—daily.
Italy (Chiasso and Milan) via Harwich, Zeebrugge and Rotterdam—twice weekly.
Sweden (Gothenburg and Stockholm) from Birmingham, Glasgow, Hull, Leeds, London and Manchester—daily.
Switzerland (Basle, Zurich and Chiasso) via Harwich and Zeebrugge—twice weekly.
Sweden (Gothenburg and Stockholm):
Daily from Manchester, Birmingham, Hull, Leeds, Glasgow.

TERMINALS USED:
(1) London International Freight Terminal, No. 2 Shed.
Telephone: 01-534 0323
Representative: R. Brooksby

(2) Container Base (Birmingham North) Ltd.
Telephone: 021-356 7421

(3) Containerbase (Leeds) Ltd.,
Telephone: 0532 73681
Representative: J. Mayes

(4) Containerbase (Manchester) Ltd.
Telephone: 061-748 9561
Representative: S. R. Addison

(5) Containerbase (Glasgow) Ltd.
Telephone: 24331
Representative: A. Muir

HOLLANDSCHE STOOMBOOT MAATSCHAPPIJ

N.V. Hollandsche Stoomboot Maatschappij,
Oostelijke Handelskade 3, Amsterdam

PO Box 566

TELEPHONE: 020-63430
TELEX: 11038

OFFICIAL:
G. L. Medendorp (*Managing Director*)

BRANCHES:
London, Felixstowe, Shoreham, Hull, Birmingham, Manchester, Liverpool

CONTAINER SERVICES:
HSM—Phoenix Line Joint Service.
Amsterdam to Felixstowe—three sailings weekly.
MacVan—Container service:
Rotterdam to Leith—weekly.
TERMINALS USED:
(1) Container Terminal Amsterdam
Telephone: 020-113333
Telex: 13623
(2) Atlantic Container Terminal, Felixstowe
Telephone: 3589

Telex: 98436
(3) Albert Dock, Leith
Telephone: Edinburgh 534-1621
Telex: 72227

CONTAINER LEASING:
Limited leasing services for customers who use routes.
STORAGE, PACKING AND UNPACKING FACILITIES:
Available at the terminals at Felixstowe, Amsterdam and Leith.

HULL EUROSCAN

Hull Euroscan Ltd.,
TELEPHONE: Hull 42182
DIRECTORS:
J. Foster, E. E. Cooper, E. Jordan, C. Dimmock, W. S. Oxendale, E. Pinder, H. Nolan.
CONTAINER ROUTES SERVED:
Hull and Gothenburg, Hull and Rotterdam, Hull and Stockholm, Hull and Aachen, Hull and Boras, Hull and Switzerland, Hull and Antwerp, Hull and Bremen, Hull and Hamburg.
CONTAINER TERMINALS USED:
London:
W. Wingate & Johnston Ltd.,

144 Spa Road,
London S.E.16.
Telephone: 01-237-2629

Liverpool:
Bishops Wharf Ltd.
Barley Castle Lane,
off Swineyard Lane,
Stretton, Nr. Warrington,
Lancs.
Telephone: 051-92-61261

Coventry:
Capels Transport Ltd.,
Balsall Common.

Nr. Coventry,
Telephone: Berkswell 2885

Glasgow:
W. Wingate & Johnson Ltd.,
63 Patterson Street,
Glasgow, C.5.
Telephone: 041-332-5887

Manchester:
Manchester Ship Canal Co.,
Bridgewater Dept.,
New Botany Shed,
Water Street,
Manchester 3.

JEURO CONTAINERLINE

Jeuro Containerline
A joint service provided by:
V/O Sojuzvneshtrans
(All Soviet External Transport Corporation)
Moscow.

MAT Transport AG
Basle
Container Transport International (Japan)

Ltd (CTI)
PO Box 52, Yokohama Naka Sumire Bldg,
9-8, 2 chome, Ohgi-cho, Naka-ku, Yokohama
TELEPHONE: (681) 5681
TELEX: 7707

SERVICE:
Yokohama, Kobe and Osaka to Nakhodka thence by Trans-Siberian Railway and via

Hungary-Austria or via Poland-Germany to European destinations using an Intercontainer service rail link. There are three services monthly in each direction.
AGENTS:
Belgium and Luxembourg:
Belgian Pakhoed N.V. Antwerp
United Kingdom:
Anglo Soviet Shipping Company, London

ICTC

ICTC Intercontinental Container Transport Co-ordination S.a.
Huidevetterstraat 38, B-2000-Antwerp, Belgium
TELEPHONE: (03) 31 24 66
TELEX: 32823

DIRECTORS:
Jacques Mathieu (*President*)
G. van Strydonck (*Director & Manager*)
Pierre de Schepper (*Sales & Leasing*)
BRANCHES:
New York, Brussels, Kortrijk, Zeebrugge

CONTAINER SERVICES:
Full Loads mainly to Africa, Near and Middle East.
LEASING SERVICES:
General agents in Belgium and Luxemburg for Sea Containers Inc.

INTER-CONTINENTAL TRAILSEA

Intercontinental Trailsea Corporation,
11 Broadway, New York, NY 10004
TELEPHONE: 425-7860 and 943-8630
OFFICIALS:
Isaac Charchat (*Chairman*)
Zecharia Sitchin (*President*)
BRANCHES AND OFFICES:
US, Canada, UK, Western Europe, Japan, Australia, Hong Kong.
SERVICES:
An intermodal container express service linking 26 countries by United Cargo Corporation, a subsidiary.

Europe to the Far East across the US using the "Land-Bridge" service operated by the Land-Bridge Corporation, a subsidiary.
MAIN UK TERMINAL:
United Cargo Containers Ltd.,
Unit 7, Thames Side Industrial Estate, London E.16
Director: D. B. Wallace.
Telephone: 01-4763346

LEASING:
Per voyage and long-term leasing offered.
(See Leasing Section).
GENERAL:
ITC is the parent company of United Cargo Corporation, a world-wide container carrier and US non-vessel operator with headquarters in New York. The basic concept of ITC is to provide an inland to inland international container transport service.
Arrangements are made with inland carriers to establish their terminals as " UCC Receiving and Distributing Terminals," linked with some 200 UCC terminals established in 26 countries.
Using the Port of New York as the gateway and adding marine tariff rates to the inland carrier's rates, the shipper can be quoted one predetermined price to cover the cost of the full movement of the cargo from the receiving terminal to the distributing terminal at destination. Because the charges are based on rates per 100 lb and because containers eliminate the need for costly export packing,

the system is particularly economic for those shipping less than a full load at a time. A further facility is the issue by UCC of a Thru Bill of Lading which expedites both the movement of the cargo and payment for the goods.

FINANCE:
Movements of cargo are further speeded up through a "cash and carry" payment plan available from an affiliate, ITC Commercial Credit Card, Inc. whose U.K. office is. Commercial Credit Card Ltd., 16, New Street, London EC2.

DISTRIBUTION:
The concept of "Total Transportation" is further enhanced through the services of International Book Services, Inc, which moves imported books from containers to book stores or individual subscribers. The company plans to provide similar service to other trades.

INTER-CONTINENTAL TRANSPORTATION

Inter-Continental Transportation Inc.,
1130 US Highway No. 1
Elizabeth, New Jersey, 07201
TELEPHONE: 201-353 7400 (N.J.)
(212) 267-3211 (N.Y.)
EXECUTIVE IN CHARGE OF CONTAINER OPERATION:
Mark Newman (*Sales & Traffic*)
John F. Haney (*Operations*)
BRANCHES:
Boston, Mass; Philadelphia, Pa; Stratford,

Conn; Springfield, Mass; Albany N.Y.

CONTAINER SERVICES:
US North Atlantic Ports to Europe via ports in the Antwerp/Hamburg range—Daily.

TERMINALS:
Boston Mass.
Telephone: 617-268-9720
Philadelphia, Pa.
Telephone: 215-533-4827
Stratford, Con.

Telephone: 203-378-0468
Springfield, Mass.
Telephone: 203-745-1648
Albany, N.Y.
Telephone: 518-HE4-3164

17 Battery Place, New York,
New York 10004
TRADING SCOPE:
Between: US ports and foreign ports in continents of Africa, Asia, Europe, Australia, Central and South America.

INTERNATIONAL CONTAINER OPERATORS

International Container Operators A-S
Europaplads 2, 8000 Århus C, Denmark
TELEPHONE: 06 123577
TELEX: 4641
DIRECTOR: Mr. Ib Hansen
This is Freight Forwarder.
BRANCHES:
International Container Operators A-S, Færgehavn Nord, 2100 Copenhagen

CONTAINER ROUTES SERVED:
One weekly round trip
Århus/Felixstowe/Malmo/Copenhagen

CONTAINER TERMINALS USED:
Quay No. 14, Århus. ICO, A-S Århus

Telephone: 123577
CONTAINER LEASING SERVICES:
Containers provided for leasing.

CONTAINER PARK FACILITIES:
Quay No. 14, Århus.

INTERSTAR

Interstar International Transport Company and Forwarding Agents
Vredeman de Vriesstraat 38
Telephone: 202122
Telex: 23374

Shipments to and from any part of the world, Chartering, Warehousing, Insurance, Regular transports by truck and tankcar throughout Western Europe.

INTERNATIONAL FERRY FREIGHT

International Ferry Freight Limited

Whiterock Warehouse
Avenue Industrial Estate,
Romford, RM3 0BY, Essex
TELEPHONE: Ingrebourne 49711
TELEX: 262383

EXECUTIVES IN CHARGE OF CONTAINER SERVICES:
Romford—V. W. Martin
Hull—J. N. A. Marshall

BRANCHES:
Hull, Middlesbrough, Rotterdam, Mannheim, Hamn, Basle.

SERVICES WITH OWN OR LEASED CONTAINERS:
Door to door services. UK to Scandinavia and Europe and v.v. Daily road and rail services using ports of Hull, Tilbury, Middlesbrough and Harwich via Rotterdam, Antwerp, Hamburg, Halsingborg and Copenhagen. ISO 20', 30', 40' containers available— standard tilt, and open top, also bulk 20 ft and 30 ft containers.

IRISH FERRYWAYS

Irish Ferryways (CIE)

Connolly Station, Amiens Street, Dublin 1
TELEPHONE: 42941
TELEX: 5153
DIRECTORS:
S. Linehan (*General Manager*)
GENERAL:
Irish Ferryways was formed by Coras Iompair Eireann and Containerway and Roadferry Ltd, the British-based unit-load operator in Europe, owned by the British National Freight Corporation. Irish Ferryways handle container freight from Ireland (Dublin, Drogheda or New Ross) to Britain, and onwards to all European countries. Their new terminal at

Tolka Quay, Dublin, is one of the most modern in Ireland. It has equipment for handling all types of containers—general refrigerated, flats and bulk liquid.
CONTAINER SERVICES:
Dublin/Preston—Daily
Drogheda/Preston—Twice weekly
Larne/Ardrossan—Daily
New Ross/Newport—Twice weekly
CONTAINER TERMINALS USED:
(1) Tolka Quay, Dublin
Telephone: Dublin 47948

(2) Albert Edward Dock, Preston
Telephone: Preston 26255

Irish Ferryways terminal at Tolka Quay, Dublin.

(3) The Quay, New Ross, Co. Wexford
Telephone: New Ross 21445

(4) East Lock, Alexandra Dock, Newport, Mon.

Irish Ferryways (Ferry Trailers Ltd.)

Tower Bridge House,
198-204 Tower Bridge Road, London SE1
TELEPHONE: 01-407-4533
TELEX: 263772
GENERAL:
See entry under Containerway.

EXECUTIVE IN CHARGE OF CONTAINER OPERATIONS:

Kersten Hunik's International Transportbedrijf NV

Westplein 2
Telephone: 114720

Kühne & Nagel Speditions—Aktiengesellschaft

REGISTERED OFFICE:
D-2800 Bremen 1,
Grosse Weserbruecke, Postf. 27
TELEPHONE: (0421) 360 51
TELEX: 0245656
HEAD OFFICE:
D2000, Hamburg 1,
Raboisen 40, Postf. 1084
TELEPHONE: (0411) 59 10 01
TELEX: 02162084
DIRECTORS:
Alfred Kühne (President, Supervisory Board)
Ludwig Rössinger (Vice-President)
Klaus-Michael Kühne (Chairman, Executive Board)
SUBSIDIARY COMPANIES OPERATING CONTAINER SERVICES:
Austria:
Kühne & Nagel Gesellschaft mbH
A-1010 Vienna, Renngasse 10/VII
Telephone: 635611
Telex: 074771
Belgium:
Kühne & Nagel pvba
Van Eycklei 14, B2000, Antwerp
Telephone: 313 860
Telex: 31305
Also at Brussels.
Canada:
Kühne & Nagel (Canada) Ltd.
1578 K Heron Road, Ottawa 8, Ont.
Telephone: (613) 7338699
Also at Calgary, Edmonton, Hamilton, Montreal, Quebec, Toronto, Vancouver, Winnipeg.
France:
Kühne & Nagel SA
28 rue du Puits Dixme, BP29, F94, Thiais
Telephone: 6776600
Telex: 20863
Germany:
Registered and Head offices given above.
Also at Berlin, Bielefeld, Bonn, Braunschweig, Bremerhaven, Cologne, Dusseldorf, Frankfurt, Hagen/Westf, Hannover, Luebeck, Mannheim, Munich, Nuernberg, Passau, Regensburg, Stuttgart, Wuppertal.
Great Britain:

Telephone: Newport 51237

(5) Ripple Road. Barking, Essex
Telephone: 592-7344

IRISH FERRYWAYS

S. Linehan (General Manager) Dublin

SERVICES WITH OWN OR LEASED CONTAINERS:
Preston to Dublin—Daily.
Newport to New Ross—Twice Weekly.
Preston to Drogheda—Twice weekly.
Ardrossan to Larne—Daily.

KERSTEN HUNIK

Telex: 22184-22190
International Carriers, International Forwarding, Grouping Service, Rhine Chartering, Storage, Insurances.

KÜHNE & NAGEL

Kühne & Nagel Ltd.
60 St. Martins Lane,
London WC2N 4JU
Telephone: 01-836 3522
Telex: 24971
Also at Birmingham, Bristol, Harwich, Liverpool, Manchester.
Hong Kong:
Kühne & Nagel (Hong Kong) Ltd.
Room 203, Lake Yew Bldg, 50/52 Queens Road Central, P.O. Box 16657
Telephone: 247027
Telex: HX3681
Iran:
Transco Express Co. Ltd.
307 Avenue Shah-Reza
Air France Bldg., PO Box 1160
Tehran
Telephone: 600611
Telex: 215447
Italy:
Kühne & Nagel S.a.R.L.
Via Cairoli 8, CP 794
1-161 24 Genoa
Telephone: 297609
Telex: 27627
Also at Ancona, Bologna, Firenze, Milan, Turin, Trieste.
Japan:
Unitrans Ltd.
No. 1, 1-chome, Nihonbashi Edobashi, Chuo-ku, Central POB 2052, Tokyo
Telephone: 2732561
Telex: 4676
Also at Osaka.
Kenya:
Kühne & Nagel Ltd.
Nakufreight Ltd.
Raherntulla Trust Bldg, Government Road, PO Box 1423, Nairobi
Also at Mombasa.
Netherlands:
Kühne & Nagel Expeditie en Scheepvaart NV
Glashaven 48/58, Post 1294, Rotterdam 1
Telephone: (010) 144422
Also at Amsterdam, Schiphol, 's-Heerenberg, Venrio.
Portugal:

(6) Harbour Street, Ardrossan, Ayrshire
Telephone: 4111
Telex: 778163

Irish Ferryways Terminal.

Kühne & Nagel Lda.
Praca Duqueda Terceira 11-2°, Lisbon 2
Telephone: 34405
Telex: 1411
Also at Oporto.
Singapore:
Nakufreight Private Ltd.
63 Robinson Road, PO Box 2795, Singapore 1
Telephone: 95652
Telex: RS320
Republic of South Africa:
Kühne & Nagel (Pty) Ltd.
601 Longsbank Building, 187 Bree Street, PO Box 11131, Johannesburg
Telephone: 51615
Telex: 550257
Also at Capetown, Durban, Port Elizabeth.
Spain:
Kühne & Nagel SA
Calle Rodriguez, San Pedro 2, 1°, Madrid 15
Telephone: 2248726
Telex: 27299
Also at Alicante, Barcelona, Bilbao, Irun, Port Bou, Valencia.
Switzerland:
Kühne & Nagel Aktiengesellschaft
CH 4002 Basle, Aeschenvorstadt 4
Telephone: (061) 237023
Also at Geneva, Zurich.
USA:
Kühne & Nagel Inc.
30 Church Street, New York, N.Y. 10007
Telephone: 732 3900
Telex: 126707
Also at Chicago, Houston, Charlotte, Los Angeles.
SERVICES USING OWN OR LEASED CONTAINERS
Inter—European
Europe—North America
Europe—Japan Via T.S.R.
Europe—Iran
CONTAINERS IN SERVICE
Dry cargo   30   20 × 8 × 8
Dry cargo   76   30 × 8 × 8
Tilt   10   20 × 8 × 8
In addition, several hundred units of various sizes and types are always on hire, mostly on a long term basis.

LANGSTAFF, EREMBERT

Langstaff, Erembert and Co. Ltd.,

Leadenhall Buildings, London, EC3
TELEPHONE: 01-626 0073
TELEX: 935629
DIRECTORS AND EXECUTIVES IN CHARGE OF CONTAINER SERVICES:
F. H. Cuttell (Managing Director)
R. E. Boyd—Bradford
G. Hodgson—Liverpool
A. Whitney—London
BRANCHES:
Liverpool

Hargreaves Buildings, 5 Chapel Street, Liverpool, 3.
Bradford
Thorpe Chambers, 12a Ivegate, Bradford, 1
Manchester
2 Mount Street, Manchester 2
Hull
Samman House, Bowlalley Lane, Hull
London Airport
Heathrow Airport—London, Hounslow, Middlesex.

Manchester Airport
Wythenshawe, Manchester, 22
SERVICES WITH OWN OR LEASED CONTAINERS:
United Kingdom to Canada, USA and Australia.
TERMINALS USED:
Hansons Ltd., Leeds Road, Huddersfield
Manchester Ship Canal Co., Water Street, Manchester.
All terminals of Express Container Transport Ltd.

LEP TRANSPORT

LEP Transport Ltd.,
Sunlight Wharf,
Upper Thames Street.
London, EC4
TELEPHONE: 01-236 5050
TELEX: 25678
DIRECTORS:
R. K. Leeper (*Chairman*)
R. J. D. Leeper (*Managing*)
D. St.J. Edwards
J. R. Braun
T. W. B. Leeper
R. W. Studer
BRANCHES:
United Kingdom:
Belfast, Birmingham, Bradford, Bristol,
Dover, Dundee, East Kilbride, Felixstowe,
Glasgow, Goole, Grangemouth, Harwich, Hull,
Ipswich, Leeds, Leicester, Leith, Liverpool,
Manchester, Middlesbrough, Newcastle-on-
Tyne, Newport (Mon.), Northampton, Not-
tingham, Sheffield, Southampton, Slough,
Stoke-on-Trent, Tilbury.
Overseas Associated Companies:
Australia, Canada, New Zealand, South
Africa, USA, Austria, Belgium, France,
Germany, Italy, Eire, Norway, Portugal,
Switzerland.
SERVICES WITH OWN OR LEASED CONTAINERS
London—Dublin Daily
Liverpool—Dublin Three to four times a
week
Birmingham—Dublin Five times a week
Bristol—Dublin—Weekly
London—Belfast Two to three times a week
Liverpool—Belfast Three to four times a
week
Birmingham—Belfast Two to three times a
week
Sheffield—Belfast weekly
Sheffield—Dublin weekly
EUROPE
All Services Feeding All Europe
London—Rotterdam Daily.
London—Dunkirk Three Times Per Week.
London—Antwerp Three Times Per Week.
London—Malmö Weekly
London—Copenhagen Twice per week.
London—Oslo Weekly
London—Boston Weekly
London—Gothenburg Twice weekly.
London—Stockholm Three times per week.
Harwich—Zeebrugge Twice Daily.
Birmingham—Rotterdam Weekly.
Birmingham—Antwerp Weekly.
Birmingham—Hamburg Twice Weekly.
Birmingham—Belfast Three times per
week
Birmingham—Cologne Weekly
Birmingham—Stockholm Weekly
Birmingham—Gothenburg Weekly
Hull—Gothenburg Three Times Weekly.
Hull—Stockholm/Norrkoping Three Times
Weekly.
Hull—Oslo Weekly.
Hull—Rotterdam Five times weekly
Goole—Antwerp Three Times Weekly.
Goole—Amsterdam Three Times Weekly

Immingham—Copenhagen Weekly.
Manchester—Aachen Twice weekly
Manchester—Basle Twice weekly.
Glasgow—Basle Weekly
Glasgow—Vienna Weekly
Glasgow—Paris Weekly
Glasgow—Milan Weekly
Glasgow—Stuttgart Weekly
Glasgow—Rotterdam Weekly
Glasgow—Gothenburg Weekly
Glasgow—Stockholm Weekly
Sheffield—Basle Weekly

Bradford—Gothenburg Weekly.
Bradford—Stockholm Weekly.

NORTH AMERICA AND AUSTRALIA
London—New York/Baltimore Weekly.
London—Freemantle/Sydney/Melbourne/
Adelaide/Brisbane Weekly.
London—Montreal/Toronto Weekly.
London—USA West Coast Ports Weekly.
Northampton—Boston Weekly
Northampton—New York Weekly.
Northampton—Chicago Weekly.
Bristol—USA and Canada Weekly.
Liverpool—USA/Canada/Australia Weekly.
Manchester—Canada and Australia
Weekly.
Birmingham—USA/Canada/Australia
Weekly.
Bradford—Boston Weekly
Sheffield—New York Weekly.

CONTAINER TERMINALS USED:
LONDON
Sunlight Wharf, (OWN)
37 Upper Thames Street, EC4
Telephone: 01-236 5050
Telex: 25678
Container Controller UK/Europe—
Mr. R. Wootton.

Charlton Freight Depot, (OWN)
Anchor and Hope Lane, SE7.
Telephone: 01-858 3261
Corney Road, (OWN)
Chiswick, W4.
Telephone: 01-995 1300
Shed No. 1 (OWN)
London International Freight Terminal,
Temple Mill Lane, E13.
Telephone: 01-534 0036
BIRMINGHAM
Dennis Road, (OWN)
Birmingham 12
Telephone: 021-449 4971
Telex: 33130
Birmingham Container Base,
College Road, Perry Barr, Birmingham 22B.
Telephone: 021-356 7952
BRADFORD:
Buck Street,
Bradford.
Telephone: 0274-22341
Telex: 51364
BRISTOL
808A Bath Road, (OWN)
Brislington, Bristol 4.
Telephone 0272-27312

GOOLE
Belgravia, (OWN)
Goole.
Telephone: 3332
Telex: 56143
HULL
Valetta Street, (OWN)
Marfleet, Hull
Telephone: 0482 36684
Representatives:
LEEDS
Leeds Container Base,
Wakefield Road, Stourton, Leeds 10
Telephone: 0532 73681
LEICESTER
Norman Road, (OWN)
Thurmaston
Telephone: 0533 4233803
LIVERPOOL
Chaloner Street, Liverpool
Telephone: 051-236 2582
Liverpool Container Base,
Orrell Lane, Bootle, Lancashire
MANCHESTER
Lyons Road, (OWN)
Trafford Park, Manchester
Telephone: 061-236 8791
Manchester Container Base,
Barton Dock Road, Manchester, M31. 2LP.
Telephone: 061-748 9511
NORTHAMPTON
Ransome Road,
Northampton, NN4. 9AA
Telephone: 0604-62123
SHEFFIELD:
Ordnance Depot,
Skew Hill Lane,
Grenoside, Sheffield
Telephone: 0742-28061
SOUTHAMPTON
c/o Container Depot,
West Bay Road, Southampton
Telephone: 0703-24586
STOKE-ON-TRENT
Willow Row, (OWN)
Longton, Stoke-on-Trent
Telephone: 0782-32296
SCOTLAND
26 Glenburn Road, (OWN)
College Milton, East Kilbride
Telephone: 0355-2 25341
Container Base Scotland,
Gartsherrie Road, Coatbridge, Lanarkshire
Telephone: 27151
Telex: 778375
CONTAINER CONTROLLER GERMANY
Mr. A. Schmirler,
Lassen & Co., Stuttgart.
Telephone: Stuttgart 297446
CONTAINER CONTROLLER SWITZERLAND
Mr. R. Naef,
Natural A.G., Basel
Telephone: Basel 345050
CONTAINER CONTROLLER AUSTRIA
Mr. Barwig
Intercontinentale A.G., Vienna
Telephone: Vienna 340606

Lep Transport Pty Ltd.
543 Little Collins Street,
Melbourne, Vic. 3000
GPO Box 2389V., Melbourne Vic. 3001
TELEPHONE: 62.6531
TELEX: AA31638
Lep Transport (N.S.W.) Pty Ltd.
352 Kent Street, Sydney, N.S.W. 2000
POSTAL ADDRESS:
GPO Box 4084, Sydney, N.S.W. 2001
TELEPHONE: 29.7845
TELEX: AA21249

BRANCHES:
South Australia:
289 Pirie Street, Adelaide, S.A. 5000
POSTAL ADDRESS:
PGO Box 453D, Adelaide, S.A. 5001
TELEPHONE: 23.6300

Western Australia:
88b Norman Street, North Innaloo, W.A.
6018
POSTAL ADDRESS:
P.O. Box 17, Doubleview W.A. 6018

TELEPHONE: 46.5865
DIRECTORS AND EXECUTIVES IN CHARGE OF
CONTAINERS:
Mr. R. C. Goodwright (*Managing Director*)
Melbourne
Mr. B. W. Dardis (*Director*) Sydney
Mr. A. W. Blissenden (*Director*) Melbourne
Mr. J. N. Fahlbusch (*Representative*)
Adelaide
Mr. D. T. Smith (*Representative*) Perth
SERVICES:
Australia to Europe, USA, Japan.

MACANDREWS

Macpak Tilt unit loaded with Spanish oranges.

A Douglas NS8 Tugmaster with U-wagon manoeuvring MacPak containers in the MacPak compound at Southampton.

Mac Andrews & Co. Limited
Plantation House, Mincing Lane. London, EC3
TELEPHONE: 01-626 1543
TELEGRAMS: MacAndrew London EC3
TELEX: 888352
CENTRAL OFFICE FOR SPAIN:
Plaza Duque Medinaceli, 5, Apartado 441, Barcelona-2, Spain
TELEPHONE: 231-37-07
TELEGRAMS: MacAndrews Barcelona
TELEX: 54752
DIRECTORS:
Hon. A. C. R. Weir (*Chairman*)
Hon. J. V. Weir
A. L. Billington
P. B. Larsen
Mogens Steincke (Danish)
K. G. Reid
OFFICIALS:
B. V. Caskie (*Manager, Macpak Container Service*)
D. Sparrowe (*Manager Container Service, Madrid and Bilbao*)
J. M. Andrade (*Manager, Bilbao*)

BRANCHES:
Bilbao (with office at Santurce), Madrid, Tarragona, Burriana, Valencia, Almeria, Malaga and Seville.

CONTAINER ROUTES SERVED:
Macpak Container Service, Bilbao—Southampton—Bilbao

Roll-on/roll-off per Swedish m.s. *Patricia* and *Hispania*.
Liverpool—Bilbao—Liverpool
Lift-on/Lift-off per *Velazquez* (Chartered).
Liverpool—Barcelona—Valencia—Liverpool
Lift-on/Lift-off *Cervantes* and *Churruca* (Chartered).

CONTAINER TERMINALS USED:
Macpack Terminal, Southampton
Representative:
MacAndrews & Co. Limited
Telephone: 27988

Macpak Terminal, Santurce (Bilbao).
Port Superintendent: S. Rushton
Mac Andrews & Co. Ltd., Santurce
Telephone: 251321
Telex: 32036

CONTAINER PARK FACILITIES AND BREAK BULK PACKING AND STORAGE AREAS:
Southampton Macpak Terminal with inland depots at Stratford, Birmingham, Manchester, Carfin, Liverpool, Swansea, Sheffield, Bradford.
Santurce Macpak Terminal (Bilbao).

MACLEOD

M. MacLeod & Co. Ltd.,
143 West Regent Street, Glasgow, C2

TELEPHONE: 041-248 4171
TELEX: 778426

OFFICIALS:

J. Ralph (*Director*)
H. J. Kennedy (*Freight Manager*)

CONTAINER SERVICES:
Glasgow to Vienna—Weekly.
Glasgow to Basle—Weekly
TERMINAL USED:
Coatbridge.

M.A.T. TRANSPORT

MAT Container Depot—Peterborough

MAT Transport Limited,
Arnold House, 36/41 Holywell Lane, London, EC2
TELEPHONE: 01-247-6500
TELEX: 883225/886384 (main office)
885136 (container dept. direct)
DIRECTORS:
R. F. Williams (*Chairman*)
P. A. Kunzler (*Managing Director*)
S. D. A. Guppy, R. W. Kunzler, G. C. T. Randall, A. Armstrong, F. A. Lenzinger, P. J. Cox, C. J. Cole, S. R. Taylor
BRANCHES:
Hull: King George V Dock, Hedon Road.
Harwich: 3 Coller Road, Parkeston Quay.
Knowle: Knowle & Dorridge Goods Station Knowle, Warwickshire.
Telephone: 056-45 4383
Manchester: MAT Transport, 42 Container Base (Manchester) Ltd
Telephone: 061 748 9417
Dover: Room 38, Southern House, Dover Marine.
Associated Companies: MAT Transport AG Basle, 50 Peter Merian Strasse.
Zurich, 88, Sihlfeldstrasse.

CONTAINER ROUTES SERVED:
Harwich—Zeebrugge, Rotterdam, Bremerhaven, Dunkirk, Esbjerg.
Hull—Rotterdam, Antwerp, Esbjerg, Gothenburg, Amsterdam, Hamburg, Bremen, Rostock.
Dover—Dunkirk.
Felixstowe—Malmo, Rotterdam, Antwerp, Helsinki, New York, Gothenburg.

CONTAINER TERMINALS USED:
Depot No. 6 London International Freight Terminal.
Morris Cowley Goods Station, Cowley, Oxford.

CONTAINER LEASING SERVICES:
MAT Transport does not lease containers, but own containers and utilise these containers in providing the through transport services to exporters and importers.

CONTAINER PARK FACILITIES AND BREAK BULK PACKING AND STORAGE:
Hull, Dover, Felixstowe plus: MAT Transit depot at Zeebrugge; MAT Transport, Popple Street, Hedon Road, Hull, Knowle and Dorridge Goods Station, Harwich and Felixstowe.

MASPED

MASPED Hungarian General Forwarding Enterprise
See entry under Hungary.

MEADOWS

Thomas Meadows & Company Limited,
36, Grosvenor Gardens,
London S.W.1.
TELEPHONE: 01-730 0266
TELEX: 27241
DIRECTORS:
S. J. Fetherston, R. J. Fetherston (*Governing Directors*)
J. M. Fetherston (*Chief Executive*)
E. J. Bishop
A. L. Boyes
W. P. Brown
A. Fetherston
F. T. Morgan (*Company Secretary*)

BRANCHES:
Overseas: including subsidiary companies: Canada, U.S.A., Australia, New Zealand, South Africa, France and Belgium
U.K.: Birmingham, Bradford, Bristol, Glasgow, Grangemouth, Hull, Ipswich, Leicester, Leith, Liverpool, Manchester, Nottingham, Northampton, Sheffield, Stoke-on-Trent.
CONTAINER ROUTES SERVED:
Full Load and Groupage Services: Canada – Montreal, Toronto, Vancouver, Winnipeg.
Italy – Chiasso, Milan
United States – New York, Boston, Baltimore
Switzerland—Basle, Zurich, Buchs
Denmark—Copenhagen, Esjberg

Sweden—Gothenburg, Stockholm
Finland—Helsinki
Ireland—Dublin
Australia—Full load and groupage to all five main ports.
France (via Paris), Austria, Northern Ireland (via Belfast), Holland, Central and Southern Germany, Norway.
Full load services to South Africa, Japan,

CONTAINER TERMINALS:
All owned by Thomas Meadows & Co. Ltd.
Name of terminal:

Export:
London South East Tel: 01-987 6208

London North West (Colnbrook, Bucks.)
   Tel: 01-964 2871
Birmingham Tel: 021 706 6122
Bradford Tel: 0274 33611
Bristol Tel: 0272 49351
Glasgow Tel: 041-887 1260
Grangemouth Tel: 03-244 2735
Hull Tel: 0482 25541
Ipswich Tel: 0473 74411
Leicester Tel: 0533 760221
Manchester Tel: 061-832 8401
Northampton Tel: 0604 62861

Meadowfreight West of London Container Depot

Nottingham Tel: 0602 51045
Sheffield Tel: 0742 40607
Liverpool Tel: 051-227 2070

In addition Thomas Meadows participate in bonded break bulk facilities in London, Birmingham, Liverpool, Manchester and Glasgow.

CONTAINER LEASING SERVICES:
Containers are available for leasing on either long term or round trip basis for use in all trades.

MID-PACIFIC FREIGHT FORWARDERS

Mid Pacific Freight Forwarders
1560 West 12th Street,
Long Beach, California 90813
TELEPHONE: (213) 775-7161
TELEX: (Cable Code) Mid Trans
OFFICIALS:
J. J. Connell (*Vice President*)
J. V. Marion (*Director Intermodal Development*)

BRANCHES:
Long Beach, Oakland, Honolulu.
GENERAL:
The Company is a subsidiary of Signal Trucking Service Ltd.
SERVICES USING LEASED CONTAINERS:
Full and consolidated loads to Hawaii, Guam, Japan and Australia by first available vessel.

AGENTS:
Mid Pacific Transportation Systems Inc.
Agana, Guam

LEASING:
Equipment leased through Signal Trucking Service Ltd.

MISSOURI PACIFIC INTERMODAL TRANSPORT

Missouri Pacific Intermodal Transport Inc.,
Room 1151, Missouri Pacific Building,
210 North 13th Street, St. Louis Missouri 63103

TELEPHONE: 314-622-0123
TELEX: 044-7105, 044-7382, 044-813

DIRECTORS AND EXECUTIVES IN CHARGE OF CONTAINER SERVICES:
Mr. D. B. Jenks (*Chairman of Board*)
Mr. C. T. Groton, Jr. (*President*)
Mr. H. A. Smith, (*Vice-President*)
Mr. H. M. Prater, (*Vice-President*)
Mr. M. M. Hennelly, (*Vice-President and General Counsel*)
Mr. R. A. Martin (*Vice-President—Sales*)
Mr. T. D. Rodman (*Controller*)

Mr. L. A. Bruns (*Treasurer*)
Mr. C. A. Rockwell (*Secretary*)

SERVICES WITH OWN orLEASED CONTAINERS:
New Orleans, Houston and Galveston to Rotterdam, Amsterdam, Antwerp, Hamburg, Bremen and London

TERMINALS:
Missouri Pacific Railroad terminals etc.
New Orleans
Telephone: 504-523-2971
Houston:
Telephone: 713-227-3151
Galveston:
Telephone: 713-227-3151

A Missouri Pacific Distribution and Consolidation Centre

MODERN INTERMODAL TRAFFIC

Modern Intermodal Traffic Corp,
1417 Clay Street, Oakland, California 94612
L. P. Sargent, (*Managing Director*)
TRADING SCOPE:
1 From: US North Atlantic Ports and Hampton Roads/Eastport, Maine Range.
To: England, Scotland, Wales, Northern Ireland, UK.
2 From: Great Britain, Northern Ireland and Eire.

To: US North Atlantic Ports and Portland, Maine/Hampton Roads Range.
3 From: US Pacific Coast Ports.
To: Japan, Hong Kong and Manila.
4 From: Ports in California, Oregon and Washington.
To: UK, Ireland, Scandinavia and Continental Europe.
5 From: US Atlantic and Gulf Ports.
To: Japan, Okinawa, Korea, Taiwan, Hong Kong, Philippine Islands, Vietnam, Cambodia

and Laos.
6 From: Antwerp, Rotterdam and Amsterdam.
To: New York, Boston, Philadelphia, Baltimore and ports in the Hampton Roads, Virginia Range.
7 From: Ports in Japan, Korea and Okinawa.
To: Pacific Coast Ports in California, Oregon and Washington.
8 From: US Pacific Coast Ports.
To: Ports in Australia and New Zealand.

MONDIA

N.V. Mondia
Kaai 259
Antwerp
TELEPHONE: (03) 42.21.20
TELEX: (03) 435

BRANCHES AND ASSOCIATED COMPANIES IN BELGIUM
N.V. Corbeel-Mondia SA
Rue Tielemausstraat 2, Brussels
  Telephone: (02) 27.98.40

Telex: (09) 337
N.V. Mondia
Wiedauwkaai 87, Ghent
Telephone: (09) 51.86.21
Telex: (09) 337

N.V. Germany-Mondia SA
Avenue Georges Truffaut 49
Liege
Telephone: (04) 62.78.50
Telex: (04) 411
N.V. Mondia
Henry Fordlaan, Genk
Telephone: (011) 53609

G. C. Morley
25 Sunbridge Road,
Bradford 1, Yorkshire
TELEPHONE: (0274) Bradford 33276
TELEX: 51134
OFFICIALS IN CHARGE OF CONTAINER
SERVICES:
G. C. Morley (*Principal*)
K. Ellik (*Sales Development and Co-ordination*)
P. Hayton (*TIR Trailers*)
A. P. Bannon (*Overseas Containers, Irish Unit Loads and Train Ferry*)
S. Warriner (*Containers, Europe*)

SERVICES WITH OWN OR LEASED CONTAINERS
Full Loads—Daily to:
Austria, Belgium, Denmark, Finland, France, Holland, Ireland, West Germany, Northern Ireland, Italy, Norway, Spain, Sweden, Switzerland, Yugoslavia.
Groupage Services daily to:
Dusseldorf, Calais, Dunkirk, Amsterdam, Rotterdam.
Groupage Services twice weekly to:
Antwerp, Basle, Brussels, Buchs, Chiasso, Dumodossola, Milan, Roubaix.

N.V. Romar SA

12, Rue des Cent Bonniers
Anderlues
Telephone: (07) 52.50.61
Telex: (07) 307

BRANCHES-EUROPE:
Basle, Bremen, Bodegraven, Duisberg,

MORLEY

TERMINAL:
City Road Depot,
Thornton Road,
Bradford 1.
Facilities include a warehouse with 46,451 m² (500,000 ft²) and a container/trailer park with an area of 6,690 m² (72,000 ft²).

EQUIPMENT IN SERVICE:
Containers:
20 ft End load box type
Full tilt containers
Side tilt containers
Side door containers
Open Top
Box type
Removable Hard Top
30 ft Box Type end loading
Full Tilt containers
Side door containers
40 ft Box type end loading Side Door containers.
T.I.R. Trailers
Box Type Soft Top
Full Tilt and Flats
10 m and 12 m
Semi-low loaders and low loaders

Eberbach, Frankfurt, Hamburg, Karlsruhe, Kehl, Köln, Ludwigshafen, Lyon, Manheim, Mainz, Milan, Nijmegen, Paris, Rotterdam, Speyer, Strasbourg.

SERVICES:
Throughout Europe
Europe-USA

BRANCHES:
Harwich:
47 King's Head Street,
Telephone: Harwich 2316
Telex: 98304
Hull:
King George Dock,
Telephone: Hull 78136
Telex: 52414
Felixstowe:
Pier House
Telephone:
Telex: 98304
Liverpool:
Irwell Chambers East,
Fazakerly Street,
Telephone: 051-236 4041
Telex:
London:
131 Wapping High Street, E1
Telephone: 01-481 1865
Telex: 884160
Manchester:
Swinton House, Cromwell Road,
Salford 6
Telephone:
Telex:

MOVERS' & WAREHOUSEMENS' ASSOC.

Movers' and Warehousemen's Ass'n, of America, Inc,
Suite 1101, Warner Bldg,
Washington, DC 20004

OFFICIALS:
Carroll F. Genovese (*Agent*)

TRADING SCOPE:
Between United States ports and foreign ports in the continents of Africa, Asia, Europe, Australia, North America, South America and foreign ports of the Islands in the oceans and seas between and adjacent to such continents.

NORTHERN IRELAND TRAILERS

Northern Ireland Trailers (Scotland) Ltd.,
85 Polmadie Road, Glasgow, C5
A member of the P & O Group of Companies
TELEPHONE: 041-429 1151
TELEX: 778461

PRINCIPAL OFFICIAL:
J. M. Campbell (*General Manager*)
BRANCHES:
Ardrossan
Telephone: 0294 3045
Telex: 77195
Larne
Telephone: 0574 2343
Telex: 74536
Belfast
Telephone: 0232 746431
Telex: 74553

Pacific Intermodal Corporation
545, Sansome Street,
PO Box 2357
San Francisco, California 94126
John H. Robinson (*President*)
TELEPHONE: (415) 433-4218
TELEX: RCA 27390

Pacific Van & Storage Co, Inc,
1415 West Torrance Blvd,
Torrance, California

Northern Ireland Trailer (Scotland) Ltd depot at Polmadie, near Glasgow
SERVICES WITH OWN OR LEASED CONTAINERS:
Scotland to Northern Ireland and Republic of Ireland—Daily.
STORAGE, PACKING AND UNPACKING FACILITIES:
Groupage facilities at Glasgow.
Storage facilities at Ardrossan.

PACIFIC INTERMODAL

Peter Gilbert (*Manager*)
TRADING SCOPE:
Between: US Ports and World Ports.

GENERAL:
The Company is part of the Harper Group.

PACIFIC VAN AND STORAGE

Henry A. Pontes (*President*)
TRADING SCOPE:
Between: US Ports and World Ports.

Seawheel container at Harwich (Parkeston quay)

Pitt & Scott Ltd.,
Eden Grove London N7
TELEPHONE: 01-607 7321
TELEX: 21857
DIRECTORS AND PRINCIPAL OFFICIALS:
D. M. Scott and M. K. Scott (*Joint Managing*)
J. W. Ellis (*in charge of Containers*)
K. Wyatt (*Manager-Container Groupage*)
Telephone: Whitehall 3.3440

PRF Group
2121 91st Street, North Bergen N.J. 07047
Puerto Rico Forwarding Co. Inc.,
European Container Service,
Virgin Islands Transport
TELEPHONE: 201-432-1212
TELEX: 126 194
OFFICIALS:
H. V. Kantzer (*President*)
Max Margolin (*Executive Vice-President and Treasurer*)
Rolfe Kuelke (*Vice-President ECS*)

TERMINALS AND BRANCHES:
Northford, Conn.
Telephone: 203-239-7007
Atlanta, Ga.
Telephone: 404-351-8780
Boston, Mass.
Telephone: 617-288-2414
Chicago, Ill.
Telephone: 312-594-7550
Cleveland, Ohio
Telephone: 216-288-3186
Jacksonville, Fla.
Telephone: 904-768-3468
Miami, Fla.
Telephone: 305-888-1457
Milwaukee, Wis.
Telephone: 414-342-4888
New York, N.Y.
Telephone: 212-524-3010
North Bergen, N.J.
Telephone: 201-861-4650
San Juan, P.R.
Telephone: 789-2183
SERVICES:
European Container Service:
USA and the United Kingdom

P.S.A. Transport Ltd.,
70 Old Broad Street, London, EC2.
TELEPHONE: 01-283 2424
TELEX: 23806
DIRECTORS AND EXECUTIVES IN CHARGE OF CONTAINER OPERATIONS:
R. Johnson (*Managing Director*)

Ranking Kuhn (Freight) Ltd.,
Cape House, 787 Commercial Road,
London E.14
TELEPHONE: 01 987 5090 (20 lines)
TELEX: 987074

Reimann Stok & Kersken's Vereenigde Expeditiebedrijven NV
Glashaven 8a
Telephone: 136010

Royalpac Corporation,
24 Stone Street, New York,
New York

PITT AND SCOTT

BRANCHES:
Pitt & Scott Ltd., 65 Birkett Street, Liverpool 3
Telephone: 051-207 3132
Pitt & Scott Ltd., 1/3 Dixon Street, Glasgow 1
Telephone: 041-248 5521
Pitt & Scott Ltd., 24 Rue du Mont Thabor, Paris
Telephone: 010 3310 733362

PRF GROUP

The PRF Depot at San Juan P.R.

USA and Austria, Belgium, Denmark, Finland, France, West Germany, Northern Italy, Norway, Luxemburg, Netherlands, Sweden, Switzerland
Weekly or more frequent services via New York.
Puerto Rican Forwarding Co. Ltd.,
USA to San Juan, Puerto Rico
Virgin Island Transport
USA via New York, Jacksonville and Miami to St. Thomas, St. Croix and St. John V.I.

PSA TRANSPORT

J. Kosinski
D. Payne

BRANCHES:
PSA Transport Ltd.
15A Manor Street, Hull, Yorks.

RANKING KUHN

DIRECTOR IN CHARGE OF CONTAINER SERVICES:
J. J. Burke
BRANCHES:
Liverpool, Great Yarmouth, Felixstowe,

REIMANN STOK & KERSKEN

Telex: 21554
Forwarding, packing, storage, road transport, airfreight, National and International groupage services, ferry transport.

ROYALPAC

Robert M. Weiss (*Executive Vice-President*)
TRADING SCOPE:
Between: US Ports and World Ports.

Pitt & Scott Corp., 55, Liberty Street, New York NY 10005
Telephone: 212-267 8884
SERVICES WITH OWN OR LEASED CONTAINERS:
All European, North American and Pacific routes

TERMINALS USED:
Participation facilities at all main port and inland container terminals.

Frequent services are operated on the above routes.
OTHER ACTIVITIES:
New England Forwarding Co, Inc.
ICC-Part IV Car loading company serving 37 US States on Import/Export traffic

The Group operates domestic freight forwarding and motor carrier services air freight operations both domestic and international.

Telephone: Hull 36639
Telex: 52517

SERVICE WITH OWN CONTAINERS:
Refrigerated containers between Poland and UK via London and Ipswich and Gdynia.

Dover, Rotterdam and Milan.

SERVICES WITH OWN OR LEASED CONTAINERS:
Groupage to Italy Switzerland, and Persian Gulf

RUYS & CO.

Ruys & Co.

Head Office, Veerhaven 7,
P.O. Box 966
Telephone: 114800
Cables: Ruys
Chartering Dept.: Telex: 21348. Cables:

Ruyscha
Liner Agents, Agents for tankers and trampers, Bunkering Agents, Chartering and Insurance Brokers, Sale and Purchase Brokers, Forwarding Agents (import, export, customs clearance, unit load operators, groupage services, warehousing), Rhine transports, Cargo Superintendents, Air Freight Agents, Con-

solidators, Passage and Travel Agents.
Branch Office: Airport, Rotterdam
Telephone: 283835
Telex: 23399
Branch Office: Europoort, Scheldeweg 5,
Rozenburg
Telephone: 01-885-3290
Telex: 23414

SCHELE, AKTIEBOLAGET TH.

Aktiebolaget Th. Schéle

Postbox 92
301 02 Halmstad 1, Sweden
TELEPHONE: 100440
TELEX: 38071

OFFICIALS:
R. Christianson (*Managing Director*)
R. Andersson
Robert Christianson
S. Jönsson
O. Georgsson

SERVICES WITH OWNED OR LEASED CONTAINERS:
Roll-on ferry TOR-Mercia/TOR-Scandia.
Halmstad — Immingham — Amsterdam—weekly.
Lift on/lift off "GOTHIA".
Halmstad—Tilbury (London)—weekly.

SCHENKERS LIMITED

Schenkers Limited
Royal London House, 13 Finsbury Square,
London, EC2
TELEPHONE: 01-628 7050
TELEX: London 886856

DIRECTORS AND PRINCIPAL OFFICIALS
F. Brash (*Managing Director*)
R. Metz (*Director and General Manager*)
A. Rustemeyer (*Sales and Development Manager*)
M. Mehta (*Container Co-ordinator*)

BRANCHES:
Belfast, Birmingham, Bradford, Bristol, Dover, Dublin, Glasgow, Goole. Harwich, Hull, Ipswich, Leith, Liverpool, London Airport. Manchester, Newcastle-on-Tyne, Newport, Cork, Galway, Limerick.

CONTAINER SERVICES:
All European routes by rail and road.

CONTAINER TERMINALS USED:
Name of London Terminal
London (Stratford) International Freight Terminal (L.I.F.T.)
Representative   *Telephone No.*
D. Luscombe   01-534 0036
STORAGE, PACKING AND UNPACKING FACILITIES:
Charlton, London
Sunlight Wharf, London
Spitalfields, (Vallance Road)
    Birmingham, Manchester, Coatbridge

SCHENKER TRANS-SIBERIAN SERVICE

Schenker Trans-Siberian Container Service
SERVICE:
Europe to and from Japan by truck to Moscow, thence Trans-Siberian Railway to Nakhodka for shipment to Japan.

SEATRANS CONSOLIDATED NZ LTD.

Seatrans Consolidated (N.Z.) Limited,
Private Bag, Mount Maunganui, New Zealand
TELEPHONE: 54-099
TELEX: NZ2285
DIRECTORS AND EXECUTIVES IN CHARGE OF CONTAINER SERVICES:
R. A. Owens (*Managing Director*)
L. J. B. Dickson
A. J. Gallagher
P. J. Trapski
A. C. Williams (*General Manager*)
W. R. Meredith (*Secretary*)
BRANCHES:
Auckland, Wellington, Christchurch, Nelson, Dunedin, Invercargill, with agents at Timaru, Napier, New Plymouth.

CONTAINER SERVICES:
Auckland to Wellington, Lyttelton, Dunedin, Wellington to Lyttelton, Dunedin, Lyttelton to Dunedin.
New Zealand Ports to Sydney and Melbourne.

CONTAINER LEASING:
The Company leases 20 ft ISO Containers and 14·4 ft refrigerated and dry containers, also flats. (See Leasing Section).

TERMINALS USED:
Swiftrail/Carr and Haslam Ltd. Depot, Sackville Street, Grey Lynn, Auckland
Telephone: 362-513
Swiftrail/Kiwi Trans tasman Ltd.,

67, Hutt Road, Wellington
Telephone: 44-054
Swiftrail/C. Williams & Son Ltd.,
Cnr Brisbane and Carlisle Street, Christchurch
Telephone: 77-663
Swiftrail, Cnr Castle Street and Anzac Avenue, Dunedin
Telephone: 79-001

CONTAINER PARK FACILITIES AND BREAK BULK AREAS:
30 acres including 3 acres of buildings entirely owned by Seatrans.
SPECIAL CONTAINER AGREEMENTS:
Special agreements with other freight-forwarders and New Zealand Railways.

SEAWHEEL LIMITED

Seawheel Limited,
Lovell House
Pelton Road, Greenwich, London, SE10
    England
(Subsidiary of Lovell's Shipping and Transport Group)
TELEPHONE: 01-858 8111
TELEX: 23114
DIRECTORS:
G. E. Lovell (*Chairman*)
D. D. Lovell
H. W. Gale
R. B. Dawbarn (*Managing*)
J. P. Lawrence (*Continental—based in Antwerp*)
P. A. D. Coles (*Operations*)
A. J. Martin
E. R. Jordan
M. J. McGrath (*Marketing*)

GENERAL:
Seawheel is an international container line operating a door-to-door service between the UK and Ireland, Belgium, Denmark, France, Germany, Holland, Italy and Luxembourg.

CONTAINERS IN SERVICE:

Type	Number
Lancashire flats, up to 27 ft in length	450
20 ft ISO flats, some of which specially constructed to carry steel coils, marble, etc.	550
30 ft ISO flats	100
20 ft ISO containers (some with twin decks, some insulated)	200
30 ft ISO containers equipped with the Joloda pallet handling system, some 8·5 ft high.	500
40 ft ISO containers equipped with the Joloda pallet handling system, some 8·5 ft high.	100
TOTAL FLEET	1,900

SERVICES:
NEAR CONTINENT:

To/From		Sailings per week each way
Felixstowe	Amsterdam	—
Felixstowe	Antwerp	5

Northern Ireland Trailers (Scotland) Ltd container being transferred to a slave trailer at Ardrossan

Felixstowe	Rotterdam	6
Harwich	Zeebrugge	12
Harwich	Rotterdam	6
Hull	Antwerp	3
Hull	Rotterdam	6
Tilbury	Antwerp	—
Tilbury	Rotterdam	—

Scandinavia:

Felixstowe	Copenhagen and Esbjerg	2
Goole	Copenhagen	1
Grimsby	Copenhagen and Esbjerg	2
Harwich	Copenhagen and Fredericia	5

Ireland:

Avonmouth/ (Bristol)		3/4
Newport	New Ross	2
Preston	Dublin	5

Other routes can be used as occasions demand.
All ports are connected with daily rail/road services to final destinations.

BRANCHES:
Belgium:
Seawheel, p.v.ba.
Frankrijklei 111, Antwerpen 1.
Telephone: 417030
Telex: 31149

Holland:
Seawheel,
Van Riemsdijkweg 14, Rotterdam 21
Telephone: (010) 292508
Telex: 23481

Germany:
Seawheel, G.M.B.H.,
Kirchfeldstrasse 71, 4000 Dusseldorf,
Telephone: 348071-73
Telex: 8587325
Denmark:
Dan Transport A/S,
Vestergade 33, 1002 Kobenhavn, K.
Telephone: Minerva 1688
Telex: 5000
Dan Transport A/S,

99 Prinsessegade, 7000 Fredericia/Jutland
Telephone: (059) 20233
Telex: 3395
Dan Transport A/S,
Englandskajen, Esbjerg/Jutland
Telephone: Esbjerg (051) 27677
Telex: 3446

Italy:
Fratelli Avandero S.A.S.,
Via Valtellina 21/27
20159 Milan
Telephone: 600 281
Telex: 31193
Fratelli Avandero S.A.S.,
Rivalta Scrivia Centre, Rooms N.150,
1520 and 154, 15050 Rivalta Scrivia
Telephone: 86062
Telex: 21445

Ireland:
Seawheel Limited,
29/30 Georges Quay, Dublin 2
Telephone: Dublin 775161
Telex: 5114
Seawheel Limited,
South Quay, New Ross, Co. Wexford
Telephone: New Ross 21330

United Kingdom:
Seawheel Limited,
c/o Freightliner Terminal,
London Street,
Birmingham 8
N Berth, Avonmouth Docks,
Avonmouth

Telephone: OBR2 4581
Telex: 44784
Seawheel Limited,
The Dock, Dock Road, Felixstowe, Suffolk
Telephone: 03942 4804
Telex: 98276
Seawheel Limited,
98 West George Street, Glasgow, C2
Telephone: Douglas 8892
Telex: 778241
Seawheel Limited,
9/12 East Dock Road,
Parkeston Quay,
Harwich, Essex
Telephone: 02555 4333-5
Telex: 98442
Seawheel Limited,
Hedon Road, King George Dock, Hull
Telephone: 0482 76282
Telex: 52449
Seawheel Limited,
1 Rumford Place, Chapel Street,
Liverpool L3 9QN
Telephone: 051-236 5126
Telex: 62107
Seawheel Limited,
Freightliner Terminal,
Westinghouse Lane,
Trafford Park, Manchester 17
Seawheel Limited,
Freightliner Terminal, Rover Way,
Pengham, Cardiff
Telephone: 0222 497101
Seawheel Limited,
Albert Edward Dock, Preston
Telephone: 0772 28334
Telex: 67691
Seawheel Limited,
111 Queen Street, Sheffield, 1.
Telephone: Sheffield 22187

SEWELL AND CROWTHER (FREIGHT) LTD.

Sewell & Crowther (Freight) Limited
City Gate House, Finsbury Square London,
E.C.2
TELEPHONE: 01-638 9591
TELEX: 887635
DIRECTORS AND EXECUTIVES IN CHARGE OF
CONTAINER SERVICES:
J. E. Harris

M. J. Williams
M. J. Cornwall

BRANCHES:
Cunard Building, Water Street, Liverpool 3
SERVICES WITH OWN OR LEASED CONTAINERS.
London/Canada—Weekly
London/Australia—every 7-10 days.

London/New York—Weekly.

CONTAINER TERMINALS USED:
Express Container Transport Ltd.,
Bugsbys Way, Anchor and Hope Lane,
Charlton, SE7.
Representative: H. J. Hooper
Telephone: 01-855 5491

SOUTHERN PACIFIC MARINE TRANSPORT INC.

Southern Pacific Marine Transport, Inc,
9 First Street,
San Francisco, California 94105
G. R. Nickerson (Agent)

TRADING SCOPE:
From: California and Oregon.
To: Ports in Japan.

SUTHERLAND INTERNATIONAL DESPATCH LTD.

Sutherland International Despatch Ltd.,
55-61 Moorgate, London, EC2
TELEPHONE: 606 4292
DIRECTORS AND EXECUTIVES IN CHARGE OF
CONTAINER SERVICES:
H. G. Waite

S. Jackson
BRANCHES:
Liverpool, Glasgow, Toronto.
SERVICES WITH OWN OR LEASED CONTAINERS:
United Kingdom to Canada

TERMINAL USED:
J. B. Woodcock & Son,
334 Beckton Road, London, E16
Representative: D. Woodcock
Telephone: 01-476 2200.

TRAFPAK (TANK CONTAINER SERVICES) LTD.

TRAFPAK (Tank Containers Services Ltd)
HEAD OFFICE:
Clarendon House, 11-12 Clifford Street,
London, W1 X2HD
TELEPHONE: 01-629 8434
TELEX: 263552
DIRECTORS:
V. King, MBE
J. M. B. Gotch
C. J. De Vriese (Dutch)
H. Luijpen (Dutch)
SALES MANAGER IN CHARGE OF CONTAINER
OPERATION:
P. Hansen
OVERSEAS REPRESENTATIVES:
ROTTERDAM:
Pakhoed NV,
Boompjes 60-68,

Rotterdam, Holland
Telephone: 30.29.11
Telex: 23023
GOTHENBURG:
Nordic Tank Storage AB,
Skeppsbroplatsen 1 tr,
Gothenburg, Sweden
Telephone: 17.29.00
Telex: 20894
MANNHEIM:
Rhein-Lloyd GmbH,
68 Mannheim 1,
Postfach 1949,
Schwarzwaldstrasse 76
Telephone: 21844
Telex: 463309
and Pakhoed offices in Hamburg, Antwerp,
Paris

Trafpak Bulk Container.

GENERAL:
TRAFPAK was the first Container Operator with ISO tank containers on the short sea routes to Europe. Specialising in the transport of bulk liquids between the United

Kingdom and all parts of Europe, Trafpak operate a variety of tanks, some of which are illustrated here, including ISO 20 foot units with stainless steel, mild steel and glass reinforced plastic tanks.

Capacities range from 3,600 to 4,465 gallons, and many special features are included according to the intended use. These include insulation; electrical or steam heating facilities; provision for discharge by gravity, suction or air pressure; safety valves; temperature control gauge.

Trafpak quote through rates for spot and contract deliveries between UK and all parts of Europe. The development of European railways container routes, and the range of shipping services from UK have greatly enlarged the scope of TRAFPAK's through transport service. Recent expansion to their specialised services includes the introduction of tanks for beer and hydrogen peroxide.

TRAFPAK is a subsidiary of Traffic Services Ltd, London and Pakhoed NV, Rotterdam.

CONTAINERS:
20 ft ISO bulk liquid tank containers and Portapak tanks—stainless steel, 1,400 gallons, 6,200 litres capacity are available for door-to-door transport.

SPECIFICATIONS:
Conforming to ISO and British Railways

Trailer Express Ltd.,
Humber Road,
    South Killingholme, Grimsby, Lincs..
TELEPHONE: Immingham 2625
TELEX: 52384
GENERAL MANAGER:
    T. Tiedemann

Trafpak unit manufactured by Container & Pressure Vessels Ltd.

freight container specifications. Capacities 3,600 to 4,465 gallons (16,360 to 20,300 litres), suitable for chemicals including hazardous liquids; edible oils, beer.

TYPES:
Stainless steel insulated tank with electrical or steam heating
Glass reinforced plastic tank with/without insulation and electrical heating

TRAILER EXPRESS LTD.

BRANCHES:
All over Scandinavia.

SERVICES WITH OWN OR LEASED CONTAINERS:
UK to Scandinavia via Immingham,

TRAFPAK. Portapak containers—loaded two to a trailer in UK—1,400 galls capacity stainless steel insulated, suitable for inflammable and poisonous cargoes.

BUILDERS:
Darham Industries Ltd, Staveleys of Atherton Ltd,
Container and Pressure Vessels Ltd.
Gloster Saro Ltd.
Grundy (Teddington) Ltd.
Hesler Heat Exchangers Ltd.

CONSTRUCTION DETAILS:
Grade 316, 304, 321 stainless steel tank, steel end frames.
Glass reinforced plastic tank, steel end frames.

Grimsby, Hull, Felixstowe, Harwich and London.

TERMINALS USED:
S.H.I.F.T., South Killingholme (details as above).

TRANSATLANTIC AND PACIFIC CONTAINER CARGO INC.

Transatlantic and Pacific Container Cargo, Inc,
21 West Street, New York,
New York 10006
OFFICIAL.
Raymond O. Dahlstrom
TRADING SCOPE:
1 Between: New York and Antwerp, Rotterdam, Bremen, Hamburg, and Ports in the UK.
2 From: Genoa, Leghorn and Naples.

To: US North Atlantic Ports of Discharge (Hampton Roads/Portland Range).
3 From: North Atlantic Ports of US.
To: Algeria, Egypt, France, Gibraltar, Greece, Italy, Lebanon, Libya, Morocco, Syria, Tunisia.
4 From: North Atlantic Ports of the US in the Eastport, Maine/Hampton Roads Range.
To: Ports of call in Antwerp, Rotterdam,

Amsterdam, Bremen, Hamburg, and the UK.
5 From: Ports of call in Antwerp, Rotterdam, Amsterdam, Bremen, Hamburg, and the UK.
To: New York, Harbour Ports of the US.
6 From: New York.
To: Copenhagen, Gothenburg, Helsinki, Oslo.
7 From: Copenhagen, Gothenburg, Helsinki, Oslo
To: New York.

TRANSCARLOADING CORPORATION

Transcarloading Corporation
(Transcarloading Container System)

744 N.E. 27th Avenue
Miami, Florida
TELEPHONE: (305) 373-5454

OFFICIALS IN CHARGE OF CONTAINER SERVICES:
M. Sola Sr. (President)
M. Sola Jr. (Vice-President)
Fabio Ruiz (Manager)
BRANCH:
PO Box 3295
Jacksonville, Fla 322206

SERVICES:
Weekly Service—Trailerloads only—between

(1) Miami and San Juan, P.R.
(2) Jacksonville and San Juan P.R.
(3) Miami and St. Thomas V.1.
(4) Miami and St. Croix V.1.
(5) Miami and Kingston, Jamaica

TRANSCONEX INC.

Transconex Inc.
For Telephone, Telex, Branches and Officials, see Transconex Jamaica Inc.
SERVICES:
Jacksonville and Puerto Rico

Miami and Puerto Rico
Miami and St. Thomas V.I.
Miami and St. Croix, V.I.
Weekly (LTL shipments only)

TRANSCONEX JAMAICA INC.

Transconex-Jamaica Inc.
990 S.E. 11th Street, Hialeah, Florida
TELEPHONE: (305) 887-1591
TELEX: Western Union 051689

OFFICIALS IN CHARGE OF CONTAINER SERVICES:
M. Sola, Jr. (President)

Roy M. Jacobs (Vice-President)
R. A. Catnichi (Treasurer)
Julig Siberio (Operations-Traffic)
Howard Melnick (Sales)
M. Sola Sr. (Accounting)
BRANCHES:
629 West 54th Street, New York NY 10019
Telephone: (212) LT-1-7210

PO Box 48 Kingston, Jamaica
Telephone: 23411

SERVICES:
New York and Kingston—weekly (LTL shipments only)
Miami and Kingston—weekly (LTL shipments only)

TRANSCONTAINER EXPRESS LTD.

Transcontainer Express Ltd.
Central House, 32-66 High Street,
Stratford, London, E15 2PP
TELEPHONE: 01-555 0121

TELEX: 896334
DIRECTORS AND EXECUTIVES IN CHARGE OF CONTAINER SERVICES:
J. L. Rees (Managing Director)

G. F. Sodeau (General Manager)

BRANCHES:
Glasgow and throughout France.

SERVICES WITH OWN CONTAINERS:
United Kingdom, France, Netherlands, Switzerland, Belgium—Daily.

CONTAINER LEASING:
Single trip leasing arrangements UK—France.

TERMINALS USED:
All public terminals in UK, France, Netherlands and Belgium.

TRANSLLOYD LTD

Translloyd Ltd,
Europe House, Hemming Street, London E1
TELEX: 24726
DIRECTORS:
M. Kaye, P. Kaye, K. Thompson, L.

Manson, P. Rosenthal

CONTAINER SERVICES:
From UK and return, New York, Montreal, Paris, Antwerp, Rotterdam, Düssel-

dorf, Milan, Stockholm, Gothenburg, Turin, Oslo, Rome, Helzinki, Bologna, Frankfurt, Cologne, Hamburg, Bremen, Basle, Zurich, Lagano, Tel Aviv, Hong Kong, Sydney, Melbourne, Adelaide.

TRANS SIBERIAN CONTAINER LINE

Trans-Siberian Container Line (TSCL)

V/O Sojuzvneshtrans
(All Soviet External Transport Corporation)
Moscow
Baltic Shipping Company
Leningrad

Far East Shipping Company
Vladivostock
SERVICE:
London, Antwerp and other European ports as the service expands, to and from Leningrad; thence via Moscow and the Trans-Siberian Railway to Nakhodka for

shipment to Japanese Ports. The service operates every two weeks.
AGENTS:
Belgium:
Transworld Marine Agency Cy., Antwerp
United Kingdom:
Anglo-Soviet Shipping Company, London

TRANSLODE UNITS LTD.

Translode Units Ltd.
Coolsingel 75
Telephone: 141533
Telex: 23237 (also at Liverpool, London,

Ferry trailer operators
International Freight forwarding Company. Operators of a specialised inter-continental warehouse to warehouse service. Shipments

arranged by sea/rail/road/ferry services and air. Containers and flats available for long- or short-term hire.

TRANSMODAL CARGOES INC.

Transmodal Cargoes Inc.
150 Broadway.
New York, NY 10038
TELEPHONE: (212) C07-4414

OFFICIALS:
H. D. Tabak (*President*)
SERVICES WITH OWN OR LEASED CONTAINERS:
All routes.

TRANSWORLD SHIPPING LTD.

Trans World Shipping Ltd.,
3 Quilp Street, London, SE1
TELEPHONE: 01-407 8731
TELEX: 21820

DIRECTORS:
W. Ernest Dettwiler   L. Trayner
S. Dettwiler   D. E. Goddard
       (*in charge of Container Services*)

SERVICES WITH OWN OR LEASED CONTAINERS:
(1) London, Bristol Liverpool, Southampton to New York, Baltimore, Boston, Philadelphia, Montreal, Toronto and West Coast Ports of North America.
(2) London to Scandinavia.
CONTAINER TERMINALS:
Ace Warehouse,
  Pickwick Street, London S.E.1.
  Telephone: 01-407 8731

Alexander Schor,
  New York
  Telephone: D14 0459
St. Arnaud and Bergevin Ltd.,
  Montreal
  Telephone: 844 1561
STORAGE, PACKING AND UNPACKING FACILITIES FOR CONTAINERS:
Ace warehouse, owned by the parent Company, is used for these operations.

TURKISH TRADING & TRANSPORT

Turkish Trading and Transport Co Ltd.
Gillies Street, Kentish Town, London, NW.5
  TELEPHONE: 01-267 3221
  TELEX: 267717
OFFICIALS:
  M. Sherif (*Managing Director*)
SERVICES:
Groupage between UK, Belgium, Netherlands, Austria, Scandinavia to Turkey and Middle Eastern destinations.
  Turkey and Iran—daily.
  Baghdad, Kuwait, Dubai, Bahrein, Saudi Arabia.
  Abu-Dhabi and other destinations as required—weekly.
  Groupage between UK, Scandinavia, Netherlands, Belgium, Germany, Austria to Poland, Czechoslovakia.

Hungary, Romania and Moscow—frequent opportunities.

AGENTS:
Turkey:
Karakoy,
  Rihtimcad 209, Istanbul
  TELEPHONE: 44.66.24
Netherlands:
Herfurth NV
  Westerstraat 42 Rotterdam
  TELEPHONE: 010-13 4500
  TELEX: 22425
Belgium:
Thomas and Ellis
  Rue Picard 48 Brussels
  TELEPHONE: 02-26 48 70
  TELEX: 21099

Austria:
Adria
  Taborstrasse 4-6 Vienna 11
  TELEPHONE: 24.35.06
  TELEX: 074587
Norway:
Globe
  Oslo 5 Astre Akerv 95
  TELEPHONE: 33 40 76
  TELEX: 11655
Germany:
Turkish Trading and Transport
  8 Munchen 75 Thalkirchnerstrasse 124
  TELEPHONE: 77 60 93
  TELEX: 529749

EQUIPMENT IN SERVICE:
  20 and 40 ft containers.

TUZCUOGLU

Tuzcuoglu

Mehmet Ali Tuzcuoglu
Gazi M. Kemal Bul. No. 74, Ankara, Turkey

TELEPHONE: 17 91 17 & 12 08 26
TELEGRAMS: Tuzcular
TELEX: 51
SUBSIDIARY COMPANIES:
H. F. Tuzcuoglu
HEAD OFFICE:
Gazi, Bulvari No. 10, Izmir

TELEPHONE: 32394 & 23034
TELEGRAMS: Hafet
TELEX: 33

Istanbul Express

HEAD OFFICE:
  Ali Süavi Sokak No. 92, Maltepe-Ankara
  P.O. Box 255, Bakanliklar
  TELEPHONE: 12 00 65
TELEGRAMS: Isteks

PRINCIPAL ROUTES:
Tuzcuoglu and its subsidiaries, Istabul Express, Sark Express and H. F. Tuzcuoglu are the main container transporters in Turkey. Containers go by road and rail via Istanbul, Izmir, Iskenderun and Mersiz to and from Iran and the Middle East.

ULSTER LINK

Ulster Link
Holme Street, Liverpool, L5 9SA
TELEPHONE: 051-207 4561
TELEX: 62374
OFFICIALS:
B. R. Davies (*General Manager*)

BRANCHES:
  Belfast, London, Preston, Dublin, Ardrossan.

CONTAINER SERVICES:
  Great Britain to Northern Ireland daily.

Door-to-Door Unit Load Services—wide variety of containers, trailers and flats available. Groupage Services for part-loads and sundry traffic between London, Liverpool, Manchester, Preston and Belfast.

UNER H.

H. Unér A/B
Aktiebolag Fleminggatan 30, Norrköping,
Sweden
TELEPHONE: 011/10 00 40
TELEGRAMS: Uner
TELEX: 64053
DIRECTORS:
G. Crafoord (*Managing Director*)

BRANCHES:
Hallstavik, Jönköping, Orebro
CONTAINER SERVICES:
Sweden—USA
TERMINALS USED:
Own terminal close to Norrköping harbour
(consolidated cargo)
Representative: H. Unér

Telephone: 011/10 00 40
LEASING SERVICES:
As agents for ACL Ltd.
complete stock of containers
Also arrange leasing services
CTI and Messrs. Freys Express
Gothenburg.

UNITED CARGO CONTAINERS LTD.

United Cargo Containers Ltd
New Street
London, EC2
TELEPHONE: 01 283 7121
TELEX: 897724
LONDON DEPOT:
J. J. Sutton Clarke (*Chairman and Managing*)
D. B. Wallace (*Operations*)
G. Fitch (*Marketing*)
E. G. Buckland (*Administration*)
Z. Sitchin
I. Charchat
G. Pohl

7 unit
Silvertown Industrial Estate
Factory Road,
Silvertown, London, E16.
BRANCHES:
Manchester, Leicester, Birmingham, Bristol
and Birstall, Yorks.
CONTAINER SERVICES:
UK to USA via New York—weekly

UK to Canada via Montreal—weekly
UK to Netherlands, Germany, Italy—as
required.
Note: The Company continue to re-organise
and the entry is therefore incomplete.
EXPORT RECEIVING DEPOTS:
United Cargo Containers (Europe) Ltd
354 Beckton Road, London, E16
Representative: A. Taylor
Telephone: Albert Dock 2200
Butlers Warehousing and Distribution Ltd.
St. Andrews Road, Avonmouth
Representative: P. J. Fuller
Telephone: Avonmouth 2371
H. W. Coates (Cosby) Ltd.
Main Street, Cosby, Nr. Leicester
Representative: T. Ellis
Telephone: Narborough 2387
Guymers (Transport) Ltd.
Ten Acres, Station Road, Rushall, Walsall
Representative: M. Poole
Telephone: Walsall 24651

J. L. Cooper Ltd.
Foxley Lane, Milton, Staffordshire
Representative: Mr. Mason
Telephone: Stoke 54264
Northern Warehouse Services Ltd.
Bradford Road, Birstall, Nr. Leeds
Representative: G. Large
Telephone: Batley 3609
Arbuckle Smith & Co. Ltd.
100 Cheapside Street, Glasgow, and
Carfin Warehouse, Motherwell
Imports—With Inland Clearance Customs
Approval:
Butlers & Colonial Wharves Ltd.,
'Z' Shed, Wapping High Street, London, E1
Representative: Mr. Nimmo
Telephone: Royal 8731
Anglo Overseas Transport Co. Ltd.,
No. 9 Shed, London International Freight
Terminal, Stratford, London, E15
Representative: J. Thorn
Telephone: 01-534 0111

UNITED CARGO CORPORATION

United Cargo Corporation,
(See Intercontinental Trailsea Corp.).

UNIVERSAL CARLOADING AND DISTRIBUTING CO LTD.

Universal Car Loading and Distributing Co.
Ltd.—Thrutainer Division
The Company is a subsidiary of United
States Freight Corporation.
THRUTAINER SERVICE
Thrutainer Division
345 Hudson Street,
New York N.Y. 10014
TELEPHONE: 212-675-5600
TELEX: ITT UCD 423282
OFFICIAL IN CHARGE OF CONTAINER OPERA-
TIONS:
M. E. Uremovich (*General Manager*)
BRANCHES:
All major US cities
SERVICES USING OWN OR LEASED CON-
TAINERS:

Operates extensive domestic forwarding
NVOC operations. Consolidates and distributes freight to and from 50 US States
under applicable ICC authority. Operates
major container service, between New York,
Norfolk, New Orleans, Houston, and UK
and North European destinations including
Scandinavia. Also similar service to and
from Japan. All services offered on a
single through bill of loading.

MAJOR TERMINALS USED
USA
Universal Car Loading and Distributing
Co. Inc. terminals at:
Chicago
977 West Cermak Road, Chicago Ill.,
Telephone 312-738-3000
Houston, Texas
1217, Prairie Street, McFadden Bldg,
Houston, Texas 77002
Telephone: (713) 223 4109
Louisville
812 W. Magnolia Street, Louisville, Ky.
40208
Telephone: 502-637-3682
St. Louis
110 Miller St., St. Louis, Mo. 63104
Telephone: 314-421-2380

New Orleans, La.
Gravier Bldg, Room 206,
New Orleans, La. 70130
Telephone: (504) 522-7137
Cincinnati
Gest and McLean Streets,
Cincinnati, Ohio 45203
Telephone: 513-241-4160
Minneapolis
401 N. St., Minneapolis, Minn. 55405
Telephone: 612-335-4191
Milwaukee
3520 W. Mill Road, Milwaukee, Wis 53209
Telephone: 414-353-3180
Grand Rapids
882 Hynes Ave. S.W., Grand Rapids,
Mich 49502
Telephone: 616-452-3284
Cleveland
1191 E. 40th St., Cleveland, Ohio 45203
Telephone: 216-361-4900
Detroit
140 12th St., Detroit, Mich. 48216
Telephone: 313-825-7600

Los Angeles
608 North Mission Blvd,
P.O. Box 60019
Los Angeles, California
Telephone: 190054

San Francisco/Oakland.
2095 7th St., PO Box 24324,
Oakland, Calif. 94623
Telephone:
New York
643 W. 59th St., NY 10019
Telephone: (212) 586-7300
Europe
Thrutainer European Office
Torstenssonsgaten 3,
11456, Stockholm, Sweden
Telephone:
Telex: 854 17777
Officials:
Count S. O. Bernadotte (*European Man-*
ager)

Thrutainers arriving at Elizabeth Terminal
Thrutainer of Sweden
Gyltenstiensgaten 4,
P.O. Box 27020, 10251 Stockholm 27
and
Packhusgaten 2B, P.O. Box 44
40120 Gothenburg 1
Thrutainer of Denmark
Nome Voldgade 6
D/C 1358 Copenhagen
Thrutainer of Holland
Statimsburg 56, The Hague
Thrutainer of Germany
Schillerstrasse 26
2 Hamburg 50
Thrutainer of Germany
4m Karlsbad 15, 1 Berlin 30

Piggypacker now in operation at Seattle,
Washington. It has 45 ton capacity, capable
of top or bottom lifting trailers or containers
20 to 40 feet in length. It is contemplated
that Denver and Salt Lake City facilities will
be similarly equipped.

Thrutainer of Belgium
Brussels and Antwerp, 17-21 Rue Vanden
Boogaerde, Brussels
Thrutainer of Switzerland
Unter Rebgasse 7
CH-4000 Basle

Thrutainer of France
24 rue Caumartin, Paris IX

Thrutainer of England
4 Lower Belgrave Street, SW1 London,
England

Japan:
Nittu Thrutainer
Nippon Express Ltd, Nittu Bldg,
No. 12-9, 3-chome, Soto-Kanda,
Chiyoda-ku, Tokyo

UNIVERSAL TRANSPORT CONTAINER SERVICE

Universal Transport Container Service
J. D. O'Hern & Co. Limited
159 Bay St., Toronto, Ontario.

SERVICES: Canada—United Kingdom
A weekly year round service with 20 ft units is given, door to door between Man-

chester, London and Southampton and Monteal, Quebec and Halifax.

UNITRANS LTD.

Unitrans Ltd.
Tokyo
GENERAL:
A Company set up jointly by:

Mitsubishi Warehouse and Transportation Co Ltd, and Kühne and Nugel Ltd.
OFFICIALS:
Kiochi Hidaka (*President*)

Horst B. Schuhmaker (*Vice-President*)
SERVICE:
Europe—Japan via Trans-Siberian Railway.

VAN GEND & LOOS

Van Gend & Loos-Holland
Postbox 779, Amsterdam
TELEPHONE: 23 86 11
TELEX: 1 25 84
Postbox 387, Rotterdam
TELEPHONE: 23 59 90
TELEX: 2 24 58
Postbox 2049, Utrecht
TELEPHONE: 2 83 11
TELEX: 4 70 36
BRANCHES:
Pakhuismeesteren, N.V.

12, Van Oldenbarneveldtstraat, P.O.B. 863,
Rotterdam
Telephone: 11 19 90
Telex: 22162 (pakhuismeesters)
Pakhuismeesteren, Amsterdam, N.V.
130, Prins Hendrikkade, P.O.B., 110,

Amsterdam
Telephone: 24 39 69
Telex: 14144 (pakmeesters asd)
Pakhuismeesteren, N.V.

1, Meirburg, Antwerp
Telephone: 31 19 20
Telex: 3376 (pakhuis antwerp)

Pakhuismeesteren, S.à.r.l
47, rue Richer, Paris
Telephone: LAF 1546
Telex: 28566 (pakhuis paris)
Pakhuismeesteren, N.V., Rotterdam
12, Uhlandstrasse, Dusseldorf
Telephone: 68 44 48
Telex: 8586656 (phm d)

WILLIAMES CONTAINER SERVICE LIMITED

Williames Container Service Limited
Belfast
TELEPHONE: 74841
TELEX: 74200
Dublin
TELEPHONE: 47641
TELEX: 5560

Preston
TELEPHONE: 728636
TELEX: 67454
BRANCHES:
London, Rotterdam
GENERAL:
The company is a subsidiary of W. E.

Williames Ltd.
SERVICES:
Belfast and Dublin—Preston Daily.
Belfast and Dublin—Rotterdam.
CONTAINERS IN SERVICE:
Some 180 20 ft dry cargo units and 30 ft flats are reported as in service.

WINGATE, W. & JOHNSTON LTD.

W. Wingate & Johnston Ltd.,
St. Mary Axe House, St. Mary Axe, London,
EC3
TELEPHONE: 01-283 8030
TELEX: 888904
DIRECTORS: I. A. Pearson (*Managing Director*)
D. G. Kinsella. G. R. McKinlay, G. A.
Griffin, Lt. Col. E. C. Easter, T. Slater,

D. A. McKee.
CONTAINER EXECUTIVE:
F. W. Pedrick

BRANCHES:
Liverpool, Manchester, Glasgow, Leeds,
Newcastle, Southampton, Birmingham,
Leicester, Ipswich, Newport

CONTAINER SERVICES WITH OWN OR LEASED CONTAINERS:
From: Depots in London, Liverpool,
Glasgow, Birmingham, Manchester and
Ipswich.

To: Baltimore, Boston, New York, Los
Angeles, Toronto, Montreal and Vancouver.

WOODCOCK GA FREIGHT LTD

G. A. Woodcock Freight Ltd,
Park House Lane, Sheffield, S9 1WY
TELEPHONE: Sheffield 40884
TELEX: 54375
A. Mosforth (*Freight Director*)
S. Brotherton (*Sales Director*)
D. L. Grundy (*Unit Load Divisional Manager*)
BRANCHES:
Birmingham, Hull, Leeds, Liverpool, London, Newcastle-upon-Tyne, Southampton,
Swansea.
SERVICES USING OWN OR LEASED CONTAINERS:
Full Load Movements:
To and from all European destinations,

Canada, USA, Australia and the Far East
(Hong Kong, Japan and Singapore).
Groupage Services—Europe:

Hull, Sheffield, Leeds and London to:
Rotterdam, Dusseldorf, Cologne, Frankfurt-am-Main, Stuttgart, Vienna, Antwerp, Brussels—Twice weekly.

Hull, Sheffield, Leeds and London to:
Copenhagen, Esbjerg, Gothenburg, Oslo,
Helsinki, Milan, Turin, Basle—Weekly.

Groupage Services—North America:
Sheffield to Quebec, Montreal, Toronto,

Hamilton—Weekly.

MEMBERS OF:
Mersey Groupage Limited
Liverpool
Midland Groupage Limited
Birmingham
Hull Euroscan Limited
Hull

SUBSIDIARY AND ASSOCIATE COMPANIES:
Rispin of Hull, Ltd.
Dairycoates, Wiltshire Road, Hull
Sheffield Packaging Services Ltd.
Mowson Lane, Worrall, Sheffield

WORLD TRANSPORT AGENCY LTD.

World Transport Agency Ltd.,
20-22 Emerson Street, London, SE1
TELEPHONE: 01-928 6996 (16 lines)
TELEX: 28401
DIRECTORS: J. E. Sommer (*Managing*),
T. H. Guard, N. Chesworth, A. F. Issberner
D. Cole
BRANCHES:
Own offices in Manchester, Birmingham,
Hull, Liverpool, Bradford, Sheffield, Stoke-on-Trent, Basle (Switzerland) and at principal
UK Airports.
CONTAINER SERVICES WITH OWN OR LEASED CONTAINERS:
UK to Switzerland/Italy, Sweden, Finland,

Netherlands, Belgium, Germany and USA/Canada.

Other continental destinations as required.
CONTAINER TERMINALS USED:
All operative UK Port and BR Freightliner Terminals. (Participation only in all instances).

STORAGE, PACKING AND UNPACKING FACILITIES:
The Company participates in most of the facilities provided at main terminals but have own facilities at:
20-22 Emerson Street, London, SE1

No. 9 Building L.I.F.T. Stratford London E15
T.E.P.S. Warehouse, 147 Wincolmlee, Hull
8-9 Warwick Place, Trafford Park, Manchester 17
26 Orgrave Close, Dove House Farm Industrial Estate, Handsworth, Sheffield, S13 9MP
Newstead Trading Estate, Trentham, Stoke-on-Trent, ST4 8HX

SPECIAL ARRANGEMENTS OR AGREEMENTS:
The Company is a member of Express Transport and E.C.G. (Harwich)

LEASING

LEASING
INTRODUCTION

The current picture of world container leasing is that there are now at least five large firms with branches in every main container- using country in the world.

The European Pool System has been developed to provide one trip only leasing.

Many manufacturers are now offering container leasing arrangements but we have listed only special leasing companies or companies offering leasing services in this section.

One way leasing has become very popular and some companies are offering special services i.e. hire of trailers, cranes and repairs.

INSTITUTE OF INTERNATIONAL LESSORS

Institute of International Container Lessors

INTERNATIONAL HEADQUARTERS:
Airwork House
35 Piccadilly
London WIV 9PB
TELEPHONE: 437 7273
TELEX: 22677

OFFICIALS:
Helmut F. H. Hansen (*President*)
James B. Sherwood (*Treasurer*)
MEMBERS:
S.S.I. Container Corporation
CTI—Container Transport International Inc.
Interpool Limited
Integrated Container Services Inc.
Sea Containers Inc.

Contrans Geselllschaft Fur Containerverkehr

GENERAL:
The Institute announced its formation at an inaugural meeting in November 1971.

It represents international container leasing companies throughout the world aiming to facilitate leasing and advising and assisting the container industry.

INTERNATIONAL OPERATORS
CONTRANS

Contrans Gesellschaft fur den Uebersee-Behalterverkehr mbH,
2000 Hamburg 13,
Rothenbaumchaussee 38
TELEPHONE: 441851
TELEX: 02 14275
DIRECTORS:
Helmut F. H. Hansen
Werner Ahsendorf
SALES MANAGERS IN CHARGE OF CONTAINER
OPERATIONS:
Peter Tiedemann
Peter Evers

REPAIR SHOP:
Hamburg-Kuhwerder,
Reiherdamm 44
Telephone: 31 68 71
GERMAN AGENCY:
Westfälische Transport-Aktien-Gesellschaft
46 Dortmund, Mallinckrodtstr. 320
GERMAN BRANCH OFFICES:
Berlin:
Westfälische Transport-Aktien-Gesellschaft
1 Berlin 20, Eiswerderstr. 18
Braunschweig:
Münsterische Schiffahrts- und Lagerhaus AG
33 Braunschweig-Hafen, Hafenstr. 32
Bremen:
2800 Bremen, Birkenstrasse 37
Bremerhaven:
Herm. Runge
285 Bremerhaven 12, Postfach 2173
Station: Bremerhaven-Kaiserhafen and Mallinckrodtstr 320
Cologne:
Westfälische Transport-Aktien-Gesellschaft
5 Köln 15, Rheinauhafen
Dortmund:
Westfälische Speditions-Gesellschaft mbH
46 Dortmund, Speicherstr. 2
Düsseldorf:
Westdeutsche Speditions- und Schiffahrts-Gesellschaft mbH
4 Düsseldorf-Hafen, Zollhof 1
Duisburg:
Westfälische Transport-Aktien-Gesellschaft
41 Duisburg-Ruhrort
König-Friedrich-Wilhelm-Str. 4
Emden:
Westfälische Transport-Aktien-Gesellschaft
297 Emden. Schweckendieckplatz 6
Frankfurt:
Westfälische Transport-Aktien-Gesellschaft
6 Frankfurt/Main
Kleine Bockenheimer Strasse 18a
Hamburg:
Contrans Gesellschaft für Containerverkehr mbH
2 Hamburg 13, Rothenbaumchaussee 38

(*Technical Depot*)
2 Hamburg-Kuhwerder, Reiherdamm 44
Hanover:
UNION—Schiffahrts- und Lagerhaus-Gesellschaft mbH
3 Hannover, Königstr. 3
Karlsruhe:
Menzinger-Fendel
Schiffahrt und Spedition GmbH
75 Karlsruhe 12, Werftstr. 9
Kehl:
Menzinger-Fendel
Schiffahrt und Spedition GmbH
764 Kehl, Hafenstr. 28
Mannheim:
Westfälische Transport-Aktien-Gesellschaft
68 Mannheim, Rheinvorlandstr. 5
Munich:
Menzinger-Fendel
Schiffahrt un Spedition Bayern GmbH
8043 Unterföhring, Müncherstr 26
Münster:
Münsterische Schiffahrts- und Lagerhaus AG
44 Münster, Hafenweg 48
Nürnberg:
Westfälische Transport-Aktien-Gessellschaft
85 Nürnberg, Breslaver Str. 370
Oldenburg:
Roelofs & Co. GmbH
29 Oldenburg, Hafenstr. 7-8
Osnabrück:
Osnabrücker Lagerhausgesellschaft mbH.
45 Osnabrück, Hafenstr. 11
Regensburg:
Westfälische Transport-Aktien-Gesellschaft
84 Regensburg-Irlmauth
Brückenstrasse 2 (Osthafen)
Stuttgart:
Menzinger-Fendel
Schiffahrt und Spedition GmbH
7141 Schwieberdinger, b. Stuttgart
Wilhelmshaven:
Wilhelmshavener Schiffahrts- und Lagerhaus-Gesellschaft mbH
294 Wilhelmshaven, Emsstrasse

FOREIGN AGENCIES:
England:
Scruttons Ltd.
Colonial House, 30-34 Mincing Lane, London. E.C.3
Sub-Agents:
Cory Storage & Distribution Service Ltd.
130-138 Minories, London, E.C.3 N1S
F. Wardell (Haulage) Ltd.
Barleycastle Lane, Appleton Thorne Warrington/Lancashire
Manston T. S. Ltd.

Leyes Road, London, E.16
S. & H. McCall Transport (Glasgow) Ltd.
161, Helen Street, Glasgow, S.W.1
Edward Nicholson Ltd.
Dock Road, Garston, Liverpool
Dagenham Storage Company Ltd.
Pooles Lane, Ripple Road,
Dagenham, Essex

Belgium:
Grisar & Velge, S.A.
13, Keizerstraat, Antwerpen 1
Depots:
Grisar & Velge
Harwrchstraat 10, 8380 Zeebrugge
De Jager-Delbere
Bahnstation: Kortrijk/Weide,
St. Lodewijk/Deerlijk
Finland:
Fennoscandia Chartering AB
Kajsaniemigatan 4A, Helsinki 10
Sweden:
Nordström & Thulin AB
Skeppsbron 34, 11181 Stockholm

Nyman & Schultz Transport AB
Box 7078, Balastgat 2,
S-402 32 Gothenburg
Nyman & Schultz Transport AB
Box 437, Skeppsbron 5,
S-201, 24 Malmo
J. Ringborg AB
Box 408, S605-05, Norrköping
Ireland:
Heyn & Sons Ltd
Dolferin Docks, Belfast
Dublin Maritime Ltd.
20 Eden Quay, Dublin 1.
Portugal:
Marcus & Harting Lda.
Rossio 40-45, Apartado 2300, Lissabon 2
Burmester & Cia.
Rue de Reboleira 49, Apartado 226
Porto
Norway:
Generalagent:
Birger Ekerjolt AS
Radhusgatan 7B, Oslo 1
Subagent:
J. Chanche Olsen
Strandgate 5, Sandnes
Det Nordenfjeldske
Dampskibsselskab, 7000 Trondheim
Norship AS
6001 Alesund
Nordenfjeldske's Ekspedisjon
5000 Bergen
Denmark:
Generalagent:
Petersen, Möller & Hoppe

Bredgade 34, 1260 Copenhagen-K
C. Breinholt
D. Lauritzenvej
6700 Esbjerg

Depots:
Knut Erichsen & Co.
Havnegade 4, 8000 Aarhus C
N. P. Hansen & Co.
Ostre Havn, 5000 Odense
Netherlands:
Contrans Nederland N.V.
Rotterdam 1, Rhoon
J. Nederveen (*Manager*)
Switzerland:
Balser Lagerhaus- und Speditionsgesellschaft
AG
Riehenstr. 157, 4021 Balse
France:
General Agent:
Moor-Genestal & Cie. SA.
Transports Internationaux et Maritimes
13, Avenue de l'opéra, Paris 1er
Depots:
Moor-Genestal & Cie. SA.
16, Rue de la République, Marseilles
Docks Industriels S.A.
Franklin Building
Rue du 120°, P.O. Box 372, 76 Le Havre
Docks Industriels S.A.
28, Place Gambetta,
P.O. Box 567 P.R., 33 Bordeaux
Docks Insustriels S.A.
1, Quai de la République
P.O. Box 68, 34 Sete
Docks Industriels S.A.
7, Quai Freycinet 1
P.O. Box 1033, Dunkirk
Docks Industriels S.A.
9, Quai de France
P.O. Box 529, 76 Rouen
Docks Industriels S.A.
92, Quai de la Fosse
P.O. Box 417, 44 Nantes
Austria:
Schenker & Co. AG.
Hoher Markt, 12, Vienna 1
Italy:
General Agent:
S.A.I.M.A.
Via Pontaccio, 13, 20121 Milan
Depots:
S.A.I.M.A.
Corso Rosselli 71, Casella Postale 490
10100 Turin
S.A.I.M.A.
Via S. Aspreno, 13, 80133 Naples
S.A.I.M.A.
Via G. Galatti, 22, 34122 Trieste
S.A.I.M.A.
Via Fieschi, 8/2, 16121 Genoa
S.A.I.M.A. s.p.a.
Spedizioni Internazionali
Via Salvatore Orlando, 20 a, Leghorn
S.A.I.M.A. Ravenna
V. le Santi Baldini, 16, 48100 Ravenna
S.A.I.M.A.
V. S. Martino, 10, 60100 Ancona
S.A.I.M.A.
Via Divisione Acqui 55
41100 Modena
TKC
Trazioni Containers Kangourou
Largo Leonardi 9A, 28100 Novara
Jugoslavia:
Fersped, Int. Spedition
Mose Pijade 39, Ljubljana
Jugosped, Int, Spedition
Terazidja 10, Beograd
Hungary:
Mahart, Ungarische Schiffahrts-AG.
Apaczai Csere J. u. 11, Budapest V
Masped, Ungarische Allgem.
Transport-Unternehmung
-V, Kristóf tér 2/3, Budapest
Czechoslovakia:
Cechofracht
Unternehmen für Seeschiffahrt und

Internatoinale Spedition
Na Prikope 8, Prague 1
Cechofracht
Unternehmen für Seeschiffahrt und
Internationale Spedition
Tr. 1, Maje 52, Liberec
Spain:
General Agent:
Unimar S.A.
Fortuny 3-5 izq., Madrid 4
J. Melia & Cia.
Calle de Colon 17, Valencia
Commercial Combalia
Sagrera S.A.
Via Layetana 15, Barcelona
E. Erhardt & Cia.
Ercilla 17, Bilbao
Anso y Cia.
Edificio del Puerto, Pasajes
Conansa S.A.
Edificio Elcano, Seville
Hijo de M. Garcia Blay
Apodaca 13/15, Tarragona
Israel:
Translloyd Ltd.
Shipping and Forwarding Agents
P.O. Box 4135, Tel Aviv
U.S.A.:
Uni-Flex Container Corp.
330, Madison Avenue,
New York, N.Y. 10017
Port. Terminals, Inc.
666, Summer Street,
Boston Massachusetts 02210
Gil-Flex Rental
4001 N.W. 29th Street,
Miami/Florida 33142
Uni-Flex Container Corp.
351, California Street—Suite 1315,
San Francisco, California 94104
Uni-Flex Container Corp.
2160, East 7th Street,
Los Angeles, California 90023
Detroit Harbor Terminals Inc.
3461 M. Jefferson,
Detroit, Michigan 48209
Ben Gutman Truck Service, Inc.
1615 North Eleventh Street,
St. Louis, Missouri 63106
Holt Hauling & Warehouse Systems, Inc.
701 North Broadway,
Gloucester City, New Jersey 08030
R. & E. Hauling Inc.
527 Chesapeake Avenue,
P.O. Box No. 2800
Baltimore/Maryland 21225
Port Container Industries,
Post Office Box No. 32,
Galena Park, Texas 77547
Houston, Texas
City Transfer Co., Inc.
Post Office Box No. 1841
Mobile, Alabama
Strachan Shipping Company
Savannah Bank & Trust Bldg.,
P.O. Box No. 9667,
Savannah, Georgia 31402
Containerization Service Inc.,
1087 W. 11th Street,
Port of Cleveland
Cleveland/Ohio 44113
Flexi-Van Service Center
1650—32nd Street,
Oakland/California 94615
Norbel Container & Drayage Service, Inc.
7020, Franklin Avenue
Post Office Box No. 8247
New Orleans, Louisiana 70122
Intermodal Container Pool Ltd.
353 St. Nicholas St.—Suite 412
Montreal 125, Quebec, Canada
Uni-Flex Container Corp.
228, La Salle Street,
Chicago, Illinois 60601
Japan:
Mitsubishi Warehouse & Transportation
Company

1-1, Edobashi, Nihonbashi, Chuo-Ku
Tokyo
Mitsubishi Warehouse Co. Ltd.
Meikai Bldg.
No. 32, Akashi-Machi, Ikuta-Ku,
Kobe
Mitsubishi Warehouse Co. Ltd.
4, 2-chome Kaigan-dori, Naka-Ku,
Yokohama
Mitsubishi Warehouse Co. Ltd.
59, 2-Chome, Hiroicho, Nakamura-Ku
Nagoya
Hong Kong:
The Hongkong & Kowloon Wharf & Godown
Company Ltd.
Hongkong
Far East:
Warehousing and Transportation (PTE)
100G Pasir Panjang Road,
P.O. Box 9, Pasir Panjang Post Office,
Singapore 5
Globe Freight Terminal Co., Ltd.
6-1 Po Ai Road,
Nuan Naun, Keelung, Taiwan
Korea:
FEMTCO Shipping Co. Ltd.
International Post Box 1134,
Suites 204-212 Bando Bldg., Séoul
Australia:
James Patrick & Co. Pty. Ltd.
33 Pitt Street,
Sydney, N.S.W. 2000
James Patrick & Co. Pty. Ltd.
Circular Quay,
Brisbane, Queensland, 4000
James Patrick & Co. Pty. Ltd.
35 William Street,
Melbourne, Victoria, 3000
James Patrick & Co. Pty. Ltd.
25 Wentworth Street
Port Kembla, N.S.W., 2505
James Patrick & Co. Pty. Ltd.
3 Todd Street,
Port Adelaide, S.A., 5015
James Patrick & Co. Pty. Ltd.
1 Mouatt Street,
Freemantle, W.A., 6160
James Patrick & Co. Pty. Ltd.
10-12 Telford Street,
Newcastle, N.S.W., 2300
Argentina:
Container Leasing S.A.
Sr. Alfredo Weiner
Viamonte 1328, Buenos Aires
Brazil:
Container Leasing Do Brasil
Av. President Antonio Carlos
No. 607, Grupo 304,
Rio de Janeiro—GB
Paraguay:
El Paraguayo S.A.
Estrella 934, Asunción
Hong Kong:
The Hongkong & Kowloon Wharf &
Godown Company Ltd.
Hongkong

CONTRANS baby container:

Equipment Available For Lease:

Containers:

UIC Containers, 5m³ and 10 m³ capacity

UIC Tank Containers, 5,000 litre capacity

ISO Standard Container, 20 ft and 40 ft

ISO Tank Likwitainers 20 ft insulated and suitable for heating

ISO Tank Containers 20 ft, high-grade steel

ISO Refrigeration Containers, 20 ft and 40ft Tampers and side wall evaporators

ISO Special Containers—Open Top—Open Side in the sizes 20 ft and 40 ft—Flats

Modules:

Baby Containers, Economist

Semitrailer-chassis:

20 ft, 40 ft and universal chassis

Load security:

Strap and board systems, packing cushions

Repair and Servicing:

All types and models of containers; large stock of spare parts, special welding, assembly service, PVC repairs, cleaning and deodorizing as well as all paint and finishing jobs, spray booths for containers up to 40 ft length all chassis and prime movers; Special rolling inspection stand. brake checks and tests officially recognized according to sec 29 as supplemented by sec 41 of the Highway Safety Code.

Inspection:

Acceptance according to ISO/DIN, Germanischer Lloyd, Deutscher Bundesbahn, Technical Inspection Service.

With the help and cooperation of the American partner, Messrs. UNIFLEX, New York, CONTRANS today disposes of more than 22,000 containers and 118 depots all over the world. CONTRANS NEDERLAND N.V. opened business on 1st April 1971, under Mr. Nederveen. By this world-wide depot organisation CONTRANS is able to offer

Country	Starting Point	No. of Days	9/10 m³ Standard Rate DM	Overcharge DM	5 m³ Standard Rate DM	Overcharge DM
Tariff at 1st May, 1971:						
Belgium	Antwerp	15	100,—	3,50	70,—	2,50
Netherlands	Rotterdam	15	100,—	3,50	70,—	2,50
Finland	Helsinki	15	100,—	3,50	70,—	2,50
Austria	Vienna	15	100,—	3,50	70,—	2,50
Switzerland	Basle	15	100,—	3,50	70,—	2,50
Jugoslavia	Belgrade	15	100,—	3,50	70,—	2,50
	Ljubljana		100,—	3,50	70,—	2,50
Denmark	Copenhagen	15				
	Aarhus		100,—	3,50	70,—	2,50
	Odense					
Sweden	Stockholm	15				
	Göteborg		100,—	3,50	70,—	2,50
Gt. Britain	London	15				
Iceland	Round trip	25	100,—	3,50	70,—	2,50
Ireland	,,	25	120,—	3,50	80,—	2,50
Norway	,,	25	120,—	3,50	80,—	2,50
Poland	,,	25	120,—	3,50	80,—	2,50
USSR	,,	25	120,—	3,50	80,—	2,50
France	,,	25	120,—	3,50	80,—	2,50
Mediterranean	,,	50	120,—	3,50	80,—	2,50
Turkey	,,	50	220,—	3,50	140,—	2,50
Morocco	,,	50	220,—	3,50	140,—	2,50
Canary Isles	,,	50	220,—	3,50	140,—	2,50
USA (East Coast)	,,	50	220,—	3,50	140,—	2,50
Canada Great Lakes	,,	50	220,—	3,50	140,—	2,50
All other Overseas places	,,	75	220,—	3,50	140,—	2,50
			300,—	3,50	220,—	2,50

Trailer Tariff

No. of Days	20 ft Standard and Open-Top Daily Rate DM	40 ft Standard Daily Rate DM	20 ft Refrigerated Daily Rate DM	20 ft Trailer High Steel Daily Rate DM	20 ft Pressure Tank Trailer Daily Rate DM
30	10,—	18,—	42,—	27,50	35,—
90	8,—	14,—	39,50	25,—	30,—
90	7,—	12,—	35,—	22,50	27,50
Minimum rate	100,—	180,—	250,—	250,—	250,—

5000-l-Trailer—Round Trip

Place	Daily Rate DM
Europe and Mediterranean	7,50
All other places	7,50

Baby Container:

No of Days	Type 1 DM	Type 2 DM
30	1,50	2,—
60	1,40	1,85
90	1,35	1,75
180	1,30	1,70
360	1,25	1,65
360	1,20	1,60

one-way traffic, which is economical for the Lessee, backed up by an extensive service system. In order to intensify activity CONTRANS at its end took over a new branch, the so-called operating service. Operating service means the execution of disposition and control of the other container pools.

Contrans is aiming to set up a European chassis leasing system for which purpose they and the *Industriewerke Transportsysteme GmbH*, Hamburg have constructed a suitable chassis. Because of the excellent outcome of tests CONTRANS decided to take over in Germany 40 units of a combination chassis for 20 ft and 40 ft containers. To commence the European chassis leasing system 360 chassis units were placed at Copenhagen, Bremen, Bremerhaven, Rotterdam, Antwerp and Le Havre and the Hamburg depot increased. Not all details regarding frontier traffic are yet clarified but CONTRANS does not only act as to planning but also for the cooperation of all parties concerned. New Inland chassis depots for delivery and redelivery will soon be created.

New 20 ft × 8 ft × 5 ft 4 in CONTRANS Likwitainer, Type 205E.

CONTRANS 20 ft Container trailer built by IWT.

CONTAINER TRANSPORT INTERNATIONAL INC (C.T.I.)

Container Transport International Inc.
17 Battery Place, New York, NY 10004
TELEPHONE: (212) 425 2828
TELEGRAMS: CTI, New York
TELEX: 222975
OFFICERS:
Jerome Slater (*President*)
Eugene R. Birchler (*Vice President*)
A. Blanco (*Vice President*)
Leonard Tarloff (*Gen. Traffic Manager*)
Benj. D. Bernstein (*Treasurer*)
F. A. Jackson (*Secretary*)
W. M. Goldman (*Comptroller*)
Fred E. Van Loenen (*Vice President*)

CTI's Per Diem Plan

This provides for instant availability of equipment at various CTI terminals throughout the world, but still maintains the economies of long term rates.

(1) The equipment covered by this plan is standard ISO 20 ft steel containers with fork-lift pockets, and standard 40 ft ISO aluminum containers.

(2) Such equipment is generally available at all CTI depots, in the US and abroad.

(3) Equipment can be returned to the CTI depot from which acquired, at any time, and without advance notice, against payment of a turn-in charge of $50.00. To avoid multiple trucking and handling charges, arrangements can be made to consider carrier's terminal facility as a CTI Depot'.

(4) The per diem rate is $1.75 for the 20 ft container, and $3.50 for the 40 ft container.

(5) In the event that the container is kept in operation for a period of one year, the turn-in charge is waived, and an additional 30 day period of use is granted without charge.

(6) Containers may be freely inter-changed between participating carriers of the CTI Interchange System, provided that:

(a) Originating carrier notifies receiving carrier as to turn-in point.

(b) The 30 day free time bonus is awarded only to carriers keeping equipment in their possession for one year.

(7) Carrier has the option, at any time, to convert from the Per Diem Plan to any Term Lease Plan at current rates as published by CTI.

(8) Similar plans are available for other types of containers and related equipment.

European Pool System

The European pool system is a system

Loading a 20 ft steel container on to a 20 ft tandem axle chassis at Port Newark.

whereby containers can be issued on lease for a minimum of 7 days on a one trip only basis. By the end of 1970 6,000 20 ft containers were in this system. A regulation charge of from 0-$25 a day is charged in areas (i.e. Portugal) where containers are likely to get stuck. The normal fee then is $2.52 per day plus regulator charge for a 20 ft container.

A bigger short term market reservoir is useful for reinforcing the long term lease agreements, but computer control is proving difficult.

1971 Developments

4,000 new containers are being constructed in Japan for the Far East Trade. Some special insulated containers are being constructed in Finland.

Finance Lease Arrangements

CTI-Container Transport International, Inc has broadened its container leasing operations to include a new instalment plan purchase programme, operated by Container Leasing Corporation, a CTI subsidiary. Under the new programme a CTI customer will be able to lease any number and variety of containers he needs for a period of from five to ten years under 'finance leases'. The payments, which will be based on the total cost of each unit

plus interest, will result in his owning the equipment at lease maturity. Head of this operation is Mr. F. Van Loenen, new Manager of the Finance Lease Department.

USA OFFICES
CHICAGO, ILLINOIS 60604:
CTI-Container Transport International Inc.
327 So LaSalle Street
Telephone: (312) 427-4283/4/5
WU Telex: 25-3136
Cables: Container Chicago
Lloyd G. Lucas (*Manager, Mid Western Operations*)
MIAMI, FLORIDA 33134:
CTI-Container Transport International Inc.
4219 S.W. 9th Terrace
Telephone: (305) 444-2679
Cables: Container, Miami
Rosemary 'Pete' Campbell (*Manager*)
NEW ORLEANS, LOUISIANA 70130:
CTI-Container Transport International Inc.
1608 Int. Trade Mart
Telephone: (504) 523-1178
WU Telex: 58-369
Lt. Col. Mike Kachmarik, USAR (ret) (*Director, South Western Region*)
NORFOLK, VIRGINIA 23510:
CTI-Container Transport International Inc.

40 ft refrigerated reefer now available for lease from CTI.   Note the Thermo King unit is completely recessed.

Law Building, 147 Granby Street
Telephone: (703) MAdison 7-7948
Gloria Campbell (*Manager*)
PHILADELPHIA, PA. 19133:.
CTI-Container Transport International Inc.
2501 Germantown Avenue
Telephone: (215) BAldwin 9-0400
Benj. D. Bernstein (*Manager*)
PORT NEWARK, N.J.07114:
CTI-Container Transport International Inc.
Building 161 Marsh Street
Telephone: (212) 425-2828 ex-296
Harry Doyle (*Manager*)
SAN FRANCISCO, CALIF. 94105:
CTI-Container Transport International Inc.
Suite 408, 105 Market Street
Telephone: (415) 391-2346/7/8/9
WU Telex: 34-228
Cables: Container, S.F.
Leonard E. Pera (*Managing Director,
Western Division*)
WASHINGTON, D.C.
Direct line Telephone: ENterprise 1-3240 to
CTI-Container Transport International Inc.,
New York
Exclusive Agent:
Merchants Storage Company of Virginia
520 South Van Dorn Street, Alexandria,
Va. 22304
Telephone: (703) 354-0400
C. A. Hite (*Vice President*)
EUROPEAN HEADQUARTERS:
CTI-Container Transport International Inc.
Eagle House, 109/110 Jermyn Street,
London, S.W.1, England
Telephone 01.930 0156/7/8
Telex: 24952 (Seavan London)
Cables: Seavan London
Cmdr. Clive Gwinner, RN (ret.) (*General
Overseas Manager*)
AUSTRALIA:
Capt. C. I. Jensen,
c/o Data Systems Management (Pty) Ltd,
50 Young Street,
Sydney, N.S.W. 2000
Telephone: 27-7696
Cables: Datamac, Sydney

BELGIUM AND LUXEMBURG:
Container Transport International (Belgium)
N.V.

9-33 Cadixstraat, Antwerp, Belgium
Telephone: 32 38 20
Telex: 31433 (Freyloo Antw)
Cables: Container, Antwerp
J. Vercammen (*Director*)

FRANCE
Container Transport International (France)
S.A.
138 Rue de Rivoli, Paris 8e, France
Telephone 359 2616
Telex: 65965 (CTI Paris)
Cables: Seavan, Paris

GERMANY:
Container Transport International (Germany)
G.m.b.H.
P.O. Box 3949
Hebelstrasse 11 (Corner Scheffelstrasse)
Frankfurt/Main 1, Germany

ITALY AND YUGOSLAVIA:
Container Transport International (Italia)
S.p.A.
Via I. Rosellini 2, 20124 Milano, Italy
Telephone: 680.548-690 469
Telex: 31147 (Paris)
Cables: Container, Milano
Mr. Gualtiero Demani (*Manager*)
JAPAN:
Container Transport International (Japan)
Ltd.
P.O. Box 52 Yokohama Naka
Sumire Building,
9-8, 2-chome, Okina-cho, Naka-ku,
Yokohama
Telephone: Yokohama (681) 5681/5
Telex: 7707 (CTIJ)

CTI Container open-top unit (above) and collapsible cargo flat (below).

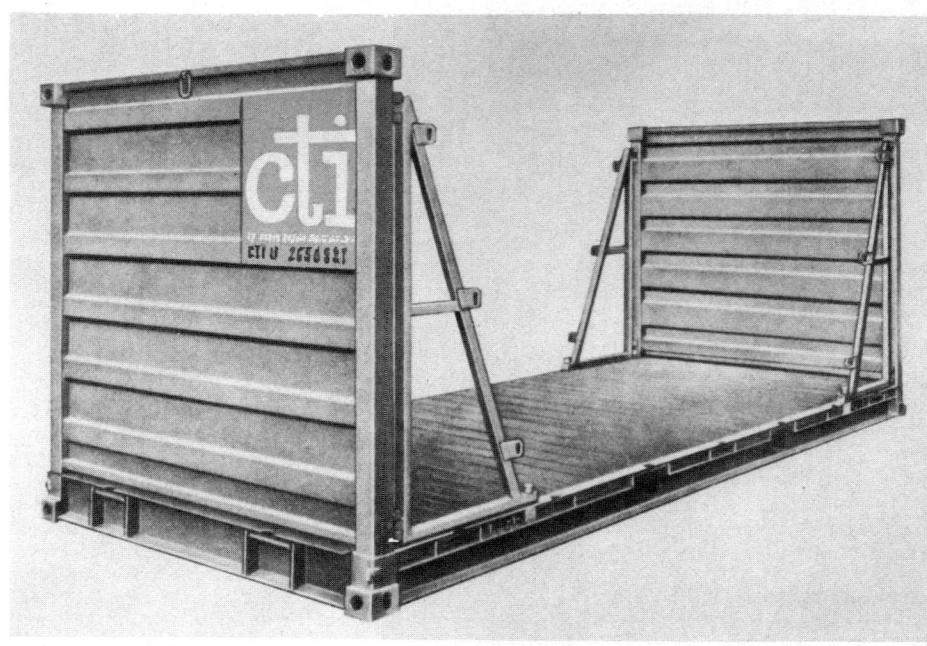

Cables: CTIJ, Yokohama
T. Miyamoto (*Exec. Vice-President*)
PANAMA:
CTI-Container Transport International
(Panama) SA
P.O. Box 895, Curundu, Panama Canal Zone
4th of July Ave. & 17A Street, Panama City
Telephone: 622011-622022
Cables: (Via Tropical) Container, Panama
Mr. David F. K. Brown (*Manager, Latin
America Division*)
SPAIN:
Container Transport International (Espana)
S.A.
Calle Murcia 10, Madrid 7, Spain
Telephone: 227 38 20
Cables: Container, Madrid
Luis Fluiters (*President*)

UNITED KINGDOM:
**Container Transport (Great Britain) Ltd.
Eagle House
109/110 Jermyn Street, London S.W.1,
England**
Telephone: 01.930 0156/7/8

Telex: 24952 (Seavan London)
Cables: Seavan London
Commander Clive Gwinner RN (ret.)
(*Managing Director*)
Agents in Principal Countries of the World
Agents and representatives have Classification Numbers as follows:
(1) Participants in the CTI Interchange
Systems and/or Container Stations
(2) Cargo Agents
(3) Household Goods Agents
Agents without Classification Numbers are equipped primarily for the handling of household goods, but may also be used for other type shipments. It is essential however that containers are returned to approved container stations only.
ALASKA:
Sig Wold Storage & Transfer Co.
802 Second Avenue, Fairbanks 99701   (3)
Smyth Overseas Van Lines Inc.
2510 Post Road, Anchorage 99501   (3)

ARGENTINA:
Lift-Van International Inc.

P.O. Box 3630
Calle Sarmiento 640, 3er Piso, Buenos Aires
Telephone: 46-5889
Cables: Liftvan, Buenos Aires
A. J. Coghlan (*Manager*)

AUSTRALIA:
LEP Transport Pty. Ltd.
543 Little Collins Street, Melbourne
Victoria 3000
Telephone: 62 6531
Cables: Depolep, Melbourne
R. Goodwright (*General Manager*)
A & E Le Mesurier Ltd.
Lipson Street, Port Adelaide
South Australia 5015
Telephone: 4 1421
Cables: Centuary Adelaide (2)
J. A. Soar (*Director*)
LEP Transport (N.S.W.) Pty. Ltd.
10, Young Street, Sydney, N.S.W.
Telephone: 27 746
P H. Norman (*Managing Director*) (2)
Wridgway Bros. (Auburn) Pty., Ltd.
2-18 Camberwell Road
Auburn, Victoria, Australia (3)
AUSTRIA:
Panalpina AG
Gigergasse 1
A-1031 Vienna
Telephone: 777 694 725
Telex: 11794
Cables: Panalpina, Vienna
F. Friedrich (*Manager*)
BAHAMAS:
McCartney Thompson Co., Ltd. (3)
P.O. Box 887
Nassau, Bahamas
Cables: Macttomco Bahamas
BELGIUM:
Container Transport International (Belgium)
N.V. (1) (3)
Agence Maritime A. Freyman and Van Loo
S.P.R.L.
9-33 Cadixstraat, Antwerp, Belgium
Telephone: 32 38 30
Telex: 31433 or 31951 (Freyloo Antw)
Cables: Freyloo, Antwerp
Mr. N. Gosselin (*Managing Associate*)
With branch offices in Brussels, Courtrai and
Ostend. Direct all traffic inquiries to the
Antwerp Office. (2)
Ets Cornelius
91-93 C. de Ninove, Brussels
Telephone: 21.02.25
Telex: 23831
Cables: Demcornelis, Brussels
Container Depots: Antwerp, Zeebrugge
BERMUDA:
Bermuda Transfer & Storage Company, Ltd.
Dundonald Street West, Hamilton
Telephone: 5900
Cables: Transferco Bermuda
W. E. Jones (*Manager*)
BOLIVIA:
Incatur, S.A.
Avenida Camacho No. 1476
Casilla 460, La Paz
Cables: Incatur, La Paz
Telex: Incatur, La Paz 5214
Robert P. Hertzog (*Manager*)
BRAZIL:
Transportes Fink S.A.
Caixa Postal 8298
Rua Barao da Itapetininga 46, Sao Paulo
Telephone: 36.1122
Cables: Transportefink, Sao Paulo
Transportes Fink, S.A.
P.O. Box 2866
Avenida Rio Branco 257, Rio de Janeiro
Telephone: 52-5959
Cables: Transportefink, Rio
BURMA:
Golden Bird Agencies Limited
P.O. Box 1298
420 Merchant Street, Rangoon, Burma
Telex: 14706 and 14899
Cables: Schwenget, Rangoon

CANADA:
Intermodal Container Pool Ltd.
353 St. Nicholas St., Suite 412, Montreal
125 P.Q. (1)
Telephone: (514) 843.887
Cables: Conpool, Montreal
L. Kendall (*Manager*)
CHILE:
S. I. T. Deca Ltda.
Casilla 2932, Agustinas 1049, Santiago
Telephone: 82662/3
Telex: 3520065 Gonchil
Cables: Decavion, Santiago
Carlos K. Stein (*Manager*)
COLOMBIA:
Aero Mar Ltda.
Apartado Aereo 6986
Avenida Jimenez 7-25, Bogota D.E.
Telephone: 436-816
Telex: 044672 Aeromar
Cables: Aeroduan, Bogota
CONGO REPUBLIC:
Agence Maritime Internationale
Matadi, Republic of the Congo
Cables: Agenmarin, Matadi
COSTA RICA:
Transportes Baxter, Ltda.
P.O. Box 5389, San Jose
Telephone: 224261
Alberto Barquero (*Manager*)
CURACAO:
Meyer Emballeer-En Transportbedrijf N.V.
Schottegatweg Oost 11, Willemstad
Telephone: 35249
A. M. Meijer (*Manager*)
DENMARK:
Team-Trailers A.S.
Sydvestvej 73, 2600 Copenhagen-Glostrup
Telephone: 96 92 44
Telex: 2856 (Teamtrail KH)
Knut E. Andrearsen (*Manager*)
DOMINICAN REPUBLIC:
Teodulo Aquino C por A
Calle 18, No. 99
(Ens. La Fe)
Santo Domingo
ECUADOR:
Metropolitan Expreso S.A.
Apartado Postal 1200, Quito
Telephone: 37700/37860
Cables: Metrotouring, Quito
Victor Hernan Cortez (*Manager*)
EL SALVADOR:
Mudanzas Suarez
12 Calle Poniente Entre 27729, Avenida Sur,
San Salvador
Telephone: 21-6118, 21-6275
Cables: Risuarez, San Salvador
Rafael R. Suarez (*Manager*)
ETHIOPIA:
Messagerie Africa S/A
P.O. Box 630
221-223 Avenue H. Selassie 1st, Asmara,
Ethiopia
Telephone: 10157
Cables: Messerit, Asmara
FINLAND:
Oy Huolintakeskus A.B.
Kalevank 7, Helsinki, Finland
Telephone: 61021
Telex: 12-530
Cables: Huolintakeskus, Helsinki (2)
G. Lindberg (*Manager*)
Oy Victor Ek, A.B.
Eltelaranta 16,
Helsinki, Finland
Telephone: 61631
Telex: 12-432
Cables: Victorek, Helsinki (3)
Container Depots: Helsinki, Lahti, Tampere
FRANCE:
CTI-Container Transport International
(France) S.A.
13 Rue Paul Baudry, Paris 8e
Telephone: 359.2616
Telex: 65965
Cables: Seavan, Paris
Guy M. Dardel (*President*)

Container Depots: Paris, Le Havre,
Bordeaux, Lyon, Marseille, Dunkirk,
Strasbourg
GERMANY:
CTI-Container Transport International
(Germany) G.m.b.H.
P.O. Box 3949
Hebelstrasse 11 (Corner Scheffelstrasse)
Frankfurt/Main 1
Telephone: (series) no.: (0611)-590188
Telex: 414283 ctid
Cables: Container, Frankfurt
Hermann Truckenmueller (*Manager*)
CTI agent and container station Hamburg:
Carl Tiedemann
Roedingsmarkt 20, 2 Hamburg 11
Telephone: Hamburg 36 14 41
Telex: 2-12524 (CT D)
Cables: Fairplay, Hamburg
Michael Hanauer (*Manager*)
Container Depots in: Bochum, Bremen,
Frankfurt, Cologne, Dusseldorf,
Ludwigsburg/Stuttgart, Mannheim, Munich,
Nuremberg
GHANA:
Watson Services Ltd.
P.O. Box 1013
Labadi Road, Accra
Telephone: 75163
Cables: Watserve, Accra
GREAT BRITAIN:
See United Kingdom
GREECE:
'Hermes' Rudolph Maslias & Co.
P.O. Box 326, 37, Fr. Roosevelt Street,
Athens 135
Telephone: 624-801
Cables: Etermis, Athens (2) (3)
GUAM:
Smith Van of Guam
P.O. Box 1094, Agana
Telephone: 722 200
Cables: Smith Co. Agana
GUATEMALA:
Caniz Van Lines
Apartado Postal No. 35, 8a Ave, 15-48,
Guatemala 1, Guatemala C.A.
Telephone: 4682 and 9815
Cables: Caniz, Guatemala City
HAITI:
Seminaire Adventiste Packing Service
P.O.B. 1725, Port au Prince
HAWAII:
Smyth Hawaiian Van Lines
B017 Vualena St., Honolulu 96819
Telephone: 808 841 6171
Cables: Shvlco, Honolulu
HONDURAS:
Juan R. Gamundi (*Manager*)
No. 310, Edificio Midence-Soto, Tegucicalpa,
D.C.
Telephone: 2-3638, 2-1333
HONG KONG:
Consolidated Container Services Ltd.
Sincere Insurance Building,
4, Hennessy Road, Hong Kong
Telephone: H-729 800; H-730 149
Telex: 4355
Cables: Conserlim, Hong Kong
B. P. Holden (*Manager*)

ICELAND:
Petur Arnason
Hagamel 35, Reykjavik
Telephone: 10195
Cables: Arnes, Reykjavik
INDIA:
Lee & Muirhead
12 Rampart Row, Fort, Bombay 1
Telephone: 251571
Cables: Lemuir, Bombay
INDONESIA:
P. T. Intra-Priok
Djl. Bangka No. 1-Pelabuhan 111
P.O. Box 7,
Tandjung Priok, Djakarta
Telephone: O.P. 29150

IRAN:
Near East Transport
126 Takht Jamshid
Tehran, Iran
Cables: Net, Tehran
IRAQ:
Levant Express Transport (Iraq) W.L.L.
Kubba Bldg., Saadoon Street
P.O.B. 3002 Saadoon, Baghdad
Telephone: 89558/59
Cables: Levantex. Baghdad
IRELAND:
R. A. Burke Ltd.
22 Eden Quay, Dublin 1
Telephone: 43650
Cables: Rabco, Dublin   (2)
Ernest Cullen & Sons, Ltd.
Henrietta Place, Dublin
Telephone: 43504-5
Cables: Haulage, Dublin   (3)
ITALY:
CTI-Container Transport International
(Italia) S.P.A.
Francesco Parisi
Via I. Rosellini 2, Milan 2541, Italy
Telephone: 688
Telex: 31147 (Parisi)
Cables: Parisi, Milan
R. Stradella (Director)
Main office in Trieste. Branch offices in
Genoa, Leghorn, Ravenna, Venice. Direct
all traffic inquiries to the Milan Office.   (2)
D. C. Stein-Roma
Via del Babuino 70, 106187 Rome
Telephone: 671 867
Container Depots: Cadenazzo, Genoa,
Milan and Leghorn
IVORY COAST:
J. P. Holmen Ets
P.O. Box 1313
Abidjan, Ivory Coast
JAMAICA:
B. L. Williams & Co.
25 Harbour Street
Kingston, Jamaica
Telephone: 25832
JAPAN:
CTI-Container Transport International
(Japan) Ltd.
P.O. Box 52 Yokohama Naka
Sumire Building, 9-8, 2-chome, Okina-cho
Naka-ku, Yokohama
Telephone: (681) 5681/5 (Yokohama)
Telex: 7707 (CTIJ)
Cables: CTIJ, Yokohama
Y. Matsumoto (Vice President)
Hawaiian Far-East Van, Inc.
117 Yamashita-cho, Naka-ku, Yokohama
Telephone: 65-2241/43
Cables: Hafevan, Yokohama
James R. Kumagai (Manager)   (2) (3)
JORDAN:
Jordan Express Co.
P.O. Box 2143
King Hussein Road, Bilbeisi Bldg.
Amman
Telephone: 22184/5
Cables: Jordex, Amman
Isa J. Majaj (Director)
KENYA:
The Express Transport Co., Ltd.
P.O. Box 433
Nairobi, Kenya
KOREA:
Yongsan Cargo Trans. Co., Ltd.
92 Kalwol-Dong, Yongsan-ku
Seoul
Telephone: 4.2733
Cables: Yongsantrasco, Seoul
KUWAIT:
Gulf Agency Co. Ltd.,
P.O. Box 589
Kuwait
LEBANON:
O.D. Debbas & Sons
Ave. Foch & Rue Du Port
Beirut

Mr. Dimitri Debbas (Manager)   (2) (3)
LIBERIA:
Alreime (Liberia) Co., Ltd.
P.O. Box 135, Monrovia, Liberia
Telephone: 21646, 21037
Cables: Freight, Monrovia
Telex: 209
LIBYA:
The Tripolitania Enterprises Co.
P.O. Box 149, Tripoli
Telephone: 41627-45489
Cables: Teco Tripoliafrica
L. Mefalopulos (Manager)   (2) (3)
Libyan Transport Company
P.O. Box 94, Benghazi   (2) (3)
Mr. A. Buzer (Manager)
LUXEMBURG:
CTI-Container Transport International
(Belgium) N.V.
9-33 Cadixstraat, Antwerp, Belgium
Telephone: 32 38 20
Telex: 31433 (Freyloo Antw)
Cables: Container, Antwerp
J. Vercammen (Director)
MALAYSIA:
Packing & Storage Ltd.
9 Jalan Gereta, Kuala Lumpur
Telephone: 85358
Cables: Packstor, Kuala Lumpur
Transport & Storage Ltd.
P.O. Box 1575, 173 Cecil Street
Cables: Transtor, Singapore
MEXICO:
Mundanzas Gou S.A. de C.V.
Apartado Postal 16126
Nuevo Santo Domingo No. 149
Tracc. San Antonio, Axcapotzalco
Mexico 16, D.F.
Telephone: 612-900
Cables: Edgousa, Mexico City
MOZAMBIQUE (PORTUGUESE EAST AFRICA)
Allen, Wach & Shepherd, Ltd.
P.O. Boxes 270, 280 and 290
Beira
NETHERLANDS:
CTI-Container Transport International
(Holland) N.V.
Boomjes 55, Rotterdam
Telephone: 139446/7
Telex: 24240 (CTI Holland Rt)
Anthony E. Kolff (Special Representative)
Container Depots: Rotterdam, Amsterdam
NEW ZEALAND:
Seatrans Consolidated (NZ) Ltd.
Rata Street (Mail Private Bag)
Mount Marganui, NZ
Telephone: 54099
Cables: Seatrain NZ
Telex: NZ 2285
A. C. Williams (Manager)
NICARAGUA:
Transportes EVICO
P.O. Box 1412, Managua
Telephone: 36-83
Ed Vidaurri (Manager)
NIGERIA:
John Holt Shipping Services, Ltd.
22 Wharf Road (P.O. Box 89) Apapa
NORWAY:
A/S Adams Express
36 Akersgatan, Oslo 1
Telephone: 33 72 21
Cables: Adams, Oslo
Telex: 6224 Oslo
K. Collins-Andersen (Manager)
OKINAWA:
Smyth Van of Okinawa
APO, 96248, San Francisco, Calif.
Telephone: 099 5261
Cables: Sivleo, Okinawa
PAKISTAN:
Dadabhoy Harmusjee & Sons
P.O. Box 4737
12, Nadir House, McLeod Rd., Karachi 2
Telephone: 236172-232837
Cables: Dadysons, Karachi
Dadabhoy B. Mama (Manager)

PANAMA:
CTI-Container Transport International
(Panama) S.A.
P.O. Box 895, Curundu, Panama Canal Zone
4th of July Ave. and 17A Street,
Panama City
Telephone: 622011-622022
Cables: (Via Tropical) Container, Panama
Air Van Pak, Inc.
P.O. Box 2005, Curundu, P.C.Z.
Telephone: PCZ2-2562
Cables: (Tropical) Baxter, Panama RP
F. S. Rudesheim (Manager)   (3)
PARAGUAY:
Estanislao H. Arce
Presidente Franco 945
Asuncion
PERU:
Garcia Baggage Transfer Agency, Inc.
Av. Tingo Maria 1601-09, Brena (Lima)
Telephone: 32062
Cables: Gabatra, Lima
Telex: Gabatralim Wla-5341
Domingo Zavala (Manager)
PHILIPPINES:
Delgado Brokerage Corp.
P.O. Box 292, Manila
Telephone: 3-85-41
Cables: Delbros, Manila
Fred B. Land, Jr. (Manager)
PORTUGAL:
A. J. Goncalves de Moraes Lda.
P.O. Box 2772
26-1° Rua De Sao Paulo, Lisbon
Telephone: 34943
Cables: Amotas, Lisbon
Telex: 296/297 Lisbon
Mr. Barros, Junior (Manager)   (2)
Empresa de Transportes Galamas, Lda
Rua da Victoria 10, Lisbon
Cables: Transgalamas, Lisbon   (3)
PUERTO RICO:
Continental Moving & Storage Corp.
P.O. Box 427, Bayamon PR 00619
Telephone: 785-9600
Cables: Conmoving, Bayamon
RHODESIA:
G. Elcombe Ltd.
6 Railway Avenue
Salisbury
SIERRA LEONE:
Union Maritime et Commerciale
P.O. Box 417
7 College Road, Cline Town
Freetown
Telephone: 33-48
Cables: Umarco, Freetown
SOUTH AFRICA:
Grindrod, Gersigny & Co. (Pty) Ltd.
P.O. Box 2161
10 Leslie Street, Durban
Telephone: 311411
Telex: 6-7267
Cables: Grindrodco, Durban   (2)
Stuttaford & Co. Ltd.
P.O. Box 69
Capetown, So. Africa   (3)
SPAIN:
CTI-Container Transport International
(Espana) S.A.
Calle Murcia 10, Madrid 7, Spain
Telephone: 227 38 20
Cables: Container, Madrid
Luis Fluiters (President)
Transportes Fluiters, S.A.
Barquillo, 12
Madrid 4, Spain
Telephone: 2315240
Cables: Fluiters, Madrid
Luis Fluiters (Director)   (3)
Container Depots: Madrid, Barcelona
Valencia, Bilbao
SUDAN:
Kastaki, Saleem, Ganbert & Sons
P.O. Box 615
Khartoum, Sudan
Telephone: 70871

SWEDEN:
CTI-Container Transport International (Scandinavia) A/B
Nybrogatan 38, P.O. Box 5206, 102 45 Stockholm
Telephone: 67 69 92/72/38
Telex: 10587 (Scancon S)
Cables: Scancontainer, Stockholm
H. G. Koschland (*Managing Director*)
Olle Wallentin (*Sales Representative*)
Kommendorsgatan, Gothenburg 6
Telephone: 641154
Telex: 21074

SWITZERLAND:
Inter-Transport Ltd.
CFF Bldg., Station La Praille, 1211, Geneva 26
Telephone: 43 88 00
Telex: 22803 (Intertrans Gve)
Cables: Intertransports, Geneva
E. Ley (*President*)
With representation in Basle, Berne and Zurich. (1) (2) (3)

A. Welti-Furrer A.G.
Mullerstrasse 16
Zurich 22, Switzerland
Telephone: 23 76 15
Telex: 52 742
Cables: Weltifurrer, Zurich (3)
Container Depots: Basle, Bad Bahnhof

SYRIA:
Dahdah Bros.
P.O. Box 127
Damascus

TAIWAN (FORMOSA):
Oriental Enterprises, Inc.
Box 1, APO 96263, San Francisco, Calif.
32-1 Chung Shan Rd. N.
2nd Section, Taipei
Telephone: 48002
Cables: Orinc Taipei
Harvey Toy (*Manager*)

TANZANIA:
Express Transport Co., Ltd.
P.O. Box 884
Dar-es-Salaam, Tanzania
Telephone: 21426/7
Cables: Express, Dar-es-Salaam

THAILAND:
Boonma Moving & Storage Co., Ltd.
P.O. Box 11/128 Phrakanong
Bangkok, II.
Telephone: 38035
Cables: Moving, Bangkok

TRINIDAD:
Henderson Shipping Service
8 Abercromby Street, Port-of-Spain
Telephone: 3-4166/67
Cables: Wilhend, Port-of-Spain
T. Nathaniel (*Manager*)

TUNISIA:
F. Pierotti
21 Avenue Barthou, Tunis
Telephone: 280.268, 284.282, 284.296

TURKEY:
Mehmet Ali Tuzcuoglu
Gazi M. Kemal Bulvari No. 86, Ankara
Telephone: 125863
Cables: Tuzcular, Ankara

UGANDA:
Excel Packing, Forwarding & Receiving Co., Ltd.
P.O. Box 3559, Kampala,
Telephone: 5361
R. Joshi (*Managing Director*)

UNITED KINGDOM
CTI-Container Transport (Great Britain) Ltd.
Eagle House, 109/110 Jermyn Street, London S.W.1, England
Telephone: 01-930 0156/7/8
Telex: 24952 (Seavan London)
Cables: Seavan, London
Commander Clive Gwinner, RN (ret.) (*Managing Director*)

MAT Transport Limited (2)
Arnold House, 36-41 Holywell Lane, Great Eastern Street
P.O. Box 251, London, E.C.2
Telephone: Bishopsgate 6500
Telex: 28404
J. L. Vaughan (*Traffic Manager*)
Container Depots: London, Liverpool, Birmingham, Glasgow, Bristol, Coventry, Derby, Hull, Manchester, Middlesbrough.

URUGUAY:
Aero Expreso Internacional Uruguayo S.A.
Mercedes y Convencion, Montevideo (R.O.U.)
Telephone: 98 24 52, 98 23 52, 98 26 28
Omar Trombotti (*Managing Director*)

VENEZUELA:
Clover International Movers C.A.
Apartado 705
Avenida San Martin, Caracas
Telephone: 41.07.45
Cables: Corin, Caracas
Ignacia Perozo Parra (*General Manager*)

VIET-NAM:
Cie. Saigonaise de Transit
67 Rue Nguyen-Du
Saigon.

VIRGIN ISLANDS:
The Viking Corp.
P.O. Box 1536, Charlotte-Amalie, St. Thomas V1 00820
Telephone: 774-1536
Cables: Viking, St. Thomas
George Lovejoy (*Manager*)

Island Transport Service
P.O. Box 879, Christiansted, St. Croix, V1 00820
Telephone: 773-0195
Cables: Porterm, St. Croix
Frank Catanach (*Manager*)
Col. Wm. Jay Fleming, USA (ret) (*Special Consultant, Caribbean Area*)

YUGOSLAVIA:
Container Transport International (Italia) S.p.A. (see Italy)

ZAMBIA:
Agence Maritime Internationale
Box 964, Lusaka

(1) Participant in CTI Interchange Agreement
(2) Cargo Agent
(3) Household Goods Agent

CONTAINER MODELS

		Cargo Capacity
20 ft	Steel Dry Cargo Container	18,140 kg (40,000 lb)
30 ft	Steel Container	22,200 kg (48,500 lb)
30 ft	Steel Container (side door)	21,968 kg (48,440 lb)
20 ft	Aluminium Seatrailer (with fork pockets)	18,594 kg (41,000 lb)
20 ft	Steel Container with Removable Steel Roof	17,879 kg (39,382 lb)
20 ft	Tank Container	23,000 kg (50,640 lb)
20 ft	Steel Semi-Insulated/ Ventilated Containers	17,730 kg (39,100 lb)
20 ft	FRP-Plywood Container	(18,290 kg (40,323 lb)
20 ft	Steel Flats	18,140 kg (40,000 lb)
20 ft	Steel Collapsible Flat with Steel side and end rails	19,170 kg (42,224 lb)
20 ft	Steel Collapsible Flat (4 ft high)	19,621 kg (43,260 lb)
20 ft	Collapsible Coil Carrier with side and end rails	*Point Loading* 18,458 kg (40,656 lb); *Distributed Loading* 22,107 kg (48,496 lb)

		Cargo Capacity
20 ft	Steel Flat with removable sides (4 ft high) and forklift pockets	22,670 kg (50,000 lb)
30 ft	Steel Tilt Container with forklift pockets	21,550 kg (47,510 lb)
20 ft and 30 ft	Steel Open Side Containers	*20 ft* 17,617 kg (38,845 lb); *30 ft* 21,496 kg (47,399 lb)
20 ft and 40 ft	Open Top Steel Container	*20 ft* 18,320 kg (40,391 lb); *40 ft* 26,530 kg (58,429 lb)
40 ft	Open Top Containers with 8 ft 6 in tunnel and swing-clear rear membrane	26,293 kg (57,969 lb)
40 ft	Steel dry Cargo Container	27,630 kg (60,912 lb)
30 ft	Steel dry Cargo Container	22,200 kg (48,500 lb)
40 ft	Aluminium Marine Container with lining	24,948 kg (55,000 lb)
40 ft	Aluminium FlexiVan	27,216 kg (60,000 lb)
40 ft	Dry Cargo Gooseneck Container, chassis and bogie, 8 ft 6 in high	*Steel* 27,380 kg (60,361 lb); *Aluminium* 27,438 kg (60,500 lb)
40 ft	Tunnel Refrigerated Container with Thermo-King (—28·9°C—26·7°C) Unit	*with fuel tank* 25,549 kg (56,275 lb)
20 ft and 40 ft	Steel Side Door Containers	*20 ft* 17,958 kg (39,598 lb); *40 ft* 27,064 kg (59,676 lb)
10 m³	Dry Cargo Container Type 410. 2·59 m (8 ft 6⅛ in) × 2·14 m (7 ft ⅜ in) × 2·09 m (6 ft 10¼ in)	5,443 kg (12,000 lb)
8 m³	Dry Cargo Container Type 357, 2·40 m (7 ft 10½ in) × 2·10 m (6 ft 10¾ in) × 2·01 m (6 ft 7 in)	5,987·4 kg (13,200 lb)

Other Items
20 ft frame and bogie
24 ft chassis and tandem bogie
20 ft coupleable chassis
20 ft frame with single axle bogie
40 ft chassis and bogie
40 ft steel flatbed trailer with sliding tandem axle bogie and eight twistlocks for 1 40 ft or 2 20 ft units, cargo capacity 25,000 kg (55,000 lb).

Smaller containers, Type 365 and 184 with cargo capacities of 5,080 kg (11,200 lb) and 4,083 kg (9,000 lb) are also available.

Bags of chemicals go through the side door of a new 40 ft container which CTI-Container Transport International Inc. has just added to its fleet. The unit has a door at one end and on one side.

AFFILIATED COMPANIES:
Container Leasing Corporation
17 Battery Place, New York, NY 10004
Telephone: (212) 425-2828
Telex: 222975
Cables: Container NY
TWX: 710 581-2932

Fred Van Loenen (*Vice President*)

US Container Stations:
The container stations at Chicago, Ill., New Orleans, La., Norfolk, Va., Philadelphia, Pa., Port Newark, NJ (Port of New York) and San Francisco should be contacted through the CTI offices listed under 'USA' offices.

BOSTON MASS:
Wiggin Terminals, Inc.
156 State Street

Boston Mass. 02129
Telephone: (617) 268 9870
Telex: 710.339.6806

CLEVELAND, OHIO:
International Development Corp.
1087 West 11th Street
Cleveland, Ohio 44113
Telephone: (216) 781-6681

DETROIT, MICHIGAN:
Capital Cartage
8585 Dearborn Ave.
Detroit, Mich. 48209
Telephone: (313) 843-8100
HOUSTON, TEXAS:
Gulf Port Crating Co.
1600 N. 75 Street
P.O. Box 2343

Houston, Texas 77001
Telephone: (713) WA 3-5551

LOS ANGELES, CALIFORNIA
Consolidated Dock & Storage Co.
1400 E. Anaheim Street
Wilmington, California 90744
Telephone: (213) 830-8181

TOLEDO, OHIO:
Jones Transfer Co.
111 Jones Avenue, Monroe, Michigan 48161
Telephone: (419) 726-2631

OAKLAND, CALIFORNIA
Containerfreight Corporation
Building No. 120, Oakland Army Base
Oakland, California 94107
Telephone: (415) 986-5121

INTERGRATED CONTAINER SERVICE INC. (I.C.S.)

Integrated Container Service, Inc (ICS)
HEAD OFFICE:
555 Fifth Avenue,
New York,
NY 10017
TELEPHONE: (212) 684 5132
TELEX: 126040
TELEGRAMS: Intconserv New York City
OFFICERS:
J. P. Thrasher (*President*)
A. Goldman (*Vice President ICSI*)
D. Kenny (*Vice President, Counsel*)
J. Davies (*Vice President, Technical Services*)
J. Needleman (*Vice President, Finance*)
GENERAL:
Integrated Container Service, Inc. is a container leasing company which provides highly specialized equipment necessary for the efficient movement of freight on a 'door-to-door' basis between continents. The ICS plan offers demountable van containers especially designed to co-ordinate and integrate rail-highway-marine shipments between the major areas of the free world. Integrated Container Service equipment is designed to achieve

maximum inter-changeability with most forms of marine and surface transportation groups and offers the flexibility of operating as a system or as an individual piece of revenue equipment thereby insuring revenue generating capability.

Equipment is available to participants in a pool plan confined mainly to selected rail, marine, and highway carriers both in the United States and abroad.

All pool participants pay for the use of equipment on a per diem basis for the period of time it is in their possession thereby minimizing equipment investments and increasing their shipper customers.

North & South American Area HQ and Region HQ
R. Strouce (*Vice President*)
P. Sirignano (*Area Coordinator*)
AMERICA-EASTERN REGION (GULF AND S. AMERICA):
G. Roof (*Manager*)
90 West Street, New York, N.Y. 10017
Telephone: (212) 684 5132

Telex: 126040 (ISC Eastern NYK)
AMERICA-CENTRAL REGION (CANADA):
M. Richmond (*Manager*)
327 South La Salle St., Suite 1548
Chicago, Ill. 60604
Telephone: (312) 939 4611
Telex: 253729 (ICS Midwest CGO)

America—Southern Region
J. Hunter (*Manager*)
Room 840—Paul Brown Buidling
818 Olive St.
St. Louis, Missouri 63101
Telephone: 314 621 0363
Telex: 447185

European Area HQ and Region HQ
Kings House,
9-10 Haymarket, London, S.W.1
Telephone: 01-839 4444
Telex: 266861
Telegrams: Icsinc London S.W.1
R. H. Finn (*Vice President, Europe*)
K. G. Happich (*Area Coordinator*)

Kings House,
9-10 Haymarket, London, S.W.1
Telephone: 01-839 4444
Telex: 266861
A. E. Curtis (*UK Manager*)
M. D. Webster (*Interchange Controller*)
MEDITERRANEAN REGION:
ANTWERP (serving Benelux)
Meirburg 1, Antwerp
Belgium
Telephone: 311145/46
Telex: 33543
A. E. Curtis (*Regional Manager*)
H. T. Elemans (*Interchange Controller*)
GENOA (serving Italy and Switzerland)
Piazza G. Matteotti 2
16123 Genoa, Italy,
Telephone: 202864
Telex: 27553
H. Lufi (*Regional Manager*)
M. Malvelli (*Interchange Controller*)
HAMBURG (serving Germany, Austria and
   Hungary)
2000 Hamburg 11,
Katharinenstrasse 33',
West Germany
Telephone: 366464
Telex: 211968
H. Grosse (*Regional Manager*)
U. Marquardt (*Interchange Controller*)
PARIS (serving France)
ICS
26 Rue de la Pepinière
Paris 8e
Telephone: 522 7910
A. Fernagu (*Manager*)
R. Prefontaine (*Interchange Controller*)-

STOCKHOLM (serving Scandinavia and
   Finland)
Skeppsbron 16,
111 30 Stockholm,
Sweden,
Telephone: 118835
Telex: 1858
P. Widlund (*Regional Manager*)
C. Wahlund (*Interchange Controller*)
LONDON (serving United Kingdom and
   Ireland)

H. Lufi (*Manager*)
ICS S.r.L.
Piazza G. Matteotti, 16123 Genoa

Italy
Telephone: 202 864-205 762
Telex: 27553 (ICS MED)
SCANDINAVIAN REGION:
P. Wildlund (*Manager*)
C. Wahlund (*Intercharge Controller*)
Integrated Container Scandinavia A/B
Skeppsbron 16, 11130 Stockholm
   Sweden
Telephone: 11 88 35-20 18 85
Telex: 17675 (ICS STO)
CENTRAL AND EASTERN EUROPEAN REGION:
H. Grasse (*Manager*)
U. Maquardt (*Interchange Controller*)
Integrated Container Service G.m.b.H.

Katharinenstrasse 33
2000 Hamburg 11, West Germany
Telephone: 36 64 64/65
Telex: 211968 (ICS CO D)
BENELUX REGION:
A. E. Curtis (*Manager*)
Integrated Container Service
Union Buildings, Meinberg 1, Antwerp
Belgium
Telephone: 323/3111 45/46
Telex: 33543

Pacific Area HQ and Region HQ

F. Fisher (*Vice President*)
W. Stenwick (*Area Coordinator*)
AMERICAN-PACIFIC REGION (JAPAN AND
   MANILLA):
W. MacIntosh (*Manager*)

601 California St., Suite 1210
San Francisco, California 94108
Telephone: (415) 421 7932
Telex: 340664 (ICS West)
   The Depots and Agents in Taiwan, Hong
Kong, Singapore and Australia (F. Strang
Pty, 121 Sussex St., Sydney) come under
this area.
JAPAN:
K. Oda (*Manager*)
c/o Kamigumi Co. Ltc.,
7-11, 3-Chome, Shibaura, Tokyo
Telephone: 452 3940
Telex: 781 0241 2516

Equipment Pool Plan

ICS Provides a comprehensive range of
pooling and leasing services to freight carriers
(shipping companies, railway companies, road
transport operators, freight forwarders and
container operators) through its world-wide
interchange office and depot system.

These facilities are available to carriers
who sign the Pool Participation Agreement
which merely provides for insurance and
repair procedures, and involves no cost or
commitment apart from this.

ICS SERVICE PLANS:
1. DEPOT PLAN:
Service
   Short term hire from ICS depots for
specified periods, for one way or round trips
to other ICS depots, arranged through ICS
offices.
Payment
   Per diem rates, usually with a minimum
charge.
Benefits
   Quick access to equipment world-wide.
   Short term hire, reducing fleet size.
   One way trips, reducing deadheading.
   Agreed termination.
2. POOL MANAGEMENT PLAN:
Service
   Flexible longer term (1 to 8 year) hires.
Participants specify the number of units they
wish to receive and/or release at a wide range
of ICS depots, and these numbers can be
varied up or down within agreed limits.
   Participants must commit to keep a
minimum of at least 25 units on continuous
hire. These need not, of course, be the same
25 units, so long as the average level of 25 or
more is maintained.
   Participants' existing units can also be
purchased then and committed to the Pool.
Payments
   Fixed per diems with termination fees
based on traffic pattern, length of hire and
quantity, or by fluctuating diem based on the
level of monthly terminations.
Benefits
   Minimisation on imbalances in traffic
pattern over a given period of time.
   Built-in variability in size and type of fleet
to meet varying requirements.
   Agreed availability and/or release at select-
ed points.
3. LEASE PLAN:
Service
   Any number of units are leased for any
period over six months.
   Purchase and lease-back to equipment can
usually be arranged.
   Options can be built in, e.g. to provide
conversion rights to new equipment, or to
transfer to Pool Management Plan.
Payment
   Fixed per diem, based on equipment cost,
quantity and length of hire.
Benefits
   Additional source of finance.
   Quick availability (e.g. for trial purposes).
   Ability to change type or increase or reduce
amount of equipment in service if require-
ments change.

EQUIPMENT AVAILABLE:
Containers Operated as at 1st May, 1971:
                               Serial Nos.
14,300 20 ft dry cargo   260,000-279,999
 4,680 40 ft dry cargo   200,000-208,999
   400 20 ft open top   460,000-460,520
Available in USA
   Chassis for 40 ft dry cargo container
   25 ft 6 in (7·7 m) Chassis
   22 ft 6 in (6·85 m) Chassis
   Frame for 20 ft dry cargo container
   Single Axle Bogies
   Tandem Axle Bogies
Available in Europe
   22 ft 6 in skeletal trailers
   40 ft skeletal trailers
   40 ft gooseneck trailers

EQUIPMENT FOR CONSIGNEES:
The 6,096 mm (20 ft) units can be coupled for
highway and rail transportation, or when
loaded to full allowable net cargo capacity
can be used as individual units. The 6,096 mm
(20 ft) units have an inside cubage of 34 m³
(1,185 cu ft); the 12,192 mm (40 ft) units have
an inside cubage of 68·38 m³ (2,415 cu ft), and
are designed for maximum payloads of
20,321 kg (44,800 lb) and 27,215 kg (60,000 lb)
respectively.

Both the 20 ft and 40 ft units are designed
to be used as over-the-road trailers 3,810 mm
(12 ft 6 in) high, with a fifth-wheel height of
1,219 mm (48 in).

All ICS equipment is 'sea-going' and is
built to standards superior to those required
for land transportation. (See design specifications.)

This equipment will perform as well or
better than the highest quality commercial
trailers or demountable container units
presently in use in domestic service either for
Piggyback' or highway trailer service.

20 ft Strick Sea-Trailer Containers

BASIC DIMENSIONS:
Overall length 6,058 mm (19 ft 10½ in)
Overall width 2,438 mm (8 ft 0 in)
Overall height 2,438 mm (8 ft 0 in)
Inside length 5,940 mm (19 ft 5⅞ in)
Inside width (6·4 mm (¼ in) lining) 2,349 mm
(7 ft 8½ in)
Inside height 2,232 mm (7 ft 3¾ in)
Rear door opening width 2,284 mm (7 ft
5⅝ in)
Rear door opening height 2,130 mm (6 ft
11⅞ in)
Inside cubage 31 m³ (1,100 cu ft)
BASIC WEIGHTS:
Tare weight 1,406 kg (3,100 lb)
Maximum payload 18,915 kg (41,700 lb)
(coupled 27,669 kg (61,000 lb))
Maximum gross weight 20,321 kg (44,800 lb)
(20 long tons), (coupled 30,481 kg (67,200 lb)
(30 long tons)).
DESIGN LOADS:
Stacking in ship's cells — Six high (coupled
—four high)
Acceleration, when lifting by crane — 2 g
Load against side panels — ·6 g at maximum
inclination at 30° from vertical
Front-aft load, imposed directly upon con-
tainer — ·4 g
Roof load — 2 men weighing 90·7 kg (200 lb)
each on 610 mm (24 in) centers, at 1·5 g
Floor load, distributed — 1,709 kg/m² (350
lb/sq ft) at 2 g
Floor load, concentrated — Lift truck with
5,443 kg (12,000 lb) front axle loading
(2,540 to 3,048 kg (2½ to 3 ton) capacity)
Payload distribution — Limited by 1,709
kg/m² (350 lb/sq ft) floor load condition only.

DESIGN CONDITIONS:
The Container conforms to ASA/ISO dimensions, design loadings and payload specifications. It is also constructed to meet TIR
requirements. The ASA/ISO corner fittings
include provision to accommodate STRICK

end to end coupling. Permitting Containers to be handled as individual 20 ft Containers or coupled as 40 ft Container or Semi-Trailer

CHASSIS

The chassis locks to the 6,096 mm (20 ft) Sea-Trailer at the corner fittings and has the necessary king pin and subframe; landing gear; anti-nose dive supports; air and electrical system; track angle to accept a wide slide bogie, and accessories to allow its use on Flexi-Van.

These chassis will be nominally 6,096 mm (20 ft) long, 2,438 mm (8 ft) wide and a maximum depth of 152 mm (6 in)

Chassis, with its container and single axle bogie will be operable as a 6,096 mm (20 ft) single axle semi-trailer. With the containers coupled, it will permit operation as a single axle or tandem axle 12,192 mm (40 ft) semi-trailer. A single chassis with bogie can also be drawn by a tractor, empty.

The bogie will be slidable along the full length of the chassis, with adjustable locations.

Two single axle bogies may be connected to a chassis so that they can be operated in tandem to meet maximum load requirements. When two chassis are end-to-end coupled through the attached containers, the single axle bogies may be positioned together to form a tandem, semi-trailer arrangement.

DIMENSIONS:

Height to pick-up-plate — 1,219 mm (4 ft)
Height to top of side rails — 1,372 mm (4 ft 6 in)
King pin location — 876 mm (2 ft 10½ in)
Axle location — 762 mm (2½ ft) from rear to 3,505 mm (11 ft 6 in) in increments of 152 mm (6 in)
Chassis weight — 1,125 kg (2,480 lb)

40 ft Strick Sea Going Containers

BASIC DIMENSIONS:
Overall length 12,192 mm (40 ft 0 in)
Overall height 2,590 mm (8 ft 6 in)
Overall width 2,438 mm (8 ft 0 in)
Inside length 12,062 mm (39 ft 6⅞ in)
Inside width (6·4 mm (¼ in) lining) 2,349 mm (7 ft 8½ in)
Inside height 2,397 mm (7 ft 10⅜ in)
Rear door opening width 2,273 mm (7 ft 5¼ in)
Rear door opening height 2,291 mm (7 ft 6⅛ in)
Inside cubage 68·38 m³ (2,415 cu ft)
BASIC WEIGHTS:
Tare weight 3,647 kg (8,040 lb)
Maximum payload 27,215 kg (60,000 lb)
Maximum gross weight 30,862 kg (68,040 lb)
DESIGN LOADS:
Stacking in ship's cells — Four high
Acceleration, when lifting by crane — 2 g
Load against side panels — ·6 g at maximum inclination at 30° from vertical
Front-aft load, imposed directly upon container — ·4 g
Roof load — Two men weighing 90·7 kg (200 lb) each on 610 mm (24 in) centers, at 1·5 g
Floor load, distributed — 1,709 kg/m² (350 lb/sq ft) at 2 g
Floor load, concentrated — Lift truck with 5,443 kg (12,000 lb) front axle loading (2,540 to 3,048 kg (2½ to 3 ton) capacity)
Payload distribution — Limited by 11,340 kg (25,000 lb) distributed over any 3,048 mm (10 ft) of container length, rest distributed evenly over balance of floor.

20' 8" × 8' ISO Strick alloy steel container with pre-painted alloy panelling, fork-lift pockets, Coupleable. Manufactured under license by IWT in Germany.

ICS containers moving into a city freightyard at Dallas, Texas.

STORAGE AND REPAIR DEPOTS:

EUROPE:

Austria	Klagenfurt; Vienna
Belgium	Antwerp
Denmark	Copenhagen
Finland	Helsinki
France	Dunkirk; Lyons; Paris; Le Havre; Bordeaux; Marseille; Strasbourg
Germany	Aachen; Berlin; Bremen; Bremerhaven; Cologne; Dusseldorf; Hamburg; Regensburg; Hanover; Lubeck; Munich; Mainz; Mannheim
Holland	Amsterdam; Rotterdam
Ireland	Dublin
Italy	Cadenazzo, Milan; Trieste; Naples; Rivalta Scrivia
Norway	Oslo
Portugal	Lisbon
Spain	Barcelona; Cadiz; Bilbao; Madrid
Sweden	Gothenburg; Stockholm
Switzerland	Basle
United Kingdom	Andover; Cumbernauld; Garstang; Glasgow; Leeds; Liverpool; Manchester; Poplar; Rochford; Sheffield; Woodville

NORTH AMERICA:

Canada	Montreal; Toronto
Mexican Gulf	Houston; New Orleans; Miami
West Coast	Indianapolis; San Francisco/ Oakland; Los Angeles
East Coast	Baltimore, Boston; Jacksonville; New York; Norfolk; Philadelphia; Savannah
US Mid-West	Chicago; Cleveland; Detroit; Moling
South Coast	Dallas; Kansas; Milwaukee; Mobile,
SOUTH AMERICA	Buenos Aires

AUSTRALASIA AND FAR EAST:

Australia	Sydney; Melbourne
Japan	Tokyo/Yokohama; Osaka/ Kobe; Nagoya
Hong Kong	

MOBILE REPAIR UNITS:

New York	Ship Tank Foot of Grace St. Secaucus, N.J. Telephone: (201) 864.0550
United Kingdom	Cravens Homalloy Ltd, Sutton Road, Rochford, Essex Telephone: Southend-on-Sea 544991

Repair depots at Garstang and Southampton.

INTERPOOL

Interpool Inc

(Subsidiary of Steadman Industries Limited Toronto)
630 Third Avenue,
New York, NY 10017

TELEPHONE: (212) 682-4975
W. L. Serenbetz (*President*)
Martin Tuchman (*General Manager and Vice-President*)
Rodney P. Adair (*Vice President, Finance*)

D. E. De Longis (*General Sales Manager*)
T. P. Birnie (*Director of Operations*)

CONTAINER LEASING:
Interpool leases containers to Members

under a variety of plans designed to suit any need, competitive with any other leasing arrangement, and competitive with the cost of ownership. There are 110 members amongst the shipping companies.

INTERCHANGE AND PER DIEM RELIEF
A true container Pool concept. Excess containers are accepted by the Pool or interchanged to other Members.
INLAND CONTAINER POOLS
Interpool Service Points and Container Pools are maintained at various inland points as required. The total pool will be about 17,500 containers by December 1971. New containers are added at a rate of nearly 1,000 per month.

TRAILER CHASSIS
Requirements are reduced drastically. Not required for inland rail moves. Available on per diem basis where needed for drayage and Motor Carrier service. Not required for storage at inland points.

MOTOR CARRIER SERVICES
Interpool leases trailer chassis to Members, making these available to Motor Carriers under Steamship Company's regular interchange agreement.
DRAYAGE SERVICES:
Interpool provides local services in Port areas and in inland points, using trailer chassis leased to Members on per diem basis.
PER DIEM COLLECTION:
Interpool collects per diem from railroads, as under Plan 2½, crediting Member's account.

CONTAINER POOL POINTS:

Europe

Drop-off Charge $ 20 ft	40 ft	Interpool Pool Point and Area Office
		London
0	0	Belfast
0	0	Birmingham
25	0	Bristol
0	0	Derby/Nottingham
25	0	Felixstowe
0	0	Glasgow
0	X	Hull
0	0	Ipswich
0	0	Leeds
0	0	Liverpool
0	0	London
0	0	Manchester/Warrington
0	X	Middlesbrough
25	X	Newport
50	25	Southampton
		Dublin
25	X	Dublin
		Amsterdam:
25	0	Amsterdam
25	0	Rotterdam
25	25	Basel
		Cologne:
0	0	Cologne
		Mannheim:
0	0	Mannheim
		Antwerp:
0	0	Antwerp
50	50	Zeebrugge
		Paris:
0	X	Bordeaux
0	X	Dunkirk
0	0	Le Havre
0	X	Lille
0	0	Marseilles
0	0	Paris
0	X	Rouen
0	X	Reims
0	X	Strasbourg
		Copenhagen:
0	X	Aarhus
25	0	Copenhagen
0	X	Odense
0	X	Esbjerg
		Oslo:
100	50	Oslo
25	X	Bergen
25	X	Stavangar
		Gothenburg:
100	50	Gothenburg
		Florence:
0	25	Genoa
0	25	Leghorn
0	0	Milan
0	X	Naples

Drop-off Charge $ 20 ft	40 ft	
0	X	Turin
		Vienna:
0	0	Vienna
0	0	Graz
		Madrid:
25	25	Madrid
25	25	Barcelona
25	25	Bilbao
25	X	Valencia
25	X	Alicante
		Lisbon:
0	X	Lisbon
		Oporto:
0	X	Oporto
		Hamburg:
0	0	Bremen
0	0	Dusselodrf
0	0	Frankfurt
0	0	Hamburg
X	X	Lubeck
0	0	Munich
0	0	Nuremberg
0	0	Stuttgart
		Helsinki:
100	100	Helsinki
		Yugoslavia:
25	25	Ljubljana

North America

20 ft	40 ft	
		Atlanta
25	X	Atlanta
0	X	Nashville
25	X	Birmingham
0	0	Jacksonville
100	X	Miami
0	0	Savannah
50	0	Morehead City
0	0	Kingsport Tenn.
		Chicago:
0	0	Chicago Ill.
0	25	Milwaukee
0	X	Peoria Ill.
0	0	St. Paul, Minn.
0	X	Waukesha
		Columbus:
—	—	Columbus O
		Detroit:
25	X	Cleveland O.
25	X	Detroit, Mich.
25	X	Toledo O.
		Montreal:
0	X	Montreal, Que.
50	X	Quebec City
50	X	Halifax N.S.
		New York:
0	X	Alentown

Drop-off Charge $ 20 ft	40 ft	
0	0	Baltimore
75	X	Boston
0	X	Buffalo, N.Y.
25	0	New York area Jersey City
0	0	Norfolk Va
25	X	Philadelphia, Pa
0	X	Rochester N.Y.
		New Orleans:
0	X	Dallas
0	0	Houston, Texas
0	0	New Orleans, La
0	0	Mobile
0	0	Memphis Tenn.
		San Francisco:
—	X	Los Angeles, Cal.
25	X	Portland Ore.
—	X	San Francisco/Oakland
50	X	Vancouver BC
		Toronto:
0	X	Toronto, Ont.
—	X	Hamilton
		Tokyo
0	X	Kobe
0	X	Tokyo
0	X	Yokohama
		Seoul:
0	X	Inchon
0	X	Pusan
		Taiwan:
0	X	Taipei
		Hong Kong:
0	X	Hong Kong
		Manila:
100	X	Manila
		Singapore:
75	X	Singapore
		Adelaide:
50	X	Adelaide
		Brisbane:
0	X	Brisbane
		Fremantle:
0	X	Fremantle
		Melbourne:
25	X	Melbourne
		Sydney:
125	X	Sydney
		Auckland:
25	X	Auckland
		Israel:
25	X	Ashdod
25	X	Haifa

CHARGES:
Basic Per Diem Charge: 20 ft Container $1·75 U.S. Funds; for all short term and one way leases.
X.—40 ft Containers not handled at this point.

INTERPOOL OFFICES:
New York:
(Head Office)
Telephone: 212-682-4975
Telex: 127999
Cable: Interpool Inc, 630 3rd Ave., New York, N.Y. 10017
T. P. Birnie (*Manager*)

Adelaide:
Freightbases Pty Ltd.
Box 75, Port Adelaide, South Australia
J. Pendrigh (*Manager*)
Amsterdam:
Interpool N.V.,
Kabelweg 53-55., Postbus 8129, Amsterdam-W2

Telephone: 142233, 142234
Telex: 13298
Mrs. Hermelink (*Manager*)
Antwerp:
Ruys & Co., N.V.
Britselel 23/25, 2000 Antwerpen, Antwerp
Telephone: 32 18 80
Telex: 31 245

M. Stevens (*Manager*)
Ashdod:
D. Raviv Co.
  P.O. Box 247, Ashdod, Israel
  Telephone: 055-32991
  Telex: 03-812
  David Raviv (*Manager*)
Atlanta: Ga
  1256 Malibu Court, Morrow Ga, 30260
  Telephone: 404-361-5723
  Jack D. Burden (*Manager*)
Auckland:
Russell & Somers Ltd.,
  79-83 Customs Street, East Auckland 1,
  N.Z. (P.O.B. 1284)
  Telephone: 361-660
  Telex: Randz 2531
  D. J. Percival, (*Asst. Gen. Manager*)
Brisbane:
B.H.G.S. Agencies
  P.O. Box 72, Hamilton Central Brisbane
  G. W. Dunsford (*Manager*)
Baltimore:
Western Maryland Railway Co.
  Port Codington, Baltimore Md.
  Telephone: 301-955-2955
  Chuck White (*Manager*)
Chicago:
  327 South La Salle St. Chicago, Ill.
  60604
  Telephone: 312-939-2945
  George Moreth (*Manager*)
Cologne:
Damco Shiffahrt Und Spedition GMBH
  5, Koelni P.O. Box 230122
  Telephone: 315021-25
  Telex: 08882503
  G. Nagelmann (*Manager*)

Columbus:
Interpool
  5697 Forrest Ash Lane, Suite A Columbus,
  Ohio 43229
  Telephone: 614-888-9904
  Code: 43229
  G. K. Owen (*Manager*)
Copenhagen:
Motorships Agencies Ltd.
  Telephone: 29 68 00
  Telex: 2293, 36 Hornemansgade,
  Copenhagen
Detroit:
Detroit Processing Terminal
  4485W Jefferson, Detroit, Mich 48209
  Telephone: 313-825-6040
  Telex: 235340
  Capt. Angus Black (*Manager*)
Dublin:
Irish Ferryways (CIE)
  Tolka Quay, Dublin, 1, Ireland
  Telephone: 47948
  Telex: 5468
  Frank Redmond (*Manager*)
Florence:
Salviati and Santori
  8 Lugarno A. Vespucci 50123,
  Florence, Italy
  Telephone: 263341
  Telex: 57238
  F. Ginepro (*Manager*)
Fremantle:
Freight Bases Pty. Ltd.
  O.P.O. Box 59, North Fremantle,
  Western Australia 6159
  Telephone: 5-4655
  Telex: 92376
  Cable: Freightbases Perth
  M.Prietorius (*Manager*)
Gothenburg:
AB Scanfreight
  P.O. Box 8873, S40272, Gothenburg 8,
  Sweden
  Telephone: 031-540140
  Telex: 2243
Hamburg:
Interpool
  Bei Den Muehren 1, 2 Hamburg 11
  Telephone: 36-40-48/49

Telex: 215313
K. Englehardt (*Manager*)
Helsinki:
FINNEXPRESS OY
  Helsinki 12, Isoroobertinkatu 4
  Telephone: 14455
  Telex: 12843
  P. Lamken (*Manager*)
Hong Kong:
New Tech Service Inc., (H.K.) Ltd.
  310 Realty Bldg., 71 Des Voeux Road, C.,
  Hong Kong
  Telephone: H-238782-H-249229
  Cable: TEKSER-HONKKONG
  Patrick Hung (*Manager*)
Jacksonville:
Transcarribean Maritime Service Inc.
  P.O. Box 515, Tallyrand Docks,
  Jacksonville, Fla 33 206
  Telephone: 904-356-3013
  Larry Duggan (*Manager*)
London:
Interpool (U.K.) Ltd.
  Princes House, 190 Piccadilly,
  London, W.1, England
  Telephone: 439-0331
  Telex: 24859
  M. K. Davis (*Manager*)
Lisbon:
L. Azevedo & Guimaraes Lda
  Av 24 de Julho 128, 1, Lisbon
  Telephone: 679044
  Telex: 1428
  F. Rocha (*Manager*)
Ljubljana:
c/o Intereuropa, Ltd.
  Ljubljana, Yugoslavia
  Telephone: 313224
  Krompotic (*Manager*)
Manila:
Aboitiz & Co. Inc.
  W. A. Paradies, Mary Bachrach Bldg,
  Port Area P.O. Box 219, Manila
  Philippine Ilds.
  Cable; ABOITIZ Manila
Mannheim:
Damco Schiffahrt Und Spedition GMBH
  68 Mannheim,
  P.O. Box 520
  Telephone: 24941
  Telex: 0462001
  N. Schramm (*Manager*)

Melbourne:
Freightbases Pty. Ltd.
  Box 286, Footscray, Victoria
  Capt. I. E. Slater (*Manager*)
Miami:
Transcarribean Maritime Service Inc.
  501 N.E. First Avenue, Miami, Fla.
  33132
  Telephone: 305-358-1790
  Telex: 519403
  Henry Suarez (*Manager*)
Mobile:
T. A. Province Co.
  1-Stuart Circle, Mobile, Alabama
  Telephone: 205-433-5424
  Les Stuart (*Manager*)
Montreal:
  P.O. Box 514, Montreal AMF, Que.
  Telephone: 514-430-2743
  Bill Aumand (*Manager*)
Madrid:
Centramares, S.L.
  Velasquez, 7, Madrid-1
  Telephone: 2257960
  Telex: 27533, 27780
  R. Trachsler (*Manager*)
New Orleans:
  324 Gateway Bldg, 124 Camp Street,
  New Orleans, La. 70130
  Telephone: 504-529-2281
  Telex: 587476
  Bill Wolfe (*Manager*)
Oslo:
Scanfreight, Norge, A.S.

Dronningensgt 22, Oslo 1
  Telephone: 208842, 202259
  Telex: 18728
  E. Margard (*Manager*)
Oporto:
Azveedo & Lima Lda,
  Av. Dos Aliados 211, S, Oporto
  Telephone: 37861
  Telex: 2730
  J. Amadeu (*Manager*)
Paris:
S.E.C.A.M.
  15 Rue de la Pepiniere, Paris 8E France
  Telephone: 387 3645
  Telex: 29205
  Mme. Remande (*Manager*)
San Francisco:
Pacific Coast Container Corp.
  12776 Neptune Ave., San Leandro, Calif.
  94577
  Telephone: 415-357-8226
  Telex: 34465
Seoul:
Korea Shipping Corp. Ltd.
  I.P.O. Box 1164 Seoul, Korea
  Telex: 2223
  Cable: Korea Ship, Seoul, Korea
  Won Suck Cho (*Manager*)
Singapore:
Orient Expediters Inc. (Singapore) Private
  Ltd. Singapore Transport Supply Service
  Private Ltd.
  409 River Valley Road, Republic of
  Singapore
  Telephone: 372 701, 371 312
  Cables: Oeising, Singapore
Singapore:
Orient Expediters Inc. (Singapore) Private
  Ltd. Singapore Transport Supply Service
  Private Ltd.
  409 River Valley Road, Republic of
  Singapore
  Telephone: 372 701, 371 312
  Cables: Oeising, Singapore
Sydney:
Freightbases Pty. Ltd.
  Miller Road, Villawood, Depot Sydney
  A. D. Elbourne (*Manager*)
Taiwan:
Orient Expediters, Inc Taiwan Ltd.
  7a Golden Mansion 31-25 Chi-Nan Road,
  Sec 2, Taipei-Taiwan
  Telephone: 3732 78
  Cable: Oeitai Peitou-Taipei
  N. W. Isbrandtsen (*Manager*)
Tokyo:
Overseas Container Express
  Kaigai Kontena Yusoo, Matsuzawa Bldg.,
  3-5-7, Ginza, Chuo-Ku, Tokyo
  Telephone: Tokyo 653-0831
  Telex: 038 22225
  K. Ueoka (*Manager*)
Toronto:
Steadman Industries Ltd.
  280 Belfield Road, Rexdale, Ont.
  Telephone: 416-677-2680
  Telex: 06-217754
  Fred Hawkins (*Manager*)
Vancouver: BC
Arrow Transfer Ltd.
  320 Seymour Blvd, North Vancouver, BC
  Telephone: 604-985-2111
  Telex: 045 08748
  C. Bouchard (*Manager*)
Vienna:
Enrico Sperco & Sohn A. G.
  Vienna 1, Kaerntnerstrasse 33
  Telephone: 524211
  Telex: 11834
USA SUB OFFICES:
Allentown:
D. F. Bast, Inc.
  1425 N. Maxwell St., Allentown, Pa 18001
  Telephone: 215-434-9461
  J. Bryer (*Manager*)
Atlanta:
  1256 Malibu Court, Morrow, Ga 30260

Telephone: 404-361,8552
Jack D. Burden (*Manager*)

Boston:
Port Terminals, Inc.
666 Summer Street, Boston Mass 02210
Telephone: 617-542-7100
B. Murphy (*Manager*)

Chicago:
(Container Pool Location)
3500 South Kedzie Avenue, Chigaco, Ill.
60632

Cleveland:
Great Lakes International Corp.
103 Erieside Avenue, Cleveland, Ohio
44114
Telephone: 216-696-6880
R. Trevisanutto (*Manager*)

Houston:
Port Container Industries
P.O. Box 32, Galena Park, Texas
Telephone: 713-672-0512
W. C. Walker (*Manager*)

Jacksonville:
Transcarribean Maritime Service Inc.
P.O. Box 515, Tallyrand Docks,
Jacksonville, Fla 33206
Telephone: 904-356-3013
Larry Duggan (*Manager*)

Jersey City:
Container Master
248 Johnston Avenue, Jersey City, N.J.

07302
Telephone: 201-432-2480
Telex: 128135

Los Angeles:
Great Western Container Freight
886 North Mission Road, Los Angeles,
Calif. 90033
Telephone: 213-223-3895
J. Potashnik (*Manager*)

Memphis:
Chickasaw Warehouse
23-50 Florida Street, Memphis,
Tenn. 38109
Telephone: 901-947-3175
Neely Mallory (*Manager*)

Milwaukee:
Kro-Flite Cartage Co.
4001 Greentree Road, Milwaukee, Wisc.
Telephone: 414-352-3514
Erv. Winkowski (*Manager*)

Mobile:
T.A. Province Co.
1 Stuart Circle, Mobile, Alabama
Telephone: 205-433-5424
Mr. Les Stuart (*Manager*)

Morehead City N.C.:
P.O. Box 648, Morehead City, N.C. 28557
Telephone: 919-726-3158
Cooley Lewis (*Manager*)

New York:
Interpool
630, 3rd Avenue, New York, N.Y. 10017
Telephone: 212-682-4975
Telex: 127999
Cable: Intpoolinc
J. Riordan (*Manager*)

Norfolk:
Container Carriers Corp.
P.O. Box 6069, Milan Station, Norfolk Va.
23508
Telephone: 703-423-5817
Cable: CONCAR

Philadelphia:
Pier 7, 701 N. Broadway, Gloucester
N.J. 08030
Telephone: 215-WA 3-5000
Art Grubbs (*Manager*)

San Francisco/Oakland:
(Office) Interpool
World Trade Center, Room 275,
San Francisco, Cal. 94111
Telephone: 415-982-3562
Telex: 34465

Savannah:
Chatham Services·
P.O. Box 2088, Savannah, Ga 31402
Telephone: 912-234-8265
Telex: 54-6460
J. J. Flynn (*Manager*)

SEA CONTAINERS INC

Sea Containers Leasing Corporation
Sea Containers Ltd.
Sea Containers Chartering Ltd.
REGISTERED OFFICE:
283 State Street, Albany, New York, U.S.A.
OPERATIONS OFFICE:
39 Park Street,
London, W.1.,
England
TELEPHONE: 499-0221
TELEX: 27553
CABLES: Seatainers, London
DIRECTORS:
J. B. Sherwood (*President*)
M. E. Gellert
J. J. Pinto
M. E. Pinto
Hamilton Robinson, Jr.
P. J. R. Schlee
W. E. Sherwood
OFFICERS:
J. B. Sherwood (*President*)
P. J. Molony (*Vice-President, Finane*)
D. J. Turner (*Vice-President, Sales*)
R. M. Riggs (*Secretary*)
DEPARTMENTAL MANAGERS:
A. de Berc (*Operations*)
A. A. Blaker (*United Kingdom*)
R. E. Kulp (*Refrigerated and Tank Containers*)
A. J. I. Poynder (*Cranes*)
J. Sinclair (*Mediterranean and Southern Europe*)
J. D. Tingle (*Engineering*)

R. S. Ward (*General Sales Manager*)
J. F. White (*Sacndinavia and Northern Europe*)
C. Knowles (*Maintenance and Repairs*)

Sea Containers' leasing programmes range from package deals comprising container ships, gantry cranes, standard and specialised containers, chassis and associated handling equipment, to leasing of, each item individually or in numbers.

Container leasing terms include one way, short term, long term and interchange programmes offered through a world-wide network of over 150 depots.

Sea Containers' fleet of equipment numbers in excess of 25,000 units, expanding at the rate of about 10,000 units per year.

Tango container gantry cranes, of which eight are already erected or under construction, are available for hire throughout the world. These cranes can be provided in many sizes to suit individual requirements.

A fleet of 25 cellular container ships is in service or under construction. The "Hustler" and "Strider" classes are lift-on, lift-off with capacities of 124 and 348 20 ft × 8 ft 6 in high equivalents. The "Tarros" and "Strider" T with capacities of 111 and 298 20 ft × 8 ft 6 in equivelants, combine the features of lift-on, lift-off and roll-on, roll-off with stern loading ramp and ship mounted gantry crane. (See Ship Leasing section).

BRANCHES:
Argentina:
Lingas SRL, San Martin 448,
Buenos Aires
Telephone: 490792
Telex. 121658
Capt. K. W. Keymer
Australia:
Chep Handling Systems,
Container Division,
283 Alfred Street,
North Sydney
NSW 2060
Telephone: 9298388
Cables: Chepquip
Mr. P. T. Williams
Depots in Sydney and Melbourne.
Austria:
Gebruder Weiss,
A-1041 Vienna, Schonbrunner Strasse 7,
Telephone: 577511
Telex: 01-1808
Mr. M. Bonomo
Belgium:
Intercontinental Container Transport Co-ordination, SA
38 Huidevetterstraat, Antwerp
Telephone: 312466 or 325091
Telex: 32823
Mr. G. Van Strydonck
Brazil:
CICON Cia. Commercial de Containers,
Av. Rio Branco, 25 S/1415

Rio de Janeiro GB
Telephone: 223-1865
Cables: Seatainers, Rio
Telex: Submuloc 318 18 Rio
Mr. Luiz Eduardo Correa da Costa
Depots at Rio de Janeiro, Santos, Fortaleza Recife, Salvador, Porto Alegre, Vitoria, Paranagu.
Canada:
Kuehne & Nagel (Canada) Ltd.
485 McGill Street,
Montreal 125 PQ
Telephone: 688 9521
Telex: 05 67568
Mr. H. W. Klaus
Branches and depots in Edmonton, Toronto, Winnipeg and Vancouver.
Denmark:
ICO International Container Operators A-S,
Faergehavn Nord, Copenhagen 2100
Telephone: 29 68 88
Telex: 6786
Mr. A. Nielsen
Branches and depots in Aarhus and Esbjerg.
Finland:
Oy Victor Ek Ab,
Eltelaranta 16, Postfack 13211,
Helsinki 3
Telephone: 61-631
Telex: 12-432
Mr. L. J. Homen

France:
SCAC
30 Quai National 92 Puteaux
Telephone: 236 47 00
Telex: 62590
Mr. C. Debuire
Depots at Le Havre, Marseille, Dunkirk, Paris, Perpignan, Strasbourg and Bordeaux.
Germany/Hungary
Gerd Buss Terminal K.G.,
2000 Hamburg 11,
Cremon 32,
P.O. Box 110244
Telephone: 36861
Telex: 212152
Cables: Bussgerd
Mr. P. Ewerth and Mrs. K. Ewerth
Branches and depots in Berlin, Bremen, Bremerhaven, Cologne, Hanover, Mannheim, Munich, Mainz, Regensburg and Budapest.
Great Britain:
Sea Containers Ltd.,
39 Park Street, London W.1.
Telephone: 499 0221
Telex: 27553
Cables: Seatainer, London
Mr. A. A. Blaker
Depots at Belfast, Birmingham, Bristol, Swansea, Glasgow, Hull, Garston, (Liverpool), Bradford, Southampton, London, Warrington, Derby, Felixstowe, Middlesbrough.

Hong Kong:
Butterfield & Swire (Hong Kong) Ltd.
Union House,
9 Connaught Road,
P.O. Box 4,
Telephone: 230011
Telex: 3206
Mr. B. Weldon
India:
Pent. Ocean Steamships Pvt. Ltd.
Fort House,
221 Dr. D. Naorogi Road,
Bombay 1
Telephone: 266797
Telex: 0112636
Cables: Sajarman
Captain J. C. Anand
Ireland:
George Bell & Co. Ltd.
Hawkins House,
Hawkins Street,
Dublin 2

Telephone: 775455 & 774316
Telex: 5115
Cables: Bell
Mr. B. Vincent
Israel:
International Forwarding Co. of Israel Ltd.
P.O. Box 29020,
Tel Aviv
Telephone: 51631
Telex: 33576
Cables: Infois, Tel Aviv
Mr. J. Carni
Depots at Haifa and Ashdod.
Italy:
Allievi S.p.A.
Via Fantoli, 28/4, 20138 Milan
Telephone: 504175
Telex: 31567
Miss I. Allievi
Depots at Genoa, Leghorn, Milan, Naples, Bologna, Trieste and Rome.
Japan:
Fuji Asano Kaiun Co. Ltd.
Yabuhara Building 14-4 2-Chome,
Hatchobori, Chuo-Ku,
Tokyo
Telephone: 552 9211
Telex: TK 2545
Mr. T. Yasuda
Depots at Kobe and Yokohama.
Morocco:
Maunter SA
48 rue Karatchi, Casablanca
Telephone: 62931
Telex: 21007
Mr. T. de la Tour
Netherlands:
Pakhoed N.V.
Boompjes 60-68,
Rotterdam
Telephone: 302911
Telex: 23023-21092
Mr. W. Persson
Depots at Rotterdam and Amsterdam.

Norway:
BNS Ltd,
P.O.B. 822,
Radhusgaten 28,
Oslo 1
Telephone: 337283
Telex: 11352
Mr. S. Neerland
Depots at Oslo, Horten, Sarpsborg, Bergen, Kristiansand, S., Stavanger, Trondheim and Drammen.
Portugal:
Campanhia de Navegaçao 'Carregadores Acoreanos',
Avenida D. Carlos 1,
42-4°, Lisbon 2
Telephone: 36 70 61 and 325515
Telex: 1424
Cables: Oraval, Lisbon
Capt. A. S. Palhares
Depots at Lisbon and Leixoes.
Singapore:
Ingram Far East Pte Ltd.
Chequers Hotel Building,
P.O. Box 3032
Singapore
Telephone: 533511
Telex: Singapore RS21536
Cable: Ingconsing
Mr. C. A. Hartnoll
South Africa:
Container Transportation Co. S.A. (Pty) Ltd.
Standard House,
Smith Street, P.O. Box 2161,
Durban
Telephone: 311411
Telex: 6-7267
Mr. B. King
Depots at Cape Town, Durban and Johannesberg.
Spain:
Sea Containers Espana S.A.
Castellana 4,

7th Floor IBM Building,
Madrid 1
Telephone: 2267620
Telex: 27542
Mr. A. Elbaz
Depots at Barcelona, Bilbao, Madrid and Valencia.
Sweden:
Freys Express AB,
P.O. Box 74,
Ringogatan, Stalvertsgatan 10,
40121 Gothenburg 1,
Telephone: 513900
Telex: 20015
Cables: Freyexpress
Depots at Gothenburg, Malmo, Stockholm
Switzerland:
Sea Containers Switzerland,
P.O.B. 19-1000 Lausanne, 6 Av. Fantaisie,
c/o D. A. Drouth
Depots at Basle, Geneva, Chavornay and Chiasso
Taiwan:
World Wide Freight Terminal Inc.
23 Chung Chan N Road,
Sec. 2.
Taipei
Mr. Y. S. Chen
Telephone: 513151
Telex: TP 256
Depots at Keelung and Kaiohshung
United States:
Agents for Eastern U.S.A. except Florida
Overseas Enterprises Inc.
82 Wall Street, New York, NY 10005
Telephone: HA 5-3185
Telex: 22252
Cables: Ewighaus
Mr. T. A. Ewig
Chicago Representative:
International Cargo Containers Inc.
78 East Madison Street,
Chicago,
Illinois 60602
Houston Representative:
Port Container Industries Inc.
8400 Clinton Drive,
Houston, Texas 77547
New Orleans Representative:
Overseas Enterprises Inc.
c/o Mid-Gulf Shipping Co. Inc.
International Trade Mart, Suite 1024
2 Canal Street, New Orleans,
Louisiana 70130
Savannah Representative:
Southeastern Maritime Corp.,
P.O. Box 2747, Savannah,
Georgia 31402
Charleston Representative:
Southeastern Maritime Corp.,
P.O. Drawer 978,
Charleston, South Carolina
Baltimore Representative:
Atlantic & Gulf Stevedores Inc.,
Pier 1 MPA, Marine Terminal,
200 South Clinton Street,
Baltimore, Maryland
Norfolk Representative:
Foley's Warehousing Inc.,
24th Morton Street,
Norfolk, Virginia
Boston Representative:
Patterson Wylde & Co. Inc.
156 State Street,
Boston, Massachuseetts 02109
Philadelphia Representative:
Atlantic & Gulf Stevedores Inc.,
Lafayette Building,
Philadelphia,
Pennsylvania 19106
Depots at all above locations plus Boston (Representative Overseas Enterprises Inc. New York).
Agents for Miami and Florida:
Chester Blackburn & Roder Inc.
1040 Biscayne Boulevard, Miami,

Florida 33132
Telephone: 305 377-3781
Telex: 810848-6535
Mr. W. Higgins
Agents for the West Coast:
California Cargo Containers Inc.
801 Maritime Street, Oakland,
California 94607
Telephone: 835-4484
Telex: 337613
Mr. V. Bayduk
Depots at Fresno, Los Angeles, Portland,
San Francisco (Oakland) and Seattle.

EQUIPMENT FOR HIRE:
Skeletal Chassis:

Sea Containers offer for lease skeletal Chassis in the United States and Europe. The current inventory includes:

20 ft single axle coupleable chassis capable of carrying a 20 ft container. Two of these chassis, coupled together, form a 40 ft tandem rig, capable of carrying two 20 ft or one 40 ft container.

40 ft straight frame chassis incorporating sliding tandem axle capable of carrying 2 × 20 ft containers on one 40 ft container—with or without gooseneck.

23 ft tandem axle chassis for carrying 20 ft containers with high payloads.

The above are available in the United States and all are suitable for United States rail piggy-back operation.

23 ft tandem axle skeletal chassis capable of carrying one 20 ft container: suitable for operation with a tractor unit operating at 30 tons gross trailer weight.

The above are available and comply with local regulations, in most European countries.

40 ft tandem axle skeletal chassis capable of carrying one 40 ft, one 30 ft or two 20 ft containers: suitable for operation with a tractor unit operating at 44 tons gross trailer weight.

The above items are available and comply with local regulations in most European countries. Units for use in other parts of the world can be made available on request.

TYPES OF CONTAINERS AVAILABLE FOR LEASE

Length	Width	Height	Type, Construction and Special features
6 ft 7 in	8 ft	7 ft 5 in	Steel 6·7 type container
20 ft	8 ft	8 ft	Frames for 3 × 6·7 types to make ISO 20 ft × 8 ft module
10 ft	8 ft	8 ft	Standard ISO steel container
20 ft	8 ft	8 ft	Standard ISO steel container
20 ft	8 ft	8 ft 6 in	Standard steel container
20 ft	8 ft	8 ft	Steel open sided ventilated container with canvas sides and steel roof
20 ft	8 ft	8 ft 6 in	Steel open sided ventilated container with canvas sides and steel roof
20 ft	8 ft	8 ft	Steel ISO open top container with canvas cover
20 ft	8 ft	8 ft 6 in	Steel open top container with canvas cover
20 ft	8 ft	8 ft	Steel open top and open side container with canvas cover
20 ft	8 ft	8 ft	Steel ISO container with 2·3 metre side doors on both sides

An ISO 8 ft 6 in 40 ft box awaiting despatch from a Japanese factory

An 8 ft 6 in high ventilated curtain-sided container especially suitable for carrying fruit and vegetables

A 5 ft 8 in high 40 ft long car carrier loaded with vehicles awaiting shipment. This unit is also ideal for carrying heavy cargo, such as steel bars and commodities in drums.

20 ft	8 ft	5 ft 8 in	Steel open top drum carrying container with end doors, with or without canvas covers
20 ft	8 ft		Steel ISO flat
20 ft	8 ft	8 ft 6 in	Steel bulk cargo container with loading and unloading hatches and end doors
20 ft	8 ft	8 ft	Stainless steel ISO tank for wines, spirits and chemicals, 18,600 litres. Insulated heated tanks also available
20 ft	8 ft	8 ft	Coldwrap refrigerated ISO container
20 ft	8 ft	8 ft 6 in	Insulated container
20 ft	8 ft	8 ft 6 in	Steel flat rack container with fixed ends and removable side stanchions
30 ft	8 ft	8 ft	Standard steel ISO container
20 ft	8 ft	8 ft 6 in	Steel container with 2·8 metre side doors on both sides
20 ft	8 ft	4 ft	Steel half height open top container with canvas cover-end doors or drop sides
20 ft	8 ft	5 ft 8 in	Steel open top drum carrying container with end doors, with or without canvas covers
20 ft	8 ft		Steel ISO flat
20 ft	8 ft	8 ft 6 in	Steel bulk cargo container with loading and unloading hatches and end doors
20 ft	8 ft	8 ft	Stainless steel ISO tank for wines, spirits and chemicals, 18,600 litres. Insulated heated tanks also available
20 ft	8 ft	8 ft	Coldwrap refrigerated ISO container
20 ft	8 ft	8 ft 6 in	Insulated container
20 ft	8 ft	8 ft 6 in	Steel flat rack container with fixed ends and removable side stanchions
30 ft	8 ft	8 ft	Standard steel ISO container

NOTES:

(i) 8 ft 6 in, 4 ft or 5 ft 8 in high, and open side types comply in all respects with ISO requirements except in height and/or side loading tests.

(ii) All ISO and 6·7 types are registered under the U.I.C. (Railways) Convention. Most non ISO types also carry this registration.

(iii) All except uncovered types are T.I.R. approved.

CONTAINER CRANE AVAILABLE FOR LEASE

The Tango crane is made to Sea Containers special requirements by Liebherr and is available for leases of five years or more (the total fixed costs of operation are unlikely to exceed US $250 per day). Spreaders and other ancillary equipment, including 30 ton general cargo hook, are provided. Various configurations and sizes are available from large size quay side versions to land gantries. Features include an unusually light corner loading, wide leg span, erection without the need for extensive civil engineering works, and extremely quick erection and dismantling.

A typical land sea version has the following specification.

Leg span	80 ft — 100 ft
Outreach	72 ft — 90 ft
Backreach	Up to 35 ft
Height below spreader	60 ft — 80 ft
Total lift	100 ft — 120 ft
Wheelgauge	65
Hoist speeds	38 ft/minute at 30 ton load
	102 ft/minute at 6 ton load
Trolley speed	250 ft/minute
Crane travel speed	120 ft/minute
Wheel loading	15-25 tons per wheel
Power supply	AC 380/440 volts, 3 phase, 50 cycles

A typical land version would have the same basic features with a span of 135 ft and an outreach of 33 ft on each side.

SEAWHEEL (INTERNATIONAL CONTAINER LINES)

Seawheel Limited:
(Subsidiary of Lovell's Shipping and Transport Group Ltd.)
Pelton Road,
Greenwich,
London, S.E.10,
England
TELEPHONE: 01-858 8111
TELEX: 23114 Officium
TELEGRAMS: Electively London

DIRECTORS:
G. E. Lovell (Chairman)
D. D. Lovell
H. W. Gale
R. B. Dawbarn (Managing)
J. P. Lawrence (Continental—based in Antwerp)
P. A. D. Coles (Operations)
M. J. McGrath (Marketing)
A. J. Martin
E. R. Jordan

GENERAL MANAGERS:
J. P. Lawrence (Continent)
G. H. C. Turner (UK)

GENERAL

Seawheel is an international container line operating a door-to-door service between the UK and Ireland, Belgium, Denmark, France, Germany, Holland, Italy and Luxemburg.

The strategic siting of offices throughout its markets ensures that Seawheel is always able to maintain a high standard of service for its customers. As one of the leading pioneers of container transport in Europe, the company is in the forefront of operational development, particularly in the sphere of rail working. Its marketing attitude is sophisticated and great store is set by the word service in all it implies. Seawheel maintains constant liaison with its customers and the company is always prepared to discuss fully their overall distribution problems.

EQUIPMENT:

Type	Number
Lancashire flats, up to 27 ft in length	450
20 ft ISO flats, some of which specially constructed to carry steel coils, marble, etc	500
30 ft ISO flats	100
20 ft ISO containers, some of which equipped with twin decks, some of which insulated, capacity approx. 30·8 cu m (1,080 cu ft)	200
30 ft ISO containers equipped with the Joloda pallet handling system, some 8 ft 6 in high, capacity approx. 48·1 cu m (1,700 cu ft)	500
40 ft ISO containers equipped with the Joloda pallet handling system, some 8 ft 6 in high, capacity approx. 63·1 cu m (2,230 cu ft)	80
Total Fleet	1,830

Under present Ministry of Transport regulations in the United Kingdom the maximum payload for most of the company's equipment is 20,320 kilos (20 long tons). However, the regulations may shortly be amended and Seawheel's equipment will accordingly be up rated to the new maximum permissible payloads.

BRANCH OFFICE ADDRESSES AND MANAGERS (S = sales office. P = port/inland terminal office)

BELGIUM:
Seawheel pvba,
Frankrijklei 111,
Antwerpen B-2000
Telephone: 316810
Telex: 31149
F. Engelen (*Manager*)   (S)

Seawheel pvba,
Havendok 6
Quay 326,
Antwerpen 2030
Telephone: 417030
Telex: 32253
G. Vleugels (*Manager*)   (P)

Seawheel N.V.
Loodswezenstraat 10
8380 Zeebrugge
Telephone: 050 54575
Telex: 19168
G. Duchene (*Manager*)   (P)

HOLLAND:
Seawheel,
Van Riemsdijkweg 14,
Rotterdam 21
Telephone: (010) 3110/292 077
Telex: 23481
P. J. C. van Veen (*Manager*)   (S)
H. de Groot (*Manager*)   (P)

GERMANY:
Seawheel GmbH,
Kirchfeldstrasse 71,
4000 Dusseldorf
Telephone: 0104-9211
Telex: 8587325
E. R. Buresch (*Manager*)   (SP)
H. J. Fischer   (P)

Seawheel GmbH
463 Bochun Langendreer
Uhlenwinkel Container Terminal
West Germany
Telephone: 02321.287169
Telex: 0825698
W. E. Wartenberg (*Manager*)

DENMARK:
Dan Transport A/S.
Vestergade 33,
1002 Kobenhavn, K
Telephone: Minerva 1688
Telex: 5000
E. Toft   (SP)

Dan Transport A/S,
99, Prinsessegade,
7000 Fredericia/Jutland
Telephone: (059) 20233
Telex: 3395
B. Andersen (*Manager*)   (SP)

Dan Transport A/S,.
Englandskajan, DK 6700
Esbjerg/Jutland
Telephone: Esbjerg (051) 27677
Telex: 3446

ITALY:
Fratelli Avandero SAS,
Via Valtellina 21/27,
20159 Milano
Telephone: 600281
Telex: 31193   (S)
Fratelli Avandero SAS,
Rivalta Scrivia Centre Rooms,
No. 150, 152 and 154,
15050 Rivalta Scrivia,
Telephone: 86062
Telex: 21445
A. Pozzolini (*Manager*)   (SP)

40 ft Seawheel Container.

IRELAND
Seawheel Limited,
P.O. Box 31A, 29 George's Quay
Dublin 2
Telephone: Dublin 775161
Telex: 5562
A. V. Dufficy (*Manager*)   (SP)
Seawheel Limited,
14 Rockfield Park
Waterford
Telephone: Waterford 5737

UNITED KINGDOM:
Seawheel Ltd,
Freightliner Terminal,
Landor Street,
Birmingham
Telephone: 021 359 3594
Telex: 339196
C. D. Payne (*Manager*)
J. Cox   (P)
Bathurst Wharf
Bristol BS99 7AS
Telephone: 0272 20336
Telex: 44167
G. A. J. Clifford   (S)
R. R. Filliter (*Manager*)   (P)

Freightliner Terminal
Rouer Way
Pengam
Cardiff CF2 2YP
Telephone: 0222.497101
Telex: 497033
L. J. Knight (*Manager*)   (SP)

Seawheel Limited,
The Dock,
Dock Road,
Felixstowe IP11 8QP
Telephone: 03942 4804
Telex: 98276
D. Turner (*Manager*)   (P)

Seawheel Limited,
98 West George Street,
Glasgow, C2
Telephone: Douglas 8892
Telex: 778241
J. Cooper (*Manager*)   (SP)

Seawheel Limited,
9/12 East Dock Road,
Parkeston Quay,
Harwich, Essex
Telephone: 02555 4333-5
Telex: 98442
E. Gibbons (*Manager*)   (P)

Seawheel Limited,
Hedon Road,
King George Dock,
Hull

Telephone: 0482 76282
Telex: 52449
M. Betts (*Manager*)   (P)

Seawheel Limited
Freightliner Terminal,
Dock Road,
Garston,
Liverpool L192 JN   (P)
F. McHale (*Manager*)

Seawheel Limited,
Richmond House,
1 Rumford Place
Liverpool L39 QN
Telephone: Central 5126
Telex: 62107
D. A. Barlow (*Manager*)   (S)

Seawheel Limited,
Freightliner Terminal,
Westinghouse Road,
Trafford Park
Manchester 17
Telephone: 061-872-5611
Telex: 668098
A. McCormick   (S)
G. Butterworth   (P)

Seawheel Limited,
Lovell House,
Pelton Road,
Greenwich, London, S.E.10
Telephone: 01-858 8111
Telex: 23114 Officium
I. Wilson-Soppitt (*Manager*)   (S)

Seawheel Limited,
111 Queen Street,
Sheffield 1
Telephone: Sheffield 22187
F. Maskell (*Manager*)   (S)
D. Cooper (*Manager*)   (P)

Sea Routes		Sailings per week each way
	To/From	
Near Continent:		
Felixstowe	Antwerp	3
Felixstowe	Rotterdam	12
Harwich	Zeebrugge	10
Harwich	Rotterdam	5
Harwich	Dunkirk	5
Hull	Antwerp	3
Hull	Rotterdam	6
		—
	Total available	56

Scandinavia:

Felixstowe	Copenhagen and Esbjerg		2
Hull	Copenhagen and Esbjerg		2
	Total available		4

Ireland:

Avonmouth/ Bristol	Dublin		4
Liverpool	Dublin		4
	Total aviable		8

Other routes can be used as occasions demand.

All ports are connected with daily rail/road services to final destinations.

ROUTES UNDER DEVELOPMENT:
Spain, Portugal, Norway, Sweden.

OTHER:
Seawheel is sole agent for Dart Container-line Limited for their container distribution in the UK for traffic to and from the terminal port of Southampton. Seawheel has also been appointed their Sales Agent for Ireland (North and South).

FRANCE
EUROTAINER

Eurotainer—Société Européenne de Containers Spéciau
25 Rue d'Aumale, Paris 9e
TELEPHONE: 285.30.00
TELEX· 65802 CLLARO
HEAD OFFICE
Paris 9°-12, rue de La Rochefoucauld
DIRECTORS
J. Courson (*Directeur*)
M. Doucet (*Secrétaire Général*)
TERMS
Short term and long term lease.

Containers operated as at 1st May 1971

Type ISO	External dimensions (Ft) length	width	height	Specifications
Tank	20	8	8	Stainless steel insulated, capacity 19,000 litres (5,000 US gall.), one compartment, working pressure 1, 5 bar/psig, steam heating system.
Insulated	20	8	8½	Insulation: polyurethane and polyester-overall. Coefficient K=O, 25Kcal/h/°C/m².
Insulated	20	8	8	
Insulated	10	8	8	
Refrigerated	20	9	8	Liquid nitrogen refrigeration system for positive or negative temperatures (+ 10°C—30°C). +
Refrigerated	20	8	8	Refrigeration unit: Thermo King PDL 55 SG, diesel and electrical power source

GERMAN FEDERAL REPUBLIC

BUSS

Gerd Buss KG
Cremon 32
P.B. 112160
G. 2000 Hamburg 11
TELEPHONE: 31 10 11 (Day)
49 97 46 (Night)
TELEX: 02.12152

Captain P. K. Ewerth (*Container System Service Manager*)
BRANCHES:
Buss represent Sea Containers and Nattrans USA on the continent
DEPOTS:
Bremen/Bremerhaven, Berlin, Cologne,

Budapest, Hamburg, Hanover, Mannheim, Mainz and Munich.
TARIFF:
20 ft Units:
Short term $1·75 per day to 90 days
Medium term $1·10 per day to one year
Long term 80c per day for 5 years

RENTCON

Rentcon
The Container Rental Service of:
CARL TIEDEMANN
Container Leasing Service
Hamburg 11,
Roedingsmarkt 20
TELEPHONE: 36 14 41
TELEGRAMS: Fairplay
TELEX: 21 25 24
DIRECTORS:
M. Hanauer
T. Vorberg

TYPES AND QUANTITY OF CONTAINERS AVAILABLE FOR LEASE:
6½ ft, 10 ft, 20 ft, 20 ft with side door, 20 ft open top, 30 ft, 30 ft with side door, 40 ft, 40 ft with side door at Hamburg, Rotterdam, Antwerp, London, etc according to current depot-list.

TERMS AND TARIFF:
One way trip hire, short-term lease, long-term lease. No minimum days charged.

Containers are hired under the RENTCON name and by a special "all-in insurance" scheme rental agreements include total coverage for a small surcharge on normal rates.

EUROPE:
Germany (FR):
Bochum, Bremen, Cologne, Dusseldorf/Neuss, Frankfurt/Main, Hamburg, Kassel, Mainz, Mannheim, Munich, Nuremberg, Osnabrueck, Regensburg, Stuttgart.
Germany (GDR):
Berlin, Dresden, Erfurt, Halle, Karl-Marx-Stadt, Leipzig, Magdeburg, Rostock.
Austria:
Vienna
Belgium:
Antwerp
Czechoslovakia:
Liberec, Lovosice, Plzen, Prague, Olomouc, Uherske-Brod.
Denmark:
Copenhagen, Fredericia
Finland:
Helsinki, Tampere
France:
Dunkirk, Le Havre, Lyons, Marseilles, Paris
Greece:
Piraeus
Hungary:
Budapest

Unloading empty Rentcon containers at Hamburg.

Italy:
Bologna, Cadenazzo, Genoa, Leghorn, Milan, Naples, Rivalta Scrivia
Malta:
Valletta
Netherlands:
Amsterdam, Rotterdam
Poland:
Gdynia
Portugal:
Lisbon
Spain:
Barcelona, Bilbao

Sweden:
Gothenburg, Malmo, Stockholm
Switzerland:
Basle
United Kingdom:
Birmingham, Bristol, Glasgow, Hull/Goole, Leeds, Liverpool, London, Tilbury, Manchester
AMERICA:
Argentina:
Buenos Aires
Brazil:
Rio de Janeiro, Santos
Canada:
Hamilton, Montreal, Toronto
U.S.A.:
Chicago, Detroit, Los Angeles, Milwaukee, New York, San Francisco, Toledo
AFRICA AND ASIA:
Hongkong:
Hongkong
Japan:
Kobe, Nagoya, Shimizu, Tokyo, Yokohama
Singapore:
Singapore
South Africa:
Cape Town, Durban, East-London, Port Elizabeth, Laurenço Marques
Taiwan:
Taipeh

RENTCON Containers for Hire

	6 ft 6 in non-standard	10 ft ISO	20 ft ISO	20 ft sidedoor	20 ft open top	20 ft flat
LENGTH outside	2,010 mm 6 ft 7 in	3,030 mm (10 ft)	6,055 mm (20 ft)	6,055 mm (20 ft)	6,055 mm (20 ft)	6,055 mm (20 ft)
inside	1,895 mm (6 ft 2½ in)	2,835 mm (9 ft 4 in)	5,900 mm (19 ft 4½ in)	5,864 mm (19 ft 3 in)	5,870 mm (19 ft 3 in)	
WIDTH outside	2,435 mm (8 ft)	2,435 mm (8 ft)	2,435 mm (8 ft)	2,345 mm (8 ft)	2,435 mm (8 ft)	2,435 mm (8 ft)
inside	2,300 mm (7 ft 6½ in)	2,325 mm (7 ft 7 in)	2,325 mm (7 ft 8 in)	2,305 mm (7 ft 6¾ in)	2,300 mm (7 ft 7 in)	
HEIGHT outside	2,265 mm (7 ft 5 in)	2,435 mm (8 ft)	2,435 mm (8 ft)	2,435 mm (8 ft)	2,435 mm (8 ft)	2,435 mm (8 ft)
inside	2,030 mm (6 ft 8 in)	2,175 mm (7 ft 1 in)	2,175 mm (7 ft 1 in)	2,233 mm (7 ft 3 in)	2,160 mm (7 ft 1 in)	
FRONT-DOOR Width	1,880 mm (6 ft 2 in)	2,253 mm (7 ft 4½ in)	2,255 mm (7 ft 4½ in)	2,287 mm (7 ft 6 in)	2,120 mm (7 ft 4 in)	
Height	1,923 mm (6 ft 3½ in)	2,130 mm (7 ft)	2,130 mm (7 ft)	2,187 mm (7 ft 2 in)	2,160 mm (7 ft 1 in)	
SIDE-DOOR width				2,500 mm (8 ft 2½ in)		
height				2,100 mm (6 ft 10½ in)		
WEIGHTS tare weight	820 kg 1,810 lb)	1,200 kg (2,666 lb)	2,150 kg (4,730 lb)	2,000 kg (4,410 lb)	2,000 kg (4,409 lb)	2,310 kg (5,094 lb)
payload	6,030 kg (13,290 lb)	8,800 kg (19,556 lb)	17,850 kg (39,270 lb)	18,000 kg (39,683 lb)	18,320 kg (40,391 lb)	18,140 kg (40,000 lb)
gross weight	6,850 kg (15,100 lb)	10,000 kg (22,222 lb)	20,000 kg (44,000 lb)	20,000 kg (44,092 lb)	20,320 kg (44,800 lb)	20,450 kg (45,094 lb)
Cubic capacity	9 m^3 (318 cu ft)	15·4 m^3 (530 cu ft)	30 m^3 (1,060 cu ft)	30 m^3 (1,060 cu ft)	29·05 m^3 (1,026 cu ft)	ca. 30 m^3 ca. 1,050 cu ft

*without refrigeration unit.

	30 ft side door	30 ft tilt-tainer	40 ft ISO	40 ft side-door	20 ft × 5 ft 4 in Tank-C Liquitainer	20 ft Kuhl-Container Reefer-Container	30 ft Kuhl-Container Reefer-Container
LENGTH outside	9,125 mm (30 ft)	9,125 mm (30 ft)	12,190 mm (40 ft)	12,190 mm (40 ft)	6,055 mm (20 ft)	6,055 mm (20 ft)	12,190 mm (40 ft)
inside	8,950 mm (29 ft 4½ in)	8,980 mm (29 ft 6 in)	12,025 mm (39 ft 6 in)	12,000 mm (39 ft 5 in)		5,115 mm (16 ft 9½ in)	11,177 mm (36 ft 7 in)
WIDTH outside	2,435 mm (8 ft)	2,435 mm (8 ft)	2,435 mm (8 ft)	2,435 mm (8 ft)	2,435 mm (8 ft)	2,435 mm (8 ft)	2,435 mm (8 ft)
inside	2,158 mm (7 ft)	2,330 mm (7 ft 7½ in)	2,325 mm (7 ft 7½ in)	2,300 mm (7 ft 6¾ in)		2,135 mm (7 ft)	2,137 mm (7 ft)
HEIGHT Outside	2,435 mm (8 ft)	2,435 mm (8 ft)	2,435 mm (8 ft)	2,435 mm (8 ft)	1,620 mm (5 ft 4 in)	2,435 mm (8 ft)	2,435 mm (8 ft)
inside	2,158 mm (7 ft)	2,110 mm (6 ft 11 in)	2,185 mm (7 ft 2 in)	2,230 mm (7 ft 4 in)		2,062 mm (6 ft 9½ in)	2,062 mm (6 ft 9½ in)
FRONT-DOOR width	2,300 mm (7 ft 6½ in)	2,285 mm (7 ft 6 in)	2,265 mm (7 ft 5½ in)	2,290 mm (7 ft 6 in)		2,125 mm (6 ft 11½ in)	2,125 mm (6 ft 11½ in)
height	2,158 mm (7 ft)	2,035 mm (6 ft 8 in)	2,130 mm (6 ft 10 in)	2,190 mm (7 ft 2 in)		1,990 mm (6 ft 6½ in)	1,990 mm (6 ft 6½ in)
SIDE-DOOR width	2,300 mm (7 ft 6½ in)			2,500 mm (8 ft 2 in)			
height	2,000 mm (6 ft 6 in)			2,100 mm (6 ft 11 in)			
WEIGHTS: tare weight	3,000 kg (6,600 lb)	3,370 kg (7,488 lb)	2,880 kg 6,360 lb)	2,936 kg (6,472 lb)	2,500 kg 5,512 lb)	2,505 kg (5,590 lb*)	4,940 kg (10,868 lb*)
payload	22,500 kg (49,500 lb)	20,000 kg (44,444 lb)	27,120 kg (59,788 lb)	27,064 kg (59,576 lb)			
gross weight	25,000 kg (56,100 lb)	23,370 kg (51,933 lb)	30,000 kg (66,138 lb)	30,000 kg (66,149 lb)	20,320 kg (44,800 lb)	20,320 kg (44,800 lb)	30,480 kg (67,056 lb)
Cubic capacity	45 m^3 (1,589 cu ft)	44 m^3 (1,554 cu ft)	61·5 m^3 (2,172 cu ft)	62 m^3 (2,189 cu ft)	19 m^3 (671 cu ft)	22·1 m^3 (785 cu ft	48·7 m^3 (1,722 cu ft)

JAPAN

Nippon International Container Service Ltd.
Shiba-Hamamatsucho 3-5 Minatoku
Tokyo

New York Liner Administration Co. Ltd.
Marunouchi 2-20-1
Chiyodaku
Tokyo
(A Division of Dymo Industries)

NETHERLANDS

CETEM

Container-en Trailer Exploitatie Mij
Reeweg 24, Rotterdam

TELEPHONE: 295078
Rental of road haulage equipment, con-

tainers, trailers, low-loaders, Kangaroo semi-
trailers, chassis and flats.

CONTAINER CLEARING

Container Clearing NV
Boompjes 57, Rotterdam
Box 2141

TELEPHONE: 134303
TELEX: 21186
Sale, lease, repair, insurance and trucking

of all types of containers, trailers and
accessories.

DTS

Dockside Trailer Service
Van Riemsdijkweg 40
Rotterdam
TELEPHONE: 29 88 66
TELEGRAMS: DTS-Holland
TELEX: DTS-Holland nv. 24764
REPAIR DEPOT:
Van Riemsdijkweg 39
M. C. Pleit (*Manager*)
Telephone: 298866 ex 6 & 7
RENT AND LEASE DEPT.:
DIRECTORS:
B. J. S. van Rijn (*President*)
A. F. Spits (*Director Rent and Lease*)
R. P. R. van Rijn (*Director Repairs*)
RENT AND LEASE DEPT.:
Alb Plesmanweg 191
Rotterdam
Telephone: (010) 298866 ex. 1
J. J. de Laat (*Manager*)
Vlothavenweg 10, Amsterdam
Telephone: 238311 ex. 242
A. Th. Balk (*Manager*)
DTS lease containers, trailers, flats and
tilttainers. They store and handle contain-
ers, provide transport and repair facilities.

Container chassis — 20 ft

— 30 ft/20 ft

— 40 ft/30 ft/20 ft

Platform trailers with twistlocks — 40 ft

Soft covered trailers — 40 ft

Vans with side door — 40 ft

Tilt-tainers — 20 ft / 30 ft

Containers — 20 ft / 30 ft O.T. / 40 ft

Flats — 20 ft

Specials

TARIFFS:
Four different rates are charged—per day,
per week (6 and 7 day), per week (3 month)
and per week (6 month). Full details are
supplied on request.

GENERAL:
DTS are increasing their fleet in 1971 to
750 trailers and containers. Terminals in

England, Belgium and Sweden are being
developed.

FURNESS

Furness Transportgroep N.V.
Van Weerden Poel marweg 14, Rotterdam
TELEPHONE: 295000

Leasing of ISO containers one way trip,
long term basis and round trip if required.

NVRK

N.V. Rederij Koenigsfeld
Willemskade 19

Rotterdam
TELEPHONE: 111 085

TELEX: 21265
Container Leasing.

NEW ZEALAND
SEATRANS

Seatrans Consolidated (N.Z.) Limited

SEATRANS
Seatrans Consolidated (N.Z.) Limited,
Private Bag,
Mount Maunganui, New Zealand
Telephone: 54-099
Telex: NZ 2285
DIRECTORS:
R. A. Owens (*Managing Director*)
A. C. Williams (*General Manager*)
BRANCHES:
Auckland, Wellington, Christchurch, Dun-
edin, Invercargill, Tauranga.

AGENTS:
Timaru, Napier, New Plymouth, Whangarei.

CONTAINERS TYPE OFFERED FOR HIRE:
20 ft ISO containers (as at 1 May, 1971):

Total	Length	Width	Height
10	4·39 m	2·4 m	2·4 m
	(14 ft 5 in)	(8 ft)	(8 ft)
20			
Refrigerated			
18	4·39 m	2·4 m	1·5 m
Flats	(14 ft 5 in)	(8 ft)	(5 ft)

Ser. Nos.
SRC-6927
—6936

SRR-698,
SRR 6910-6913
SRR 701-703
SRR 705-7015
SRR 7101
SRO 693-697
SRO 6914-6926

CONTAINER SERVICES:
New Zealand/Australia
New Zealand/Japan

CONTAINER TERMINALS:		
Name of Terminal (*Leased*)	*Representative*	*Telephone No.*
Swiftrail/Carr & Haslam Ltd, Depot Westmorland St, Greylynn Auckland	E. R. Schmidt	30-129
Swiftrail/Kiwi Trans Tasman Ltd. 57 Thorndon Quay, Wellington	P. A. Russo	44-054
Swiftrail/C. Williams & Son Ltd Cnr Brisbane & Carlisle St, Christchurch	J. S. Morrison	77-663
Swiftrail (N.Z.) Ltd 14 Crawford Street, Dunedin	R. W. Shaw	79-001

CONTAINER PARK FACILITIES AND BREAK BULK AREAS:
Thirty acres including three acres of buildings entirely owned by Seatrans.

SPECIAL CONTAINER AGREEMENTS:
Special agreements with other freight—forwarders and N.Z. Railways.

TERMS AND TARIFF:
Refrigerated containers:
$6·50 per day, short term.
$5·50 per day, long term.

ADDITIONAL EQUIPMENT AVAILABLE FOR LEASING
Port of Mount Maunganui:
17 Fork Trucks 35,264 kg (16,000 lb) to

44,080 kg (20,000 lb) capacity.
10 Fork Trucks 8,816 kg (4,000 lb) to 17,632 kg (8,000 lb) capacity.
4 Log Handling Machines of 132,240 kg (60,000 lb) capacity.
1 Log Handling Machine of 198,360 kg (90,000 lb) capacity (with adaptations for other uses).
1 Crane 10 ton capacity.
1 Crane 3½ ton capacity (tower type).
Port of Auckland:
1 Fork Trucks 11,020 kg (5,000 lb) capacity.
Port of Dunedin:
1 Log Handling Machine 88,160 kg (40,000 lb) capacity.
2 Fork Trucks 8,816 kg (4,000 lb) and

11,020 kg (5,000 lb) capacity.
1 Log handling machine 35,264 kg (16,000 lb) capacity.
Port of Nelson:
1 Log Handling Machine 88,160 kg (40,000 lb) capacity.
2 Log handling machines 35,264 kg (16,000 lb) capacity.
Port of Whangarei:
1 Log Handling Machine 66,120 kg (30,000 lb) capacity.
1 Fork Truck 35,264 kg (16,000 lb) capacity.
Port of Bluff:
1 Fork Truck 11,020 kg (5,000 lb) capacity
All log handling machines listed above are capable of adaptation to fork lift uses.

UNITED KINGDOM
BROWN JENKINSON

Brown, Jenkinson & Co Limited,
Dunster House,
17/19 Mark Lane,
London, EC3
(see also UK Freight Forwarders)
BRANCHES:
Brown, Jenkinson & Co (Shipping) Ltd.
565, Sefton House,
Exchange Buildings, Liverpool 2
Telephone: 051 236 3742/6
Telex: 62219
M. Browning (*Director*)
Brown, Jenkinson & Co. (Shipping) Ltd.
75, Harborne Road, Birmingham 15
Telephone: 021 454 5751
Telex: 338 185
D. Deighton (*Director*)
Brown, Jenkinson & Co. (Shipping) Ltd.
Phoenix Wharf, Commissioners Road,
Rochester, Kent
Telephone: 0634 79881
Telex: 96226
J. Everett
Brown, Jenkinson & Co. (Shipping) Ltd.
Trelawny House, The Dock,
Felixstowe
Telephone: 03942 3878
Telex: 98345
I Robertson (*Director*)
(*Offices in Bradford and Manchester opening shortly*)
As business continues to improve, it has been decided to form a group of associates all trading under the name of "Container Clearing International". These are situated in Antwerp, Bremen, Copenhagen, Hamburg, Paris, Rotterdam:
PARIS—J. Davis
Container Clearing International,
Medafret S.A.
6, Rue Mayran, Paris IX
Telephone: 878 73-69
Telex: 29760

BREMEN—W. Scheling
Container Clearing International GMBH,
28 Bremen 1, Postfach 122,
Martinistrasse 26
Telephone: 32 34 76
Telex: 244487
ANTWERP—J. v. d. Broek
Container Clearing International,
S. A. Kennedy, Hunter & Co. Ltd.,
2 Orteliuskaai, Antwerp
Telephone: 3259 30
Telex: 32265/6
HAMBURG—C. Hagemann
Container Clearing International, GMBH
Theodor & F. Eimbcke,
"Eimbcke Haus",
2000 Hamburg 1
Telephone: 339181
Telex: 02161725
COPENHAGEN—J. Skjellerup, Mr Rasmussen
Container Clearing International,
Messrs. Lehmann Junior
Baltikavej, DK 2100 Copenhagen
Telephone: RY 9575
Telex: 6012
ROTTERDAM:—F. C. L. van Vugt
Container Clearing International,
Boompjes, 57
P.O. Box 2141, Rotterdam
Telephone: 134303
Telex: 21186

General
Ship, freight, air and insurance brokers, Brown, Jenkinson & Co Ltd also offer shippers extensive facilities for the leasing, hiring or purchasing of containers and act as 'Container Brokers'.
Among the services available are hire/leasing of most types of equipment, steel, alloy, alloy/steel, small, medium or large, for long or short periods, i.e. as little as two weeks, up to seven years or even longer, also on a

one-way basis for some areas, that means, picking up at one point and re-delivering at another, without the hirer having to find a return load.
For hire periods exceeding 6 months, containers can be supplied with the hirer's own livery markings.
Special fleet-hire and lease-purchase plans are available for the larger user whilst through its wide associations, the Company is regularly able to offer used equipment for purchase or sale.
Facilities for the maintenance and valeting of equipment are available in the United Kingdom, on the Continent and in Scandinavia and the USA. Elsewhere, arrangements can be made.

Shipping Companies Represented
Bugsier Line, Consortium Line, Combi Line, C de N'Carregadores Acoreanos' SARL, Delta Line, Deutsche Ost-Afrika Line, Europe-Canada Lakes Line, Gracechurch Line, Hapag Lloyd AG, Hoegh Line, Pakistan SL, A Kirsten-Hamburg-London Line, Rhine-London Line, South Africa Line, Svea Line.

UNIT TYPES FOR HIRE:
Type 40 ft 40 ft × 8 ft × 8 ft ISO
40 ft × 8 ft × 8 ft ISO
end door/end and side door.
40 ft × 8 ft × 8 ft 6 in
dry cargo and refrigerated.
Type 30 ft 30 ft × 8 ft × 8 ft end door/end
and side doors/full side access.
30 ft × 8 ft × 8 ft
tilt containers.
30 ft × 8 ft × 8 ft refrigerated.
30 ft × 8 ft × 8 ft open top.
30 ft × 8 ft Lancashire flats.

Type 20 ft   20 ft × 8 ft × 8 ft ISO
              20 ft × 8 ft × 8 ft 6 in
              20 ft × 8 ft × 8 ft ISO
              open top and tilt containers.
              30 ft × 8 ft × 8 ft ISO
              refrigerated containers.
              20 ft × 8 ft × 8 ft ISO
              bulk tanks.

Commercial Finance (Containers) Limited

HEAD OFFICE:
Old Exchange Chambers,
6 St. Ann's Passage,
King Street,
Manchester, M26AE
TELEPHONE: 061-834 5393 and 6411

BRANCH:
Commercial Finance (South Lancs) Ltd,
104 Upper Parliament Street,
Nottingham
Telephone: 0602 42318

DIRECTORS:
D. D. Hall
F. L. Hall

SECRETARY:
V. West

            20 ft × 8 ft × 8 ft ISO
            module stackable and collapsible
            flats.
            20 ft × 8 ft × 4 ft ISO
            module stackable and collapsible
            flats.
Type T/2   8 ft × 7 ft 9 in × 7 ft 7 in
            (400 ft³)

CFC

TYPES AND QUANTITY OF CONTAINERS
AVAILABLE AT 1st MAY, 1971:
Standard ISO Dry:
845 20 ft
 25 40 ft
 20 70 ft
Insulated
 30 20 ft
Lancashire Flats
 25
ISO Flats
 85
   A number of polystyrene and fibreglass Air
Freight Containers are also available.
DEPOTS:
   Wigan, Glasgow and Manchester.

GENERAL:
   CFC make provision for mid-quarterly

Type T/3   8 ft × 7 ft × 6 ft 10 in
            8·664 m³ (306 ft³)
Type A36   8 ft 6 in × 6 ft 3 in × 6 ft 10½ in
            8·35 m³ (295 ft³)
Type A35   7 ft 10½ in × 6 ft 11 in × 6 ft 7 in
            8·01 m³ (283 ft³)
Type T/1   7 ft 9 in × 6 ft 3 in × 6 ft 8 in
            7·362 m³ (260 ft³)

payments. The hirer can claim some of his
money back for his enterprise before he
has to start paying out. An associate
company Commercial Finance (South Lancs)
Ltd can help with industrial and business
finance queries.
   CFC customers include operators like
Manchester Liners, OCL, ACT, Inter, Ferrymasters, Ronagency, Edmundsons, N.C.L.,
Irish Shipping, Jenkinsons, Escombe, Dart,
Lep, Hallfreight, Greenore and Cork Ferry
Services. The firm has already achieved
export orders exceeding a quarter of a
million dollars. CFC containers manufactured in the U.K. are on lease to overseas
clients based in Belgium, Denmark, Germany,
North America, Portugal and Spain.
TERMS AND TARIFF:
Daily, short and long-term leasing. Minimum
period 30 days.

CONTAINERMASTERS

Containermasters Limited

68 Willow Walk,
London S.E.1
TELEPHONE: 01.237.6666
TELEGRAMS: Flexhill-London
TELEX: 888 567 Flexshipco Ldn

DIRECTORS AND PRINCIPAL OFFICIALS:
T. H. Flexen (*Director*)
R. B. Fairhead

BRANCHES:
Flexhill (Air) Ltd., Middx.
Faron Ltd., London
Flexhill Shipping Co. Ltd., London
Flexhill Shipping Co. (Liverpool) Ltd., Liver-
pool
Flexhill (Air) Ltd., Manchester
Richards Haulage Ltd.

MAIN CONTAINER ROUTES SERVED:
London—Dublin
Manchester—Dublin
London—Paris
London—Oslo
London—Gothenburg—Stockholm
Hull—Bremerhaven—Hamburg
London—Antwerp
Manchester—Paris
London—Rotterdam—Frankfurt—
Munich—Vienna
London—Rotterdam—Frankfurt—Basle-
Milan—Rome
London—Bremen—Berlin—Warsaw—
Moscow
London—Bremen—Prague
London—Bremen—Vienna—Belgrade
London—Bremen—Vienna—Budapest
London—Bremen—Vienna—Bucharest
London—Bremerhaven—Hamburg
Paris—Bordeaux
Paris—Toulouse
Paris—Marseilles
Paris—Lyon
Paris—Milan—Rome

RECEIVING AND DISTRIBUTING DEPOTS AT:

Manchester	Bremen	Cologne
Leeds	Vienna	Mannheim
Hull	Rotterdam	Stuttgart
Oslo	Paris	Antwerp
Gothenburg	Milan	Dortmund
Stockholm	Basle	Dusseldorf
Copenhagen	Dublin	Hanover

SERVICES:
Groupage and unit loads and full trailer or
container loads

EQUIPMENT AVAILABLE:
TIR trailers 8, 10 and 12·5 m (28, 29 and
37 ft) sizes, 7, 10, 12, 16 and 20 ft non-
standard containers, 30 and 40 ft ISO con-
trainers, non-standard flats, 20, 30 and 17½ ft
sizes and special removable roof 20 ft ISO
containers.

Containermasters TIR van trailer.

UK CONTAINER TERMINALS:

Name of Terminal.	Representative	Telephone No.
International Freight Terminal 18 Crimscott Street London S.E.1	J. Forbes	01.237.666

EUR

European Unit Routes Ltd.
15 St. Helen's Place,
London, E.C.3
England
TELEPHONE: 01-588 1344
TELEX: 885844

European Unit Routes Ltd. was the first company to open regular all-container services between Tilbury and the Continent. It is a subsidiary of the General Steam Navigation Co. Ltd. and a member of the P. & O. Group.

The service caters for the sea terminal-sea terminal movement of privately owned 20 ft, 30 ft and 40 ft units.

DIRECTORS:
D. L. J. Mortelman, OBE (*Chairman*)
W. M. Lang (*Director*)
D. E. Grover (*Director*)

Offices
LONDON (Headquarters):
(Admin. Technical & Sales)
Address as above
Marketing Manager: S. D. Sussex

Port Offices
TILBURY:
European Unit Routes Ltd.
No. 43 Berth, Tilbury Dock
Telephone: 0375-82 4191
Telex: 897251

ANTWERP:
European Unit Routes Ltd.
416-418 Berth, Noord Natie Terminal
Churchill Dock
Telephone: 413730 & 413739
Telex: 32984

DUNKIRK
European Unit Routes Ltd
Freycinet 13, Dock 6
Telephone: 66.58.74
Telex: 82953

ROTTERDAM
European Unit Routes Ltd.
Unitcentre N.V., Zaltbommelstraat,
Waalhaven Pier 7
Telephone: 29.89.44 and 29.86.52
Telex: 24225

HAMBURG
European Unit Routes Ltd.
Euro-Kai Terminal
Griesenwerder Damm
Telephone: 740.2704 and 36.141843
Telex: 213872

Service
EUR offers the following regular container shipping services between U.K. and the Continent:- Tilbury-Antwerp, Tilbury-Dunkirk, Tilbury-Rotterdam, Tilbury-Hamburg. In addition to carrying EUR-owned containers, 8 ft 6 in height containers can be accepted subject to pre-advice to the Terminal. A stock of EUR Galvanised End Door ISO containers are available for hire at a nominal fee for short or long term trips.

ECONOMY
The EUR terminal/terminal rates incorporate double handling at each terminal and are inclusive of all normal port charges.

SECURITY
Containers are sealed immediately on receipt into EUR custody and remain secure against pilferage. Seal numbers are strictly controlled.

ROTTERDAM:
Deliveries can be made via road and rail in one day to most major conurbations in France, Holland, Germany and Belgium. Direct rail connections are available to Austria, Switzerland and Italy.

All EUR terminals have excellent trunk road connections with the hinterland.

TILBURY:
Freightliner connected. Rail rates are inclusive of delivery to or collection from EUR Terminal.

Loading a ship at the EUR berth, Tilbury.

Sea Terminals
**43 Container Berth
Tilbury Docks, Essex**

BERTH OPERATORS:
The Port of London Authority

Telephone: 0375-82-3444
OPERATING HOURS:
Mon/Sat 0700-2100 hours
Collection and delivery can be made during the night subject to prior arrangement with EUR/PLA.
PORT OFFICE:
European Unit Routes Ltd., No. 43 Berth
Telephone: 0375-82-4191
Telex: 897251
H.M. CUSTOMS:
At No. 43 Berth
Telephone: 0375-82-4121, ext. 21
Landing Officers
Telephone: 0375-82-4121, ext. 24

416-418 Berth, Noord Natie Terminal
Churchill Dock, Antwerp
BERTH OPERATORS:
Noord Natie N.V.
Churchill Dock
Telephone: 41.70.79
OPERATING HOURS:
Monday to Friday 0800-1600 hours
Saturday 0800-1200 hours

Freycinet 13, Dock 6
Dunkirk
BERTH OPERATORS:
Jokelson & Handtsaem S.A.
8 Place des Nations
Telephone: 010.33.20
OPERATING HOURS:
Monday to Saturday 0800-1800 hours

Euro-Kai Terminal
Griesenwerder Damm, Hamburg
BERTH OPERATORS:
Euro-Kai K.G.
Telephone: 36.14.18.27
OPERATING HOURS:
Monday to Saturday 0600-2300 hours

Zaltbommelstraat
Waalhaven Pier 7, Rotterdam
BERTH OPERATORS:
Unitcentre N.V.
Telephone: 29.35.88
OPERATING HOURS:
0730 Monday to 1530 Saturday

Container Hire
EUR have a stock of ISO containers available at the sea terminals for leasing by merchants and forwarders. The minimum hire period is 30 days, and shipment must be confined to vessels and services owned or operated by or specifically approved by EUR.

The rates of hire vary according to size and type of unit required, and the duration of the leasing period.

Containers taken on hire may be returned on termination of hire to any EUR Terminal.

Example.—Dry cargo unit externally measuring 20 ft × 8 ft × 8 ft. Short term hire (min. 30 days) £1 per day, permitting the hirer to return the unit to any EUR sea terminal on termination of hire.

20 FT CONTAINER
DATA PLATE INFORMATION
Gross weight rating 20 tons
Payload rating 18 tons 1 qr
Tare weight: 1 ton 19 cwt
Cubic capacity 30·44 m³ (1,075 cu ft)
All containers are built and tested to British Standards (1967), Lloyds requirements, and the relevant Technical Annexes of the TIR Carnet (1959), the Customs Convention on Containers (1956) and to UIC requirements (592 OR).

LEASING CHARGES FOR EUR DRY CARGO END DOOR LOADING CONTAINERS (1.7.1970):

	20 ft	30 ft	40 ft
Minimum period 30 days	20/- per day	29/- per day	49/- per day
Minimum period 1 year	17/6 per day	26/- per day	44/- per day
Minimum period 2 years	15/- per day	22/- per day	37/- per day
Minimum period 3 years	12/6 per day	18/- per day	30/- per day

Monthly Turnover Rebates are allowed against the consolidated total of the monthly Freight and Leasing accounts on the following scale:

All accounts below £1,600	7½% Rebate	£2,500 and over	12½%
£1,600 and over	8%	£2,600 and over	13%
£1,700 and over	8½%	£2,700 and over	13½%
£1,800 and over	9%	£2,800 and over	14%
£1,900 and over	9½%	£2,900 and over	14½%
£2,000 and over	10%	£3,000 and over	15%
£2,100 and over	10½%	£3,500 and over	16%
£2,200 and over	11%	£4,100 and over	17%
£2,300 and over	11½%	£4,800 and over	18%
£2,400 and over	12%	£5,600 and over	19%
		£6,500 and over	20%

This rebate is only allowed if accounts are paid within 15 days of presentation.

THE GENERAL STEAM NAVIGATION CO. LTD.

The General Steam Navigation Co. Ltd.,
Three Quays, Tower Hill, London, E.C.3
TELEPHONE: 01-623 3000
TELEGRAMS: Glyconic, London, E.C.3
TELEX: London 886007

GENERAL:
G.S.N. are rethinking their policy on containers and have withdrawn from leasing operations.

HULL EUROSCAN

Hull Euroscan
Brighton Road
Heswell, Hull, Yorkshire
DIRECTORS:
N. H. Bryan
E. E. Cooper
E. Jordan
S. Tinegate

W. S. Oxendale
E. Pinder
N. Nolan
TERMINAL REPRESENTATIVE:
A. Fordon
CONTAINERS FOR HIRE:
20 ft ISO units

IMM

International Marine Management Inc.
18 Finsbury Circus
London E.C.2
TELEPHONE: 01.628.6651
TELEX: 885604
DIRECTORS:
H. J. Burley Smith (*President*)
R. Ochshorn (*Vice President*)
SALES MANAGER i/c CONTAINER OPERATIONS:
J. C. Lewis
BRANCH:
Felixstowe
EQUIPMENT:
Auto Perch car carrying frames for 40 ft ISO containers.
GENERAL DESIGN:
(i) Cradle frames, with integral tie down provisions, designed to support the rear wheels at the optimum height and supported by vertical side members constitute the essentials: a front wheel support stop completes the picture.
(ii) The design was evolved round the premiss that no structural alternative should

be made to the container, that the frames should be light in weight, small in volume and man portable. Further the design has allowed for any side loading stresses to be transferred not to the container side wall but to its main longitudinal strength members instead.
(iii) Adequate overall clearance to be maintained between the automobile, the support frames and the container side walls, roof and floor.
SPECIFIC POINTS:
(i) The integral structure has been specifically designed to absorb 2·5 g in any plane across the range of masses to found in America and European passenger cars.
(ii) Latches in the vertical frames are automatically closing during the loading made and have to be specifically opened on demanning. Accidental release in transit is thereby precluded. Samples have been tested to destruction and can absorb 100% overload on the design stress without collapse.
(iiii) Lfting in the present series is designed

to be done by a conventional fork lift truck with overshoes. The overshoes are provided with safety catches to preclude the vehicle slipping off during the lifting operation.
(iv) Operators are not required to go under a fork suspended load at any time.
(v) Any length of vehicle can be accommodated as the frames are infinitely variable in position.
(vi) Tie down facilities are integral with the front and rear frames, they can be conventional chain tensioners or toelyne webbing strap holders which ever is most convenient.

TERMS AND TARIFF:
Trip lease arrangements for trial moves. Negotiable leases available for longer term.

GENERAL:
Port agents for b line and U.S. Lines at Felixstowe.

STAR CONTAINER SERVICES

Star Container Services
Sidney House, Long Lane,
Halesowen, Worcs., England
TELEPHONE: 021-559 1243/2578/3162
DIRECTORS:
M. R. Everton (*Managing Director*)
L. A. Thomas
A. Jaquiss
M. J. Jones (*Executive Director*)
U.K. AGENTS:
Birmingham:
Star Container Services Ltd.
Sidney House, Long Lane
Halesowen Worcs.
Liverpool:
Taylors Transport Ltd
331/337 Derby Road
Bootle, Liverpool

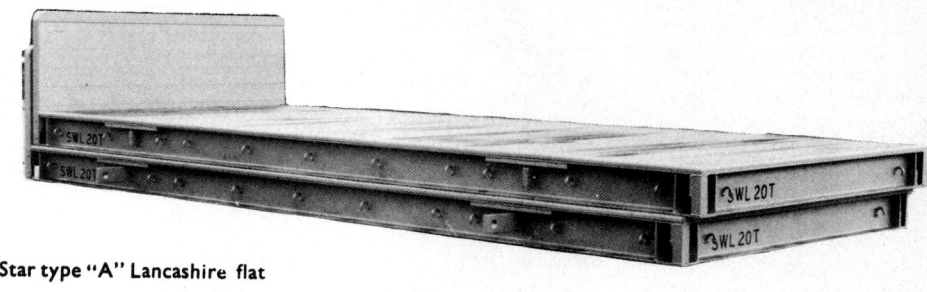

Star type "A" Lancashire flat

Southampton:
Containercare Ltd.
  Ryde Terrace, Chapel, Southampton
Scotland:
Star Container Services Ltd.
  Whitburn, West Lothian
Tilbury:
British & Northern Shipping Agency Ltd.
  26 Tilbury Dock, Tilbury, Essex
Yorkshire:
Hewson Bros. (Howden) Ltd.
  Thorpe Road, Howden, Goole, Yorks.
OVERSEAS AGENTS:
Belgium:
CIE. Dens-Ocean S.A.,
  Maria-Theresialei. 7, Antwerp
Denmark:
E. A. Bendix & Co. Ltd.
  St. Kongonsgade, Copenhagen
Germany:
Rabien & Stadtlander,
  Sogestrasse 31/33, Bremen

Holland:
D. Burger & Zoon,
  P.O. Box 149, Westerstraat, 7-13,
  Rotterdam
Italy:
Ideal Container,
  Via XX Settembre, 34/7,
  16121 Genova
Norway:
Skandinavisk Bilspedition A/S
  Ulvenveien 82 Postboks 53
  Økern Oslo 5

GENERAL:
Facilities offered by the company include: Container leasing, Groupage services, Storage and Repair services.

The STAR PLAN provides a completely flexible leasing service for Containers and Lancashire Flats designed to meet the needs of unit load equipment users. Special attention is given to unusual requirements.

The equipment is available for lease at immediate notice on a daily basis or on short or long term contracts.

Equipment is to full ISO standards and special attention has been given to the development of the STAR LANCASHIRE FLAT, type A is illustrated above.

One way services are available to certain

30 ft Star Container Services Ltd. container.

20 ft Star containers.

destinations—these services are expanding all the while and particulars are available on application.

Available in 20 ft, 30 ft and non-standard sizes, this flat combines maximum strength with lightness, and can be supplied painted in the customers' own livery.

LEASE RATES:
  Available on request.

TRANSCONTAINER EXPRESS

Transcontainer Express Ltd.
Central House, 32-66 High Street, Stratford
London, E15 2PP
TELEPHONE: 01-555.0121
TELEX: 896-334 Transcon Ldn
DIRECTORS:
J. L. Rees
W. Fraser
J. B. Palmer
GENERAL MANAGER:
G. F. Sodeau

OPERATING MANAGERS:
N. M. Geddes
J. H. Spalding
BRANCH OFFICE:
Trafalgar House, 72 Hope Street, Glasgow C.2
R. P. Wood (*Manager*)
CONTAINER SERVICES OFFERED:
UK, France, Holland, Belgium
Many times daily—own containers

TERMS AND ROUTES:
Single trip leasings, UK to France
Specialist service with one nett price, door to door
CONTAINER TERMINALS USED:
Fifty terminals in France and UK
CONTAINERS OPERATED at 1st MAY, 1971:
  200   30 ft ISO Dry
1,700   20 ft ISO Dry
   10   20 ft ISO Tanks for wines and spirit

WINNIC

Winn International Containers Limited
HEAD OFFICE:
Winn International Containers Limited,
London Scottish House,
London Road,
Barking, Essex, England
TELEPHONE: 01-594 4641
TELEGRAMS: Winnic Barking
TELEX: 262852
HEADQUARTERS, REPAIR AND
MAINTENANCE DIVISIONS AND EASTERN
OFFICE:
Winn International Containers Ltd.
Station Road, Parkeston,
Harwich, Essex
Telephone: Harwich 4313

Telex: 98456
NORTHERN OFFICE:
J. P. Wilson (*Area Manager*)
Winn International Containers Ltd.
1 St Mary's Road, Riddlesden,
Keighley, Yorks.
Telephone: Keighley 3498
Telex: 51519

HEADQUARTERS, CONTINENTAL DIVISION:
R. Visser (*General Manager*)
Winnic N.V.
  Calandstraat 49/51, Rotterdam 3002
  Holland
  Telephone: (010) 146510
  Telex: 24374

Winnic V.V.
  Bunschotenweg 131, 1E, Eemhaven
  Rotterdam 22, Zuid
  Telephone: 146510
  Telex: 24374
ITALIAN OFFICE:
O. Garofalo (*Area Manager*)
Winn International Containers Ltd.
  Via M. Macchi 26
  20124 Milan, Italy
  Telephone: 27 89 57
  Telex: 31 412
DIRECTORS:
G. C. Howard (*Chairman*)
H. C. Hobbs (*Managing Director*)
M. A. Knight

R. Visser
F. C. Margetts CBE
MANAGERS IN CHARGE OF CONTAINER OPER-
ATIONS:
T. A. Goodwin (*Controlling Executive, Main-
tenance and Repair*)
R. Goode (*General Manager Maintenance and
Repair Division, Harwich*)
R. Visser (*General Manager, Containers
(Continent)*)
L. M. Boorer (*Sales Manager, UK*)
J. P. Wilson (*Northern Area Manager*)
A. Tilley (*Depot Manager, Hull*)
R. Schneider (*General Manager, Repair
Depot Rotterdam*)

TYPES AND QUANTITY OF CONTAINERS
AVAILABLE FOR LEASE AND WHERE AVAILABLE

20 ft and 30 ft Standard Boxes (steel or
alloy), 20 ft and 30 ft Open Top Boxes, 20 ft
30 ft and 40 ft Sydors (containers with
hinged doors in the centre of each side
giving partial side access, as well as twin
rear doors), 20 ft and 30 ft Fulldoors (containers with multiple-hinged doors along one
or both sides, giving full unrestricted side
access, as well as twin rear doors), 20 ft and
39 ft tilts (either soft-top or hard-top), as
well as 20 ft and 30 ft flats, insulated containers and other specialised types.

Stocks of most of the above types are
usually readily available at Winnic depots,
distributed throughout Europe (see list
below), although quantities of each type
available vary from day to day.

SPECIFICATIONS:

Containers conform to ISO, BSI and BR
specifications and TIR, UIC and Lloyds
Registrations where appropriate.

BRIEF DESCRIPTION OF TERMS AND TARIFF:

The Winnic Container Leasing Service is
comprehensive and for UK and European
routes the rates are inclusive of maintenance
and repair facilities and also the provision
of replacement units together with third
party insurance.

The cost of leasing a Winnic is fixed—there
are no unexpected bills to meet for repair
costs—thus enabling the entire costs of
container usage to be incorporated into
customers' tariffs.

Non-comprehensive terms are available on
request.

WINNIC DEPOTS:

The locations of all Winnic depots presently
in use are listed below but Winnic are
rapidly extending their range and one trip
hire arrangements will be available to and
from each new depot as it becomes operational. Customers should telephone Winnic
for delivery to an area not listed.

BRANCHES:
U.K. WORKSHOPS:
Winn International Containers Limited,
   Station Road, Parkeston, Harwich
   Telephone: Harwich 2414/5
   Telex: 98456
Winn International Containers Limited
   B.R.S. Depot, Leads Road, Hull, Yorks.
   Telephone: Hull 74371
   Telex: 52115
Winn International Containers Limited
   c/o Austins of East Ham,
   Centenary Works, London Road, Barking,
   Essex
   Telephone: 01-594-4641
   Telex: 262852
DEPOTS:
Birmingham:
Winnic Depot Birmingham
   c/o J. Hickman & Son (Brierley Hill) Ltd.,
   P.O. Box 21, Pensnett Trading Estate,
   Pensnett, Brierley Hill, Staffs.
Bradford:
Winnic Depot Bradford
   c/o G. C. Morley
   International Freight Warehouse
   City Road, Bradford, Yorkshire

Side loading containers at Winnic Repair Depot, Parkeston.

Glasgow:
Winnic Depot Glasgow
   c/o Scott Packing & Warehousing Ltd.
   Woodilea Industrial Estate,
   Kirkintilloch, Dumbartonshire,
   Scotland
Harwich:
Winnic Depot Harwich
   Station Road, Parkeston, Harwich,
   Essex
Hull:
Winnic Depot Hull
   c/o B.R.S. Ltd.,
   Leads Road, Hull, Yorks.
Liverpool:
Winnic Depot Liverpool
   c/o Edward Nicholson Ltd.,
   Dock Road, Garston, Liverpool 19
London:
Winnic Depot London (East)
   c/o Austins of East Ham,
   Centenary House, London Road,
   Barking, Essex
Warrington:
Winnic Depot Warrington
   c/o Wardell Warehousing Co. Ltd.
   Barley Castle Lane, Appleton,
   Warrington, Lancs.
WINNIC IRELAND:
Irish Representatives:
Alltransport Ltd.,
   14, Hawkins Street, Dublin 2
   Telephone: 773188/9
   Telex: 5602
DEPOTS:
Dublin:
Winnic Depot Dublin
   c/o Alltransport Ltd.,
   Williames Container Service Ltd.,
   Tolka Quay, Dublin 1
WINNIC NETHERLANDS:
Headquarters, Continental Division:
Winnic N.V.
   Calandstraat 49/51, Rotterdam 3002,
   Z. Holland, Nederlands
   Telephone: 366316
   Telex: 24374.

DEPOTS:
Rotterdam:
Winnic Depot Rotterdam
   Bunschotenweg 131, 1e, Eemhaven
   Rotterdam 22—Zuid, Netherlands
WINNIC BELGIUM:
Belgian Representatives:
   F. Lanslots & Co.,
   Oude Steenweg 10/12, Antwerp,
   Belgium
   Telephone: 410661
   Telex: 32261
DEPOTS:
Antwerp:
Winnic Depot Antwerp

Patched container at Winnic Repair Depot,
Parkeston
   c/o F. Lanslots & Co.,
   Kaai 172, Antwerp, Belgium
WINNIC SPAIN:
Spanish Representatives:
Commercial Abengoa S.A.
   Avenida de Carlos V, No. 20,
   Seville, Spain
   Telephone: 25.48.36
   Telex: 72121
DEPOTS:
Barcelona:
Winnic Depot Barcelona
   c/o Mapor Container Terminal,
   Muelle Poniente, Barcelona,
   Spain
Bilbao:
Winnic Depot Bilbao
   c/o Termasa Terminales—Maritimes,
   Santure Puerte, Bilbao, Spain
WINNIC AUSTRIA:
Austrian Representatives:
Karl Herber Transportgesellschaft mbH
   Blumauervergasse 6,
   Postfach 85, A 1021 Wien,
   Austria
   Telephone (Wien) 24 854
   Telex: 74612
DEPOTS:
Salzburg:
Winnic Depot Salzburg
   c/o Station Salzburg—Hauptbanhof,
   Anschlusgleis—Anlage Wildenhofer,
   Salzburg, Austria

Vienna:
Winnic Depot Wien
c/o Karl Herber Transportgesellschaft mbH
Wien Nordwest Bahnof Gleis 30a,
Containerplatz Obenhalb des Gleissehuhes,
Vienna, Austria
WINNIC FRANCE:
French Representative:
P. Sykes Esq.,
54, Rue de Seine, 75—Paris (6e),
France
DEPOTS:
Dunkirk:
Winnic Depot Dunkerque
c/o P.S.C.
Chassée des Darses, 59—Dunkirk,
France
Le Havre:
Winnic Depot Le Havre
c/o P.S.C.
Quai de Floride, Terre Plein Hangar 12,
76—Le Havre, France
Lyons:
Winnic Depot Lyon
c/o P.S.C.
4, Av. Lionel Terray—Meyzieu,
69—Lyons, France
Marseilles:
Winnic Depot Marseille
c/o Soc. Franchise Y. Serris et Cie
60, Rue de Joliette,
13—Marseilles (2e), France
Paris:
Winnic Depot Paris
c/o C.G.T.,
Bassin No. 2,
92—Port de Gennevilliers,
France
WINNIC ITALY:
Italian Office:
Winnic, S.R.L.
Via M. Macchi 26, 20124 Milan
Italy
Telephone: (02) 27.89.57
Telex: 31412
Area Manager: O. Garofalo
DEPOTS:
Milan:
Winnic Depot Milano
c/o Messrs. Allievi,
Via Fantoli 28/4, 20100 Milan
Italy

Milan South:
Winnic Depot Milano (di Sud)
c/o Folli Gobbi,
Via Ripamonti 280, Milan,
Italy
Naples:
Winnic Depot Naples
c/o S.O.A. International Container Terminal F.S.
100 Via Emanuele Gianturco,
(per ferrovie—Scalo di Napoli—Traccia),
80142 Naples, Italy
Rome:
Winnic Depot Roma
c/o Roma Terminal Containers S.P.A.
Roma Monterotondo,
Scale Ferroviario, Rome,
Italy

WINNIC DENMARK:
Danish Representatives:
Lehmann Junion
3 Malmøgade, 2100 Copenhagen,
Denmark
DEPOTS:
Aarhus:
Winnic Depot Aarhus
c/o Danlast A/S,
Aarhus, Jylland, Denmark
Copenhagen:
Winnic Depor Copenhagen
c/o Canlast A/S,
Sydvestvej 73, DK 2600 Glostrup,
Sjaelland, Denmark
Odense:
Winnic Depot Odense
c/o Danlast A/S,
Odense, Fyn, Denmark
WINNIC W. GERMANY:
German Representatives:
Collico G.m.b.H.
Bahnstrasse 10,
565 Solingen—Ohligs,
Nordrhein, Germany
Telephone: Solingen (02122)—74243
DEPOTS:
Bremen:
Winnic Depot Bremen
c/o Uhlmann und Co,
Bremerhavenstrasse 265, Bremen,
Germany

Cologne:
Winnic Depot Kolne
c/o West-Friesland Eurotransport G.m.b.if
Stapelkai,
5 Kolne (Niehl-Hofch),
Nordrhein, Germany
Dusseldorf:
Winnic Depot Düsseldorf
c/o Deutsche Bundesbahn Container Terminal
Station Dusseldorf—Bilk,
4 Dusseldorf, Nordrhein,
Germany

Frankfurt:
Winnic Depot Frankfurt
c/o Deutsche Bundesbahn Container Terminal
Station Frankfurt/Main—Ost.,
6 Frankfurt/Main,
Hessen, Germany
Hamburg:
Winnic Depot Hamburg
c/o Collico Kantor Hamburg (Karlheinz Born),
Container Depot Burchardkai,
Hamburg Waltershof,
2 Hamburg, Germany
Hanover:
Winnic Depot Hanover
c/o Deutsche Bundesbahn Container Terminal
Hannover—Linden,
Hannover, Germany
Mannheim:
Winnic Depot Mannheim
c/o Mannheim H.G.B.F.
Schiebebuhne 10, 68 Mannheim,
Baden—Wurttenburg, Germany
Munich:
Winnic Depot Munchen
c/o Deutsche Bundesbahn Container Terminal
Station Munchen—HBF, 8 Munchen,
Bayern, Germany
Stuttgart:
Winnic Depot Stuttgart
c/o Deutsche Bundesbahn Container Terminal,
c/o Station Ludwigsburg,
714 Ludwigsburg,
Baden—Wurttemburg, Germany

WOOLLEY

W. B. Woolley & Co Ltd,
24/25 Mark Lane,
London, EC3 R7 DH
TELEPHONE: 01-623 5871
TELEGRAMS: Wooly Ldn
TELEX: 888050 Wooly Ldn
DIRECTOR:
H. L. Vaughan
CONTAINER TERMINALS:
Name of Terminal
(Participating Member)

Archibald Young (Storage) Ltd,
1 Meadowside St,
Renfrew, Scotland
Mr. Higgins   041-886-2356

Containerbase (B'ham) North, Ltd,
College Rd, Perry Bar,
Birmingham 22

SUBSIDIARY COMPANY:

W. B. Woolley (Scotland) Ltd,
Royal London House,
54 West Nile Street,
Glasgow, C1, Scotland
Telegrams: 'Worldwide Glasgow'
Telex: 77219 'Wooly Glasgow'
Telephone: 041-248-2929
I. S. Todd (*Scotland*)

Mr. H. L. Vaughan   067.63.3753

CONTAINER ROUTES:
Europe:
France, Germany, Holland, Belgium, Switzerland, Italy
USA:
Eastern Seaboard
TYPES AVAILABLE FOR HIRE:
575 gallon Thompson Portable Tanks
575 gallon Grundy Portable Tanks
20 ft, 30 ft and 40 ft Containers (all types)

UNITED STATES OF AMERICA
ADVANCE

Advance Distribution Company
351 California Street,
San Francisco, Calif 94104

CALIFORNIA

California Cargo Containers
801 Maritime Street,
Oakland, California 94607
TELEPHONE: 835 4484
(A Division of Dymo Industries
BRANCH:
440 Banning Blvd,
Wilmington,
California
Telephone: 834 2564

CONTAINER MANAGER:
James Pepper

Crusader 400-B container made by California.

CONTAINERS FOR HIRE:

Series and Serial Number	Type	Outside Dimensions			Internal Volume		Tare		Weight Max Gross		Door Opening	
		L	W	H	m³	cu ft	Kg	lbs	Kg.	lbs	W	H
Crusader 160	Dry	1·27 m	2·16 m	2·05 m	4·7	168	453·5	1000	4081·5	9000	1·81 m	1·73 m
		(4 ft 2 in)	(7 ft 1½ in)	(6 ft 9 in)							(5 ft 11¾ in)	(5 ft 8½ in)
Crusader 160-B	Dry	1·27 m	2·16 m	2·05 m	4·8	170	431·0	950	4058·9	8950	2·94 m	1·82 m
		(4 ft 2 in)	(7 ft 1½ in)	(6 ft 9 in)							(6 ft 8½ in)	(6 ft)
Crusader 250	Dry	1·81 m	2·16 m	2·05 m	7·02	248	498·8	1100	5942·0	13,100	1·88 m	1·73 m
		(5 ft 11½ in)	7 ft 1½ in	(6 ft 9 in)							(6 ft 2½ in)	(5 ft 8½ in)
Crusader 400	Dry	2·43 m	2·43 m	2·05 m	10·5	374	807·3	1780	6250·4	13,780	2·08 m	1·75 m
		(8 ft)	(8 ft)	(6 ft 9 in)							(6 ft 10 in)	(5 ft 8¾ in)
Crusader 400-B	Dry	2·43 m	2·43 m	2·05 m	10·2	363	680·2	1500	6123·4	13,500	2·31 m	1·82 m
		(8 ft)	(8 ft)	(6 ft 9 in)							(7 ft 7½ in)	(6 ft)
Atlas 550 ASA/ISO	Dry	2·98 m	2·43 m	2·43 m	15·3	542	1142·8	2520	10,228·4	22,520	2·28 m	2·15 m
		(9 ft 9¾ in)	(8 ft)	(8 ft)							(7 ft 6 in)	(7 ft 1 in)
Atlas 2000 Series 2000-2149	Dry	6·07 m	2·43 m	2·43 m	31·36	1108	1927·7	4250	19,277·7	42,500	2·28 m	2·15 m
		(19 ft 10½ in)	(8 ft)	(8 ft)							(7 ft 6 in)	(7 ft 1 in)
Series 2150-2349	Dry	6·07 m	2·43 m	2·43 m	31·61	1117	1859·7	4100	20,003·4	44,100	2·28 m	2·15 m
		(19 ft 10½ in)	(8 ft)	(8 ft)							(7 ft 6 in)	(7 ft 1 in)
Series 2350 (A)-2401 (A)	Areoquip	6·07 m	2·43 m	2·43 m	31·37	1109	2086·5	4600	20,250·2	44,600	2·29 m	2·15 m
		(19 ft 10½ in)	(8 ft)	(8 ft)							(7 ft 6½ in)	(7 ft 1 in)
Series 2402-2549 (Upwards)	Dry	6·07 m	2·43 m	2·43 m	31·61	1117	1959·5	4320	20,103·1	44,320	2·29 m	2·15 m
		(19 ft 10½ in)	(8 ft)	(8 ft)							(7 ft 6½ in)	(7 ft 1 in)

CAMBEIS

Cambeis Trucking Co Inc
312 Third Avenue,
Brooklyn, New York, NY 11215

COMPASS

**Whittaker Corporation
Compass Container Division**
1015 Market Avenue
Richmond California 94804
TELEPHONE: (415) 237 5122
TELEGRAMS: Compass
DIRECTORS:
Don Brandow (*Manager*)
A. A. Burda (*General Manager*)
BRANCH:
266 J.F.K. Boulevard,
Bayonne, N.J. 07002
TELEPHONE: (201) 437 74 31
Jeff Czarnecki (*Manager*)
M. J. Harr (*Sales Manager in charge of Container Operations*)
AVAILABILITY:
Compass containers are available in Japan, Singapore, Hong Kong, Taiwan, New York, **Los Angeles, San Francisco, Chicago.**

TERMS AND TARIFF:
Available *per diem*, trip leases, short or long term leases
STANDARDS: USASI ISO.
CONTAINERS FOR HIRE:
Dry: 20 ft ISO, 20 ft × 8½ ft, 40 ft ISO
Refrigerated: 20 ft ISO, 40 ft × 8½ ft
Flat Rack: 20 ft × 8 ft × 9 ft
Chassis: 26 and 27 ft
LEASING ARRANGEMENTS:
Pickup/Delivery Service is available at additional cost, long term lease rates available and aeroquip track provided as required.
Containers may be picked up/returned at the following depots:

Container Care Corporation.
440 Banning Blvd.
Wilmington, California
Telephone: (213) 834-1701

Greene Container Transport, Inc.
3500 South Kedzie Avenue
Chicago, Illinois
Telephone: (312) 247-27774
Warehousing & Transportation Ltd.,
100G Pasir Panjang Road,
Singapore
Hong Kong & Kowloon Wharf & Godown Co.,
Hong Kong
Hungtai Engineering Services,
No. 82 Min Sheng East Road,
Taipei, Taiwan
Sumitomo Warehouse Co.
21 Yamashita-cho, Naka-ku
Yokohama, Japan
Sumitomo Warehouse Co.,
No. 57, Naniwa-cho, Ikuta-ku, Kobe, Japan.
Roberts Warehouse,
55 Goodrich Street, Mariners Harbour,

Staten Island, NY 10303
Telephone: (212) 447.1800
Rentcon
Carl Tiedemann,
Rodingsmarkt, 20/26,
Hamburg 11, W. Germany
Star International,
P.O. Box 12264, St Louis, Missouri
Telephone: (314) 231.6220

E. R. Collings Trucking Co. Inc.,
6939 Old Clinton Road, Houston, Texas
Telephone: (713) 675.8251
Fleetways Transport Services Pty. Ltd.,
61 Bertie Street, Port Melbourne,
Victoria 3207, Australia
Gulf Ports Crating Company,
Box 51972, New Orleans, La 70150
Telephone: (504) 525.9936

J. V. M. Kean Ltd.,
Columbus House,
14-18 Customs Street East,
Auckland N.Z.

REPAIR FACILITIES:
Compass containers can be repaired at main headquarters. Minor repairs can be undertaken by agents.

CONTINENTAL TRAILER-ATC LEASING

Continental Trailer—ATC Leasing
(A subsidiary of Wells Industries)
Stephen Vyn (*President*)
Bruce Fowler (*General Manager*)
ATC GENERAL HEADQUARTERS:
4346 E. Sheila St. Los Angeles Calif 90023
TELEPHONE: (213) 268-2593
TELEX: 910-321-4401
(A DIVISION OF:
Continental Transportation Systems
13231 Lakeland Road (P.O. Box 2910)
Santa Fe Springs, Calif. 90670
TELEPHONE: (213) 685-6426
TELEX: 910-586-1634)

AGENTS:
Atlanta:
Intermodal Transportation Systems Inc.
    Telephone: (404) 577-6691
Chicago:
Intermodal Ground Services Inc.
    Telephone: (312) 586-5980
Honolulu:
ATC Pacific Rentals Inc.
    Telephone: (808) 845-6606
Houston:
Missouri Pacific Intermodal Transport Inc.
    Telephone: (713) 227-3151 ext 620
Kansas City:
Missouri Pacific Intermodal Transport Inc.
    Telephone: (816) 483-0525
Los Angeles:
ATC Leasing
    Telephone: (213) 268-2593
New Orleans:
Missouri Pacific Intermodal Transport, Inc.
    Telephone: (504) 523-2971
New York/New Jersey Metropolitan Area:

Intermodal Ground Services Inc.
    Telephone: (201) 792-5333
Oakland/San Francisco:
Haslett Company
    Telephone: (415) 834-6346
Portland:
Wilhelm Trucking Company
    Telephone: (503) 227-0561
Seattle:
Northern Pacific Transport Co.
    Telephone: (206) 725-2111
St Louis:
Missouri Pacific Intermodal Transport, Inc.
    Telephone: (314) 621-1000
REPAIR DEPOT:
    9634 Santa Fe Springs Road
    California 90670
FACTORY:
    13231 Lakeland Road
    Santa Fe Springs
    California 90670
ATC Leasing Corporation has established a mobile ground support network in USA. This network provides a pool of trailers and storage yards in all the major transportation centres in the United States. Units can be picked up at one depot and left at another. Each of these trailer pool areas is operated by an ATC franchised agent. ATC agents are companies such as the Burlington Northern Railroad Intermodal Transportation Systems Missouri Pacific Railroad Haslett Warehouse etc.
    The services each agent is required to provide are as follows:

1. LEASING:
Each ATC agent's fleet consists of van trailers,

flatbeds and various sizes and styles of container chassis equipment. These units are available for lease.
    Per Diem
    Weekly monthly or long term
    "One Way Trip" this is the "pick it up here-leave it there" concept.
Note: With ATC's tailored leasing plans the customer has units available when, where and for the exact amount of time he needs them.
2. STORAGE:
ATC's yards are all fenced, paved and illuminated to provide proper protection to trailers or containers that are stored. Plans include per diem storage of containers. ATC can store a customers container/chassis combination while in the turn around stage waiting for new freight.
3. MAINTENANCE & REPAIR:
All locations are able to perform inspections, clean out service, preventative maintenance programmes, major repairs, etc, on trailers, containers or chassis. Service plans are available in various forms to best suit the customer.
4. CARTAGE:
All locations can supply power to pick up or deliver trailers and chassis. ATC can supply the actual freight movement from shipper to rail if requested.
5. COMPUTER CONTROL:
ATC, Los Angeles is the key to the pool network. The entire operation is computer controlled so as to provide customers with immediate information about any services they are using within the ATC Agency Network.

EWING

Carl F. Ewing Inc.
82 Wall Street, New York, NY
    Dry and tank containers available. Smallest size 9·06 m³ (320 cu ft). Steel, aluminium or plywood construction.

GENERAL AMERICAN

General American Transportation Co.
135 South La Salle St., Chicago, Ill. 60690
    Standard size containers, dry and tank type available.

GREAT DANE

Great Dane Trailers Inc.
Lathrop Ave. P.O. Box 67, Savannah, Ga. 31402
TELEPHONE: 912-232.4471
DIRECTORS:
C. Hammond Jr.
B. Reeve Jr.
E. R. Moir
F. J. Melius
SALES MANAGER IN CHARGE OF CONTAINER OPERATIONS:
C. F. "Kit" Hammond

USA BRANCHES:
Great Dane Trailers, Inc.
    1219 Bankhead Hwy.,
    West Birmingham, Ala. 35204
    Telephone: (205) 251-9285
    Jerry O. Davis (*Manager*)

Great Dane Trailers, Inc.
    3160 W. Beaver St. P.O. Box 6732
    Jacksonville, Fla. 32205
    Telephone: (904) 387-3541
    W. E. Voiselle (*Manager*)
Great Dane Trailers, Inc.
    3130 NW 79th Avenue

Miami, Fla. 33152
    Telephone: (305) 635-0943
    Harry E. Yallelus (*Manager*)
Great Dane Trailers, Inc.
    6710 E. Buffalo Ave.
    P.O. Box 11146 Tampa, Fal. 33619
    Telephone: (813) 626-2147
    R. S. Vaughn (*Manager*)
Great Dane Trailers, Inc.
    660 University Ave., S.W. Atlanta, Ga. 30310
    Telephone: (404) 758-4611

A. S. Langston (*Vice President*)
Great Dane Trailers, Inc.
    3800 North I-85 P.O. Box 1966
    Charlotte, N.C. 28201
    Telephone: (704) 596-3721
    R. W. Saussy (*Manager*)
Great Dane Trailers, Inc.
    P.O. Box 3577
    2702 Deepwater Terminal Rd.
    Richmond Va. 23234
    Telephone: (703) 233-9875
    F. C. Anderson (*Manager*)

Great Dane manufactures marine ASA/ISO dry and refrigerated containers in all sizes from 10 ft to 40 ft × 8 ft × 8·5 ft in stainless steel or aluminium but do not maintain a pool or keep units in stock. They operate long term leases only. (See also Manufacturers' Section).

INTERCONTINENTAL

Intercontinental Trailsea Corporation
11 Broadway, New York, N.Y. 10004

TELEPHONE: 943-8630 425 7860
OFFICIALS:
Isaac Charchat (*Chairman*)
Zecharia Stichin (*President*)
D. Murphy (*Vice President*)
W. Van Ersden (*Vice President*)

BRANCHES:
USA, Canada, UK, Western Europe, Japan, Australia and Hong Kong.
ALLIED COMPANIES:
United Cargo Corporation
International Book Service Inc.
The Land-Bridge Corporation
Intercontinental Trailsea Corporation (Maine)
ITC Commercial Credit Card Inc.

CONTAINERS AVAILABLE FOR LEASE AT 1st MAY 1971:
1,000 20 ft and 40 ft ISO Dry on long term per diem rates.
ROUTES:
Door to door—world wide. Express container service by United Cargo Corporation.
Europe to the Far East across the US using the "Land-Bridge" service operated by the Land-Bridge Corporation.
MAIN UK TERMINAL:
United Cargo Containers Ltd.,
Unit 7, Thames Side Industrial Estate, London E.16
Director: D. B. Wallace
Telephone: 01.476.3346
ITC is a subsidiary of the United Cargo Corporation, a world wide container carrier with headquarters in New York. The basic concept of ITC is to provide an inland to inland international container transport service.

Arrangements are made with inland carriers to establish their terminals as "UCC Receiving & Distributing Terminals", and linked with some 200 UCC terminals established in 26 countries. Using the Port of New York as the gateway and adding marine tariff rates to the inland carrier's rates, the shipper can be quoted one predetermined price to cover the cost of the full movement of the cargo from the receiving terminal to the distributing terminal at destination. Because the charges are based on rates per cu. ft and because containers eliminate the need for costly export packing the system is particularly economic for those shipping less than a full load at a time. A further facility is the issue by UCC of a Thru Bill of Lading which expedites both the movement of the cargo and payment for the goods.

(See also Non Vessel Operators Section).

INTERMODAL

Intermodal Contrailer Inc
711 Second Street,
Hoboken, NJ 7030

NORTH AMERICAN INTERNATIONAL

North American International
P.O. Box 201, New Haven, Indiana
CONTAINERS FOR HIRE:
Steel containers dry only, including 20 ft refrigerated available. Smallest size 4·24 m³ (150 ft³).

SMYTH

Smyth Worldwide Mover Inc
Container Div.
11616 Aurora Ave N,
TELEPHONE: EM44000 Seattle

Washington 98103
TELEGRAMS: Smythco
TELEX: 032-442
Aluminium dry containers available of

2·2 m × 1·4 m × 2·1 m (7 ft 4 in × 4 ft 8 in × 7 ft) only.
MANAGER MILITARY DIVISION:
G. R. Hansen

STONE DOWNER

Stone & Downer Co.
131 State Street,
Boston, Mass 02109

TELEPHONE: 617 523-3800
TELEGRAMS: Demander
OFFICIALS:
James Low (*President*)

Paul K. Laroque (*Vice President*)
R. Perkins (*Secretary*)

BRANCHES:
Air Cargo Section
Logan International Airport
East Boston, Mass.

ROUTES:
All routes
TERMINALS:
Represented at all Boston Terminals
LEASING:
Can be arranged
PARKING FACILITIES:
At all terminals

T.M.

T.M. Leasing
Trailmobile (A Div)
200 South Michigan Ave,
Chicago, Ill 60604
TELEPHONE: 312: 939 : 1350

SALES MANAGER: W. J. Deck
T. M. Leasing was started in January 1969 as a long term truck and trailer leasing company. It has 5,000 trailers on lease.

CONTAINERS FOR HIRE:
Steel, aluminium and plastic-coated plywood containers, dry or tank, refrigerated and insulated to ANSI and ISO standards.

TRANSPORT POOL

Transport Pool
7th and Maritime Streets,
Oakland, Calif

UNIFLEX

UNI-FLEX Container Division
(A Division of Flexi-Van Inc, A subsidiary of Gilbert Flexi-Van Corp.)
330 Madison Avenue, New York, N.Y.
TELEPHONE: 212 682 7888
C. W. Henkels (*President*)

BRANCH:
64 Kingsway, London WC2

Telephone: 242.2411
O. Plascow (*UK Manager*)

BRANCHES AND DEPOTS:
United States:
New York, Boston, Philadelphia, Baltimore, Norfolk, Miami, New Orleans, Houston, Chicago, Los Angeles, San Francisco, Detroit, Cleveland, St. Louis, Oakland,

Savannah.
South America:
Asuncion, Paraguay and Rio de Janeiro, Brazil.
Europe:
AUSTRIA: Vienna.
BELGIUM: Antwerp.
DENMARK: Aarhus, Copenahagen, Odense
ENGLAND: Greenford, London, Warrington,

HUNGARY: Budapest.
ISRAEL: Tel Aviv.
ITALY: Genoa, Milan, Naples, Trieste, Turin.
NETHERLANDS: Rotterdam.
NORWAY: Oslo.
PORTUGAL: Lisbon, Oporto.
SCOTLAND: Glasgow.
SPAIN: Barcelona, Bilbao, Madrid, Valencia
SWEDEN: Stockholm.
SWITZERLAND: Basle.
YUGOSLAVIA: Belgrade, Ljubljana.

Asia:
JAPAN: Kobe, Nagoya, Tokyo, Yokohama.
TAIWAN: Keelung, Taipai.
SINGAPORE:, HONG KONG: Kowloon.
Australia:
Brisbane, Fremantle, Melbourne, Newcastle,
Port Adelaide, Port Kembla, Sydney.
LEASING ARRANGEMENTS:
One 4-way, round trip or short term to suit
customers requirements.
GENERAL:
Uni-Flex Container Division is the con-

tainer and chassis rental organisation of
Flexi-Van, Inc.
Flexi-Van, Inc. is the transportation
equipment and leasing subsidiary of Gilbert
Flexi-Van Corporation. Uni-Flex, along
with five other sister companies, provides
rental and leasing of all types of transportation equipment, including truck-tractors,
highway trailers, intermodal containers,
chassis and specialized transportation vehicles
Flexi-Van, Inc., was formed in 1957 to hold
the basic patents of the Flexi-Van container
system. This system was the first practical
method of moving containers on specially
designed flat cars and as highway trailers.
From being a pioneer in the development of
containerisation, Flexi-Van has moved into
the broad range of providing all types of
transportation equipment at strategic locations throughout the world.
Uni-Flex Container Division with offices
and agents in six continents provides intermodal containers and chassis for rental on a

one-way trip or term lease. The units
available for lease have all passed the stringent inspection of the firm's engineering staff
and are considered to represent the finest
design and equipment specifications. The
firm's major depots in the United States are
Oakland, California and Secaucus, New
Jersey. On these locations, Flexi-Van Service Center provides repair and preventive
maintenance for cargo containers prior to
redispatching on international voyages. In
Europe and the U.K. Uni-Flex, though a
joint operational agreement with CON-
TRANS, offers containers and chassis at all
CONTRANS' locations. The reciprocal agreement provides that Uni-Flex rents
CONTRANS' equipment at all of its facilities
in the United States, South America and the
countries of Asia. The combined efforts of
the two firms enable them to operate one of
the world's largest container fleets and
provides a most diversified type and size of
equipment.

WORLD WIDE

World Wide Containers
26 Journal Square,
Jersey City, NJ

XTRA

XTRA, Inc.

TELEPHONE: 617-523 8070
TELEX: 94552
HEAD OFFICES:
150 Causeway Street,
Boston,
Massachusetts, 02114 USA
and
222 St. John Street,
Portland, Maine 04102, USA

BRANCHES:
Chicago, Illinois; Atlanta, Georgia; Balti-
more, Maryland; Newark, New Jersey; New
Orleans, Louisiana; San Francisco, California;
Saint Louis, Missouri.
Max Uhlig & Co,—Agent
Hamburg, Germany and Yokohama, Japan.

DIRECTORS:
J. Prendiville
R. Kieran
S. Kudisch
F. Ventre
C. Kaye
H. Streeter
E. Roberts
T. Richmond
C. Bockstoce
G. Donaldson

SALES MANAGER IN CHARGE OF CONTAINER
OPERATIONS:
William H. Sarakenoff (*Vice President of
Customer Service, Chicago, Illinois*)

TYPES AND QUANTITY OF CONTAINERS
AVAILABLE FOR LEASE:
20 ft and 40 ft dry freight containers both
steel and aluminium

Available in all major ports in USA and
Europe

20 ft container fleet—1,600
40 ft container fleet—485
20 ft open top steel—200
Serial Nos.
XTRU 810000—811599
XTRU 870000—870484
XTRU 610003—610202
   2 27 ft
   2 22 ft
497 25 ft   Tandem Chassis
 52 26 ft
487 40 ft
994 20-40 ft Chassis

BRIEF DESCRIPTION OF TERMS AND TARIFF:
Short or long term leases or daily per diem
rates of $2.00/day per container for 20 ft
containers and $3.50/day for 40 ft containers.
All rates are subject to change.

SHIP CHARTERERS
AND
NON OPERATING
SHIP OWNERS

SHIP CHARTERERS AND NON-OPERATING SHIP-OWNERS

ACT (Australia) Ltd.
136 Fenchurch Street,
London EC3
UK

Asmar Lineas
c/o Equimar Maritima SA
Ercilla 1
Bilbao
Spain
SHIPS ON LEASE TO CONTENEMAR LINES:
Beatriz del Mar (133 20 ft)
Mercedes del Mar (133 20 ft)
Helmut Bastian
4/5 Altenwall,
28 Bremen,
W. Germany

Bauer & Hauschildt K.G.
11 Katharinenstrasse,
2 Hamburg 11
W. Germany
Ship for lease:
Buxtehude II
(78 20 ft)
Odd Berg
P.O. Box 1366 Vika,
Oslo,
Norway
Ships on lease to Atlantic Lines Ltd:
Panatlantic (33/30 35/40 ft trailers)
Pancaribe (33/30 35/40 ft trailers)
Panamerica (33/30 35/40 ft trailers)
Under construction:
2 *Ships*
Arnold Becker
Hauptstrasse 73,
2151 Konigriech
W. Germany
Ship on lease to Bell Line
Bell Valiant (65 20 ft)
Belcan NV
c/o Ubem SA, NV
150 Mechelse Steenweg,
Antwerp,
Belgium
SHIPS ON LEASE TO FEDERAL ATLANTIC
LAKES LINES:
Federal St. Laurent (400 20 ft)
Federal Schelde (400 20 ft)
G. Bell (Chartering) Ltd
Hawkins House,
Dublin
Ireland
Ship on lease to Bell Line
Bell Combat (over 100 20 ft)
Blaesbjerg & Company
BP-Huset Europaplads 2
8100 Aarhus C,
Denmark
SHIPS ON LEASE TO B-LINE:
Unit Scan (80 20 ft) and two ships under
construction.
Heinrich Block
Fahrenkrön 10,
2 Hamburg 71,
W. Germany
Ship for Lease:
Klaus Block (71 20 ft)
**Johann M. K. Blumenthal
Reederei**
See under "Orion"
Blue Star Line Ltd.
Albion House
34 Leadenhall Street,
London EC3,
U.K.
UNDER CONSTRUCTION:
2 ships for Scanstar Ltd.

Blue Star, Port Line and Ellerman Lines
Albion House
34 Leadenhall Street,
London EC3,
U.K.
SHIPS ON LEASE TO ACT:
ACT I (1,223 20 ft)
ACT II (1,233 20 ft) (see Ship Operators
section).
Aug. & Wm. Bolten
Müller's Nachfolger
Maltentweite 8,
2 Hamburg 11
W. Germany
Ships on lease to Swedish Lloyd
Barbel Bolten (155 20 ft)
Marietta Bolten (150 20 ft)
Teesland (75 20 ft)
Jürgen Breuer
Heinrich K. G.
Augustenhöh 4a
2000 Hamburg 50
W. Germany
Ships on lease to Bellferry
Bell Vanguard (65 20 ft)

Bristol City Line of Steamships Ltd.
129 Cumberland Road,
Bristol BS1 6UY
U.K.

British Yukon Ocean Services Ltd
Standard Building (Floor 12)
510 West Hastings Street,
Vancouver 2, B.C.
Canada
*Ship on lease to British Yukon Navigation
Co.*
Frank H. Brown (200 20 ft)

Cardigan Shipping Co
c/o Blandford Shipping Co.
33 Bury Street,

London EC3
Bravo Contender (55 30 ft)
Containership Chartering Service
Sea-Land Services
P.O. Box 2000
Elizabeth
N.J.
USA
Ships on lease to Sea-Land Service Inc
Chicago (609 35 ft)
Houston (395 35 ft)
St. Louis (609 35 ft)
**Compagnie Maritime Belge (Lloyd Royal),
S.A.**
Member of the Dart Containerline Company
Limited
St. Katelijnevest 61, Antwerp
TELEPHONES: 33.88.90 — 32.18.90 —
32.19.10
TELEGRAPHIC ADDRESS: COMARBEL
Antwerp
TELEX: Agenmarin An 31366
DIRECTORS:
Baron de Spirlet (*Chairman and Managing
Director*)

The *Panamerica*, length 78.6 m (258 ft 7 in), beam 13.6 m (44 ft 9 in), draught 3.14 m (10 ft 4 in) capacity 33-35 ft trailers or 30-40 ft trailers. Owned by Oddberg of Oslo.

Capt V. Rasquin (*Marine Superintendent*)
*Ship on lease to Dart Containerline Company
Limited*
Dart Europe (1,556 20 ft)

Common Brothers (Management) Ltd
Exchange Buildings,
Quayside,
Newcastle-on-Tyne,
NE1 3AB
U.K.
Ships on lease to Caribbean Trailer Express:
Caribbean Enterprise (51 30 ft)
Caribbean Venture (51 30 ft)
Ships on lease to Svea Line
Nimos (Lift/on Lift/off and Roll/on-Roll-off
vessel)

Under Construction:
Two ships.

ACL's Atlantic Causeway.

Compagnie Generale Transatlantique
6 Rue Auber,
Paris 9e,
France
SHIPS ON LEASE TO ACL
Atlantic Champagne (966 20 ft)
Atlantic Cognac (232 20 ft)

Compagnie des Messageries Maritimes
12 Boulevard de la Madeleine,
Paris 8e
France
SHIPS ON LEASE TO SCTC:
Kangourou (1,492 20 ft) and two ships under
construction.

Concord Line Aktieselskab
Hellerupvej 14
Hellerup
Copenhagen
Denmark
TELEPHONE: Hellerup 8068 (Office)
Ordrup 8730 (Private)
TELEX: 5568
DIRECTORS:
Ian Fenger
J. D. Lauritzen
Ships for lease:
Sylvia Cord (160 20 ft and 64 10 ft)
Margaret Cord (160 20 ft and 64 10 ft)

Containership Chartering Service
Sea-Land Services
P.O. Box 2000
Elizabeth
N.J.
USA
New Yorker (190 17 ft)

Cunard Brocklebank Limited
Cunard Building,
Liverpool L3 1DY
U.K.
TELEPHONE:
TELEX:
Ships on lease to ACL:
Atlantic Causeway (966 20 ft)
Atlantic Conveyor (966 20 ft)

Donmac Corporation
P.O. Box 1050
Elizabeth, NJ
Ship on lease to Sea-Land Services Inc:
Bienville (452 35 ft)

Peter Döohle
Maltenweite 5-7.
2 Hamburg 11
W. Germany
TELEPHONE: 36.26.46
TELEX: 02 14666
Ships on lease to Sea-Land Services Inc
Albert Frieseike (63 35 ft)
Arosia (133 20 ft)

to European Unit Routes:
Impala (63 20 ft)
Isabella (133 20 ft)

Reederei Erich Drescher
2 Hamburg 11
Alter Fischmarkt 11
TELEPHONE: 33.93.11
TELEX: 021.61395 Wilhansen
Ship on lease to Fabre Line:
Ede Sottorf (264 20 ft)
Under Construction:
One ship.

Equimar Maritima SA
Ercilla 1,
Bilbao,
Spain
SHIPS ON LEASE TO CONTENEMAR LINES:
Tatiana Del Mar

Hefried Fahje
Fahje, Otto & Son,
2 Hamburg-55
W. Germany
TELEPHONE: 86.03.24
Ship on lease to EUR, London:
Eland (63 20 ft)

Fearnley & Eger
P.O. Box 355
Radhusgt 23
Oslo 1,
Norway
SHIPS ON LEASE TO BARBER LINES A/S:
Fernlake (132 20 ft)
Fernview (132 20 ft)

James Fisher & Sons Ltd.
PO Box 4,
Fisher House,
Barrow-in-Furness
Lancashire
SHIPS ON LEASE TO TRANSPORT FERRY
SERVICE:
Orwell Fisher (116 20 ft)
Solway Fisher (116 20 ft)

Flensburger Schiffs-Partenvereinigung AG
Rathausstrasse 41
239 Flensburg
W. Germany
Ship on lease to Dart Containerline:
Juno (192 20 ft incl 10 20 ft reefers)

H. M. Gehrkens
P.O. Box 933
Beimneuen Krah 2
2 Hamburg 11
W. Germany
Ship on lease to Team Line:
Wasa (Ro/Ro ship)

Greyhound Leasing & Finance Corp
c/o S. Atlantic & Caribbean Line Inc
808 N.E. 2nd Avenue,
Miami
Fla 33132
USA
Ship on lease to S. Atlantic & Caribbean Line:
Sacal Borincano (40 40 ft Ro/Ro ship)

Günter Graebe
Osterwisch & Graebe
Vorsetzen 41
2 Hamburg 11
W. Germany
Ship on lease to EUR, London:
Caribou (100 20 ft inc 10 20 ft reefers)
Ship on lease to Macpak Container Service:
Velasques (102 20 ft)

**Hamburg South America Line.
Dampfschiffahrts-Gesellschaft
Eggert und Amsinck**
PO Box 1540
2000 Hamburg 11,
W. Germany

COLUMBUS LINE:
Columbus America
Columbus Australia
Columbus New Zealand

Heinrich Kahrs
2161 Gräpel über Himmeliforten,
Hamburg,
W. Germany
SHIP ON LEASE TO BELL LINE LTD.
Bell Vigour (95 20 ft)

**Nederlandsch-Amerikaansche Stoomvaart-
Maatschappij**
Holland Amerika Lijn
Wilhelminakade 86
Rotterdam,
Netherlands
Ships on lease to Atlantic Container Line Ltd:
Atlantic Crown (569 20 ft)
Atlantic Star (569 20 ft)

Holland Stoomboot Maatschappij NV
O Handelskade 3
PO Box 566,
Amsterdam,
Netherlands
SHIP ON LEASE TO CPS LTD:
Emstroom

Hudson Waterways Corporation
c/o Transeastern Ass. Inc.,
1 Chase Manhattan Plaza,
New York,
N.Y. 10005
USA
Ships on lease to Seatrain Lines Inc
(Each 170-177 40 ft)

Seatrain Carolina	*Seatrain Maryland*
Seatrain Delaware	*Seatrain Ohio*
Seatrain Florida	*Seatrain Puerto Rico*
Seatrain Maine	*Seatrain San Juan*
	Seatrain Washington

Under Construction:
Seven ships in course of conversion (1,600
20 ft)

Island Navigation Corporation
20 Exchange Place,
New York,
NY 10005
U.S.A.
SHIPS UNDER CONVERSION FOR ORIENT
OVERSEAS CONTAINER LINE:
*Hong Kong Beauty, Hong Kong Surity,
Hong Kong Truth,* (350 20 ft).

Ernst Jacob
Rathausstrasse 20
239 Flensburg,
W. Germany
TELEPHONE: 7041
TELEX: 022 864
Ship on lease to Fabreline:
Helene Roth (245 20 ft)

Atlantic Crown owned by Holland America Line.

Joaquin Davila CIA S.A.
Plaza Compostela 22,
P.O. Box 80,
Vigo,
Spain
SHIPS ON LEASE TO UNION MARITIMA ESPANOLA:
Isla Del Atlantico (150 20 ft)
Isla Del Mediterraneo (150 20 ft)
UNDER CONSTRUCTION:
Two ships.

Johannes Bos
Buchenweg 21
295 Loga,
W. Germany
SHIPS ON LEASE TO ELLERMAN'S WILSON LINE:
Tasso: (60 20 ft)
Truro (60 20 ft)
SHIP ON LEASE TO MACPAK CONTAINER SERVICE:
Valdes (71 20 ft)

Johan Kahrs Jr
(See under **Johns Thode**)

Hans Kruger GmbH
Mattentwiete 5
2 Hamburg 11
W. Germany
TELEPHONE: 36.61.44
TELEX: 021.2733
Ship on lease to Dart Containerline:
Joerg Krueger (202 20 ft)
Britta Krueger (202 20 ft)

Litton Industries Leasing Corporation
P.O. Box 1050
Elizabeth,
New Jersey,
USA
Ships on lease to Sea-Land Service Inc:
Afoundria (225 35 ft inc 60 reefers)
Anchorage (354 35 ft inc 60 reefers)
Arizpa (225 35 ft inc 60 reefers)
Beauregard (226 35 ft inc 60 reefers)
Charleston (360 35 ft inc 63 reefers)
Elizabethport (476 35 ft inc 56 reefers)
Long Beach (609 35 ft inc 100 reefers)
Los Angeles (476 35 ft inc 56 reefers)
Oakland (609 35 ft inc 100 reefers)
Panama (609 35 ft inc 100 reefers)
San Francisco (476 35 ft inc 56 reefers)
San Juan (476 35 ft inc 56 reefers)
Seattle (354 35 ft inc 48 reefers)
Summit (238 35 ft inc 60 reefers)
Trenton (609 35 ft inc 100 reefers)
Wacosta (225 35 ft inc 63 reefers)
Warrior (225 35 ft inc 61 reefers)
Boston (360 35 ft inc 60 reefers)
Detroit (62 35 ft and 460 autos)
Houston (302 35 ft inc 63 reefers)
Mayaguez (274 35 ft inc 60 reefers)

Madison Transportation Co Inc
P.O. Box 1050
Elizabeth,
New Jersey,
USA
Ship on lease to Sea-Land Services Inc:
Jacksonville (332 35 ft inc 63 reefers)

Mathies Reederei KG
Baumwall 3
P.O. Box 929
2 Hamburg 11
W. Germany
Ship on lease to Team Line:
Hansa (Roll/on/Roll-off ship)

Midsea Containership Inc
Belvedere Building,
P.O. Box 907
Hamilton,
Bermuda
Ships for lease:
Ida Isle (150 20 ft)
Gretchen Isle (150 20 ft)

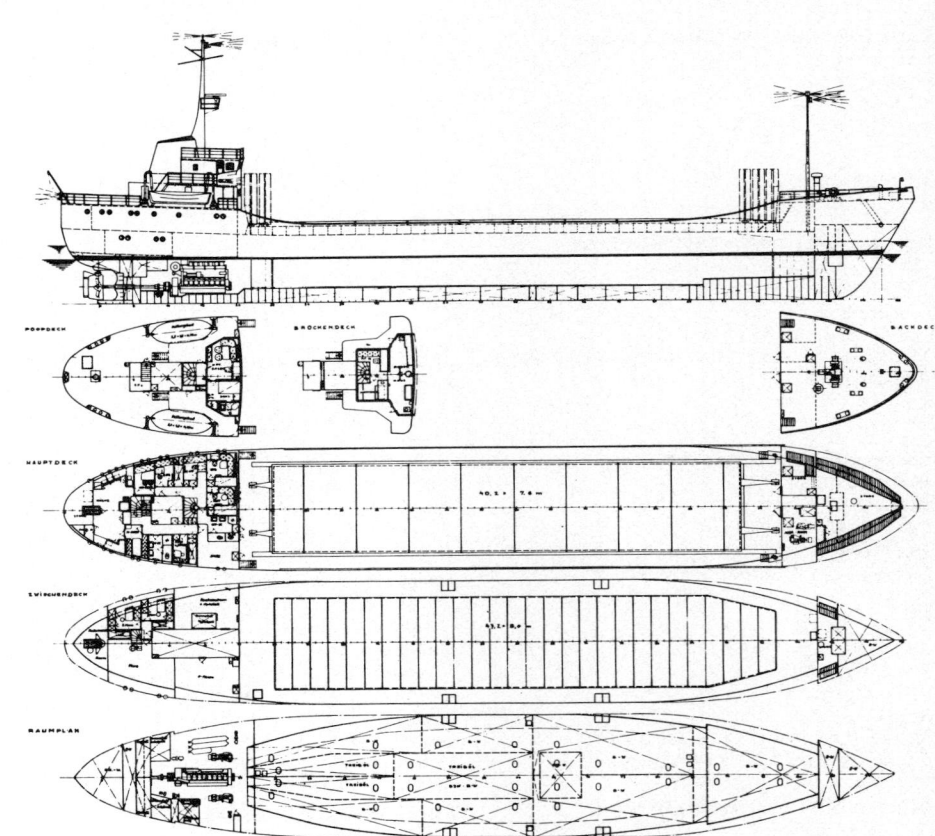

Eland

The Joerg Krueger.

Hope Isle (150 20 ft)
Ellen Isle (150 20 ft)
Sally Isle (150 20 ft)
Waser Isle (150 20 ft)
Isla del Mediterrano (140 20 ft)
Isla del Atlantico (140 20 ft)
Kormoran Isle (98 20 ft)
Ship on lease to Scandinavian Container Services
Christine Isle (86 20 ft)
to Amerind Shipping Corporation:
Gwendolen Isle (86 20 ft)
Hother Isle (316 20 ft)
Under construction:
3 ships (436 20 ft)
2 ships (280 20 ft)

Meyer-Brake
P.O. Box 69
Buhnhofstrasse 7
Brake 288
W. Germany
Ships for lease:
Tegelersand (121 20 ft)
Seefeldersand (121 20 ft)
Burhaversand (121 20 fyt)

Stollhammersand (121 20 ft)
Fedderwardersand (121 20 ft)
Accumersand (121 20 ft)
Beckumersand (121 20 ft)
Mellumersand (single deck fitted for some containers)
Borkumersand (single deck fitted for some containers)
Baltrumersand (single deck fitted for some comtainers)
Langwardersand (80 20 ft)
Einswardersand (80 20 ft)
Rugwardersand (80 20 ft)
Eckwardersand (70 20 ft)
Boitwardersand (70 20 ft)

Torrey Mosvold
P.O. Box 52
Kristiansand S
Norway
Ships on lease to Sea-Land Service Inc:
Mosbay (300 35 ft)
Mosgulf (300 35 ft)
Mosengen (300 35 ft)
Mostangen (300 35 ft)
To Central Gulf Steamship Corp:
Acadia Forest (1,650 20 ft or 73 barges)
Atlantic Forest (1,650 20 ft or 73 barges)

W. H. Müller & Co
(Batavier) N.V.
P.O. Box 795
St. Jobsweg 20
Rotterdam,
Holland
Ship on lease to Zeeland Steamship Co:
Domburgh (77 20 ft)

Otto Nagel
Durrstrasse 11,
   Lubeck Karlshof
W. Germany
SHIP ON LEASE TO HOLLAND CONTAINER
LINE:
Zaanstroom (Roll-on Roll-off)

Narwhol Ltd.
PO Box 378
   Nassau NP
Bahamas
SHIP ON LEASE TO ATLANTIC LINES LTD:
Jamacian Provider (Roll-on Roll-off)

Nile Steamship Co
Manchester Liners House,
St. Ann's Square,
Manchester 2
U.K.
Ship on lease to Manchester Liners Ltd:
Manchester Courage (548 20 ft)
Under construction:
Manchester Crusade

Nordstjernan Rederi A/B
A. Axelson Johnson
Stureplan 3
P.O. Box 7196
Stockholm 7
Sweden
Ships on lease to Johnson Line:
Annie Johnson (620 20 ft and 62 40 ft)
Buenos Aires (122 20 ft)
Margaret Johnson (620 20 ft and 62 40 ft)
Rio de Janeiro (122 20 ft)
San Francisco (620 20 ft and 62 40 ft)
Axel Johnson (560 20 ft and 62 40 ft)
Bahia Blanca (152 20 ft)
Brasila (152 20 ft)
Montevideo (152 20 ft)
Rosario (152 20 ft)
Santos (152 20 ft)
Under construction:
3 ships

Ocean Fleets Ltd. (designers)
(Subsidiary of Ocean Steamship Co.
Ltd.—owners)
Navigation House
   One Aldgate,
London EC3,
U.K.
SHIPS ON LEASE TO OCL:
   Botany Bay, Encounter Bay, Finders Bay,
Jervis Bay, Discovery Bay, Moreton Bay all
(1,300 20 ft) see Ship Operators section).

D. Oltman
Martinistrasse 21
28 Bremen 1
W. Germany
TELEPHONE: 3.60.61
TELEX: 024.5132
Ships on lease to Canadian Pacific Steamship
Ltd, until Autumn 1971
Beaverrando (170 20 ft)
Beavermondo (170 20 ft)

"Orion" Schiffahrts-Gesellschaft Reith & Co
and J. M. K. Blumenthal
Palmaille 118
2 Hamburg 50
W. Germany
TELEPHONE: 39 12 61/65
TELEX: 021 2759
Ships on lease:
Meta Reith (260 20 ft)
Willi Reith (260 20 ft)
Ida Isle (150 20 ft)
Gretchen Isle (150 20 ft)

Bellatrix (240 20 ft)
Beterginze (240 20 ft)
Under construction:
Three ships of 240/260 20 ft capacity to be
ready in Sept and Nov 1971 and March 1972.
They will be equipped with ship cranes.

Osterwich & Son
Vosltzen 41
2 Hamburg 11
W. Germany

TELEPHONE: 364112
Ship on lease to Nordström & Thulin AB:
Adda (50 20 ft)
To Currie Line Ltd:
Destel (63 20 ft and deck stowage)
To Brit Don Unit Services Ltd:-
Don Ricardo (50 20 ft)
To Bo Norrman Shipping AB:
Lubbecke (128 20 ft and deck stowage)
To Compagnie Maritime Belge SA:
Twiehausen (128 20 ft and deck stowage)
Under Construction:
Osterland (63 20 ft and deck stowage)
Bomberg (128 20 ft and deck stowage)
To Sea-Land Service Inc:
Ragna (62 35 ft)

J. A. Reinecke
2 Hamburg 36
Hoe Bleichen 11
West Germany
SHIPS ON LEASE AT MAY 1972:
Falcon (ex *Fuldatal*) (196 20 ft)
Saaletal (114 20 ft)
Donautal (110 20 ft)
Neckartal (114 20 ft)
Norcape (ex *Rhonetal*) (128 20 ft)
Isartal (114 20 ft)
Travetal (70 20 ft)
Travetal 361 (196 20 ft)

L. Remeeus N.V.
c/o Norfolk Line,
Keizerstraat 2
Scheveningen
Holland
Ship on lease to Norfolk Line:
Duke of Holland (25 33 ft Trailers)
Duchess of Holland (11 40 ft Trailers, Roll-on
Roll-off)
Under Construction:
Duke of Norfolk (33 33ft Trailers, Roll-on
Roll-off)

Gerd Ritscher
c/o Kustenschiffahrt
Baver & Hausschidlt KG
11 Katharinenstrasse
2 Hamburg 11
W. Germany
Ship on lease to Bellferry:
Bell Victor (80 20 ft)

Dietrich Sander
Bereederungs GmbH
28 Bremen

Am Wall 128-134
Ships on lease to Bell Line Ltd, Dublin
Gabriela (36 20 ft)
Michaela (36 20 ft)
Daniela (36 20 ft)

Scandinavian Motorships AB
Osthammavigatar 70
   Stockholm N
Sweden
UNDER CONSTRUCTION:
   Four ships for Wallenius Lines.

Scarsdale Shipping Co. Ltd.
c/o 595 River Road,
   Edgewater
NJ 07020
U.S.A.

Gerhard Schepers
Emmelner strasse 12,
4472 Haven/Ems
W. Germany
Ships on lease to Sea-Land Services Inc:
Mare Jada, Nicarao (fitted with ship cranes,
total 35 ft unit capacity unknown)
Stadt Aschendorf (62 35 ft)
Under construction:
one ship

Schepers Rhine Sea Line
Tausendfensterhaus
P.O. Box 41 1844
41 Duisburg-Ruhrort
W. Germany
Ship on lease to Iberian Container Line Ltd:
Isar (63 20 ft)
Ship on lease to EUR:
Donav (63 20 ft)

Schulte & Bruns
Burgermeister Suid
Strasse 82
28 Bremen
W. Germany
Ship on lease to Washbay Lines:
Lynn (80 20 ft incl 10 reefers)

Sea Containers Chartering Ltd.
39 Park Street,
London W.1.
U.K.
TELEPHONE: 499.0221
TELEX: 27553
Ship on lease to Ellerman and Papayanni
Lines Ltd:
Minho (120)
Taqus (124)
Tormes (124)

MS *Duke of Holland* of the Norfolk Line.   Capacity 25 trailers.   Owner L. Remeeus NV.

Tamega (124)
Tua (124)

Under construction:
Eleven "Hustler" class ships with stern ramps and deck mounted gantries. All Sea Container ships can carry 8 ft 6 in high containers.

Ships on lease to Transport Ferry Service:
Curran (60 20 ft)
Moyle (60 20 ft)

To Ellerman Lines Ltd:
Tiber (124)
To Currie Line Ltd:
England (120)

Sea Containers Chartering Ltd.
39 Park Street,
London W.1.
U.K.
Ship on lease to Ellerman Lines Ltd:
Tronto (124)
Ship on lease to Tarros Line Ltd:
Vento di Scirocco (110)
Launched 31 January 1971 the first of 7 Tarros ships for the Northern Adriatic Service.

Ship on lease to CPS Ltd:
Weser Isle (152 20 ft)

SSM Transport NV
Veer Kades 5
P.O. Box 1284
Nieuwland (81 20 ft)
Rotterdam, Netherlands
Ship on lease to Macvan:
Niewland (81 20 ft)

Shamrock Shipping Co Ltd
(C. S. Brown)
The Harbour,
Larne,
Northern Ireland
TELEPHONE: Larne 2227
TELEGRAMS: Jack, Larne
TELEX: 747104

Shelbourne Shipping Co
Dublin Ireland
Ships on lease to B + 1 Steam Packet Co Ltd:
Kildare (74 20 ft)
Tipperary (74 20 ft)

Shin Yei Steamship Co.
1, 2-chome,
Muromachi,
Chuo-ku
Tokyo,
Japan
SHIP ON LEASE TO SEA LAND ORIENT LTD.:
Otowasan Maru (256 35 ft)

Shosen Mitsui Kinkai K.K.
3-3, 5 chome Akanaka
Minato-ku,
Tokyo,
Japan
SHIP ON LEASE TO MITSUI OSK LINES:
Tarumaezan Maru (106 20 ft)

Goffried Steinmeyer Co.
Schlachte 19/20
Bremen
W. Germany
SHIPS ON LEASE TO AFRICATAINER LINE:
Amanda (133 20 ft)
Anja (130 20 ft)

Sun Leasing Co.
c/o 358 St. Marks Street,
Staten Island,
New York,
U.S.A.
SHIPS ON LEASE TO TRANSAMERICAN TRAILER TRANSPORT INC:
Eric K. Holzer (244 40 ft trailers)
Ponce de Leon (244 40 ft trailers)

MV Minho, first series of "Hustler" Class vessels. Chartered by Ellerman and Papayanni Lines Ltd; seen here working at Gladstone Dock, Liverpool.

Swedish American Lines
Packhusplatsen 6
PO Box 2185
Gothenburg C
Sweden
SHIP ON LEASE TO ACL:
Atlantic Saga (580 20 ft)

Tarros Spa.
Piazza de Marini 1
16123 Genoa
Italy
SHIPS ON LEASE TO GRENDI TARROS LINE:
Vento del Golfo, Vento di Levante (31 20 ft Roll-on Roll-off)
Vento di Tramontana (160 20 ft Roll-on Roll-off)

Johs. Thode
Kohlbrandtreppe 2
2 Hamburg 50
W. Germany
SHIPS ON LEASE TO AFRICATAINER LINE:
(Hugo Bartels & Sohn KG)
Andrea (133 20 ft) *Anita* (133 20 ft)
SHIPS ON LEASE TO BELL LINE:
(J. Bos)
Bell Vision
SHIPS ON LEASE TO FINSKA ANGFARTYGS AB:
(K. H. Danz)
Iris (72 20 ft)
SHIP ON LEASE TO SVEA LINE:
(H. Freudenberg)
Bele (72 20 ft)
SHIP ON LEASE TO UNITED BALTIC CORP:
(J. Kahrs)
Baltic Concorde (63 20 ft)
SHIPS AVAILABLE TO LEASE:
(H. Wulff) *John Wulff* (63 20 ft)
(M. Lesitikow) *Seamaid* (72 20 ft)
(J. Bos) *Freja* (63 20 ft)

Torm A/S
Dampskibsselskabet
Holmens Kanal 42
Copenhagen K .
Denmark
Under Construction:
Three ships.

Triport Shipping Co.
120 St. Vincent Street,
Glasgow C2,
Scotland
SHIPS ON LEASE TO TOR LINE:
Tor Mercia (175 20 ft)
Tor Scandia (175 20 ft)

Tynedale Shipping Co
c/o Clarke Traffic Services Ltd.,
1155, Dorchester West Blvd.,
P.O. Box 730,
Montreal 102

Ulster Steamship Co. Ltd.
PO Box 108,
10/14 Victoria Street,
Belfast,
N. Ireland
SHIPS ON LEASE TO HEAD DONALDSON LINE:
Inishowen Head (400 20 ft)

Vinke & Zoonen
Parklaan 28
Rotterdam 2
Netherlands
SHIP ON LEASE TO AMERIND SHIPPING CO:
Jasmine (81 20 ft)

Wallenius Bremen GmbH
Postfach 1924
Bremen 28
W. Germany
SHIP ON LEASE TO ATLANTIC CONTAINER LINE:
Atlantic Cinderella (966 20 ft)
SHIP ON LEASE TO WALLENIUS LINES:
Undine (100 20 ft)

Bernhard Warrings
2941 Carolinensiel
Neve Strasse 7
Germany
Ship on lease to Cawoods Containers
Craigavad (74 20 ft and 4 40 ft reefers)
Ship on lease to CPS Ltd:
Weser Isle (152 20 ft)

W. Wilhelmsen
PO Box 1359
Oslo 1
Norway
SHIPS ON LEASE TO BARBER LINES A/S:
Tagaytay, Tai Ping, Tarantel, Traviata, (168 20 ft)
UNDER CONVERSION:
Five ships for ScanAustral
UNDER CONSTRUCTION:
Three Ships.

Jonny Winter
2101 Hamburg 96
Fährdeich 160
TELEPHONE: 745.9422
Ship on lease to Bell Line:
Bell Venture: (69 20 ft)
Under construction:
Class 100A4E3 (145 20 ft incl 20 reefers)

H. Wurthmann
Oberrege 3
2287 Elsfleth
W. Germany
SHIP ON LEASE TO CPS LTD:
Hope Isle (152 20 ft)

CONTAINER MANUFACTURERS

CONTAINER MANUFACTURERS

ACKERMANN

Ackermann Fahrzeugbau AG
56 Wuppertal-Vohwinkel
Postfach 17
Germany (Federal Republic)
TELEPHONE: (02121) 78 01 01-09
TELEX: 08591/754
CONTAINERS:

Units suitable for the transport of standard European railway pallets offering an **extra** 1,000 mm in length, about 60 mm in width and about 200 mm in height over the standard ISO 20 ft container dimensions. They are part of a demountable body system known as Eurotainers. Units in the system have optional box-type or flatbed superstructures. The outer frames are fitted with standard grab tackle recesses and corner castings compatible with 20 ft ISO dimensions.

The Ackermann Eurotainer demountable body system uses box units which though of non-ISO dimensions are equipped with ISO corner castings positioned as for 20 ft container.

ADAMSON AND HATCHETT

An Adamson & Hatchet 20 ft all-steel end-loading general cargo container.

Adamson & Hatchett Ltd.
Dukinfield,
Cheshire
(One of the Acrow Group of companies)
TELEPHONE:061-330-2822
TELEGRAMS: Adhat Dukinfield
TELEX: 66240
DIRECTORS:
W. A. de Vigier (*Chairman*)
G. A. Flint (*Managing*)
S. Shenton
J. Bonallack

Containers
Dry freight in aluminium alloy and all-steel, open top, tilt and side-loading in steel, refrigerated and insulated in aluminium alloy. To 20 ft, 30 ft and 40 ft lengths.

Design Standards
ISO, BS 3951, TIR, UIC, Lloyds, Bureau Veritas, American Bureau of Shipping.

Construction
Steel containers are welded and in alloy are riveted. Manufactured under licence from Great Dane in USA and sub-licence granted to Acrow (Australia) Ltd.

Production
Principle owners of Adamson & Hatchett containers are: Sea Containers Ltd, Associated Container Transport, Overseas Containers Ltd, SSI Container Corporation, MacAndrews & Co.

The following table shows production of standard ISO and other containers for 1970 and 1971:

Adamson & Hatchett container production 1970–71

Type		Quantity Manufactured 20 ft	30 ft	40 ft
Dry goods	1970	1,828	—	—
	1971	3,250	—	100
Insulated	1970	—	—	—
	1971	—	—	—
Refrigerated	1970	—	—	—
	1971	—	—	—
Open top	1970	—	—	—
	1971	550 4 ft 3 in high		
		800 8 ft and 8 ft 6 in high		

Adamson & Hatchett range of Containers Dry Freight or (General Purpose) Containers

Type by ISO or other Recognised Standard Dimensions	Main Materials of Construction (See space below for notes on additional materials and methods of construction)	Internal			Internal Measurements of End door openings		
		Length mm ft in	Height mm ft in	Width mm ft in	Height mm ft in	Width mm ft in	Cubic Capacity m³ ft³
20 ft × 8 ft × 8 ft	Steel	5,906 19' 4½"	2,223 7' 3½"	2,350 7' 8½"	2,337 7' 8"	2,134 7' 0"	31 m³ 1,095 ft³
	Aluminium	5,918 19' 5"	2,223 7' 3½"	2,337 7' 8"	2,134 7' 0"		31 m³ 1,095 m³
	Timber and Plastics	5,899 19' 4½"	2,235 7' 4"	2,337 7' 8"	2,134 7' 0"		31 m³ 1,095 ft³
40 ft × 8 ft × 8 ft	Steel	12,040 29' 6"	2,223 7' 3½"	2,337 7' 8"	2,286 7' 0"	2,134 7' 0"	62·3 m³ 2,208 ft³
	Aluminium	12,040 39' 6"	2,223 7' 3½"	2,337 7' 8"	2,286 7' 6"	2,134 7' 0"	62·3 m³ 2,208 ft³

BRAIDESI

Braidesi ISO Standard 20 ft., 30 ft., and 40 ft containers manufactured in 1968/69.

Costruzioni Meccaniche Braidesi S.p.A.
Via XXIV Maggi 10
12042 B R A (Cuneo), Italy
TELEPHONE: 43611
DIRECTORS:
P. I. Giovanni Saglietti (*General Manager*)
P. I. Renato Foietta (*Production Manager*)
Dott. Ettore Piacentino (*Container Sales Manager*)
Rag. Remo Burdese (*Administrative Manager*)

DESIGN STANDARDS: ISO
PRODUCTION:
Production figures for 1968 and 1969 are shown in the table. The company additionally produced 150 twenty foot containers in the first part of 1970.
CONTAINERS:
Steel dry freight containers including open and tilt varieties.

Type		Quantity Manufactured		
		20 ft	30 ft	40 ft
Dry goods	1968	200	50	—
	1969	600	300	—
Insulated	1968	—	—	
	1969	—	—	
Refrigerated	1968	—	—	
	1969	—	—	
Specials*	1968	—	50	—
	1969	150	350	—

*Tilt-Tainer, Open-Top, Tilt-Side, Opening- Side.

BRAIDESI CONTAINERS:

Type	Main Material of Construction	Internal			End door openings		Cubic Capacity
		Length	Height	Width	Width	Height	
20 ft × 8 ft × 8 ft	Steel	5,885 mm 19 ft 2 in	2,245 mm 6 ft 10 in	2,330 mm 7 ft 8 in	2,262 mm 7 ft 5 in	2,140 mm 7 ft 0½ in	30·70 m³ 1,094 ft³ (approx.)
30 ft × 8 ft × 8 ft	Steel	8,950 mm 29 ft 4 in	2,225 mm 7 ft 3 in	2,330 mm 7 ft 8 in	2,262 mm 7 ft 4 in	2,120 mm 6 ft 11½ in	46·30 m³ 1,624 ft³ (approx.)
20 ft × 8 ft × 8 ft 6 in	Steel Open-Side	5,880 mm 19 ft 2 in	2,310 mm 7 ft 9 in	2,285 mm 7 ft 8 in	—	—	31·03 m³ 1,095 ft³ (approx.)

BREDA

Ferroviaria Breda Pistoiesi S.p.A.
Viale Sarca 336
Milano, Italy
TELEPHONE: 6967
TELEX: 31050 Ferbreda
DIRECTORS:
Dr. Ing. Braguzzi (*Managing*)

Dr. Ing. Pietro Callerio
CONTAINERS:
Dry freight, insulated and refrigerated
DESIGN STANDARD:
ISO, Lloyd's Register, American Bureau of Shipping, Registro Italiano Navale, U.I.C.

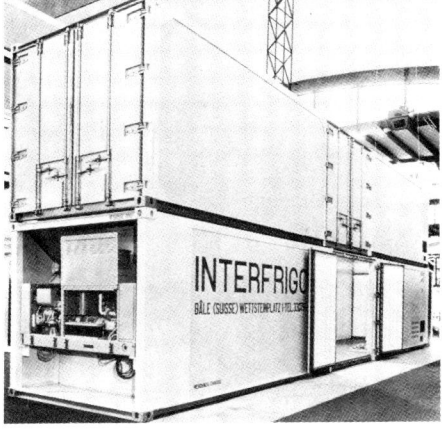

Typical Breda refrigerated containers.

BRITISH RAIL

British Rail Engineering Ltd.

Melbury House, Melbury Terrace, London NW1, England
TELEPHONE: 01 262 3232 (Ext. 5756)
TELEX: Rail HQ 24678

DIRECTORS:
J. M. W. Bosworth (*Chairman*)
L. W. Ibbotson M.B.E.
P. G. James C.B.E.
Dr. Sydney Jones
T. C. B. Miller M.B.E.
L. F. Neal
A. E. Robson (*Managing*)

LICENCES GRANTED OVERSEAS:
Freight Containers (Africa Pty) Ltd.
40 Commissioner Street,
PO Box 9616,
Johannesburgh, South Africa.

CONSTRUCTION, MATERIALS AND METHOD:
All Steel Containers. All welded steel construction, corrugated steel, side fixed end and roof panels. Metal faced plywood or corrugated steel doors. Plywood or plank floor.
Double Skin Container. Welded steel framework, Aluminium bodyside, fixed end and roof panels riveted to steel frame. Plywood floor and interior lining. Metal faced plywood doors.

PRODUCTION:
As shown in table. Of the 419 special 20 ft units made in 1969, 284 were of the flat type, 16 of the soft top type and 119 of the tilt type. Of the 249 special 30 ft units made in 1969, 100 were flat, 16 soft tops, 130 tilt types and 3 curtain sided. Ninety one 8 ft 6 in high containers have been made of which 54 were 30 ft long and 39, 40 ft long.

CONTAINERS:
All steel, aluminium alloy, glass fibre/plywood, steel with plywood lining.

Freightliner container for liquids in bulk

20 ft All Steel Covered Containers End Doors Only
20 ft All Steel Covered Containers End & Side Doors
20 ft Glass Fibre Faced Plywood Container End Door only
20 ft Tilt Container (Soft Top & Hardtop)
20 ft All Steel Soft Top Container
20 ft Insulated Container
20 ft Double Skin Covered Container
20 ft Mk IV Open Container (ISO location and securing facilities, lifting bracket for grappler type lift)
30 ft All Steel Container End & Side Doors
30 ft Tilt Containers (Hard & Soft Top)
30 ft All Steel Soft Top
30 ft Mk IV Open Container (ISO location & securing facilities lifting bracket for grappler type lift).
40 ft All Steel End and Side Doors
40 ft All Steel End Doors Only

DESIGN STANDARDS:
ISO, BS 3951, Lloyds, U.I.C.
Glass fibre/Plywood containers. Welded steel framework, glass fibre faced plywood bodyside, fixed end and roof panels riveted to steel framework. Glass fibre faced plywood doors. Plywood or plank floors.

Mark IV Open Containers. All welded steel construction, Headboard corrugated steel, removable steel mesh panels at sides and end.

British Rail Engineering Range of Containers Dry Freight or (General Purpose) Containers

Type by ISO or other Recognised Standard Dimensions	Main Materials of Construction (See space below for notes on additional materials and methods of construction)	Internal Length mm ft in	Internal Height mm ft in	Internal Width mm ft in	Internal measurements of End door-openings Width mm ft in	Internal measurements of End door-openings Height mm ft in	Side Opening		Cubic Capacity m³ ft³
20 ft × 8 ft × 8 ft	Steel (soft top)	5,924 19′ 5 1/4″	2,200 7′ 2 5/8″	2,350 7′ 8 1/2″	2,350 7′ 8 1/2″	2,144 7′ 0 13/32″			30·6 m³ 1,081 ft³
	Aluminium and all steel	5,924 19′ 5 1/4″	2,200 7′ 2 5/8″	2,313 7′ 7 3/32″	2,350 7′ 8 1/2″	2,144 7′ 0 13/32″	2,144 8′ 0″	2,140 7′ 0 1/4″	30·4 m³ 1,073 ft³
	Timber and Plastics Double skin	5,944 19′ 6 1/32″ 5,920 19′ 5 1/16″	2,216 7′ 3 7/32″ 2,199 7′ 2 9/32″	2,370 7′ 9 5/16″ 2,324 7′ 7 1/2″	2,350 7′ 8 1/2″ 2,350 7′ 8 1/2″	2,144 7′ 0 13/32″ 2,144 7′ 0 13/32″			30·3 m³ 1,070 ft³ 30·2 m³ 1,068 ft³
30 ft × 8 ft × 8 ft	Steel (soft top)	8,992 29′ 6″	2,199 7′ 2 19/32″	2,350 7′ 8 1/2″	2,350 7′ 8 1/2″	2,144 7′ 0 13/32″			46·4 m³ 1,641 ft³
	All steel	8,996 29′ 6 5/32″	2,085 6′ 10 3/32″	2,312 7′ 7 1/32″	2,386 7′ 6″	1,982 6′ 6 1/32″	8,788 28′ 10″	1,954 6′ 4 15/16″	43·3 m³ 1,531 ft³
40 ft 8 ft × 8 ft	Steel	12,063 39′ 6 29/32″	2,216 7′ 3 7/32″	2,339 7′ 8 1/16″	2,350 7′ 8 1/2″	2,144 7′ 0 13/32″	2,438 8′ 0″	2,140 7′ 0 1/4″	67·5 m³ 2,385 ft³

LA BRUGEOISE

S.A. La Brugeoise et Nivelles,

8200 Brugge 2,
Belgium
TELEPHONE: 050 30721—51
TELEX: 191.22 Brugeoise Brge.

DIRECTORS:
O. J. Bronchart (*Managing Director*)
M. Simonart (*General Manager*)
P. Vande Sijpe (*Plant Manager*)
J. Barbier (*Chief Engineer, Containers*)
L. Monbaliu (*Office Manager, Containers*)

CONTAINERS:
General purpose containers in corrugated steel with or without interlocking corner castings. General purpose containers in aluminium as per STRICK specifications and licence. Insulated and refrigerated containers. Open top and flat containers, the latter may be with or without removable ends. Containers in steel or aluminium may be 8 ft 6 in high. Open top containers in steel may be 4 ft high.

Door openings at end:
Clear width 2,286 mm (7 ft 6 in)
Clear height 2,159 mm (7 ft 1 in)

General purpose. Crusader 160B
External dimensions:
Length 2,172 mm (7 ft 1 1/2 in)
Width 1,270 mm (4 ft 2 in)
Height 2,057 mm (6 ft 9 in)

LICENCES HELD:
For Strick aluminium containers.

PRODUCTION:
The company produced 1,000 20 ft aluminium containers in 1971 as against 100 steel units in 1970. Fifteen hundred steel and 500 aluminium 40 ft containers were made in 1971 as against 1,400 steel and 150 aluminium in 1970.

DESIGN STANDARD:
ISO

CONSTRUCTION—MATERIALS AND METHOD:
Aluminium containers of exterior and interior post design.

Steel containers and container-flats: all-welded construction

Aluminium-containers: riveted construction.

Steel containers in corrugated sheets without interior posts and with specially designed roofs.

Main specifications for standard containers are as in the table and in the case of 10 ft units and specials as follows.

La Brugeoise and Nivelles 40 ft container supplied to Atlantic Container Line on BN skeletal trailer type PC-20 3.

Principal Owners:
ACL (Atlantic Container Line) Hamilton—Bermuda
Belgo-Anglaise des Ferry-Boats—Zeebrugge
Blohm & Voss—Hamburg
CMB (Belgian Line—New York—Antwerp
CMCR (Cie Maritime des Chargeurs Réunis)—Paris
COCAM Rental System—Brussels—Antwerp
CTI (Container Transport International) New York—Paris—Antwerp.
DART Line—Hamilton—Bermuda.
Finn Lines—Helsinki.
ICS (International Container Service) New York—London
Carl Tiedemann—Hamburg
Tor Line—New York—Gothenburg.
TIP (Transport International Pool) Rotterdam.
Transport Pool Inc.—Fairless Hills—Pennsylvania.

La Brugeoise Range of Containers Dry Freight (or General Purpose) Containers

Type by ISO or other Recognised Standard Dimensions	*Main Materials of Construction (See space below for notes on additional materials and methods of construction)*	*Internal*			*Internal Measurements of End door openings*		
		Length mm ft in	*Height mm ft in*	*Width mm ft in*	*Width mm ft in*	*Height mm ft in*	*Cubic Capacity m³ ft³*
20 ft × 8 ft × 8 ft	Steel	5,915 19′ 5″	2,230 7′ 3¾″	2,330 7′ 7¾″	2,300 90 13/16″	2,310 84″	30·73 m³ 1,085 ft³
	Aluminium	5,920 19′ 5″	2,211 7′ 3″	2,349 7′ 8½″	2,284 89 15/16″	2,130 83⅞″	30·75 m³ 1,085 ft³
30 ft × 8 ft × 8 ft	Steel	9,010 29′ 6¾″	2,200 7′ 2⅝″	2,335 7′ 7 15/16″	2,300 90 9/16″	2,140 84¼″	46·28 m³ 1,634 ft³
40 ft × 8 ft × 8 ft	Steel	12,040 39′ 6″	2,390 7′ 10⅛″	2,330 7′ 7¾″	2,310 90″	2,286 90 1/16	67·05 m³ 2,368 ft³
	Aluminium	12,061 39′ 6⅞″	2,362 7′ 9″	2,349 7′ 8½″	2,284 89 15/16″	2,284 89 15/16″	66·91 m³ 2,363 ft³

Each of these types can be delivered with an external height of 8′ 6″ (2590 mm) giving a greater volume.

BUTTERFIELD

W. P. Butterfield (Engineers) Ltd.
PO Box 38, Shipley, Yorks
TELEPHONE: Shipley 52244
TELEGRAMS: Tanks, Shipley
TELEX: 51583

DIRECTORS:
W. P. Butterfield (*Chairman*)
G. M. D. Anderson (*Managing*)
M. L. Beardall

PRODUCTS:
Road and Storage Tanks
Cryogenic Equipment, Chemical & Industrial Plant
CONTAINER TYPES:
20 and 30 ft ISO tank containers
PRINCIPAL USERS:
Shipping companies and international hauliers.

General purpose. Type 20 ft Tank
External dimensions:
Length 6,096 mm (20 ft 0 in)
Width 2,438 mm (8 ft 0 in)
Height 2,438 mm (8 ft 0 in)
Capacity 4,000 gallons

General purpose. Stainless Steel Type 30 ft Tank
External dimensions;
Length 9,144 mm (30 ft 0 in)
Width 2,438 mm (8 ft 0 in)
Height 2,438 mm (8 ft 0 in)
Capacity 5,000 gallons

CALIFORNIA

California Cargo Containers Inc.
(A Division of Dymo Industries)
801 Maritime Street, Oakland,
California 94607

TELEPHONE: 835-4484 (Oakland, California)
CABLES: Calcargo

BRANCHES:
Agents in: Yokohama and Kobe, Japan; New York City, New York; Los Angeles, California

DIRECTORS:
Victor Bayduk (*General Manager*)
James A. Pepper (*Sales Manager*)
CONTAINERS:
Crusader 160B, 160, 250, 400B and 400
Atlas 2000
TYPES:
Dry Cargo type containers of various sizes. No refrigerated or insulated containers
DESIGN STANDARD:
8 ft × 8 ft × 10 ft and 8 ft × 8 ft × 20 ft to USASI and ISO specifications. Various size small containers (not to any standards)

CONSTRUCTION:
Steel frame and understructure with glass-fibred plywood panels
PRINCIPAL OWNERS OF CONTAINERS:
California Cargo Containers

General purpose. Atlas 2000
Internal dimensions:
Length 5,963 mm (19 ft 6¾ in)
Width 2,375 mm (7 ft 9½ in)
Height 2,235 mm (7 ft 4 in)

Internal dimensions:
Length 2,121 mm (6 ft 11½ in)
Width 1,186 mm (3 ft 11 in)
Height 1,892 mm (6 ft 2½ in)
Door openings at side (hinged):
Clear width 2,045 mm (6 ft 8½ in)
Clear height 1,829 mm (6 ft 0 in)

General purpose. Crusader 160
External dimensions:
Length 2,172 mm (7 ft 1½ in)
Width 1,270 mm (4 ft 2 in)
Height 2,108 mm (6 ft 11 in)
Internal dimensions:
Length 2,121 mm (6 ft 11½ in)
Width 1,173 mm (3 ft 10½ in)
Height 1,892 mm (6 ft 2½ in)
Door openings at side (hinged):
Clear width 1,810 mm (5 ft 11¼ in)
Clear height 1,740 mm (5 ft 8½ in)

General purpose. Crusader 250
External dimensions:
Length 2,172 mm (7 ft 1½ in)
Width 1,816 mm (5 ft 11½ in)
Height 2,057 mm (6 ft 9 in)

Door openings at side (hinged):
Clear width 1,822 mm (5 ft 11¼ in)
Clear height 1,740 mm (5 ft 8½ in)

Internal dimensions:
Length 2,121 mm (6 ft 11½ in)
Width 1,753 mm (5 ft 9 in)
Height 1,892 mm (6 ft 2½ in)

This model available with or without top loading hatch.

40 ft × 8 ft × 8 ft 6 in STRICK inner post design container with aluminium outer skin

General purpose. Crusader 400B
External dimensions:
Length 2,438 mm (8 ft 0 in)
Width 2,438 mm (8 ft 0 in)
Height 2,057 mm (6 ft 9 in)
Internal dimensions:
Length 2,388 mm (7 ft 10 in)
Width 2,350 mm (7 ft 8½ in)
Height 1,835 mm (6 ft ¼ in)
Door openings at side (hinged):
Clear width 2,324 mm (7 ft 7 in)
Clear height 1,829 mm (6 ft 0 in)

General purpose. Crusader 400
External dimensions:
Length 2,438 mm (8 ft 0 in)
Width 2,438 mm (8 ft 0 in)
Height 2,057 mm (6 ft 9 in)
Internal dimensions:
Length 2,388 mm (7 ft 10 in)
Width 2,330 mm (7 ft 7¾ in)
Height 1,905 mm (6 ft 3 in)
Door openings at side (hinged):
Clear width 2,083 mm (6 ft 10 in)
Clear height 1,746 mm (5 ft 8¾ in)

CANADIAN CAR TRAILERS

Canadian Car Division, Hawker Siddeley Canada Ltd.
P.O. Box 67, Station "F",
Thunder Bay, Ontario
TELEPHONE: 807-622-5351
TELEX: 033-260
SALES MANAGER:
W. J. Russell

LICENSEES ABROAD:
None
CONTAINERS:
All sizes
SPECIFICATIONS:
Custom built
TYPES:
Model 5 000-SR insulated container is

available in 20, 27, 30 and 40 ft lengths. There is an extensive range of options.

DESIGN STANDARD:
ISO

CONSTRUCTION—MATERIALS AND METHOD:
To customer requirements using assembly line techniques.

CODER

Société Nouvelle de Gestion des Etablissements Coder
(S.N.G.E.C.) 71 Quai National
92 Puteaux, France
TELEPHONE: (1) 772.24-05
TELEX: 62.120
DIRECTORS:
J. J. Joseph

LICENSEES ABROAD:
Tramaes (Spain)

CONTAINERS:
Stainless steel tank containers, heated and insulated, designed to carry a wide range of hazardous and non-hazardous liquids from highly corrosive chemicals to foodstuffs, oil and beverages, by sea, rail and road transport.
Framework is of all welded construction using high yield strength steel rectangular box sections and mild steel tubular sections. Cast steel corner fittings are to ISO recommendations to permit top lifting with spreaders and six high stacking.
Filling is via one 18 in (450 mm) dial full opening 4 point or 6 point fixing manhole. Discharging is via outlet pipes terminating with ball, dual gate or butterfly valve and screw plug. Pressure discharge is by means of an air inlet connection with ball valve and pressure gauge, and by pressure vacuum

DIMENSIONS AND RATINGS OF CODER ISO TANK CONTAINERS:		
Model CR 20:		
External measurements	Gross weight:	Capacity:
Length 6,054 mm (19 ft 10⅜ in)	20,321 kg (44,800 lb)	Mini 12,601 litre (2,772 gal)
Height 2,438·4 mm (8 ft)		Maxi 19,198 litre (4,223 gal)
Width 2,438·4 mm (8 ft)		
Model CR 30:		
External measurements:	Gross weight:	Capacity:
Length 9,125 mm (29 ft 11¼ in)	25,400 kg (56,000 lb)	Mini 20,680 litre (4,487 gal)
Height 2,438·4 mm (8 ft)		Maxi 26,778 litre (5,895 gal)
Width 2,438·4 mm (8 ft)		

relief valve.

PRODUCTION:
Sixty-one 20 ft and eighteen 30 ft tank containers in 1970.

SPECIFICATIONS:
10 ft—20 ft—30 ft ISO Standard

DESIGN STANDARD:
ISO; TIR approved, complying with ADR/RID and latest IMCO draft recommendations for hazardous loads.

The SNGEC ISO 20 ft × 8 ft × 8 ft stainless steel tank container. Capacity: 4,224 gal. Single compartment. Pressure discharge incorporated.

CONSTRUCTION—MATERIALS AND METHOD:
Stainless steel—Top hat patented CODER
design

PRINCIPLE OWNERS:
Eurotainer, France; Sea Containers Inc.,
UK; Marcevaggi-Merzario, Italy; Ehrhardt
Spedition, West Germany; Sabaton.

The SNGEC ISO 30 ft × 8 ft × 8 ft stainless steel
tank container is heated and insulated. Capacity:
5,895 gals. Single compartment. Pressure
discharge incorporated.

COMET

Comet Corporation
N. 3808 Sullivan Road, Spokane,
Washington 99216, USA
TELEPHONE: (509) 924-4800
DIRECTORS:
Thoburn Brown (*President*)
N. T. Thompson (*Vice President and General
Manager*)

CONTAINERS:
Dry freight and refrigerated.

DESIGN STANDARD:
ISO standards as well as individual customer
specifications.

CONSTRUCTION:
Aluminium extrusion and sheet, fabricated
steel, glassfibre, glassfibre reinforced plywood,
urethane foam, laminated wood. All welded
and riveted.

PRINCIPAL USERS:
Matson Navigation Co., Alaska Steamship,
Arctic Terminals, Alaska Railroad, XTRA
Inc., American Mail Line, Seatrain Lines,
American President Lines.

One of a recent order for 1,000 Comet containers. The containers measure 27 ft long,
8 ft wide and 9½ ft high.

Comet 20 ft container for Xtra, Inc.

Containers Made by Comet Corporation in 1970-71				
Type		Quantity Manufactured		
		20 ft	24 ft	27 ft
Dry goods	1970	62		500
	1971	1,000		
Insulated	1970			
Refrigerated	1971	50		

Refrigerated Containers supplied by Comet								
20 ft	Steel	5,806	2,133	2,253	2,253	2,682	35·25 Btu's per hr per at (F°)	27·9 m³
×	Aluminium	19′ 0¾″	7′ 0″	7′ 4¾″	7′ 4¾″	6′ 10″		987 ft³
8 ft × 8 ft	Steel, Fiberglass, Plywood	5,791	2,108	2,208	2,208	2,682	34·49 ,, ,, ,, ,, ,,	26·9 m³
		19′ 0″	6′ 11″	7′ 2⅞″	7′ 2⅞″	6′ 10″		951 ft³
30 ft	Steel	8,858	2,133	2,253	2,253	2,682	50·50 ,, ,, ,, ,, ,,	42·6 m³
×	Aluminium	29′ 0¾″	7′ 0″	7′ 4¾″	7′ 4¾″	6′ 10″		1,505 ft³
8 ft × 8 ft	Steel, Fiberglass, Plywood	8,839	2,108	2,208	2,208	2,682	49·98 ,, ,, ,, ,, ,,	41·0 m³
		29′ 0″	6′ 11″	7′ 2⅞″	7′ 2⅞″	6′ 10″		1,452 ft³
40 ft	Steel	11,944	2,133	2,253	2,253	2,682	65·75 ,, ,, ,, ,, ,,	57·4 m²
×	Aluminium	39′ 2¼″	7′ 0″	7′ 4¾″	7′ 4¾″	6′ 10″		2,029 ft³
8 ft × 8 ft	Steel, Fiberglass, Plywood	7,981	2,108	2,208	2,208	2,682	65·47 ,, ,, ,, ,, ,,	55·4 m³
		39′ 1½″	6′ 11″	7′ 2⅞″	7′ 2⅞″	6′ 10″		1,592 ft³
Other Sizes	Steel	7,962	2,590	2,253	2,253	2,540	47·48 ,, ,, ,, ,, ,,	46·6 m³
	Aluminium	26′ 2¼″	8′ 6″	7′ 4¾″	7′ 4¾″	8′ 4″		1,959 ft³
Length 27′ 0″	Timber and Plastics	7.962	2,565	2,514	2,208	2,540	48·0 ,, ,, ,, ,, ,,	45·0 m³
Height 9′ 6″		26′ 1¼″	8′ 5″	7′ 2⅞″	7′ 2″	8′ 4″.		1.646 ft³
Width 8′ 0″								

Containers Made by Comet Corporations Dry Freight or (General Purpose) Containers

Type by ISO or other Recognised Standard Dimensions	*Main Materials of Construction (See space below for notes on additional materials and methods of construction)*	*Internal* Length mm ft in	*Internal* Height mm ft in	*Internal* Width mm ft in	*Internal Measurements of End door openings* Width mm ft in	*Internal Measurements of End door openings* Height mm ft in	*Cubic Capacity*
20 ft	Steel	5,930	2,250	2,356	2,286	2,195	Optional by customer Specification 31·3 m^3
×	Aluminium	19′ 5½″	7′ 4⅜″	7′ 8¾″	7′ 6″	7′ 1″	1,108 ft^2
8 ft × 8 ft	Steel, Fiberglass, Plywood	5,947	2,260	7,372	2,286	2,159	,, ,, ,, ,, 31·8 m^3
		19′ 6⅛″	7′ 5″	7′ 9⅜″	7′ 6″	7′ 1″	1,126 ft^3
30 ft	Steel	5,978	2,253	2,356	2,286	2,159	,, ,, ,, ,, 47·4 m^3
×	Aluminium	29′ 5½″	7′ 4¾″	7′ 8¾″	7′ 6″	7′ 1″	1,677 ft^3
8 ft × 8 ft	Steel, Fibreglass, Plywood	8,991	2,260	2.372	2,286	2,159	,, ,, ,, ,, 48·2 m^3
		29 6⅛″	7′ 5″	7′ 9⅜″	7′ 6″	7′ 1″	1,703 ft^3
40 ft	Steel	12,065	2,256	2,356	2,286	2,159	,, ,, ,, ,, 63·8 m^3
×	Aluminium	39′ 7″	7′ 4⅜″	7′ 8⅜″	7′ 6″	7′ 1″	2,256 ft^3
8 ft × 8 ft	Steel, Fiberglass, Plywood	12,078	2,260	2,372	2,286	2.159	,, ,, ,, ,, 64·7 m^3
		39′ 7⅝″	7′ 5″	7′ 9⅜″	7′ 6″	7′ 1″	2,287 ft^3
Other Sizes	Steel	8,069	2,679	2,356	2,286	2,565	,, ,, ,, ,, 51·6 m^3
	Aluminium	26′ 6½″	8′ 9½″	7′ 8¾″	7′ 6″	8′ 5″	1,804 ft^3
Length 27 ft	Steel, Fiberglass, Plywood	8,117	2,717	2,372	2,286	2,616	,, ,, ,, 52·3 m^3
Height 9′ 6″		26′ 7⅝″	8′ 11″	7′ 9⅜″	7′ 6″	8′ 7″	1,848 ft^3
Width 8′ 0″							

COMPASS

Compass Container Company
(Subsidiary of Whittaker Corporation)
1015 Market Avenue,
Richmond, California 94804, USA
TELEPHONE: (415) 237 5122

DIRECTORS:
A. A. Burda (*General Manager*)
Donn Brandow (*Manager*)
Michael J. Harr (*Manager, Sales*)

PRINCIPAL OWNERS:
American President Lines, State Lines, American Isbrandtsen, Pacific Far East Line.

CONTAINERS:
Eighteen different types, mostly of plywood and glassfibre construction

Standards: ABS, ASA and ISO

The technique uses flat panels of plywood faced with fibreglass—reinforced plastic, the panels being attached to a steel framework.

The containers are designed and constructed for all modes of transportation including marine handling and features weathertightness, resistance to handling damage as well as ease of repair by means of Fibreglass Patch Kit.

In addition to the range of ISO containers listed below the company manufactures a series of intermodal small containers which fit in side ISO units.

A Compass side door container

Compass ISO Containers manufactured in 1970-71

Type		Quantity manufactured 20 ft	30 ft	40 ft
Dry goods	1970	500		50
	1971	500		500
Insulated	1970			
	1971			
Refrigerated	1970	50		25
	1971	50		50-100
Specials*	1970	200		
	1971	300		

*Convertible Tops, Flat Racks

Standard Dry

Standard ISO
Type 6,055 mm (20 ft) Dry
Inside length 5,956·3 mm (234½ in)
Inside width 2,374·9 mm (93½ in)
Inside height 2,273·3 mm (89½ in)
Outside length 6,057·9 mm (238½ in)
Outside width 2,438·4 mm (96 in)
Outside height 2,438·4 mm (96 in)
Inside cube 32,339·3 cu m (1,142·0 ft³)
Door opening width 2,298·7 m (90½ in)
Door opening height 2,159 mm (85 in)

20 ft Dry Freight Convertible Top

Standard ISO
Type, 20 ft Dry, Convertible Top
Inside length 5,943·6 mm (234 in)
Inwide width 2,413 mm (93 in)
Inside height 2,260·6 mm (89 in)
Outside length 6,057·9 mm (238½ in)
Outside width 2,438·4 mm (96 in)
Outside height 2,438·4 mm (96 in)
Top opening length 5,664·2 mm (223 in)
Top opening width 2,184·4 mm (86 in)
Inside cube 31·55 cu m (1,114 cu ft)
Door opening width 2,311·4 mm (91 in)
Door opening height 2,311·4 mm (91 in)
Door opening height 2,159 mm (85 in, header in)
Removable door header
Removable top

20 ft Side Door Unit

Standard ISO
Type Dry—20 ft Side Door

Inside length 5,943·6 mm (234 in)
Inside width 2,374·9 mm (93½ in)
Inside height 2,260·6 mm (89 in)
Outside length 6,057·9 mm (238½ in)
Outside width 2,438·4 mm (96 in)
Outside height 2,438·4 mm (96 in)
Inside cube 31,603·1 cu m (1,126 in³)
End door opening width 2,292·35 mm (90¼ in)
End door opening height 2,159 mm (85 in)
Side door opening width 2,292·35 (90¼ in)
Side door opening height 2,159 (85 in)

Compass Container Side Door

Standard ISO
Type Dry—20 ft Side Door
Inside length 5,943·6 mm (234 in)
Inside width 2,349·5 mm (92½ in)
Inside height 2,413 mm (95 in)
Outside length 6,057·9 mm (238½ in)
Outside width 2,438 mm (96 in)
Outside height 2,590·8 mm (102 in).
Inside cube 33·8 cu m (1,196·0 in³)
End door opening width 2,298·7 mm (90½ in)
End opening door height 2,311 mm (91 in)
Side door opening width 1,905 mm (75 in)
Side door opening height 2,273·3 mm (89½ in

Compass Container Side Door

Standard ISO
Type Dry—20 ft Side Door
Inside length 5,892·8 mm (232 in)
Inside width 2,374·9 mm (93½ in)
Inside height 2,235·2 mm (88 in)

Outside length 6,057·9 mm (238½ in)
Outside width 2,438·4 mm (96 in)
Outside height 2,438·4 mm (96 in)
Inside cube 31·28 cu m (1,104·7 ft³)
Door opening width, End 2,292·35 mm (91¼ in) Side 1,828·8 mm (72 in)
Door opening height, End 2,159 mm (85 in) Side 2,133·6 (84 in)

Compass Container 40 ft Side Door

Standard ISO
Inside length 12,005 mm (39 ft 7 in)
Inside width 2,374·9 mm (93½ in)
Inside height 2,247·9 mm (88½ in)
Outside length 12,192 mm (40 ft)
Outside width 2,438·4 mm (8 ft)
Outside height 2,438·4 mm (8 ft)
Inside cube 65·64 cu m (2,318 ft³)
End door opening width 2,286 mm (90 in)
End door opening height 2,159 mm (85 in)
Side door opening width 2,286 mm (90 in)
Side door opening height 2,159 mm (85 in)

20 ft Refrigerated Container

Standard ISO
Type 20 ft Reefer
Inside length 5,334 mm (210 in)
Inside width 2,209·8 mm (87 in)
Inside height 2,108·2 mm (83 in)
Outside length 6,057·9 mm (238½ in)
Outside width 2,438·4 mm (96 in)
Outside height 2,438·4 mm (96 in)
Usable inside cube 22·65 cu m (846·0 cu ft)
Door opening width 2,247·9 mm (88½ in)
Door opening height 2,108·2 mm (83 in)

CONCARGO

Concargo Limited

Winterstoke Road,
Old Mixon,
Weston-super-Mare,
Somerset
TELEPHONE: Weston 28221
TELEX: 449173
DIRECTORS:
   D. Knightly
   C. M. Wilmot
   J. Nuttall
SPECIFICATIONS:
   BS 3951, Lloyds, TIR, British Rail, UIC
TYPES:
   Insulated, Refrigerated and Heated/Ventilated
DESIGN STANDARD:
   ISO Recommendation, Australian Department of Health
CONSTRUCTION:
   Metal frame, plywood coated glass reinforced polyester with polyurethane insulation.
PRINCIPAL USERS:
   ACT (Australia) Ltd.; National Freight Federation; East Asiatic Co., Manchester Liners Ltd.; VNS/Hapag Lloyd; Freightliners Ltd.

CONTAINERS:
   Shipping, road, rail and air freight containers. A typical ISO Freeze 20 container as illustrated would have the following internal dimensions:
   Length 5,821 mm (19 ft 1¼ in)
   Internal width 2,260 mm (7 ft 5 in)
   Internal height 2,202 mm (7 ft 2¾ in)
   Cubic capacity 28·7 m³ (1,014 cu ft)
   Rating 20,321 kg (20 tons)
   Tare weight 2,286 kg (2 tons 5 cwts)
   Insulation, Polyurethane Foam
   Heat loss 15·8 kilo-cal/°C (43 BTU/hr/°F)

Three typical 20 ft ISO Insulated Containers by Concargo.

CONSTRUCCIONES Y AUXILIAR DE FERROCARRILES

Construcciones y Auxiliar de Ferrocarriles S.A.

Paseo Calvo Sotelo 27-6°
Madrid 4, Spain
TELEPHONE: 4196200
BRANCH ADDRESSES:
C.A.F., Apartado 2, Beasain, Guipuzcoa, Spain
Talleres Irun, Barrio Anaca, Irun, Spain.
Talleres Madrid, Cerro de la Plata, Madrid
M.M. y C., Escoriaza y Fabros, 71-73, Zaragoza

DIRECTORS:
P. Ardaiz San Martin
J. Elosegui Labadia
J. Luis Betegon Arnal
DESIGN STANDARDS:
ISO, RENFE, UIC

CONTAINERS:
Twenty foot all welded steel containers. The containers can be stacked six high. Open sided and closed box versions are

available. 8 ft 6 in high units are also made.

METHOD OF CONSTRUCTION:
Containers are constructed in accordance with ISO Standard and TIR requirements using cold rolled sections and plate welded together. High toughness corner casting and fork lift pockets for empty and fully laden containers are fitted.

The closed box models are made of all welded steel using the CO² process. Hot rolled steel plates are shot blasted and primed prior to welding.

FLOOR:

Arc welded steel sections lined with grooved and tongue impregnated wood screwed to lower cross steel sections.

In the closed box container one piece impregnated wood boards are screwed to lower cross sections.

In the open sided container, the frame made of welded steel sections, is provided with two removable posts and two hinged steel doors which support four rows of wooden slats. Three collapsible wooden doors, steel framed and PVC ventilated and secured by plastic covered tables, complete the side structure.

SIDE WALLS:

Corrugated 1·5 mm thick steel plate and transomes welded to inside face of the steel plates.

REAR DOORS:

One front double wing, rubber sealed door with double cam locking device. Four steel hinges with stainless steel lubricated pins allow for a 270° opening. The locking devices can be secured by padlocks and are prepared for customs seals.

ROOF:

Butt welded steel plates supported by channel section members intermittently welded to roof plate.

LINING:

Upon customer's request a lining can be fitted.

FINISH:

Containers are prime coated with long life anti-rust Epoxy resin and a final coat of chlorinated-rubber paint reaching 125 microns. Mandatory inscriptions are included.

MAIN USERS:

Sea Containers Inc, RENFE, Contenemar Lines.

CAF ALL STEEL ISO CONTAINER DIMENSIONS:

Exterior:			Interior						
Length	Width	Height	Length	Width	Height	Approx. tare weight	Gross load	Capacity volume	
6,055 mm (19 ft 10½ in)	2,435 mm (8 ft 0 in)	2,435 mm (8 ft 0 in)	5,870 mm (19 ft 3 in)	2,335 mm (7 ft 8 in)	2,173 mm (7 ft 1 in)	2,160 kg (4,760 lb)	20,000 kg (44,100 lb)	30 m³ (1,060 cm fl)	

CAF ALL STEEL CLOSED BOX CONTAINER

DIMENSIONS: External Dimensions			Internal Dimensions			Estimated Tare	Gross Load	Capacity
Length	Width	Height	Length	Width	Height			
8 ft × 8 ft			19 ft 5 in	7 ft 7⅛ in	7 ft 1½ in	4,620 lb	44,800 lb	1,070 cu ft
8 ft × 8 ft 6 in			5,920 mm	2,314 mm	2,172 mm	2,100 kg	20,320 kg	30 m³
19 ft 10½ in	8 ft 0 in	8 ft 0 in	19 ft 5 in	7 ft 7⅛ in	7 ft 1½ in	4,750 lb	49,000 lb	1,140 cu ft
6,055 mm	2,435 mm	2,435 mm	5,920 mm	2,314 mm	2,324 mm	2,160 kg	22,160 kg	32 m³
19 ft 10½ in	8 ft 0 in	8 ft 6 in						
6,055 mm	2,435 mm	2,578 mm						

A—20 ft × 8 ft × 8 ft ISO Container
B—20 ft × 8 ft × 8 ft × 6 in Container

CAF ALL STEEL OPEN SIDED CONTAINER DIMENSIONS:

Internal Dimensions			Side Openings		Estimated Tare	Gross Load	Capacity
Length	Width	Height	Width	Height			
19 ft 3¾ in	7 ft 5⅛ in	7 ft 5⅛ in	18 ft 0⅜ in	7 ft 3 in	6,692 lb	51,496 lb	1,070 cu ft
5,886 mm	2,265 mm	2,262 mm	5,502 mm	2,210 mm	3,035 kg	23,355 kg	30 m³

CONTAINERS & PRESSURE VESSELS

Containers & Pressure Vessels
Clones,
Co. Monaghan,
Republic of Ireland
TELEPHONE: Clones 90 & 101
BRANCH ADDRESS:
90 Gatwick Road,
Crawley,
Surrey

Telephone: Crawley 26762

DIRECTORS:
P. J. O'Hare
J. Brady
C. Boyle
H. Collins
D. O. Neill (*Managing*)
L. E. Draisey (*U.K. Sales*)

CONTAINERS:

ISO tank containers of frameless construction. Tanks of stainless steel. Light weight for hazardous conditions. Insulation to customer requirements. The company also make semi ISO soft steel coil flats.

DESIGN STANDARDS:
ISO and semi ISO.

COOLTAINER

International Cooltainer AB
Sandhamnsgatan 38,
115 28 Stockholm, Sweden
TELEPHONE: 60 30 51/52
TELEX: 10894
DIRECTORS:
Janis Teteris (*Managing*)
Ing. Rune Lysen (*Technical*)
Bjorn Y. Hakanson (*Sales Promotion and Marketing*)
DESIGN STANDARDS: ISO, Lloyds
PRINCIPLE USERS: Firgor, C.T.I.
CONTAINERS:

Twenty foot and forty foot refrigerated containers.

PRODUCTION:

Two hundred and twenty 20 ft containers and one hundred 40 ft units were made in 1969.

METHOD OF CONSTRUCTION:

Frame: The frame is a welded construction made of profiled tubes. Rigid and compact body is supporting all extra forces during transport, trucking and lifting.

Floor: Constructed in four layers and glued together under pressure.

The lower layer is made of steel sheets 1·5 mm thick. St 52—3.

The layer between is made of Conticell 60-75 mm (2·4-3 in) thick, an insulating foam with specific weight of 60 kg/m³ and a thermal conductivity of 0·030 kcal/mh°C at 10°C recording to DIN 52612.

The upper layer is made of W.B.P. (Weather and boil proof) plywood, 20 mm (0·12 in) thick.

The top layer is 3 mm (0·12 in) plastic coat, and surface treated with special sand to prevent slipping.

Side walls, forward and wall: outside plates are 1·5 mm (0·06 in) thick St 52—3 steel with corrugated cross section. Forward and wall consists of 1·5 mm thick St 52—3 steel plates, stiffened by welded bars from the inside. The roof consists of 1·5 mm thick St 52—3 steel plates without any stiffeners.

Insulation protection consists of 5 mm thick polyester. The polyester insulation protection is built with a corrugated cross section The 103 mm space between the outside wall and insulation lining is filled with polyurethane foam (specific weight 40 kg/m³), forming a strong sandwich system unit.

Insulation: The polyurethane, used for the insulation, is foamed up with light pressure so that a specific weight of 38—42 kg/m³ is assured. A special procedure of foaming makes a very good sticking between the polyurethane steel and polyester.

Door: The two handing doors are built on a frame, outside covered with steel plates, inside formed polyester and between plyourethane, 80 mm thick. The tightening is provided with three steps of rubber packing between the container, the frame and the doors. Each door is hung by four hinges and locked with two fasteners. The door can be opened in 270°.

Clear door opening:
  height 2,120 mm
  width 1,969 mm

Other equipment: standardized corner fittings; fork lift tunnels, height 120 mm, width 300 mm; straddle carrier rails.

Painting: Steel work is protected with two layers anti-rust primer plus one layer finish paint.
  Inside is not painted.

Refrigerating plant 2 MK 15 CT: The refrigerating plant is especially built for the container in order to maintain prescribed temperature.

Gas compressor recif. mach. 2 cyl.	54 × 38 mm
Nominal cooling capacity	4,600 kcal/h at +25°C/−10°C
At rpm	1,400 kcal/h each
Ambient temperature	+40°C max.
Container temperature	−25°C min.
Refrigerant	R-12
Compressor oil	Shell Clavns 33
Electric power supply	380 V, 50 Hz
Power consumption	2·45 KW each refrigerating plant

Dimensions of the Cooltainer range of refrigerated containers

5,262	2,072	2,210	2,120
17′ 3¾″	6′ 9⅝″	7′ 3″	6′ 11″
11,327	2,235	2,095	
37′	7′ 3¼″	6′ 8″	
1,972	0·064 Btu/f2 hr degree		
6′ 4½″	0·32 Kcal/m² hr degree C.		
2,083	0·64 Btu/f² hr degree		
6′ 7″	0·32 Kcal/m² hr degree C.		
24·10			
52			

Dimensions of the Cooltainer range of refrigerated containers

Type by ISO or other Recognised Standard Dimension	Main Materials of Construction (See space below for notes on additional materials and methods of construction)	Internal			Internal Measurements of End door openings		Approx. heat gain in BTUs/hr or K-cals/hr	Cubic Capacity m³ ft³
		Length mm ft in	Height mm ft in	Width mm ft in	Width mm ft in	Height mm ft in		
20 ft × 8 ft × 8 ft	Aluminium	5,262 17′ 3¾″	2,072 6′ 9⅝″	2,210 7′ 3″	2,120 6′ 11″	1,972 6′ 4½″	0·64 Btu/f² hr degree 0·32 Kcal/m² hr degree C.	24·10
30 ft × 8 ft × 8 ft	Aluminium							
40 ft × 8 ft × 8 ft	Aluminium	11,327 37′	2,235 7′ 3¼″	2,095 6′ 8″		2,083 6′ 7″	0·064 Btu/f2 hr degree 0·32 Kcal/m² hr degree C.	52

CRANE FRUEHAUF

Crane Fruehauf Containers Ltd,
649/655 London Road, Isleworth, Middlesex, England
TELEPHONE: 01-568 0041
TELEX: 262051
DIRECTORS:
D. R. Marsh (*Chairman*)
J. K. Thompson (*Managing Director*)
R. Thompson
W. I. Green
J. Paterson
B. Widdowson
R. J. Jervis

CONTAINERS:
Smooth skin dry freight, exposed post, insulated and refrigerated containers. Tiltainers, Bulktainers, container tanks, hopper container tanks. Skeletal semi-trailers. See Crane Fruehauf entry in the Container Handling section.
DESIGN STANDARD:
ISO, TIR. Lloyd's, UIC, BS 3951

Crane Fruehauf General Purpose Smooth Skin Container. (KA and KB Models)

Constructed of aluminium with steel end frames. With an airtight outer shell, Crane Fruehauf containers possess sufficient strength to withstand and counter all load handling and shipment stress, but are sufficiently light in weight and construction to provide maximum payload within total gross weight. The internal lining can be cleaned easily, wears well and will not shrink or swell with moisture changes. Flooring is watertight, and able to withstand fork-lift truck loading. Door seals, of special Crane Fruehauf design, are watertight.

Crane Fruehauf General Purpose Exposed Post Container. (KF and KG Models)

The exposed post container is similar in construction to Crane Fruehauf's smooth skin

Crane Fruehauf Tank Container.
Built to the standard 20 ft × 8 ft × 18 ft, this Crane Fruehauf Bulk Liquids Tank Container has a capacity of 4,200 gallons gross. The tank is of single compartment design, constructed of stainless steel.

model, made of aluminium with steel end frames.

Dimensions:
Models KA2, KB2, KF2 and KG2, 10 ft

Capacity 15·29 cu m (540 cu ft)
Tare weights:
  KA2 (Aluminium alloy) 1,029 kg (2,270 lb)
  KB2 (Aluminium alloy/steel) 1,156 kg (2,550 lb)
  KF2 (Aluminium alloy) 1,029 kg (2,270 lb)
  KG2 (Aluminium alloy/steel) 1,156 kg (2,550 lb)

General purpose. Models KA2, KB2, KF2, and KG2, 20 ft

Capacity 31·15 cu m (1,100 cu ft)
Tare weights:
  KA2 (Aluminium alloy) 1,687 kg (3,720 lb)
  KB2 (Aluminium alloy/steel) 1,837 kg (4,050 lb)
  KF2 (Aluminium alloy) 1,687 kg (3,720 lb)
  KG2 (Aluminium alloy/steel) 1,837 kg (4,050 lb)

General purpose. Models KA2, KB2, KF2 and KG2, 30 ft

Capacity 47·00 cu m (1,660 cu ft)
Tare Weights:
KA2 (Aluminium alloy) 2,173 kg (4,790 lb)
KB2 (Aluminium alloy/steel) 2,449 kg (5,400 lb)
KF2 (Aluminium alloy) 2,173 kg (4,790 lb)
KG2 (Aluminium alloy/steel) 2,449 kg (5,400 lb)

General purpose. Models KA2, KB2, KF2 and KG2, 40 ft

Capacity 63·43 cu m (2,245 cu ft)
Tare weights:
KA2 (Aluminium alloy) 2,662 kg (5,870 lb)
KB2 (Aluminium alloy/steel) 3,061 kg (6,750 lb)
KF2 (Aluminium alloy) 2,662 kg (5,870 lb)
KG2 (Aluminium alloy/steel) 3,061 kg (6,750 lb)

Crane Fruehauf Insulated/Refrigerated Containers

Designed to take mechanical or liquid gas refrigeration units and still maintain the overall ISO dimensions. The containers are available with two levels of insulation, both achieved by in-situ foamed non-inflammable urethane. Doors are fully sealed by Crane Fruehauf multi-wedge cushion seals in the door bevels, and vinyl plastic double seal round the edges. The front wall of the container is recessed to allow mechanical refrigeration unit to be fitted within the container length module.

Insulated/Refrigerated Reefer Type KA2 20 ft
.Tare weights:
(Aluminium alloy) 2,340 kg (5,150 lb)
Insulated/Refrigerated Reefer Type KA2 40 ft
Tare weights:
(Aluminium alloy) 3,570 kg (8,585 lb)

Crane Fruehauf Plastic/Plywood PP2 General Purpose Containers

Constructed with steel framing and plastic faced plywood panelling on fixed end, doors, sides and roof, no interior lining necessary. Insulation/Reefer kits can be fitted.

PP2 20 ft
Nominal Capacity 31·70 cu m (1,120 cu ft)
Tare weight 2,015 kg (4,480 lb)
PP2 30 ft
Nominal Capacity 47·80 cu m (1,690 cu ft)
Tare weight 2,720 kg (5,995 lb)
PP2 40 ft
Nominal Capacity 64·40 cu m (2,271 cu ft)
Tare weight 3,410 kg (7,500 lb)

Crane Fruehauf Open Top Containers OKA/OKB/OKF/OKG

Overall dimensions are similar to box type KA/KB/KF/KG above but top cover is by detachable tilt and roof bows.

Crane Fruehauf Open-Frame 'Tiltainer' Flat

Designed for ease of loading from the sides or top, the container consists of a platform with container ends and removable roof-bows and roof-rails. The load is protected by a 'tilt'. It is designed for operators wanting to use containerisation for the shipment of heavy and bulky equipment such as machinery, which would present loading difficulties with standard totally enclosed containers.

Crane Fruehauf Trailers Ltd, have introduced a number of Dockside Mobile Repair Service units for the repair and maintenance of damaged containers, trailers and tractors passing through the various ports at which these units are established. These include Felixstowe, Tilbury, Southampton and Liverpool. Designed to provide transport operators with an efficient "on the spot" repair service, these Dockside Repair outfits supplement the growing number of Crane Fruehauf repair/modification/overhaul service depots and branch offices located in the U.K.

Crane Fruehauf are also able to offer a genuine international service network by calling on their Fruehauf Associates' depot facilities throughout the world.

Crane Fruehauf 40 ft dry freight containers at Felixstowe Container Terminal.

Crane Fruehauf OKB2-SRT open-top containers, specially designed for Seatrain Lines. They measure 40 ft × 8 ft × 8 ft 6 in high and incorporate an underfloor tunnel arrangement to reduce overall height during transport.

Tilt covered open-frame containers are available in the same sizes as Crane Fruehauf's ISO containers—20 ft, 30 ft and 40 ft—and have standard container corner fastenings. Lashing rings are fitted in the floor and at the side of the platform, various types of side superstructure can be fitted.

Dimensions:
Tiltainer Type 20 ft (Nominal (Type 1C)
Height variable
Tare weight 2,080 kg (4,600 lb)
Tiltainer Type 30 ft Nominal (Type 1B)
Height variable
Tare weight 3,628 kg (8,000 lb)

Crane Fruehauf Container Tank

18,184 litres (4,000 gallons), single compartment stainless steel tank designed to conform to the standard 20 ft × 8 ft × 8 ft basic container module. The container framework is constructed of mild steel tubular and channel section material and welded to the tank via hat section rings. The framework is of all welded construction and provides adequate strength for stacking loaded containers six high.

Crane Fruehauf 'Bulktainer'

An open top container complying to ISO standards for the transportation of bulk loads. Constructed from steel throughout with Roof Bows for supporting a TIR tilt. Load discharge can be made through a large single tail door hinged at its top or twin vertically hinged doors. ISO corner castings are located at all corners to enable stacking and lifting operation as for conventional containers.
Dimensions:
Bulktainer Type 20 ft. Nominal (Type 1C)
Bulktainer Type 30 ft. Nominal (Type 1B)

Crane Fruehauf 20 ft refrigerated containers.

Crane Fruehauf Hopper Containers

Overall dimensions to comply with ISO Hopper details to suit loads.

Crane Freuhauf open frame 'Tiltainer' flat designed for the shipment of heavy and bulk equipment.

DAVIDSON

Davidson & Co. (Coach Builders) Ltd.
Church Road, Edge Lane, Liverpool 13
TELEPHONE: 051-228 6377
DIRECTORS:
W. I. Campion
J. Wardle
T. Tippin

CONTAINERS:
Built to ISO and TIR requirements, mainly specials to customers requirements. Self-contained exhibition unit 8 ft × 8 ft × 30 ft sealed for transport and customs clearance but opening out to double the width. Twenty built in 1967 and 30 in 1968. Manufactured in light alloys. Six have been built 2·59 m (8 ft 6 in) high overall

MAIN CUSTOMERS:
Shipping companies.

DORSEY

Dorsey Trailers, Inc.,
Hickman Avenue
Elba, Alabama 36323, USA
TELEPHONE: Area Code (205) 897-2241
DIRECTORS:
George L. Collier (*President*)
T. K. Dorsey (*Executive Vice-President and Director of Sales*)
Sam Collier (*Vice-President, Finance and Administration*)
Roy Belcer (*Vice-President, Engineering and Manufacturing*)

Joe De Vane (*Manager of Distribution Sales*)

PRODUCTS:
Containers and container chassis (see container handling equipment section).

TYPES:
Van Containers-Dry Freight. insulated and refrigerated, platform containers, gondola containers.

PRODUCTION:
550 30 ft dry goods containers were made in 1971.

DESIGN STANDARD:
ANSI M H 5.1. ISO

CONSTRUCTION MATERIALS:
Steel, aluminium, composite, fibre glass reinforced plywood and fibreglass.

CONTAINERS:
Aluminium skin interior post for marine container service. Twenty foot and forty foot models available.
Steel dry freight containers. All welded steel post. Twenty foot and forty foot models are available.
Composite dry freight containers using fibre glass clad plywood panels. Twenty foot and forty foot models.
Aluminium insulated freight containers. Twenty and forty foot models.
Refrigerated platform and gondola containers.

A Dorsey insulated container.

Two 20 ft Dorsey dry-freight containers mounted on Dorsey couplable semi-trailers.

DURAMIN

Duramin Engineering Co. Ltd.

Harbour Road, Lydney, Glos. GL15 4EN, England
TELEPHONE: Lydney 2371-6

TELEGRAMS: Duramin Lydney
TELEX: 43289

DIRECTORS:
D. D. Williams (*Chairman*)
E. Horritt (*Managing Director*)
D. Lloyd Jones
G. A. H. Watts
A. J. Watts
J. Elliot Bown

LICENSEES ABROAD:
Rubery Owen and Kemsley Pty. Ltd;
Kingsbury, Woodville, South Australia;
Etablissements Industriels de Soule
Bagnères de Bigorre, Haute Pyrenée, France;
Eskal Duna de CYR de Boques SA
Factoria de Madrid, Carretara, Villa Verde
Vallecas 18, Madrid 21, Spain

CONTAINERS:

Manufacturing and marketing licenses granted in respect of patented process for manufacturing insulated and refrigerated containers.

Dry freight, removable roof, side opening, bulk, bulk/side opening dual purpose and open top.

SPECIFICATIONS:
ISO, BS 3951, Lloyds

CONSTRUCTION—MATERIALS AND METHOD

All Duramin containers feature an exterior steel frame. 'Internal dimensions' and 'BTU's per hour heat gain' in the case of insulated and refrigerated containers relate to units in standard form only and are variable according to customer requirements. In the dry freight range the 'Maxi' container has natural insulating properties and is variable to customers needs.

PRODUCTION CAPABILITY:
5,000 × 20 ft modules per annum of which about ¼ are insulated.

Duramin Series GP/EP Flush Interior (external pillars)
Duramin Series GP/IP Flush Exterior (internal pillars)

DESCRIPTION:
Shell: High-yield steel frame laced with extruded high-tensile alloy pillars. Base Frame:

Duramin " Jumbo " side-loader is illustrated in this **40 ft ISO container for MAT Transport.**

All welded high-yield steel. Floor: 27mm (1 $\frac{1}{16}$ in) plywood. Sides and Fixed End: Extruded alloy pillars clench-bolted to roof and floor frame. Cladding: 16 SWG NS4 half-hard aluminium alloy, lap-jointed and riveted. Door Frame: Steel box frame construction. Double doors: 25 mm thick one-piece plywood, clad aluminium outside, galvanised steel inside, hinged to swing flush with container sides. Retaining catches, rubber sealing, positive closure.

NON-STANDARD EXTRAS (and/or alternatives) incorporated to special requirements.
'Freightliner'-type base. Exterior Plywood cladding. Open roof with detachable bearers). Side loading access. Recessed shackles for alternative lift. Second deck and fittings. Load restraint lining and fittings. Recessed rails in floor (for pallet loading). Bulk-tipping adaptations. UIC certification.

Description:
Duramin patent construction embodies the use of insulated panels composed of a core of polyurethane, bonded and skinned on all surfaces with reinforced glassfibre by a special vacuum process. The panels, produced as complete homogeneous slabs, which largely eliminate internal bracing, are housed and bonded in a high-yield steel structure and base frame, which absorbs all stresses imposed by handling and stacking.
External corner frame: High-yield steel sections. Shell: Sides, roof, floor, front end, doors, each formed in one piece. Sandwich construction with foam core polyurethane insulation and reinforced glassfibre skins. Thickness 4 in all round. Floor: Specially reinforced with a plywood lamination. Surface coated with grit-impregnated material, abrasion resistant, non-slip. Doors: Sealed double

doors, each fitted with two locking bars. Hinged to swing flush with container sides. Finish: Smooth surface interior and exterior. Lifting facilities: ISO corner castings

Duramin Series RE Refrigerated Containers

Of the same basic construction and specification as the insulated series, Duramin refrigerated containers are fitted with proprietary refrigerating units of the required capacity. A special compartment built integrally with the shell of the container accommodates a mechanical refrigeration unit operated from an external d.c. or a.c. electricity mains supply, or alternatively from an independent built-in i.c. engine. Alternative refrigeration can be incorporated consisting of liquid nitrogen or liquid carbon dioxide systems. Clear door-opening (all models): 2,195 mm (86·5 in) 2,055 mm (81 in). The heat loss from a 20 ft container with 4 in of polyurethane insulation is approx. 30 BTU/hr/°F.

STANDARD EXTRAS (and/or alternatives)
Insulated panels, variation in thickness. Light alloy fluted floor. Fork lift tunnels. Leg pockets for jacking. TIR certification.

NON-STANDARD EXTRAS (and/or alternatives) to special requirements
Freightliner'-type base. Roof-hanging rails. Second decks and fittings. Load restraint lining and fittings. Circular apertures and plugs in bulkhead for cold air ducting attachments. Provision for clip-on refrigeration units. Dry ice bunker. Side loading access. Recessed shackles for alternative lift. UIC certification.

PRINCIPAL USERS:
Associated Container Transportation (Australia) Limited
Geo. Bell and Co. Ltd.

Dry Freight (General Purpose) Type by ISO or other recognised Standard Dimensions	Main Materials of Construction	Internal Dimensions: Length mm ft in	Internal Dimensions: Height mm ft in	Internal Dimensions: Width mm ft in	End Doors: Width mm ft in	End Doors: Height mm ft in	Internal Measurements of other types of opening	Cubic Capacity
20 ft × 8 ft × 8 ft	Aluminium and steel	5,930 19 ft 5½ in	2,254 7 ft 4¾ in	2,336 7 ft 8 in	2,336 7 ft 8 in	2,145 7 ft 0½ in	(a) Removable roof combined with hinged and/or removeable header rail.	31·1 m³ 1,100 ft³
	MAXI—composite	5,930 19 ft 5½ in	2,254 7 ft 4¾ in	2,336 7 ft 8 in	2,336 7 ft 8 in	2,145 7 ft 0½ in		31·1 m³ 1,100 ft³
	G.R.P./Plywood	5,930 19 ft 5½ in	2,253 7 ft 4¾ in	2,358 7 ft 8¾ in	2,336 7 ft 8 in	2,145 7 ft 0½ in	(b) Side opening	31·50 m³ 1,112 ft³
30 ft × 8 ft × 8 ft	Aluminium and steel	8,985 29 ft 5¾ in	2,254 7 ft 4¾ in	2,336 7 ft 8 in	2,336 7 ft 8 in	2,145 7 ft 0 ½in	(c) Bulk adaptation, featuring roof and fixed end or door end hatches.	47·3 m³ 1,671 ft³
	MAXI—composite	8,985 29 ft 5¾ in	2,254 7 ft 4¾ in	2,336 7 ft 8 in	2,336 7 ft 8 in	2,145 7 ft 0½ in		47·3 m³ 1,671 ft³
	G.R.P./Plywood	9,000 29 ft 6¼ in	2,253 7 ft 4¾ in	2,358 7 ft 8¾ in	2,336 7 ft 8 in	2,145 7 ft 0½ in	(d) Combination of (b) and (c).	47·8 m³ 1,688 ft³
40 ft × 8 ft × 8 ft	Aluminium and steel	12,051 39 ft 6½ in	2,254 7 ft 4¾ in	2,336 7 ft 8 in	2,336 7 ft 8 in	2,145 7 ft 0½ in		63·3 m³ 2,238 ft³
	MAXI—composite	12,051 39 ft 6½ in	2,254 7 ft 4¾ in	2,336 7 ft 8 in	2,336 7 ft 8 in	2,145 7 ft 0½ in		63·3 m³ 2,238 ft³
	G.R.P./Plywood	12,060 39 ft 5¾ in	2,253 7 ft 4¾ in	2,358 7 ft 8¾ in	2,336 7 ft 8 in	2,145 7 ft 0½ in		64·1 m³ 2,257 ft³
20 ft × 8 ft × 4 ft	Steel with composite removable hard top roof	5,923 19 ft 5¼ in	1,041 3 ft 5 in	2,346 7 ft 8⅜ in	2,346 7 ft 8⅜ in	863 2 ft 10 in	Features end doors and removable one piece hard top roof combined with hinged and/or removable header rail.	14·35 m³ 510 ft³
20 ft/30 ft/40 ft × 8 ft 6 in × 8 ft		As 8 ft × 8 ft units detailed above, but internal height increased by 5½/6 in.						
Insulated and refrigerated							Approx. heat gain in Btu's/hr or K.Cals/hr.	
20 ft × 8 ft × 8 ft	Steel, timber and G.R.P. composite	5,791 19 ft 0 in	2,133 7 ft 0 in	2,235 7 ft 4 in	Door width generally as interior width.		40	27·6 m³ 975 ft³
30 ft × 8 ft × 8 ft	Steel, timber and G.R.P. composite	6,406 29 ft 0¾ in	2,133 7 ft 0 in	2,235 7 ft 4 in	Door height fractionally less than internal height.		56	42·2 m³ 1,492 ft³
40 ft × 8 ft × 8 ft	Steel, timber and G.R.P. composite	11,924 39 ft 1½ in	2,133 7 ft 0 in	2,235 7 ft 4 in			73	56·8 m³ 2,008 ft³

All internal dimensions given based on "standard" units, but these can vary according to insulation rating required.

British Rail
Dart Container Lines
Ellerman Wilson Ltd
Eurotransport Limited
Hamburg-Sudamerikanische
International Ferry Freight Limited
MAT Transport Ltd
Manchester Liners Limited
Overseas Containers Limited
Northern Ireland Trailers Ltd

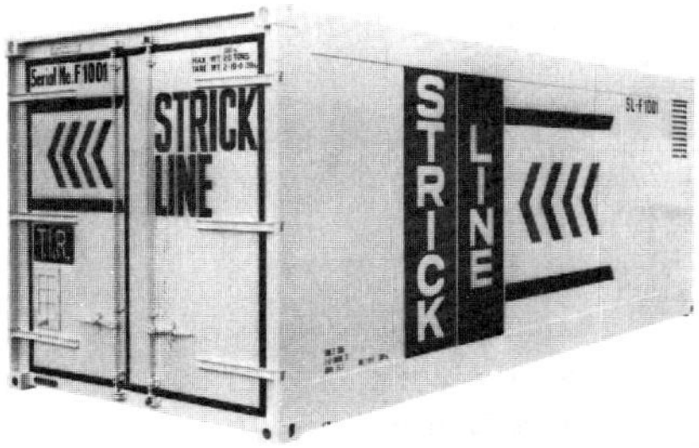

20 ft refrigerated container by Duramin for Strick Line Ltd.

USERS *cont.*

Transport Holdings Co Ltd
Road Services (Caledonian) Ltd
Seawheel Limited

Duramin Containers, double stacked.

Duramin 30 ft ISO Container with side-loading facility and 'Salwall' lining (for multi-position load anchorage)

ENSCOTE

Ensecote Ltd.
Thorncliffe, Sheffield, S30 4YP

TELEPHONE: Ecclesfield 3171
TELEX: 54-220

DIRECTORS:
A. H. Kynaston (*Chairman*)
A. Cunningham
PRODUCTION:
In 1968, the company produced 46 containers measuring 10 ft × 8 ft × 8 ft.

CONTAINERS:
Special units for the transport of hazardous and dutiable cargo.

MAIN USERS:
Birt Potter Westray, George Gibson & Co.

FIAT

Fiat S.p.A.
Corso Marconi 10/20—10125 Turin (Italy)
TELEPHONE: 6565
TELEX: Fiatsede; 21025, 21026, 21029, 21056, 21425
CONTAINERS: Dry and insulated containers.
CONSTRUCTION:
Steel frame and aluminium panelling
PRINCIPAL OWNERS OF CONTAINERS:
Tarros S.p.A., Piazza De Marini 1, Genoa (Italy), Ignazio Messina, Tarros S.p.A., Traghetti del Mederteraneo, C.T.I., LOCAT, Zust Ambrossetti S.p.A., Merzario S.p.A., Montecatini Edison, Fiat, SAUI, S. Cristoforo. SLPUIA.
DESIGN STANDARDS:
ISO

ISO Van Container (Dry Types)
DESCRIPTION:
Framed in high yield steel with panelling in corrosion-proof light aluminium alloy. Sides are reinforced by extruded posts of aluminium light alloy. Roof of pressed light alloy panels. Assembly: steel parts by welding; aluminium sheets and posts riveted together and riveted or bolted to the steel structure. All steel to aluminium facing surfaces are carefully insulated to prevent electrolytic corrosion. Lifting, stacking, base frame resistance, floor,

Two Fiat IC containers mounted on Fiat truck model 690N3 and combination trailer

sides, doors and roof according to the specifications recommended, so far, by the ISO Committee.
DIMENSIONS:
Fiat containers are presently built in the following international lengths: Type 1A—

40 ft, 1B—30 ft, 1C—20 ft, 1D—10 ft, 1E—6.5 ft.
BASE FRAME:
Two box-like steel side-rails with tubular cross members welded to them.
CORNER FITTINGS of special cast steel as the

latest ISO recommendations.

FLOOR formed from sandwich elements of fir-wood and beech-wood treated with phenolic resins. In conformity with the ISO specifications, it allows the passage of a fork-lift truck having a maximum load of 5,460 kg (1,203 lb) on the front wheels.

SIDES: Sheets reinforced by extruded top-hat-section posts, all in aluminium light alloy. Only the container size 1D has aluminum sheets reinforced by corrugated light alloy in lieu of aluminium extruded posts.

FRONT-END: Two vertical box-like steel posts and two steel cross members welded to the four corner fittings; wall of aluminium plate reinforced by a riveted corrugated aluminium light alloy sheet.

REAR END: As front-end frame with hinge doors.

DOORS: Double doors of beech ply-wood treated with resins (Rexilon) coated each side by aluminium light alloy plates. Hinged to swing round against container sides, with retaining catches. Fitted with four locking bars and a special sealing to prevent water entering container between doors and frame.

ROOF: Two box-like steel side-rails welded to upper corner fittings and cross members. The special aluminium light alloy pressed roof panels with stiffening ribs are supported by top-hat-section steel cross members.

WATERPROOFING: Special sealing compound, used on all panelling joints etc.

FINISH: All steelwork is treated with several corrosion-proof prime coats plus finish coats of special marine-corrosion-resistant paint. No paint on the aluminium surface.

ISO Classification	External dimensions			Internal dimensions		
	L	W	H	L	W	H
	m	m	m	m	m	m
1A 40' x 8' x 8'	12.190 (39 ft 11 59/64 in)	2.435 (7 ft 11 55/64 in)	2.435 (7 ft 11 55/64 in)	12.03 (39 ft 5 5/8 in)	2.33 (7 ft 7 47/64 in)	2.24 (7 ft 4 3/16 in)
1B 30' x 8' x 8'	9.125 (29 ft 11 1/4 in)	2.435 (7 ft 11 55/64 in)	2.435 (7 ft 11 55/64 in)	8.96 (29 ft 4 3/4 in)	2.33 (7 ft 7 47/64 in)	2.24 (7 ft 4 3/16 in)
1C 20' x 8' x 8'	6.055 (19 ft 10 25/64 in)	2.435 (7 ft 11 55/64 in)	2.435 (7 ft 11 55/64 in)	5.91 (19 ft 4 43/64 in)	2.33 (7 ft 7 47/64 in)	2.24 (7 ft 4 3/16 in)
1D 10' x 8' x 8'	2.990 (9 ft 9 23/32 in)	2.435 (7 ft 11 55/64 in)	2.435 (7 ft 11 55/64 in)	2.85 (9 ft 4 13/64 in)	2.33 (7 ft 7 47/64 in)	2.24 (7 ft 4 3/16 in)
1E 6.5' x 8' x 8'	1.965 (6 ft 5 23/64 in)	2.435 (7 ft 11 55/64 in)	2.435 (7 ft 11 55/64 in)	1.83 (6 ft 0 3/64 in)	2.33 (7 ft 7 47/64 in)	2.24 (7 ft 4 3/16 in)

ISO Classification	Door clearway W	Door clear H	Useful internal volume	Tare	Max capacity	Gross Weight (II)
	m	m	cu. m.	kg	kg	kg
1A 40' x 8' x 8'	2.22 (6 ft 7 17/32 in)	2.15 (7 ft 0 41/64 in)	62.8 (2,218 cu. ft.)	2,840 (6,259 lbs)	27,640 (60,918 lbs)	30,480 (67,177 lbs)
1B 30' x 8' x 8'	2.22 (6 ft 7 17/32 in)	2.15 (7 ft 0 41/64 in)	46.8 (1,653 cu. ft.)	2,240 (4,937 lbs)	23,160 (51,044 lbs)	25,400 (55,981 lbs)
1C 20' x 8' x 8'	2.22 (6 ft 7 17/32 in)	2.15 (7 ft 0 41/64 in)	31.0 (1,095 cu. ft.)	1,500 (3,306 lbs)	18,820 (41,479 lbs)	20,320 (44,785 lbs)
1D 10' x 8' x 8'	2.22 (6 ft 7 17/32 in)	2.15 (7 ft 0 41/64 in)	14.9 (526 cu. ft.)	950 (2,093 lbs)	9,100 (20,056 lbs)	10,160 (22,392 lbs)
1E 6.5' x 8' x 8'	2.22 (6 ft 7 17/32 in)	2.15 (7 ft 0 41/64 in)	9.7 (342 cu. ft.)	790 (1,741 lbs)	6,310 (13,907 lbs)	7,110 (15,670 lbs)

FRANGECO SA

Frangeco S.A.

71, Quai National
92—Puteaux, France
TELEPHONE: Paris (1) 772.24-05
TELEX: Frangeco 62.120

DIRECTORS:
J. J. Joseph (*Managing*)
A. J. de Senneville (*Director, container Department*)

DESIGN STANDARDS:
ISO, TIR, SNCF/UIC, AFNOR, Bureau Veritas

PRODUCTION:
In 1970, 100 twenty foot ISO dry goods containers were produced against 105 in 1969. Two hundred 30 ft units were produced in 1970, none in 1969. Three hundred 40 ft units

were produced in 1970, two hundred in 1969. Some 200 specials were produced in 1970 including tilt containers and half height open top units. One hundred 40 foot refrigerated units were made in 1971

PRINCIPLE USERS:
C.T.I., C.N.C., Carl Tiedemann, M.D.F.

REPAIR FACILITIES:
Besides factories at Maubeuge and Villefranche—S/Saone, there are three depots in France where Frangeco containers can be repaired: at Le Coudray, Bassens and Vitrolles.

CONTAINERS:
Dry freight, refrigerated and bulk liquid containers to ISO recommendations.

CONSTRUCTION:
Two methods are used: 1. All welded, press folded, half hard high yield strength steel.

2. plywood panels overlaid on both sides with glass reinforced polyester used with a steel frame. Floors may be made from pine boards or plywood. Locking devices are of the power brace type.

All Steel 8 ft × 8 ft × 20 ft

Construction: All welded, of press folded half hard high yield strength steel.

Structure: A frame at each end, top siderails, bottom siderails (incorporating built in facilities for handling by straddle carrier or "Travelift"), roof bows, floor cross members and lower bodyrails, formed from press folded steel.

Corner Fittings: Eight cast steel corner fittings as recommended by ISO to permit top lifting with spreaders, hooks or slings, as well as stacking (6 high fully laden).

Type by ISO or other Recognised Standard Dimensions	Main Materials of Construction (See space below for notes on additional materials and methods of construction)	Internal			Internal Measurements of End door openings		Cubic Capacity
		Length mm / ft in	Height mm / ft in	Width mm / ft in	Width mm / ft in	Height mm / ft in	m³
20 ft × 8 ft × 8 ft	Steel	5,904 / 19' 4 7/16"	2,209 / 7' 3"	2,334 / 7' 5"	2,290 / 6' 11 7/8"	2,230 / 6' 11 7/8"	30,600 / 1,080
	Timber and Plastics	5,940 / 19' 5 7/8"	2,245 / 7' 9 7/16"	2,373 / 4' 4 3/8"	2,290 / 7' 5"	2,130 / 7' 0"	31,600 / 1,116
		8,975	2,209 / 7' 9"	2,334 / 7' 8"	2,290 / 7' 5"	2,130 / 6' 11 7/8"	46,300
40 ft × 8 ft × 8 ft 6"	Steel	12,040 / 39' 6"	2,360 / 7' 8 3/8"	2,334 / 7' 7 7/8"	2,290 / 7' 5"	2,282	66,500

The range of containers made by Frangeco

Floor: Constructed of scarfed fir boards assembled with plastic seal to insure watertightness. They are secured to the underframe with self-tapping screws.

Roof: Plain high yield strength steel.

Side and End Walls: Made of vertical castellated press folded high yield strength steel. Four ventilation devices, two on each side. An internal cargo securing system, consisting of two flat bars welded along each sidewall.

Doors and Locks: Double doors, each leaf composed of:—A frame of press folded high yield strength steel—A panel of vertical castellated press folded high yield strength steel—Four hinges of die steel operating in antirust bushings (three for side doors)—One steel "antirack" pressure cam locking mechanism, bracing the whole structure and maintaining the door shut tight on continuous ETP type seals. Retaining catches are provided on container sides. Doorlocks are capable of being sealed, in conformity with T.I.R. requirements.

Finish: Sandblasting. Painting, to the user's choice colour. Markings.

Optional:
Side doors. Fork lift tunnels.
Leg pockets for jacking.

All steel dry freight 8 ft × 8 ft × 30 ft

CONSTRUCTION:
All welded, of press folded half hard high yield strength steel.

STRUCTURE:
A frame at each end, top siderails, bottom siderails (incorporating built in facilities for handling by straddle carrier), roof bows, floor cross members and lower body rails, formed from press folded steel

CORNER FITTINGS:
Eight cast steel corner fittings as recommended by ISO to permit top lifting with spreaders, hooks or slings, as well as stacking (6 high fully laden).

FLOOR:
Plywood floor, secured to the underframe with self-tapping screws.

ROOF:
Plain high yield strength steel.

SIDE AND END WALLS:
Made of vertical castellated press folded high yeild strength steel. Four ventilation devices, two on each side. An internal cargo securing system, consisting of two flat bars welded along each sidewall.

DOORS AND LOCKS:
Double doors, each leaf composed of: A frame of press folded high yield strength steel —A panel of vertical castellated press folded high yield strength steel—four hinges of die steel operating in anti-rust bushings (three for side doors)—two steel "antirack" pressure cam locking mechanisms (one for side doors)—one continuous EPT type seal. Retaining catches are provided on container sides. Doorlocks are capable of being sealed, in conformity with TIR requirements. Plywood side doors on option: Double doors, each leaf composed of: A frame of GRP-overlaid plywood—four hinges of die steel operating in stainless steel bushings—two steel "antirack" pressure cam locking mechanisms—one continuous EPT type seal. Retaining catches and sealing.

FINISH:
Sandblasting. Painting, to the user's choice colour. Markings.

OPTIONAL:
Side doors. Fork-lift tunnels.

DIMENSIONS AND RATINGS:
External measurements:
Length 9,125 mm (30 ft 0 in)
Width 2,438 mm (8 ft 0 in)
Height 2,438 (8 ft 0 in)

FRANGECO/TITAN. Stainless steel 30 × 8 × 8 tank container for carriage of drinks and chemical products. Capacity 5,719 gallons. Three compartments. Available too in 3,700 gallon single compartment tank or 4,400 gallon three-compartment tank within a 20 × 8 × 8 module.

Internal measurements:
Length 8,975 mm (29 ft 5⅜ in)
Width 2,330 mm (7 ft 7¾ in)
Height 2,206 mm (7 ft 2⅞ in)
Cubic capacity 46,131 m³ (1,629 cu ft)
Door opening:
Rear doors
Width 2,290 mm (7 ft 6⅛ in)
Height 2,130 mm (7 ft 0 in)
Steel side doors
Width 2,260 mm (7 ft 5 in)
Height 2,130 mm (7 ft 0 in)
Plywood side doors
Width 2,800 mm (9 ft 2¼ in*)
Height 2,130 mm (7 ft 0 in)
Gross weight: 254,240 kg (56,000 lb.)
Tare weight: 2,800 kg (6,173 lb)
Payload: 22,600 kg (49,827 lb)
*In this case, container, inside width is 7 ft 6⅛ in

MD 40 Ac 1 All steel 8 ft × 8 ft 6 in × 40 ft

Construction: All welded, of press folded half hard high yield strength steel.

Structure: A frame at each end, top siderails, bottom siderails (incorporating built in facilities for handling by straddle carrier or "Travelift"), roof bows, floor cross members, lower bodyrails and braces, formed from press folded steel.

Corner Fittings: Eight cast steel corner fittings as recommended by ISO to permit top lifting with spreaders, as well as stacking (6 high, fully laden).

Floor: Constructed of scarfed fir bcards assembled with plastic seals to insure watertightness. They are secured to the underframe with self-tapping screws.

Roof: Plain high yield strength steel.

Side and End Walls: Made of vertical castellated press folded high yield strength steel. Six ventilation devices, three on each side. An internal cargo securing system, consisting of two flat bars welded along each sidewall.

Door and Locks: Double rear door, each leaf composed of:—A frame of press folded high yield strength steel—A panel of vertical castellated press folded high yield strength steel—Four hinges of die steel operating in antirust bushings—Two steel "antirack" pressure cam locking mechanisms, bracing the whole structure and maintaining the door shut tight on continuous ETP type seats. Retaining catches are provided on containers sides. Doorlocks are capable of being sealed, in conformity with T.I.R. requirements.

Finish: Sandblasting. Painting to the user's choice colour. Markings.

Alternative: 40 ft × 8 ft × 8 ft 6 in container, fitted or not with a tunnel (gooseneck opening).

MD 20 P12 8 ft × 8 ft × 20 ft Plywood and plastic Dry Freight

Construction: Plywood panels, overlaid on both sides with glass fibre reinforced polyester (GRP)—Welded high tensile steel frame.

Structure: The frame at each end, top siderails, bottom siderails (incorporating built in facilities for handling by straddle carrier or "Travelift" as well as four forklift tunnels for forklifting the container empty or fully loaded) and floor cross members are formed from press folded steel and are electrically welded.

Corner Fittings: Eight cast steel corner fittings as recommended by ISO to permit top lifting with spreader or hoods, as well as stacking (6 high fully laden).

Floor: Constructed of longitudinal scarfed fir boards assembled with plastic seals to insure watertightness. They are secured to the underframe with self-tapping screws.

Roof, Side and End Walls: Manufactured from GRP-overlaid plywood.

Door and Locks: Double end door, each leaf composed of: A frame of GRP-overlaid plywood—Four hinges of die steel operating in stainless steel bushings—Two steel "antirack" pressure cam locking mechanisms, bracing the whole structure and maintaining the door shut tight cn continuous ETP type seals. Retaining catches are provided on container sides. Doorlocks are capable of being sealed, in conformity with T.I.R. requirements.

Finish: All steel parts are degreased, sandblasted, antirust coated, topcoated to the user's choice colour.

Optional: Plywood floor.

Hard top 30 ft × 8 ft 6 in × 8 ft 6 in tilt container

Structure: End frames, roof bows, floor cross members, are formed from press folded high yield strength steel, top and bottom siderails of weldable mild steel.

Standard ISO corner fittings: 8 cast steel corner fittings, to latest ISO recommendations designed for lifting with spreaders as well as for stacking.

Rear doors and locks: Double doors of castellated press folded high yield strength steel. Each door is fitted with four hinges with stainless steel pins and bushes. Four pressure cam locking mechanisms, bracing the whole structure, maintain the doors shut tight on continuous EPT type seals.

Front fixed end: Made of vertical castellated press folded high yield strength steel.

Roof: Plain high yield strength steel.

Sides: Full side access both sides. Each drop side door consists of two horizontally hinged panels. The bottom panel, of mild steel, is fitted with three hinges which allow the door to be opened and folded down along the bottom siderail. The top panel is of fir board, similar to the removable boards inserted in the corner posts and stanchions above dropside doors. Two bolts lock the door in the closed position. Stanchions are detachable. Polyester side tilt cover, to TIR requirements, is permanently fixed along the top siderail. To facilitate access, the tilt cover can be raised over the roof. TIR wire ropes, rivetted to top siderail, are customs sealed at the centre of bottom rail.

Floor: Plywood floor, secured to the underframe with self-tapping screws.

Cargo Securing Devices: Lashing rings are fitted to the floor. A cargo securing device is provided on each stanchion.

Assembling: All steel parts are electrically welded.

Finish: All steel parts are sandblasted, antirust coated and externally top coated to the user's choice colour. Timber boards remain unpainted.

Markings: Regular inscriptions. Private livery to customer's requirements.

DIMENSIONS AND RATINGS:
External measurements:
   Length 9,125 mm (29 ft 11¼ in)
   Width 2,438 mm (8 ft)
   Height 2,591 mm (8 ft 6 in)
Internal measurements:
   Length 8,937 mm (29 ft 5¼ in)
   Width 2,290 mm 7 ft 6⅛ in)
   Height 2,254 mm (7 ft 4¾ in)
   Cubic capacity 51·6 m³ (1,823 ft³)
Floor:
   Height 278 mm (10 15/16 in)
Rear door opening:
   Width 2,290 mm (7 ft 6⅛ in)
   Height 2,176 mm (7 ft 1¾ in)
Maximum clear side opening:
   Length 8,145 mm (26 ft 8 11/16 in)
   Height 2,184 mm (7 ft 2 in)
Gross weight 249,700 kg (55,115 lb)
Tare: 4,000 kg (8,818 lb)
Payload: 21,000 kg (46,297 lb)

CB3 30 Ac 2 8 ft × 8 ft × 30 ft Bulk Liquid
Construction: Z8.CNDT 18/12 stainless

steel for the tank. Press folded half hard high yield strength steel and mild steel for the framework and tank mountings. All component units are electrically welded.

Tank: 5,700 gallon three-compartment tank, for transport of drinks and chemical products, composed of:—One cylindrical shell and four bulkheads of Z8.CNDT 18/12 stainless steel.—Three 18 in filling manholes located on top centre of each compartment— Three 2¾ in stainless steel discharge pipes terminating at the rear of the tank with a 3 in bronze plug valve complete with cap and chain (MACON screwed end connection).

Ancillary equipmnet: A mild steel ladder provides access to the top of the tank. Three non-skid mild steel walkways admit to the three manholes.

Frame: Tank is housed in a 30 ft × 8 ft × 8 ft framework consisting of:—Bottom siderails, corner posts and forklift tunnels of press folded high yield strength steel. Bottom siderails incorporate built-in facilities for handling by straddle carrier or "Travelift" and are provided with two tunnels for forklifting the container empty or fully loaded—Cross members, top siderails, middle posts and tie-rods of mild steel rectangular box section.—Gusset plates of steel sheet— Eight cast steel corner fittings built to ISO recommendations permitting top lifting with spreaders or hooks, as well as stacking (6 high fully loaded).

Mild steel tank mountings: Two transversal cradles, welded to tank and middle posts. Two longitudinal brackets supported by bottom siderails. Z8.CNDT 18/12 stainless steel parts are used to provide a means of attachment of those supporting members to the tank shell.

Finish: Stainless steel tank remains self-colour. Remaining steel parts are degreased, sandblasted, antirust coated and topcoated to the user's choice colour. Markings.

Other Capacities: Tanks with capacities of 17,000 litres (3,700 gal) and 20,000 litre (4,400 gal) are also available within the 20 ft × 8 ft × 8 ft module.

All steel general purpose freight container 40' × 8' × 8' 6" with side door.

20 ft All Steel container with side door.

Frangeco ISO 30 ft × 8 ft × 8 ft dry freight container manufactured from high tensile steel. Staggered side doors allow goods to be loaded at an angle through both doors together.

FREIGHT BONALLACK

Freight Bonallack Ltd.

Paycocke Road, Basildon, Essex, England
TELEPHONE: Basildon 20481
TELEX: 99401
BRANCH ADDRESSES
Norwich Division-Fifers Lane, Norwich,
   NOR 18A, Norfolk
   Telephone: 4924
Lancing Division-Churchill Industrial Estate,
   Lancing, Sussex
   Telephone: 62481
Wakefield Division-Alverthorpe, Wakefield,
   Yorkshire
   Telephone: 71141
DIRECTORS:
Sir Richard Bonallack (*Chairman*)
D. R. Peters
R. J. Dean
L. F. Anderson
A. L. Coles
W. W. Kee
M. F. Bonallack
D. F. Dartnell
N. Lyons A.C.W.A.
H. Bills

Design Standards

ISO, USASI, Lloyd's Register of Shipping, BS 3851, TIR, RENFE, SNCF.

Containers

Insulated refrigerated and dry freight.

Dry Freight Containers: Aluminium alloy with all-welded end frames of BS 968 steel.

Bonallack "Coldsaver" 30 ft ISO insulated container fitted with I/C engine powered refrigeration unit

Other framing in aluminium alloy with alternative of BS 968 steel. End frames welded, other framing components secured by high tensile bolts or huckbolts. Panels riveted at close pitch. Interior linings in aluminium alloy, resin bonded ply or glass reinforced plastic.

The alloy longitudinals of this Bonallack container are riveted to spurs on the corner castings, all panels and cross-member rivets being easily removable. The extrusions are also designed to protect bolt and rivet heads and panel edges from damage.

Insulated/refrigerated containers

These are built in patented 'Coldsaver' construction, a unique modular method that uses sandwich alloy/insulant framework

Freight Bonallack Container production 1970-1				
		Quantity manufactured		
Type		20 ft	30 ft	40 ft
Dry goods	1970	Under 100	Singles	Singles
	1971	Under 100	Singles	Singles
Insulated	1970	Over 1,200	Under 100	Singles
	1971			
Refrigerated	1970	Over 2,000	Under 100	Singles
	1971			

pillars to provide a complete thermal break between skins. Any internal or external lining material may be used, and insulation is of the thickness necessary to achieve the designed thermal performance. All maximum Heat Gain figures are guaranteed. Fabricated BS 968 steel end frames are used with aluminium alloy or steel longitudinals allowing easy replacement of any panel without disturbing the load or affecting structural rigidity. Any type of refrigeration system can be fitted or the container can be used in conjunction with a ship's central system, or a clip-on unit. A Coldsaver was the first 20 ft insulated ISO container to receive full Lloyd's approval, and Bonallack were the first company to build over 1,000 insulated containers under Lloyd's certification scheme.

The new "Coldsaver" Mk VI container range had just been introduced at the time of going to press.

Licences granted Abroad

Sanchez Quinones, S.A. Madrid, Spain
Container Fabricators, Auckland, New Zealand

Main Users

ACT, P & O, Coast Lines, Shaw Saville, Adams Butter, Scottish Shire Line, Plessey, LEP Transport, Northern Ireland Trailers, Shell International, John Russell (Grangemouth), London Welsh Transport, Norman Gledhill, Road Services (Caledonian), Vauxhall Motors, British Channel Islands Shipping, Commodore Shipping, Interglas SA, Channelflow Freight Services, Blue Star Line.

REPAIR FACILITIES:

Spare parts stockists being appointed in Germany, Belgium, New Zealand, Hong Kong and Singapore.

Heavy duty hinges carry each door of this 20 ft ISO Bonallack 'Coldsaver' and additional resistance to deformation is provided by four sets of locking gear and four vertical anti-racking devices which also protect the locking fastenings.

Bonallack "Coldsaver" 20 ft ISO unit fitted with electric refrigeration equipment

Bonallack "Coldsaver" 40 ft ISO container, refrigerated with diesel/electric unit, container provided with full internal air ducts

The Freight Bonallack range of freight containers

Clear Internal Dimensions

	Length			Width			Height		
	Ft in		mm	Ft in		mm	Ft in		mm
20 × 8 × 8 Insulated	19 ft 0 in		5791	7 ft 4 in		2235	6 ft 10½ in		2095
20 × 8 × 8 ft 6 in Insulated REFRIGERATED	19 ft 0 in		5791	7 ft 4 in		2235	7 ft 4 in		2235
20 × 8 × 8 Electric	17 ft 11 in		5460	7 ft 4 in		2235	6 ft 10½ in		2095
20 × 8 × 8 liq. nit.	17 ft 1 in		5206	7 ft 4 in		2235	6 ft 10½ in		2095
20 × 8 × 8 I.C. engine	17 ft 3 in		5258	7 ft 4 in		2235	6 ft 10½ in		2095
20 × 8 × 8 "clip on" Insulated	18 ft 8 in		5690	7 ft 4 in		2235	6 ft 10½ in		2095
30 × 8 × 8	92 ft 0 in		8839	7 ft 4 in		2235	6 ft 10½ in		2095
40 × 8 × 8 I.C. engine	36 ft 6 in		11125	7 ft 4 in		2235	6 ft 10½ in		2095
40 × 8 × 8 ft 6 in Diesel/electric	36 ft 1 in		10998	7 ft 2 in		2184	7 ft 0 in		2134

Clear Internal Dimensions

	Door Opening						Maximum Heat Gain		Bale capacity		complete	
	Width			Height			50°F	IMT				
	Ft in		mm	Ft in		mm	BTU/ hr/°F	Kcal hr/°C	cu ft	cu m	Tons	kg
20 × 8 × 8 Insulated	7 ft 4 in		2235	6 ft 10 in		2083	45	20·6	958	27·1	2·3	2340
20 × 8 × 8 ft 6 in Insulated REFRIGERATED	7 ft 4 in		2235	7 ft 4 in		2235	48	21·9	1021	28·9	2·5	2540
20 × 8 × 8 Electric	7 ft 4 in		2235	6 ft 10 in		2083	46	21·1	897	25·4	2·7	2740
20 × 8 × 8 liq. nit.	7 ft 4 in		2235	6 ft 10 in		2083	40	20·1	860	24·4	2·8	2845
20 × 8 × 8 I.C. engine	7 ft 4 in		2235	6 ft 10 in		2083	46	21·1	855	24·2	2·9	2945
20 × 8 × 8 "clip on" Insulated	7 ft 4 in		2235	6 ft 10 in		2083	44	20·1	940	26·6	2·3	2340
30 × 8 × 8 40 × 8 × 8 I.C. engine	7 ft 4 in		2235	6 ft 10 in		2083	62	28·4	1462	41·4	3·8	3860
	7 ft 4 in		2235	6 ft 10 in		2083	75	34·4	1840	52·1	5·2	5280
40 × 8 × 8 ft 6 in Diesel/electric	7 ft 2 in		2184	7 ft 0 in		2134	63	28·8	1810	51·3	6·0	6100

FREIGHTER

Freighter Limited,
Warrigal Road,
Moorabbin Victoria 3189
Australia
TELEPHONE: 95-0366
TELEX: Thoroughbuilt
BRANCHES:
Lord St., Botany, N.S.W.
Rocklea, Brisbane, Queensland
Osborne Park, West Australia
Seaton, South Australia
Launceston, Tasmania
Lae, New Guinea
DIRECTORS:
K. O. Humphries (*Chairman*)
J. A. Locarnini (*Managing*)
N. Nixon
Sir Barton Pope
H. W. Shilcock

T. H. King
AFFILIATES ABROAD:
Hino Motors (Japan)
Trailmobile International (U.S.A.)

International Containers Ltd.
Hong Kong (Containers)
IST Consolidated
Steadman Industries (Canada)
Transicold Corporation (U.S.A.)
CONTAINERS:
20 ft × 8 ft × 8 ft. All types and custom-built.
TYPES:
Dry Freight, Insulated, Refrigerated, Containers. Also, collapsible, open-top, flat-trays, container systems, etc.

SPECIFICATIONS:
ISO Standard, Standards Assn., of Australia, Lloyds Register of Shipping.

DESIGN STANDARD:
As for specifications above
CONSTRUCTION—MATERIALS AND METHOD:
Aluminium, corrugated-steel, flat panel steel, glassfibre, plywood. Riveted and/or welded construction
PRINCIPAL OWNERS OF CONTAINERS:
Commonwealth Railways
Western Australian Railways
Trans-Ocean Containers
Associated Steamship Co.
Overseas Containers

PRODUCTION:
In 1969, 1,500 dry goods, 150 insulated, 100 refrigerated and 1,800 special containers all 20 ft long were produced. . Of the special containers 1,700 were of the folding type and 100 open top.

Freighters Ltd. Containers Available Dry Freight or (General Purpose) Containers

Type by ISO Standard Dimensions	Main Materials of Construction	Internal			Internal measurements of End door openings		Approx. heat gain in BTUs/hr or K-cals/hr	Cubic Capacity
		Length	Height	Width	Width	Height		
20 ft × 8 ft × 8 ft	Steel	5,892 232 "	2,210 87"	2,337 92"	2,337 92"	2,134 84"		30·3 1,070
	Aluminium	5,892 232"	2,235 88"	2,337 82"	2,337 92"	2,134 84"		30·6 1,080
	Plywood	5,918 233"	2,235 88"	2,362 93"	2,337 93"	2,134 84"		31·2 1,200
10 ft × 8 ft × 8 ft		2,819 111"	2,210 87"	2,337 92"	2,337 92"	2,134 84"		14·4 510

Refrigerated Containers

Type by ISO Standard Dimensions	Main Materials of Construction	Internal			Internal measurements of End door openings		Approx. heat gain	Cubic Capacity
20 ft × 8 ft × 8 ft	Steel	5,436 214"	2,083 82"	2,235 88"	2,235 88"	2,083 82"	50 Btu/hr	25·3 895
	Aluminium	5,436 214"	2,083 82"	2,235 88"	2,235 88"	2,083 82"		25·3 895

Insulated Containers

Type by ISO Standard Dimensions	Main Materials of Construction	Internal			Internal measurements of End door openings		Approx. heat gain	Cubic Capacity
20 ft × 8 ft × 8 ft	Steel	2,921 223"	2,083 82"	2,235 88"	2,235 88"	2,083 82"	50 btu/hr	26·3 930
	Aluminium	2,921 223"	2,083 82"	2,235 88"	2,235 88"	2,083 82"		

FRIGOR

Frigor Koleanlaeg, Tage W. Nielsen A/S
Holstebrovej, DK-8800 Viborg,
Denmark
TELEPHONE: (06) 623900
TELEGRAMS: Frigor Viborg

TELEX: 6 62 09
DIRECTORS:
T. W. Nielsen
C. Sonderskov
K. J. Jensen

F. S. Hoffmann (*Manager Container Department*)
CONTAINERS:
GRP steel and aluminium insulated containers.

FRUEHAUF DIVISION

Fruehauf Division

Fruehauf Corporation,
10900 Harper Avenue,
Detroit, Michigan 48232
USA
TELEPHONE: (313) 921 2410
TELEX: 23 5256
DIRECTORS:
T. J. Reghantis (*Vice-President and General Manager*)
D. R. McCleary (*Vice-President and Sales Manager*)
C. E. Abbot (*Vice-President Container Sales*)
PRODUCTS:
All lengths and types of tank, dry freight,

refrigerated and open top containers. Containers are made from aluminium, plywood or steel panels. A typical plywood container would have roof, sides and front end panels made from a single sheet of ⅜ in plywood coated with 1/16 in fibre glass reinforced plastics for maximum protection against corrosion. Corner fittings are USASI/ISO standard. Corner posts allow six-high stacking. Cross members are made from 4½ in steel I/beam on 15 in centres. Doors are 1 in solid plymetal with 24 ga. zinc coated steel skin inside. The floor is made from 1⅛ in T & G laminated hardwood.

General specification of Fruehauf 20 ft and 40 ft open top containers are as follows:

CORNER FITTINGS: ISO Standard.
CORNER POSTS: Standard Six-High Stacking on 40 ft containers. Higher rated capacities available.
CROSSMEMBERS: Extruded aluminium 4 in I-Beam on 15 in Centres.
DOORS: 1 in solid plymetal with ·040 ga. pre-painted aluminium exterior skin, patented anti-rax door brackets and lock flange door mounting—reinforced to meet ISO door strength requirements.
FLOOR: 1⅛ in T & G laminated hardwood—three screws (two on 20 ft containers) each board at each crossmember.
FRONT CORNERS: Square inside and outside, 60 in swing radius with 36 in King Pin.

PAINT: Steel parts aluminium. Aluminium extrusions natural—exposed interior parts painted. In all cases where dissimilar metals may contact, they are protected from galvanic corrosion by an electrolytic insulating tape.

PANELS: Choice of ·050 ga. aluminium or white colour pre-painted aluminium panels.

POSTS: 5½ in wide extruded aluminium body posts on 24 in centres.

REAR HEADER: Swinging removable type.

SPREADER BARS: On 36 in centres.

TARP: 20 oz. vinyl covered nylon. Light green colour both sides—12 in minimum overlap on all edges, constructed per T.I.R. requirements. Equipped with ⅛ in × 2 in nylon web strap with corrosion resistant hardware to maintain tension on web strap, prevents tarp from sagging between bows.

TARP BOWS: ⅞ in dia steel welded to each spreader bar.

TARP LOOPS: Steel—spaced at 7½ in centres—welded to steel top rail and rear doors.

TIE DOWN ROPE: Single piece plastic covered with steel wire core in centre—rope ends meet at rear doors and fitted with metal end pieces with hollow rivets to secure customs seal.

UPPER RAILS: Recessed to provide tarp protection and additional side wall strength.

Fruehauf tank containers are capable of handling a wide variety of chemicals including alcohol at low pressure with proper venting as well as dry bulk products including plastic pellets. The inner vessel is available in stainless steel, carbon steel or aluminium. Other optional features include a variety of vessels and linings to suit specialised hauling needs. Small forklift pockets for empty handling are also available. Standard features are a patented vent assuring an unusually high degree of product retention and a special butterfly valve actuator which serves both as an emergency valve and a standard discharge valve. These containers also feature corner casting restraint for lashing, sling lift capabilities, dynamic restraint for rail transport, coupling for operation as

20 ft Fruehauf Division dry freight pre-painted aluminium containers being unloaded in New York

40 ft over the road or shipboard units, offset lower rail to accomodate straddle lift carriers. The frame permits the container to be tipped to unload dry flowable products.

Fruehauf reefer containers use corrosion resistant pre-painted aluminium panels as standard for outer shell material. Foamed in place sanifoam insulation completely fills all wall, ceiling and floor cavities. Floors are of extruded aluminium with welded seams. A one piece aluminium roof sheet is bonded to the roof bows. Corner posts and latching hardware are specially designed to prevent racking out of the doors.

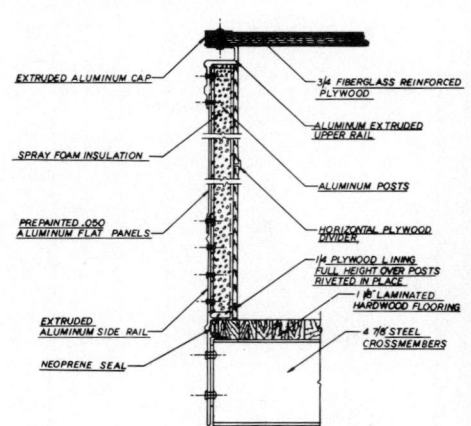

How Fruehauf reefer containers are insulated

FRUEHAUF FRANCE

Fruehauf France
2 Avenue de L'Aunette
91 Ris-Orangis (Essonne)
France
TELEPHONE: 906.12.94
TELEGRAMS: Ris-Orangis Telex Fruefrance
TELEX: Fruehauf Risor 69967

DIRECTORS:
Raoul Massardy (*Chairman and Managing Director:*
François Godbille (*Joint Managing Director*)
François Godbille (*Assistant Managing Director*)
François Gressin (*General Secretary responsible for Containerisation*)
Bruno Chabert (*Container Department*)
Louis Parmentier
Patrick Massardy
Pierre Leboucher
Pierre Douilhet
Jean Gaschard
Marc Van Laer

PRODUCTION:
Total capacity for between 8,000-10,000 containers/year including at least 100 40 ft units per month.

PRINCIPAL USERS:
A.C.L., Fabre Line, SNCF, Eurocontainer, Sea Land Service Inc., Seatrain, United States Lines, East Asiatic Company, Messageries Maritimes, Eurotainer, Nippon Yusen Kaisha Line.

REPAIR SERVICES:
Survilliers, Ris Orangis, Auxerre, Lyon,

Fruehauf France 40 ft × 8 ft × 8 ft 6 in CONTAINER with all steel frame and prepainted and riveted aluminium alloy panels. Front gooseneck tunnel. Anti-rack device ISO gross weight: 30.480 metric tons—tare: 3.429 metric tons. Capacity: 68 cubic metres. The Fruehauf "Marsquin" straight model for transport of all containers: 40' — 30' — 2 × 20' —or one fully loaded 20'. Gross weight: 35/38 metric tons—Tare 4.500 metric tons. The container can also be transported by a "Squale" gooseneck model chassis allowing decreased overall height.
The container is being loaded in the spacious storing area of the Auxerre Fruehauf France factory which manufactures 400 40' and 200 20' containers per month, or their equivalant

Lille, Nancy, Bordeaux, Marseille, Coger Le Havre, Sud Container Marseille, Brostroms Göthenburg (Sweden).

CONTAINERS:
Range consists of steel, aluminium alloy and glass reinforced plastic plywood units as well as tank containers, refrigerated units and flat and tilt types.

The 40 ft × 8 ft × 8 ft 6 in container with ISO tunnel is rapidly increasing its share of the market. The present most used model comprises a steel frame with smooth outside panel cladding of prepainted aluminium alloy.

The 20 ft × 8 ft × 8 ft container comes in three designs: steel, aluminium alloy or glass reinforced plastic plywood the frame being of steel in every case. Although not a recognised ISO standard the 8 ft 6 in high 20 ft container is used by several shipping companies.

Recent additions to the Fruehauf France range are:

A 40 ft × 8 ft × 8 ft 6 in open top container of prepainted and riveted steel with tarpaulin (tilt sheet). This is now in mass production.

A 40 ft × 8 ft × 8 ft 6 in refrigerated container with polyurethane insulation and a metric heat co-efficient of K = 0·22.

A 20 ft × 8 ft × 8 ft 6 in container with completely opening sides recommended for industrial use.

STANDARD FRUEHAUF FRANCE CONTAINERS:

Dry freight closed top
Pre-painted and riveted steel
Aluminium alloy
plain or pre-painted
GRP Plywood
20 ft × 8 ft × 8 ft
20 ft × 8 ft × 8 ft 6 in
40 ft × 8 ft × 8 ft
40 ft × 8 ft × 8 ft 6 in
with tunnel
VARIANTS:
Side door-Code . . -02
2 or 4 fork lift pockets (on 20 ft)
Aluminium cross members
Light insulation
40 ft × 8 ft × 8 ft 6 in without tunnel
Code 42·00
Special non ISO tunnels

Open top with removable tarpaulin and removable rear header
Pre-painted and riveted steel
Aluminium alloy
plain or pre-painted
20 ft × 8 ft × 8 ft
20 ft × 8 ft × 8 ft 6 in
40 ft × 8 ft × 8 ft
40 ft × 8 ft × 8 ft 6 in
with tunnel
VARIANTS:
2 or 4 fork-lift pockets (on 20 ft)
40 ft × 8 ft × 8 ft 6 in
without tunnel
or with non ISO tunnel

Dry freight closed top
Pre-painted and riveted steel
Aluminium alloy
GRP Plywood
10 ft × 8 ft × 8 ft
30 ft × 8 ft × 8 ft
35 ft × 8 ft × 8 ft 6 in
with tunnel
VARIANTS:
2 fork-lift pockets (on 10 ft)
Side door on (30 ft)-Code . . -02
Outside posts (on 35 ft aluminium)
Completely opening side
(on 30 ft)-Code . . -65
also possible on 20 ft

Open top with tarpaulins and removable rear header
Pre-painted and riveted steel
Aluminium Alloy
30 ft × 8 ft × 8 ft
35 ft × 8 ft × 8 ft 6 in

A Freuhauf France Container being removed from the storing area of the Auxerre factory

with tunnel
40 ft × 8 ft × 8 ft
40 ft × 8 ft × 8 ft 6 in
with tunnel
20 ft × 8 ft × 4 ft
20 ft × 8 ft × 4 ft 3 in
VARIANTS:
2 or 4 fork-lift pockets (on 20 ft)
Outside posts (on 35 ft)
Half height containers
with fixed header
and without rear door
(high density loads)
Code . . -50

Insulated and refrigerated 'reefer' type containers
Construction of refrigerated container:
—Outside skin:
    Glass reinforced plastic
—Lining: Glass reinforced
    plastic or stainless steel
—Insulation: Foamed polyurethane
Cooling of refrigerated container:
—by electro-mechanical unit
—by cryogenic liquid
10 ft × 8 ft × 8 ft
20 ft × 8 ft × 8 ft
20 ft × 8 ft × 8 ft 6 in
30 ft × 8 ft × 8 ft
30 ft × 8 ft × 8 ft 6 in
40 ft × 8 ft × 8 ft
40 ft × 8 ft × 8 ft 6 in
VARIANTS:
Meat bars for hooks
2 or 4 fork-lift pocket (on 10 ft - 20 ft)
Heated container-Code . . -24

Tank container
Stainless steel
SHAPE:
—Cylindrical
—Elliptical
Most usual capacities
—20 ft × 8 ft × 8 ft   18,000 l
—20 ft × 8 ft × 4 ft   9,000 l
20 ft × 8 ft × 8 ft
20 ft × 8 ft × 4 ft
20 ft × 8 ft × 4 ft 4 in
30 ft × 8 ft × 8 ft
40 ft × 8 ft × 8 ft

VARIANTS:
Insulation
Several compartments
For non hazardous edible products
For hazardous chemical products
Different stainless steel grades

Flat and tilt type platforms
Steel
20 ft × 8 ft × 8 ft   20·60
30 ft × 8 ft × 8 ft   30·60
VARIANTS OF FLAT/TILT TYPE BODYWORKS:
Side slats
Hinged sidewalls and TIR
Tilt Sheet
Fork-lift pockets (on 20 ft)

Bulk containers gravity discharge
Steel
Stainless Steel
20 ft × 8 ft × 8 ft   20·80
30 ft × 8 ft × 8 ft   30·80
40 ft × 8 ft × 8 ft   40·80

Options on Various Models
Air vents in wall panels to reduce inside condensation; Anti-rax device for test at 15·7 tons, i.e. higher than ISO recommendations (patented); Full length upper or lower lashing bars allowing tie down at all points; Recessed lashings rings welded to rear corner posts; Lashing rings spaced over full length and fixed to lower rails; Large size lashing rings recessed into the floor and fixed to the crossmembers for heavy unit loads; Wood treatment to Australian/New Zealand, Commonwealth Health Department requirements; Marine plywood lining, full height or half height (except · on GRP/plywood containers); Couplable corner fittings on 10 ft and 20 ft containers, either of ISO model (Fruehauf patent) or of special large size type; Frames of "muffler grade" stainless steel; Loading or lashing equipment: e.g. Joloda; or Aeroquip or similar types; Straddle carrier lift provision on lower rails; Intermediate road frame equipment for removable running gears (on 20 ft and 40 ft).

GRAAF

Niedersachische Waggonfabrik
Joseph Graaff G.m.b.H., Elze (Han.)
West Germany
TELEPHONE: (05124)-2041
TELEX:0927168
LICENSEES ABROAD:
Thomas McArdle Ltd.,
Dundalk, Ireland
Juan Tiktin, Marquinaria Para Obras,
Alcala 76, Madrid 9 Spain

CONTAINERS:
Dry cargo, insulated, refrigerated, top loading and tank containers to ISO and other standards, also cargo flats. Specially designed containers and pallets to individual requirements.

DESIGN STANDARDS:
ISO, ASA and BS 3951 MH 51

CONSTRUCTION, MATERIALS and METHOD:
All steel, all welded. GRP plastic coated plywood in steel frame. Tank containers in chromium-nickel-steel or mild steel.

PRINCIPAL OWNERS:
Hapag Lloyd Container Linie, Hamburg 1, Ballindam 25
Contrans Gesellschaft für Ubersee-Behältredienst mbH, Hamburg 13, Rothenbaumchaussee 38.

PRINCIPAL OWNERS:
Hapag-Lloyd Container Lines who have recently placed a further order for 3,600 40 ft × 8 ft × 8 ft 6 in containers with the GRP-plywood panels and steel frames.

One of the order for 1,200 20 ft containers placed with Graaff by Hapag Lloyd. The containers have GRP plywood panels and steel frames.

DIMENSIONS:

External measurements Length—width—height	40 ft × 8 ft × 8 ft		40 ft × 8 ft × 8 ft 6 in		20 ft × 8 ft × 8 ft		20 ft × 8 ft × 8 ft 6 in	
Max Gross-Weight	30,480 kg	67,200 lb	30,480 kg	67,200 lb	20,320 kg	44,800 lb	20,320 kg	44,800 lb
Tare weight app.	3,300 kg	7,257 lb	3,500 kg	7,710 lb	1,900 kg	4,190 lb	1,980 kg	4,365 lb
Payload	27,180 kg	59,925 lb	26,980 kg	59,490 lb	18,420 kg	40,610 lb	18,340 kg	40,435 lb
Cubic capacity app.	64·7 m³	2·286 cu ft	68·8 m³	2·530 cu ft	31·8 m³	1·123 cu ft	33·8 m³	1·194 cu ft
Overall sizes								
Length	12,190 mm	40 ft	12,190 mm	40 ft	6,055 mm	19 ft 10½ in	6,055 mm	19 ft 10½ in
Width	2,435 mm	8 ft	2,435 mm	8 ft	2,435 mm	8 ft	2,435 mm	8 ft
Height	2,435 mm	8 ft	2,587 mm	8 ft 6 in	2,435 mm	8 ft	2,578 mm	8 ft 6 in
Inside dimensions								
Length	12,069 mm	39 ft 7$\frac{5}{32}$ in	12,069 mm	39 ft 7$\frac{5}{32}$ in	5,935 mm	19 ft 5$\frac{43}{64}$ in	5,935 mm	19 ft 5$\frac{43}{64}$ in
Width	2,373 mm	7 ft 9$\frac{7}{16}$ in	2,373 mm	7 ft 9$\frac{7}{16}$ in	2,373 mm	7 ft 9$\frac{7}{16}$ in	2,373 mm	7 ft 9$\frac{7}{16}$ in
Height	2,259 mm	7 ft 4$\frac{15}{16}$ in	2,405 mm	7 ft 10$\frac{11}{16}$ in	2,295 mm	7 ft 4$\frac{15}{16}$ in	2,405 mm	7 ft 10$\frac{11}{16}$ in
Door opening								
Width	2,335 mm	7 ft 8 in	2,335 mm	7 ft 8 in	2,335 mm	7 ft 8 in	2,335 mm	7 ft 8 in
Height	2,145 mm	7 ft 0$\frac{7}{16}$in	2,292 mm	7 ft 6¼ in	2,145 mm	7 ft 0$\frac{7}{16}$ in	2,292 mm	7 ft 6¼ in

GRANGES ESSEM

Granges Essem
S-730 50 Skultuna
Sweden
GENERAL SALES AGENT:
Hans H. Grosse & Co.
2000 Hamburg 11
Katharinenstrasse 33
Germany (Federal Republic)
TELEPHONE: 33 60 96
TELEX: 211 968 ISCOD
CONTAINERS:
Aluminium combined bulk cargo and dry freight container.
Aluminium bulk container.

Combined bulk and dry freight containers with bearing surfaces for straddle carriers
Corner Fittings:
Made of aluminium extrusions welded together according to a patented procedure and meeting the ISO requirements for 40 ft containers.
Tested by Bureau Veritas, Det Norske Veritas, and Albury Testing Laboratories.
Inside:
Vertical corners rounded. Sharp corners at roof and floor. Baffle plates guiding the bulk material towards the outlet.
Floor:
Impregnated birch plywood, the upper surface covered with a hard layer of glass fibre polyester lamination. The floor is supported by aluminium extrusions attached underneath. The floor is divided into easily replaceable parts. All joints are protected by a sealing compound. The floor is designed in accordance with TIR-requirements.
Side Walls:
Aluminium plate stiffened by vertical extrusions which are spot welded to the sides. One of the side walls is fitted with doors.
End Walls:
Aliminium plate stiffened by horizontal extrusions spot-welded to the walls. One end is provided with a discharge gate, the lower edge of which is level with the inside floor.

Roof:
Aliminium plate stiffened with extrusions which are welded on continuously. The roof is provided with one or two manholes, or one hatch with two separate hatch covers, and one control inlet.
Ventilation:
Holes for ventilation near roof corner fittings can be provided.
Doors:
The doors are made of 26 mm waterproof plywood with fibre glass reinforcements on both sides, fitted with extruded aluminium profiles. Each door is attached to the door posts by four hinges. The doors can be opened fully (180 degrees) and locked in open position. Each door is provided with two heavy-duty locking bars which can bear loads horizontally as well as vertically. Locking bars are provided for customs sealing in accordance with TIR-requirements.
Testing:
    (a) Density test of the container.
    (b) Strength tests according to Lloyd's and ISO requirements.

Type B/C 20 ft × 8 ft × 8 ft M1
Gross weight: 20,320 kg (44,800 lbs)
Tare weight: 1,650 kg (3,640 lb)
Payload: 18,670 kg (41,160 lb)
Overall length: 6,058 mm (20 ft)
Overall height: 2,438 mm (8 ft)
Overall width: 2,438 mm (8 ft)
Cubic capacity: 27·5 m³ (27·5 m³)

Type B/C 30 ft × 8 ft × 8 ft M1
Gross weight: 25,400 kg (56,000 lb)
Tare weight: 2,000 kg (4,410 lb)
Payload: 23,400 kg (51,590 lb)
Overall length: 9,125 mm (30 ft)
Overall height: 2,438 mm (8 ft)
Overall width: 2,438 mm (8 ft)
Cubic capacity: 41·7 m³ (41·7 m³)

Bulk Container
Corner Fittings:
Made of aluminium extrusions welded together according to a patented procedure

and meeting the ISO requirements for 40 ft containers.
Tested by Bureau Veritas, Det Norske Veritas, and Albury Testing Laboratories.
Inside:
Completely smooth surfaces with rounded corners. Baffle plates guiding the bulk material towards the outlet.
Floor:
Aluminium plate supported by extrusions which are welded on.
Side Walls:
Aluminium plate stiffened by vertical extrusions spot-welded to the sides.
End Walls:
Aluminium plate stiffened by horizontal extrusions spot-welded to the walls. One end is provided with a discharge gate, the lower edge being level with the inside floor.
Roof:
Aluminium plate stiffened with extrusions which are welded on continuously. The roof is provided with one or two manholes and one control inlet.
Ventilation:
Holes for ventilation near roof corner fittings can be provided.
Testing:
Density test of the container. Strength tests according to Lloyd's and ISO requirements

Type B 20 ft × 8 ft × 8 ft M1
Gross weight: 20,320 kg (44,800 lb)
Tare weight: 1,240 kg (2,730 lb)
Payload: 19,080 kg (42,007 lb)
Overall length: 6,058 mm (20 ft)
Overall height: 2,438 mm (8 ft or 8 ft 6 in)
Overall width: 2,438 mm (8 ft)
Cubic capacity: 30 m³ (30 m³)
Gross weight: 25,400 kg (56,000 lb)
Tare weight: 1,510 kg (3,330 lb)
Payload: 23,890 kg (52,670 lb)
Overall length: 9,125 mm (30 ft)
Overall height: 2,438 mm (8 ft or 8 ft 6 in)
Overall width: 2,438 mm (8 ft)
Cubic capacity: 45 m³ (45 m³)

GREAT DANE

Great Dane Trailers, Inc.
(Subsidiary of United States Freight Co.
New York)
(*See also entry in leasing Section*)
HEAD OFFICE:
PO Box 67,
Savannah,
Ga, 31402
USA.
TELEPHONE: (912) 232-4471
SALES OFFICES:
Savannah, Atlanta, Jacksonville, Fla., Charlotte, NC., Miami Fla., Birmingham, Ala.,
Knoxville, Tenn.; Richmond, Va.
DIRECTORS:
Christopher F. Hammond (*Director*)
Brooke Reeve, Jr. (*Executive Vice President*)
G. R. Moir
F. Melius
Henry T. Skipper (*Vice President Sales*)
Kit Hammond (*Manager, Railroad and Marine Sales*)
UK BRANCH:
Adamson & Hatchett, Dukinfield, England
PATENT LICENCES:
Licences have been granted by the company for overseas manufacture to:
Adamson & Hatchett, Dukinfield,
England.
Van Hool et Fils, Belgium.
SPECIFICATIONS:
ASA and ISO
TYPES:
Dry cargo and refrigerated containers.
Dry freight trailers, refrigerated trailers,
piggy back trailers
CONSTRUCTION:
Aluminium, stainless steel, steel
PRINCIPAL OWNERS OF CONTAINERS:
United States Lines,
Grace Lines
K-Line
PRODUCTION:
Two hundred 40 ft dry freight and fifty
40 ft refrigerated in 1970.
CONTAINERS:
From 8 ft × 8 ft × 10 ft to 8ft 6 in × 8 ft ×
40 ft
all ASA and ISO sizes

**Great Dane Model 440. Dry Cargo Container.
40 ft**
External dimensions:
Length 12,192 mm (40 ft 0 in)
Width 2,438 mm (8 ft 0 in)
Height 2,438 mm (8 ft 0 in)
Internal dimensions:
Length 12,039 mm (39 ft 6 in)
Width 2,336 mm (7 ft 8 in)
At 8 ft 6 in overall height the internal
heights become:

	Internal height	Cubic capacity
40 ft	2·41 m	68·10 m³
	7 ft 11 in	2,406 ft³
20 ft	2·41 m	33·45 m³
	7 ft 11 in	1,181 ft³

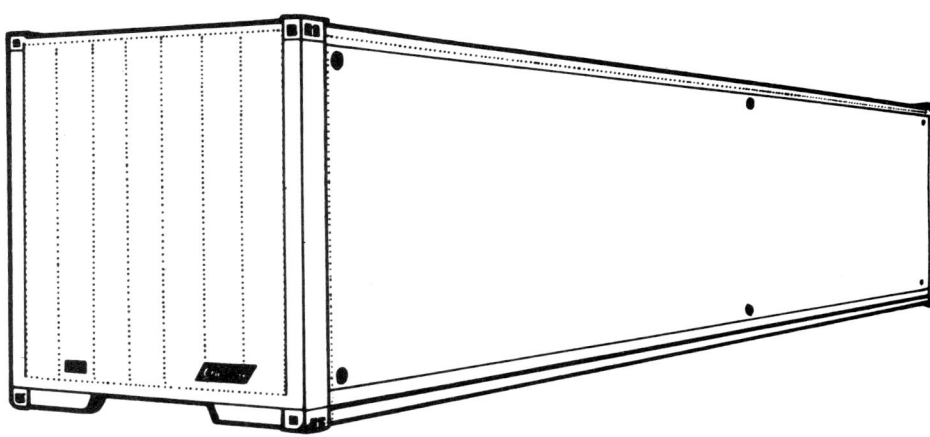

Great Dane cargo container Model 440

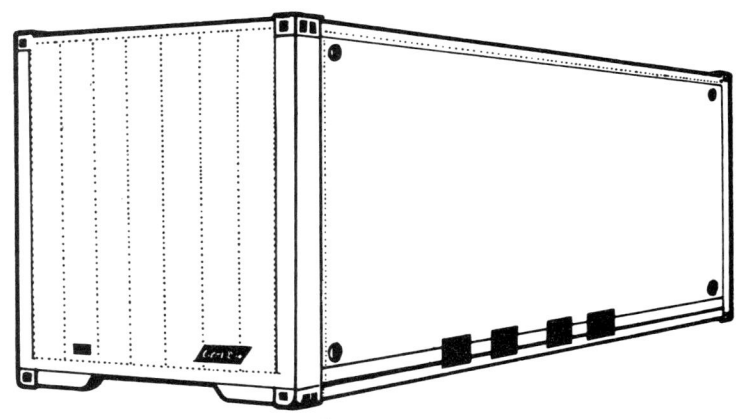

Great Dane cargo container Model 420

Internal Dimensions of Great Dane container range:

ISO	Length	Width	Height	Cubic Capacity
Dry Freight	12·04 m	2·34 m	2·26 m	63·72 m³
40 ft	39 ft 6 in	7 ft 8 in	7 ft 5 in	2,254 ft³
Dry Freight	5·92 m	2·34 m	2·26 m	31·43 m³
20 ft	19 ft 5 in	7 ft 8 in	7 ft 5 in	1,107 ft³

No internal dimensions are available for insulated and refrigerated containers as these vary according to the thickness of insulation and typical examples are not stated. The insulating medium is normally polyurethane.

TESTING FACILITY:
Great Dane tests container construction methods with a specially built testing facility. All tests meet or exceed ASA-ISO requirements for strength and design.

40 ft refrigerated container of aluminium alloy construction by Great Dane. Model 440Z—I

Stacking Tests: A hydraulic press loads the corner posts and corner castings to in excess of the weight the container will receive. Deflection of the posts is measured.

Top and Bottom Lifting Tests: Overloaded containers are suspended for five minutes from the top corner castings to simulate actual lift conditions. They are lifted, also, by the bottom corner castings. Deflection of the bottom rails is measured.

Restraint Test: The container is anchored at one end and pulled or compressed hydraulically from the other end. Both the welding of the castings and the bottom rails are checked in this manner.

Floor Load Testing: A heavily loaded fork truck is driven across the unsupported floor, side to side and front to back, to test floor construction strength.

Tests are also carried out on side walls, end walls, weather proofness, roof strength and in the case of refrigerated containers—air distribution, air-leakage, and cooling and heat loss tests.

Great Dane 40 ft stainless steel refrigerated container. Model 940Z—I.

HANSA

Hansa Waggonbau GmbH
28 Bremen 11
Pfalzburger Strasse 251,
Postfach 110 109
TELEPHONE: 45 40 11
TELEX: 0244423
DIRECTORS:
Hans Peter -Weinhardt
PRODUCTION:
2,000 20 ft containers in 1970. In 1971 3,000 20 ft units and 1,280 40 ft units plus 200 40 ft open top units.
MAIN USERS:
Hapag Lloyd
Integrated Container Services
Hamburg Südamerikanische Dampfschiff-fahrts-Gesellschaft (HSDG)
Johnson Line
CONTAINERS:
Dry freight steel and steel and plywood ISO containers.

All steel dry freight 40 ft × 8 ft × 8 ft 6 in
Type 1 A ISO
Inside length 12,010 mm (39 ft 5 in)
Inside width 2,337 mm (7 ft 8 in)
Inside height 2,399 mm (7 ft 10½ in)
Door width 2,335 mm (7 ft 8 in)
Door height 2,290 mm (7 ft 6 in)
Volume 67·3 m³ (2,483 ft³)
This container is also available with side doors.

Open-top All Steel 40 ft × 8 ft × 8 ft 6 in
Type 1 A ISO
Inside length 12,010 mm (39 ft 5 in)
Inside width 2,337 mm (7 ft 8 in)
Inside height 2,350 mm (7 ft 8½ in)
Door width 2,335 mm (7 ft 8 in)
Door height 2,290 mm (7 ft 6 in)
Volume 65 m³ (2,295 ft³)

Steel and Plywood Container 20 ft × 8 ft × 8 ft
Type 1 C ISO
Inside length 5,937 mm (19 ft 5¾ in)
Inside width 2,373 mm (7 ft 9⅖ in)
Inside height 2,259 mm (7 ft 4¾ in)
Door height 2,145 mm (7 ft 0½ in)
Door width 2,335 mm (7 ft 8 in)
Volume 31·8 m³ (468 ft³)

Steel and Plywood 20 ft × 8 ft × 8 ft 6 in
Type 1 C ISO
Inside length 5,937 mm (19 ft 5¾ in)
Inside width 2,373 mm (7 ft 9⅖ in)
Inside height 2,410 mm (7 ft 11 in)
Door height 2,290 mm (7 ft 6 in)
Door width 2,335 mm (7 ft 8 in)
Volume 33·9 m³ (475 ft³)

HOLVRIEKA

Verenigde Holvrieka Bedrijren N.W.
Europalaan 97, Utrecht, Netherlands
TELEPHONE: 030-882811
TELEX: 47291 holvr nl

DIRECTORS:
W. de Waard

CONTAINERS:
Stainless steel tank containers including flat bed tank containers, steel and aluminium tank containers, insulated and electrically heated units.
PRODUCTION:
In 1970 5 20 ft and 10 30 ft tank containers were produced. At the time of going to press, 100 20 ft and 5 30 ft units had been manufactured.
PRINCIPLE OWNERS:
Rijba-France, Le Havre, France; G. S. v. d. I Jssel, Netherlands; van Rulten's Transport-en, Netherlands.

Holvrieka 30 ft tank container

HUNGARIAN SHIPYARDS

Hungarian Shipyards and Crane Factory,
Budapest, XIII, Váci út 202
LETTERS:
Budapest 62. POB 280
TELEPHONE: 200–800
TELEX: 3600
CABLE: Ship and crane, Budapest
DIRECTORS:
László Maracskó (*General Director*)
András Hanusz (*General Director*)
Dr. Lászlo Gardos (*Deputy Commercial Director*)

CONTAINERS:
This organisation in 1968 started to manufacture transcontainers, on licence from Strick, USA. It also produces a wide range of all steel and steel and aluminium containers, of the closed and open top variety and stainless steel tank container.

DESIGN STANDARD:
ISO, TIR, Federal German Railway acceptance standards.

Type S 20 S
20 ft Steel container, couplable.
Built under licence from Strick.
Gross weight: 20,000 kg (44,000 lb)
Tare weight approx.: 2,160 kg (4,752 lb)
Payload: 17,840 kg (39,248 lb)
Cubic capacity: 30 m^3 (1,060 cu ft)
INTERNAL DIMENSIONS:
Length: 5,900 mm (19 ft 4$\frac{1}{3}$ in)
Width: 2,325 mm (7 ft 8 in)
Height: 2,175 mm (7 ft 1 in)

Door Opening:
Inside width: 2,255 mm (7 ft 4$\frac{25}{32}$ in)
Inside Height: 2,130 mm (6 ft 11$\frac{7}{8}$ in).

METHODS AND MATERIALS:
Floor Assembly:
Electrically welded, light steel sections. Wooden floor with tongue-and-groove joints, impregnated with anti-fouling preservative. Made splash-proof by securing with countersunk screws.
Corner Posts:
Steel sections.
Walls:
Vertically profiled steel sheets of 1·5 mm thickness with sliding bars and lashing bars welded on inside.
Roof:
Light steel sections with sheet-metal covering.
Corner Fittings:
Made of high quality steel in form of couplable corner fittings according to Strick Licence. Two 20 ft containers can be coupled to make up a 40 footer.
Doors:
Double doors with profiled rubber seal and double cam-type locking bars. Each door can be opened to 270 degrees and can be locked in that position. When doors are open almost the whole container cross-section is clear for loading and unloading. Sheet-metal clad steel frames impart the necessary rigidity to the doors. Each door is supported by four steel hinges provided with stainless steel hinge pins which can be lubricated.
Fork Lifter and Straddle-Carrier Transport:
Through-type fork lift pockets arranged transverse to longitudinal axis for fork lifters and special hoisting gear. Longitudinal floor beams designed for straddle carrier transport.
Stacking capability, six high.

Type S 20 A
20 ft container of composite steel and aluminium construction, couplable, built under licence for Strick.
Gross Weight: 20·000 kg (44,000 lbs)
Tare Weight approx. 1·860 kg (4,092 lbs)
Payload: 18·140 kg (39,908 lbs)
Cubic capacity: 30 m^3 (1,060 cu ft)
INTERNAL DIMENSIONS:
Length: 5,899 mm(19 ft 4 $\frac{5}{16}$ in)
Width: 2,315 mm (7 ft 7$\frac{1}{8}$ in)
Height: 2,185 mm (7 ft 2 in)
DOOR OPENING:
Inside Width 2,255 mm (7 ft 4$\frac{3}{4}$ in)
Inside Height 2,130 mm 6 ft 11$\frac{7}{8}$ in)
METHODS AND MATERIALS:
Frame and Floor Assembly:
Electrically welded, high tensile steel. Wooden floor with tongue-and-groove joints, impregnated with anti-fouling preservative. Made splash-proof by securing with countersunk screws.
Walls:
Sea water-resistant aluminium strengthened by mounted hat sections. Surfaces touching steel frame insulated by polyethylene foil. Full-height, plywood lining inside. Two steel panels running longitudinally, each with rope rings.

Roof:
Roof sheet bonded with roof bows by permanently flexible sealing compound. Extra sealing along longitudinal roof beams by hook-shaped sealing strips.
Corner Fittings:
High quality, cast steel welded into frame. Made in form of couplable corner fittings according to Strick Licence. Two 20 ft containers can be coupled to make up a 40 footer.

Doors:
Double doors with rubber sealing strips and 2 double cam-type locking bars. Each door can be opened to 270 degrees and can be locked in that position. When doors are open almost the whole container cross-section is clear for loading and unloading. Doors are supported by 4 steel hinges provided with stainless steel hinge pins which can be lubricated. The doors are of plymetal construction with Multiplex panels enclosed by aluminium sections.
Fork Lifter and Straddle Carrier Transport:
Through-type fork lift pockets arranged transverse to longitudinal axis for fork lifters and special hoisting gear. Suitable for straddle lifting through appropriate construction of longitudinal floor beams.
Stacking Capability six high (uncoupled).
Sealing and Plain Finish:
Extra sealing of joints between steel and aluminium by permanently flexible sealing compound. All steel parts are sand blasted and coated with zinc chromate primer. Top coating upon request of customer.

Two-partition tank container made of stainless steel, type TE-20.02
External dimensions:
Length 6,055 mm (19 ft 10$\frac{3}{8}$ in)
Width 2,435 mm (7 ft 11$\frac{49}{64}$ in)
Height 2,435 mm (7 ft 11$\frac{49}{64}$ in)
Tank dimensions:
Length 5,650 mm (19 ft 8$\frac{7}{16}$ in)
Dia. 2,200 mm (7 ft 2$\frac{5}{32}$ in)
Capacity 2 × 10,000 litres (2 × 2,200 gal)
Dia of manholes 450 mm (17$\frac{23}{32}$ in)
Dia. of discharge stub 80 mm (3$\frac{9}{64}$ in)
Weights:
Empty weight of container 3,400 kg (7,500 lb)
Total gross weight 20,000 kg (44,100 lb)
Payload 16,600 kg (36,600 lb)

One-compartment tank container made of stainless steel, type TE-20.01
External dimensions:
Length 6,055 mm (19 ft 10$\frac{3}{8}$ in)

On exhibition and photographed stacked 5-high these 20 ft all-steel containers were built by the Hungarian Shipyard.

Width 2,435 mm (7 ft 11$\frac{7}{8}$ in)
Height 2,435 mm (7 ft 11$\frac{7}{8}$ in)
Tank dimensions:
Length 5,600 mm (18 ft 4$\frac{15}{32}$ in)
Dia. 2,200 mm (7 ft 2$\frac{5}{32}$ in)
Capacity 20,000 litres (4,399·5 gal)
Dia. of manhole 450 mm (17$\frac{23}{32}$ in)
Dia. of discharge stub 80 mm (3$\frac{9}{64}$ in)
Weights:
Empty weight of container 3,000 kg (6,614 lb)
Total gross weight 20,000 kg (44,100 lb)
Payload 17,000 kg (37,479 lb)

20 ft steel container type C.20J. with enlarged inside dimensions
Principal dimensions:
The principal dimensions and load capacity of the container complies with the internationally approved ISO-recommendations and the rules of the American Bureau of Shipping.
External dimensions:
Full length 6,055 mm (19 ft 10$\frac{3}{8}$ in)
Full breadth 2,435 mm (7 ft 11$\frac{7}{8}$ in)
Full height 2,435 mm (7 ft 11$\frac{7}{8}$ in)
Internal dimensions:
Length 5,900 mm (19 ft 4$\frac{13}{32}$ in)
Breadth 2,330 mm (7 ft 7$\frac{47}{64}$ in)
Height 2,240 mm (7 ft 4$\frac{3}{16}$ in)
Dimensions of door-way:
Breadth 2,290 mm (7 ft 6$\frac{5}{32}$ in)
Height 2,130 mm (6 ft 11$\frac{53}{64}$ in)
Weight:
Total weight with cargo 20,320 kg (44,798 lb)
Empty weight of container 2,305 kg (5,082 lb)
Payload 18,015 kg (39,716 lb)
Internal working volume 30·8 m^3 (1,094·7 ft^3)

20 ft steel container, type S20S SIS
External dimensions:
Overall length 6,055 mm (19 ft 10$\frac{3}{8}$ in)
Overall width 2,435 mm (7 ft 11$\frac{7}{8}$ in)
Full height 2,435 mm (7 ft 11$\frac{7}{8}$ in)
Internal dimensions:
Inside length 5,900 mm (19 ft 4$\frac{13}{32}$ in)
Inside width 2,325 mm (7 ft 7$\frac{17}{32}$ in)
Inside height 2,175 mm (7 ft 1$\frac{5}{8}$ in)
Dimensions of the Door opening:
Inside width 2,225 mm (7 ft 3$\frac{19}{32}$ in)
Inside height 2,130 mm (6 ft 11$\frac{55}{64}$ in)
Weight:
Total weight with load 20,000 kg (44,092 lb)
Empty weight of container 2,160 kg (4,762 lb)

Payload 17,840 kg (39,330 lb)

20 ft Steel container, type S.20.B with enlarged interior dimensions

Main dimensions:

The main dimensions of the container and carrying capacity are corresponding to the ISO recommendations and to DIN 1519 1c standard.

External dimensions:
- Length overall 6,055 mm (19 ft $10\frac{3}{8}$ in)
- Breadth overall 2,435 mm (7 ft $11\frac{7}{8}$ in)
- Height overall 2,435 mm (7 ft $11\frac{7}{8}$ in)

Interior dimensions:
- Length 5,905 mm (19 ft $4\frac{15}{32}$ in)
- Breadth 2,340 mm (7 ft $8\frac{1}{8}$ in)
- Height 2,246 mm (7 ft $4\frac{27}{64}$ in)

Dimensions of the door-clearance:
- Breadth 2,340 mm (7 ft $8\frac{1}{8}$ in)
- Height 2,134 mm (7 ft $0\frac{1}{64}$ in)

Weight:
- Total weight loaded 20,000 kg (44,092 lb)
- Dead load 2,130 kg (4,696 lb)
- Interior useful load 17,870 kg (39,496 lb)
- Interior useful cubic capacity 31·1 m^3 (1,098·3 ft^3)

20 ft Steel Container Open Top
- Gross weight 20,320 kg (44,800 lb)
- Tare weight approx. 2,225 kg (4,905 lb)
- Payload 18,095 kg (39,895 lb)
- Cube 29·2 m^3 (1,031 ft^3)
- Overall length 6,055 mm (19 ft $10\frac{1}{2}$ in)
- Overall width 2,435 mm (8 ft)
- Overall height 2,435 mm (8 ft)
- Inside length 5,885 mm (19 ft $3\frac{45}{64}$ in)
- Inside width 2,305 mm (7 ft $6\frac{47}{64}$ in)
- Inside height 2,115 mm (6 ft $11\frac{1}{4}$ in)

Door opening:
- Inside width 2,255 mm (7 ft $4\frac{25}{32}$ in)
- Inside height 2,130 mm (6 ft $11\frac{7}{8}$ in)

20 ft Steel Container Open Side
- Gross weight 18,000 kg (39,700 lb)
- Tare weight 2,480 kg (5,470 lb)
- Payload 15,520 kg (34,220 lb)
- Cube 28·3 m^3 (1,000 ft^3)
- Overall length 6,055 mm (19 ft $10\frac{1}{2}$ in)
- Overall width 2,435 mm (8 ft)
- Overall height 2,435 mm (8 ft)
- Inside length 5,885 mm (19 ft $3\frac{45}{64}$ in)
- Inside width 2,275 mm (7 ft $5\frac{19}{32}$ in)
- Inside height 2,110 mm (6 ft $11\frac{7}{64}$ in)

Side wall opening:
- Length 2,650 mm (8 ft $8\frac{11}{32}$ in)
- Height 2,040 mm (6 ft $8\frac{11}{32}$ in)

Door opening:
- Inside width 2,255 mm (7 ft $4\frac{25}{32}$ in)
- Inside height 2,070 mm (6 ft $9\frac{1}{4}$ in)

Opening or folding board panel:
- Length 5,420 mm (18 ft $2\frac{9}{32}$ in)
- Height 2,040 mm (6 ft $8\frac{11}{32}$ in)
- Height of board panel 600 mm (2 ft)

20 ft Cargo Flat
- Gross weight 25,000 kg (55,125 lb)
- Tare weight 2,330 kg (5,125 lb)
- Payload 22,670 kg (50,000 lb)
- Overall length 6,055 mm (19 ft $10\frac{1}{2}$ in)
- Overall width 2,435 mm (8 ft)
- Overall height 1,200 mm (3 ft $11\frac{1}{4}$ in)
- Inside length 5,870 mm (19 ft $3\frac{7}{64}$ in)
- Inside width 2,239 mm (7 ft $4\frac{11}{64}$ in)
- Inside height 810 mm (2 ft $\frac{25}{32}$ in)
- Centre of pockets 840 mm (2 ft $0\frac{31}{32}$ in)
- Centre of pockets 2,080 mm (6 ft $9\frac{7}{8}$ in)
- Inside Dimensions
  - 120 × 300 mm ($4\frac{3}{32}$ in × $11\frac{13}{16}$ in)
- Inside dimensions
  - 120 × 360 mm ($4\frac{23}{32}$ in × $14\frac{11}{64}$ in)

20 ft Stainless steel Tankcontainer, couplable,

External dimensions:
- Overall length 6,055 mm (19 ft $10\frac{25}{64}$ in)
- Overall width 2,435 mm (7 ft $11\frac{49}{64}$ in)
- Overall height 2,435 mm (7 ft $11\frac{49}{64}$ in)

Dimensions of the tank:
- Length 5,600 mm (18 ft $4\frac{15}{32}$ in)
- Diameter 2,000 mm (6 ft $6\frac{3}{4}$ in)
- Volume 16,700 litres (4·4 gal)
- Dia. of manhole 450 mm ($17\frac{23}{32}$ in)
- Dia. of discharge stub 80 mm ($3\frac{9}{64}$ in)

Weights:
- Empty weight of container 3,200 kg (70·55 lb)
- Gross weight, max. 20,000 kg (44,090 lb)
- Payload 16,800 kg (37,038 lb)

6 ft 6 in All-Steel Container
- Gross weight 6,850 kg (15,100 lb)
- Tare weight approx. 820 kg (1,810 lb)
- Payload 6,030 kg (13,290 lb)
- Cube 9 m^3 (318 ft^3)
- Overall length 2,435 mm (8 ft)
- Overall width 2,010 mm (6 ft 7 in)
- Overall height 2,265 mm (7 ft 5 in)
- Inside length 2,300 mm (7 ft $6\frac{1}{2}$ in)
- Inside width 1,895 mm (6 ft $2\frac{1}{2}$ in)
- Inside height 2,030 mm (6 ft 8 in)

Door opening:
- Inside width 1,880 mm (6 ft 2 in)
- Inside height 1,923 mm (6 ft $3\frac{23}{32}$ in)

10 ft Steel Container
- Gross weight 10,160 kg (22,400 lb)
- Tare weight approx. 1,225 kg (2,700 lb)
- Payload 8,935 kg (19,700 lb)
- Cube 14·1 m^3 (500 ft^3)
- Overall length 2,990 mm (9 ft $9\frac{3}{4}$ in)
- Overall width 2,435 mm (8 ft)
- Overall height 2,435 mm (8 ft)
- Inside length 2,815 mm (9 ft $2\frac{53}{64}$ in)
- Inside width 2,305 mm (7 ft $6\frac{47}{64}$ in)
- Inside height 2,175 mm (7 ft 1 in)

Door opening:
- Inside width 2,255 mm (7 ft $4\frac{25}{32}$ in)
- Inside height 2,130 mm (6 ft $11\frac{7}{8}$ in)

Hungarian Shipyards and Crane Factory type S20S steel container

20 ft Steel Container
- Gross weight 20,320 kg (44,800 lb)
- Tare weight approx. 2,150 kg (4,740 lb)
- Payload 18,170 kg (40,060 lb)
- Cube 29·5 m^3 (1,040 ft^3)
- Overall length 6,055 mm (19 ft $10\frac{1}{2}$ in)
- Overall width 2,435 mm (8 ft)
- Overall height 2,435 mm (8 ft)
- Inside length 5,885 mm (19 ft $3\frac{45}{64}$ in)
- Inside width 2,305 mm (7 ft $6\frac{47}{64}$ in)
- Inside height 2,175 mm (7 ft 1 in)

Door opening:
- Inside width 2,255 mm (7 ft $4\frac{25}{32}$ in)
- Inside height 2,130 mm (6 ft $11\frac{7}{8}$ in)

20 ft Steel/Aluminium Container, couplable
- Gross weight 20,000 kg (44,000 lb)
- Tare weight approx. 1,860 kg (4,092 lb)
- Payload 18,140 kg (39,908 lb)
- Cubic capacity 30 m^3 (1,060 ft^3)
- Overall length 6.055 mm (19, ft $10\frac{1}{2}$ in)
- Overall width 2,435 mm (8 ft)
- Overall height 2,435 mm (8 ft)
- Inside length 5,899 mm (19 ft $4\frac{5}{16}$ in)
- Inside width 2,315 mm (7 ft $7\frac{1}{8}$ in)
- Inside height 2,185 mm (7 ft 2 in)

Door opening:
- Inside width 2,255 mm (7 ft $4\frac{3}{4}$ in)
- Inside height 2,130 mm (6 ft $11\frac{7}{8}$ in)

PRINCIPAL OWNERS

IWT/Industriewerke Transportsystem, Hamburg and Sea Containers Ltd.
Johnson Line
ICS

INTERCONSULT LTD.

Kockum Interconsult AB
Box 95, S-311 01 Falkenberg 1
Fack, S-201 10 Malmö 1, Sweden
TELEPHONE: 0346-140 10
TELEX: 38087 Inter S

BRANCH ADDRESS:
AB Interconsult, Box 95 S-311 00, Falkenberg, Sweden
TELEPHONE: 0346-14010
TELEX: 3587 Interconsult FBG
DIRECTOR:
Jochum Beckman (*Managing*)

ASSOCIATED COMPANY:
Kokum Industries Ltd, Gresham Road, Buckingham Avenue, Trading Estate, Slough, Bucks, England

TELEPHONE: Slough 20839 and 26191
TELEX: Slough 8422

Interconsult insulated containers

CONTAINERS:
All types— 20 ft, 30 ft and 40 ft.
Dry freight, including open top and container flats. Insulated and refrigerated. Bulk powder and liquid tank containers.
CONSTRUCTION—MATERIALS AND METHOD:
All welded steel.
Steel frame and stainless steel tank.
Steel frame and glassfibre walls sandwich construction. Reinforced plastics.
CONSTRUCTION—FRAME:
Framework: Special profile section in steel—all welded construction with integral corner castings at base only.
CONSTRUCTION—TANK:
Tank: Mild steel plate—all welded. Hemispherical ends and internal cones.
Testing is carried out in accordance with

Interconsult Container Flats, 10 ft × 8 ft × 4 ft or 8 ft ends—20 ft × 8ft × 4 ft or 8 ft ends

ISO requirements.

The Interconsult foldable flat container.

Range of Interconsult Containers:
Dry Freight or (General Purpose) Containers

Type by ISO or other Recognised Standard Dimensions	*Main Materials of Construction*	*Internal* Length mm ft in	*Internal* Height mm ft in	*Internal* Width mm ft in	*Internal measurements of End door openings* Width mm ft in	*Internal measurements of End door openings* Height mm ft in	*Approx. heat gain in BTUs/hr or K-cals/hr*	*Cubic Capacity*
20 ft × 8 ft × 8 ft	Steel	5,870 19′ 3⅛″	2,223 7′ 3¾″	2,305 7′ 6¾″	2,305 7′ 6¾″	2,136 7′ 0 1/16″		30·2m³ 1,066·5 ft³
40 ft × 8 ft × 8 ft	Steel	11,902 39′ 4½″	2,235 7′ 4″	2,299 7′ 6½″	2,305 7′ 6¾″	2,136 7′ 0 1/16″		61·7m³ 2,179 ft³
Refrigerated Containers								
20 ft × 8 ft × 8 ft	Glass fibre reinforced plastics	5,251 17′ 2¾″	2,023 6′ 7⅝″	2,169 7′ 1⅛″	2,194 7′ 2¾″	2,023 6′ 7⅝″	14·2—16 Kcal hr °C	23m³ 812·25 ft³
40 ft × 8 ft × 8 ft	Glass fibre reinforced	11,204 26′ 9⅛″	2,023 6′ 7⅝″	2,194 7′ 2⅜″	2,194 7′ 2⅜″	2,023 6′ 7⅝″	26·4—30·0Kcal hr °C	49·2m³ 1,737·25 ft³
Insulated Containers								
20 ft × 8 ft × 8 ft	Reinforced plastics	5,825 19′ 1 5/16″	2,178 7′ 1¾″	2,254 7′ 4¾″	2,254 7′ 4¾″	2,130 6′ 11⅞″	14·9 Kcal hr °C	28m³ 989 ft³
30 ft × 8 ft × 8 ft	Reinforced plastics	5,769 18′ 11⅛″	2,144 6′ 11¼″	2,194 7′ 2⅜″	2,194 7′ 2⅛″	2,023 6′ 7⅝″	14·2—16·0 Kcal hr °C	26·7m³ 943 ft³
40 ft × 8 ft × 8 ft	Reinforced plastics	11,903 39′ 0⅝″	2,114 6′ 11¼″	1,294 7′ 2⅜″	2,194 7′ 2⅜″	2,023 6′ 7⅝″	26·4—30·0 Kcal °C	55·2m³ 1,949·5 ft³

INTERNATIONAL CONTAINERS

International Containers Ltd. (ICL)
Fung House, Hong Kong
TELEPHONE: H236193
DIRECTORS:
Albert Cheng (*Director*)
R. H. Ash (*General Manager*)

The Company is 50 per cent owned by Hong Kong Chiap Hua Manufacturing Company, Comalco (Asia) Ltd, a subsidiary of an Australian Company, which have a 40 per cent interest and Freighter Industries Ltd, another Australian company has a 10 per cent share.

PRODUCTION:
First orders from OCL for 20 ft dry cargo units are in production. It is hoped to have an annual production of 3,000 to 4,000 units per year which depending upon orders could be increased to a maximum of about 9,000 units per year.

REPAIRS:
The factory, situated alongside a quay wall, is well placed to receive containers requiring repairs from all over the harbour by lighters.

KOCKUM

Kockum Industries Ltd
Gresham Road, Buckingham Avenue,
Trading Estate, Slough, Bucks, England
TELEPHONE: Slough 20839 and 23743
TELEX: 84314
DIRECTORS:
G. Kockum (*Chairman*)
J. D. Shapland (*Managing*)
A. Hogman
SALES MANAGER:
S. G. Medcraft
PARENT COMPANY:
Kockum Mechaniska Verkstads AB, Malmo
ASSOCIATE COMPANY:
Subsidiaries of Kockum M/V, Malmo
CONTAINERS:
Bulk powder rail and road tanks and B.R.
Freightliner "Prestank"
SPECIFICATIONS:
ISO and Freightliner

Kockum Industries modular tank

LEX TILLOTSON

Lex Tillotson (Containers)
Swinemoor Lane
Beverley, HU17 0JZ
England
TELEPHONE: 0482 882293
TELEX: 52343
DIRECTORS:
J. F. Parslow
B. Cherry
C. R. Pape
CONTAINERS:
Dry freight, Tilt-tainers, Open tops, Side door

and Collapsible.
DESIGN STANDARDS:
ISO, BS 3985, UIC, Lloyds, TIR.

MATERIALS:
Frames of steel and aluminium alloy.
Cladding of steel, alloy or stainless steel.

PRODUCTION:
In 1970, 6 30 ft dry freight containers were
made. One 40 ft refrigerated unit was made.
122 20 ft, 75 30 ft and 3 40 ft special units
(including tiltainers, side door units, half

heights etc) were made.
MAIN USERS:
MAT Transport Ltd.
International Ferry Freight
Dart Containerline,
Manchester Liners
Metric Line
Crowe & Co. Ltd.
REPAIR FACILITIES:
Available at Beverley (Hull), Southampton,
and Burnley (Preston, Manchester, Liver-
pool).

LITEWATE

Litewate Transport Equipment Corp.,
4220 South 13th Street, Milwaukee, Wisconsin
53221 USA
TELEPHONE: 414-281-5070
DIRECTORS:
Edward R. Boedeker (*President*)
LICENSEES ABROAD:
Thompson Bros., Gloucester, England

Isocontainer, GmbH & Co Kg Hamburg,
Germany
DESIGN STANDARD:
ISO, USASI, ABS
CONTAINERS:
Insulated and refrigerated containers only
of resin reinforced fiber-glass, integrally

moulded in one piece. Insulation is of
polyurethane.

PRODUCTION:
120 20 ft, 170 27 ft and 3 40 ft units
were produced in 1970. In 1971 122 20 ft
units and 100 27 ft units had been manufactured at the time of going to press.

Litewaite Containers available

Type by ISO or other Recognised Standard Dimensions	Main Materials of Construction (See space below for notes on additional materials and methods of construction)	Internal			Internal measurements of End door openings		Approx. heat gain in BTUs/hr or K-cals/hr	
		Length mm ft in	Height mm ft in	Width mm ft in	Width mm ft in	Height mm ft in		Cubic Capacity m³
20 ft × 8 ft × 8 ft	FRP	5,842 230"	2,159 85"	2,286 90"	2,286 90"	2,159 85"	27/Btu/hr	28·8 1,018
27 ft × 9 ft 6 in × 8 ft	FRP	7,950 314"	2,565 101"	2,286 90"	2,280 90"	2,515 99"	63/Btu/hr	44·6 1,575

Insulated Containers

40 ft × 8 ft 6 in × 8 ft	FRP	11,913 469"	2,159 85"	2,286 90"	2,286 90"	2,159 85"		
5 ft × 6 ft 3 in × 8 ft	FRP	1,303 51½"	1,575 62"	2,311 91"	2,311 91"	1,575 62"	12/Btu/hr	4·8 168
*Built to Aero Space Standards SAE (AS-832)								

LUCHAIRE S.A.

Luchaire S.A.
Departement Containers
180 Boulevard Haussmann,
Paris Vlll, France
TELEPHONE: 924.63.44
TELEX: 65.372 Paris
DIRECTORS:
J. J. Wilmot-Roussel (*Chairman and Managing Director*)
J. C. Quilhot (*Director, Metal Working Division*)

PRODUCTION:
1,000 unit production schedule for 1971.

CONTAINERS:
This company has only just entered the container field. It produces 20 ft and 40 ft all steel containers 8 ft and 8 ft 6 in high. Corrugated iron panels are used for end walls, roofs and sidewalls. There are 270 degree opening doors. Australian treated hardwood or plywood floors are provided.

The Luchaire range of dry freight containers

	20 ft		40 ft	
Overall length	6,055 mm	20 ft	12,187 mm	40 ft
Overall width	2,435 mm	8 ft	2,435 mm	8 ft
Overall height	2,435 mm	8 ft	2,588 mm	8 ft 6 in
Inner length	2,325 mm	19 ft 5 in	2,325 mm	39 ft 5 $\frac{33}{64}$ in
Inner width	5,917 mm	7 ft 7$\frac{1}{2}$ in	12,027 mm	7 ft 7$\frac{9}{16}$ in
Inner height	2,243 mm	7 ft 4$\frac{4}{25}$ in	2,392 mm	7 ft 10$\frac{13}{64}$ in
Width opened doors	2,305 mm	7 ft 6$\frac{3}{4}$ in	2,305 mm	7 ft 6$\frac{3}{4}$ in
Height opened doors	2,146 mm	7 ft 0$\frac{12}{25}$ in	2,191·5 mm	7 ft 2$\frac{5}{16}$ in
Volumetric capacity	30·7 m³	1,084 ft³ 267 in³	66·88 m³	2,363 ft³
Maximum payload	18,220 kg	40,170 lb	26,910 kg	59,310 lb
Tare	2,100 kg	4,630 lb	3,570 kg	7,868 lb
Gross weight	20,320 kg	44,800 lb	30,480 kg	67,178 lb

LUTHER

Luther GmbH & Co.
3300 Braunschweig,
Frankfurter Strasse,
Postfach 526,
Germany (Federal Republic)
TELEPHONE: 221091
TELEX: 213571 lwhh d
DIRECTOR:
E. Schmidt

CONTAINERS:
Tank containers for hazardous and non-hazardous uses.

Stainless Steel Type TC 16/1
CONTENTS:
Net: 16,380 litre; 3,600 Imp gallon; 4,330 US gallon.
Gross: 17,200 litre; 3,790 Imp gallon; 4,545 US gallon.
WEIGHT:
Gross. 20,320 kg; 44,780 lb.
Tare. 3,550 kg; 7,826 lb.
DIMENSIONS:
Length: 6,055 mm; 19 ft 10$\frac{1}{2}$ in.
Width: 2,435 mm; 8 ft.
Height: 2,435 mm; 8 ft.
TANK:
Length: 5,850 mm ;19 ft 2 in.
Diameter: 2,000 mm; 6 ft 6$\frac{7}{10}$ in.;
Working pressure: 3 kp/cm²; 42 psi.

Test pressure: 4·5 kp/cm²; 64 psi
Working temperature: 100°C; 212°F.
Filling:
1. With a hose through man-hole.
2. With a hose connected to the gravity emptying device.
3. With filling pipe (additional device for hazardous chemicals).
Discharging:
1. Gravity discharge through 3 in ball-cock,
   (a) with 3 in NPT connection thread
   or
   (b) 3 in-150 lb ASA flange blind-flanged.
2. With filling pipe (additional device).

McARDLE LTD.

Thomas McArdle Ltd.
Industrial Estate,
Coe's Road,
Dundalk
Republic of Ireland
TELEPHONE: (042) 5533
TELEX: 4572 MCA El
DIRECTORS:
T. J. McArdle (*Chairman and Managing Director*)
M. McArdle
F. McArdle
N. V. McCann
W. Schattschneider
J. H. D. Ryan
R. Mulholland

PRODUCTION:
As shown in table below, including 500 20 ft containers 8 ft 6 in high, 100 30 ft units and 600 40 ft units of that height.

CONTAINERS:
Principal products at present include 40 ft × 8 ft 6 in high steel dry freight containers.

Works facilities include two shot-blasting plants and test rigs for carrying out prototype and production batch structural tests.

PRINCIPLE USERS:
British & Irish Steampacket Co.
Coras Iompair Eireann
Greenore Ferries Ltd.
Meri Shipping Co. (Helsinki)
Manchester Liners Ltd.
Sea Containers Ltd.
Associated Container Transport Ltd.
Ben Line Steamers Ltd.
Australian National Line
France, Holland, Ireland Line
Ulster Ferries
George Bell Ltd.

Type		Quantity manufactured			
		20 ft	30 ft	40 ft	10 ft
Dry goods	1970	91	26	42	—
	1971	280	—	896	—
Insulated	1970	30	—	—	6
	1971	130	—	—	—
Refrigerated	1970	—	—	—	—
	1971	—	—	20	—
Collapsible Flats Specials*	1970	537	80	—	—
Open Tops & Tiltainers	1971	180	200	140	—
Half Heights	1970	37	—	—	—
	1971	650	—	—	—

McArdle 8 ft. 8 in. high 40 ft. container.

Dennison Trailers Ltd.
Anglo Irish Transport Ltd.
Hudig & Vieder Ltd.
Lep Transport Ltd.

MAFI

MAFI-Fahrzeugwerke
7015 Korntal-Stuttgart
Steinbeisstrasse. 9
W. Germany
TELEPHONE: 88 11 21-27
TELEX: 7-23 391

MANUFACTURERS OF:
containers, flats, handling equipment for containers and roll-on/roll-off, special transport vehicles

DIRECTORS:
M. Fiala
W. Fiala
H. Fiala

CONTAINERS:

1. Dry Cargo
2. Open Top
3. Insulated
4. Tilt-Container
5. Open Side Container
6. ISO Flats
7. Other Flats

DESIGN STANDARD:
ISO, American Bureau of Shipping, Germanischer Lloyd, TIR, UIC

PRINCIPAL USERS:
Atlantic Containers Line Ltd., Stockholm
Leco Container Leasing AG, Zug/Switzerland Flexi-Van Inc., New York
Johnson Line, Stockholm
Tiger Line, Wilmington
Fabre Line, Paris

40 ft Steel-Container 1 A, Type OTA and 40 ft × 8 ft × 6 ft 8 in tunnel type

Base:
Steel-weld-construction.
Additional characteristics of tunnel-type: At the front area the floor group has a tunnel as clearance for the frame of suitable semi-trailer. Fittings for the tie-down clambs of the chassis are provided at the front and rear end.

Corner fittings:
Cast-iron corners made of GS 52 as per latest prescriptions of ISO/TC 104.

Endframe construction:
Mode of box sections with high rigidity. Admissible stacking load: 6-high. Admissible anti-rack-load: 15 tons.

Doors:
Two-wing-plymetal-door coated with galvanized steel plates on both sides, at one headboard. Angle of aperture 270° each. Per door wing 4 galvanized hinges with stainless bushings and bolts.

Door lock:
One twin-cam-antirack-lock type DL per door wing and one cam-lock type GS, system Power Brace.

Door sealing:
Infinite overlap sealing made of seawater-proof and weather-resistant rubber with Neoprene.

Side and headboards:
Corrugated sheet metal.

Roof:
Outward corrugated sheet metal, reinforced around the corner castings.

Indoor ventilation:
One each side wall one ventilation opening each is provided, which are diagonally arranged and protected against spray-water

Floor:
Pinewood planks, top quality in grove-and spring design, longitudinally planked and impregnated.

Surface treatment and painting:
Anti-rust preservation of the surface by shock-proof, resistant to aging and seawater-proof painting.

Dimensions:

40 ft Steel-Container 1A, Type OTA:
Admissible total weight 30,480 kg (30 tons)
Dead weight ca. 3,200 kg (7,055 lb)
Outside measurements l × w × h 12,190 × 2,435 × 2,435 mm ($479\frac{7}{8}$ in × $95\frac{7}{8}$ in × $95\frac{7}{8}$ in)
Inside measurements l × w× h 12,050 × 2,335 × 2,240 mm ($474\frac{3}{8}$ in × 92 in × $81\frac{3}{16}$ in)
Door opening w × h 2,285 × 2,139 mm (90 in × $84\frac{1}{4}$ in)
Cubic contents ca. 63 m³ (2,225 ft³)

40 ft × 8 ft × 8 ft 6 in tunnel type
Admissible total weight 30,480 kg (30 tons)
Dead weight ca. 3,400 kg (7,496 lb)
Outside measurements l ×w × h 12,190 × 2,435 × 2,590 mm ($479\frac{7}{8}$ × $95\frac{7}{8}$ × 102 in)
Inside measurements l× w × h 12,050 × 2,335 × 2,395 mm ($474\frac{3}{8}$ × 92 × $94\frac{1}{4}$ in)
Door opening w × h 2,285 × 2,300 mm (90 × $90\frac{1}{2}$ in)
Cubic contents ca. 67·4 m³ (2,380 ft³)

Additional Equipment:

1. Lashing devices, such as lashing strips, lashing rings etc.
2. Holder for transport papers.
3. Built in plates.
4. Design acc. to the regulations of the Australian Health Authority.
5. Individual inscription.

20 ft Steel-Container

Base:
This has longitudinal beams with rebound for elevating vehicles with grab jaws. Alternatively 2 or 4 continuous forklift pockets.

Corner fittings:
Cast-iron-corners made of GS 52 as per latest prescriptions of ISO/TC 104.

Endframe construction:
Made of box sections with high rigidity.
Admissible stacking load: 6-high.
Admissible anti-rack-load: 15 tons.

Doors:
Two-wing-plymetal-door coated with galvanized steel plates on both sides, at one headboard. Angle of aperture 270° each. Per door wing 4 galvanized hinges with stainless bushings and bolts.

Door lock:
One twin-cam-antirack-lock type DL per door wing and one cam-lock type GS, system Power Brace, galvanized.

Door sealing:
Infinite overlap sealing made of seawater-proof and weather-resistant rubber with Neoprene.

Side- and headboards:
Corrugaret sheet metal

Roof:
Outward corrugated sheet metal, reinforced around the corner castings.

Indoor ventilation:
On each side wall one ventilation opening each is provided, which are diagonally arranged and protected against spray-water.

Floor:
Pinewood planks, top quality in grove and spring design, longitudinally planked and impregnated.

Surface treatment and painting:
Anti-rust preservation of the surface by shock-proof, resistant to aging and seawater-proof painting.

Dimensions:

Container Size 1 *C:*
Admissible total weight 20,320 kg (20 tons)
Dead weight approx. 1,850 kg (4,076 lb)
Outside measurements l ×w × h 6,055 × 2,435 × 2,435 mm ($283\frac{3}{8}$ × $95\frac{7}{8}$ × $95\frac{7}{8}$ in) (20 ft × 8 ft × 8 ft)
Inside measurements l × w × h 5,920 × 2,332 × 2,224 mm (233 × $91\frac{3}{4}$ × $87\frac{7}{8}$ in)
Door opening w × h 2,285 × 2,121 mm (90 × $83\frac{1}{2}$ in)
Cubic contents ca. 30·8 m³ (1,088 ft³)

Additional Equipment:

1. Lashing devices, such as lashing strips, lashing rings etc.
2. Holder for transport papers
3. Built in plates.
4. Design acc. to the regulations of the Australian Health Authority.
5. Individual inscription.

Open-Top-Container

Basic frame:
Made of bevelled longitudinal and rolled double-T cross beams. With size 20 ft two or four continuous forklift pockets are possible.

Corner fittings:
Cast steel corners, quality at least GS 45 acc. to the latest prescriptions of ISO.

Endframe construction:
Made of box sections with high rigidity.
Admissible stacking load: 6-high
Admissible anti-rack-load: 15 tons.

Doors:
At one front wall two-wing plymetal door coated with galvanized steel plates on both sides. Angle of aperture 270° each. Per door wing 4 galvanized hinges with stainless bushings and pins.

Door lock:
One twin-cam-antirack-lock type DL per door wing and one cam-lock type GS system Power Brace, galvanized.

Door sealing:
Infinite overlap sealing made of seawater proof and weather resistant rubber with Neoprene.

Side and head wall:
Corrugated sheet metal.

Roof:
Removable, towards above buckled hoops made of hollow sections. The roof frame above the door can be removed, too. The roof is covered by a PVC-tarpaulin according to TIR requirements. Securing the of tarpaulin is by a plastic coated steel rope.

Floor:
Pine wood planks 35 mm thick, impregnated (anti sepric).

Surface treatment and painting:
A prime coat is applied on a clean surface. Then a top coating is applied consisting of single-component plastic lacquer.
Thickness of coat, dry, approx. 100 my.

Dimensions:

MAFI Container size 1 *C, type open top 20 ft × 8 ft × 8 ft*
Admissible total weight 20,320 kg (20 tons)
Dead weight, approx. 2,050 kg (4,520 lb)
Outside measurements, l × w × h 6,055 × 2,435 × 2,435 mm ($238\frac{3}{8}$ × $95\frac{7}{8}$ × 95 in)
Inside measurements, l × w × h 5,920 × 2,332 × 2,213 mm (233 × 91x × $87\frac{1}{8}$ in)
Door opening, w × h 2,285 × 2,090 mm (90 × $82\frac{1}{4}$ in)
Loading volume, about 30·5 m³ (1,077 ft³) with 2 or 4 forklift pockets.

MAFI Container size 1 *A, type open top 40 ft × 8 ft × 8ft high*
Admissible total weight 30,480 kg (30 tons)
Dead weight, approx. 3,900 kg (8,598 lb)
Outside measurements. l × w × h 12,190 × 2,435 × 2,434 mm ($479\frac{7}{8}$ × $95\frac{7}{8}$ × $95\frac{7}{8}$ in)
Inside measurements, l × w × h 12,055 × 2,332 × 2,213 mm ($474\frac{5}{8}$ × $91\frac{3}{4}$ × $87\frac{1}{8}$ in)
Door opening, w × h 2,285 × 2,090 mm (90 × $82\frac{1}{4}$ in)
Loading volume ,about 62·3 m³ (2,200 ft³)

MAFI Container size 1 *A, open top 40 ft × 8 ft × 8* ft *6 in*
Admissible total weight 30,480 kg (30 tons)
Dead weight, approx. 4,100 kg 9.029 lb)
Outside measurements, l × w × h 12,190 × 2,435 × 2,580 mm ($479\frac{7}{8}$ × $95\frac{7}{8}$ × $101\frac{1}{4}$ in)
Inside measurements, l × w × h 12,055 × 2,332 × 2,352 mm ($474\frac{5}{8}$ × $91\frac{3}{4}$ × $92\frac{5}{8}$ in)
Door opening, w × h 2,285 × 2,245 mm (90 × $88\frac{3}{8}$ in)
Loading volume, about 66 m³ (2,331 ft³)

Tilt-Container 20 ft-30 ft

Base:
Frame construction, welded of rolled steel

sections, with 2 continuous forklift pockets and pick-up ledges for elevating vehicles with clamps.

Corner fittings:

Cast-iron corners made of GS 52 as per latest prescriptions of ISO/TC 104.

Corner columns:

Hollow profiles, admitting stacking 4-high.

Front wall:

Made of corrugated sheet metal.

Rear wall:

Alternatively corrugated sheet metal, as used for the front wall or doors with antirack locks and removable roof beam.

Side walls:

With firmly welded roof beams and removable middle columns.

The side boards consist of sheet metal, 700 mm high. Above the side boards 3 planks, insertable in equal distances are provided.

Roof:

Removable hoops with a buckling of 50 mm. To prevent a dent of the tarpaulin, in the middle a strap is provided endwise.

Floor:

Weatherproof glued plywood planks, impregnated as per requirements.

Cover:

Roof and side walls as per TIR-prescriptions are covered by a PVC-tarpaulin. Locking of the tarpaulin by PVC-coated steel rope with customs seals.

Painting:

Weatherproof, monochromatic, colour as per option.

Dimensions:

Til -Conıainer 20 ft

Capacity 18,000 kg (39,683 lb)
Dead weight, about 2,200 kg (4,435 lb)
Outside dimensions 6,055 × 2,435 × 2,435 mm (238⅜ × 95⅞ × 95⅞ in)
Inside dimensions, 5,880 × 2,245 × 2,120 mm (20 × 8 × 8 ft)
Cubic contents, about 29 m³ (1,024 lb)
Height of mount base 255 mm (10⅜ in)
Height of side board 700 mm (27½ in)
Front wall, sheet metal, 1·35 mm thick ($\frac{3}{64}$ in)
Floor cover, plywood, 25 mm thick (6$\frac{3}{64}$ in)
Tarpaulin, PVC-coated in quality 4050, TIR approved.

Tilt-Container 30 ft

Capacity 20,000 kg (44,092 lb)
Dead weight, about 3,350 kg (7,386 lb)
Outside dimensions 9,125 × 2,435 × 2,435 mm (30 × 8 × 8 ft)
Inside dimensions 8,950 × 2,315 × 2,090 mm (253⅜ × 90⅛ × 82¼ in)
Cubic contents 43 m³ (1,519 ft³)
Height of mount base 256 mm (10⅜ in)
Height of side board 700 mm 27½ in)
Front wall, sheet metal, 1·25 mm thick ($\frac{3}{64}$ in)
Floor cover, plywood, 25 mm thicjk ($\frac{43}{64}$ in)
Tarpaulin, PVC-coated in quality 4050, TIR-approved.

Additional Equipment:

1. Lashing devices, such as lashing strips, lashing rings etc.
2. Holder for transport papers.
3. Documents-pocket for TIR-certificate.
4. Special inscription.

20 ft Plywood-Container

Mount base:

Bevelled respectively rolled longitudinal and crossbeams. Outer longitudinal beams with rebound for elevating vehicles with grab jaws. Alternatively 2 or 4 continuous forklift pockets if required.

Corner fittings:

Cast-iron-corners made of GS 52 as per latest prescriptions of ISO/TC 104.

Endframe construction:

Made of box sections with high rigidity. Admissible stacking load: 6-high.

Doors:

Two-wing-plymetal-door at one headboard coated with zincplated steel metal on both sides. Angle of aperture 270° each. Per door wing four zinced hinges with stainless bushings and bolts.

Door lock:

Per door wing one twin-cam-antirack-lock type DL and one cam-lock type CS, system Power Brace, zinced.

Door sealing:

Infinite overlap sealing made of seawater-proof and weather-resistant rubber with Neoprene.

Roof, side and headboards:

Plywood panels, coated on both sides with synthetic resin, the outside of the panels is smooth. The plates are riveted to the framework by use of "Huckbolt"-rivets in connection with a sealing compound.

Floor cover:

Plywood panels made of Finnish birch, waterproof laid and impregnated, in the door area reinforced by means of a sheet metal.

Painting of the framework:

1. Sandblasted
2. Primed
3. Finish on artificial bases (colour as per option).

Dimensions Size 1C:

Admissible total weight 20 tons
Dead weight approx. 2,005 kg (4,420 lb)
Outside measurements, l × w × h 6,055 × 2,435 × 2,435 mm (20 ft × 8 ft × 8 ft)
Inside measurements, l × w × h 9,512 × 2,372 × 2,299 mm (19 ft 5⅞ in × 7 ft 9⅜ in × 7 ft 3¾ in)
Door opening, w × h 2,266 × 2,129 mm (7 ft 6 in × 7 ft 11 $\frac{7}{16}$ in)
Cubic contents approx. 31·4332 m³ (1,110 ft³)

Additional Equipment:

1. Lashing devices, such as lashing strips, lashing rings etc.
2. Holder for transport papers.
3. Design acc. to the regulations of the Australian Health Authority.
4. Individual inscription.

Reefer-Container

Base:

Bevelled rolled longitudinal and cross-beams. Outer longitudinal beams with recess for elevating vehicles with grab jaws. Alternatively 2 or 4 continuous forklift pockets.

Corner fittings:

Cast-iron-corners made of St 45.2 (minimum quality) as per prescriptions of ISO/TC 104.

Endframe construction:

Made of sectional steel with high rigidity. Admissible stacking load 6-high. Admissible anti-rack-load: 15 tons.

Doors:

Two wing wood door at one headwall externally coated with galvanized steel metal. Angle of aperture 270° each. Per door wing 4 galvanized hinges with stainless bushings and bolts.

Door lock:

One twin-cam-antirack-lock type DL per door wing and one cam-lock type GS, system Power Brace, galvanized.

Door sealing:

Double sealing with altogether 4 sealing lips made of seawater-proof and weather-resistant rubber with Neoprene.

Side- and headboards and roof:

Sandwich panels. Exterior layer cosist-ing of plastic-coated plywood, medium layer polyurethane foam, interior layer consisting of polyester reinforced with glassfibre with grooves for air ciruclation.

Floor:

Aluminium T-profile, spaced for air circulation laid out in longitudinal direction on a plywood cover. Under the floor cover insulation with ployurethane foam. A fork-lift truck can drive on the floor, as specified by ISO.

Surface treatment and painting:

Anti-rust preservation or parts in steel with shock-proof, resistant to ageing and sea-water-proof painting.

Dimensions, Container Size 1 C

Admissible total weight 20,320 kg (20 tons)
Dead weight without refrigerator, approx. 2,350 kg (5,181 lb)
Outside measurements l × w × h 6,055 × 2,435 × 2,435 mm (238⅜ × 95⅞ × 85⅞ in)
Inside measurements, l × w × h 5,650 × 2,185 × 2,090 mm (222½ × 85 × 82¼ in)
Door opening w × h 2,185 × 2,090 mm (86 × 82¼ in)
Cubic contents approx. 25·8 m³ (911 ft³)

Additional Equipment:

1. Refrigerator
2. Individual inscription etc.

Other designs and sizes upon request.

20 ft Flat

Basic frame:

Frame construction, welded of rolled steel sections, as standard equipped with 2 continuous forklift pockets and pick-up ledges on either side for lifting with elevating vehicles equipped with clamps.

Superstructure:

Consisting of head walls and lateral diagonal doors for supporting the head walls. The following variants are possible:

(a) insertable head walls
(b) collapsible head walls
(c) insertable and collapsable head walls

Corner fittings:

Cast steel corners of GS 52 according to the latest prescriptions of ISO/TC 104.

Dimensions:	F 20 SA insertable super-structre	F 20 FA collapsible super-structure	F 20 OA without super-structure
Capacity	20 tons	20 tons	20 tons
Dead weight ca.	2,310 kg 5,093 lb)	2,250 kg (4,960 lb)	1,790 mm 1,790 kg
Length	6,055 mm (238⅜ in)	6,055 mm (238⅜ in)	(3,946 lb) 6,055 mm
Length	5,854 mm (230½ in)	5,854 mm (230½ in)	(238⅜ in) —
Width	2,435 mm (95⅞ in)	2,435 mm (95⅞ in)	2,435 mm
Width	2,258 mm (88⅞ in)	2,258 mm (88⅞ in)	(95⅞ in) —
Height 8 ft	2,435 mm (95⅞ in)	2,435 mm (95⅞ in)	285 mm
Height	2,150 mm (84⅝ in)	2,10 mm (84⅝ in)	(11¼ in) —
Alternatively:			
Height 4 ft	1,212 mm (47¾ in)	1,212 mm (47¾ in)	
Height	927 mm (36½ in)	927 mm (36½ in)	

Head walls:

Compact walls of bent hollow profiles and laterally corrugated sheet steel.

Side walls:

Inward and outward tiltable diagonal frames with clamping devices.

Floor:

Impregnated solid wood cover, laid in segments.

10 ft Flat

Basic frame:

Made of bent plate-profiles, welded together with the cover sheet to form a box section, with 2 continuous forklift pockets, crane bolts and 'pick-up edges on the outside girders for handling the flats with elevating vehicles equipped with clamps.

Head walls:

Frame of square tube with corrugated sheet metal plates and stacking pins. The head walls are fixed by diagonal members mounted on gimbals. When collapsing the headwalls, the members are tilt inward and locked. On each corner column 3 clamping devices for lashing the load are provided.

All lockings are simple plug connections which can easily be operated.

Dimensions:

Capacity 10,000 kg (2,204 lb)
Dead weight ca. 800 kg (1,764 lb)
Total weight 10,800 kg (23,810 lb)
Total length 2,990 mm (117¾ in)
Total width 2,435 mm (95¾ in)
Total height, folded out 1,435 mm (56½ in)
Stacking height 1,375 mm (53¼ in)
Total height, collapsible 255 mm (10 in)
Surface treatment lacquered, colouring optional.

Bin-Container

Base:

Steel-weld-construction, made of bent or rolled longitudinal- and cross-beams. Alternatively with forklift pockets and longitudinal rebound for elevating vehicles with clamps.

Corner fittings:

Cast-iron-corners made of GS 52.3 as per latest recommendations of ISO.

Endframe construction:

Made of box sections with high rigidity. Admissible stacking load: 6-high.

Side- and headboard:

Corrugated sheet steel. One headboard as lowerable flap, serving in lowered position as ramp. On the bottom-end the ramp is pivoted and on top locked with both corner columns by means of 2 slide pins. In lowered position a forklift (meeting the ISO-recommendations) can drive over the ramp. Turned up the ramp withstands an equally distributed load of 7·5 tons.

Floor cover:

Pinewood planks, 40 mm thick impregnated according to requirements. At the ramp the floor is additionally reinforced by a sheet metal plate. The planks are fixed with screws, enabling easy exchange of damaged planks.

Surface treatment and Painting:

1. All profiles and plates sandblasted before assembly.
2. Side- and head plates are double pickled.
3. Cleaning and degreasing of the container after assembly.
4. Single component epoxyd resin, paint thickness, dry: 100 microsec, colour tone: oxide-red.

The Mafi Trac-Porta-Lift with prime mover attached, incorporating the new automatic top-lift spreader for containers from 20 ft to 40 ft.

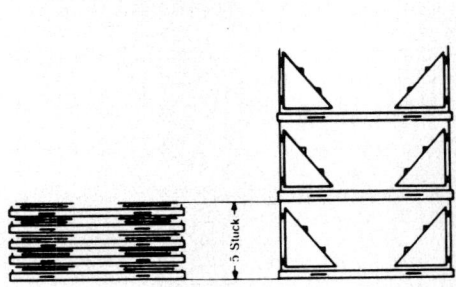

Diagram of MAFI Flats F10/KA with collapsible head and side boards. Showing five collapsed stacked to height of one erected

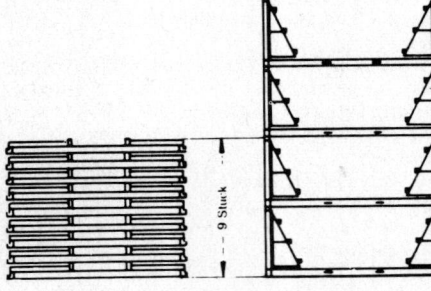

Diagram of F20/SA MAFI flats showing nine collapsed stacked to equivalent height of two erected

Illustrating the robust top end frame member of the Mafi open-top container.

A batch of all-steel 20 ft containers.

MAFI Flat 10 ft

A Mafi 40 ft open-top container.

Technical data:
20 ft × 8 ft × 4 ft Bin Container:

Admissible total weight 20,320 kg (20 tons)
Dead weight approx. 1,650 kg (3,638 bb)
Outside dimensions, l × w × h × 6,055 × 2,435 × 1,212 mm (238⅜ × 95⅞ × 47¾ in)
Inside dimensions, l w × h × 5,928 × 2,333 × 1,025 mm (233⅜ × 91⅞ × 40⅜ in)
Width:
Between the corner columns 2,285 mm (90 in)
Between the upper longitudinal beams 2,063 mm (81¼ in)
Loading capacity approx. 14·2 m³ (501·5 ft³)

20 ft × 8 ft × 4 ft 3 in
Admissible total weight 20,320 kg (20 tons)
Dead weight approx. 1,680 kg (3,704 lb)
Outside dimensions, l × w × h 6,055 × 2,435 × 1,288 mm (238⅜ × 95⅞ × 50¾ in)
Inside dimensions l × w × h 5,928 × 2,333 × 1,100 mm (233⅜ × 91⅞ × 43⅜ in)
Width:
Between the corner columns (2,285 mm (90 in)
Between the upper longitudinal beams 2,063 mm (81¼ in)
Loading capacity approx. 15·2 m³ (536¾ ft³)

40 ft × 8 ft × 4 ft 3 in
Admissible total weight 30,480 kg (30 tons)
Dead weight approx. 3,320 kg (7,319 lb)
Outside dimensions, l× w × h 12,190 × 2,435 × 1,288 mm (479⅞ × 95⅞ × 50¾ in)
Inside dimensions, l × w × h 12,070 × 2,333 × 1,100 mm (475¼ × 91⅞ × 43⅜ in)
Width:
Between the corner columns 2,285 mm (90 in)
Between the upper longitudinal beams 2,063 mm (81¼ in)
Loading capacity approx. 32·5 m³ (1,148 ft³)

M.A.N.

Maschinenfabrik Augsburg Nürnberg AG.,
Werk München 8000 München 50,
Dachauer Strasse 667
TELEPHONE: 14801
TELEX: 05-28333
CONTAINERS:
ISO/DIN—Dry freight Containers 20/40 ft
DESIGN STANDARD:
ISO/DIN
CONSTRUCTION—MATERIALS AND METHOD:
Aluminium/Steel

MARSHALL

Marshall of Cambridge (Engineering) Ltd
Motor Bodies Division

Airport Works, Cambridge England
TELEPHONE: Cambridge 56291
TELEX: 81208
DIRECTORS:
A. G. G. Marshall
M. J. Marshall
Mrs. M. M. Fry
R. Lane
J. H. Huntridge
R. D. Horsbrough
M. St. Clair Marshall
P. D. N. Hedderwick
CONTAINERS:
Dry freight; open top; side door
CONSTRUCTION—MATERIALS AND METHOD
Steel; light alloy; ply/glassfibre;
Welding; and all riveting
DESIGN STANDARD:
ISO, BS 3951, Lloyds Approval, Ministry of Transport, TIR, British Rail, UIC
Production capacity continues at a rate of 1,000 per annum.

INTERNAL DIMENSIONS:

ISO	Internal		
	Length	Width	Height
40ft Dry Freight	12.02m 39ft 5¾ins	2.33m 7ft 7¾ins	2.32m 7ft 7⅜ ins
30ft Dry Freight	8.97m 29ft 5½ins	2.33m 7ft 7¾ins	2.32m 7ft 7⅜ins
20ft Dry Freight	5.91m 19ft 4¾ins	2.33m 7ft 7¾ins	2.32m 7ft 7⅜ins

PRINCIPAL USERS:
Overseas Containers Ltd.
Alfred Holt
Associated Container Transportation Ltd.
Ben Line
Blue Star Line
Star Container Services Ltd
Seawheel Ltd.
European Unit Routes Ltd
New Zealand Shipping Co.
Transport Development Group
Transcontainer Express
Translode Units Ltd.
Currie Line Ltd.
National Physical Laboratory
Winn International Containers Ltd.
Pitt & Scott Ltd.
B.R.S.
Pickfords
Associated Ferry Transport
Containerway and Road Ferry
AUL
Ocean Management Services
World Transport Agency
Capital City Waste
B.A.C.
R.T.I.T.B.
B.D.H. Chemicals Ltd
Regiment of Transport (M.O.D.)

MASCHINENEXPORT

Maschinenexport
Volkseigener Aussenhandelsbetrieb der DDR
DDR—108 Berlin, Mohrenstrasse 61.
EDITOR'S NOTE:
All information on containers, cranes and other container handling equipment will be readily available from Maschinenexport in East Berlin, but it is not to be understood that they undertake manufacture being solely a buying and selling organisation.

MICKLEOVER

Mickleover Transport Ltd.
Part of Unigate Ltd.
Twyford Works, Whitby Avenue,
Park Royal, London, N.W.10, England

TELEPHONE: 01-965 7788
L. W. Lawrence (*Commercial Manager*)
CONTAINERS:
Railway transport containers. ISO freight containers, 20 ft. Stainless steel container tanks. GRP containers to customers' specifications.

Refrigerated Container
GOOD BACON HAS
DANISH
WRITTEN ALL OVER IT
Direct from Denmark

MILLER TRAILERS

Miller Trailers, Inc,
333 Sixth Ave, West,
Bradenton, Florida, USA
TELEPHONE: (813) 746-6145
TELEGRAMS: Miltrail
CONTAINERS:
Manufactures 20 ft and 40 ft ISO dry goods
and insulated containers, either of aluminium
alloy throughout or of composite steel and
aluminium construction.

INTERNAL DIMENSIONS:

	Length
20 ft	5·92 m
	19 ft 5 in
40 ft	12·01 m
	39 ft 5 in

Licences to manufacture containers abroad
have been granted in Peru, Colombia,
Jamaica, Venezuela and Honduras.

In 1969 250 twenty foot dry goods containers, 450 forty foot dry containers and 60
twenty foot insulated containers were manufactured.

MAIN USERS:
K Line, New York Inc,
South Atlantic and Caribbean Lines, Inc,
Sears, Roebuck & Co

MORTEO SOPREFIN

Morteo Soprefin S.p.A.
16128 Genoa, Corso Andrea Podesta, 8. Italy
TELEPHONE: 58 76 52
TELEGRAMS: Morteosoprefin, Genoa
TELEX: Morteo 27570
PRODUCTS:
Dry-freight, liquid and refrigerated con-
tainers to ISO standards
DESIGN STANDARDS: ISO
CONSTRUCTION:
All steel. Specials of 20 ft length have
walls, roof and doors of stainless steel.
stainless steel.

Four Morteo Sporefin containers being shipped
to Yugoslavia in 1969.

A Morteo-Soprefin container during testing in Southern Italy.

INTERNAL DIMENSIONS:

Type	Internal			Door Opening		Cubic Capacity	Tare
	Length	Width	Height	Width	Height		
Dry Freight 20ft Steel	5904mm 19ft 4¼ins					30.6 cu.m. 1081 cu.ft.	1900 kg 4189 lbs
Dry Freight 30ft Steel	8972mm 29ft 5ins	2333mm 7ft 7¾ins	2220mm 7ft 3¼ins	2290mm 7ft 6in	2130mm 6ft 11¾ins	46.5 cu.m 1642 cu.ft.	2700 kg 5952 lbs
Dry Freight 40ft Steel	12012mm 39ft 4½ins					62.2 cu.m. 2196 cu.ft.	3600 kg 7937 lbs
Refrigerated 20ft 2 Cyls : Nitrogen	5731mm 18ft 9½ins					26 cu.m. 918 cu.ft.	2450 kg 5401 lbs
Refrigerated 20ft 3 H.P. Unit	5371mm 17ft 7½ins	2201mm 7ft 2¾ins	2096mm 6ft 10¼ins	2201mm 7ft 2½ins	2057mm 6ft 8¼ins	25.5 cu.m. 900.5 cu.ft.	2240 kg 4938 lbs
Refrigerated 20ft 5 H.P. Unit	5251mm 17ft 2½ins					24.2 cu.m. 854.6 cu.ft.	2300 kg 5071 lbs
20ft Dry Freight Open Top	5904mm 19ft 4¼ins	2333mm 7ft 7¾ins	2120mm 6ft 11½ins	2290mm 7ft 6in	2130mm 6ft 11¾ins	29.2 cu.m. 1031 cu.ft.	1830 kg 4034 lbs
20ft Dry Freight ½ height open top	5904mm 19ft 4¼ins	2333mm 7ft 7¾ins	1050mm 3ft 5¼ins	2290mm 7ft 6in	903mm 2ft 11½ins	14.5 cu.m. 508.5 cu.ft.	1290 kg 2844 lbs

MURFITT

R. Murfitt Ltd.
Sandall Road
Wisbech
Cambridgeshire, PE13 2RR
TELEPHONE : (0945) 2351/4
TELEX : 32241
DIRECTORS :

Alexander Dunn-Stark (*Managing*)
Frederick Stothard

CONTAINERS :
This company is developing a special tank container for powders of the type incorporated inside an ISO framework. The object is to allow re-use on a return journey without the need for cleaning. The container, which will consist of two compartments, is designed to accept bags which fit round the inside of the tank and are fastened to the container at one point only. A vacuum created between the outside of the bags and the walls of the container causes the bags to be sucked up against the inside of the compartments forming a lining ready for filling. Air pressure inserted between the lining and the container walls rolls the material inside the bags towards the end outlet in each compartment.

Murfitt Special tank container

NETAM

N.V. Nederlandse Tank Apparaten-en Machine fabriek 'Netam'
van Helmontstraat 33,
Rotterdam,
Nederlands

TELEPHONE : 010-254880
TELEX : 22596
DIRECTORS :
B. A. van Rijn Ing (*Director*)
A. Wiegman Ing (*Sales Manager*)

CONTAINERS :
The Fruehauf range of containers and tilt containers.
PRINCIPLE USERS :
Sealand, Seatrain, Meyer Line, Moore McCormack, Anker.

NORDVERK

AB Nordverk,
Uddavalla,
Sweden
TELEPHONE : 0522 14100
TELEX : 5297
TELEGRAMS : Nordverk

DESIGN STANDARDS :
ISO
CONTAINERS :
Cargo flats or open containers in the following measurements: 10 ft × 8 ft × 4 ft, 20 ft × 8 ft × 8 ft, 30 ft × 8 ft. The first three units mentioned have side and end walls which fold. They are designed to stack 6 units high in a cellular system or 2 units high free standing. They may be handled by corner fittings or fork lift channels.

NORTH WESTERN TRAILER

North Western Trailer Co. Ltd.
Sandhurst Avenue
St. Annes-on-Sea
Lancs.
TELEPHONE: St. Annes 26717
DIRECTORS:
T. Howe
D. E. Howe
G. B. Johnson

L. Atkinson
D. Howe
PRODUCTS:
All types of 20 ft, 30 ft and 40 ft general purpose rigid and folding containers.
DESIGN STANDARD: ISO and non ISO.
MATERIALS AND METHODS:
Steel angles and sections electrically welded on a production line basis.
OUTPUT:
Increased capacity following expansion programme.

MAIN USERS: Most major shipping lines and haulage contractors.

CONTAINERS:
purpose rigid, tilt, half height and folding containers. 20 ft, 30 ft and 40 ft containers have been manufactured to the 8 ft × 8 ft 6 in profile.

REPAIR FACILITIES:
These are available at the Company's branch address at Marsh Lane, Preston, Lancs.

PAASKE

C. Paaske
23 Bygdø Alle, Oslo 2,
Norway
TELEPHONE: (024) 44 18 60
TELEX: 18050
CONTAINERS:
Producers both of containers and refrigerating systems. The insulated and refrigerated "Finsam" containers made by this company are constructed from welded steel with external cladding of cold rolled steel sheets. Internal cladding is of aluminium or stainless steel. Insulation is by means of high grade rigid polyurethane-foam expanded in place. Refrigeration is tailor made.
Typical Finsam containers
20 ft insulated ISO steel container

External dimensions:
Length 6,055 mm (19 ft 10½ in)
Width 2,435 mm (8 ft)
Height 2,435 mm (8 ft)
Internal dimensions:
Length 5,830 mm (19 ft 0½ in)
Width 2,263 mm (7 ft 5 in)
Height 2,175 mm (7 ft 2 in)
Tare weight 2,500 kg (5,730 lb)
Capacity ca. 29 m³ (ca 1,025 cu ft)
20 ft refrigerated ISO steel container
External dimensions:
Length 6,055 mm (19 ft 10½ in)
Width 2,435 mm (8 ft)
Height 2,435 mm (8 ft)
Internal dimensions:

Length 5,390 mm (17 ft 8 in)
Width 2,263 mm (8 ft)
Height 2,175 mm (7 ft 2 in)
Tare weight 2,900 kg (6,394 lb)
Capacity ca 26·5 m³ (ca. 940 ft³)
40 ft refrigerated ISO steel container
External dimensions:
Length 12,190 mm (40 ft)
Width 2,435 mm (8 ft)
Height 2,435 mm (8 ft)
Internal dimensions:
Length 11,296 mm (37 ft 1 in)
Width 2,230 mm (6 ft 11 in)
Height: 2,165 mm (7 ft 1 in)
Tare weight 5,300 kg (11,686 lb)
Capacity ca. 54·6 m³ (ca. 1,928 ft³)

RAGHENO

Usines Ragheno S.A.
Motstraat 54
Mechelen (Belgium)
TELEPHONE: (015) 422.03 and 454.35
TELEX: 22538
DIRECTORS:
J. Pieters (*Managing Director, President of the Board*)
H. Demeter (*Technical Manager*)
CONTAINERS:
All containers according to ISO recommendations or special specifications wanted by customers
PRINCIPAL OWNERS
Ministere Belge des Communications
Direction de la Marine

12·19 m (40 ft) I.S.O. container built in Usines Ragheno S.A. works

RHEINSTAHL

**Rheinische Stahlwerke Transporttechnik,
SEAG-Waggonbau**
5931 Netphen-Dreis-Tiefenbach
Germany (Federal Republic)
TELEPHONE: 0271/7171
TELEX
0872843 seag sieg
DIRECTORS:
H. König, K. Ueber
CONTAINERS:
ISO—and other containers with sliding roofs
and sliding walls
SPECIFICATIONS:
Standards of German Federal State Railways
and others
TYPES:
ISO, UiC and others
CONSTRUCTION—MATERIALS AND METHOD:
All-steel, all-aluminium or mixed construc-
tion and/or plastic and timber.

General Purpose 40 ft
Door openings: at end
    Clear width 2,250 mm (7 ft 4½ in)
    Clear height 2,050 mm (6 ft 8¾ in)
Door openings: at side
(Sliding)
    Clear width 5,160 mm (16 ft 11¼ in)
    Clear hight 2,050 mm (6 ft 8¾ in)
Roof opening: sliding cover
    Clear length 5,740 mm (18 ft 10 in)
    Clear width 2,160 mm (7 ft 1 in)

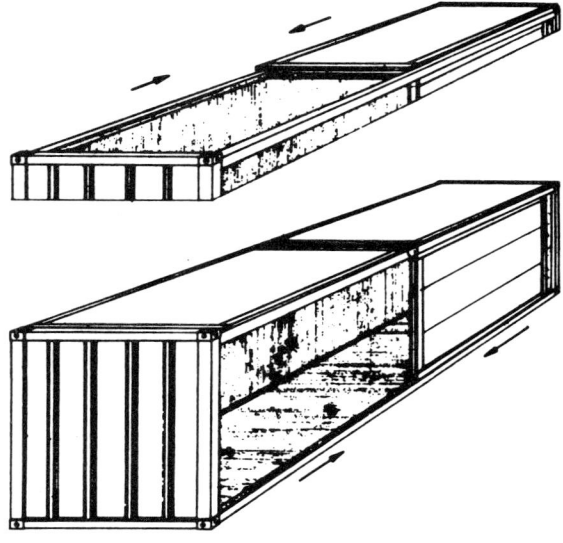

Rheinstahl 40 ft Container with sliding roof and sliding sides

PRINCIPAL OWNERS OF CONTAINERS:
German Federal Railway

RUBERY OWEN

Rubery, Owen & Co. Ltd.,
Container Division

Kings Hill Works,
Darlaston Road,
Wednesbury, Staffs. England
TELEPHONE: 021-556-1221
TELEX: 338236/7

DIRECTORS:
Sir Alfred Owen, C.B.E. (Ch.), A. D. Owen,
J. E. Owen, H. Jean, B. Stanley, J. A. Glover,
W. Holmes, R. G. Houston, J. T. Plumley

CONTAINERS:
Dry freight (standard designs ISO or custom
built), side loading, open top, bulk tipping

cargo flats for general freight, plain flats for
sheeted loads or with detachable sides for
packaged goods. Vehicle transporter flats for
lashed-on cars and light vans for shipping.
TYPES:
10 ft, 20 ft, 30 ft and 40 ft
DESIGN STANDARD:
ISO

S.I.C.

Societe Intercontinentale Des Containers
6 Rue Daru, 75 Paris 8e, France
TELEPHONE: 924.07.29
TELEX: 65.515
DIRECTORS:
Pierre Detanger (*Président-Directeur Général*)
CONTAINERS:
    Dry freight, 20 ft, 30 ft and 40 ft, an opening
roof 20 ft container and smaller containers
to UIC dimensions.
PRODUCTION:
    In 1970, 5,200 20 ft, 500 30 ft and 1,500
40 ft dry goods containers were made against
3,000 20 ft, 400 30 ft and 600 40 ft units in
1969. The 40 ft units were 8 ft 6 in high
and 50 of the 20 ft units were 8 ft 6 in high.
300 20 ft and 200 40 ft units with open tops
had been made in 1971 at the time of going to
press.
PRINCIPLE USERS:
Container Transport International,
Chargeurs Réunis-Fabre Line, Coast Line.
CONSTRUCTION:
All-steel and welded.
GENERAL DATA:
ISO 40 ft.
Length 12,017 mm (39 ft 5⅛ in)
Width 2,345 mm (7 ft 8²¹⁄₆₄ in)
Height 2,229 mm (7 ft 9⁴⁵⁄₆₄ in)
Door Opening:
    Width 2,337 mm (7 ft 8 ins)
    Height 2,165 mm (7 ft 1¹⁵⁄₁₆ in)
Gooseneck 40 ft (8 ft 6 in high)
Internal dimensions:
    Length 12,017 mm (39 ft 5⅛ in)
    Width 2,345 (7 ft 8²¹⁄₆₄ in)
    Height 2,380 mm (7 ft 8½ in)
Door opening:
    Width 2,337 mm (7 ft 8 in)
    Height 2,317 mm (7 ft 7⁷⁄₃₂ in)

ISO 30 ft with side door
Internal dimensions:
    Length 8,952 mm (29 ft 4⁷⁄₁₆ in)
    Width 2,345 mm (7 ft 8²¹⁄₆₄ in)
    Height 2,229 mm (7 ft 0¾ in)
Door opening:
    Width 2,337 mm (7 ft 8 in)
    Height 2,165 mm (7 ft 1¹⁵⁄₆₄ in)
Side door opening:
    Width 2,337 mm (7 ft 8 in)
    Height 2,158 mm (7 ft 1¹⁵⁄₆₄ in)
ISO 20 ft
Internal dimensions:
    Length 5,900 mm (19 ft 4¹⁵⁄₆₄ in)
    Width 2,345 mm (7 ft 8²¹⁄₆₄ in)

Height 2,229 mm (7 ft 3¾ in)
Door opening:
    Width 2,337 mm
    Height 2,165 mm (7 ft 1¹⁵⁄₆₄ in)
ISO 20 ft with side door
Internal dimensions:
    Length 5,900 mm (19 ft 4⁹⁄₃₂ in)
    Width 2,345 mm (7 ft 8²¹⁄₆₄ in)
    Height 2,229 mm (7 ft 1¹⁵⁄₆₄ in)
Door opening:
    Width 2,337 mm (7 ft 8 in)
    Height 2,165 mm (7 ft 1¹⁵⁄₁₆ in)

The SIC 40 ft Gooseneck container,
8 ft 6 in overall height.

Side door opening:
 Width 2,300 mm (7 ft 6½ in)
 Height 2,000 mm (6 ft 6¾ in)
 Fork lift pockets are optional on this container.

ISO 20 ft with opening roof
Internal dimensions:
 Length 5,880 mm (19 ft 4¾ in)
 Width 2,310 mm (7 ft 6⁶¹⁄₆₄ in)
 Height 2,190 mm (7 ft 2⅛ in)
Door opening:
 Width 2,300 mm (7 ft 6½ in)
 Height 2,130 mm (6 ft 11¾ in)
Roof opening:
 Length 5,626 mm (18 ft 5 in)
 Width 2,300 mm (7 ft 6½ in)
 Opening of hinged lintel 1,840 mm (6 ft 0½ in)

ISO 10 ft
Internal dimensions:
 Length 2,835 mm (9 ft 3³²⁄₆₄ in)
 Width 2,345 mm (7 ft 8²¹⁄₆₄ in)
 Height 2,229 mm (7 ft 3¾ in)
Door opening:
 Width 2,337 mm (7 ft 8 in)
 Height 2,165 mm (7 ft 1¹⁵⁄₆₄ in)

Interlocking modular containers
The Trans 9
 The particularly strong construction of the Trans 9 container allows it to be used on conventional ships in all conditions.

 The Trans 9 is designed to be used for the fractioning of goods which when carried out in 20 ft containers presents problems of redistribution and cancels a part of the advantages of containerisation.

 A group of three Trans 9 containers when locked on to a platform have exactly the same dimensions as an ISO 1C 20 ft container and can thus be inserted in container ships.

 The platform consists of a metal frame equipped with twist locks which serve to secure the Trans 9 containers by means of the external corners fittings.

 The Trans 9 structure gives the same resistance as a standard 20 ft container.

External dimensions:
 Length 2,435 mm (8 ft)
 Width 2,000 mm (6 ft 6⁴⁷⁄₆₄ in)
 Height 2,265 mm (7 ft 5¹⁵⁄₆₄ in)

Silverdale Motor Bodies Ltd.
York Road, Birmingham, 28.
TELEPHONE: 021-777 4466/7/8
BRANCH ADDRESS:
70A Long Lane, Smithfield, London, EC1
DIRECTORS:
F. Fitzpatrick

THE SIC 20 ft opening roof container.

Internal dimensions:
 Length 2,310 mm (7 ft 6¹⁵⁄₆₄ in)
 Width 1,880 mm (6 ft 2 ¹⁄₆₄ in)
 Height 2,050 mm (6 ft 8⁴⁵⁄₆₄ in)
Door opening:
 Width 1,872 mm (6 ft 1⁴⁵⁄₆₄ in)
 Height 1,966 mm (6 ft 5¹³⁄₃₂ in)
The Trans 19 with side door:
External dimensions:
 Length 4,027·5 mm (13 ft 2³⁵⁄₆₄ in)
 Width 2,435 mm (8 ft)

 Height 2,265 mm (7 ft 5¹¹⁄₆₄ in)
Internal dimensions:
 Length 3,852·5 mm (12 ft 7 ²¹⁄₃₂ in)
 Width 2,310 mm (7 ft 6⁶¹⁄₆₄ in)
 Height 2,050 mm (6 ft 8⁴⁵⁄₆₄ in)
Door opening:
 Width 2,300 mm (7 ft 6³⁵⁄₆₄ in)
 Height 1,960 mm (6 ft 5⁵⁄₃₂ in)
Side door opening:
 Width 1,500 mm (4 ft 11¹⁄₁₆ mm)
 Height 1,900 mm (6 ft 2¹³⁄₁₆ in)

SILVERDALE

J. Fitzpatrick

PRODUCTS:
 Insulated and refrigerated vehicle bodies and containers to customers requirements, mainly to accommodate meat loads hung from roof-rails.

METHODS AND MATERIALS:
 Twin alloy framed with fibre-glass spacers to break down metal to metal contact. Extruded aluminium alloy sections and sheet are used, insulation with polystyrene sheet or high density 'in situ' polyurethane foam.

S.N.A.V.

Societe Nouvelle des Ateliers de Venissieux
Chemin du Génie
69 Vénissieux, P.O. Box 4,
France
BRANCH ADDRESS:
Industrial Development and Procurement Inc
600 Old Country Road,
Garden City, Long Island,
New York 11 530
TELEPHONE: 34 603 F
TELEX: Snav-Lyon
DESIGN STANDARDS:
ISO, UIC and TIR
PRODUCTION:
 2,800 20 ft, 300 30 ft and 400 40 ft dry freight containers were made in 1970. 500 20 ft and 150 30 ft specials were made.
LICENCES:
 Hold the exclusive licence to manufacture Strick products in France.
CONTAINERS:
Steel, Aluminium, Plywood, Open-top, Insulated and Refrigerated. 20 ft, 30 ft and

40 ft × 8 ft and 8 ft 6 in high. Also skeletal semi-trailers for transporting containers—see Container Handling Section.
PRINCIPAL USERS:
 ICS, Sea Containers, CTI, Uniflex and other leasing companies; Coast Lines, Fabre Lines, Torm Line, A.C.L. CNC, SNTI, Calberson N.C.H.P. etc.

The Steel Container
 General purpose containers manufactured in the full range of ISO series I dimensions, and 8 ft 6 in high.

 Front and rear frames in folded high-tensile steel with crossmembers protecting locking system. Each frame separately tested to 30 tons before assembly. Top and bottom rails in folded high-tensile steel sheet. Front and side panels in corrugated steel sheet. Internal side panels supplied with flat steel cargo securing tracks.

 Steel end doors (plymax optional) featuring full 270° opening along side panels. Five large steel hinges with stainless steel pins and

self-lubricating bushings. Four full height antirack bars pressure arm locks and keepers squeeze doors tight on a double lip seal.

 Floor in laminated hardwood 1⅛ in thick impregnated with chemical preservative (Australian Regulations optional) and fastened to each closely spaced crossmember with special self-tapping cadmium plated steel screws. Whole underside of the floor, sills and inside bottom rails undercoated with antirust to prevent corrosion and preserve watertightness.

 All steel components carefully sand-blasted before passivation and priming. All parts receive then two coats of oven-backed paint, guaranteed for three years against peeling.

The Aluminium Container
 Manufactured in the full range of ISO series I dimensions and 8 ft 6 in high.

 The corner post sections in steel are the same as those used in the steel container, as are the corner castings and their method of attachment.

The side and end walls are of aluminium sheet assembled with ship-lap joints, riveted together. The ribs are of top-hat section extruded aluminium alloy and the container may have either internal or external post design.

Watertightness is ensured by a double-seal door sheet section of special design.

Floor in laminated hardwood 1⅛ in thick impregnated with chemical preservative (Australian Regulations optional) and fastened to each closely spaced crossmember with special self-tapping cadmium plated steel screws. Whole underside of the floor, sills and inside bottom rails undercoated with antirust to prevent corrosion and preserve watertightness.

One piece aluminium roof. Top hat section aluminium alloy roof ribs. Attachment of the roof sheet is by adhesion under pressure. The rivets attaching the roof sheet to the top and end frame members are quite outside the interior loading space and even if a rivet should fail there will be no ingress of water into the container.

At all points where steel and aluminium are in contact, a layer of insulating material is placed between the surfaces as a protection against corrosion.

The interior is lined to prevent damage to the external panelling from clumsy handling of goods inside the container. Equipment (e.g. Aeroquip-Salwall) for load lashing or to accept a second deck may be attached.

SNAV RANGE OF CONTAINERS

Type	Model	Material	Fork lift pockets	Internal Dimensions Length mm	Height mm	Width mm	End Door Open Height mm	Width mm	Side doors opening Height mm	Width mm	Cubic cap. m
20 ft × 8 ft × 8 ft	Dry	steel	4	5,893	2,209	2,318	2,130	2,300	—	—	30·2
				19 ft 4 in	7 ft 3 in	7 ft 7¼ in	84 in	90½ in			1,057 ft³
20 ft × 8 ft × 8 ft	Dry	steel	—	5,893	2,224	2,318	2,131	2,300	—	—	30·3
				19 ft 4 in	7 ft 3½ in	7 ft 7¼ in	84 in	90½ in			1,070 ft³
20 ft × 8 ft × 8 ft	Dry	steel	4	5,912	2,221	2,318	2,131	2,300	—	—	30·5
				19 ft 4¾ in	7 ft 3½ in	7 ft 7¼ in	84 in	90½ in			1,077 ft³
20 ft × 8 ft × 8 ft 6 in	Dry	steel	4	5,893	2,361	2,318	2,254	2,300	—	—	32·2
				19 ft 4 in	7 ft 9 in	7 ft 7¼ in	88½ in	90½ in			1,057 ft³
20 ft × 8 ft × 8 ft 6 in	Dry	steel	—	5,893	2,376	2,318	2,283	2,300	—	—	32·5
				19 ft 4 in	7 ft 9½ in	7 ft 7¼ in	90 in	90½ in			1,077 ft³
20 ft × 8 ft × 8 ft 6 in	Side doors	steel	—	5,893	2,376	2,318	2,283	2,300	2,229	2,800	32·5
				19 ft 4 in	7 ft 9½ in	7 ft 7¼ in	90 in	90½ in	87¾ in	110¼ in	1,057 ft³
20 ft × 8 ft × 8 ft	Open top	steel	4	5,893	2,147	2,318	2,029	2,300	—	—	29·2
				19 ft 4 in	7 ft 0½ in	7 ft 7¼ in	80 in	90½ in			1,032 ft³
20 ft × 8 ft × 8 ft	Open top	steel	—	5,893	2,162	2,318	2,044	2,300	—	—	29·5
				19 ft 4 in	7 ft 1 in	7 ft 7¼ in	80½ in	90½ in			1,042 ft³
20 ft × 8 ft × 8 ft 6 in	Open top	steel	4	5,893	2,229	2,318	2,181	2,300	—	—	31·3
				19 ft 4 in	7 ft 3¾ in	7 ft 7¼ in	85¾ in	90½ in			1,105 ft³
20 ft × 8 ft × 8 ft 6 in	Open top	steel	—	5,893	2,314	2,318	2,196	2,300	—	—	31·5
				19 ft 4 in	7 ft 7 in	7 ft 7¼ in	86½ in	90½ in			1,112 ft³
20 ft × 8 ft × 8 ft	Open side	steel	—	5,935	2,252	2,308	2,132	2,300	2,132	5,639	30·2
				19 ft 10½ in	7 ft 4¾ in		84 in	90½ in	84 in	222 in	1,057 ft³
30 ft × 8 ft × 8 ft	Dry	steel	—	8,958	2,224	2,318	2,131	2,300	—	—	46·2
				28 ft 8¾ in	7 ft 3½ in	7 ft 7¼ in	84 in	90½ in			1,596 ft³
30 ft × 8 ft × 8 ft 6 in	Dry	steel	—	8,958	2,376	2,318	2,283	2,300	—	—	49·3
				28 ft 8¾ in	7 ft 9½ in	7 ft 7¼ in	90 in	90½ in			1,741 ft³
30 ft × 8 ft × 8 ft 6 in	Side doors	steel	—	8,958	2,376	2,318	2,283	2,300	2,229	2,800	49·3
				28 ft 8¾ in	7 ft 9½ in	7 ft 7¼ in	90 in	90½ in	90½ in	110¼ in	1,741 ft³
30 ft × 8 ft × 8 ft 6 in	Open side	steel	2	8,958	2,235	2,308	2,132	2,300	2,132	5,639	46·2
				28 ft 8¾ in	7 ft 4 in		84 in	90½ in	84 in	222 in	1,632 ft³
40 ft × 8 ft × 8 ft 6 in	Dry	steel	—	12,020	2,376	2,318	2,283	2,300	—	—	66·2
				39 ft 5¼ in	7 ft 9½ in	7 ft 7¼ in	90 in	90½ in			2,338 ft³
40 ft × 8 ft × 8 ft 6 in	Side doors	steel	—	12,020	2,376	2,318	2,283	2,300	2,229	2,800	66·2
				39 ft 5¼ in	7 ft 9½ in	7 ft 7¼ in	90 in	90½ in	90½ in	110¼ in	2,338 ft³

D. SOULE

Etablissements Industriels D. Soulé

Bagnères-de-Bigorre
65 France

Telephone: 95-07-31
Telegrams: Soulé Bagnères-de-Bigorre

Telex: 57.879 SOULÉ-BAGNB

Branch Office:
2 Rue de la Baume, Paris, 8me,
  Telephone: 359 83.60

Depots:
59, Rue de Nanterre, Asnières

Telephone: 733.04.40
113 Rue Mazenod, Lyon

Telephone: 62.03.44

Containers:
Fibre glass insulated and refrigerated units.

A container made by D. Soulé in use by S.T.E.F.

SPITZER

Ludwig Spitzer Sen. KG.,
Silofahrzeuge, Mosbach/Baden,
Bei Heidelberg,
Germany (Federal Republic)
TELEPHONE: 06261/3041
TELEX: 04-66123
CABLES: spitzersen mosbachbaden
DIRECTORS:
R. F. Heidemann (*Sales*)
CONTAINERS:
Dual purpose 'Combi-containers' and 'Universal' tipping containers for the transport of discrete items and bulk goods and tank containers both to ISO measurements.

The Combi-Container

For the transport of discrete items or powdered or granulated materials. It is equipped with flexible and collapsible outlets for discharging by gravity (without tipping). There are air tight doors at the rear for loading piece goods. Manholes of 400 mm (15⅜ in) are provided for loading bulk materials. The range is as follows:
Type:
C 40/60 40 ft (12,190 × 2,430 × 2,430 mm)
C 30/45 30 ft (9,125 × 2,430 × 2,430 mm)
C 20/29 20 ft (6,055 × 2,430 × 2,430 mm)
C 10/14 10 ft (2,990 × 2,430 × 2,430 mm)
Capacity app. 60 m³ (2,100 ft³) dead weight
45 m³ (1,570 ft³)
29 m³ (1,015 ft³)
14 m³ (490 ft³)

Combi Container

Has twin doors and man-holes. It can be tipped to discharge goods. The tipping angle is up to 50°. The walls are slightly convex to withstand the pressure of liquids. The range is as follows:
Type:
U 40/57 40 ft (12,190 × 2,430 × 2,430 mm)
U 30/42 30 ft (9,125 × 2,430 × 2,430 mm)
U 20/26 20 ft (6,055 × 2,430 × 2,430 mm)
U 10/11 10 ft (2,990 × 2,430 × 2,430 mm)
Capacity app. 57 m³ (2,000 ft³) dead weight
42 m³ (1,470 ft³)
26 m³ (915 ft³)
11 m³ (386 ft³)

Kipp Container

For the bulk transport of powdered and granulated goods. Discharge is by compressed air. The range is as follows:
Type:
P 40/32 40 ft (12,190 × 2,430 × 2,430 mm)
P 30/24 30 ft (9,125 × 2,430 × 2,430 mm)
P 20/16 20 ft (6,055 × 2,430 × 2,430 mm)
P 10/ 8 10 ft (2,990 × 2,430 × 2,430 mm)
Dead weight 5,200 kg
4,000 kg
2,900 kg
2,000 kg
Capacity app. 32 m³ (1,130 ft³)
24 m³ (850 ft³)
16 m³ (565 ft³)
8 m³ (280 ft³)

Spitzer Combi-Container

Spitzer Kipp Container

STANDARD

Standard Railway Wagon Co., Ltd.
HEAD OFFICE:
Reddish, Stockport, England

TELEPHONE:
Stockport 4222/3
Heywood 60237/8
MAIN WORKS:
Reddish, Stockport

DIRECTORS:
T. R. Bell (*Managing and Chairman*)
Sir Stanley Bell
L. T. Reddy
S. G. Errington

CONTAINERS:
Special purpose, 20 ton, steel coil.
DESIGN STANDARD:
ISO/'Freightliner'
CONSTRUCTION—MATERIALS
All steel
PRINCIPAL OWNERS:
Containerway and Road Ferry Ltd.

Coil Carrying Container 20 ft

SPECIFICATIONS:
Floor: 12 mm (½ in) plywood.

Freightliner Locating Pockets are fitted. Two Fork Lift Pockets.
Headboard.

Internal dimensions:
Length 6,052 mm (19 ft 10¼ in)
Width 2,362 mm (7 ft 9 in)
Depth with headboard 1,384 mm (4 ft 6½ in)
Depth without headboard 470 mm (1 ft 6½ in)
Depth of well 247 mm (0 ft 9¾ in)
Width of well 1,117 mm (3 ft 8 in)
Maximum weight of coil 18,797 kg (18½ tons)

STF

Salvatore Trifone & Figli
Via Robecco 10/12 Magenta (MI)
20013
Italy
TELEPHONE: 972108
DIRECTORS:
Franco Trifone
Antonino Trifone
PRODUCTION:
95 20 ft and 12 30 ft dry freight containers were made in 1970. 15 20 ft and 10 30 ft tank units were made. In 1971 130 20 ft and 25 30 ft dry freight units were on order. 20 20 ft and 20 30 ft tank units were on order.
CONTAINERS:
General purpose and tank containers. Tank containers are made in 10 ft, 20 ft and 30 ft lengths.

STF RANGE OF CONTAINERS:		Internal measurements		
		Height	Width	Length
10 ft × 8 ft × 8 ft	Steel	2,240 mm	2,335 mm	2,850 mm
		88 in	92 in	112¼ in
6 ft 6 in × 8 ft × 8 ft	Steel	2,220 mm	2,270 mm	1,885 mm
		87½ in	89¼ in	74¼ in
20 ft × 8 ft × 8 ft	Steel	2,245 mm	2,347 mm	5,920 mm
		88½ in	92½ in	233 in
20 ft × 8 ft × 8 ft	Aluminium	2,245 mm	2,347 mm	5,920 mm
		88½ in	92½ in	233 in
30 ft × 8 ft × 8 ft	Aluminium	2,333 mm	2,240 mm	8,960 mm
		91¼ in	88 in	352¾ in

STRICK

Strick Corporation
US Highway No. 1,
Fairless Hills, Pa. 19030
TELEPHONE: 215-949-3600
TELEX: 84-3412

BRANCHES:
Strick Chicago,
5300 West 73rd Street,
Chicago, Illinois 60649
Strick Charlotte
4525 S. Interstate 85,
Charlotte, N.C. 28208
Strick Los Angeles,
2790 Atlantic Blvd.,
Bell, California 90201
Strick North Jersey,
2480 Secaucus Road,
North Bergen, N.J. 07047

DIRECTORS:
Sol Katz (*Chairman of the Board*)
Phil Orzeck, (*President*)
Harry Shapiro (*Vice President, Marketing*)
Robert Hitch (*Vice President, Engineering and Manufacturing*)
Sherwin Gaines, (*Vice President, Sales*)
Jack Greenberg (*Executive Vice President*)
Len Barkan (*Vice President and General Counsel*)
SALES MANAGER IN CHARGE OF CONTAINER OPERATIONS:
Howard Marx,
2480 Secaucus Road,
North Bergen, N.J. 07047
Tel: 201-864-1215

SVENSKA METALLVERKEN

AB Svenska Metallverken
Skultunaverken,
730 50 Skultuna, Sweden
TELEPHONE: Västerås 021 750 80
TELEGRAMS: skultunaverken, västeras
TELEX: 4737 essemsk s
CONTAINERS:
Bulk and dry freight units. The company specialises in the Parator 20 ft and 30 ft aluminium and fibre glass reinforced plywood containers.

The Parator-Container
The container is made with a frame of high strength extruded aluminium profiles with walls and roof of fibreglass reinforced plywood panels. Smooth inner and exterior walls and roof surfaces, plus counter sunkhead rivets offer protection against "hooking incidents". There are no inside roof bows or side ports.
The frame: The frame elements, made of high strength extruded aluminium, are connected together by MIG-TIG welding. The frame consists of corner posts, top and bottom side rails, front and rear header, front sill, rub rail and bottom cross members.

Walls and roof: The fibreglass reinforced waterproof plywood panels are made to withstand sudden and heavy impacts.
The material meets all the British Standard specifications BS 1455: 1956 including the requirement that it must be able to withstand a tropical climate.
The floor: The Parator-Container's floor constructed of impregnated 24 mm (1 in) thick Finnish birch plywood (BS 1455:1956) covered on the upper surface with a hard diamond-patterned layer of fibreglass polyester lamination. The floor is made up of four equal sized sections, easy to replace, under which are 21 bottom cross members.
The first five cross members are spaced only 177 mm (7 in) apart to give extra protection to the floor nearest the door opening where it has to bear the brunt of knocks when the container is being loaded and unloaded by fork-lift trucks.

Corner fittings: The container's corner fittings are made from extruded aluminium profiles in an Al-Zn alloy which has good stress properties and a high yield point. Special attaching devices ensure an extremely good welding connection. The top corner fittings protrude a minimum 6 mm (¼ in) above the top face of the top side rail, and the bottom corner fittings lie 8 mm (⅓ in) below the bottom side rails.

The doors: They are also made of fibreglass reinforced waterproof Finnish birch plywood panels mounted in aluminium profiles. Each door has four hinges. The doors can be fully opened (270 degrees) and locked in the open position.
Each door is provided with two heavy duty locking bars of high quality plated steel. They are able to bear both horizontal and vertical loads.
Locking bars are provided for customs sealing—and the hardware is supplied with customs seal cover in accordance with TIR requirements. In addition, one door is provided with a document pocket with protective cover.

WAGGONFABRIK TALBOT

Waggonfabrik Talbot
51 Aachen, Julicherstr. 213-237,
Postfach 1410
Germany (Federal Republic)
TELEPHONE: 4681
TELEX: 832845
DIRECTORS:
Richard Talbot
Herbert Talbot
Heinz-Dieter von Wittgenstein
Kurt Capellmann
Dr. Dold
CONTAINERS:
Special containers were developed in 1970 of which 239 30 ft units had been made in 1971 at the time of going to press.

THYSSEN

Thyssen Industrie GmbH
4 Dusseldorf 1
Thyssenhaus, Postfach 7928
Germany (Federal Republic)

Containers formerly manufactured by Mannesmann are now made by the company following a merger of the two companies on Oct 1 1970.

TOKYU

Tokyu Car Manufacturing Co.
1 Kamariya-cho,
Kanazawa-ky,
Yokohama,
Japan
TELEPHONE: (045) 701-5151

SALES DEPARTMENT:
Yaesu-Mitsui Bldg.,
7, 5-chome, Yaesu,
Chuo-ku,
Tokyo

CONTAINERS:
Dry freight and insulated ISO containers and flats and tank containers. This company supplies containers to the Japanese railways.

All Steel Containers
External dimensions:
Length 6,055 mm (20 ft)
Width 2,435 mm (8 ft)
Height 2,435 (8 ft)
Internal dimensions:
Length 5,888 mm (232¼ in)
Width 2,320 mm (91⅓ in)
Height 2,208 ,mm (87 in)
Door opening:
Width 2,273 mm (89½ in)
Height 2,130 mm (83¾ in)
Inside volume: 30·16 m^3
Tare weight: 2,150 kg

Stainless Steel Unit (Dry freight)
External dimensions:
Length 6,055 mm (20 ft)
Width 2,435 mm (8 ft)
Height 2,435 mm (8 ft)
Internal dimensions:
Length 5,899 mm (212¼ in)
Width 2,340 mm (92⅛ in)
Height 2,231 mm (87¾ in)
Door opening:
Width 2,343 mm (92¼ in)
Height 2,138 mm (84⅛ in)
Inside volume: 30·8 m^3 (1,341·9 cu ft)
Tare weight 1,740 kg (3,836 lb)

Aluminium Dry freight
External dimensions:
Length 6,055 mm (20 ft)
Width 2,435 mm (8 ft)
Height 2,435 mm (8 ft)
Internal dimensions:
Length 5,917 mm (232¾ in)
Width 2,341 mm (92¼ in)
Height 2,240 mm (88⅛ in)
Door opening:
Width 2,284 mm (89⅞ in)
Height 2,135 mm (84 in)
Inside volume: 31·0 m^3 (1,094·7 cu ft)
Tare weight: 1,660 kg (3,659·6 lb)

ISO IC Dry Cargo Container 20 ft
External dimensions:
Length 6,055 mm (20 ft)
Width 2,435 mm (8 ft)
Height 2,435 mm (8 ft)
Internal dimensions:
Length 5,890 mm (231¾ in)
Width 2,320 mm (91⅓ in)
Height 1,295 mm (86½ in)
Door opening:
Width 2,273 mm (89½ in)
Height 2,152 mm (84¾ in)
Inside volume: 30·07 m^3 (1,085 cu ft)
Tare weight 2,240 kg (4,938·4 lb)

40 ft × 8 ft × 8 ft 6 in Gooseneck Dry Cargo Container
External dimensions:
Length 12,190 mm (40 ft)
Width 2,435 mm (8 ft)
Height 2,590 mm (8 ft 6 in)
Internal dimensions:
Length 12,027 mm (473½ in)
Width 2,317 mm (91¼ in)
Height 2,396 mm (94 ⅓ in)
End door opening:
Width 2,286 mm (90 in)
Height 2,315 mm (91⅛ in)
Side door opening:
Width 2,500 mm (98½ in)
Height 2,257 mm 88⅛ in)
Inside volume: 66·76 m^3 (2,578 cu ft)
Tare weight: 3,200 kg (7,054·7 lb)

Flat with fixed end supports
External dimensions:
Length 6,055 mm (20 ft)
Width 2,435 mm (8 ft)
Height 2,435 mm (8 ft)
Tare weight: 2,400 kg (5,291 lb)

Flat with collapsible end supports
External dimensions:
Length 6,055 mm (20 ft)
Width 2,435 mm (8 ft)
Height 2,435 mm (8 ft)
Tare weight: 2,500 kg (5,511·5 lb)

TRAILCO

Trailco Mfg. & Sales Co.
(A Subsidiary of Vernitron Corporation)
Hummels Wharf, Pennsylvania 17831
USA
TELEPHONE: 717-743-1261
Trailco-Greenville Corporation
(A Subsidiary of Vernitron Corporation)
Greenville, Mississippi 38701
USA
TELEPHONE: 601-335-5231
DIRECTORS:
J. R. Cunningham (*President*)
Charles G. Ellsworth (*Vice-President*)
Roger E. Seal (*Controller*)
DESIGN STANDARDS:
USASI-ISO MH5.
PRODUCTION:
In 1969, 1,000 twenty ft dry goods containers were produced as against 1,100 in 1968. Seven hundred 40 ft units were produced as against 900 in 1968. Two hundred 20 ft containers and 400 forty ft containers 8 ft 6 in high were made by the company.
CONTAINERS:
High tensile steel, aluminium alloy, fiberglass reinforced plywood. Aluminium side sheet, aluminium top and bottom rail-front and rear frame from hi-tensile steel.

Container Vans
One of the manufacturers of semi-trailers in the USA, Trailco was one of the pioneers in the application of aluminium for the design and construction of semi-trailers and has been a major contributor to the growth of bulk materials handling with its Bulk Van semi-trailer units.

Base Model CV-2088 Demountable Type
Size USASI-ISO-TIR dimensional specifications for standard Group 1 demountable type container.
. Capacity USASI-ISO-TIR load and design specifications for standard Group 1 demountable type container. Roof: walk-on load
Front and Rear Frame 4·8 mm ($\frac{3}{16}$ in) hi-tensile steel, primed and painted aluminium before assembly.
Corners—square
Rubrail—extruded aluminium

A 40 ft Group/Demountable type Trailco container mounted on a 40 ft Trailco chassis.

Cross Members—127 mm (5 in) steel on 305 mm (12 in) centres
Floor—127 mm (1⅛ in) laminated oak
Body Posts:
Front—28·5 mm (10 gauge) hi-tensile steel, 50 mm (2 in)depth hat section.
Sides—Extruded aluminium 127 mm (5 in) wide × 30 mm (1⅜ in) depth hat section, on 475 mm (18 in) centers.
Body Panels:
Front—·063 ($\frac{1}{16}$ in) aluminium, smooth
Sides—·050 ($\frac{3}{64}$ in) aluminium smooth
Caprail sides—Extruded aluminium
Roof bows—hi-tensile steel on 457 mm (18 in) centres.
Roof sheet—·063 ($\frac{1}{16}$ in) aluminium, one piece, bonded to bows.
Rear Doors—19 mm (¾ in) plywood core, four hinges each door, two cam locks each door, rubber gasket seal. Inner door face: 22 gauge galvanized steel. Outer door face: aluminium. Complete door encased by aluminium extrusion.
Lining:
Front—12·7 mm (½ in) plywood, full height
Sides—6·4 mm (¼ in) plywood, full height
Paint—all steel parts primed and painted aluminium.
Internal dimensions:
Length 5,912 mm (19 ft 4¾ in)
Width 2,343 mm (7 ft 8¼ in)
Height 2,259 mm (7 ft 4$\frac{13}{16}$ in)
Door openings at end:
Clear width 2,286 mm (7 ft 6 in)
Clear height 2,159 mm (7 ft 1 in)
Tunnel type containers also available.

TRAILMOBILE

40 ft open-top exterior post aluminium container.

Trailmobile
200 So. Michigan Ave,
Chicago, Ill. 60604.
USA
TELEPHONE: 312-939-1350
TELEGRAMS: Trailco Chicago
BRANCH ADDRESS:
Over 100 through continental USA and Canadian Trailmobile Limited,
PO Box 848,
Brantford, Ontario, Canada
Trailmobile de Mexico,
Apartado Postal No. M-10297,
Administracion de Correos No. 1,
Mexico 1, DF
Trailor
110 Avenue de la Republique
Paris X1 me, France
CONTAINERS:
Steel, aluminium and plastic clad plywood containers of all types including dry freight, open top, insulated and refrigerated, platform, tank, and other special designs. Capability to manufacture to all existing standards including ISO, USASI, and ABS.

20 ft Fibre glass reinforced plywood refrigerated container
Length, overall 6·06 m (19 ft 10½ in)
Length, inside 5·47 m (17 ft 11 7/16 in)
Height, overall 2·44 m (8 ft 0 in)
Height, inside 2·08 m (82 in); 1·98 m (78 in) to the loading line
Width, overall 2·44 m (8 ft 0 in)
Width, inside (2·18 m) (85⅞ in)
Clear rear opening, height 2·16 m (85 in) header to bolster
Clear rear opening, width 2·29 m (90 in) post to post
Cubic capacity 25·79 m³ (876 cu ft) to ceiling; 23·59 m³ (833 cu ft) to loading line
Load capacity 17,145 kg (37,800 lb) when fitted with refrigeration unit
Estimated weight 2,547 kg (5,550 lb); 3,175 kg (7,000 lb) with refrigeration unit
Gross load 20,320 kg (44,800 lb)
UNDERFRAME:
Type flush bottom
Lower outer rails 8-gauge high-tensile steel
Crossmembers 10·80 cm (4¼ in) deep extruded 6061-T6 aluminium I-Beams on approximate 33·02 cm (13 in) centres
Lift pockets four, formed high-tensile steel, two on 2·08 m (82 in) centres, two on ·86 m (34 in) centres; 10·16 cm × 30·48 cm (4 in × 12 in) clear tine openings
BODY:
Side walls 1·91 cm (¾ in) laminated panels, (1·59 cm (⅝ in) plywood cores
Front walls complete perimeter of 10-gauge high-tensile steel
Corner posts, front special design tubular high-tensile steel, designed for 6-high stack load; meet ANSI requirements
Corner posts, rear 6·35 mm (¼ in) high-tensile steel, designed for 6-high stack load; meet ANSI requirements; full-height hinge protection
Corner fittings cast steel; conform to latest ANSI/ISO design
Top outer rail 10-gauge high-tensile steel, full length
Roof 1·59 cm (⅝ in) laminated panel; 1·27 cm (½ in) plywood core
Rear doors 2·06 cm (13/16 in) plymetal, 24-gauge metal both sides
Insulation 7·62 cm (3 in) foamed-in-place polyurethane in front, sides and roof; 6·99 cm (2¾ in) block foam in floor; 7·62 cm (3 in) block foam in rear doors
Floor 5·08 cm (2 in) CROSS-FLO extruded aluminium T-sections with welded longitunidal seams; two 2·54 cm (1 in) drains each in front and rear gutters
Loading line 2·54 cm (1 in) bright red strip 10·16 cm (4 in) below ceiling
Lining white Trailmobile SUPERLINER on sides and rear doors; Trailmobile white flat fibreglass on roof and perimeter of front opening
Wood treatment all wood pressure treated against insect infestation; no treated wood exposed inside container
Undercoat heavy duty ·76 mm (0·30 in) thick on understructure and bottom of floor underpan
Finishing exterior steel surfaces shot-blasted and coated with "Zinc-Lock # 351" finished with white "Zinc-Lock # 900"

20 ft Fibreglass-reinforced plywood dry freight container
GENERAL:
Length overall 6·06 m (19 ft 10½ in)
Length, inside 5·93 m (19 ft 5 5/16 in)
Height, overall 2·44 m (8 ft 0 in)
Height, inside 2·26 m (89 in)
Width, overall 2·44 m (8 ft 0 in)
Width, inside (2·38 m (93⅝ in)
Clear rear opening height 2·15 m (84 9/16 in)
Clear rear opening, width 2·29 m (90 in)
Cubic capacity 31·92 m³ (1,128 cu ft)
Load capacity 18,512 kg (40,813 kg)
Estimated weight 1,808 kg (3,987 lb)
Gross load 20,320 kg (44,800 lb)
UNDERFRAME:
Type flush bottom
Bottom rails 8-gauge high-tensile steel
Crossmembers 10·8 cm (4¼ in) deep extruded 6061-T6 aluminium I-beams, on approximate 30·48 cm (12 in) centers
Fork lift pockets four, 10·16 cm × 30·48 cm (4 in × 12 in) full width
BODY:
Front and side walls 1·91 cm (¾ in) thick fibreglass-reinforced plywood, 1·59 cm (⅝ in) exterior grade plywood core
Corner posts, front 4·76 mm (3/16 in) high-tensile steel; designed for 6-high stack load; meet ANSI requirements
Corner posts, rear 6·35 mm (¼ in) high-tensile steel; designed for 6-high stack load; meet ANSI requirements
Corner fittings cast steel, conform to latest ANSI design
Corner protection 12-gauge high-tensile steel plates over roof panel at all four corners
Top outer rail 10-gauge high-tensile steel, full length
Roof 1·59 cm (⅝ in) thick fibreglass-reinforced plywood, 1·27 cm (½ in) exterior grade plywood core
Rear doors 2·70 cm (1 1/16 in) steel-faced plymetal
Rear door locks two, T/M anti-rack type; all hardware hot-dipped galvanized
Floor 2·86 cm (1⅛ in) thick solid fir, shiplap joints
Lining none (natural woven roving)
Undercoat ·76 mm (·030 in) heavy duty
Corrosion protection, all exterior steel surfaces coated with "Zinc-Lock # 351"
Finishing, gray gel coat on outsides of panels and roof

40 ft aluminium dry freight container
Length, overall 12·2 m (40 ft 0 in)
Length, inside 11·65 m (39 ft 6½ in)
Height, overall 2·59 m (8 ft 6 in)
Height, inside 2·38 m (93⅞ in) floor top to bottoms of roof bows
Width, overall 2·44 m (8 ft 0 in)
Width, inside 2·35 m (92½ in) at lining
Clear rear opening, height 2·28 m (89 9/16 in)
Clear rear opening, width 2·29 m (90 in)
Cubic capacity 67·41 m³ (2,382 cu ft)
Load capacity 27,555 kg (60,750 lb)
Estimated weight 2,925 kg (6,450 lb)
Gross load 30,481 kg (67,200 lb)
UNDERFRAME:
Type Gooseneck tunnel-bottom section
Bottom rails Extruded 6061-T6 aluminium
Crossmembers Aluminium I-beams 12·38 cm (4⅞ in) deep, on 30·48 cm (12 in) centres
Outriggers 10-gauge Z-shaped, on 30·48 cm (12 in) centres
Tunnel area 1·03 m × 3·12 m (40½ in × 10 ft 3 in) long, welded high-tensile steel
Tunnel rails 4·76 mm (3/16 in) thick, 1·03 m (40½ in) apart
Tunnel floor section 4·76 mm (3/16 in) thick, steel channel-section reinforcements beneath

BODY:
Front and side walls 1·27 mm (·050 in) 5052-H291 aluminium sheets, pre-painted
Front and side posts 17·78 cm × 3,175 cm deep (7 in × 1¼ in deep) hat-shaped extruded 6061-T6 aluminium, on 60·96 cm (24 in) centres on sides
Front and rear frames designed for 6-high stack load; meet ANSI/ISO requirements
Outer headers integral with roof protectors
Front sill steel box-section reinforced member full width over tunnel
Rear sill high-tensile steel, enclosed, tubular-shaped
Corner fittings cast steel; conform to latest ANSI/ISO design
Top outer rail Extruded 6061-T6 aluminium, recessed exterior flange for riveting roof sheet
Roof One-piece, 1·02 mm (·040 in) 3003-H14 aluminium sheet
Roof bows 8·89 cm wide × 2·54 cm deep (3½ in wide × 1 in deep) hat-shaped extruded 6061-T6 aluminium, on 60·69 cm (24 in) centres
Roof protectors 12-gauge high-tensile steel

full width of container × 48·26 cm (19 in)

Roof fastening, rivets on 2·54 cm (1 in) centres entire periphery outside of body; roof bonded to roof bows with adhesive

Rear doors plymetal; all hardware hop-dipped galvanised

Rear door locks four, T/M heavy duty anti-rack type

Floor 2·86 cm (1⅛ in) laminated hardwood, shiplap joints, 3 screws per board at each crossmember

Lining 6·35 mm (¼ in) 3-ply exterior grade A-C plywood

Undercoat ·76 mm (·030 in) heavy duty

Corrosion protection, steel parts shop-blasted and coated with "Zinc-Lock # 351"; steel surfaces electrolytically protected from aluminium

LICENSEES:
Freighters Industries Limited,
Warrigal Road, Moorabbiz S20,
Australia
SITM—'La Helvetica', SA,
Bv. Centenario 1202, Canada de Gomez,
Santa Fe, Argentina
MAN Postfach 114 8000 Munich 3, Germany
Rinaldo Piaggio, S.p.A.,
Viale Brigata Bisagno, 14,
Genoa, Italy 16100
Nippon Trailmobile Co, Ltd.,
160 Shimoto-cho
Atsuta-ku
Nagoya, Japan

Stainless steel tank container 8 ft × 8 ft × 20 ft. Capacity: 5,000 gallons.

Van der Ploeg's Fabrieken,
'Pacton' N.V.,
Groenendijk 84,
Nieuwerkerk a/d Ijssel,

The Netherlands
Bus Bodies (S.A.) Ltd.
PO Box 4008
Port Elizabeth, South Africa

40 ft dry freight container, exterior post design.

20 ft dry freight container of fibre-glass reinforced plywood.

40 ft dry freight container of aluminium construction. 8 ft 6 in high.

TRAILOR

Trailor (Trailmobile International)
110 Avenue de la Republique,
Paris 11e
TELEPHONE: 357.68.30
TELEX: 22 746 F
DIRECTORS:
R. More
P. Ripert
P. Jackson
R. Druilhe
CONTAINERS:
Typical Trailor containers are as follows:—

20 ft Standard ISO Aluminium Dry Freight

This is built with interior or exterior posts. It can be adapted to various requirements.
Length overall 6,058 mm (19 ft 10½ in)
Width overall 2,438 mm (8 ft 0 in)
Height overall 2,438 mm (8 ft 0 in)
Cubic capacity 31,492 m³ (1,112 cu ft)
Estim. weight 1,647 kg (3,630 lb)
Load capacity 18,675 kg (41,170 lb)

40 ft Standard ISO Aluminium Dry Freight with tunnel

The basic dry freight unit in the range. This is also available with interior or exterior post design.
Length overall 12,192 mm (40 ft 0 in)
Width, overall 2,438 mm (8 ft 0 in)
Height overall 2,592 mm (8 ft 6 in)
Cubic capacity 67,451 m³ (2,382 cu ft)
Estim. weight 2,926 kg (6,460 lb)
Load capacity 27,556 kg (60,750 lb)

VALMET

Valmet Oy
Valmet Building, Punanotkonk 2
PO Box 13155 Helsinki 13, Finland
TELEPHONE: 11441
TELEGRAMS: Valmet Helsinki
TELEX: 12 427 valpk sf
BRANCE ADDRESS:
Valmet Oy Pansio Works, Turku 15, Finland
    Telephone: 921-303 322
    Telex: 62211
DIRECTORS:
Olavi J. Mattila (*Commercial Director*)
Henrik Solin (*Commercial Director*)
T. M. Kaipainen

Jorma Tissari
U. Lahteenkorva
Yrjo Rantala

OVERSEAS:
    Sales UK and Western Europe—Price & Pierce (Machinery) Ltd,
51 Aldwych, London W.C.2
    Telephone: 01-240 2494
    Telex: 28551
CONTAINERS:
Steel and plywood, Fiberglass covered.

DESIGN STANDARDS:
ISO, TIR, UIC, Lloyds, American Bureau of Shipping.
PRODUCTION:
    In 1968, 300 twenty foot containers were built against 550 in 1969. In addition to those 550 conventional dry goods units, 125 were built in 1969 with side door access, 150 containers 8 ft 6 in high have been built.

PRINCIPAL OWNERS:
CTI, OCL, Ben Line, Finnish Steamship Company, Finnish Railways.

CONSTRUCTION:

The Valmet Container is constructed with patented plywood panels bolted to a steel frame. The wall panels are bolted to the steel frame. They consist of two plywood sheets separated by vertical plywood ribs at 2 in (50 mm) centres. Total thickness $1\frac{3}{16}$ in (30 mm). Interior surface are coated with 40 g/m² paper impregnated with phenolic reisn. The exterior surfaces are coated with a 10·1 polyester resin/glass fibre compound to a thickness of 660 g/m².

The floor is bolted to the base frame. It is a self-supporting plywood panel consisting of two sheets separated by a cellular plywood rib construction.

Total floor thickness is 4 in (100 mm), top and bottom surfaces are impregnated with a phenolic resin grained to provide a nonslip surface.

The roof is a single 9 mm plywood panel. Interior and exterior coatings are identical to the walls. The doors are 40 mm thick and of similar construction to the walls.

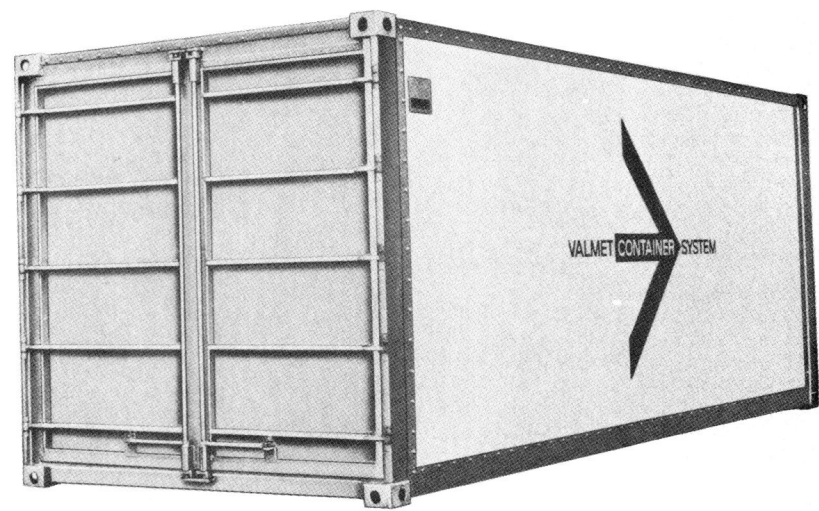

A 20 ft container of plywood-steel construction by Valmet, the G.20

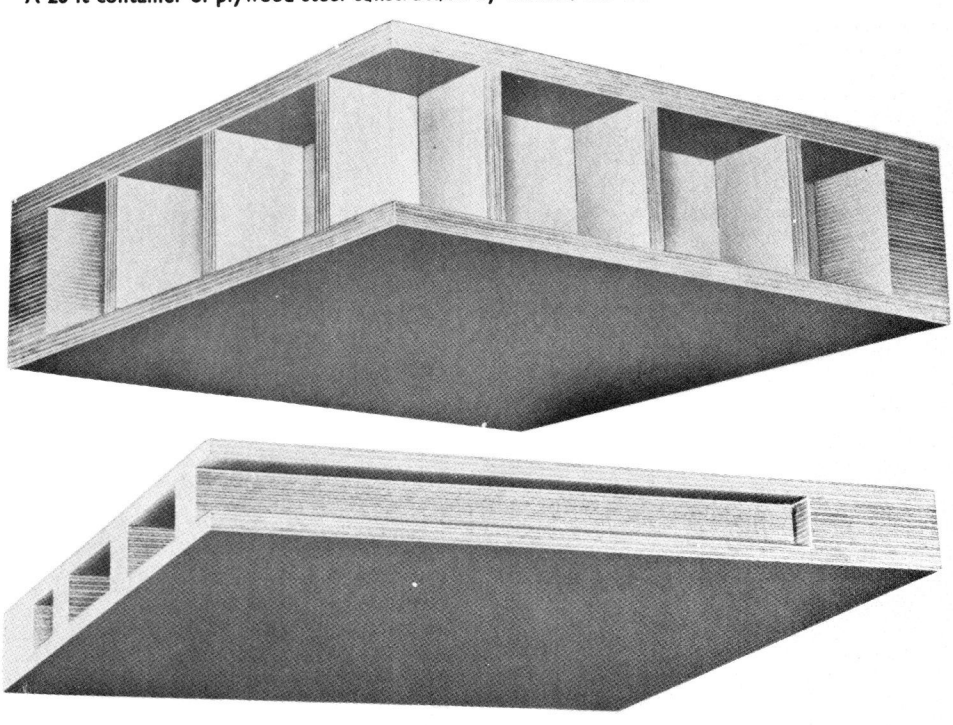

Valmet G.20 Container sections. The walls and floor of the container are built of these plywood-structured units

Range of Valmet plywood containers
Dry Freight or (General Purpose) Containers

Type by ISO or other Recognised Standard Dimensions	Main Materials of Construction (See space below for notes on additional materials and methods of construction)	Internal			Internal measurements of				Cubic Capacity
					End door openings		Side door Openings		
		Length	Height	Width	Width	Height	Width	Height	
20 ft × 8 ft × 8 ft	Plywood sandwich	5,905 mm 19′ 4½″	2,267 mm 7′ 5¼″	2,342 mm 7′ 8 3/16″	2,335 mm 7′ 0⅞″				31·3 m³ 1,105 ft
	Plywood sandwich	5,960 mm 19′ 6 41/64″	2,400 mm 7′ 10½″	2,250 mm 7′ 4 9/16″			2,340 mm 7′ 8⅜″	2,280 mm 7′ 5 13/16″	33 mm 1,165 ft³

VASO MISKIN

Vaso Miskin CRNI
Zivka Josila 2,
POB 732
Sarajevo, Yugoslavia
TELEPHONE: Centrala 41-222, 41-234, 41-343
Director 40-493
TELEGRAMS: Miskin CRNI Sarajevo
CONTAINERS:
Closed and open UIC, closed UIC 10 ton, open UIC.

General purpose. Closed and Open Container
External dimensions:
Length 5,000 mm (16 ft 5 in)
Width 2,300 mm (7 ft 6½ in)
Height 2,000 mm (6 ft 6¼ in)
Max. width with legs retracted 2,460 mm (8 ft ¼ in)
Max. width with legs extracted 3,030 mm (9 ft 11 in)

General purpose. Closed Container
External dimensions:
Length 4,800 mm (15 ft 9¼ in)
Width 2,160 mm (7 ft ⅞ in)
Height 1,770 mm (5 ft 9¼ in)
Door openings at end:
Clear width 1,773 mm (5 ft 9¾ in)
Clear height 2,185 mm (7 ft 1¼ in)
Cubic Capacity 18·4 m³ (652 cu ft)

General purpose. Open Container
External dimensions:
Length 4,770 mm (15 ft 7½ in)
Width 2,160 mm (7 ft ¾ in)
Height 1,840 mm (6 ft ¼ in)
Tipping door openings at end:
Clear width 2,160 mm (7 ft ¾ in)
Clear height 1,100 mm (3 ft 7½ in)
Cubic capacity 18·9 m³ (670·7 cu ft)

S.20 General purpose Closed Container

External dimensions:
Length 6,055 mm (21 ft 3 15/16 in)
Width 2,435 mm (7 ft 11 11/16 in)
Height 2,435 mm (7 ft 11 11/16 in)
Inside dimensions:
Inside length 5,862 mm (19 ft 0½ in)
Inside weight 2,315 mm (7 ft 6 15/16 in)
Inside height 2,157 mm (7 ft 0⅝ in)

Veenema & Wiegers Incorporated,
241 North Tenth,
Patterson, New Jersey 07508 USA
TELEPHONE: 201-684—6558
CONTAINERS:
40 ft, 30 ft, 20 ft and 10 ft and custom sizes
DESIGN STANDARD:
ISO, USASI
CONSTRUCTION—MATERIALS AND METHOD:
Aluminium, aluminium and glassfibre
CONTAINERS:

Dimensions:	
Container nominal:	Minimum capacity
40 ft	2,270 cu ft
30 ft	1,716 cu ft
20 ft	1,120 cu ft
10 ft	539 cu ft

Custom sizes available on request.
CONSTRUCTION:
Frame—Steel and aluminium.
Corner Castings—ISO-USASI.
Panels—Front, side, door: 1·5 mm
(·060 in) polyester glassfibre seam-
less sheets sandwiched over 19 mm
(¾ in) exterior grade plywood (roof
is glassfibre over 12·7 mm (½ in)
plywood).
Floor—edge-grained, laminated
finish 28·5 mm (1⅛ in) oak.

Inside clear dimensions:
Length 5,931 mm (19 ft 5½ in)

Snia Viscosa S.p.A.
Via Montebello,
18-20121 Milan,
Italy
TELEPHONE: 6332
TELEGRAMS: Viscosnia—Milano
TELEX: 31389 Snia

Transferring a container from an FAP MOD 1516 truck to one of the flatcars adapted by Vaso Miskin Crni for container work.

Inside door measurements:
Weight 2,255 mm (7 ft 0½ in)
Height 2,127 mm (6 ft 11½ in)
Gross weight 20,300 kg (44,754 lb)

A Vaso Miskin car container.

Payload 2,030 kg (4,475 lb)
Maximum load 18,250 kg (40,200 lb)
Cubic capacity 29·31 m³ (1,030 ft³)

VEENEMA AND WIEGERS

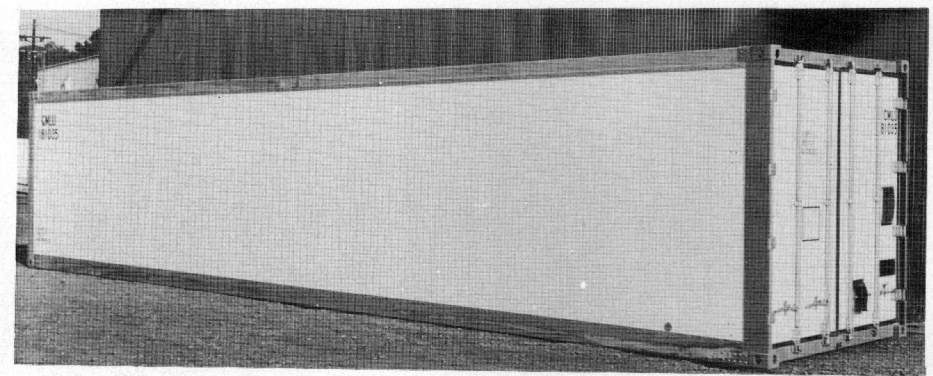

40 ft Veenema & Wiegers container

Width 2,375 mm (7 ft 9½ in)
Height 2,254 mm (7 ft 4¾ in)
Door opening dimensions:
Width 2,286 mm (7 ft 6 in)
Height 2,159 mm (7 ft 1 in)
Tare weight 1,678 kg (3,700 lb)
Capacity 31·7 m³ (1,120 cu ft)

PRINCIPAL OWNERS OF CONTAINERS:
American Export Isbrandtsen Lines, Moore
McCormack Lines, Container Marine Lines,
Contrans, Hapag-Lloyd, United States Lines,
Grancolombiana, Sea Train, Xtra Incorpora-
ted, United States Navigation Co., West
India Line.

VISCOSA

DIRECTORS AND MANAGERS:
Ing. Giovanni Masera (*General Manager*)
Ing. Giovanni Chistoni (*Assistant General Manager*)
CONTAINERS:
Refrigerated containers built with glass
fibre reinforced polyester resin.

V. & W. Gondola container

Viscosa container

Westerwalder Eisenwerk
Dr. Paul Gerhard KG,
5241 Weitfeld/Sieg,
Germany (Federal Republic)
TELEPHONE: (02747) 571 & 572
TELEX: 0875323
DISTRIBUTORS:
UK Ports and Terminals Consultants Ltd.
Graham House, Pannells Court,
Guildford, Surrey

WEW

CONTAINERS:
Rectangular bulk containers for the
transport and storage of liquids and granular
bulk-solids.

The largest capacity for 40 feet length is
27·50 m³ (971·25 ft³). Smaller volumes are
obtainable by subdividing the length and
reducing the height, leaving the width constant at 8 feet.

Four stacking-load-bearing, buckling- resistant corner supports are welded together
each with four sides and four cross beams via
eight cast steel ISO corner fittings to form
a closed frame.

The side beams are additionally connected
by internal cross beams horizontally and by
internal supports vertically depending on the
length.

63843

New WEW Likwitainer claimed to be the first pressure resistant square section ISO liquid container

The base side beams can be fitted according to ISO with retaining edges for straddle carrier handling.

The actual container is formed by welding the outward curving cambered wall panels to the frame sections. Frames are made from mild steel and the tanks from stainless steel.

The resistance of the frame to distortion is increased along both centre lines by the curvature of the wall panels. The side walls are therefore rigid supports preventing undesirable deflection of the container under full load.

A recent addition to the range has been a pressure resistant unit claimed to be the first pressure resistant square section ISO tank container.

STANDARDS:
ISO, SNCF/UIC, LLOYDS, Bureau Veritas, TIR.

The WEW range of Likwitainers

Type	Length	Width	Height	Nominal Capacity		
				m³	US gal.	Im. gal.
5 t	(2,220)	(1,796)	(1,450)	4·41	1,165	970
65	6 ft 6 in (1,965)	8 ft (2,435)	5 ft 4 in (1,620)	5·60	1,480	1,230
104	10 ft (2,990)	8 ft (2,435)	4 ft (1,217)	6·20	1,640	1,360
105	10 ft (2,990)	8 ft (2,435)	5 ft 4 in (1,620)	8·70	2,300	1,920
204	20 ft (6,055)	8 ft (2,435)	4 ft (1,217)	13·50	3,570	2,970
205	20 ft (6,055)	8 ft (2,435)	5 ft 4 in (1,620)	19·00	5,020	4,180
304	30 ft (9,125)	8 ft (2,435)	4 ft (1,217)	20·10	5,310	4,420
305	30 ft (9,125)	8 ft (2,435)	5 ft 4 in (1,620)	27·30	7,210	6,010
354	35 ft (10,660)	8 ft (2,435)	4 ft 3 in (1,260)	24·00	6,340	5,280*
404	40 ft (12,190)	8 ft (2,435)	4 ft 3 in (1,260)	27·50	7,270	6,050*

*These nominal capacities are increased by about 8 % in absence of the gooseneck tunnel.

WRIGHT

Norman R. Wright Containers Pty. Ltd.,
20 Dixon St.,
Royal Park,
South Australia
TELEPHONE: 4 1815

CONTAINERS:
General purpose and refrigerated containers and flats to ISO specifications but a large number of custom built containers are produced.

YEWCO

Yorkshire Engineering & Welding Co. Ltd.
Friars Works,
Bradford Road,
Idle,
Bradford, Yorks.
TELEPHONE: Bradford 612471 (S.T.D. OBR4)
TELEGRAMS: Yewco, Bradford
TELEX: 51176
DIRECTORS:
V. W. Wood (Chairman)
S. G. Wood (Managing)
G. F. Wood
G. T. Chambers
PRODUCTS:
Bulk liquid steel and stainless steel container tanks, insulated and uninsulated. Units are made in the 20 ft 20 ton module and may

also be in the 30 ft 35 ton module. The proprietory name 'Isotank' is used. The containers are designed to carry a wide range of hazardous and non hazardous liquids. Altogether there are 36 standard models with capacities up to 20,000 litres (4,400 Imp. gall.)

Yewco Isotanks Standard A Stainless Steel

The Tanks are of acid resisting stainless steel to BS. EN58J (BS 1449 316S16) and are of single compartment. (4,400 I.G. cap. max.)

The units are designed for the carriage of hazardous goods by road, rail and sea transportation.

Two manlids are fitted one each end of the 'Isotank' for ease of access, inspection and cleaning purposes. Each manlid is of the pressure type, hinged and incorporates a

vacuum/vent valve. Pressure release is 30 psig. Vacuum release is set within a range— 5 psig (10 in HG) to 1 psig (2 in HG) determined by the commodities to be carried. 3 in A.S.A. flanges are provided for closed fill or dip purposes.

A top operated footvalve connecting pipework, and quick action cone valve permit discharge at the rate of 4,000 I.G. in 23 minutes for water at 7·2°C (45°F).

The ISO framework is of mild steel and high yield steel rectangular hollow sections, and of folded sections electrically welded together. Lifting and securing points for B.R. Freightliner straddle carrier are incorporated together with ascent ladders and top spillage collection system.

Tank interiors are normally to "dull polished" standards with welds ground and polished to the condition of the parent metal. The exterior of the tank and framework are blasted. Mild steel work is given two coats of special primer paint capable of accepting any finishing coat nominated by Customers, or recommended finish treatments. The dull matt surface of the tank is normally left in the blasted condition where aggressive chemicals may be carried. but may be finish painted to Customer's choice if required.

The tanks are built under Lloyds Survey and certified accordingly. E.C.E. Customs approval plates are fitted. Customer identification plates in compliance with ISO regulations are also fitted.

Insulation if required, is a combination of lightweight low "K" value materials with a cladding of (a) Glass reinforced plastics, (b) Stainless steel sheet, (c) Aluminium alloy sheet.

Heat breakers are interposed between all the faces to prevent transfer of heat to the framework from the tank. The overall heat leak of the fully insulated units is determined by its size, but in each case, corresponding to a 'U' value not greater than ·045 BTU/hr. ft² deg. F. Heat gain/loss is less than ·15 deg. F per hour in a temperature differential of 150°F (·0625°C per hr in a temperature differential of 65·56°C) using water.

Heating may be electrical on 110v/220v/ 415v 50 cycles A.C. supply 3 phase/single phase, with or without neutral. The controls give the widest range of temperature applications up to 98·3°C (200°F). Thermostats automatically regulate the heat input to whatever limits are required by the commodity, either during transit or before discharge.

Steam heating facilities may be fitted if required, usually to the exterior of the tank skin, and terminating in a screwed connection to the steam supply.

Temperature Gauges to measure the commodity may be fitted, usually one is sufficient located at the discharge end of the tank.

Baffles or compartmentation baffles or separate compatrments for the carriage of dis-similar commodities may be fitted together with separate outlets as required.

Polishing of interiors where foodstuffs are concerned, i.e. milk, chocolate, beers, wines etc., interior polishing to Yewco No. 1. standard provides for such commodities, a safe interior condition. Risks of contamination of cargoes are reduced and cleaning simplified.

Yewco Hazardous Goods (Isotanks)

Single compartment, 2 manlids and covers, one outlet, dull polished interior, exterior blasted. Mild steel painted two coats primer. Certified by Lloyds. E.C.E. plate and ISO plates fitted.

Extras if required:—Interior baffle or baffles; Interior bulkheads with additional outlet or outlets; Insulation and clad in glass reinforced plastics, colour impregrated; Insulation and clad in stainless steel sheet; Insulation and clad in aluminium sheet; Fork lift pockets to Customers, or ISO centres as preferred; Thermometer and cowl; Inert gas infusion system for loads which deteriorate in contact with air or oxygen etc; Interior polished to No. 1 standards; Calibration to Customer's or H.M. Customs requirements; Painting and artwork above that stated; Top discharge only for certain hazardous loads; Heating: Electric or steam.

Fully insulated and refrigerated units

This 'Isotank' is fully insulated, and without further fittings may be used to cool a cargo, or hold cargoes at almost any temper-ature by means of CO² (Carbon Dioxide).

9 cu ft (1·88 cu m) of bunker space is available (more if required) for blocks of CO² incorporated in the Isotank manwalk.

Each block as manufactured by ICI weighs approximately 25 lb (11·3 kg) and has a heat extraction rate of 274 Btu's per lb. (154·3 K.cal per kg) at a temperature of 32°F (·5°C), or 246 Btu per lb, (135 K.cal per kg) at —109°F (—78·33°C). The object of refrigeration is to help cool the vapour space of some highly inflamables and some foods; i.e. milk, beers, or liquid egg, where exposure to solar radiation on the Isotank and high ambient temperatures make such commodities deteriorate or become dangerous.

A Thermometer 0°C—100°C provides adequate readings.

The 'Isotank' is of 4,040 I.G. (18,350 litres) Gross.

Tank:—Stainless Steel,

EN58J	British Specification
316	American Specification
24	Udeholm Specification
832SK	Avesta Specification

Design pressure 30 P.S.I.G. (2,109 kg/cm²)
Test pressure 45 P.S.I.G. (3·1635 kg/cm²)
Vacuum 2 in H.G. (—70·3 gm/cm²)

One manlid 18 in diameter (457 mm) incorporates Duplicated combined pressure relief/vacuum valves, and a 1½ in BSP plug connection (38·1 mm).

One outlet at the rear, with internal foot valve and an effective hygienic plug valve connect to a 3 in ASA (76·2 mm) flange.

DESIGN STANDARDS:
ISO: BS3951: Lloyds Register Tanks Certification Scheme; Dept Labour and Industry New South Wales, Australia; United States Coast Guard Dept of Transportation; IMCO; ADR; RID; BOT; HO; MOT; ECE; TIR; UIC; BR; C & E.

YORK

York Trailer Company Limited
Container Division, Corby,
Northants, England
TELEPHONE: 05366-3561
TELEX: 34516 Cables: Yorktra
FACTORY BRANCHES:
Warrington, Glasgow, Cardiff, Northallerton, Rainham, nr. Tilbury (Essex), London (Watford), Doncaster, Cannock, Bristol.
OFFICES:
London, Rotterdam, Toronto
DIRECTORS: F. Davies
CONTAINERS:
York CG series of all-steel containers
SPECIFICATIONS:
ISO, BS 3951, Lloyd's
TYPES:
BG10, BG20, BG30 and BG40.

Construction Details—General purpose Containers

SIDE WALLS, FRONT BULKHEAD, ROOF: All welded, all steel, frameless construction: 16 gauge steel panels continuously welded. Vertical corrugations pressed into panels at 152 mm (6 in) centres form integral posts. Roof construction similar to sides and front. Corrugations form transverse drain gulleys, shed water through drain holes in hi-tensile formed steel top rail. Withstands loads well in excess of loadings specified in BS 3951.

General Purpose. Type CG10 (10 ft)
Internal dimensions:
Length 2,858 mm (9 ft 4½ in)
Width 2,350 mm (7 ft 8½ in)
Height 2,223 mm (7 ft 3½ in)
Door openings at end:
Clear width 2,337 mm (7 ft 8 in)
Clear height 2,159 mm (7 ft 1 in)

General Purpose. Type 5CG20 (20 ft)
Internal dimensions:
Length 5,926 mm (19 ft 5¼ in)
Width 2,350 mm (7 ft 8½ in)
Height 2,223 mm (7 ft 3½ in)

Door openings at end.
Clear width 2,337 mm (7 ft 8 in)
Clear height 2,159 mm (7 ft 1 in)

General Purpose. Type CG30 (30 ft)
Internal dimensions:
Length 8,991 mm (29 ft 6 in)
Width 2,350 mm (7 ft 8½ in)
Height 2,223 mm (7 ft 3½ in)
Door openings at end:
Clear width 2,337 mm (7 ft 8 in)
Clear height 2,159 mm (7 ft 1 in)

AL Series 20 ft aluminium alloy and steel general purpose ISO container.

General Purpose. Type CG40 (40 ft)

Internal dimensions:
   Length 12,060 mm (39 ft 6¾ in)
   Width 2,350 mm (7 ft 8½ in)
   Height 2,223 mm (7 ft 3½ in)
Door openings at end:
   Clear width 2,337 mm (7 ft 8 in)
   Clear height 2,159 mm (7 ft 1 in)

York OT Series

In steel or aluminium. Basically as standard units, but with roof replaced by reinforced steel top frame and removable roof bows. Fitted tarp roll-back cover is to TIR requirements. Door frame has swing-away rear headrail.

Lengths: 10 ft, 20 ft, 30 ft and 40 ft.
"Half height" version also available.

York AL Series

Aluminium clad steel-framed container. An exceptionally light unit.

York Bulktainer

Standard York ISO containers can be modified for use as bulk carriers with tipping skeletal trailers. 18 in square hatches in roof permit hopper loading of granular or powder loads. The load can be dumped by means of either an 18 in × 34 in or a 5 ft 9 in × 9 in hatch built into the front end of the container, or through a discharge chute via four hatches in the rear doors. The York bulktainer is available in lengths of 20 ft, 30 ft and 40 ft.

York Tunnel Type Containers

All York general purpose and OT series containers are now available at 2,590 mm (8 ft 6 in) exterior height. Tunnels built into base frame permit their carriage on gooseneck skeletals ensuring minimum height operation.

An 8 ft 6 in high York open top container carried on a York gooseneck skeletal container carrier. The gooseneck trailer is specially designed to carry 8 ft 6 in high containers within the overall height restrictions.

OT Series open top 20 ft container.

A standard York all steel general purpose container.

CONTAINER HANDLING EQUIPMENT

Container Component Manufacturers

Container Filling and Associated Services

Container Repair, Testing and Cleaning Services

CONTAINER HANDLING EQUIPMENT

AABACAS

10 ton capacity Aabacas double girder cranes at Morris & David Jones, Huyton, Liverpool.

Aabacas Engineering Co. Ltd.
Kelvin Road,
Wallasey, Cheshire, England
TELEPHONE: 051-638-5932
TELEGRAMS: Aabacas, Wallasey
DIRECTORS:
V. L. M. Orrell
N. E. J. Fraser
G. K. Clayton
C. F. H. G. Vaughan
PRODUCTS:

Double girder four point lift cranes, suitable for container terminals, manufactured in spans ranging from 25 ft to 80 ft and in safe working load capacities from 10 tons to 20 tons.

The equipment can be built with varying spans throughout the above range and with a wide range of operating speeds and lifting heights.

AERO-GO INC

20 ton capacity ships cargo container on Aero-Go, Inc. Model T20 Transporter or dockside and ships hold positioning.

Aero-Go, Inc.
5800 Corson Avenue South,
Seattle, Washington 98108

TELEPHONE: RO 3-9380.   Area Code 206
DIRECTORS:
K. G. Wood
H. J. Eckert
PRODUCTS:

Air pallets with capacities of up to 100 tons and above, air turntables and air conveyor systems for heavy loads.

Aero-Go Container Turntables and Conveyors

Permanently installed air turntable and conveyor systems operate in a similar manner to standard air pallets except the orientation is inverted. The Aero-Castors are installed "face" up in the floor and air is supplied through floor manifolds to the castors. The smooth, non-porous bottom surface of the cargo container "floats" upon the inflating castors. Since a thin film of air separates the container from the castors, damage and wear to the container bottom is minimized.

Normally, available space allows use of greater numbers of Aero-Castors which can utilize low pressure air in the range of 10 psig or less. Air volume consumption is limited by orifice size from the manifold to individual castors.

The air supply to the turntable or conveyor section is actuated and shut off by trip valves in the floor ahead of and after the operating section. As a container enters a section, the float valve opens to permit air flow to the castors to support the load. After the container floats off the support area, a second trip valve cuts the air supply. As the load is free floating with a coefficient of friction of less than $\frac{1}{2}$ per cent one or two men can move multi-ton loads with relative ease.

For containers having irregular bottom surfaces, a smooth steel plate interface is used to move with the load. Various control and power accessories are used with the air flotation system to provide an integrated materials management system.

Aero-Go Air Pallets

Air pallets are load carrying platforms supported by a thin-film of air flow. The platforms can be moved by fork truck to position freight containers on dockside, in terminals, and ships' holds. Load capacity of individual pallet is made to specification. Compressed air, usually under 25 psig, is introduced into the several nylon-reinforced neoprene Aero-Castors under the pallet through an air inlet fitting and integral manifold. Air is evenly distributed within the assembly, inflating the Aero-Castors and lifting the platform approximately one inch. The air is allowed to escape in a continuous flow through orifices in the castors, providing a thin film of air several thousandths of an inch deep between the castors and the deck to float the load.

The volume of air required to float the castors is governed by the surface to be traversed. A standard 'Aero Castor' operating on a smooth surface such as sealed concrete, metal deck, or vinyl tile will consume approximately 5 SCFM of air per castor. Rougher or more porous surfaces will increase air consumption. Thin sheet metal or plastic overlays can be used to cover rough surfaces or bridge cracks.

Typical coefficient of friction of 'Aero-Castors' upon a smooth surface is less than $\frac{1}{2}\%$. A 10,000 lb load can be moved with a push of 50 lb or less. Air supply sources include plant air stepped down to under 25 psig, portable compressor/accumulators, low pressure centrifugal blowers, or self-generating units attached to the pallet. The castors are self regulating providing vibration free stable operation.

AERO LIFT

Aero Lift Corporation

ADDRESS:
1732 4th Avenue South, Seattle, Washington, 98134 USA
TELEPHONE: 206-MA-3-0063
TELEGRAMS: Western Union

DIRECTORS:
Gene Tuura (*President*)
M. Tuura (*Secretary and Treasurer*)

PRODUCTS:

The Con-Stow Fork-Lift Truck Attachment

This attachment enables a fork-lift truck with only 4536 kg (10,000 lb) capacity to handle loads of 22680 kg (50,000 lb). Utilisation is limited to low ceiling heights such as 'wings' where head-room is critical. An 8 ft high container can be handled in an overall height of 2·64 m (8 ft 8 in). The deck pressure under load is less than imposed by the wheels of the

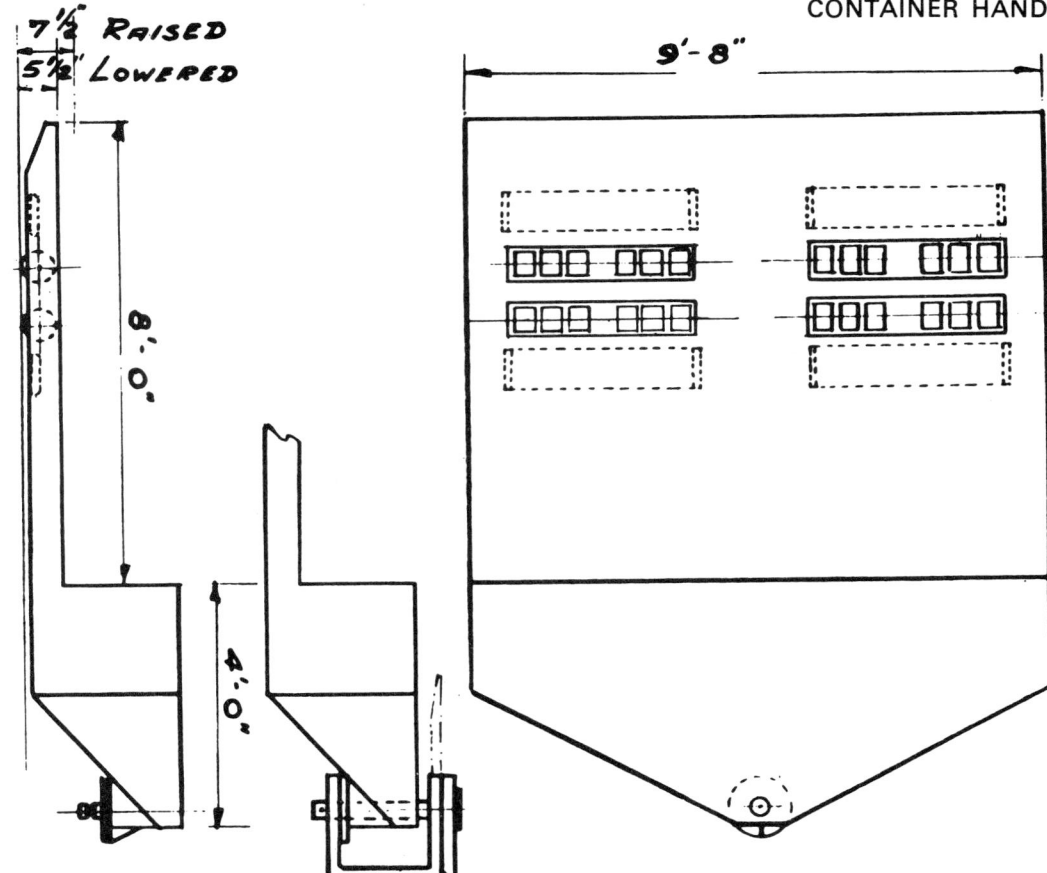

7½" RAISED
5½" LOWERED

8' 0"

4' 0"

9'-8"

fork lift truck and the unit can be used for short distances on tarmac or wood floors. The under-clearance is 15·875 mm (⅝ in). It will turn a 20 ft container in a 8·53 m (28 ft) right-angle.

Water is used for the hydraulic lift and the unit is powered by a 36 volt DC motor. Batteries and a charging unit are integral with the Con-Stow and there is a power capability for 150 lifts before it is necessary to recharge the battery.

Aero Lift Modular Support System for Jumbo Aircraft

This uses ISO containers as the support medium. AS-832 containers for "in flight" use will be handled by same equipment. The system will be custom built, depending on functions required by individual airlines, such as use with lower lobe LD1 and 2, plus supplementary functions as in transport of igloos to present family of airframes.

Electroleg Container Jack System

Jacks for supporting ISO or AS-832 containers, lifting and lowering by means of the corner castings. A vehicle can back under a container so lifted.

Four tripods of tubular steel construction take the weight of the container. Each jack is fitted with a lift motor, a screw drive and a lift screw.

The constant speed of the 3-phase short circuit motors guarantees an even lift. Each motor has an integral brake which automatically locks up when the electrical supply to the motor is cut off. The extra light rotation lift screw is fitted with a hardened special nut which runs on recirculating ball bearings. The support bearing of the screw allows a limited swing of the screw to compensate minor ground irregularities, thus avoiding undue stresses.

Lifting capacity 20 tons
Lifting height 1,600 mm (63 in)
Lifting time, loaded 2·5-3 min
Weight, one jack only 63 kg (135 lb)
Motor performance 0·62 kW (1 HP)

LIFTING SHOES:

The lifting shoes engage with the lower corner casting when they are rotated 90° from the horizontal. The nut of the lift screw is placed in the fork of the shoe so that the ball-shaped faces contact each other and therein allow for slight errors in alignment.

Weight, one shoe only 16 kg (35 lb)

CONTROLS:

A portable control box, a relay box, and rubber-insulated cables from control box to relay box, and from relay box to each jack, are used for the control of the equipment. The cables have snap-on connectors and the switches and relays are enclosed in boxes for protection against damage and dampness. The six press buttons of the control box are: up and down buttons and the four buttons for individual operation of each jack. Colour codes are used on each cable to simplify connection.

Operating voltage 3-phase AC 380/220 C
Current draw 8 A
Current draw at start, stall 40 A
(Motors for other voltages are supplied on special request against factory approval).

TRANSPORT:

The set can easily be transported to the place of operation.

ALLEN

A. H. Allen & Co. Ltd.

HEAD OFFICE:
Spencer Bridge Works, Northampton, NN5 7DT, England
TELEPHONE: 52242
DIRECTORS:
E. Waller (*Chairman*)
K. C. Allen (*Managing Director*)
K. E. Willers
M. J. McAllister
A. B. Norrey
J. A. Buckle,
PRODUCTS:
Goliath type rail mounted container cranes. Lattice type and welded box construction. Capacity up to 40 tons. Lifting and spreader frames of all types with manual electrical and hydraulic operation.

Type 040 Container Crane at Chrysler (U.K.) Ltd, Coventry as illustrated

25 tons S.W.L.
30 ft long ISO containers.

The Allen twin-leg Goliath container crane

All weather cab control.
Joy stick controllers.
Height of lift: 17 ft 6 in under containers.
Hoist and lower: 30 ft/min
Cross traverse: 95 ft/min.
Long travel: 500 ft/min.
Railcars: 52 ft.

Split level crab, giving slewing, levelling and tilting facilities.
Two-way radio communication system.
Remote control lifting frame.
Standard range: Type 030, 41 ft rail span to type 060, 75 ft 6 in rail span, Up to 40 tons S.W.L.

The Anderson-Grice Co. Ltd.
Taymouth Engineering Works,
PO Box No. 1, 2 Anderson Street, Carnoustie,
Angus, DD7 6YA, Scotland
TELEPHONE: Carnoustie 2214-5-6
TELEGRAMS: 'Diamond, Carnoustie'
DIRECTORS:
J. R. Pate (*Managing*)
J. Laing
L. W. Strand
PRODUCTS:
Three motor electric derrick cranes with capacities up to 35 tons and jib lengths up to 150 ft, lifting full load at 75% jib length and half load at 96% jib length.
Two-speed or three-speed hoisting with speeds to suit individual requirements.
TOPLIS LEVEL LUFFING:
Installations of electric or toplis level luffing cranes are at the following Docks:—Tilbury, Liverpool, Ipswich, Manchester, Bristol and Waterford, also electric overhead travelling cranes with capacities up to 40 tons, with span, speeds, height of lift, etc., to suit individual requirements. Cage or floor control.
Photograph shows typical installation at Garston Docks, Liverpool, where a 32 ton electric derrick (British Transport Docks Board) is handling containers in conjunction with an overhead travelling crane (Irish Sea Ferries Ltd.).

The Anderson-Grice container crane.

Anderston Clyde Engineers Ltd.
P.O. Box 11, Ince, Near Wigan, Lancs.
TELEPHONE: 44055
TELEX: 67603

ASEA Mechanical Products Division,
Fack, Helsingborg, Sweden
TELEPHONE: Helsingborg (042) 13 93 00
TELEGRAMS: ASEA Helsingborg
TELEX: 72 330 (asea hbg)
PRODUCTS: Electric deck cranes, container handling cranes.

ASEA 45 ton Quay Crane
This crane is designed primarily to handle two 6·09 m (20 ft) containers simultaneously with special twin-lift spreaders, but it may also be used for 9·14 or 12·19 m (30 ft or 40 ft) containers. The portal frame and boom are of welded box-girder construction. The boom is hinged and may be raised to the stowed position to clear ships' superstructure. In the working position the boom is suspended from steel bars, which are linked together at about half their length so that they will fold when the boom is raised. The boom is raised by steel wire ropes running over the top of the portal to machinery at the rear of the fixed girders, where a concrete counterweight is

Lattice Type Container Cranes
The unit comprises two standard Allen Goliath Cranes, tied in such a manner that the control cab and main panel are sited between the structures, to give the operator a clear view over the road and rail tracks.

The crane is mounted on double flanged crane wheels, with tracks of 52 ft centres spanning three rail tracks and one roadway. The long travel transmission is effected by two main slip-ring motors with steps of rotor resistance for speed control and a squirrel cage pony motor to give a single creep speed characteristic.

ANDERSON GRICE

ANDERSTON CLYDE

PRODUCTS:
Manufacturers of Colossus gantries with capacities up to 30 tons and hand or electric hoist units.

ASEA

also located. Electrical interlocking prevents the raising of the boom unless the trolley is in its parked station between the legs of the portal. However, the trolley can work the length of the fixed girders once the boom has been raised.
Apart from the slip-ring motor driven derricking machinery, all drives are powered by d.c. motors with high efficiency, thyristor static converter control equipment, giving fine, accurate speed control, high reliability, and a minimum of maintenance.
All motions are fully protected by limit

This version of the ASEA 25 ton deck crane is one of five units supplied to Scandiships "Talarah" and "Woollhara", built by Eriksbergs Mek. Verkstad for the Transatlantic S.S. Co. of Gothenburg. The cranes on these ships have no driver's cab or controllers on the crane itself, but are operated solely from shoulder-borne portable controllers, which may be plugged in at three stations at each pair of hatches

Four special hoist units carry an electro-hydraulic grappler frame on 16 falls of rope, eight falls being reeved to a compensating beam at one end of the frame and the other eight reeved to a fixed beam at the other end. Levelling, overhoist and overlower limit switches are incorporated in the hoist control.
Safe working load is 30 ton; hoist speed, 8 ft/min; cross-travel speed, 30 and 90 ft/min; long travel, 20-200 ft/min; lift height 12 ft 6 in to underside of container.
Lattice type constructed Container Cranes are in use at Freightliner Depots at Edinburgh, Newcastle, Hull, Kings Cross-London, and Cardiff.

switches, end stops and interlocks, where necessary.

The portal runs on a total of 32 wheels, half of which are individually driven.

The trolley has four travel drives and carries two sets of hoisting machinery, which may be operated individually or coupled. The operator's cab is suspended from the trolley and contains controls for all functions of the crane, excepting derricking.

The twin spreaders may be operated individually or coupled, and when they enter their respective cell structures on board, automatic disengagement takes place. The distance between the spreaders can be adjusted during the handling cycle to suit any difference between the spacing aboard and ashore. Tilting to compensate for list and trim is also arranged. The hoisting motion is rendered inoperable unless all twist locks on the spreaders have fully engaged or disengaged the corner fittings of the containers.

A feature of the crane installed at Sydney Harbour, Australia is that the landward legs of the portal are pin-jointed and this together with special pivoted bogies allows the crane to negotiate curves in the track.

Characteristics

Hoisting capacity on spreaders 45 tons
Lift height over quay level 21·3 m (70 ft)
Plumbing depth below quay level 10·7 m (35 ft)
Outreach from seaward rail 33·5 m (110 ft)
Quay rail centres 15·24 m (50 ft)
Hoist speed, full load 36 m/min (120 ft/min)
Hoist speed, light spreader 90 m/min (300 ft/min)
Crab speed 150 m/min (500 ft/min)
Portal speed 39 m/min (128 ft/min)
Time to raise or lower boom 7 minutes

ASEA 25 ton Deck Crane

ASEA's 25 ton deck crane is expressly designed for handling containers or flats. The lifting capacity has been selected so that a 6·09 m (20 ft) (20 ton) container can be hoisted with a spreader. 9·14 or 12·19 m (30 or 40 ft) containers can be accommodated by operating the crane in combination with an adjacent 5 or 10 ton crane and using an equalising beam. When a spreader is not employed the full 25 ton capacity is available and for loads of eight tons and below a high speed gear can be engaged.

The crane body is a compact, welded stressed skin structure set up on a slewing gear-ring, which evenly distributes the axial loads and tilting movements and transfers them to the crane mount.

Each motion of the crane is driven by two motors through spur and helical gearing. The hoist drives are mechanically connected, while the luffing and slewing drives are balanced electrically.

The motors are of totally enclosed, deck-watertight, marine type with integral disc brakes. They are supplied from a Ward-Leonard set consisting of an a.c. drive motor with single and multi-circuit generators built as one unit.

Operation is normally from a portable controller. The operator can thus move around freely and follow the complete handling cycle. A driver's cab with fixed controllers can be fitted, if required.

The crane embodies the short minimum outreach principle, which allows the hook to plumb close to the crane body, thus eliminating the need to move cargo horizontally in the hold.

Second generation Asea quay crane at the Skane Terminal, Port of Helsingbourg, Sweden. A similar crane is in use at the Port of Oxeløsund.

Asea 30.5 tonne terminal crane

Asea container handling bridge crane with 36.5 ton lift on spreader

Asea tandem deck crane

Asea gantry container crane

30.5-tonne Container Handling Cranes at The Skandia Terminal, Gothenburg

The crane is of the single girder type with underslung trolley, the trolley-travel wheels running on the top of the girder.

A feature of this crane is that it can negotiate a curve in the track with an inner radius of 50 m. Pin-jointed legs on the landward side with a transverse member of special design, together with pivoted bogies and the possibility of driving the wheels on each side at different speeds, facilitates this manoeuvre.

Suspended from the trolley are two sheave assemblies which are designed to suit a telescopic spreader for handling containers up to 40 ft in length. An equalising beam with a ramshorn hook at the centre for 45 tons can also be fitted.

The portal frame and boom are of box-girder construction for strength and ease of maintenance. The boom is hinged and in the working position is suspended from double steel straps, which are linked together so that they will fold when the boom is raised to the stowed position. Electrical interlocking prevents the boom from being raised unless the trolley is in its parking station on the fixed section of the girder.

The trolley has four travel drives and carries two sets of hoisting machinery, which may be operated independently or coupled. The operator's cab is suspended from the trolley and contains controls for all functions of the crane except derricking. D.C. motors with high efficiency thyristor converter control equipment are employed on the hoisting drives. The crane and trolley-travel drives are powered by slip-ring motors controlled by thyristor voltage regulators, electrical braking being by a patented system. The derricking machinery is driven by a contract-or-controlled slip-ring motor.

The portal runs on a total of 16 flanged wheels, and 16 plain wheels. One of each wheel-pair is driven.

All functions are fully protected by limit switches, end stops and interlocks, where necessary.

PERFORMANCE:
Hoisting capacity:
  on spreader 30·5 tons
    on hook 45 tons

Hoist speed:
  full load 40 m/min
  no load 100 m/min
  Trolley speed 120 m/min
Portal speed 45 m/min
Time to raise or lower boom 6 minutes

Customer	No. of cranes	Type	Location	Delivery
Overseas Containers Ltd. London	1	45-ton, twin boom design, fitted with twin-lift spreaders for handling two 20 ft containers at the same time	OCL Container Terminal, Berth No. 39, Tilbury Docks UK	1968
Maritime Services Board, N.S.W. Australia	1	,,	White Bay Berth, Sydney Harbour, Australia	1969
Helsingborg Harbour Authority	1	45-ton, single boom, underslung trolley design with telescopic spreader to handle containers up to 40 ft in length	Skåne Terminal Helsingborg, Sweden	1969
Gränges TGOJ Eskilstuna, Sweden	1	35-ton, single boom, underslung trolley design for handling containers up to 40 ft in length	Port of Oxelösund, Sweden	1970
Gothenburg Harbour Authority	2	45-ton, single boom, underslung trolley design for handling containers up to 40 ft in length	Skandia Terminal, Gothenburg Sweden	1970
Keelung Harbour Bureau Central Trust of China, Taiwan	1 1	35-ton, single boom, underslung trolley design with telescopic spreader for containers up to 40 ft in length	Keelung Harbour, Taiwan	1972
La Spezia Harbour, Italy	1	25-ton single boom, underslung trolley design for 20 ft containers in co-operation with Italian manufacturer	La Spezia, Italy	1971
Palermo Harbour, Italy	1	35-ton single boom, underslung trolley design for 40 ft containers in co-operation with Italian manufacturer	Palermo, Italy	1972
Maritime Services Board, N.S.W., Sydney, Australia	2	35-ton single boom, underslung trolley design for handling containers up to 40 ft in length	Glebe Island, Sydney, Australia	1972

CONTAINER-HANDLING BRIDGE CRANE

This rail-running crane for container handling and heavy lifts at Odense is one of three similar units supplied to the Danish State Railways.

It is of single box-girder design, with the trolley running on top of the bridge and extending on either side to give the necessary spread between the hoisting falls. One of the vertical members is specifically designed to afford lateral flexibility so that minor deviations in rail span can be accommodated. The crane runs on six flanged wheels, two of which are driven.

The control gear for the crane-travel drives together with the cable reeling unit is fitted on one of the end carriages. The end carriages are provided with rubber buffers, rail scrapers and storm locks.

The trolley consists of a welded steel frame, which carries the hoisting and traversing drives as well as the associated control-gear cubicles. The hoisting motor drives two barrels through helical reduction gearing. The travel machinery is located on one side of the trolley and drives two wheels. Anti-tilting protection is provided on both sides of the trolley. Supply to the trolley is via flexible cables suspended from cable-trolleys.

All motors are of the slip-ring type. The hoisting motor is thyristor regulated, which means that a specific speed is obtained at each controller position irrespective of the load, the feedback reference signal being obtained from a tachometer generator connected to the input shaft of the hoisting reduction gear. The travel motors have normal reversing switchgear.

Operation of the three motions takes place from a pendant controller suspended from the trolley. A platform for the operator is provided on one of the end carriages and provision for fitting a driver's cab to the trolley, if required at some later date, has been made.

PARTICULARS:
Lifting capacity:
　On hook 36·5 tons
　On spreader 30·5 tons
Speeds:
　Hoisting 4·5 m/min
　Trolley travel 15 m/min
　Crane travel 60 m/min
Track gauge: 13 m

Container Gantry

The gantry structure is of welded box-girder design, stiffened with diaphragms. Fore-and-aft travel is by pinion and rack drives, the gantry wheels running on rails located outboard of the hatch coamings. Powered reels are fitted for the supply cables to the gantry.

The trolley travels through pinion and rack drives on top of the gantry girders and out over the ship's side on the outriggers. Electrical interlocks and mechanical stops prevent trolley travel beyond the gantry girders until the outriggers are locked in position. Supply to the trolley is by cable tender. All handling operations are controlled from the driver's cab suspended from the trolley. Swinging out as well as stowing of the outriggers takes place from stations adjacent to the hinges.

High quality, totally enclosed gearing of ASEA manufacture is used on all drives.

Thyristor regulation of squirrel-cage motors is employed for all main drives. This static-state control system affords fine speed regulation and low maintenance.

The cranes are fitted with Sideliner programmed-operation equipment to facilitate rapid and safe handling with a minimum of driver fatigue.

	Forward Crane	Aft Crane
S.W.L. on spreader	20	30 tons
Hoist speed, full load	45	30 m/min
Trolley speed	90	90 m/min
Crane speed	15	15
Motor ratings:		
Hoist	2 × 100	2 × 100 kW
Trolley travel	2 × 65	2 × 65 kW
Crane travel	2 × 20	2 × 20 kW
Auxiliary hoist:		
S.W.L.	10	10 tons
Hoisting speed, full load	30	30 m/min
Hoist motor rating	65	65 kW

Tandem Deck Cranes

The ASEA tandem arrangement comprises two deck cranes mounted on a common platform, which can rotate through 360°. This arrangement affords the following operation alternatives.:
—Independent operation, working two holds fore-and-aft of the mount
—Independent operation, working the same hold from both sides of the ship.
—Parallel operation, with both cranes at a fixed slew angle and with rotation taking place at the platform.

Each crane is equipped for independent operation from its cab. When the cranes are to be used in tandem, operation takes place from the cab of one of the cranes, while the other crane functions as a slave unit, automatically following the motions of the master unit. The cranes are designed to operate with the ship at 5° heel and 2° angle of trim.

AUTOLAVA

Autolava Oy
Raisio
Finland
TELEPHONE: 921-783 408
TELEX: 62-117
DIRECTORS:
Matti Paatela (*Managing*)
Matti Posa (*Export Manager*)
PRODUCT:
Hydraulic tipping system suitable for freight containers. The system is known as 'Multilift'. It has many uses outside container handling particularly in the waste disposal and construction industries.
OVERSEAS AGENTS:
Multilift agents who import the system from Finland are to be found in: Austria, France and Luxemburg, Holland, Italy, Spain, Norway, The Republic of South Africa, Sweden, Switzerland, West Germany.

Autolava tipping system used for a freight container

BELOTTI

Belotti S.p.A.
FACTORY: Via Poiré, 16010 Manesseno (Genova)

EXPORT OFFICE: Via Mangili 38/A, I 00197

Roma
TELEPHONE: Genova 406752-3-4, Roma 875291

TELEGRAMS: 'Belottigru-Genova'

'Belottigru-Roma'
DIRECTORS:
Giovanni Belotti
Ing. Silvano Pavesi
PRODUCTS: 30 ton capacity straddle crane.

Straddle Crane with Side Lift

A range of self-propelled straddle cranes available in versions for either two or three-row stacking. The B/67 lifts centrally placed loads of up to 30 tons and lateral loads of up to 20 tons.

It operates over level, solid surfaces at speeds up to 25 km/h (15·5 mph).

Power is supplied by a 200 hp diesel driving four hydraulic motors, each of which operates one wheel through a chain transmission. All four wheels are steerable. The rear wheels can be steered in either the same or the opposite direction as the front one. This permits the vehicle to be turned in its own length.

Two hydraulically actuated outriggers stabilize the vehicle during lateral lifting operations.

The Belotti Crane B 69 C. Maximum capacity 22 tons. Suitable for 20 ft containers. The automatic spreader can be hydraulically turned clockwise or anti-clockwise through 180°. Equipped with normal block and hook the B 69 C is a traditional crane.

The Belotti B/67b Straddle Crane. This crane has been specially developed to handle containers. 20 ft containers can be lifted laterally, transplanted and stacked three high. 40 ft containers can be lifted axially, transported and stacked two high. There is a smaller version (B/67) suitable for stacking two high only.

BENNES MARREL

Bennes Marrel

ADDRESS:
13 rue Pierre Copel 42—Saint-Etienne
TELEPHONE: (77) 33-45-95
TELEGRAMS: Marreleva St-Etienne
TELEX: 33 657
DIRECTORS:
J. d'Assignies (*Chairman and Managing Director*)
P. Colonna (*Joint Managing Director*)

PRODUCTS:

The Marrel 'Rolltainer' is a device for loading or unloading containers, whether loaded or empty, on to rigid or semi-trailer commercial vehicles. It will operate with 20 ft or 30 ft ISO containers. The transporting vehicle is equipped with a twin-ram tipping sub-frame, tipping to 22°. A low speed and high torque hydraulic winch 1,000 m-kg (7,240 ft-lbs) at 10 r.p.m. drives a double cable to winch containers on or off the vehicle when tipped and operating through the corner fittings. The bottom side frames rest on two caterpillar assemblies at the rear end and large bearing surfaces ensure only low stresses are imparted to the lower part of the containers.

A roller stabiliser is lowered to the ground from the rear end of the chassis to reduce stress on the rear suspension and to ensure the front end of the vehicle does not lift. All the operations of the hydraulic servo-mechanisms, the winch, the roller drive and the sub-frame tilting are controlled from the driver's cab.

The "Rolltainer" system in operation.

A 20 ft container mounted on a rigid 6-wheel chassis equipped with the "Rolltainer" loading-unloading system.

A close-up of the rear end of a commercial chassis equipped with the "Rolltainer" device.

BETHLEHAM

Bethlehem Steel Corporation
Bethlehem, Pennsylvania 18016 U.S.A.
TELEPHONE: 694-2424 Area Code 215
DIRECTORS:
John G. White. Jr., *Manager of Sales*, railroad product sales division, Sales Department.
PRODUCTS:

Special and standard railroad freight cars of all descriptions as well as car components. Main materials used: Steel.

Bethlehem's standard 89 ft 4 in completely flush deck flat car with end of car cushioning, is suitable for attachment of container securing devices to accommodate containers of any length.

Of special interest is the retractable pedestal for containers on Bethlehem Steel Corporation's prototype trailer-container flat car. Twelve such pedestals on the car provide container securement and cushioning, allowing 14 inches of travel in either direction.

Bethlehem flush deck flat car with container securing devices.

BODEN

Boden Trailers Ltd
Royton, Oldham, Lancashire
TELEPHONE: 061-624 9551
TELEX: 66648
DIRECTORS:
R. G. Hooker (*Chairman*)
L. H. Allwood (*Vice Chairman*)
D. R. Marsh (*Managing Director*)
A. S. Aranyos (USA)
D. E. Bernstein (USA)
J. L. B. Crane,
B. K. Day
W. E. Grace (USA)
R. J. Jervis
R. R. Pickering (FCA)
R. D. Rowan (USA)
R. Taylor
J. K. Thompson
K. D. Vick

Mark 3 Boden Skeletal and Platform Skeletal Semi-Trailers for Container Transportation by Road

The Mark 3 Boden range of Skeletal semi-trailers, either Decked (PSK) or Undecked (SK), are specifically designed for Container transportation.

The multi-purpose Mark 3 Boden Decked Skeletal has been designed for the general haulier who is also called upon to transport containers. It incorporates all the advantages of the Mark 3 Boden Skeletal together with a flush-surfaced deck for the haulage of general freight.

Dynamic stress requirements of container transportation are fully met by tremendously strong outriggers, which pierce the deck to finish flush with the platform surface. Straight through I-beam cross members are added to support conventional loads.

Designed for dual-purpose operation, the Mark 3 Boden PSK embodies the design principles of their specialised SK skeletal model and is decked to provide a flush surface for the transport of general freight. It provides increased flexibility for the general haulier who is also called upon to transport containers. Nine standard models are available to cope with the varying numbers and lengths of container modules made to ISO specifications.

Fitted with a modified rave to provide an effective compromise between the requirements of the two types of load, the Mark 3 Decked Skeletal also features the patented Boden Twistlock.

Cost differential between the conventional tandem axle platform semi-trailer and the specialised Mark 3 Boden Decked Skeletal is less than 10% on standard models.

Already proved for operation at 15 metres overall length, the Group SK and PSK semi-trailers each provide a range of 9 standard models to cope with varying numbers and lengths of containers produced to ISO recommendations; all these models are individually designed to obtain correct king-pin and bogie reactions. All Mark 3 Skeletals benefit from technological know-how and

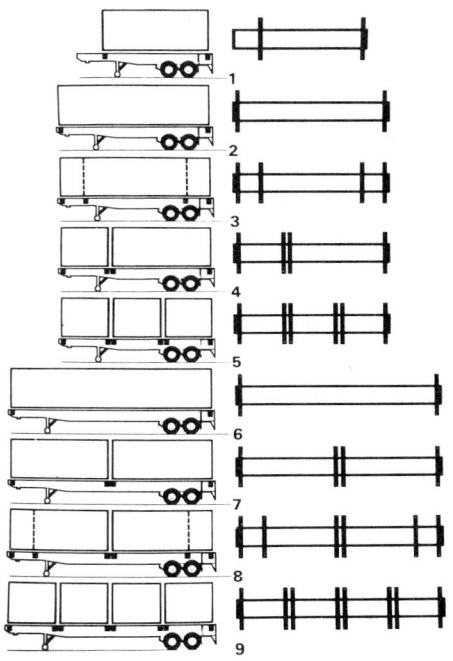

Nine standard skeletal and platform skeletal models are available in the Mark 3 Boden ranges of specialist container carrying semi-trailers. Fitted with either removable or retractable twistlocks, these are designed to meet the requirements of transporting any container or combination of containers built to ISO recommendation.

flow-line production techniques proved and perfected at the Group's Oldham Division.

BOLLNÄS

Bollnäs Verkstads Ab
Box 61,
821 01 Bollnäs
Sweden
TELEPHONE: 0 278/200 00
PRODUCTS:

Prime movers and semi trailer systems for handling containers and other units at ports and terminals.

Bollnäs also make container transporters incorporating hoist units to give lift. The 1469 is principally used for lifting and transporting containers 40 ft long, but which can also be used with 20 ft units. It normally has six hoist units. The standard transporter is built for lifting to a height of

approximately 1,750 mm (69 in). It can also be made to lift to a height of 2,750 mm (110 in) and wide enough to straddle rail trucks. It is designed to be towed by a prime mover. Other transporters are types 1484 and 1485. These have 4 hoist units and can be operated from the cab of a prime mover.

BOWER AND SPAYNE

Bower & Spayne Ltd.
Airport Estate,
Fifers Lane
Norwich
Norfolk NOR 57A
England
TELEPHONE: 43477
Telegrams: Metals Norwich
DIRECTORS:
P. M. R. Bower
R. Spayne
P. D. Spayne
I. E. Bower
PRODUCTS:

Top-lift frames for handling containers by fork-lift truck, side loader, or crane: 10 ft, 20 ft, 30 ft, 40 ft sizes, up to 30 ton max. loading, with lifting hooks or twist locks; manual/hydraulic operation.

The 'BOSUN': 20 Ton Mobile Gantry for handling containers and other loads.

Corner Wheel Fittings for containers, easily attached, to render containers mobile.

Stillages, pallets, etc., as internal equipment for containers.

Mobile Ramp for fork-lift and other truckage access and egress to and from containers.

The Bosun 20·5 Mobile Gantry

Design Purpose: loading and unloading road or rail transport. Containers up to 20 ft × 8 ft × 8 ft dimensions, up to 20 tons weight from the equalising slings. Other loads up to 5 tons weight using single point slinging from the load beam. Bosun is the 1970's version of the common lift anything mobile gantry, having an ISO container capability and designed as a low cost, safe unit for the low to medium volume throughput user. Many potential users in this market do not have 17 ft clear height doors thus the gantry frame is designed to raise and lower in direct proportion to the load, minimum overall height being 11 ft 8 in, maximum 17 ft 10 in.

Design Features: Frame—fabricated from rectangular hollow section steel to material requirements of BS 4360: 1968, Weldable Structural Steels. Assembly end weld in two fixtures—accuracy at low cost. Overall length has been designed bearing in mind the traffic acts relating to indivisible loads and Bosun can thus be delivered, at low cost, fully assembled and ready for work. Designed with an 8 in dominant dimension producing co-ordinated appearance. Basically the frame consists of two lower sections each with travelling masts, the masts being joined by a very rigid load beam. One of the lower sections carries all control equipment. Mast bearings are alloy steel rollers and housings are fully adjustable to ensure maximum bearing life. Load beam carries two equalising sling units and either central shackle or load trolley to customers choice.

Bower & Spayne 40 ft. container lift frame.

All four 16 in diameter wheels have 360° swivel and 4 way directional locks—fully manoeuvrable and capable of being towed from either end. Polyurethane wheels standard, cast iron optional. Slings supplied as standard in 75 grade alloy steel and sized for 20 ft 20 ton ISO container.

Hydraulic and control—74 in lift is provided by two hydraulic cylinders, one in each lower frame section. Cylinders are supplied by hydraulic system consisting of 25 gallon reservoir, pressure regulator and gauge, filter, gear pump and simple manual control valve. Cylinder synchronisation is by flow sensing and dividing valve under full flow conditions, tilt switches and restrictors under acceleration. Safety items include a circuit providing normal rate of descent in event of hose or pipe breakage and a circuit providing a 1° tilt limit to frame. Standard power source for pump is a 3 phase mains electric motor—battery electric motor, diesel engine, compressed air/hydraulic pump are optional.

Operating Features: the effect of out of balance loads can be cancelled by use of the two equalising units. The units allow the centre of gravity of a load to be located manually, automatically locking in position when load is lifted. Load can be lifted parallel to ground or at any desired angle of tilt. Towing eyes are standard at both ends of gantry but the Bosun can be manoeuvred by manpower under no load conditions. Although primarily designed as a mobile lifting/lowering machine, it can be towed fully loaded at low speed on a reasonably smooth surface providing the load is supported by the optional toe steady beams. Under full load conditions the wheels project a stress intensity of 12,800 lbs to a floor area of approx 6 sq in. An eight wheel version is available to suit ground construction unable to accept this loading.

PRINCIPAL DIMENSIONS/SPECIFICATION:
SWL with container slung from equalising units—20 tons.
SWL with load slung from single point on load beam—5 tons.
Overall gantry length—9 ft 5¾ in.
Overall gantry width—11 ft 9½ in.
Clear width between uprights—9 ft 9 in.
Overall gantry height—mast lowered—11 ft 8 in.
Overall gantry height—mast raised—17 ft 10 in.
Wheelbase—variable between 8 ft 0½ in and 9 ft 1½ in.
Track—10 ft 8 in.
Wheels—16 ft diameter × 5 in width.
Towing—continuous drawbar pull required, full load—1,150 lbs.
Towing—intermittant drawbar pull required, full load—2,400 lbs.
Manual—effort required to maintain movement, no load—150 lbs.
Manual—effort required to start movement, no load—300 lbs.
Hydraulic reservoir capacity—25 imp gallons.
Hydraulic operating pressure, normal—2,000 psi.

BROMMA SMIDES

AB Bromma Smides & Mek Verkstad
Krossgatan 31-33,
162 26 Vällingby, Stockholm, Sweden
TELEPHONE: Stockholm (08) 380030
TELEX: 10224 conquips
CABLES: Backtemanmek Stockholm
PRODUCTS:

Fixed and telescopic spreaders, electrically or hydraulically operated for all sizes and types of container. Container lashing systems for ships, decks. Elevating roller stand bridge to facilitate container lashing on board ship. 'Conlock' automatic container lashing system.

Conlock Automatic Container Lashing

A fitting primarily for use on board ship to simplify the problem of lashing containers to decks. Double acting twist locks, the rotation of which is activated by a pretensioned spring, are placed either into the deck locating sockets or top corner castings of a container. The weight of the container releases the tensioning of the spring permitting the twist lock to revolve through 90 deg into a locked position. To release a container you operate a push button which releases the twist lock for an additional 90 deg rotation into the unlocked position.

Elevating Travelling Bridge for Deck Lashing

This is designed to help personnel lash containers up to 4 high on shipdeck. The bridge is supported by a telescopic mast and ladder. It has a centre section with extension arms on either side. The extension arms have movable pulleys equipped with davit gear for hoisting or lashing top fittings and wires. The track running trolley on which the device runs is powered by a geared electric brake motor.

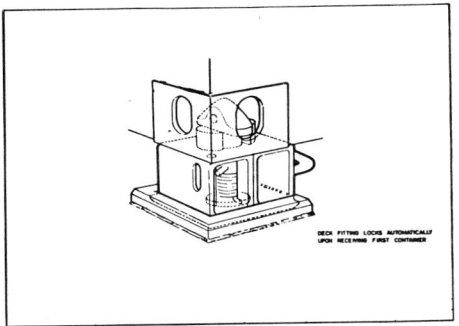
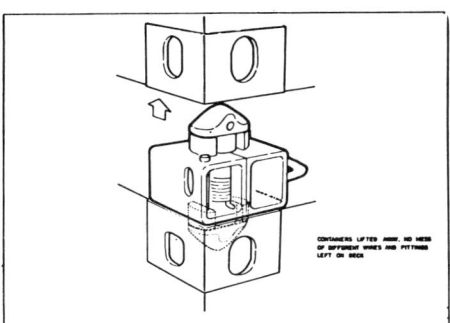
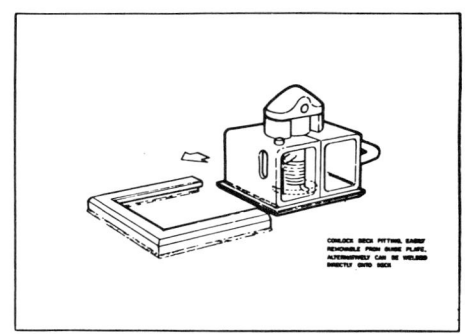

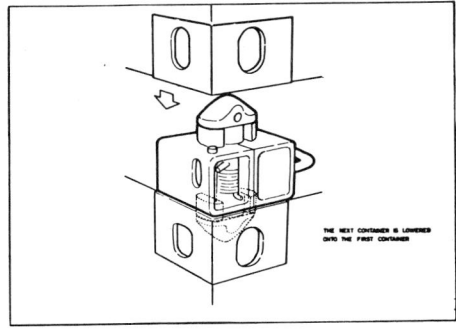
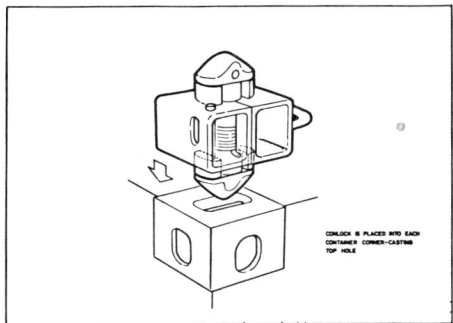
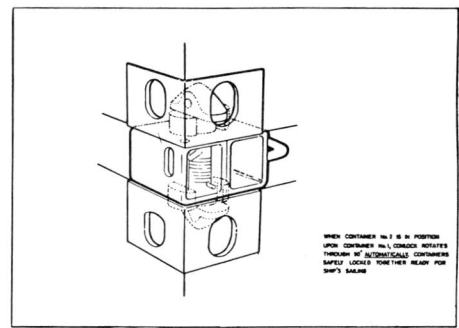

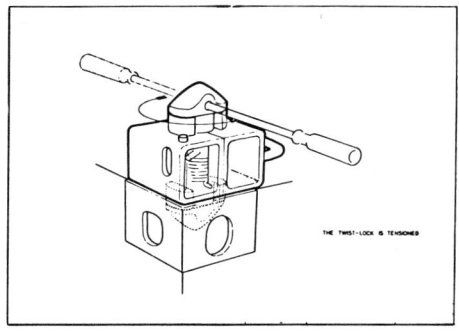
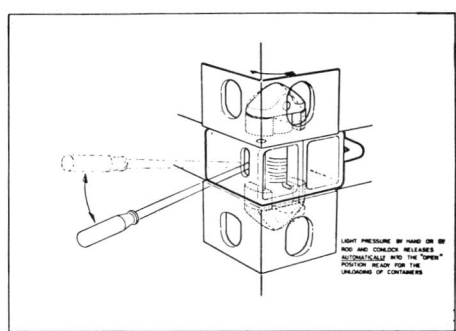

How the Conlock system works.

The Bromma Smides travelling bridge for lashing containers up to 4 high on shipdeck.

LA BRUGEOISE

S A La Brugeoise et Nivelles

8200-Brugge 2 (Belgium)
TELEPHONE: 050 30751
TELEX: 191.22
DIRECTORS:
O. J. Bronchart (*Managing*)
M. Simonart (*General Manager*)
P. Vande Sijpe (*Plant Manager*)
J. Sarteau (*Marketing Manager*)
J. L. Barbier (*Chief Engineer*)
L. Morrbaliu (*Office Manager Containers*)

PRODUCTS:
Skeletal semi-trailers for container transport,
*Type PC.*16.3
For 20 ft containers.

*Type PC.*20.3
For transport of all types of containers,
(e.g. 40 footers or 2 20 ft and optionally for

The PC. 20.3 for one 40 ft or two 20 ft containers or optionally for 30 ft or 35 ft units.

30 ft or 35 ft containers).
Tilt trailer (Savoyarde Model)

The La Brugeoise 16·3 semi-trailer for 20 ft containers.

TTP-36—a trailer which is adaptable for containers.

CARRUTHERS

J. H. Carruthers & Co Ltd
HEAD OFFICE:
College Milton, East Kilbride, Glasgow
TELEPHONE: East Kilbride 20591
TELEGRAMS: Hoisting, East Kilbride, Glasgow
TELEX: 77782
DIRECTORS:
R. L. Davidson (*Chairman*)
W. G. Cowan (*Managing*)
T. Lister (*Works*)
J. A. T. Pairman
J. G. Harte
PRODUCTS:
Monobox travelling gantry, Goliath and semi-Goliath cranes, modular crane control gear. The Containamaster special purpose Goliath crane.

Monobox Electric Travelling Cranes

The Carruthers monobox cranes are of single box girder construction with the trolley mounted at the side, as distinct from the conventional twin girder crane with the trolley mounted between the rails on the tops of the girders. With the girder loaded in torsion by the side mounting of the trolley a high capacity/weight ratio is achieved, which reduces appreciably the loading on the gantry structure.

Cranes up to 10 tons capacity having a standard height of lift of 30 ft and those over 10 tons capacity 40 ft. Designs for single box girder cranes of 200 tons capacity and 130 ft span have been prepared. Many of the working parts on the standard series of cranes are interchangeable which allows the stocking of a minimum number of spares in factories where a number of cranes of this series is in service.

Over 600 "Monobox" cranes are now working in factories, warehouses and freight terminals throughout the world. The largest Goliath crane manufactured is 61 m (200 ft) wide and is located at Woolwich. Many of these cranes are in operation at container handling depots including Ardrossan, Larmer Preston.

The cantilever extensions of these cranes enable containers to be handled directly between the central stacking areas and vehicles on the roads at the sides.

Containamaster Goliath Container Crane

The "Containamaster" will handle 8 ft by 8 ft containers of any length up to the 40 ft long ISO standard. It will stack them three high and will pass a fourth container over the stack. It will slew (rotate) containers. It will cover a container park up to 180 ft of width and of any length.

It will hoist a payload of 28 tons at 40 ft a minute, it will traverse it across the park at 200 ft per minute, and simultaneously, will travel it the length of the park at 400 ft per minute, and, incidentally, it will slew containers at a rate of 2 minutes per revolution.

It will operate at slower speeds, if required. There is a choice of speeds for each of the three basic motions of the crane and the best combination can be selected for a particular requirement.
Length:
Any length up to 180 feet overall; rail centres are available to suit almost any site.
Height:
55 feet overall. This allows for a moving container to pass over a 3-high stack.
Payload:
Any loaded container up to a maximum of 27 tons.
Speeds:
There are 4 basic motions on the "Containamaster" crane; hoisting, slewing (rotating), traversing and travelling. You have a choice of speeds and you can select the best com-

25-Ton Carruthers Monobox Goliath Crane at 39 ft span (11·9 m), 16 ft Cantilever (4·88 m) and height of lift 27 ft 2 ins (8·28 m). Supplied to Containerways, Ardrossan.

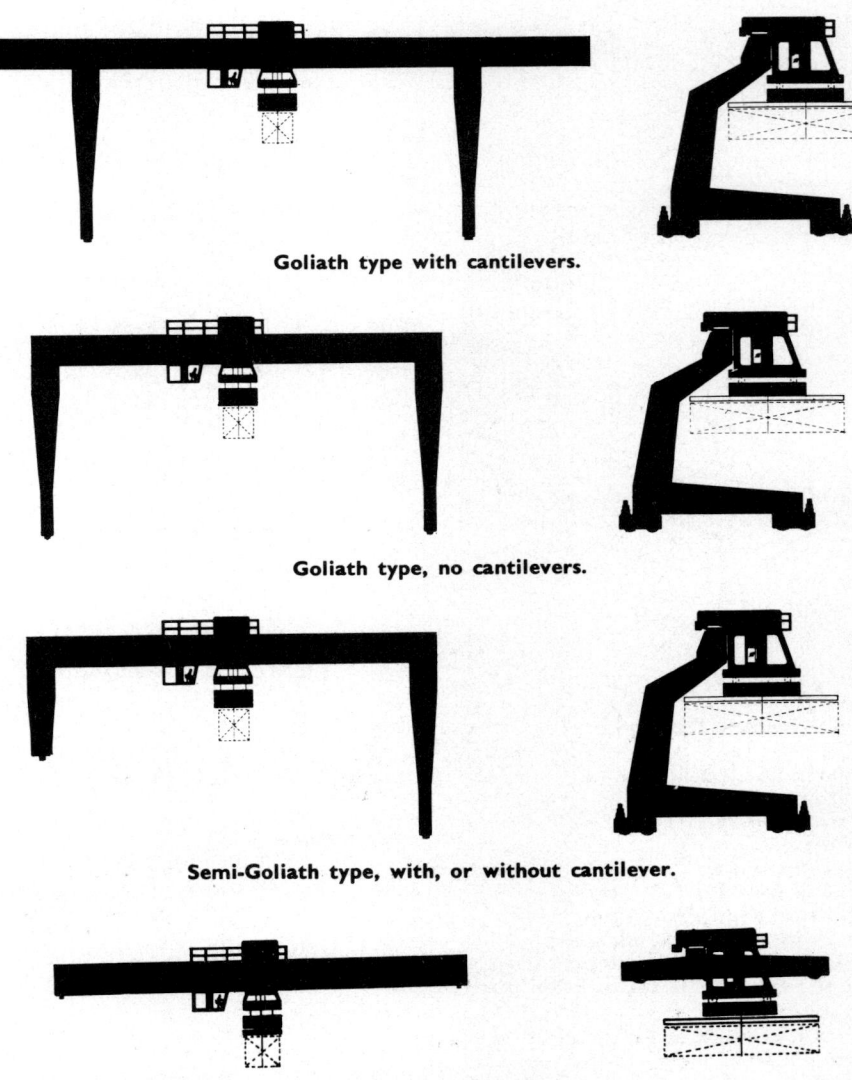

Goliath type with cantilevers.

Goliath type, no cantilevers.

Semi-Goliath type, with, or without cantilever.

Overhead.

Variations of the Carruthers "Containamaster" theme. There is a choice of any of these versions in a variety of overall lengths.

bination of all to suit your own special requirements.
(a) Hoist either 20 or 40 feet per minute.
(b) Slewing (rotating) fixed at 1 revolution in 2 minutes.
(c) Traversing either 100 or 200 feet per minute.
(d) Travelling 200, 300 or 400 feet per minute.

Classification:
There are two choices of classification as prescribed in the British Standard for cranes of this type. Either Class II or Class IV. Class II is defined as 2,000 working hours per year.
Class IV is defined as 4,000 working hours per year, or more.

Simple chain-hook system.

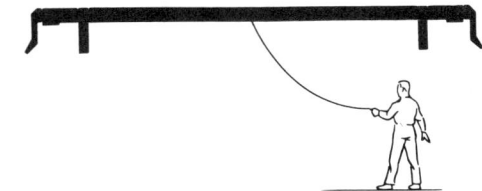
Automatic engagement, manual release; one frame for each container length.

Automatic engagement, automatic release; one frame for each container length.

Automatic engagement, automatic release; adjustable (from cabin) to suit varying lengths of container.

Standard attachments for the Carruthers "Containermaster".

CLARK

Clark International Marketing S.A.
Industrial Truck Division, PO Box 1320, Battle Creek, Michigan 49016 USA
TELEPHONE: Area Code 616 964-5543
TELEGRAMS: 810-276-2200
DIRECTORS:
W. E. Schirmer (*Chairman of the Board*)
J. F. Bechtel (*President*)
L. N. Owen (*Vice President and Director of Marketing*)
OVERSEAS MARKETING OFFICE:
Clark International Marketing SA, 2 Place du Champ de Mars, Brussels 5, Belgium
SALES OFFICE IN UNITED KINGDOM:
Clark Equipment Limited, Industrial Truck Division, Pump Lane, Hayes, Middlesex
P. O. Richards (*Product Sales Manager, Containerisation*)
PRODUCTS:
Clark Van Carriers Series 512, 520 and 521. Clarklift CY525, CY625 and CY700 forklift trucks suitable for container handling. The latter have capacities of 52,500 lb, 62,500 lb, and 70,000 lb all at 48 in load centres.

Clark Van Carriers
The Series 512 Van Carrier is a six-wheel machine having capacity of 30 tons. It can stack 20 ft containers three high and 40 ft containers two high. It can also place container rows close together since it requires only 3 ft 10 in between rows to straddle a container unit.

The Series 520 Van Carrier is an eight-wheel machine having capacity of 30 tons. In all other respects its capability is the same as the Series 512.

The Series 521 Van Carrier is an eight-wheel machine having capacity of 40 tons. It can stack 40 ft containers three high.

Frame
Tubular side members reinforced at stress points, tubular corner housings and rear cross members all electrically welded.

Hoist Mechanism
Lift frame is hydraulically hoisted and stabilized within the carrier frame. Mechanical hydraulic hoist equalization system is provided. This system will automatically compensate for differences in longitudinal C.G. of container up to a 45% to 55% ratio.

Lifting Frame
Main lifting frame is rectangular fabricated structure suspended from hoist mechanism at four points by one strand of 2¼ in pitch roller chain. Main lifting frame designed to handle 20 ft containers. Auxiliary lifting frame for handling 40 ft containers is a rectangular fabricated structure and is suspended from the main lifting frame by means of main lifting frame latch mechanism and quickly detachable couplings. Main lift frame is guided at two points within the carrier frame. Main lift frame and auxiliary lift frame is equipped with four ISO type hydraulically

Clark Series 512 Van Carrier

operated latches mounted at each corner.

Electrical interlock provided for main lift frame and auxiliary lift frame by use of two separate systems. Each system will consist of four mill grade limit switches in series. Indicator lights at operator position show green when properly engaged, red if not secure to container. This system will signal when picking up 20 ft containers, the auxiliary lift frame and auxiliary lift frame containers.

Clark Series 520 Van Carrier handling containers at the ECT berth at Rotterdam.

CLARK CHAPMAN

Clark Chapman Crane & Bridge Division
Woodeson House, Rodley, Leeds, LS13 1HN
TELEPHONE: Pudsey 79001
TELEX: 55159
TELEX ANSWER BACK CODE: Cranes Rodley
TELEGRAMS: Cranes Rodley

PRODUCTS:

Container transporter cranes, Goliath transporter cranes, all types of bridge cranes and other cranes.

The Crane & Bridge Division of the Clarke Chapman Group incorporates Clyde Crane & Booth Ltd., Sir William Arrol & Co. Ltd., and Wellman-Cranes Ltd., all three companies producing container handling cranes. In addition the Division includes Cowans Sheldon & Co. Ltd., and John Boyd Engineers (Annan) Ltd.

Clyde-Booth Container Transporter Cranes

Clyde Crane & Booth Ltd. built the first container transporter crane to be commissioned in the United Kingdom. Two identical 25 ton cranes were supplied to the port of Grangemouth, Scotland, and the first of these was put into service in June 1967, within eight months of the order being placed by the British Transport Docks Board.

There are currently three designs of 30-ton capacity Clyde-Booth rigid container handler transporter cranes – Mark V, VI and VII. These are built to handle containers up to 40 ft long, can be adjusted to suit site conditions in respect of height, outreach, rail centres and wheel loading (by adding more wheels) but the basic design remains constant. All three designs have the following features: Rack operated traversing gear driven by a motor through Ward Leonard control; trolley position indicator and a container levelling device.

The Clyde-Booth container crane above is one of two identical 25 ton units supplied to the port of Grangemouth, Scotland. Commissioned in June 1967, it was the first container crane to be put into service in the United Kingdom.

LOADING PARTICULARS:

Maximum loading:
Weight of loaded container

Mark V	*Mark VI*	*Mark VII*
30 tons	30 tons	30 tons
(67.200 lbs)	(67.200 lbs)	(67.200 lbs)

Allowance for weight of spreader beam and fittings.

8·tons	8 tons	8 tons

Total weight on rope system.

38 tons	38 tons	38 tons

Maximum outreach from centre of waterside rail.

21·03 m	24·993 m	35·05 m
(69 ft 0 in)	(82 ft 0 in)	(115 ft 0 in)

Distance from edge of quay to centre of waterside rail.

1·21 m	2·133 m	3·04 m
(4 ft 0 in)	(7 ft 0 in)	(10 ft 0 in)

Range of lift.

30·784 m	30·48 m	33·52 m
(101 ft 0 in)	(100 ft 0 in)	(110 ft 0 in)

Maximum working wheel load i.e. fully loaded machine plus a wind load equivalent to 5 lb/ft^2

24 tons	35 tons	29 tons

Approximate total weight of transporter in working order but excluding container.

330 tons	390 tons	475 tons

SPEEDS OF OPERATION:

Hoisting with full load

18·288 m/min	35·05 m/min)	35·05 m/min.
(60 ft/min)	(115 ft/min)	(115 ft/min)

Slow speeds available down to approximately 10% of full load speed.

Traverse with full load

45·72 m/min	121·9 m/min	121·92 m/min
(150 ft/min)	(400 ft/min)	(400 ft/min)

Long Travel with full load
Slow speeds available down to approximately 12% of full load speed.

45·72 m/min	45·72 m/min	45·72 m/min
(150 ft/min)	(150 ft/min)	150 ft /min)

Boom Hoist. Boom raised from horizontal to stowed position in

7 minutes	7 minutes·	7 minutes

Tilting. Longitudinal tilting of container either way to a maximum of 3°

Arrol Goliath Container Cranes

Sir William Arrol and Company Ltd., have built 2-6-2 and 2-6-3 road/rail goliath cranes for eight British Rail Freight liner terminals. These cranes are able to handle about 35 containers/hour, of 10, 20, 30 and 40 ft. length and up to 30 tons weight. The cranes are of welded steel box design. All the main motions are controlled by thyristor equipment with pre-selection for automatic trolley positioning over the rail tracks.

Wellman Container Transporter Cranes

Wellman-Cranes Ltd., have built five of these large container cranes for the British Rail Freightliner service into Ireland, two each for Holyhead and for Dublin and one for Belfast, the latter to join a Clyde Booth crane already in service.

The entire structure of these Wellman transporter cranes is of welded box plate form, the main booms being of torsion-box construction. On large rail span machines, full triangulation of the upper structural elements achieves minimum deflection of the luffing boom when the trolley and load are at maximum outreach.

Special attention has been taken to the ease with which mechanical parts can be maintained. The trolley runs on the top of the main booms, thus giving access to all parts which require regular checking. The trolley can also be traversed back under the machinery house, enabling complete overhauls to be carried out under cover. Maintenance is further simplified by accommodating all the mechanical and electrical assemblies in a single machinery house.

Thyristor control equipment is used on all motions, except for the boom hoist, which is conventional slip ring control. Electric power is carried to the operator's cabin,

Clyde Crane 30 ton extensible automatic spreader beam. The telescoping motion, the retraction of the corner guides and operation of the latching mechanism are all electrically operated. This particular unit was supplied to British Rail at Belfast.

suspended from the underside of the trolley frame, by means of the Wellman-BEWA flexible cable carrier looped system. Trolley traverse is rope operated, the drive being by two motors and twin rope barrels. The container rope hoist drive, consists of a single motor driving two barrels and both the traverse and hoist drives have deflector pullies to enable the hoist and traverse rope systems to operate when the boom is raised.

The Clarke Chapman Crane & Bridge Division have built over thirty ship to shore and goliath container handling cranes.

British Crane & Excavator Corporation Ltd
Steel House
Eastcote, Pinner, Middlesex
TELEPHONE: 01-866 5881
TELEGRAMS: Britcranex, Pinner
TELEX: 21619
DIRECTORS:
A. G. Howe (*Chairman*)
D. Hassall (*Managing*)
L. Archer
L. Bullen
V. J. Canham
T. I. K. Dunlop
R. L. E. Keates
R. L. Lester
A. D. Steel
PRODUCTS:
Coles mobile cranes.

The following Coles mobile cranes, when equipped with appropriate spreaders, are suitable for handling freight containers in ports, rail yards and inland container terminals:
Adonis C—Capacity 11 ton, max jib length 40 ft.
Adonis—15 tons, max jib 85 ft (including fly jib).
Dominant—17·5 tons, max jib 95 ft (including fly jib).
Endurance—30 tons, max jib 140 ft (including fly jib).
Conqueror—60 tons, max jib 200 ft (including fly jib.)
Vigorous—35 tons, max jib length 180 ft (including fly jib.)

Conlift Container Hebegerate GmbH & Co.
6982 Freudenberg/Main,
Josef-Haamann-Strasse 1-4
Germany (Federal Republic)
TELEPHONE: 09375/273

COLES

Coles 'Endurance' mobile crane.

CONLIFT

TELEX: 06 89 224

PRODUCTS:
Mobile and fixed container stilts and transporters.

CONTINENTAL

Continental Trailer Corporation
13231 Lakeland Road
Box 2910
Santa Fe Springs
California 90670 U.S.A.
TELEPHONE: (213) 685-6426
A subsidiary of Wells Industries Corp
DIRECTOR: Stephen C. Vyn (*President*)
PRODUCTS:

Semi-trailers, skeletals especially designed to carry containers which conform to USASI-MH-5.1 specifications, the new chassis features a monocoque design which results in savings of 600 lb over conventional container chassis and 1,000 lb lighter than conventional flatbeds often used in hauling containers.

Besides light weight, the new model features patented twist-centre locks, the middle set of which can be lowered in order to receive 24 ft containers.

These chassis are reinforced for piggyback service and are manufactured with T-1, steel fabricated frames. These Continental Model CC-6627 chassis come in standard 27-ft lengths with Timken axles, three-leaf Hutchins springs with 'no-hop' attachments.

In addition to saving weight, the revolutionary, new monocoque construction facilitates maintenance because of the ease with which

650A1 Model Travelift (30 tons capacity) handling containers—at Glasgow

landing gears and axle assemblies can be serviced. Empty trailer weight is 6,000 lb, the payload capacity is 50,000 lb.

The 'Travelift'

The 'Travelift' is also designed to handle containers and heavy industrial loads. The difference between the two machines is that the 'Travelift' can straddle up three lines of containers plus the vehicle being loaded and can traverse the container from one stack to another whilst travelling up and down the lines. They are used extensively by British Rail in their Freightliner terminals at London, Manchester, Liverpool and Glasgow and by numerous stevedoring companies.

The 'Travelift' is self powered and is operated by the driver seated in an enclosed cab with a clear view of the load being handled. It is not confined to a specific track, allowing complete flexibility when planning storage areas, and yard extensions can be undertaken without additional cost.

COSTAMASNAGA

Officine Di Costamasnaga S.P.A.
22041 Costamasnaga (Como) Italy
TELEPHONE: 85.51.92 TELEX: 38184
DIRECTORS:
Carlo Magni (*General Manager*)
Ing. P. Liverani (*Technical Manager*)
Ing. Giuseppe Broggi (*Factory Manager*)
Ing. Bramanti (*Production Manager*)
Dott. Gaetano Fumagalli (*Administration Manager*)
Ida Magni (*Commercial Manager*)
Gianni Bernadi (*Commercial Manager*)
PRODUCT:
Container handling crane for rail and sea terminals

Costamasnaga 30 ton Gantry Crane

An 0-6-0 gantry crane has recently been installed by the company at Milano Rogoredo container terminal. The crane covers an area of 366 m (1,201 ft) by 20 m (66 ft).

The gantry moves on the guide rails at speeds up to 120 m/min. Lifting speed is 5 m/min (16 ft/min) and speed of transfer with loaded containers is up to 30 m/min (98 ft/min). Containers can be stacked three high. The spreader beam, which moves on a platform guided by a vertical column, can make turns of up to 60 degrees and can be inclined in all directions to accommodate irregularly placed containers or awkward loads. Capacity of the machine is 30 tons and operation is by one man.

An automatic weighing device is incorporated in the standard model. A radio-telephone system linking the crane driver with shunting control centre can also be provided.

The 'Costamasnaga' spreader is automatically adjustable to accept containers at 20 ft, 30-ft, 35 ft and 40 ft. The adjustment is by mechanical control effected through a geared motor and rack. Automatic lock pins ensure maintenance of the selected length. Hydraulic jacks control the lock-pins and rotation of the container seizing tangs. All the handling requirements are push-button, remote control.

Costamasnaga 0-6-0 Type Crane with mobile gantry, covers a working area of 86,000 m² (925,700 sq. ft) and has a working height of 7·50 m (24 ft 7 in) which allows the passage of a third container over two already superimposed on the ground. Capacity 30 tons.

CRANE FRUEHAUF

Crane Fruehauf Trailers Ltd
HEAD OFFICE:
655 London Road, Isleworth, Middlesex
TELEPHONE: 01-568 0641
TELEX: 262051
DIRECTORS:
E. G. Hooker (*Chairman*)
L. H. Allwood (*Vice Chairman*)

D. R. Marsh (*Managing Director*)
A. S. Aranyos (USA)
D. E. Bernstein (USA)
J. L. B. Crane, MA (Cantab.)
B. K. Day
W. E. Grace (USA)
R. J. Jervis
R. D. Rowan (USA)

R.-Taylor
J. K. Thompson
K. D. Vick
PRODUCTS:

Crane Fruehauf skeletal and platform skeletal semi-trailers for container transportation by road.

The range of Crane Fruehauf semi-trailers

for carrying containers comprises nine standard SK models, fitted with either removable or retractable twistlocks, and these are designed to meet the requirements of transporting any container or combination of containers built to ISO recommendations. Main frame is of two-member I-beam construction with special outrigger support points to meet the dynamic stress imposed by the container's corner castings.

Designed for dual-purpose operation the Crane Fruehauf PSK embodies design principles of the specialised SK skeletal model, decked to provide a flush surface for the transportation of general freight. It provides increased flexibility for the general haulier who is also called upon to transport containers, and nine standard models are available to cope with the varying numbers and lengths of all container modules manufactured to ISO recommendations. Fitted with either removable or retractable twistlocks, the Crane Fruehauf PSK models provide a rugged main frame of two-member I-beam construction, with special outrigger support points to meet the dynamic stress imposed by the container's corner castings. Straight through I-beam cross-members, decked, support conventional loads, and the difference in cost between the dual-purpose Crane Fruehauf PSK models and ordinary platform semi-trailers is less than 10 per cent on standard models.

Other skeletal semitrailer models have been tailor made by Crane Fruehauf for specialised requirements, including tipping skeletals developed for use with Crane Fruehauf's bulk solids container, goose necked skeletals for use with containers incorporating an underfloor tunnel arrangement, and step frame skeletals to reduce overall weight when travelling.

Crane Fruehauf tipping skeletal semi-trailer developed for operation with the CF 20 ft 'Bulktainer' bulk solids container at 28 tons G.C.W.

Crane Fruehauf platform skeleton semi-trailer for dual-purpose of containers by road.

40 ft Crane Fruehauf skeleton semi-trailer for the transportation of containers by road.

A new Crane Fruehauf skeletal. Special features include Crane Fruehauf F2 EWH wide spread bogie suspension and dual king pins to conform with British and Dutch regulations when operating with maximum permissible weights

Above and Left.

These new Crane Fruehauf gooseneck skeletal semi trailers are designed to reduce overall height during transport by road

Van Doorne's Automobielfabrieken N.V.
Eindhoven,
Holland
TELEPHONE: OVO 149111
TELEX: 51085
DIRECTORS:
W. A. V. van Doorne

DAF

PRODUCTS:
Special semi-trailers for the transportation of 20, 30, 35 and 40 ft containers.
Universal semi-trailers for containers and general cargo tractors and semi-trailers for the transportation of containers at terminals and roll-on roll-off services.

DAF tractor and container semi-trailer

DAYBROOK-OTTAWA

Division Gulf & Western Metals Co.
Daybrook-Ottawa
1313 North Hickory Street,
Ottawa, Kansas 66067 USA.
TELEPHONE: Area Code 913 242-2200

DIRECTORS:
Frank H. Vivian (*Vice President and General Manager*)
PRODUCTS:
The company produces a range of six yard

tractors. The Commando Thirty is used for hauling trailers in yard terminals and ramp loading on seagoing vessels. The Commando Mark III is used for piggy packing in railroad yards.

DEMAG

Demag Industrial Equipment Ltd.,
Turriff Building, Great West Road,
Brentford, Middlesex England
TELEPHONE: 01-560-2188
TELEGRAMS: Demag Hounslow
TELEX: 24153
GERMAN ADDRESS:
Demag Aktiengesellschaft, Postfach 13
5532 Jünkerath/Rhld
Germany

DIRECTORS:
E. A. Volkmar
D. F. Heyman
F. A. Blake (*Secretary*)

PRODUCTS:
Straddle Loader TJ 203/3
Capacity: 40 tons. To stack 8 ft/8 ft 6 in/ 9 ft high ISO containers, 20/30/35/40 ft long and 2 × 20 ft, three-high. The spreader can also be lowered to handle demi (4 ft high) containers.
Wheels: Eight road wheels all steered, four driven via hydrostatic drive.
Road speed: Max. 29 km/h (18 mph).
Lifting speed: 12·2 m (40 ft) per min.

Straddle Loader TJ 203/2
Capacity: 40 tons. To stack 8 ft/8 ft 6 in/9 ft high ISO containers 20/30/35/40 ft long and 2 × 20 ft, two-high.
The spreader can also be lowered to handle

demi (4 ft high) containers.
Wheels: Eight road wheels all steered, 4 driven via hydrostatic drive.
Road speed: Max. 29 km/h (18 mph).
Lifting Speed: 12·2 m (40 ft) per min.

Straddle Loader TJ 203/1
Capacity: 30 tons. To lift 8 ft/8 ft 6 in/9 ft high ISO containers 20/30/35/40 ft long high enough to load or unload road/rail vehicles.
The spreader can also be lowered to handle demi (4 ft high) containers.
Wheels: Six road wheels all steered, 2 driven via hydrostatic drive.
Road speed: Max. 29 km/h (18 mph).
Lifting speed: 12·2 m (40 ft) per min.

DOBSON

W. E. & F. Dobson Ltd.
Colwick Industrial Estate, Colwick, Nottingham, NG4 2BT.
TELEPHONE: Nottingham 241341
TELEGRAMS: Hyprop, Nottingham
TELEX: 37132
DIRECTORS:
J. Godfrey
A. T. Marr
M. T. McHugh
A. Shutt
G. F. H. Le Roy
L. W. Taylor
P. E. Woodhead
PRODUCTS:
Mobile hydraulic lifting legs for handling ISO containers, maximum designed lifting load per set of 4 legs is 22½ tons, petrol, diesel or electric power pack giving an operating lift speed of 3 ft/min.
Heavy duty mobile hydraulic lifting legs for handling ISO containers with lateral alignment facility, designed lifting load per set of 4 legs is 35 tons. Diesel or Electric power pack giving an operating lift speed of 3 ft/min.

Mobile Hydraulic Lifting Legs (20 ton)
A hydraulically operated system developed for use in the handling of ISO containers or custom built bodies fitted with suitable

Body unlocked and chassis rams extended, lifting body or flat-bed clear of vehicle.

bottom corner castings. It comprises 4 trolley mounted hydraulic legs each embodying a suitable corner casting with a lock mechanism, quick release hose couplings and a corner braced fitting to give additional stability.

The mobile hydraulic legs are positioned at each corner of the container and the hoses from the mobile power unit connected to each leg. The power unit is actuated, raising the legs to the required height. The legs are then locked on to the corners of the container and the container raised clear of the chassis, or trailer.

The vehicle may then be driven away and is, therefore, available for other operations.

The container can now be lowered to the ground, the legs unlocked, hoses disconnected and the mobile legs wheeled away. The equipment is suitable for lifting from both flat-bed and skeletal trailers.

A deadman's handle control valve ensures that all hydraulic circuits are locked should the operator release the controls with power unit running. Pressure is automatically locked into a leg should the flexible hose be inadvertently damaged. Maximum designed lifting load is 20 tons per set of four legs.

Mobile Hydraulic Lifting Legs (35 tons)

These are similar in principle to the lower capacity lifting legs referred to above. Lateral shift is provided to allow alignment of a container over a vehicle chassis.

Hydraulic Body Handling System —Type 41

The system is readily acceptable to either rigid or articulated chassis. It may be fitted as an accessory to both new and existing chassis. All the hydraulic lifting equipment is mounted on the vehicle chassis with the body or container supported on a subframe to which is attached four manually operated mechanical legs.

The equipment on the chassis comprises hydraulic rams, control valve, oil tank, relief valve and all necessary pipework. Hydraulic pressure is by means of a power take-off pump driven from the vehicle gearbox. A relief valve is incorporated in the system to protect the equipment from hydraulic overload. The subframe fits on the chassis by means of conical spigots on the chassis and mating pieces on the subframe. The subframe is locked to the chassis with 4 mechanical locks having a 90° twist action and of a design which ensures no possibility of being accidentally unlocked during transit. All mechanical locks employed for securing the legs in position, both when stowed or extended, are of the "safety catch" principle to obviate

Mechanical legs having been adjusted and hydraulic rams retracted, body is free standing.

Vehicle driven clear of body or flat-bed and freed for other work.

Vehicle ready for the road with body or flat-bed mechanically locked in position.

possibility of accidental release.

On arrival of a vehicle at its unloading point, the body is unlocked, the legs are withdrawn, swung into position and automatically locked in place.

By operating one control valve only, the rams are extended, lifting the subframe clear of the chassis, level lift being ensured by means of special valves built into the hydraulic circuit. The legs are then adjusted to within approx. 1 inch from the ground, the hydraulic rams are retracted and the subframe left standing free on the mechanical legs. The vehicle is now free for other work.

To replace the subframe on the chassis, the

vehicle is positioned underneath, the hydraulic rams extended, lifting the frame and allowing the legs to be retracted and stowed beneath the frame. Correct positioning of the frame on the chassis is assured by the conical guides. The rams are lowered, the frame locks engaged and the vehicle is ready for the road.

DORSEY

Dorsey Trailers, Inc.
Elba, Alabama 36323
TELEPHONE: Area Code (205) 897-2241
DIRECTORS:
George L. Collier (*President*)
Frank A. Mularz (*Vice President, Sales*)
Sam Collier (*Vice President, Finance*)
Roy Belcer (*Vice President, Engineering*)
PRODUCTS:

A complete line of job tested container hauling chassis and container hauling platform.

The Couple-able DX 20-40 is a recent innovation that is already seeing service for several major operators, providing utmost flexibility in the movement of 20 ft containers either separately or in pairs. It was developed and patented by Dorsey and Xtra, Inc.

The two units coupled together into a single 40 ft. tandem axle unit.

The system has several features that are unique in the field:

Two identical single axle 20 ft chassis can be coupled to form one 40 ft tandem unit with load equalizing suspension. Either chassis can serve at either front or rear of the coupled assembly.

A close-up view of the equalizing suspension on couplable chassis.

A new version of Dorsey Trailers' Couple-able chassis handles all types of 40 ft as well as the 20 ft containers for which it has been used for several years.

Even when coupled the 40 ft unit supports the load completely and no connecting of containers is required. Any make or model container with ANSI-ISO corner castings can be handled. The coupled chassis can operate empty or with one 20 ft or 30 ft container.

F. L. Douglas (Equipment) Ltd.

Village Road,
Arle,
Cheltenham, Glos.
TELEPHONE: Cheltenham 27921
TELEGRAMS: Dougquip Cheltenham
TELEX: 43182
DIRECTORS:
E. M. Maxwell
J. Carroll
W. E. Wyman
T. L. Douglas
PRODUCTS:
The 'Tugmaster' range of tractor vehicles. The N.S.7 and N.S.8 have been specially designed for Roll-on/Roll-off ferry operation.
(1) N.S.70　　12 tons on 5th wheel
Max speed　25 mph
(2) N.S. 8/M　　17 tons ,,　　,,
,,　,,　30 mph

Fenwick-Manutention

7 Rue Curie,
69 Lyons 6
France
TELEPHONE: 52 04 77
TELEX: 33 137
PRODUCTS:
The 'Liftainer' mobile gantry for container

Fruehauf France

2 Avenue de l'Aunette,
91 Ris-Orangis,
France
TELEPHONE: 906 12 94/906 24 02
TELEX: 69 967
DIRECTORS:
Raoul Massardy (*Chairman and Managing Director*)

Fruehauf Division

Fruehauf Corporation,
10900 Harper Avenue,
Detroit,
Michigan 48232

TELEPHONE: (313) 921 2410
TELEX: 23 5256
DIRECTORS:
T. J. Reghanti

PRODUCTS:
Container chassis for all lengths of container and combinations of length.
Fruehauf's new gooseneck chassis is designed to accommodate 40 ft ISO sanctioned tunnel type containers.

Gentili Brighi & Co, SpA,

20151 Milan
Via Inverigo, 14, Italy
TELEPHONE: 306.941

Upon coupling, the front and rear suspension hangers lock automatically into a load-equalizing tandem instead of as two independent single axles. The suspension moves on sliders and can be located at 120 in setting.

DOUGLAS

(3) N.S.8	20 tons ,,	,,
,, ,, 24 mph		
(4) N.S.8 Container	22 tons ,,	,,
Base		
,, ,, 29 mph		
(5) N.S.8 Terminal	28 tons ,,	,,
Tractor		
,, ,, 22 mph		

Specification details of the NS8 Container Base chassis:
OVERALL DIMENSIONS:
Length: 198 in
Width: 98 in
Height: 94 in
Wheelbase: 105 in
Lowered 5th Wheel height· 45 in
Raised 5th wheel height: 75 in
Approx. weight: 6 tons 13 cwt
Engine: GM 466 Diesel
Hydraulic Fifth wheel

FENWICK-MANUTENTION

handling and short distance transport. It is mounted on four rotating castors and is suitable for towing either empty or with an empty container. It has a capacity of 20,000 kg (44,100 lb) being intended to handle 20 ft containers. Two hydraulically-operated lifting jacks operate

FRUEHAUF FRANCE

François Godbille (*Assistant Managing Director*)
François Gressin (*General Secretary responsible for Containerisation*)
Bruno Chabert (*Container Department*)
PRODUCTS:
Container semi-trailers designated 'Mar-

FRUEHAUF

Coupling on unlevel ground is facilitated by a new locking system: a pair of chasses will lock automatically even if alignment is off as much as 10° horizontally, and height differs as much as 5 inches.

Standard Douglas 22 ton capacity hydraulic elevating fifth wheel with hydraulic rams trunnion mounted in chassis. Maximum fifth wheel travel 30 in. Lifting arms fitted with guide channels to minimize side loading of rams. Fifth wheel release air pressure operated from drivers cab.

Douglas *NS 8* Con-BaseTractor illustrating the elevating 5ª wheel, which has a maximum lift of 30 in (762 mm) and a capacity of 22 tons.

via two beams to which chains are attacked to lift containers. The lift height is 1,750 mm The gantry may be electric, diesel or petrol powered.
The Swedish LMV range of forklift trucks and sideloaders for container lifting and transport are also supplied by Fenwick.

souin' for the transport of all containers— 40 ft, 30 ft and 2 × 20 ft fully loaded.
The 'Narval' container chassis with gooseneck has an extra low platform for the transport of 20 ft × 8 ft × 8 ft 6 in containers.
(See also Container Section).

Fruehauf's new gooseneck container chassis (top) is designed to accommodate 40 ft ISO sanctioned tunnel type containers. Bottom left—full width front bolster is equipped with pin through lock securing devices to handle any type corner fitting in service. Three-eight inch thick high strength steel shroud protects glad hands, lights, wiring and securing devices. Bottom right—Lights and twist lock handles are recessed into the rear bolster for maximum protection

GENTILI BRIGHI

TELEX: 32567 (Brigenti)
In association under licence with Harnishfeger Corporation, Milwaukee, USA

PRODUCTS:
Container Gantry Cranes.
To lift all sizes of containers up to 40 ft.

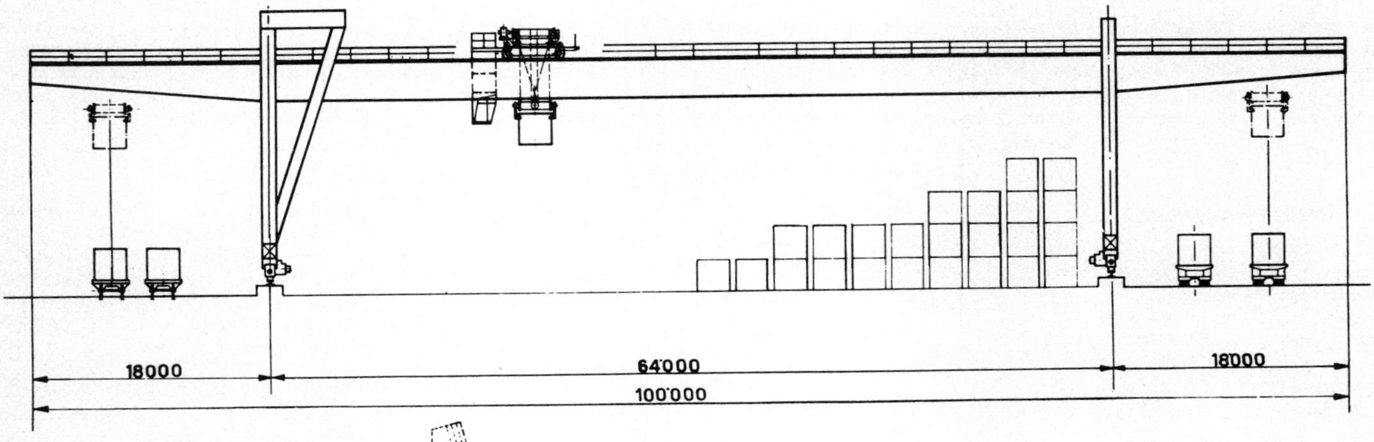

18000   64000   18000

100'000

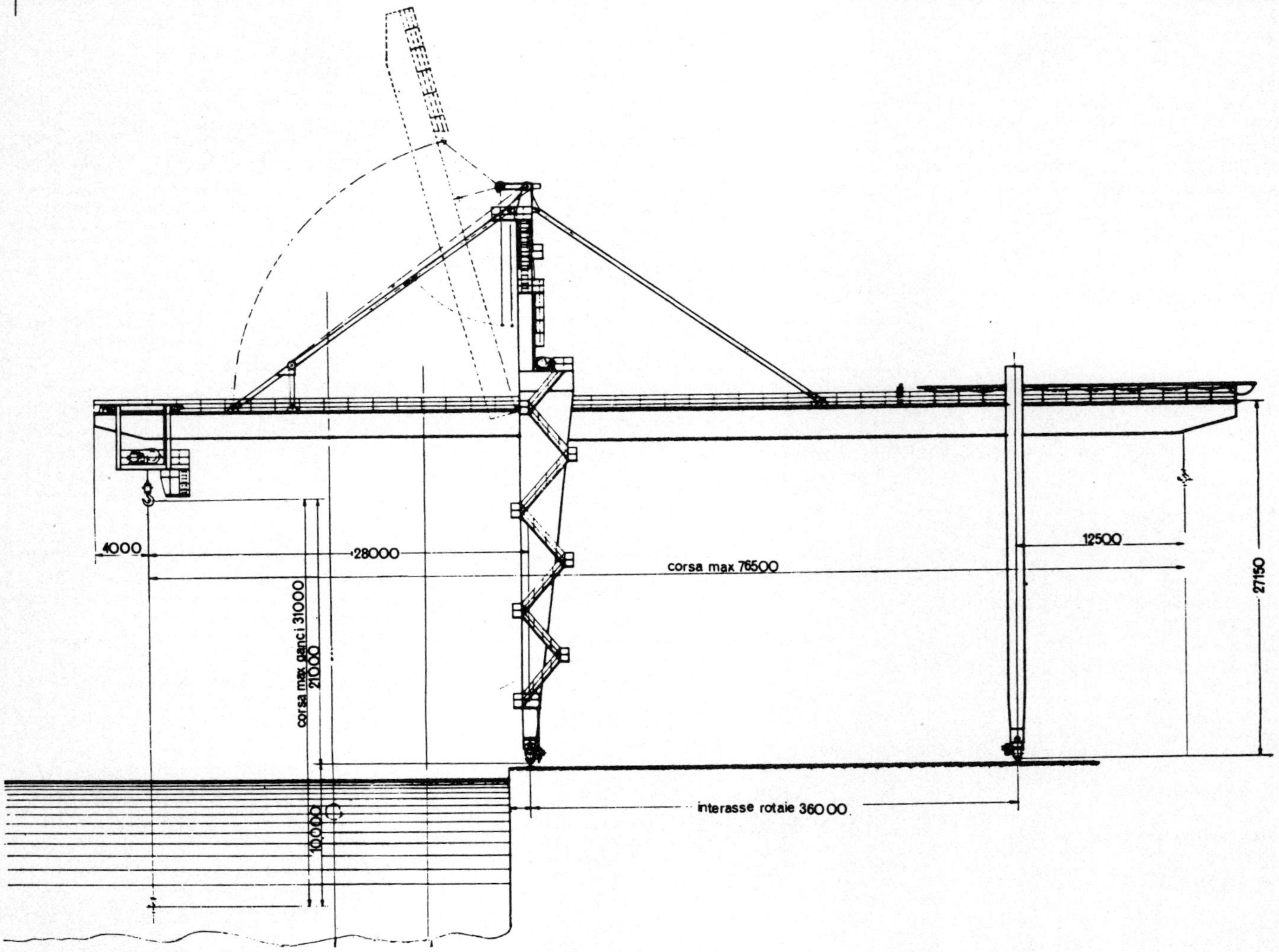

4000   28000   corsa max 76500   12500   27150

corsa max ganci 31000   21000

interasse rotaie 360 00

GOLDHOFER

Goldhofer KG

8940 Memmingen
Germany (Federal Republic)

TELEPHONE: Memmingen (08331) 6024
TELEGRAMS: Goldhofer Memmingen
TELEX: 054547

DIRECTORS:
Alois Goldhofer
Dr. Ing. Prabhaker
R. Khirwadkar

MARKETING ARRANGEMENTS:
UK, Europe and Africa—Clarke International Marketing S.A. US and Canada, Clarke Equipment Co.

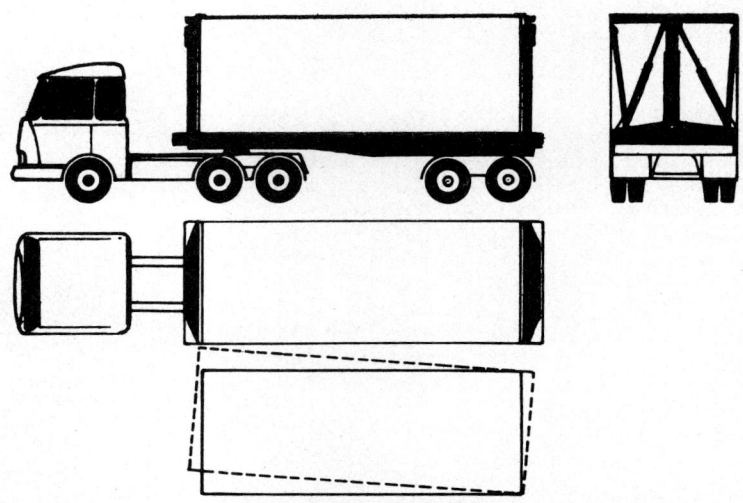

Inaccuracy in the approach of the **Swinglift**-vehicle can be overcome 200 mm sideways and 400 mm longitudinally. This gives a quick grasp and lift of the load.

PRODUCTS:

A hydraulic sideloading device, mounted on a truck or semi-trailer, for transferring containers, flats, pallets or single loads between road and rail or between the ground or a loading platform and the vehicle which supports the transfer device. Known as the 'Swinglift', it is designed to operate in ports and rail terminals and in industry generally. It can handle containers up to 40 ft in length and loads weighing up to 30 tons. Optional modifications to suit different loads—i.e. different sizes of container or single loads—may be made. Spreaders and other special lifting devices for prefabricated parts and other heavy loads are available. A reduction in price is offered if a "Swinglift" is required to operate on one side only.

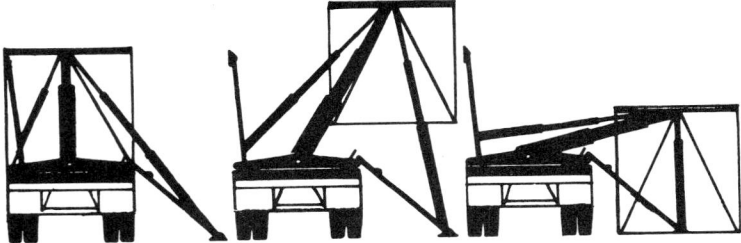

Swing action shows supporting, lift-off and setting-down of the load. The hydraulic steering works mostly automatic, though manual operation is possible. Through this, stacking can be done. Lift-on operation takes place the other way round.

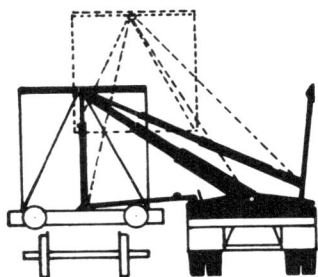 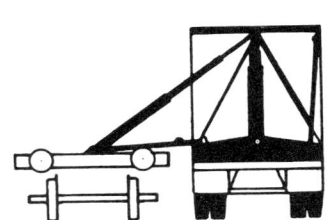

Unloading railcars with the **Swinglift**-vehicle is quick and safe. Transfer loading to a transport-vehicle starts the rolling of the container to the customer.

Use of the **Swinglift** to operate flats, — here loaded with prefab elements. It is possible through combined operations (for containers, flats as well singular loads) to exploit the **Swinglift** to it's maximum capability.

Goldhofer—swinglift with hydraulic spreader extendible from 20 ft to 40 ft mounted on extendible semi-trailer.

Goldhofer—swinglift with spreader for 20 ft container mounted on a semi-trailer.

GRAAFF

Niedersachische Waggonfabrik Joseph Graaff GmbH
Elze (Han) West Germany
TELEPHONE: 05124-2041

TELEX: 0927 168
PRODUCTS:
Semi-trailers, and skeletal semi-trailers for container transport.

HARNISCHFEGER

Harnischfeger Corporation,
4400 West National Ave,
Milwaukee,
Wisconsin, USA 53246
TELEPHONE: 414-671-4400
TELEX: 026724
CABLES: HARNINCO
DIRECTORS:
Henry Harnischfeger (*Chairman of the Board and President*)
R. D. Teece (*Executive Vice President*)
W. L. Carter (*Vice President, Finance*)
G. D. Schmus (*Treasurer*)
G. B. Knight (*Secretary*)

J. A. Mezera (*Vice President, Construction and Mining Group*)
PRODUCTS:
P&H (trade mark) 2650-TC Truck Crane.
Capacity: 250 short tons.
Container capacity with 150 foot boom: 30 short tons at 100 foot radius.
Loading speed: 25 containers per hour on deck, 17-19 per hour below deck.

Container Gantry Cranes.
Ship's container cranes.
These cranes are manufactured in Europe by Gentili Brighi & Co of Milan, Italy (qv).

Harnischfeger 6250-TC truck crane using container handling boom with two hook lines and 30 ft high operator's cab

HATLAPA

Uetersener Maschinenfabrik Hatlapa

HEAD OFFICE:

Uetersen (Holst.) near Hamburg, W. Germany

P.O. Box 27

TELEPHONE: 04122/7111

TELEGRAMS: Hatlapa Uetersen

TELEX: 218510 htlued

DIRECTORS:

Hans-Heinrich Hatlapa

Rolf Hatlapa

PRODUCTS:

Hatlapa have developed the twin derrick system especially for semi-container vessels enabling the handling of containers of 20 to 35 tons with parallel working derricks, and the handling of normal general cargo using the union purchase system, both with the small auxiliary winches working automatically according to the Hatlapa/AEG Patent. This system has proved to be very economic on more than 200 vessels. Without wasting time, the derricks can be put into any position so reducing considerably the berthing time.

The Hatlapa 'Crane Derrick' for 3, 5, 10, 20 or 40 tons lift was designed for container handling and can be used for loading general cargo as well without requiring much re-rigging. Only three winches are necessary.

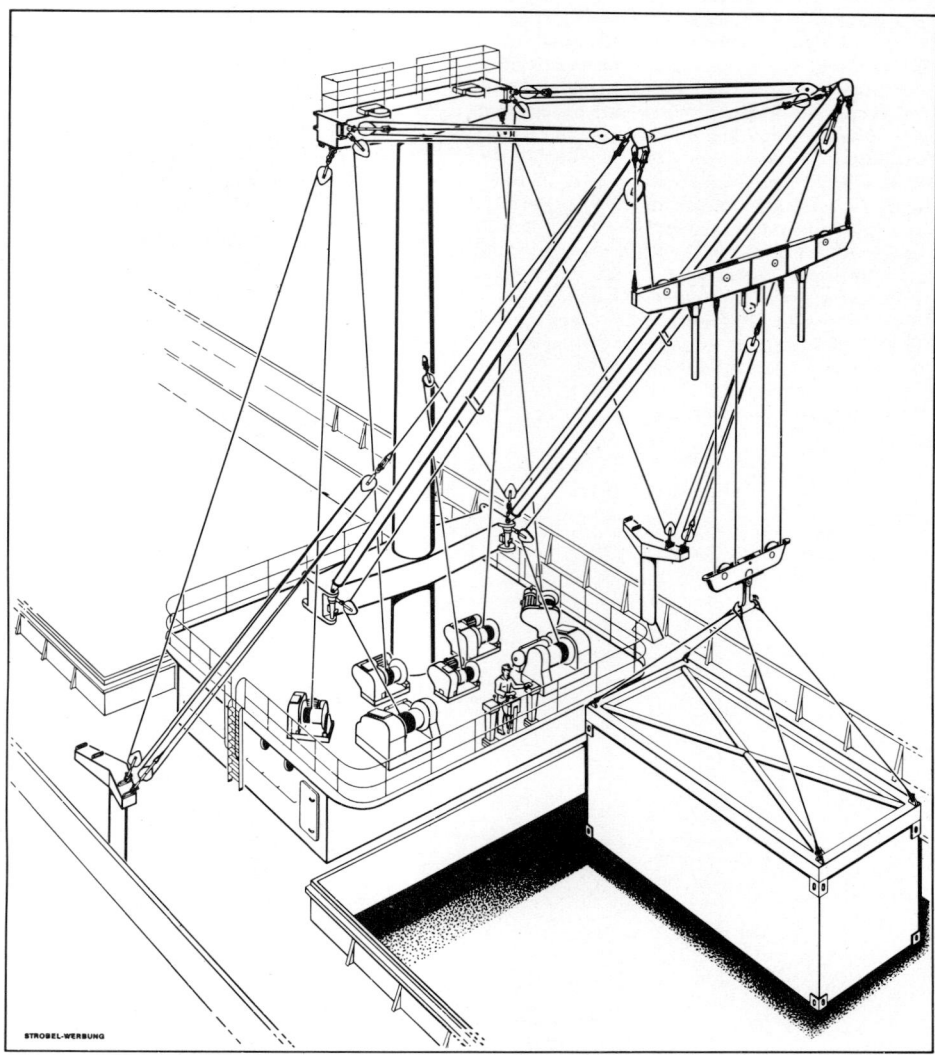

The Hatlapa "Crane Derrick"

HENLEY

Henley Forklift Co. Ltd.

Newbridge Road Industrial Estate,

Pontllanfraith,

Blackwood, Mon., NP2 2XF

TELEPHONE: Blackwood 2671 and 3731

TELEX: 49655

DIRECTORS:

Fortes Hayes (*Chairman*)

E. Holmes (*Deputy Chairman*)

D. C. Hardwick (*Managing Director*)

C. R. Stanger (*Technical*)

B. H. Dorricot (*Sales*)

P. Bentley (*Works*)

C. S. Taylor

G. B. Taylor

T. Compton (Sales Manager)

PRODUCTS:

A range of counterbalanced forklift and sideloading trucks from 4,000 lb (1,814 kg) up to 68,000 lb (30,800 kg) capacity.

Hercules and Hermes front loading forklifts

Hercules series, 15,000 lb (6,800 kg) to 26,000 lb (11,800 kg) capacity at 24 in (610 mm) load centres with automatic transmission, hydrostatic steering, 10 ft lift mast, load guard, power brakes, full instrumentation, fully adjustable seat, high efficiency silencer, twin hydraulic pump, 2704E Ford engine and spiral bevel drive axle are fitted as standard equipment.

Hermes series, 45,000 lb (20,400 kg) to 68,000 lb (30,800 kg) capacity at 48 in (1,220 mm) load centres with automatic transmission,

Henley " Hermes ".

hydrostatic steering, load guard, 10 ft lift mast, air brakes, full instrumentation, suspension seat, high efficiency silencer, triple hydraulic pump, 200 bhp Leyland engine and heavy duty double reduction drive axle are fitted as standard equipment.

The Midas Sideloader

Midas sideloader, 56,000 lb (25,800 kg) at 48 in (1,220 mm) load centres with automatic transmission, hydrostatic steering, 8 ft lift mast, load guard, power brakes, full instrumentation, suspension seat, high efficiency silencer, twin hydraulic pump, 200 b.h.p. Leyland engine, cab, tail, side and stop lights and heavy duty double reduction drive axle are fitted as standard equipment.

Thirty ton capacity Henley 'Hermes' forklift working alongside a Henley 'Hercules'.

HILGERS

HILGERS AG

5456 Rheinbrohl, W. Germany
TELEPHONE: (02635) 74
TELEX: 086 291 43
DIRECTORS:
Dipl. Kfm. Wilhelm Fehter
Dipl. Ing. Karl Lange
Dipl. Ing. Gerhard Schreier
PRODUCTS:
Container gantry and portal cranes.

Container Handling Gantry Crane

This has an automatic spreader of telescopic type for taking 10 ft, 20 ft, 30 ft and 40 ft containers to ISO-Standard and 35 ft containers of Sea-Land Transport GmbH as well as for loading of piece goods.

SPECIFICATIONS:

capacity at spreader	35 tons
capacity at hook	40 tons
span	15·0 m
wheel base	16·0 m
reach at water side	35·0 m
reach at land side	21·0 m
height of lift	35·0 m
lifting speed	40·0 m/min.
lowering speed	60·0 m/min.
crab travel speed	100 m/min.
crane travel speed	40·0 m/min.
weight	400 tons

Interlocking of containers is effected at top corner castings by means of special T-head bolts. Lateral guides of suitable design are provided for centering spreader in line with containers. These guides can be turned upwards automatically when the spreader is lowered into a ship's container guides. All drives for T-head bolt interlocking, shifting of telescopic parts and interlocking devices are of electro-mechanical design. Control of the individual positions and movements is done through limit switches. For current supply between rotary crab and spreader two motor cable drums are installed on the crab. A socket connection is provided between cables and spreader.

Rocking Type Crane

This is specially suitable for use at smaller depots. It is designed for handling 10 ft, 20 ft, 30 ft and 40 ft containers to ISO-Standard and 35 ft containers of Sea-Land Transport GmbH, for loading and unloading piece goods, and any standard-containers. It is equipped with two rocker arms with mechanical or hydraulic drive and a connecting traverse of rotary design with trolleys and electric hoists for taking the end piece of a spreader. Crabs can be adjusted without difficulty to standard dimensions of individual containers.

SPECIFICATIONS:

Total capacity	40 tons
capacity of each crab	20 tons
hoisting speed	4 m/min.
slow motion hoisting speed	0,4 m/min.
crab travel speed	10 m/min.
period for one rocking motion	approx. 5 seconds

Portal Crane

This has an overhead double-rail crab, calculated for a maximum container load of 35 tons; special crab for handling 20 ft, 30 ft and 40 ft containers to ISO Standard as well as 35 ft containers of Sea-Land Transport GmbH and for movement of piece goods.

SPECIFICATIONS:

max. load capacity at spreader		35 tons
excentrical ratio of load distribution		2/5 : 3/5
span		
wheel base of portal		22 m (20 m)
crane track rail	approx.	8 m
max. wheel pressure of portal		S 49
lifting height from top of rail to lower edge of spreader	approx.	26 tons (without wind)
lifting speed	approx.	8,0 m
crab travel speed	approx.	5,0 m/min. slow motion 1 : 10
crane travel speed	approx.	20 m/min. slow motion 1 : 10
slewing speed	approx.	50 m/min. slow motion 1 : 10
control with frequency changer.	approx.	1/2 min. for 180° range of slewing

HUNTER

G. Hunter (London) Limited
Gumley Road, Grays, Essex RM16 1XT
TELEPHONE: Grays Thurrock 5155
TELEGRAMS: Hunter Grays
TELEX: 28747
DIRECTORS:
  Dennis Hunter
  P. S. Underwood (*Sales Director*)
  E. K. Thoupos
  E. J. Hunter
  G. J. Hunter
  W. F. Swallow
PRODUCTS:
  Container handling gantries, container
lifting hooks, scissor lifts, chains.

The Hunter container hook has a swivel pin similar in shape to the recess on the container is set parallel with the main body of the 'hook'. This is inserted and when angled for lifting turns so that it is locked into position and unable to slip out.

Hunter handling gantry

Hunter Container Gantries

These are specifically designed for the smaller users of containers and for handling containers on and off trailers in places inaccessible to cranes.

They are completely mobile and can be pushed or towed for re-siting.

An Exo International block is mounted centrally on the main beam and an extended operating shaft enables the operator to stand clear of the container. Electric hoists may be fitted if required.

Special container handling lifting slings (bottom lift) together with a spreader beam are supplied with the gantry.

The adaptor hooks for locating in the container bottom lifting holes are designed so that they cannot be dislodged while lifting or lowering is taking place.

Load capacity: from 3-tons.

Hunter Container Hook

The Hunter container hook has a swivel pin similar in shape to the recess on the container and set parallel with the main body of the 'hook'. This is inserted and when angled for lifting turns so that it is locked into position and unable to slip out. Because of the design of the hook, it is easy and quick to locate in the lifting recesses provided on the container.

The shape of the body of the hook is designed so that it does not put undue stress on the body of the container being lifted.

It overcomes the problems inherent in using a normal hook for lifting, such as damage to the container caused by high stress points, and damage to the crane hooks with the resultant deterioration in their safe working load and the possibility of a failure causing an accident.

The Hunter container hooks can be used with any container lifting tackle.

Hunter container hooks are used primarily with containers meeting BS 4228 1967.

HUTSONS

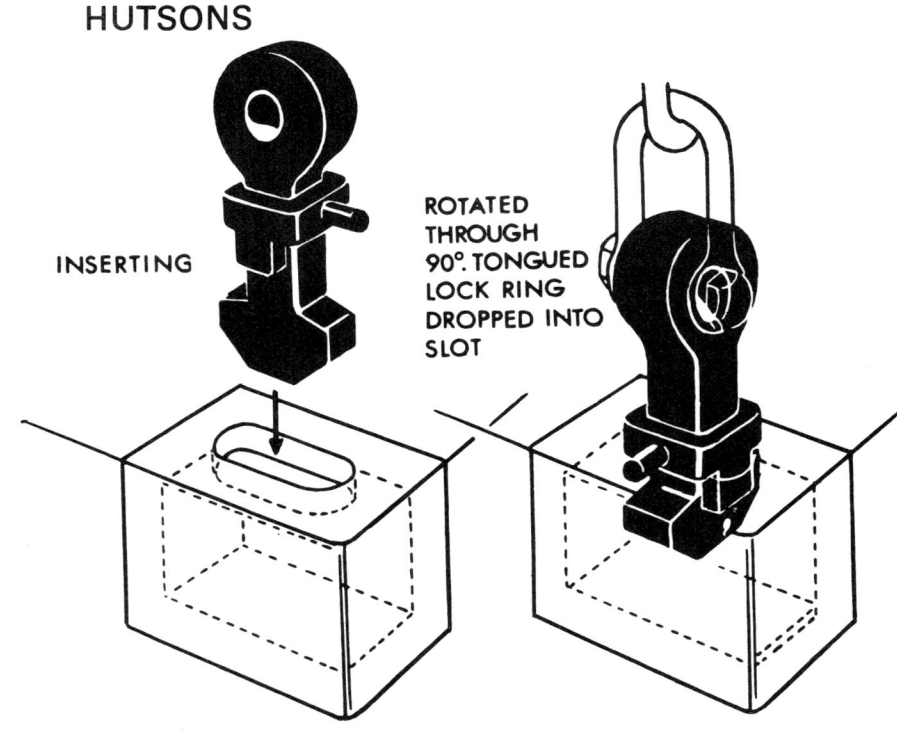

INSERTING

ROTATED THROUGH 90°. TONGUED LOCK RING DROPPED INTO SLOT

Hutsons Ltd.
Kelvinhaugh Engine Works, Glasgow, C3
TELEPHONE: 041-221 3714/5/6
TELEGRAMS: CAMAND
DIRECTORS:
H. Evans
A. Evans
A. C. London
G. Staines
I. Craig

PRODUCTS:

Top and bottom lifting devices for use with chain—40 ton capacity. Mark III bottom lifting camlocks are for attachment to a container's lower corner castings eliminating the need for hooks.

Mark II top lifting camlocks consist of special self-locking lugs for attachment to the top corners. Both types can be attached and detached in a moment by one man.

Top Lifting Camlock Mk. II.

HYMO

Hymo Lift Ltd.
16-18 Clarendon Road,
Watford,
Herts, WD1 1JY
England

TELEPHONE: 21262
TELEX: 923008
DIRECTORS:
Brian Reavell (*Managing*)
D. W. Edney (*Sales*)

C. Bjornemark

PRODUCTS:
Scissor Lift Tables. Capacities up to 50 ton. Lifting speeds 10 ft/min nominal.

HYSTER

Hyster Overseas
Turriff Buildings,
Great West Road,
Brentford, Middlesex
TELEPHONE: 01-568 9292
TELEGRAMS: Hyster London, Telex
TELEX: London 25870

PRODUCTS:

Lift Trucks, Straddle Carriers, Mobile Cranes, Trailers specifically produced for handling containers.

Challenger Lift Truck Range

Forklifts with lifting capacities of 23,800 kg and 29,000 kg (52,000 lb and 62,000 lb) at 1,200 mm (48 in) load centres, for handling loaded containers with spreader attachment. Top travel speed forward and reverse is 36·2 km/hr. Lifting speeds without load is 14·28 m/min (47 ft/min) and with rated load is 11·85 m/min (39 ft/min).

The Hyster H520 landing a 20 ft container using the top corner castings.

IHI

Ishikawajima-Harima Heavy Industries Co. Ltd.
2-1, 2 chome, Otemachi
Chiyoda-Ku, Tokyo, Japan
TELEPHONE: (03) 270 9111
TELEX: IHICO TK2232
IHICO TK4239
CABLES: Ihico Tokyo
DIRECTORS:
T. Yamagata (*Manager, Transportation Equipment Section No. 4 Machinery Export Dept.*)

PRODUCTS:
Dockside and shipboard container cranes, stabil-o-matic spreader and anti-swaying systems

IHI Dockside Container Crane
Designed exclusively for container handling, the IHI dockside crane is of box-girder construction and has a rope-trolley system. Containers of all sizes from 20-40 ft can be handled according to the spreader in use. A Ward-Leonard control system is installed to ensure smooth operation, and the crane is also equipped with IHI's stabil-o-matic anti-sway, attitude adjusting, spreader system.

An IHI Container Crane

IHI Shipboard Container Crane

The Type CS crane normally handles one 20 ft container. A 40 ft container can be handled by two cranes of this type positioned adjacently. Both cranes are coupled electrically and operated by a driver seated in either one of the two cabs. All the twist lugs at four corners of the spreader function automatically and an indicator light in the cab confirms the locking of the twist lugs. An alarm system sounds when the ship trims beyond 1 degree or lists over 6 degrees to ensure safety of operation.

Specifications of IHI Standard Type Container Crane as follows:

Rated capacity 40 LT
Hoisting speed 100 ft/min
Traversing speed 400 ft/min
Travelling speed 150 ft/min

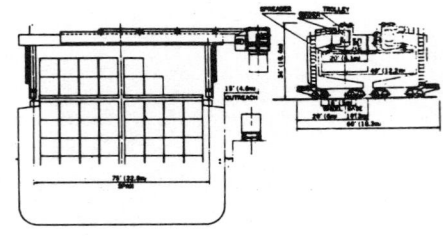

IHI Type CS Shipboard Container Crane.

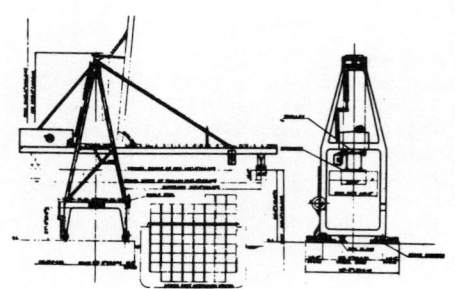

IHI Dockside Container Crane Type CD-1.

JAPAN CONTAINER ASSOCIATION

Japan Container Association

Room No. 802-A Yaesu-Mitsui Bldg.,
7,5-Chome, Yaesu, Chuo-Ku,
Tokyo, Japan
TELEPHONE: 274-2641
TELEGRAMS: Japan container

Some of the handling equipment in use in Japan

JONES

Jones Cranes Limited

Letchworth,
Herts., England
TELEPHONE: Letchworth 2360
TELEGRAMS: Jones, Letchworth
TELEX: 82112
DIRECTORS:
Jack A. Wellings (*Chairman*)
Peter Bonner (*Managing Director*)
A. M. Gray
V. L. Hamilton
I. MacLeod Smith
Percy R. Levy
R. Reynolds
G. Innes

PRODUCTS:
Mobile and truck-mounted cranes with lifting capacities up to 45 tons.

DETAILS:
Hoisting and lowering speeds, 5 tons on single fall 36·5 m/min (120 ft/min), 40 tons

Jones 851 mobile crane with 50 ft jib will stack containers up to three high.

Jones 15·30 mobile crane with 45 ft (13·716 m) main jib and 20 ft (6·09 m) fly jib (also reeved to handle general cargo)

on eight falls, 4·5 m/min (15 ft/min). Slewing speed (continuous circle in either direction) 2 rpm laden. Derrick speed (maxminimum radius) 60 seconds. Travelling speeds (mobile) 12·8 km/h (8 mph), (truck mounted) 56·3 km/h (35 mph).

Jones 851 truck mounted crane has the travel speed to service several depots over a wide area

KAMAG

Kamag Transporttechnik GmbH & Co.

79 Ulm/Donau,
Daimlerstrasse 18,
Germany (Federal Republic)

TELEPHONE: 0731/1731
TELEX: 0712728
DIRECTORS:
F. X. Kögel
Karl Weinmann

PRODUCTS:
Trailers for roll-on/roll-off traffic. Special tractors for moving the trailers which are known as 'Rolltrailers'.

KEIENBURG

Karl Keienburg
Hebezeug-und Kranbau
D 43 Essen 1
Postf. 988
TELEPHONE: 02141 23 72 53-56
TELEGRAMS: Krankeienburg
TELEX: 857 314
DIRECTOR:
Ing. S. Keienburg
PRODUCTS:
Container Portal Cranes. A particular feature of the Keienburg cranes is that they are of tubular construction. The standard container crane has a maximum lift of 30 tons to a height of 5,000 mm (16 ft 6 in). The span is 8,000 mm (26 ft 3 in). A spreader with four lifting chain hooks can be supplied with the crane and can be hand-adjusted to suit 20 ft, 30 ft or 40 ft containers.

The Keienburg Portal container crane.

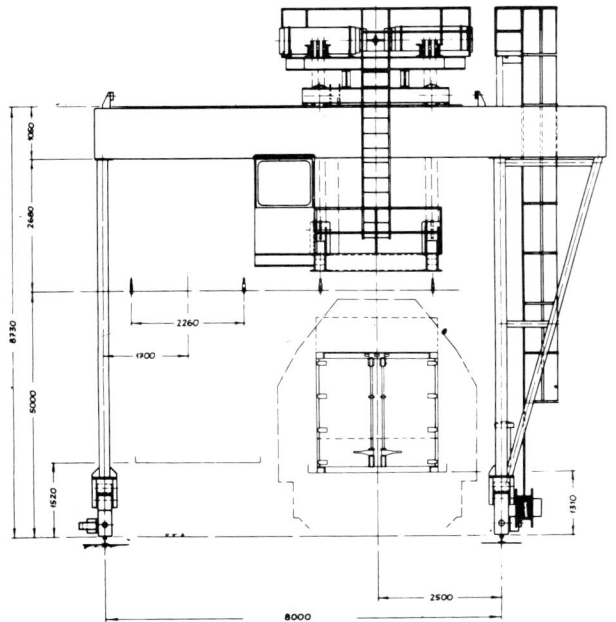
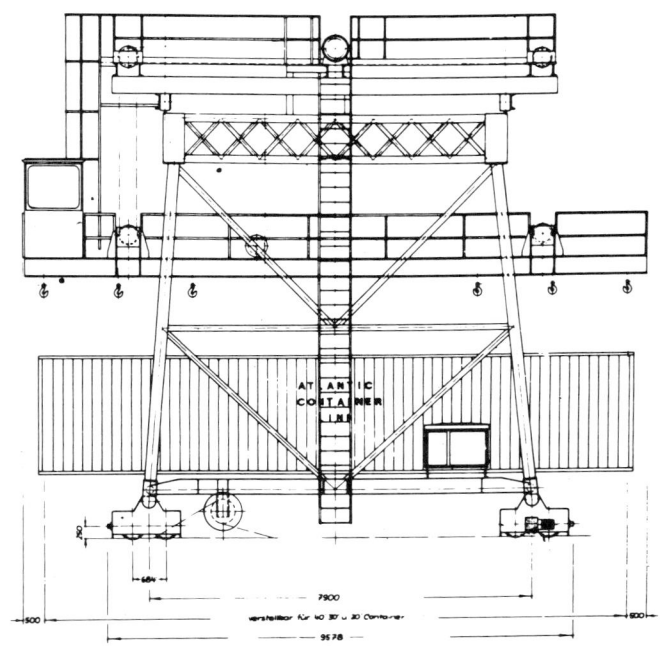

Front and side elevations of the Keienburg Portal container crane.

KLAUS GmbH

Klaus GmbH Fahrzeug-u-Maschinenfabrik

LICENSEES:

Sole distribution and manufacturing rights for the UK and certain Commonwealth countries have been granted to Sheppard Fabrications Ltd., Barnham, Norfolk. See under Sheppard.

PRODUCTS: Klaus Kran-Mobil twin crane for container trailers.

Klaus Kran-Mobil

The Klaus Kran-Mobil is a self-contained transporter crane system designed for the loading, stacking and carriage of containers from 10 to 40 ft in length and up to 30 tons in weight. The crane will handle single containers set 60 mm (2¾ in) apart from a 4 m (13 ft 0 in) high vehicle. Stability while loading and off-loading is provided by hydraulically operated stabilizers which reach beneath the carrying vehicle. The max permissible loaded weight of the vehicle is 46 tons.

The basic model operates from one side and it is capable of handling 20 ft and 30 ft ISO containers. It can unload or load containers from rail cars, road vehicles etc. and it can double stack containers up to 30

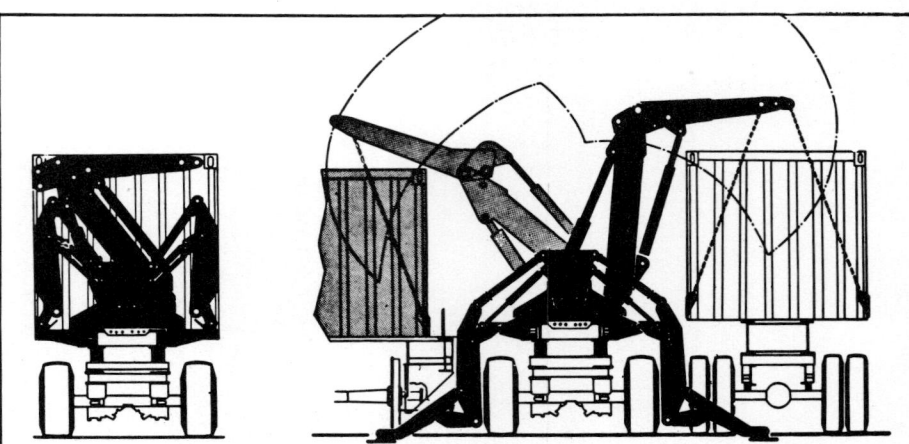

Klaus Kran-Mobil twin crane—end view

tons capacity. Other models are available to handle containers of 10 ft and 40 ft. So too are machines which load to either side.

Klaus Kran-Mobil—side view

KLOCKNER FERROMATIK

Klöckner-Ferromatik GmbH

462 Castrop-Rauxel 2,
Wartburgstrasse 21-25
Postfach 665
Germany (Federal Republic)
TELEPHONE: (02305) 1741
TELEX: 08 229 514 KWCR
DIRECTORS:
Dieter F. Pracht
Karl-Heinz Wehner
Gunter Ziesenhenne
PRODUCTS:

Container stilts for loading containers on to vehicles and for supporting containers. The equipment operates with containers of all sizes. It avoids the need for a gantry or other handling equipment.

The equipment consists of four light-metal cylinders with a bore of 1,600 mm and a load capacity of 8 Mp each. They are provided with a wheeled chassis for easy handling and the portable electrically or diesel-engine driven pump unit as well as the high pressure hoses equipped with

bayonet couplings. The cylinders are fastened to the corner fittings of the longitudinal walls of the container through framed constructions in the distance of these and are bolted.

After the high pressure hoses have been attached to the cylinders, the container is hydraulically lifted from the truck or waggon so far that the vehicle can be moved. Then the container is placed down on the ground or on another vehicle. When the container is loaded on a truck, the cylinders being in a space of 3,310 mm make it possible for the truck easily to under-run the lifted container.

The cylinders are equipped with non-return valves. It is impossible for the load to sink down when the pipe and hose lines are damaged, and the bayonet couplings close automatically when the hoses are disconnected. The base plates of the cylinders are so designed that all standard containers (up to 40 ft (12·1 m) of length) can be handled in loaded condition. Rough ground is levelled

Klöckner-Ferromatik container lifting stilts.

by the spherical joint between piston rod and base plate.

On request mountings can be attached to the pump unit for the cylinders with the framed constructions and for the hoses, for laying aside these parts when transporting the loading mechanism for containers.

KONE

Kone Oy Crane Division, Hyvinkaa, Finland

HEAD OFFICE:
Munkkiniemen Kartano, Helsinki 33
Finland
TELEPHONE: Hyvinkää 13700
TELEGRAMS: Kone
TELEX: 15-122 or 12-466

BRANCH: Kone (Industrial) Ltd., Suite 901
1010 St. Catharine Street West, Montreal,
Quebec, Canada.
Telephone: 861-2190.

DIRECTORS:
Heikki H. Herlin (*Chairman*)
Pekka Herlin (*General Manager*)
Lars Eriksson (*Director of Materials Handling Group*)
Arno Saraste (*Director of the Kone Lift Group*)
PRODUCTS:
General purpose and container cranes, Spreaders.

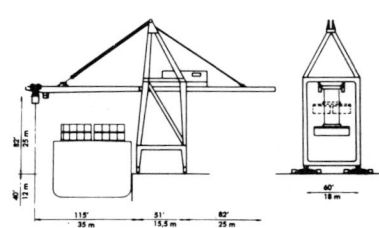

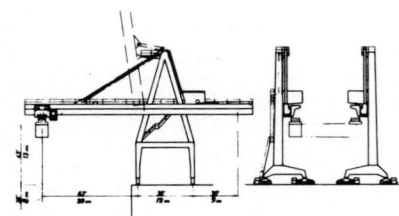

A characteristic of the Kone Twin Crane is that each crane can handle 20 ft containers separately while both together can deal with 30, 35 and 40 ft ones. By replacing the container landing device by a hook or grab each crane can be used separately to deal with both general cargo and bulk goods.

Kone Multi-Purpose Crane and Spreader

For harbours where facilities for so-called terminal traffic do not exist and where investment must be made in accordance with traffic and resources.

The crane can be used to handle containers as well as general cargo and bulk goods. With a multi-purpose crane investment costs remain as small as possible, and the crane

can be put to work from the very start even if container traffic is still slight.

The first crane of this type was recently delivered to the port of Malmö, Sweden. It is equipped with three interchangeable loading devices: a spreader for containers, a grab for bulk goods, and a hook.

The crane can lift 30-ton containers with an automatic spreader. The spreader can be adapted to handle easily all container sizes between 20 and 40 feet. The specially constructed double lever jib and the adjustment of the suspension cables keep containers in a horizontal position during conveyance, irrespective of radius. The loading device can be revolved round the vertical axis, enabling the container to be placed in the position required relative to the pier. This facility thus speeds up particularly loading and unloading work to and from trucks. Containers can be kept in a small space by the pier area side by side and on top of one another; for example, it is possible to store nearly 400 20-ft containers along a stretch of a hundred meters.

The spreader can easily be adjusted to handle all lengths between 20 and 40 ft. If the container is eccentrically loaded, the spreader shifts the centre of gravity to the suspension point of the cables hoisting the container. When required, a container can be tilted, thus facilitating loading and unloading on a sloping deck. Swinging resulting from the hoisting height has been checked effectively with a hydraulic swing suppressor.

The crane's average handling speed is 30 containers per hour.

For handling general cargo, the crane has been equipped with 10-ton and 50-ton hooks. A four-cabled grab is used to deal with bulk cargo—this can be released and fitted quickly to the crane's cables. The hoisting capacity with the grab is 16 tons, giving a possible handling capacity of 400 tons per hour.

Kone Twin Crane

Smaller than the multi-purpose crane this is suitable for average harbours dealing with transfer traffic. It is generally used in pairs and each crane can handle 20 ft containers separately, while both together can deal with 30, 35 and 40 ft ones. For combined hoisting the cranes are automatically linked to each other, their motions being electrically synchronized with one another.

Manoeuvring takes place from the cab of one of the cranes. The crane's combined hoisting capacity is 2 × 25 metric tons. It is also possible to fit out the crane with a twin machine for grab work.

By replacing the container handling device by a hook or a grab each crane can be used separately to deal with both general cargo and bulk goods. With a hook the hoisting capacity is 25 metric tons; with a grab, 12·5 metric tons. When equipped with a special loading device the crane can also deal with lumber bundles, paper rolls and bulky bales.

Kone Twin-loader Crane

A very large capacity is demanded of container cranes in large ocean terminals. For this purpose a twin loader crane was developed, whose long outreach makes the loading and unloading of the largest container vessels possible, using two loading devices.

20 ft containers can be lifted separately from the same 40 ft cell inside the container vessel or from a series of cells. After this, the loading devices can be driven together and linked in the air to form a 'train'. Combined hoisting and transfer can be done very quickly.

In this operation the crane's maximum handling capacity in simultaneous discharging and loading (pendulum movement) can reach almost 80 containers an hour. This represents 800 tons, assuming an average container load of 10 tons.

Because of their telescopic construction the same loading devices can be used to handle containers more than 20 ft long. In this method the loading devices are fixed together in the air to form one rigid structure, and one container is handled at a time. This gives a handling capacity of 40 containers per hour.

Kone container quay crane at the Port of Helsinki. It handles containers from 20 ft- 40 ft long with an automatic spreader. Maximum hoisting capacity is 40 tons.

Container Gantry Crane

Designed principally for use in railway terminals the crane reaches over one or several tracks depending on the size of its handling capacity.

The crane's hoisting movement is controlled by servo-eddy current control. The traversing movement can be controlled by SCR so that precise control of the container is possible at all stages of handling. The container can be revolved round its vertical axis ± 6°, and can be tilted along its longitudinal axis to facilitate positioning on the platform of a truck.

Kone multi-purpose crane for handling containers—bulk and general cargo maximum load is 20 tons.

Railway terminal crane for handling 20 ft to 40 ft containers with an automatic spreader as by Swedish State Railways.

Lancer Boss Limited

Leighton Buzzard,
Bedfordshire,
England
TELEPHONE: Leighton Buzzard 2031
TELEGRAMS: Sideloader Leighton Buzzard
TELEX: 82235
DIRECTORS:
G. N. Bowman-Shaw
T. Bowman-Shaw
J. A. F. Luttrell
J. Kinross
E. Monkhouse
OVERSEAS MARKETING:
With Allis Chalmers of Milwaukee, USA.
PRODUCTS:

Lancer 2500 Series Container Handling
Truck designed to handle 20 ft ISO containers
with hydraulically operated toplift attachment. These can now stack 20 ft containers
3 high. Lift is sufficient to deal with 8 ft
6 in high as well as 8 ft high containers.
Empties can be stacked up to three high
without the need to put down stabilising
jacks.

Lancer 3,500 Series Container Handling
Truck designed to handle 20, 30 and 40 ft
containers with hydraulically operated top-
lift attachment.

Boss D Series Mark III frontlift trucks
designed to handle ISO containers to a gross
weight of 20 tons with a hydraulically
operated toplift attachment stacking up to
three high with inverted forks.

Boss B Series Mark III frontlift truck with
simplified handling attachment for dealing
with empty containers.

Sideloader 2500 Series

The 2500 series is designed to handle 20 ft
long, 20 ton gross weight ISO containers,
stacking two-high with a toplift attachment

Lancer 2500 Sideloader with traversing cab handling 20 ft ISO container.

The Lancer 3500 Sideloader operated at Unit Centre, Rotterdam, by Heyplatt NV the Dutch
stevedoring company. The illustration shows the 3500 stacking 40 ft United States Lines containers
two high.

Boss D series Mark III front lift truck with
hydraulically operated top lift attachment.
Stacking a 20 ft filled container—Lancer
Boss Ltd.

or three high with inverted hooks. The chassis and cab are of all-welded steel construction. Traversing cab is mounted forward and moves across the full width of the machine to give maximum visibility to the operator at all stages of the handling cycle.

Motor is a 6 cylinder Cummins NH250 diesel developing 240 bhp at 2,100 rpm. Maximum torque 740 lb/ft at 1,500 rpm. Transmission comprises a heavy duty industrial torque convertor with hydraulically operated full power shift gearbox. No normal clutch or gearchange is involved. Brake and accelerator are in the normal automotive position. Torque convertor forward/reverse, and speed controls are positioned for easy-operation. There are independent controls for the operation of jacks, mast traverse and cab traverse. A single joystick controls toplift attachment, slew, reach and tilt. Safety interlocks are fitted as standard to prevent lifting of the stabilising jacks when the load is traversed out, and to prevent interlocking the twistlocks when the load is suspended. There is no drive until the jacks are retracted, to ensure complete safety throughout all stages of the handling cycle.

Sideloader 3500 Series

The 3500 series handles 20 ft, 30 ft and 40 ft ISO containers to a gross weight of 35 tons with a hydraulically operated telescopic toplift attachment stacking 2 high, or 3 high with inverted forks.

Power for the standard model is a Cummins NT380 turbo-charged six-cylinder, 855 cu in developing 380 bhp at 2,300 rpm. Maximum torque 950 lb/ft at 1,650 rpm. The chassis and its forward-mounted low level traversing cab are of all welded steel construction.

The transmission comprises a heavy-duty industrial torque converter with hydraulically operated full power shift gearbox.

Final drive transmits power via heavy-duty all-roller triple Triplex chain totally enclosed in heavy-duty oil bath protected from dirt and damage. Shafts are mounted on bearings in eccentric hubs for chain adjustment. Flexible coupling to gear box and drive axle for twin rear wheel drive.

STEERING:
Twin front wheel steer with full hydrostatic power steering.

BRAKES:
Air power operated brakes on all wheels. Front four 496 × 180 mm (19½ in × 7 in). Rear two 496 × 204 mm (19½ in × 8 in). Fail safe air-operated parking brake.

HYDRAULICS:
Low pressure triple-filtered system.
Gear type pumps direct mounted to torque converter, with constant drive power take off. Control valves of the parallel spool type. Double acting cylinders for stabilising jacks, mast traverse, fork tilt, and steering. Large diameter single acting type for lift.

MAST AND CARRIAGE:
Extra heavy-duty fabricated mast of roller construction. Full width main rollers with paired sealed self-lubricating ball bearings.

FORKS AND FORK TILT:
Twin cylinders tilt the carriage and forks 6 degrees up and 4 degrees down—controlled from the driver's cab.

MAST TRAVERSE:
Two heavy-duty roller chains—either side of the mast—ensuring alignment. Chains are activated by two sprockets, keyed to heavy-duty traversing shaft, rotated by patented flexible chain rack system, operated by two double-acting hydraulic cylinders.

CONTROLS:
Brake and accelerator in normal automotive positions on right-hand side. All hydraulic controls (independent levers for safe op-

Lancer 3500 Series sideloader, shown here transporting a 40 ft 30 ton container, is now available with telescopic toplift attachment designed to handle, 20, 30 and 40 ft containers in any required sequence, extension or retraction of the toplift taking less than 30 seconds and the adjustment can be carried out in any case while the truck is travelling to the next pick-up point.

Newest model of the Lancer 2500 Series container handling sideloader features a stylish, roomy cab which exploits to the full the visibility gained through the cab-traversing action, and a light-weighted H-type toplift attachment for handling containers weighing up to 20 tons.

eration) to driver's right hand. Torque converter forward/reverse selector control positioned in front. Warning horn fitted as standard to warn against travel whilst jacks are down.

ELECTRICAL EQUIPMENT:
24 volt circuit. Four 6 volt heavy-duty batteries in series. Heavy-duty alternator ensures ample charge at low engine speeds. Twin head, side, rear/stop lights, trafficators, parallel windscreen wiper, starter, warning horn and normal operating gauges standard. Solenoid operated engine stop. Optional electrical equipment includes flood and working lights.

TANK CAPACITIES:
Engine fuel tank—80 gallons; hydraulic fluid tank—120 gallons.

ATTACHMENTS:
Hydraulically operated Lancer designed toplift attachment for handling standard 20 ft, 30 ft and 40 ft ISO containers.

MAIN USERS:
There are approximately 150 Lancer Boss sideloaders of the Series 3500 and 2500 in use throughout the world.

LIEBHERR

Liebherr Building Machinery Ltd
Travellers Lane,
Welham Green,
Hatfield, Herts.
TELEPHONE: 65381.
TELEGRAMS: Liebherr Hatfield
TELEX: 261 271

BRANCHES:
In UK: Edinburgh,
Whitehall Industrial Estate,
Bathgate, West Lothian
Overseas: Germany, Eire, France, Austria,
South Africa

DIRECTORS:
H. Schauwecker (*Managing*)
J. M. Matthews, M.B.E.
PRODUCTS:
Container Gantry Cranes, dockside cranes,
deck cranes.

Two Liebherr 30 ton container gantry cranes owned by Bristol Steam Navigation Ltd, at Avonmouth. The cranes have a S.W.L. of 30 tons and have been tested at 37½ tons (25% overload). Span is 122 ft with a 42 ft overhang over the ship, with luffing arrangement. Total height is 70 ft and the cranes run on a 300 ft travel. A special interlock device prevents the cranes colliding. There is a radio link between cab and the ground.

LUTHER-WERKE

Luther-Werke Braunschweig

2 Hamburg 22, Schwanenwik 36
TELEPHONE: 224150
TELEX: 2 161 315

DIRECTOR: E. Schmidt
PRODUCTS:
Container carrying chassis.

MAFI

**MAFI-Fahrzeugwerke GmbH & Co.
International
D-7015 Korntal-Stuttgart,
Germany (Federal Republic)**
TELEPHONE: (0711) 8802-1
TELEGRAMS: mafi korntalwurt
TELEX: 7 23391
DIRECTORS:
Martin Fiala
Winfried Fiala
Helmut Fiala
OVERSEAS COMPANIES:
Mafi (UK) Ltd.
Graham House, Pannells Court, Guildford
Surrey. Telephone: 76815. Telex: Mafi
Guildford 85457
PRODUCTS:
Terminal tractor and trailer systems
lifters and transporters.
Container Lift
This is for loading, unloading and transport
of containers and similar loads.
The chassis consists primarily of an
extendable main frame allowing containers
of different lengths to be handled. The
capacity of the crane unit is 30 tons and the

Mafi Fahrzeugwerke Porta lift.

maximum load length is 40 ft (see also Mafi UK).

Rolltrailer system

This is for loading roll-on/roll-off ships. It consists of low loaders with detachable goosenecks operated by 'Tugmaster' tractor units or forklifts used as tractors.

Porta Lift

This has been developed for the transport, handling and stacking of containers and flats within terminal areas. Two basic designs are manufactured:

The 'Porta-Lift' for pivoting on a fifth wheel prime mover.

The 'Trac-Porta-Lift' with integral prime mover.

Both are available either in different sizes for 20 ft, 30 ft, or 40 ft containers with rope lashing and automatic top-spreader, or with telescopic spreaders for 20 ft-30 ft or 20 ft-30 ft-40 ft units.

U type lift transporter

This elevating trailer is specially designed for the horizontal transport of containers and flats. The lift height of 700 mm (2 ft 7½ in) also allows loading and unloading of low platform trailers. Tractors with hydraulic fifth wheel couplings or forklifts with carrying capacity of at least 5 tons can be used as prime movers. Control of the hydraulic lift cylinders is operated remotely from the prime movers' cab. If the prime mover is not equipped with sufficient power to operate the hydraulic equipment, it is possible to install the equipment in the transporter together with an internal combustion engine to power it.

Mafi Fahrzeugwerke Roll Trailer system.

Mafi Fahrzeugwerke U type elevator.

MAFI U.K.

Mafi (UK) Ltd.,

Graham House, Pannells Court, Guildford
Surrey
TELEPHONE: 76815
TELEX: Mafi Guildford 85457
DIRECTORS:
Dr. F. Hofstetter (Swiss)
R. Dubach (Swiss)
D. W. Bews
PRODUCTS:

Terminal tractors and trailer systems, lifters and transporters.

The Rolltrailer System

This consists of a semi-trailer, a tractor with an elevating fifth wheel and a gooseneck which couples with the trailer. The coupling system is patented. The system as a whole is designed for moving containers on and off roll-on/roll-off ships and for terminal and quay traffic. The range of 'Rolltrailers' available is shown in the following table.

Mafi Fahrzeugwerke The Container lift.

Rolltrailers—technical data

Capacity	12 t	20 t	25 t	30 t	40 t	55 t
Length approx.	20 ft	20 ft	30 ft	40 ft	40 ft	40 ft
	6,100 mm	6,100 mm	9,150 mm	12,200 mm	12,200 mm	12,200 mm
Width approx.	8 ft	8 ft	8 ft	8 ft	8 ft	8 ft
	2,500 mm	2,500 mm	2,500 mm	2,500 mm	2,500 mm	2,500 mm
Total weight approx	14·3 t	22·5 t	28·8 t	35·0 t	46 t	65 t
Fifth wheel load approx. (gooseneck included)	7·5 t	10·3 t	13·7 t	15 t	15 t	17 t
Axle load	9 t	14 t	17 t	11 t	16·5 t	25 t
Wheel load	2·25 t	3·5 t	4·25 t	2·75 t	4·1 t	6·25 t

A semi-trailer 20 ft-40 ft

CHASSIS:

Frame made of precision telescopic tubes, adjustable for loading lengths of 20 ft, 30 ft and 40 ft with cross-beams for support of containers. Adjusting device for control cables.

SADDLE SUPPORT:

To be operated mechanically.

LOCKING OF CONTAINER:

4 fixed twistlocks.

KING PIN:

2 in king pin screwed on a slide plate.

RUNNING GEAR:

Unsteered tandem axle-aggregate.

BRAKE DEVICE:

All-wheel compressed air-brake acc. to national regulations for road traffic. Hand spindle brake as parking brake.

UNDERCARRIAGE PROTECTION:

Rigid undercarriage protection over the whole width at the rear end.

FURTHER EQUIPMENT:

Two fenders on full length, mounted on rigid supports. A drag shoe with security-chain at the rear end of the chassis. Tool box.

ELECTRICAL SYSTEM:

Electrical system with 12 Volt alternatively 24 Volt tension. Two large tail-lights, the left one with licence-plate lighting. Connecting cable to the truck-tractor.

FINISH:

On artificial resin basis, monochromatic. Colour as per option.

Superstructure

CONSTRUCTION:

The containerlift is installed on both ends of the semi-trailer and consists of:
(a) a swingable telescopic tube for support on the ground.
    The supporting legs are steerable individually.
(b) A crane-aggregate for vertical and horizontal movement of the container.

FOLLOWING OPERATIONS CAN BE MADE:

Reloading of containers from one vehicle to another one.

Lifting of containers and putting them down on the ground.

Stacking of 2 containers.

Picking out of a particular container from several ones standing closely together with a gap corresponding to the standard.

HYDRAULIC CYLINDERS:

Double-acting cylinders with ball and socket joints and hard chromium plated piston rods.

STEERING:

Magnetic valves for lifting, transloading and putting down of containers as well as for extending and swivelling of the support are being actuated from a portable control device. Connection possibilities of the control device at the front and rear of the semi-trailer.

LOADING DEVICE:

Steel ropes with locking device for hanging into the container corners.

Additional Equipment:

HYDRAULIC AGGREGATE:

Hydraulic system with twin-piston pump and gasoline engine completely assembled in the semitrailer.

Technical data of Mafi-Containerlift Type LSC 20/40 with unsteered tandem axle:

Payload (inclusive of containers dead weight): 30,000 kg (66,139 lb) approx.

Dead weight of semitrailer, approx: 13,000 kg (28,660 lb)

Total weight of semitrailer: 43,000 kg (24,799 lb)

Required fifth-wheel load: 17,000 kg (37,479 lb

Axle load: 2 + 13,000 kg (28,660 lb)

Total weight of truck tractor: 26,000 kg (57,320 lb)

Truck-trailer combination total weight: 52,000 kg (114,640 lb)

Tyres: 8 × 12·00-20 PR 18

Top speed: 80 km/h (50 mph)

Frame height, laden: 1·460 mm (57½ in)

Technical data of Mafi-Containerlift Type SCL 20/40 with three-axles aggregate:

Payload (inclusive of containers dead weight): 28,000 kg (61,729 lb) approx.

Dead weight of semitrailer, approx.; 16,000 kg (35,274 lb)

Total weight of semitrailer: 44,000 kg (97,003 lb)

Required fifth-wheel load: 17,000 kg (37,479 lb)

Axle load: 3 × 9,000 kg (1,984 lb)

Total weight of truck-tractor: 26,000 kg (57,320 lb)

Truck-trailer combination total weight: 53,000 kg (116,848 lb)

Tyres: 12 × 10·00-20 PR 14

Top Speed: 80 km/h (50 mph)

Frame height, laden: 1,460 mm (57½ in)

MISKIN

Vaso Miskin Crni

Transport Equipment and machine factory
Zivca Josila 2
POB 732, Sarajevo
Yugoslavia
TELEPHONE: 41 222
TELEGRAMS: Miskin Crni Sarajevo

TELEX: 41 116

PRODUCTS:

All types of road vehicles for container transport tipping skeletal trailers including road/rail transfer and stilt system. Rail flats for container transport.

MECHANISATION PRODUCTS

Mechanisation Products
5 Walworth Road,
Hitchin,
Herts.
TELEPHONE: 4119

TELEGRAMS: Mechan-Hitchin

DIRECTORS:
Eric Salmons
Kenneth S. Moore

PRODUCTS:

Container lifting attachments including 'modular' system suitable for forklift trucks and sideloaders and adaptable to all sizes of ISO containers.

HERBERT MORRIS

Herbert Morris Ltd

HEAD OFFICE:

PO Box 7, Loughborough, Leicestershire England TELEPHONE: Loughborough 63123
TELEGRAMS: Comorris Loughborough
TELEX: 34408 (Comorris Loboro)

DIRECTORS:
F. M. Morris (*President*)
P. W. Lawson (*Chairman*)
H. Flavell (*Group Managing Director*)
S. Gardner (*Home Sales*)
D. B. Mirk
K. J. Jennings
T. L. Hill
E. P. McTighe
J. R. Dobson
R. R. Woolcott
J. Gill

PRODUCTS: Goliath Freightliner cranes. single and double road handling units, double Goliath container handling cranes, stacking cranes, Quay cranes, ten lone Goliaths, sliding-boom container cranes.

Morris 0-6-0 Electric Goliath Crane

The Morris 0-6-0 Goliath crane handles containers up to 30 tons capacity in any of the standard British Rail "Freightliner" or ISO sizes up to 40 ft long. The crane spans two rail tracks and four roadways, transferring loaded containers from rolling stock on to road transport or vice-versa. One cycle of operation (pick up, transfer and put down) has an average duration of three minutes and the crane can handle up to 360 containers per day. This crane is similar to the 30 smaller 0-4-0 electric Goliath cranes supplied to British Rail for the Freightliner depots.

Five motions are provided including tilt and slew so that loads can be correctly and quickly positioned on to road trailers which may be sloping or inaccurately parked, and a special feature is the rigid hoist mast which moves on rollers and guides in the crab frame. This arrangement gives a truly vertical lift and maximum stability of the load under all operating conditions.

All motions of the crane are controlled by a driver without assistance from the ground. The cabin is suspended from a stalk on the crab structure so that the driver has the best possible view of the load. A high standard of comfort is provided, and all crane movements are controlled from joy-stick control levers.

The grapple was designed by British Rail to handle all types of container, and has comprehensive interlocks to prevent lifting from taking place until all twist-locks or lifting arms are properly engaged in the pockets of the container being lifted. Control buttons in the operator's cab select the correct twist-lock centres for "Freightliner" or ISO containers and for 10 ft, 20 ft and 30 ft loads. A special sub-frame is attached to the grapple to handle 40 ft loads.

Ward-Leonard motor-generator control of the main motions gives, in addition to the normal speeds, a creep speed together with high speeds at reduced loads. The crane normally takes its power from 380/440 volts 3-phase a.c. reeled flexible conductors located at ground level, or from an enclosed conductor system. Where power supplies are not conveniently available a diesel unit can be carried on the crane to generate its own power.

The rope drum is driven by a motor through spur reduction gearing enclosed in an oil-tight steel gear box.

Container size 12·19 m (40 ft 0 in)
Container capacity 30 tons
Test load 37½ tons
Span (centre to centre of track rails) 15·85 m (52 ft 0 in)
Height of lift to underside of container 5·18 m (17 ft 0 in)
Hoist speed (full load) 6·1 mpm (20 fpm)
Crab travel (full load) 30·49 mpm (100 fpm)
Main travel (full load) 91·4 mpm (300 fpm)
Slewing range 15° total
Slewing speed ¼ rpm
Maximum slope of tilt 1 in 18
Tilt speed full range in ½ minute
Weight of crane 95 tons approx
Maximum wheel loading 23·5 tons
Rating heavy duty
(All figures approximate)

Morris Sliding-boom Container Crane

The three Morris designed cranes ordered by Seatrain Lines Inc. for their Weehawken (New Jersey) dock complex are of sliding-boom construction so as to serve both sides of a finger pier. The boom can project 33·5 m (110 ft) either side of the main structure, which itself spans 100 feet, giving the crane a working area some 97·5 m (320 ft) wide. This area includes ships either side of the quay, road and rail loading areas and also container storage facilities. The operating distance of the cranes is virtually unlimited as self-propulsion by diesel generators, totalling over 1,100 h.p., eliminates current delivery problems. The need for back-up cranes is also removed.

Use of all three cranes intensively on one ship is expected to give record turnaround times during which containers up to 40 feet in length and weighing 40-tons (45 US tons) will be handled.

Features of the crane reflect these intended working conditions. Steel fabrication techniques developed by Morris when pioneering box section crane structures have now been applied to hoist drums, gearboxes and bogies which are all welded steel structures. High precision spherical roller bearings support wheels, gears, hoist drums and grapple sheaves —minimizing power requirements throughout the crane. All wheels are one piece steel castings.

Multiple motor drives on the main travel, crab travel and hoist allow limited use of the crane at reduced speed in the event of a motor breakdown.

MAIN TRAVEL MOTION

An outstanding feature of this crane is the 32 wheel main travel drive arrangement. Complete articulation of the bogies is given by pivoted connections between bogies, spreaders and the main structure, ensuring even load distribution and effective drive from the 16 powered wheels. These are driven by eight motors via reduction gearboxes and offer very high tractive effort even when full extension of the boom gives minimum designed wheel loadings on one side of the crane and during adverse weather conditions.

MAIN STRUCTURE

Welded box section beams, suitably braced with diaphragms, are securely bolted together to form the main structure.

The boom is supported on two portal frames connected by horizontal members, and all the main members are of hollow box construction. As well as providing a light and strong structure, this gives safe covered access for inspection and maintenance of all machinery and control gear.

CRAB AND HOISTING MACHINERY

Crab drive on the crane is self-contained within the crab and consists of two motor/spur gearbox units driving all four crab wheels through "live" axles. Final spur gear drives

Morris sliding boom crane recently erected for Seatrain Lines Inc. at their Weehawken (New Jersey) dock complex

to the wheels, often difficult to protect completely, are thus eliminated. This form of drive gives an unusually high maximum crab travelling speed of 122 m (400 ft) per minute and has many advantages over systems using ropes reeved along the boom, including reduced stretching, rope wear and noise. Two motors drive the twin hoisting drums via a common spur gear reduction box. This arrangement gives a full load hoisting speed of 53·1 m (175 ft) per minute and also allows limited hoisting to continue at half normal speed if one motor fails. Very fast hoisting, with speeds up to 106·7 m (350 ft) per minute, is possible with lighter loads. The twin drum arrangement gives inherent stability to the load during movement.

BOOM AND BOOM TRAVEL

The boom structure has two rails along the underside of its main girders which run on four two-wheel bogies fixed to the main structure adjacent to the corner uprights. Electric actuators lift and lower the bogies which in turn raise or lower the boom, allowing it to be moved to the desired position at a speed of 75 ft/min. Once in position the bogies are lowered and the boom rests on rigid supports to give stability during hoisting and other motions.

CAGE

Comfort and simplicity of crane control are offered by the cage which is attached to the crab unit by a short stalk girder. All round vision through tough anti-glare glass (including a floor mounted window), close proximity to the load, and joystick controls make accurate load and grapple positioning straightforward. The cage is heat insulated and

fully air conditioned to maintain a pleasant working temperature. Access is by a hinged door at the rear, approached by properly illuminated walkways and ladders which are largely enclosed in the leg girders. A voice communication system and pushbutton klaxon alarm are fitted. For additional safety, warning bells on the crane sound at ground level when main travel movement begins.

POWER SUPPLY AND CONTROL

A 1000 hp diesel engine drives dc generators to supply current to the main travel, crab travel and hoisting motors.

These motions are controlled by sophisticated multi-notch Ward-Leonard control units which give creep speeds for fine positioning during loading, unloading and stacking operations, and also increased maximum hoisting speeds for less than full loads.

The boom winch and boom lift actuators receive power from a diesel alternator unit which also supplies ac power for floodlights, lighting, air conditioning, etc.

Both diesel units are situated in a completely weatherproof housing which is approached by ladders and walkways enclosed in a leg and cross girder.

BRAKES

In addition to the regenerative braking action on all main motions, effective when speed controllers are moved to slower notches, all motor units on the crane are fitted with automatic braking systems. Where multiple motors are featured (main travel, crab travel and hoist) the safety of several independent brakes is included.

Electromagnetic disc brakes are fitted to

the extended tailshafts of the main travel and boom winch motors. Braking on the crab travelling gear is by electro-hydraulic drum brakes operating on the motor-gearbox couplings.

The hoisting machinery features electro-

magnetic drum brakes acting on the motor-gearbox couplings.

LUBRICATION

The complete enclosure of gears by steel fabricated or cast boxes allows oil bath lubrication of the gears and supporting

bearings. All other bearings and bogie articulation swivels are grease lubricated through nipples grouped together on battery plates which are conveniently positioned for access.

This simplifies regular maintenance procedure.

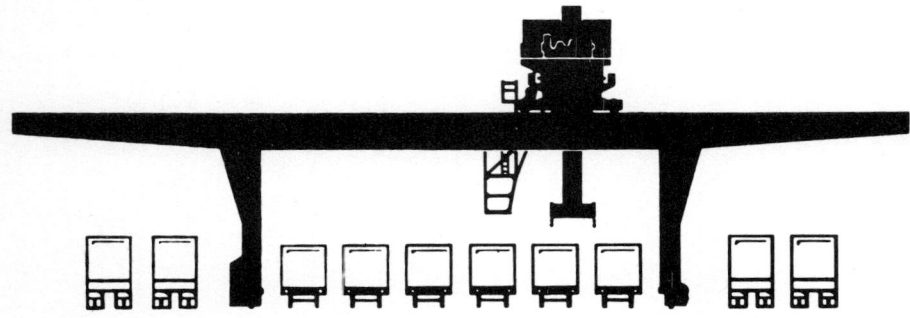 

Morris 10-lane Goliath Container Handling Crane

MUNCK

Munck International A/S

HEAD OFFICE:
PO Box 652, N-5001 Bergen, Norway
TELEPHONE: Bergen 98030
TELEX: 2025-2247 (Norway)
BRITISH COMPANY:
Munck (UK) Ltd., 77 Uxbridge Road, London W.5.
TELEPHONE: 01-579-4141
TELEX: 262979
DIRECTORS:
O. A. Munck, (Chairman Norwegian)
T. A. Munck, BSc, AIEE (Norwegian)
F. J. Munck, BSc, ARTC (Norwegian)

The company has factories in Belgium, Sweden, USA, Brazil, Canada, United Kingdom and Norway.

PRODUCTS: Munckloader, Rolling Gantry, Ships Cranes for containers.

Munckloader

Munckloader rolling gantry ship's cranes travel on rails along the deck and have hinged jibs which project over the ship's sides during operation. The load is suspended from a trolley which travels athwartship, and carries the hoist and travel machinery. During the voyage the cranes are parked on special stowage brackets. About 15 minutes are needed for parking or rigging. During loading and unloading all movements are controlled from the operator's cab, suspended from the trolley. No labour is required in the hold. Electrical power is supplied to the cranes from the ship's supply (440 volts, 3 phase 50 or 60 cycles) via a special cable boom.

Special handling devices such as electro-hydraulic grabs, vacuum lifting heads, electro mechanical bale clamps and electro hydraulic lumber forks can be provided to take advantage of the very fast loading/unloading cycle, and the cranes are equally well suited for handling containers by means of a container spreader.

The cranes are designed to fit the vessel, and the lifting capacities and operating speeds are chosen to suit owner's requirements. A special crane for handling containers was installed on the M/V Frank H. Brown and M/V Klondike (6,780 tons dwt) in 1965 and 1969 respectively. These cranes are designed for lifting 27,180 kg (60,000 lb) containers and are also equipped with a strong-back for handling loads up to 40 tons. The electrical machinery is dimensioned for placing 25 containers on board and removing a further 25 in 75 minutes. Main characteristics are:

Hoist speed at no load, 73 m/min (240 ft/min); at 60,000 lb 30 m/min (100 ft/min); at 80,000 lb 24 m/min (80 ft/min)
Travel trolley speed, 67-85 m/min (220/280 ft/min)
Gantry travel speed, 30 m/min (100 ft/min)
Crane rail span, 17 m (58 ft)
Safe working load at 49 ft outreach, excluding weight of spreader bar, 36,240 kg (80,000 lb)

Safe working load at 60 ft outreach, excluding weight of spreader bar, 27,180 kg (60,000 lb)

Total weight of crane, including trolley, 190 tons.

Six vessels each of 27,450 dw t have been built for the Star Bulk Shipping Company, Each has been equipped with two 25 ton swl Munckloaders, and handling devices provided for loading and unloading containers as well as ore, scrap iron, packaged timber, wood pulp bales and newsprint rolls. The cranes are roofed to permit loading and unloading to continue regardless of weather conditions. The main characteristics of these cranes are:

Lifting capacity (swl), including weight of lifting device/container spreader, 25 tons
Hoist speed, 32 m/min (107/200 ft/min)
Trolley travel speed, 90 m/min (300 ft/min)
Gantry travel speed, 24 m/min (80 ft/min)
Crane rail span, 24·0 m (79 ft)
Maximum outreach from ship side, 8·0 m (26 ft)
Total weight of crane, including trolley, 180 tons.

A series of 12 ships similar to above are being equipped with two 25 ton Munckloaders each.

A NEW PRODUCT FROM THE MUNCK-GROUP: MUNCK standard container crane of Goliath electric travelling type, on steel rails for handling of containers in railway yards.

The crane is equipped with standard spreader bar for ISO containers from 10 to 40 ft lengths, and will be able to handle the containers in whatsoever position they will have been lined up along the railway cars.

Max lifting capacity: 33 metric tons
Max lifting height: 8 m
Max lifting speed: 6 m/min
Max trolley speed: 30 m/min
Max bridge speed: 40 m/min
Control from weather proof cabin on crane bridge.

The Munck Goliath container crane is built for outdoors service and its transport capacity will be from 8-10 containers per hour, depending on the average travel length.
Recent installations are as follows:
Two Munck Portloaders for handling ISO containers by means of Munck automatic universal spreaders, at Ferry Boats, Zeebrugge, Belgium.
Span: 31·5 m (103 ft 4 in)
Max. outreach:
over ship: 35·5 m (116 ft)
over land: 23·0 m (75 ft)
Payload: 45 tons
Lifting capacity: 55 tons
Max. lift above quay: 22 m
Total weight of each installation: 750 tons
Max. transport capacity: 30 containers/hour

Two Munck goliath cranes for handling ISO containers and palletized loads by means of Munck manual spreaders for Norwegian Railways (NSB).
Span: 14-17 m (46-56 ft)
Payload: 30 tons
Lifting capacity: 35 tons
Max. lift above rails: 6 m (20 ft)

Total weight of each installation: 60 tons
Max. transport capacity: 10 containers/hour
One Munck goliath crane for handling of ISO containers and palletized loads by means of Munck automatic universal spreader and turn table for Norwegian Railways (NSB).
Span: 22 m (72 ft)
Payload: 30 tons
Lifting capacity: 40 tons
Max. lift above rails: 8 m (26 ft)
Total weight of each installation: 100 tons
Max. transport capacity: 30 containers/hour

NEBBIM

N.V. Nederlandse Bedrijfsauto Import Maatschappij Nebbim

Postbus 1203
Binckhorstlaan 209-219
's-Gravenhage
Holland
Telephone: (070) 81 40 51
Telex: 32004
Directors:
M. H. Panhuyzen
R. Meijer
Products:
Bollnäs Hoist Units are intended to be used for lifting and moving containers, flats, exchangeable platforms and all other load units, provided with ISO-corner fittings.

Lifting heights up to 1·75 or 2·75 m. Lifting speed approx 5 cm/sec with pump capacity of 25 litres/1,500 revs and 140 kp/cm². This speed can be raised with higher pump capacity to a maximum of 9·4 m/sec. The hoist unit has to be combined with a terminal tractor, delivering the required hydraulic pressure and supporting this kangaroo at the king pin. With the help of the tractor the hoist unit can be driven along the container or other unit, that has to be picked up from a truck or to be placed on it. Bollnäs hoist units can be delivered for all sizes of containers and flats. Lifting capacity 20 tons.

Nebbim Böllnas hoist unit taking over a load with a Böllnas terminal tractor

NELLEN

Nellen Machenfabrik constructiewerkplaats en Technisch bureau NV

Sluisjesdyk 20-34,
Rotterdam
Holland
Telephone: 010 297955
Telex: 21003
Directors:
A. H. Nellen
W. A. de Geus
P. C. Kreft

Products:
Mobile cranes and spreaders suitable for handling freight containers. The N 125-L has a lifting capacity of 25 tons at 4,700 mm radius with a 10 m jib. The N-150-L has a lifting capacity as follows:
35 tons at 9 m radius (main jib)
12·7 tons at 20 m radius (main jib)
4 tons at 26 m radius (fly jib).

Nellen mobile Crane W-150-L for containers and piece goods. Provided with hydraulically operated outriggers

NETAM-FRUEHAUF

Netam-Fruehauf

N.V. Nederl. Tank-, Apparaten en Machinefabriek 'Netam'
Telephone: 010-254880
Telex: 22596
Head office:
'Netam', van Helmontstraat 33, Rotterdam, Netherlands
Works:
Leek, Rotterdam
Associated companies:
Dockside Trailer Service
Van Riemsdijkweg 39,
Rotterdam
Telephone: 295221
Directors and sales manager:
B. A. van Rijn, Ing. (Director)
A. Wiegman, Ing. (Sales Manager)
Products:
Netam is the fully licensed associate of Fruehauf for the Benelux countries and produces a full range of container handling equipment including skeletons, bogies, adaptor frames, dollies, barrows, doubles and suspensions.

Netam-Fruehauf Skeleton

Depending on the container type used, a choice can be made out of two types, Straight Frame or Gooseneck.
The overall length changes with the dimension of the container:
12·192 m   40 ft (40 ft)   container
10·668 m   35 ft (35 ft)   container
9·144 m   30 ft (29 ft 11¼ in)   container
6·058 m   20 ft (19 ft 10½ in)   container

The width is maximum 2·50 m (8 ft 2⅜ in)
The height varies from 1·26 m (4 ft 1⅜ in) to 1·480 m (4 ft 10¼ in)
In container locking devices there is a choice

Netam Fruehauf skeletal trailer for 20 ft containers or flats

Netam Fruehauf skeletal trailer for one 40 ft or two 20 ft containers or flats

Type	Internal			Capacity	Tare	Max. pay-load
	Length	Width	Height			
NFT 20	5920 19ft 5ins	2260 7ft 5ins	2135 7ft 0ins	29.2 cu.m. 9.58 cu.ft.	2600kg 2½ tons	17720kg 17½ tons
NFT 30	8990 29ft 6ins	2260 7ft 5ins	2000 6ft 6¾ins	41.5 cu.m. 1,360 cu.ft.	3850kg 3¾ tons	21525kg 20 tons

in the twist lock system and the bolster clamp system. Under-construction, king pin location, braking system and lights change with customers' requirements, and road regulations of various countries.

HYDRAULIC FIFTH WHEEL

The Netam-Fruehauf 34 in hydraulic fifth wheel matches a terminal truck to either container skeletons or terminal trailers fitted with a 2 in SAE king pin, without using the support legs.

Features: king pin load 10,700 kg
weight 580 kg (1,278 lb)
40 ft chassis
35 ft chassis
29 ft 11¼ in chassis
22 ft or 22 ft 3 in chassis

TERMINAL DOLLIES

Features: king pin load 10,000 kg adjustable height + 0·20 m

TERMINAL TRAILERS

Type	Under-Construction	Locking Device
20 ft Term TR	F1—Fixed	Twist lock
40 ft Term TR	F2—Fixed	Twist lock
40 ft Term TR	F2—Fixed	Twist lock

GVW	Tare	Payload
20,000 kg	2,100 kg	17,900 kg
30,000 kg	2,700 kg	27,300 kg

Container chassis

Type		Chassis	Under-Constr.	Locking Device	GVW	Dead Weight Excl. Cont.	Payload Incl. Cont.
20 ft	Skeleton	Straight	F1		20,000 kg	2,650 kg	17,350 kg
			F2	Twist lock	26,000 kg	3,200 kg	22,800 kg
			F2		26,000 kg	3,500 kg	22,500 kg
30 ft	Skeleton	Straight	F2W	Twist lock	30,000 kg	4,000 kg	26,000 kg
			F2W		30,000 kg	3,500 kg	26,500 kg
35 ft	Skeleton	Gooseneck	F2W	Bolster clamp	30,000 kg	4,250 kg	25,750 kg
40 ft	Skeleton	Straight	G. Lelt/20	Twist lock/ bolster clamp	30,000 kg	5,000 kg	25,000 kg
			F2W		30,000 kg	3,950 kg	26,050 kg
		Gooseneck	G.Lelt/20		30,000 kg	4,700 kg	25,300 kg
40 ft/2 × 20 ft Skeleton		Straight	F2W		30,000 kg	4,450 kg	25,550 kg
			G.Lelt/20	Twist lock	30,000 kg	5,200 kg	24,800 kg
20 ft full Trailer		Straight	F1	Twist lock	20,000 kg	3,500 kg	16,500 kg
			F2		26,000 kg	4,250 kg	21,750 kg
Single Bogie			F1	Pins in siderail	20,000 kg	1,800 kg	18,200 kg
			F2W		30,000 kg	3,300 kg	26,700 kg
Tandem Bogie			G.Lelt/20	Pins in siderail	30.000 kg	4,050 kg	25,850 kg

(10,000 kg = 22,040 lb)

NICOLAS

Nicolas, Manix
89 Champs-sur-Yonne,
France
TELEPHONE: (86) 52 00 09
PRODUCTS:
   Electro-hydraulic container lifting stilts

which can be transported by a container carrying road vehicle and which can be operated off the vehicle's batteries. If necessary special extra batteries can be used for intensive use.

NORDVERK

Ab Nordverk
Uddavella,
Sweden
TELEPHONE: 0522 14100
TELEX: 5297
TELEGRAMS: Nordverk
PRODUCTS:
   Bogie systems for use with forklift trucks to enable relatively light duty forklifts to shunt containers and flats weighing up to 40 ton into position.

Cont-Roll

This consists of a fork attachment plate

which needs to be tailor made to suit any truck, a hydraulic system operated from the driver's seat and available for 40 ton or 20 ton gross loads and an 8-wheeled bogie for 40 ton or 20 ton gross loads. The forklift which need have only half the capacity of the load it is moving, lifts the container by means of the near sides of the top corner castings and one set of bogies is positioned. The same procedure is followed at the other end of the container to convert it into a rolling unit. Ground clearance is 350 mm (13¾ in).

Jack Wagon

There are two types. 20 BL and 20 BH. The 20 BH is designed to transport containers and flats by means of the bottom corner fittings. The 20 BL picks up and transports by gripping the side rails of a container. Both units consist of wheel mounted frames like semi trailers with attachments for fitting to fork carriage of a forklift truck. Maximum load which can be handled is 20 ton and maximum length of unit is 20 ft. Using the Jack Wagon a 5 ton forklift can transport a container weighing 20 tons or a 3 ton forklift one weighing 10 tons.

NORVAD

Norvad Equipment Limited,
P.O. Box No. 14, Passey Place, Eltham,
London, S.E.9. England

TELEPHONE: 01-850 0367
TELEGRAMS: Norvad, London S.E.9
DIRECTORS: R. Gorman, L. M. Gorman, J. Gorman
PRODUCTS: Norvad SF Safety Hooks.

SF Safety Hooks

This is a self-closing hook made in chrome nickel steel. Hook 3204, with eye, has a breaking load of 42 tons, giving an SWL of 6-7 tons. It fits the ISO container corner fitting and many hooks of this type are now used for container handling.

Each hook is tested and marked with the permissible working load in tons.

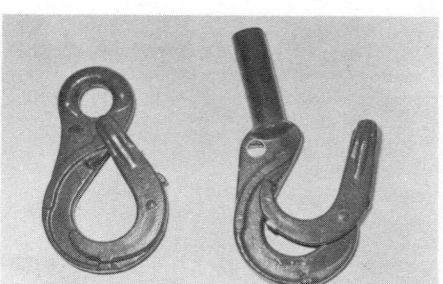

Two Norvad SF safety hooks, eye type (*left*) and with unmachined shank (*right*). The hooks form a closed pear-shaped loop that can be opened and automatically closed and secured.

ORENSTEIN-KOPPEL

Orenstein & Koppel Aktiengesellschaft

Lübeck Works, 2400 Lübeck, Einsiedel-strasse 6 Germany

TELEPHONE: 45011

TELEX: 2 6 823

DIRECTORS:

Karl W. Bach
Dr.-Ing. Alfred Welte
Dr. Ing. Helmut Heusler
Dr. Heinz-Gunter Kohlen

PRODUCTS: Single and Gemini deck cranes for containers, general cargo and bulk materials by motor-grab operation.

Gemini Deck Crane

The Gemini deck crane consists of two separate cranes, each of which can be slewed individually through 210°. Both are mount-ed on a common main turntable slewable through 360°. Each crane can work inde-pendently of the other from the same or different hatches. In dual operation with double load the same outreach can be achieved as when used independently.

Different types from 5 to 25 tons as single cranes and 2 × 5 to 2 × 25 tons are available, with maximum outreaches from 14 to 22 m minimum outreach about 10% of maximum outreach.

Optional extras: remote control, pro-gramming attachment, hook turning device, motor-grab, mobile gantries with appropriate cranes.

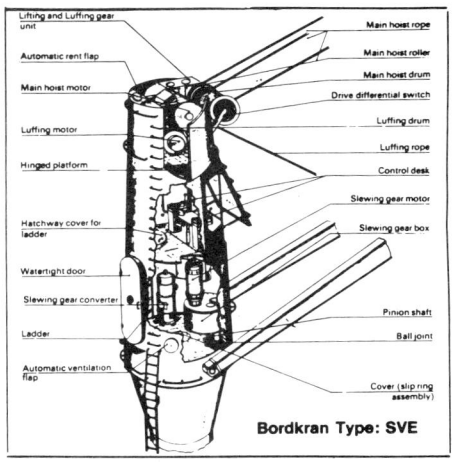

Exploded view of cabin and operating mechan-ism of the Orrenstein - Koppel ship's crane.

Bordkran Type: SVE

ORI

Oficine Rimorchi Industriali
48019 Granarolo Faentino,
Casella Postale 1,
Italy

TELEPHONE: (0546) 41041

PRODUCTS:
Scissor lifts suitable for container lifting.

PACECO

PACECO, a Division of Fruehauf Corp.

HEADQUARTERS:
2350 Blanding Avenue,
Alameda, California 94501
TELEPHONE: (415) 522-6100
TELEX: 325-399
EUROPEAN SALES OFFICE:
Paceco International Limited
Millbank Tower, Millbank,
London, S.W.1
TELEPHONE: 01-828-7777
TELEX: 27921
PACECO LICENSEES:
Australia:
Vickers Hoskins Pty, Limited
   Post Office Box 51,
   Bassendean,
   Western Australia
   Telephone: 791-683
Canada:
Paceco-Canada, Limited
   640 West Hastings Street,
   Vancouver 2, British Columbia
   Telephone: (604) 681-9101
France:
Ateliers et Chantiers de Bretagne
   Prairie-au-Duc,
   P.O. Box 165,
   44 Nantes
India:
Braithwaite & Co., Ltd.
   Hide Road, 5
   Calcutta 43,
   Telephone: Chandernagore 326
   Cable: BRO MKIRK
Italy:
Reggiane O.M.I., S.p.A.
   Via Vasco Agosti 27,
   42100 Reggio Emilia
Japan:
Mitsui Shipbuilding & Engineering Co. Ltd.
   6-4 Tsukiji 5-chome
   Chuo-Ku Tokyo
   Telephone: (214) 543-3111
   Telex: TK 2821, 2924
South Africa:
Dorman Long (Africa) Limited
   6th Floor Norwich Union House,
   91 Commissioner Street,
   P.O. Box 2997
   Johannesburg,
   Republic of South Africa

Two 40 ton Transtainers, which feature 360° rotating trolleys and control cab which moves with the load, operating at Penn Central Terminal, Chicago, Illinois.

Paceco Vickers container crane in action at Bellport, Newport, Monmouthshire.

Spain:
Fruehauf S.A.
   Plaza de Salamanca 10
   Madrid 6
United Kingdom:
Vickers Limited

Vickers House, Millbank Tower,
Millbank,
London S.W.1
Telephone: 01-828-7777
Telex: 27921

PRODUCTS: Shoreside, shipboard and yard gantry cranes, lifting beams and top and bottom lift container spreaders.

Paceco Transtainers

Transtainers are self-propelled gantry cranes designed for the rapid handling of containers. Rubber tyred and rail mounted units are available and both can handle loads up to 50 tons.

Transtainers are built to heavy duty crane standards and are of all-welded rigid frame, box construction.

Rubber-tyred units are equipped with low pressure earthmover tyres operating at 115 psi.

Conduit, wiring and pipes are concealed for clean appearance and weather protection. Cables and drums have large diameter machined drums that eliminate overwrap. Wheel yokes are welded steel sections for maximum strength and the axle is integrally welded to wheel. All operating machinery is equipped with anti-friction bearings.

Hoist and travel motions are powered by DC stepless, variable voltage systems. Automatic field weakening allows a light spreader or container to move at twice its loaded speed to pick up quickly another payload and reduce operating time.

Rail mounted units are available in configurations to serve up to six tracks. The 6-track model is of cantilever design to permit unhindered vehicular movement outside the gantry legs. The operator's cab travels with the trolley, which rotates through 360°.

Paceco Universal Lifting Spreader

This handles both containers and trailers. Spreader arms swing out when positioning for lift. Wide, wood-covered lift shoes span under deck reinforcing beams to prevent excessive loading on side body panels. Lifting beam retracts 80° for empty clearance over trailers or rail trucks. Spreader has top-lift capability for fast container handling and is expandable to handle 20 ft through 40 ft container or piggyback sizes.

PACECQ Portainer.

Paceco Shipstainer

The Paceco Shipstainer has an articulating boom with 31 ft 6 in outreach and can serve two lanes of traffic on either side of the ship to permit simultaneous loading and unloading. When retracted for sailing, it stows flush with the side of the ship, entirely above deck-level, only 47 ft 6 in high. Capacity is up to 40 tons; loaded hoist speed is 100 fpm, gantry travel is 130 fpm.

Paceco Portainer

Pierside container handling crane, available in ten basic designs. Paceco standard Portainer has a 30 ton capacity, hoist speed 120 fpm loaded and 205 fpm unloaded, trolley travel is 410 fpm. Other models include the Twin Lift Portainer, Long Span Portainer and Low Profile 'Portainer' with a choice of capacity and operational features. Pictured is the new Twin Lift Paceco Portainer at Los Angeles.

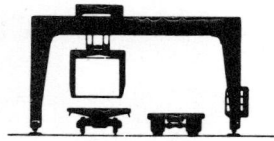

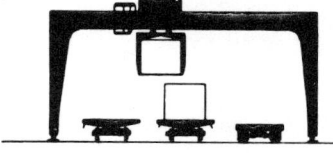

Paceco rail mounted Transtainers

PACTON

Van der Ploeg's fabrieken Pacton N.V.
Nieuwerkerk a/d Ijessel,
Holland
TELEPHONE: 01803-3144

TELEX: 24023 PACTONL
PRODUCTS:
Container semi-trailers.

PEINER

Peiner Maschinen-und Schraubenwerke AG
ADDRESS:
315 Peine, PO Box 46, Western Germany
TELEPHONE: (05171) 431
TELEGRAMS: Peinerag Peiner
TELEX: 09 2662/63 peine d
DIRECTORS:
Richard Bühring (Sales)
Dr.-Ing Peter Ferling (*Administration*)
Hans Vobkötter (*Design and Manufacture*)
PRODUCTS: Peiner container cranes; PPH 30 straddle carrier; spreaders, harbour and wharf cranes, heavy load cranes, tower and climbing cranes, etc.

Peiner Container Cranes

Peiner container cranes are designed to handle containers outside as well as inside

Peiner Telescopic Spreader

Peiner PPH30 Straddle Carrier

the track gauge of the crane. They can be used for loading and unloading of vessels and also for the handling of containers on the land side storage area.

Cranes with a capacity of 32 tons can lift 45 tons at a reduced radius. The cranes can be equipped for twin operation, that is, handling of two 20 ton containers which can be lifted separately and placed diagonally separately, provided that the crane is equipped with self travelling Peiner trolley on which the hoist units and corresponding trolleys are arranged.

Peiner container cranes can also be equipped with the following:

Peiner Special Spreader

This is for the horizontal placing of unsymmetrically loaded containers by means of chain pull and central control of the twist-locks. Suspension with high quality chains can be used for all spreader frames from 20 to 40 ft.

Peiner Telescopic Spreader

The Peiner Telescopic Spreader can be adapted to containers with a length between 20 and 40 feet. This adaption is made by remote controlled motors. The twist-locks and flippers are also controlled from the crane driver's cabin.

A Peiner container crane in Antwerp.

Peiner PPH 30 Straddle Carrier

This is designed for containers of all usual lengths (20, 30 and 40 feet) as well as semi-containers. Travelling speed, 17 mph (28 km/h), capacity 30 tons; 40 km/h with a load up to 20 tons; maximum climbing ability, 3% gradient, Servo-steering, small curve radius. The spreader can be moved to the side. The Straddle Carrier runs forward, backwards and sideways. Wheels are separately sprung.

PENGCO

Pengco (Transport Systems) Ltd.
Oxney Road,
Peterborough, England
TELEPHONE: 0733 68315/6/7
TELEX: 32267
DIRECTORS:
R. J. Rowley, R. J. Ashling, J. H. Davies

PRODUCTS:
Load-O-Matic demountable body systems. Designed for speed interchange of loaded or empty bodies on rigid chassis, this system introduces many of the benefits of articulation to the rigid chassis. Suitable for all popular chassis with bodies from 4·2 m (14 ft) to 7·3 m (24 ft), it will handle loads up to 15 tons, can be used to transport standard ISO or Freightliner type containers. Load-O-Matic is completely self-contained with all lifting equipment fitted to the chassis. Operated by driver only, body changing can be effected in 2-3 minutes.

TIPPING CONTAINERS:
Also Pengco tipping equipment for tipping ISO containers when fitted to skeletal trailers.

Pengco Load-O-Matic demountable body system depositing 20 ft ISO container for loading at customer's premises

Pengco skeletal tipping semi trailer showing 30 ft ISO container in tipped position. This vehicle is also available with self contained pneumatic discharge equipment to enable bulk pulverant loads to be discharged into silos without the need for site conveying equipment at delivery points

PFAFF

Pfaff-Silber Blau
Windenfabrik Gottfried Schober,
89 Augsburg 2, Postfach 309 (POB),
W Germany
TELEPHONE: (0821) 29255
TELEGRAMS: Pfaffwinde
TELEX: 053760
DIRECTORS:
August Pfaff
Walter Pfaff
PRODUCTS:
Container Lifting Jacks.

One set consists of four movable jacks with attached lifting beam and electrical control panel. Jacks can be operated individually or simultaneously. In case of failure of one jack, the electrical supply is automatically cut off to avoid further operation of the remaining jacks. The lifting beams which are placed against the top corner fittings are connected with lifting arm by means of a swinging beam. The containers are hanging on steel wire ropes with a special bolting attachment for the bottom corner fittings. The steel wire rope is connected to the lifting beam.

The containers are hanging on the ropes in pendulum fashion and thus avoiding side thrust and any possible tension on the jacks. To obtain a lateral movement of the contai ers for precise lowering onto the carrying vehicle two jacks on one side are slightly lowered.

Suitable for 20 ft and 40 ft containers. The jacks are also available in a manually operated version.

TECHNICAL DATA:

Cat. No.		58020
Capacity per set of 4 jacks	tons	20
Permissible maximum load per jack	tons	6
Closed height	mm	2720	(8 ft 11 in)
Lift	mm	1700	(5 ft 7 in)
Lifting speed	mm/min	430	(17 in/min)
Motor	220/380V	3,6KW
Weight per complete set	kg	2150	(4,740 lb)

POWER LIFTS LTD

Power Lifts Limited
ADDRESS:
   Colnebrook Works, Lower High Street, Watford, Herts. England
TELEPHONE: Watford 27724/5
TELEGRAMS: Power Lifts Ltd., Watford
DIRECTORS:
   Charles Pither
   Ron Hyde, AMIMechE
   John Pither
   John Atkins

PRODUCTS:
A heavy duty 30 ton capacity power lift for container handling.
Lift has a platform size of 9·14 m (30 ft) × 3·6 m (12 ft) with a closed height of 0·6 m (2 ft) and elevates to a maximum height of 6·09 m (20 ft) in 1¾ minutes.
Other sizes can be made to suit customer's requirements.

PRICE AND PIERCE

Price & Pierce Machinery Ltd.
51 Aldwych, London, WC2
TELEPHONE: 01-240 2494
TELEGRAMS: Timber London WC2
TELEX: London 28551
DIRECTORS:
S. B. G. Johansson (*Managing*)
J. G. Rustad
D. G. Mitchell
PRODUCT:
Contake Container Crane, capacity 25 tons. Spreader with bottom lift suitable for 10 ft to 40 ft containers. Operating from fixed central point with 360° traverse. Total traverse time 30 seconds. Total cycle time 4 minutes.

Contake 20 ft container crane about to lock on to corner castings.

F. W. D. Wagner Inc.
4427 N.E. 158th Ave.,
Portland, Oregon 97220
P.O. Box 20044
TELEPHONE: Area Code 503 252 5531
EXPORT DISTRIBUTORS:
Columbia Exporters Inc., 345 N.E. 8th
Avenue, Portland Oregon 97232
PRODUCTS:
Container handling forward reaching lift
trucks which can also handle trailers. An ex-
panding spreader suitable for use with dock
and ship- loading cranes which can handle
trailers measuring between 20 ft and 40 ft.

Piggy Packers
There are two models—the P 80 and the
PC 90. Both are equipped with spreader
attachments which allow containers or trailers
to be lifted from above or below. To handle
a trailer or container from below, four folding
arms drop down and grip from underneath.
The PC 80 can lift and carry a maximum load
of 80,000 lb at 48 in load centres. The PC
90 can bottom lift and carry 90,000 lb at 48 in
load centres and top lift and carry 60,000 lb.
There is a carriage side shift of 9 in to right
and left on both machines.

RAY-GO WAGNER P-80

ENGINE: (Package)	Standard	Option
Make	Allis Chalmers or	Cummins
Model	16000 Series H	N-855-C
Max. H.P.	238 @ 2100 RPM	240 @ 2100 RPM
	Sea Level @ 60 F	Sea Level @ 60 F
Governed RPM	2100	2100

POWER TRAIN:
Torque converter and power shift transmission.
Full reversing type — 4 speeds.
Travel speeds up to 18 MPH.

DRIVE AXLE: (Ratio 25.322:1)
Type ..... Planetary Drive
Brakes ..... Air Actuated

STEERING:
Full power hydraulic with 50 G.P.M. pump, engine
driven, operating 2 double acting cylinders controlled
by valve with conventional steering wheel in cab;
system protected by relief valve.

TIRES:
Drivers (Tubeless) ..... 29.5 x 35; 40 PR
Tailwheel (Tubeless) ..... 16.00 x 25; 24 PR
(Jumbo Stems in Tailwheel Tires for Hydro-flation)

ELECTRICAL SYSTEM: (12 Volt)
Charging system ..... 12 Volt
— Alternator ..... 60 AMP
Circuit breakers (lights) ..... 30 AMP
Circuit breakers (access) ..... 20 AMP
Battery (2) (12 Volt) 205 AMP Hour (ea.)
Starter ..... 12 Volt High Torque

MEASUREMENTS AND DIMENSIONS:
Width overall outside carriage ..... 28'5"
Height overall with carriage ..... 17'0"
Height without cab (chassis) ..... 13'0"
Height with cab (chassis) ..... 14'9"
Wheel base ..... 23'0"
Width outside of tires ..... 12'4"
Width inside of tires ..... 6'10"
Length, ground level ..... 40'6"
Height, inside head ..... 12'6"
Width, inside head ..... 8'1"

WEIGHT:
Complete Machine ..... 98,500 lbs.
Tailwheel ..... 36,300 lbs.

TURNING RADIUS:
Inside ..... 6'4"
Outside carriage ..... 29'0"
Tail swing ..... 28'7"

CAPACITIES:
Cooling system with heater ..... 18 gals.
Crankcase with filter ..... 11 gals.
Hydraulic tank ..... 350 gals.
Fuel tank ..... 450 gals.

LIFT CAPACITY:
Bottom lift and carry (48" load center) ..... 80,000 lbs.
Carriage side shift — 9" right
9" left of center

PC-90

ENGINE:
Make ..... Allis Chalmers or Cummins
Model ..... 16000 Series H N-855-C
Max. H.P. ..... 238 @ 2100 RPM 240 @ 2100 RPM
Sea Level @ 60 F Sea Level @ 60 F
Governed RPM 2100 2100

POWER TRAIN:
Torque converter and power shift transmission.
Full reversing type — 4 speeds.
Travel speeds up to 18 MPH.

DRIVE AXLE: (Ratio 29.559:1)
Type ..... Planetary Drive
Brakes ..... Air Actuated

STEERING:
Full power hydraulic with 40 G.P.M. pump, engine
driven, operating 2 double acting cylinders controlled
by valve with conventional steering wheel in cab;
system protected by relief valve.

TIRES:
Drivers (Tubless) ..... 33.5 x 33; 44 PR
Tailwheel (Tubeless) ..... 23.5 x 25; 24 PR
(Jumbo Stems in Tailwheel Tires for Hydro-flation)

ELECTRICAL SYSTEM: (12-24 Volt)
Charging system ..... 12 Volt
— 60 AMP alternator
Circuit breakers (lights) ..... 30 AMP
Circuit breakers (access) ..... 20 AMP
Battery ..... 2-D8 205 AMP Hour (ea.)

MEASUREMENTS AND DIMENSIONS:
Height without cab ..... 14'6"
Height with cab ..... 15'0"
Wheel base ..... 26'0"
Width outside of tires ..... 13'1"
Width inside of tires ..... 7'4"
Length, ground level ..... 44'6"
Height, inside head ..... 13'0"
Width, inside head ..... 8'1"

WEIGHT:
With 27 feet expandable spreader ..... 122,500 lbs.
With 40 feet expandable spreader ..... 125,750 lbs.

TURNING RADIUS:
Inside ..... 10'4"
Outside carriage ..... 25'10"
Tail Swing ..... 31'10"

CAPACITIES:
Cooling system with heater ..... 18 gals.
Crankcase with filter ..... 11 gals.
Hydraulic tank ..... 350 gals.
Fuel tank ..... 450 gals.

LIFT CAPACITY:
Bottom lift and carry (48" load center) ..... 90,000 lbs.
Top lift and carry (48" load center) ..... 60,000 lbs.
Carriage side shift — 9" right
9" left of center

ROLLALONG

Rollalong Ltd
Southampton Road
Ringwood, BH24 1JB Hampshire, England
TELEPHONE: Ringwood 2116/7/8
DIRECTORS:
Sir Ian Yeaman (*Chairman*)
D. M. Lindner (*Managing Director*)
Murray Lindner
G. Norrish

Maj. Gen. D. R. Horsfield
J. C. Booker
J. C. Powell
C. C. Truscott
PRODUCTS:
Universal container trolley-gantry, up to

22 ton capacity; container chain sling adjuster.
Universal Trolley-Gantry
This equipment has been designed specifically
for the handling of containers at warehouses
and distribution centres.

Universal Mobile Gantry

It is of welded construction, manufactured from 8 in × 4 in RHS to BS4 Pt.2. 1965, and is equipped with a self-contained hydraulic system. The power unit provides hydraulic pressure of 1,000 psi, the pump giving a flow rate of 17 gal. per min. for a lifting speed of approximately 6 ft per min. The hydraulic fluid used should be one of those recommended in maintenance instructions.

The two hydraulic cylinders comprise 6 in bore cylinders with 3 in dia. rams connected to a horizontal lifting beam, giving a range of vertical movement of 6 ft 4 in. Under load the rams are self-adjusting to ensure even lifting.

The whole is mounted on four Flexello EH fabricated steel castors with opposed taper roller bearings. They are Superthane tyred and have a diameter of 16 in and a tread width of 5 in giving a floor loading, at 24 tons gross, of 1,625 lb per sq in . Each castor is lockable in any one of four positions, facilitating movement in any desired direction, and enabling the machine to be turned within its own diagonal dimension.

Spreader beams of strong triangulated construction enable an unladen container to be stabilised during movement, whilst the main weight is sustained by the chain slings and lifting beam.

The machine is a development of an original idea to provide a cheap, simple and reliable method of mounting and de-mounting bulk loads to and from vehicles, and has been designed to provide great strength and simplicity of operation with a minimal maintenance requirement.

It has been designed and developed to provide an easily movable means of lifting, for example, a fully laden 20 ft ISO container or flatbed clear of a road vehicle, and then lowering it to the ground at that position. All four castors are lockable in any one of four positions, and provision is made for attaching the towbar at either end of the gantry, so that any manoeuvring is kept to a minimum.

The chain sling adjusters enable an end-heavy load to be lifted without any tilt if required, or will enable a load to be lifted at an angle to suit the rake of the vehicle involved. They are not automatic in operation, but they enable the sling lengths to be varied without the necessity for unshackling, etc. They operate on the principle that when no tension is on the chain slings they are free to roll through the adjusters, over the pulleys. As soon as lifting is commenced and the chain slings come under tension, the central pulley is firmly locked and no further movement is allowed. Therefore, with an end-heavy load if the gantry is positioned, either by moving it slightly, or, if the container is on a vehicle, by moving the vehicle slightly, so that the lifting beams and rams are in line with the estimated centre of gravity of the load, the slings will then, on lifting, lock in the correct ratios to provide a level lift. With a container on the ground, a little practice and experience will enable an operator to position the gantry so that it may be lifted at an angle suitable to a coupled semi-trailer so that, on lowering, the four bottom corner castings seat on the twistlocks at the same moment.

The ex-works price includes all fittings, etc. The trailing lead for the power supply to the motor, so that, when connected to the power supply, lifting operations may commence, can be supplied as an extra; to customer's own specification if so desired.

The diesel hydraulic version uses a Ford 3 cylinder 16 bhp water-cooled diesel engine to drive the hydraulic pump.

The electro hydraulic version uses a 15 hp 380 to 440 volt/three phase drive proof electric

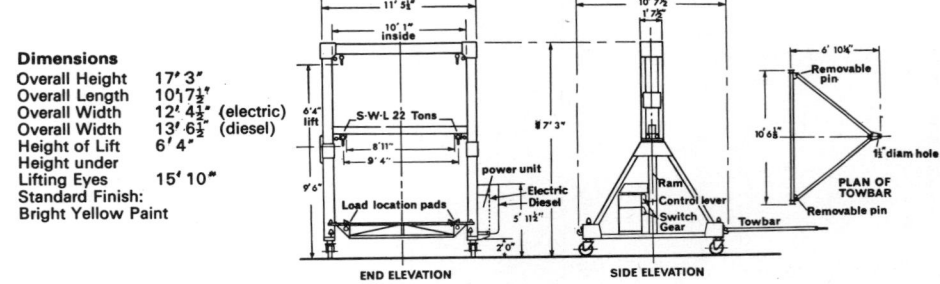

Dimensions

Overall Height	17' 3"
Overall Length	10' 7½'
Overall Width	12' 4¼' (electric)
Overall Width	13' 6½' (diesel)
Height of Lift	6' 4"
Height under Lifting Eyes	15' 10"
Standard Finish: Bright Yellow Paint	

Dimensions of the Rollalong Universal Mobile Gantry (drawing)

The diesel powered 22 ton Rollalong Mobile Gantry with one castor motorised for movement and steering when unladen

The Rollalong electro hydraulic turn lift gantry specially developed to handle ISO tank bodies with liquid loads

motor mounted on a 30 gallon hydraulic fluid version.

For lifting and lowering loads in excess of 20 ft in length and with a gross weight of more than 20 tons two gantries can be used.

Rollalong chain-sling adjuster

The purpose of the adjuster is to enable loads up to 10 tons capacity, to be lifted horizontally

Rubery Owen & Company Ltd. (Contracts Division)

Darleston, PO Box 10, Wednesbury, Staffs., WS10 8JD
TELEPHONE: 021-526 3131
TELEGRAMS: Ruberowen Telex Darleston
TELEX: 338236
DIRECTORS:
Sir Alfred Owen (*Chairman*)
F. Lee (*Contracts Division General Manager*)
PRODUCTS:
Rubery Owen Contracts Division market the Owen 'Travelift' straddle transporter and 'Karricon' straddle carrier, which are designed for the handling and transporting of containers in marshalling yards and container parks.

The Karricons

A range of straddle carriers capable of handling standard ISO containers up to 40 ft in length as well as non-standard 8 ft 6 in units.

There are two machines, the 'Karricon 3042', which can handle containers up to 40 ft in length and stack 2 high and the 'Karricon 3043' for handling containers up to 40 ft long, three high.

These machines are of modular construction, a feature which gives a flexible design specification in which height, width and length can be varied to overcome specialist handling problems.

Both machines incorporate the latest telescopic spreader frame with automatic twist locks which engages in container corner castings. On completion of a change, the centres are mechanically locked and the control selector is isolated until the frame is engaged with the container and all weight is removed from the hoist system. The two hoists are powered by hydrostatic motors and the system includes a safety feature to stop and hold the full rated load should a power failure occur. The hoists can be operated independently to allow the frame to be tilted or levelled.

One of the inherent tasks of a machine of this type is the precise positioning of the heavy container during stacking, combined with high-speed travel whilst conveying the load from the container park to the quayside. This is achieved by optional two or four wheel drive giving two speed ranges, one for fast travel and the other for close-quarter manoeuvring in confined spaces the hydrostatic drive providing a fine degree of 'inching' control for the accurate positioning of the load.

Power is supplied by two Perkins 6·354 diesel engines directly coupled to the hydraulic pump units. Each unit forms a power module which can be removed *en-bloc* for servicing and exchange.

Top speed is 15 mph. Lifting capacity up to 30 tons and hoist speed 29 ft per minute.
Principal users of the equipment are:
Freight container Handling Shipping Authoriser, Dockside to Storage Compound.
e.g. Skandiaterminalen, Gothenburg, Sweden.
Halterm, Halifax, Nova Scotia, Canada.
Containerbase Federation Ltd., Leeds and Coatbridge.
T. Wallis-Smith, Coggins Ltd, Tilbury.
Transport & Ferry Services, Ltd, Felixstowe.

even if the weight is not evenly distributed between the points at which the chain sling is attached.

When no load is carried by the chain sling, the chainwheel is free to rotate, but when the sling is supporting a load the projecting ends of the pulley pins engage on internal projections and hold the pulley against rotation. If therefore the chain sling is applied to a load

and, on lifting, it is found that the load assumes a tilted position, the load can be lowered to relieve the chain sling of its weight, thus freeing the pulley. This enables the crane hook carrying the adjuster to be moved in the appropriate direction causing the chainwheel to rotate and shifting the point at which the lifting force is applied, so that the load remains untilted when lifted.

RUBERY OWEN

Owen Karricon model 3043 loads a 20 ft container on to a trailer.

A Karricon 3043 transfers a 30 ft container to the stack.

SCAMMELL

Scammell Lorries Ltd,
Watford WD1 8QB,
Herts,
England
TELEPHONE: 44211
TELEX: 261760
TELEGRAMS: Twelfton Watford Telex
PRODUCTS:

Container trailers. These are based on the 'Challenger' trailer series. They are designed to carry 20 ft, 30 ft or 40 ft ISO containers. There are skeletal and dual purpose models both of which can be fitted with additional outriggers or fixing posts to take other ISO container sizes. The dual purpose model enables an operator to conduct container and general haulage business. Specifications of the three main types of Scammell container trailers are as follows:

Auto-Coupling Container Trailers

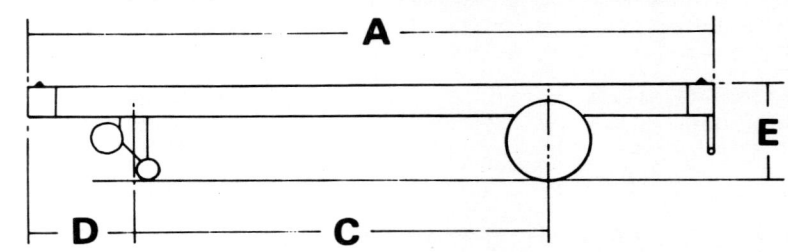

A LENGTH	B WIDTH	C WHEELBASE	D OVERHANG	E HEIGHT UNLADEN	I.S.O. CONTAINER SIZE WITH 9.00 x 20 TYRES FITTED	CALCULATED WEIGHT CHASSIS ONLY	CALCULATED WEIGHT WITH PLATFORM
							T CWT
21ft 0in	8ft 0in	14ft 6in	2ft 0in	4ft 3¼in	20ft	1.16.0.0	2. 2.0.0
31ft 0in	8ft 0in	23ft 0in	2ft 0in	4ft 3¼in	30ft	2. 3.0.0	2.12.0.0

Challenger Container Trailers

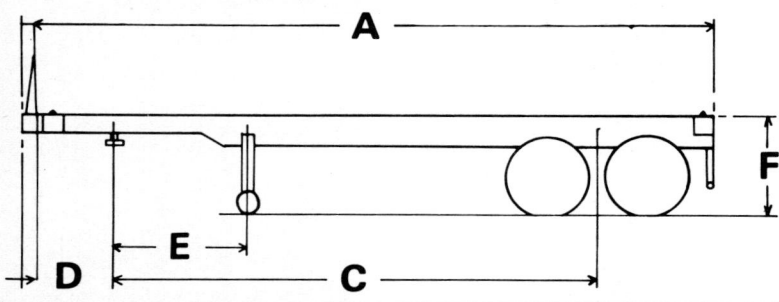

A LENGTH	B WIDTH	C WHEELBASE	D KING PIN	E LANDING GEAR	F HEIGHT UNLADEN AT BOGIE CENTRE LINE WITH 9.00 x 20 TYRES FITTED	I.S.O. CONTAINER SIZE	CALCULATED WEIGHT
							T CWT
7.01m (23ft 0in)	2.43m (8ft 0in)	4.87m (16ft 0in)	0.75m (2ft 6in)	7ft 3in	4ft 3¼in	20ft	3. 2.0.0
9.39m (30ft 10in)	2.43m (8ft 0in)	6.85m (22ft 6in)	0.76m (2ft 6in)	7ft 3in	4ft 3¼in	30ft	3.10.0.0
12.47m (40ft 11in)	2.43m (8ft 0in)	8.68m (28ft 6in)	0.76m (2ft 6in)	7ft 3in	4ft 8¼in	40ft	4. 4.0.0

Dual Purpose Container Trailers

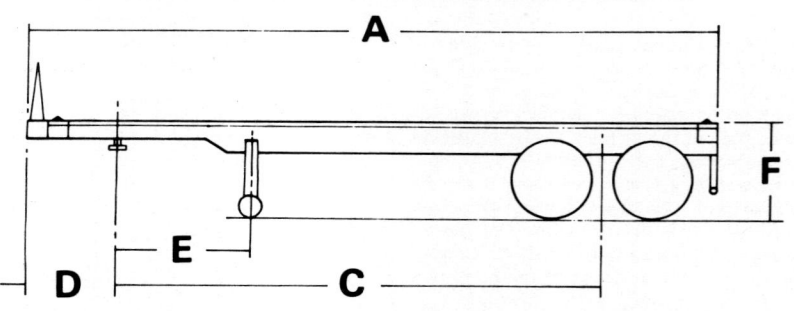

A LENGTH	B WIDTH	C WHEELBASE	D KING PIN	E LANDING GEAR	F HEIGHT UNLADEN AT CENTRE LINE OF BOGIE WHEN 9.00 x 20 TYRES FITTED	I.S.O. CONTAINER SIZE	CALCULATED WEIGHT
							T CWT
30ft 0in	8ft 2in	22ft 6in	2ft 6in	7ft 3in	4ft 3¼in	30ft 0in	4. 6.0.0
33ft 0in	8ft 2in	23ft 6in	2ft 6in	7ft 3in	4ft 3¼in	30ft 0in	4. 9.2.0
34ft 0in	8ft 2in		2ft 6in	7ft 3in	4ft 8¼in		
36ft 0in	8ft 2in		2ft 6in	7ft 3in	4ft 8¼in		
38ft 0in	8ft 2in		2ft 6in	7ft 3in	4ft 8¼in		
40ft 11in	8ft 2in	28ft 6in	2ft 6in	7ft 3in	4ft 8¼in	40ft 0in	5. 5.0.0

SHAW

Joshua Shaw & Sons Ltd.

Bradford Road, Batley Yorks
TELEPHONE: 4444
TELEX: 5574 12
BRANCH OFFICE:
Shaw Sideloaders (Export) Ltd.
    16 Stratford Place, London W1 N9AF
    Telephone: 01-629-6243
    Telex: 262906
PRODUCTS:
    The Shawloader 560C. A heavy-duty side-loader with top lift attachment to handle 20 ton containers of 20 ft, 30 ft and 40 ft length. All operations hydraulically controlled from the driver,s cab. Capacity (with attachment) 45,000 lb or 56,000 lb less the attachment.
    Leyland 6-cylinder diesel engine.
    The Shawloader 670 becomes available in late 1971. This is designed to top lift 20 ft, 30 ft or 40 ft containers weighing up to 30 tons. Unlike the Shawloader 570, the 670 model has an underslung cab mounted to the front of the chassis. This may be fixed to the chassis, and be equipped with a swivel seat or may extend the entire width of the machine having two fixed control points and a traversing seat.

General Data on Shaw 560 Sideloader

Capacity (less attachment):
    25,400 kg at 1,220 mm (56,000 lb at 48 in)
Capacity (with attachment):
    20,500 kg at 1,220 mm (45,000 lb at 48 in)
Lift height—standard:
    5490 mm (18 ft)
Lift height—optional:
    7920 mm (26 ft)
Lift speed—laden: 12 m/min (40 fpm)
    unladen 15 m/min (50 fpm)
Traverse speed:
    15 m/min (50 fpm)
Travel speed (forward and reverse) 40 kph (25 mph)
Tyres 14·00 × 24·22 ply. Wheels: 4 pce, 16 stud.
Fork section 255 × 125 mm (10 in × 5 in)
Maximum laden gradeability 12½% (1 in 8)
Unladen weight—with attachment and standard mast 41,700 kg (92,000 lb)

General data on Shaw 670 Sideloader

Fork capacity (over 12 ft lift load derates)
    36,800 kg (81,000 lb)

Shinko Electric Company Ltd.
Asahi Building,
No. 5, 3-chome,
Edobashi, Nihibashi,

The largest model in the Shaw sideloader range. Lifting capacity is 20,410 kg (45,000 lb) at 1,219 mm (48 in) load centres. The unit, which has a hydraulic spreader, can stack 20 ft containers three high.

Capacity of the Shaw 670—with container attachment		
40 ft × 8 ft × 8 ft container beam:		Max capacity
20 ft mast drop forks stacking 2 high		30,500 kg (67,200 lb)
20 ft mast inverted forks stacking 2 high		30,500 kg (67,200 lb)
20 ft mast inverted forks stacking 3 high		20,320 kg (44,800 lb)
12 ft mast inverted forks stacking 2 high		30,500 kg (67,200 lb)
30 ft × 8 ft × 8 ft container beam		
Drop or inverted forks stacking 2 high		30,500 kg (67,200 lb)
20 ft mast inverted forks stacking 3 high		20,320 kg (44,800 lb)
20 ft × 8 ft × 8 ft container beam		
Drop or inverted forks stacking 2 high		30,500 kg (67,200 lb)
20 ft mast inverted forks stacking 3 high		20,320 kg (44,800 lb)

Load centre on forks, 1,219 mm (4 ft 0 in)
Platform width, 2,515 mm (8 ft 3 in)
Lift height:
    standard 6,096 mm (20 ft 0 in)
    optional 3,658 mm (12 ft 0 in)
Lift speed—laden 15 m/min (50 ft/min)
Traverse speed, 15 m/min (50 ft/min)
Travel speed—laden 40 km/hr (25 mph)
Tyres, 28 ply (1,600 × 25)
Wheels—4 front, 4 rear, 5 piece 14 cleat fixing
Fork section 304 × 127 mm (12 × 5 in)

Maximum laden gradeability 12½% (1 in 8)
Unladen weight with 40 ft container attachment 66,900 kg (147,500 lb)

Mast data

Lift height		Overall height	
		Mast lowered	Mast raised
12 ft 0 in		12 ft 2 in	18 ft 2 in
3,658 mm		3,708 mm	5,537 mm
20 ft 0 in		16 ft 2 in	26 ft 2 in
6,096 mm		4,928 mm	7,975 mm

SHINKO

Chuo-ku,
Tokyo, Japan

PRODUCTS:
    Sideloaders suitable for container handling.

SHEPPARD

Sheppard Fabrications Ltd.
Barnham, Thetford, Norfolk
TELEPHONE: Elveden 291
TELEX: 81396
PRODUCTS:
    The Sheppard-Klaus sideloading container crane.
OVERSEAS LICENCES HELD:
    Sheppard Fabrications hold the UK licence to sell and manufacture the Klaus sideloading crane made by Klaus GmbH (see under Klaus).

A Sheppard Klaus sideloading crane being demonstrated at British Rail's Gosford Green sidings.

SILENT HOIST

Silent Hoist & Crane Co.
841-899 63rd Street,
Brooklyn, N.Y. 11220, USA
TELEPHONE: (212) 238-2525
TELEGRAMS: Silentoist New York
DIRECTORS:
Dr. J. W. Wunsch (*President*)
Eric Martin Wunsch (*Executive Vice-President*)

PRODUCTS:
Silent Hoist 'Liftruks', 18,120–45,300 kg (40,000-100,000 lb) capacity, and Toplift handler 22,650 kg (50,000 lb) capacity.

Fork Lift Trucks
The five models in the company's range have lift capacities from 40-100,000 lb. Features include front wheel drive, rear-wheel power.

steering, hydraulic lifting and tilting mechanism and air power service brakes with mechanical drive shaft brake for parking. Chassis are built in heavy duty welded steel.

Toplift Handler
The Toplift Handler will lift standard 20-40 ft containers and has a capacity of 50,000 lb. The top lift cradle has full floating and self aligning power-guided lock-on at each of the four corners. Safe lock-on indicators are monitored by the operator in the cab. A power side shifter permits accurate spotting. The vehicle can be quickly converted for use as a fork lift truck when required.

Silent Hoist Toplift Handler has a 50,000 lb capacity. Safe lock-on indicators are installed in the operator's cab.

SIPRO-KELLER

Societe Sipro-Keller
41 Montrichard, France
TELEPHONE: 266

PRODUCT:
The Mocoprek container loading and unloading system which comprises four powerful screw-jacks, one attached to each corner post by a pair of hinged arms. The jacks are hydraulically operated. The hydraulic pump is mounted on the fixed end-wall

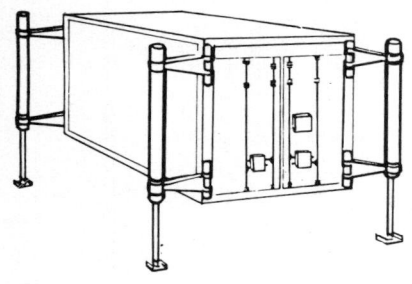

and may be driven electrically or by a small petrol engine. It is push-button remote control operated. The arms are folded back for transport but spread-out for unloading where their wide spread of 3·60 m (11 ft 8 in)

A feature of Transmaterial Mocoprek system for self-demountable containers is the wide-spread of the lifting legs allowing adequate room to manoeuvre the transporting vehicle.

facilitates positioning of the transport vehicle. The Mocoprek system enables a container to be mounted or unloaded from a vehicle in three minutes. Maximum lift 22 tons.

The Mocoprek system fitted to an ISO type container. A feature of this system is that there is plenty of room between the supports for a vehicle to enter.

S.N.A.V.

Societe Nouvelle des Ateliers de Venissieux
Chemin du Genie
69, Vénissieux, France
DIRECTORS:
Pierre Bonnin (*Chairman*)
Charles Louwet (*Managing Director*)
TELEPHONE: (78) 72.85.21
TELEX: 34 603 F

PRODUCTS:
Skeletal semi-trailers specifically designed to transport containers.

Within the weight limitations of the road regulations, containers up to 40 ft length can be carried on tandem axle semi-trailers.

All 40 ft SNAV semi-trailers have three positions for the king-pin.

SNAV 40 ft semi-trailer

SNAV 40 ft semi-trailer

The SNAV 40 ft Skeletal semi-trailer enables the transport of either a 40 ft container, or 2 non-coupled 20 ft containers, or a 30 ft container, or even a 35 ft one.

Its three position kingpin makes hitching to many types of road tractor possible.

The twist locks are mounted on screw jacks which can be height-adjusted. Thus, perfect clamping of the corner casting is obtained.

The empty weight of this semi-trailer is 4,875 kg for a carrying capacity of 23,550 kg.

SNAV 20 ft semi-trailers

These semi-trailers are produced either with single-axle or with two axles.

SNAV 2 axle 20 ft semi-trailer

SOUTHERN IRON

Southern Iron & Equipment Company, 5522 New Peachtree Road, Chamblee, Georgia 30005, U.S.A.

TELEPHONE: 404/457-3176

DIRECTORS: Tom C. Campbell (President)

PRODUCTS: Southern Iron and Equipment Co. builds a 50 ton capacity gantry crane for the loading of containers or trailers.

It will handle 20–40 ft containers and trailers up to 50 ft length.

The crane has a weighing system and it parks trailers at 35° angle making it possible to place four trailers contiguous, to and within the length of, an 89 ft flat car.

Southern Iron Equipment Company's Piggyback trailer slewing lift.

STAR IRON

Star Iron & Steel Co

326, Alexander Avenue,
Tacoma, Washington 98421 USA
TELEPHONE: (206) 627-9131
MANUFACTURERS OVERSEAS:
Canada:
Canada Iron Foundries Ltd
Western Bridge Division
Japan:
Kawasaki Electric & Machine Co. Ltd
PRODUCTS:
The Starporter series of container cranes

33.5-Ton Fixed Tower Luffing Boom Container and General Cargo Crane and Handling System for Feeder Port Facility.

40-Ton Container and General Cargo Crane with Extra Back Reach & Load Handling with Apron Luffed — South Carolina State Ports.

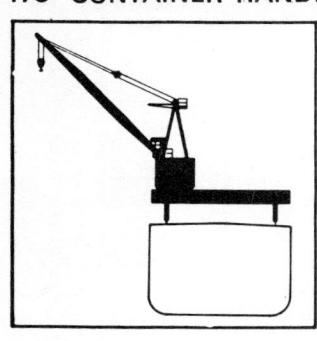

30-Ton Ship or Barge Mounted Container and General Cargo Crane.

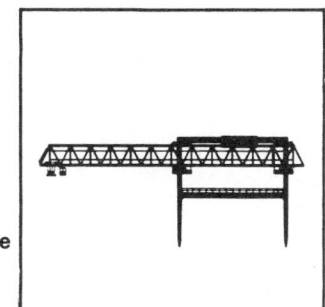

40-Ton Container and General Cargo Crane with Horizontally Extendable and Retractable Boom.

40-Ton Container and General Cargo Crane with Rope Trolley — I.T.O. Elizabeth, N. J.

STEADMAN

Steadman Industries Ltd.
280 Belfield Road, Rexdale,
Toronto, Canada
TELEPHONE: 416-677-2680
TELEX: 06-217754
TELEGRAMS: Steadind
PRESIDENT: Gabriel Alter
BRANCHES:
European Affiliate—Klockner-Steadman Container GmbH, Troisdorf, West Germany
UK—Interpool, Ltd., 799-1611, 30 Westminster Palace Gardens, Artillery Row, London, SW1
Australia—Freighter Ltd., Warrigal Road, Moorabbin S20, Victoria

Subsidiary and associated companies—Interpool Inc., 630 Third Ave., New York, N.Y. 10017. Interpool N.V. Corsicaweg 10, Amsterdam, West Haven, Nederlands.
PRODUCTS:
Containers: Railtainers (patented) containers with added features for side transfer, 20 ft, 30 ft and 40 ft, ASA/ISO. Side transfer semi-trailers; Railtainers and universal type; truck mounted side transfer units; Railtainer system adaptors for standard ASA/ISO containers; truck, trailer and rail car bolsters; container legs, demountable or built-in retractable; self lifting trailers. Side transfer units for transferring any ISO container.

Railtainer System
The Railtainer systems were developed to replace expensive single purpose machinery for inter modal container transfers with low-cost multi-purpose vehicles, and to free the container from wheels wherever practicable.

In Canada, the railroads (both CPR and CNR) use Railtainer containers, identical in size and in corner fittings to the ocean-going containers, to provide savings in handling and rehandling, and in equipment cost.

A Railtainer side-transfer unit added to a delivery trailer chassis costs $3,000 and requires no construction work or high capital cost as do permanent terminal gantries.

The same Railtainer side-transfer unit also has the ability to put a container on legs and to pick it up from legs.

Railtainer equipment is designed to operate with Railtainer containers. The Railtainer container meets all of the internationally established standards including size, corner fittings etc. However, certain additional features are built into the Railtainer container: (a) the tooth rack; (b) smooth end sills built for side-transfer, and (c) leg receptacles. Most containers now in use do not include these features, but as facilities are being increasingly provided to handle Railtainer containers, demand for containers built in this way can be expected to grow. However, one category of adaptors supplied by Steadman can be attached to any container when it reaches port, and will provide all of the required features. This adaptor remains attached to the container as long as it is inland, and is removed from the container before it is again loaded aboard a vessel. Another type of adaptor can be attached to many containers prior to making a transfer, and removed after the transfer. The adaptor in this case is kept with the transfer unit. Using this adaptor the transfer can be made, but receptacles for demountable legs are not

Universal Side Transfer Unit, a new development by Steadman Industries Limited transfers any ISO Container to or from Rail-Cars, Delivery Trailers, or Storage Racks.

Carrier 69 NK clip on refrigeration unit

provided. In this way, with almost no limitation, every container in the world can be handled on Railtainer equipment, but unless originally equipped with Railtainer features, the costs of such handling are somewhat higher.

The Railtainer system gives complete choice of truck, piggy back or C.O.F.C.

Latest Railtainer
The new corner-pull side-transfer unit accomplishes four major objectives.

(a) Corner-pull from ISO corner castings eliminates any possible claims of container stress or distortion during transfer.

(b) Easily adapted for use with any ISO size container—20 ft, 30 ft, 40 ft, or with 24 ft, 27 ft or 35 ft units in special operations.

(c) Maintains transfer speed of original Railtainer side-transfer trailer-less than two minutes actual transfer.

(d) No space required under bolster thus reducing height on rail cars or trailers by minimum of three inches.

The reduction in height, particularly important for British, Continental and Japanese railroads, adds to effectiveness of side-transfer by reducing overhead clearance problems. It is particularly significant in avoiding interference with electric wires on electrified rail lines which constitute a danger in top-lift methods of handling.

Special importance is attached to this unit by its ability in transferring from flat surfaces not equipped with bolsters while still remaining fully compatible with all existing side-transfer bolster equipped rail cars or road trailers.

Consistent with previous development of low cost Railtainer equipment the 20 ft corner-pull side-transfer unit may also be used as a delivery trailer chassis when not engaged in transfer operations.

STEPHEN

Alexander Stephen Container. Handling Equipment Limited
Botany Estate
Sovereign Way,
Tonbridge,
Kent.
Telephone: 63377/8/9
Telex: 77596
Directors:
J. F. Stephen (*Chairman*)
G. J. McGhee (*Managing*)
A. F. Saunders (*Sales*)
R. Kemp
E. E. Toon
K. J. Wheeler
Products:
Dockside tractors, shipborne and dockside
trailers and Conjack lifters/transporters

Dockside Tractors

The Shipcharger Mk. II/6/04 dockside
tractor, powered by a Ford 2704E engine
with Brockhouse 3-speed forward and 3-
speed reverse torque transmission, together
with elevating fifth wheel plate and sliding
cab, besides being a power unit for Conjacks,
can safely and efficiently handle trailers used
in container Roll-on/Roll-off and marshalling
yard operations.

Trailers

A wide range of dockside and shipborne
trailers and semi-trailers are available.

Standard units are as follows:

(i) 20 ft, 30 ft and 40 ft low-level Shiploader semi-trailer with detachable, folding or
fixed goosenecks for dockside use, container
carrying, etc., skeletal or decked, payloads
up to 40 tons.

(ii) 40 ft × 60 ft ton Shiploader trailers.

(iii) 20 to 40 ton capacity straight frame
semi-trailers for dockside use, container-
transporting etc., decked or undecked.

(iv) Independent 4-wheel dockside trailers.

Non-standard custom built dockside or
shipborne trailers designed to order.

Conjack Lifters/Transporters

The Conjack is a container lifting device
with top lift spreader capable of transporting
ISO 8 ft × 8 ft containers of 20 ft or 30 ft
length, for use on the dockside and in container parking areas or between the two, and
can be used to move containers from, or
place on to, articulated trailers, flat-beds,
etc. for transport by road. The DL Conjacks
also have the ability to stack one container
upon the other, having a 9 ft lift.

Four models are presently available—the
20 SL, the 20 DL, the 30/20 DL and the
30/20 DLW. The last model mentioned has
an extra width 'U' frame. The Conjacks are
designed to be towed, powered and controlled
by a Stephen Shipcharger tractor or similar
power unit.

The Conjack basic frame adopts a 'U'
configuration in the plan view and is constructed in box section members for maximum
rigidity and torsional stiffness. This frame
provides the mountings for the hydraulic
rams, wheels, axles and fifth wheel pin.

The Conjack spreader frame is a basic
mattress equipped such that the attachment
and lift of containers is by means of hydraulically operated twist locks located at the
corners. In the case of the 30/20 DL the
extreme ends are used for 30 ft containers,
and twist locks are fitted for 20 ft containers
equi-spaced about the centre line. All
spreader operations are controlled by the
operator from the Shipcharger cab. Limit
switches are incorporated in the twist lock
assemblies which give visual indication by
means of a lamp panel to the driver that the
spreader is (a) locked correctly and (b) that all
twist locks are safely engaged before lifting is
attempted. The spreader is raised and lowered
by the operation of four hydraulic rams

The 30/20 DL Conjack loads a semi-trailer at Stratford Freightliner Terminal.

20 DL Conjack stacking containers.

Shipcharger Mk. II Tractor.

Technical Data:

Carrying capacity	20 ton for containers 20 ft
Lifting height	2·9 m (9 ft 6 in)
Lifting speed	5·5 m/min (18 ft/min)
Travelling speed	20 km/h (12·4 m/h)
Travelling drive	hydrostatically
Driving machine	diesel engine 6 VD 14·5/12·1 SRW permanent output $N_2 = 150$ hp
Height of device at stacking	5,750 mm (226⅜ in)
Height of device at transporting	4,500 mm (177⅛ in)
Width of device	5,235 mm (206⅛ in)
Length of device	9,420 mm (370⅞ in)
Aisle width for rectangular curve drive	8·8 m (28 ft 11 in)
Turning radius	7·8 m (25 ft 7 in)
Lateral adjustability of the container	±250 mm (9⅞ in)
Longitudinal inclination of the container	2·8°

connected to the spreader by means of a
balance chain/pulley assembly at each corner.
Asymmetrically loaded containers are catered
for by a balancing mechanism, in which
three of the hydraulic jacks are arranged as
position servos to slave from the fourth. The
Conjack spreader can also cater for angular
disparity between the top of the container
and the Conjack.

Facility for bottom lifting non-ISO containers or flats is provided for by chains
attached to the spreader by 'D' shackles.

All DL Conjacks are capable of slewing,
controlled by the driver from the cab to
enable accurate positioning of a container on
to a vehicle or another container.

All Conjack models are fitted with Michelin
tyres mounted in single formation, eliminating
tyre scrub.

Brakes are fitted to both wheels of all
Conjack models operated by a Westinghouse
two line air system and an air release mechanical spring brake.

Connection of the tractor vehicle is by
standard SMM & T 2 in fifth wheel pin.
When disconnected from the tractor the Conjack stands upon a hydraulically retractable
two speed landing gear by Davies Magnet.

The hydraulic system is a 20 gpm 1,800 psi
service from the tractor for the 20 SL and DL,
and 30 gpm for the 30/20 models.

The electrical system for the solenoid
operated valves, signal lamp circuit and
other facilities, is 12 volt.

Container transporter and lifter trailer

This is intended for the infrequent movement of containers. It picks up, places on
the ground and transports containers with
the help of a tractor. It is suitable for 10 ft
and 20 ft containers. It is designed for a
travel speed of 10 km/hr (6 mph). Operation
is through a compressed air link. Lifting is
hydraulically powered. Lift height is 2·9 m
(9 ft 6 in).

Stephen Goliath Container Hoist for 8 ft-9 ft high containers

The 'Goliath' Container Hoist is a mobile lifting unit designed to load and unload all sizes of containers. The unit is hydraulically operated and may be towed (unladen) on castor wheels.

Specification:
Height of lift 5 ft 6 in (1·6764 m)
Speed of lift 6 ft 0 in per minute (1·8288 m)
Overall height 17 ft 0 in (5·1816 m)
Overall width 15 ft 0 in (4·5720 m)
Overall length 17 ft 0 in (5·1816m)
Clearance between legs 12 ft 0 in (3·6576 m)
Maximum S.W.L. 35 tons
Maximum container length 40 ft 0 in
Electrical supply 400/440 volts 3 phase 50 cycles/Diesel power unit optional.
Maximum hydraulic pressure 2,000 psi

Operation:
1. The hoist is towed into position over the container.
2. The electrical supply is connected by multi-pin plug or diesel unit started.
3. The hoist is then raised by 4 hydraulic jacks so that the support bases may be swung into position.
4. The hoist is then lowered on to the support bases by raising the 4 hydraulic jacks.
5. The 4 lifting ropes are engaged into the bottom pockets of the container. (A separate set of lifting ropes is supplied for 20 ft 0 in, 30 ft 0 in, and 40 ft 0 in containers).
6. The container is then raised by operating the 2 control levers on the hydraulic power pack. The container may be levelled by operating these levers in turn should the load in the container be out of balance.
7. The lorry can then be driven away from under the container which is then lowered

to the ground.
8. After lowering the 4 ropes are disengaged, the hoist is raised and the support bases swung into the parked position so that it can then be lowered on to the wheels

for towing away.

The Container Hoist above is a typical model but slight modifications can be made should they be required to suit special purposes.

UEB UTA straddle carrier and stacker for 20 ft containers.

STOTHERT AND PITT

Stothert & Pitt Ltd.
HEAD OFFICE:
P.O. Box 25, Bath, BA2 3DJ
TELEPHONE:
   Bath 63401
TELEGRAMS: Stothert, Bath
TELEX: 44311

DIRECTORS:
Sir Richard Clarke KCB, OBE (*Chairman*)
Dr W. H. Darlington, MBE, (*Managing Director*
T. W. Y. Alderton
P. Thomson-Walker
T. E. R. Torrance
R. P. Green
G. T. Cantlay
G. Foster
R. C. Saloway
S. Wainwright

PRODUCTS:
Container handling transporter and goliath cranes for dockside and marshalling duties. Stothert & Pitt have produced a number of container handling cranes for varying duties. Among those on order is one with a 45-ton capacity. Stothert & Pitt also produce a range of spreaders for use with container handling equipment. The range includes the telescopic fixed length and twin lift types.

One of two 30-ton container handling transporter cranes supplied by Stothert & Pitt to British Rail at Parkestone Quay, Harwich.

30 ton capacity container handling Goliath Crane operating in British Rail marshalling compound. The crane is equipped with a rigid mast design of hoisting gear so as to avoid undue swing of the containers during rapid acceleration and deceleration of the cross traversing and rail travelling motions.

STRACHAN AND HENSHAW

Strachan & Henshaw Ltd.
PO Box 103, Ashton Vale Road,
Bristol BS99 7TJ
TELEPHONE: 664671
TELEGRAMS: 'Stelhoist' Bristol
TELEX: 44170
DIRECTORS:
R. Bellinger (*Managing*)
E. J. Hutchinson

A. W. Johnson
J. A. Sperring
PRODUCTS:
Telescopic spreader with electro-hydraulic operation to adapt the 20 ft, 30 ft and 40 ft ISO containers. The twist locks and corner guides are remotely controlled from the crane cabin. The capacity of the spreader is 30 tons.

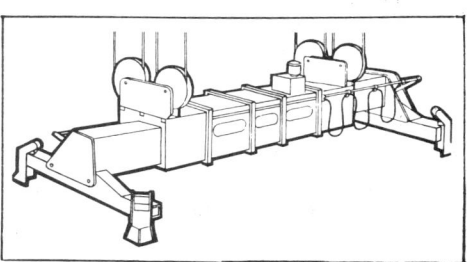

Strachan and Henshaw telescopic spreader.

TAKRAF

VVB Takraf
701 Leipzig,
Germany (Democratic Republic)
TELEPHONE: 7 92 20
TELEX: 051577
PRODUCTS:
Container transporters and stackers. Side-loading inter transport transfer devices. Rail flats.
Semi-trailer mounted unloading device
This system allows containers to be unloaded where other handling equipment is not available. The device, as illustrated is

mounted on a semi-trailer. It enables containers to be picked up from and placed on the ground. The process is remote controlled and the handling cycle is about 10 minutes. Containers and flats with a maximum weight of 20 tons and a maximum length of 20 ft can be carried.
Straddle carrier
VEB VTA Leipzig have developed the self-propelled container stacker for this special purpose. Driven by a 150 hp diesel engine it picks up a 20 ft container and carries it at a speed of up to 20 km/h (12 mph) to the

place where it is to be deposited. The apparatus can also stack 2 containers, one on top of the other. The lifting height of 2·9 m combines with a carrying capacity of 20 ton.

The stacker can also be used for placing containers on to and removing them from road vehicles. It matters little how the container is set down.

Special control devices are available to compensate for lateral shifting and longitudinal inclination.

TASKERS

Taskers Trailers Limited
Anna Valley, Andover, Hants, England
TELEPHONE: Andover 238J
TELEX: 47539
DIRECTORS:
H. Booker (*Chairman*)
L. A. C. Fuller (*Director and Manager*)
A. E. Wisewell (*Production*)
H. R. Haigh (*Works*)
R. R. G. Worth (*Financial*)
PRODUCTS:
Taskers container trailers are available in single and tandem or triaxel form to accept multiples of ISO containers. The 40 ft models can be provided with dual kingpins for all alternative tractor couplings and are designed to operate at all gross train weights. Offered as skeletal in its basic form, a wide

Taskers 20 ft skeletal chassis designed to carry one 20 ft ISO container variety of options are available. Extra intermediate bolsters can be fitted to carry containers in varying lengths. Wood or alloy checker floors at the rear end can be provided, side guard rails can be fitted or the trailer can be supplied as a dual purpose unit for both containers or general cargoes. In its standard form 20 ft trailers are equipped with fixed twistlocks whilst the 30 ft and 40 ft versions have retractable type twistlocks to suit customers' requirements. A wide range of alternative running gears are available. Air suspension is optional on all models. Box frame members give torsional rigidity and strength to the whole trailer and braking and electric circuits fully conform to the latest regulations.

Taskers 40 ft skeletal for one 40 ft or two 20 ft units. The trailer has widespread suspension and a two position kingpin

TITAN

Titan, Departement Route de Frangeco
71 Quai National
92 Puteaux
France
TELEPHONE: 1 772.24-05
TELEGRAMS: Frangeco-Puteaux
TELEX: Frangeco 62.120
DIRECTORS:
J. J. Joseph (Managing)

PRODUCTS:
Range of straight frame 'I' beam trailers for transporting containers by road. There are basically two types as follows:

G.V.W.23T
Constructed with 2 cross members to support a 20 ft container.

Titan 29/32 S2 PC Container semi-trailer
This unit is designed to transport one 40 ft container, two 20 ft containers or one 20 ft unit in the centre of the chassis.

G.V.W. 29,4T or 29/32T
With 4 cross members for 20 ft and 30 ft container. An optional rear access platform

G.V.W. 23 T for one 20ft container

G.V.W. 29,4 T or 29/32 T for a 20ft and a 30ft container

G.V.W. 29,4 T or 29/32 T for one 40ft or two 20ft containers

is provided for 20 ft container. The same designation applies to the trailer with 3 crossmembers for one 40 ft or two 20 ft containers. Optionally there may be 2 cross members for 30 ft container and a rear access platform.

TOOLBRIDGE

Tollbridge Engineering Ltd.
30 High St., Lymington, Hampshire
England
TELEPHONE: 2252
DIRECTORS:
J. B. Smith
R. Butler
G. Chiverton
F. J. Hancock

20-ton Dock Side Container Trailer
Has turntable steering and hand parking brake on front wheels. Operating speed 5 mph. Carrying platform (20 ft × 8 ft) fitted with wooden cross members allowing fork lift trucks to lift any type of load whether or not fitted with specialised lifting slots.

30-ton Dock Side Container Trailer
Has turntable steering and hand parking brake on front wheels. Operating speed 5 mph. Carrying platform (40 ft × 8 ft) fitted with wooden cross members allowing fork lift trucks to lift any type of load whether or not fitted with specialised lifting slots.

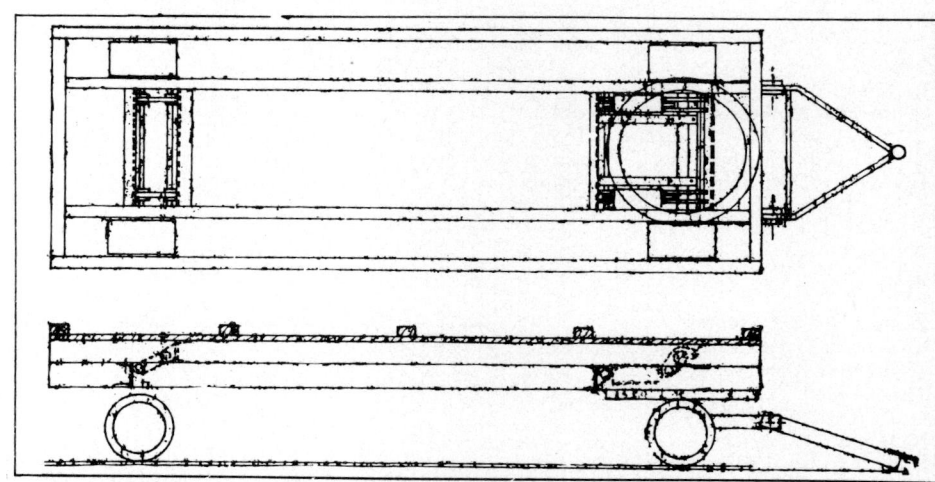

A Tollbridge Trailer with a hydraulic lifting platform

20-ton Hydraulic platform Trailer
Has turntable steering and hand parking brake on front wheels. Operating speed 5 mph. The width of this 20 ft trailer may be varied at users request to fit between concrete supports onto which containers may be rested. This trailer is fitted with hydraulically lifting platform which enables container to be lowered onto plinths.

LE TOURNEAU

R. G. Le Tourneau, Inc
P.O. Box 2307
Longview, Texas 75601, USA
TELEPHONE: 214 753-4411
CABLES: Bobletorno

PRODUCTS:
Straddle Cranes and the 'Side Porter' handling equipment for containers and piggyback trailers.

The Side-Porter Range:
SP70:
Maximum capacity 31,752 kg (70,000 lb)

SP 90:

Maximum capacity 40,823 kg (90,000 lb).

The units are powered with a diesel engine, with DC and AC generators supplying power for the (DC) electric wheels for traction power, eliminating transmission and torque converter, and (AC) for all other operating functions. Two-wheel drive is standard, although four-wheel drive can be supplied. The tongs have an adjustment range of 24 ft, with the ability to move sideways to adjust the lifting centres, from 14 to 24 ft. The unit lifts its maximum capacity on a straight vertical lift.

The Side Porter permits a cycle time of 2 minutes 5 seconds per trailer or container handled. An important feature of the system is that it can lead containers as well as trailers

Le Tourneau model SP-70 side porter.

with an exclusive top and bottom pick capability. In tests, it has unloaded four 8 × 8 × 24 ft containers from a flatcar in five minutes. The unit can stack containers two high on the ground.

Besides the small turning radius (23 ft) and versatility of the tongs, the system has a fine adjustment so that trailers can be easily manoeuvered into the exact positions over the fifth wheel stanchions on flatcars.

Straddle Hoist, SHL 80

Maximum rated capacity 36,288 kg (80,000 lb). To handle containers of 20, 30 and 40 ft nominal length. The cranes feature top and bottom lift capabilities.

The design provides an exclusive torsion beam configuration with combination top or bottom pick and full rotation. These features make it possible to traverse the full distance from one cantilever to the other, since the load may be rotated past the box beam upright structure.

Variations in lifting capacities and in portal height and width are available, and the units are also available with or without the cantilever extension.

Steering is two-wheel automotive, or four-wheel with 90 degree angle of travel.

Safety guards are located at each wheel, and when the guard meets an obstacle the travel brake is applied instantly.

The operator control centre can be in either of the two upright box sections. If desired, dual controls can be provided. Operator visibility is provided in all directions, as the seat and control console swivel so he can face the direction of his work.

For mobility, each electric wheel is a prime mover, with a DC motor and gear unit mounted in the rim. Speed is variable from 0 to 5 mph in forward or reverse. A diesel engine provides power to AC and DC generators that power all functions.

Large, low-profile, wide-base tyres furnish

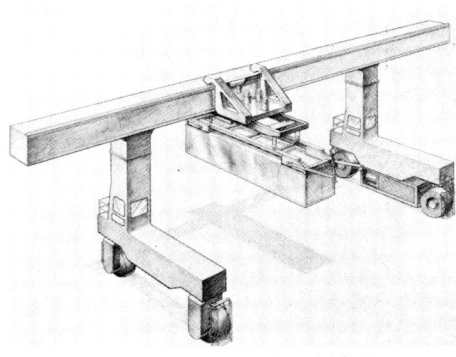

Le Tourneau model SHL-80 Strad-I-hoist.

support for operation over stabilized soil, not necessarily paved.

TOWER CRANES

Tower Cranes Ltd

Cold Blow Lane,
London SE 17
TELEPHONE: 01732 0113
TELEGRAMS: Towercranes Soeast London
CABLES: Towercranes London

DIRECTORS:
W. F. Vonck (Dutch)
W. F. Vonck, jr. (Dutch)
PRODUCTS:
The Keienburg Portal Crane. This has been a specialised development of Karl Keienburg of Essen for the past 40 years. For full details of the products see entry under Keienburg in this section. Also, tower cranes suitable for storage of empty and full containers.

TOWMOTOR

Towmotor Corporation

16100 Euclid Avenue,
Cleveland 44112
USA

UK SALES OFFICE: PO Box 162,
Glasgow, Scotland
TELEPHONE: (216) 451 0900
TELEGRAMS: (UK) Caterpillar Glasgow
TELEX: (UK) 77721

SALES OFFICE (Europe):
Caterpillar Overseas SA,
PO Box 408,
118 Rue du Rhone,
1211 Geneva 3, Switzerland

WORKS: Cleveland, Ohio and Dallas, Oregon, USA

LICENSEE: Brodrene Vestergaard,
Copenhagen, Denmark

AGENCIES ABROAD: World Wide Dealership Organization

DIRECTORS:
Bob Fairbank (*President*)

Towmotor AH-52 Fork Lift Truck with container top-handling attachment. This truck can stack 20 ft ISO containers, weighing up to 20 tons, three high.

PRODUCTS :	Lifting Capacity		Lift Height	Container Size	Operating Speed	
					(Lift loaded)	(Travel)
Top handling attachment for model AH-52 lift truck	21545 kg at 1.24m 47,500 lbs at 49 ins		5.5m 18 ft	6.10m 20 ft	8.4 mpm 27.5 fpm	20.9 kph 13 mph
Side handling attachment for model AH-52 lift truck (empty or partially loaded containers)	21545 kg at 1.22m 47,500 lbs at 48 ins		5.5m 18 ft	6.10m 20 ft	8.4 mpm 27.5 fpm	20.9 kph 13 mph
End handling attachment for models B-20, B-22, and B-25 lift trucks (empty containers)	2358.7 kg at 3.05m 5,200 lbs at 120 ins		3.05m 10 ft	6.10m 20 ft	15.2 mpm 50.0 fpm	34.1 kph 21.3 mph

TRAILMOBILE

Trailmobile Division
Pullman Incorporated,
200 So. Michigan Avenue,
Chicago, Ill. 60604 USA
TELEPHONE: 312 939 1350
TELEGRAMS: 'Trailco' Chicago
PRODUCTS
Container chassis
(See also entry in
Container Manufacturing section)
Six Main Points of Construction:
1. Unitised High tensile steel frame chassis (20 ft and 40 ft).
2. Lightweight suspension (single and tandem axle).
3. All Welded Hi-Tensile Steel Crossmembers and Bumper.
4. Two-Speed, Squareleg Landing Gear distributes load evenly onto main rails and is adaptable to all tractor fifth wheel heights.
5. Corrosion Resistant Wiring is enclosed in metal conduit.
6. Seven-Way Weatherproof Ata Electrical Connector.
Options—gooseneck frame, USASI corner casting, and inboard cam operated locks etc.

35 ft twin-barrelled stainless steel tank container 8,000 gallon capacity, mounted on Trailmobile semi-trailer chassis.

Trailmobile 40-foot Universal Container Chassis

Trailmobile's universal container chassis will carry a tunnel-bottom or flush-bottom container without modification to either container or chassis.

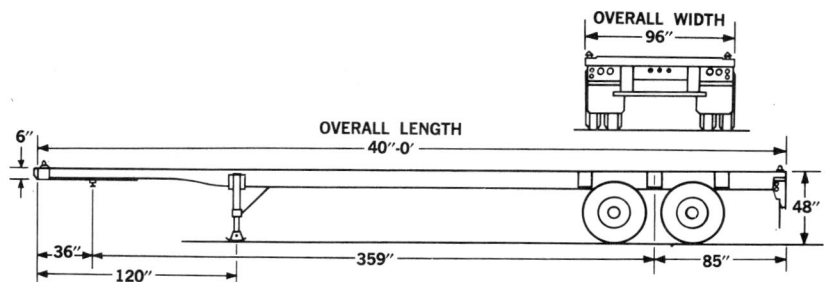

Basic Specifications:

Length, overall	40 ft 0 in (12,19 m)
Frame height, front	53¾ in (1,37 m) at kingpin, 47½ in (1,21 m) coupler height
Frame height, rear	48 in (1,22 m) at centreline of suspension
Width, at front and rear bolsters	95½ in (2,43 m)
Width, at rails	42 in (1,07 m)
Estimated weight	6,135 lbs (2,783 kg)

TRAILOR

Trailor
110 Av. de la République
Paris XI
TELEPHONE: 355 67 00
TELEX: 22 746 F

DIRECTORS:
M. R. More
P. Ripert
P. Jackson
R. Druilhe

PRODUCTS:
All types of container chassis including terminal and telescopic chassis. A speciality is a removable twistlock.

The Trailor range of container chassis:

	20ft	2×20ft	30'ft	35ft (Ht 8ft 6in)	40ft	40ft (Ht 8ft 6in)	Flexi-van	Plate-lage AR
Single axle 20ft skeletal semi trailer — 6050	▨						20'	
Tandem axle 20ft skeletal semi trailer — 6720	▨						20'	
Drop frame for low level loading of a 20ft container — 8880	▨						20'	
20ft and 30ft tandem axle chassis — 9118	▨		▨				20'	✱
Special Sea Land 35ft container chassis — 10880				▨				
Tandem axle 40ft goose-neck chassis for tunnel container — 12235						▨		
Tandem axle skeletal chassis for containers 1×20ft-2×20ft-1×30ft-1×40ft-Flexivan — 12238	▨	▨▨	▨		▨	▨	20' 40'	✱
Telescopic multi-purpose skeletal semi-trailer for container 1×20ft-2×20ft-1×30ft 1×35ft-1×40ft Flexivan. — 12238	▨	▨▨	▨	▨	▨	▨	20' 40'	✱

TREWHELLA

Trewhella Bros (UK) Ltd.
Rolfe Street,
Smethwick,
Warley
Worcs.
TELEPHONE: 021 558 0093
DIRECTORS:
R. G. Horton
M. Graham
G. S. McNab

B. H. Trewhella
W. G. A. Russell
G. W. Tailor
PRODUCTS:
Trewhella empty container transporter units mark 1 and 2 formerly marketed by Vickers Cargo Handling Division. The unit consists of wheels which fasten on to the ISO corner castings of containers allowing the containers to be pushed or towed.

Trispan mobile gantry

TRISPAN

Trispan Handling (Whitchurch) Ltd.
Whitchurch
Hants.
TELEPHONE: 2280
DIRECTORS:
W. R. Watkinson
G. H. Robins
W. Stepien

PRODUCTS:

Trispan mobile gantry.
    5-ton Capacity lifting speed 25 ft/min.
    12-ton Capacity lifting speed 15 ft/min.
    20-ton Capacity lifting speed 15 ft/min.
    Hydraulic or diesel power lift
    Power traction and steering available.

Trewhella empty container transporter unit

TUCHSCHMID

Gebr. Tuchschmid AG Frauenfeld
8500 Frauenfeld,
Bahnhofplatz,
Switzerland
TELEPHONE: 054 72471

PRODUCTS:
    Mocoprek hydraulic container stilts which are fitted to containers and folded during transport. Lift height is 1,700 mm (66·9 in). The hydraulic cylinders are supported by hinged arms which move through 180 degrees. When the stilts are required the arms are extended and the cylinders operated to raise the container. The hinged arms allow a distance of 3,800 mm (149·6 in) between two sets of stilts so that the system can be used with rail as well as road vehicles. Lift capacity is 20 tons.
    Mocopik container lifting frame with hydraulic jacks. This is a mobile unit powered for travel when in the lower position. It can thus be operated by one man. A container is held in place by wire rope fitted with bolts which interlock with ISO corner castings. The unit can be used with road and rail vehicles.

VALMET

Valmet OY
Tampere Works,
PO Box 185, 331000 Tampere 10
Finland
TELEPHONE: 62622
TELEX: 22-112 valle sf
(*See also entry for Yale*)

DIRECTORS:
Lauri Nurmiaho (*Assistant General Manager*)
Ilkka Lapinleimu (*Works Manager*)
Pekka Heikkilä (*Manager, Materials Handling Equipment Dept.*)
PRODUCTS:
    Container 2-high stacking straddle carriers with expandable 20-40 ft spreader, 30 ton capacity. Max. speed loaded 25 km/h. Container handling straddle carriers with spreader or swing shoes from 10 to 30 ton capacity, max. speeds loaded 30-40 km/h. Special straddle carriers for Ro/Ro and other operations from 10 to 30 ton capacity

available. Max speeds loaded 25-40 km/h. Mobile Gantry Cranes with spreader from 25 to 30 ton capacity. Max travel speed 9 km/h.

Fork lift Trucks with 20 ft spreader and sidelift frame. Basic capacity rating 25 ton/ 1,250 mm. Max. speed loaded 30 km/h.

The Top-Lift attachment for container handling is suitable for 20 ft containers weighing up to 20 tons. It has ±150 mm sideshift and ±50 mm tilt. It pivots ±9·5 deg. The attachment is said to be able to pick up a bent container thanks to the free movement of its spindles in the horizontal.

Standard Straddle Carriers

The range of straddle carriers offered by Valmet most of which are suitable for container handling include the 10 ton capacity 200 series, the 13 ton 300 Series, the 18 ton 400 Series, the 23 ton 500 Series, the 30 ton 650 Series and the 50 ton 1,100 Series. Dual control cabs are offered at extra cost on all models. An innovation is a stacking straddle carrier which allows two high stacking (see below). So far the company has not made any units designed to stack containers three high but since the company was a pioneer in the design of straddle carriers there is no doubt that units of the high stacking kind could be produced if required.

Tailor-made Straddle Carriers and Container Vans

The Tampere Works of Valmet Oy, Finland, will be delivering twelve special straddle carriers and two container vans of an entirely new type to Pacific Australian Direct Line. This special equipment will be used for roll-on/roll-off ship-loading and unloading, which will be starting a service on the PAD-line in 1971.

During a 60 day round trip (Australia-USA West Coast/British Columbia) the vessels will call at about twenty different ports and a quick despatch is therefore extremely important. Since all ports do not have all technical requirements, the Transatlantic decided to equip the ships with special carriers for cargo handling. Each ship will have two different straddle carrier models and one container van aboard for handling pulp lumber bundles, steel sheets, tubes and 40 feet containers.

The straddle carriers, which are of 13¼ and 25 ton capacity, have a maximum height of less than 3 metres yet a lifting height of 0·7 metres. Instead of the standard lifting shoes the straddle carrier is equipped with four forks which can be turned 90° inwards to transport loads without a pallet or stickers (strapped lumber etc.). For transport of steel sheets the 25 ton carriers can be equipped with an electromagnetic attachment, which can handle steel sheets bundles up to 18,000 kg (40,000 lb) in weight. Mounting of this attachment requires only 1-2 minutes, due to the snap-on connectors.

Two Container Vans of an Entirely New Type

While 40-feet containers form an important part of the loads to be handled, the Tampere Works also designed a new container van for Pacific Australian Direct Line which achieves an 80-90% cube utilisation of hold space. The container van, with a driving height of only 2,900 mm, can enter practically any place in the vessel and stack containers two high in a headroom only few inches higher than the container van. This new system totally eliminates the need of expensive rolltrailers of any kind.

The container van grips the containers from the top corner castings at both ends. The twist-locks enter the corner castings through the openings at both container ends and not from above as in the case of a top-lift. Although the overall height of the container van is small the lifting height is extremely

The Valmet TD 2512 Fork Lift Truck with automatic container top handling attachment.

The Valmet TD 2512 Forklift

PERFORMANCE:

Lifting capacity	25,000 kg (55,000 lb)
Load centre	1,250 mm (49 in)
Rating from centre of axle	6,125,000 kg/cm (530,000 in/lb)
Driving speed: loaded/unloaded	60/36 km/h (19/22½ mph)
Lifting speed: loaded/unloaded	0·25/0·27 m/s (0·82/0·89 ft/s)
Lowering speed: loaded/unloaded	0·35/0·35 m/s (1·12/1·12 ft/s)
Intersecting aisle width	5,700 mm (18 ft 9 in)
Turning radius	6,350 mm (20 ft 10 in)

DIMENSIONS:

Length without forks	6,800 mm (22 ft 4 in)
Width	3,250 mm (10 ft 8 in)
Ground clearance:	
minimum	300 mm (11¾ in)
at centre	435 mm (17⅛ in)
Weights:	
standard truck without mast	28,500 kg (62,700 lb)
standard truck (A25055)	38,705 kg (85,150 lb)
weight on drive axle (A25055) loaded	59,200 kg (130,240 lb)
weight on steer axle (A25055) loaded	4,505 kg (9,910 lb)
standard carriage	2,450 kg (5,390 lb)
side-shift carriage	3,400 kg (7,480 lb)
Wheel base	5,000 mm (16 ft 6 in)
Wheel track: front/rear	2,761/2,440 mm ((9 ft 1 in/8 in)
Distance from drive axle centre to face of forks (D):	
standard carriage	1,200 mm (47 in)
side-shift carriage	1,240 mm (49 in)
Tyres, front and rear	16.00—25 in/28 ply
Number of tyres, front/rear	4/2
Fork thickness	120 mm (4¾ in)
Fork weight:	
2,200 mm (87 in)	1,000 kg (2,200 lb)
2,500 mm (98½ in)	1,070 kg (2,354 lb)
3,100 mm (122 in)	1,200 kg (2,640 lb)

MASTS:

Type		A25027	A25036	A25055	A25070
Minimum height	A mm/in	3,250/128	3,700/145½	4,650/183	5,400/212½
Height of lift	B mm/in	2,700/106¼	3,600/141¾	5,500/216½	7,000/275½
Maximum height	C mm/in	5,080/200	5,980/235½	7,880/310¼	9,380/369¼
Weight	kg/lb	4,330/9,525	4,630/10,185	5,615/12,350	6,303/13,865

Safety coefficient: 1·4 with standard carriage
1·3 with side-shift carriage

high and it can stack 8 ft × 8 ft 6 in × 40 ft containers two high. The lifting height without increase in overall height of container van is 300 mm (approx. 12 in). The four wheels of the container van can be turned 90° in motion and on spot or locked to any position in between for crab steering of the container van. The capacity of the container van is 30,000 kg (66,000 lb).

Valmet Stacking Straddle Carrier

The "stacking straddle carrier" is designed for harbour handling of 20 ft, 30 ft and 40 ft containers. It can stack two 9 ft high containers.

This model is of low chassis construction, which means it can be driven straight into warehouses with about 5-metre high doors. Most stacking straddle carriers need a 7-metre door-opening. In a low-slung straddle carrier the centre of gravity is low, so the driver has good control on his vehicle. The carrier has hydrodynamic transmission. This power transmission system gives top speed and good gradability.

A "telescopic" chassis low chassis construction possible. Two horizontal hydraulic cylinders handle the actual primary lifting, raising the container into the transport position. Their action is linked to both ends of the top-lift by tracks. The mechanical link-up shafts at the ends assure simultaneous, smooth lifting action.

Four vertical cylinders—one at each corner of the carrier-deal with the lift. They lift the inside of the carrier chassis, supported by needle-bearing rollers, into the stacking position. The cylinder action is also mechanically controlled, with each cylinder travelling identical lifting distances.

The top-lift, hydraulically extendable for lifting 20 ft, 30 ft and 40 ft containers, can be side-shifted to give a easier grip on the container. The grip is handled by automatically turning twistlock spindles.

The power source comprises two Perkins 6,354 diesel engines, one on either side of the straddle carrier. Transmission goes to the straddle carrier rear wheels via an Allison

A Valmet 23 ton container straddle carrier loading a 40 ft container on to a vehicle chassis.

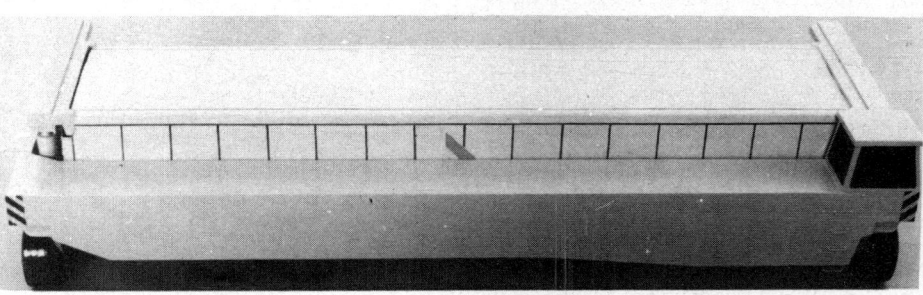

Model of the Valmet C Van

TRT 2220-3 automatic gear system, angle gear and finally a chain. There are two forward gears and two reverse gears.

The four-wheel steering uses the Orbitrol ysstem. Each wheel is double-sprung, with the springs located inside the chassis. There is no need to remove the wheel fork and steering rod when changing the springs. The straddle carrier wheel also has two shock absorbers to stabilize the spring action. The

The gantrycrane and straddle carrier together guarantee an effective handling at the terminals.

tyres are large: 16·0-25 in. Each wheel has air-boosted power brakes. The handbrake is the drum brake of the gear system takeoff shaft.

New Users

In 1971, Valmet Oy made an agreement with the Australian big enterprise The Broken Hill Proprietary Co Ltd for the supply of 14 straddle carriers. The straddle carriers will be delivered to the customer during 1972. These 30 ton straddle carriers will handle steel industry products in harbours and at steel works. Some of them will be stationary on board.

Except to Australia, Valmet exports straddle carriers to the USA, Scandinavia and the rest of Europe.

Valmet stacking straddle carrier

WILD

M. B. Wild & Co. Ltd.
Wharton Street, Nechells, Birmingham
B7 5TS
TELEPHONE: 021-327 2041
TELEGRAMS: Hauling Birmingham
DIRECTORS:
A. A. Marks (*Chairman*)
A. H. Davies (*Managing*)
M. J. Wild (*Tehcnical/Works*)

PRODUCTS:

Portal container crane of 10, 20, 30 and 40 tons capacity. Spans up to 46 m (153 ft). Height of lift up to 30 m (98 ft).

Maximum speeds related to size of crane:
Hoist 18 m/min (60 ft/min)
Cross Traverse 50 m/min (160 ft/min)
Long Travel 61·0 m/min (200 ft/min)
Creep speeds: optional. Slewing: optional.

The main structure is built from high quality steel tube welded together to form standard sections. The steel tubular construction enables a high strength and relatively light structure to be obtained besides improved wind-load characteristics. The units are constructed on specially designed welding jigs and are completely interchangeable.

Hoist Unit

This consists basically of a slipring motor, driving through a high efficiency spur-gear box to a machine grooved steel drum. The load is held securely should there be a power failure. There is a four fall rope system with a 6:1 safety factor.

The creep speed unit is fitted to the hoisting mechanism which operates in a similar way to that used for the bogie drive.

Traverse gear is fitted to the hoist unit to enable the hoist to be traversed along the main beam, the creep speed attachment is also provided to enable precise movements to be obtained.

The hoist unit is also provided with a patented overload preventer unit which comes into effect when the load has exceeded a predetermined value.

Controls

These are in the form of two joystick controllers only, each fitted with automatic spring return to the 'off' position. The first notch on each controller operates the creep speed. On the travelling motions this means that smooth starts can be obtained and wheel spin eliminated. Timers are provided to ensure an automatic sequence of the resistances. All motors are suitably protected electrically and interlocked, the main protection panel with control fuses, etc., is mounted inside the cabin. The hoist control panel being mounted above the cabin.

All contractors and control equipment are selected to give a life of three million operations without contact attention or renewal.

Cabin

This is of the high visibility type fitted with anti-glare toughened glass mounted inside rubber mouldings complete with a fully adjustable seat and escape apparatus.

Bogies

These are of the twin-wheel type, the wheels being cast-steel double flanged, with taper roller bearings. A central jack is built in as an integral part to enable the bogie to be swivelled through 360°. In addition to this, the bogie is flexible in the vertical direction in order to encounter any possible irregularities in the track.

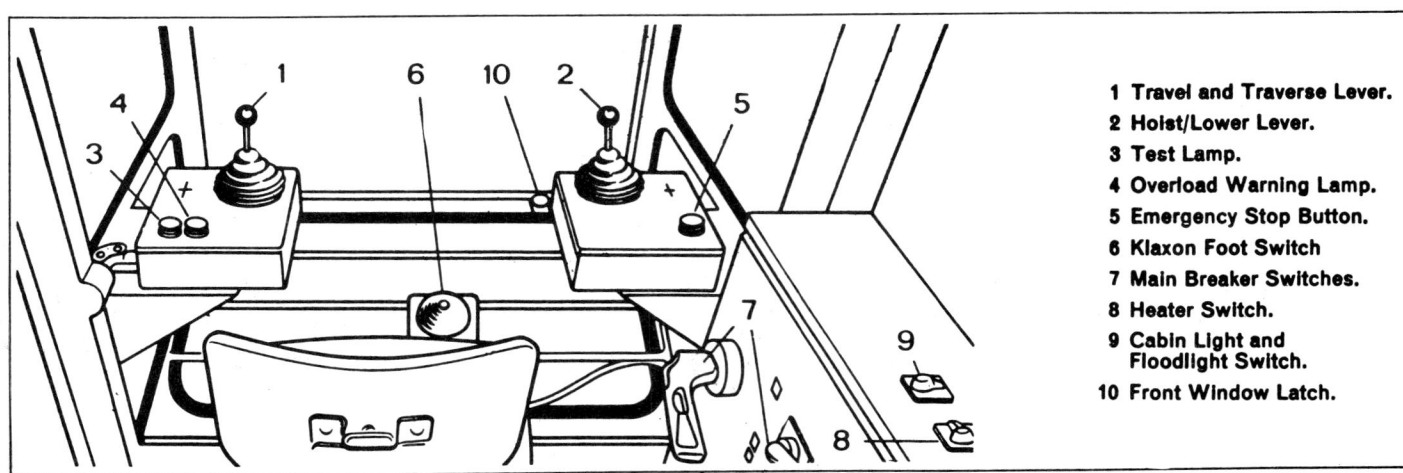

1 Travel and Traverse Lever.
2 Hoist/Lower Lever.
3 Test Lamp.
4 Overload Warning Lamp.
5 Emergency Stop Button.
6 Klaxon Foot Switch
7 Main Breaker Switches.
8 Heater Switch.
9 Cabin Light and Floodlight Switch.
10 Front Window Latch.

Yale Materials Handling Equipment
Wednesfield, Staffordshire, England
TELEPHONE: Willenhall 66955
TELEX: 338133
LONDON OFFICE:
207-211, The Vale, London W3,
TELEPHONE: 01/985/1200
TELEX: 27798
PRODUCTS: Valmet container straddle carriers, container jacks, fork-lift trucks, etc. See Valmet's entry for details.

YALE

The Yale DP180 fork lift truck of 18,000 lb capacity.

York Trailer Co Ltd,
Corby, Northants
TELEPHONE: 05366-3561
TELEX: 34516
CABLES: Yorktra
FACTORY BRANCHES:
Warrington, Glasgow, Cardiff, Northallerton, Rainham Nr Tilbury (Essex), London (Watford), Doncaster, Cannock, Bristol.
OFFICES:
London, Rotterdam, Toronto
DIRECTOR:
F. Davies
PRODUCTS:
Semi-trailers, including skeletals especially designed for the road-transport of containers.

York make trailers to carry all types and makes of ISO containers. There are SK Skeletals for 20, 30 or 40 ft containers, PSK platform container carriers, TSK tipping skeletal carriers and Gooseneck skeletal trailers for tunnel containers.

YORK

York PSK platform skeletal container carrier.

York Trailer

CONTAINER COMPONENTS

COMPONENT MANUFACTURERS

AVON RUBBER

Avon Rubber Company Ltd.,
Industrial Products Division
HEAD OFFICE:
Abbey Mills, Church Street, Bradford-on-Avon, Wiltshire
TELEPHONE: Bradford-on-Avon 2191
TELEGRAMS: Moulton, Bradford-on-Avon
TELEX: 44856
DIRECTOR:
Peter Fisher (*Director and General Manager, Industrial Products Division*)

SALES MANAGER: L. J. Flower.

PRODUCTS:
Flexible Container Door Seals.
Standard extruded sections are available for sealing container door. Non-standard sections also provided and a design service is available for developing improved seals for container manufacturers.

Avon offer a standard range of door seals internationally, and a design service for new seals to all container manufacturers.
Materials include:
Neoprene, Neoprene sponge, Ethylene Propylene and PVC
Twin hardness extrusions
Seals can be supplied in complete frames (moulded corners) or in straight lengths.

BLAIR

J. N. Blair Ltd.
Riverside,
Market Harborough,
Leicestershire
TELEPHONE: 0645 4853
TELEGRAMS: Blairprod, Market Harborough
TELEX: 34529
EUROPEAN SALES:
Blair Products SA,
Boulevard St. Georges 72, 1205 Geneva
Telephone: 43 66 14
Telex: 23308
DIRECTORS:
J. N. Blair, BSc
D. I. R. Blair
J. B. Dawson
I. R. Valentine (*Marketing Manager*)
C. Imhoff (*Sales Manager, Europe*)
OVERSEAS MANUFACTURING LICENCES HELD:
Miner Enterprises Inc. for 'Power Brace' container door fasteners (see below).
PRODUCTS: Container Hardware.
The range of Lloyds approved and tested products includes:

The patented '*Power Brace*' *door gear* with over-centre cam action is weldable forged, cast and pressed low temperature steel with fittings suitable for either bolt-on or weld-on construction, hot dip galvanised to BS.729 Part 1 as standard.
Non-creep, high tensile, corrosion resistant plastic '*Contal*' *bushings* to provide a near frictionless bearing for container door gear, stable down to —40°C.
Heavy-duty X-L hinges in weldable forged steel, properties retained down to —40°C. Hinges are also to individual customer specifications. 'Contal' or stainless steel bushes.
Stainless or mild steel hinge pins.
Heavy duty *tipper gate fasteners* with over-centre action cams in weldable forged steel. Complete assemblies are supplied to customer specifications.
Retractable and removable *twistlocks* of weldable steel plate tube and forged steel.
Nylon *selector pins* of simple operation-rugged design, for maintenance free operation.

'*Enterprise*' *discharge devices* in cast and pressed steel for discharging a wide range of products in bulk from containers as well as railway wagons and road vehicles.
Designs for controlled and un-controlled gravity discharge, vacuum discharge, fluidization, air pressure or electric.
Plastic *meat hooks* for carrying chilled carcass meat in insulated containers. They are corrosion resistant. low friction and lightweight, easily handled when fully loaded and hygienic and steam cleanable.
Corner castings in weldable forged steel. These are Lloyds and ISO approved close tolerance castings for use with 'Twistlock', stacking fittings, corner ties, etc.
Venesta '*Plymax*' *door panels*—25 mm Douglas fir plywood faced with aluminium/steel or steel/steel. Tested panels are available conforming to Department of Health impregnation laws for operation in Australia and New Zealand, to BS.1355 CSA 0121 and all international certificate standards.

BLOXWICH LOCK AND STAMPING

The Bloxwich Lock & Stamping Co. Ltd.
Container Products Division, Victoria Road, Hednesford, Staffs.
REGISTERED OFFICE:
Alexander Works, Bloxwich, Nr. Walsall, Staffs, England
TELEPHONE: 3551
TELEGRAMS: Stampings Bloxwich
TELEX: Chamcom 338212

DIRECTORS:
H. A. Squire (*Managing*)
E. L. S. Sanders (*Deputy Managing*)
G. Wallis (*Executive Sales Director*)
A. E. Lax (*General Manager, Container Division*)

PRODUCTS:
Locking gear, hinges and other ancillary

container fittings.

DESIGN STANDARDS:
ISO Lloyds.

MATERIALS:
Steel. All parts are made from steel guaranteed to withstand temperatures down to minus 40 degrees Centrigrade.

BRITISH OXYGEN

The British Oxygen Company Ltd.
Hammersmith House,
London W6
TELEPHONE: 01 748 2020
TELEX: 22833
'Pelican': the latest BOC non-mechanical liquid nitrogen refrigeration equipment.

Simple to install, it is suitable for use in small vans. Like the Polarstream all that is required is a source of liquid nitrogen when a refill is necessary.

PRODUCTS:
Polarstream non-mechanical liquid nitrogen refrigeration systems for most kinds of

transport operations. The system can be adapted for refrigerated containers where different temperatures are required in different areas of a container, as for example where fresh and frozen foods are transported in one container.

BRITISH STEEL

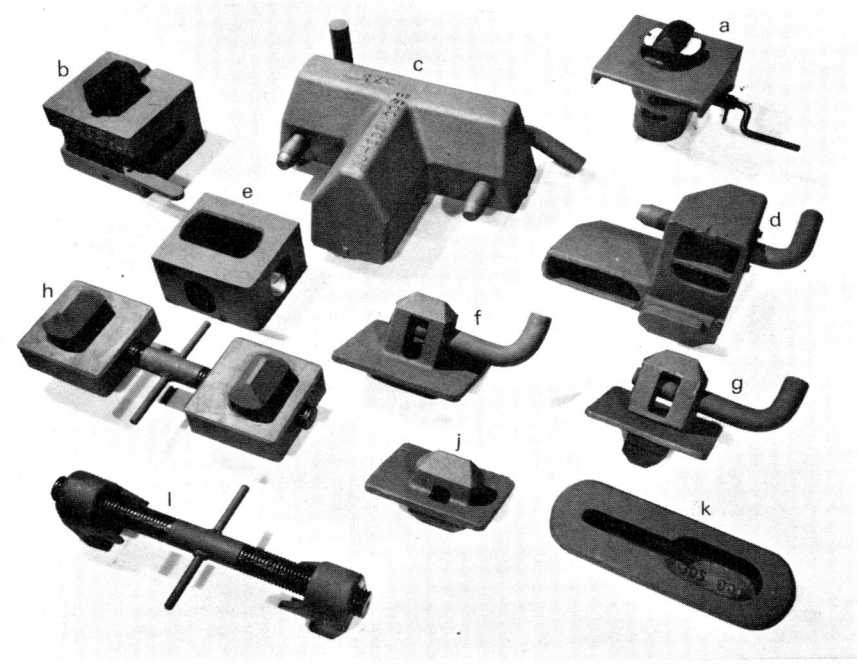

Range of container fittings produced by the River Don and Associated Works, Special Steels Division.

British Steel Corporation
Forges Foundries and Engineering Group
River Don and Associated Works
Sheffield S9 2RZ
England
TELEPHONE: 49071 (STD 0742)
TELEX: 54185

PRODUCTS:

A full range of cast steel components for use with containerisation including road and rail vehicles and marine applications.

Road and Rail Vehicles

Twistlock securing studs are mounted at the outboard end of each outrigger, providing longitudinal and lateral restraint to withstand 'g' forces of acceleration and deceleration. The centre stud affords some gathering during the final lowering operation, this allowing speedy loading. When the container is seated correctly, each twistlock centre stud is rotated through 90° by means of a handle to impose vertical restraint on the container.

Three types of twistlock are available:

1. Fixed Twistlocks—for use on vehicles designed to carry one standard size of container.
2. Removable Twistlocks—where the centre stud can be removed and secured adjacently or stowed. This type is for use when carrying 1 × 40 ft or 2 × 20 ft containers. These can be interconnected to facilitate operation from one side of the vehicle.
3. Retractable Twistlocks—for use on multipurpose full decked trailers. The centre stud may be retracted to provide an unobstructed trailer surface for carrying non-containerised cargo.

Any combination of the above three types is possible for a completely flexible system.

Marine Applications

To accommodate deck stowage of containers, the hatch cover is generally equipped to carry containers over all the available area. Combinations of fittings can be used to provide rigid (for one size of container) or completely flexible (all container sizes within standard) securing systems. The flexible system requires the welding of deck inserts into the hatch cover during manufacture to coincide with the four corner bearings of the container. Securing studs are placed in the inserts and have an angled face to guide the container into position. Also provided is a locking pin which passes through the end aperture of the corner casting and into the stud, its function being to combat vertical forces resulting from tipping moments created when the vessel rolls excessively. This arrangement is guaranteed for single stacked containers.

When stacks are higher, lashing fittings and a combination of stacking cones, stacking adaptors and interbridge connectors are necessary.

British Steel Corporation provides a package deal so that on receipt of a vessel's specification at tender stage, determination and recommendation of all fittings and equipment necessary for safe stowage of containers can be undertaken.

CARGOCAIRE

Cargocaire Ltd.

2 Glebe Road, Huntingdon
TELEPHONE: 51201
TELEX: 32106
TELEGRAMS: Cargocaire Huntingdon

DIRECTORS:
P. L. Grant, BSc, MRINA
J. R. Chappell
Capt. R. E. Baker (*Marine Sales Manager*)

PRODUCTS:
(a) 'Drytainer' Unit. A self-contained dehumidifier for dewpoint control inside containers.

(b) Ship-installed central dehumidification systems for container cells.
The system employs a unique rotary-bed type chemical dehumidifier with continuous reactivation.

CARRIER OVERSEAS CORPORATION

Carrier Overseas Corporation
385 Madison Avenue
New York, N.Y. 10017
USA
TELEPHONE: (212) 759-5000
TELEX: 126250

DIRECTORS:

Americo Silvero (*Vice-President, Export Sales*)

PRODUCTS:

Refrigeration-heating units for containers, trucks and semi-trailers. Air conditioning units for truck cabs. The system used is mechanically operated forced air refrigeration. The range of units extends up to 10,080 K-cal/hr (40,000 BTU/hr) at 17°C (110°F) ambient. Units designed for container refrigeration are electrically driven. All units have 230 volt, A/C, three phase 60 cycle power supplies.

The 69NK Clip-on Refrigeration Unit

The 69NK is a self-contained, one piece, clip-on refrigeration unit ready to operate when externally mounted to the front end of an insulated container. It is designed for quick demounting at dockside prior to shipboard loading of the container. It may be carried attached to the container on railroad flat cars or over-the-road for inland transport service.

A Carrier 5F20 compressor is directly driven by an Onan DJBA, 2 cylinder, diesel engine. A fuel tank having a capacity of 70 US gallons is integral with the unit. Marine finishes and stainless hardware are used to protect the unit from the corrosive effects of salt atmospheres.

The net cooling capacity of the system using Refrigerant 22 is a minimum 7500 Btuh (1891 Kcal/h) at —10°F (—23·3°C) return air to the evaporator and 100°F (37·8°C) ambient air to the condenser. The heating

Carrier 69 NK clip on refrigeration unit

capacity is a minimum 6000 Btuh (1512 Kcal/h). Air discharges from the bottom of the unit at the container's floor level. It returns at the top of the unit having first provided an envelope of refrigerated air around the frozen cargo in the container.

Thermostatic capacity control is employed using a simple hot gas bypass system. Evaporator coil defrost is automatic.

The 69NK is equipped with fork lift pockets for positioning on the container. It is retained at only four mounting locations with quick disconnect devices. It weighs 2,400 lbs (1,089 kg) and is a nominal 22 inches (559 mm) in depth.

COOLCHAIN

Cool-Chain Inc.
Division of Frigitemp Corporation
7445 Girard Ave.,
PO Box 226, La Jolla,
California 92037
TELEPHONE: 714-459-8293
TELEX: Rathco
DIRECTORS:
Eric Rath (*President*)
John A. Batcher (*Vice President, Marketing*)
Mel Silver (*Executive Vice President*)
PRODUCTION:
Production only began in 1970, no figures yet available.

PRODUCTS:
Climate control and refrigeration units for

containers. Claimed to be the only system which is designed to ship fresh fruit, vegetable and meat over long distances as well as frozen foods. The Cooltainer transport refrigeration system has the following general specification.

Dual compressors, dual condensers and other system components—for in-transit back-up and reserve capacity.

Two 3 hp sealed condensing units. Total CFM 6,000.

Separate evaporator coils for each condensing unit.

Condensing units are all copper type, and treated for Marine use.

Oversize evaporator coil means low product/coil temperature differential which helps prevent dehydration.

Easy access for repair and service.

Precooling is possible at 34,000 BTU per hour at 1·7°C (35°F).

Power requirements: 220/60/3, 30 amperes. The aim of the system is to provide precise critical control of all environmental elements needed to protect perishables. It drives moist air under pressure to the centre of the load, where heat build up is greatest. A constant relative humidity of between 85% and 90% is thus maintained.

DAIKIN

Daikin Kogyo Co. Ltd.
Fuji Building, 5 Yaesu 2-Chome,
Chuo-Ku, Tokyo,
Japan
TELEPHONE: 272-3211
TELEGRAMS: TKYDAIKINOKAY
TELEX: 222-2839
DIRECTORS:
Chuichiro Tamura

PRODUCTS:
Air conditioning and refrigerating equipment. The company's wide range of such products includes marine type refrigeration

equipment for containers suitable for transport by land and sea. The equipment is suitable for 20 ft and 40 ft containers. The heat gain for 20 ft units is 10,700 BTU/hr at —18°C (+35°C) ambient temperature. For 40 ft units it is 16,900 BTU/hr at the same temperatures. All pumps are electric powered.

PRODUCTION:
In 1968 Daikin produced 200 units for container use. In 1969 that figure grew to 300. It became 500 in 1970.

Container fitted with Daikin refrigeration unit.

Standard specifications of Daikin Container Refrigeration Units

Model	LK501D	LK801D
Type	Dual voltage one unit type, air/water cooled	Dual voltage one unit type, air/water cooled
Storage temperature setting limit	—28°∅+26°C	—28°∅+26°C
Casing	Anti-corrosive aluminium	Anti-corrosive aluminium
Power source	3 phase 440V 60 Hz, 415V, 380V 50 Hz	3 phase 200V 50/60 Hz, 220V 60 Hz 3 phase 440V 60 Hz, 415V, 380V 50 Hz
Refrigeration capacity Kcal/hr	2,700	4,250
Air volume Indoor side m³/min Outdoor side m³/min	60 50	90 75
Compressor Type Model Cia. mm × stroke mm × cyl number Motor rating output Kw	Semi-hermetic type 2HC 58LA-R 58 × 60 × 2 3·75	Semi-hermetic type 8 HC 58LA-R 58 × 60 × 3 5·5
Fan Type Model Motor rating output Kw Number	Propeller type P 250 0·2 (2p. Single phase 200V 50/60 Hz, 220V 60 Hz) Single phase 440V 60 Hz 415V, 380V, 50 Hz 4 (Each 2 for indoor and outdoor sides)	Propeller type P 250 0·2 (Single phase 200V 50/60 Hz, 220V 60 Hz, Single phase 440V 60 Hz, 415V, 380V 50 Hz) 6 (Each 3 for indoor and outdoor sides)
Condenser Air cooled condenser Water cooled condenser	Cross fin coil (Copper tubes and copper fins) Horizontal shell and finnished tube type, CH 1705	Cross fin coil (Copper tubes and copper fins) Horizontal shell and finned tube type CH1705
Cooler	Cross fin coil (Copper tubes, aluminium fins)	Cross fin coil (Copper tubes, aluminium fins)

Standard specifications of Daikin Container Refrigeration Units

Electric heater		
Both for heating and dehumidifying	650W × 6 pcs	1000W × 6 pcs
For drain pan	250W × 2 pcs	250W × 2 pcs
For drain piping	80W × 2 pcs	80W × 2 pcs
Refrigerant control		
Switching method from air cooled to water cooled and vice versa	Expansion valve Condenser fan starts and stops automatically due to cooling water pressure	Expansion valve Condenser fan starts and stops automatically due to cooling water pressure
Defrosting		
On	When detecting cooler pressure difference	When detecting cooler pressure difference
Off	When detecting cooler temperature	When detecting cooler temperature
Water piping		
Cooling water inlet	1B 1 way Male quick joint	1B 1 way Male quick joint
Cooling water outlet	1B 2 way Female quick joint	1B 1 way Female quick joint
Drain piping	50ø O.D.	50ø O.D.
Accessories for cold districts operation	Crank case heater condensing press regulating system at air cooled operation (Automatic condenser fan cut system)	Crank case heater condensing press regulating system at air cooled operation (Automatic condenser fan cut system)
Cooling water volume l/min	26·5 (Max water temp. 36°C) Flow volume is regulated by water regulating valve due to condensing temperature	40 (Max water temp. 36°C) Flow volume is regulated by water regulating valve due to condensing temperature.
Protection devices	No fuse breaker, Over-current relay, Motor protection thermostat, Dual pressure switch, Oil pressure protection switch, Fuse metal, Over-heat protection	No fuse breaker, Over-current relay, Motor protection thermostat, Dual pressure switch, Oil pressure protection switch, Fuse metal, Over-heat protection
Refrigerant	R-12	R-12
Lubricant	SUNISO 3GS-D1	SUNISO 3GS-D1
Designed weight		
Total weight	580 kg	780 kg
Parts for work on the spot kg	Approx. 5	Approx. 5
Power transformer	—	—

Note: Refrigeration capacity and air volume are based on the following conditions. Storage temp. —18°C

Power source 3 phase 200V, 60Hz Ambient temperature during the air cooled operation is 35°C.

Water temperature and water volume during the water cooled operation are 36°C and 26·5 (40) l/min respectively.

ENSECOTE

Ensecote Ltd.
Thorncliffe, Sheffield, S30 4YP

TELEPHONE: Ecclesfield 3171
TELEX: 54-220

DIRECTORS:
A. H. Kynaston (*Chairman*)
A. Cunningham

PRODUCTS:
Special lining units for the transport of hazardous and dutiable cargo.

MAIN USERS:
Birt Potter Westray, George Gibson & Co.

FRIGOR

Frigor Køleanlaeg
Tage W. Nielsen A/S,
Holstebrovej,
DK-8800 Viborg
Denmark

TELEPHONE: (06) 623900
TELEGRAMS: Frigor Viborg
TELEX: 6 62 09
DIRECTORS:
Tage W. Nei'lsen
C. Sønderskov
K. J. Jensen
F. S. Hoffmann (*Manager, Container Dept.*)
PRODUCTS:
Clip-on refrigeration units.

Clip-on Refrigeration Units
These have been specially developed to meet the container transport requirements of all perishable foodstuff from —25°C (—11°F) through to +13°C (+55°F).

The system is combined electrical and diesel-electrical in operation, designed for 3 × 380 V AC, 50 cycles or 3 × 440 V, 60 cycles. Thus the unit is equipped with its own power plant, but can also operate entirely electrically by connection to the mains.

To control the BTU/hs output of the system a constant crankcase pressure regulator valve is utilised. This valve limits the output by high suction temperatures and secures that the difference of temperature is always correct.

For carriage of fruit, there is a fresh air intake provided with a sampling test cock fitted in the air-return for checking of CO_2 contents.

The units are equipped with special devices for joining them to the corner fittings of the container. Mounting and dismounting is a matter of a few minutes. Flexible gaskets ensure a leak-tight joint between the system and the container inlet/outlet connection apertures.

The steel framing and all steel components are protected against corrosion for marine use. All covers are of seawater resistant aluminium or stainless steel. All electrical equipment under water tight covers.

The system is designed to withstand a dynamic loading of 2 "G's" in all directions and operate at a permanent list of 20° and continue to operate for 13 seconds during a roll of 30° from vertical.

GALT

Galt Equipment Ltd.,
47 Marie Victorin Blvd.,
Candiac, Montreal,
Canada
TELEPHONE: (514) 659-9107

TELEGRAMS: Springer Montreal
DIRECTORS:
J. C. Springer (*President*)
J. K. Foessl (*Executive Vice-President, General Manager*)
M. Beaudet
PRODUCTION:
Units fitted in 1971—262.
In 1972—300 (forecast).

PRODUCT:

Clip-on refrigeration equipment.
Container cooler cartridges.
Container heater cartridges.

Heater and Cooler Cartridges

Containers are semi-insulated to have a heat loss or gain of 100 to 200 B.T.U./hr and have a built in receptacle to receive cartridge.

Both heater and cooler cartridges and future dehumidifier or venting unit are all of the same size and thus interchangeable.

Average total time to extract cartridge from outbound container and re-insert it into inbound is approximately 2½ minutes.

Most movement of semi perishable-or protected cargo not requiring heating or cooling at sea, cartridges are pulled from outbound container and slipped in inbound, thus a ratio of one cartridge for 3 containers will provide a protected cargo movement.

The cube loss inside the container is approximately 45 cubic feet or less than 5%. This is less than space generally lost in dry freight containers because of high density of most cargoes.

HOLT WILLIAMS AND CO LTD

Holt Williams & Co. Ltd.
Woods Lane,
Cradley Heath,
Warley,
Worcs.
TELEPHONE: Cradley Heath 60611
TELEGRAMS: Holt Williams, Cradley Heath
TELEX: 338916
DIRECTORS:
J. I. Bills
J. R. Williams
M. Fall
PRODUCTS:

ISO freight container locating and restraining equipment.

Retractable container locating and restraining device

This retractable container locating and restraining device, manufactured from B.S. 592 Grade 'A' mild steel casting, will help container operators to eliminate accidents that occur when containers are poorly located and carelessly handled. This device eliminates any chance of damage on impact with the container as it retracts should the unit be left in the locked position. It also eliminates the need for deck lashings because of its positive locking action. It can be welded to chassis members with mild steel welding rods. Fitted at strategic positions on the trailer it allows the operator to carry any length of freight container without having to dismantle and stow loose parts.

The device is supplied in left and right hand actions, ensuring that the operating lever is always neatly stowed away when the device is in the fully locked position

1. Holt Williams retractable container locating and restraining device in the open locked position when the unit is ready to accept a container. Position of the lever gives warning that the pin is still unlocked.
2. In the locked position with the lever stowed inboard. The container is now secure.
3. The unit in the locked and retracted position. The pin would naturally return to this position should it suffer any impact while in position 2.

during transportation. Manufactured from the highest quality steels, electronically tested for weakness to ensure maximum strength and durability, all parts on the unit are fully interchangeable with replacement mechanisms easily obtainable.

Locating and restraining device

This non-retractable locating and restraining device provides a positive locking action by means of the sturdy locking locating pin and a visual check by the locking lever that the pin is actually locked into the container corner unit. The unit is supplied in left and right hand actions to ensure that it is always neatly stowed away when the container is in the fully locked position during transportation.

Twistlocks—double locking stacking adaptor HW-1090

This unit has been developed to provide positive location and locking of ISO containers during vertical stacking operations inboard ship or free standing on quayside. This device ensures maximum safety during these operations. The Holtite Double locking adaptor has no loose parts and the

operating lever with positive push pull action gives visual indication when locked or unlocked.

Container stacking adaptors

Holtite manufacture two types of container stacking adaptors. The first, the single stacking adaptor, is designed for the stacking of containers at deck, quay or floor level whilst the other, the double stacking adaptor, enables containers to be stacked one on top of the other whilst at quay, deck, or floor level.

ISO Freight Liner container locating pin

Designed specifically for use on the new rail freight liners this locating pin ensures positive and easy location during loading which is invaluable when used in conjunction with the Holtite retractable container locating and restraining device.

ISO Freight container (corner unit)

This corner unit is manufactured and conforms to the latest international standards and can be used in conjunction with all standard locating, lifting and restraining devices, including the Holtite retractable locating and restraining device.

LUKE

Luke Systems
A division of K. G. Luke Group Industries Ltd.

PO Box 64, Mitcham, 3132
Victoria, Australia
PO Box No. 64
TELEPHONE: 874 0333
TELEX: KGLUKE AA 31704
DIRECTORS:
John S. Bellamy (Sales Supervisor)
PRODUCTS:

Container refrigeration systems. Features include all-electric, forced convection a temperature range —20°C (—5°F) to 12·8°C (55°F) and Lloyds approved design. The equipment is entirely self-contained.

"Packaged", integral and "Clip-on" container refrigeration systems. Also "packaged" truck refrigeration systems. All container models now use "Air flow floor" methods of air distribution resulting in improved conditions.

Luke Series 1220

All electric, forced convection, the Luke Series 1200 Clip-On system is designed for 380/440 volt, 50 cycle, 3 phase power supplies. Operating range is —5°F to +55°F at 37·8°C (100°F) ambient. As an alternative for 60 cycle power supplies, the Series 1220

A group of containers some of which fitted with Luke clip-on refrigeration systems. Note how the containers with clip-ons can be stacked in the same way as those fitted with integrals.

Model 120 system is available at a slight extra cost, but otherwise the specification is as for the Series 1220.

Controls are fully automatic, all electric, with pilot lights indicating the actual phase of operation at all times. Circuitry is protected by the provision of fail-safe devices. A circular chart recorder is fitted as standard.

To assist in the control of CO_2 build-up within the container due to the heat of respiration developed when fresh fruit or vegetables are being carried, an air intake ability is provided, together with a sampling test cock in the return air line to permit the use of a portable CO_2 indicator.

A constant crankcase pressure regulating valve is utilised to control the BTU/hr output of the system for transport of foodstuffs at container temperatures over $6.7°C$ ($+20°F$) and up to $10°C$ ($50°F$). The system is completely self-contained with all components being fully protected against saltwater and atmospheric corrosion.

A further major feature is that the system is designed to permit operation in conditions of permanent list of 20° off the vertical and to continue to operate for 13 seconds during a roll of 30° either side of the vertical. Logs kept by operators show operation and maintenance costs of up to 50% less over a 12 month period than with any other similar system available.

Luke Clip-on container refrigeration system attached to a 20 ft ISO container. The system is now known as the Luke series 1220, Model 100.

Luke Series 2000 Integral Systems

These are of similar specification and all use the "Air flow floor" method of air distribution.

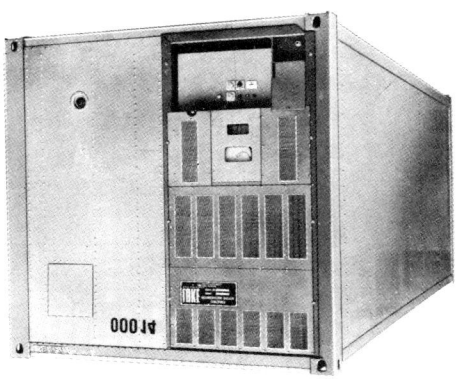

A Luke series 2000 all electric, forced convection packaged 'integral' container refrigeration system, shown installed in a typical ISO 20 ft container. Air distribution follows the well proven 'Air flow floor' system.

A Luke series 1220 all electric forced convection 'packaged' container refrigeration system —clip on type. It is designed to be readily attached to the corner fittings of insulated ISO containers, yet can still permit handling of the whole unit in the usual way by cranes or mobile equipment.

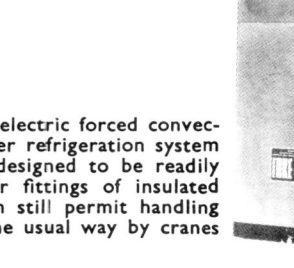

MET-L-WOOD

Met-L-Wood Corporation
6755 W. 65th Street
Chicago, Illinois 60638
USA
Telephone: 312/585-7575
Sales Manager:
D. Otto Williamson

PRODUCTION:

In 1970, ten thousand containers using Met-L-Wood products were made.

PRODUCT:

Metal bonded to plywood and other structural laminates including 'Sea-Lok' (R)

container doors. The latter have hermetically sealed panels and provide positive water seal for container door openings. Met-L-Wood laminate from which the doors are made, consists of a core of plywood with metal facings—steel or aluminium—bonded together by a special process.

MUNK

Munk Industria AB
Fredsgatan 18
703 62 Orebro
Sweden
Telephone: 019-12 47 20
Telegrams: munkab

TELEX: 73 367

PRODUCTS:

Munk-Essem aluminium corner fittings. designed in accordance with ISO and other standards. The following mechanical properties are guaranteed:
Yield strength: 261 p/mm² (37,000 psi)
Tensile strength 31 kp/mm² (44,000 psi)
Elongation 11%
All openings are machined in order to satisfy the close tolerances stipulated.

PARTLOW

The Partlow Corporation
New Hartford, New York 13413
Telephone: (315) 797-2222

DIRECTORS:
H. W. Partlow, Jr., (*President and General Manager*)

Wayne A. McGrew, (*Executive vice-President*)
Lawrence C. Curtis (*Sales Manager*)

PRODUCTS:

Temperature controllers for refrigerated transport—rail, truck, container, marine—which are dominant in the world today—i.e. virtually 100% of US, Canadian rail carriers; most of US long-haul trucking; most of US marine containership, along with Australian, Far East, West German, etc.

There are approximately 60,000 temperature controllers in service throughout the world today, some of which originated 15 years ago.

The instruments derive their basic simplicity and efficiency from the unique 'Piston-Pak' (US Patent No. 3,103,818) mercury-filled thermal element, an integral part of every Partlow temperature controller.

The Non-Indicating Model ZCQA

Designed to deliver a snap-acting pneumatic signal to provide on-off liquid valve operation in a nitrogen refrigeration system.

Operation—The control mechanism, actuated by the temperature-responsive thermal element, opens or closes a small pilot valve to the pneumatic relay. When the thermal element reflects temperatures below control set temperature, the pilot valve opens, bleeding pressure from under a relay diaphragm. This causes the relay to relieve gas pressure to the liquid N_2 valve dome and permits it to close.

On temperature rise above set point, the pilot valve closes, pressurising the gas line to the liquid valve dome and opening it. The relay is so constructed that its valves snap either full open of closed in response to the pilot valve signal, with no intermediate position possible.

The control has been made a standard for the Linde Polarstream nitrogen refrigeration system.

Series DWC Recording Version

The recording version of the indicating Series DWC incorporates up to three snap-acting switches to provide regulation of three electrical circuits on a rise or fall of temperature.

Operation—The control is set at desired temperature by turning a knob located inside the hinged cover. This moves a red set pointer across the calibrated chart and simultaneously positions the control switches in proper relation to the actuating mechanism.

Standard range: —30°C to +25°C (—20° to +80°F), with protection to 170°F.

Temperature is recorded on an 8-inch chart. Either pen and ink or a stylus and pressure-sensitive paper marking system is available. All standard rotations to 31-day available. Chart drives are spring, electric or battery-powered.

Thin-line Recorder—To accommodate increasing demands for smaller components in marine container refrigeration units, a two-switch modification of the Model RDWC has been developed. Designated the Model RLW, the control is only 121 mm (4¾ in) deep (compared to 169 mm (6¼ in) for the three-switch control).

Non-Freezing Throttling valve

The company's development of a non-freezing throttling valve for regulating the flow of liquid nitrogen in transport ended the fumbling trial and error approach. Further developments have produced controllers for completely shutting-off the flow of gas as an alternative to throttling.

The Model 15 liquid nitrogen valve was designed to respond to a pneumatic signal to throttle the supply of liquid nitrogen in transport refrigeration applications. Its original design and construction precludes freezing under the low-temperature conditions produced by the cryogenic liquid it throttles.

Pneumatic signal pressure is 10 psi max. Valve starts to open at 5 to 5¼ psi; is fully open at 6 to 6½ psi, and is fully closed at 4½ psi. Maximum liquid pressure is 80 psi.

Operation: The Model 15 valve is used in conjunction with a Partlow pneumatic temperature controller. Gaseous nitrogen, drawn from the top of the liquid nitrogen tank, is piped through the pneumatic controller to the Model 15 valve. It provides the operating power to position the valve, providing a controlled flow of liquid nitrogen in direct relationship to the thermal requirements of the equipment.

The valve is completely compatible with the Partlow LFA pneumatic indicating temperature controller.

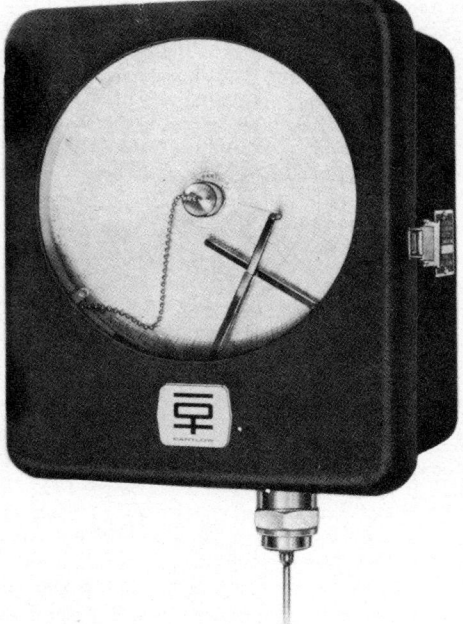

One of the RDW Series Partlow control units.

Model 15—Pneumatically-operated Liquid Nitrogen Valve.

Model ZCQA Partlow non indicating pneumatic on-off control for nitrogen refrigeration.

PETTER

Petters Ltd.

Hamble, Southampton, SO3 5NJ, England
TELEPHONE: Hamble 2061
TELEGRAMS: Petter Hamble Telex
TELEX: 47626
Types Petter models KL SG and PDL 55 SG.
DIRECTORS:
R. G. M. Cawson (*Director & General Manager Petters Ltd., Hamble*)
H. R. Priestley (*General Sales Manager, refrigeration*)

PRODUCTS:
Transport and sea-going refrigeration equipment.

Mechanically operated refrigeration equipment for sea going containers. The all electric, extra slim, PS and PSL Petter refrigeration units are specifically designed for cooling or heating cargo areas in 20 ft insulated containers. Petter KL Medium/heavy duty and PDL heavy duty sea-going units are all driven by power from the ship's electrical system and some models are fitted with petrol or diesel engines · · ·

A PS 245 sea-going refrigeration unit manufactured by Petters Ltd.

Model	Engine Drive	Electric Drive A.C.	Electric Drive D.C.	Refrigeration	Heating
PS240		X		X	
PS245		X		X	X
PSL5-45		X		X	X
KL20 SG-AC	X	X		X	
KL40 SG-AC		X		X	
KL45 SG-AC		X		X	X
KL55 SG-AC	X	X		X	X
KL20 SG-DC	X		X	X	
KL40 SG-DC			X	X	
KL45 SG-DC			X	X	X
KL20 SG-DC/AC	X	X	X	X	
PDL55 SG-AC	X	X		X	X

Petter Model PDL 55 SG-AC refrigeration unit for sea-going containers.

independent operation on land. Petter units are designed to withstand the most arduous conditions of service at sea and comply with the requirements of Lloyd's Register of Shipping.

Nominal Refrigeration Capacities
PS Series (Electrical supply-60 H²)
7,000 Btu/h at 0°F box temperature and 100°F ambient.
1,800 Kcal/h at —20°C box temperature and 30°C ambient.
PSL (Electrical supply-60 Hz)
10,500 Btu/h at 0°F box temperature and 100°F ambient.
2,650 Kcal/h at —18°C box temperature and 38°C ambient.
KLSG (Ergine drive)
8,000 Btu/h at 0°F box temperature and 100°F ambient.
2,100 Kcal/h at —20°C box temperature and 30°C ambient.
PDL55SGAC (Engine Drive)
18,600 Btu/h at 0°F box temperature and 100°F ambient.
4,400 Kcal/h at —20°C box temperature and 30°C ambient.

P.V.C. PRODUCTS

PVC Products (Ireland) Ltd.
Dundalk,
Ireland (Republic)
TELEPHONE: 5000

DIRECTOR:
H. P. O'Neil (*Managing*)
PRODUCTS:
PVC nylon container covers.

THERMO KING

Thermo King Corporation
314 West 90th Street,
Minneapolis,
Minnesota 55420
TELEPHONE: 881 2601
TELEX: 910-576-2822

PRODUCTS:
Refrigeration, heating units and generator sets for containers. Available models are as follows:

SROL 50-SG
One piece, self-contained unit equipped with its own engine and standby electric motor. The evaporator section extends into the container and the unit is fastened with six bolts. Installation or removal can be done without entering the container. Cooling or heating is thermostatically controlled. The aluminium frame is of special design to withstand the stress of road operation. Seagoing specifications have been applied in the design of this unit.
CAPACITY:
System net cooling capacity at 100°F (37·8°C) ambient.

Return Air to Evaporator	btu/hr (Kcal/h)	440V Amp. Draw
Electric Operation:		
0°F (—17·8°C)	16,000 (4,032)	17·5
35°F (1·7°C)	32,000 (8,064)	19·5
Engine Operation:		
0°F	15,000 (3,780)	
35°F	29,500 (7,433)	

System net heating capacity:
10,500 Btu/hr (2,646 kcal/hr)

Air flow:
Condenser fan, 4,350 CFM
Evaporator fan, 2,900 CFM

SL 50-45
All electric, two piece unit designed for sea-going containers. It mounts flush with the front face of the container. It requires a suitable outside source of electric power. The condensing section takes only 12 inches of the box depth. The evaporator section is mounted inside the container alongside the condensing unit, and is only 12 inches deep. There is thermostatic control of heating or cooling operations. The standard unit has an air cooled condenser for above deck operation. Water cooled condenser for below deck operation is optional at extra cost, or a unit is available with both types of condensers. Water pressure to water cooled condenser automatically turns off the air cooled condenser fans.
CAPACITY:
System net cooling capacity at 100°F (37·8°C) ambient.

Return Air to Evaporator	btu/hr (Kcal/h)	220V Amp. draw
0°F (—17·8°C)	10,500 (2,646)	16·5
35°F (1·7°C)	21,000 (5,292)	19

Condenser fan air flow: 1,800 CFM
Evaporator fan air flow: 1,600 CFM

EL 75-45
All electric, one piece unit designed to fit flush in the end of the container. The unit completely fills the end space but is only 12⅝″ deep. It mounts on the recessed, insulated front wall, and is readily demount-
able. A suitable external electric power source is required for this high capacity heating and cooling unit. In all aspects, the EL 75-45 is designed for container operations on land or aboard ship.
CAPACITY:
System net cooling capacity at 100°F (37·8°C) ambient.

Return air to evaporator	btu/hr (Kcal/h)
0°F (—17·8°C)	17,000 (4,284)
55°F (1·7°C)	32,000 (8,064)

System heating capacity, 30,000 Btu/hr (7,560 Kcal/h)

NCE 50-45 and NCE 75-45
All electric, one piece units. The evaporator extends into the container through an opening in the front wall. The front of the unit is flush with the front of the container. A separate control box is mounted next to the unit.
External electric power source is required. This may be a Thermo King GS1250DN generator mounted under the unit or a GS1250DU mounted under the trailer chassis. There should be a dockside or shipboard power source.
CAPACITY:
System net cooling capacity at 100°F (37·8°C) ambient.
Model NCE 50-45

Return air to evaporator	btu/hr (Kcal/h)	220 V. Amp. draw
0°F (—17·8°C)	12,000 (3,024)	17 max.
35°F (1·7°C)	25,600 (6,451)	21 max.

Model NCE 75-45

	btu/hr (Kcal/h)	
0°F (—17·8°C)	19,000 (4,788)	22 max.
35°F (1·7°C)	36,500 (9,198)	26 max.

System net heating capacity 13,800 (3,450)
Condenser air flow:
NCE50-45 3,200 CFM
NCE75-45 3,500 CFM
Evaporator fan air flow:
NCE50-45 1,860 CFM
NCE75-45 2,250 CFM

NWD 50-SG

A large capacity unit powered by diesel engine and standby electric motor. It is one piece, self-contained, factory tested and ready to operate. The evaporator section fits into opening in front of the container, and the unit fastens with six bolts. The corrosion resistant aluminium frame is painted with weatherproof enamel. After initial start, the engine operates continuously, maintaining temperature automatically. The unit operates at "high speed cool" until thermostat setting is reached, then at "low speed cool" until more refrigeration is called for. If outside temperature falls below thermostat setting, the unit operates at "low speed heat" or at "high speed heat" as required.

CAPACITY:
System net cooling capacity at 100°F (37·8°C) ambient.

Van der Giessen-De Noord N.V.
Alblasserdam,
Holland
TELEPHONE: 01859 2844 TELEX: 23629

Return air to evaporator	btu/hr (Kcal/h)
0°F (—17·8°C)	18,500 (4,662)
35°F (1·7°C)	36,500 (9,198)

CWE 50-45 and CWE 75-45

A one piece, all electric, front mount unit. The front of the unit is flush with the front of the container. The condensing section and evaporator section are side by side. The condensing section contains the motor-compressor, condensor coil, fan and controls. The insulated evaporator section contains the evaporator coil, fan, heat exchanger, expansion valve, electric heaters for defrosting and heating operations.

An external electric power source is required. This may be dockside or shipboard power; or a generator mounted under the unit.

CAPACITY:
System net cooling capacity at 100°F (37·8°C) ambient.

Model CWE50-45

Return air to evaporator	btu/hr (Kcal/h)	220V Amp. draw
0°F (—17·8°C)	10,000 (2,520)	18
35°F (1·7°C)	19,000 (4,788)	21

Model CWE75-45

Return air to evaporator	btu/hr (Kcal/h)	220V Amp. draw
0°F (—17·8°C)	17,000 (4,284)	20
35°F (1·7°C)	32,000 (8,064)	23

Condenser fan air flow:
CWE50-45 2,000 CFM
CWE75-45 4,500 CFM
Evaporator fan air flow:
CWE50-45 1,600 CFM
CWE75-45 2.600 CFM

CGS 1250-DU and CGS 1250-DN Generator Sets

Custom designed 15 KW diesel generators, to supply current for Thermo King electric powered refrigeration units. The generator units include engines, generators, battery charging alternators, control boxes and gauges. The units are available for 220V or 440V, 3 phase, 60 cycle operation in sea-going or standard versions.

Model CGS1250DU: Mounts under a trailer chassis. There is a welded steel frame with aluminium doors. The radiator guard is at the forward end. The 75 gallon fuel tank is fastened to the unit frame.

Model CGS1250DN is designed for mounting on the container under the Thermo King refrigeration unit. A special 85 gallon fuel tank is available to support the generator set. There is a welded aluminium frame and aluminium doors.

VAN DER GIESSEN

DIRECTORS:
J. U. Smit
P. J. van der Giessen

PRODUCTS:
Licence held from Flexo Plywood, London for the production of container panels for 20 ft, 30 ft and 40 ft containers.

WESTINGHOUSE

Westinghouse Electric International Co.
200 Park Avenue, New York, NY 10017, USA
TELEPHONE: (212) 692 3224
TELEX: 224719/420569
PRODUCTS:
Thermo King mechanical refrigeration units for containers, trucks and trailers.

The unit is a self-contained nose (or front) mounted refrigeration plant complete with its own power pack. Normally electrically powered the unit comprises automatic cool/heat/defrost. Units are manufactured with capacities suitable for 20 ft up to 40 ft containers and units may be powered from ship or dock electricity supply. 220 V, 380 V, 440 V 3-phase, 50 or 60 cycle.

Thermo-King Power Pack, GS 1250D Undermount.
Fully automatic diesel engine powered generator set that supplies current for the operation of an electric powered refrigeration unit. It is mounted underneath the trailer chassis and contains all the necessary equipment to produce an ample supply of electric energy.
Inside the frame is the engine, generator, batteries, battery charging alternator, control box, and gauges. The fuel tank is integrally mounted on the unit frame.

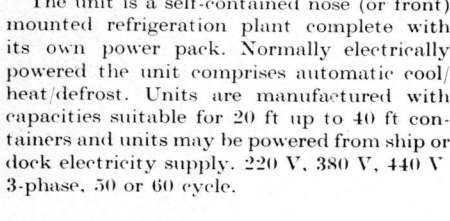

Thermo-King model NWE-75-45 M9SG & M10SG.
Compact, all-electric, front-mount, one-piece refrigeration/heating unit for large containers. Completely self-contained unit operates from electric power at all times. Electric power is provided from diesel-engine generator for over-the-road or from shipboard or dockside plug-in power source. Automatically controlled temperature at all times. Available for operation on 220 or 440 V, 3-phase, 60 cycles.

Thermo-King model SL-5.
Two-piece, flush mount unit for sea-going containers. Five h.p. motor compressor. All-electric unit provides cooling and heating service. A suitable outside source of electric power is required. The front of the condensing section is flush with the front of the container, and is only 12½ in deep. The evaporator section mounts inside the container, alongside the condensing section on the front wall, and is 12½ in deep. The unit is equipped with a semi-hermetic compressor and electrically driven fans. Air cooled or water cooled condensers available or both are provided in one unit.

CONTAINER FILLING AND ASSOCIATED SERVICES

CONTAINER FILLING AND ASSOCIATED SERVICES

ALLIS CHALMERS

Allis-Chalmers,
Material Handling Division
Box 471, Harvey,
Illinois 60426, USA
TELEPHONE: 312 : 331 : 0500

PRODUCTS:
Forklifts suitable for container loading.
Allis-Chalmers are USA agents for Lancer Boss sideloaders.

BLEREAU - PEG

Blereau-Peg
16 bis Rue Champs-Lagarde,
Versailles 78
France

TELEPHONE: 950.72.40
PRODUCTS:
Forklift trucks suitable for container filling.

P.C. & C.K. Chase Ltd.
113 Oyster Lane,
Byfleet,
Surrey
TELEPHONE: 42121
DIRECTORS:
The Viscountess Boyd
The Rt. Hon. Viscount Boyd of Merton C.H.
The Hon. S. D. R. Lennox-Boyd
P. C. Chase
P. R. Chase
I. S. S. Ferris
PRODUCTS:
Bridge plates, container loading ramps and 'Long ramps'.

Chase loading ramp.   Long ground to vehicle model

CLARK

Clark Equipment Co.,
Industrial Truck Division
525 North 24th St., Battle Creek

Michigan 49016
BRANCHES:
Agents or subsidiary companies are to be found in most countries in the world.
PRODUCTS:
Forklift trucks suitable for container filling.

COLT

Colt Staplers Ltd.,
30 Lower Addiscombe Road
Croydon CR9 6AY
TELEPHONE: 01 686 2931
DIRECTORS:
L. J. Smith (*Managing*)
S. W. Lurcuck
PRODUCTS:
Comprehensive range of load control equipment.

The Safeguard Nylon Load Retaining Strap
The latest version of this equipment is fitted with a cadmium-plated, quick release buckle of improved design and heavier construction than the original model. The Mk I buckle was released by pushing a tongue inwards and, to prevent accidental release, a locking pin had to be engaged after the strap had been tensioned. On the Mk II buckle, release is effected by pulling the tongue upwards so that the risk of accidental operation is virtually eliminated and the strap is simply pulled tight to ensure secure load location.

The straps are made from proofed nylon webbing and the width has been standardised at 1¾ in. A variety of end fittings can be supplied for the straps to suit differing applications.

The manufacturers have also introduced perforated channel sections for mounting in the container body to give a choice of anchorage position for the straps. The sections are made in interlocking 762 mm 2 ft 6 in lengths and can be quickly attached.

CONVEYANCER

Conveyancer Fork Trucks, Ltd.
P.O. Box 24, Liverpool Rd.,
Warrington, Lancs.
TELEPHONE: 35922
TELEX: 62145
TELEGRAMS: Hydraulics Warrington

DIRECTORS:
Miles Beevor
Sir Alfred Owen C.B.E. (*Chairman*)
R. A. Young (*Managing*)
A. D. Owen

T. C. Wright
A. W. Veness
PRODUCTS:
Forklift trucks suitable for container loading.

COPPERLOY

Copperloy International
8901 East Pleasant Valley Road,
Cleveland, Ohio 44131
USA
UK and European Suppliers:
Keyzar Farnworth Packaging Ltd.,
Burlington Parade, 68 High Street,
Chiselhurst, Kent BR7 5AQ, UK
Telephone: 01 467 0111
Telex: 21394
J. J. Farnworth (*Manager*)
PRODUCTS:
Mobile yard ramps suitable for loading trailer mounted containers. Yard ramps are 9·1 m-10·9 m (30 ft-36 ft) long and 7,257 kg-

11,340 kg (16,000 lb-25,000 lb) in capacity. All units are 1,778 mm (70 in) wide. A range of smaller units also 1,778 mm (70 in) wide and 6 m to 8 m (20 ft-26 ft) long is also available. In both ranges there are two types offered: a pallet loading type for horizontal entry to the container being filled and a straight type giving a continuous grade right up to the tail of the vehicle on which the container rests. Maximum grade

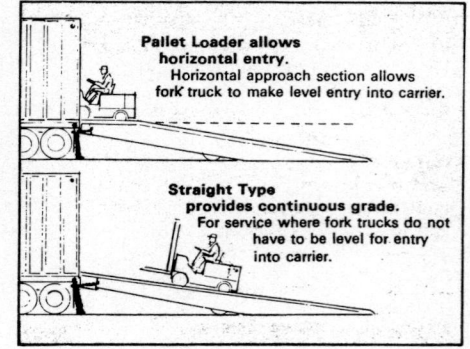

Pallet Loader allows horizontal entry.
Horizontal approach section allows fork truck to make level entry into carrier.

Straight Type provides continuous grade.
For service where fork trucks do not have to be level for entry into carrier.

on the pallet loader yard ramp is 8½° (15%), 9° (15½%) on the 9 m (30 ft) straight type and 7½° (13%) on the 11 m (36 ft) straight type. Maximum grade on the Bantam ramp is 10° (17½%) on the pallet loader type and 9½° (13½%) on the straight type. Built-in hydraulic hand pumps equipped with overloading by-pass valves quickly adjust the top ends of ramps with the vehicle decks within a range of 889 mm-1,549 mm (35 in-61 in).

Coubro & Scrutton (M & I) Ltd.
430 Barking Road,
London E.13
TELEPHONE: 01 476 4477

COUBRO & SCRUTTON

TELEGRAMS: Coubro London E.13
DIRECTORS:
J. W. Scrutton (*Chairman*)
D. V. Tattoo (*Managing*)

J. F. H. Baker (*Sales*)
H. W. H. Ellis (*Financial*)
PRODUCTS:
    Securings in steel.

COVENTRY CLIMAX ENGINES

Coventry Climax Engines Ltd.,
Widdrington Road,
Coventry CV1 4DX
TELEPHONE: (0203) 24100
TELEGRAMS: Climax Coventry Telex
TELEX: 31632
DIRECTORS:
Sir William Lyons
L. P. Lee
R. P. Lister
F. G. Carter
P. W. Cooper
W. T. F. Hassan
H. W. M. Fleury
E. W. Baston
W. E. Phipps
PRODUCTS:
    Climax Universal type 50-EC electric fork-lift trucks equipped with high-free-lift masts for standard ISO container filling.

The Climax 50-EC battery-powered fork lift truck designed for container stuffing. Up to 5,000 lb (2,266 kg) capacity, yet still complying with ISO floor-loading requirements. Fitted with Climax SCR 72 electronic control system for efficiency in operation. Available with low silhouette and high-free-lift mast for operation both in and out of containers.

CROWN CONTROLS

Crown Controls Ltd.,
Armdale Road,
Feltham,
Middlesex
TELEPHONE: (01 890 0191)
PRODUCTS:
    Battery electric forklift trucks suitable for container loading.

A Crown low profile forklift truck loading a container.

Deutsche Reichsbahn
Forschungs und Entwicklungswerke WIB
372 Blankenburg (Harz)
Germany (Democratic Republic)
TELEPHONE: 61
TELEX: 088 451
TELEGRAMS: Forschung Blankenburg (Harz)

B. Dixon-Bate Ltd.
Cargo Control Division
HEAD OFFICE:
Bridge Works, Tarvin Road,
Chester CH3 5NA
TELEPHONE: Chester 24034
TELEGRAMS: Trail, Chestre
TELEX: 61317

DIRECTORS:
Barry D. Bate (*Managing*)
Dennis D. Bate
A. D. W. Good (*Sales Manager/Cargo Control Division*)
PRODUCTS:
'Shorfast' cargo and container control equipment, consisting of nylon webbing lashing straps, tubular steel spring-loaded shoring bars and beam brackets to support 4 in × 2 in transverse timber beams to act as bearers for intermediate decking or shoring

DEUTSCHE REICHSBAHN

DIRECTOR: Helmut Meier
PRODUCTS:
Elevating stilts for containers. Four units are used one for each corner of a container. They are used to remove a container from a semi-trailer by interlocking with the corner

DIXON-BATE

or partitioning. Recent additions to the range include a heavy duty spring shoring bar of 2 in square steel tube and also a garment rail specifically for carrying clothes on hangers. This in conjunction with the 'Shorfast' track installation, provides full space utilisation irrespective of garment length. 'Shorfast' claims to be the only system of its type of British origin and manufacture.
In addition to the standard range, special equipment can be produced to meet individual requirements.

All three elements of the Shorfast Modular System—Lashing, Shoring and Decking— applied to a mixed container load.

castings and allowing the trailer to be drawn out from under the container. They can then lower the container to ground level for loading and lift it again to allow a semi-trailer to be backed underneath it for transport.

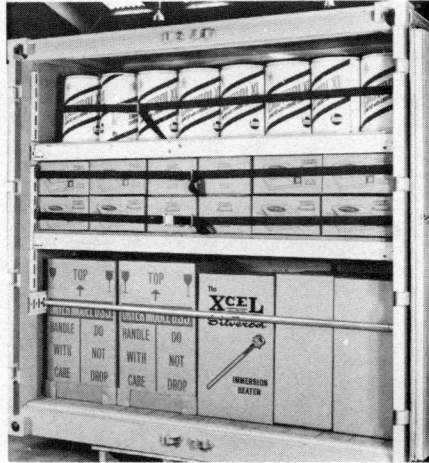

DOBSON

W. E. & F. Dobson Ltd.,
Colwick Industrial Estate,
Colwick,
Nottingham
TELEPHONE: 249251

TELEX: 37132
PRODUCTS:
Forklift trucks suitable for container loading.

DRIX

Drix Plastics Ltd.
Richmond Gardens,
Portswood,
Southampton SO2 1RZ,
England
TELEPHONE: 59666
DIRECTORS:
D. E. Phelips
R. H. Trower
R. F. Bannister
R. V. Henderson
PRODUCTS:
Drix disposable container liners developed

in conjunction with ICI Ltd. for the bulk carrying of powders, granules, grain or pellets.
Two main types of liner are in standard production.
Gravity Filled:
The liner is provided with filling sleeves which correspond to the hatches in the container top.
Pump Filled:
Fitted with a filling sleeve high up at one

end through which the cargo is pumped.
Both types are emptied by tipping the container contents into a silo or hopper. If it is thought necessary, the liner is made with a discharge chute but normally the liner is slashed to empty.
Before being filled the liner is inflated with air and correctly positioned within the container. (The gravity fed liner is provided with eyelets around the top sides for correct positioning).

DURAMIN

Duramin Engineering Co. Ltd.
Harbour Road, Lydney, Glos.
TELEPHONE: Lydney 2371-6 (STD 05944)
TELEGRAMS: Duramin Lydney
TELEX: 43289
DIRECTORS:
D. D. Williams (*Chairman*)
E. Horritt (*Managing*)
D. Lloyd-Jones
A. J. Watts
G. A. H. Watts
J. Elliot Brown
P. Guthrie
P. B. Conolly (*Sales Manager*)
PRODUCTS:
The 'Aerola' and 'Palletaire' loading systems (See also Container section). These are patented systems allowing for easy, speedy loading and discharge of goods into and out of containers and vehicles.

Aerola
'Aerola' is basically four sets of heavy duty rollers housed in channels recessed into the vehicle floor. The rollers are elevated by compressed air above floor level ready for a load of pallets which are easily and smoothly rolled into position over the track which has an extremely low co-efficient of friction. When the vehicle is loaded the air is exhausted and the pallets are gently lowered onto the

The Duramin "Aerola" system in use.

floor. The rollers return below floor level.

The four sets of longitudinal rollers comprise two tracks which are capable of elevating a full vehicle load consisting of single stacked pallets each weighing approximately 1 ton. It will operate at an air pressure of 2·5 kg/cm²-2·8 kg/cm² (35-45 lb/in²) although if heavier loads have to be lifted the system is perfectly safe at a pressure of 5·6 kg/cm²-7 kg/cm² (80-100 lb/in²). Future developments of this system include facility to remove complete loads as one.

Fenwick Manutention
65 Rue du Dr Bauer,
93 St. Ouen,
France

Fiat Om
25100 Brescia,
Via Volturno 62,

Hayes and Bishop Limited
Devonshire Works, Dukes Avenue
Chiswick, London W4
TELEPHONE: 01-994 7827
DIRECTOR:
J. S. Sieder
PRODUCT:

Air-operated rolling stillage system for container packing and unpacking.
The system incorporates:—

1. Two pneumatic slippers, or a line of slippers inter-connected and inflated or deflated from a central point simultaneously.

   An air supply of the low pressure type (this may be a fixed system, portable or wall compressor, or a bottled supply if the work load is light; alternatively it could be driven from a vehicle vacuum pump).

2. A set of steerable and fixed slippers.
3. The pallet or stillage type unit load base itself, which must be capable of being lifted by chain or sling and nested.
4. A scissor lift dock leveller (this may be of the travelling type on rails if more than one container at a time is handled, or fixed if only one bay is needed).

The stillage unit load base is of the wooden type for cheapness. constructed with lateral cross timberboards and mounted on three longitudinal timber supports two at the extreme edges and one in the centre. The approximate depth of gap required for easy entry and to allow for all inequalities in floors etc. is five inches.

As can be seen from the diagrams the method of procedure for unloading a vehicle is thus:

The pneumatic slippers are placed under the load and inflated to carry the load on the free running rollers. (N.B. when the slippers are deflated their castors are automatically brought into position for easy transportation).

The scissor lift (if required) is elevated to the level of the vehicle deck and the requisite load is trundled by hand onto its rollers.

The lift is positioned at floor level and the load is pushed, first onto the steerable slipper, and then onto the fixed one.

The load is then ready for hand manoeuvre anywhere in the warehouse.

The system is reversed for loading of vehicles; the air supply is carried either in the warehouse or in the vehicle (20 p.s.i. max req) and any part of a load can be manoeuvred separately.

In this system the pneumatic slippers are fixed in wells below the deck level of the vehicle and air is supplied from the vehicle's own compressor.

When inflated they take the load on their

Palletaire
'Palletaire' is a specially narrow wheeled robust trolley the length of a pallet running on two simple unobtrusive flat guide rails. An ingenious built-in air operated lifting mechanism controlled by a pedal enables the operator to elevate a pallet clear of the vehicle floor and move it into position. When the air is exhausted the pallet is lowered smoothly to rest on the firm base and the trolley frees itself for the next load. For unloading the procedure is reversed.

FENWICK

TELEPHONE: 076.37.59
PRODUCTS:
Forklift trucks suitable for container filling.

FIAT

Italy
PRODUCTS:
Forklift suitable for container filling.

HAYES AND BISHOP

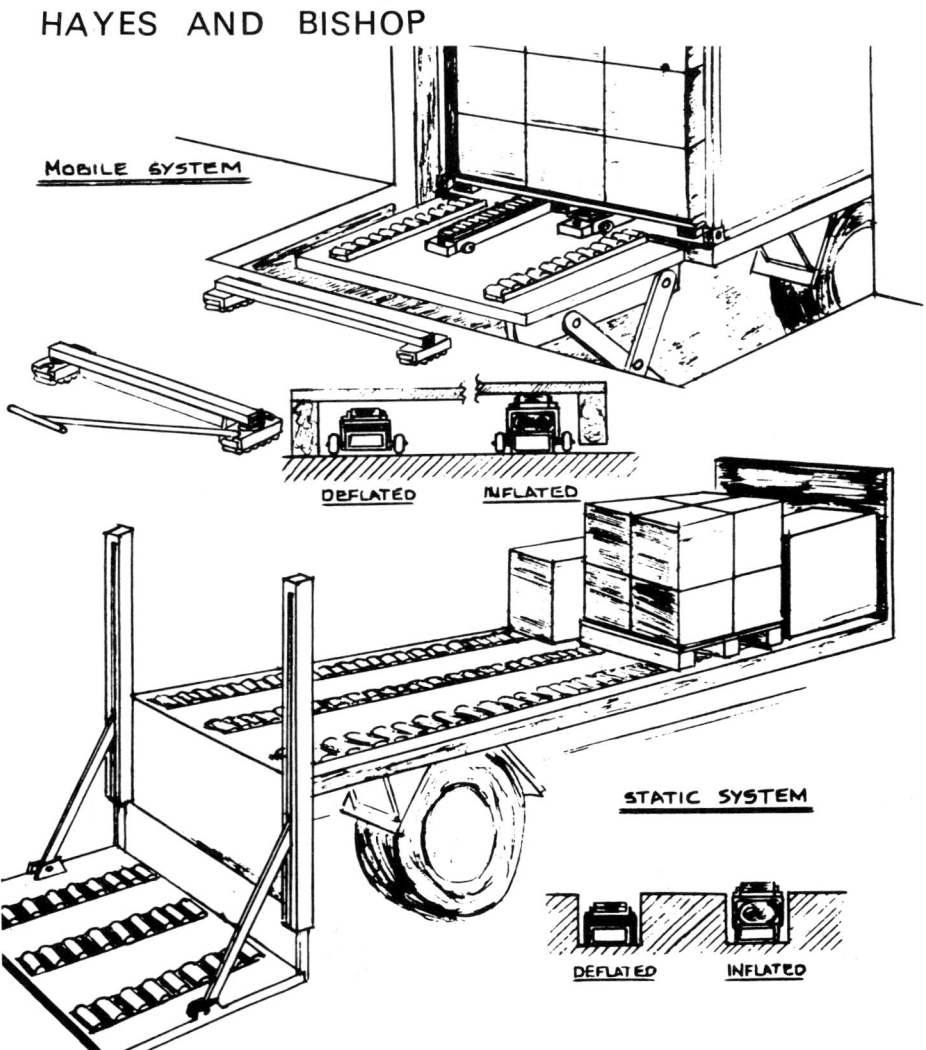

A feature of the 'Palletaire' system is the automatic nozzle through which a reservoir on the trolley is charged so that the lifting mechanism may be operated in any part of a vehicle or on a warehouse floor without the need for the trolley to be in actual contact with the source of supply of compressed air at the moment of operation.

This unit is capable of elevating a loaded pallet of average size weighing approximately 1 ton and designs are available for larger loads.

rollers for easy hand manoeuvreability.

The tailboard of the vehicle is of the elevateable type and carries rollers on which the load, or any part of the load, can be manoeuvred.

Fixed and steerable solid slippers can be utilised for transport within the warehouse if required.

Hayes and Bishop, the patentees, are ready to recommend and supply systems to suit any requirements or conditions for dealing with containers or separate packaged loads of any type.

After a container has been loaded with the Hayes and Bishop loading system the air is released from the pneumatic slippers which can be withdrawn leaving the load on the floor of the container

HENLEY FORKLIFT

Henley Forklift Co. Ltd.
Newbridge Road Industrial Estate,
Pontllanfraith,
Blackwood, Mon. NP2 2XF
TELEPHONE: Blackwood 2671 and 3731
TELEX: 49655
SERVICE DIVISION:
263 Bromford Lane, Birmingham 8

Telephone: 021-327-4961
Telex: 338621
DIRECTORS:
Forbes Hayes (*Chairman*)
E. Holmes (*Deputy Chairman*)
D. C. Hardwick (*Managing Director*)
C. R. Stanger (*Technical Director*)
B. H. Dorricott (*Sales Director*)

P. Bentley (*Works*)
C. S. Taylor
G. B. Taylor
T. Compton (*Sales Manager*)
PRODUCTS:
Diesel forklift trucks suitable for container filling. Front lift and sideloading.

FARBWERKE HOECHST

Farbwerke Hoechst AG,
6230 Frankfurt/M80
Germany (Federal Republic)
TELEPHONE: 0611 3055833
PRODUCTS:
Trevira container liners for the transport of bulk products in dry freight containers.

HUNTER

G. Hunter (London) Ltd.
Gumley Road, Grays,
Essex RM16 1XT
TELEPHONE: Grays Thurrock 5155
TELEX: 28747
DIRECTORS:
Dennis Hunter
P. S. Underwood
E. K. Thoupos
E. J. Hunter
G. J. Hunter
PRODUCTS:
Dock levellers and scissor lifts. A retractable dock leveller, specially designed for servicing lorry mounted containers, has been developed by this company. Hunter also make a swing lip unit which allows vehicle or container doors to close in front of a loading lock.

Called the "Retracta" it has been developed to give access to a container wherever it is placed on a vehicle. It overcomes the problem of dealing with a container loaded on to a chassis longer than the container. The "Retracta" has a capacity of 10 tons and will withstand a single axle load of nine tons. Electro-hydraulically powered, the leveller extends from a loading bank against which a vehicle has been backed and reaches into a container on the vehicle deck.

Safety features are built into the equipment to avoid damage to containers, vehicles or operators. The leveller is suitable for servicing side-loading vehicles and refrigerated containers.

This is how it works:
1. Container vehicle backs to loading bank. Dock leveller in retracted position.
2. Dock leveller raised to full height by press button control and tapered lip is extended to position just inside container threshold. The tapered lip is designed to give smooth transfer of load from dock leveller to the container floor.
3. Press button control lowers dock leveller on to container floor, allowing it to float with the vehicle suspension as the container is loaded or unloaded.
4. Servicing of container is carried out. If the vehicle is driven away during this operation the leveller automatically locks in position.
5. Press button control lifts leveller clear of container floor and retracts the lip fully into the bank.

The new Hunter "Retracta" dock leveller during on-site trials. It is said to be the first dock leveller in the world designed specifically for loading containers.

A new Hunter dock leveller is the swing lip. This is particularly suitable for installation where vehicle doors are closed in front of the loading bank or where the area in front of the loading bank is used for overnight parking and a projecting lip could be a hazard.

A driver can park his lorry flush to the bank whatever time he arrives with a load—even in the middle of the night—because the dock leveller can be raised and brought into use without the vehicle being moved again.

The leveller is installed so that the leading edge of the platform is flush with the front of the bank. In the basic counterbalanced model, the lip is made to swing upwards by operation from the top of the bank. The platform is operated on the counterbalance principle and is raised and lowered by lifting the side handles. When these are lifted they withdraw the locking bolts which hold the platform level with the bank when not in use. This enables cross traffic to treat the dock leveller as a normal part of the bank when it is not being used for loading or unloading.

As the springs on the vehicle raise or lower the vehicle bed (according to whether the

container is being loaded or unloaded) the leveller automatically 'floats' with the vehicle to provide a constantly smooth platform between the loading bank and vehicle bed.

There are two basic versions of the new swing lip dock leveller available—the counterbalanced and electro-hydraulic models. Both have standard swing lip over the full platform width. However, it can be provided 1 ft 8 in (500 mm) narrower, with hinged flaps on either side.

COUNTERBALANCED:
Three movements are required to operate the counterbalanced swing lip dock leveller. (1) the platform is raised in the normal manner using the side handles, and the side locking bolts are retracted; (2) the forward handle is raised and the lip swung upwards; (3) resting on the deck of the vehicle it is locked by its own weight.

ELECTRO-HYDRAULIC:
Operation is by hydraulic ram, connected to the dock leveller power pack. A push button, wall mounted control station controls the up/down movement of the leveller and the up/down action of the swing lip.

The leveller is available in three, six and ten ton capacities and a variety of sizes to meet differing requirements.

HYMO LIFT

Hymo-Lift Ltd.
16-18 Clarendon Road,
Watford,
Herts,
England

TELEPHONE: 21262
TELEX: 923008
PRODUCTS:
Scissor lifts suitable as aids for container filling.

Hyster Company
Industrial Truck Operations
PO Box 847
Danville, Illinois 61832

Hyster Overseas,
Turriff Buildings,
Great West Road,
Brentford, Middlesex,
England.

International Marine Management
18 Finsbury Circus,
London E.C.2
TELEPHONE: 01 628 6651
TELEGRAMS: Expofrate
TELEX: 885604
DIRECTOR AND PROJECT MANAGER:
H. J. Burley-Smith (*President*)
C. T. Robinson (*Project Manager*)

PRODUCT:
The 'Auto Perch' system for stowing motor cars in containers.

Joloda Transport Equipment Limited
205 Menlove Avenue, Liverpool, 18, England
TELEPHONE: 051-428 1621
TELEGRAMS: Joloda
DIRECTORS:
G. B. Johnstone
G. K. Johnstone
J. P. Barker (*Managing*)
J. Waller (*Sales Manager*)
J. Pickavance

PRODUCTS:
Pallet loading equipment known as "Joloda" in high tensile steel for use inside freight containers and vehicles. Capacities are up to 20 tons for hydraulic models and 1½ tons for mechanical models.

HYSTER

USA
PRODUCT:
Fork lift trucks suitable for container loading.

HYSTER OVERSEAS

TELEPHONE: 01 568 9292
TELEGRAMS: Hyster London
TELEX: London 25870
PRODUCTS:
Forklift trucks for container filling.

I. M.M.

International Marine Management's "Auto Perch" system.

JOLODA

Following loading, the equipment is removed for re-use.

The Joloda
This is a system consisting of a pair of elevating roller trolleys running in tracks set in or laid on an existing general purpose freight floor. The units run below floor level when down and are raised above floor level by a single movement of a simple tommy bar. One pair of "Jolodas" can handle any number of pallets.

The mechanical model lifts up to 1½ tons per pair. Hydraulic models move up to 20 tons per pair and both have a high safety

One of 20 engines loaded with the aid of a Joloda into containers bound for Australia

The Joloda channels may be extended through the open door of the container to accept the load.

The above photograph shows a 14 ton single pallet load, 5·9 m 19 ft 6 in long being lifted and rolled into a 20 ft ISO container in less than one minute at a demonstration given to Alfred Holt Shipping Lines of Liverpool.

The tracks are simply placed directly on the floor of the container, and either cross linked or held in parallel by simple floor attachments.

The tracks may also be extended out of the container within reach of a fork-lift truck, where the container may be placed some distance from the end of the vehicle on which the container is being carried.

The Joloda portable track sections may be removed after loading or reinserted for unloading, thus making it possible to pallet load or unload any number of containers with only one set of this equipment at each terminal point.

factor with manual and overriding automatic braking control and cannot crash the headboard or overrun the tail.

Standard 'Jolodas' are in 914 mm (36 in), 1,016 mm (40 in) and 1,219 mm (48 in) lengths. 'Jolodas' are also made in various forms and capacities to meet customers particular requirements.

Joloda top hat section 10 swg steel track, 238 m/ton (780 ft per ton) is supplied in lengths from 4·3 m to 7·9 m (14 ft to 26 ft) which are readily extended, without welding, to any further length which may be required.

Automatic retractable brake trip stops (one per track at rear of vehicle) are an optional alternative to a fixed bolt head and are intended to operate in the event of the operator failing to apply the manual control.

KORNYLAK

Kornylak Corporation
400 Heaton St., Hamilton,
Ohio 45011
TELEPHONE: 513 894 7171
TELEGRAMS: Kornylak

PRODUCTS:
Conveyor and other handling equipment which could be used for the filling of containers and the marshalling of goods intended for container transport.

LANCER BOSS

Lancer Boss Ltd.,
Leighton Buzzard,
Bedfordshire LU7 8SR
TELEPHONE: 2031
TELEX: 82235
DIRECTORS:
G. N. Bowman-Shaw
T. Bowman-Shaw
J. A. F. Luttrell
J. Kinross A.M.I.M.E.
E. Monkhouse

PRODUCTS:
Electric forklifts with low profile suitable for container filling and emptying.

Lancer Boss. P Series Electric 4,000 lb capacity Truck. Fitted with Boss Westinghouse SCR Suptronic control system.

LANSING BAGNALL

Lansing Bagnall Ltd.
Kingsclere Road,
Basingstoke
Hants, England
TELEPHONE: 3131
TELEGRAMS: Bagnallic, Basingstoke
TELEX: Bagnallic Basingstoke 85120
DIRECTORS:
E. Kaye (Governing)
S. R. Harbour
R. S. Odd
H. A. Richardson
V. A. G. Lambert
J. B. Peat
D. A. Larkins
A. R. Wright
Peter Watson
PRODUCTS:
FOER 9 'CONTAINER FREIGHT-LOADER'
This truck embodies all the inherent features of the standard FOER 9 range, together with several new characteristics which make the truck suitable for container loading applications. This truck is based on the standard FOER 9/4,000 lb model.

The mast unit fitted to the Container Freight-Loader has an overall nested height of only 77 in and embodies a full free lift of 49½ in. This enables the truck to enter the container and double stack pallet loads, without increasing the overall height of the masts. These can be supplied in Twin or Triple versions and have extended lift heights of 112 in and 165 in respectively.

Magline Inc.,
Pinconning,
Michigan 48650,
P.O. Box 86

MAGLINE

USA
PRODUCTS:
Mobile ramps suitable for filling trailer mounted containers by forklift truck.

MEHLER

Val. Mehler Aktiengesellschaft
64 Fulda,
Germany (Federal Republic)
TELEPHONE: 0661 8031
TELEX: 049 852
PRODUCTS:

Container liners which make it possible to use standard dry freight containers for bulk commodities.

The liners are made of Valmex laminated fabric coated in three different ways so as to be resistant to chemicals, food-proof, and suitable for neutral commodities.

The self supporting design makes additional support unnecessary. The liner can be fitted into a standard container within minutes by means of the screws which are fitted between the sidewalls of a container.

Filling holes are provided according to requirements. Zips can be fitted for pneumatic discharge.

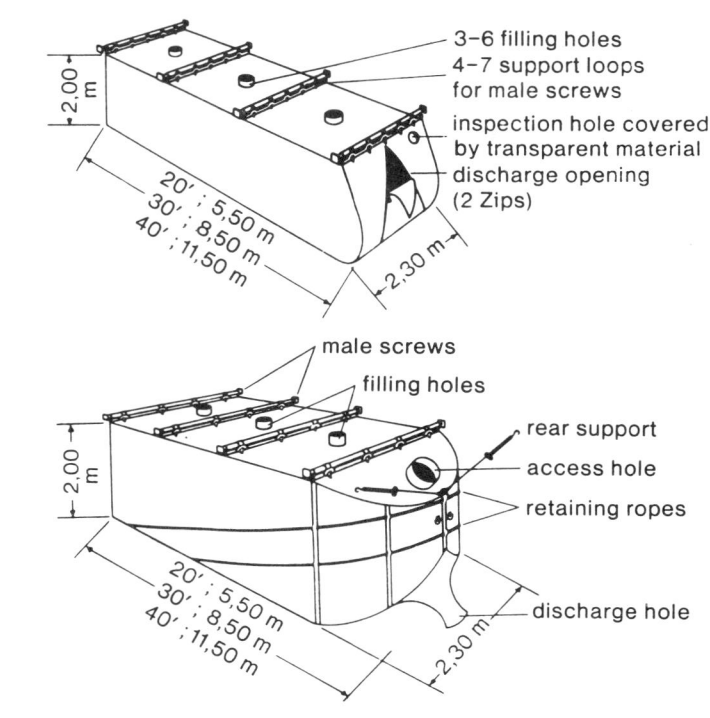

3–6 filling holes
4–7 support loops for male screws
inspection hole covered by transparent material
discharge opening (2 Zips)

male screws
filling holes
rear support
access hole
retaining ropes
discharge hole

Standard sizes and weights (approx.) of Mehler container liners

Container	length	width	height	vol.	Empty weight
20 ft	5·50 m	2·30 m	2·00 m	24 m³	80 kg
30 ft	8·50 m	2·30 m	2·00 m	36 m³	110 kg
40 ft	11·50 m	2·30 m	2·00 m	48 m³	140 kg

MONTGOMERIE REID

Montgomerie Reid Ltd.,
Bramley, Basingstoke
Hants, England
TELEPHONE: Bramley Green 444
TELEGRAMS: Emmar Bramley Hants

TELEX: 85199
DIRECTORS:
I. T. Henderson (*Chairman*)
M. A. H. Walford (*Vice Chairman*)
H. P. Beaumont (*Managing*)

F. D. Weston (*Secretary*)
J. P. Barker (*Marketing*)
PRODUCTS:
Range of seven electric forklifts of which at least two are suitable for container filling.

NEWLAND ENGINEERING

Newland Engineering Co. Ltd.
Johnson Brook Foundry, Birch Lane,
Dukinfield, Cheshire
TELEPHONE: 061 368 1906
DIRECTORS:
C. H. Greasley
I. F. C. Beswick
B. N. Greasley
S. Beswick
PRODUCTS:
Mobile belt and slat loading machines with capacities up to 1,000 lbs.

Newland Cantilever Loader

This model has a long cantilever outreach for loading containers and Freightliners. A grip surface belt conveyor discharges the goods on to a roller conveyor system, giving the optimum handling flexibility at the take-off point. Both sections have hydraulic incline adjustment units which act independently of each other so that the goods flow down to the operator at the height required, or back to the belt for unloading, according to the setting of the adjusters. Standard chassis suspension is on four heavy duty roller bearing swivel wheels. Equipment will carry packages of up to 6 cwt, 14 ft into container. Currently under development by the company is a heavy-duty long reach conveyor for container loading/unloading and this is expected to have a penetration of 22-24 ft (6·7 m-7·31 m).

The Newland Mark II/A Container Loader

Recently introduced to facilitate the filling and emptying of containers, the Newland Mark II/A Container Loader has a cantilever outreach of 20 ft entirely supported from the conveyor chassis, without any subsidiary support from the container.

An hydraulic pump unit operating tandem

The Newland Mark II A. container loader.

Newland Cantilever Loader Carrier packages of up to 6 cwt into a container.

hydraulic rams gives quick and easy adjustment to any desired operating height within the container.

Roller bearing wheels mounted on ball bearing turnplates with a 360° swivel action ensure ease of movement and slewing.

The special belt with treaded tough rubber surface runs on ball bearing rollers and will handle goods of practically any type, with the added advantage that any risk of damage to goods of a fragile nature is minimised.

Cantilever Loader Model 23
Outreach—4·26 m (14 ft)
Capacity—453 kg (1,000 lbs) distributed
Made by Newland Engineering Co. Ltd.

Full control is provided at both ends of the machine by push button units having "Forward", "Reverse", and "Stop" push buttons.

The reversing feature renders the machine equally effective for both loading and unloading.

The standard conveying speed is 80 ft min but the use of stock interchangeable reduction gear units enables a wide range of alternative speeds to be offered at the customer's option, depending on the application.

The standard operating current is 400/440 volt 3 phase 50 cycles but the design of the drive unit is such that the machine can be supplied to operate on practically any alternative electrical supply.

The Newland Type T.C./33 Container Loader

Overall length with boom extended—40 ft (12·2 m).

"Inward" and "outward" adjustment of the telescopic boom is power driven and operated by a simple control at the delivery end of the machine.

The heavy duty 24 in (609 mm) grip surfaced belt runs on ball bearing rollers and is in one continuous length, extending and retracting to conform to the telescopic boom adjustment.

The machine is self-supporting from the counterbalanced chassis, and additional stabilising wheels are provided. Heavy duty roller bearing chassis castors with directional locks on the forward pair ensure easy movement.

Two independent sets of hydraulic rams and pumps adjust the contour of the machine so that it is equally effective for loading/unloading containers on the floor, or from the top of a raised loading bank, in addition to the more usual application illustrated.

The drive unit incorporates an electric motor of the standard frame size and voltage applicable to the country or conditions in which the machine will be operating, the most usual being 380/440 volt 3 phase 50 cycles. Single phase drives available to order.

The standard fixed conveying speed is 100 ft/min (30·5 m/min), but the reduction gearbox is available in a wide range of ratios, and thus alternative speeds can be supplied without any difficulty simply by exchanging the unit.

The push button starter incorporates a severser for unloading. Standard feed height—2 ft (609 mm). Capacity—14 cwt (712 kilos) distributed; 2 cwt (101·6 kilos) packages or sacks.

H. K. Porter Company (Great Britain) Ltd.,
Cameron Street,
Hillington,
Glasgow S.W.2

PORTER

TELEPHONE: 041 883 8771
PRODUCT:
Cargo control systems for restraining loads inside containers.

The Raymond Corporation
4016 Madison St.,
Greene,

RAYMOND

N.Y. 13778, USA
PRODUCTS:
Forklift trucks suitable for container filling.

G. E. & L. V. Rich Ltd.
Oakfield Road,
London S.E.20

TELEPHONE: 01 778 4203

RICH

PRODUCT:
Dock levellers. Among several different kinds of extension lip to span the gap between dock leveller and rear of vehicle the company provides a "Packaway" or retractable lip for closed container or sideloading.

Rite Hite Corporation
6011 S. Pennsylvania Ave.,
Cudahy, Wisconsin 53110
USA

RITE

PRODUCTS:
Dock levellers suitable for loading trailer mounted containers from loading docks.

Salev S.A.
28 Rue Escudier,
92-Boulogne,
France

SALEV

TELEPHONE: 605-64-40
PRODUCTS:
Forklift trucks suitable for container filling.

Seasafe Transport AB
Torstenssonsgatan 3,
S-114 56 Stockholm
Sweden
TELEPHONE: 67 92 55

SEASAFE

TELEGRAMS: Seasafe
TELEX: 10139 Seasafe-S

DIRECTORS
P. O. Trostad (*Managing*)

PRODUCTS:
Lashing equipment for cars, trailers, general cargo and containers. Chain lashing equipment is made of alloy steel.

St. Clare Engineering Ltd.
HEAD OFFICE:
St. Clare Engineering Ltd.

ST CLARE

Bridge Road Works
Lymington, Hants
TELEPHONE: Lymington 3288

DIRECTORS:
W. J. Ryden
L. St. C. Byrne

Toyo Umpanki Co Ltd.,
15-5, 1-Chome, Nishi-Shimbashi,
Minato-ku, Tokyo,
Japan

TOYO UMPANKI

TELEGRAMS: Toyoumpanki tokyo
PRODUCTS:
Forklifts suitable for container loading.

Industrial Truck Division,
Eaton Yale & Towne Inc.,
Suite 800,
Foxcroft Square Pavillion,

EATON YALE

Jenkintown, Pa 19046,
USA
PRODUCTS:
Forklift trucks suitable for container filling.

Yale Industrial Truck and Hoist Division
Wednesfield, Staffs,
England
TELEPHONE: Willenhall 66955
TELEX: 338133
PRODUCTS:
Forklift trucks suitable for container filling.

YALE

The "Grab-O-Matic" drum handling attachment makes it possible to pick up drums from behind rather than from the side as becomes necessary with clamps. Thus space in a container can be more effectively used.

WESSEX

Wessex Industries Ltd.,
Market St., Poole,
Dorset
TELEPHONE: 2626
TELEGRAMS: Industries Poole
TELEX: 41327
DIRECTORS:
K. H. Willis (*Chairman*)
L. A. Snook (*Managing*)
J. T. Taylor
R. H. MacWilliam

PRODUCTS:

Container loading trucks, fork lift trucks and tractors. The range includes:

EFC 30-24 battery electric container loading truck with a capacity of 3,000 lb at 24 in centres.

EFCM 155 battery electric container loading truck with a capacity of 1,500 kg at 500 mm centres.

EF and FE range of lift trucks from 625 kg (1,300 lb) to 9,000 kg (20,000 lb).

ET range of tractors up to 20 tons capacity.

A Wessex container truck is fitted with full free lift, side shift and is available both in English and Metric versions (EFC 30-24—3,000 lb at 24 in centres, EFCM 155—1,500 kg at 500 mm centres).

CONTAINER REPAIR, TESTING AND CLEANING SERVICES

CONTAINER REPAIR, TESTING AND CLEANING SERVICES

Reference should also be made to the Ports Section for Container Repair Organisations.

AUSTRIA
INTERNATIONAL TESTING STATION

International Testing Station
Arsenal, Vienna, Austria
   Set up ten years ago by UIC the Arsenal station tests rolling stock and containers for effects of freezing conditions, for k-valve stresses, roller-rig and wind tests.

BELGIUM
ICCS

International Containers and Chassis Service
Churchilldok 420
B-2030 Antwerp
TELEPHONE: (03) 41.70.31/39
C. Tombeur (*Service Manager*)
   Official after-sales service agents for Van Hool, Brugeoise et Nivelles and Strick containers.
   Service agents for Fruehauf Corporation. Repairs to chassis, rolling stock and all types of containers are carried out.

Floor repairs being carried out at ICCS depot, Antwerp.

Re-welding a nearly repaired container at ICCS depot, Antwerp.

SATI
Société Anonyme de Transports Isothermes
Quay 121, Albert Dock, Antwerp
TELEPHONE: 41.06.37 (day)
                  30.83.35 (night)
TELEX: Refribel 31 139

SATI
   Repair shops and mobile units on Antwerp and Zeebrugge Terminals.
   CRANE FRUEHAUF Container and Trailer spares and Maintenance Dealers for Belgium.

DENMARK

Thor Jorgensen A/S
57/71 Toldbodgade
DK-12153 Copenhagen K

TELEPHONE: 01.115101 (day)
                  01.851256 (night)
TELEX: 2548/49
   Member of Container Aid International.

FRANCE
TERGNIER

Centre National de Tergnier
Aisne, France
   The centre for testing ISO containers in France. It comes under the control of OTUA and applications for testing should be addressed to the director at:
Office Technique pour l'Utilisation de l'Acier,
15 rue d'Astorg
Paris, 8e
TELEPHONE: 265.7280

STIM

STIM
Societe de Travaux et Industries Maritime
12 Blvd. de la Madelaine
Paris 9e

TELEPHONE: 742.21.89 (24 hours)
TELEX: 21.740
   Member of Container Aid International.

GERMANY

Gerd Buss, K.G.
Cremon 32
P.B. 112160
G.2000 Hamburg 11

TELEPHONE: 31.10.11 (day)
                  49.97.46 (night)
TELEX: 02.12152
   Member of Container Aid International and see also leasing section.

ITALY

Fratelli Avandero SAS
Container Repair Service
Via Valtellina 21-27, Cas. Post. 3763
Milan

TELEPHONE: 69.55
TELEX: MI 31193
G. Boschetti (*Director General*)

   The Rivalta Scrivia repair depot has been closed and Milan is now the centre of Avandero's operations.

NETHERLANDS

Netam Repair Depot
71 Vievhavenstraat,
Rotterdam
WINNIC
   (See U.K. entry).

TELEPHONE: 25.48.80
and at:
33 Van Helmenstraat,

Rotterdam
TELEPHONE: 25.58.80
TELEX: 22596

SWITZERLAND

Container Aid AG
4133 Pratteln, Nr Basle
TELEPHONE: 061.81 5511
TELEX: 62 386
GENERAL:

Container Aid AG was founded in June 1968, to repair, maintain, wash and inspect containers. Small repairs are carried out by mobile van. Large repairs are given to the nearby Schindler Carriage and Wagon Company.

Container Aid AG's mobile repair van.

UNITED KINGDOM
ALBURY

Albury Laboratories Ltd.
Container Test Centre
Albury,
Guildford, Surrey
TELEPHONE: Shere 2041
DIRECTORS:
Arthur Tebby (*Managing and Sales*)
R. Heap
A. N. Hurst
SERVICE:

Albury tested the first 20 ft, 30 ft and 40 ft dry freight containers to be Lloyd's approved; now facilities are available for every standard test procedure and also for research and development work on new designs.

The main loading rig accommodates containers of any length and is capable of applying loads far in excess of current requirements, to provide information for development, in addition to the basic tests: roof strength, floor strength, stacking, lifting, (top and bottom), racking ($12\frac{1}{2}$ tons), restraint end and door strength, side wall strength, watertightness.

The Laboratories are completely independent of government departments, industrial interests or standards authorities.

All work is rigorously confidential to clients.

Special tests to assist prototype development can be arranged at short notice.

A leading thin wall structures expert is retained to advise on complex design problems.

Additional test facilities are available for: customs security, corrosion resistance, durability, weathering, local impact, general impact, marking, welding, corner castings, door furniture, cleansing and pressure testing.
TESTING STANDARDS:

All ISO international standards and consortium requirements are met for the testing of dry freight and bulk liquid containers. The list includes: ISO, Lloyds, BSI, UIC, OCL, ACT, ACL, American Standards, Bureau Veritas, Australian Department of Shipping.

A Svenska Metallverke 30 ft lightweight aluminium van undergoing end wall tests at the Albury Container Test Centre.

BIRCH

J. S. & L. Birch (Engineering) Ltd.
5 Neville Road,
Waterloo,
Liverpool L22 ONJ
TELEPHONE: 051 928 2292

DIRECTORS:
J. F. Birch (*Managing*)
L. A. Birch
A. P. Stirling
F. D. Bateson

PRODUCTS:
Washing units for vehicles and containers.
An interior and exterior washing and disinfecting plant for containers is available.

BRITISH RAILWAYS

British Rail Engineering Ltd.
222 Marylebone Road,
London, NW1

TELEPHONE: 01 262 3232
BRANCHES:

Derby:
British Rail Engineering Limited,
Litchurch Lane, Derby
Telephone: Derby 42442 ext. 2801
Telex: 37422
J. R. Stables (*Manager*)

Eastleigh:
British Rail Engineering Limited,
Eastleigh, Hampshire
Telephone: Southampton 23838 ext. 7301
Telex: 47579
L. I. Sanders (*Manager*)

Glasgow:
British Rail Engineering Limited,
130 Springburn Road, Glasgow
Telephone: 041-332 9811 ext. 2782
Telex: 77716
J. F. Elliott (*Manager*)

Horwich:
British Rail Engineering Limited,
Horwich, Lancashire
Telephone: Horwich 66801 ext. 201
Telex.: 63104
E. T. Butcher (*Manager*)

London:
British Rail Engineering Limited,
Ruckholt Road, Leyton, London E10
Telephone: 01-534 4500 ext. 5300
Telex: 261391
W. A. Robertson (*Manager*)

Wolverton:
British Rail Engineering Limited,
Wolverton, Buckinghamshire
Telephone: Wolverton 2381 ext. 4201
Telex: 82228
G. W. G. Tew (*Manager*)

York:
British Rail Engineering Limited,
Holgate Road, York
Telephone: York 53022 ext. 3201
Telex: 57828
W. H. Sykes (*Manager*)

CLYDE WHARF

Clyde Wharf Ltd.
(A member of the Tate and Lyle Group)
28 North Woolwich Road
London E.16
TELEPHONE: 01 476 5671
J. Hicks (*Managing Director*)

Repairs, servicing, fumigation and TIR conversions of containers and trailers.
Vehicle Testing Station
Arsenal
Vienna III
  Austria

International testing station for temperature and speed control. Regulated by the Office for Research and Experiments (ORE) of the International Union of Railways (UIC).

CONTAINERCARE

Containercare (Southern) Ltd.
Ryde Terrace
Chapel
Southampton
Hants.

TELEPHONE: 0703 24186
          0703 25924
          0703 59601 (after hours)
TELEX: 47629
R. S. Blanchard (*Manager*)

SERVICES:
Depots at Western Docks, Southampton; Cardiff; Martelsham; Glasgow; Liverpool and Dublin with an overseas depot et Rotterdam. Services include storage, shot blasting, painting, cleaning and an 'official Repair Establishment is being established, which will incorporate testing equipment.

CONTAINER WORKSHOPS LTD

Container Workshops Ltd.,
Trafford Wharf Road,
Manchester 17

TELEPHONE: 061 872 1094

SERVICES:
Major repairs are carried out in the workshops in Trafford Park where testing facilities and makers' spares are available. Minor repairs can be done on site by a mobile

repair unit. Regular inspections and surveys are carried out to keep containers up to standard.
Cleaning, washing and painting services are also offered.

CRANE-FRUEHAUF

Crane Fruehauf Trailers Ltd.   (Service Depot)
Walton Avenue
Felixstowe
Suffolk

TELEPHONE: 03942 4725/6060
P. Stone (*Manager*)
Repair services for all sizes and makes of containers.

EUROCLEAN

Euroclean
(Speed-O-Klene Equipment Co. Ltd.)
178 Bedford Road,
Kempston
Bedford
TELEPHONE: (02305) 3531
TELEGRAMS: SPOK Kempston
DIRECTORS:
  H. A. J. Silley
  F. R. W. Schumacher
  C. Granville
  P. G. Bystedt
  J. M. Gardner
  J. J. M. Glasse
HIGH PRESSURE WASHING SYSTEMS FOR CONTAINERS:
The basic Euroclean machine is a stylish,

portable high pressure unit equipped with two injection channels, designed for use with Euroclean chemicals.
The high pressure pump is flange mounted directly to the power unit and operates at a pressure of 50 atmos (710 lbf/in).
The twin injection systems are easily adjusted to give the accurate range of dilutions required for the appropriate Euroclean system. Specific programmes are available covering all aspects of container cleaning on or off the transporter.
The programmes for the interior, cover a very wide variety of impurities such as

animal and vegetable fats, mineral oils and greases, sugars, resins, cement and concrete residues—disinfectants can also be applied.
The programmes for the exterior include aluminium cleaning and deoxidisation, rust removal, as well as normal maintenance cleaning to remove traffic impurities and road salts using the Euroclean wax barrier systems.
The systems are all applied with the same pressure unit, which is simple to operate, cheap to run, and will result in substantial reductions in man hours and turn-round time.

MAINTENANCE CLEANING OF CONTAINERS:
(USED FOR THE TRANSPORT OF ANIMAL
CARCASSES OR OFFAL):

BASE MATERIALS:
Galvanized iron
Fibre glass, asbestos, rubber
Aluminium or similar alloys

IMPURITIES:	PREDILUTION:	CHEMICALS:
Chicken offal and feathers,	1 : 1-4 before injection	Euroclean 205
Animal fats, blood, urine, etc.	1 : 1-4 before injection	Euroclean M5
	1 : 1 before injection	Euroclean DES 251

METHOD USING EUROCLEAN HIGH PRESSURE
EQUIPMENT:

1. Pre-rinse with water to remove excess dirt.
2. Apply Euroclean 205 acid to all areas and allow to act for not less than 5 minutes. Operator safety precautions must be strictly observed—see Information Bulletin on Euroclean 205.
3. Neutralize acid by applying Euroclean M5 alkali throughout.
4. Clean all areas thoroughly with Euroclean M5.
5. Rinse very thoroughly with water.
6. Apply Euroclean DES 251 lightly to all areas and leave. Do not rinse off.

Costs (based on 200 litre prices at 9 litres/min)			per minute
Euroclean 205	(pre-diluted 1 : 2)	injected at 2 %	2 np
Euroclean M5	(pre-diluted 1 : 2)	injected at 2 %	1 np
Euroclean DES 251	(pre-diluted 1 : 1)	injected at 2 %	2 np

MVEE

Military Vehicles and Engineering Establishment (MVEE)

Christchurch
Hants. BH23 2BB
TELEPHONE: Christchurch 4431
D. Cardwell (*Director*)
E. R. Copage (*Officer in charge of Container Testing*)

Since the first ISO containers were made in the UK, the facilities of the MVEE Bridge Testing Rig have been used for carrying out tests on them to both International and National Specification requirements.

The Bridge Testing Rig, which has a capacity of 5mN and an ability to accept structures up to 10·5 m (34 ft 10 in) wide, 8 m (26 ft) high and 184 m (600 ft) long, is occasionally still used to carry out tests on some specialised types of containers, but the majority of containers are now tested in a new covered structural test facility in test rigs specifically designed for the purpose. The new rigs can accept all sizes of containers, and are capable of accepting non-standard versions up to 3 m high for stacking test loads up to 1·1mN/column, transverse rigidity test loads up to 150kN (in tension and compression) as well as the normal test loads for the lift tests, restraint, and end and side wall tests.

The dynamic test rig was designed to meet the ISO and BSI requirements for the restraint and end wall tests for IC freight containers, and is still used for tests on restraint systems. It can be made available for dynamic tests on tank containers if these should be required.

Since MVEE, Christchurch (formerly MEXE) has been involved in a wide range of civil and military structural tests for over fifty years, the establishment is uniquely equipped to deal with abnormal tests required for non-standard containers. More detailed information on the entire range of testing facilities available to industry may be obtained on request. Applications for test should be addressed to the Head of the Engineer Equipment Division at Christchurch.

REPCON

REPCON
Head Office
30-38 Canal Street
Bootle
L20 8MP Lancashire
TELEPHONE: 051-922 8761/5
TELEX: 62356
D. L. Reevel (*Director*)
W. R. Atherton (*National Sales Manager*)
G. Moreton (*Chief Engineer*)
J. Swinscoe (*Quality Controller*)
E. Rankin (*Controller, Containers*)
J. McCormack (*Controller, Trailers*)
Note: At time of going to press Repcon are operating from 6/8 Forth Street, Bootle, Lancashire.
Telephone: 051-922 8761

North West Division
The North West Division covers an area extending as far North as Fleetwood and includes Manchester, Merseyside, and Ellesmere Port
Mr. W. H. Griffiths (*Divisional Manager*)
Telephone: 051-922 8761/5
After hours: 051-334 5511
MAJOR WORKSHOP:
Canal Street,
Bootle, Lancashire

Telephone: 051-922 8761/4
After hours: Scarisbrick 369
B. McKibbin (*Works Superintendent*)
Mr. R. W. Jackson (*Main Stores Superintendent*)
(Internal and outside sales of container and trailer parts).

CONTAINER WORKSHOPS:
Containerbase (Aintree) Ltd.
Orrell Lane
Liverpool
B. Atkinson (*Foreman*)
Telephone: 051-525 7461 Ext. 43
After hours: 051-226 5941
H. Riley (*North West Area Manager*)
Telephone: 051-922 8761/4
After hours: 051-226 5941
Chain Caul Road
Albert Edward Dock
Preston
Lancashire
Containerbase (Manchester) Ltd.
Barton Dock Road
Barton Dock Estate (West)
Urmston
Lancashire N31 2LP
Telephone: 061-748 7001
After hours: 051-226 5941

Gladstone Container Terminal
Liverpool 5
F. Hunter (*Foreman*)
Telephone: 051-922 3905
After hours: 051-226 5941
Containerbase (Warrington)
Barley Castle Lane
Appleton
Warrington
B. Johnson (*Foreman*)
Telephone: 92 6135

North East Division
The area includes Leeds, Middlesbrough and its hinterland, the Humber ports including Hull, Bradford, Huddersfield and Sheffield.
MAJOR WORKSHOPS:
Mr. J. R. Armitage (*North East Area Manager*)
John O'Gaunt Industrial Estate
Pontefract Road
Rothwell
Near Leeds
Telephone: Rothwell 3716/7
After hours: 048-483 3657
CONTAINER WORKSHOP:
Containerbase (Leeds) Ltd.
Wakefield Road,
Stourton

Leeds 10
Telephone: 0532 75702
After hours: 0532 645542

Scottish Division

Repcon's operations in Scotland cover the area round Glasgow port, and includes Greenock, Coatbridge Containerbase, Grangemouth and Leith.
A. Blair (*Scottish Area Manager*)
Repcon Limited
15 South Bridge Street
Airdrie
Scotland
Telephone: 02366 66755
After hours: 035-52 23703
CONTAINER WORKSHOP:
Containerbase (Scotland) Ltd.
Gartsherrie Road
Coatbridge
Lanarkshire
J. Steel (*Foreman*)
Telephone: 0236-27260
After hours: 035-52 23703

GREENOCK CONTAINER TERMINAL:
J. Peat (*Foreman*)
Telephone: 0236-27260
After hours: 035-52 23703

Repcon South-East Ltd.
J. G. Lansdale (*Director*)
W. L. Collard (*Director*)
Magnet Road,
London Road,
West Thurrock,
Greys, Essex

Southern Division

Centred on Southampton, this division also serves the Portsmouth area, Reading,

Oxford, Bristol and the Bristol Channel ports. Sykes and Trimmer Ltd. is part of the Repcon organisation. In addition to container and trailer repairs Sykes and Trimmer Ltd. also handle van and lorry bodywork repairs, and fibreglass repairs of all types.
MAJOR WORKSHOP:
J. Trimmer (*Divisional Manager*)
Sykes & Trimmer Ltd.
Millbrook Trading Estate
Southampton
Telephone: 0703 76891/4
After hours: 096-271 2612
E. G. C. Trimmer (*Workshop Manager*)
Telephone: 0703 76891/4
After hours: 042-18 4021
(internal and outside sales of container and trailer parts)
W. J. Taylor (*Stores Superintendent*)
Telephone: 0703 76891/4

Repcon & Sykes & Trimmer
SERVICES AVAILABLE:
1. Refrigeration plant. Repair and Maintenance.
2. Major repairs to containers of all types.
3. T.I.R. repairs—including patch repairs to plastic tilts.
4. Testing (a) Tension test to corner posts
   (b) Light test
   (c) Water test
   (d) Air leakage
5. Mobile vans for in-situ repairs.
6. Washing and cleaning.
7. Fumigation.
8. Repairs and maintenance of trailers.
9. Air test of refrigerated and insulated containers.
10. Unit body construction.
11. Composite body construction.

Branch 1	Liverpool	1, 2, 3, 4, 5, 6, 7, 8, 9 (10 and 11 available at new works)
Branch 3	Leeds	2, 3, 4* (b) (c), 5, 6, 7, 8, 9.
		* (a) obtainable on loan from Liverpool.
	Middlesborough	5.
	Hull	5.
Branch 4	Manchester	2, 3, 4 (b) (c), 5, 7, 8, 9. (any services not covered, obtainable from Liverpool).
Branch 5	Aintree	As Branch 4.
Branch 6	Preston	2, 4, (a) (b) (c), 5, 8, 9. (other services obtainable at Liverpool).
Branch 7	Scotland	2, 3, 4 (a) (b) (c), 5, 6, 7, 8, (no undercover premises) 9.
Branch 8	Mobiles	Service as Liverpool.
Branch 9	Sykes & Trimmer	1, 2, 3, 4 (a) (b) (c), 5, 6, 7, 8, 9, 10, 11.
Branch 10	Repcon South-East Ltd	2, 4 (a) (b) (c), 5, 6, 7, 8, 9.

OVERSEAS BRANCHES:
Repcon are the founders of Container Aid International and in addition to numerous European branches have set up repair facilities in Hong Kong and Singapore.

TRANS—INDUSTRIAL

Trans-Industrial Services Ltd.
26 Kensington Gardens,
Ilford,
Essex
TELEPHONE: 01-554-1081

R. P. M. O'Hanlon (*Managing Director*)
PRODUCT:
Mobile repair and maintenance facilities for containers.

ULTRASONIC

Ultrasonic Vehicle Washing Systems
A Division of Ultrasonic Machines Ltd.,
352 Bath Road, Slough, Bucks,
England.
TELEPHONE: Burnham (Bucks) 4455
TELEX: 84677
BRANCHES:
Ultrasonic Machines (Nederland) NV
Ultrasonic Machines GmbH, Germany (Federal Republic)
Ultrasonic Machines SA, Belgium
PRODUCT:
System for cleaning vehicles and containers.
This is how it works:
The vehicle is first sprayed with a negative antistatic chemical. The jet spray pulsates many thousands of times a minute, giving a wave form on the vehicles to allow the liquid to achieve high density penetration of the dirt very quickly. In a matter of seconds, the whole vehicle is saturated. The chemical etches thoroughly into the dirt, and physically repels all those particles carrying a negative charge. It loosens the dirt structure by breaking down the dirt particles.
The vehicle is sprayed again with a second chemical, this time a positive antistatic

chemical. Its effect is to repel all positively charged particles. It works its way round the etched particles and breaks the bond between these particles and the vehicle.
A third spray, this time of water, rinses the vehicle. Encrusted dirt, now freed from its electrostatic bondage, streams off. In a few seconds the vehicle is clean. It dries without water marks, and leaves an anticorrosive finish with a bright appearance. Windows, too, are bright and clear.
After a vehicle has been washed, its surface remains neutralised for a period of time, depending on local conditions. It is dirt resistant. Regularly used, the system keeps the vehicle clean *between* washes. This also has an important bearing on the operating cost of the system when half the amount of chemical is used.

The system consists of 2 main units:
1. The Console containing:
   (a) The simple control panel
   (b) The water reservoir and pump unit
   (c) Reservoir tanks for the unique Ultrasonic Chemicals.

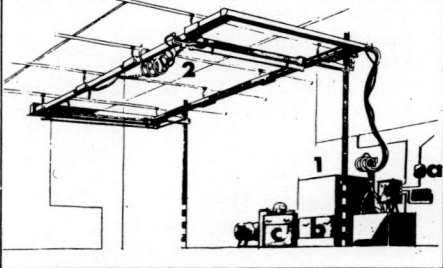

2. The Elevator Spray Frame is the part that does the actual washing. It is a rectangular frame of extruded aluminium the length of which is determined by the customer's requirements. Vehicles of any size can be washed with equal efficiency, economically using only the amount of chemical relative to the size of the vehicle to be washed. The same system will wash the Chairman's car or a 60 ft tanker. For articulated vehicles, the frame can be provided with a cross-spray system to wash the front of the trailer and the rear of the cab.

WINNIC

Winn International Containers Limited

Winn International Containers Ltd.
London Scottish House,
London Road, Barking, Essex
TELEPHONE: 01-594 4641/2/3/4
TELEGRAMS: Winnic Barking
TELEX: 262852
Head Office & Headquarters
Maintenance & Repair Division
MAINTENANCE & REPAIR DEPOTS,
UNITED KINGDOM:
Winn International Containers Ltd.
Station Road,
Parkeston,
Harwich, Essex
TELEPHONE: 02555 2414/5
TELEX: 98456
Winn International Containers Ltd.
London Road,
Barking, Essex
TELEPHONE: 01-594 4641/2/3/4
TELEGRAMS: Winnic Barking
TELEX: 262852
Winn International Containers Ltd.
Leads Road (B.R.S. Depot),
Hull, Yorkshire
TELEPHONE: 0482 74371
            0482 75121
TELEX: 52115

CONTINENTAL:
HEADQUARTERS, MAINTENANCE AND REPAIR DIVISION:
Winnic N.V.,
Calandstraat 49/51,
3002 Rotterdam.
Holland
TELEPHONE: (010) 146510
TELEX: 24374
Netherlands:
Winnic N. V.
Bunschotenweg 131,
1E, Eemhaven,
Rotterdam, 22. Zuid.
TELEPHONE: 146510
TELEX: 24374
Italy:
Winn International Containers Ltd.
Via M. Macchi 26,
20124 Milan, Italy
TELEPHONE: 27 89 57
TELES: 31412
GENERAL:
Comprehensive network of United Kingdom and Continental mobile service, agencies and storage depots, with further Maintenance and Repair depots imminent.
MAINTENANCE AND REPAIR DIVISION MANAGEMENT:
T. A. Goodwin (*Maintenance & Repair Executive, Barking Head Office*)

R. Goode (*General Manager, Harwich*)
A. Tilley (*Manager, Hull Depot*)
R. Visser (*General Manager, Continent, Rotterdam Office*)
R. Schneider (*Manager, Rotterdam Depot*)
SERVICE AND FACILITIES GENERALLY AVAILABLE:
Centred on the service developed for the successful Winnic Comprehensive and Non-Comprehensive Container and Semi-Trailer leasing organisation operating throughout the United Kingdom and the Continent, the Winnic Maintenance and Repair Division offers a service incorporating years of practical experience operating under modern management.

Efficient depot workshops and mobile service undertake the whole range of Container and Semi-Trailer maintenance and repair from the smallest item to major re-builds including T.I.R. Tilt Cover repair.

The Winnic fleet of fully equipped modern vans and skilled personnel operate as a mobile service available in readiness to deal with P.V.C. Tilt Cover repairs, glades of secondary structure/panel damage and minor repair details to Containers and Semi-Trailers at transit points throughout the United Kingdom and the Continent and including quay operations based at Parkeston, Harwich.

UNITED STATES OF AMERICA

MINER

Miner Enterprises Inc.
Research and Development Division
1001 E. 87th Street,
Chicago
Illinois 60619
TELEPHONE: 312/374-7400
W. E. Wiltall (*President*)
GENERAL:
The only independent, commercially available testing facility in USA, the Research and Development Division custom engineers test programmes to customer specifications, as well as to comply with standards set up by regulatory authorities or industry bodies. This includes the following tests: stacking, racking, lifting, restraint through bottom fittings, floor and roof strength, end wall, side wall and door strength, weather tightness, dimensional checks and, for insulated or refrigerated containers, air leak, heat transfer, cooling and heat rise.

In addition, the Miner facility includes a modern test track for impact testing of containers and loading under actual operating clonditions.

All tests are electronically monitored and recorded, and completely documented, unbiased reports issued to the customer.

A 40 ft stacking tent at Miner Enterprises Inc.

40 ft end wall test at Miner Enterprises Inc.

STCC

Ship Tank Container Corporation
Foot of Grace Street,
Secaucus, N.J. 07094
TELEPHONE: 201 864 0500
OFFICIAL:
Manuel Garcia Jr. (*President*)

Stone Downer Co.
See also list of USA maintenance firms given in the New York port section.

BRANCH:
419 W 22nd Street,
Norfolk, Va. 23517
Telephone: 622 2520
James Drews (*Manager*)

MAIN ACTIVITIES:
Repair and maintenance of freight containers at the two locations.

INTERNATIONAL ROAD
AND
INTERNATIONAL RAIL

INTERNATIONAL ROAD

International Road Transport Union (IRÙ)
Centre International
1-3, Rue de Varembé, 1202 Geneva, Switzerland
TELEPHONE: (022) 34 13 30/34 13 39/34 13 38
TELEX: 27107

P. Groenendijk (*Secretary General*)
M. de Gottrau (*Deputy*)
A Tarnowski (*Deputy*)
Dr. R. Schober (*President, W. Germany*)
L. Raucamp (*Vice-President, W. Germany*)
P. Baragiola (*Vice-President, Italy*)
J. Richard Deshais (*Vice-President, France*)
Cl. Leblanc (*Vice-President, France*)
H. Van der Berg (*Vice-President, Netherlands*)
K. C. Turner (*Vice-President, United Kingdom*)
C. Auderet (*Vice-President, Switzerland*)
Dr. A. De Muynck (*Vice-President, Belgium*)

Section I (Passenger Transport)
   President: P. Baragiola (*Italy*)
Section II (Freight transport)
   President: L. Raucamp (*W. Germany*)
Section III (Private transport)
   President: Dr A. De Muynck (*Belgium*)

General
IRU, founded in Geneva on March 23, 1948, is an international non-governmental organization of national federations for road transport. They are active members of this Union which also comprises associate members (groups and undertakings interested in its activities). It has consultative status in the UN (1949) and the Council of Europe (1959).

Its main objective is to contribute to the development and the prosperity of national and international road transport in all countries and to defend the interests of road transport.

To attain these objectives IRU endeavours to solve problems connected with its purpose and particularly those in the fields of economic, social, legal and technical development.

IRU Members
ASSOCIATE MEMBERS

IRU has 22 associate members in Europe (including groups of transport undertakings and manufacturers of commercial vehicles) and four in countries outside Europe.
Brazil:
Associaçao Nacional das Emprêsas de Transportes Rodoriarios de Carga
Av. Beira Mar, 262, Rio de Janeiro
Canada:
Canadian Trucking Associations Inc,
251 Bank Street, Ottawa 4
India:
AIMUC, Asaf Ali Road 16-A, New Delhi-1
Japan:
Japan Trucking Association,
No. 2, 3-Chome, Yotsuya Shinjuku-ku, Tokyo
ACTIVE MEMBERS:

IRU has 47 active members in Europe and five outside Europe: i.e. those engaged in professional transport of passengers and goods by road and private transport.
ALBANIA:
Association Nationale des Entreprises de Transports Routiers (ANALTIR),
Ministère du Commerce, Tirana

WEST GERMANY (DR)
Bundesverband des Deutschen Personenverkehrs (BDP),
Ravensteinstrasse 2, 6-Frankfurt/Main
Bundesverband des Deutschen Güterfernverkehrs (BDF),
Haus des Strassenverkehrs—
   Breitenbachstrasse, 1,
   6-Frankfurt (M) 93

Deutsche Industrie und Handelstag (DIHT)
Adenauerallee, 148 Bonn 53
EAST GERMANY (FR)
Arbeitsgemeinschaft zur Förderung und Entwicklung des Internationalen Strassenverkehrs in der Deutschen Demokratischen Republik eV (AIST),—Mauerstrasse, 53-Berlin 108
AUSTRIA:
Arbeitsgemeinschaft Internationaler Strassenverkehrsunternehmer Osterreichs (AISO),
Bauernmarkt, 13—A-1011 Vienna
BELGIUM:
Fédération Nationale des Exploitants d'Autobus et d'Autocars (FNEAA),
Rue Léon Lepage, 4—Brussels 1
Fédération Nationale Belge des Transporteurs Routiers (FNBTR),
Rue Picard, 69—Brussels 2
Union Professionnelle des Transporteurs Routiers Internationaux (UPTRI),
Rue Picard, 69—Brussels 2
Fédération des Industries Belges (FIB),
Rue Ravenstein, 4—Brussels 1

BULGARIA:
Association des Entreprises Bulgares des Transports Routiers Internationaux,
Rue Rezbarska, 10—Sofia
DENMARK:
Turistvognmaendenes Landsorganisation
Puggaardsgade, 15—1575 Copenhagen V
Landsforeiningen Danske Vognmaend (LDV),
Jens Kofodsgade, 1—1268 Copenhagen K

Landsforeningen Danske Vognmoend
Jens Kofodsgade 1,
Copenhagen K, Denmark
TELEPHONE: Byen 7646
TELEX: 82219
The members of this road transport association who operate containers beyond Danish national borders are:
ROLAND MUNCH
Jagtvej 71,
6700 Esbjerg
KNUD NYBORG
7322 Farre
K. E. CHRISTESEN
Oster Vedsted pr.,
6760 Ribe

DAN TRANSPORT
Vestergade 33,
1456 Kobenhavn K
EKSATRANS A/S
Kongelysvej 10-12
2820 Gentofte
HOLGER HANSEN
Haderslevvej 145,
6000 Kolding
LARS VEDSTESEN
Fynsgade 24,
6700 Esbjerg
TRANSPORTAKTIESELSKABET HAUSTEIN
6340 Krusaa
FERRYMASTER A/S
Ravnsborggade 6,
2200 Kobenhavn N

DE FORENDE VOGNMANDSFORRETNINGER
Haraldsgade 15,
2200 Kobenhavn N
PAUL LEHMANN
Flensborgvej 11
6340 Krusaa
KNUD HANSEN
Bengtasvej 11,
2900 Hellerup
A. E. GRODT
Europavej 3,
6100 Haderslev

WALTHER HANSEN
W. Hansen-Transport A/S,
Ndr. Toldbod 21
2100 Kobenhavn 0
SPAIN:
Sindicato Nacional de Transportes y Comunicaciones (SNTC),
Paseo del Prado, 18-20—Madrid 14
Consejo Superior de las Camaras Oficiales de Comercio Industria y Navegacionde Espana,
Calle Claudio Coello, 19-1°—Madrid 1
FINLAND:
Suomen Kuorma Autoliitto r.y.
Ammattiautollija, Luotsikatu, 7A4
   —Helsinki 16
FRANCE:
Fédération Nationale des Loueurs de Voitures de Place à Taximètre (FNLVT)
129 rue Jules-Guerde, 92 Levallois-Perret,
Fédération Nationale des Transports Routiers (FNTR),
Rue de la Bienfaisance, 44—Paris 8e
Union des Usagers de Véhicules de Transport Privé (UVTP)
Rue de Stockholm, 5—Paris 8e
GREECE:
Bund der LKW-Automobillisten Griechenlands,
Rue Lycocrgov 9, Athens
HUNGARY:
Association des Transporteurs Routiers Internationaux en Hongrie (ATRIH),
Lenin krt 96—Budapest VI (62)
IRELAND:
Lastas Eireann Teoranta (LET),
Lansdowne House, Ballsbridge, Dublin 4
ITALY:
Associazione Nazionale Autoservici in Concessione (ANAC),
Via Cavour, 71—00184 Rome
Associazione Nazionale delle Imprese dei Trasporti Automobilistici (ANITA),
Via Plebiscito, 102—00186 Rome
Consociazione Nazionali Federazioni Autotrasporti (CNFA)
Via del Plebiscito, 102—00186 Rome
Confederazione Generale dell'Indistria Italiana
Piazza Venezia, 11—00187 Rome
LUXEMBURG:
Association des Enterpreneurs Luxembourgeous de Ligneso Autobue (AELLA)
Rue Jean Origer, 5, Luxembourg-Gare
NORWAY:
Norges Lastbilier Forbundet (NLF)
—Fagerheimgt, 18—Oslo 5
NETHERLANDS:
Koninklijke Nederlandse Vereniging van Transport Ondernemingen (KNVTO),
Van Stolkweg, 29a—The Hague
Nationale Organisatie voor het Beroepsgoederenvervoer Wegtransport (NOB),
Vervoershuis—Huis te Landelaan, 492, Rijswijk (zH)
Stichting Nederlandse Internationale Wegvervoer Organisatie (NIWO),
Koninginnegracht 93/94—The Hague
Algemene Verladers-en Eigen Vervoerders Organisatie (EVO)
Stadhouderslaan 162, The Hague

POLAND:
Association des Transporteurs Routiers Internationaux en Pologne (Zrzesznie Miedzynarodowych Przewoznikow Drogowych w Polsce) (ZMPD)
—Grojecka ul 17—Warsaw 22
PORTUGAL:
Grémio dos Industriais de Transportes em Automoveis (GITA),
Rua Dr Antonio Candido, 8—Lisbon 1

ROMANIA:
Association roumaine pour transports routiers internationaux, Romtrans
Calea Rahovei, 196—Bucarest

UNITED KINGDOM:
Passenger Vehicle Operators Association Ltd, (PVOA)
Emerald Street, 12, London, W.C.1
Road Haulage Association Ltd, (RHA),
22, Upper Woburn Place, London, W.C.1
Freight Transport Association Ltd, (FTA),
Sunley House, Bedford Park,
Croydon CR9 1XU

SWEDEN:
Svenska Busstrafikförbundet (SBF)
Nybrodatan, 7—5-114-34 Stockholm
Svenska Akeriförbundet (SA)
Valhallavägen, 66—Stockholm O
Svenska Taxiförbundet (STF),
Radmansgattan 48, Ztr. 11357 Stockholm

SWITZERLAND:
Fédération Suisse de l'Industrie des Transports Automobiles (TAG),
Seftigenstrasse, 26-3007 Berne
Association Suisse des Propriétaires d'Auto-camions (ASPA),
Sulgenauweg, 26-3007 Berne

CZECHOSLOVAKIA:
Association des Transports Routiers Internationaux Tchécoslovaques (CESMAD),
Hybernska, 32—Prague I

TURKEY:
Union of Chambers of Commerce, Industry and Commodity Exchanges of Turkey,
Union of Chambers of Commerce Industry and Commodity of Exchanges of Turkey,
Ataturk Bulvari 149,—Ankara

YUGOSLAVIA:
Centre du Transport International par Vehicules Automobiles (CMA)
Terazije, 23/V—Belgrade
Overseas:
ARGENTINE:
Association latinamerica del transporte automotor por carreteras (ALATAC)
Arenida Belgrano, 1870 Buenos Aires
IRAN:
Iran Chamber of Commerce, Industries and Mines
Avenue Takst—Jamshid 254, Tehran
ISRAEL:
Israel Trucking Board
12 Ben Zion Boulevard, Tel Aviv
USA:
American Trucking Asscn. Inc.
1616 P Street NW, Washington DC 20036
Equipment Interchange Asscn. (EIA)
1616 P. Street NW, Washington DC 20036

T.I.R. REGULATIONS

The Customs Convention on the International Transport of Goods by Road, 1959

PURPOSE AND SCOPE:
The purpose of the Convention is to enable goods to travel in Customs-sealed road vehicles or in Customs-sealed containers carried on road vehicles across one or more national frontiers with the minimum of Customs interference. Goods entering the procedure in countries which are parties to the Convention may normally pass through the territory of any other member country without payment of, or security for, Customs duties and other taxes and without Customs examination provided that:

(a) the goods are transported in road vehicles or containers previously approved in accordance with the requirements laid down by the Convention;
(b) the goods are documented on a TIR carnet; and
(c) the TIR carnet is issued by an association approved in accordance with the terms of the Convention.

The Convention applies notwithstanding that the road vehicles are carried for *part* of the journey by another means of transport, e.g. on a roll-on/roll-off ferry between the United Kingdom and the Continent. An ECE Resolution recommends Contracting Parties to extend the use of TIR carnets to containers carried for *part* of their journey by other means of transport *without being loaded on a road vehicle*. The United Kingdom along with most, but not all, other countries concerned has accepted this recommendation. TIR Carnets will therefore be accepted by the United Kingdom Customs to cover goods carried in containers however they arrive in or leave the United Kingdom and however they are carried whilst under Customs control within the United Kingdom.

The Convention is aimed at the overall facilitation of the international movement of goods carried in road vehicles and containers, but, in order to minimise and expedite formalities at frontiers some additional controls are necessary in the country of departure. Customs are ready to accept the extra work involved when an export cargo, which would normally require little or no control, is first brought within the TIR procedure in the United Kingdom, in the expectation that by doing so they will speed the flow of British exports through other countries. Carriers are however asked to ensure that carnets are fully and accurately completed and that sufficient time is allowed for completion of the necessary formalities, particularly before sailing of scheduled ferry services.

Countries in which the Convention operates

In addition to the United Kingdom the Convention operates in Austria, Belgium, Bulgaria, Czechoslovakia, Denmark, Federal Republic of Germany, Finland, France, Greece, Hungary, Italy, Liechtenstein, Luxemburg, Netherlands, Norway, Poland, Portugal, Republic of Ireland, Romania, Spain, Sweden, Switzerland, Turkey, the United States of America and Yugoslavia. Japan is about to adhere to the convention.

Definition of 'road vehicle' and 'container' for the purposes of the Convention

For the purposes of the TIR Convention, the term "road vehicle" includes any trailer or semi-trailer designed to be drawn by a road vehicle or tractor. The term "container" means an article of transport equipment (lift van, movable tank or other similar structure) strong enough to be suitable for repeated use, specially designed to facilitate the carriage of goods by any means of transport without intermediate unloading and having an internal volume of one cubic metre (approximately 35 cubic feet) or more.

Approval of vehicles and containers

Under the Convention a vehicle or container must be approved by the competent authority of the country in which the owner or carrier is resident or established to ensure that it meets the necessary constructional requirements.

Carriers are advised to ensure that their vehicles and containers continue to be maintained to the approved structural standards, since Customs authorities here and abroad will refuse to allow unsatisfactory vehicles or containers to proceed under TIR carnets.

TIR Plates

Road vehicles operating under the system are required to carry removable plates, capable of being sealed, measuring 250 mm × 400 mm (9·8 in × 15·7 in) with the white letters TIR on a blue background. The plates should be affixed to the front and rear of the vehicle in such a position that they are clearly visible. Trailers, semi-trailers and containers should be similarly marked at the front and rear, where necessary the plates being placed on the upper part so as to be clearly visible over the cab of the lorry or of the tractor.

The TIR Carnet

A carnet is issued by a guaranteeing association normally in the country where the holder of the carnet is established or resident or, in certain circumstances, in the country in which the TIR journey commences. It is valid for one complete journey only and covers the goods carried on one vehicle or normally in one container. It may also cover goods in more than one container provided the containers are loaded on a single road vehicle and remain on that vehicle throughout their journey and provided the goods manifest of the carnet clearly distinguishes the contents of each container.

The carnet comprises a set of pairs of vouchers (with corresponding counterfoils) bound in a cover. Each pair consists of a Voucher No. 1 for control at the office of departure or at offices of entry en route and a Voucher No. 2 for control at offices of exit en route or at offices of destination. Except as indicated in paragraph 111, a pair of vouchers is necessary for the country of departure, for the country of destination and for each country traversed. Carnets normally consist of three or seven pairs of vouchers

The constituent parts of the carnet are used as follows:
(a) Cover:
(i) Page 1 is completed by the guaranteeing association and the international organisation to which it is affiliated. The initials of the latter will appear on this page; there are three such organisations:
IRU—Union Internationale des Transports Routiers
FIA—Federation Internationale de l'Automobile
AIT—Alliance Internationale de Tourisme.
(ii) Page 2 is a declaration and undertaking which must be completed by the holder or his agent.
(iii) Page 3 sets out rules for the use of the carnet.
(iv) Page 4 is for the recording of accidents en route.
(b) Vouchers:
(i) Each voucher includes a goods manifest and all the manifests in the carnet are completed by the holder or his agent in the language of the country from which the goods are exported before the carnet is presented to the Customs office in the exporting country. Translations may be required by countries en route.
(ii) The vouchers are detachable and are for retention by the various Customs offices through which the vehicle or container passes. To each voucher there is a corresponding counterfoil which is completed and stamped by each Customs office and left in the carnet for the information of other Customs offices.
The carnet is printed in French but

additional pages may be inserted giving a translation in the language of the country of issue. This translation generally takes the form of a yellow voucher preceding those referred to above; this translation is for information only and is not detached by Customs.

The guaranteeing associations

The guaranteeing associations, which are each affiliated to at least one of the international organisations referred to above, issue carnets to their members and guarantee any duty or tax due on goods travelling under carnet. The guaranteeing associations in the United Kingdom are:

RHA—Road Haulage Association Ltd.
72 Upper Woburn Place,
London WC1
Telephone: 01.387.9711
FTA—Freight Transport Association Ltd.
Sunley House, Bedford Park,
Croydon, CR9 IXU
Telephone: 01.686.0731
For overseas associations, the IRU will supply full details.

Special arrangements for heavy or bulky goods

In addition to goods transported in approved vehicles and containers the benefits of the Convention may also apply to heavy or bulky goods. The term "heavy or bulky goods" means any object which in the opinion of the Customs of the exporting country cannot readily be dismantled for transport and of which

(a) the weight exceeds 7,000 kg (15,428 lb); or
(b) one dimension exceeds 5 m (16·4 ft); or
(c) two dimensions exceed 2 m (6·5 ft); or
(d) the height, taking account of the loading position, exceeds 2 m.

The Customs Officer must be satisfied that such an object (with any accessories) can be easily identified by reference to the description given in the goods manifest, or can be provided with identifying marks or can be sealed so that it cannot be replaced in whole or part by other goods or anything be removed from it. To assist in the identification the Officer may require packing lists, photographs, blue prints, etc., to be attached to the carnet and in such a case the procedure outlined in Rule 4(c) in Rules for the use of the TIR carnet (Appendix to this Notice) should be followed. The Customs Officer must also be satisfied that the carrying vehicle contains no hidden spaces where goods can be concealed.

Where such goods are carried under TIR carnet, the cover and all the vouchers of the carnet should bear the endorsement "Heavy or bulky goods" in bold red letters in the language in which the carnet is printed.

Offices of departure and destination and offices en route

The holder of the TIR carnet must specify on the vouchers the offices of departure and destination and the offices en route to be used on the particular journey for which the carnet has been issued. Customs offices of departure and destination are defined in the Convention as the inland or frontier Customs offices of a Contracting Party where the system provided by the Convention begins or ceases to apply to an international transport by road vehicle or container of a load or part load. A Customs office en route is defined as any frontier Customs office of a Contracting Party which a vehicle or container merely passes through in the course of an international transport under the system provided by the Convention. Details of offices approved by the Contracting Parties can be ascertained from the guaranteeing associations.

In the United Kingdom, all ports and land boundary stations may act as offices of departure and destination, as may approved Inland Clearance Depots and certain approved Inland Rail Depots provided that in the latter case the containers are removed between them and the ports by rail. Wharves and airports approved under the inter-port removal arrangements and bonded warehouses approved for the examination of beer and wine imported in containers are also approved as offices of destination. Bonded warehouses approved for the loading of beer and wine in containers are offices of departure. Where goods are removed within the United Kingdom to or from one of the inland places referred to above or in transit from, say, the Republic of Ireland to the Continent of Europe, the ports or land boundary stations are regarded as offices of entry or exit en route.

Loading and unloading at more than one place

The Convention provides for a single TIR carnet to cover goods loaded or unloaded at several offices of departure or destination, subject to the following rules:

(a) The Customs offices of departure must all be situated in the same country;
(b) the Customs offices of destination must be situated in not more than two countries; and
(c) the total number of Customs offices of departure and destination must not exceed four.

In the case of heavy and bulky goods the TIR carnet may not involve more than one office of departure and one office of destination.

Where more than one office of departure or destination is involved, the carnet must include an extra pair of vouchers for each additional office. In the goods manifest in every voucher of the carnet the goods loaded at each office of departure or destined for each office of destination should be clearly separated.

REGULATIONS ON TECHNICAL CONDITIONS APPLICABLE TO ROAD VEHICLES WHICH MAY BE ACCEPTED FOR INTERNATIONAL TRANSPORT OF GOODS UNDER CUSTOM SEAL.

General

Approval for the international transport of goods by road vehicle under Customs seal may be granted only for vehicles constructed and equipped in such a manner that:

(a) Customs seals can be simply and effectively affixed thereto;
(b) no goods can be removed from or introduced into the sealed part of the vehicle without obvious damage to it or without breaking the seals;
(c) they contain no concealed spaces where goods may be hidden.

The vehicles shall be so constructed that all spaces in the form of compartments, receptacles or other recesses which are capable of holding goods are readily accessible for Customs inspection.

Should any empty spaces be formed by the different layers of the sides, floor and roof of the vehicle, the inside surface shall be firmly fixed, solid and unbroken and incapable of being dismantled without leaving obvious traces.

Structure of Loading Compartment

The sides, floor and roof of the loading compartment shall be constructed of plates, boards or panels of sufficient strength, of adequate thickness, and welded, riveted, grooved or jointed in such a way as not to leave any gaps in the structure through which access to the contents can be obtained. The various parts shall fit each other exactly and be so arranged that it is impossible either to move or remove them without leaving visible traces or damaging the Customs seals.

Where assembly is effected by means of rivets, the latter may be seated on the inside or outside; rivets joining the essential parts of the sides, floor and roof shall pass through the parts joined. Where assembly is effected otherwise than by means of rivets, those bolts or other joining devices which hold the essential parts of the sides, floor and roof shall be seated on the outside, protrude on the inside and be properly bolted, riveted or welded, while the other bolts or joining devices may be seated on the inside, provided that the nut is welded in a satisfactory manner on the outside and is not covered with non-transparent material. The assembly or metal plates or panels may also be effected by the curving or folding of their edges towards the inside of the vehicles, and these edges may be joined

either by rivets, bolts or other joining devices passing through the edges thus curved or folded and through the devices (if any) connecting them;

or by metal strips curved under pressure to form clamps at the same time as the edges of the parts to be assembled and ensuring permanent compression of the joints thus made (see Sketch A).

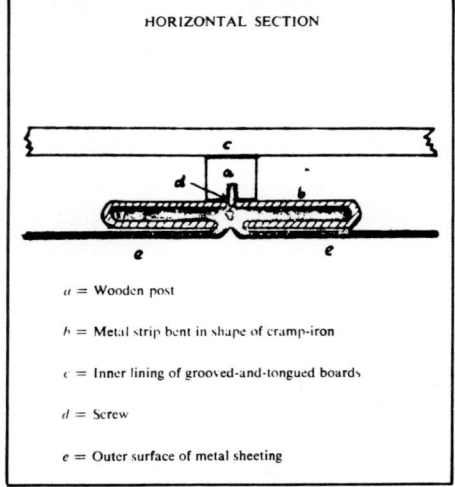

HORIZONTAL SECTION

a = Wooden post

b = Metal strip bent in shape of cramp-iron

c = Inner lining of grooved-and-tongued boards

d = Screw

e = Outer surface of metal sheeting

fig A

Apertures for ventilation shall be allowed provided their longest side does not exceed 400 mm. If they permit direct access to the interior of the loading compartment, they shall be covered with metal gauze or perforated metal screens (maximum dimension of holes: 3 mm in both cases) and protected by welded metal lattice-work (maximum dimensions of holes: 10 mm). If they do not permit direct access to the interior of the loading compartment (for example, by means of multiple-bend air ducts), they shall be provided with the same protective devices but the dimensions of the holes may be increased to 10 mm and 20 mm respectively (instead of 3 mm and 10 mm). It shall not be possible to remove these devices from the outside without leaving visible traces. Metal gauze shall be of wire at least 1 mm in diameter and so made that single strands cannot be pushed together and that the size of individual holes cannot be increased without leaving visible traces.

Windows shall be allowed provided that they comprise a fixed glass and metal grill which cannot be removed from the outside. The holes of the grill shall not exceed 10 mm across.

Openings made in the floor for technical purposes, such as lubrication, maintenance and filling of the sand-box, shall be allowed only on condition that they are fitted with a cover capable of being fixed in such a way as to render the loading compartment inaccessible from the outside.

Closing Systems

Doors and all other closing systems of vehicles shall be fitted with a device which shall permit simple and effective Customs sealing. This device shall either be welded to the side of doors where these are of metal, or secured by at least two bolts, riveted or welded to the nuts on the inside.

Hinges shall be so made and fitted that doors and other closing systems cannot be lifted off the hinge-pins once shut; the screws, bolts, hinge-pins and other fasteners shall be welded to the outer parts of the hinges. These requirements shall be waived, however, where the doors and other closing systems have a locking device inaccessible from the outside which, once it is applied, prevents the doors from being lifted off the hinge-pins.

Doors shall be so constructed as to cover all interstices and ensure complete and effective closure.

The vehicle shall be provided with a satisfactory device for protecting the Customs seal, or shall be so constructed that the Customs seal is adequately protected.

Vehicles for Special Use

The foregoing conditions shall apply to insulated vehicles, refrigerator vehicles, tank vehicles and furniture vehicles in so far as they are not incompatible with the technical requirements which such vehicles must fulfil in accordance with their use.

The flanges (filler caps), drain cocks and manholes of tank wagons shall be so constructed as to allow simple and effective Customs sealing.

Sheeted Vehicles

Where applicable, the provision of articles 2 to 4 above shall apply to sheeted vehicles. However, the system of closing and protecting the ventilation apertures mentioned in article 2, paragraph 3, may consist externally of a perforated metal screen (maximum dimension of holes 10 mm) and internally of metal gauze or some other very strong gauze (maximum dimension of meshes: 3 mm), the strands being such that they cannot be pushed together without leaving visible traces), the screen and the gauze being fixed to the sheet in such a way that their assembly cannot be altered without leaving obvious traces. In addition, sheeted vehicles shall conform to the following conditions.

The sheet shall be either of strong canvas or, provided it is not dark in colour of plastic-covered or rubberised cloth, non-tensile and of sufficient strength. It shall be fashioned in one piece or of strips in one piece. It shall be in good condition and made up in such a way that once the closing device has been secured, it is impossible to gain access to the load without leaving obvious traces.

If the sheet is made up of several strips, their edges shall be folded into one another and sewn together with two seams at least 15 mm apart. These seams shall be made as shown in sketch B attached to the present Regulations; however, where in the case of certain parts of the sheet, such as flaps at the rear and reinforced corners, it is not possible to assemble the strips in that way, it shall be sufficient to fold the edge of the top section and made the seams as shown in sketch C attached to these regulations. The threads used for each of the two seams shall be plainly different in colour; one of the seams shall be visible only from the inside and the colour of the thread used for that seam shall be plainly different from the colour of the sheet itself. All seams shall be machine-sewn.

If the sheet is of plastic-covered cloth, and is made up of several strips, the strips may also be welded together in the manner shown in sketch D attached to these Regulations. The edges of the strips shall overlap by at least 15 mm. The strips shall be fused together over the whole width of the overlapping parts. The edge of the outer sheet shall be covered with a band of plastic at least 7 mm wide, affixed by the same welding process. The plastic band and a width of at least 3 mm on each side shall have a well-marked uniform relief stamped on it. The strips shall be welded in such a way that they cannot be separated and then rejoined without leaving obvious traces.

Repairs shall be made in accordance with the method described in sketch E attached to these Regulations; the edges shall be folded into one another and sewn together with two visible seams at least 15 mm apart; the colour of the thread visible from the inside shall be different from that of the thread visible from the outside and from that of the sheet itself; all seams shall be machine-sewn. Nevertheless, sheets of plastic-covered cloth may also be repaired in accordance with the method described above.

Securing rings shall be so fitted that they cannot be removed from the outside. Eyelets in the sheet shall be reinforced with metal or leather. The interval between eyelets or rings shall not exceed 200 mm.

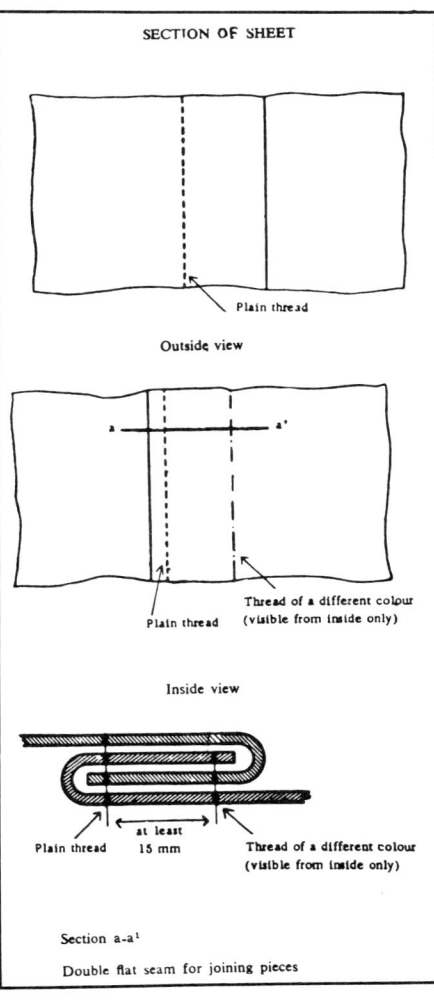

fig B

The sheet shall be so fixed as to render the load quite inaccessible. It shall be supported by at least three lengthwise bars or laths resting at the ends of the loading platform either on hoops or on the end walls of the platform; where the loading platform is more than 4 metres long, at lease one intermediate hoop must be provided. The hoops shall be fixed in such a way that it is impossible to alter their position from the outside.

The following types of fastening shall be used:

(a) steel wire rope of at least 3 mm diameter; or

(b) hemp or sisal rope of at least 8 mm diameter encased in a transparent non-tensible plastic sheath; or,

(c) iron bars at least 8 mm in diameter.

Steel wire ropes shall not be covered, except with a transparent non-tensible plastic sheath. Iron bars shall not be coated with non-transparent material.

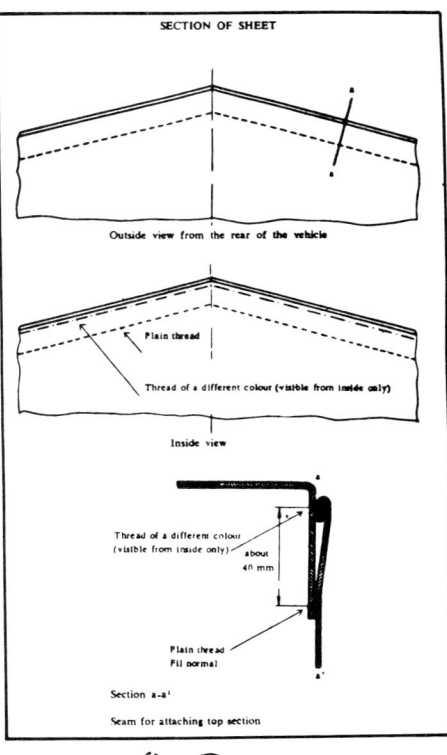

fig C

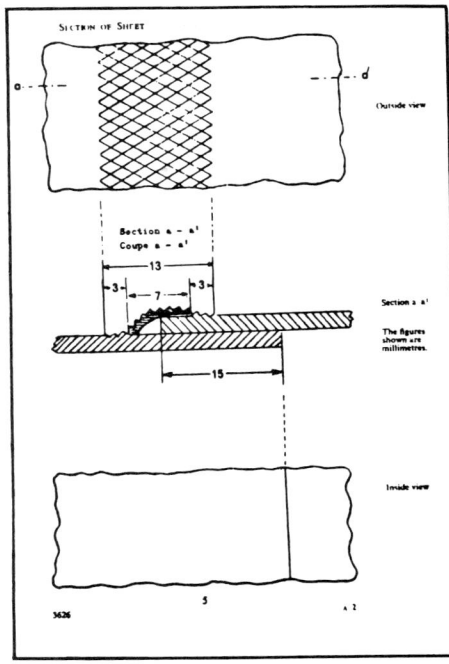

fig D

Each wire rope or hemp or sisal rope shall be in one piece and have a metal end piece. The fastener of each metal end piece shall include a hollow rivet passing through the rope so as to allow the introduction of a string of the Customs seal. The rope shall remain visible on either side of the hollow rivet

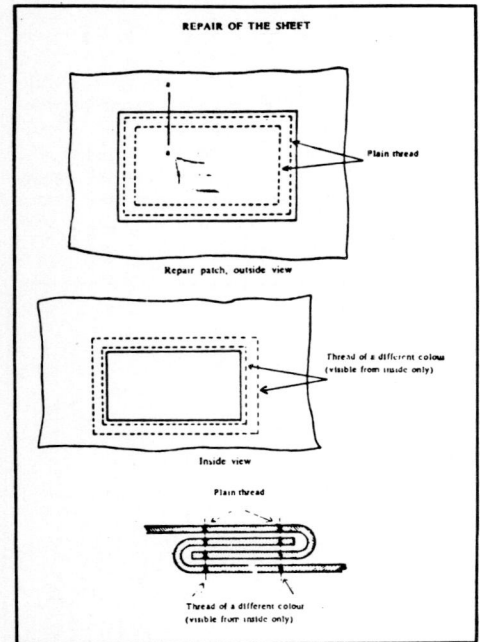

REPAIR OF THE SHEET

Repair patch, outside view

Plain thread

Inside view

Thread of a different colour (visible from inside only)

Plain thread

Thread of a different colour (visible from inside only)

fig E

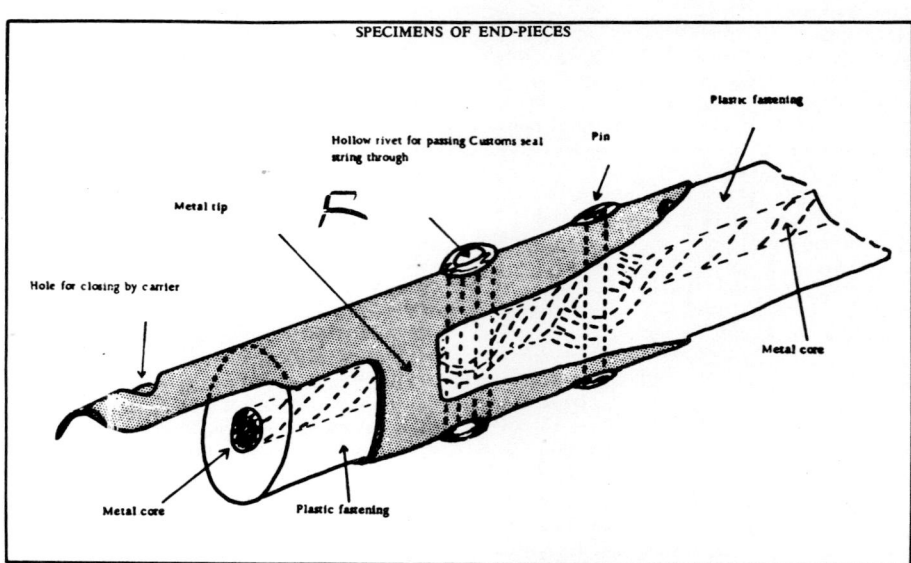

SPECIMENS OF END-PIECES

Hollow rivet for passing Customs seal string through

Pin

Plastic fastening

Metal tip

Hole for closing by carrier

Metal core

Metal core

Plastic fastening

fig F

so that it is possible to ascertain whether the rope is in one piece. (See sketch F.)

Each iron bar shall be in one piece. It shall have a hole at one end to take the closing device and, at the other end, a head forged to the bar and so constructed as to make it impossible for the bar to turn on its axis.

When ropes are used the sides of the vehicles shall be at least 350 mm high and the sheet shall cover the sides to a depth of at least 300 mm.

At the openings used for loading and unloading the vehicle, the two edges of the sheet shall have an adequate overlap. They shall likewise be fastened by a flap attached to the outside and sewn in accordance with paragraph 3 of this article. The fastenings shall be either those provided for in paragraph 8 or thongs at least 20 mm wide and 3 mm thick made of leather or non-tensible rubberised cloth. These thongs shall be attached inside the sheet and fitted with eyelets to take the wire rope or iron bar mentioned above.

SIZE AND WEIGHT LIMITS—EUROPE

Maximum permitted lengths, widths, heights, and weights Europe	Width			Height			Length			Weight tons
	m	ft	in	m	ft	in	m	ft	in	
Austria	2·5	8	2½	3·8	12	5½	18	59	1	38
Belgium	2·5	8	2½	4·0	13	2	18	59	1	40
Bulgaria	2·5	8	2½	4·0	13	2	18	59	1	40
Czechoslovakia	2·5	8	2½	3·8	12	5½	22	72	3	38
Denmark	2·5	8	2½	3·6	11	10	18	59	1	32
Eire	2·5	8	2½	—	—		16·5	54	1½	32
Finland	2·5	8	2½	3·8	12	5½	18	59	1	17·5*
France	2·5	8	2½	—	—		18	59	1	35
Germany, E	2·5	8	2½	4·0	13	2	18	59	1	—
Germany, W	2·5	8	2½	4·0	13	2	18	59	1	38
Greece	2·5	8	2½	3·8	12	5½	18	59	1	25+
Hungary	2·5	8	2½	4·0	13	2	18	59	1	36
Italy	2·5	8	2½	4·0	13	2	18	59	1	36
Netherlands	2·5	8	2½	4·0	13	2	18	59	1	50
Norway	2·2†	7	3	—	—		—			—
Poland	2·5	8	2½	3·8	12	5½	18	59	1	48
Portugal	2·45	8	0½	4·0	13	2	14	46	0	35
Spain	2·5	8	2½	4·0	13	2	16·5	54	1½	32
Sweden	2·5	8	2½	—	—		—			—
Switzerland	2·3†	7	7	4·0	13	2	18	59	1	26
Turkey	2·5	8	2½	3·8	12	5½	18	59	1	32·5
United Kingdom	2·5	8	2½	—	—		15	49	2½ × 32	

*Higher weights are permitted in Finland depending on the total length
+Up to 32 tons allowed on certain Greek roads

× Articulated motor vehicles. Rigid is 11 m (36 ft 1 in)
†On some main roads 2·35 (7 ft 8 in) is allowed in Norway, 2·5 (8 ft 2½ in) in Switzerland

SIZE AND WEIGHT LIMITS— ASIA, AUSTRALIA

Maximum permitted lengths, widths heights and weights Asia, Middle East, Far East and Australasia	Width			Height			Length			Weight tons
				m	ft	in	m	ft	in	
China (Taiwan)	2·5	8	2½	3·8	12	5½	14	46	0	20
Hong Kong	2·44	8	0	3·2	10	6	10	32	10	4·58 ×
Iraq	2·6	8	6½	3·8	12	5½	20	65	8	50
Israel	2·5	8	2½	3·8	12	5½	18	59	1	40·7
Japan	2·5	8	2½	3·5	11	6	24	78	9	40
Korea	2·5	8	2½	3·5	11	6	10	32	10	20
Lebanon	2·5	8	2½	3·5	11	6	18	59	1	35
Malaysia	2·29	7	6	N R*	N R*		12·19	40	0	— +
Saudi Arabia	N R*	N R*		N R*	N R*		N R*		N R*	
Syria	2·5	8	2½	3·8	12	5½	19	59	1	35
Thailand	2·5	8	2½	—	—		10	32	10	—
Australia	2·44	8	0	4·27	14	0½	15·24	50	0	47·24
	2·5	8	2½	4·42	14	6	21·64	71	0	47·24
New Zealand	2·44	8	0	4·27	14	0½	18·29	60	0	38·61

+Varies according to different highways
*N R = No Regulations
'Australian regulations vary by states. Figures indicate variations in maximum limits. Tasmania is excluded.

× Unladen. The Commissioner of Police can authorise increases.

INTERNATIONAL RAIL

EUROPEAN CONTAINER RAIL ORGANISATIONS

C.N.C.
Compagnie Nouvelle de Cadres
(*See entry under France for domestic operations*)
OPERATIONS: French rail container transport company. Arranges local collection and delivery at terminals.

HEAD OFFICE:
Direction Genérale, 20 Boulevard Diderot, Paris 12 ème 75, France.
Telephone: 345 322 0
Telegrams: Cadrofer, Paris.

Telex: Cadrofer, Paris 22500.
Jean Daudemard-Gregnac (*Director General*)
Henri Megoeuvil (*Director*)
J. J. Jouve (*Commercial Director*)

Agencies and Depots Villes	Addresses	Telephone:
Agen	Gare d'Agen Cour Marchandises, B.P. 43 R.P.	66.26.18
Angers	Gare SNCF Marchandises, B.P. 10 R.P.	88.67.34
Angouleme	Gare d'Angouleme, Rue Leclerc Chauvin, B.P. 7 Angouleme-L'Houmeau	95.12.12
Armentieres	Gare SNCF B.P. 45 Armentieres 59	77.30.78
Avignon	Gare Marchandises, Boulevard St- Dominique, B.P. 85	81.44.48
Bayonne	Gare SNCF Marchandises, Quai de Lesseps-B.P. 149	25.25.83
Beaune	Gare SNCF, B.P. 34	926
Belfort	Gare SNCF, Rue de Mulhouse, B.P. 88	28.00.27
Beziers	Gare SNCF, Cour Gare Voyageurs, Bd. de Verdun	28.30.50
Bordeaux	Gare Bordeaux-Bastide, Avenue Abadie, B.P. 30, Bordeaux-Bastide	92.81.70 / 92.81.71 / 92.81.72
Brive	Gare SNCF-Marchandises, Rue Moisan, B.P. 23, Brive	24.21.95
Caen	Gare SNCF Marchandises B.P. 20-06, 14-Caen	82.12.49
Chalon S/Saone	Gare SNCF, B.P. No 170	48.31.33
Clermont-Ferrand	Gare SNCF Marchandises, Avenue Edouard Michelin B.P. 415	92.96.31
Cognac	Gare SNCF Marchandises, 16-Cognac	82.23.68
Dieppe	Gare SNCF, B.P. 73 R.P.	84.32.41

Agencies and Depots Villes	Addresses		Telephone:
Dijon	Gare SNFC de Dijon-Porte-Neuve, Avenue Junot, B.P. 232 R.P.		32.47.12 3⸱.18.09
Dunkirk	Gare SNCF, Marchandises, B.P. 2103	Local Port	66.57.41 66.45.73
Elbeuf	Gare SNCF, B.P. 7 St-Ausbin-Les-E⸱⸱, ᶜ		77.11.70
Epinal	Gare d'Epinal SNCF, Cour Marchandises, Avenue Dutac, B.P. 119 R.P.		82.44.22 82.49.70
Grenoble	Gare SNCF Marchandises, Rue Pierre Semard		96.72.52
Le Havre	Gare SNCF, 6, rue Turgot	Local Port	42.23.33 48.27.28
Hendaye	Gare SNCF, Cour de la Bidassoa		26.70.09
Libourne	Gare de Libourne		51.02.55
Lille	Gare Lille-St-Sauveur, 25, Bd J. B. Lebas, B.P. 1346 R.P.		53.24.82 53.2⸱⸱
Limoges	Gare SNCF de Limoges Montjovis Pl. des Charentes, B.P. 110		77.36.91
Lorient	Gare SNCF, Boulevard Cosmao Dumanoir		21.00.28
Lyon	Gare Lyon-Guillotiere-Scaronne, 11, Av. Leclerc (7e)		72.85.71
Lyon Venissieux	Chantier de Venissieux Groupage Centre, Chemin de Charbonnier, B.P. 80 Pal 69 St-Priest		70.03.95
Macon	Gare SNCF Marchandises, B.P. 224 R.P.		38.28.48
Marseille	Gare Marseille Canet, 29, Bd de Lesseps, B.P. 44 Saint Barthelemy (14e)		50.24.68
Marseille FOS	CNC Chantier de FOS Container Terminal		05.02.02

Agencies and Depots	Addresses	Telephone:	Agencies and Depots	Addresses	Telephone:
	13 Golfe de FOS		Toulon	Gare SNCF Extérieure	92.82.60
Metz	Gare SNCF METZ-Marchandises, Rue de l'Amphitheatre, B.P. 236 R.P.	68.01.86		B.P. 136	
			Toulouse	Gare SNCF Toulouse-Matabiau-Raynal,	48.42.16 48.42.17
Montlucon	Gare SNCF, rue Stéphane Servant	05.37.20		37, Avenue de Lyon, B.P. 159 R.P.	84.42.18
Montpellier	Gare de Montpellier SNCF, 5, rue Jules Ferry, B.P. 1223	72.92.00	Tourcoing	Gare SNCF Tourcoing Marchandises, Rue du Levant, B.P. 0-46 R.P.	74.70.79
Mulhouse	Gare SNCF Mulhouse Nord, Marchandises, B.P. 412	42.00.28 42.02.28	Tours	Gare SNCF Saint Pierre-des-Corps, B.P. 68	05.06.47
Nancy	Gare SNCF Nancy Ville, Rue Gabriel Mouilleron, B.P. 3046 Porte Saint Nicolas	27.00.84 27.19.84	Valence	Gare SNCF de Valence, Rue Denis Papin, B.P. 45	43.31.14
Nantes	Gare Nantes Etat, Boulevard de la Prairie au Duc, B.P. 663 R.P.	71.57.33	**ALGERIA** Algiers	25, Boulevard Colonel Amirouche, B.P. 1146, Algiers	64.98.58 et 59 Cables: Cadrofer, Alger
Nice	Gare Nice St Roch, Porte A	89.11.93	Annaba	Compagnie Nationale Algérienne de Navigation (C.N.A.N.), Cours de la Révolution, B.P. 19 Annaba	55.55
Nimes	Gare SNCF Nimes Marchandises, Rue Sully, B.P. 136	67.58.32	Bejaia	Société Nationale des Chemins de Fer Algériens (S.N.C.F.A.), Gare de Bejaia	
Nuits-sous-Ravieres	Gare SNCF	72 à Nuits-Sur-Armencon	Constantine	Monsieur Cernon, Transports Rapides Carre, Hall P.V. Gare de Constantine	
Paris	CNC Agence de Paris, 127 Arc Ledru Rollin, Paris 11e Bureaux: 20, Bld Diderot, B.P. 55, Paris 12e	355.94.54 345.32.20	Mostaganem	Agence Remaci & Benguettat, Quai Bordes, Post n° 1 Bureaux n° 26-28	622.96
Pau	Gare SNCF, Avenue Gaston Lacoste, B.P. 73	27.86.12	Skikda	Société Algérienne de Navigation Charles Schiaffino & Cie, Port de Skikda, Quai Sud	56.24
Perpignan (1)	Gare SNCF Marchandises, Bld St Assiscle, B.P. 436	34.42.80	**TUNISIA** Tunis	Société Commerciale Tunisienne (S.O.C.O.T.U.), 5, Avenue Dag Hammarskjoeld B.P. 162, Tunis	242.999 Telex: 106
Reims	Gare SNCF Reims Marchandises, Place de la République B.P. 224	47.68.61	**MOROCCO** Casablanca	42, Avenue de l'Armée Royale	689-17 & 734-22
Rennes	Gare SNCF de Rennes, Ave. Chardonnet, B.P. 502 R.P.	36.47.90	**SENEGAL** Dakar	Regie des Chemins de fer du Senegal, Division Commerciale 38, Boulevard de la République, B.P. 265, Dakar	317.46 á 48 Cables: Fersenegal Dakar
Roanne	Gare SNCF Marchandises, Rue Pierre Sémard, B.P. 112	71.42.35	**CORSICA** Ajaccio	Comptoir Insulaire de Transit, 15, Blvd Roi Jérome, B.P. N° 10	21.36.98
Roubaix	Gare SNCF Marchandises, Rue de l'Ouest, B.P. 132	73.48.37	Bastia	Compagnie Generale Trans-mediterraneenne, Hotel de la Chambre de Commerce	0.57-5. 40 et 7. 53
Rouen	Gare SNCF de Rouen-Rive-Gauche, Rue de Seine, B.P. 1063, Rouen-St-Sever	71.21.27 71.32.03	Calvi	Société Tramar, Quai Landry	8
St-Etienne	Gare SNCF de Etienne-Chateaucreux, B.P. 158	34.14.07	Ile Rousse	Société Tramar, Avenue Calizi, B.P. 14, Ile Rousse	35 Cables: Tramar/ Ile Rousse
St-Quentin	Gare SNCF de St-Quentin, Cour P.V.	62.56.13	Porto Vecchio	Société d'Acconage Porto-Vecchiaise, Hangars, Chambre de Commerce	41
Sete	Gare SNCF de Sete Mediterranee, Place Mangeot, B.P. 119	74.17.94	Propriano	Agence Maritime Sorba	6 Cables: Sorba-Propriano
Strasbourg	Gare SNCF de Strasbourg-Cronenbourg, 48, Chemin Haut-BP, B.P. 10	30.38.40 30.33.65			
Tarbes	Gare SNCF Tarbes, P.V. Rue Robert Destarac, B.P. 11	93.25.35			

CONTAINERS IN USE:
  Standard ISO 10 ft, 20 ft, 30 ft and 40 ft units are in common use and CNC also has 30 ft tiltainers, and a number of new 6·057 m (20 ft) × 2·438 m (8 ft) × 1·200 m (4 ft) container units with covered tops.

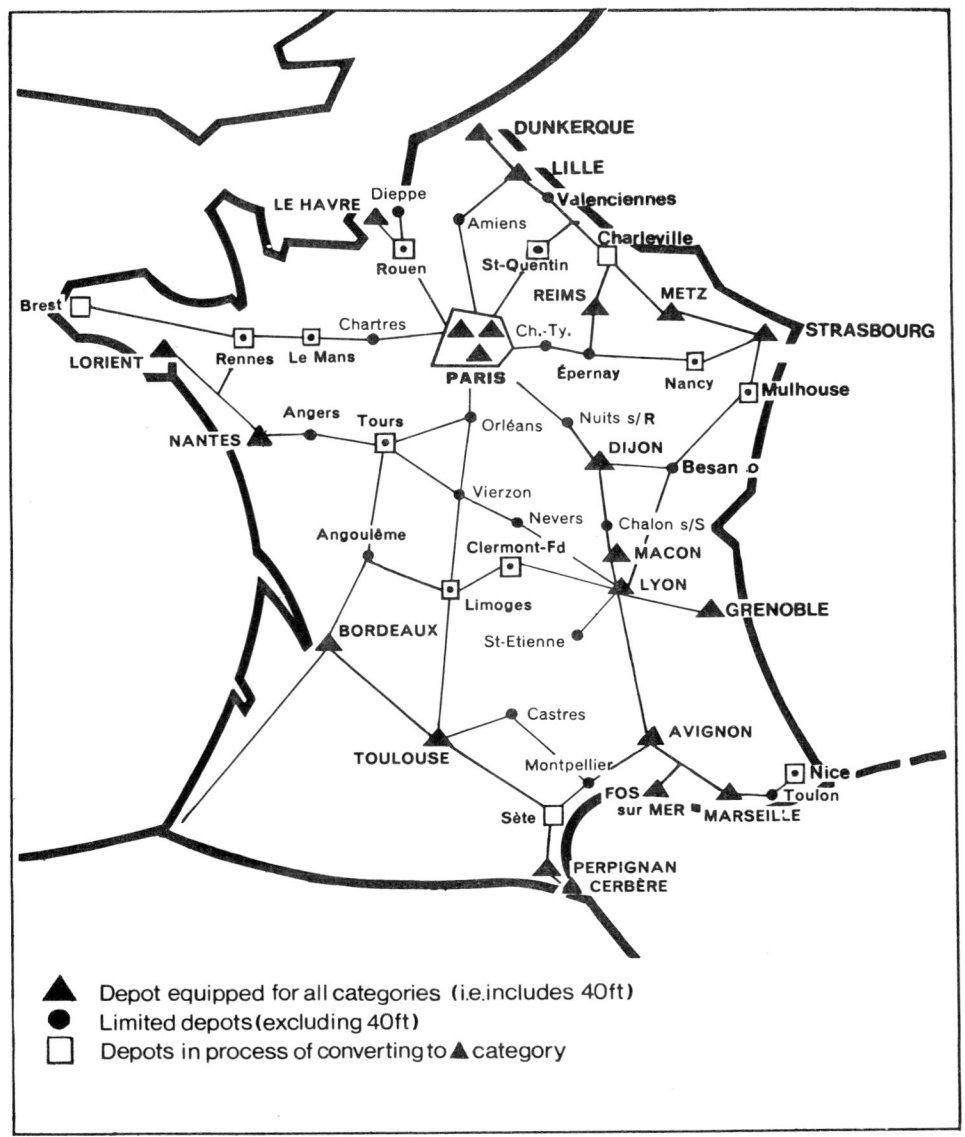

▲ Depot equipped for all categories (i.e.includes 40ft)
● Limited depots (excluding 40ft)
☐ Depots in process of converting to ▲ category

NOVATRANS
(Societe Norevelle de Exploitation de Transports Combines)
HEAD OFFICE:
21 Rue du Rocher 75, Paris 8 eme,
Tel: 387.41.79. Telex: 656265

Edmond Renaud (Chairman)
R. Mazeaud (Director)

In April 1967, the Novatrans freight operating system was set up by the two French piggyback operators GTTM and STEMA

It is expected that eventually Novatrans will be incorporated with CNC, but at the moment the Kangaroo, UFR and MC.22 systems have the advantage of being able to use the roll/on roll/off ferry network to the UK.

International Company for transport by Transcontainers

(*Société Internationale pour le Transport par Transcontainers*)

CH-400 Basle, Switzerland
TELEPHONE: 22 25 25
TELEX: 62298
CABLES: Transcofer Basle
General Manager: G. Fléchon

General

The national railway administration of the following 20 European participants in the Company for International Transport by transcontainers, known as 'INTERCONTAINER':

Austria	Irish Republic
Belgium	Italy
Denmark	Jugloslavia
Finland	Luxembourg
France	Netherlands
Germany DB	Norway
Germany DR	Portugal
Greece	Spain
Great Britain	Sweden
Hungary	Switzerland

The INTERFRIGO Company is also participating.

The general role of INTERCONTAINER may be defined as that of a 'common commercial agency' of the above Railways representing them collectively in matters of international transport of transcontainers. The Company therefore presents a unified agency at the service of the clientele who are interested in transport in all the above countries and provides contact with all the transport enterprises involved, including terminal authorities and road services. INTERCONTAINER makes contracts with these various agencies and is thus able to ensure door-to-door operations.

It seeks particularly to serve transit and forwarding agents, shipping lines, container operators and other undertakings specialising in international transport.

The special objectives of INTERCONTAINER are to ensure transits under the best possible conditions in those cases where logically and economically they should be carried out by rail for trunk haulage.

In order to achieve this the Company is developing a network of regular, rapid block-train workings without intermediate shunting by virtue of which it is able to offer competitive prices.

Intercontainer is a co-operative society based on Belgian Law and with the general management in Basle. Intercontainer is represented by the railways of each country or by an agency specialising in railway administration.

Train Services

Containers can be forwarded on any international routes, according to the customer's needs. Two kinds of train services exist.

Container Handling Equipment

Handling equipment at terminals varies from country to country, as terminal operations are carried out entirely by the different railway administrations.

All major terminals have gantry cranes equipped with spreaders which can handle containers of 20 ft, 30 ft and 40 ft (and in most cases 35 ft) length, weighing up to 30 tons. However, road restrictions in many countries impose shorter permitted lengths or lighter permitted gross weights.

Containers and Wagons

The containers with which INTERCONTAINER are primarily concerned are 8 × 8 × 20 ft, 30 ft, 40 ft standard ISO types known as 'transcontainers'. Others varying somewhat from these sizes, such as the 8 ft wide maritime containers 8 ft 6 in high ×

INTERCONTAINER

35 ft long, can also be accommodated.

INTERCONTAINER does not own any transcontainers nor does it intend to do so in the near future. However, it may hire out transcontainers in connection with certain block-train services, as for example Paris-Cologne, and Paris-Antwerp-Rotterdam

Rail Vehicles

INTERCONTAINER uses flat wagons of various types for its transcontainer operations. In addition, in 1971 555 special 60 ft wagons will be constructed for its own use.

Terminal Services

INTERCONTAINER uses terminals operated by the railways or by private companies for the transfer of containers between rail and road. For collection and delivery by road INTERCONTAINER uses lorries or trailers provided by the railways or by local road hauliers. Customers may, however, provide their own road vehicles for this purpose if they so wish.

Expansion of the "Trans-Europ-Container-Express" network therefore depends on the installation of container terminals all over Europe. These terminals are rapidly increasing in number: there were 38 in October 1968, more than 100 by the end of 1971 and further terminals are planned.

Refrigerated Containers

It is appropriate to mention the very close cooperation established between INTERCONTAINER and INTERFRIGO. The latter is entrusted with the organisation and development of international, controlled-temperature transports. It is owned by 19 railway companies and is a founder member of INTERCONTAINER.

Under the policy adopted between the two companies INTERFRIGO maintains both commercial and technical management of all controlled-temperature container transport. This traffic being of a kind involving services differing from those of pure and simple carriage, INTERFRIGO supplies ventilated or refrigerated transcontainers and their regular servicing. Address: Interfrigo Company, Wettsteinplatz, 1, Basle, Switzerland. Telephone: 061-330750. Telex: 63372.

Documentation

Intercontainer uses a single consignment note and the currency is based on the Swiss Franc.

Traffic

The traffic at September 1970 amounts to 15,000 containers of all types or 18,500 20 ft units, including 26% empties. Traffic figures can be divided into 76·3% port, 17·6% through traffic to Great Britain and 6·1% continental traffic.

National Representatives

AUSTRIA
Generaldirektion der
Österreichischen Bundesbahnen
Kommerzielle Direktion
Abteilung IV/4
Gauermanngasse 4
A-1010 Vienna
Telephone: 5650
Telex: 12104

BELGIUM
Société Anonyme INTERFERRY
Noorderplaats 2
2000 Antwerpen
Telephone: 313916/323658
Telex: 32529

DENMARK
DANSKE STATSBANER
Generaldirektoratet
Salgskontoret for Godstransport
Sølvgade 40
DK 1349 Copenhagen K
Telephone: 140400 int. 2265
Telex: Copenhagen 2225

FINLAND
Valtion Rautatiet
Rataitieballitus
Betriebsabteilung
Vilhontatu 13, Helsinki
Telephone: 717777
Telex: 1230151

FRANCE
CNC
(Compagnie Nouvelle de Cadres)
20 Boulevard Diderot
Paris XII
Telephone: 3453220
Telex: 22500

GERMANY (DB)
TRANSFRACHT GmbH
Gutlertstrasse 160/4
Frankfurt (Main)
Telephone: 230351
Telex: 41.45.45

GERMANY (DR)
VEB-DEUTRANS
Internationale Spedition
Otto-Grotewohl-Strasse 25
DDR-108 Berlin
Telephone: 22 01 21
Telex: 112331/113312
Telegrams: Deutranscontainer Berlin

GREAT BRITAIN
(Harwich Terminal)
British Railways Board
Shipping & Int. Services Division
Liverpool Street Station, London EC2
Telephone: 01-283 7535

Telex: 886821 LND
(Freightliner Terminals)

FREIGHTLINERS LTD.
43 Cardington St.
London NW1
Telephone: 3879400
Telex: 24743

GREECE
Org. da Chemins de fer Héllénique
Rue Eolou 102
Athens 131
Telephone: 31.53.87
Telex: 215.187

HUNGARY
MAVTRANS
Speditionsbüreau der MAV
Budapest V
Telephone: 382-324
Telex: 3434

IRISH REPUBLIC
Coras Iompair Eireann
Office of the Commercial Manager
Connolly Station
Amiens Street
Dublin 1
Telephone: Dublin 42941
Telex: CIE Dublin 5153

ITALY:
CEMAT SpA
Via Savoia. 19
Rome 00198
Telephone: 865.484
Via Valtellina 5/7
Milan
Telephone: 68.87.551
Telex: 33629

LUXEMBURG
Société Nationale des Chemins
de fer Luxembourgeois
Service Technique Général
Division Commerciale
Place de la Gare 9
LUXEMBURG
Telephone: 49901
Telex: 288

NETHERLANDS
NV Nederlandse Spoorwegen
Dienst van Economische Zaken
le Afdeling, Secte Containers

Moreelsepark 1
Utrecht
Telephone: 030/15871 Int. 754
Telex: 47257

NORWAY
Norges Statsbaner
Hoved Administrasjonen
Salgsaudeliagen
Storgaten, 33
Oslo 1
Telephone: 20.95.50 ex 2103
Telex: 11168

PORTUGAL:
Companhia Dos Caminos De Ferro Portugueses
Commercial Department
Servico de Transportes Complementares
Estacao de Santa Apolonia
Lisbon 2
Telephone: 86 41 81-9; 86 41 01-10
Telex: 1382

SPAIN
Proconsa
Promotores del Conteredor SA
Direction Commercial RENFE
Paseo del Reg 32, Madrid
Telephone: 2467652
Telex: 27632

SWEDEN
STATENS JÄRNVÄGAR
Centralförvaltningen
Mäster Samuelsgaten 70
Stockholm C
Telephone: 226000 Int. 1564
Telex: 1410, Statsbanan
Telegrams: Ka Sthlm

SWITZERLAND
Chemins de fer Fédéraux Suisses
Service Commercial
Trafic Marchandises SB
Mittelsttasse 43

Güterverkehr
3000 Berne
Telephone: 031/60 11 11
Telex: 32500

YUGOSLAVIA
Zajednica Jugoslovenskih
Zeleznica

Kommerzieller Dienst
Nemanjina 6/11
Beograd
Telephone: 22701 ext. 5122
Telex: 11.166

Future Activities and TECE

Intercontainer is developing special shuttle service block trains, the first two being the Paris-Cologne train and the Rotterdam-Antwerp-Paris train. The latter connects with Bordeaux, Toulouse, Lyons and Marseilles. These services come under the heading of Trans-Europ-Container Express (TECE) and there are 6 departures a week in each direction.

Much of the traffic goes by TEEM, and the following table shows the progress to date of loaded containers.

May '68—Nov '68	2,650	
Dec '68—Nov '69	8,400	20 ft units
Dec '69—Nov '70	13,750	
Dec '70—March '71	17,600	

A "Block train" chartered by Intercontainer. It operates on a regular shuttle service between Basle (Switzerland) and Chiasso, Italy, regardless of the weather conditions.

INTERFRIGO

Société Ferroviaire Internationale de Transports Frigorifiques (INTERFRIGO)
Wettsteinplatz 1
CH-4005 Basle, Switzerland
TELEPHONE: (061) 33 07 50
TELEX: 62231
GENERAL:

INTERFRIGO was set up in 1949 to provide a pool of refrigerated wagons for European Railway operators and to ensure that these wagons were temperature controlled en route from consignor to consignee. In 1967 the organisation became a founder member of Intercontainer and concluded an agreement by which Interfrigo retained the task of developing and marketing international rail transport for refrigerated containers belonging to private operators, the railways or to Interfrigo. Intercontainer arranges the actual carrying operation.
INTERFRIGO CONTAINER SERVICES:

Interfrigo offers to traders the following services for containers fitted for controlled temperature.
Service No. 1 (insulated transport):

This service applies to all transcontainers supplied by traders and coming within one of the following categories:
—insulated or utilised as such
—empties of all types
—loaded with goods not requiring controlled temperature.

This covers only transport by fast services which INTERFRIGO will supervise.
Service No. 2 (mechanically refrigerated transport):

This service applies to all loaded self-refrigerating transcontainers of the mechanically refrigerated type, when supplied by traders, and loaded with goods requiring a controlled temperature.

The service offered by INTERFRIGO for such stock includes:
—transport by fast and priority services
—supervision of the working of the

machinery and level of the temperature required during transport, excluding the supply of fuel and refrigerating materials, which can only be obtained by special agreement.
Service No. 3 (transport with supply of electrical energy):

This service applies to transcontainers of the mechanically refrigerated type, not self-refrigerating, supplied by traders loaded with goods requiring a controlled temperature, and which necessitate a source of electrical energy for the working of their machinery.

The service offered for such stock includes:
—transport by fast and priority services
—supervision of the working of the machinery and level of the temperature required during transport
—supply of electrical energy during transport.
Service No. 4 (transport with supply of a transcontainer):

This service applies to the transcontainers made available by INTERFRIGO.

The service offered for such stock includes:
For transcontainers loaded with goods requiring a controlled temperature
—supply of a transcontainer of the mechanically refrigerated type
—transport by fast and priority services
—supervision of the working of the machinery and level of the temperature required during transport as well as supplying fuel for the machinery.
For transcontainers loaded with goods not requiring a controlled temperature or insulated transport
—supply of a transcontainer of any type
—transport by fast services.
Supplementary Services subject to special agreement:

In addition to the preceding services Nos. 1-4 and within the limits of its capabilities INTERFRIGO can offer supplementary

Interfrigo Refrigerated Wagons,

services for which special agreements must be concluded.
CONTAINER FLEET:

In 1970 INTERFRIGO owned 71 40 ft and 15 20 ft refrigerated units. It is anticipated that by 1972 181 40 ft units and 163 20 ft units will be in operation.

NATIONAL REPRESENTATIVES:
Austria:
General Representation for Austria:
Dipl. Ing. Josef Rain
Maria Treu-Gasse 2, A-1080 Wien
Postfach 52,
Telephone: 42 47 70
Belgium:
N. V. Interferry
Noorderplaats 2, B-2000 Antwerpen,
Telephone: (03) 31 50 55, (03) 31 50 56
Telex: 32529
Bulgaria:
U.E.E. "BDZ" Transports frigorifiques ferroviaires Bureau Central INTERFRIGO
Rue Ekzarh Jossif 30, Sofia
Telephone: 87 59 67
Telex: 423
Czechoslovakia:
"CSD INTRANS"/Skupina INTERFRIGO
Praha Liben-Horni-Nadrazi

Telephone: 830 519 or 2124 (ext. 4953)
Telex: 1286

Denmark:
Danske Statsbaner
Sølvgade 40, DK-1349 Kobenhavn K
Telephone: (01) 140 400
Telex: 5654

France:
Stef, 93, bd Malesherbes
F-75 Paris 8e
Telephone: 522-8894
Telex: 28969

Germany (FR):
Operating Representation Deutsche Bundesbahn-Zentrale Transportleitung-Gñterwagendienst,
Hedderichstrasse 55,
D-6 Frankfurt-am-Main 70
Telephone: 265/5926
Telex: 0411124
Commercial Representation:
Transthermos GmbH, Holler Allee 85
D-28 Bremen 1, Postfach 1217
Telephone: 34 00 41
Telex: 0244457

Germany (DR):
Deutsche Reichbahn
Ministerium für Verkehrswesen—INTER-FRIGO Büro,
Voss-Strasse 33, DDR-108, Berlin 8
Telephone: 53 02 01
Telex: 112250

Great Britain:
General operating representation:
British Railways Board
Continental Rolling Stock Department
222, Marylebone Road, London, N.W.1
Telephone: AMBassador 32 32 (ext. 5865 or 5209)
Telex: 21971 and 21976
General commercial representation (National representation):
British Rail
Shipping and International Services Division,
Liverpool Street Station,
London, E.C.2
Telephone: 01-283 7535
Telex: 886821
Commercial and operating representation for inland transports only in mechanically refrigerated transcontainers:

Freightliners Ltd.
43 Cardington Street,
London, N.W.1
Telephone: 01-387 9400
Telex: 24743

Greece:
Organisme des Chemins de fer Helléniques S.A.
102 rue Eolou, Athènes (131)
Telephone: 315 382
Telex: 215187

Hungary:
Chemins de fer de l'Etat Hongrois 1/8
Groupe INTERFRIGO
Nepköztarsasag Utja 73, Budapest VI
Telephone: 220 660
Telex: 641

Italy:
Ferrovie Italiane dello Stato
Direzione Generale (for transports in refrigerator wagons)
Piazza della Croce Rossa, I-00161 Roma
—Servizio Movimento
Telephone: 4670/31743-31346
Telex: 61089
—Servizio Commerciale e del Traffico
Telephone: 4670/2644
Telex: 97030
Instituto Nazionale Trasporti (for transports in mechanically refrigerated wagons and transcontainers),
Via Savoia 19, I-00198 Roma
Telephone: 861 851

Luxembourg:
Chemins de fer Luxembourgeois
Service Technique Général—Division commerciale
Place de la Gare
Luxembourg
Telephone: 49901
Telex: 288

Netherlands (The):
N. V. Nederlandse Spoorwegen
Moreelsepark 1, Utrecht
Telephone: 030-29 403
Telex: 47257

Norway:
Norges Statsbaner (NSB)
Hovedadministrasjonen
Storgaten 33, Oslo
Telephone: 20 95 50
Telex: 1168

Romania:
Chemins de fer Roumains (CFR)
Services des transports internationaux frigorifiques INTERFRIGO
Bulevardul Dinicu Golescu 38, Bucuresti
Telephone: 17 20 60
Telex: 047425

Spain/Portugal
Transfesa
Bravo Murillo No. 38-2°
Apartado 3225, Madrid (3)
Telephone: 224 87 35
Telex: 07745 or 07663

Sweden:
Statens Järnvägar (SJ)
Centralförvaltningen—Driftavdelningen
S-105 50 Stockholm C.
Telephone: 22 64 20
Telex: 1410

Switzerland:
Frigosuisse
Chemins de Fer Fédéraux Suisses, CH-3000 Bern
Service commercial—Marchandises
Telephone: (031) 60 25 90
Telex: 32500
Division de l'Exploitation—Section 6
Telephone: (031) 60 22 86
Telex: 32500
Bahnhof Kühlhaus AG
CH-4002 Basel
Telephone: (061) 35 55 90
Telex: 62271
Société de Gares Frigorifiques et Ports Francs de Genève
CH-1227 Carouge
Telephone: (022) 43 87 60
Marco Celoria S.A.
CH-6830 Chiasso
Telephone: (091) 4 26 02

Turkey:
TCDD—Turkiye Cumhuriyeti Devlet Demiryollari
1 inci Isletme Müdürlügü
Haydarpasa-Istanbul
Telephone: 26 71 10 (ext. 127 or 147)

Yugoslavia:
Zajednica Jugoslovenskih Zeleznica
Odelenje za operativne poslove, Grupe INTERFRIGO
Nemanjina 6/11, Beograd
Telephone: 29 427
Telex: 11166

SECTION SEVEN

AIR FREIGHT

AIR FREIGHT
INTRODUCTION

AIR CARGO TRENDS

Using statistics to guide future planning decisions has a major drawback. It is the limitation imposed by the time-gap between completion of an activity and the publication of figures which record events in that activity. Because of this interval industry early-warning signals emerge slowly and often too late to change decisions based on earlier information.

Nowhere is this inertia effect more evident than in aviation. In an industry with complicated airborne and ground equipment involving huge investments, long lead times on orders are normal. In stable growth conditions of the past, gestation gaps of two, three and four years were relatively unimportant. The main effect of delay was to outdate the equipment slightly.

In 1971 airfreight growth levelled off as international trade became less buoyant. Manufacturers with spare productive capacity and better able to meet delivery dates, turned back to surface transport as the cheaper alternative to air. Moves like this produced a plateau on air freight growth charts which appeared to have taken most operators by surprise—almost as if they expected it never to happen. At the end of 1970, whilst analysts were waiting for the year's figures, a number of experts bravely continued to predict air cargo growth rates of the 15 per cent per annum order in spite of clear evidence of industrial pessimism. Although some may have felt that growth figures needed qualifying there were few, if any, voices raised against what had become fairly standard predictions.

Yet there were plenty of external signs that inflation, in particular, had got the better of Western economies. Rapid rises of wages in all developed countries produced runaway costs. The fast rise in prices of every commodity and manufactured product effectively blunted demand across the world. Wages bought less, factory production slowed, less transport was needed. All through 1970 major US airlines caught in this spiral reported huge losses as their traffic slumped. Their purchases of extra aircraft to meet predicted demand proved to be astronomically expensive as the transports were operated with substantial spare space. By early 1971 it was clear that the impetus behind the upward thrust of cargo growth had lost its power.

Summarising these effects in 1970 the International Civil Aviation Organisation (ICAO) said "Negative factors, in particular a general softening of the economy in the United States of America and an increasing inflationary trend in many countries of the world have played a greater determining role than in recent years in the development of the air transport industry. Business traffic and air freight seem to have been affected and rising costs have cut into the operating profits of some airlines just at a time when the large capacity aircraft are being introduced creating problems of excess capacity. In the US in 1970 a number of major airlines reduced personnel, cut back schedules and postponed or even cancelled some aircraft orders".

Results in the current year appear to be no better as giant airlines struggle to balance their books. Against TWA's background of a large first-half loss of $34·8-m (£14·5-m) (in 1970 the first half loss was $45·2-m (£18·8-m)), for example, its president and chief operating officer Mr F. C. Wiser said that he did not expect an early financial recovery. He described the 1971 drop in business as "an air traffic recession—the most serious we have had in our industry's history".

Because of the need for long term planning of capacity and the sensitivity of this space to traffic changes most airlines in 1971 have found themselves with a good deal more unsold space that they could accept comfortably. Nowhere was this situation more obvious than on the North Atlantic—the world's busiest long-haul air route.

During 1970 cargo carried across the Atlantic by IATA members in passenger aircraft with cargo space (combination aircraft) was only 2 per cent above the total weight of the previous year. This small gain was more than offset by a 5·7 per cent decline in results from scheduled all-cargo carriers. Overall the traffic of both types of operator added up to 2·8 per cent decline in N Atlantic cargo compared with 1969. Revenue was improved by a 4 US cents per kilogram increase on both specific commodity and general rates during the year, representing rises from 1·5 to 11 per cent.

Another rate increase, but not one that benefitted airlines, took place in the USA where the American Government imposed transport taxes increasing, among other costs, waybill charges by 5 per cent and putting up jet fuel costs. In addition several all-cargo operators, facing heavy losses, filed several increases of rates with CAB. All are to be investigated in a general air freight rate investigation. Australia raised its domestic cargo rates by 6 per cent in August, and pushed them up by a further 3 per cent in September. One New Zealand carrier was allowed to increase its rates by 15 per cent.

World wide, according to ICAO, cargo tonne-km on international routes went up by only 8·3 per cent and this figure includes, retrospectively, data from Aeroflot. The USSR joined ICAO on 14th November 1970 bringing the Organisation's membership to 120. Domestic cargo of the 120 members increased by only 7·2 per cent. A year before the increases had been 32·6 per cent internationally, 9·9 per cent domestically.

In the US, domestic traffic growth dropped to 6·1 per cent (9 per cent in 1969) and on international routes it was 17·4 per cent. Among European carriers a slackening of expansion was considerable. 1970 growth was only 5 per cent compared with 34·6 per cent in the year before.

In the Far East the growth pattern looked a little more healthy with an 11·5 per cent growth internationally and 15·2 per cent domestically. Another region which looked more cheerful was South America. International cargo results went up 22·7 per cent but only 3·9 per cent domestically. Oceania got 14·1 per cent increase internationally and 7·5 per cent domestically. Africa had a strong domestic growth at 34·0 per cent.

With the general growth picture—passenger and cargo—blurred by uncertainty it was inevitable that some world airline giants discussed amalgamations. Two airlines which received US Presidential approval to purchase were Northwest to buy Northeast. American Airlines and Western Airlines eyed each other and so did Eastern and Caribair. Some Supplementary carriers have considered merger plans, among which is the acquisition of American Flyers by Universal Airlines.

Some airlines are blaming overcapacity on the B747, although its arrival and a worldwide fall in traffic is a chicken and egg situation. The B747 was ordered in quantity long before the present airline slump began to show itself.

Airlines

One result of the slip in scheduled traffic has been the focussing of attention on the activities of charter operators. Scheduled airlines have not been slow to accuse them of taking traffic from regular flights with attractive, low-cost special rates, sometimes half those of the normal IATA fares. The non-scheduled operators' retort is that the traffic would not be available at IATA rates.

The parcels storage lanes at BOAC Cargo centre London-Heathrow with their Rapistan conveyors give some idea of the investment required for a modern air cargo terminal

For some years a number of IATA airlines have run Associate companies to undertake charter and non-IATA type-traffic. This trend has increased recently—BOAC has formed British Overseas Air Charter Ltd, BEA has had Air Tours for Inclusive Tour work since 1970 and has announced its intention to bid for cargo charters, offering its fleet of Merchantmen.

These moves may well result eventually in an excess of charter capacity. World airline statistics have been affected by the release of US supplemental carriers from Vietnam. In America the civil charter market results grew 40 per cent in 1969 compared with 1968 and this increase must have had some effect on scheduled operations These US supplementals using modern long-range jets introduced a new dimension to non-scheduled operations and helped to open big US travel and cargo potentials. Their activities have produced passenger-kilometer figures equal to 5 per cent of the total *world* scheduled pass-km (ICAO respondents). In the freight market the US independent operators are very active. But, as with the scheduled carrier, all is not well with every one of these operators. In 1970 the US supplementals lost $18·20-m (£7·6-m).

European charter operators seem confident about the future. There are fundamentally two types of operators, the privately financed and independent companies and those affiliated to scheduled IATA airlines and members of the European Air Charter Group. They are Austrian Air Transport (Austria), Sobelair (Belgium), Kar-Air (Finland), Aero-maritime and Air Charter International (France), Condor (FR Germany), Societa

Aerea Mediterranea (Italy), Martinair (Netherlands), Scanair (Denmark), Aviaco (Spain), Balair (Switzerland), Air Yugoslavia (Yugoslavia).

It can be said fairly that most airlines were caught unprepared for the current cargo slump. Some appear to have been thrown into confusion. Their disarray was evident at the 4th Biannual Composite Cargo Conference held at Singapore this year. Called to review and set world-wide rate patterns for two years ahead the results of these meetings normally fairly predictable. This year however, very little emerged at the end of a full month of discussion between representatives of over 100 airlines. Mr H. Don Reynolds IATA's Assistant Director General-Traffic who chaired the Conference, described it as "undoubtedly the most difficult cargo rates negotiations undertaken in the history of the scheduled international transportation industry".

There appeared to have been a total disagreement among delegates over rates for Pacific routes. Eventually the Conference declared a "terminated situation" which leaves all major questions over the region unresolved. There was strong argument too, over N. Atlantic rates but carriers were generally agreed on their ultimate goal.

One objective of ITA's Singapore Conference was to improve the low yield from cargo. Rates are still based largely on fill-up traffic designed to attract freight to the belly holds of passenger aircraft. Air cargo business began its growth from these small spaces under cabins until it burst their capacity bounds. Then freighters took over. Now the pendulum is swinging back again

Underfloor spaces in the wide-body jets will take large quantities of cargo and most operators want to see this capacity filled first because their operation is cheaper. If cargo rates can be raised the inevitable difficulties facing large fleets will be decreased.

One reason for operator nervousness at Singapore could well be the dramatic fall-off in revenue yield in 1970. Returns from cargo traffic which has been increasing by 20-30 per cent each year for some time past, averaged in 1970 for the 119 members an average of 2-8 per cent.

Airports

A total of 880 airports offering facilities to international standards were available to operators in 1970. A number of events conspired during the year to push up the costs of running these organisations. They included increased security measures to isolate weapons and explosives, and to ensure that parked aircraft were protected. In addition, more than ever before public attention has been drawn to the effects of aircraft on their environment. This has caused reviews of plans for new and existing airports to ensure that they have the least effect on the public and these charges are not inconsiderable.

Extra costs of these types are reflected in extra charges to airlines. Mr Knut Hammarskjöld Director General IATA said "The continuing upward trend in airport and air navigation charges is a matter of growing concern to the airlines in view of their relative importance in total airline costs. At present these charges account for five per cent of airline operating costs on an industry basis, compared to four per cent in 1966. For

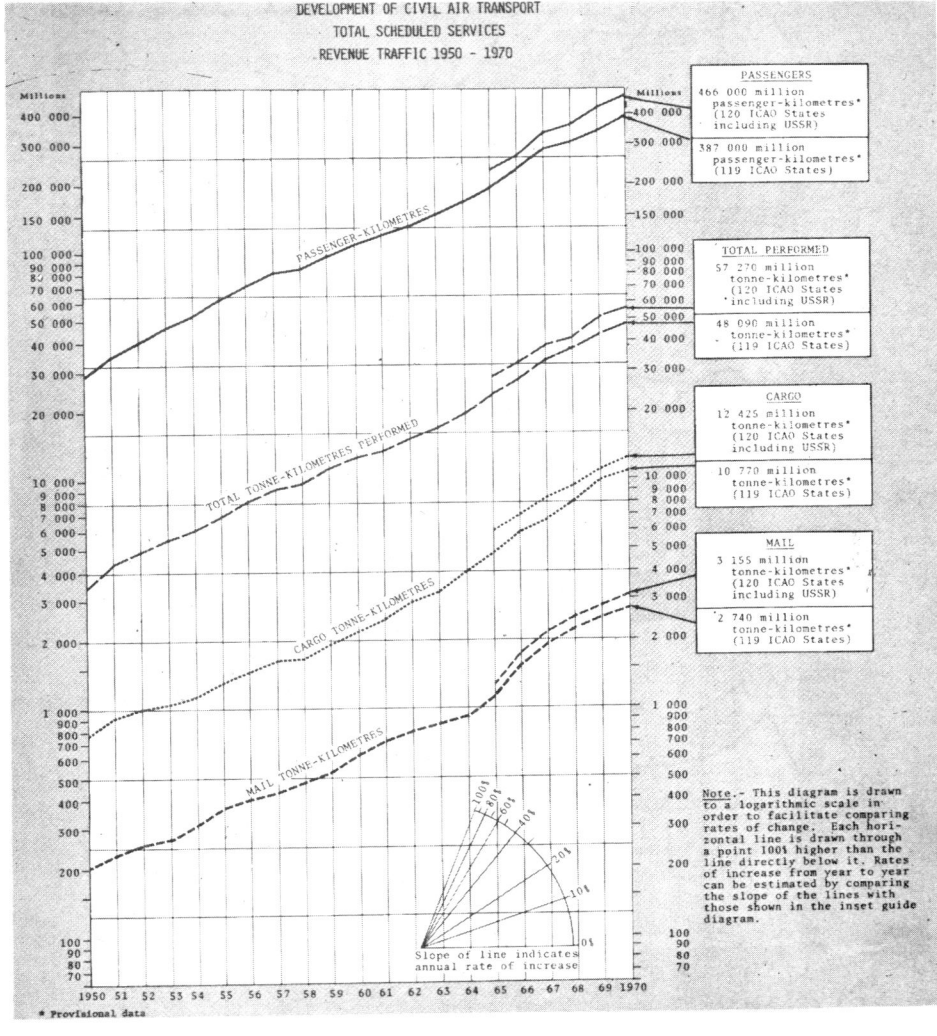

DEVELOPMENT OF CIVIL AIR TRANSPORT
TOTAL SCHEDULED SERVICES
REVENUE TRAFFIC 1950 - 1970

some short-haul operators these charges are as high as 10 per cent of operating costs.

"Unfortunately the outlook is not good and charges are therefore likely to become an increasingly significant cost element in airline operation. For example, the 20 member states of the European Civil Aviation Conference (ECAC) have agreed in principle that the revenue previously accruing from the airport passenger service charge should be a direct levy on the airlines with effect from 1 April 1971. The same 20 states have also agreed in principle to co-ordinate the introduction of en route facility charges with effect from 1 November 1971, aiming at the recovery of at least 15 per cent of the total allocable costs against civil aviation plus one per cent for administrative costs. It is not known how many of the ECAC States will actually implement the agreements in principle, but the minimum impact of the additional costs to the airlines in the first instance is estimated at US$55-m per annum

"The major thrust of our efforts to stem the rise in charges, which must inevitably be passed on to passengers and shippers, has been through the IATA Charges Working Group (CWG) which has presented the airline industries' view on this problem to various international civil aviation bodies governmental agencies and airport authorities. Our objective is to obtain a standardization of procedures and rationalization in the imposition of charges. The CWG has had some success in its negotiations. In some cases responsible authorities have agreed to defer increases in charges; in others they have reduced the proposed level of increases, while in yet other cases the authorities have agreed to recover these charges using internationally accepted guidelines".

One of the first major airports to issue 1970 figures was Amsterdam-Schiphol Europe's best designed and most up-to-date facility with a fully automatic cargo handling terminal. In March the airport reported that the 35,383-tonne 1969 increase over 1968 dropped to 14,827-tonnes in 1970. Scheduled carriers using the airport reported an increase in tonnage but non-scheduled operators on intra-European routes reported a disastrous drop in traffic.

Aircraft

When BEA announced this year, that for cargo carrying it was placing passenger aircraft first in its marketing strategy it was only putting into words a philosophy now adopted by most airlines. Pure freighters are out of fashion. After the heady 1960s expansion of freight traffic which made necessary the purchases of all-cargo aircraft, most airlines have rethought the wisdom of tying capital in single purpose aircraft. The trend was assisted on long haul routes by the advent of a new generation of wide bodied jets, personified by the Boeing 747. Its large underfloor holds take as much cargo by weight as a 707 freighter and companies are making use of the space with new types of underfloor containers suitable for 747s, DC-10s and L-1011s.

General 1970 statistics for the North Atlantic show this particular trend although there were relatively few 747s operating the route during that year. (Pan American made the first 747 commercial flight across the Atlantic, in January 1970). Figures for the route show that during 1970 cargo weight carried in passenger (combination) aircraft rose by 2 per cent but weight carried in scheduled all-cargo aircraft fell by 5·7 per cent. It was the charter operators who took the biggest knock. Their traffic dropped by over a half, by minus 52·7 per cent.

Moves to use big passenger jets is likely to continue well into the 1970s until traffic recovers sufficiently or transport costs are brought down low enough to allow the big true-cargo carriers of the B747 and L-500 freighter type to be brought into serivce.

Having said that, there are two airlines which appear to be swimming against the tide. Most important of them, Lufthansa, is known for its caution but has persisted in planning for operations with at least one B747 freighter. At present the German airline timetable sees its single giant-size freighter in service by early 1972 and a great deal of theoretical work has been undertaken to ensure that it is used profitably on a six times weekly Frankfurt-New York service. It will be able to lift 100 tons over this distance and offer a volume equal to three times that of the 707. For the first time an airline is talking in earnest about using standard sized 8 × 8 section containers which will be interchangeable with surface transport.

Whether the second operator of 747 freighters, Korean Airlines, about which little is known, has such ambitious plans remains to be seen. It intends to use its one large cargo carrier on Pacific services.

OUTLOOK

In spite of a levelling off of demand for aircraft cargo capacity, airlines today are handling very large loads. For some time ahead they have to adapt themselves to a policy of retaining their share of the market instead of continually reaching for new business. The disadvantage of this second strategy is that so long as there is more new traffic, customers needs may have to take second place. A steady market condition should see a return to policies in which the customer is right.

Just how long the present halt in trade expansion is likely to last cannot be predicted. Some forecasters believe that the worst is over but effects of the slump will be felt for at least another year. Whether their summary is right or wrong matters very little to most airlines who after an unprecedented 25 years of growth now face for the first time serious reversals. For some time ahead now they face difficult times but from them should emerge a more mature approach to the whole business of marketing air cargo.

THE INTERNATIONAL AIR TRANSPORT ASSOCIATION (IATA)

This Association is the organisation of the world's scheduled airlines. It is devoted to providing safe, regular and economical transport of both passengers and freight and works constantly towards technological, operational and procedural improvements throughout the industry.

IATA was founded in 1945 and is a non-governmental and private trade Association with its headquarters in Montreal, Canada. Its member airlines—now numbering over 100—carry more than 90 per cent of world airline traffic, so that the Association, through its Traffic Committees, Working, and Special Groups functions as an international pool and centre for the exchange of information and experience. The main international agreements are reached through IATA Traffic Conferences and, as a direct result of the increasing importance of freight operations, there have been separate passenger and freight conferences since 1964. All rates, rules and regulations must have unanimous acceptance by member airlines—each having one vote—and all agreements must be subsequently approved by interested governments.

The present system of IATA standard containers was adopted at Cargo Traffic Conference in San Juan, Puerto Rico, and mandatory design criteria and test requirements came into force on 1st October, 1967.

The main objectives of the container programme are to unitize multiple packages into a single, larger unit load and through standardisation of dimensions and equipment, to acheive maximum cube utilisation of the aircraft space. To this end incentives have been developed to encourage shippers to use IATA registered unit load devices for the carriage of air freight, thereby effecting efficiencies to both the shipper and carrier.

Seventeen container sizes were developed by the IATA Containers Board, for registration by shippers and container manufacturers. All are modular to standard size aircraft pallets and conform to the fuselage loading contours of the aircraft types now in world-wide mixed traffic and all-cargo service. Forklift entries and tie-down insets are provided in all sizes—which range from one-eighth to full-pallet size 224 × 274 cm and 224 × 318 cm (88 × 108 in and 88 × 125 in) and have volumes from ⅓ m³ (18 cu ft) to 11·5 m³ (405 cu ft). This range also covers the door and hold size restrictions in the belly-holds of passenger carrying aircraft.

Bulk Unitization:

Further encouragement was given to shippers prepared to use unitized load devices at the 1969 third IATA cargo conference held at Athens. From 1st October, 1969, the new programme provided flat rates on a point-to-point basis for shippers who load and unload aircraft unit load devices off-airport. The units can be owned either by member airlines or by shippers. Shipper owned units must be registered with IATA and conform to standard IATA Interline Specifications. Such shipper owned units have a lower bulk charge than those applicable to airline owned units and enjoy a tare weight allowance. The units involved are:

(i) Full size aircraft pallets with aircraft net or igloo, sizes 224 × 318 cm (88 × 125 in) and 224 × 274 cm (88 × 108 in) with maxi-

mum height up to 218 cm (86 in).

(ii) Half size lower deck containers for high capacity aircraft. 158 × 233 × 163 cm (62 × 92 × 64 in).

(iii) Half size aircraft pallets, nets and igloos, sizes 224 × 155 cm (88 × 61 in) and 224 × 135 cm (88 × 53 in) with maximum heights up to 218 cm (86 in) and 193 cm (76 in) respectively. (On North Atlantic routes only).

(iv) B-747 full pallet with net or igloo 224 × 318 × 163 cm (88 × 125 × 64 in).

For shippers who wish to use airline-owned equipment, empty units can be obtained from a Member airline for loading and unloading by shipper/consignee free of charge but are subject to a demurrage charge after 48 hours from midnight of the day of release at destination. Normal pick-up and delivery charges for empty units to and from airports shall apply.

Loading must conform to contours established by the airlines to fit the interior cabin configurations of their aircraft. Each airline will provide guidance on such contours when their equipment is used. Shipper owned units will have standard contours controlled by rigid shells as part of the assembly in the Interline Specifications.

Rating Incentives:

For Bulk Unitization, consignments carried in Member owned units are charged at the actual net weight of the shipment. Empty Member owned units are offered free-of-charge, subject to demurrage. Non-Member owned units are charged at their actual gross weight less a fixed tare weight allowance.

Registered non-aircraft containers (i.e. units designed to be carried on or in aircraft unit load devices) owned by non-Members can be subject to rating incentives based on an IATA agreed formula. It is associated with the volume occupied by an aircraft unit load device (ULD)—a unit which attaches direct to an aircraft and requires no further restraint—regardless of the length of haul. Only IATA registered standard size, non-aircraft containers owned

by non-Members (i.e. shippers and container manufacturers) are eligible for discount.

Incentives are calculated in two ways; first by a Unitization formula of US $ discount

$$= \frac{External\ Vol\ in\ ft^3\ minus\ 2.}{4}$$

A second discount of 5 % for Cube Utilization is granted on standard size unit load devices above 1·821-m³ (63·44-ft³).

Rules covering this programme include, in brief: no discount to be greater than 10 % of the charges: a minimum chargeable weight based on 142·55-kg/m³ (8·9 lb/ft³) shall apply to all unit load devices: a tare weight allowance is made. The method of calculating a charge is to take the gross weight (or volume) of the consignment less the tare weight allowance of the ULD multiplied by the applicable airfreight rate, less the ULD discount: provided that the ULD discount shall not exceed 10 % of applicable charges and also provided that the chargeable weight of the consignment shall not be less than the minimum weight for the ULD.

Comprehensive publications are available from IATA on all unit load devices. They can be obtained from the International Air Transport Association, 1155 Mansfield Street, Montreal 2, Quebec, Canada, or in Britain from Aerad Publications Ltd, Hayes Road, Southall, Middlesex, England.

These publications are issued on behalf of the following airline members and their associated airlines. The two letter code which follows the company name and head office location in parentheses is used in the new IATA Markings and Identification Codes explained later.

Aerial Tours PTY Ltd.	**TI**
Aer Lingus Teoranta (Dublin)	**EI**
Aerlinte Eireann (Dublin)	**IN**
Aerolineas Argentinas (Buenos Aires)	**AR**
Aerolineas Peruanas S.A. (Lima)	**EP**
Aeronaves de Mexico S.A. (Mexico City	**AM**
Aerovias Nacionales de Colombia, S.A. (AVIANCA) (Bogota)	**AV**
Air Afrique (Abidjan)	**RK**
Air Algerie (Algiers)	**AH**
Air Canada (Montreal)	**AC**

Northwest Airlines based at Minneapolis-St. Paul Airport, Minnesota has 15 Boeing 747s in service or on order. Here IATA specification LD-3 containers (now coded AVE) built by Goodyear are being loaded into the aft container compartment

Air Ceylon (Colombo)	AE
Air Congo (Kinshasa)	QC
Air France (Paris)	AF
Air Guinee (Conakry)	GI
Air-India (Bombay)	AI
Air Malawi (Blantyre)	QM
Air Mali (Bamako)	MY
Air New Zealand Ltd. (Auckland)	TE
Air Siam Air Co Ltd. (Bangkok)	VG
Air Vietnam (Saigon)	VN
ALIA—The Royal Jordanian Airlines (Amman)	RJ
ALITALIA—Linee Aeree Italiane (Rome)	AZ
American Airlines Inc. (New York)	AA
Ansett Airlines of Australia (Adelaide)	AN
Ansett Airlines of Papua, New Guinea (Lae)	PN
Ariana Afghan Airline Co. Ltd. (Kabul)	FG
Austrian Airlines (Vienna)	OS
Braniff International (Dallas)	BN
British European Airways Corp. (London)	BE
British Overseas Airways Corp. (London)	BA
British West Indian Airways Ltd. (Trinidad)	BW
British Caledonian Airways (Horley)	BR
CP Air (Vancouver)	CP
Ceskoslovenske Aerolinie (Prague)	OK
Chicago Helicopter Airways Inc. (Chicago)	CH
China Air Lines (Taipei)	CI
Commercial Airways (PTY) Ltd. (Johannesburg)	MN
Compania Ecuatoriana de Aviacion S.A. (Quito)	EU
Compania Mexicana de Aviacion S.A.	MX
Continental Air Lines Inc. (Los Angeles)	CO
Cyprus Airways Limited (Nicosia)	CY
Delta Air Lines Inc. (Atlanta)	DL
Deutsche Lufthansa AG (Cologne)	LH
Direccao de Exploracao dos Transportes Aereos "DETA"	TM
Direccao de Exploracao dos Transportes Aereos "DTA" (Lourenco Marques)	DT
East African Airways Corp. (Nairobi)	EC
Eastern Air Lines Inc. (New York)	EA
Eastern Provincial Airways (1963) Ltd. (Gander)	PV
East-West Airlines Ltd. (Tamworth)	EW
EL AL Israel Airlines Limited (Tel Aviv)	LY
Empresa Consolidada Cubana de Aviacion (Havana)	CU
Ethiopian Airlines S.C. (Addis Ababa)	ET
FINNAIR Oy (Helsinki)	AY
Flugfelag Islands H.F. (ICELANDAIR) (Reykjavik)	FI
Flying Tiger Line Inc. (The (Los Angeles)	FT
P.N. Garuda Indonesian Airways (Djakarta)	GA
Ghana Airways, Corp. (Accra)	GH
IBERIA, Lineas Aereas de Espana, S.A. (Madrid)	IB
Indian Airlines (New Dehli)	IC
Iran National Airlines Corporation (Teheran)	IR
Iraqi Airways (Baghdad)	IA
Japan Air Lines Co. Ltd. (Tokyo)	JL
Jugoslovenski Aerotransport (JAT) (Belgrade)	JU
KLM Royal Dutch Airlines (Amsterdam)	KL
Kuwait Airways Corp. (Kuwait)	KU
Libyan Arab Airlines (Tripoli)	LN
Linea Aerea del Cobre Ltda. (Santiago)	UC

TAP, Lisbon operates three cargo and quick-change (QC) versions of the Boeing 727

Linea Aerea Nacional de Chile (Santiago)	LA
Malta Airlines, The (Sliena)	MG
Middle East Airlines Airliban (Beirut)	ME
Mohawk Airlines Inc. (Utica)	MO
National Airlines Inc. (Miami)	NA
New York Airways Inc. (New York)	NY
New Zealand National Airways Corporation (Wellington)	NZ
Nigeria Airways Limited (Lagos)	WT
Northwest Airlines Inc. (St. Paul)	NW
Olympic Airways S.A. (Athens)	OA
Pakistan International Airlines Corporation (Karachi)	PK
Pan American World Airways Inc. (New York)	PA
Philippine Air Lines Inc. (Manila)	PR
Polish Airlines "LOT" (Warsaw)	LO
Qantas Airways Ltd. (Sydney)	QF
Quebecair Inc. (Montreal)	QB
Saudi Arabian Airlines (Jeddah)	SV
Scandinavian Airlines System (Stockholm)	SK
Servicos Aereos Cruzeiro do Sul S.A. (Rio de Janeiro)	SC
Societe Anonyme Belge d'Exploitation de la Navigation Aerienne (SABENA) (Brussels)	SN
South African Airways (Johannesburg)	SA
Sudan Airways (Khartoum)	SD
Suidwes Lugdiens (Eiendoms) Beperk (Windhoek)	SW
Swiss Air Transport Co Ltd. (Zurich)	SR
Syrian Arab Airlines (Damascus)	RB
Territory Airlines PTY Ltd.	GV
Trans-Australia Airlines (Melbourne)	TN
Trans-Mediterranean Airways (Beirut)	TL
Trans World Airlines (New York)	TW
Transportes Aereos Portugueses S.A.R.L. (TAP) (Lisbon)	TP
Tunis Air (Tunis)	TU
Turk Hava Yollari (Istanbul)	TK
Union de Transports Aeriens (Paris)	UT
United Air Lines Inc. (Chicago)	UA
United Arab Airlines (Cairo)	MS
VARIG, S.A. (Viacao Aerea Rio-Grandense) (Porto Alegre)	RG
Venezolana Internacional de Aviacion S.A. (Caracas)	VA
Viacao Aerea Sao Paulo S.A. (Sao Paulo)	VP
Zambia Airways Corp (Lusaka)	QZ

Air Freight Terms

The following terms are those in constant and international use. They are reproduced from the IATA Register of Containers and Pallets. The meanings quoted are the accepted interpretations of the terms in IATA air freight regulations.

Air Cargo—which is equivalent to the term "goods", means any property carried or to be carried under the terms of an international postal convention, baggage or property of the carrier; provided that baggage moving under an air waybill is cargo.

Air Waybill—which is equivalent to the term air consignment note, means the document entitled Air Waybill/Consignment Note' made out by or on behalf of the shipper which evidences the contract between the shipper and carrier(s) for carriage of goods over the route(s) of the carrier(s).

Aircraft Unit Load Device—a unit that interfaces directly with an aircraft restraint system and meets all restraint requirements without the use of supplementary equipment. As such it can be either a combination of components (e.g. an aircraft pallet plus net plus non-structural igloo), or pallets plus structural igloo; or one complete structural unit (e.g. a lower hold cargo/baggage container).

Avoirdupois—an English and American system of weights based on a pound of 16 ounces and a ton of 2,000 pounds.

Base—the bottom of a container, that may sometimes be a pallet, which comes in contact with the floor.

Belly—general term describing lower portion of an aircraft.

Belly-Hold—lower deck or lower compartment in an aircraft used for stowing baggage mail or bulk loaded cargo.

Cargo-Hold—an area in the front and aft sections of the aircraft below the passenger deck used to contain cargo or unit load devices.

Carriage—which is equivalent to the term transportation, means carriage of goods by air on an airport-to-airport basis, including all services of the carrier incidental thereto.

Carrier—includes the air carrier issuing the Air Waybill and all air carriers that carry or undertake to carry the goods under such Air Waybill, or to perform any other services related to such air carriage.

Compression Test—The downward forces or stresses imposed upon a unit load device to simulate either stacking in a warehouse or top loading and gravity pull during flight.

Consignee—means the person whose name appears on the Air Waybill as the party to whom the goods are to be delivered by the carrier.

Consignment—which is equivalent to the

term shipment, means one or more pieces of goods accepted by the carrier from one shipper at one time and at one address, receipted for in one lot and moving under one Air Waybill to one consignee at one destination address.

Consignment Piece—a piece within a consignment means boxing, using crates, bags, barrels, banding and strapping or similar devices in order to derive a piece.

Consignor—which is equivalent to the term shipper, means the person whose name appears on the Air Waybill as the party contracting with the carrier(s) for carriage of the goods.

Container—a receptacle used to group individual items or packages into a single larger unit load. (See also non-aircraft container).

Contoured—a contoured container is one which is specifically designed to aircraft loading contours in order to utilize the maximum cubic space available in aircraft cabins or holds, subject to practical loading limitations.

Cube Utilization—means maximum use of available space in an aircraft.

Deflection:—the change in shape (bulge) of a sidewall or panel of a container or igloo (or component parts thereof) when subjected to compression loads.

Delamination—the separation of the layers of bonded materials.

Demurrage—a charge for storage in a warehouse or on airline premises, which accrues after a specified period of time.

Density—the relationship of weight to volume in a unit, i.e. lb per cu ft or kg per cu m.

Depth—measured fore and aft into the aircraft lengthwise.

Dimensions—the measurements of an object. The length, width and height of a container measured parallel to each of its axes and expressed in this order. As used herein, intended to mean the extreme external measurement of the unit load device. However, the dimensions of aircraft contours are related to the extreme internal measurement of the aircraft fuselage cross-section.

Disposable—a fibreboard unit load device which meets the IATA compression test requirements for single use.

Distortion—the permanent bulge or bowing of a panel beyond its original shape.

Dynamic Load Test—means that the completely assembled and closed container is positioned on a platform scale and a moving platen is brought into position to apply a continually increasing pressure up to the limit required.

Empty—to remove goods from a unit load device.

End—the walls of the container which, when loaded into an aircraft, are fore and aft.

Envelope—the interior cabin cross-section of an aircraft.

External Dimensions—the extreme outside measurement, including any handles or other protrusions, on a unit load device.

External Volume—the amount of space that unit load device occupies in an aircraft. Calculated upon the extreme dimensions of the unit.

Fibreboard, Solid or Corrugated—defined as a fabricated material used in container manufacture which is made from wood pulp, straw, waste papers, or any combination thereof, pressed and held together to form a semi-rigid board, and which may be in solid form, consisting of two or more plies glued together, or in corrugated form in which one or more fluted pieces are glued between alternate flat facings. Both types may or may not be lined on one or both faces with laminated paper, metal foil, plastic, or kraft or similar paper.

Fill—to insert (load) goods into or onto unit load device.

Floor Bearing—the maximum weight that

This large, automatic Air Canada pallet loader moves on two rails from the airline cargo terminal to two-level lorries waiting outside at Montreal International airport. Platform of the loader can be raised to meet the floor level of any truck or transporter.

A marine diesel engine loading into an Air New Zealand DC-8. Company's routes join New Zealand with the US, Australia, Singapore and Japan in addition to a number of important Pacific islands.

the aircraft floor is capable of withstanding. The distribution of weight evenly over the aircraft floor to meet weight and balance requirements.

Floor Load—static and dynamic loads imposed on the floor by the payload.

Footprint—the amount of flat bottom surface on an aircraft unit load device that comes in direct contact with the aircraft floor (or in the case of a non-aircraft container, the part that comes in contact with the aircraft pallet).

Igloo/hootl—is a bottomless shell made of fibreglass, metal or other suitable material. Its shape conforms to aircraft cargo compartment contours. It covers the maximum usable area of an aircraft pallet to which it is secured during flight.

Identification Code—the IATA markings on a unit that indicates the type, size, category, serial number and registrant.

Imperial Measure:—an English and American method of measurement e.g. 12 inches to one foot.

Leasing—management by a third party, or group of parties, of the supply of aircraft unit load devices to airliners or to shippers.

Length—in relation to aircraft unit load devices, measured fore and aft into the aircraft.

Loading—stowing loaded aircraft unit load devices or bulk cargo inside the aircraft.

Loading Contour—the maximum aircraft envelope for purposes of stowage inside the aircraft, having taken into account the necessary clearances between the aircraft wall and the load.

Markings—the IATA registration markings on a unit load device to indicate the detailed characteristics of the unit.

Maximum Aircraft Envelope—the maximum space available in the interior fuselage minus a one inch tolerance from the airframe manufacturer's constant cross-section contour to compensate for manufacturing variations and minor interior lining modifications made by carriers.

Maximum Net Weight Permissible—the maximum net weight permissible is the manufacturer's declared rating for the unit load device i.e., the maximum weight of contents which the manufacturer states the unit load device is capable of carrying for the purpose of registration with IATA.

Maximum Gross Weight Permissible—the maximum gross weight permissible is the sum of the tare weight and the maximum net weight permissible of the unit load device.

Minimum Design Criteria—the technical criteria as established by IATA for the purposes of designing a non-aircraft container to meet the minimum air freight requirements.

Non-Aircraft Container—a box, either contoured or rectangular, primarily made of fibreboard or plywood but sometimes permanent metal or fibreglass materials, designed to be carried on or in an aircraft unit load device.

Non-Member—Any entity other than an IATA Member airline, e.g. shipper or container manufacturer.

Aircraft Pallet—is a platform with a flat under surface and with standard dimensions used for assembling goods into unit loads thereby permitting rapid loading and unloading of aircraft equipped with mechanical handling systems. It is designed to restrain loads aboard the aircraft through the use of nets, straps or other tie-down equipment. As such, it is a component of the aircraft loading and restraint system.

Integral Pallet—a double layered platform, commonly made of wooden materials, forming the floor or attached to a container to provide forklift capability (see also Warehouse Pallet).

Warehouse Pallet—is a platform or flat surface made of solid, slatted or intersticed material, with or without fixed attachments, and designed to provide forklift capability. Its main function is to facilitate handling by grouping individual items into a single larger unit load.

Puncture Test—the BEACH puncture test, as employed in the IATA Container Programme, determines the resistance of fibreboard materials to withstand damage from sharp objects from within or from outside the box. The test is conducted on machines employed for this purpose. One BEACH unit is equivalent to 0·265-in-lb or 0·305-cm-kg.

Rating Incentive—means a discount and *Tare Weight Allowance* given to shippers for using *Registered Unit Load Devices* under the IATA Container Programme.

Registered—endorsement that complete data on a unit has been provided to IATA for the purpose of participating in any unitisation/containerisation programmes involving rating incentives, or that a unit meets specific standards.

Registrant—a unit manufacturer who has registered their IATA standard unit with IATA.

Shipper—see Consignor.

Side (of a Container)—the walls of a container which, when loaded in an aircraft, face the port or starboard wall of the fuselage.

Single Use—movement of a consignment, or any part thereof, in an IATA registered unit load device to final destination under one Air Waybill, regardless of carriage over more than one carrier.

Stacking—placing one unit on top of another, or in multiples, either in a warehouse or in an aircraft, for purposes of saving floor space.

Standardisation—uniformity of design. As used herein, intended to mean types of unit

Alitalia's mechanised cargo terminal at Rome-Fuimicino airport has cost over £1,300,000. In 1970 it handled more than 76,000-tons of air cargo

DIAGRAM OF STANDARD SIZES

CONTAINER NO. 1

CONTAINER NO. 2

CONTAINER NO. 4

CONTAINER NO. 5

CONTAINER NO. 6

CONTAINERS NOS. 3 AND 7 TO 17 incl.

Note: Height Dimensions on Base are forklift entry clearance, not Height of Pallet.

load devices that can be used universally in various types of aircraft.

Static Load Test—the completely assembled and closed container is positioned on a platform scale whereafter a stationary mass weight shall be evenly distributed over a plate of sufficient size to cover the surface of the container and remain there over a given period of time.

Tare Weight—the tare weight is the actual weight of the unit load device in an empty condition. It includes all liners and/or partitions and/or fittings, etc., when these are required by the container specification as registered with IATA.

Tare Weight Allowance—is free weight allowance per cubic foot of *Registered Unit Load Device* given to shippers under the IATA Container Programme.

Tare Weight Objective—a recommended but not mandatory weight target for materials to be used in the construction of a unit load device.

Unitization—means to consolidate multiple packages or items into a single load.

Unit Load Device—is any combination of *Container and Warehouse Pallet* or *Igloo and Aircraft Pallet* or the individual units. Its function is to facilitate handling of consignments by grouping individual items or packages into a single larger unit load.

Volume—the cubic capacity of a unit based on the external (or internal) dimensions.

Wall Deflection—horizontal bulge of a container wall under compression.

Width—in relation to containers, measured across the aircraft.

IATA CONTAINER PROGRAMME

Purpose

The main objectives of the IATA Container Programme introduced by the Member airlines of the International Air Transport Association (IATA) are to unitize multiple packages into a single larger unit load and through standardization of dimensions and equipment to achieve maximum cube utilization of aircraft space. To this end, incentives have been developed to encourage shippers to use IATA registered unit load devices for the carriage of air freight, thereby effecting efficiencies to both the shipper and carrier. The mandatory standards specified hereafter apply to non-Member owned IATA registered containers used under this programme.

Standard Sizes

The IATA Container Programme is geared to standard size containers, with integral warehouse pallet. Standard size means modular to aircraft pallets, i.e. 224 × 274 cm (88 × 108 in) or 224 × 318 cm (88 × 125 in).

Minimum Design Criteria

(a) All standard size unit load devices shall have an integral pallet, or similar provisions for handling by mechanical equipment. Such pallets, or lifting devices shall be designed so as to distribute the weight over the aircraft pallet and/or flat floor of the aircraft in approximately a uniform manner and shall be considered an integral part of the container.

(b) Notwithstanding Paragraph (a) above, Standard Size Numbers 16 and 17 may be registered with or without a pallet. These containers may be designed without an integral pallet when registered for a maximum gross weight permissible of 227 kg (500 lb) or less.

(c) The maximum floor loading requirements for all unit load devices shall be 0·097 kg per sq cm (200 lb per sq ft) of floor bearing surface (footprint). Floor loading shall be calculated by dividing the total area of the undersurface of the integral pallet which comes in direct contact with the aircraft floor, into the maximum gross weight permissible.

(d) Contact with the aircraft pallet or floor shall be provided by either a single plane surface or by skids/stringers. Stringer parts must be parallel and in unbroken contact with the floor for their full length and may extend to the extreme dimensions of the container base. Legs or blocks are not acceptable (see diagram).

(e) The floor, as an integral part of the container, shall be capable of withstanding the load uniformly distributed over the entire floor when supported solely by the fork tines.

(f) Forklift entry clearances shall be at least 30 cm (12 in) wide and between 6·4 cm (2¼ in) and 10 cm (4 in) high on all unit load devices, except standard sizes No. 1 to 3 which require heights of 10 cm (4 in). Forklift entry shall be provided from at least two opposite sides, although four-way entry is preferred.

(g) Unit load device measurements shall state the extreme dimensions in an empty condition and shall include any integral pallet, handles or other external fittings.

(h) For purpose of manufacture, the maximum variation of measurements shall be plus 0, minus 2·5 cm (1 in) from such stated measurements.

(i) Containers shall be constructed to permit air flow in and out of the container for pressure equalization.

Test Requirements

(1) *Compression Test*

The compression test requirements as outlined below shall apply to all unit load devices owned by non-Members, regardless of materials used in the construction. This test simulates resistance to weights, such as would be applied when stacking in an aircraft or warehouse, or other conditions normally incident to air transportation.

(a) The compression test shall be performed on the fully assembled unit under registration. All unit load devices shall be tested in an empty condition, securely closed, including liners, partitions, pallets as required, etc. which are an integral part of the structural design, and shall be subjected to the compression test requirements outlined below.

(b) The minimum compression test loads for all materials are specified in the IATA Compression Test Tables (over) which are expressed in total lb or kg to be placed on top surface and is based on dynamic loading.

(c) When dynamic loading is not possible, and static loading is used, the static load shall be applied for a period of five minutes at a value of 85 per cent of the dynamic load required.

(d) A record shall be made of the amount the container walls have deflected horizontally under the maximum force applied in the stacking direction. The test load recorded shall be at least that stated in the Tables. The results shall be submitted in the manner prescribed in the Application Form for Registration of Unit Load Devices.

(e) The deflection of the walls of the container under compression for the width and the length separately shall not bulge more than 2 per cent or 3·2 cm (1¼ in) whichever is

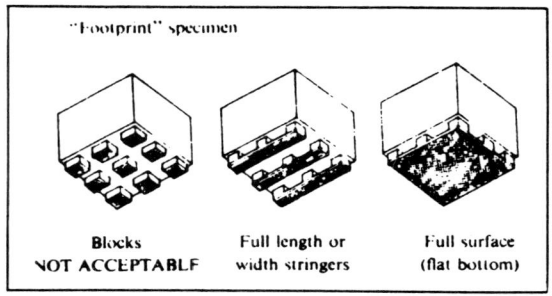

"Footprint" specimen

Blocks
NOT ACCEPTABLE

Full length or width stringers

Full surface (flat bottom)

greater, e.g. 254 cm long by 127 cm wide (100 × 50 in) can deflect to 259 × 130 cm (102 × 51¼ in). Vertical deflection is not measured in this test since this measurement is required for determination of maximum width and length dimensions of the loaded container in relation to the perimeter limitation of the aircraft pallet and net.

(f) Fibreboard unit load devices should be preconditioned for 48 hours under the prescribed atmospheric conditions prior to testing. The test load values shown in the Tables are based on the assumption of dynamic test loading of fiberboard containers preconditioned at a temperature of 73·4°F ± 5° and an atmosphere of 50 per cent relative humidity ± 2 per cent or at 20°C ± 2° at 65 per cent ± 2 per cent relative humidity.

Dynamic Test Loading means that the completely assembled and closed container is positioned on a platform scale and a moving platen is brought into position to apply a continually increasing pressure up to the limit required.

Static Test Loading means that the completely assembled and closed container is positioned on a platform scale and a stationary mass weight is evenly distributed over a plate of sufficient size to cover the surface of the container and shall remain there over a given period of time.

(2) *Puncture Test* (for fiberboard material)
To protect the contents from external hazards, the container material must have resistance to puncture. For fiberboard, this resistance

shall be measured by means of a *Beach* puncture test. The minimum requirement will be 400 *Beach* units for fiberboard containers. One *Beach* scale unit of puncture equals 0·305 cm–kg or 0·265 in–lb (or 0·946428 in–ounces per in of tear).

Performance Criteria
In addition to their basic function of containing loads up to their maximum weight capacity, IATA registered containers tendered to Member airlines will also be expected to perform adequately during air transportation when handled, stacked or top loaded as follows:
Handling
Individual container handlings and numbers of trips will vary widely. A typical trip will include the following:
(a) Shipper loading contents.
(b) Transfer to temporary storage.
(c) Transfer from storage to truck.
(d) Transfer from truck to airline roller conveyor.
(e) Transfer from roller conveyor to temporary terminal storage.
(f) Transfer from terminal storage to aircraft pallet.
(g) Transfer to aircraft.
(h) Stowage on board aircraft.
The above order will be reversed when aircraft reaches destination airport.

Time Element
A typical flight will last up to 48 hours but

Livestock continues to offer steady rewards to operators who invest in special equipment. The Invicta International DC-4 has comfortable stabling for 10 horses.

some cases may be stored up to 14 days The number of trips for each type of container may be:
(a) Disposable fiberboard—one trip.
(b) Multi-use fiberboard—five trips.
(c) Other material—unspecified.
Climatic Ranges
Insofar as atmospheric conditions may effect the performance of the unit load device or any part thereof, it should be taken into account that during air transportation, these conditions range from +30°C to −35°C (+95°F to −30°F) with relative humidity from 20 per cent to 85 per cent. These are the mean temperature and humidity figures world-wide without taking into account extremes in temperatures such as those experienced in arctic, sub-polar, or desert regions. This, however, is not a test requirement.

The incentives given for IATA standard sized non-Member unit load devices are tabled opposite:

Note. There is a compatibility between Nos. 5, and 9 IATA with ATA domestic containers B, and D—which is of interest to shippers of consignments to and from points in the US.

IATA STANDARD
CONTAINERS

Standard Size No	Tare Weight Allowance (or actual, whichever is less)		Minimum Chargeable Weight		Container Rebate US$
	lb	kg	lb	kg	
1	537	244	3183	1444	93·40
2	607	275·5	3598	1632	105·60
3	335	152	1986	901	58·10
4	257	116·5	1520	689·5	44·30
5	297	135	1760	798·5	51·40
6	231	105	1368	620·5	39·90
7	191	87	1130	512·5	32·80
8	132	60	779	353·3	22·50
9	96	44	565	256·5	16·20
10	106	48	628	285	18·00
11	265	120·5	1575	714·5	46·00
12	133	60·5	788	357·5	22·70
13	57	26	507	230	13·80
14	45	20·5	394	179	10·60
15	44	20	390	177	10·50
16	32	14·5	283	128·5	7·50
17	18	8·5	160	72·5	4·00

INCENTIVES

TABLE I
(Imperial Measure and Avoirdupois)

Size No	Inches			External Volume (cu ft)	Top Surface Area (sq ft)	Minimum Compression Test Load (lb) Other Material	Single lb	Fibreboard‡	Multiple lb
	Length	Width	Height						
1	84	102	76/66/45*	357·55	6048	2782	2782		2782
2	84	119	76/45*	404·23	6048	2782	2782		2782
3	84	102	45	223·13	8568	5998	5998		5998
4	84	58	74/39	170·78	1134	552	552		552
5	84	58	76/45*	197·70	3024	1391	1391		1391
6	84	42	76/66*	153·71	3024	1391	1391		1391
7	84	58	45	126·88	4872	3411	3411		3411
8	84	40	45	87·50	3360	2352	4704		9408
9	42	58	45	63·44	2436	1706	3412		6824
10	42	50	58	70·49	2100	1071	2142		4284
11	84	52	70	176·94	4368	2010	4020		8040
12	42	52	70	88·47	2184	1005	2010		4020
13	42	52	45	56·88	2184	1529	3058		6116
14	42	52	35	44·24	2184	1857	3714		7428
15	42	40	45	43·75	1680	1176	2352		4704
**16	42	29	45	31·72	1218	853	1706		3412
**17	42	29	25·5	17·97	1218	1218	2436		4872

**May be registered without integral pallet when gross permissable weight is 227 kg (500 lb) or less.

*Contoured

‡Preconditioned at 73·4°F ± 5° at 50 per cent ± 2 per cent RH.

TABLE II
(Metric)

Centimetres Size No.	Length	Width	Height	External Volume (cu m)	Top Surface Area (sq cm)	Minimum Compression Test Load (kg) Other Material	Fibreboard‡ Single	Multiple
1	214	259	193/168/115*	10·154	39,162	1253·5	1253·5	1253·5
2	214	303	193/115*	11·513	39,162	1253·5	1253·5	1253·5
3	214	259	115	6·374	55,426	2716	2716	2716
4	214	148	188/99*	4·837	7,316	236·5	236·5	236·5
5	214	148	193/115*	5·645	19,688	630	630	630
6	214	107	193/168*	4·379	19,688	630	630	630
7	214	148	115	3·642	31,672	1552	1552	1552
8	214	102	115	2·510	21,828	1070	1855·5	3,711
9	107	148	115	1·821	15,836	776	1346	2,692
10	107	127	148	2·011	13,589	462	815·5	1,631
11	214	132	178	5·028	28,248	904	1610·5	3,221
12	107	132	178	2·514	14,124	452	805	1,610
13	107	132	115	1·624	14,124	692	1200·5	2,401
14	107	132	89	1·257	14,124	847·5	1539·5	3,079
15	107	102	115	1·255	10,914	535	928	1,856
**16	107	74	115	0·911	7,918	388	673	1,346
**17	107	74	65	0·515	7,918	562·5	990	1,980

**May be registered without integral pallet when gross permissable weight is 227 kg (500 lb) or less.

* Contoured

‡ Preconditioned at 20°C ± 2° at 65 per cent ± 2 per cent RH

MARKINGS AND IDENTIFICATION CODES:
In May 1971 IATA issued details of its new system of coding for unit load devices. Designed as an informative method of identification a broad description of each unit can be obtained from its alphanumeric groupings. These have to be clearly marked on each unit.

The IATA Identification Code (ID Code) is made up by nine alphanumeric characters arranged in a pre set order.

Digit	Character	Description
1	Alphabetic	Equipment Catagory (e.g. P = aircraft pallet)
2 and 3	Alpha/ numeric	Type and size (e.g. 1 = 88 × 125-in pallet.
4, 5, 6 & 7	Alpha/ numeric	C = Full size contours 88 × 125-in) Serial number (These are to be assigned by the owner).
8 and 9	Alpha/ numeric	Owner or registrant (e.g. Air Canada = AC)

Code lists
Equipment Category (Digit 1) etc., etc.
For details of new IATA alpha/numeric code please see IATA style tables and diagrams on pages 584, 585, 586, 587 and 588.

INTERNATIONAL LIST OF MANUFACTURERS OF IATA REGISTERED CONTAINERS

Owner Registrant Code
Owner/Registrant Code follows company name. IATA style letter in parenthesis follows Equipment Category e.g. COS (K).

ARGENTINE
Schcolnik S.A.I.C. (2S)
Venezuela 4269
Buenos Aires
COS(A)
AUSTRALIA
Adelaide Fibre Box Pty. Ltd. (2F)
22 Hanson Road North,
Wingfield, S.A. 5013
COS(K)
Broons Containers (N.S.W.) Pty, Ltd (4B)
274 Victoria Road,
Rydalmere, N.S.W.
COR(K), COS(K)
512-520 Geelong Road,
Brooklyn,
Victoria
COS(A)

Carlton Box Co Pty, Ltd (2F)
228 Hall Street,
Spotswood, Victoria 3015
COS(K)
Cartons & Corrugated Papers Pty Ltd (2F)
9 Kent Road,
Mascot, NSW 2020
COS(K)
CHEP Handling Systems (1C)
(Brambles Holdings Ltd)

Waterloo, NSW
COE(-), COJ(-), COK(-), COM(-), COP(-), COQ(-), COR(J), COS(J)
Fibre Containers Limited (2F)
McCauley Street,
Matraville, NSW
COS(K)
Fibre Containers (Tas.) Pty. Ltd (2F)
17 Pitcairn Street,
Glenorchy, Tasmania 7010
COS(K)
Hercules Fibre Containers (2F)
249 Middleborough Road,
Box Hill, Victoria 3128
COS(K)
Perth Fibre Box Pty Ltd (2F)
344 Scarborough Beach Road,
Osborne Park, W.A. 6017
COS(K)

Tri-Wall Containers Pty. Ltd.
1-7 Spring Street
Chatswood N.S.W.
COH (–), COJ (A), COK (–), COL (–), CON (A), COP (A) COQ (A), COR (A), COS (A).

AUSTRIA
Neusiedler AG Fur Papierfabrikation (1N)
Schottenring 21
A-1013 Vienna
COR(A)- COS(A), COM(L), CON(L), COP(L)
Rondo Vorarlberger, (4R)
Papierhandels-Ges,
6820 Frastanz, Vorarlberg
COQ(J), COR(J), COS(A)

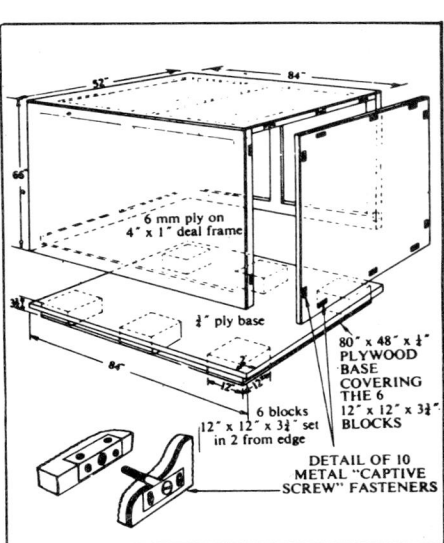

Typical plywood container made and used by members of the Federation of International Furniture Removers, COL (P)

Schelling Interwell GmbH (3S)
4054 Nettingsdorf,
Oberösterreich
COQ(J), COR(A) (J), COS(A)
Wiener Wellpappe GmbH (3W)
Brunner Strasse 75,

1235 Wein (Liesing)
COQ(J), COR(J)J, COS(A)

BELGIUM
N.V. Bowater-Philips (3P)
100 New Orleansstraat,
Ghent
COP(-), COS(-)
**Federation of International Furniture Remov-
ers (1F)**
81a rue de la Loi, Brussels 4
COL(P), COM(P)
Weyerhaeuser Belgium S.A. (2W)
Ghlin-Les-Mons
COS(K)

CANADA
Consolidated Bathurst Packaging Ltd (4D)
635 Dorchester Blvd.,
Montreal, P.Q.
COS(A)
1035 Hodge Street,
St. Laurent, Quebec
COS(A)
1000 Gerrard Street East,
Toronto,
Ontario
COS(A)
P.O. Box 910,
Whiteby, Ontario
COS(A)
Cavell Ave.,
Hamilton, Ontario
COS(A)
1155 Talbot Street,
St. Thomas, Ontario
COS(A)
450 Dawson Road,
St. Boniface, Manitoba
COS(A)
Dever Road,
Lancaster N.B.
COS(A)
Macintyre Wood Products Ltd (2MO)
P.O. Box 247,
Smiths Falls, Ontario
COG(O), COH(O), COJ(O), COK(O), COL(O),
COM(O), CON(J), COP(A), COQ(J), COR(A),
COS(A)
Smith Packaging Ltd (8S)
111 Eastside Drive,
Toronto 18, Ontario
COG(O), COH(O), COJ(O), COK(O), COL(O),
COM(O), CON(A), COP(A), COQ(A), COR(A)

Tri-Wall Containers (Canada) Ltd.
310 Keele Centre
530 Keele Street
Toronto, Ontario
COM (–), COJ (A), COR (–), COL (–), :
CON (A), COP (A), COQ (A), COR (A),
COS (A)

DENMARK
IB. S. Christiansen GmbH (5C)
1 Gl Amtsvej
DK 3450
Allerod
COJ(P), COQ(P), COS(P)
Colon Emballage A/S (2D)
Tagensvej 135
2200 Kobenhavn, N.
CON(J), COS(J)
FINLAND
Enso-Gutzeit, OY, (2E)
Finish Paper & Board,
Lahti Mills, Lahti
CON(L), COP(L), COR(A)
**Finnish Paper and Board Converters' Associa-
tion (3F)**
Fabianinkatu 29,
P.O. Box 13035,
Helsinki 13
CON(L), COP(L), COR(A)
FRANCE
Societe F. Beghin (1B)
68 Kaysersberg
COE(L), COJ(L), COP(A)(J), COR(A),
COS(A)

A	Certified lower deck aircraft container.
B	Certified main deck aircraft container.
C	Non-aircraft container.
D	Non-certified lower deck aircraft container.
E	Non-certified main deck aircraft container.
N	Aircraft pallet net.
P	Aircraft pallet.
R	Refrigerated or temperature controlled units.
S	Structural igloo.
U	Igloo (non-structural).

Type and Size (Digits 2 and 3)

1.   These digits are intended to fully describe the unit and therefore combine the factors for external dimensions (base size), contour, specification and airworthiness certification.

2.   Maximum aircraft envelopes have been developed for each type of cargo-carrying aircraft currently in operation. The specific aircraft contours are shown in Section II of the Aircraft Unit Load Devices Manual. The shapes show the available loading space of the cabin cross-section. These Loading Contours determine the patterns of the built-up pallet loads, or the igloo contours, according to the flexibility desired in interchanging between different types of aircraft. The Loading Contours have been sequentially numbered, and the individual aircraft unit load devices will be coded and marked according to the variety of aircraft in which they can be carried.

3.   The Legend for the Type and Size digits is as follows and the assigned combined codes for non-aircraft containers are listed thereafter. The detailed codes for aircraft units are published in the Aircraft Unit Load Devices Manual.

LEGEND

1 Series	88 x 125" pallets
2 Series	88 x 108" pallets
3 Series	Miscellaneous full size pallets (e.g. 88 x 121, 88 x 118, etc.)
4 Series	Miscellaneous sized pallets (e.g. 76 x 70", 60 x 53", 108 x 54" etc.)
5 Series	Half size pallets
6 Series	96 x 125" pallets
7 Series	8 x 10, 20, 30, 40 ft. base/pallets
8 Series	Lower deck half size pallet 60.4 x 61.5"
9 Series	Lower deck full size pallet 60.4 x 125"
A, B, C Series	Full size contours 88 x 125"
D, E, F Series	Full size contours 88 x 108"
G, H, J Series	Miscellaneous full size contours 88 x 121, 88 x 118" etc.
K, L Series	Miscellaneous size contours 76 x 70", 60 x 53" etc.
M, N Series	Miscellaneous Main deck containers
P Series	Half size contours
Q Series	96 x 125" contours
R, S, T, U Series	8 x 8 foot containers
V Series	Lower deck half size containers
W Series	Lower deck full size containers
O Series	Non-aircraft containers, standard sizes
X Series	Non-aircraft containers, non-standard (Member owned)

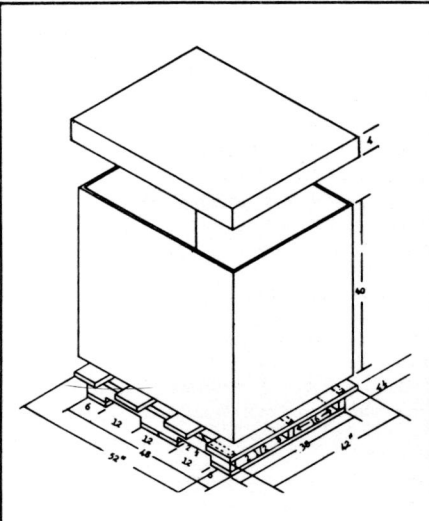

Triple-wall corrugated fibreboard and wood container with wooden pallet, by Macintyre Wood Products Ltd., CON (J)

Half-width contoured Igloo built by Tridair Ltd. for Seaboard World Airlines.

Walton et Place S.A. (1W)
78 rue de Crimee
Paris 19e
COP(L)
GERMANY
Hans Adelmann (2A)
Hauptstrasse 65,
Heroldsberg B, NBG
COB(P)

**Europa Carton Aktiengesellschaft Wellpappen-
work Hamburg (3E)**
Tilsiter Strasse 144,
2 Hamburg 70
COJ(-), COP(A), COR(A), COS(A)
Klingele Papierwerke K.G. (2K)
7067 Grunbach,
Stuttgart, Postfach 20
COQ(L), COR(M), COS(A)
Seyfert Wellpappe, (5S)
7313 Reichenbach/Fils,
Ulmer Strasse 58
COR(K), COS(A)

Hch. Sieger GmbH (6S)
Neumarkt 12,
500 Koln
COR(A)

Thimm-Wellpappen K.G. (3T)
P.O. Box 41
3410 Northeim/Han
COH(M), COJ(M), CON(M), COP(M),
COQ(M), COR(A)(M), COS(A)

Zellstoffabrik Waldof (1Z)
Zewa Faltikstenwerk
Karlstrasse 51
495 Minden/Westfalen
COH(A), COJ(A), COM(-), COP(A), COQ(A),
COR(A), COS(A)(E)

**West German distributors for
Compagnie de Kaysersberg, France.**

Fa. Knipp & Co.,
6050 Offenbach,
Kaiserstrasse 32-34.

Fa. A. Brenner,
8 Munchen,
Euckenstrasse 2.

Fa. Alex Breuer,
5 Koln 17,
Postfach 47.

Moderne Verpackung,
Hans J. R. Huwald,
2 Hamburg,
Rauchenstrasse 45.

Fa. Karl Koeppen Chg.,
1 Berlin SW 61,
Wassertorstrasse 9.

Fa. H. J. Lichtenberger,
68 Mannheim,
Hafenbahnstrasse 30.

Rheinische Papiermanufaktur,
Hans Mehwald,
4 Dusseldorf,
Oberbilker Allee 199.

'Papyrus',
Kurt Klutentreter,
85 Nurnberg,
Wandererstrasse 103/7.

Fa. Tillmann & Co.,
6052 Muhlheim/Main,
Friedensstrasse 146/148.

Karl Heuchemer,
5427 Bad Ems,
Wilhelms Allee 55.

Fa. Weihrauch & Co.,
3014 Misburg-Hannover,
Buchholzstrasse 81.

Gustav Wondrak & Sohn,
895 Kaufbeuren-Neugablonz,
Postfach 1062.

GREECE

"Vis" Containers Manufacturing Co Ltd (2V)
54 Athens Street Neon Phaliron
Athens 53
COS(A)

HONG KONG

Amoycan Corrugated Carton Factory (4A)
N.K.I.L. 53,
Ngau Chi Wan,
Kowloon
COS(A)

ISRAEL

Tri-Wall Containers (Israel) Ltd (6T)
10 Lipsky Street
Tel-Aviv
COH(-), COJ(A), COK(-), COL(-), CON(A),
COP (A) COQ(A), COR(A), COS(A)

General Packaging Ltd (3G)
Tel-Aviv
COE(-), COJ(-), COK(-), COM(-), COP(-),
COQ(-), COR(-), COS(J)

ITALY

Italo Gatti S.P.A. (8I)
via Privata Lorenzetti 15,
Monza, Milan
COS(A)

Bruno Gualdi (4G)
Imballaggi Industriali,
Via San Bernardino da Siena No. 41,
Carpi (Moderna), 41012

(Miscellaneous Non-Aircraft, Non-standard sized units — Member Owned)

The word "small" is used to mean less than quarter pallet size and less than 25 cu.ft. (0.7 cu.m.). Since the dimensions vary considerably, the terms "full, half and quarter pallet sizes" are used in a general sense and it is intended to mean 1 on a pallet, 2 on a pallet and 4 on a pallet, but not necessarily modular to the total usable space on the pallet.

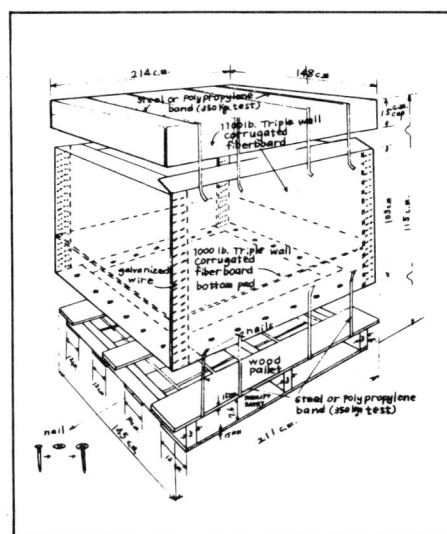

A collapsible corrugated, fibreboard and wood 2·96 m³ (103·6 cu. ft) container built by Yamada Danbouru Co. Ltd, Tokyo COG (J)

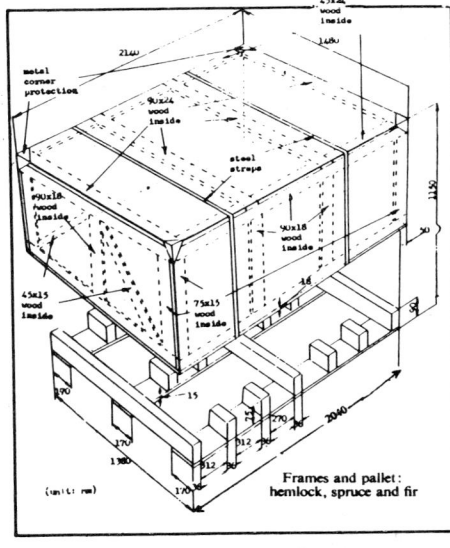

Manufactured by Mabuchi Kensetsu Co. Ltd. this container is plywood, wood and metal, on a wood pallet. COG (D)

COR(A), COS(A)

Soc. Italiana Imballaggi (7I)
W.A.R. de Donde A & C
Via Cantu 1, Vigevano (Pavia)
COR(A), COS(A)

S.P.A. Francesco Pisani & Figli (5P)
Arpino,
Province Frosinone
COR(A), COS(A)

Unicontrans (1U)
Universal Containerized Transport
Via Torricelli 23

37100 Verona
COA(P), COC(P), COG(P), COJ(P)

Vosa, SpA (3V)
Novi Ligure (AL)
Strada Serravalle 30
COJ(L), COK(J), COM(L), COQ(J), COR(A)
(J), COS(A)

IRELAND

Mar-Loe Packing Co Ltd (4M)
19 Allen Park
Shannon Airport,
Co. Clare

COE(P)
JAPAN
Araki Woods Works (1C)
Container Div,
2-3-11 Chuo,
Edogawake, Tokyo
COE(-), COJ(-), COK(-), COM(-), COP(-),
COQ(-), COR(J), COS(J)

Canon Camera Co Inc (1D)
3-30-2 Shimomaruko,
Ohta-ku, Tokyo
COG(P)

Chiyoda Shikogyo Co Ltd (4C)
48-2 Higashiimazato-cho
Higashinari-ku,
Osaka
COJ(N)(J), COR(J)

Japan Container Packing Co. Ltd., Fty (1J)
181-4 chome,
Yamamoto-cho,
Naka-Ku, Yokohama,
COP(A), COR(A), COS(A)

C. E. Kridle In (3K)
Tokunaga Bldg.,
82 Yamashitacho,
Nakaku,-
Yokohama
COJ(P)

Mabuchi Kensetsu Co. Ltd. (1M)
Tokyo Plant,
1-4 Edagawa-cho,
Fukagawa, Koto-ku,
Tokyo
(COG(P)

Mitsubishi Shoji Kaisha Ltd (5M)
2-20 Marunouchi,
Chiyoda-ku,
Tokyo
COG(J), COJ(J), COR(J), COS(A)

Nippon Hi-Pack Co. Ltd. (2N)
700 Nyoisarucho,
Kasugai City,
Aichi Pref.
COJ(J), CON(J), COQ(J), COR(J), COS(J)

Rengo Shiki Co. Ltd. (2R)
4-18 Hiranomachi,
Higashi-ku,
Osaka
COJ(N), COK(N), COM(N), CON(N), COP(N),
COQ(N), COR(L), COS(A)

Yamada Corrugated Containers Co. (1Y)
1-6 Nihonbashi Moncho,
Chuo-ku,
Tokyo
COG(J), COH(A), COJ(A), COK(J), CON(A),
COP(A), COQ(A), COR(A), COS(A)

NETHERLANDS
N.V. "Mercurius" Golfcartonindustrie (5G)
Kostverlorenweg,
Soest
COJ(L), COR(A), COS(A)

XA	Full pallet size container — contoured
XB	Full pallet size container — rectangular
XC	Half pallet size container — contoured. Metal or Fiberglass
XD	Half pallet size container — contoured. Plywood or Fiberboard
XE	Half pallet size container — rectangular. Metal or Fiberglass
XF	Half pallet size container — rectangular. Plywood or Fiberboard
XG	Quarter pallet size container — contoured. Metal or Fiberglass
XH	Quarter pallet size container — contoured. Plywood or Fiberboard
XJ	Quarter pallet size container — rectangular. Metal or Fiberglass
XK	Quarter pallet size container — rectangular. Plywood or Fiberboard
XL	Small metal or fiberglass boxes — less than 1/4 pallet size
XM	Small plywood or fiberboard containers — less than 1/4 pallet size
XN	Small fabric, cloth or vinyl bags — less than 1/4 pallet size
XP	Insulated boxes — half pallet size — rectangular
XQ	Insulated boxes — quarter pallet size — rectangular
XR	Insulated boxes — less than 1/4 pallet size
XS	Insulated packs or bags — fabric/plastics
XT	Temperature controlled containers — Full pallet size, contoured
XU	Temperature controlled containers — Half pallet size, contoured
XV	Garmet racks
XW	Seat packs or seat containers
XY	
X1	
X2	

Serial Number (Digits 4, 5, 6 and 7)

The sequential serial numbers are to be assigned by the Owner and the four characters can be either numeric or alphabetic or a combination of both.

The assignment of the four-digit alpha/numeric serial number incorporated into the ID Code is the prerogative of the manufacturer and his customers. The combination of letters and figures allows sufficient scope to prevent duplication of serial numbers in any one type of unit for a considerable period of time. The letters OIXZ should not be used. The Serial number is not required for non-Member owned non-aircraft containers but the reserved positions in the ID Code should be maintained and blocked off in the manner given by IATA at the time of registration.

Owner/Registrant Code (Digits 8 and 9)

The last two digits in the ID Code will show the Owner if the unit is airline owned, or the Registrant if owned by a shipper or leasing agent.

For airline owned units, the two-letter airline designator shall be shown.

Non-Member owned units are registered by manufacturers who in turn make them available to shippers world-wide. Since it would be impractical to attempt to keep a central record of every shipper who purchases unit load device from every manufacturer, the last two digits in the ID Code, for non-Member non-airline units will be assigned to the manufacturer (Registrant) at the time of registration of the unit with IATA. This code shall be alpha/numeric. Shippers or leasing agent owners should paint their name conspicuously elsewhere on the unit.

In due course when a system of third party ownership has been established, two numeric characters will indicate leasing/pooling operator ownership.

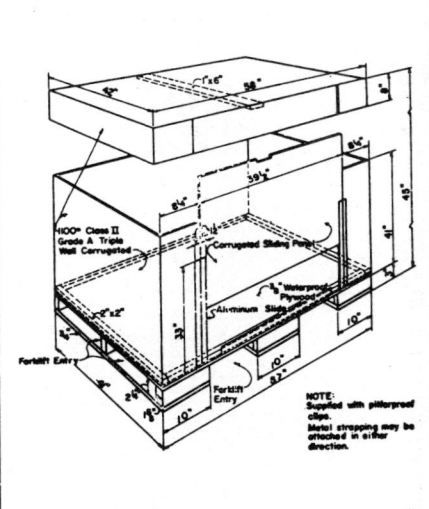

Cargo Packers Inc., triple-wall fibreboard unit to IATA Size 9 and Type 'D' ATA Domestic Container Programme. COJ (–)

N.V. Movi (3P)
99 Stadionweg,
Rotterdam
COP(-), COS(-)

N.V. Philips (3P)
Eindhoven,
COP(A), COS(A)

Tri-wall Containers (Europa) N.V. (6T)
SJC Van Merkenlaan
Rijswijk (Z-H),
COH(-), COJ(A), COK(-), COL(-), CON(A),
COP(A), COQ(A), COR(A), COS(A)

Contoured, framed, plywood container of 2,931 lb (1,329·5 kg) capacity, by Chicago Mill & Lumber Company. IATA Size 5, ATA type 'B'. COJ (9)

SOUTH AFRICA
Containair Africa (Pty) Limited (1C)
P.O. Box 105
Strand, K.P./C.P.
COE(-), COJ(-), COK(-)(J), COM(-), COP(-),
COQ(-), COR(-)(J), COS(J)

SPAIN
Pagusa, Papeleras Del Guadalquivir, S.A. (2P)
Carretera Amarilla s/n,
Apartado 297,
Seville
COQ(L), COR(M), COS(A)

This IATA size 16 container, now recoded COR, will be one of a number of sizes due to be phased-out of service in 1972, because of a small demand.

SWEDEN
Broderna Nordgren AB (4N)
820 13 Runemo,
COR(P)
Fredells Travaru AB
Hammarbyvagen 75,
S-10460 Stockholm,
COS(P)
Kinnawell AB (1K)
S-511 04 Kinna 4
COS(J)
Munksjo Aktie Bolag (9M)
Box,
Jönköping
COP(J), COQ(J), COR(J), COS(J)
Ab Hugo Nordgren (3N)
181 20 Lidingo, Fack
COR(L), COS(I)
Robert Skarstedt (7S)
P.O. Box 13056,
Gothenburg 13
COS(K)
Thimgren & Co. (2T)
Box 2015,
127 02 Slarholmen 2
COS(-)
SWITZERLAND
Container License Ltd (5D)
Alpenstrasse 12, Zug
COQ(J), COR(J), COS(A)
Model Limited (7M)
Weinfelden
COK(A), COL(A), COQ(J), COR(J), COS(A)
E. H. Schelling Ltd (4S)
CH 8153, Rümlang
COR(I), COS(A)
UNITED KINGDOM
E. Abrahams & Co Ltd (1A)
11a Pearson Street,
Kingsland Road,
London, E.2
COM(P)
Alliance Box Co. (Scotland) Ltd. (3A)
29 Saracen Street,
Glasgow, N.2
COM(L), COP(L)
Ashton Containers Limited (7A)
Winterstoke Road,
Bristol 3
COM(L), COP(L), COS(A)
The Banner Church Organisation Ltd. (1C)
South Street,
Reading,
Berks
COE(-), COJ(-), COK(-), COM(-), COP(-),
COQ(-), COR(-), COS(J)
Bowater Packaging Limited (3B)
Gunnels Wood Road,
Stevenage, Herts.
COM(-)
Instant Shut Box Co. Ltd. (4I)
71A Fairfield Road,
Bowy London, E.3
COM(P), COP(P)
MacMillan Bloedel Containers Limited (3M)
24/30 King Street
Watford, Herts.
COR(M)
Reed Corrugated Cases Ltd. (1R)
Reed House,
82 Piccadilly
London W.1
COM(L), COP(-), COQ(L), COR(A)(K)(L),
COS(A)
Duaboard Unit
New Hythe,
Maidstone, Kent
COG(L), COH(L), COJ(L), COK(L), CON(L),
COP(L), COR(A), COS(A)
Hugh Stevenson & Sons Ltd. (9S)
Alexandra Docks,
Newport,
Mon.
COR(N), COS(A)
Sumacon Ltd. (0S)
Stanhope Works,
Kings Langley, Herts
COJ(P), COM(P), COP(P)

The Owner/Registrant code is assigned as follows:—

Two Alphabetic characters	— airline owned
One alphabetic and one numeric, in either sequence	— non-Member Registrant (not airline owned)
Two numeric characters (Reserved for future)	— third party, leasing/pooling operator

The present list of Registrants of non-aircraft unit load devices follows overleaf.

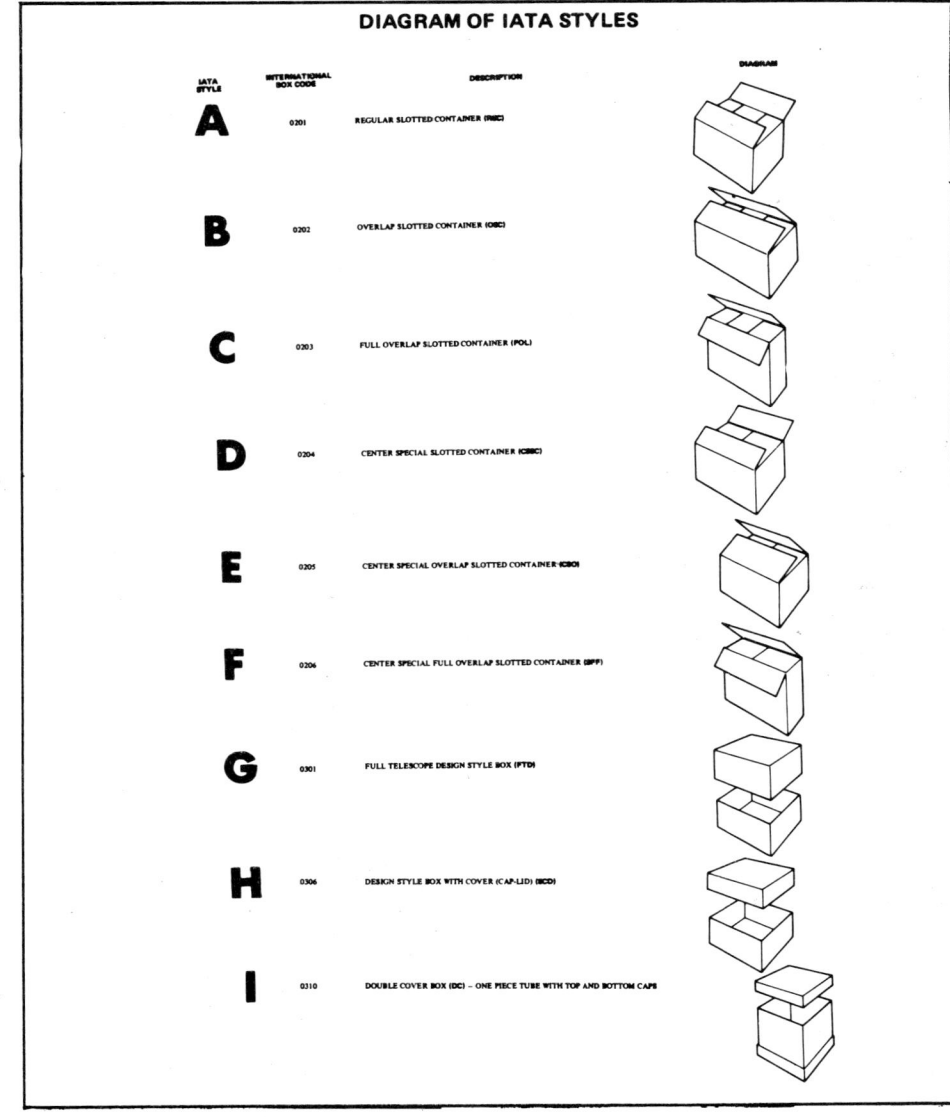

DIAGRAM OF IATA STYLES

IATA STYLE	INTERNATIONAL BOX CODE	DESCRIPTION	DIAGRAM
A	0201	REGULAR SLOTTED CONTAINER (RSC)	
B	0202	OVERLAP SLOTTED CONTAINER (OSC)	
C	0203	FULL OVERLAP SLOTTED CONTAINER (FOL)	
D	0204	CENTER SPECIAL SLOTTED CONTAINER (CSSC)	
E	0205	CENTER SPECIAL OVERLAP SLOTTED CONTAINER (CSO)	
F	0206	CENTER SPECIAL FULL OVERLAP SLOTTED CONTAINER (SFF)	
G	0301	FULL TELESCOPE DESIGN STYLE BOX (FTD)	
H	0306	DESIGN STYLE BOX WITH COVER (CAP-LID) (SCD)	
I	0310	DOUBLE COVER BOX (DC) – ONE PIECE TUBE WITH TOP AND BOTTOM CAPS	

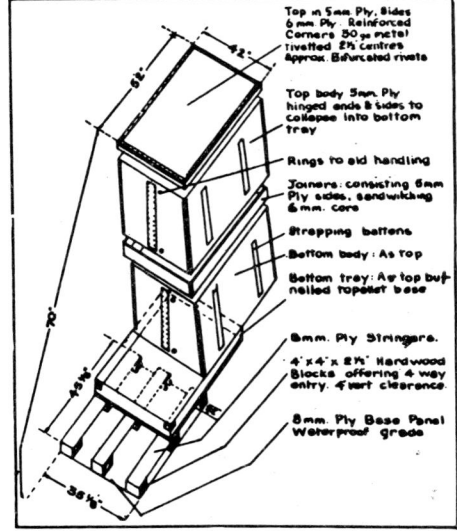

IATA Size 12 Sumacon container Plywood and metal construction, collapsible, multiple-use unit. COM (P)

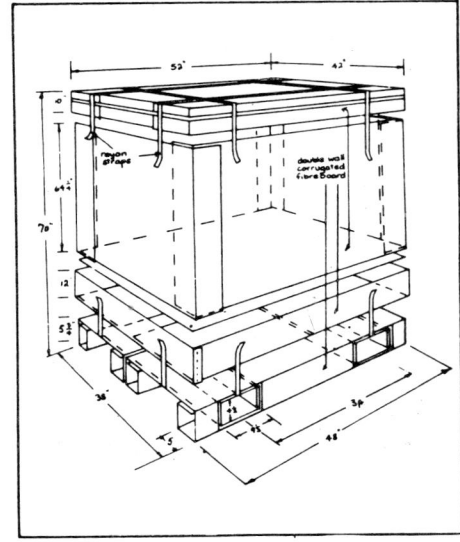

Ashton Containers Ltd., double-wall, fibreboard container. Seven-piece unit, collapsible, with cap lid or removable front panel. IATA Size 12. COM (−)

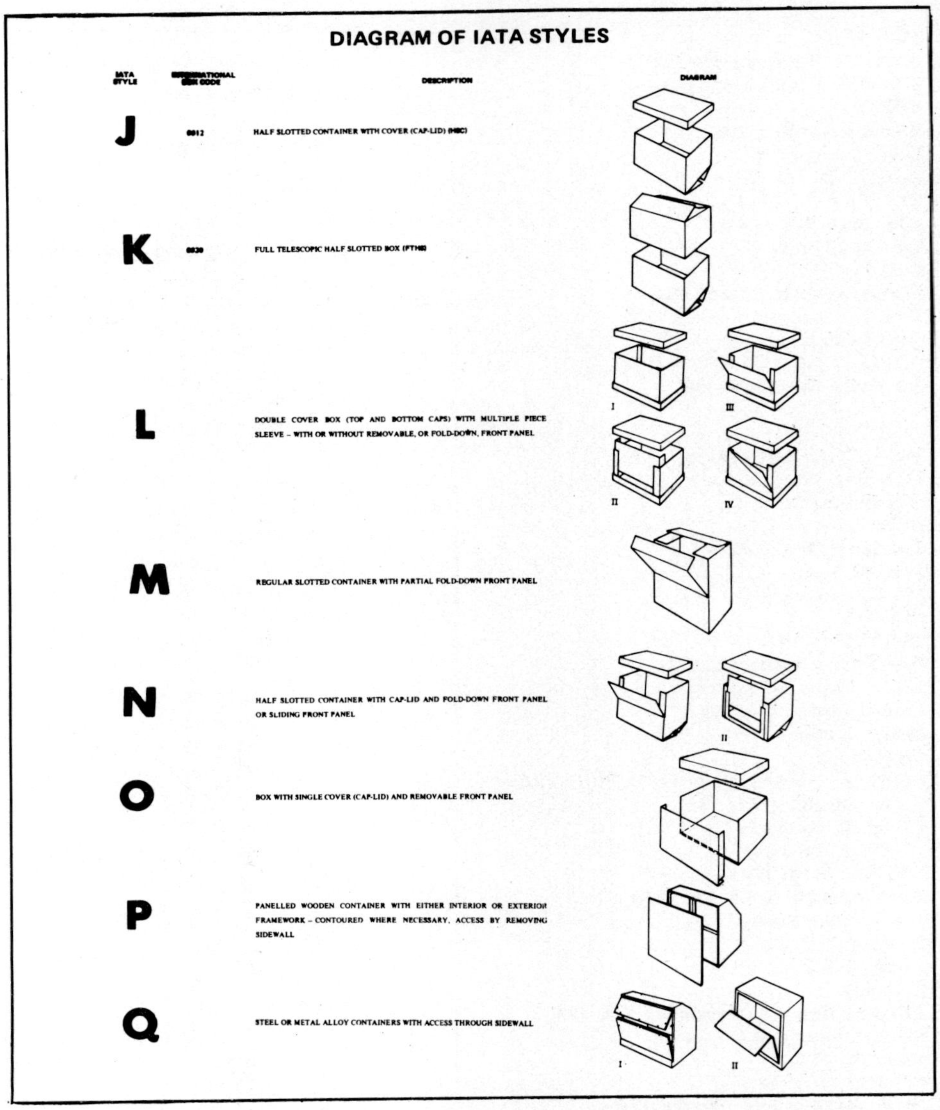

Thames Case Limited (1T)
Purfleet,
Essex, RM16 1RD
COR(A), COS(A)
Tillotsons Corrugated Cases Ltd (4T)
Burwell CB5,
Cambridge OAJ
COQ(J), COR(J), COS(A)
Tri-Wall Containers Ltd. (6T)
1 Mount Street,
London W1Y 5AA
COL(-), CON(A), COP(A), COQ(A),
COR(A), COS(A)

**United Kingdom distributors—with names of
manufacturers represented quoted in
parenthesis after each address.**
Martin Ferrey Ltd.,
Gordon Mill,
Arden Street, Halliswood,
Oldham, Lancashire.
(Hugh Stevenson & Co. Ltd.)
A. Latter & Co. Ltd.,
Orchard Works,
Toddington, near Cheltenham,
Glos.
(Reed Corrugated Cases Ltd.)
(Ashton Containers Ltd.)
A. Latter & Co. Ltd.,
43 South End,
Croydon. CR9. IAN.
(Reed Corrugated Cases Ltd.)
(Ashton Containers Ltd.)
T. G. Nuttall Ltd.,
Grange Works,
Beech Road, Chorlton-cum-Hardy,
Manchester 21.
(Reed Corrugated Cases Ltd.)
Peter Sayce Associates Ltd.,
Westminster Bank Chambers,
16 Kingsway,
Altrincham, Cheshire.
(Reed Corrugated Cases Ltd.
(Ashton Containers Ltd.)
Peter Sayce Associates Ltd.,
c/o J. Hickman & Son (Brierley Hill) Ltd.,
Saltwells Road, Cradley Heath,
Warley, Worcs.
(Reed Corrugated Cases Ltd.)
(Ashton Containers Ltd.)
Yorkshire Box Co. Ltd.,
Gloucester Street,
Leeds 10.
(Ashton Containers Ltd.)

UNITED STATES OF AMERICA
Ampex Corporation (5A)
Audio/Video Communications Div
401 Broadway,
Redwood City,
California 94063
COE(Q), COJ(Q)
Banner Metals Inc. (1C)
Containair Div.,
2959 E. Victoria Street,
Compton,
Calif. 90224
COE(-), COJ(-), COK(-), COM(-), COP(-),
COQ(-), COR(-)(J), COS(J)
Boise Cascade Corporation (2B)
P.O. Box 200,
Boise,
Idaho 83701
COQ(J), COR(J), COS(J)
J. I. Case Limited (2C)
701 State Street,
Racine,
Wisconsin 53404
COJ(L)
Chicago Mill and Lumber Company (3C)
P.O. Box 1400,
Greenville,
Mississippi, 38701
COE(P), COG (P), COJ(P), COL(P)
Helena, Arkansas
COE(P), COG(P), COJ(P), COL(P)
Tallulah, Louisiana

COE(P), COG(P), COJ(P), COL(P)
Cheraw, South Carolina
COE(P), COG(P), COJ(P), COL(P)
Cincinnati Industrial Packaging Corp. (6C)
5210 Wooster Road,
Cincinnati,
Ohio 45226
COG(L), COJ(L)
Connelly Containers Inc. (3D)
Bala Cynwyd
Pennsylvania 19004
COR(A), COS(A)
Containair of Michigan Inc. (1C)
Detroit,
Michigan 48239
COE(-), COJ(-), COK(-), COM(-), COP(-),
COQ(-), COR(J), COS(J)
Containair Systems Corp.
Containair Division,
145-80 228th Street,
Springfield Gardens,
New York 11413
COE(-), COJ(-), COK(-), COM(-), COP(-),
COQ(-), COR(J), COS(J)
Container Corporation of America (7C)
38 South Dearborn Street,
Chicago, Illinois 60602
COJ(L), COR(A), COS(A)
Anderson, Indianna 46011
COJ(L), COR(A), COS(A)
Fernandina Beach,
Florida 32034
COJ(A), COR(A), COS(A)
P.O. Box 60447, 8440 Tewantin Street,
Houston, Texas 77060
COJ(L), COR(A), COS(A)
P.O. Box 5067,
Fountain City,
Knoxville, Tennessee 37918

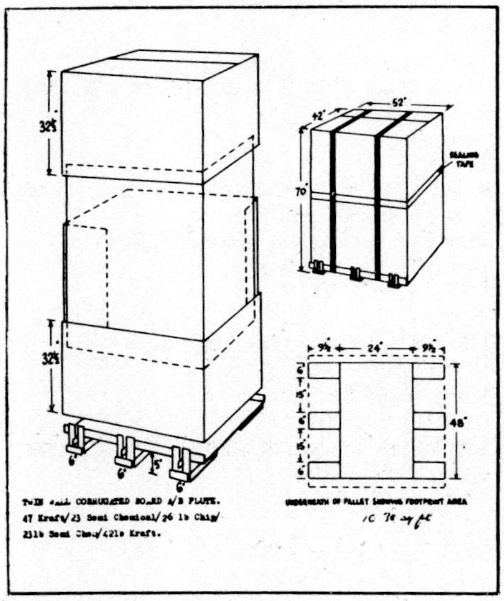

DIAGRAM OF IATA STYLES

Bowater Packaging Ltd., two-tier unit with
inner sleeve liner. Capacity 1,874 lb (850 kg).
COM (–)

COJ(L), COR(A), COS(A)
2601 South Malt Avenue,
Los Angeles, California 90022
COJ(L), COR(A), COS(A)
P.O. Box 858,
Muskogee, Oklahoma 74402
COJ(L), COR(A), COS(A)
Quentin Avenue and Wright Place
New Brunswick,
New Jersey 08901
COJ(L), COR(A), COS(A)

4549 Horton Street,
Oakland, California 94608
COJ(L), COR(A), COS(A)
12005 North Burgard Street,
Portland, Oregon 97203
COJ(L), COR(A), COS(A)
690 Mill Street,
Rock Island, Illinois 61201
COJ(L), COR(A), COS(A)
6 Goddard Avenue,
Chesterfield, Missouri 63017
COJ(L), COR(A), COS(A)
4624 E. Marginal Way South,
Seattle, Washington 98134
COJ(L), COR(A), COS(A)
P.O. Box 1441,
2617 West 7th Street,
Fort Worth, Texas 77060
COJ(L), COR(A), COS(A)

Control Data Corporation (sc)
8100 34th Avenue South,
Minneapolis,
Minn. 55440
COJ(L)

Eckol Corporation (1E)
Sand Road,
Doylestown, Pennsylvania
COE(P)

Eckol Container Systems Inc.
2636 W. Mt. Carmel Avenue
Glenside Pennsylvania
COE(P), COG(P), COJ(P), COK(-), COL(P),
COM(-), COP(-), COQ(-), COR(J), COS(J)

Gaylord Container Div. (6G)
Crown Zellerbach
One Bush Street,
San Francisco,
California
COJ(L)

General Box Company (1G)
1825 Miner Street,
Desplaines,
Ill. 60016
COE(L), COJ(L)

General Packaging Corporation (2G)
13400 Harry Hines Boulevard,
Dallas,
Texas 75234
COJ(A), CON(A), COP(A), COQ(A), COR(A),
COS(A)

Hutchinson Products Inc. (1C)
Container Div.
Hutchinson, Minnesota 55350
COE(-), COJ(-), COK(-), COM(-), COP(-),
COQ(-), COR(J), COS(J)

IBM Corporation
Office Products Div.,
New Circle Road,
Lexington 40507,
Kentucky
COP(K)

IBM World Trade Corp. (2I)
East Fishkill Facility, Route 52,
Hopewell June, New York 12533
CON(I), COP(I), COR(I), COS(I)

Inland Container Corp. (3I)
120 E. Market Street,
Indianapolis,
Indiana
COR(A), COS(A)(B)

International Paper Co. (5I)
220 East 42nd Street,
New York, N.Y. 10017
COJ(L)

Irvin Industries Inc. (6I)
15001 S. Figueroa St.,
Gardena,
California 90247
COJ(Q)

C. E. Kridle Inc. (3K)
131A South 1st Street,
Richmond,
California,
COJ(P)
1535 Grove Street,
Berkeley,
California
COJ(P)

Mizpah Container Co. (6M)
2026 Abalone Street,
Torrance,
California 90501
COG(P)

Modern Packaging Inc (8M)
600 Niles Avenue,
South Bend, Indiana 46622
COR(A), COS(A)

Modern Packaging of Peru Inc. (8M)
734 North Chili,
Peru, Indiana 46970
COR(A), COS(A)

North American Container Corp. (5N)
Container Div.,
P.O. Box 11914,
Atlanta, Georgia, 30305
COE(P), COJ(-), COK(-), COM(-), COP(-),
COQ(-), COR(J), COS(J)
3455 Welcome All Road,
Atlanta, Georgia 30331
COG(P)

Ockerlund Wood Products Inc.
Forest Park
Illinois 60130
COE(-), COJ(-), COK(-), COM(-), COP(-),
COQ(-), COR(J), COS(J)

Packaging Corporation of America (IP)
470 Market Avenue SW
Grand Rapids,
Michigan 49502
COS(A)

Dan Robb (3R)
1239 McKeoene
Cincinnati,
Ohio 45205
COE(P), COG(P), COJ(P)

St. Regis Paper Co. (3E)
P.O. Box 4449
Pittsburg,
Pa. 15205
COJ(L)

The 7 Brothers International Inc. (Santini Bros. Inc.) (1S)
57-48 49th Street,
Maspeth,
New York
COG(J), COH(J), COJ(J), COK(J), COL(J)
COM(J)

Time Container Corporation
5303 West 74th Place,
Chicago,
Ill. 60638
COS(A)

Tri-Wall Containers Inc. (6T)
One Dupont Street,
Plainview, L.I.,
New York 11803
COH(-), COJ(A), COK(-), COL(-), CON(A),
COP(A), COQ(A), COR(A), COS(A)
Wassaic, New York 12592
COH(-), COJ(A), COK(-), COL(-), CON(A),
COP(A), COQ(A), COR(A), COS(A)
Butler, Indiana 46721
COH(-), COJ(A), COK(-), COL(-), CON(A),
COP(A), COQ(A), COR(A), COS(A)
7447 N. Blackstone Ave.,
California 93650
COH(-), COJ(A), COK(-), COL(-), CON(A),
COP(A), COQ(A), COR(A), COS(A)

Union Camp Corporation (2U)
233 Broadway,
New York, N.Y. 10007
COJ(-), COR(A), COS(A)
P.O. Box 1608,
Lakeland,
Fla. 33802
COJ(-), CQR(A), COS(A)
P.O. Box 570,
Savannah,
Ga. 31402
COJ(-), COR(A), COS(A)
500 Pine Tree Street,
Forest Park,
Atlanta, Ga. 30050
COJ(-), COR(A), COS(A)
P.O. Box 645,
Morristown,

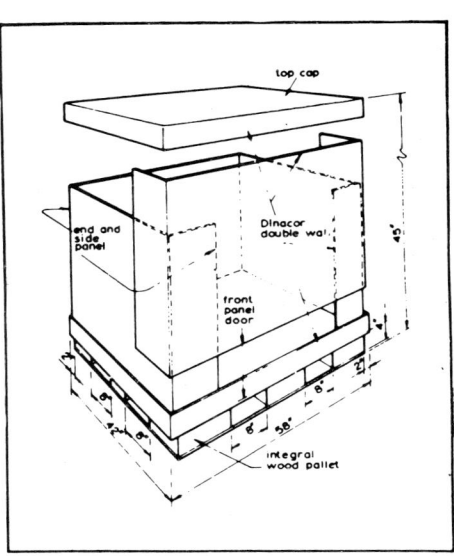

Produced by various manufacturers in USA, South America, Germany, Italy and Netherlands. Four-piece Dinacar double-wall fibreboard container to IATA Size 9, ATA type 'D'. COJ (L)

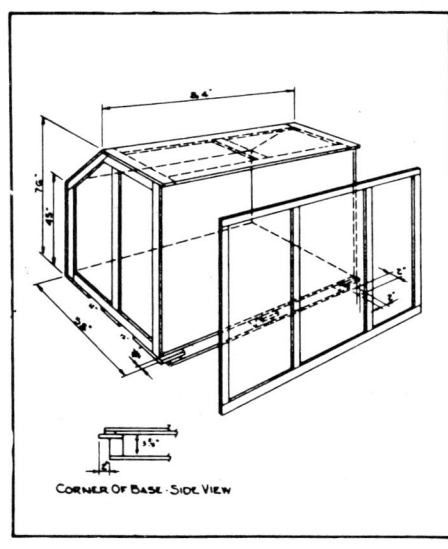

Contoured, wood-framed, plywood unit suitable for outside storage. IATA Size 5, ATA type 'B' and made by Eckol Corporation. COE (P)

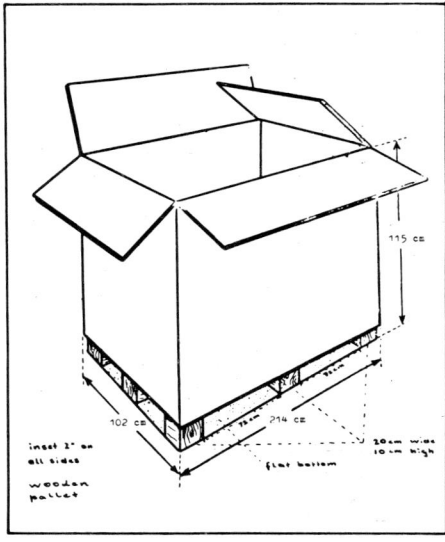

Triple-wall corrugated fibreboard and wood container, by Zellstofffabrik Waldhof, Zewa-Faltkistenwerk. COH (A)

Tenn. 37814
COJ(-), COR(A), COS(A)
P.O. Box 327,
Jamestown, N.C. 27282
COJ(-), COR(A), COS(A)
P.O. Box 5292,
Spartanburg,
S.C. 29301
COJ(-), COR(A), COS(A)
P.O. Box 2040,
Trenton, N.J. 08609
COJ(-), COR(A), COS(A)
P.O. Box 258,
Washington, Pa. 15301
COJ(-), COR(A), COS(A)
P.O. Box 1567,
Lancaster, Pa. 17601
COJ(-), COR(A), COS(A)
P.O. Box 41004
Sharonvill, Ohio 45241
COJ(-), COR(A), COS(A)
P.O. Box 1789,
Cleveland,
Ohio 44105
COJ(-), COR(A), COS(A)
P.O. Box 588,
Monroe,
Michigan 48161
COJ(-), COR(A), COS(A)
P.O. Box 2253,
Kalamazoo,
Michigan 49001

AIR CARGO PALLETS USED BY IATA MEMBER AIRLINES

All the pallets described below are registered with IATA and are in service with member airlines. They may be considered as the present standard cargo stacking bases, used either with nets or straps to restrain the loads or, increasingly, hood/igloo type covers to form contoured, enclosed containers. With certain exceptions for specific aircraft types, they conform to the standard 88 × 108 in (224 × 275 cm) and 88 × 125 in (224 × 318 cm) external dimensions, and have built-in provision for net attachments and aircraft floor anchorages.

Loading is carried out in the air cargo terminals and the pallets are ground transported by means of ball/roller floor equipped vehicles. All-freight and QC aircraft are similarly equipped, so that inter-continental large jets regularly operate to turn-round times of 45 minutes or less.

Pallets which have been used only in the main cabins of first generation long-haul jets are now also used in the lower-lobe spaces of Boeing 747s.

The following specifications are listed in IATA sizes.

IATA ID Code P1A
TRANS WORLD AIRLINES, INC.
General merchandise. Online use. Manufacturer: Brownline Corp., U.S.A. External length, width and height. including fittings: 88 × 125 × 0·63 in (224 × 318 × 1·5 cm). Internal length, width and height: 84 × 121 × 0·63 in (214 × 308 × 1·5 cm). Tare weight: 280 lb (127 kg). Max net perm. weight: 8,000 lb (3,629 kg). Plywood faced on both sides with lebanex. 3 in (5·7 cm) aluminium frame riveted to plywood. Plastic cover over load and tie-down nets secure load to pallet. Multiple use. Airworthiness Cert: FAA 707C.

IATA ID Code P1A
**AMERICAN AIRLINES
BRITISH OVERSEAS AIRWAYS
   CORPORATION
DEUTSCHE LUFTHANSA
QANTAS
SAUDI ARABIAN**

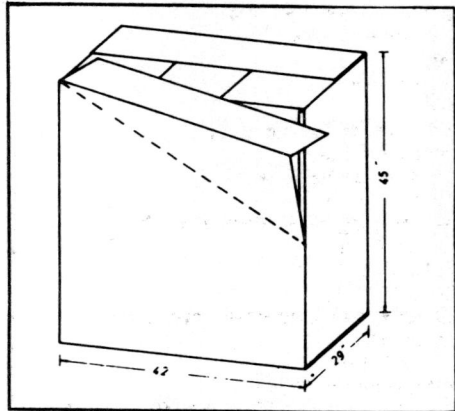

Double-wall fibreboard container, with top opening and fold-down front panel. IATA Size 16, 482 lb (219 kg) capacity. By Klingle Papierwerke KG and Pagusa Papeleras Guadalquivir. (DSC-256)

COJ(-), COR(A), COS(A)
100 E. Oakton Street,
Des Plaines,
Illinois 50018
COJ(-), COR(A), COS(A)

General merchandise. Online use. Manufacturer: Brownline Corp. USA. External length: width and height, including fittings: 88 × 125 × 0·63 in (224 × 318 × 1·5 cm). Tare weight: 253 lb (115 kg). 9G pallet of balsa core faced with Phenolic. Aluminium net attachments riveted to frame. Each corner is a stainless steel block. Plastic sheet placed over load and overthrow nets secure load to pallet. Multiple use. Max net perm weight: 10,000 lb (4,536 kg). Airworthiness Cert: FAA 707-320-C.

IATA Reg. No. P-29
BRITISH OVERSEAS AIRWAYS CORPORATION
Manufacturer: Trianco. Construction materials: polyurethane foam, aluminium. Size: 88 × 125 × 1·63 in (224 × 318 × 4·1 cm) Tare weight: 248 lb (112·5 kg) Weight limitations: 10,000 lb (4,536 kg). Airworthiness Cert: ARB 707C.

IATA ID Code P1A
QANTAS
Manufacturer: Tridair. Construction materials: aluminium, plywood and phenolic. Size: 88 × 125 × 0·70 in (224 × 318 × 1·7 cm). Tare weight: 249 lb (113 kg). Weight limitations: 13,300 lb (6,032 kg). Airworthiness Cert: FAA TC707-320C.

IATA ID Code P1A
AER LINGUS
Manufacturer: Tridair. Construction materials: aluminium and balsa. Size: 88 × 125 × 0·70 in (224 × 318 × 1·7 cm). Tare weight: 199 lb (90 kg). Weight limitations: 10,000 lb (4,536 kg). Airworthiness Cert: ARB C-316, B707, B727, B737.

IATA ID Code P1A
AER LINGUS
Manufacturer: Tridair. Construction materials: aluminium and balsa. Size 88 × 125 × 0·70 in (224 × 318 × 1·7 cm) or tied-down at 88 × 108 × 0·70 in (224 × 274 × 1·7 cm). Tare weight: 199 lb (90 kg). Weight limitations: 10,000 lb (4,536 kg) or 8,000 lb 3,629 kg). Airworthiness Cert: FAA B-737-348.

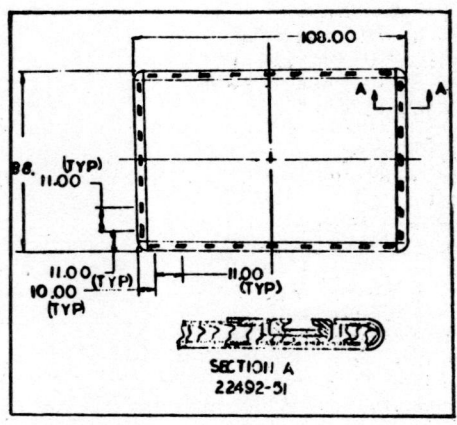

Three inch (7·5 cm) aluminium frame rivetted to plywood pallet, faced on both sides with lebanex. (P-3).

Villaume Industries Inc. (IV)
76 West Indiana,
St. Paul,
Minnesota 55107
COE(P)

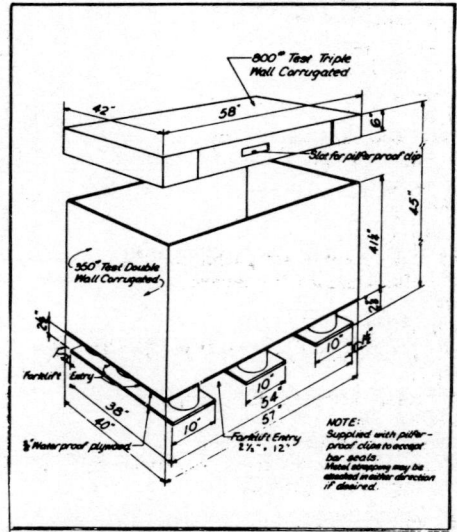

IATA Size 9, ATA type 'D', fibreboard/plywood container by Cargo Packers Inc. Cap lid 1,536 lb (696·5 kg) capacity. COJ(-)

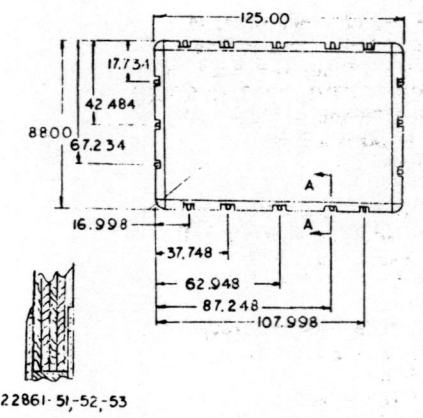

9G pallet of balsa core faced with Phenolic, with aluminium net attachments riveted to frame. Each corner is a stainless steel block (P1A).

IATA ID Code P1B
EASTERN AIR LINES INC
Manufacturer: Heath. Construction materials: aluminium and balsa. Size 88 × 125 × 0·80 in (224 × 318 × 2·00 cm). Tare weight: 225 lb (120 kg). Weight limitations: 10,000 lb (4,536 kg). Airworthiness Cert: FAA 727-25C, 727-51C, 707-351C.

IATA ID Code P1B
AIR FRANCE
EASTERN AIR LINES INC
PAN AMERICAN WORLD AIRWAYS
General merchandise. Online use. Manufacturer: Brownline Corp., U.S.A. External length, width and height, including fittings: 88 × 125 × 0·63 in (224 × 318 × 1·5 cm). Internal length, width and height: 84 × 121 × 0·63 in (214 × 308 × 1·5 cm). Tare weight: 225 lb (102 kg). Max net perm. weight: AF 10,000 lb (4,536 kg), PAA 8,000 lb (3,629 kg). Constructed of plywood faced on both sides with Lebanex. Aluminium framing of 3 in around outside of pallet, united to plywood and Lebanex sheets. Rubberized envelope covers load, tie-down nets secure load. Multiple use. Airworthiness Cert: FAA 707-320C.

IATA ID Code P1B
SCANDINAVIAN AIRLINES
BRANIFF INTERNATIONAL
Manufacturer: Brownline Inc, U.S.A. Construction materials: plywood, lebanite and aluminium. Size 88 × 125 × 0·7 in (224 × 318 × 1·7 cm). Tare weight: 265 lb (120 kg). Weight limitation: 12,500 lb (5,670 kg). Airworthiness Cert: FAA 707-320C, Scandinavian CAA DC-8F.

IATA ID Code P1B
NORTHWEST AIRLINES
EASTERN AIR LINES INC
Manufacturer: Brownline Corp. U.S.A. Construction materials: Plywood in an aluminium frame with IATA 85/60 tie-downs. Size 88 × 125 × 0·63 in (224 × 318 × 1·5 cm). Tare weight: 225 lb (102 kg). Weight limitation: 10,000 lb (4,536 kg). Airworthiness Cert: FAA 707-320C 727-151C.

IATA ID Code P1B
EASTERN AIR LINES INC
Manufacturer: Tridair. Construction materials: aluminium and balsa. Size 88 × 125 × 0·63 in (224 × 318 × 1·5 cm). Tare weight: 225 lb (102 kg). Weight limitations: 13,300 lb (6,032 kg). Airworthiness Cert: FAA B707C, 727.

IATA ID Code P1C
ALITALIA
DEUTSCHE LUFTHANSA
Manufacturer: Irvin. Construction materials: plywood, phenrock and aluminium. Size 88 × 125 × 0·78 in (224 × 318 × 1·9 cm). Tare weight: 240 lb (109 kg). Weight limitations: 10,000 lb (4,536 kg). Airworthiness Cert: RAI Italy.

IATA ID Code P1C
BRITISH OVERSEAS AIRWAYS CORPORATION
QANTAS
DEUTSCHE LUFTHANSA
SCANDINAVIAN AIRLINES SYSTEM
Manufacturer: Brownline-Tridair. Construction materials: balsa and aluminium. Size: 88 × 125 × 0·62 in (224 × 318 × 1·58 cm). Tare weight: 240 lb (109 kg). Weight limitations: DLH 10,000 lb (4,536 kg), SK 12,500 lb (5,660 kg) BA 13,300 lb (6,032 kg). Airworthiness Cert: FAA 707C, 727C. FAA and Scand. CAA DC-8F (50 & 60), DC-9F.

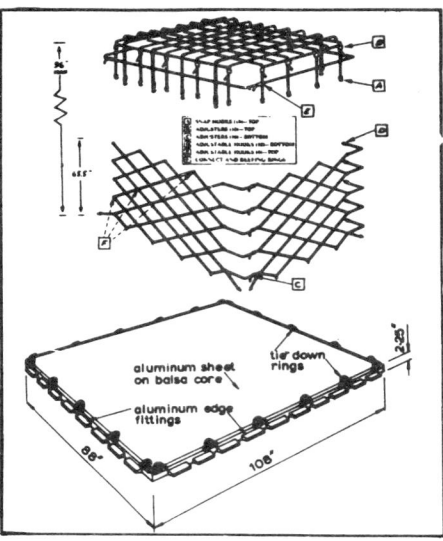

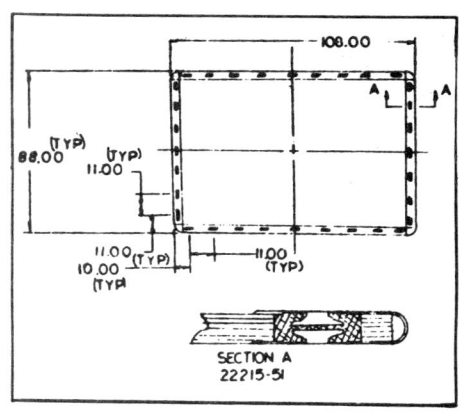

Layout of Tridair aluminium / balsa laminated, 88 × 108 × 2·25 in (224 × 274 × 5·7 cms) pallet used by BOAC, showing arrangement of 9G net assembly (P-2F)

IATA ID Code P1D
UNITED AIR LINES INC
Manufacturer: Brooks Perkins. Construction materials: aluminium and balsa. Size: 88 × 125 × 0·75 in (224 × 318 × 2·00 cm). Tare weight: 225 lb (102 kg). Weight limitations: 13,300 lb (6,033 kg). Airworthiness Cert: FAA 727-22C, DC-8F-54.

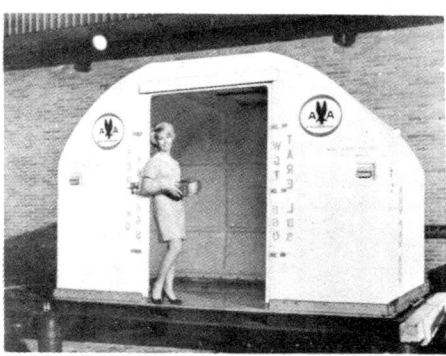

This pallet-mounted, fibreglass Igloo of American Airlines is waterproof and lockable. Company has Boeing 707-323C convertible and 707-323 freighter aircraft but does not interline its Igloos.

All the Quantas fleet of 707s are fitted with cargo doors and can be converted to mixed cargo-passenger aircraft if required

SAS has DC-9F freighters in service. Here a hooded pallet is about to be loaded and the train of towed dollies inched up to the

IATA ID Code P1D
UNITED AIR LINES INC
Manufacturer: Brooks Perkins. Construction materials: aluminium and balsa. Size: 88 × 125 × 0·75 in (224 × 318 × 2·00 cm). Tare weight: 225 lb (102 kg). Weight limitations: 13,300 lb (6,033 kg).

IATA ID Code P1D
AIR CANADA
Manufacturer: Brooks Perkins. Construction materials: aluminium and balsa. Size: 88 × 125 × 0·70 in (224 × 318 × 1·7 cm). Tare weight: 225 lb (102 kg). Weight limitations: 10,000 lb (4,536 kg). Airworthiness Cert: FAA DC-8F-54, (29/1/70).

IATA ID Code P1D
AIR CANADA
Manufacturer: Heath. Construction materials: aluminium, plywood and phenrock. Size: 88 × 125 × 0·70 in (224 × 318 × 1·7 cm). Tare weight: 225 lb (102 kg). Weight limitations: 9,000 lb (4,083 kg). Airworthiness Cert: DC-8F-54 & 55.

IATA ID Code P1D
AIR CANADA
UNITED AIR LINES INC
Manufacturer: Heath. Construction materials: aluminium and balsa. Size: 88 × 125 × 0·70 in (224 × 318 × 1·7 cm). Weight limitations: AC 10,000 lb (4,536 kg), UA 12,500 lb (5,670 kg). Airworthiness Cert: FAA DC-8F-54 & 55.

IATA ID Code P1D
UNITED AIRLINES INC
Manufacturer: Irvin. Construction materials: aluminium and balsa. Size: 88 × 125 × 0·75 in (224 × 318 × 2·00 cm). Tare weight 225 lb (102 kg). Weight limitations: 13,300 lb (6,033 kg).

IATA ID Code P1D
VIASA
Manufacturer: Marino. Construction materisla: aluminium and balsa. Size: 88 × 125 × 1·8 in (224 × 318 × 0·73 cm). Tare weight: 275 lb (125 kg). Weight limitations: 12,500 lb (5,670 kg). Airworthiness Cert: FAA DC-8F-55 & 63. B707-345C.

IATA ID Code P1D
KLM ROYAL DUTCH AIRLINES
SCANDINAVIAN AIRLINES SYSTEM
SEABOARD WORLD AIRLINES
General merchandise. Online use. Manufacturer: Brownline Corp., U.S.A. External length, width and height, including fittings: 88 × 125 × 0·7 in (224 × 318 × 1·7 cm). Internal length, width and height: 82 × 119 × 0·7 in (208 × 302 × 1·7 cm). Tare weight: 225 lb (102· kg). Max net perm. weight: 12,500 lb (5,670 kg). Constructed of plywood and faced on both sides with $\frac{3}{32}$ in (·23 cm) paper phenolic laminate, aluminium framing of 3 in (7·5 cm) around outside of pallet and united to plywood and facing sheets. Plywood sides can be placed around pallet inside aluminium framing. Loaded pallet covered with tie-down net, secured to anchor plates set in perimeter of pallet. Multiple use. Airworthiness Cert: FAA DC8.

IATA ID Code P1D
VIASA
UNITED AIR LINES INC
Manufacturer: Brownline. Construction materials: aluminium and balsa. Size: 88 × 125 × 0·70 in (224 × 318 × 1·7 cm). Tare weight: VA 230 lb (104 kg), UA 225 lb

A self-powered belt conveyor helps unload Peruvian produce from the belly-hold of an Aerolineas Peruanas (APSA) aircraft

Six US Mail boxes fit snugly into a 747 under-floor container owned by TWA.

Seven Finnair igloos and one of the Finnish national airline's Boeing 707-320Cs

(102 kg). Weight limitations: 12,500 lb (5,670 kg). Airworthiness Cert: FAA STC DC-8-50 & 60F, 727-22C.

IATA ID Code P1D
UNITED AIR LINES, INC.
General merchandise. Online and interline. Manufacturer: Brownline Corp., U.S.A. External length, width and height, including fittings: 88 × 125 × 0·63 in (224 × 318 × 1·5 cm). Internal length, width and height: 84 × 121 × 0·63 in (214 × 308 × 1·5 cm). Tare weight: 225 lb (102 kg). Max net perm. weight: 12,400 lb (5,625 kg). Plywood core

with lebanite facing in 4 in aluminium frame. Tie-down nets secure load to pallet and tie-down attachments pallet to aircraft floor. Multiple use. Airworthiness Cert: FAA DC-8.

IATA ID Code P1D
UNITED AIR LINES INC
Manufacturer: Tridair. Construction materials: aluminium and balsa. Size: 88 × 125 × 0·75 in (224 × 318 × 2·00 cm). Tare weight: 225 lb (102 kg). Weight limitations: 13,300 lb (6,033 kg). Airworthiness Cert: FAA DC-8F-54, 55, 63, B727-22C.

IATA ID Code P1F
SEABOARD WORLD AIRLINES INC
General merchandise. Online use. Manufacturer: Brownline Corp., U.S.A. External length, width and height, including fittings. 88 × 125 × 0·70 in (224 × 318 × 1·7 cm); Internal length, width and height: 82 × 119 × 0·63 in (208 × 302 × 1·5 cm). Tare weight 235 lb (106·5 kg). Max net perm 707-320C, DC-8-55F, DC-8-63F.

IATA ID Code P1F
JAPAN AIR LINES
FLYING TIGER LINE INC
Manufacturer: Brownline Inc, U.S.A. Construction materials: balsa, and aluminium. Size: 88 × 125 × 0·08 in (224 × 318 × 2 cm). Tare weight: 274 lb (124·5 kg) FT 220 lb (100 kg). Weight limitations: 12,500 lb (5,670 kg). Airworthiness Cert: DC-8-63F.

IATA ID Code P1F
FLYING TIGER LINE INC
JAPAN AIR LINES
Manufacturer: Brownline. Construction materials: aluminium and balsa. Size: 88 × 125 × 0·7 in (224 × 318 × 1·7 cm). Tare weight: FT 220 lb (100 kg) JL 230 lb (104 kg). Weight limitations: 12,500 lb (5,670 kg). Airworthiness Cert: FAA DC-8-63F, DC-8-55F & 62F.

IATA ID Code P1G
DEUTSCHE LUFTHANSA
SCANDINAVIAN AIRLINES SYSTEM
KLM ROYAL DUTCH AIRLINES
Manufacturer: Bruggemann & Brand. Construction materials: balsa and aluminium; 3g continuous seat track. Size 88 × 125 × 0·74 in (224 × 318 × 1·88 cm). Tare weight: LH 209 lb (95 kg), KL 231 lb (105 kg). Weight limitations: 10,000 lb (4,535 kg), 13,300 lb (6,033 kg). Airworthiness Cert: LBA Germany 707C, 727C, 737C, 747, 747B, DC-8F.

IATA ID Code P1G
SABENA
Manufacturer: Sabena. Construction materials: multiplex wood, beech backelised aluminium, 3g continuous seat track. Size: 88 × 125 × 0·80 in (224 × 318 × 2 cm). Tare weight: 240 lb (109 kg). Weight limitations: 13,300 lb (6,033 kg). Airworthiness Cert: Belgium AA 707-329C, 727-QC, 747.

IATA ID Code P1G
SABENA
Manufacturer: Sabena. Construction materials: multiplex wood, beech backelised aluminium. Size 88 × 125 × 0·80 in (224 × 318 × 2·00 cm) variable to 88 × 108 × 0·80 in (224 × 274 × 2·00 cm). Tare weight: 264 lb (120 kg). Weight limitations: 13,300 lb (6,033 kg) and 10,000 lb (4,530 kg). Airworthiness Cert: Belgium AA B707, B727QC, B747.

IATA ID Code P1G
SABENA
Manufacturer: Sabena. Construction materials: multiplex wood, beech backelised aluminium. Size: 88 × 125 × 0·80 in (224 × 318 × 2·00 cm) variable to 88 × 108 × 0·80 in (224 × 274 × 2·00 cm). Tare weight: 258 lb (117 kg). Weight limitations: 10,000 lb (4,536 kg). Airworthiness Cert: Belgium AA B707, B727QC.

Heavy valves of this type, being nudged into a Martinair, DC-9, are concentrated loads that require the weight to be well spread even on a cargo floor

Cargo reservations departments are increasingly assisted by computers and other rapid response electronic equipment. In this Swissair Zurich office staff uses closed circuit TV, electronic adding machines, Telex systems and pneumatic tubes for fast transfer of documents among other aids.

IATA ID Code P1G
FLYING TIGER LINE INC
Manufacturer: Tridair. Construction materials: balsa and aluminium; 3g continuous seat track. Size 88 × 125 × 0·64 in (224 × 318 × 1·6 cm). Tare weight 220 lb (100 kg). Weight limitations: 12,500 lb (5,670 kg). Airworthiness Cert: FAA DC8-63F.

IATA ID Code P1G
AIR CANADA
Manufacturer: Tridair. Construction materials: aluminium and balsa; 3g continuous seat track. Size: 88 × 125 × 0·64 in (224 × 318 × 1·6 cm). Tare weight: 225 lb

Two large pieces of machinery wait on roller conveyors to be collected for one of Iberia's DC-8 convertible aircraft.

The interior of a BEA Merchantman converted by Aviation Traders (Engineering) from one of the airline's fleet of passenger Vanguards. In the foreground is an HSA/light alloy cargo pallet. Eventually BEA will have nine Merchantmen.

(102 kg). Weight limitations: 10,000 lb (4,356 kg). Airworthiness Cert: FAA DC-8F-54.

IATA ID Code P1G
BRITISH OVERSEAS AIRWAYS CORPORATION

Manufacturer: Tridair. Construction materials: aluminium and balsa; 3g continuous seat track. Size: 88 × 125 × 0·80 in (224 × 318 × 2·00 cm). Tare weight: 230 lb (104·5 kg). Weight limitations: 13,300 lb (6,033 kg). Airworthiness Cert: FAA 707C, 727C.

IATA ID Code P1K
FLYING TIGER LINE INC

Manufacturer: Brownline. Construction materials: aluminium and balsa. Size: 88 × 125 × 0·63 in (224 × 318 × 1·7 cm) (segmented). Tare weight: 260 lb (118 kg). Weight limitations: 12,500 lb (5,670 kg). Airworthiness Cert: FAA DC-8-63F.

IATA ID Code P2A
SABENA

Manufacturer: Sabena. Construction materials: multiplex beech, backelised aluminium. Size: 88 × 108 × 0·63 in (224 × 274 × 1·5 cm). Tare weight: 183 lb (83 kg). Weight limitations: 8,208 lb (3,723 kg). Airworthiness Cert: Belgium AA 707, 727QC.

IATA ID Code P2A
AIR INDIA

General merchandise. Manufacturer: Tridair. External length, width and height: 88 × 108 × 0·63 in (224 × 274 × 1·5 cm). Constructed of plywood and phenrock with IATA 04/03 tie downs. Tare weight: 165 lb (75 kg). Max. net perm. weight 8,000 lb (3,629 kg). Airworthiness Cert: FAA 707-320C.

IATA ID Code P2A
BRANIFF INTERNATIONAL
SABENA
AER LINGUS
AEROLINEAS ARGENTINAS
ETHIOPIAN
BRITISH OVERSEAS AIRWAYS CORPORATION
ICELANDAIR
QANTAS
VARIG
CHINA

General merchandise. Outline and interline use. Manufacturer: Tridair. External length, width and height, including fittings: 88 × 108 × 0·63 in (224 × 274 × 1·5 cm). Internal length width and height: 86 × 106 × 0·63 in (219 × 269 × 1·5 cm). Tare weight: 200 lb (91 kg). Max net perm. weight: 8,000 to 10,000 lb (3,629 to 4,536 kg) depending on airline. Plywood faced with phenolic in aluminium frame with steel corners. 9G pallet. Polythene sheet placed over load and nets secure load to pallet. Multiple use. Airworthiness Cert: FAA 707-320C.

IATA ID Code P2A
NORTHWEST AIRLINES
AIR INDIA

Manufacturer: Tridair. Construction materials: balsa, aluminium. Size: 88 × 108 × 0·75 in (224 × 274 × 1·9 cm). Tare weight: 200 lb (91 kg). Weight limitation: 10,000 lb (4,536 kg). Airworthiness Cert: FAA 707-320C.

IATA ID Code P2A
IRAN NATIONAL AIRLINES CORPORATION
CHINA AIR LINE

Manufacturer: Tridair. Construction materials: aluminium and balsa. Size: 88 × 108 × 0·78 in (224 × 274 × 2·00 cm). Tare

Both DC-8 and DC-9 freighters are used by Alitalia to sustain its world network of all-cargo routes

Bulk freight offered-up to the door of an Indian Airlines HS748 for a compartment in the rear of the aircraft

weight: 190 lb (86 kg). Weight limitations: 8,000 lb (3,629 kg). Airworthiness Cert: FAA STC B707-320C, 727C.

IATA ID Code P2B
AIR FRANCE

General merchandise. Online use. Manufacturer: Tridair. External length, width and height, including fittings: 88 × 108 × 0·63 in (224 × 274 × 1·5 cm). Internal length, width and height: 80 × 100 × 0·63 in (204 × 254 × 1·5 cm). Tare weight: 177 lb (80 kg). Max net perm. weight: 7,716 lb (3,500 kg). Plywood faced with lebanex in aluminium frame with 3G and 9G tie-down attachments. Rubberized envelope covers load. Restraint nets secure the load. 3G/9G tie-downs attach pallet to aircraft floor. Airworthiness Certs. FAA 707-320C. Multiple use.

IATA ID Code P2C
AIR INDIA

Manufacturer: Bruggemann & Brand. Construction materials: aluminium and balsa. Size: 88 × 108 × 0·63 in (224 × 274 × 1·7 cm). Tare weight: 199 lb (90 kg). Weight limitations: 10,000 lb (4,536 kg). Airworthiness Cert: FAA B-707.

IATA ID Code P2F
BRITISH OVERSEAS AIRWAYS CORPORATION

General merchandise. Online use. Manufacturers: Tridair. External length, width and height, including fittings: 88 × 108 × 2·25 in (224 × 274 × 5·7 cm). Internal length, width and height: 84 × 014 × 2·25 in (214 × 264 × 5·7 cm). Tare weight: 309 lb (140 kg). Max net perm. weight: 10,000 lb (4,536 kg). Balsa core in aluminium sheet top and bottom with aluminium fittings. 22 rings around periphery for tie-downs. Tie-down rings for strain of 7,500 lb/3,400 kg. 9G net assembly restrains load. Multiple use. Airworthiness Cert: 707C.

IATA ID Code P2G
FINNAIR
BRANIFF INTERNATIONAL
PAN AMERICAN
TRANS-MEDITERRANEAN AIRWAYS

General merchandise. Online and interline use. Manufacturer: Tridair. External length, width and height including fittings: 88 × 108 × 0·63 in (224 × 274 × 1·5 cm). Tare weight: 210 lb (95·5 kg). Plywood core with lebanex facings on both sides. 3 in (7·5 cm) aluminium frame riveted to plywood. A net and overthrow strap is provided to tie down the load. Multiple use. Weight limitation 7,000 lb (3,175 kg). Airworthiness Cert: FAA 707-320C, DC-8-62F.

IATA ID Code P2G
SEABOARD WORLD AIRLINES

General merchandise. Online use. Manufacturer: Tridair. External length, width and height, including fittings: 88 × 108 × 0·63 in (224 × 274 × 1·5 cm). Internal length, width and height: 85 × 105 × 0·63 in (216 × 266 × 1·5 cm). Tare weight 185 lb (84 kg). Max net perm. weight: 8,000 lb (3,629 kg). Constructed of plywood and faced on both sides with $\frac{3}{32}$ in (·23 cm) paper phenolic laminate, aluminium framing of 3 in (7·5 cm) around outside of pallet and united to plywood and facing sheets. Plywood sides can be placed around pallet inside aluminium framing. Loaded pallet covered with tie-down net secured to anchor plates set in perimeter of pallet. Multiple use. Airworthiness Cert: FAA DC-8.

Pallets on roller topped loading dollies are moved up in a train to one of the Qantas fleet of Boeing 707-338Cs. These aircraft serve the Australia/Europe route via SE Asia and also cross the Pacific to the US.

Northwest Igloo

IATA ID Code P2G
AIR CANADA
ALITALIA
JAPAN AIR LINES
KLM ROYAL DUTCH AIRLINES
SCANDINAVIAN AIRLINES SYSTEM
SWISSAIR

General merchandise. Online use by AC, AZ, KLM, SAS, SR. Online and interline use by JAL. Manufacturer: Tridair. External length, width and height, including fittings: 88 × 108 × 0·63 in (224 × 274 × 1·5 cm). Tare weight: 180 lb (88 kg). Plywood faced on both sides with lebanex in 7·5 cm (3 in) aluminium frame. Cargo tie-down facilities IATA type code 90/70. Bearing load limits 970 kg sq in (200 lb sq ft); weight limits 8,000 lb (3,629 kg). Airworthiness Cert: FAA DC-8.

IATA ID Code P2G
AIR CANADA

Manufacturer: Brooks Perkins. Construction materials: aluminium and balsa. Size: 88 × 108 × 0·63 in (224 × 274 × 1·5 cm). Tare weight: 185 lb (84 kg). Weight limitations: 8,000 lb (3,629 kg). Airworthiness Cert: FAA DC-8-54F.

IATA ID Code P2J
SCANDINAVIAN AIRLINES SYSTEM
KLM ROYAL DUTCH AIRLINES
DEUTSCHE LUFTHANSA

Manufacturer: Bruggemann. Construction materials: aluminium and balsa; 3g continuous seat track. Size: 88 × 108 × 0·74 in (224 × 274 × 1·9 cm). Tare weight: 199 lb (90 kg). Weight limitations: 10,000 lb (4,536 kg). Airworthiness Cert: FAA DC-8F/DC-9RC at 8,000 lb (3,629 kg) and LBA Germany 707C.

IATA ID Code P2J
AIR CANADA

Manufacturer: Tridair. Construction materials: aluminium and balsa; 3g continuous seat track. Size: 88 × 108 × 0·64 in (224 × 274 × 1·6 cm). Tare weight: 185 lb (84 kg). Weight limitations: 8,000 lb (3,629 kg). Airworthiness Cert: FAA DC-8F-54.

IATA ID Code P2J
SCANDINAVIAN AIRLINES SYSTEM
SWISSAIR

Manufacturer: Tridair. Construction materials: balsa and aluminium; 3g continuous seat track. Size 88 × 108 × 0·63 in (224 × 274 × 1·5 cm). Tare weight: 216 lb (98 kg). Weight limitations: 8,000 lb (3,629 kg). Airworthiness Cert: FAA and Scand. CAA DC-8F (50 & 60), DC-9F.

IATA ID Code P2J
DEUTSCHE LUFTHANSA

Manufacturer: VFW GmbH, Germany. Construction materials: balsa and aluminium; 3g continuous seat track. Size: 88 × 108 × 0·68 in (224 × 274 × 1·73 cm). Tare weight: 196 lb (89 kg). Weight limitations: 10,000 lb (4,536 kg). Airworthiness Cert: LBA Germany 707C, 727C, 737C, 747, 747B, 747F.

IATA OD Code P2M
BRITISH EUROPEAN AIRWAYS

Manufacturer: Hawker Siddeley. Construction materials: light metal alloys. Size: 88 × 108 × 2·00 in (224 × 274 × 5·00 cm). Tare weight: 264 lb (120 kg). Weight limitations: 8,000 lb (3,629 kg). Airworthiness Cert: ARB Argosy 200.

IATA ID Code P2N
DEUTSCHE LUFTHANSA, AG

Tubular steel rack for hanging garments. Collapsible, screw-on fittings, adjustable height. Multiple, online use. Rented. External length, width and height, including fittings: 41·5 × 22 × 52 in (105 × 55 × 132 cm). Tare weight: 33 lb (15 kg). Max net perm. weight 265 lb (120 kg).

IATA ID Code P3T
AER LINGUS

Manufacturer: Tridair. Construction materials: aluminium and balsa. Size: 80 × 108 × 0·63 in (203 × 274 × 1·7 cm). Tare weight: 174 lb (79 kg). Weight limitations: 8,000 lb (3,629 kg). Airworthiness Cert: ARB B737.

IATA ID Code P4L
EAST AFRICAN AIRWAYS

Manufacturer: British Aircraft Corporation. Construction materials: balsa, plywood and steel with IATA 4/3 rings. Size 60 × 53 × 1·25 in (153 × 135 × 4 cm). Tare weight: 146 lb (66 kg). Weight limitation: 1,455 lb (660 kg). Airworthiness Cert: ARB Super VC-10.

IATA ID Code P4Q
FLYING TIGER LINE INC
Manufacturer: Brooks & Perkins. Construction materials: aluminium and balsa. Size: 61·5 × 177 × 2·25 in (156 × 450 × 6·00 cm). Tare weight: 360 lb (163 kg). Weight limitations: 7,000 lb (3,180 kg). Airworthiness Cert: FAA DC-8-6F3.

IATA ID Code P5B
SEABOARD WORLD AIRLINES INC
Manufacturer: Tridair. Construction materials: aluminium and balsa. Size 88 × 61·5 × 0·63 in (224 × 156 × 1·7 cm). Tare

UNIT LOAD DEVICES OWNED BY IATA MEMBER AIRLINES

The containers and pallets listed in this section are those currently in airline service and registered with IATA. Including the hood/igloo containers used by many major operators for their all-freight and mixed traffic services, the list contains many specialised units, e.g. insulated boxes and bags, hanging garment racks, high security and chemical containers. Their availability somewhat reflects the areas of operations, and some revenue sources of the individual airlines but, in general, operators are able to handle any load which they are allowed to carry and which will fit into the aircraft.

The following cross-reference table indicates the IATA reference numbers of the containers, "C" numbers and Igloos "U" numbers, owned by individual operators. The main specifications are in IATA number order—as some units are owned by more than one airline—and these are followed by an international list of container manufacturers.

IATA ID Code COD LH
DEUTSCHE LUFTHANSA (LH)
Moulded contoured fibreglass-polyester; double floor, 4-way forklift entry. Schulz 267150. External dimensions: 84 × 58 × 74/39 in (214 × 148 × 188/89 cm). Internal vol. 156·8 ft³ (4,431 m³). Tare weight: 291 lb (132 kg). Max net perm weight: 3,530 lb (1,601 kg).

IATA ID Code COE
SEABOARD WORLD AIRLINES INC (SB)
DEUTSCHE LUFTHANSA (LH)
Materials: Triplewall corrugated fibreboard and plywood. External dimensions: 84 × 58 × 76/45 in (214 × 148 × 193/115 cm). External vol. 197·7 cu ft (5,645 m³). Tare weight: 297 lb (135 kg). Max net perm. weight 5,000 lb (2,268 kg).

IATA ID Code COE PA
PAN AMERICAN WORLD AIRWAYS INC (PA)
Corrugated aluminium, base aluminium and balsa sandwich panels in high strength aluminium extrusions, four hand holds on doors. Brooks & Perkins 17228-100. External dimensions: 84 × 58 × 76/45 in (214 × 148 × 193/115 cm). Internal vol.: 166·0 ft³ (4·7 m³). Tare weight: 338 lb (153·5 kg). Max perm net weight: 3,500 lb (1,587·6 kg)

IATA ID Code CXC LH
DEUTSCHE LUFTHANSA (LH)
Materials: Fibreglass. Schultz 1030201. External dimensions: 82·5 × 59 × 80·5/44·2 in (210 × 149 × 205/112 cm). External vol. 180·77 cu ft (5·12 m³). Tare weight: 293·2 lb (133 kg). Max net perm. weight: 3,528 lb (1,600 kg).

weight: 190 lb (86 kg). Weight limitations: 5,520 lb (2,380 kg). Airworthiness Cert: FAA DC-8-63F.

IATA ID Code P5F
SWISSAIR
SCANDINAVIAN AIRLINES SYSTEM
Manufacturer: Brownline Inc, U.S.A. Construction materials: balsa, aluminium, 3g continuous seat track. Size 88 × 53 × 0·63 in (224 × 135 × 1·5 cm). Tare weight: 115 lb (53 kg). Weight limitations: 2,500 lb (1,134 kg). Airworthiness Cert: FAA and Scand. CAA DC-8F (50 & 60), DC-9F.

OPERATOR	IATA REG UNIT LOAD DEVICE
Aer Lingus Teoranta (EI)	P1A, P2A, P3A, UJT
Air Canada (AC)	P1D, P1G, P2G, P2J, UAD, UDC, AVM
Air France (AF)	P1B, P2B, UAB, CXE, CXK, CXN, CXV
Air India (AI)	P2A, P2C, UDF, CXR, CXS
Alitalia (AZ)	P1C, P2C, AVM
Aerolineas Argentinas (AR)	P2A
British European Airways (BE)	P2M
British Overseas Airways (BA)	P1A, P1C, P1G, P2A, P2F, UAB, AVK CXV
Braniff International Airways (BN)	P1B, P1F, P2A, P2G, UAC, UDA
China Air lines (CI)	P2A
Eastern Air Lines (EA)	P1B, UAC, UAE
East African Airways (EC)	P4L
Ethiopian Airlines (ET)	P2A, UAJ, UDG, UDH
Finnair (AY)	P2G, UCD
Flying Tiger Line (FT)	P1F, P1G, P1K, P4Q, UAA
Iranair (IR)	P2A
Japan Air Lines (JL)	P1F, P2G, UAA, U, UDB, AVL, AVM
KLM (KL)	P1D, P1G, P2G, P2J, UAK, UAL, UDD CXM, RXT
National Airlines (NA)	AVE
Northwest Airlines (NW)	P1B, P2A, UAG, AVE
Deutsche Lufthansa (LH)	P1C, P1G, P2J, P2N, UA3, UAK, UAL, AVH AVM, COD, COE, CXC, CXE, CXM, CXS, CXV, CXW
Icelandic Airlines	P2A
Pakistan International Airline (PK)	
Pan American World Airways (PA)	P1B, P1F, P2G, UAB, UAD, UAF, AVF, AVG, COE, CXR
Qantas (QF)	P1A, P1C, P2A
Sabena (SN)	P1G, P2A, U, UDH, AVM, BMA, RXT
Saudi Arabian Airlines (SV)	P1A
Scandinavian Airlines System (SK)	P1B, P1C, P1D, P1G, P2G, P2J, P5F, P5K, UD7, UPP, CXK
Seaboard World Airlines (SB)	P1D, P1F, P2G, P5B, UA1, UAA, UPE, COE, CXC, CXE, CXG, CXJ, CXV
Swissair (SR)	P2G, P2J, P5F, UDC
Trans Mediterranean Airways (TL)	P2G
Trans World Airlines (TW)	P1A, UAB, UAH, AVE, CXC, CXE
United Air Lines (UA)	P1D, UAA, UAC, UAE, AVE, SAA, RAH
VIASA (VA)	P1D
VARIG (RG)	P2A

IATA ID Code CXC LH
DEUTSCHE LUFTHANSA (LH)
Material: Fibreglass. Schultz 2011. External dimensions: 82·5 × 60 × 80·5 in (210 × 152 × 205 cm). External vol: 180·77 cu ft (5·12 m³). Tare weight: 293·2 lb (133 kg). Max net perm. weight: 3,528 lb (1,600 kg).

IATA ID Code CXC LH
DEUTSCHE LUFTHANSA (LH)
Materials: Fibreglass. Schultz 2012. External dimensions: 82·5 × 60 × 80·5 in (210 × 152 × 205 cm). External vol: 180·77 cu ft (5·12 m³). Tare weight: 369·6 lb (168 kg). Max net perm. weight 3,528 lb (1,600 kg).

IATA ID Code CXC TW
TRANS WORLD AIRWAYS, INC (TW)
Contoured, rectangular container. Bonded corrugated sandwich panel sections, extruded framing, side opening removable doors. Inside tie-down of seat track sections spaced around container, 32 in (81 cm) above floor.

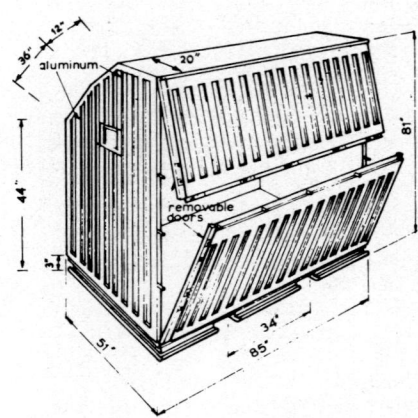

Contoured container by Fruehauf Corp. for PanAm and TWA. Bonded, corrugated alloy panels with side-opening doors. 3,912 lb (1774·5 kg) capacity. (CXC TW)

Forklift. External length, width and height: online by TWA, online and interline by PAA.

Rented. External length, width and height: 85 × 51 × 81 in (216 × 130 × 206 cm). Internal length, width and height: 83 × 49 × 78 in (211 × 125 × 198 cm). External cube: 178·95 cu ft (5·068 m³). Internal cube: 161 cu ft (4·508 m³). Tare weight: 348 lb (158 kg). Max net perm. weight: 3,912 lb (1,774·5 kg). Foot print: 28·2 sq ft (151 lb sq ft).

IATA ID Code CXC
SEABOARD WORLD AIRLINES (SB)
TRANS WORLD AIRLINES, INC (TW)

Contoured, rectangular container. Bonded corrugated sandwich panel sections, extruded framing, side opening removable doors. Inside tie-down of seat track sections spaced around container, 32 in (81 cm) above floor. Forklift base openings. External length, width and height: 85 × 51 × 74 in (216 × 130 × 188 cm). Internal length, width and height: 83 × 49 × 71 in. (211 × 125 × 180 cm). Tare weight: 323 lb (147 kg). Max net perm. weight: 3,680 lb (1,669·6 kg). Foot print: 28·2 sq ft (141·9 lb sq ft).

IATA ID Code CXE SB
SEABOARD WORLD AIRLINES, INC (SB)

Rectangular container. Aluminium panelled with steel channel reinforcement. Hinged sides to fold inside. Nine castors, forklift clearance under. Detachable, lockable, top cover. Ring bolts at corners. Multiple use, online and interline. Rented. External length, width and height: 79 × 57 × 37 in (201 × 145 × 94 cm). Internal length, width and height: 77 × 55 × 32 in (196 × 140 × 81 cm). External cube: 96·42 cu ft (2·740 m³). Internal cube: 78·43 cu ft (2·223 m³). Tare weight: 229 lb (104 kg). Max net perm. weight: 2,000 lb (907·5 kg).

IATA ID Code CXE
DEUTSCHE LUFTHANSA A.G. (LH)
SEABOARD WORLD AIRLINES, INC (SB)
TRANS WORLD AIRLINES, INC (TW)

Rectangular container on 7 castors. All aluminium, beaded and reinforced. Split side panel opens up and down. Ring bolts at edges. Ply/metal shelf. Multiple use, online and interline. External length, width and height: 84 × 42 × 63 in. (214 × 107 × 160 cm). Internal length, width and height: 80 × 40 × 59 in (203 × 102 × 150 cm). External cube: 128·63 cu ft (3·664 m³). Internal cube: 109·26 cu ft (3·106 m³). Tare weight: 210 lb (95·5 kg) without shelf. Max net perm. weight: 2,000 lb (907·5 kg) without shelf.

IATA ID Code CXE AF
AIR FRANCE (AF)

Rectangular container. Beaded aluminium panels riveted to channel framing. Side opening with hinged upper door and removable lower panel, 8 wheels, forklift entry, lockable, ring bolts at edges. Multiple use, online and interline. Rented. External length, width and height: 84 × 42 × 63 in (214 × 107 × 160 cm). Tare weight: 220 lb (100 kg). Maximum net perm. weight: 1,763 lb (800 kg).

IATA ID Code CXE SB
SEABOARD WORLD AIRLINES, INC (SB)

Rectangular container for belly hold of Canadair CL-44 aircraft. Aluminium panelled in channel framework, top opening with 2 hinged flaps (47·5 × 46 in: 121 × 117 cm) lockable, ring bolts at corners, forklift entry under. Multiple use, online and interline. Rented. External length, width and height: 79 × 46 × 33 in (201 × 117 × 84 cm). Internal length, width and height: 77·5 × 44 × 31·5 in (197 × 112 × 80 cm). External cube: 69·40 cu ft (1·976 m³). Internal cube: 62·17 cu ft (1·766 m³). Tare weight: 123 lb (56 kg). Max net perm. weight: 1,653 lb (750 kg).

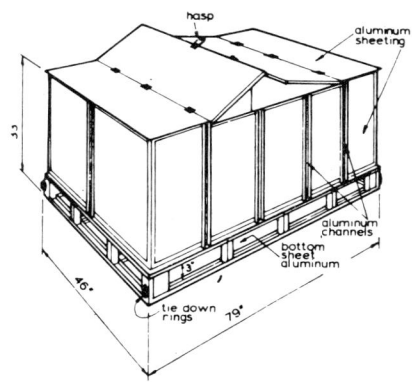

Deutsche Fruehauf GMBH unit for CL-44 aircraft belly holds. All aluminium construction. Used by Seaboard World Airlines. (CXE SB)

This model of Lufthansa's new cargo terminal at Frankfurt shows how the unit load devices are routed from the terminal to any one of nine loading points. Nose loading of 747 freighters or side door-loading is possible

IATA ID Code CXG SB
SEABOARD WORLD AIRLINES, INC (SB)
Contoured container, corrugated aluminium sandwich sections bonded and riveted to extruded framing. 4-way forklift entry. Front opening, removable doors. Multiple use, online and interline. External length, width and height: 51 × 41·5 × 74 in (130 × 105 × 188 cm). Internal length, width and height: 49 × 39·5 × 71 in (125 × 100 × 180 cm). External cube: 81·90 cu ft (2·320 m³). Internal cube: 71·50 cu ft (2·025 m³). Tare weight: 214 lb (97 kg). Max net perm. weight: 2,000 lb (907 kg).

IATA ID Code CXJ SB
SEABOARD WORLD AIRLINES, INC (SB)
Rectangular container. Tubular steel frame. aluminium sheet sides covered wire mesh. Top opening, collapsible, may be sealed/locked, 6 braced legs with 4 tie-down rings. Multiple use, online and interline. External length, width and height: 47·5 × 39·5 × 45·5 in (120 × 100 × 116 cm). Internal length, width and height: 46 × 38 × 39·5 in (117 × 96 × 100 cm). Internal cube: 39·96 cu ft (1·124 m³). Tare weight: 65 lb (29·5 kg). Max net perm. weight: 800 lb (363 kg).

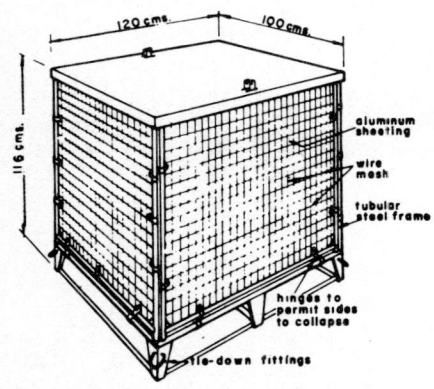

Seaboard World Airlines collapsible unit in tubular steel, wire mesh and aluminium sheet. (CXJ SB)

IATA ID Code CXJ SB
SEABOARD WORLD AIRLINES, INC (SB)
Rectangular container, smooth aluminium with steel channel reinforcing, hinged sides, top opening with removable cap lid, collapsible, ring bolts at corners, lockable, 4 wheels. Multiple use, online and interline. External length, width and height: 58 × 39 × 38·5 in (147 × 99 × 98 cm). Internal length, width and height: 57 × 38 × 34·5 in (145 × 97 × 88 cm). External cube: 50·4 ft³ (1·43 m³). Tare weight: 99 lb (45 kg). Max. net perm. weight: 882 lb (400 kg).

IATA ID Code CXJ SB
SEABOARD WORLD AIRLINES, INC (SB)
Rectangular container, aluminium sheet reinforced with channel sections, removable lid, hasp closing, tie-down rings at corners, forklift provision. Multiple use, online and interline. Rented. External length, width and height: 58·5 × 39 × 38·5 in (148 × 99 × 98 cm). Internal length, width and height: 56 × 37 × 31·5 in (143 × 94 × 80 cm). Internal cube: 37·77 cu ft (1·08 m³). Tare weight: 111 lb (50 kg). Max net perm. weight: 1,654 lb (750 kg).

IATA ID Code CXK SK
SCANDINAVIAN AIRLINES SYSTEM (SK)
Rectangular container. Birch plywood, metal reinforced, smaller side panels removable. Top opening, lockable, collapsible. Skids under for forklift. Multiple use, online and interline. Rented. External

length, width and height: 43·5 × 31·5 × 28 in (111 × 80 × 71 cm). Internal length, width and height: 42·5 × 30·5 × 25·5 in (108 × 77 × 65 cm). Internal cube: 19·13 cu ft (0·541 m³). Tare weight: 62 lb (28 kg). Max net perm. weight: 2,200 lb (1,000 kg).

IATA ID Code CXK AF
AIR FRANCE (AF)
Triple-wall, corrugated fibreboard, rectangular container. Top opening, collapsible. Multiple use, online by AF, online and interline by KLM. External length, width and height: 42 × 25·5 × 33 in (107 × 65 × 84 cm). Internal length, width and height: 41 × 24·5 × 31 in (104 × 62 × 79 cm). Tare weight: 22 lb (10 kg). Max net perm. weight: 478 lb (217 kg).

IATA ID Code CXK AF
AIR FRANCE (AF)
Rectangular container, two layers corrugated fibreboard covered by linerboard, top opening, collapsible. Multiple use, online. Rented. External length, width and height: 43 × 26·5 × 34·5 in (109 × 67 × 87 cm). Internal length, width and height: 42 × 25·5 × 33 in (107 × 65 × 84 cm). Tare weight: 16 lb (7·5 kg). Max net perm. weight: 353 lb (160 kg).

IATA ID Code CXM
DEUTSCHE LUFTHANSA AG (LH)
KLM ROYAL DUTCH AIRLINES (KL)
Rectangular bag container, p.v.c. covered polyester, carrying handles, collapsible. String sealed. Multiple use. Online and interline. External length, width and height: 19·5 × 19·5 × 15·5 in (50 × 50 × 40 cm). Internal length, width and height: 19·5 × 19·5 × 15·5 in (50 × 50 × 40 cm). Tare weight: 5 lb (2 kg). Max net perm. weight: 220 lb (100 kg).

IATA ID Code CXN AF
AIR FRANCE (AF)
Rectangular container in fire and waterproof linen with chlorofibre (rhovyl) lining. Top opening, strap closings, adjustable height, 4 tie-down rings, collapsible. Multiple use, online. External length, width and height: 37·5 × 19·5 × 29 in (95 × 50 × 74 cm). Internal length, width and height: 36 × 18·5 × 28·5 in (92 × 47 × 72 cm). Tare weight: 20 lb (9 kg). Max net perm. weight: 111 lb (50 kg).

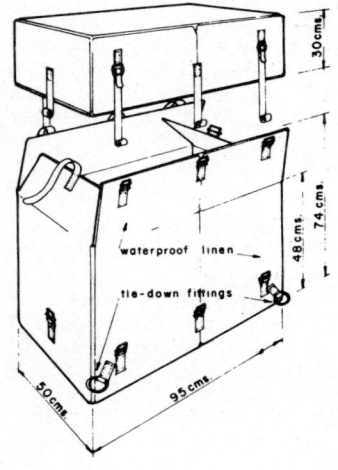

Fire and waterproof linen, collapsible container with removable top. Made by Comptoir Linier for Air France. (CXN AF)

A loaded pallet is transferred from a dolly to the mobile transporter which will move it to the elevating platform for delivery at sill height to the 747 lower-lobe compartment

IATA ID Code CXR P A
PAN AMERICAN WORLD AIRWAYS (PA)
Construction materials: aluminium and polyurethane. Size: 40 × 32 × 22 in (102 × 81 × 56 cm). External volume: 16·3 cu ft (0·46 m³). Tare weight: 75 lb (34 kg). Max net perm. weight: 1,000 lb (454 kg).

IATA ID Code CXR AI
AIR INDIA (AI)
Construction materials: thermocole, aluminium and teakwood. Size: 52·5 × 24 × 16·5 in (134 × 61 × 42 cm). External volume: 12·03 cu ft (0·34 m³). Tare weight: 75 lb (34 kg). Maximum net perm. weight: 220 lb (100 kg).

IATA ID Code CXS AI
AIR-INDIA (AI)
Insulated container. Rectangular, top opening, plastic and nylon with fibreglass insulation, collapsible. Carrying straps. Multiple, online use. External length, width and height, including fittings: 37 × 26 × 26 in (94 × 66 × 66 cm). Internal length, width and height 36 × 24 × 24 in (91 × 61 × 61 cm). Tare weight: 24 lb (11 kg). Max net perm. weight: 110 lb (50 kg).

IATA ID Code CXS LH
DEUTSCHE LUFTHANSA, AG (LH)
Insulated rectangular bag container. PVC coated polyester fabric with polyether-foam insulation, top opening, strap fixings, 4 wooden skids, folds flat. Multiple use, online. External length, width and height: 39 × 29 × 29·5 in (98 × 73 × 75 cm). Internal length, width and height: 37·5 × 27·5 × 27·5 in (95 × 70 × 70 cm). Tare weight: 31 lb (14 kg). Max. net perm. weight: 220 lb (100 kg).

IATA ID Code CXV LH
DEUTSCHE LUFTHANSA, AG (LH)
Tubular steel rack for hanging garments. Collapsible, screw-on fittings, adjustable height. Multiple, online use. Rented. External length, width and height, including fittings: 41·5 × 22 × 52 in (105 × 55 × 132 cm). Tare weight: 33 lb (15 kg). Max net perm. weight 265 lb (120 kg).

IATA ID Code CXV
BRITISH OVERSEAS AIRWAYS CORPORATION (BA)
SEABOARD WORLD AIRLINES, INC (SB)
Rack for hanging garments. Tubular steel frame with 4 castors. Plastic dust cover. Collapsible. Multiple use, online and interline. Rented. External length, width and height: 54 × 18 × 60 in (137 × 46 × 152 cm). Tare weight: 18 lb (8·5 kg). Max net perm. weight: 110 lb (50 kg).

IATA ID Code CXV AF
AIR FRANCE
Rack for hanging garments. Tubular steel frame, pin locked. Collapsible, adjustable height, plastic dust cover. Multiple use, online and interline. Rented. External length, width and height: 24 × 22 × 53 in (61 × 56 × 135 cm). Tare weight: 19 lb (9 kg). Max net perm. weight: 150 lb (68 kg).

IATA Code CXV AF
AIR FRANCE (AF)
Rack for hanging garments. Welded tubular steel, collapsible, adjustable height, pin locked. Plastic dust cover. Multiple use, online and interline. Rented. External length, width and height: 48 × 22 × 53 in

Tow-carts in the Alitalia cargo terminal Rome require no human assistance. They are directed automatically to their destinations.

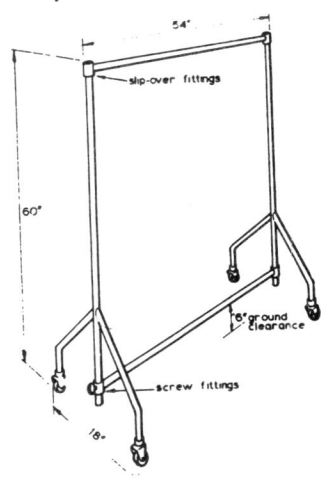

Tubular steel framed, wheeled, collapsible garment rack used by BOAC and Seaboard World Airlines. 110 lb (50 kg) capacity. (CXV)

(121 × 56 × 135 cm). Tare weight: 25 lb (11·5 kg). Max net perm. weight: 300 lb (130 kg).

IATA ID Code CXW LH
DEUTSCHE LUFTHANSA
Bag-shaped to fit the space between two passenger seats. Restrained by webbing. Nylon cotton duck with top opening; collapsible. Multiple Online use. Rented. External dimensions: 54·9 × 47·6 × 53 in (139·5 × 121 × 135 cm). Tare weight: 16 lb (7 kg). Max net perm. weight: 480 lb (218 kg).

IATA ID Code RXT SN
SABENA BELGIAN WORLD AIRLINES (SN)
Contoured container for chemicals, etc. Fibreglass sandwich panels, insulated with plastic foam. Temperature indicator. Hinged front door, lockable. (Dow P/N Qx 2292·2). Used on 88 × 108 in pallet. Multiple, online use. External length, width and height: 83 × 96 × 70 in (211 × 244 × 178 cm). Internal length, width and height: 76·5 ×

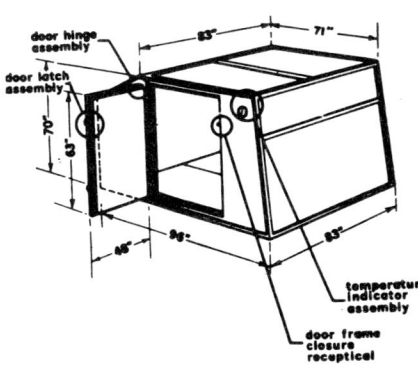

Insulated, sealed, indicating thermometer equipped, contoured container by Dow Chemical Company, for Sabena Belgian World Airlines. Used on 88 × 108 in pallet. (RXT SN)

89 × 63 in (194 × 226 × 160 cm). External cube: 300 cu ft (8·496 m³). Internal cube: 230 cu ft (6·513 m³). Tare weight: 613 lb (278 kg). Max. net perm. weight: 7,480 lb (3,393 kg).

IATA ID Code RXT KL
KLM ROYAL DUTCH AIRLINES (KL)
Construction materials: riveted sheets of aluminium forming with polyurethane foam sandwich insulated wall panels. Size 83·5 × 104 × 74 in (213 × 264 × 188 cm). External volume: 352 cu ft (9·97 m³). Tare weight 1,300 lb (590 kg). Max net perm. weight: 5,300 lb (2,410 kg).

IATA ID Code RXT SN
SABENA
Construction materials: fibreglass sandwich panels joined with epoxy adhesives; insulated with plastic foam and metal door hinges and closures. Size 83 × 96 × 74 in (211 × 244 × 188 cm). External volume: 304 cu ft (8·6 m³). Tare weight: 684 lb (310 kg). Max net perm. weight: 7,480 lb (3,393 kg).

IATA ID Code UA1
SCANDINAVIAN AIRLINES SYSTEM
Manufacturer: Tridair BL008. Fibreglass, polyester IATA Contour No. 1. Size: 224 × 318 × 203 cm (88 × 125 × 80 in). Tare weight: 233 kg (514 lb). Max perm. gross weight: 6,033 kg (13,300 lb). Volume: 11·97 m³ (422·7 cu ft).

IATA ID Code UA3
DEUTSCHE LUFTHANSA
KLM ROYAL DUTCH AIRLINES
Manufacturer: R. F. Schulz 1011200. Fibreglass, polyester (2 halves) IAIA Contour No. 3. Size: 224 × 318 × 203 cm (88 × 125 × 80 in). Tare weight: 205 kg (452 lb). Max perm gross weight: 4,536 kg (10,000 lb). Volume: 11·45 m³ (404·4 cu ft

IATA ID Code UAA
JAPAN AIR LINES
Manufacturer: Suzuei SD-08-1. Fibre, reinforced plastic. Size: 224 × 318 × 203 cm (88 × 125 × 80 in). Tare weight: 238·5 kg (526 lb). Max perm. gross weight: 5,670 kg (12,500 lb). Volume: 12·29 m³ (434·12 cu ft).

IATA ID Code UAA
JAPAN AIR LINES
Manufacturer: Suzuei Sangyo. Construction materials: fibreboard reinforced plastic shell. Size: 224 × 318 × 205 cm (88 × 125 × 81 in). Units used in combination: Pallets BL 22630-51; Nets BL 22758-51. Tare weight 231·5 kg (511 lb). Max perm. gross weight: 5,776·5 kg (12,735 lb). Volume: 12·2 m³ (428·63 cu ft).

IATA ID Code UAA
UNITED AIR LINES
Manufacturer: Tridair 22594-52. Construction materials: fibreglass. Size: 224 × 318 × 207/122 cm (88 × 125 × 81·5/48 in). Units used in combination: Pallets BL 23224-51; Nets BL 22672-51. Tare weight: 247 kg (545 lb). Max perm. gross weight: 5,917 kg (13,045 lb). Volume: 12·94 m³ (457 cu ft).

IATA ID Code UAA
FLYING TIGER LINE, INC
SEABOARD WORLD AIRLINES INC
Manufacturer: Tridair 24655-51. Construction materials: aluminium and balsa. Size: 224 × 318 × 206 cm (88 × 125 × 81·25 in). Units used in combination: Pallets BL 40160; Nets BL 22672-52. Tare weight: FT 261 kg (575 lb), SWA 267 kg (590 lb). Max perm. gross weight: 5,670 kg (12,500 lb). Volume: 12·94 m³ (457 cu ft).

IATA ID Code UAA
UNITED AIR LINES INC
Manufacturer: Tridair 41170-101. Fibreglass and vinyl/nylon. Size: 224 × 318 × 204 cm (88 × 125 × 81·25 in). Tare weight: 272·5 kg (600 lb) Max perm. gross weight: 5,670 kg (12,500 lb). Volume: 12·94 m³ (457 cu ft).

IATA ID Code UAB
PAN AMERICAN WORLD AIRWAYS
Manufacturer: Heath Tecna AC-10064-1. Reinforced, polyester. Size: 224 × 318 × 218/196/117 cm (88 × 15 × 86/77/46 in). Tare weight: 244 kg (540 lb). Max perm. gross weight: 6,033 kg (13,300 lb). Volume: 12·6 m³ (445 cu ft).

IATA ID Code UAB
PAN AMERICAN WORLD AIRWAYS
Manufacturer: Ranger Boat RB-1001. Reinforced polyester. Size: 224 × 318 × 218/196/117 cm (88 × 125 × 86/77/46 in). Tare weight: 134 kg (295 lb). Max perm. gross weight: 6,033 kg (13,300 lb). Volume: 12·6 m³ (445 cu ft).

IATA ID Code UAB
AIR FRANCE
Manufacturer: Tridair 22659-51. Construction materials: fibreglass. Size 244 × 318 × 218 cm (88 × 125 × 86 in). Units used in combination: Pallets BL 22864-51; Nets BL 22364-51. Tare weight: 218 kg (480 lb). Max perm gross weight: 4,528 kg (9,982 lb.). Volume 13·17 m³ (465 cu ft).

IATA ID Code UAB
BRITISH OVERSEAS AIRWAYS CORPORATION
Manufacturer: Tridair 22743-51. Construction materials: fibreglass. Size 224 × 318 × 218 cm (88 × 125 × 86 in). Units used in combination: Pallets BL 22371-51; Nets BL 23119-51. Tare weight: 225 kg (495 lb). Max perm. gross weight: 4,652 kg (10,253 lb). Volume 13·17 m³ (465 cu ft).

IATA ID Code UAB
TRANS WORLD AIRLINES INC
Manufacturer: Tridair 23216-51. Construction materials: fibreglass. Size: 224 × 318 × 218 cm (88 × 125 × 86 in). Units used in combination: Pallets BL 22252-51; Nets BL 23564-51. Tare weight: 272·5 kg (600 lb). Max perm. gross weight: 3,629 kg (8,000 lb). Volume: 13·17 m³ (465 cu ft).

IATA ID Code UAB
TRANS WORLD AIRLINES INC
Manufacturer: Dortech, U.S.A. Construction materials: fibreglass. Size: 224 × 318 × 219/198/108 cm (88 × 125 × 86/78/42·5 in). Units used in combination: Pallets BL 22252-51; Nets BL 22180-51 & BL 22181-51. Tare weight 249·5 kg (550 lb). Max perm. gross weight: 3,629 kg (8,000 lb). Volume 13·17 m³ (465 cu ft).

IATA ID Code UAC
UNITED AIR LINES
Manufacturer: Brownline Inc., U.S.A. Construction materials: fibreglass. Size 224 × 318 × 203/124 cm (88 × 125 × 80/48·5 in). Units used in combination: Pallets BL 23224-51; Nets BL 23143-51. Tare weight: 236 kg (520 lb). Max perm. gross weight: 4,772 kg (10,520 lb). Volume: 11·3 m³ (397 cu ft).

IATA ID Code UAC
BRANIFF
Manufacturer: Brownline Inc. U.S.A. Construction materials: fibreglass. Size: 224 × 318 × 206/125 cm (88 × 125 × 81/49 in). Units used in combination: Pallets BL 22864-52; Nets BL 22364. Tare weight: 247 kg (546 lb). Max perm gross weight: 3,876 kg (8,545 lb). Volume: 11·38 m³ (401·9 cu ft).

IATA ID Code UAC
EASTERN AIR LINES INC
Manufacturer: Heath Tecna AC-10636-1. Fibreglass. Size: 224 × 318 × 202 cm (88 × 125 × 79·6 in). Tare weight 236 kg (520 lb). Max perm. gross weight: 4,536 kg (10,000 lb). Volume: 11·33 m³ (400·1 cu ft).

IATA ID Code UAD
PAN AMERICAN WORLD AIRWAYS
Manufacturer: Brownline Inc., U.S.A. Construction materials: fibreglass. Size: 224 × 318 × 250/193/109 cm (88 × 125 × 80·5/76/43 in). Units used in combination: Pallets BL 22864-51; Nets BL 22364-51. Tare weight: 263 kg (580 lb). Max perm. gross weight: 3,892 kg (8,580 lb). Volume: 12·07 m³ (426 cu ft).

IATA ID Code UAD
AIR CANADA
Manufacturer: Atlantic Bridge FD 1662. Fibreglass. Size: 224 × 318 × 198/170/114 cm (88 × 125 × 78/67/45 in). Tare weight: 242·5 kg (534 lb). Max gross perm. weight: 4,536 kg (10,000 lb). Volume: 11·53 m³ 406·94 cu ft.

IATA ID Code UAE
UNITED AIR LINES INC
Manufacturer: Tridair 40808-101. Fibreglass and vinyl/nylon. Size: 224 × 318 × 202 cm (88 × 125 × 79·6 in). Tare weight: 256·5 kg (565 lb). Max perm. gross weight: 5,670 kg (12,500 lb). Volume: 11·44 m³ (397 cu ft).

IATA ID Code UAE
EASTERN AIR LINES INC
Manufacturer: Tridair 23147-51. Construction materials: fibreglass. Size: 224 × 318 × 206 cm (88 × 125 × 81 in). Units used in combination: Pallets BL 22864-51 & BL 23223-51; Nets BL 22364-51 & BL 23215-51. Tare weight: 247 kg (545 lb). Max perm. gross weight: 3,877 kg (8,545 lb). Volume: 11·45 m³ (401 cu ft).

IATA ID Code UAF
Manufacturer: Tridair 23340-51. Construction materials: fibreglass. Size: 224 × 318 × 202/115 cm (88 × 125 × 79·5/45 in). Units used in combination: Pallets BL 22864-51; Nets BL 22364-51. Tare weight: 305 kg (672 lb). Max perm. gross weight: 3,934 kg (8,672 lb). Volume: 10·62 m³ (375 cu ft).

IATA ID Code UAG
NORTHWEST AIRLINES INC
Manufacturer: Dortech, U.S.A. Construction materials: fibreglass. Size: 216 × 308 × 206/180/145/38 cm (85 × 121 × 83/71/57/15 in). Units used in combination: Pallets BL 23223-51; Nets BL 23618-51. Tare weight: 263 kg (580 lb). Max perm. gross weight; 4,536 kg (10,000 lb). Volume: 11·61 m³ (410 cu ft).

IATA ID Code UAH
TRANS WORLD AIRLINES INC
Manufacturer: Tridair 23632-51. Construction materials: fibreglass. Size: 224 × 318 × 204/107 cm (88 × 125 × 80/42 in). Units used in combination: Pallets BL 22252-51; Nets BL 23652-51. Tare weight: 297·5 kg (656 lb). Max perm. gross weight: 3,926 kg (8,000 lb). Volume: 11·18 m³ (394·7 cu ft).

IATA ID Code UAJ
AER LINGUS TEORANTA
Manufacturer: Tridair BL 012. Fibreglass and vinyl. Size: 224 × 318 × 198 cm (88 × 125 × 77 in). Tare weight: 229 kg (505 lb). Max perm. gross weight: 4,536 kg (10,000 lb). Volume: 10 m³ (353 cu ft).

IATA ID Code UAK
DEUTSCHE LUFTHANSA
KLM ROYAL DUTCH AIRLINES
Manufacturer: Schulz 264020. Fibreglass (2 halves). Size: 224 × 318 × 157 cm (88 × 125 × 63 in). Tare weight: 197 kg (434 lb). Max perm. gross weight: 3,629 kg (8,000 lb). Volume 10·00 m³ (353·00 cu ft).

IATA ID Code UAL
DEUTSCHE LUFTHANSA
KLM ROYAL DUTCH AIRLINES
Units used in combination: Pallets LH BB 210412 or BL 24076-51; Nets BB 2220bb. KL BB 210412. Tare weight: LH 200 kg (440 lb), KL 212 kg (467 lb). Max perm. gross weight: 4,536 kg (10,000 lb). Volume: 11·2 m³ (396 cu ft).

IATA ID Code U
SABENA
Manufacturer: Sabena. Fibreglass. Size: 211 × 308 × 201/138/81 cm (83 × 121 × 79/54·5/32 in). Tare weight: 270 kg (595 lb). Max perm. gross weight: 6,033 kg (13,300 lb). Volume: 11·00 m³ (392·00 cu ft).

IATA ID Code U
JAPAN AIR LINES
Manufacturer: Suzuei SB-72-3. Fibre, reinforced plastic. Size: 214 × 308 × 201 cm (84 × 121 × 79 in). Tare weight: 227 kg (500 lb). Max perm. gross weight: 5,670 kg (12,500 lb). Volume: 11·38 m³ (402·00 cu ft).

IATA ID Code UD7
SCANDINAVIAN AIRLINES SYSTEM
Manufacturer: Tridair 40803. Fibreglass, polyester IATA Contour No. 7. Size: 224 × 274 × 193 cm (88 × 108 × 76 in). Tare weight: 205 kg (452 lb). Max perm. gross weight: 4,536 kg (10,000 lb). Volume: 9·77 m³ (345·1 cu ft).

IATA ID Code UDA
BRANIFF
Manufacturer: Tridair 23127-51. Construction materials: fibreglass. Size: 224 × 274 × 206/148/123 cm (88 × 108 × 81/58/48·5 in). Units used in combination: Pallets BL 22862-51; Nets BL 23125-51. Tare weight 240·5 kg (530 lb). Max perm. gross weight: 3,869·5 kg (8,530 lb). Volume: 10·61 m³ (374·7 cu ft).

IATA ID Code UDB
JAPAN AIR LINES
Manufacturer: Fujimoto Sangyo. Construction materials: fibre reinforced plastic. Size: 224 × 274 × 206 cm (88 × 108 × 81 in). Units used in combination: Pallets BL 22492-51; Nets BL 21710-51. Tare weight: 207·5 kg (457 lb). Max perm. gross weight: 3,629 kg (8,000 lb). Volume: 10·76 m³ (379 cu ft).

IATA ID Code UDC
AIR CANADA
Manufacturer: Atlantic Bridge FD1728. Fibreglass. Size: 224 × 274 × 198/170/114 cm (88 × 108 × 78/67/45 in). Tare weight: 219 kg (483 lb). Max perm. gross weight: 3,639 kg (8,000 lb). Volume: 10·21 m³ (3,605 cu ft).

IATA ID Code UDC
FINNAIR
Manufacturer: Schulz 2650. Fibreglass (2 halves). Size: 224 × 274 × 199 cm (88 × 108 × 78·5 in). Tare weight: 180 kg (397 lb). Max perm. gross weight: 3,450 kg (7,606 lb). Volume: 10·15 m³ (358·3 cu ft).

IATA ID Code UDC
SWISSAIR
Manufacturer: Tridair 23426. Construction materials: fibreglass. Size: 224 × 274 × 206 cm (88 × 108 × 81 in). Units used in combination: Pallets BL 22492-51 Nets BL 21970-51 & 2. Tare weight: 220 kg (485 lb). Max perm. gross weight: 3,500 kg (7,716 lb). Volume: 10·5 m³ (370·79 cu ft).

IATA ID Code UDD
KLM ROYAL DUTCH AIRLINES
Manufacturer: Schulz 101140. Fibreglass (2 halves). Size: 224 × 274 × 207 (88 × 108 × 81·5 in). Tare weight: 190 kg (419 lb). Max perm. gross weight: 3,639 kg (8,000 lb). Volume: 10·6 m³ (375 cu ft).

IATA ID Code UDF
AIR INDIA
Manufacturer: Bruggemann and Brand. Construction materials: fibreglass (2 halves). Size: 224 × 274 × 205 cm (88 × 274 × 81 in). Units used in combination: Pallets Bruggemann 2105-11b; Nets BB 2217bb or BL 22362-51. Tare weight: 183·5 kg (404 lb). Max perm. gross weight: 4,536 kg (10,000 lb). Volume: 9·575 m³ (338·10 cu ft).

IATA ID Code UDG
AER LINGUS TEORANTA
Manufacturer: Tridair BL 014. Fibreglass and vinyl. Size: 224 × 274 × 196 cm (88 × 108 × 77 in). Tare weight: 196 kg (432 lb). Max perm. gross weight: 3,639 kg (8,000 lb). Volume 9·56 m³ (336·00 cu ft).

IATA ID Code UDH
SABENA
Manufacturer: Sabena. Construction materials: fibreglass. Size: 224 × 274 × 204 cm (88 × 108 × 80 in). Units used in combination: Pallets BL 22862-51 (ET) & 1-7551; Nets BL 22362-51. Tare weight: 250 kg (551 lb). Max perm. gross weight: 3,384 kg (8,452 lb). Volume: 9·94 m³ (351 cu ft).

IATA ID Code UJT
AER LINGUS TEORANTA
Manufacturer: Tridair BL 015. Fibreglass and vinyl. Size: 204 × 274 × 201 cm (80 × 108 × 79 in). Tare weight: 118 kg (415 lb). Max perm. gross weight: 3,638 kg (8,000 lb). Volume: 8·64 m³ (305·00 cu ft).

IATA ID Code UPE
SEABOARD WORLD AIRLINES INC
Manufacturer: Tridair 41598-101. Figreglass Size: 224 × 156 × 208 cm (88 × 61·5 × 82 in). Tare weight: 168 kg (370 lb). Max perm. gross weight: 2,380 kg (5,250 lb). Volume: 6·15 m³ (217·00 cu ft).

IATA ID Code UPP
SCANDINAVIAN AIRLINES SYSTEM
Manufacturer: Tridair 40803. Fibreglass, polyester. Size: 224 × 143 × 193 cm (88 × 53 × 76 in). Tare weight: 120 kg (265 lb). Max perm. gross weight: 1,134 kg (12,500 lb). Volume: 4·72 m³ (166·6 cu ft).

AIRCRAFT CONTAINER UNIT LOAD DEVICES
OWNED BY IATA MEMBER AIRLINES

IATA ID Code AVE
UNITED AIR LINES INC
Manufacturer: Goodyear. Materials: aluminium and balsa. External dimensions: 200·7 × 153·4 × 162·5 cm (79 × 60·4 × 64 in). External volume: 4·7 m³ (166 ft³). Tare weight: 168 kg (370 lb). Max gross weight perm: 1,587 kg (3,500 lb). Airworthiness Cert: FAA B-747.

IATA ID Code AVE
TRANS WORLD AIRLINES INC
Manufacturer: GATX. Materials: sheet metal balsa, core clad aluminium. External dimensions: 200·7 × 153·4 × 162·6 cm (79 × 60·4 × 64 in). Tare weight: 168 kg (370 lb). Max gross weight perm: B-747 1,284 kg (2,830 lb) L-1011 1,474 kg (3,250 lb). Airworthiness Cert: FAA B-747.

IATA ID Code AVE
NATIONAL AIRLINES INC
NORTHWEST AIRLINES INC
Manufacturer: Goodyear. Materials: aluminium. External dimensions: 200·4 × 153·4 162·3 cm (78·9 × 60·4 × 63·9 in). External volume: 4·7 m³ (166 ft³). Tare weight: 199 kg (262 lb). Max gross weight perm: B-747 1,284 kg (2,830 lb), DC-10 1,587 kg (3,500 lb), L-1011 1,474 kg (3,250 lb). Airworthiness Cert: FAA B-747, DC-10, L-1011.

IATA ID Code AVE
UNITED AIRLINES INC
Manufacturer: Brooks & Perkins. Materials: aluminium. External dimensions: $200.7 \times 153.4 \times 162.6$ cm ($79 \times 60.4 \times 64$ in). External volume: 4.7 m³ (166 ft³). Tare weight: 168 kg (370 lb). Max gross weight perm: $1,587$ kg ($3,500$ lb). Airworthiness Cert: FAA B-747.

IATA ID Code AVF
PAN AMERICAN WORLD AIRWAYS INC
Manufacturer: Brooks & Perkins. Materials: aluminium and wood. External dimensions: $223.5 \times 153.3 \times 162.5$ cm ($87.97 \times 60.4 \times 63.97$ in). External volume: 5.02 m³ (177.3 ft³). Tare weight: 106.5 kg (235 lb). Max gross weight perm: $1,284$ kg ($2,830$ lb). Airworthiness Cert: FAA B-747.

IATA ID Code AVG
PAN AMERICAN WORLD AIRWAYS INC
Manufacturer: Goodyear. Materials: aluminium. External dimensions: $233 \times 153.4 \times 162.3$ cm ($91.8 \times 60.4 \times 63.9$ in). External volume: 5.34 m³ (188.5 ft³). Tare weight: 95 kg (209 lb). Max gross weight perm: $1,284$ kg ($2,830$ lb). Airworthiness Cert: FAA B-747.

IATA ID Code AVH
DEUTSCHE LUFTHANSA
Manufacturer: Avio-Diepen Fokker. Materials: fibreglass, PVC foam and balsa. External dimensions: $233 \times 153.4 \times 160$ cm ($91.7 \times 60.4 \times 63$ in). External volume: 5.2 m³ (183 ft³). Tare weight; 118 kg (260 lb). Max gross weight perm: $1,284$ kg ($2,830$ lb). Airworthiness Cert: FAA B-747 (5.1.70).

IATA ID Code AVH
ALITALIA
Manufacturer: Irvin. Materials: aluminium and balsa. External dimensions: $233.7 \times 153.4 \times 160$ cm ($92 \times 60.4 \times 63$ in). Ex-

ternal volume: 5.2 m³ (183 ft³). Tare weight: 145.5 kg (320 lb). Max gross weight perm: $1,284$ kg ($2,830$ lb). Airworthiness Cert: FAA B-747.

IATA ID Code AVH
DEUTSCHE LUFTHANSA
Manufacturer: Sell-Haus. Materials: aluminium and sheet metal. External dimensions: $233.4 \times 153.4 \times 160$ cm ($91.9 \times 60.4 \times 63$ in). External volume: 5.2 m³ (183 ft³). Tare weight: 129.5 kg (285 lb). Max gross weight perm: $1,284$ kg ($2,830$ lb). Airworthiness Cert: LBA B-747.

IATA ID Code AVK
BRITISH OVERSEAS AIRWAYS CORPORATION
Manufacturer: Goodyear. Materials: aluminium. External dimensions: $232.6 \times 144.3 \times 162.2$ cm ($91.6 \times 56.4 \times 63.9$ in). External volume: 4.9 m³ (174 ft³). Tare weight: 154 kg (340 lb). Max gross weight perm: $1,284$ kg ($2,830$ lb). Airworthiness Cert: FAA B747.

IATA ID Code AVL
JAPAN AIR LINES CO LTD
Manufacturer: Showa. Materials: aluminium honeycomb sandwich. External dimensions: $234 \times 153 \times 163$ cm ($92 \times 60 \times 64$ in). External volume: 5.3 m³ (188 ft³). Tare weight: 127 kg (280 lb). Max gross weight perm: $1,284$ kg ($2,830$ lb). Airworthiness Cert: JCAB B-747.

IATA ID Code AVM
AIR CANADA
Manufacturer: Brooks & Perkins. Materials: aluminium, balsa sandwich. External dimensions: $200.7 \times 153.4 \times 162.6$ cm ($79 \times 60.4 \times 64$ in). External volume: 4.84 m³ (171 ft³). Tare weight: 141.4 kg (312 lb). Max gross weight perm: $1,474$ kg ($3,250$ lb). Airworthiness Cert: FAA B-747 (pending).

IATA ID Code AVM
JAPAN AIR LINES CO LTD
Manufacturer: Showa. Materials: aluminium honeycomb sandwich. External dimensions: $200.7 \times 153.4 \times 162.6$ cm ($79 \times 60.4 \times 64$ in). External volume: 4.85 m³ (171.4 ft³). Tare weight: 145 kg (320 lb). Max gross weight perm: B-747 $1,284$ kg ($2,830$ lb). L-1011 $1,474$ kg ($3,250$ lb), DC-10 $1,587.5$ kg ($3,500$ lb). Airworthiness Cert: JCAB & FAA B-747.

IATA ID Code AVM
SABENA
Manufacturer: Sabena. Materials: aluminium and fibreglass. External dimensions: $200 \times 149.5 \times 162.5$ cm ($79 \times 58.5 \times 64$ in). External volume: 4.6 m³ (160.7 ft³). Tare weight: 100 kg (220 lb). Max gross weight perm: $1,284$ kg ($2,830$ lb). Airworthiness Cert: Belgian Authority B-747.

IATA ID Code AVM
DEUTSCHE LUFTHANSA
Manufacturer: Brooks & Perkins. Materials: aluminium and balsa sandwich. External dimensions: $199.97 \times 153.34 \times 162.4$ cm ($78.7 \times 60.37 \times 63.9$ in). External volume: 4.6 m³ (163 ft³). Tare weight: 123 kg (271 lb). Max gross weight perm.: B-747 $1,284$ kg ($2,830$ lb), L-1011 $1,474$ kg ($3,250$ lb). Airworthiness Cert: FAA & LBA B-747 (pending).

IATA ID Code BMA
SABENA
Manufacturer: Sabena. Materials: aluminium, fibreglass and vinyl. External dimensions: $317.5 \times 96.5 \times 152.4$ cm ($125 \times 38 \times 60$ in). External volume: 4.37 m³ (154.3 ft³). Tare weight: 110 kg (243 lb). Max gross weight perm: 795 kg ($1,753$ lb). Airworthiness Cert: Belgian AA B-747.

MANUFACTURERS OF IATA MEMBER OWNED
UNIT LOAD DEVICES

Aircraft Pallets
Aircraft Igloos
Aircraft Structural Igloos
Aircraft Refrigerated or insulated igloos
Aircraft Containers
Non-aircraft Containers
ID Code P
ID Code U
ID Code S
ID Code R
ID Codes A & B
ID Codes CD, CX & RX
BELGIUM
Sabena,
Brussels Airport
RXTSN, AVMSN, BMASN, P1GSN, P2ASN, USN, UDH (ET, SN)
CANADA
Laprairie Aircraft Ltd.,
Laprairie,
Quebec
CXVAF
FRANCE
Comptoir Linier,
79 rue de Tocqueville,
Paris 17e
CXN AF
GERMANY (Federal Republic of)
Brüggeman & Brand KG,
5802 Wetter, Ruhr 2

CXWLH; P1G (LH, SK, KL); P2CAI, P2J (SB, KL, LH); UDFAI
Deutsche Fruehauf GmbH & Co.,
8306 Schierling, NDB
CXE SB, CXJSB
Deutsche Lufthansa, AG
1 Claudiusstrasse,
Cologne,
CXV LH
Felten & Guilleaume & W. Sanner & Co.
Georgstr. 5a,
5 Koln,
CXS LH
Firma Giesemann,
Oldenburg i.O.
CXM
Seaboard World Airlines, Inc.,
Frankfurt
CXE SB, CXJ SB
Sell-Haus und Kuncheintechnik,
6348 Herborn/Hessen
CXE AF, AVHLH
R. F. Schulz
CODLH, CXCLH, UA3 (LH, KL), UAK (LH, KL), UAL (LH, KL), UDCAY, UDDKL
VFW-Fokker GmbH
28 Bremen, W. Germany
Hünefeldstrasse
P2JLH

Accepting freight for sorting at the Lufthansa freight centre, Frankfurt airport. Packages travel upwards on loading belts to the main conveyor where consignments are sorted semi-automatically.

INDIA
Venus Steel Industries,
30c Pharucha Compound, Pais Str,
Bombay 11
CXR AI

JAPAN
Fuji Motor Corp.,
1 42-1 Imokubo,
Yamatomachi,
Kitatama-gun, Tokyo
UDBJL
Showa Aircraft Industry Co. Ltd.,
1-12-chome, Nihombashi,
Muro-machi, Chuo-ku, Tokyo
AVLJL, AVMJL
Suzuei Sangoyo Co. Ltd.
15-10, 1 chome,
Uchisawai-cho,
Chiyoda-ky, Tokyo
UAAJL, UJL
NETHERLANDS
Avio-Diepen Fokker,
Ypenburg, The Hague
AVHLH
Paul & Van Weelde NV
Nieuwerkerk A/D Ijssel
RXT KL
SWEDEN
Wedaverken,
Sodertalje
CXK SK
UNITED KINGDOM
British Aircraft Corporation,
100 Pall Mall,
London SW1
P4LEC
Hawker Siddeley Group Ltd,
32 Duke Str, St. James's,
London SW1
P2MBE
Tridair Industries Ltd,
Tamian Way, Green Lane,
Hounslow, Middlesex
(See Tridair Industries, Cargomatic **Div**
USA)
Latex Upholstery Ltd.,
41 Lonsdale Road,
London, W.2.
CXS AI
UNITED STATES OF AMERICA
Atlantic Bridge,
UADAC, UDCAC

Atlantic Container Corporation,
Long Island,
City N.Y.
CXK AF

Brooks & Perkins Inc,
Suite 750, Honeywell Centre,
17515 W Nine Mile Road,
Southfield,
Michigan 48075
P1D (UA, AC); P2GAC; P4QFT; AVEUA;
AVFPA; AVMAC; AVMLH; COEPA

Brownline Corporation,
2500 Compton Blvd.,
Redondo Beach,
California
PIA (TW, BA, QF, SV); P1B (AF, PA, EA,
SK, BN, NW); P1C (DL, SV, BA, QF);
P1D (KL, SK, SB, VA, UA); P1F (BN, JL,
PA, SB, FT); P1T (FT); P5F (SK, SR);
UAC (UA, BN); UAD (PA)

Containair Systems Corp,
Containair Div,
145-80 228th Street,
Springfield Gardens, NY 11413
COELH & SB

Dortech Incorporated,
Stamford,
Connecticut
UAGNW

Tradewinds

Dow Chemical Company,
Midland,
Michigan
RXT SN

Fruehauf Corporation,
Cargo Systems Division,
5137 S. Boyle Avenue,
Los Angeles 58,
California
CXC TW, CXC, CXG SB

GATX Boothe Corp.,
Alcoa Bld, 560 Battery Str.,
San Francisco, Calif. 94111
AVETW

Goodyear Aerospace Corp.,
1210 Massillon Rd.,
Akron,
Ohio 44315
AVE (UA, NA, NW); AVGPA; AVKBA

Grumman Aircraft Corporation,
Farmingdale,
Long Island,
N.Y.
CXE

Heath Tecna Corp.,
Machined Products Div.,
19819 8th Avenue S. Kent,
Washington 9031
P1BEA, P1D (AC, UA); P1FPA; UABPA;
UACEA

Irvin Industries Inc.,
15001 S. Figueroe Str.,
Gardena, California 90247
P1CAZ; P1DUA; AVHAZ

Marino Systems Inc.,
1545 Fifth Industrial Ct.,
Bay Shore, LI, NY 11706
P1DVA

Ranger Boat,
UABPA

Tridair Industries, Cargomatic Div.,
717 Main Str.,
Westbury, L.I.
New York 11590

P1BEA; P1G (FT, AC, BA); P2A (AI, AR,
ET, BN, BA, FI, QF, SN, RG, CI, EI, NW,
IC, AF); P1DUA; P2FBA; P2G (BN, PA,
TL, AY, SB, AC, AZ, JL, KM, SA, SR);
P2J (AC, SK, SR); P2NLH; P3TEI; P5BSB;
UA1SK; UAA (UA, FT, SB); UAB (AF, BA,
TW); UAE (UA, EA); UAFPA; UAHTW;
UAJEI; UD7SK; UDABN; UDCSR; UD
GEI; UJTEI; UPESB; UPPSK; SAAUA;
RAHUA

Sal-Fax Corporation
212 Drexel,
Hot Springs,
Arkansas 71901
CXR PA

Tri-Wall Containers Inc.,
799 Washington Street,
New York 14, N.Y.
CXK AF

Major air exports for Israel are agricultural produce, day-old chicks and textiles which moved in increasing quantities by air from the end of 1969 aboard El Al's convertible 707-320Cs

Contoured, refrigerated, air freight container of all-metal construction with fork lift entry under. This multi-use unit is built by Paul and Van Weelde NV, Nieuwerkerk a/d Ijssel, The Netherlands.

A cargo pallet ball-table, rollers and tie-down points make a spartan interior in this SAS freighter

This baggage and cargo container for an Air France Super B Boeing 727-200 lower holds can carry 25 large pieces of luggage or the equivalent amount of cargo.

Fully loaded, weather protected and netted a pallet is moved from the make-up pit to one of several storage positions on the airside of Alitalia's Rome cargo terminal.

For more than six years cargo manifests have been prepared automatically for Swissair, Zurich on this IBM printer from data abstracted from punch cards. A manifest covering all essential details up to 40 shipments can be printed in a few seconds and then duplicated.

Igloos built by Air Logistics Corp being tested in service with Pan American

One of BEA's nine Merchantmen discharges two of its pallets at the airline's London-Heathrow Cargocentre.

MAJOR CARGO CARRYING AIRLINES

Every airline is capable of carrying quantities of small-parcel, bulk-cargo in its fleet but not all can accept the modern, major, unit load devices. This list covers national and international operators both scheduled and non-scheduled (charter) which accept major-ULDs (pallets, igloos and large containers). Where some doubt exists ULDs are not specified.

Aer Lingus Teoranta
Irish International Airlines, Dublin Airport, Ireland
FLEET: 6 B737-248; 2 B737-248QC; 4 BAC One-eleven-200.
MAJOR CARGO TERMINALS: Dublin, London
ULDs: Pallets; Igloos; containers.
SENIOR CARGO STAFF:
O. Boden (*Cargo Manager*)
L. Ward (*Assistant Cargo Manager*)

Aerlinte Eireann
Irish International Airlines, Dublin Airport, Ireland
FLEET: 2 B747-148; 6 B707-320C.
ULDs: Pallets; Igloos; Containers, B747 containers and pallets.
SENIOR CARGO STAFF:
O. Boden (*Cargo Manager*)
L. Ward (*Assistant Cargo Manager*)

Aeroflot
Leningradsky Prospekt 37, Moscow A-167, USSR
FLEET: No official figures available.

Aerolineas Argentinas
Paseo Colon 185, Buenos Aires, Argentina
FLEET: 4 B707-387B; 2 B707-387C; 4 B737-287; 2 B737-287C; 3 Caravelle; 9 HS748. On order: 2 B707-387C
ULDs: 707 belly hold pallets; containers.
SENIOR CARGO STAFF:
Oscar E. Venarotti (*System Cargo Manager*)
Luis E. T. Rodriquez (*System Cargo Sales Manager*)

APSA
Aerolineas Peruanas SA, Jiron Cuzco 177, Lima, Peru
FLEET: 3 CV990A; 1 DC8-52; On order 1 L100-20 Hercules.
ULDs: Pallets.
SENIOR CARGO STAFF:
Roberto Loayza (*Manager Cargo Sales*)
Enrique de Romaña (*Manager Cargo Promotion*)

Aero Spacelines Inc.
Santa Barbara Airport, California 93102,
USA (Charter operator)
FLEET: 1 B377 Mini Guppy; 1 B377 Pregnant Guppy; 1 B377 Super Guppy; 1 Guppy 201.

Aero Trasporti Italiani SpA
(ATI), Capodichino Airport, 80144 Naples, Italy
FLEET: 8 DC9-30; 13 F27 Friendships (three with special doors).

Avianca
Aerovias Nacionales de Colombia SA, Carrera 7a, No 16-84, Bogota, Colombia
FLEET: 2 B707-359B; 4 B720-059B; 4 B727-59; 2 B737-59; 2 HS748; 13 DC4; 11 Hyper DC3.

Air Afrique
Société Aériénne Africaine Multinationale BP 21017, Abidjan, Ivory Coast.
FLEET: 1 DC8-30; 3 DC8-50; 1 DC-863; 2 Caravelle 11R; 2 YS11A-300; 3 DC4; 1 DC 3. On order 3 DC10-30.

Air Canada
1 Place Ville Marie, Montreal 113, Quebec, Canada
FLEET: 2 B747; 11 DC8-40; 9 DC8-50; 6 DC8-61; 12 DC8-63; 36 DC9-32; 25 Viscount-700; 8 Vanguard.
MAJOR CARGO TERMINALS: London; Montreal Toronto; Winnipeg.
ULDs: Pallets; Igloos; Containers.
SENIOR CARGO STAFF:
John Eden (*Director Cargo Sales and Services*)
R. L. Alexander (*Manager Cargo Sales and Services*)

Air France
1 Place Max Hymans, Paris 15e, France
FLEET: 5 B747-128; 18 B 707-320; 7 B707-320B; 8 B707-320C; 17 B727-200; 42 Caravelle. On order: 6 B747-128; 3 B727-200.
MAJOR CARGO TERMINALS: Paris-Orly, London-Heathrow, New York-JFK.
ULDs: Pallets; Igloos: Containers; B747 containers.
SENIOR CARGO STAFF:
P. Stoekel (*System Cargo Sales Manager*)

Air Fret
110 Boulevard Pereire, Paris 17e, France (Charter operater)
FLEET: 1 L1049 Constellation; 1 DC7BF; 2 C54E (Cargo).
SENIOR CARGO STAFF:
Gérard Boyault
Fabien Nordmann

Air-India
218 Backbay Reclamation, Nariman Point, Bombay 1, India
FLEET: 2 B747-B; 3 B707-337B; 2 B707-337C; 5 707-437. On order 2 B747B (1972)
ULDs: Pallets; Igloos; Containers.
SENIOR CARGO STAFF:
E. Pereira (*Commercial Manager Cargo*)

Airlift International Inc.
P.O Box 525, Miami International Airport, Florida 33148, USA (Charter operator)
FLEET: 4 DC8-63F; 2 B707-372C; 2 B727-172C.
SENIOR CARGO STAFF:
Leo Stevens (*General Sales Manager*)

Air New Zealand Ltd.
Airways House, 101-3 Custom Street E, Auckland, New Zealand
FLEET: 5 DC8-52; 2 Electra. On order: 3 DC10-30.
SENIOR CARGO STAFF:
D. G. Patterson (*Cargo Superintendent*)
R. P. Thomas (*Shipping and Customs Controller*)
H. A. Tros (*Chief Cargo Officer*)

Alaska Airlines Inc.
Seattle-Tacoma International Airport, Seattle Washington 98158, USA (Charter operator)
FLEET: 3 B727-100C; 2 Hercules; 3 CV240; 2 Twin Otter; 3 Catalina; 2 L1649; 10 Goose.
SENIOR CARGO STAFF:
John G. Billings (*Assistant V.P. Cargo and Charter Sales*)

Alitalia
Linee Aeree Italiane SpA, Palazzo Alitalia, 00144 Roma Eur, Rome, Italy
FLEET: 12 DC8-43; 7 DC8-62; 2 DC8-62F; 33 DC9-32; 3 DC9-32F; 15 Caravelle; 4 B747.
MAJOR CARGO TERMINALS: Rome; London.
ULDs: Pallets 88 × 125; Igloos; B 747 underfloor LD-1 and LD-3.
SENIOR CARGO STAFF:
F. Trento (*Manager Freight and Postal Services*)
W. Conti (*Manager Freight Planning*)
A. Scalcione (*Manager Sales Promotion*)

American Airlines Inc.
633 Third Avenue, New York, NY 10017, USA
FLEET: 16 B747-123; 51 B707-123B; 20 B707-323; 10 B707-323B; 16 B707-323CF; 16 B720-023B; 57 B727-023; 41 B727-223; 27 BAC One-Eleven-400; 1 DC10. On

order: 24 DC10.

MAJOR CARGO TERMINALS: New York and
other main US cities.

ULDs: Pallets; Igloos; Containers; B747 and
DC10 LD-3 containers.

SENIOR CARGO STAFF:

O. A. Becker (*Senior V.P. Freight Marketing*)

T. P. Gallagher (*Assistant V.P. Freight
Sales and Advertising*)

Ansett Airlines of Australia
489 Swanston Street, Melbourne, Victoria,
Australia

FLEET: 4 B727-77; 2 B727-77QC; 12 DC9-30;
6 F28; 3 Carvairs; 17 F27-200; 5 F27-
400QC; 3 Electra; 1 DC3; 3 DC4 freighter.

ULDs: Pallets; Igloos; Containers

SENIOR CARGO STAFF:

L. C. Warton (*General Freight Manager*)

A. Hatton (*Assistant General Freight
Manager Operations*)

J. Corcoran (*Cargo Marketing Manager*)

Braniff International Inc.
P.O. Box 35001, Exchange Park, Dallas,
Texas 75235, USA

FLEET: 1 B747-127; 4 B707-138B; 7 B707-
327C; 5 B720-027; 3 B727-227; 14 B727-
27; 18 B727-27QC; 6 DC8-62; 1 DC8-62CF;
13 BAC One-Eleven-203.

ULDs: Pallets; Igloos; Containers; B747
Containers.

SENIOR CARGO STAFF:

Steven Facsko (*Director Freight Sales*)

British Air Ferries Ltd.
Southend Airport, Southend-on-Sea, Essex,
England (Scheduled/Charter operator)

FLEET: 5 Carvairs.

ULDs: Pallets; Containers.

SENIOR CARGO STAFF:

Barry Pawsey (*Cargo and Charter Manager*)

Terry Bassam (*Cargo Superintendent*)

British Caledonian Airways
London-Gatwick Airport, Horley, Surrey,
England

FLEET: 7 B707-320C; 4 BAC VC10; 12 BAC
One-Eleven-500; 8 BAC One-Eleven-200.

ULDs: Pallets; Containers.

SENIOR CARGO STAFF:

David Gerrard (*Cargo Sales Manager*)

BEA
British European Airways Corporation, Bea-
line House, Ruislip, Middlesex, England

FLEET: 21 HS Trident 1C; 15 HS Trident 2E;
4 HS Trident 3B; 2 Comet 4B; 18 BAC
One-Eleven-510; 12 BAC Vanguard; 7
Merchantmen. On order: 22 HS Trident
3B; 2 Merchantman.

MAJOR CARGO TERMINALS: London-Heathrow, Manchester, Paris.

ULDs: Pallets; Containers.

SENIOR CARGO STAFF:

John Guy (*Cargo Director*)

Capt. H. A. Hooper (*Cargo Operations*)

Harry Smallman (*General Manage Cargo*)

BOAC
British Overseas Airways Corporation,
Speedbird House, London-Heathrow Air-
port, Hounslow, Middlesex, England

FLEET: 6 B747-36; 18 B707-436; 8 B707-
336B; 3 B707-336B; 11 BAC VC10;
16 BAC Super VC10. On order: 6 B747 36.

MAJOR CARGO TERMINALS: London-Heathrow, New York-JFK, Montreal, Manchester
Prestwick.

ULDs: Pallets; Igloos; Containers; B747
LD-7 and Pallets.

SENIOR CARGO STAFF:

R. M. Hilary (*Commercial Director*)

W. D. Koster (*Cargo Manager Europe*)

C. Rix (*Cargo Marketing Manager*)

British West Indian Airways Ltd.
Kent House, Maraval, Trinidad, WI

FLEET: 6 B707-138B; 4 Visount-700.

Capitol International Airways Inc.
Metropolitan Airport, Nashville, Tennessee
37217, USA

FLEET: 2 DC8-31; 3 DC8-55F; 3 DC8-63CF,

SENIOR STAFF:

Jesse F. Slattings (*Chairman Bd. and
President*)

Mack H. Rowe (*Execituve V.P.*)

Cargolux Airlines International SA
76 avenue de la Liberté, Luxemburg,
(Charter operator)

FLEET 3 CL44 with swingtail and roller beds.

ULDs: Pallets.

SENIOR CARGO STAFF:

E. Olafsson (*General Manager*)

R. Arendal (*Sales Manager*)

Continental Air Lines Inc.
Los Angeles International Airport, California
90009, USA

FLEET: 4 B747-24; 11 B707-324; 2 B707-
320C; 8 B720-024B; 19 B727-200; 19
DC9-15F. On order: 1 DC10.

ULDs: B707 pallets, containers; B747 LD-3
and LD-7 containers.

SENIOR CARGO STAFF:

O. Lee Slay (*Staff V.P. Cargo Sales and
Service*)

William E. Williams (*Manager Cargo Sales*)

M. E. Marquis (*Manager Cargo Service*)

CP Air
1281 West Gorgia Street, Vancouver 5, BC,
Canada

FLEET: 4 DC8-63; 6 DC8-40/50; 1 DC8-55F;
4 B727-100; 7 B737-200.

MAJOR CARGO TERMINALS: Vancouver.

ULDs: Pallets; Containers.

SENIOR CARGO STAFF:

A. Kramer (*Manager Cargo Sales Int'l*)

H. L. Yeomans (*Manager Air Mail and
North American Cargo Sales*)

Delta Air Lines Inc.
Continental Colony Parkway, Atlanta,
Georgia, USA

FLEET: 1 B747; 5 DC8-61; 13 DC8; 28 CV880;
16 DC9-32; 58 DC9; 15 L100-20 Hercules.

SENIOR CARGO STAFF:

John Pogue (*Manager Cargo*)

East African Airways Corp.
P.O. Box 19002, Nairobi Airport, Kenya.

FLEET: 5 Super VC10; 3 DC9-30; 4 F27;
4 Twin Otter; 6 DC3.

ULDs: Pallets; Containers.

SENIOR CARGO STAFF:

Mr. Wanjara (*Cargo Sales Manager*)

Eastern Air Lines Inc.
10 Rockerfeller Plaza, New York, NY 10020,
USA

FLEET: 16 DC8-20/50; 17 DC8-61; 6 DC8-63;
8 DC9-10; 72 DC9-30; 50 B727-25; 25
B727-25QC; 26 B727-225; 20 Electra;
3 B747. On order 250 L1011.

SENIOR CARGO STAFF:

J. Schorr (*Director Cargo Marketing Division*)

A. N. Koppen (*Director Cargo Services*)

Eastern Provincial Airways (1963)Ltd.
Gander. Newfoundland, Canada

FLEET: 2 Carvair; 3 HP Herald; 3 B737-200.

El Al—Israel Airlines,
P.O. Box 41, Lod Airport, Israel

FLEET 3 B707-320B; 2 B707-320C; 3 B707-
420; 2 B720B; On order: 2 B747B

SENIOR CARGO STAFF:

D. Adiv, (*Dir Mktg Div*)

Ethiopian Airlines SC
P.O. Box 1755, Addis Ababa, Ethiopia

FLEET: 2 B707-320C; 2 B720B; 2 DC6B;
6 DC3; C47.

ULDs: Pallets.

SENIOR CARGO STAFF:

Hailu Ibssa (*Associate Cargo Programmes*)

Daniel Bahta (*Chief Transportation Agent*)

Finnair O Y
(Cargo Office), Kauppiaankatu 3, Helsinki 16,
Finland

FLEET: 3 DC8-62CF; 8 Super Caravelle;
4 DC9-10; 2 DC6B; 1 DC6B (Swing tail);
On order: 2 DC9-15 and 2 DC10 probably
with accommodation for passengers and
pallets.

ULDs: Pallets; Containers.

SENIOR CARGO STAFF:

Lauri Oksanen (*Manager Cargo*)

Lars Ekman (*Vice-Manager Cargo*)

Veikko Salonen (*Manager Sales*)

Flying Tiger Line Inc.
7401 World Way W, Los Angeles International Airport, California 90009, USA.
(Charter operator)

FLEET: 16 DC8-63CF.

SENIOR CARGO STAFF:

J. J. Healy (*V.P. and General Manager
Terminals*)

Iberia
Lineas Aereas de Espana SA, Valazquez 130,
Madrid 6, Spain

FLEET: 2 B747; 5 DC8-63; 1 DC8-63F;
6 DC8-50; 1 DC8-55F; 24 DC9-30; 13
Caravelle 6R; 6 Caravelle 1OR; 2 Caravelle
11R; 8 F27; 3 F28; 13
CV440; On order: 1 B747; 11 DC9-30.

SENIOR CARGO STAFF:

Lazaro Ros (*Director and General Manager*)

Icelandair
Flugfelag Islands HF, Baendahollin, Haga-
torg, Reykjavik, Iceland

FLEET: 1 B727-108C; 1 BAC Viscount 759;
2 DC6B; 2 F27; 2 DC3.

SENIOR STAFF:

Orn O. Johnson (*General Manager*)

Indian Airlines
Airlines House, 113 Gurdwara Rakabganj
Road, New Dehli 1, India

FLEET: 7 B737-200; 7 Caravelle VIN;
14 HS748; 8 F27-100; 2 F27-200; 1 F27-
400; 9 Viscount 700 Series.

SENIOR CARGO STAFF:

R. G. Jamalabad (*Deputy Managing
Marketing*)

J. F. Tarachand (*Deputy Commercial
Manager (Rates)*)

B. S. Gupta (*Assistant Commercial Manager
(Cargo)*)

International Jetair Ltd.
Calgary International Airport, PO Box 3190,
Station B, Calgary 67, Alberta, Canada

FLEET: 9 L188 Electra with freight doors.

ULDs: Container D type.

SENIOR CARGO STAFF:

R. T. Moore (*President*)

Invicta International Airlines Ltd.
Manston Airport, Kent, England (mainly
Charter cargo operator)

FLEET: 1 BAC Vanguard 959 freighter;
2 DC4F. On order: 1 BAC Vanguard 952
freighter.

ULDs: IATA Pallets size 3 DC4 and size 7
Vanguard. Container Size 13 Vanguard.

SENIOR CARGO STAFF:

C. E. Jackson (*Commercial Manager*)
(Panton House, 25 Haymarket, London
SW1);

S. J. Atkinson (*Cargo Services Manager*)
(Manston)

Japan Air Lines
Tokyo Building, 2-chome, Marunouchi,
Chiyoda-Ku, Tokyo, Japan

FLEET: 3 B747; 7 DC8-62; 2DC8-26F;
6 DC8-61; 11 DC8-50; 3 DC8-50F; 4 DC8-
30; 14 B727-100; 3 B727-100QC; 2 YS11.
On order: 13 B747B; 3 DC8-62; 3 DC8-
62F; 6 DC8-61.

MAJOR CARGO TERMINAL: Tokyo Airport.

SENIOR STAFF:

Shizuo Asada, (*Effect. V.P.*)

KLM Royal Dutch Airlines
Amsterdamseweg 55, Amsterlveen, Netherlands

FLEET: 7 B747-206B; 4 DC8-33; 7 DC8-53;
5 DC8-55F; 11 DC8-63; 4 DC9-15; 9 DC9-
32; 7 DC9-33RC; 1 F27. On order:
6 DC10-30.

MAJOR CARGO TERMINAL: Schiphol Airport.

ULDs: Pallets; Igloos; Containers; B474
Container LD-1.

SENIOR CARGO STAFF:

J. H. Timmers;

W. G. Fluitsma

A. Postma
J. J. Warnaar

Libyan National Airways SAL (Linair)
18 Sclara Ennasser, Triploi, Libyan Arab Republic
FLEET: 3 F27-600; 5 DC3-C47 (all aircraft fitted with freight doors).
SENIOR CARGO STAFF:
P. W. Bakker (*General Manager*)

Loftleidir
Icelandic Airlines, Reykjavik, Iceland
FLEET: 2 CL-44; 2 DC8-63.
SENIOR CARGO STAFF:
F. Thedorsson (*Cargo Sales Manager*)

Lufthanas
Deutsche Lufthansa Aktiengesellschaft, 5 Koln 21, Von-Gablenz Str 2-6, West Germany
FLEET: 4 B707-430; 10 B707-330B; 6 B707-330C; 9 B727-30; 11 B727-30C; 2 B727-230; 22 B727-130; 6 B737-230C; 4 B747-130. Cargo aircraft on order: 3 B727-230; 1 B747-230B; 1 B747-230F; 4 DC10.
MAJOR CARGO TERMINALS: Frankfurt; New York-JFK; London-Heathrow.
ULDs: B747 lower lobe containers LD-1 and LD-3; IATA Containers.
SENIOR CARGO STAFF:
H. F. Klumpp (*General Manager Cargo*)
W. Lower (*Cargo Operations*) (Frankfurt)

Luxair
Société Anonyme Luxembourgeoise de Navigation Aériénne, P.O. Box 2203, Luxembourg Airport, Luxembourg
FLEET: 1 B707-344; 1 Caravelle 6R; 1 Viscount 815; 3 F27.
SENIOR STAFF:
Roger Sietzen (*General Manager*)

Martin's Aircharter Co.
MAC Building, Schiphol Centre, Netherlands (Charter operator)
FLEET: 2 DC8-55F; 1 DC8-33; 3 DC9-33RC; 1 DC9-32; 2 C640; 1 F28 Fellowship.
ULDs: IATA Pallets.

Middle East Airlines Airliban SA
P.O. Box 206, Beirut International Airport, Lebanon
FLEET: 3 B707-320C; 5 B720-120B; 3 CV-990A; 1 Comet 4C; 1 Caravelle 6R. On order: 4 B720-120B.
ULDs: Pallets; Containers.
SENIOR CARGO STAFF:
Samir Boustany (*Freight Manager*)

Monarch Airlines Ltd.
Luton Airport, Luton, Bedfordshire, England (Charter operator)
FLEET: 5 Britannia-312; 1 Britannia-309; 1 Britannia-308 freighter.
SENIOR CARGO STAFF:
D. H. Scott (*Sales Manager*)
(Manfield House, 376 Strand, London WC2)

New Zealand National Airways Corp.
P.O. Box 96, Wellington C1, New Zealand
FLEET: 3 B727-219; 5 BAC Viscount 800; 13 F27. On order: 1 B737-200.

Nordair Ltd.
Montreal International Airport, Dorval, Quebec, Canada
FLEET: 3 B737-242C; 1 DC4; 3 C46T; 6 DC3; 1 Short Skyvan. On order: 1 B737-242C; 1 FH227E.
MAJOR CARGO TERMINAL: Montreal.
ULDs: Pallets; Igloos.
SENIOR CARGO STAFF:
Jim Powell
Leo Jodoin

Northwest Airlines Inc.
Minneapolis/St Paul International Airport, St. Paul, Minnesota 55111, USA.
FLEET: B727-100; B727-200; B720B; B707-320B; 26 B707-320C; 15 B747 delivered or on order.
ULDs: Pallets; Igloos; B747 Containers LD-1 and LD-3.
SENIOR CARGO STAFF:
D. H. Welton (*Director Cargo Services*)

J. A. Foster (*Director Cargo Sales*)
B. D. Hannigan (*Manager Cargo Services*)

Olympic Airways
6 Othonos Street, Athens 118, Greece
FLEET: 2 B707-384B; 4 B707-384C; 5 B727-284; 5 YS11; 7 DC6B; 2 Short Skyvan. On order: 3 YS11A.
SENIOR CARGO STAFF:
V. Skoulakis (*Director Cargo and Traffic*)

Overseas National Airways Inc.
Kennedy International Airport, New York, NY, USA (Charter operator)
FLEET: 4 DC8-63CF; 1 DC8-50F; 7 DC9-30F; 8 Electra Freighters. On order: 3 DC10F.
SENIOR CARGO STAFF:
Martin Train (*V.P. Cargo Services*)

Pakistan International Airlines Corp.
PIA Building, Karachi Airport, Pakistan
FLEET: 9 B707-340C; 3 B720-040B; 6 Twin Otter-6; 12 F27.
ULDs: Pallets; Containers.
SENIOR CARGO STAFF:
B. B. MacNeelance (*Cargo Sales Manager*)

Pan American World Airways Inc.
Pan Am Building, New York, 10017, USA
FLEET: 30 B747; 5 B707-121B; 16 B707-321; 59 B707-321B; 32 B707-321C; 9 B720B; 20 B727-21; 4 B727-QC. On order: 2 B747.
MAJOR CARGO TERMINALS: New York-Kennedy, London-Heathrow and major US gateway cities.
ULDs: Pallets; Igloos; Containers: B747 containers and pallets.
SENIOR CARGO STAFF:
C. Orders (*V.P. Cargo*)
D. Creswell (*Staff V.P. Cargo Sales*)

Qantas Airways Ltd.
Qantas House, 70 Hunter Street, Sydney, NSW 2000, Australia.
FLEET: 1 B747; 21 B707-338C; 2 DC4; 2 DC3; 2 HS125. On order 5 B747-239B.
MAJOR CARGO TERMINALS: Sydney, Melbourne, Perth, San Fransciso.
ULDs: Pallets; Igloos; Containers.
SENIOR CARGO STAFF:
G. G. Badgery (*Cargo Marketing Manager*)
J. T. Swann (*Manager Cargo Market Planning*)
R. J. Funnell (*Manager Cargo Sales Dept.*)

Sabena
Belgian World Airlines, 35 Rue Cardinal Mercier, Brussels 1, Belgium
FLEET: 2 B747; 6 B707-329; 6 B707-329C; 2 B727-29; 3 B727-29QC; 10 Caravelle; 1 DC6B; 1 F27.
SENIOR CARGO STAFF:
Y. Goossens (*Deputy V.P. Cargo Sales*)

SAS
Scandinavian Airlines System, Ulvsundavägen 193, Stockholm-Bromma, Sweden
FLEET: 1 B747B; 5 DC8-63; 6 DC8-55; 1 DC8-33; 19 DC9-41; 10 DC9-21; 15 Caravelle 3 (SE-210); 10 Metropolitan CV-44; 1 DC8-62AF; 1 DC8-62CF; 2 DC9-33AF.
ULDs: Containers (LD-1). On order LD-3.
SENIOR CARGO STAFF:
Frede Ahlgren Erihsen (*Director Cargo Marketing*)
Sven A. Heiding (*Manager Cargo Product and Sales Analyses*)
Helge Wimtborn (*Manager Cargo Sales Dev.*)

Seaboard World Airlines
JFK International Airport, Jamaica, New York 11430, USA
FLEET: 11 DC8-63CF; 3 DC8-55CF
ULDs: IATA Pallets; Igloos; Containers.
SENIOR CARGO STAFF:
John H. Mahoney (*V.P. Sales*)
Norman P. Blake (*V.P. Europe*)
(Berkley Square House, Berkley Square, London W1.)

SAM
Sociedad Aeronautica de Medellin Consolidada S.A., Cale 51, No. 53-54 Medellin, Colombia
FLEET: 6 Electra; 2 DC4.

South African Airways
SA Airways Centre, Johannesburg, South Africa.
FLEET: 2 B707-344A; 2 B707-344B; 4 B707-344C; 6 B727-44; 3 B727-44QC; 6 B737-244; 7 BAC Viscount 800; 3 HS748. On order: 3 B747B.
MAJOR CARGO TERMINALS: Johannesburg-Jan Smuts.
ULDs: Pallets; Containers.
SENIOR CARGO STAFF:
M. Louw (*Dept. Sales Manager Cargo*)
H. Wewege (*Assistant Cargo Sales Manager*)

Southern Air Transport Inc.
P.O. Box 1266, Miama, Floridi 33148, USA
FLEET: 2 DC6-A/B; 3 L100-20 Hercules.
SENIOR CARGO STAFF:
David Williams (*Sales Manager*)
Clyde Hart (*Cargo Manager*)

Swissair
Swiss Air Transport Company Ltd., PO Box 8058, Zurich, Switzerland.
FLEET: 2 B747-257B; 6 DC8-62; 1 DC8-62F; 1 DC8-53; 7 Convair CV990-30A; 21 DC9-32; 1 DC9-33F. On order: 6 DC10-30.
ULDs: IATA Pallets; Containers.
SENIOR CARGO STAFF:
W. Speck (*General Manager Cargo*)
W. Steinmann (*Cargo Manager*) (UK)

Texas International Airlines
P.O. Box 60188, Houston, Texas 77060, USA
FLEET: 25 Convair 600; 15 DC9.
SENIOR CARGO STAFF:
S. E. Smith (*Director Cargo Sales*)

Thai Airways International Ltd.
1043 Phaholyoithn Road, P.O. Box 1075, Bangkok 4, Thailand
FLEET: 2 DC8-33; 4 DC9-41.
SENIOR CARGO STAFF:
S. Thavithavat
I. Theander

Tradewind Airways Ltd.
Gatwick Airport, Horley, Surrey, England
FLEET: 6 Canadair CL-44.
ULDs: Pallets.
SENIOR CARGO STAFF:
Capt. E. J. Parker (*Director Operations*)
C. Jones (*Operations Superintendent*)

Trans Australian Airlines
(TAA), 50-56 Franklin Street, Melbourne, Victoria 3000, Australia.
FLEET: 6 B727-76; 8 DC9-30; 3 Electra; 16 F27; 10 Twin Otter; 10 DC3; On order: 4 B727-276; 4 DC9-30.
SENIOR CARGO STAFF:
D. D. Laurie (*General Cargo Manager*)

Trans Mediterranean Airways SAL
(TMA), P.O. Box 3018, Hamra Street, Beirut, Lebanon (Charter operator)
FLEET: 3 B707-320C; 5 DC6A/B; 1 DC-4.
MAJOR CARGO TERMINALS: Beirut.
ULDs: Pallets; Containers.
SENIOR CARGO STAFF:
Joe Hissen (*V.P. Traffic*)
Sammy Haddad (*Assistant V.P. Sales Europe*)

Transmeridian Air Cargo Ltd.
Stansted Airport, Essex, England (Charter Operator)
FLEET: 1 Conroy CL44-0; 4 Canadair CL44; On order: 1 CL44.
ULDs: Pallets; Containers.
SENIOR CARGO STAFF:
L. L. Orr (*Cargo Manager*)
D. Young (*Cargo Sales*)

Transportes Aeroes Portugueses
SARL (TAP), Rua Conde Redondo 79, Lisbon, Portugal
FLEET: 6 B707-382B; 2 B727-82QC; 1 B727-82C; 3 B727-82; 3 Caravelle; On order: 2 B747-282B.

ULDs: Pallets; Igloos; Containers.
SENIOR CARGO STAFF:
J. Fonseca Pinto (*Manager Sales*)
F. Carreira (*Manager Cargo Traffic Operations*)

Trans World Airlines Inc.
605 Third Avenue, New York, NY 10016, USA
FLEET: 17 B747-31; 56 B707-131/B; 48 B707-331/B; 15 B707-331C; 35 B727-31/QC; 37 B727-231; 19 DC9-15; 25 CV880. On órder: 2 B727-231; 22 L1011.
MAJOR CARGO TERMINALS: London-Heathrow; Frankfurt, Paris-Orly, Rome-Chiampino, New York-Kennedy, Los Angeles, Chicago, San Francisco, St. Louis, Kansas City, Boston, Philadelphia.
ULDs: Pallets; Containers; Structural; Garment Hanger and Refrigerated Igloos; B747 LD3 and LD7.

SENIOR CARGO STAFF:
M. L. Requa (*Staff V.P. Cargo Marketing*)
C. N. Cooke (*Director Freight Sales*)
Union de Transports Aeriens
(UTA), 50 Rue Arago, 92 Puteaux, France
FLEET: 4 DC8-62; 2DC8-55; 1 DC8-55F; 3 DC8-30; 2 Caravelle 10R. On order: 4 DC10-30.
MAJOR CARGO TERMINALS: Paris-Le Bourget.
SENIOR CARGO STAFF:
M. d'Aumery (*Director Freight and Past*)
United Air Lines
(UAL), P.O. Box 66100, Chicago-O'Hare International Airport, Illinois, 60666. USA
FLEET: 9 B747-22; 59 DC8; 30 DC8-61; 10 DC8-62; 15 DC8F; 29 B720-22; 86 B727-22; 36 B727-22QC; 28 B727-222; 74-B737-222; 16 Caravelle. On order: 9 B747-22; 22 DC10-10.
MAJOR CARGO TERMINALS: Chicago-O'Hare.
SENIOR CARGO STAFF:
Jack Misselhorn (*V.P. Cargo Sales*)

United Arab Airlines
(UAA), Cario International Airport, UAR
FLEET: 4 B707-466C; 4 Comet 4C; 3 Ilyshin 1118; 3 Anotov An-24B.
Viacao Aerea Sao Paulo S.A.
(VASP), VASP Building, Aeroporto de Congonhas, San Paulo, Brazil
FLEET: 2 BAC One-Eleven-422; 4 Viscount 827; 5 B737-200; 6 YSIIA-200.

Wien Consolidated Airlines Inc.
Box 3009, Fairbanks Airport, Alaska 99701, USA
FLEET: 3 B737-200C; 6 F27; 4 Twin Otter; 2 Short Skyvan; 2 DC3.
World Airways Inc.
Oakland Airport, California 94614, USA (Charter operator)
FLEET: 9 B707-373C; 6 B727-173QC; 3 DC8-36CF.
SENIOR CARGO STAFF:
R. L. Hindmarsh (*Director Cargo Dev.*)

MANUFACTURERS OF AIR CARGO EQUIPMENT

Abel Systems Ltd.
255 Coventry Road, Sheldon, Birmingham 26, England
Telephone: 021-743-0351
Demountable freight carrying bodies for road vehicles. Abel-loaders designed for BOAC to carry four standard freight pallets loaded by a 5-ft (1·52 m) tail loader.
Access Equipment Ltd.
Maylands Avenue, Hemel Hempstead, Herts, England
Telephone: 0442-2311
Hydraulic lifting cables.
Aero-Lift Corp.
1732-4th Avenue S, Seattle, Washington 98134, USA
Telephone: 206 3-0063
A low-cost method of handling aircraft containers using four portable electrically driven lifting legs.
L'Aiglon
BP 236, 49 Angers-France, St Barthélémy, France
Telephone: 88-72-94
Pallet nets, special nets, retention slings, tensioning buckles, strap hooks, fittings.
W. & T. Avery Ltd.
Soho Foundry, Birmingham 40, England
Telephone: 021-558-1112
Weighing equipment; automatic and manual; load-cell and bridge types for unit load devices and bulk parcels.
Aviation Traders (Engineering) Ltd.
Southend Municiple Airport, Essex, SS2 6XZ, England
Telephone: 0702-49471
Dual purpose turntable dollies Type S, mobile conveyors CKC 600, custom built elevators, transporters, Hylo freight loaders, Company builds Cochran Western Corp, California equipment under licence. Units in world-wide service.
Bagshawe & Co. Ltd.
Dunstable, Bedfordshire, England
Telephone: 0582-64141
Cargo terminal conveyor systems, including Tilt-Tray parcel sorting.
Barbieri Construzioni Meccaniche
Via Morane 264, 41100 Modena, Italy
Telephone: 059 30.00.18
Apron bulk loading equipment. Supplied to Alitalia.
Berthelat
BP 1, Plessis-Trevise 94, France
Elevators for pallets and containers.
BMA Braunschweigische Maschinenbauanstalt
33 Braunschweig, Am Alten Bahnhof 5, Postfach 295, Germany
Telephone: 0531 82011
Type TC 0301 Container transporter.

Container and pallet transporter, elevators of up to 15-ton (15·3-tonnes) capacity.
Brüggemann & Brand KG
5802 Wetter, Ruhr 2, W Germany, Bachsrt 22-26
Telephone: 2335-4081
Air cargo equipment in association with Transequip Inc. USA (which see).
CAE Industries Ltd.
PO Box 6166, Montreal 101, Canada
Telephone: 514 341-6780
Volumeter instrument giving instant indication of cargo unit's volume and weight.
J. Collis & Sons Ltd.
32-34 St Johns Wood Road, London NW8, England
Telephone: 01-286-8661
Roller and ball conveyors for supporting pallets, igloos and B747 lower hold containers. Wheels and rollers are acetal copolymer, balls stainless steel.
Cisa Italo Svizzera
Pero, (Milano) Italy
Telephone: 35.31.848
Manual and automated storage ano retrieval systems.
Daimler-Benz Aktiengesellschaft
700 Stuttgart 60, Postfach 202, W Germany
Special vehicle bodies for aircraft cargo ground support.
Dexion Handling Technology Ltd.
Dexion House, Empire Way, Wembley, Middlesex, England
Telephone: 01-902-1281
Storage system, pallet racking and all types of conveyors.
F. L. Douglas (Equipment) Ltd.
Village Road, Arle, Cheltenham, Glos, England
Telephone: 0242-27921
Towing tractors for freight and aircraft.
Douglas-Rownson Ltd.
Daneshill West Industrial Estate, Rutherford Road, Basingstoke, Hants, England
Telephone: 0256-3262
Cargo conveyors and sorting equipment.
Dunlop Belting Division
PO Box 7, Liverpool, L24 1UY, England
Telephone: 051:486-4551
Belts for all types of cargo conveying.
H. W. Edghill Equipment Ltd.
Hook, Nr. Basingstoke, Hants, England
Telephone: 025-672-2121
Self-propelled and towable powered belt elevators for loading bulk cargo.
Flexello Castors & Wheels Ltd.
Bath Road, Slough, Bucks, England
Telephone: 75-24121
Rollers, castors, wheels for conveyor systems and dollies, etc.
FMC Corporation, John Bean Div.

1115 Coleman Avenue, San Jose, California, USA
Telephone: 408 289-2342
B747 container, pallet loaders ordered by Swissair, KLM and SAS.
Fouche Lanquepin Carel
55 rue d'Amsterdam, Paris 8e, France
Lower hold B747 cargo and baggage containers.
Frech Bros.
Sissach, Basle, Switzerland
Telephone: 061-85-11 11
Self-propelled and towable B747 bulk cargo compartment loaders ordered by Swissair, KLM and SAS. Also dollies.
GEC-Elliott Mechanical Handling Ltd.
Beanacre Road, Melksham, Wilts, England
Telephone 02215-3481
Design and building of complete terminal cargo handling systems including a range of conveyors, retrieval equipment, etc.
Gicam
26 rue de la Pepiniere, Paris 8e, France
Telephone: 522-01-25
Design and production of terminal freight handling equipment based on the products of Cie Générale d'Enterprises Electrique, Fenwick Manutention, Gailet et Cie, Réel SA, Teleflex, Coupe, Hugot, Soretex and Levage.
Goodyear Aerospace Corporation
Akron, Ohio, USA
Cargo containers including those for B747 lower holds.
Telephone: 216 794-3893
Gough Econ Ltd.
Clough Street, Hanley, Stoke-on-Trent, ST1 4AP, England
Telephone: 0782-24401
Industrial lifts and conveyors including the Kornylak Armorbelt and belt conveyors.
Halifax Tool Co. Ltd.
West Lane, Southowram, Halifax, Yorks, England
Telephone: 0422-63441
Reliance battery and i.c. engine powered towing tractors.
Hawker Siddeley Group Ltd.
32 Duke Street, St. James's, London SW1, England
Telephone: 01-930-6177
Light alloy pallets produced for BEA.
Houchin Ltd.
Garford Works, Ashford, Kent, England
Telephone: 0233-23211
Apron freight handling equipment including pallet and igloo transporters with powered rollers, pallet dollies, and 12,000-lb (5,450-kg) capacity self-propelled elevators.

Klockner-Humboldt-Deutz AG
5 Koln 80, Postfach 80 05 09, W. Germany
Telephone: Koln 02 21
Generating sets for refrigerating containers.

Kornylak Corp.
400 Heaton Street, Hamilton, Ohio 45011 USA
Telephone: 513-863-1277
Conveyors, metal belt, wheel, roller; aircraft load/unload systems. Transdisc floor mounted clusters of plastic wheels for all-direction movement of pallet etc.

Fried-Krupp GmbH
414 Rheinhausen, Postfach 1960, W Germany
Design and building of complete cargo terminals.

Lamson Engineering Co. Ltd.
Hythe Road, London NW10, England
Telephone: 01-969-2424
Conveyors, chutes, rollers, etc.

Lancer Boss Ltd.
Leighton Buzzard, Bedfordshire, England
Telephone: 052-53-2031
Manufacturers of frontlift fork-trucks with diesel, LP gas, petrol, and electric power. Capacity range from 4,000 to 100,000 -lb (1,814 to 45,360-kg). Units in service at airports throughout the world.

Lansing Bagnall Ltd.
Kingsclere Road, Basingstoke, Hants, England
Telephone: 0256-3131
Electric fork-truck and tow tractors supplied to principle European airports. Distributors in over 60 countries.

Light Hovercraft
Felbridge Hotel, East Grinstead, Sussex, England
Air cushion pedestrian pallets, lifting up to 350-lb (160 kg).

Lintrol Systems (UK) Ltd.
Empress Road, Loughborough, England
Telephone: 050-93-4052

Lintrol Systems (France) S.a.r.l.
5 Place de Rio de Janerio, Paris 8e, France
Telephone: 227-08-60
Two associated companies formed by Herbert Morris Ltd and Jeumont-Schneider SA to develop and apply linear thrust motors. These units are installed at London-Heathrow Cargocentre.

R. A. Lister & Co. Ltd.
Dursley, Gloucestershire, England
Telephone: 048-96-2371
Diesel and electric towing trucks, mobile conveyors for bulk cargo. Equipment in service world-wide at airports.

Manufacturers Equipment Co. Ltd.
Sutton Road, Hull, HU8 ODR, England
Telephone: 0482-71791
A member company of the Rapistan Group (USA) (which see).

Marshall Handling Equipment Ltd.
Carlton, Nottingham NG4 3DY, England
Telephone: 0602-249271
Freight conveyors of advanced design using belts and rollers and lifts, including an accumulating conveyor designed to prevent parcels jamming. Portable light conveyor for bulk loading. Equipment used in four British airports.

Masters Equipment (Pty) Ltd.
53 Willarong Road, Caringbah, NSW 2229, Australia
Telephone: 524-5651
Cargo pallet transporters, conveyors and hoists for semi-automated warehouses. Equipment purchased by Qantas, Ansett, TAA, PAA, MSA, SAA and Jardines of Hong Kong.

Matbro Ltd.
Matbro House, Horley, Surrey, England
Telephone: 029-34-5522
Fork trucks with capacities from 3,000 to 45,000-lb (1,360 to 20,000-kg) built at Horley, Frome and in Northern Ireland have been supplied to nine British airports.

Mercury Truck and Tractor Co. Ltd.
Guildford, Surrey, England

Telephone: 0483-71271
Towing tractors powered by i.c. engines.

Otis Elevator Co. Ltd.
St. Claire House, 30-33 Minories, London EC3, England
Telephone: 01-481-1291
Industrial lifts and conveyors.

E. P. Pinon
54 rue Pasteur, 94 Frontenay-sous-Bois, France
Telephone: 873-10-40
Cargo dollies with fixed or roller beds and fixed or rotating platforms for powered handling of B747 containers.

Power Lifts Ltd.
Colnebrook Works, Lower High Street, Watford, Herts, England
Telephone: 92-41721
Mobile pallet build-up and lorry loading devices.

Rapistan Incorporated
507 Plymouth NE, Grand Rapids, Michigan 49505, USA
Telephone: 616 451-6200
(Branches and associated companies all over the world).
Planning and development of complete cargo terminal handling systems, including roller, wheel and belt conveyors, pallet pits, sorters, etc. Installations at London-Heathrow, Schiphol, New York-Kennedy, Paris-Orly.

Réalisations Métalliques
33 rue Jules Guesde, 92 Levallois, France
Telephone: 737-96-21
Pallet build-up equipment, dollies or self-propelled transporters, elevators.

Redman Fisher Engineering Ltd.
PO Box 12, Birmingham New Road, Tipton, Staffs, England
Telephone: 090-73-4141
Flowstack and automatic warehousing stacking and retrieving system at heights up to 60-ft (18·3-m). Automated cargo warehouses installed for Qantas.

RFD-GQ Ltd.
Catteshall Lane, Godalming, Surrey, England
Telephone: 048-68-4122
Inflatable building with air-tube structure suitable for temporary cargo storage.

Rheinische Stahlwerke Geschaftsbereich Transporttechnik
35 Kassel 2, Postfach 786, West Germany
Telephone: 0561-8011
Mobile and stationary cargo handling equipment.

Sadler Conveyor & Equipment Ltd.
1845 William Street, Montreal 105, Quebec, Canada
Telephone: 931-4271
Warehouse transport system including conveyors, strapping tables, two or three way roller transporter and mobile belt conveyors.

Carl Schenck Maschinenfabrik GmbH
D-61 Darmstadt, Postfach 4018, West Germany
Telephone: 06151-8821
Terminal parcel conveying systems.

Sechilienne
234 rue du Faubourg St. Honore, 75 Paris 8e, France
Telephone: 227-85-26
Tracma tractors are now in service at over 50 airports and airfields. They range from 23-hp (23CV) to 90-hp (90CV). Company also markets the large Dennis-Mercury aircraft towing vehicles.

Sovarrel, GIE
8 avenue d'Alouette, 37-Tours-01, France
Telephone: 53-40-94 Tours
Ground handling equipment including high loaders, and lifting platforms, transporters, dollies.

Transequip Ltd.
5438 West 104th Street, Los Angeles, California 90045, USA
Telephone: 213-641-3847

European Head Office: Transequip Ltd.
Browells Lane, Feltham, Middlesex, England
Telephone: 01-890-0788
Pallet racks; truck roller platforms, container dollies, pallet dollies, tie-down equipment.

Trastecnica
20093 Cologno Monzese (Milano), Via Brunelleschi 7, Italy
Telephone: 91-23-816
A member of the company of the Rapistan Group (USA). Conveyors installed at Rome-Fiumicino, and Milan-Malpensa.

C. F. Taylor (Metal Workers) Ltd.
Molly Millars Lane, Wokingham, Berks, RG11 2RY. England
Telephone: Wokingham 2500
On-board cargo hoist lifts standard pallets without external aid. Designed for use with military 707s the system can be adapted for commercial aircraft.

Teleflex Manutention
BP No. 29, 94 Ivry-sur-Seine, France
Telephone: 672-45-87
Diploducus conveying system for parcels

Towers (Sunderland) Ltd.
Framwellgate Moor, Durham, England
Telephone: 0385-5114
Patented B747 container transporter pallet with roller top deck and transporter.

Trepel Airport Equipment
6202 Wiesbaden-Biebrich, Am Schlosspark 54a, West Germany
Telephone: Wiesbaden 65799

Trepel Systems Inc.
1 Congress Square, Portland, Maine, USA 04101, USA
Telephone: 207-722-1973
Cargo hydraulic platform trucks; special fixed aircraft loaders terminal lifting-aids, rollers, etc. Company equipment in built in Britain, Italy and Spain. Products in world-wide service.

Tridair Industries (Cargomatic Division)
717 Main Street, Westbury, L.I. New York, 11590, USA
Telephone: 516-333-9510

Tridair Industries Ltd.
Tamain Way, Green Lane, Hounslow, Middlesex, England
Telephone: 01-572-0321
Cargomatic pallet and container loaders, transporters, dollies, trailers, for all aircraft including wide bodied jets. Ball mats, roller systems, pallets, igloos, baggage containers, nylon webbing restraints, service trucks. Design and manufacture of cargo terminal system and equipment. Products in world-wide service.

Tri-Wall Containers Ltd.
1 Mount Street, London W1, England
Telephone: 01-493-4311
Fibreboard IATA containers.

Vereinigte Flugtechnische Werke-Fokker GmbH
28 Bremen 1, Hunefeldstr 1/5, West Germany
Telephone: 0421-5181
Airgate, pallet and container fixed roller track, transporters dollies, lower hold containers.

Wessex Industries Ltd.
Market Street, Poole, Dorset, England
Telephone: 020-13-2626
Electric operated towing and fork lift vehicles, pallet dollies.

Wollard Aircraft Equipment Inc.
6950 NW 77th Court, Miami, Florida 33166, USA
Telephone: 305-885-4741
Loading equipment for aircraft including the low-cost CLT-581 standard vehicle adaption for B747 lower lobe containers; TM-563 standard vehicle transporter and self-propelled baggage and bulk cargo conveyors. Units in world-wide service.

A number of publications and essential documents are available to shippers of goods by air. A cross section of these, together with other documents of interest to shipping departments, are given below. Addresses of publishers are grouped at the end of the review.

GENERAL:

Economics of Air Cargo Carriage and Service Published by IATA effective Jan. 1970. Price $5.00 from IATA Chief Economist's Office, Geneva, Switzerland. A discussion by the IATA Financial and Economic studies sub-committee on the economic factors influencing air cargo transport.

The Freight Forwarder. Published by the Economic Development Committee for the Movement of Exports and available from Her Majesty's Stationary Office price 55½p which includes UK inland postage only. A report of studies made on British Shipping and Forwarding Agents.

Metrication of UK Overseas Trade, Tariffs, Documents and Statistics. Free from the National Economic Development Office. An examination of the problems involved in the effect of metrication on the UK overseas trade.

Air Cargo Distribution by Paul Jackson and William Brackenridge. Published by Gower Press price £4.00. Two airline cargo consultants discuss the marketing benefits of air freight.

World Air Transport Statistics. Published by IATA. Contains figures, mainly on an airline by airline basis, of cargo and passenger traffic.

SITPRO Report 1970. Published by

Printed Material of Interest to Air Shippers

SITPRO. Available from Her Majesty's Stationary Office, UK postage paid £1.10½. A report on a 2-year study of the affect of documentation on International Trade.

Safety Restricted Articles Regulations (14th Edition). Published by IATA, effective June 1 1971. In English and French. Available from: French Edition IATA, Montreal, $US 6.00. English Edition from International Aeradio Ltd, £2.70. Both charges cover postage and amendments. This document details packing methods, internationally accepted labelling minimum net quantity per package and handling requirements for 2,000 commodities likely to cause damage if they escape through inadequate packing or because of the effect of high altitude and temperature change.

Quick Reference Guide. Radioactive Materials (3rd Edition). Published by IATA effective June 1 1970. IATA price $US1.00 or from International Aeradio Ltd, 43p.

Labels for Restricted Articles. Purchaseable from International Aeradio Ltd and from the US Bureau of Explosives. For afixing to consignments of restricted goods as required by the IATA Restricted Articles Manual.

Manual on the Carriage of Live Animals by Air. (2nd Edition). Published by IATA, effective December 1970. IATA price $US3.50 or from International Aeradio £1.75. Both charges cover postage and amendments. This manual is concerned with the safety, welfare and care of all animals when conveyed by air.

UNIT LOAD DEVICES

Register of Container & Pallets (4th Edi-

tion). Published by IATA, effective May 1 1970. Available from IATA price $US 6.00 or from International Aeradio Ltd, £2.75. Both charges cover postage and amendments. This document lists the different types of Unit Load Devices used by IATA member airlines of those registered by users. It provides detailed information on non-aircraft containers (units for which individual restraints are not provided in the aircraft) available to non-member—manufacturers, agents, shippers etc.

Aircraft Unit Load Devices Manual. Published by IATA, price $US6.00. Detailed information of Aircraft Unit Load Devices. Those lock into aircraft restraint systems.

ADDRESSES:

Bureau of Explosives, 1920 L Street NW, Washington DC 20036, USA.

Economic Development Committee for Movement of Exports. (See National Economic Development Office below).

Gower Press Ltd, 13 Bloomsbury Square, London WC1, England.

Her Majesty's Stationary Office, High Holborn, London WC1, England.

International Aeradio Ltd, Aeradio House. Hayes Rd, Southall, Middlesex, England.

International Air Transport Association, 1155 Mansfield St, Montreal, Quebec, Canada.

National Economic Development Office, Milbank Tower, 21/41 Milbank, London SW1, England.

SITPRO (UK Committee for the Simplification of International Trade Procedures), Thames House, Milbank, London SW1, England.

TRANSPORT AIRCRAFT

Among the many air cargo trends which were emerging at the turn of the decade the direction of freighter aircraft purchasing proved to be a negative one. Ordering of special cargo-only or convertible versions of long-range jets almost halted. The reasons were simple enough. By 1969/70 airlines had assessed, with some accuracy, the effect of the new generation wide-bodied jets on future cargo carrying capacity when set against the likely growth of business. They found that for some time ahead the new generation passenger transports due to enter service increasingly on world routes through the 70s would be able to absorb much of the expected new cargo traffic. There was little need for further specialised freighter aircraft for a few years.

Most operators of the new jets did not want to get involved in additional expenditure whilst they still had to find about £9 million for each Boeing 747, for example. They were anxious that space in this aircraft and in the slightly smaller DC-10 and L-1011 should be fully employed. All airlines needed a rapid return on their investments.

All three types have large underfloor (called the lower-lobe by Boeing) holds which can be filled quickly with prepacked cargo containers. A 747 can carry in its lower-lobe spaces about half the total payload of all-cargo 707s. The impact of the wide-bodied jets will, therefore, be considerable when by the mid-70s they are serving international routes in large numbers.

For many airline cargo departments the new jets have provided a second wind. Investment in special cargo equipment, new ground equipment and buildings has been fairly heavy. But more to the financial point the freighters almost without exception lose money. As a result there has, for some

This South African Airways' cargo lift with a capacity of 5,900 kg (12,000 lb) is about to be raised to accept a full pallet load from Boeing 707 'Port Elizabeth' at Johannesberg.

time been a move to get cargo operations back wholly into passenger aircraft holds where operating costs are shared and therefore not so frightening.

The new jets will make a considerable impact on this philosophy. One study claims that a 747 can be flown across the Atlantic without passengers and still cover its operating costs with full cargo spaces. Statements

of this type whilst needing some qualification give an impression of the value of cargo in modern aircraft operations.

Development of cargo aircraft orders during the coming years can be expected to follow a traditional pattern set by the early jets. Airlines will be content with their large-hold passenger versions now coming into service until their capacity becomes inadequate for the business on offer. Then convertible and cargo versions of the 1960 generation jets will appear again followed by convertible and cargo versions of the new aircraft. The speed at which this happens will depend largely on the rate of trade recovery.

This should lead to the next stage when first of the new generation of large capacity true jet freighter is introduced. At the moment there is only one serious contender for this title, the Lockheed L-500 a commercial version—yet to be built—of the big US military C-5A freighter. Lockheed has been hard at work selling the civil aircraft partly in the hope of continuing production on a reasonable scale after the present USAF order for 81 tapers off. This large aeroplane weighing 374 tonnes (364 tons) fully loaded was designed uncompromisingly as a military freighter. It requires little change, Lockheed considers, to produce from it the world's first true long-range, high capacity commercial jet freighter.

Current Types

There has been little innovation among current types of aircraft in the past year. BEA may have established a trend in its conversion of nine of its turboprop passenger Vanguards to cargo carrying Merchantmen. These largely written-down aircraft are being modified at a cost of about £200,000. Fitted with a large side loading door and strengthened floor the Merchantman can carry 20 tons over medium distances.

The Pan American cargo staging area at Kennedy Airport, New York, was designed and built by Dexion Inc, the USA subsidiary of Dexion-Comino International Ltd. The system has a capacity of 252 containers in 18 conveyor lanes

Some new life may be given to the ageing Canadair CL-44s with a conversion by Conroy Aircraft Corporation of California. With a structurally simple modification to the fuselage the company provides twice the volume in the cabin. This extra capacity should overcome one difficulty often experienced by aircraft operators. With many commodities their volume fills the aircraft long before reaching its permitted payload.

With the Conway conversion there should be plenty of room to take light bulky loads in the 64 kg/m³ (4 lb/ft³) class and reach a reasonable payload.

In summary the current cargo aircraft market is in a hiatus. It is unlikely to pick up until world trade improves as air cargo begins to spill over from the wide bodied passenger jets.

TRANSPORT AIRCRAFT IN SERVICE

The following offers a catalogue of the major transport aircraft in commercial service world-wide, and which aircraft are engaged in day-to-day mixed-cargo or all-cargo operations on an increasing scale. The catalogue follows the same form as in our first edition, but has been amplified and updated. Our catalogue is intended to serve as a guide to these aircraft and does not contain detailed specifications, for such detailed information is to be found, of course, in our fellow volume *Jane's All the World's Aircraft*, which requires no further description here.

Only those aircraft designed before the advent of the wide-bodied jets, as freighters or convertible cargo/passenger types are included in this survey. New large capacity aircraft of the Boeing 747, Lockheed 1011 and McDonnell Douglas DC-10 although not conforming strictly to the convertible or cargo rule are included because their underfloor (lower lobe) cargo capacity is very large and it will accept goods on standard pallets or in special containers.

FOUR ENGINES—TURBOJET

Boeing 707-320C Series
THE BOEING COMPANY (USA)

This cargo or convertible cargo/passenger version of the long-range Boeing 707 is in operation with many airlines round the world. Its large cargo door can be fitted with a self-loading device of Boeing design. Max payload (all cargo) 41,657 kg (91,839 lb). Econ cruise speed 886 kmh (550 mph). Range for max payload with no reserves 6,317 km (3,925 miles).

BRITISH AIRCRAFT CORPORATION LTD (UK) BAC VC-10

Several of the Standard and Super versions of this long-range jet have been fitted with large cargo doors for commercial use. Super VC-10s with these doors were built for East African Airways and details below are for the Model 1154 as supplied to that airline. This version has the floor strengthened from forward of the wing for mixed cargo/passenger operation. Typical cargo payload in main cabin with 12 half-pallets is 9,070 kg (20,000 lb). Econ cruise speed 886 kmh (550 mph). Range with max payload 7,600 km (4,720 miles).

Freight being loaded on Aer Lingus-Irish Boeing 707 St. Brigid at Dublin Airport.

McDonnell Douglas DC-8F

DOUGLAS AIRCRAFT COMPANY, DIVISION OF McDONNELL DOUGLAS CORPORATION (USA)

A long range jet transport in service with airlines round the world. Five variants, Models 54, 55, 61 62, and 63 are available as combination or all cargo versions and these are fundamentally similar to the DC-8-50 and DC-8-60 Series passenger versions. Details below are for Model 55 freighter. Max payload capacity 43,219 kg (95,282 lb). Hold has provision for quick loading of 13 pallets. Max cruise speed 932 kmh (579 mph). Max still air range, no payload, 11,410 km (7,090 miles).

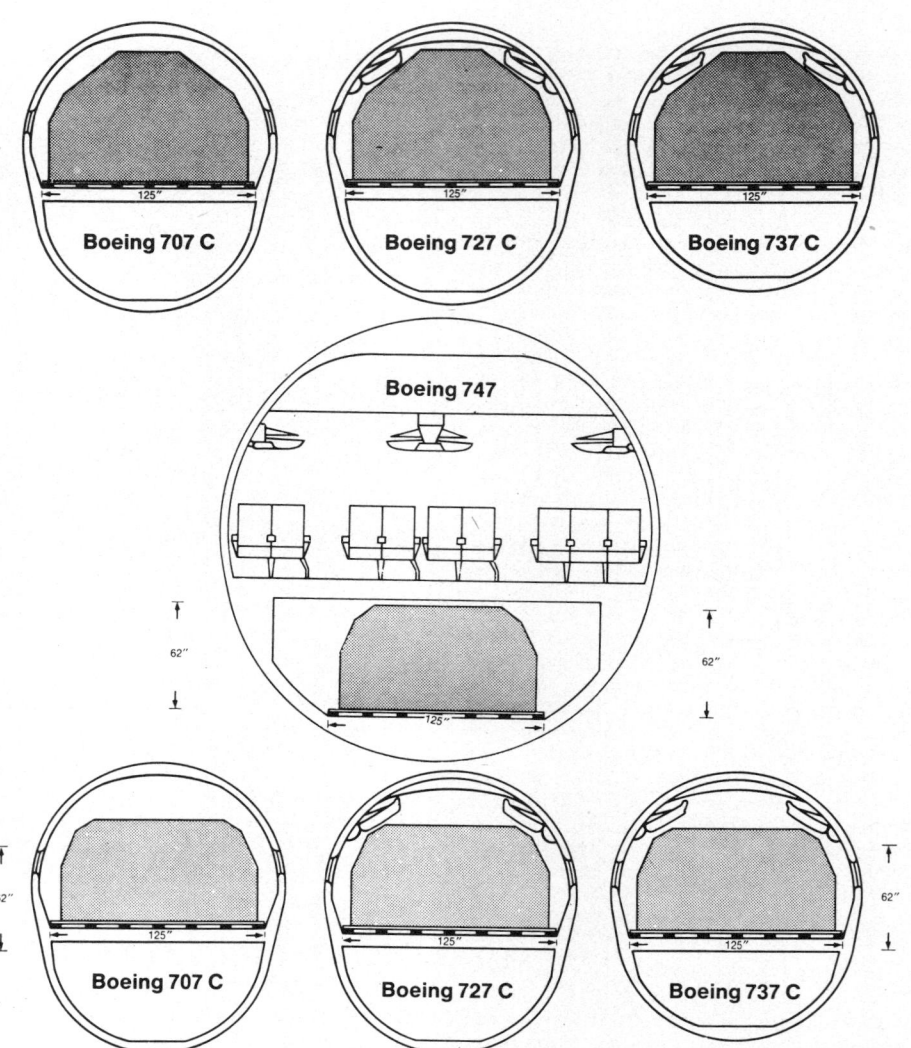

The importance of standard load carrying devices is illustrated by these drawings showing in the top three sections how a 224 cm × 317.5 cm (88 in × 125 in) pallet is used by Lufthansa in its unit cargo carrying Boeing 707C, 727C and 737C aircraft with a 203 cm (80 in) height. In lower illustration the same size pallet is shown with a 157.5 cm (62 in) load height in a 747 lower-lobe hold and in the 707C, 727C and 737C.

Modern air cargo terminals have taken all the heavy humping out of warehouse work. As goods arrive at Eastern Airlines Atlanta terminal ramp servicemen—in white—read essential information from each box and type the details in to a computer memory. In the foreground a console operator keeps check on the correct operation of the terminal.

Japan Air Lines operates a fleet of five all-cargo DC-8's in addition to a mixed fleet of Douglas, Boeing and Convair passenger jets. The airline has also ordered eight Boeing 747's.

Most airlines tend to schedule their freighters for night operations as this view of Lufthansa's Boeing 727-30C "Hagen" shows as an Igloo full of boxes is moved to the terminal.

As the world's first commercial operator of Boeing 747s Pan American is also the most experienced at handling their baggage and freight containers. Quick turnround of these wide bodied jets calls for heavy expenditure on ground equipment. Here dolly trains and transporters are delivering half-width lower lobe containers to Clipper Red Jacket.

Lightweight Brooks & Perkins containers capable of carrying nearly 800 kg ((1 759 lb) are run from their dollies to the lower hold of an Eastern Air Lines DC-8

First of the automatic air cargo terminals to be opened in Europe the SAS building at Stockholm covers 12,700 m² (139,000 sq ft) and can handle 600 tons a day.

FOUR ENGINES—TURBOPROP

Antonov AN-11

(USSR)

Freight carrying version of the An-10 with an entirely re-designed rear fuselage and tail unit. Loading ramp for freight and vehicles built-in to rear fuselage. Loading gantry with 2,300 kg (5,070 lb) capacity built-in. Max payload 20,000 kg (44,090 lb). Normal cruising speed 550 kmh (342 mph). Range with 10,000 kg (22,050 lb) cargo plus one hour reserve, 3,400 km (2,110 miles).

Cargo "igloo" being loaded aboard Seaboard World DC-8F Jet Trader series.

The Aviation Traders' pallet transporter will carry up to 15,000 lb (6 804 kg)

A Houchin pallet lift alongside one of BEA's Merchantmen.

Tridair Industries developed the Cargomatic 1140, a 747 container loader for lower-lobe baggage and cargo. It lifts 4,536 kg (10,000 lb) a distance of 3.34 m (11 ft).

BAC Vanguard

BRITISH AIRCRAFT CORPORATION LIMITED (UK) Short/medium-range transport. in service with BEA. Max payload 16,783 kg (37,000 lb). Econ cruising speed 676 kmh (420 mph) Range with max payload, no reserves, 2,945 km (1,830 miles). Nine of BEA's fleet of Vanguard passenger aircraft are being converted by Aviation Traders Ltd and BEA to all-cargo aircraft named *Merchantman*. The first *Merchantman* conversion flew for first time late 1969. Large cargo doors are being fitted to the port side of the fuselage, together with strengthened cargo flooring. The hydraulically-operated freight door is 3·48 m (11 ft 7 in) long by 2·03 m (6 ft 8 in) deep. Max freight load is 19,504 kg (43,000 lb).

BAC Britannia

BRITISH AIRCRAFT CORPORATION LIMITED (UK) Medium/long-range transport used for passenger, mixed-traffic and all-cargo services. Some aircraft incorporate side-loading cargo doors. The Aviation Traders conversion of the 300/310 Series Britannia introduced a large hydraulically-operated door, measuring 1·93 m (6 ft 4 in) × 3·12 m (10 ft 3 in). The cargo handling system accepts pallets, and the total volume available is approx 133 m³ (4,700 cu ft). Max disposable load 30,750 kg (67,890 lb).

Based in Beirut, Trans-Mediterranean Airways provides one of the most successful air tramping and scheduled freight services in the world. Its fleet of piston-engined DC-6s and DC-4s has been supplemented by a Boeing 707 320 Cs

Aero Spacelines Guppy Series
AERO SPACELINES INCORPORATED (USA)

This company has specialised in the development of Boeing B-337 Stratocruiser aircraft turning them into freighters capable of carrying large single-items of cargo unacceptable to other aircraft. Typical of these loads are rocket motors and aircraft wings. Details are for the Commercial Super Guppy. Nose is hinged to give access. Max payload 18,597 kg (41,000 lb). Cruise speed 450 kmh (280 mph).

ANTONOV AN-12 (USSR)

A medium range cargo version of the AN-10 this aircraft has been supplied to a number of airlines. A freight loading ramp is incorporated in the underside of the rear fuselage. Max payload 20,000 kg (44,090 lb). Floor max loading 1,500 kg/m² (307 lb/sq ft). Normal cruise speed 550 kmh (342 mph). Range with reserves and half max cargo load 3,400 km (2,110 miles).

Freight being loaded on a Aer Lingus-Irish Boeing jet at Shannon Airport.

BAC Viscount
BRITISH AIRCRAFT CORPORATION (WEYBRIDGE) LTD (UK)

Although this aircraft has been used as a pure freighter from time to time after removing passenger seats it could hardly be called a convertible or freighter until Aer Lingus contracted Scottish Aviation Ltd to modify four 808s as cargo/or cargo/ passenger carriers. A 2·26 m (7·4 ft) cargo opening has two doors, floor members and forward fuselage are strengthened and pallet rollers fitted. Up to nine pallets can be carried each measuring 1·35 m × 2·24 m (53 in × 88 in) and each having a load capacity of 1,074 kg (2,368 lb). Max freight load limited by zero fuel weight is 6,750 kg (14,900 lb). Two of the Aer Lingus aircraft were sold to Air Commerz in mid-1970.

Canadair Forty Four (CL-44)
CANADAIR LIMITED (CANADA)

Long-range transport aircraft, based on the Britannia design but fitted with swing-tail for rear loading of large loads. One or two side-loading cargo doors. Cargo capacity, 28,725 kg (63,272 lb). Cruising speed 621 kmh (386 mph). Max range with 27,970 kg (61,664 lb) payload and reserves, 5,254 km (3,260 miles). Unit-load containers for the belly-hold of this aircraft are used by some operators.

Bagshawe tilt-tray parcel sorting conveyor at the BEA Cargocentre London-Heathrow. Electronically controlled pneumatic discharge mechanisms automatically route a parcel to its selected chute

HS Argosy
HAWKER SIDDELEY AVIATION LIMITED (UK)

Short/medium-range all-cargo aircraft with nose and tail "straight-through" loading. Max payload 14·095 kg (31,080 lb). Econ. cruising speed 451 kmh (280 mph). Range with max payload and allowances 780 km (485 miles). HS "Rollamat" pallet/roller conveyor loading system is used by some operators.

The McDonnell Douglas DC-10 will be one of the American "airbuses" now under development, another being Lockheed's 1011 Trister. One version, the DC-10F, will be equipped with an 8½ ft × 11½ ft cargo door which swings up on the fuselage to permit large unit loading. The cabin will hold 27 standard 88 × 108 inch cargo pallets.

BEA carries more cargo within Europe than any other airline. Most of its flights are scheduled for the dark hours

Lockheed L 188 Electra
LOCKHEED AIRCRAFT CORPORATION (USA)

This short/medium haul aircraft is being produced as a convertible or pure cargo version by Lockheed Aircraft Service Co, California. Airframe is strengthened to increase the no-fuel weight by 1,814 kg (4,000 lb) to a maximum of 40,823 kg (90,000 lb). A renewed floor structure accepts pallet loading to 15,875 kg (35,000 lb) or high weight concentrated bulk cargo.

Cargo being loaded into one of Northwest Orient's Boeing 727's.

Lockheed L100 Hercules
LOCKHEED-GEORGIA COMPANY (USA)

Medium/long-range transport. In service with all-cargo operators. Rear, "straight-through" loading. Integral loading ramp. Details are for L100-20 which is a current production version with fuselage stretched by 2·53 m (8 ft 4 in). **Max payload with standard fuel 22,370 kg (49,317 lb). Max cruising speed 603 kmh (375 mph). Range with max payload, with reserves 4,120 km (2,560 miles). This aircraft is capable of transporting standard 8 ft × 8 ft road-rail containers.**

The American firm Aero Spacelines was founded for the sole purpose of transporting large and unwieldy items, and in particular rocket and space vehicle casings. The success of the company has come from contracts from the National Aeronautics and Space Agency, to fly Saturn and other rocket parts to Cape Kennedy in the specially-modified stratocruiser aircraft. Re-designed and rebuilt stratocruisers, named Guppy, Mini Guppy and Super-Guppy have made this air transport operation feasible. A Mini Guppy is pictured being loaded with body panels for the Boeing 747 aircraft, to be transported to the assembly plant at Everett, Washington.

FOUR ENGINED-PISTON

ATL-98 Carvair
AVIATION TRADERS (ENGINEERING) LIMITED (UK)

Short/medium-range, nose-loading transport designed by Aviation Traders and based on the Douglas DC-4 (C-54) passenger transport. Used for car-ferry and general cargo/charter work. **Max payload 8,444 kg (18,615 lb). Econ cruising speed 334 km (207 mph) at 10,000 ft. Range with max payload, no allowances, 3,700 km (2,300 miles).**

Douglas DC-4, Douglas DC-6, Douglas DC-7
THE DOUGLAS AIRCRAFT COMPANY COMPONENT OF MCDONNELL DOUGLAS CORPORATION (USA)

A series of transport aircraft developed from the original Douglas DC-4 design, but of increasingly greater overall dimensions, power, performance and capacity. Large numbers of these aircraft are in service all over the world for mixed-traffic and all-cargo operations. The final Douglas piston-engine transport variant was the DC-7F Speed-freighter, which was a factory conversion using the airframe and engines of the DC-7 Series. This aircraft has two large cargo doors and a strengthened floor. **Max payload 17,237 kg (38,000 lb) at 563 kmh (350 mph).**

Fork-lift trucks make light work of cargo from Pont d'Avignon one of the British Air Ferries Carvairs.

Lockheed Constellation, Super Constellation, Constellation Starliner
THE LOCKHEED AIRCRAFT CORPORATION (USA)

As with the Douglas series of piston-engined transports, numerous developments of the Constellation were produced and large numbers of the type remain in service. Performance and capacity vary considerably according to variant, but some Constellations have two large side-loading cargo doors and can lift loads of over 20 tons. Max cruising speed (L-1049G), 595 kmh (370 mph); L-1649A Starliner, 550 kmh (342 mph). Range, up to a max of 11,585 kmh (7,200 miles).

THREE ENGINES—TURBOJET

Boeing 727

THE BOEING COMPANY (USA)

The short/medium range three engine jet is produced in several versions including a freighter, a quick change and a convertible. A large number have been sold to operators all over the world. Details are for Series 100 QC (Quick Change). Passenger seats and gallies are palletised to enable conversion from all passenger to pure freighter to be made in less than 30 minutes. Max payload (structure) 19,958 kg (44,000 lb). Econ cruise speed 917 kmh (570 mph). Range with max payload including reserves 3,058 km (1,900 miles). Boeing models 707-320C, 727-100C and 727-100QC utilise the same pallets and handling systems. The 727-100 Series accepts 8 pallets.

Loading air cargo into Icelandair Boeing 727C at Glasgow Airport.

TWIN ENGINED—TURBOJET

Boeing 737

THE BOEING COMPANY (USA)

Short-range transport in large-scale service. Again, various series of the basic aircraft are available, including convertible and QC (quick change) variants. Details are for the 737-200QC which has a fuselage lengthened by 1·93 m (6 ft 4 in). Max payload 15,820 kg (34,880 lb). Max cruising speed 915 kmh (568·5 mph). Econ cruising speed at 9,150 m (30,000 ft) Mach 0·78. Range with max payload, including reserves 3,435 km (2,135 miles). The C and QC versions of the Boeing 737 are able to carry the standard pallets and utilise the standard loading systems for the Boeing 727 and 707 aircraft. The QC aircraft are quickly converted from passenger to cargo by means of palletised passenger seats and galleys.

One of Alitalia's two DC8 freightliners

BAC One-Eleven

BRITISH AIRCRAFT CORPORATION LTD (UK)

BAC has completed work on the design of a 304·5 cm wide × 178 cm high (120 × 80 in) hydraulic freight door which can be retrofitted to all One Elevens. In addition a removable 820 kg (1,807 lb) overlay floor which connects to existing seat attachments points makes it possible for any operator to convert current aircraft into convertible versions relatively quickly without special floor strengthening. The following details are for converted 500 series. Seven standard 224 × 274 × 137 cm (88 × 108 × 54 in) pallets can be carried to give a loaded capacity of 11,900 kg (26,190 lb) in 7·8 m³ (276 cu ft). A moveable bulkhead allows increased operating flexibility with mixed cargo/passenger layouts a typical one is for 54 seats plus 2,850 kg (6,280 lb) in 10 containers. Empty operating weight 24,300 kg (53,482 lb); total freight payload main cabin plus underfloor holds, 11,900 kg (26,190 lb); range at max load 1,705 km (1,060 miles).

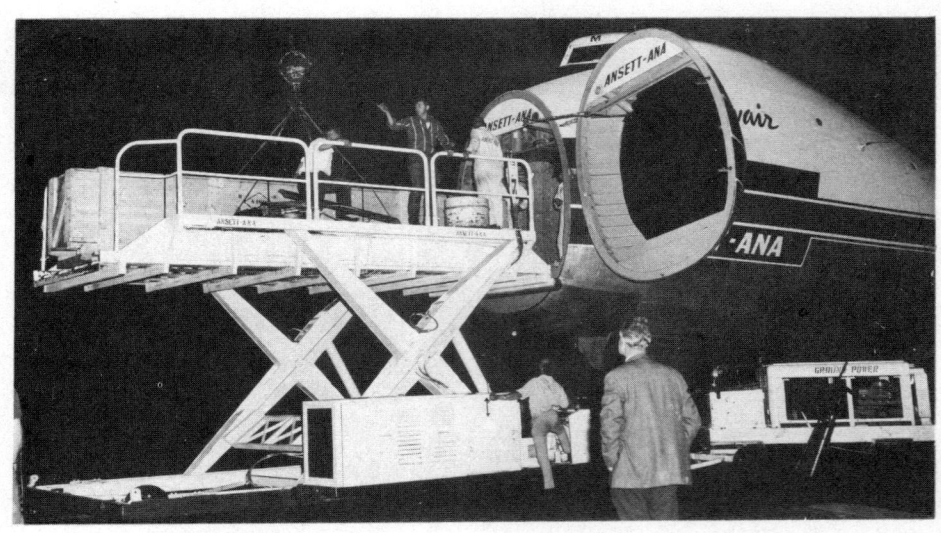

Ansett-ANA has three Carvair freighters in regular service between Sydney, Melbourne and Adelaide. Largest single consignment carried in Australia, a 6,720 kg (14,785 lb) crankshaft, was carried 2,850 km (1,770 miles) by one of these aircraft.

Douglas DC-9

THE DOUGLAS AIRCRAFT COMPANY COMPONENT OF MCDONNELL DOUGLAS CORPORATION (USA)

Short/medium-range transport in wide-scale operation. Several series are in service, including all-cargo, mixed-traffic and convertible types. The Series 30 and 40 have longer fuselages. Details are for Series 40, Max payload 15,510 kg (34,195 lb). Max cruising speed 903 kmh (561 mph). Range with reserves 1,918 km (1,192 miles). The Series 40 cargo version is able to carry eight full cargo pallets and two half pallets.

SE 210 Caravelle and Super Caravelle

SOCIÉTÉ NATIONALE INDUSTRIELLE AEROSPATIALE:

Short/medium-range transport in large-scale service. Passenger and mixed traffic versions are operated. Details are for Caravelle 11R. Max payload 9,095 kg (20,050 lb). Max cruising speed 800 kmh (500 mph). Range with max payload including reserves 2,300 km (1,430 miles). The Caravelle 11R has a specially strengthened fuselage with 9 m (29 ft 6 in) of floor strengthened to 1,000 kg/m² (205 lb/sq ft) and seven cargo attachment rails.

TWIN ENGINED —TURBOPROP

Antonov An-24
(USSR)

Short-range feeder-line transport. Several versions in service, of which the An-24T is equipped as a specialised freighter. Loading via belly freight door at rear of cabin with powered winch of 1,500 kg (3,300 lb) capacity. Max payload 4,612 kg (10,168 lb). Cruising speed 450 kmh (280 mph). Range with max payload, with reserves 1,300 km (807 miles).

DHC-6 Twin Otter
THE DE HAVILLAND AIRCRAFT OF CANADA LIMITED (CANADA)

Short-range STOL transport. A true utility aircraft, available in both land and float plane configurations, and in world wide service. Details are for Series 300. Max payload for 160 km (100 miles) range, more than 2,313 kg (5,100 lb). Max cruising speed 338 kmh (210 mph). Range with max fuel, including reserves, 1,521 km (945 miles).

Fokker F.27 Friendship
FOKKER-VFW N.V.

Short/medium-range transport in world wide service. Some versions fitted with quick-change interior with roller tracks, palletised seats and large cargo door for side-loading. Details are for the F.27 500/600. Max payload (weight limited) 5,565 kg (12,270 lb). Cruising speed 470 kmh (292 mph). Range with max payload, included reserves, 870 km (540 miles).

Fairchild Hiller F-27/FH-227
FAIRCHILD HILLER CORPORATION (USA)

This series of aircraft consists of versions of the Fokker F.27 built under licence. Dimensions and performance figures are generally similar to those quoted for the F.27 but the aircraft differ slightly in fuselage length, position of cargo door, etc.

FH-227D

This latest development of the 227 Series was certificated December 1967 and is a convertible version with a large electrically operated cargo door (dimensions as for F-27). A freight door kit is available for retrofit to earlier 227 models. Max payload is approximately 12,600 lb (5,715 kg) depending on configuration.

HS 748 SERIES 2C-1
HAWKER SIDDELEY AVIATION LIMITED (UK)

Short/medium-range transport in large scale service. Alternative internal layouts for mixed traffic or all-cargo. Max payload 5,910 kg (12,963 lb). Max cruising speed 462 kmh (287 mph). Range with max payload, including reserves, 1,110 km (690 miles).

LET L-410
LET NARODNI PODNIK (Let National Corporation (Czechoslovakia)

A light short range turboprop transport designed for passenger or freight services. Max payload 1,853 kg (4,085 lb). Max cruise speed 375 kmh (233 mph). Range with 1,400 kg (3,085 lb) payload 760 km (470 miles).

NAMC YS-11
NIHON KOKUKI SEIZO KABUSHJKI KAISHA (JAPAN)

Short/medium-range transport in production and service. Passenger, mixed-traffic and all-cargo configurations are available. Details apply to the YS-11A-300 mixed-traffic type. Max payload, 6,190 kg (13,646 lb). Max cruising speed, 469 kmh (291 mph). Range with max payload, no reserves, 1,090 km (680 miles). The all-cargo YS-11A-400 has a volume of 81 m³ (2,860 cu ft), a reinforced floor and a 3·05 m (10 ft 0 in) wide × 1·83 m (6 ft 0 in) high cargo door in the port side of aft fuselage.

Fokker Friendships are used all over the world for mixed passenger/cargo and all-cargo duties. Several cargo versions of the aircraft are built, including the Combiplane cargo or combined cargo/passenger craft.

Eastern Airlines' staff unpack baggage from a 747 underfloor container.

Aérospatiale N262

SOCIÉTÉ NATIONALE INDUSTRIELLE AÉRO-
SPATIALE

Short-haul light transport aircraft in production and service. Cruising speed 375 kmh
(233 mph). Max payload 3,270 kg (7,209 lb).
Range with max payload, including reserves,
915 km (565 miles).
cluding reserves, 915 km (565 miles).

Short SC.7 Skyvan

SHORT BROS & HARLAND LIMITED (NORTHERN
IRELAND)

Light transport. In service and quantity production. This aircraft features a full-width,
rear cargo door for "straight through"
loading, and is cleared for use on unprepared
airstrips. Max payload 2,085 kg (4,600 lb).
Max cruising speed 323 kmh (201 mph).
Range with 1,815 kg (4,000 lb) payload
including reserves, 296 km (184 miles).
The Skyvan is capable of accepting palletised
loads on a roller floor and is adaptable for
mixed cargo-passenger operations.

Braniff has a fleet of 26 jet freighters or QC versions.

TWIN ENGINED PISTON

Beechcraft Model 99

BEECH AIRCRAFT CORPORATION (USA)
Light passenger, mixed-traffic or freight
transport in service with commuter and
charter operators. A large cargo door can be
fitted. Range with max fuel and 816 kg
(1,800 lb) payload, 1,770 km (1,100 miles).

An optional under fuselage baggage/cargo
pod with a volume of 1·01 m³ (35·5 cu ft) and
structural capacity of 363 kg (800 lb) is
available. Normal cruising speed 406 kmh
(252 mph).

BN-2A Islander

BRITTEN-NORMAN LTD (UK)
Light feeder-line transport in large-scale
production and service. Max payload 1,043
kg (2,300 lb). Range with max payload,
including reserves, 670 km (425 miles).
Econ cruising speed, 249 kmh (155 mph).

To these types must be added the very large
numbers of single and twin piston-engined
aircraft—AN-2, DC-3, Martin 202, Convair
240/440, Commando, Otter, Il-14 and so on·
which are in service with domestic and charter
operators. The part played by these aircraft

is considerable in terms of traffic and trade.
General aviation is expanding in many
parts of the world and a new breed of larger
and higher performance twins has been
developed for the commuter, feeder line and
charter markets. Types such as the Twin

Otter, Islander, Beech 99, Cessna 402, Navajo,
Jetstream and Skyvan offer better economics,
short and rough field capability and extra-
ordinary commercial versatility. Their cargo
capacity is considerable and they are able to
cope with many of the IATA containers.

FUTURE TRANSPORT AIRCRAFT

There is little doubt that a 'new age' commenced with the introduction of the first of
the ultra-large capacity jet transport aircraft
in 1969–70. This seemingly ponderous statement can be explained by simply saying that
for the first time in air transport history really
large cargo capacity will be offered to shippers,
and for the first time also the airborne container will come into its own.

For all-cargo loads the immense cabin and
under-floor volume of the type will offer
transport and marketing possibilities hitherto
impossible. Lufthansa, which carrier will
pioneer the all-cargo 747F, has indicated what
can be done. On the New York–Frankfurt
route, the capacity of the aircraft will be
200,000 lb or 3 times the capacity of the
cargo jets currently in use (707s). It will carry
containers in the lower holds and containers
and cargo pallets on the main deck. To expedite loading, the nose of the aircraft will swing
up, and a mechanised system in the aircraft
will permit three men to unload and load
cargo in 30 minutes.

The following notes provide information
on the forthcoming big jets, again, as a guide
to their general characteristics. Developments have been made with all models during
the past year which reflect the commercial
awareness of their makers.

Picture for "Future Transport Aircraft"
Lockheed L-1011 Tristar has underfloor space for 18 LD-3 containers. No freighter version is
yet planned

Boeing 747

Out of 206 orders announced by August
1971 for the Boeing 747 series of 'Jumbo jets',
2 were for the 'F' all-cargo version.

Passenger versions do not have the nose-
loading facilities of the cargo type, but the
capacity of the under-floor holds, 177·0 m³
(6,250 cu ft), is such that a considerable

balance for cargo will remain after passenger baggage requirements are met. The all-cargo version has a 137·5 tons (275,000 lb) payload capacity for transcontinental and US/Hawaii services, more than triple that of the 707-320C, and its break-even load factor is substantially lower. Completely automated handling systems for upper and lower decks will enable three men to unload and load them in under 30 minutes. The aircraft is designed to cope with a random mix of existing 707, 727 and DC-8 pallets, igloos and containers, or will carry up to 26, 2·44 × 2·44 × 3·05 m (8 × 8 × 10 ft) containers, plus lower deck cargo. In addition to the two containerised lower deck holds which total 148·7 m³ (5,250 cu ft), provision is made for 28·3 m³ (1,000 cu ft) of bulk-load freight.

The first 747 passenger aircraft entered service with Pan American World Airways on January 21, 1970.

Lockheed L500 Galaxy

This civil development of the Lockheed C-5A, designated L500-114MA Galaxy, has a higher take-off weight and zero-fuel weight which, with the removal of military equipment, allows a greater payload and longer range than is possible with the USAF aircraft.

The very large volume and weight-lifting capability of the L500 enable it to carry three layers of cargo, including the largest standard containers. Loading is via a visor-type, straight-in, nose-door with full width integral ramps. Additionally, 50·9 m³ (1,800 cu ft) of bulk-loading space is available at the after end of the main deck, with its own cargo door. Two cargo doors, size 2·40 m high × 3·05 m wide (7 ft 10 in high × 10 ft 0 in wide), on the port side, provide access to the top deck. All pallets are interchangeable with those carried in Boeing 707 or Douglas DC-8 aircraft. Alternatively the L500 Galaxy can handle loads too large for any other type now in production, on its 43·60 × 5·97 wide × 4·18 m high (143 ft 0 in × 19 ft 7 in wide × 13 ft 8½ in high) main cargo deck. Total unitised volume available on both decks is 854·8 m³ (30,200 cu ft) plus 50·9 m³ (1,800

Livestock is a normal and regular export from Kenya and here one of the many specie of plains' deer awaits transport in an East African Airways DC-3 freighter.

cu ft) bulk. Max payload, 144,900 kg (319,450 lb). Max cruising speed at 7,600 m (25,000 ft) is 892 kmh (554 mph) and range with max payload 4,785 km (2,975 miles).

No civil orders have yet been announced for the L500.

Douglas DC-10

The DC-10 is a 3-jet, all-purpose, commercial transport designed for economic operation over stage lengths of 480 to 5,150 km (300 to 3,200 miles) and able to carry up to 334 passengers over 4,625 km (2,875 miles). A convertable freight, the DC-10F, will carry 71,668 kg (158,000 lb) of cargo on US domestic transcontinental routes.

Lockheed L1011 Tri Star

A 3-jet short/medium haul transport which

flew in November 1970. In its initial form it is a passenger aircraft with up to 345 seats in a cabin almost 5·95 m (19 ft 6 in) wide, plus a lower-deck galley and 91·3 m³ (3,228 cu ft) of containerised, mechanically handled, baggage/freight capacity. Main performance figures include:—Max take-off weight 185,520 kg (409,000 lb); max payload, 39,460 kg (87,000 lb); max cruising speed at 22,000 ft, 945 kmh (587 mph) and range with max payload, 5,188 km (3,224 miles).

The long-range version, the 1011-8, will carry 280 passengers, their baggage and 2,270 kg (5,000 lb) of cargo over 8,000 km (5,000 miles) stages non-stop. Eventual gross weight may reach 270,130 kg (595,000 lb).

INTERNATIONAL
CONTAINER FITMENTS

INTERNATIONAL CONTAINER STANDARDS

INTRODUCTION

International Organisation for Standardisation (ISO)—
1 rue de Varembé, 1211 Geneva 20
Switzerland
TELEPHONE: 34 12 40
SECRETARY GENERAL:
Olle Sturen
GENERAL:

The aim of ISO is to promote the development of standards in the world to facilitate the international exchange of goods and services and to develop mutual co-operation in the spheres of intellectual, scientific, technological and economic activity.

The standardisation work of ISO is handled in its Technical Committees on which each Member Body interested in a subject has the right to be represented. Member Bodies who decide to take an active part in the work of a Technical Committee are known as (P) Members (participating) of that Committee; those Member Bodies who only wish to be kept informed of the work are known as (O) Members (observers) and have the right to attend meetings but not to vote. One of the (P) members designated by the ISO Council acts as the Secretariat.

The Technical Committee may work with Sub-Committees or Working Groups set up to report upon specific aspects of the subject. These sub groups report in the form of preliminary draft proposals for consideration by the full committee. Any draft submitted to the (P) members of a Technical Committee for study which is intended eventually to become an ISO Recommendation is called a draft proposal; a given subject may figure in several successive draft proposals.

A draft proposal which receives substantial support from the (P) members of the Committee is transmitted to the central secretariat for registration as a Draft ISO Recommendation and circulation to all the (P) members for letter ballot and to all Member Bodies for approval. A Draft ISO Recommendation which has been adopted by a majority of the (P) Members of the Technical Committee and 60 per cent of the ISO Member Bodies is submitted to the Council for acceptance as an ISO Recommendation.

The Council may decide that the Recommendation should be resubmitted to Member Bodies with a view to adoption as an ISO Standard; if no Body opposes the proposal the Recommendation becomes an ISO Standard. It should be noted that this latter procedure has never been applied so far.

ISO TECHNICAL COMMITTEE No. 104—FREIGHT CONTAINERS:

This Committee was set up in 1961 with the USA Member Body as Secretariat. To enable it to tackle the main problems of external dimensions and ratings; Testing and Marking; and to deal with Terminology the Committee formed three working groups. Participating Members are Australia, Austria, Belgium, Brazil, Bulgaria, Czechoslovakia, Finland, France, Germany, Hungary, Israel, Italy, Japan, Netherlands, Poland, Portugal, Romania, Switzerland, Sweden, Turkey, United Kingdom, and USSR. Observers are Canada, Chile, Colombia, Cuba, Denmark, Eire, Greece, India, Iran, Mexico, New Zealand, Norway, Pakistan, Peru, South Africa and Spain.

The work of the Committee is reported in the text which follows. These extracts are reproduced by kind permission of the British Standards Institution, 2 Park Street, London, W1, England. It should be noted that all this material is copyright by the International Organisation for Standardisation and may not be reproduced without consent.

At the plenary meeting of the Committee held in October 1969 in Morristown, New York, USA the structure of TC 104 (Secretariat USA) was given a major overhaul and the two rather cumbersome Working Groups B and C which had done some first class work were disbanded. In 1961 the work had concentrated on the problems associated with the Series 1 closed containers to enable them to travel internationally by road, rail or sea. Working Group B (Secretariat Australia) was charged with setting up suitable dimensions and ratings whilst Working Group C (Secretariat UK) attended to specification, Testing and Marking. There was also Working Group 'A' (Secretariat Belgium) in charge of definitions and terminology. A summary of its work appears at the end of this section, headed DR 1055.

Under the new structure a number of sub-committees were formed with clearly defined areas of work. They in turn have sub-divided into smaller working groups which have been meeting in less formal conditions than hitherto and as the members have been chosen mainly for their specialised knowledge of the problems under consideration progress has improved in the last twelve months in spite of the increased complexity created by the introduction of many special purpose containers.

Sub Committee 1 (Secretariat France)
Dimensions, Specification and Testing Series 1 General Purpose Containers.

Sub Committee 2 (Secretariat UK)
Dimensions, Specification and Testing Specific Purpose Containers. Series 1 and 2.

Sub Committee 3 (Secretariat USSR)
Dimensions Specification and Testing Series 3 Containers.

Working Group 1 (Secretariat Belgium)
Terminology.

Working Group 2 (Secretariat Sweden)
Handling and Securing.

Working Group 3 (Secretariat USA)
Marking.

SERIES 1:

Precise definitions of Series 1 and Series 2 containers are stated in R 668 (the first document immediately following this introduction) but they may be generalised and simplified by saying that Series 1 Freight Containers are of 8 ft by 8 ft cross-section of 40 ft, 30 ft, 20 ft, and 10 ft length. The addition of the 40 ft × 8·5 ft high, half height open top etc, should also be noted as being included in the Series 1 Group. In order to take account of the various specialised units within Series 1 it has been suggested that to aid specifications containers should be grouped as follows:

General Cargo—Closed
     Open top
     Open top-open sides
     Open top-open sides-open ends
Thermal —Insulated
     Refrigerated
     Heated
Tank   —Bulk liquid
     Compressed gas
Dry Bulk —Gravity discharge
     Pressure discharge
Flat
Collapsible
Others

SERIES 2:

Series 2 are smaller metric-sized containers still in use in large numbers on the European railway systems.

SERIES 3:

Series 3 containers are a fairly recent addition and are small containers with a gross weight up to 5 tons. They are in use in large numbers on some of the railway systems Eastern Europe. No ISO Recommendations have been published so far. However, it has been suggested that Series 3 containers should have external width and heights of 2,100 mm and 2,400 mm (6·89 ft and 7·87 ft) respectively.

Type 3A will have a maximum gross weight of 5 tons and a length of 2,650 mm (8·69 ft).

Type 3B will have a maximum gross weight of 5 tons and a length of 1,325 mm (4·34 ft).

Type 3C will have a maximum gross weight of 2·5 tons and a length of 1,325 mm (4·34 ft).

One of the most difficult areas of work is covered by the new Working Group 3 (Secretariat USA) with the deceptively simple title of "Marking". In fact this Working Group is trying to standardise a numeric code to be shown on the sides of containers to identify their type, country of origin, size, rated load and so on which may be used for data processing container movements by computer on an international scale. Computers originally bought for costing and wages calculations are being used for container tracking and many companies, unable to wait for international agreement, have been developing their own codes. Customs and other legislative procedures are all involved in this problem which demands urgent solution because with technological improvements it is possible for the goods to arrive ahead of the paperwork.

The USA has recently published a national standard ANSI MH 5·3 entitled Specifications for Identification and Marking of Cargo Containers which is reproduced later in this edition.

AIR-FREIGHT CONTAINERS:

A number of different committees and working groups are working on the problem of suitable standards for air-freight containers. TC 104 (Freight Containers) are considering the fully inter-modal (surface/air transport) container adapted to air-freight in respect of strength and tare, and the United States leads a working group examining air containers suitable for surface transport. Perhaps such a container could be given a lower stacking requirement with correspondingly reduced sections for the corner posts to reduce the unladen weight. On the other hand aircraft restraint systems are stressed to 9g which suggests containers might need to be considerably stronger in some areas with a corresponding weight penalty.

TC 20-W.G.9 (Air Cargo) is considering an air/land container to make it lighter than one capable of being sea-borne. The air-freight industry recognises the value of a container which could integrate with the Series 1 ISO freight containers and pressures of demand may force a solution to the problem.

The International Air Transport Association's (IATA) requirements for air freight containers are published in the Air Freight section of the book.

DIMENSIONS AND RATINGS OF FREIGHT CONTAINERS
ISO RECOMMENDATION R668

2nd Edition   October 1970
This 2nd edition supersedes the first edition published in 1968

BRIEF HISTORY:

The ISO Recommendation R 668, *Dimensions and ratings of freight containers*, was drawn up by Technical Committee ISO/TC 104, *Freight Containers*, the Secretariat of which is held by the American National Standards Institute (ANSI).

Work on this question led to the adoption of Draft ISO Recommendation No. 804, which was circulated to all ISO Member Bodies for enquiry in May 1965. It was approved by 20 Member Bodies. Five Member Bodies opposed the approval of the Draft (Australia, France, Ireland, Poland and the U.S.S.R.).

The Draft ISO Recommendation was then submitted by correspondence to the ISO Council which decided, in *February* 1968, to accept it as an ISO Recommendation.

BRIEF HISTORY RELATING TO THE 2ND EDITION:

The revision of ISO Recommendation R 668-1968 was undertaken in 1969 and consists of minor modifications and of the addition of a supplementary container height in table 3. It was approved by the majority of the P-Members of ISO/TC 104, and, in an abbreviated procedure, was submitted direct to the ISO Council, which decided to accept it as the second edition of ISO Recommendation R 668; the first edition of which is cancelled.

1. DEFINITIONS:
1.1 A *freight container* is an article of transport equipment.
 (a) of a permanent character and accordingly strong enough to be suitable for repeated use;
 (b) specially designed to facilitate the carriage of goods, by one or more modes of transport, without intermediate reloading;
 (c) fitted with devices permitting its ready handling, particularly its transfer from one mode of transport to another;
 (d) so designed as to be easy to fill and empty;
 (e) having an internal volume of 1 m³ (35·3 ft³) or more.

The term *freight container* includes neither vehicles nor conventional packing.

1.2 *Rating*, means the maximum gross weight and is the maximum permissible combined weight of the freight container and of its contents.

CLASSIFICATION AND DESIGNATION OF FREIGHT CONTAINERS:
2.1. Two series of freight containers are approved:
—those of series 1, having a uniform cross-section of 2,435 mm × 2,435 mm (8 × 8 ft) are shown in Table 1;
—those of series 2, having a uniform height of 2,100 mm (6 ft 10½ in), are shown in Table 2.

The actual dimensions of both series 1 and series 2 freight containers, and their tolerances, are given in Table 3.

TABLE 1—*NOMINAL DIMENSIONS OF SERIES 1 FREIGHT CONTAINERS*

Freight Container designation	Height mm	ft	in	Width mm	ft	Nominal length* mm*	ft	in
1A	2,435	8		2,435	8	12,000**	40**	
1AA	2,591***	8	6	2,436	8	12.000**	40**	
1B	2,435	8		2,435	8	9,000	30	
1C	2,435	8		2,435	8	6,000	20	
1D	2,435	8		2,435	8	3,000	10	
1E	2,435	8		2,435	8	2,000	6	8
1F	2,435	8		2,435	8	1,500	5	

* The exact lengths in millimetres are shown in Table 3.
** In certain countries there are legal limitations to this length.
*** In certain countries there are legal limitations to this height.

TABLE 2—*NOMINAL DIMENSIONS OF SERIES 2 FREIGHT CONTAINERS*

Freight container designation	Height* mm	ft*	in	Width* mm	ft*	in	Length* mm	ft*	in
2A	2,100	6	11	2,300	7	7	2,920	9	7
2B	2,100	6	11	2,100	6	11	2,400	7	11
2C	2,100	6	11	2,300	7	7	1,450	4	9

* The exact dimensions in feet are shown in Table 3.

3. OVERALL DIMENSIONS AND RATINGS
3.1. The overall external dimensions, tolerances and ratings are given in Table 3.
3.2. The dimensions and tolerances apply when measured at the temperature of 20°C (68°F); measurements taken at other temperatures should be adjusted accordingly.

TABLE 3—*ACTUAL DIMENSIONS, PERMISSIBLE TOLERANCES AND RATINGS*

Freight container designation	Height mm	Tolerances mm	ft in	Tolerances in	Width mm	Tolerances mm	ft in	Tolerances in	Length mm	Tolerances mm	ft in	Tolerances in	Rating (max gross weight) kg (1 ton = 2,240 lb)	tons
1A	2,438	0 / —5	8	0 / —0·1875	2,438	0 / —5	8	0 / —0·1875	12,192	0 / —10	40	0 / —0·375	30,480	30
1AA	2,591	0 / —5	8 6	0 / —0·1875	2,438	0 / —5	8	0 / —0·1875	12,192	0 / —10	40	0 / —0·375	30,480	30
1B	2,438	0 / —5	8	0 / —0·1875	2,438	0 / —5	8	0 / —0·1875	9,125	0 / —10	29 11·25	0 / —0·375	25,400	25
1C	2,438	0 / —5	8	0 / —0·1875	2,438	0 / —5	8	0 / —0·1875	6,058	0 / —6	19 10·5	0 / —0·25	20,320	20
1D	2,438	0 / —5	8	0 / —0·1875	2,438	0 / —5	8	0 / —0·1875	2.991	0 / —5	9 9·75	0 / —0·1875	10,160	10
1E	2,438	0 / —5	8	0 / —0·1875	2,438	0 / —5	8	0 / —0·1875	1,968	0 / —5	6 5·5	0 / —0·1875	7,110	7
1F	2,438	0 / —5	8	0 / —0·1875	2,438	0 / —5	8	0 / —0·1875	1,460	0 / —3	4 9·5	0 / —0·125	5,080	5
2A	2,100	0 / —5	6 10·5	+0·1875 / 0	2,300	0 / —5	7 6·5	+0·1875 / 0	2,920	0 / —5	9 7	0 / —0·1875	7,110	7
2B	2,100	0 / —5	6 10·5	+0·1875 / 0	2,100	0 / —5	6 10·5	+0·1875 / 0	2,400	0 / —5	7 10·5	0 / —0·1875	7,110	7
2C	2,100	0 / —5	6 10·5	+0·1875 / 0	2,300	0 / —5	7 6·5	+0·1875 / 0	1,450	0 / —5	4 9	+0·0625 / —0·125	7,110	7

MINIMUM INTERNAL DIMENSIONS GENERAL PURPOSE SERIES 1 FREIGHT CONTAINERS ISO RECOMMENDATION No. 1894

October 1970

BRIEF HISTORY:

The ISO Recommendation R 1894, *General purpose series 1 freight containers—Minimum internal dimensions*, was drawn up by Technical Committee ISO/TC, *Freight containers*, the Secretariat of which is held by the American National Standards Institute (ANSI).

Work on this question led to the adoption of Draft ISO Recommendation No. 1894, which was circulated to all the ISO Member Bodies for enquiry in August 1969. It was approved, subject to a few modifications of an editorial nature, by the following Member Bodies:

Australia	Korea, Rep. of	Thailand
Belgium	Netherlands	Turkey
Chile	New Zealand	U.A.R.
Czechoslovakia	Norway	United Kingdom
Germany	Romania	U.S.A.
Greece	South Africa, Rep. of	U.S.S.R.
Israel	Spain	
Japan	Sweden	

The following Member Bodies opposed the approval of the Draft:

France
Switzerland

This Draft ISO Recommendation was then submitted by correspondence to the ISO Council, which decided to accept it as an ISO RECOMMENDATION.

1. SCOPE:

This ISO Recommendation sets out the minimum internal dimensions of ISO Series 1 general purpose freight containers (designated 1A, 1AA, 1B, 1C, 1D, 1E and 1F in ISO Recommendation R 668, *Dimensions and ratings of freight containers*).

NOTE: It is not intended that containers of specified internal dimensions should be suitable for transport of all types of refrigerated merchandise: the internal dimensions of these containers are being studied. However, to the extent that insulation can be installed without encroachment upon the minimum internal dimensions shown below, this ISO Recommendation may also apply to insulated freight containers as well as non-insulated general puprose freight containers.

2. DIMENSIONS:

The minimum internal dimensions for ISO Series 1 general purpose freight containers should comply with the following table:

Freight container designation	*Minimum width* *mm*	*in*	*Minimum height*	*Minimum length* *mm*	*ft*	*in*
1A	2,299	$90\frac{1}{2}$		11,998	39	$4\frac{3}{8}$
1AA	2,299	$90\frac{1}{2}$		11,998	39	$4\frac{3}{8}$
1B	2,299	$90\frac{1}{2}$		8,931	29	$3\frac{5}{8}$
1C	2,299	$90\frac{1}{2}$	Nominal container	5,867	19	3
1D	2,299	$90\frac{1}{2}$	external height	2,802	9	$2\frac{5}{16}$
1E	2,299	$90\frac{1}{2}$	minus 241 mm ($9\frac{1}{2}$ in)	1,780	5	$10\frac{1}{16}$
1F	2,299	$90\frac{1}{2}$		1,273	4	$2\frac{1}{8}$

NOTE: For the 2,438 mm (8 ft) nominal height container, the minimum internal height is 2,197 mm ($86\frac{1}{2}$ in). For the 2,591 mm (8 ft 6 in) nominal height container of nominal 12,000 mm (40 ft) length, it is 2,350 mm ($92\frac{1}{2}$ in).

The dimensions apply when measured at a temperature of 20°C (68°F). Measurements taken at other temperatures should be adjusted accordingly.

Where a top corner fitting projects into the internal space specified by the Table, the part of the corner fitting projecting into the container should not be considered as reducing the size of the container.

SPECIFICATIONS AND TESTING OF SERIES 1 FREIGHT CONTAINERS ISO RECOMMENDATION 1496

November 1970

BRIEF HISTORY

The ISO Recommendation R 1496, *Specifications and testing of series 1 freight containers*, was drawn up by Technical Committee ISO/TC 104, *Freight containers*, the Secretariat of which is held by the American National Standards Institute (ANSI).

Work on this question led to the adoption of Draft ISO Recommendation No. 1496, which was circulated to all the ISO Member Bodies for enquiry in April 1968. It was approved by the requisite majority of ISO Member Bodies.

However, as technical modifications have been made in the Draft, the ISO/TC 104 Secretariat drew up a second Draft ISO Recommendation No. 1496, which was circulated to all the ISO Member Bodies for enquiry in August 1969. It was approved, subject to a few modifications of an editorial nature, by the following Member Bodies.:

Australia	Israel	Sweden
Austria	Japan	Switzerland
Belgium	Korea, Rep. of	Thailand
Chile	Netherlands	Turkey
Czechoslovakia	New Zealand	U.A.R.
France	Norway	United Kingdom
Germany	Romania	U.S.A.
Greece	South Africa, Rep. of	U.S.S.R.
Hungary	Spain	

No Member Body opposed the approval of the second Draft.

This second Draft ISO Recommendation was then submitted by correspondence to the ISO Council, which decided to accept it as an ISO RECOMMENDATION.

1. SCOPE

This ISO Recommendation sets out basic requirements for the specifications and testing of ISO series 1 freight containers (designated 1 AA, 1A, 1B, 1C, 1D, 1E and 1F in ISO Recommendation R 668, *Dimensions and ratings of freight containers**), which are suitable for international exchange and for conveyance by road, rail and sea, including interchange between these forms of transport.

This ISO Recommendation should be read in conjunction with ISO Recommendations R 790, *Marking of series 1 and series 2 freight containers*, R 1161, *Specification of corner fittings for series 1 freight containers*, and R 1894, *General purpose series 1 freight containers—Minimum internal dimensions*.

2. DIMENSIONS AND RATINGS

The overall external dimensions and tolerances and the maximum gross weight of the freight containers covered by this ISO Recommendation are those established in ISO Recommendation R 668.

No part of the container should project beyond these overall external dimensions.

3. DESIGN FEATURES

3.1 General

Each freight container should be weatherproof and, when carrying its maximum permissible load, should be capable of fullfilling the following operating requirements:

3.1.1 STACKING: Being stacked six high, within overall limits of eccentricity of 25·4 mm (1 in) laterally and 38 mm ($1\frac{1}{2}$ in) longitudinally.

3.1.2 LIFTING FROM TOP CORNERS:

—For series 1AA, 1A, 1B and 1C containers, the lifting forces applied vertically.

—For series 1D, 1E and 1F containers, the lifting forces applied at any angle between the vertical and 30° to the vertical.

3.1.3 LIFTING FROM BOTTOM CORNERS: For series 1AA, 1A, 1B, 1C and 1D containers, being lifted from the bottom at the corners with the lifting forces applied at any angle between the vertical and 30° to the horizontal. The lifting should be performed in such a manner that the side walls are not loaded by the lifting device.

The line of action of the lifting load and the outer face of the corner fitting should be no further apart than 38 mm ($1\frac{1}{2}$ in).

3.1.4 RESTRAINT (IN TRANSIT): External restraint under dynamic load conditions of 2 g (that is, 19·62 m/s^2 or 64·4 ft/s^2) applied in a horizontal plane, longitudinally in the case of containers designated 1AA, 1A, 1B, 1C and 1D. For containers designated 1E and 1F, the load should be applied in a horizontal plane both longitudinally and transversely.

3.2 Floor

The floor of the freight container should be capable of withstanding a uniformly distributed load of not less than the maximum gross weight of the container.

For series 1AA, 1A, 1B, 1C and 1D containers, the floor should, in addition, be capable of withstanding a wheel load of not less than 2,730 kg (6,000 lb) per wheel, applied to a contact area not greater than 142 cm^2 (22 in^2), assuming a wheel width of not less than 180 mm (7 in) and a distance between wheel centres of 760 mm (30 in).

3.3 Roof

The roof of the freight container should be capable of withstanding a uniformly distributed load of not less than 200 kg (440 lb) on an area of 600 mm × 300 mm (24 in × 12 in). The load includes a dynamic factor of 50 per cent applied to the static requirement.

3.4 Walls

Each end wall of series 1AA, 1A, 1B, 1C and 1D freight containers should be capable of withstanding a uniformly distributed load of not less than 0·4 times the maximum payload. Each side wall (length dimension) should be capable of withstanding a uniformly distributed load of not less than 0·6 times the maximum payload. For series 1E and 1F freight containers, both end and side walls should be capable of withstanding a uniformity distributed load of not less than 0·6 times the maximum payload.

3.5 Corner Fittings

All series 1 freight containers should be equipped with corner fittings at the top corners. Series 1AA, 1A, 1B, 1C and 1D containers should, in addition, be equipped with corner fittings at the bottom corners.

The upper faces of top corner fittings should protrude above the top of the container by a minimum of 6 mm ($\frac{1}{4}$ in)

The container structure should not protrude below the base plane of the bottom corner fittings at the time of maximum deflection under maximum payload.

NOTE: The dimensional requirements for corner fittings for series 1 freight containers are given in ISO Recommendation R 1161.

3.6 Fork lift pockets

Fork lift pockets may be provided as optional features in series 1D, 1E and 1F freight containers. The dimensional requirements for such pockets are specified in Appendix Y.

NOTE: Fork pockets for containers 1AA, 1A, 1B and 1C are being studied within TC 104, where the view is held that fork pockets are not recommended for 1AA, 1A and 1B containers and when installed in 1C containers may only be employed when the containers are unladen.

3.7 Provisions for bottom lifting by means of straddle carriers and similar equipment

Provisions for bottom lifting all series 1 freight containers by means of straddle carriers and similar equipment may be provided as optional features. The dimensional requirements for such provisions are specified in Appendix Z.

NOTE: The requirements of section 3 do not preclude the provision of additional facilities for lifting, either from the top, or at the base of the freight container.

3.8 Door Opening

Each freight container should be provided with a door opening at least at one end, except in the case of series 1E and 1F containers, where the opening may be provided in a side wall.

Door openings should be as large as possible.

General freight containers designated 1AA, 1A, 1B, 1C and 1D should have a door opening preferably having dimensions equal to those of the internal cross-section of the container, and in any case not less than:

Door height : nominal container external height, minus 305 mm (12 in).

Door width : 2,286 mm (90 in).

For the 2,435 mm (8 ft) nominal height container (1A, 1B, 1C and 1D), the minimum door height should be 2,134 mm (84 in).

For the 2,590 mm (8 ft 6 in) nominal height container (1AA) of nominal 12,000 mm (40 ft) length, the minimum door height should be 2,286 mm (90 in).

4. TESTING:

4.1 General

Freight containers complying with the operating requirements described in section 3 should not be inferior to containers which have met the tests described in clauses 4.2 to 4.10 inclusive. It is recommended that the test for weatherproofness (Test No. 9) be made last.

Unless otherwise stated, the following test requirements should apply:

4.1.1 The symbol R denotes the maximum gross weight of the freight container, and the symbol P denotes the maximum payload of the container under test, i.e. the tare weight subtracted from the maximum gross weight.

4.1.2 The test load within the container should be uniformly distributed.

4.2 Test No. 1—Stacking

4.2.1 PROCEDURE. The freight container under test should be placed on four level pads, one under each bottom corner fitting or equivalent corner structure. The pads should be centralised under the fittings and be substantially of the same plan dimensions as the fittings. The container should be loaded so that its total weight is equal to 1.8 R.

4.2.1.1 Five containers of the same dimensions and maximum gross weight, and each uniformly loaded so that its total weight is equal to 1.8 R, should be stacked on top of the container under test. The five containers should be stacked flush in relation to each other, but offset from the container under test by 25·4 mm (1 in) laterally and 38 mm ($1\frac{1}{2}$ in) longitudinally.

4.2.1.2 Alternatively, the container under test as specified in clause 4.2.1.1 may be subjected to a load of 9 R applied through four pads of the same plan area as the corner fittings, the load being equally divided among the four corner fittings. Each pad should be offset in the same direction by 25·4 mm (1 in) laterally and 38 mm ($1\frac{1}{2}$ in)

longitudinally.

4.2.2 REQUIREMENTS. After completion of the test the container should not show any permanent deformation or abnormality which would make it unsuitable for use, and the tolerance requirements affecting handling, securing and interchange should be satisfied.

4.3 Test No. 2—Lifting from the top:

4.3.1 PROCEDURE. The freight container under test should be loaded so that its total weight is equal to $R2$, and carefully lifted from all four top corners in such a way that no noticeable acceleration or deceleration forces are applied.

For series 1AA, 1A, 1B and 1C containers, the lifting forces should be applied vertically.

For containers designated 1D, 1E and 1F, lifting should be by means of slings, the angle of each leg being at 30° from the vertical.

After lifting, the container should be suspended for not less than 5 minutes and then lowered to the ground.

4.3.2 REQUIREMENTS. After completion of the test the container should not show any permanent deformation or abnormality which would make it unsuitable for use, and the tolerance requirements affecting handling, securing and interchange should be satisfied.

4.4 Test No. 3—Lifting from the bottom:

4.4.1 GENERAL. This test should be carried out on series 1AA, 1A, 1B, 1C and 1D containers. It should also be carried out on series 1E and 1F containers if they are equipped with bottom corner fittings.

4.4.2 PROCEDURE. The container under test should be loaded so that its total weight is equal to $2R$ and carefully lifted from all four bottom corners in such a way that no noticeable acceleration or deceleration forces are applied.

As far as possible, lifting forces should be applied using one spreader under the roof.

For series 1AA, 1A, 1B, 1C and 1D containers, the angle of the lifting force should be 30° from the horizontal.

For series 1E and 1F containers, lifting should be by means of slings, the angle of the slings being at 30° from the vertical.

Lifting containers at the bottom should be performed in such a way that the side walls are not subjected to lifting forces. The container should be suspended for not less than five minutes and then lowered to the ground.

NOTE: The container should not be lifted using rings fitted for restraint purposes only.

4.4.3 REQUIREMENTS. After completion of the test the container should not show any permanent deformation or abnormality which would make it unsuitable for use, and the tolerance requirements affecting handling, securing and interchange should be satisfied.

4.5 Test No. 4—Restraint:

NOTE: The following test is to meet the operating requirements for restraint in transit as specified in clause 3.1.4.

4.5.1 PROCEDURES. The freight container should be restrained longitudinally by securing the bottom corner fittings at one end to suitable anchor points. Each end should be tested.

4.5.1.1 *Static Test.* The freight container, loaded so that its total weight is equal to R, should be secured to rigid anchor points through the bottom apertures of the bottom corner fittings at one end of the container. A force equivalent to a load of 2·5 R should be applied longitudinally to the container, equally divided through the bottom aperture of the other bottom corner fittings, first in compression and then in tension.

4.5.1.2 *Dynamic Test.**

4.5.2 REQUIREMENTS. After completion of the test the container should not show any permanent deformation or abnormality which would make it unsuitable for use, and the tolerance requirements affecting handling, securing and interchange should be satisfied.

4.6 Test No. 5—End wall strength:

4.6.1 PROCEDURES. The freight container should have each end wall tested when one end wall is blind and the other equipped with doors.

4.6.1.1 *Static Test.* Series 1AA, 1A, 1B, 1C and 1D freight containers should be loaded with a weight equal to 0·4P. Series 1E and 1F freight containers should be loaded with a weight equal to 0·6P.

It is recommended that water be used as the test load for static testing.

The container should be placed face down on the wall being tested, with the load applied to the full cross-section of the wall and uniformly distributed as far as practical.

NOTE: This test procedure covers both the end and side wall strength of the series 1E and 1F freight containers.

4.6.1.2 *Dynamic Test**.

4.6.2   REQUIREMENTS.   After completion of the test the container should not show any permanent deformation or abnormality which would make it unsuitable for use, and the tolerance requirements affecting handling, securing and interchange should be satisfied.

*A dynamic form of test has not been included in this ISO Recommendation pending further development of specifications for a satisfactory and reproducable test as an alternative to the static test.

4.7 Test No. 6—Side wall strength (Series 1AA, 1A, 1B, 1C and 1D)

4.7.1   PROCEDURE.   The freight container should be loaded to its maximum payload with material which as far as possible occupies the whole internal capacity.   It is recommended that water be used as the test load for static testing.   The container should then be tilted first to one side and then to the other side to an angle of 45°.

Alternatively, the above procedure may also be met if a side load, uniformly distributed and equivalent to $0·6P$, is applied by mechanical means.

4.7.2   REQUIREMENTS.   After completion of the test the container should not show any permanent deformation or abnormality which would make it unsuitable for use, and the tolerance requirements affecting handling, securing and interchange should be satisfied.

4.8 Test No. 7—Roof Strength

4.8.1   PROCEDURE.   A load of 300 kg (660 lb) should be uniformly distributed over an area of 600mm × 300 mm (24 in × 12 in) located at the weakest area of the roof of the freight/container.

4.8.2   REQUIREMENTS.   After completion of the test the container should not show any permanent deformation or abnormality which would make it unsuitable for use, and the tolerance requirements affecting handling, securing and interchange should be satisfied.

4.9 Test No. 8—Floor strength:

4.9.1   GENERAL.   The test applies only to series 1AA, 1A, 1B, 1C and 1D freight containers.

4.9.2   PROCEDURE.   An industrial truck equipped with tyres loaded to an axle weight of 5,460 kg (12,000 lb), including the weight of the truck or 2,730 kg (6,000 lb) per wheel applied to a contact area of 142 cm² (22 in²) assuming a wheel width of 180 mm (7 in) and a distance between wheel centres of 760 mm (30 in), should be manoeuvred over the entire floor area of the freight container in a longitudinal direction.   The test should be made with the base of the container resting on firm level ground.

4.9.3   REQUIREMENTS.   After completion of the test the container should not show any permanent deformation or abnormality which would make it unsuitable for use, and the tolerance requirements affecting handling, securing and interchange should be satisfied.

4.10 Test No. 9—Weatherproofness:

4.10.1   PROCEDURE.   A stream of water should be applied on all exterior joints and seams of the freight container from a nozzle of 12·5 mm (0·5 in) inside diameter, at a pressure of about 1·0 bar (corresponding to a head of about 10 m (33 ft) of water).   The nozzle should be held at a distance of 1·5 m (5 ft) from the container exterior joints and seams, and have a rate of travel of 100 mm (4 in) per second.

4.10.2   REQUIREMENTS.   After completion of the test, the container should be free from penetration of water.

Dimension conversion table

mm	in		
20	0·79	32	1·26
100	3·94	51	2·01
120	4·72	80	3·15
300	11·81	120	4·72
350	13·78	600	23·64
625	24·61	2,500	98·40
6	0·24	4,876	192·00
12	0·48	5,476	215·70

APPENDIX 'Y' TO ISO RECOMMENDATION 1496:

Optional provisions for handling by means of fork lift trucks
(see clause 3.6)

Figure 1 illustrates two alternative fork lift pocket arrangement for series 1 and 2 freight containers.   The dimensions of the pockets, which are optional features on series 1D, 1E and 1F containers, should be as follows:

—height of opening — 100 mm (4 in approx.) minimum
—width of opening — 300 mm (12 in approx.) minimum
                           350 mm (14 in approx.) maximum

The distance between the outer edge of the opening and the centreline of the container should be 625 mm (24½ in) approx.

The fork lift pockets may be enclosed or open at the bottom, but in each case should be located below the level of the floor. For the closed design, the distance between the bottom of the container and the bottom edge of the pocket should be 20 mm (¾ in) minimum.   For the open design, the distance from the top edge of the pocket to the bottom of the container should be 120 mm (4¾ in) minimum.

APPENDIX Z TO ISO RECOMMENDATION 1496

OPTIONAL PROVISIONS FOR BOTTOM LIFTING BY MEANS OF STRADDLE CARRIERS AND SIMILAR EQUIPMENT:
(see clause 3.7)

Figure 2 defines the positions and the dimensions of slots intended for the handling of containers 1AA, 1A, 1B, 1C and 1D by straddle trucks or similar devices.

The slots may either have the form of a C or be open at the base. These devices are optional.

Z.1 Length of Slot:
For containers 1AA, 1A, 1B and 1C, the slots may extend from one corner fitting to another.   They should have a minimum length of 5,476 mm, and be equipped with small runners of a minimum length of 600 mm.

Should the length of the slot exceed 5,476 mm (see Fig. 2), the additional slot length should be provided with transverse slots of the same section.

Z.2 Transverse Section of Slot:
See Section I-I on Figure 2.

Z.3 Specified Requirements for Sturdiness:
The slots should, at least where equipped with runners, withstand the lifting forces corresponding to the gross weight of the container when lifted with four lifting devices having a support surface of 32 mm × 254 mm (1¼ in × 10 in) (see Fig. 2).

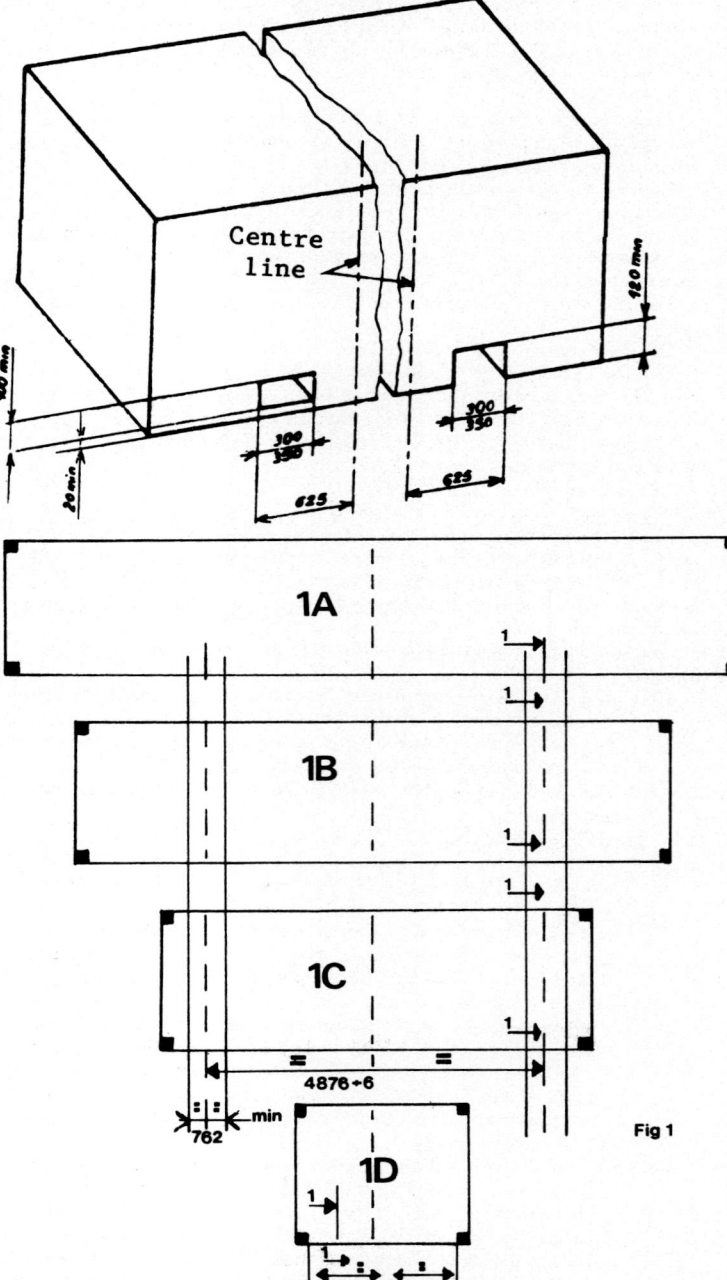

Fig 1

SPECIFICATION OF CORNER FITTINGS FOR SERIES 1
FREIGHT CONTAINERS
ISO RECOMMENDATION R1161

BRIEF HISTORY:

The ISO Recommendation R 1161, *Specification of corner fittings for series 1 freight containers*, was drawn up by Technical Committee ISO/TC 104, *Freight containers*, the Secretariat of which is held by the American National Standards Institute (ANSI).

Work on this question led to the adoption of a Draft ISO Recommendation.

In March 1968, this Draft ISO Recommendation (No. 1019) was circulated to all the ISO Member Bodies for enquiry. It received the necessary majority for approval. However, since technical modifications had been made in the Draft, ISO/TC 104 Secretariat submitted a second Draft ISO Recommendation No. 1019, in January 1970, to all ISO Member Bodies for enquiry.

This second Draft was approved, subject to a few modifications of an editorial nature, by the following Member Bodies:

Australia	Israel	Romania
Austria	Italy	South Africa, Rep. of
Belgium	Japan	Sweden
Brazil	Netherlands	Switzerland
Czechoslovakia	New Zealand	Thailand
Germany	Norway	Turkey
Greece	Peru	U.A.R.
Hungary	Poland	U.S.A.
India	Portugal	U.S.S.R.

Two Member Bodies opposed the approval of the second Draft:

France
United Kingdom

This second Draft ISO Recommendation was then submitted by correspondence to the ISO Council, which decided, in January 1970, to accept it as an ISO RECOMMENDATION.

INTRODUCTION:

This ISO Recommendation on corner fittings represents the efforts of technical and operational personnel drawn from all phases of transportation industry. The drawings describe the fittings for the top and bottom corner of series 1 freight containers which will provide compatibility in interchange between transportation modes. Care has been taken to limit consideration only to those details vital to this function.

The location, size and configuration of corner fitting apertures are specified. The faces of the corner fittings having apertures for the engagement of handling and securing devices have prescribed thickness and tolerances as shown in Figures 2, 3, 4 and 5.

The thickness of the blank walls is not prescribed since they are not involved in the engagement of the handling and securing devices, as long as their inner surfaces do not protrude into the corner fitting cavity reserved for the engaging devices. Examples of handling and securing devices are shown in Annex A.

The purpose of this ISO Recommendation is to define those details of design vital to container interchange in automatic, semi-automatic and conventional systems. Examples of the use of corner fittings are shown in Annex B.

The criteria used in determining the design are given in Annex C.

Note: The requirements of this ISO Recommendation do not preclude the provision of additional facilities for lifting either from the top or at the base of the freight container.

1. SCOPE

This ISO Recommendation establishes the basic dimensions and the functional and strength requirements of corner fittings for series 1 freight containers which conform to ISO Recommendation R 668, *Dimensions and ratings of freight containers*.

2. DIMENSIONS

The dimensions and tolerances of the corner fittings shall conform to the drawings, Figures 2, 3, 4 and 5. Each container will have two right-hand top corner fittings (on the right as the observer faces the container) and two left-hand top corner fittings which are the mirror opposite of the right-hand fittings (see Figure 1). When bottom corner fittings are required, a similar configuration would exist. The corner fitting drawings illustrate right-hand (RH) top and bottom corner fittings only; for the left-hand (LH) corner fittings the dimensions are simply transposed.

After assembly and installation of the corner fittings, the perpendicularity or trueness of the assembled fittings shall be determined by measuring the difference between dimensions D_1 and D_2 between D_3 and D_4 and between D_5 and D_6 illustrated in Figure 6. The maximum allowable differences, expressed as "K_1 max." and "K_2 max." in the Table shall not be exceeded.

3. STRENGTH REQUIREMENTS

The corner fittings shall be designed and constructed in such a manner and of such materials as to enable them to pass the operating and testing requirements which are covered in ISO Recommendation R 1496, *Specification and testing of series 1 freight containers*.

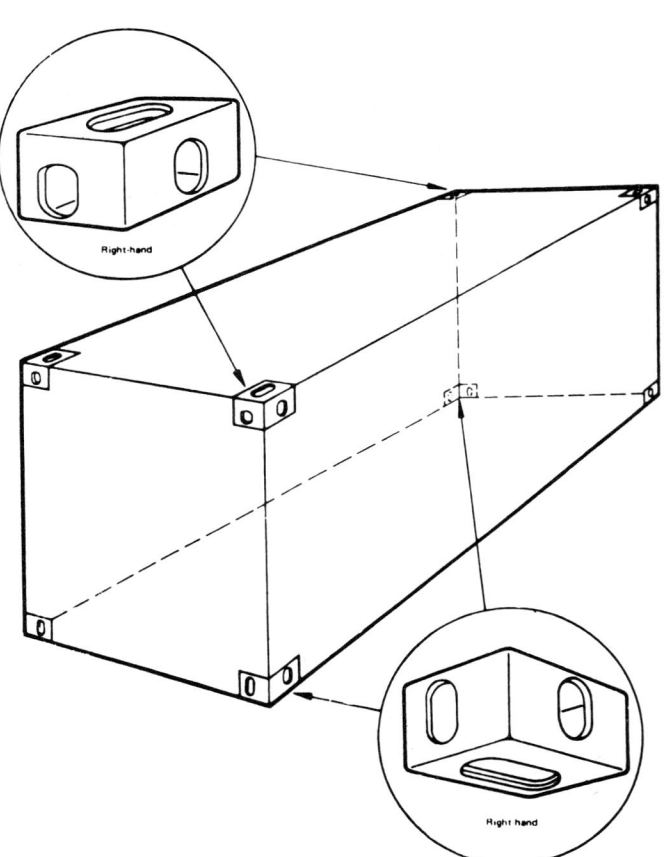

FIG. 1 - Diagrammatic sketch showing corner fitting locations

NOTES

1. Solid and dotted lines (—— and – –) show surfaces and contours which must be physically duplicated in the fitting.

2. Phantom lines (— — — —) show optional walls, which may be used to develop a box-shaped fitting.

3. Outside and inside corner radii where sharp corners are shown must be 3 mm maximum except as noted.

4. Four fittings are required per container : two right-hand and two left-hand.

FIG. 2 - Top corner fitting – Dimensions in millimetres

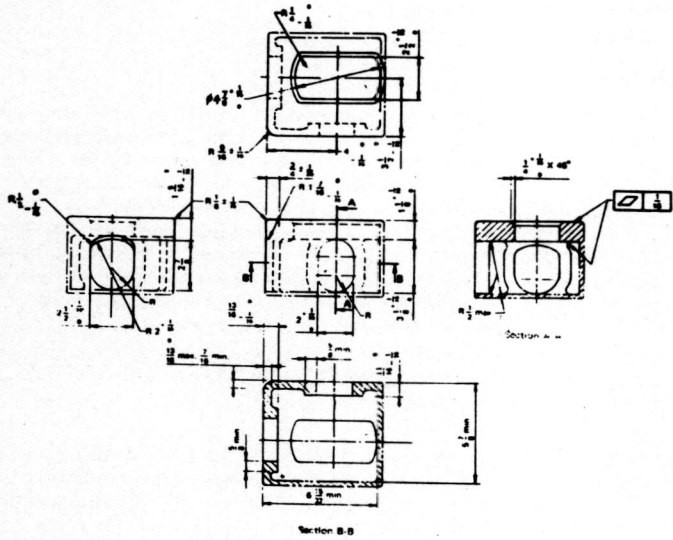

NOTES

1. Solid and dotted lines (—— and ––→) show surfaces and contours which must be physically duplicated in the fitting.

2. Phantom lines (——·——·) show optional walls, which may be used to develop a box-shaped fitting.

3. Outside and inside corner radii where sharp corners are shown must be $\frac{1}{8}$ in maximum except as noted.

4. Four fittings are required per container : two right-hand and two left-hand.

FIG. 3   Top corner fitting – Dimensions in inches

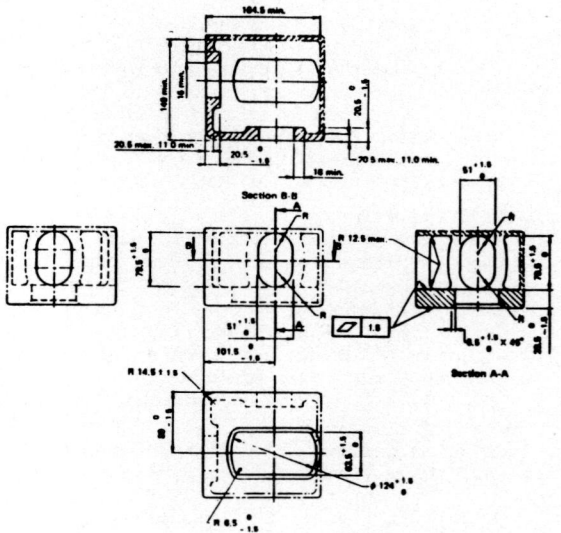

NOTES

1. Solid and dotted lines (—— and ––→) show surfaces and contours which must be physically duplicated in the fitting.

2. Phantom lines (——·——·) show optional walls, which may be used to develop a box-shaped fitting.

3. Outside and inside corner radii where sharp corners are shown must be 3 mm maximum except as noted.

4. Four fittings are required per container : two right-hand and two left-hand.

FIG. 4 – Bottom corner fitting – Dimensions in millimetres

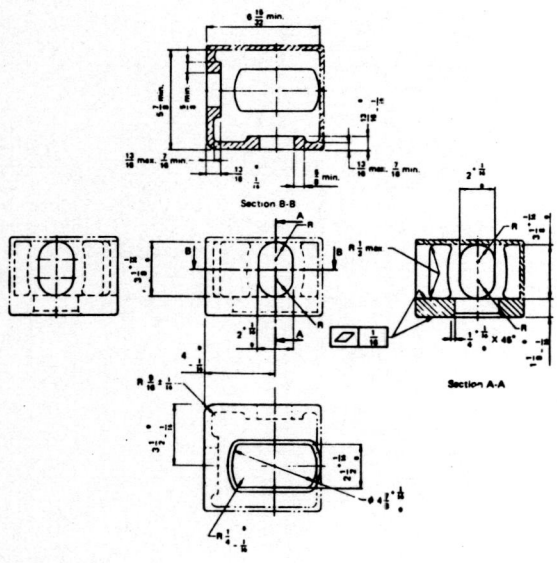

NOTES

1. Solid and dotted lines (—— and ––→) show surfaces and contours which must be physically duplicated in the fitting.

2. Phantom lines (——·——·) show optional walls, which may be used to develop a box-shaped fitting.

3. Outside and inside corner radii where sharp corners are shown must be $\frac{1}{8}$ in maximum except as noted.

4. Four fittings are required per container : two right-hand and two left-hand.

FIG. 5 – Bottom corner fitting – Dimensions in inches

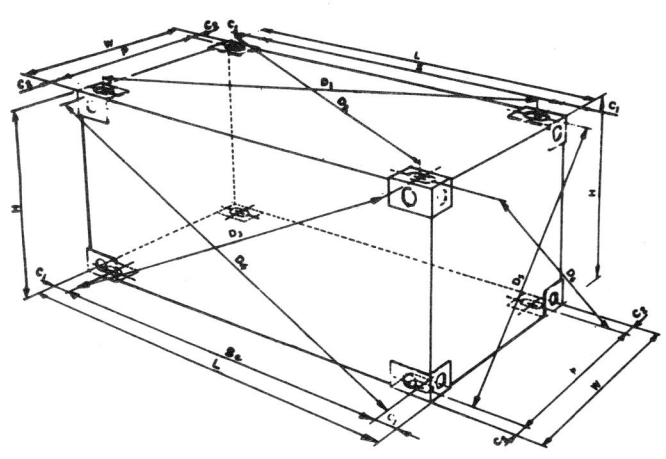

S = Length between centres of apertures in corner fittings

P = Width between centres of apertures in corner fittings

C_1 = Corner fitting measurement $101.5 \; _{-1.5}^{0}$ mm $\left(4 \; _{-1/16}^{0} \text{ in} \right)$

C_2 = Corner fitting measurement $89 \; _{-1.5}^{0}$ mm $\left(3\frac{1}{2} \; _{-1/16}^{0} \text{ in} \right)$

L = External length of the container

W = External width of the container

D = Distance between centres of apertures, or projected reference points therefrom, of diagonally opposite corner fittings, resulting in six measurements : D_1, D_2, D_3, D_4, D_5 and D_6

K_1 = Difference between D_1 and D_2 or between D_3 and D_4 ; i.e. $K_1 = |D_1 - D_2|$ or $K_1 = |D_3 - D_4|$

K_2 = Difference between D_5 and D_6 ; i.e. $K_2 = |D_5 - D_6|$

H = Overall height

FIG. 6 - Assembled corner fittings – Diagonal tolerances
(see Table opposite page)

ANNEX A

TYPICAL HANDLING AND SECURING DEVICES

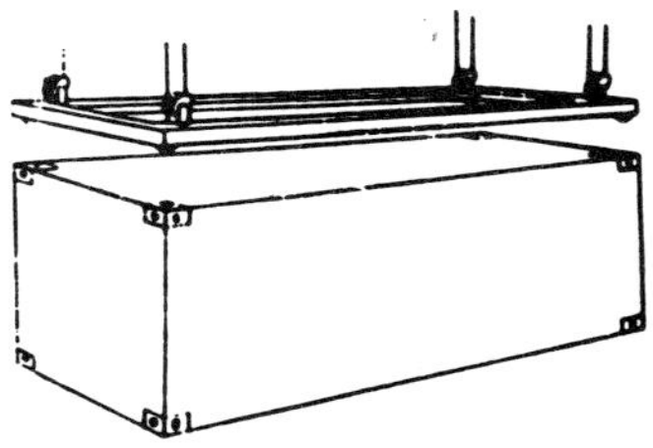

(a) Top lift automatic by means of spreader twist locks

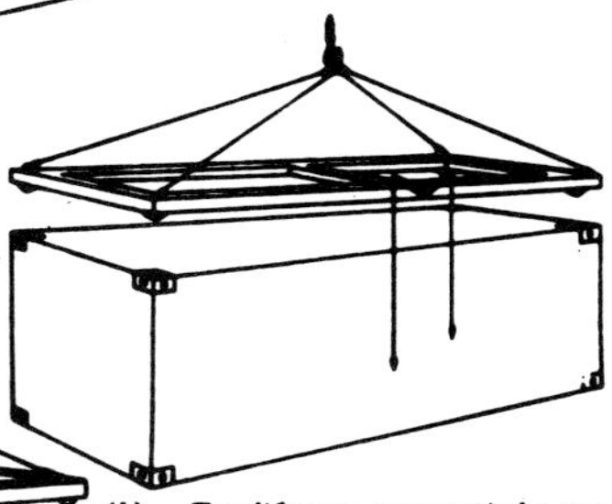

(b) Top lift semi-automatic by means of spreader twist locks

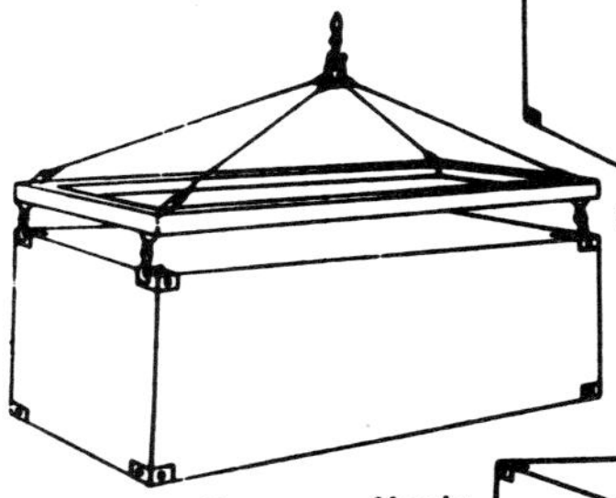

(c) Top lift manual by means of hooks or clevis

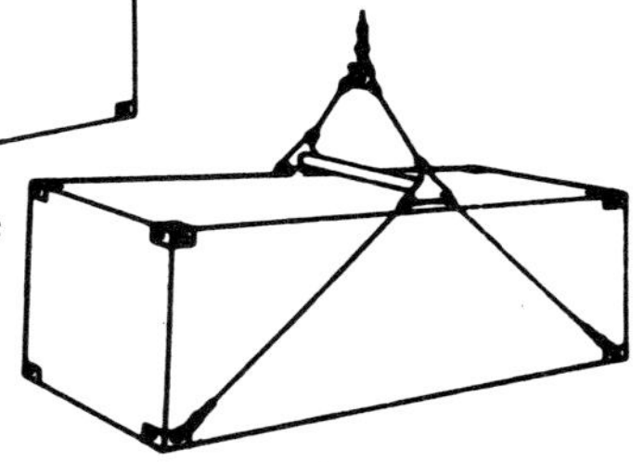

(d) Bottom lift by means of slings

FIG. A.1 Examples of methods of lifting containers by corner fittings

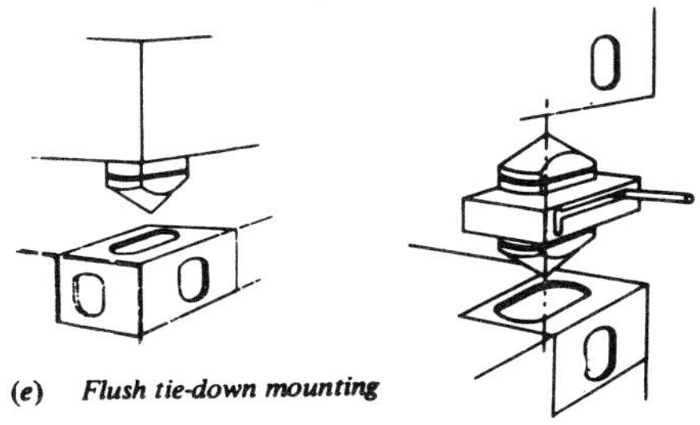

(e) Flush tie-down mounting

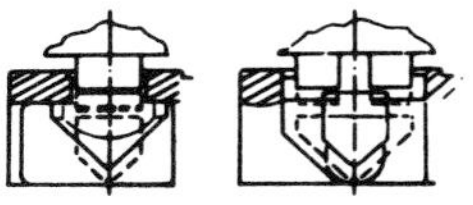

(f) Bolster with throw-bolt lock from front or side

(c) Tie-down fitting

(d) Tie-down with corner guidance

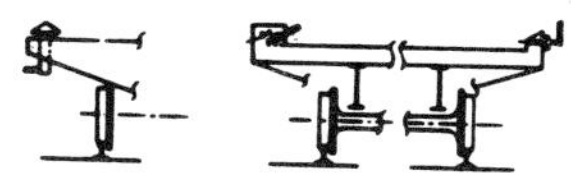

(a) Spreader twist lock

(b) Stacking fitting
Application of twist lock tie-down fitting (shown inverted with respect to drawing (c)) and stacking fitting.

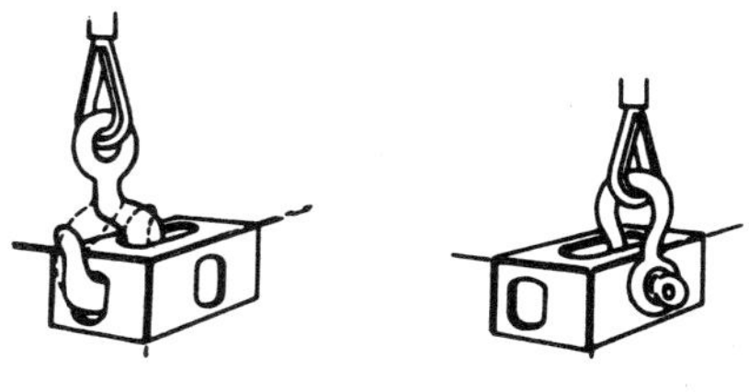

(g) Hook engagement

(h) Clevis engagement

FIG. A.2 - Examples of corner fitting engaging, lifting and securing devices

ANNEX B

TYPICAL HANDLING AND SECURING METHODS

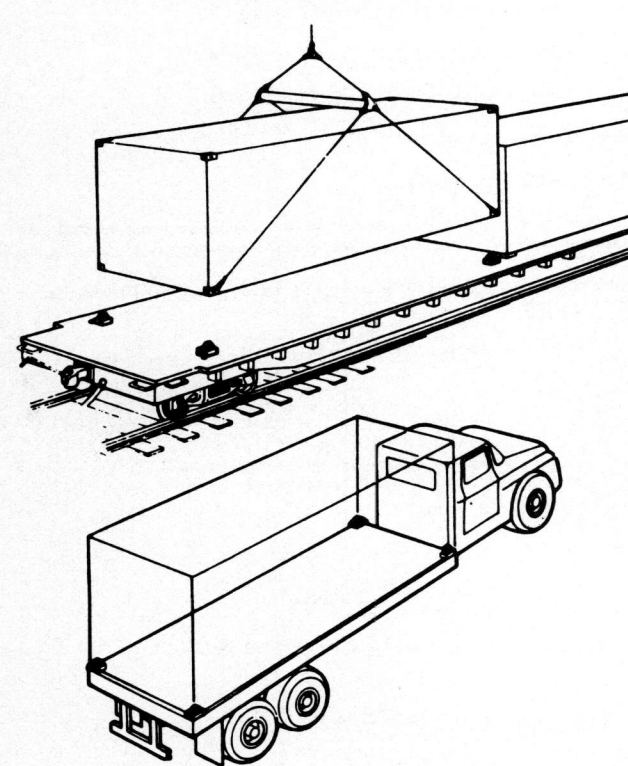

FIG. B.1   Example of use of corner fittings in railway
and road vehicle applications

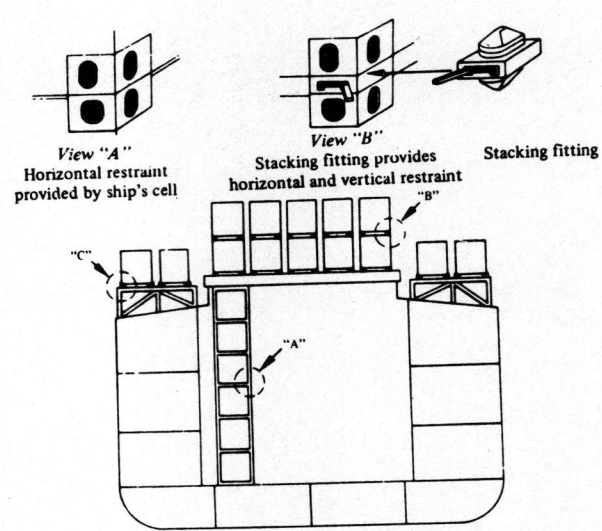

View "A"
Horizontal restraint
provided by ship's cell

View "B"
Stacking fitting provides
horizontal and vertical restraint

Stacking fitting

Example of container ship cross-section

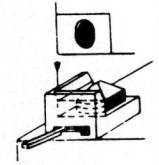

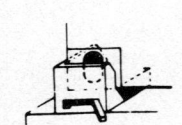

View "C"
Example of deck securing fitting which provides
gathering plus both horizontal and vertical restraint

FIG. B.2   Examples of use of corner fittings on ships
(In vertical container cells and on deck)

ANNEX C
Corner Fitting Design Criteria

The following design criteria were used in establishing the dimensional design of corner fitting specified in this ISO Recommendation.

C.1.   GENERAL CONSIDERATIONS

The designer of corner fittings should consider

(a) the tensile strength of the material to be used;

(b) the loads which the fittings will have to withstand;

(c) the dimensions of the fittings.

A knowledge of any two of these factors allows the third factor to be deduced.

C.2.   DEFINITIONS OF LOADS

Corner fittings for series 1 freight containers should withstand the loads calculated for the 1A container, as listed in the following clauses.

C.2.1.   Stacking

	Design load service conditions	Design load test conditions
Top corner fitting (Superimposed load offset 25·4 mm (1 in) laterally and 38 mm (1½ in) longitudinally	680 kN (69,000 kgf or 68 tonf)	680 kN (69,000 kgf or 68 tonf)
Bottom corner fitting (resting on flat support)	810 kN (82,000 kgf or 81 tonf)	810 kN (82,000 kgf or 81 tonf)

Bottom corner fitting

(of No. 5 container offset 25·4 mm (1 in) laterally and 38 mm (1½ in) longitudinally with respect to No. 6 container)	680 kN (69,000 kgf or 68 tonf)	680 kN (69,000 kgf or 68 tonf)

NOTE: It is considered unnecessary to increase the test load above the operational load in view of the low probability of the operational load being encountered.

C.2.2   Lifting

Top corner fitting (twist lock, hook or shackle)	75 kN (7,600 kgf or 7·5 tonf)	150 kN (15,200 kgf or 15 tonf)
Bottom corner fitting: sling at 30° to horizontal	150 kN (15,200 kgf or 15 tonf)	300 kN (30,400 kgf or 30 tonf)

NOTES:

Bottom corner fitting lifting

1. The line of action of the sling load is assumed to be parallel to and not more than 38 mm (1½ in) from the outer face of the corner fitting.

2. The load values quoted are for slings at the angles stated, but it is recognised that slings may be used at any angle between the angle stated and the vertical.

C.2.3 Restraint

	Design load service conditions	Design load test conditions
Bottom corner fittings	300 kN (30,400 kgf or 30 tonf)	380 kN each (38,100 kgf or 38 tonf each)
(2 fittings carrying load)	$(2g \times R)$	$(2g \times 1\cdot25\ R)$

C.2.4 Deck lashing

Deck lashings should be so designed that loads imparted at front and side holes of both top and bottom corner fittings do not exceed 300 kN (30,400 kgf or 30 tonf) vertically and 150 kN (15,200 kgf or 15 tonf) horizontally, both forces being in a plane parallel to the face of the corner fitting to which attachment is made, and the said plane should not be more than 38 mm ($1\frac{1}{2}$ in) from the outer face of the corner fitting. (See Fig. C.1.).

C.2.5 Misgather (localized loading of bottom corner fittings caused by lowering of container onto locating fittings which are not gathered into the hole).

Bottom corner fittings should be subjected to a test load of 150 kN (15,200 kgf or 15 tonf) applied normally to the contact area 25 mm (1 in) × 6 mm ($\frac{1}{4}$ in) on the bottom face. (See Fig. C.2.).

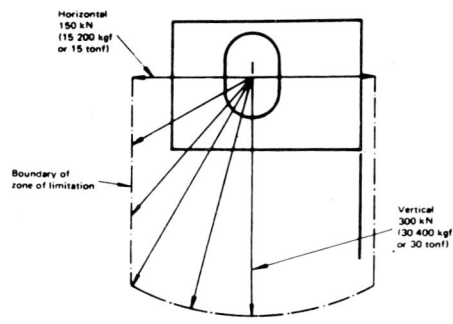

FIG. C.1 — Limits of deck lashing loads

C.3. DESIGN OF FITTINGS

C.3.1. Compulsory walls or faces in the corner fittings

C.3.1.1. *Top corner fittings*
—the top face
—the side wall
—the end wall

C.3.1.2. *Bottom corner fittings*
—the bottom face
—the side wall
—the end wall

C.3.2. Top corner fitting

C.3.2.1.   0   0

The top face should be 28·5 - 1·5 mm ($1\frac{1}{8}$ - $\frac{1}{16}$ in) thick throughout.

C.3.2.2.   0   0

The side wall should be 20·5 -1·5 mm ($\frac{13}{16}$ - $\frac{1}{16}$ in) thick for 16 mm ($\frac{5}{8}$ in) all around the side hole.

C.3.2.3.   0   0

The end wall should be 20·5 -1·5 mm ($\frac{13}{16}$ - $\frac{1}{16}$ in) thick for 16 mm ($\frac{5}{8}$ in) all around the side hole

C.3.3. Bottom corner fitting

C.3.3.1.   0   0

The bottom face should be 28·5 -1·5 mm ($1\frac{1}{2}$ - $\frac{1}{16}$ in) thick throughout

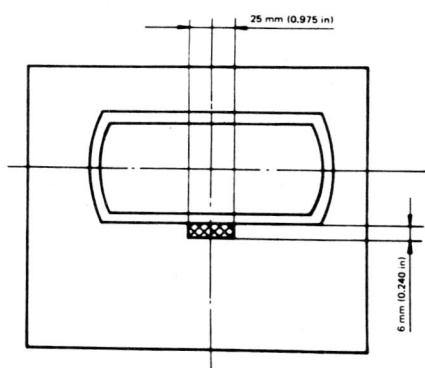

FIG. C.2 - Bottom view of bottom corner fitting
showing contact area (shaded) for misgather (push-up) test

C.3.3.2.   0   0

The side wall should be 20·5 -1·5 mm ($\frac{13}{16}$ - $\frac{1}{16}$ in) thick for 16 mm ($\frac{5}{8}$ in) all around the side hole

C.3.3.3.   0   0

The end wall should be 20·5 -1·5 mm ($\frac{13}{16}$ - $\frac{1}{16}$ in) thick for 16 mm ($\frac{5}{8}$ in) all around the side hole.

APPENDIX Y
RELEASE OF PATENTS

The basic patent considered pertinent to the function of a corner fitting handling, securing and lifting system is U.S.A. Patent No. 3 042 227 assigned to Sea-Land Service, Inc., who have released this patent on a royalty-free basis for its use in creating an international standard.

The recommended design of an engaging device used for lifting containers includes U.S.A. Patent No. 2 963 310 assigned to the Strick Trailer Company and this has also been released for use in the development of an international standard.

APPENDIX Z
PRECAUTIONARY NOTE ON END-TO-END COUPLING

A clarification of the patent position with regard to end-to-end coupling of freight containers is deemed pertinent.

End-to-end coupling of freight containers is subject to the rights granted by the issuance of U.S.A. Patent No. 3 004 772 to the Strick Trailer Company.

Because of the proprietary nature of end-to-end couplings of containers, this function could not be included in the design of the corner fittings recommended herein. However, if this function is desired, permission for its use must be obtained from the patent holder. In such circumstances, designers are cautioned to follow all the prescribed requirements for the fittings given in this ISO Recommendation.

TABLE: Dimensions and tolerances in millimetres and in feet and inches

Freight container designation	Length (external) mm	ft	—	in	S mm	ft	in	P mm	ft	in	K_1 max mm	in	K_2 max mm	in
1A	12,190 +2 −8	40	0	0 −$\frac{3}{8}$	11,985	39	3$\frac{7}{8}$	2,259	7	4$\frac{31}{32}$	19	$\frac{3}{4}$	10	$\frac{3}{8}$
1B	9,125 0 −10	29	11−	0 −$\frac{1}{4}$	8,918	29	3$\frac{1}{4}$	2,259	7	4$\frac{31}{32}$	16	$\frac{5}{8}$	10	$\frac{3}{8}$
1C	6,055 +3 −3	19	10$\frac{1}{2}$	0 −$\frac{1}{4}$	5,853	19	2$\frac{7}{16}$	2,259	7	4$\frac{31}{32}$	13	$\frac{1}{2}$	10	$\frac{3}{8}$
1D	2,990 +1 −4	9	9$\frac{3}{4}$	0 −$\frac{3}{16}$	2,787	9	1$\frac{23}{32}$	2,259	7	4$\frac{31}{32}$	10	$\frac{3}{8}$	10	$\frac{3}{8}$

Width (external)—Containers 1A, 1B, 1C, 1D: 2,435 +3mm (8 ft 0   0 in)
                                        −2   −$\frac{3}{16}$

Height (external)—Containers 1A, 1B, 1C, 1D: 2,435 +3 mm (8 ft 0   0 in)
                                         −2   −$\frac{3}{16}$

NOTE: Attention of manufacturers is drawn to the vital importance of accurately maintaining the reference dimensions of S and P. The tolerance to be applied to S and P are governed by the tolerances shown for the overall length and width in this ISO Recommendation and in ISO Recommendation R 668.

MARKING OF FREIGHT CONTAINERS SERIES 1 AND 2
ISO RECOMMENDATION 790
(REVISED TEXT)

1. SCOPE

This ISO Recommendation sets out requirements for the marking for identification purposes of Series 1 and Series 2 freight containers.

It should be noted that consideration is being given to the preparation of a code for the marking of freight containers in order to facilitate documentation by data processing methods. Until such time as acceptable methods of coding have been adopted as ISO Recommendations, it is recommended that the following requirements should be marked in 'clear', (i.e. uncoded), language.

2. MARKING

Each freight container should carry at least the markings presented in this ISO Recommendation and at the locations indicated (see Fig. 1).

All markings should be in characters not less than 100 mm (4 in) high, the characters being of proportionate width and thickness. They should be durable and in a colour contrasting with that of the container.

2.1. DOOR (at the top right-hand corner)

Owner's mark and serial number, with space provided for at least seven characters (see Fig. 1, item 1).

Maximum gross weight in kilogrammes and in short tons (see Fig. 1, item 2).

* At present Draft ISO Recommendation No. 1496.

**At present Draft ISO Recommendation No. 1497.

Tare weight in kilogrammes and in short tons (see Fig. 1, item 3).

Characters for maximum gross weight and tare weight should be not less than 50 mm (2 in) high.

The ton referred to in this ISO Recommendation is equal to 2,240 lbs approximately 1,016 kg.

2.2. END OR SIDE WALL OPPOSITE TO THE DOOR (at the top right hand corner)

Owner's mark and serial number (see Fig. 1, item 1).

2.3. ROOF (at diagonally opposite corners).

Owner's mark and serial number (see Fig. 1, item 1).

2.4. SIDE WALLS (on the remaining side walls at the top right-hand corner).

Owner's mark and serial number (see Fig. 1, item 1).

A single code letter for external overall dimensions of the freight container (see Fig. 1, item 4).

A two-digit code number for the type of freight container (see Fig. 1, item 5).

A character to indicate that it is a freight container (see Fig. 1, item 6).

The country of ownership in a code of up to three letters (if required) (see Fig. 1, item 7).

3. CARRIAGE OF DOCUMENTS

A pocket for the carriage of documents should be provided.

Note.—It is recommended that on each side wall, at the bottom right-hand corner, a label holder, recessed if necessary, should be located 200 mm (8 in) above the base (see Fig. 1, item 8). In addition, a transit marking plate or area, where practicable, having dimensions of 350 mm (14 in) wide by 500 mm (20 in) long, may be located above this label holder and recessed if necessary (see Fig. 1, item 9).

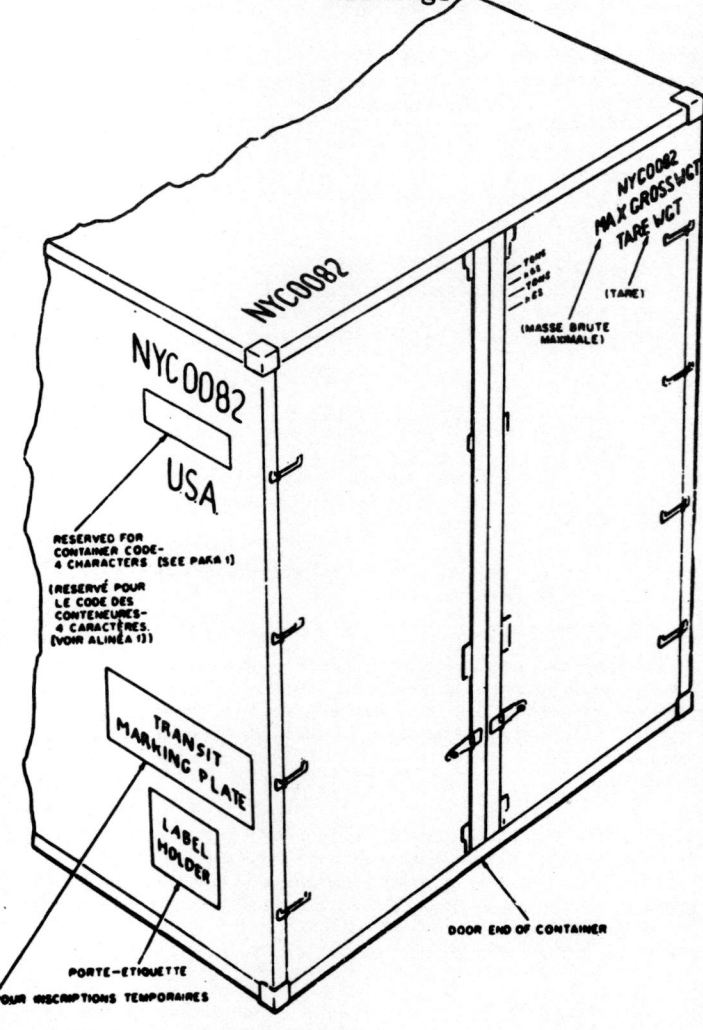

Fig. 1 Diagram showing location of markings

Fig 2 Example of typical marking

SPECIFICATIONS FOR IDENTIFICATION AND MARKING CARGO CONTAINERS
American National Standard: ANSI MH 5.3 1970

It should be noted this is a National Standard and not an ISO document. It has been extracted from American National Standard Specifications for Identification and Marking Cargo Containers, ANSI MH 5.3—1970, with the permission of the publisher, The American Society of Mechanical Engineers, United Engineering Center, 345 East 47th Street, New York, N.Y., 10017.

FOREWORD:

This standard relates to an identification marking system for cargo containers and is intended to provide information on containers for efficient routing, handling, interchange and tracing of containers. The marking information is developed in such a manner so as to be informative to operating personnel upon visual inspection and lend itself to modern data processing techniques.

Following submittal by the sponsor organisations, The American Society of Mechanical Engineers and the International Material Management Society, the standard was approved by ANSI on 31 March, 1970.

1. SCOPE AND PURPOSE:

1.1 The Scope of the Identification and Marking Standard Specifications provides a system through which cargo containers moving in international and/or domestic service, can easily be identified as to owner's name and serial number, type and size of container and country of registration. The acceptance of these standard specifications by all parties concerned will prevent duplication in marking.

1.2 The purpose of these specifications is to:

(1) provide a uniform base for marking and identifying containers for intermodal use

(2) provide a functional tool for operating personnel

(3) provide a system that will lend itself to modern data processing techniques

The standard code also provides the basis for efficient routing, handling, interchange and tracing of containers, and provides the basis for a centralised registry of cargo containers.

2. IDENTIFICATION CODE SPECIFICATIONS:

2.1 Owner's Identification code shall contain four (4) alphabetic characters which will designate ownership of the container. Example: CCLU Cary Container Leasing System.

2.2 Unit Serial Number Specifications. The unit serial number will contain six (6) numeric digits (123456). If the unit serial number requires less than six digits (1234), the numbers will be left-hand indexed with zeros (001234). The primary use of this number is to facilitate identification of the unit. These specifications do not attach any symbolic meanings to these numbers.

2.3 Type and Size Code Specifications. Two numeric digits will be assigned to both type and size, creating a numerical code. Example: Type Code 20—General Purpose (dry cargo) Cargo Container with doors at end. Size Code 20—Normal container size, 20 × 8 × 8 ft (see 3.5.3. and 3.5.4).

2.4 Gross and Tare Weights Specifications. The gross weight of the container will be represented in pounds and its metric equivalent. The tare weight of the container will be represented in pounds and its metric equivalent.

2.5 Country of Ownerships Code Specifications. The country code will consist of three (3) alphabetic characters (USA). It is proposed that the existing alphabetic code used to indicat the country of registration of vehicles used in international road traffic will be used as the basis for country of ownerships marking. If only one or two letters are used to designate a country (Costa Rica—CR, Belgium—B) the use of the letter X will be required to fill out the code i.e. CRX, BXX.

2.6 Order of Identification Code Characters

Owner Company	4 code letters
Owner's Serial Number	6 code numbers
Country of Origin	3 code letters
Type	2 code numbers
Size	2 code numbers

Total—17 characters—7 alpha, 10 numeric.

2.7 Example of Identification Code

CCLU 123456 2020 USA

Owner (Cary Container Leasing System) CCLU.

Owner's Serial Number—123456.

Type* (General Purpose, dry cargo)—20.

Size* (Nominal Size, 20 × 8 × 8)—20.

Country of Registration* (United States of America)—USA.

*Required only in international Interchange Service.

3. TYPE CODE FOR CARGO CONTAINER:

The first digit of each code will signify the generic type of container, i.e. 6—Tank Cargo Container. Unless otherwise specified, the second digit beginning with the number 1 through number 8 will signify the specific sub-type. (For example, the code 68 could represent an end loading, end discharging tank container).

NOTE: Code numbers 00 to 10 are reserved for the present generation of air containers).

3.1 General Purpose (dry cargo) Cargo Containers (code 20)
20 Doors at End
21—28 Code to be developed
29 Open Code
3.2 Platform (flatbed) Cargo Containers (code 30)
31—38 Code to be developed
39 Open Code
3.3 Open Top Cargo Containers (code 40)
41—48 Code to be developed
49 Open Code
3.4 Mechanically Refrigerated Cargo Containers (code 50)
Codes to read 50—58 (coding to await further inputs from Task Force on Refrigerated Containers).

59 Open Code
3.5 Tank Cargo Containers (code 60)
61—68 Code to be developed
69 Open Code
3.6 Insulated Cargo Containers—Ventilated Cargo Containers (code 70)
71—78 Code to be developed
79 Open Code
3.7 Open Frame or Rack Cargo Containers (code 80)
81—88 Code to be developed
89 Open Code
3.8 Special Containers i.e. Cattle Carriers, Auto Carriers, etc. (code 90)
91—99 Code to be developed

4. Size Code for Cargo Containers

(All containers 8 ft in width unless otherwise specified)
4.1 Containers under 10 ft Long
03 containers 5 ft in length and 8 ft in height
04 containers 5 ft in length and less than 8 ft in height
05 containers 5 ft in length and more than 8 ft in height
06 containers 6¾ ft in length and 8 ft in height
07 containers 6¾ ft in length and less than ft in height
08 containers 6¾ ft in length and more than 8 in height (includes ISO Series IE)
01, 02, and
09 other containers less than 10 ft in length (open codes)
4.2 Containers 10 ft and under 20 ft long
10 10 ft containers 8 ft in height
11 10 ft containers less than 8 ft in height
12 10 ft containers more than 8 ft in height
13—18 Other container lengths between 10 and 20 ft
19 open code
4.3 Containers 20 ft and under 30 ft long
20 20 ft containers 8 ft in height
21 20 ft containers less than 8 ft in height
22 20 ft containers more than 8 ft in height
23 24 ft container 8 ft in height
24 24 ft containers less than 8 ft in height
25 24 ft containers more than 8 ft in height
26—28 other container lengths between 20 ft and 30 ft
29 open code
4.4 Containers 30 ft and under 40 ft long
30 30 ft containers 8 ft in height
31 30 ft containers less than 8 ft in height
32 30 ft containers more than 8 ft in height
33 35 ft containers 8 ft in height
34 35 ft containers less than 8 ft in height
35 35 ft containers more than 8 ft in height
36—38 other container lengths between 35 and 40ft
39 open code
4.5 Containers 40 ft and over in length
40 40 ft containers 8 ft in height
41 40 ft containers less than 8 ft in height
42 40 ft containers more than 8 ft in height
43—48 other containers 40 ft and over in length
49 open code

5. MINIMUM MARKING SPECIFICATIONS FOR CARGO CONTAINERS:

5.1 Marking Location (see diagram).

5.1.1 Owners' Identification Code. The owner's identification code shall appear in four locations on the container. The four character alphabetic code (ABCD) will be marked on both sides and on both ends of the unit.

NOTE: Additional code locations may be used as an optional requirement.

5.1.1.1 Side Location. The approximate location of the code when placed on the sides will be the upper ½ of the unit. The forward ½ of the unit also.

5.1.1.2 End Location. The approximate location of the code when placed on the ends would be the upper right hand corner, direction of travel, upper left-hand corner, facing rear or door end.

5.1.2 Unit Serial Number. The unit serial number will follow in sequence after the owners' identification code (ABCD123456) and will be located on the unit in the same approximate area as the owner's identification code.

5.1.3 Type and Size Code. The approximate location will be the rear end (door end) and left-hand panel, when facing rear end of container. The order of appearance will be type code first (1st), and size code second (2nd).

5.1.4 Gross and Tare Weight. The approximate location of the gross and tare weight markings will be directly beneath the type and size code.

5.1.5 Country of Ownership. The country of ownership code (USA) will be located on the left panel rear end of the container (door end) and will follow in sequence after the type and size code (i.e. 2020USA).

6. IDENTIFICATION PLATE SPECIFICATION:

Content: The plate will contain the following information in order of appearance:

Owner's Identification Code and Unit Serial No CCLU 001213
Type and Size Code and Country of Registration
2020 USA
Maximum Gross Weight   lb   kg
Tare weight   lb   kg
Inside Volume ft³   m³
Manufacturer's Name and Location
   Premium Container Corp.
Aurora, Utah
Manufacturer's Serial Number

Serial No. 1356789
Date of Manufacture
3/65

6.1 The identification data plate will measure 3 in × 5 in and will contain ¼ in lettering embossed in permanent fashion upon the plate. (see exhibit).

6.2 The identification plate shall be placed on the lower corner and forward end right side direction of travel, of the container.

7. SIZE OF MARKING:

Markings shall be in characters not less than four inches high and of proportional width and thickness*. All markings should be durable and in a colour contrasting with the container.

*The markings required for gross and Tare Weight shall be in characters not less than two inches high and of proportional width and thickness.

8. MODIFICATIONS OF MARKING LOCATION AND SIZE:

For certain types of rack, platform, tank, etc. containers alternative marking locations may be required to accommodate the markings specified above, and different sizes of characters may be required under varying circumstances.

9. ADDITIONAL MARKING REQUIREMENTS:

9.1 Stacking Limitations. Air containers that are not capable of being stacked should be marked to indicate this limitation. Air/Land Only or Not to be Stacked should be clearly labelled on the top and both sides.

9.2 Additional marking requirements are required in the movement of hazardous cargoes.

APPENDIX
COUNTRY CODE DESIGNATIONS

Note: The following codings are based on the International Convention of Road Traffic. Where less than three letters are provided in the Code, the Code should be filed out to three letters by the addition of X's.

Albania, ALX; Algeria, DZX; Andorra, AND; Angola, PAN; Argentina, RAX; Australia, AUS; Austria, AXX; Bahrein, BRN; Barbados, BDS; Bechuanaland, BPX; Belgium, BXX; Botswana, RBX; Brazil, BRX; Bulgaria, BGX; Burma, BUR; Cambodia, KXX; Canada, CDN; Central African Republic, RCA; Ceylon, CLX; Chile, RCH; China, RCX; Colombia, COX; Congo (Brazzaville), RCB; Congo (Democratic Republic of), CGO; Costa Rica, CRX; Cuba, CXX; Curacao, CUX; Cyprus CYX; Czechoslovakia, CSX; Dahomey, DYX; Denmark, DKX; Dominican Republic, DOM; Dominica, WDX; Ecuador, ECX; Ethiopia, ETH; Finland, SFX; France, FXX; Gambia, WAG; Germany, DXX; Ghana, GHX; Greece, GRX; Guatemala, GGA; Guayana, BRG; Haiti, RHX; Holy See, VXX; Hungary, HXX; Iceland, ISX; India, IND; Indonesia, RIX; Iran, IRX; Iraq, IRQ; Ireland, IRL; Isle of Man, GBM; Israel, ILX; Italy, IXX; Ivory Coast, CIX; Jamaica, JAX; Japan, JXX; Jordan, HKJ; Kenya, EAK; Kuwait, KWT; Laos, LAO; Lebanon, RLX; Lesotho, LSX; Liechtenstein, FLX; Luxembourg, LXX; Malagasay Republic, RMX; Malawi, MWX; Malaysia, PTM; Mali, RMM; Malta, MXX; Mexico, MEX; Monaco, MCX; Morocco, MAX; Mocambique, MOC; Netherlands, NLX; Surinam, SME; Netherlands Antilles, NAX; New Zealand, NZX; Nicaragua, NIC; Niger, NIG; Nigeria, WAN; Norway, NXX; Pakistan, PAK; Panama, PAX; Paraguay, PYX; Peru, PEX; Philippines, PIX; Poland, PLX; Portugal, PXX; Romania, RXX; Rwanda, RWA; San Merino, RSM; Senegal, SNX; Sierra Leone, WAL; Singapore, SGP; Somalia, SPX; South Africa, ZAX; South West Africa, ZWA; Spain, EXX; Sweden, SXX; Switzerland, CHX; Syria, SYR; Thailand, TXX; Togo, TGX; Trinidad and Tobago, TTX; Tunisia, TNX; Turkey, TRX; Uganda, EAU; USSR, SUX; United Arab Republic, ETX; United Kingdom, GBX; Aden, ADN; Alderney, GBA; Bahamas, BSX; British Honduras, BHX; Brunei, BRU; Guernsey, GBG; Gibraltar, GBZ; Jersey, GBJ; Hong Kong, HKX; Mauritius, MSX; Province Wellesley, SSX; Seychelles, SYX; Southern Rhodesia, RSR; Swaziland, SDX; Windward Islands: Grenada, WGX; St. Lucia, WLX; St. Vincent, WVX; United Republic of Tanzania: Tanganyika, EAT; Zanzibar, EAZ; United States, USA; Uruguay, UXX; Urundi, RUX; Vatican, SCV; Venezuela, YVX; Viet-Nam (Republic of), VNX; Western Samoa, WSX; Yugoslavia, YUX; Zambia, ZXX.

TERMINOLOGY ISO RECOMMENDATION NO. 830

1. DEFINITIONS:

1.1 Freight Container

By *freight container* is meant an article of transport equipment.

(a) of a permanent character and accordingly strong enough to be suitable for repeated use;

(b) specially designed to facilitate the carriage of goods, by one or more modes of transport, without intermediate reloading;

(c) fitted with devices permitting its ready handling, particularly its transfer from one mode of transport to another;

(d) so designed as to be easy to fill and empty;

(e) having an internal volume of 35·3 ft³ (1 m³) or more.

The term *freight container* does not include vehicles or conventional packing.

1.2 General Purpose Freight Container

Freight container of rectangular shape, weatherproof, for transporting and storing a number of unit loads, packages or bulk material; that confines and protects the contents from loss or damage; that can be separated from the means of transport, handled as a unit load and transhipped without rehandling the contents (see Fig. 1 and 2).

2. CHARACTERISTICS OF FREIGHT CONTAINERS:

2.1 Non-Collapsible Freight Container

Freight container of rigid construction, the components of which are permanently assembled.

2.2. Collapsible Freight Container

Freight Container of rigid construction, the major components of which can easily be folded or dis-assembled and then re-assembled.

3. FREIGHT CONTAINER WEIGHTS:

3.1 Maximum Gross Weights

Maximum allowable total weight of freight container and its payload.

3.2 Tare Weight

Weight of empty freight container.

3.3 Maximum Payload

Maximum allowable weight of payload (maximum gross weight less tare weight).

3.4 Actual Gross Weight

Total weight of the freight container and its payload.

3.5 Actual Payload

Difference between the actual gross weight and the tare weight of the freight container.

4. FREIGHT CONTAINER STATIC AND DYNAMIC LOADS:

4.1 Floor Load

Static and Dynamic loads imposed on the floor by the payload and the wheels of handling equipment when used.

4.2 End Load

Static and dynamic loads imposed by the payload and the freight container walls and doors which are perpendicular to the longitudinal axis of the freight container.

4.3 Side Load

Static and dynamic loads imposed by the payload on the freight container walls and doors which are parallel to the longitudinal axis of the freight container.

4.4 Roof Load

External static and dynamic loads imposed on the roof of a freight container.

4.5 Superimposed Load

External static and dynamic loads imposed vertically downwards on the structure of the freight container.

5. FREIGHT CONTAINER DIMENSIONS AND VOLUME:

5.1 Dimensions

Height, width and length of a freight container, measured parallel to each of its axes and expressed in this order.

5.2 Overall External Dimensions

Maximum external overall dimensions of a freight container, including any permanent attachment.

5.3 Displacement

Volume of a freight container as determined by the multiplication of its overall external dimensions.

5.4 Internal Unobstructed Dimensions

Dimensions determined on the greatest unobstructed rectangular parallelepiped that can be inscribed in the freight container, discounting corner fittings.

5.5 Unobstructed Capacity

Volume determined by the multiplication of the internal unobstructed dimensions.

5.6 Capacity

Total internal volume.

6. FREIGHT CONTAINER COMPONENTS:

6.1 Corner Structures

Vertical frame component located at the corners of the freight container, integral with the corner fittings and connecting the roof and floor structures (see Fig. 3).

6.2 Corner Fittings

Fittings located at the corners of the freight container which normally provide means for handling, stacking and securing the freight container (see Fig. 3 and 4).

6.3 Lifting or Securing Eye

System attached to the freight container consisting essentially of rings or loops intended to facilitate its lifting or its securing (see Fig. 2).

6.4 End Frame

Each of the structures of the freight container perpendicular to its longitudinal axis consisting of the corner structures and the end members of the base and of the roof (see Fig. 5).

6.5 End Wall

Assembly surrounded by the end frame which encloses either end of the freight container (see Fig. 5).

6.6 Side Frame

Each of the structures parallel to the longitudinal axis of the freight container, consisting of the corner structures and of the bottom side rails and roof rails (see Fig. 6).

6.7 Side Wall
Assembly surrounded by the side frame either side of the freight container (see Fig. 6).

6.8 Roof Rails
Longitudinal structural members situated at the top edge on either side of the freight container (see Fig. 6).

6.9 Bottom Side Rails
Structural members situated on the longitudinal sides of the base (see Fig. 6).

6.10 End Door
Door located in an end wall (see Fig. 7).

6.11 Side Door
Door located in a side wall (see Fig. 8).

6.12 Roof
Assembly forming the top closure of the freight container limited by the end frames and the roof rails (see Fig. 6).

6.13 Base
Assembly of which the principal components are:
(a) the two bottom longitudinal members,
(b) the two bottom end members,
(c) the floor, and
(d) possibly, the cross members.
(see Fig. 9).

6.14 Cross Members
Transverse components attached to the bottom side rails and supporting the floor (see Fig. 9).

6.15 Floor
Component supporting the payload (see Fig. 9).

6.16 Skids
Beams on which certain freight containers are mounted to facilitate handling (see Fig. 2).

6.17 Fork Pockets
Openings arranged for the entry of the forks of handling devices (see Fig. 2).

General purpose freight container

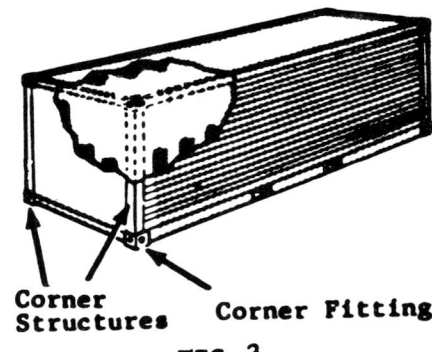
Corner Structures   Corner Fitting
FIG 3

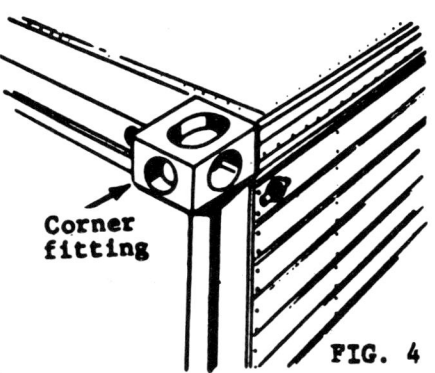
Corner fitting
FIG. 4

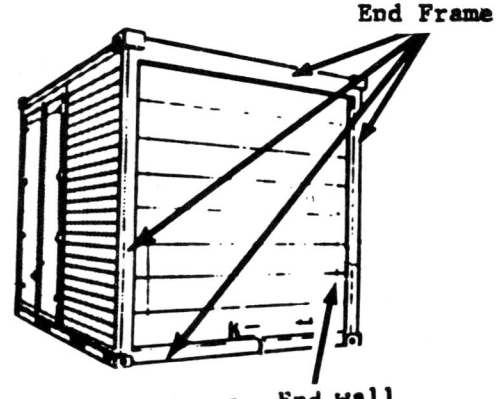
End Frame
FIG. 5   End wall

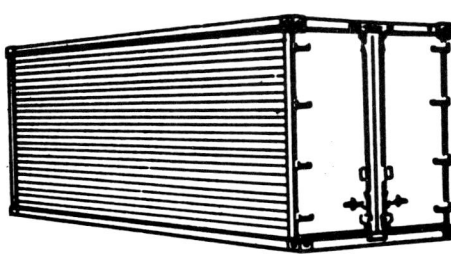
FIG. 1

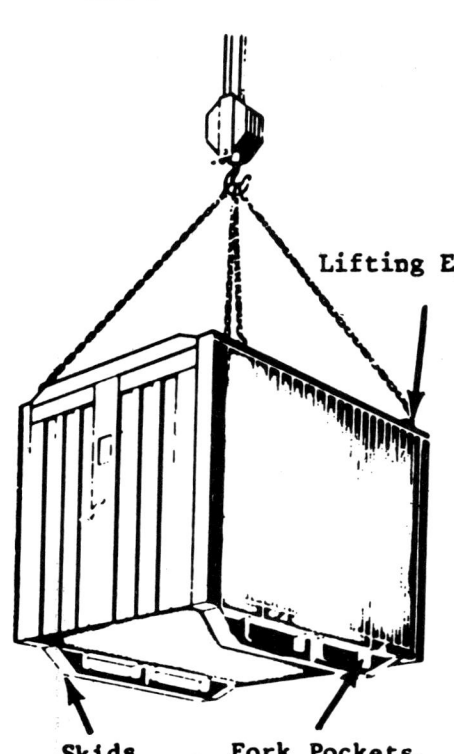
Skids   Fork Pockets.
Lifting Eye
FIG. 2

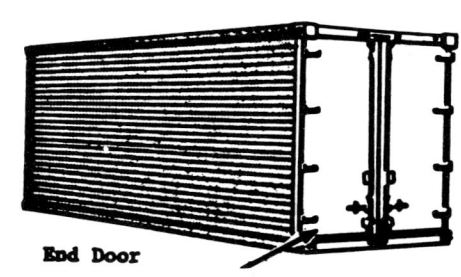
Side frame   Roof   Roof Rails   side wall   bottom side rails
FIG. 6

End Door   FIG. 7

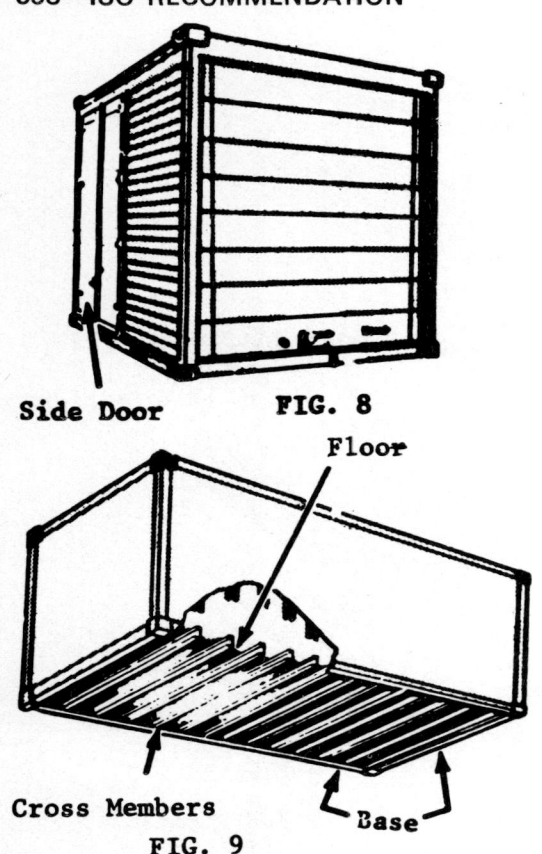

Side Door   **FIG. 8**

Floor

Cross Members   **Base**

FIG. 9

Minimum Marking Locations for Container Moving in International Trade

1.   Owner's Identification Code and Unit Serial Number (CCLU 123456).

2.   Identification Plate (See Data Plate below).

3.   Type and Size Data, Country of Ownership and Gross and Tare Weights expressed in pounds and kilograms.

NOTE: Additional Code locations may be used as an optional requirement.

Data Plate

CCLU001213 (Owner's Identification Code)

20 20 USA (Type, Size, Country of Ownership)

Max Gross Weight,   lb,   kg

Tare Weight,   lb,   kg

Inside Volume   ft³,   m³

Premium Container Corporation (Manufacturer's Name, and Location)

Manufacturer's Serial Number 1356789

Date of Manufacture 3/65

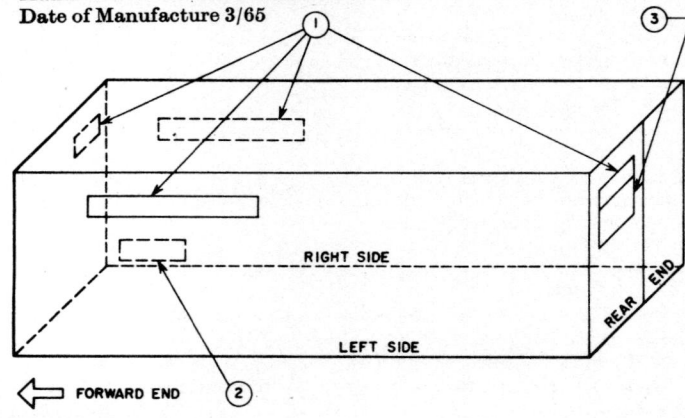

A PROPOSAL FOR AN OPTIONAL GOOSENECK TUNNEL IN A TYPE 1AA CONTAINER

The 40 ft container of 8 ft 6 in height creates problems of overall height when mounted on a semi-trailer for road transport. A tunnel in the front end of a container to accommodate a gooseneck-crank in the semi-trailer chassis frame above the king-pin and coupling plate is being studied as a Device to reduce the overall height by approximately $4\frac{3}{4}$ inches. In simple terms the tunnel is formed by cutting away the first six (say) floor bearers where they pass over the crank in the chassis and fitting a strong, unsupported floor above the tunnel.

The dimensions and sketches appearing below are from an SC1 working document and should NOT BE TAKEN AS A STANDARD but even if variations are made before a draft ISO Recommendation is published they cannot greatly affect the dimensions which are largely controlled by the geometry of the container itself.

It will be easier to read the diagram (fig. 1) if it is understood that the rectangle (half of which is dotted) represents the corner casting and the bottom line to which dimensions B & C are taken is not a construction line but the plane of the bottom corner fitting protrusion below the base of the container.

The sectional drawing (fig. 2) culled from an earlier USA proposal has been included to illustrate the end-on arrangement

Length	Lt_1	3,156 mm	$124\frac{1}{4}$ ins
	D	6 ± 1 mm	$\frac{1}{4} \pm \frac{1}{32}$ ins
Width	At	$1,029 + 3$ mm -0	$40\frac{1}{2} + \frac{1}{8}$ ins -0
Heights	B	$132.5 + 3.5$ mm -1.5	$5\frac{3}{16} + \frac{1}{8}$ ins $-\frac{1}{16}$
	C	$12.5 + 5$ mm -1.5	$\frac{1}{2} + \frac{3}{16}$ ins $-\frac{1}{16}$
	Bt	$120 + 0$ mm -1.5	$4\frac{23}{32} + 0$ ins $-\frac{1}{16}$
	Bt_1	120 mm (max)	$4\frac{23}{32}$ ins (max)

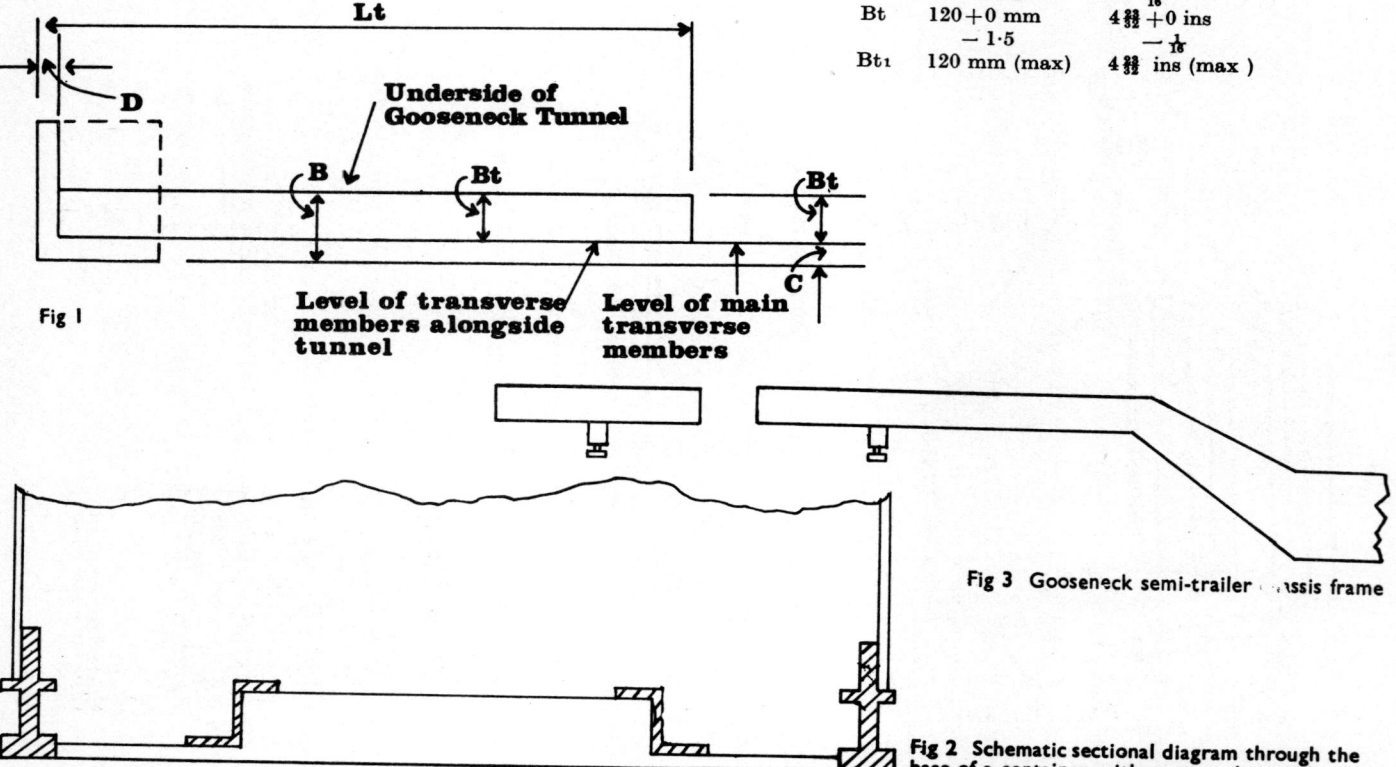

Fig 1

Lt

Underside of Gooseneck Tunnel

B   **Bt**   **Bt**

C

Level of transverse members alongside tunnel   **Level of main transverse members**

Fig 3 Gooseneck semi-trailer chassis frame

Fig 2 Schematic sectional diagram through the base of a container with gooseneck tunnel.

ISO MEMBER BODIES

AUSTRALIA (SAA)
Standards Association of Australia, Standards House, 80-86 Arthur Street, North Sydney, NSW 2060
Telephone: 929-6022   Telegrams: Austandard
Mr. A. L. Stewart (*Director*)

AUSTRIA
Oesterreichisches Normunginstitut, Leopoldsgasse 4, A1020 Wien
Telephone: 33 55 19   Telegrams: Austrianorm   Telex: 42 35
Ing. Franz J. Mayer (*Director*)

BELGIUM
Institut Belge de Normalisation, 29 Av de la Brabançonne, Bruxelles 4
Telephone: 34 92 05   Telegrams: Benor
M. M. Vanpée (*Directeur*)

BRAZIL
Associação Brasileira de Normas Técnicas, Caixa Postal No. 1680, Rio de Janeiro
Engo. Felix Ernest Stefan von Ranke (*Director Secretario General*)

BULGARIA
Institut de Normalisation, Mesures et Appereils da Mesure, 8 rue Sveta Sofia, Sofia
Telephone: 7-41-16   Telegrams: Ismiu
M. Ing K. Koer (*Director*)

CANADA (CSA)
Canadian Standards Association, 178 Rexdale Blvd, Rexdale 603, Ontario
Telephone: (416) 244-zo51
Mr. B. G. Tebo (*Director*)

CENTRAL AMERICA (ICAITI)
(Costa Rica, El Salvador, Guatemala, Honduras, Nicaragua, Panama)
Instituto Centroamericano de Investigación y Technologia Industrial 4a, Calle y Avenida la Reforma, zona 10, Apartado Postal 1552, Guatemala

CEYLON
Bureau of Ceylon Standards, 53 Dharmabòla Mawotha, Colombo 3
Dr. Ronald T. Wijewanthe (*Director*)

CHILE (INDITECNOR)
Instituto Nacional de Investigaciones Tecnologicas y Normalización, Plaza Bulnes 1302, Of. 62, Casilla de Correo 995, Santiago
Telephone: 82 854   Telegrams: Inditecnor   Telex: STGOCH
Mr. Ing. Hugo Brangier M. (*Director*)

Columbia (ICONTEC)
Instituto Colombiano de Normas Técnicas, Apartado Aereo: 14237 Bogota D.E.
Telegrams: Icontec
Mr. Ing. Javier Henao L. (*Director Ejecutivo*)

CUBA
Dirección de Normas y Metrologia, Ministerio de Industrias, Reina 408, Habana
Telephone: 6-6814
Mr. Franklin Gomez del Campo (*Director*)

CZECHOSLOVAKIA (CSN)
Urad pro normalizaci a mereni, Václavské námésti 19, Praha-1-Nové Mesto
Telephone: 238 441-3

DENMARK (DS)
Dansk Standardiseringsraad, Aurehøjvej 12, DK-2900 Hellerup
Telephone: Hellerup 9315
Mr. O. Weincke (*Managing Director*)

FINLAND (SFS)
Suomen Standardisoimisliitto r.y., Bulevardi 5. A. 7, Helsinki
Telephone: 64 34 22

FRANCE (AFNOR)
Association Française de Normalisation, Cedex 7, 92 Paris La Défense
Telephone: (I) 788-11-11
M. R. Frontard (*Directeur Général*)

GERMANY (DNA)
Deutscher Normenausschuss, 4-7 Burggrafenstrasse, 1 Berlin 30
Telephone: 1 38 21   Telex: 1 84 273
Mr. N. Ludwig, Dipl. Ing. (*Director*)

GHANA (ISIG)
National Standards Board, PO Box M245, Accra
Telephone: 63 899
Mr. E. Lartey (*Director*)

GREECE (ENO)
Ministry of Industry, Direction of Standardisation, Kanigos Street, Athens
Telephone: 629-947
Mr. Ger Kabitsis (*Director General*)

HUNGARY (MSZH)
Magyar Szabványügyi Hivatal, Ulloi-ut 25, Budapest IX
Telephone: 189-800   Telex: 948
Dr. Joseph Olajos (*Président*)

INDIA (ISI)
Indian Standards Institution, "Manak Bhavan", 9 Bahadur Shah Zafar Marg, New Dehli 1
Telephone: 27 36 11-17 .
Dr. A. N. Ghosh (*Director General*)

INDONESIA (DNI)
Jajassan "Dana Normalisasi Indonesia", Djalan Braga 38 Atas, Bandung
Telephone: 4220
Mr. M. E. E. Gandi (*Secretary*)

IRAN (ISIRI)
Institute of Standards and Industrial Research of Iran, Ministry of Economy, PO Box 2937, Teheran
Telephone: 62 22 02
Dr. Reza Shayegan (*Director General*)

IRAQ (IOS)
Iraqi Organizarion for Standards, Ministry of Industry, PO Box 11185, Baghdad
Telephone: 84106
Dr. Adnan H. Awni (*Secretary General*)

IRELAND (IIRS)
Institute for Research and Standards, Ballymun Road, Dublin 9
Telephone: 37 51 81
Mr. Martin J. Cranley (*Director General*)

ISRAEL (SII)
Standards Institution of Israel, University Street, Tel Aviv
Telephone: 44 31 51
Mr. Aharon Gilat (*Director*)

ITALY (UNI)
Ente Nazionale Italiano di Unificazione, Piazza Armando Diaz 2, I 20123 Milano
Telephone: 876 914
Dr. Ing Albino Zamboni (*Directeur*)

JAPAN (JISC)
Japanese Industrial Standards Committee, Agency of Industrial Science and Technology, Ministry of International Trade and Industry, 3-1, Kasumigaseki 1, Chiyodaku, Tokyo
Mr. Buzaemon Shindo (*President*)

KOREA, DEMOCRATIC PEOPLE'S REPUBLIC OF (CSK)
Committee for Standardization of the Democratic People's Republic of Korea, Pyongyang
Mr. Li Soon Ryul (*President*)

KOREA, REPUBLIC OF (KBS)
Korean Bureau of Standards, Ministry of Commerce and Industry, PO Box Kwanghwamoon 282, Seoul
Telephone: 73-5052
Mr. Jong Myong Choi (*Director*)

LEBANON (LIBNOR)
The Secretariat, Lebanese Standards Institution, PO Box 2806, Beirut

MALAYSIA
Standards Institution of Malaysia, 1st Floor MIDF Bldg, 117 Jalan Ampang, PO Box 544, Kuala Lumpur
Telephone: 28 572   Telegrams: Simsec
Dr. Leong Kwok Onn (*Director*)

MEXICO (DGN)
Dirección General de Normas, Av. Cuauhtémac No. 80, Mexico 7. DF
Telephone: 13-0671
Mr. Ing. José Rentería Gomez (*Director General*)

MOROCCO (SNIMA)
Service de Normalisation Industrielle Marocaine, Direction de l'Industrie, Sous-Secrétariat d'Etat à l'Indistrue et aux Mines, Rabat

NETHERLANDS (NNI)
Nederlands Normalisatie-Instituut, Polakweg 5, Rijswijk (ZH)-2016
Telephone: (070) 90 68 00   Telex: 32123
Dr. T. Dijs (*Director*)

NEW ZEALAND (SANZ)
Standards Association of New Zealand, Private Bag, Wellington 1
Telephone: 556-189
Mr. G. H. Edwards (*Director*)

NORWAY (NSF)
Norges Standardiseringsforbund, Haakon VII's gt. 2, Oslo 1
Telephone: 41 68 20
Mr. Gudbrand Jenssen (*Managing Director*)

PAKISTAN (PSI)
Pakistan Standards Institution, 39 Garden Road, Sadder, Karachi-3
Mr. A. H. Khan (*Director*)

PERU (INANTIC)
Instituto Nacional de Normas Técnicas Industriales y Certificación, Apartado No. 145, Av. Republica de Chile 698, Lima
Mr. Alfonso Lopez Ore (*Directeur*)

PHILIPPINES (KP)
Bureau of Standards of the Philippines, PO Box 3719, Manila
Telephone: 3-89-56, 3-89-13
Mr. R. E. Racela (*Director*)

POLAND (PKN)
Polski Komitet Normalizacyjny, Ul. Swietokrzyska 14, Warszawa 51
Telephone: 26 52 51

M. B. Adamski (*Président*)
PORTUGAL (IGPAI)
Repartição de Normalização, Avenida de Berna 1, Lisboa 1
Telephone: 77 00 82/3
M. Fausto Carreira (*Inspecteur Général*)

ROMANIA (OSS)
Institut Roman de Standardizare, Casata Postale 10, Bucarest 1
Telephone: 14 60 27
Mr. Ing Constantin Tuzu (*Directeur Général*)
SINGAPORE (SIRU)
Singapore Institute of Standards and Industrial Research, PO Box 2611, Singapore
Telephone: 71975
SOUTH AFRICA, REPUBLIC OF (SABS)
South African Bureau of Standards, 191 Private Bag, Pretoria
Telephone: 3-0851   Telex: 44-626 PR
Mr. R. F. J. Teichmann (*Director General*)
SPAIN (IRATRA)
Instituto Nacional de Racionalización del Trabajo, Serrano 150, Madrid 6
Telephone: 2 61 70 00
M. Fermin de la Sierra (*Directeur*)
SWEDEN (SIS)
Sveriges Standardiseringskommission, Box 3 295, S-103 66 Stockholm 3
Telephone: (08) 23 04 00
Jan Ollner (*Director*)
SWITZERLAND/SUISSE (SNV)
Association Suisse de Normalisation, Kirchenweg 4, 8032 Zurich
Telephone: (051) 47 69 70
M. W. Kuert (*Secrétaire*)
THAILAND (CTNSS)
Centre for Thai National Standard Specifications, Applied Scientific Research Corporation of Thailand, 196 Phahonyothin Road, Bangkhen, Bangkok

Group Captain Prasit Prabhasnóbol (*Director*)

TURKEY (TSE)
Türk Standardlair Enstitüsü, Necatibey Caddesi 118 Bakanliklav, Ankara
Telephone: 17 91 24
M. Velid Isfendiyar (*Secrétaire Général*)
UNITED ARAB REPUBLIC (EOS)
Egyptian Organisation for Standardization, 2 Latin America Street, Garden City, Cairo-Egypt
Telephone: 80 98 11
Dr. Ahmad Geneidy (*Director General*)
UNITED KINGDOM (BSI)
British Standards Institution, 2 Park Street, London W.1
Telephone: 01-629 9000   Telex: 266933
Mr. H. A. R. Binney, CB (*Director*)
USA (ANSI)
American National Standards Institute, Inc., 1430 Broadway, New York, NY 10018
Telephone: (212) 868-1220
Mr. Donald L. Peyton (*Managing Director*)
USSR (GOST)
Komitet Standartov, Mer i Izmeritel'nyh Priborov pri Sovete Ministrov SSSR, Leninsky Prospekt 9B, Moskva M49
Telephone: 236 40 44
Prof. Dr. techn. sc. V. V. Boitsov (*President*)
VENEZUELA (COVENIN)
Comisión Venezolana de Normas Industriales, Dirección de Industrias, Ministerio de Fomento, Officina 653, Torre Sur, Centro Simon Bolivar, Caracus
Mr. Ing. Carlos Rodriguez Sotó (*President*)
YUGOSLAVIA (JZS)
Jugoslovenski zavod za Standardizaciju, Cara Urosa ul, 54, Post pregr. 933, Beograd
Telephone: 26-563
M. Slavoljub Vitorovic, Dipl. Ing. (*Directeur*)

SECTION NINE

TRENDS FOR THE FUTURE

AIRCRAFT
SHIPS
CONTAINERS
AUTOMATED STORAGE SYSTEMS

TRENDS FOR THE FUTURE

INTRODUCTION

In this section an attempt has been made to gather together information on the current ideas and projects in the transport field that, although seemingly ambitious, nevertheless appear to be feasible.

In compiling this section it was not the intention of the editors to act as innovators, but rather to provide an impression of the kind of thinking that could bring about significant changes in the world of freight transport within the next decade, and certainly before the turn of the century. The ideas, design studies and projects mentioned in this section have been gathered from both published and unpublished sources through the aid of correspondents in many countries. Where possible, source references are given.

The container-carrying role of hovercraft has not been included in this year's section as the whole field is adequately covered in the current edition of *Jane's Surface Skimmers: Hovercraft and Hydrofoils* 1971-72. Of particular interest in this field are the developments by: Aerojet-General; Arctic Engineers and Constructors; Bell Aerospace; Enfield Marine; Hovermarine Transport; Transport Technology; and Vosper Thorneycroft.

AIRCRAFT
AIRSHIPS

General

The airship, regarded as a transport medium of the past since the late 1930s, is now undergoing a complete reappraisal that may result in its establishment as a major transport system of the future.

Research into airship design is in an advanced stage in several European countries, with the Soviet Union in the lead. That the airship is not an anachronism has been proved in theory, but has yet to be proved in practice. The designers and advocates of the airship from many countries have promised benefits from its use that have attractions for many sectors of society. Among these benefits are the relatively low level of atmospheric and noise pollution of an airship transport system, and the low cost site-to-site transport of heavy objects which could ease crowded road conditions and aid the future planning of new towns and industrial centres. The advantages seemingly offered by the revival of the airship are so numerous that finance and public opinion would seem to be the only remaining obstacles. The fear that the disasters of the 1930s will be repeated still holds wide currency, and must be overcome before the airship rises phoenix-like from the ashes of the *R*.101 and the *Hindenburg*.

The following list is a descriptive inventory of almost all the current developments in the lighter-than-air craft field that could have any bearing on freighting operations in the future. Helium would be used to provide lift for all of these airships, being completely safe; colourless, tasteless, odourless, non-toxic, non-flammable, light and completely inert at standard atmospheric conditions. Helium is found in small percentages in natural gas fields in Texas, the North Sea, the Sahara, and in Dutch and Soviet natural gas fields. A few pictures of historical interest have been included to illustrate certain points.

A broadside view of the ill-fated *R.101* moored to the tower at Cardington. Modern airship designers are planning airships much bigger than this (*Courtesy RAE Cardington*).

An interior view of the naval-styled control car of the *R.101*. Modern airship designers propose to replace these archaic navigation aids with computers and sophisticated aviation equipment (*Courtesy RAE Cardington*).

A general view of a rigid airship downship from the bow, showing the complicated internal structure. A monocoque hull would be lighter and probably stronger (*Courtesy RAE Cardington*).

A front view of the sheds at Cardington showing the *R.100* and *R.101* (October 1930). Finding suitable accommodation to construct modern airships is one of the major problems confronting contemporary designers (*Courtesy RAE Cardington*).

Airship Loading Methods

Aeroplanes and helicopters working in close cycle have been suggested as methods of loading and unloading rigid cargo airships. The high capital expenditure and cost of maintaining these forms of lighterage would be prohibitive. Until recently the only alternative method for executing this task was the hydraulic container-warehouse-lift-terminal, tentatively suggested in the last edition of JANE'S FREIGHT CONTAINERS. This loading system would have many design problems, but these, of course, could be

Aerazur Constructions Aéronautics

58 boulevard Gallieni
92-Issy-les-Moulineaux
TELEPHONE: 644-50-70
TELEX: 27887 F
This company manufactures some of the

overcome. The main fault of the system lies in the airship, which would be subjected to considerable stress due to wind pressure, etc., although a resourceful engineer could overcome this difficulty, but at considerable cost.

Perhaps the most suitable solution to the loading problem could be found in applying the principles of aerostatics to a loading system. The possible methods are: (a) using small non-rigid airships to load containers on to a larger, rigid airship. The use of

this method would of course result in a number of complex weight compensation problems; (b) the most sensible solution would seem to be an adaption of the Soviet timber-carrying blimp system (q.v.). This probably would be the most economical system, both in cost and by being transportable by the cargo airship; the added weight of the blimp winching machinery being compensated to a certain extent by the lift provided by carrying one or more blimps.

FRANCE

biggest captive balloons in the world, and has had experience in aerostatics since 1928. Some of the balloons it makes have a volume as great as 530,000 cubic feet (15,000 m³) and are used mainly for research purposes. The company believes that airships are a

viable means of future transport, and has announced that it has the theoretical and technical experience to make a successful break-through in airship design in the near future.

GERMANY (DEMOCRATIC REPUBLIC)

Delphin Luftschiff

One of the most interesting and advanced designs to emerge recently comes from East Germany. The design, for a 'Dolphin-Airship', was published in the August 1970 edition of *Flieger Revue*. It was stated in an article by Dipl. Volkswirt Ulrich Queck, the head of the K.D.T. board for research into modern airship design, and Dr. Ing. W. Schmidt that they had designed an airship that combined both aerodynamic and aerostatic principles. The airship, it was said, would be able to fly at over 500 kmh by using a propulsion system and hull configuration based on research carried out on bird-flight and fish locomotion. The dolphin (*Cephalorhynchus*) was the main object of study, being a remarkably fast and efficient swimmer, with a tail similar to that of lunate-tailed fish, although dolphins are in fact mammals. Dolphins and whales, however, swim by up-and-down movements of their tails, unlike the side-to-side tail motion of lunate-tailed fish. The lunate tail was of particular interest to the designers of the airship's propulsion system, for it casts off vortices that induce a jet-like streamlined pattern of forward motion. Another factor which influenced the propulsion design was the strong resemblance of a dolphin's tail to certain aeroplane wing configurations.

The analogy drawn between the thrust developed by the carangiform motion of certain fish, cetacean mammals and various aspects of bird flight, such as undulating flight patterns and gliding, (the latter was referred to by the K.D.T. as the Knoller-Betz effect), was applied in designing a suitable propulsion system from the airship. This propulsion system consists of an arrangement of flaps and rotating shafts at the stern of the airship, which duct air through a set of variable pitch vanes for forward thrust. Greater aerodynamic lift is obtained by a complementary set of rotating shafts on the airship's bows, which duct air over the laminar hull surface, lubricating its passage through the air. The propulsion system was described by the K.D.T. researchers as an 'undulating wave-impulse propulsion system' that creates the minimum of turbulence in the wake of the airship, allowing it to travel at maximum speed without wasting energy.

The K.D.T. officials claim that the 'Dolphin-Airship' would be viable within the next two decades, and could be used for transporting containerised goods, passengers, and for military purposes. Alternative applications would be as an oceanographic and meteorological research vessel. It was also claimed that the airship would displace conventional aircraft and sea-going vessels as a means of 'mass passenger travel' in less than a hundred years.

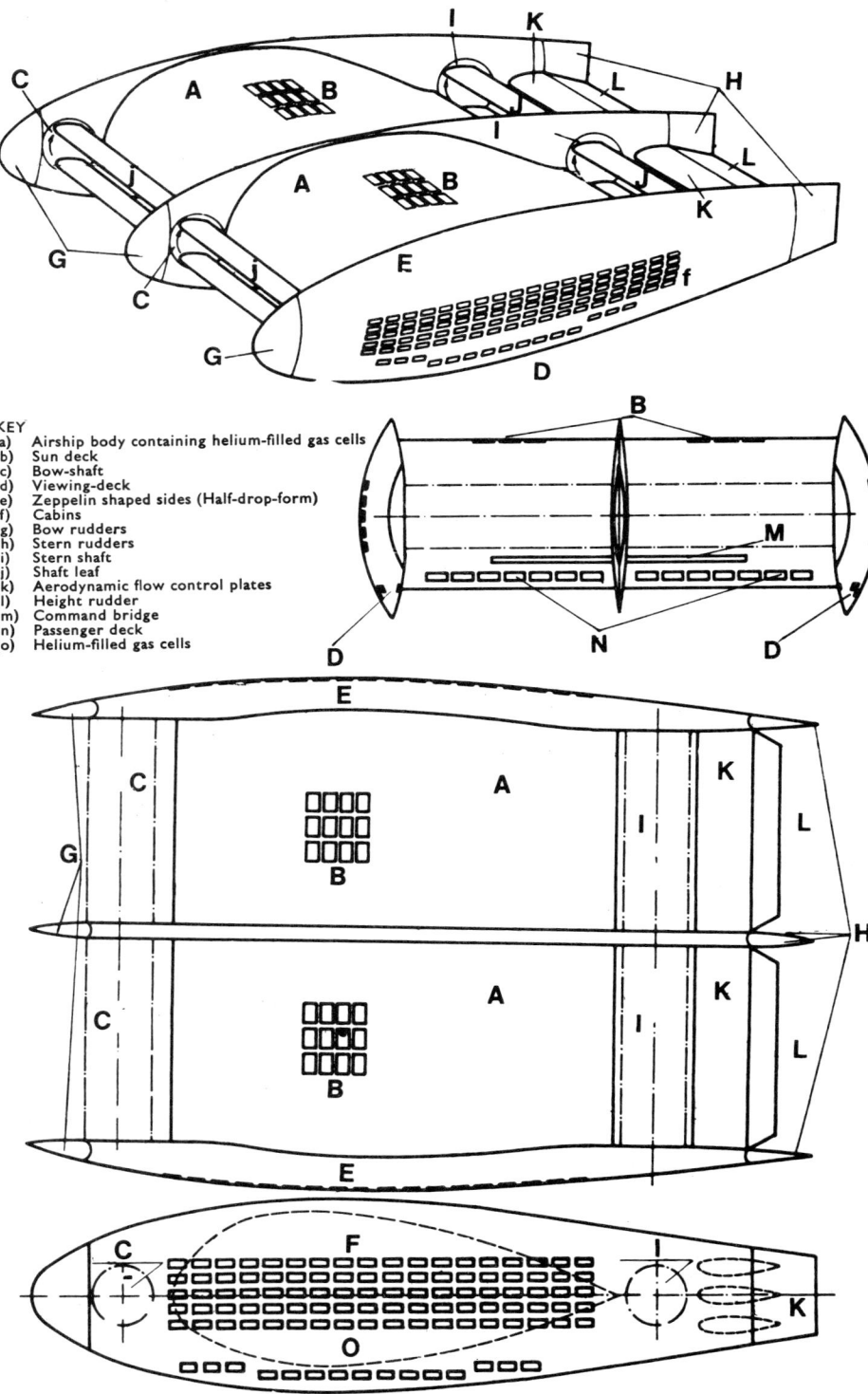

KEY
(a) Airship body containing helium-filled gas cells
(b) Sun deck
(c) Bow-shaft
(d) Viewing-deck
(e) Zeppelin shaped sides (Half-drop-form)
(f) Cabins
(g) Bow rudders
(h) Stern rudders
(i) Stern shaft
(j) Shaft leaf
(k) Aerodynamic flow control plates
(l) Height rudder
(m) Command bridge
(n) Passenger deck
(o) Helium-filled gas cells

A four-view drawing of the 'Dolphin-Airship' (*Delphin-Luftschiff*).

GERMANY (FEDERAL REPUBLIC)

Westdeutsche Luftwerbung KG
Am Flughafen D-433 Essen-Mülheim/Ruhr

Westdeutsche Luftwerbung (WDL), at present operating the *Braun Sixtant* for Deutsche Luftschifffahrt, plans to develop its own airship for commercial operation by 1973/74. Under the guidance of Theodor Wullenkemper, the director, and Richard Grunder, the chief engineer, the company's team of airship experts is planning to build four airships. The first airship scheduled to be built is to undergo flying tests late in 1971 or early in 1972. This airship, the WDL 1, will be the first built in Europe since the *Braun Sixtant*. The envelope will be filled with the inert gas helium to obtain lift. The main purpose of the WDL 1 will be to help in developing a technology for building larger airships, and to evaluate suitable methods of operating a fully commercial fleet of airships. The WDL 1 will be followed by three other so-called 'Prall-Luftschiffe'.

Technical details of the WDL non-rigid airship programme:

Airship Type	WDL 1 Experimental	WDL 2 Experimental	WDL 3 Experimental	WDL 4 Commercial design
Expected Completion	1971	1972	1973	?
Volume (m³ helium)	6,000	13,000	20,000	64,000+
Length oa. (m)	55	70	80	120
Max. diameter (m)	14·5	18	20	28
Gross weight (kg)	6,300	13,650	21,000	21,000— (65,000?)
Useful load (payload kg)	1,500	5,000	10,000	30,000
(„ tons)	(1·5)	(4·5)	(9)	(30)
Envelope weight (kg)	1,600	3,200	4,500	11,000
Power plant (hp)	2 × 180	2 × 350	2 × 400	2 × 700
Max speed (kmh)	100	120	140	140
Range (operating radius) (km)	400	1,000	1,800	2,600+

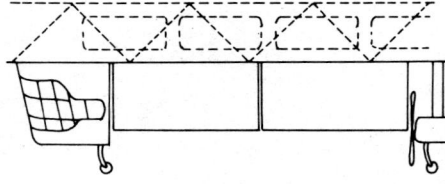

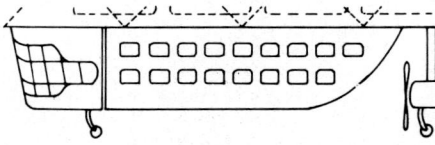

Two diagrams of the WDL gondola system showing the positioning of containers (*top*) and operation as a passenger craft (*bottom*).

WDL are only developing non-rigid airships because, they claim, rigid airships of the Zeppelin type had one important disadvantage. This was that the size and weight of a rigid airship was out of all proportion to the possible payload, because of the heavy framework needed for a rigid construction. This meant that the payload was approximately only twenty to thirty per cent of the airship's own weight. The proposed WDL non-rigid airship, with a volume of sixty to seventy million cubic metres, would, it is claimed, be more economical to operate, with its payload capability of more than fifty per cent of the total unladen weight.

The standard production model of the WDL programme will have many commercial applications. One important use will be as a container carrier (see diagram), and a special gondola carrying-system has been designed for this purpose. The other commercial applications of the WDL 4 are envisaged as: a passenger carrier; a heavy-load transporter; a rescue craft; and as a stable platform for scientific observation or military surveillance.

The *Braun Sixtant* (or *D-Lemo*) was the first airship to be inflated with helium in Europe. It made its first flight as the *Trumpf* from Stüttgart in 1958.

THE NETHERLANDS

Holland Amerika Lijn
Wilhelminakade 86
Rotterdam
TELEPHONE: 010-17 25 60
TELEX: 21172
(For other details see under Ship Operators)

This company is carrying out a study for a passenger/cargo airship that is envisaged as a means of bridging the gap between sea-going craft and the aeroplane. Their economic evaluation of airship transport is based on the costs of the movement of high-value goods by aircraft such as the Boeing 747 freight carrier. Holland-Amerika Lijn believe that freighting by airships on a Europe-United States service would be more economical than operating a Boeing 747 on the same route. They also believe that airships operating on a European service would offer even greater economic advantages as the reduction in fuel requirements would mean an increased cargo capacity.

Earlier this year Mr. R. Harthoorn, of the Holland-Amerika Lijn, announced in *Holland Shipbuilding* that the company's projected airship would have a maximum payload of 268 tons, and fly at a speed of 100 knots. This airship would cost the same as a Boeing 747, and would offer a reduction of thirty per cent on the per ton-mile cost compared with a Boeing 747, travelling at 600 mph with a payload of 80 tons.

UNITED KINGDOM

General

Of significance to Britain is the formation of an Airship Association for the serious study of contemporary airship design. In the minds of sceptics this may have conjured up a picture of enthusiastic cranks suffering from misguided nostalgia, but the announcement that a Parliamentary Committee was being formed must at least have dispelled some of these misconceptions. Another important factor, in the eyes of the advocates, was that Sir Barnes Wallis, who was originally opposed to the revival of the airship, is to design a Liquid Natural Gas-carrying airship for a British petroleum company.

Airfloat Transport Ltd

Assay House
28 Greville Street
London EC1N 8SU
TELEPHONE: (01)-242 1100
DIRECTORS:
Lord Ventry
E. Mowforth
L. P. Richards
J. Parry
B. R. V. Hughes

Airfloat Transport was formed in November, 1970, to develop a heavy-lift airship to provide factory-to-site transport of indivisible loads weighing from 50 to 300 tons for long journeys, and to carry short-range payloads of 400 tons. Alternative applications for the airship have been suggested. Many of the uses fall within the indivisible load category; for example the load frame could be replaced by a 200 ft (61 m) module to carry containerised freight or passengers. The loads would be attached to a frame consisting of parallel trusses 20 ft deep, 200 ft long and 35 ft apart. Load transfer would be carried out in hovering flight. Ballast will be carried in ISO type containers, to be let down when loading or for weight compensation when off-loading. The load transfer gear incorporates a turntable mounting for hoisting cargo in alignment with the wind, thus giving the airship a greater operational flexibility.

An airship design was announced by Airfloat Transport in *The Aeronautical Journal* of the Royal Aeronautical Society, Vol. 75, No. 723, in March 1971, but this design has been superseded by subsequent research, which resulted in a modified design being announced. Two new design factors required an increase in the size of the original projection. They were the introduction of a modified hoisting device and the requirement that the airship should be capable of remaining aloft, under static lift only, following the collapse of any one gas cell. This condition necessitates the carriage at all times of a sufficient quantity of water ballast to compensate for this loss, partly by dropping ballast and partly by transferring ballast forward and aft to restore pitching trim.

To cover the increase in lift, the airship length and diameter have been enlarged to

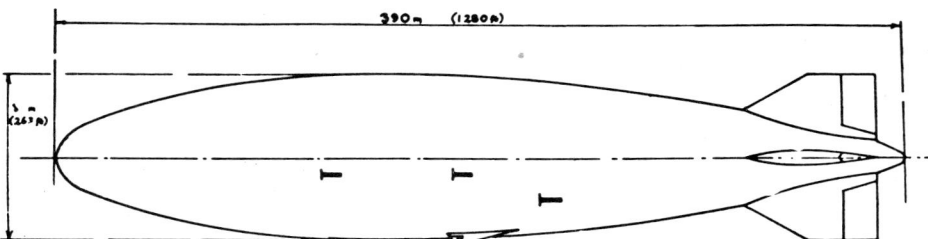

The diagram shows the variable airship geometry used by Airfloat Transport for current design analysis.

390 m (1,280 ft) and 80 m (263 ft) respectively giving a gas (helium) capacity of approximately 1,000,000 m³ (35,000,000 ft³). The profile of the airship is based upon that of the *R.101*, with the length and diameter ratio decreased by approximately ten per cent.

The airship could be powered by nuclear, gas turbine, reciprocating diesel, or reciprocating petrol, engines. Nuclear power is regarded as essentially for second or third generation airships, while reciprocating petrol engines are regarded as having an uneconomical fuel consumption rate for the airship envisaged. The choice of propulsion, therefore, appears to lie between the gas turbine propeller unit and the reciprocating diesel engine. The speed range of the airship makes it suitable for conventional propellers, though it is thought desirable to develop large low-speed types to combine optimum efficiency with a noise level acceptable for low altitude operations over populated areas.

Airfloat Transport envisage their projected airship being operated as an investment by a consortium of users who would have priority for the use of the airship over customers outside the group. This appears to be a most sensible approach to the operation of a craft that will obviously prove extremely expensive to build. Indeed, the soberness of Airfloat Transport's whole approach to the problem of airship design suggests the very seriousness of their interest.

Cargo Airships Ltd

(A subsidiary of Manchester Liners Ltd.)
141 Praed Street
London W2
TELEPHONE: (01)-723-0771
DIRECTORS:
M. Rynish (*Managing Director*)
W. A. L. Roberts (*Board Member*)
M. Pattinson (*Board Member*)
C. W. Meadowcroft (*Board Member*)
P. C. Barnes (*Board Member*)
The company was formed in 1970 to design and develop large container-carrying airships

for use in a totally air-orientated cargo transport system. However, in spite of their present extensive design developments, they do not intend manufacturing airships as part of the development programme. The airship designs evolved will be put out for tender, or licensed internationally. Cargo Airships plan ultimately to operate full control of the designs put to use.

At the present Cargo Airships is engaged in the design of a vessel with a payload of 500 tons, which will be carried in fifty ten-ton ISO type containers. The operational airspeed of the airship will be approximately 100 mph. Containers will be ferried to and from the airship by straddle helicopter, while the airship remains airborne. (It is interesting to speculate on the type of cargo to be carried to obtain a payload of 10 tons in a 10 ft box, as a standard general cargo mix will make approximately 5 tons deadweight).

Cargo Airships prefer a monocoque type of structure. With this kind of design the airship's strength would be in an outer shell made from stiff lightweight alloys or carbon fibre composites, rather than a skeletal framework of girders of the type used in the Zeppelins, and in the early British and American airships. Monocoque structures are thought to be stronger and more streamlined than any other type of structure, having less 'drag' and consequently needing less engine power and fuel for propulsion.

Cargo Airships are now developing a new design which departs radically from the design illustrated. This airship would do away with the helicopter ferry system and use a new method for taking on containers. It is worthwhile noting here that an alternative method was proposed and described in the 1970/71 edition of JANE'S FREIGHT CONTAINERS. The proposal was for a container warehouse/lift terminal; this method is favoured by some German and Soviet airship designers.

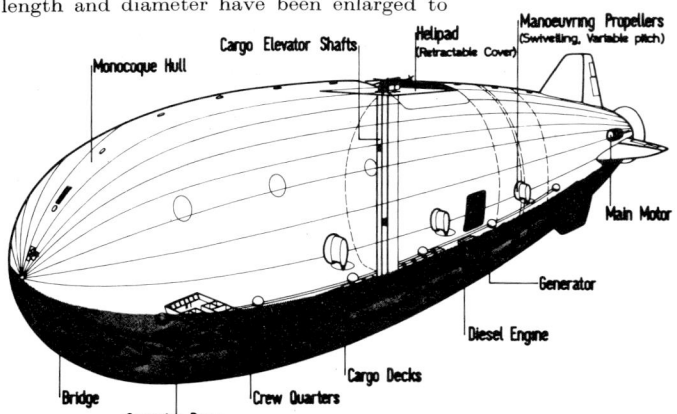

Cargo Airships' projected layout, showing some of the features that could be incorporated.

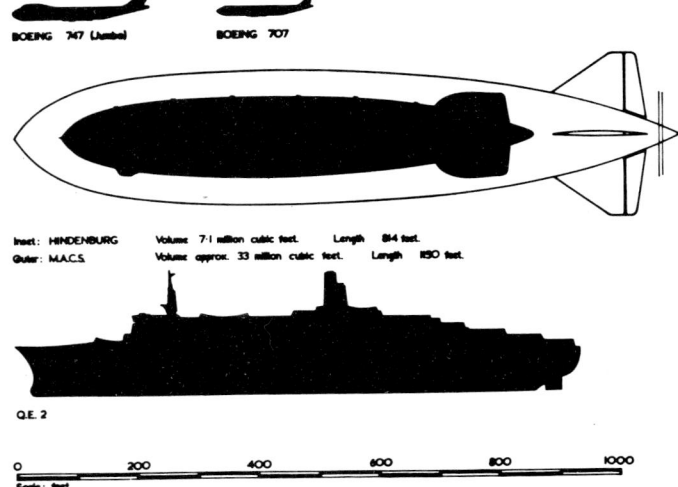

The relative sizes of a Boeing 747, a Boeing 707, the Q.E.2, the *Hindenburg* and a cargo airship are shown in the above scale drawing.

The Goodyear Tyre & Rubber Co. (Great Britain) Limited
Wolverhampton
TELEPHONE: 22321
TELEX: 33771

Since the *Bournemouth* flew in 1952 there has not been an airship in English skies. Faith in this mode of transport was destroyed by the crash of the *R.101* airship in France in 1930 which killed 36 people and by the death of 46 passengers when the *Hindenburg* caught fire and was destroyed in 1937. What is not generally realised is that the gas used in these aircraft was hydrogen, which is extremely inflammable, and rapidly becomes explosive when mixed with air. However, the airship *Europa*, to be built by Goodyear, will use helium, a completely inert gas. It is fair to say that if helium had been available in commercial quantities, giant airships like the *Hindenburg* and the *R.101* would perhaps still be gracing our skies. Unfortunately in the days of the *R.101* and the *Hindenburg*, helium was so scarce and so expensive that it was not considered an economic proposition to import it from America. However, the use of helium will make the *Europa* so safe that it would be possible to smoke while working on the envelope with absolutely no danger of fire or explosion.

The Airship Europa
Construction of the first airship to be seen over Britain for over twenty years will begin soon at the Royal Aircraft Establishment at Cardington, Bedfordshire. A team of technicians of the Goodyear Tyre and Rubber Company will build the airship which is expected to be ready for test flights in April, 1972.

This new airship, which will be named *Europa*, will be 192 feet long, 59 feet high and 50 feet wide and will be inflated with helium supplied by the British Oxygen Company Limited. Power during flight will be provided by twin six-cylinder 210 h.p. engines giving the airship a 500 mile range. Cruising speed will be 35 m.p.h. with a maximum of 50 m.p.h. The normal flying altitude will be between 1,000 and 3,000 feet with a ceiling of 7,500 feet. The airship

will have a 23 ft long cab and will be able to carry six passengers in addition to the pilot.

Goodyear has constructed more lighter-than-air craft than any other company in the world; this will be the 300th built by the company. Of this number 55 have been civil airships, the others were built for military use.

Three of the civil airships, *America*, *Columbia* and *Mayflower*, are currently in use in the United States. They travel some 100,000 air miles a year on goodwill flights and display public service announcements. When fully certificated the *Europa* is expected to fly throughout the United Kingdom and other European countries.

Mr. J. E. Pucell, Chairman and Managing Director of Goodyear Great Britain Limited, recently said, Goodyear will spend some £1¼ million on the building of the *Europa* airship and the provision of the necessary ancillary services. He further said: 'We are delighted that the first Goodyear airship to be constructed outside the United States should be built at Cardington. We expect considerable interest in this project, both from the public and from those involved in news and sports coverage, for the airship will be a unique platform for the television cameras which will be included in its special equipment'. He also said that Goodyear airships are equipped with navigational and safety devices comparable to those found in modern light aircraft and that over a million people in America have flown in them without incident.

Like its sister ships, the *Europa* will be manned and maintained by specially trained flying and ground crews. The permanent multinational crews attached to the *Europa* are expected to number 22, including five pilots and a number of engineers and maintenance specialists. They will have a fleet of five vehicles to support the airship's operations, including a vehicle to carry the main mast, spare parts and supplementary equipment; a T.V. laboratory vehicle; a coach which will serve as the crew's transport and communication centre; an estate vehicle and a minibus for ground liaison work.

All the vehicles will be linked by radio with each other and with the airship.

SPECIFICATION OF THE EUROPA:
Model: GZ20A-Non-Rigid
Manufacturer: Goodyear
Registration Number: N2A

OVERALL DIMENSIONS:
Length 58·674 m (192·50 ft)
Width 12·24 m (50·00 ft)
Height 18·13 m (59·54 ft)

ENVELOPE (HULL) DIMENSIONS:
Volume 5,739·86 m³ (202,700 cu ft)
Length 58·012 m (190·28 ft)
Max. Diameter 14·011 m (45·92 ft)
Fineness Ratio 4·14
Ballonet Volume 1,662·2 m³ (58,700 cu ft)

CAR DIMENSIONS:
Overall length 6·9 m (22·75 ft)
Width at ceiling 2·13 m (7·00 ft)
Width at floor 1·32 m (4·30 ft)
Height 2·47 m (8·10 ft)
Height including landing gear 3·66 m (11·80 ft)

WEIGHTS:
Maximum Design Gross Weight 5,824·13 kg (12,840 lbs)
Empty Weight 4,252·43 kg (9,375 lbs)

PROPULSION:
Engines (2) 210 h.p. 6 cyl: Continental 10-360-D Spec 22
Propellers: Hartzell BHC-92WF-3L LW8-447A-6R, 6 ft 6 in dia, reversible pitch.

FUEL SYSTEM:
Capacity—Regular Tanks   138 gals
         Auxiliary Tanks   158 gals
                   Total   296 gals

AIRSHIP PERFORMANCE CHARACTERISTICS:
Maximum Airspeed 50 m.p.h.
Normal Cruise 35-40 m.p.h.
Maximum rate of climb 2,400 ft/min
Maximum rate of descent 1,400 ft/min
Maximum Pitch Angles + 30°

CAPACITY:
(a) Minimum Crew One pilot
(b) Maximum (including crew) Seven

ENDURANCE—NORMAL CRUISE:
Regular Tanks Only Approx 10 hours
With Auxiliary Tanks Approx 23 hours

LIFTING GAS:
Non-inflammable Helium

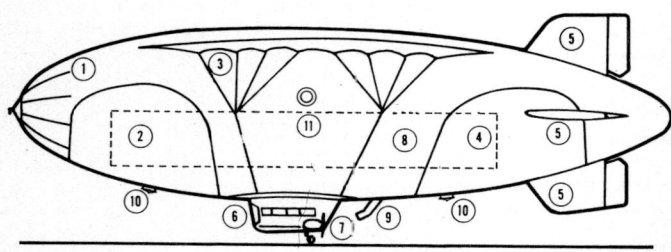

COMPONENTS OF AN AIRSHIP
1. Nose Cone Battens (supports)
2. Forward Ballonet (air bag inside envelope)
3. Catenary Curtain and Suspension Cables (inside envelope)
4. Aft Ballonet
5. Control Surfaces (rudders and elevators)
6. Car — Passenger Compartment
7. Engines
8. Night Sign Lamps
9. Air Scoops (channel air to ballonets)
10. Air Valves (regulate air in ballonets)
11. Helium Valve

The above diagram shows the basic component parts of a Goodyear airship.

One of the three Goodyear airships at present in use in the United States. The airship *Europa*, to be built at Cardington, will be the same size as the *Columbia*, which is used with her sister ships the *America* and the *Mayflower* for goodwill flights, and for advertising purposes.

UNITED STATES OF AMERICA

Aereon Corporation
1 Palmer Square,
Princeton
New Jersey 08540
TELEPHONE: 609-921-2131
CABLES: Dynairships

Airships have been operated in America since 1863, when the Aereon dirigible of Dr. S. Andrew flew successfully several times over New York. Since that time over a hundred airships have flown with the occurrence of only three major accidents. The Aereon Corporation is still in existence and hopes to produce a large rigid airship in several years time, although William McE. Miller, the President of Aereon, has stated that it would be premature to be certain of this.

Goodyear Aerospace Corporation
1210 Massillon Road
Akron
Ohio 44316

Goodyear is another American company involved in the airship business, and at present operates a fleet of non-rigids for advertising purposes. They have announced plans to build a small airship at Cardington airfield in England, and have it in operation early in 1972 (q.v.). This airship will operate in Europe in a similar manner to that of the rest of the Goodyear fleet.

Boston University

Professor Francis Morse of Boston University drew up plans for a Zeppelin-type airship with a nuclear propulsion system and presented his preliminary findings in the *New Scientist* of April 1966. He has since drafted amendments to his design, which have recently been published. Professor Morse's airship design is thought to be one of the best to have been developed. He has proposed an aeroplane as a passenger/cargo shuttle; this is based on the well tried aircraft carrying operation of the U.S. Navy airship *Akron*. However, it is thought that this type of ground-to-airship ferry would be even more expensive to operate than the helicopter method proposed by Cargo Airships Ltd.

Note

Finally, it is worth noting that a giant spherical balloon, 47 million cubic feet in volume, is to be constructed for experimental purposes in the U.S.A. The balloon, known as the '*Schjaldahl*', will provide useful information on aerostatic lift and gas cell stresses, amongst other things, that may have a bearing on the future of the airship in the United States.

A Goodyear airship with its crew and ground vehicles.

UNION OF SOVIET SOCIALIST REPUBLICS

During the past two years many reports have appeared in the Western press relating to airship construction in the U.S.S.R., but so far no one has been able to substantiate them with any definite evidence, at least not publicly. The following report, which is based on information released by the Novosti Press Agency, and on articles that have appeared in a number of East European journals over the last few years, makes some attempt at remedying the situation. The most recently published mentions of Soviet interest in the revival of the airship appeared in *Flieger Revue*, No. 6, 1970, and in *Militärtechnik*, No. 7, 1971. The reports so far mention that development is taking place in the design and construction of airships for carrying containers, heavy unit-loads, liquid natural gas, oil, and as troop and passenger transports.

In 1969 Vladimir Kyucharyants, writing in a leading Soviet newspaper, reported that the Soviet Ministry of Aviation was still opposed to the re-introduction of airships, although certain developments in that field were taking place. He further stated that in contrast to the apparent official line, academics and technologists in Moscow, Leningrad, Kiev and Novosibirsk had produced airship designs resulting in widespread interest being shown by scientific and commerce development organisations. Eventually official approval was given for several schemes to be fully explored. The one known project which has finally reached fruition is described below.

The airship design group in Kiev has built and is testing a cigar-shaped airship, known as the D-1, which is 84 m long and 25 m in diameter. The D-1 is of a double-skinned semi-monocoque construction, the hull lining being of fibre-glass, the space between the inner and outer walls being filled with a plastic foam (probably expanded polystyrene). The airship is fully rigid with four transverse frames and four stringers installed inside the lining. One of the stringers has been re-inforced to function as a corridor between the cabins, which are located in the bow, tail and centre, below the fuselage of the airship.

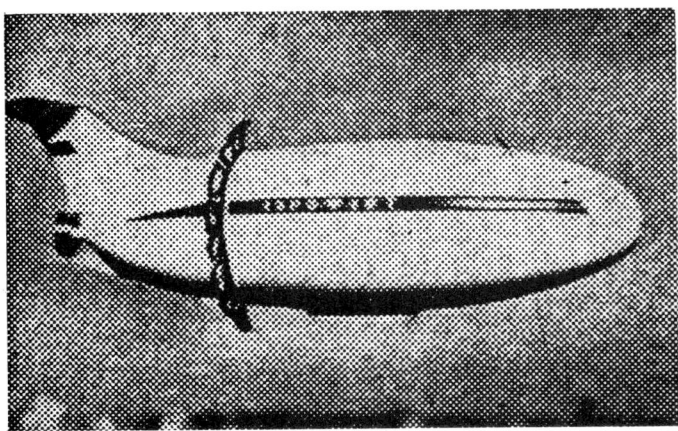

This airship conforms in some details to the specifications given for the D-1 airship which was built in Kiev in 1969. The unusual girdle and VC 10 tail configuration point to a totally different type of construction from that of the D-1 (*Courtesy Novosti Press Agency*).

This small non-rigid airship is probably used for forestry inspection work in the Soviet Union (*Courtesy Novosti Press Agency*).

Lift will be obtained by using helium, contained in bags of a thin synthetic material. An automatic compression device has been designed to regulate the gas volume so as to adjust the lifting power and thereby control the altitude at which the airship will fly. The D-1 will be able to lift cargo and passengers to a height of 7,000 m and to travel non-stop over distances in excess of 3,000 km. Aerial crane duties will also be a possibility, and all operations will be carried out in almost all weather conditions. This will be possible through the use of special de-icing equipment and of a special outer fabric which is impermeable to frost or any other atmospheric phenomena.

A turbofan aircraft engine mounted at the tail of the D-1 will enable the airship to travel at a speed ranging from 170 to 200 kmh in high winds. It is also claimed that the airship will be able to cope with moderate cross-winds when landing.

The provision of a tricycle undercarriage will ensure a safe landing operation, and keep the airship stable when moored. A low-level rotary mooring system has been developed as a provisional measure until a mooring mast with a revolving platform is available.

A photograph released by the Novosti Press Agency (see above) shows an airship similar to the one described, except that the illustrated airship seems to have a much bulkier hull form and a tail fin configuration like that of a VC 10. Another strange characteristic is the girdle apparently situated well aft; the purpose of this girdle can only be guessed since it has no counterpart in the West. Suggestions have ranged from a brace for lifting gear to a test rig for an air ducting system. The engine positioning represented by the dark shape under the tail corresponds to the particulars given for the D-1. The number of characters on the 'flash' along the hull of the airship add up to the number of characters in Aeroflot (АЭРОФЛОТ) the name of the Soviet airline company. The other photograph shows a small airship of the non-rigid type, which is probably used for forestry inspection work.

Airship designers in Leningrad were reported to be working on plans for a double-hulled rigid airship. The work is being carried out under the supervision of an aeronautical commission sponsored by the Soviet Geological Society. A number of regional and central government planning departments have expressed an interest in using this airship as a heavy-duty crane on major construction projects. This airship group, known as the Ziolkowski Commission after the Russian professor who pioneered airship design and construction in the Soviet Union, is also developing a programme of airship construction specifically for use in the almost impenetrable Taiga region of Siberia. The airship projected for this purpose is also of the double hulled type, and when built is expected to have a 200-ton lifting capacity for carrying timber (about 200 m³) over a distance of 1,000 km in ten hours.

This particular scheme is for an airship that would dispense with the traditional ballast/cargo exchange system; instead the hot exhaust gases from the engines would be used to warm certain parts of the hull in order to heat and expand the helium, thus providing greater lifting power. Valentin Murytshev, the leader of the Commission, estimates that a 2 per cent increase in the volume of the projected airship would be sufficient to enable the craft to climb approximately 160 m. Cold air would be ducted over the gas cells to reverse the process, cooling the gas and thus contracting it to bring the airship down without venting any valuable helium.

This giant airship would probable work in conjunction with a blimp and pulley log carrying system that is in general use in certain areas of the Soviet Union. This system was first announced in the Soviet journal *Smena* in 1967. The article reported that blimps (aerostatic captive balloons) were being used near the town of Khody-zhensk in the North Caucasus as aerial timber carriers. Employing blimps for this purpose meant that timber could be obtained from mountainous regions inaccessible to ground transport. (One-sixth of the timber forests in the U.S.S.R. are reported to be situated in such regions.) The system has since been put into wider use, being cheaper than previous methods of timber transportation, and possessing a further advantage in that soil erosion is prevented by dispensing with the heavy tracked vehicles previously used.

The renaissance of the airship would present a unique method of opening up the vast undeveloped areas of the U.S.S.R. That it would also be a cheap and efficient means of transporting equipment, supplies and men has been admitted at some high official levels. Proof of this can be found in an article published in *Literaturaya Gazeta* in 1969. S. Goryunov, the Soviet Minister of Geology, writing in the journal, said: 'Airships could greatly alleviate the life and working conditions of geological prospectors and improve the overall efficiency of geological prospecting work . . . .' The Novosibirsk Geology Department calculate, the minister said, that two small airships, with fifteen specialists aboard each, could do as much work in one year (in seismic reconnaissance), in Siberia, as is done by two thousand men equipped with helicopters in two or three seasons. This, together with the announcement of a saving of 20,000 million roubles over a ten year period on all fronts, forecast by the Leningrad group, must make the airship a very tempting proposition in the eyes of the Soviet planners.

A Soviet work-balloon in operation. Blimps are reported to be in use in Canada for the same type of function (*Courtesy Novosti Press Agency*).

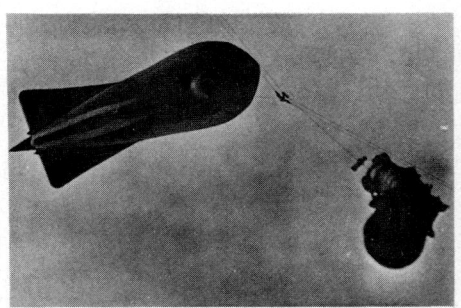

A Soviet aerial timber carrier, working on a system of cables between the felling and the storage areas (*Courtesy Novosti Press Agency*).

The advocates of the airship revival in the U.S.S.R. maintain that since engines, instruments and equipment to be used in the airships are already used on conventional aircraft, and since strong synthetics and light metal alloys have been developed, what is necessary at the initial stage is solely a desire and need to build airships.

However, it is thought that the development of a full scale airship construction industry in the U.S.S.R. would be premature, since many technical problems have yet to be solved, and as yet there are not enough trained personnel to build or fly the advanced designs being developed.

A Soviet work-balloon being prepared for a timber hauling-operation (*Courtesy Novosti Press Agency*).

Technicians working on the engine nacelle of a Soviet airship. Synthetic materials are used throughout the airship giving a light yet strong construction (*Courtesy Novosti Press Agency*).

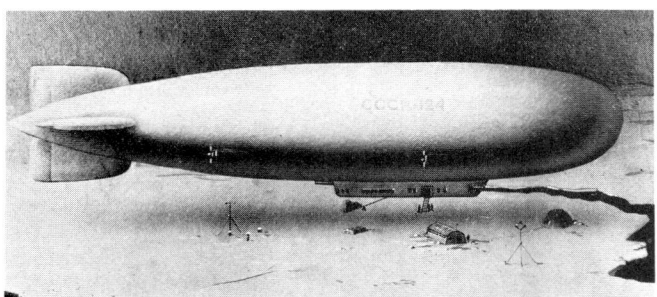

A twin hulled heavy-lift airship, *USSR L-215*, is envisaged for operation on construction projects in the Soviet Union.

This projected tanker airship, *USSR L-157*, has a counter-part in Britain being designed by Sir Barnes Wallis .

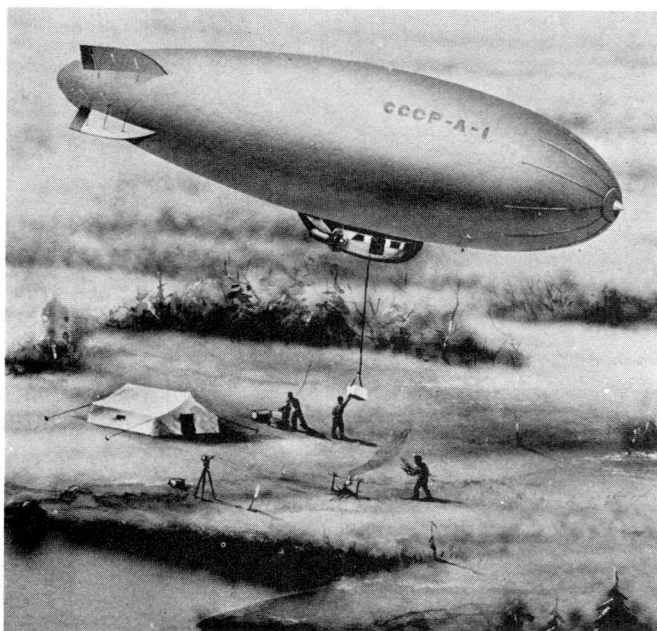

The *USSR-124* is envisaged as a research vessel for Arctic exploration work.

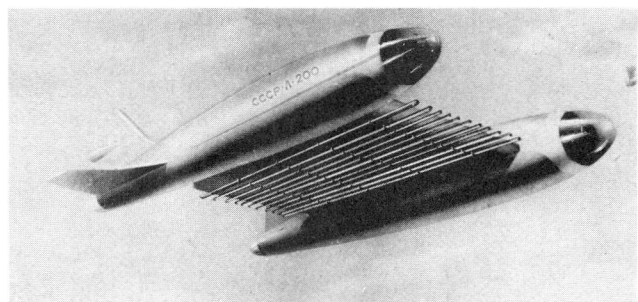

The airship *USSR L-200*, intended for transporting and laying natural-gas pipelines and railway lines in Siberia.

The Soviet Ministry of Geology plans to use small rigid airships similar to the projected *USSR L-1* for transporting fully equipped scientific expeditions to remote regions of the Soviet Union.

When built the large rigid airship *USSR LP-180* will join the small fleet of non-rigid airships that are at present employed in forestry work. Non-rigid airships are believed to have been in operation in the Soviet Union since the early 1960s.

Projects for airships with 1-, 5-, 10-, 25-, 50-, 100-, and 200-ton lifting capacities are under consideration for development in the Soviet Union. The above artist's impressions depict some of the roles envisaged for these airships. (*All seven ilustrations by courtesy of Novosti Press Agency*).

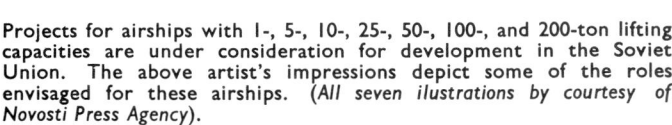

High-voltage pylons and oil-derricks could be transported and erected as part of the *USSR L-100*'s heavy-lift role.

CONTAINER CARRYING HELICOPTERS

General

The use of helicopters for lightering containers to and from sea-going vessels has been under investigation by the research departments of the U.S. Armed Forces since the late 1950s. From 1959 to the present day a series of prototypes and production models have undergone extensive and successful tests. The results of a recent series of combined services evaluation tests have proved that the helicopter might well play a significant container handling role in the future, as container-ships will probably account for a large part of the U.S. Naval transport and supply fleet within the next decade.

A number of crane helicopters have been in operational use for some time, nearly all of them have the capability to carry containers, although only a few were designed especially with that purpose in mind. The Boeing Vertol CH-47 Chinook and the Sikorsky S-64 series are just a few examples of this type of helicopter that are available in the West. Boeing Vertol are at present developing a heavy lift-helicopter, with a 22·5-ton payload capability as a multi-service support aircraft. It is envisaged as the largest helicopter in the West for the foreseeable future.

The Mil Mi-10 (NATO code-name: (V-10) Harke) and the Mi-10K flying-crane versions of the Mi-6, and the recently developed Mi-12 (NATO code-name: (V-12) Homer), that was first shown at Le Bourget in May, 1971, are Soviet helicopters capable of carrying unit payloads. The maximum payload of the Mi-10 is approximately 15 tons.

An extensive series of tests were conducted by the Sikorsky Aircraft Company in conjunction with Container Marine Line on a helicopter delivery system. An S-64A was used to transport containers from a shore-base to the *SS Container Despatcher*, over a distance of five miles. Some details of this test were reported in JANE'S FREIGHT CONTAINERS 1970-71. A more detailed account of this experiment is given below.

While it is obvious that a system such as this has a military rather than a commercial significance, it was thought that such a system could have a commercial application where other forms of transport could not operate. This has since proved to be the case as has been shown by recent experiments. It is worth noting, however, that the cost of operating this kind of service will be extremely high, for example, the cost of operating S-64 types E/F are reported to be £1,170 per day.

Boeing Vertol Heavy-Lift Helicopter

The Boeing Company's Vertol division has been awarded a $76 million contract to design, develop and build an advanced technology heavy-lift helicopter for the United States military services. The project, which began in 1968, is primarily for the development of a prototype by 1974-75. When the tests are completed the U.S. Department of Defense expects to place a substantial order for operational helicopters.

The heavy-lift helicopter is to be developed as a second line transport aircraft. It will have an external cargo system consisting of single or dual payload suspension points. The underside of the fuselage will be flattened so that containers can be carried between the straddle legs of the undercarriage.

The main task of a heavy-lift helicopter during peace-time will probably be to load and unload commercial container-ships, and to work together with underway replenishment ships of the U.S. Navy. In the latter capacity they will provide vertical replenishment to ships in a task force spread over a wide area.

Helicopter-Container Evaluation Tests

An exercise in the operational evaluation of loading and unloading standard containers was recently carried out off the coast of Virginia using Boeing CH-47 Chinooks and Sikorsky S-64A machines. The American Export Industries' *Container Despatcher* anchored five miles off-shore from Fort Story, and sixty 20 ft containers, seventy-five container chassis and twenty M52 tractors were used in the project.

The occasion, which was attended by many top level U.S. military personnel, was to evaluate the operation of loading and unloading standard containers, each measuring 8 ft × 8 ft × 20 ft and weighing ten thousand pounds apiece, from the container-ship to the shore base, and vice versa. The suitability of the containers for air transport, the weather, wind, sea conditions, types of equipment, the loading and unloading techniques were all factors included in the evaluation.

The successful exercise, which was a joint U.S. Army and Navy operation, included tests using helicopters lowering containers by means of one and two point suspension systems into the ship's hold, where they were stacked six deep.

Since container ships will probably comprise a significant part of the future U.S. merchant fleet, the test was felt to be extremely important for the development of methods for handling containers at sea.

Helicopters in a semi Commercial Operation

The marine division of the Canadian Department of transportation recently delivered sixteen 20 ft containers by helicopter to Canadian Eskimo settlements on the fringe of the arctic. In all, over a thousand tons of containerised, palletised and bulk cargo were delivered, from the *Sir Robert Crosbie*, a conventional bulk cargo vessel, to settlements on Baffin and Southampton Islands.

Winter supplies can only be delivered to these settlements during a period of ninety days before winter sets in, so the time factor is of major importance. Delays were caused by hoisting containers from the ship's main hold, although they could have been avoided if a purpose-built ship had been used. As there are no suitable docking facilities on these islands, the usual method of delivering bulk supplies consists of a two-phase operation. First the supply ship is anchored off-shore and the cargo is lightered to a beach at high water. Then the cargo is painstakingly transported over the difficult terrain to its final destination.

Operation Skylift-1970, a more recent trial than that mentioned above, has been carried out successfully in the Canadian Arctic by the Canadian Ministry of Transportation/Marine Operations Planning Division. Others participating in the experiment were Canada Steamship Lines, Eastern Canada Stevedoring Co. Ltd., Sikorsky Aircraft and United Aircraft of Canada. Eighteen days of the 32-day trial were required for the off-loading cycle, in which 4,570 tons of cargo were carried. A Sikorsky S-64E Skycrane transported the cargo from the m.v. *Fort St. Louis* to five remote settlements on Baffin and Cornwallis Islands. The settlements, Resolute Bay, Arctic Bay, Pond Inlet, Clyde River and Frobisher Bay, were chosen for their unique characteristics that make cargo discharge difficult.

Canadian officials have reported that Operation Skylift-1970 was the fastest discharge of cargo in the history of Arctic re-supply, and as a result of the experiments conducted a new and better system of cargo discharge has been developed for servicing remote Arctic settlements. (A detailed report of Operation Skylift-1970 was given in *ICHCA Monthly Journal*, October, 1971).

The success of these trials has proved beyond a shadow of doubt that a helicopter system for unloading container-ships has definite commercial applications in the right circumstances.

An impression of the Boeing tandem-rotor heavy-lift helicopter. The tall tricycle undercarriage will be variable in height and retractable.

SHIPS
MULTI-PURPOSE SHIPS

The United States Military Sealift Command proposes to construct ten multi-purpose cargo ships to replace the 29 old dry-cargo ships now in service. These ships will cost approximately $25,000,000 each. As proposed, these ships will be built by private industry for exclusive military use, being chartered to the Military Sealift Command for ten years with renewal options. With the security of the ten-year charter, private financing would be encouraged and the operators would have fully amortised and relatively modern ships after ten years of operation. This has already been done with the roll-on/roll-off ship *Admiral William M. Callaghan.*

These ships are of an advanced design, being fully convertible for carrying either break-bulk, or roll-on/roll-off, or container cargo, or a mixture of all three types. It has been suggested that pallets could also be carried if slight modifications were made to the cargo handling systems. Each ship will be capable of carrying a maximum of 1,044 standard freight containers (8 ft × 8 ft × 20 ft) or 2,015,000 cubic ft of dry cargo or have 149,000 square feet of deck space available for vehicles. Cargo handling will be facilitated by side and stern ramps and a helicopter deck, one boom with a 210-ton capacity, eight with 26-ton capacities, and six with 42-ton capacities.

When in operation the multi-purpose ship will have a complement of 36 officers and men. The dimensions will be length 650 ft

An artist's impression of a multi-purpose ship showing a container-carrying helicopter, a vehicle ferry and a hover-barge in attendance. The ship is designed to be self-sustaining and can be used to unload other ships which have lesser capabilities (*Courtesy United States Navy*).

overall, beam 100 ft, depth 64 ft, draught 28 ft and the displacement when fully loaded will be 28,958 tons. Top speed will be 21·6 knots and each ship will have a cruising radius of 13,000 miles.

If these multi-purpose ships are to be adopted by commercial shipping lines their versatility must be fully exploited to make the project commercially viable. Consider, for example, the advantageous employment of helicopters (q.v.), indispensable for cargo handling where no shore facilities exist or for underway freight transfer at sea. Many other attributes are inherent in the design, which, undoubtably, will enable this type of ship to lend itself readily to a normal mercantile marine role in the future. Moreover, it can be seen that the combination of both recently developed and well tried transportation and cargo handling techniques have produced a ship design, which is desirable in concept, and is almost certain to be economical in operation on most major shipping routes.

CATAMARANS

Catamarans, which have been in operation as ferries in Japan since the early 1950s, have only recently been regarded with any seriousness for large capacity cargo roles. The main reason for this has been the problems of breadth associated with multi-hulls, which pose docking and berthing difficulties; also structural problems in securing the two hulls together would probably limit the size. On the other hand, the catamaran offers a large deck area on a moderate deadweight, and a relatively shallow draught coupled with a high degree of initial transverse stability. The catamaran would not offer a high speed or reduced powering, but this would be of secondary importance as the sphere of operation would be on inland waterways and on short sea routes.

Catamarans, for a multitude of purposes, have been in series production in the U.S.S.R. during the last few years. This fact, together with the announcement that the U.S.S.R. Ministry of Merchant Marine has formed a Container Carriage Department in the Soviet Sovfrakht Association (Sovfrakht handles all Soviet seaborne foreign trade), leads one to believe that container carrying catamarans will be extensively used in the Soviet Union in the future.

The development of catamarans is also well under way in the West, and at least one project is expected to come to fruition within the next few years.

Bacat

Bacat is an acronym for the barge-aboard-catamaran concept being developed by an Anglo-Danish shipping group. A 2,700 dwt catamaran, costing £2,000,000, is under construction at a Frederikshaven shipyard, and will be commisioned for service in 1973.

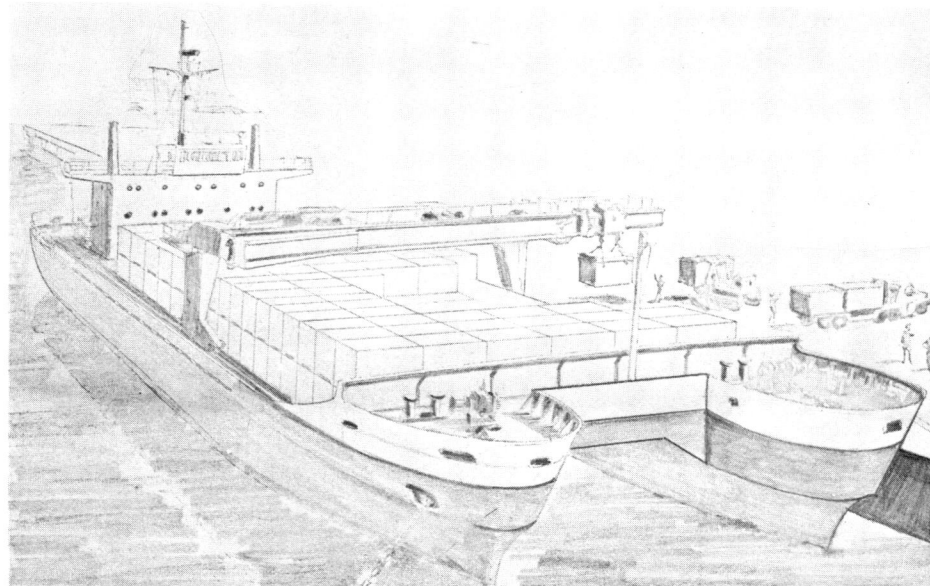

An impression of a shallow draught catamaran container-ship that could operate on short sea routes and inland waterways.

The vessel, with a single bow and catamaran hull, will carry eighteen barges, each with approximately 140 tons capacity.

The Anglo-Danish group has placed an order with the Yorkshire Dry Dock Company for fifty-seven barges. The Bacat barge Module of 17 m by 4·7 m corresponds to the dimensions of the barges used by the British Waterways Board. A system of hydraulically loading the barges from the stern of the catamaran will be used, which is similar to the method employed on Lash ships.

The British Waterways Board is backing the scheme (two 300-bhp twin-screw Schottel-powered pusher tugs have already been constructed), as they envisage Bacat as a vital element in expanding the use of the British commercial canal network. The Bacat barges will begin operations on the Trent Navigation, the Aire and Calder, and the South Yorkshire canals. This will serve to link an important industrialised part of Britain, through the Humber, with the waterways of Northern Europe.

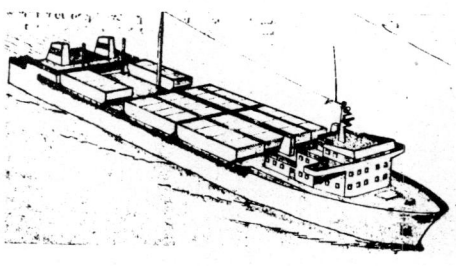

An artist's impression of the 13-knot, 2 700-ton barge carrier (Bacat) that is expected to be in operation on North Sea routes by 1973 (*Courtesy The Motor Ship*).

A cargo catamaran with a container carrying potential, in use on the Moscow-Gorki-Saratova service.

Catamaran Development in the U.S.S.R.

Catamaran freighters have been plying the Soviet waterways for the last few years as part of an extensive programme of multi-hull testing. The experimental stage seems to have been passed, as Soviet catamarans are now being mass produced. This development is part of a plan to adopt unit-cargo methods of freighting on a vast scale, thus efficiently exploiting the intricate network of navigable rivers and canals that are so vital to the internal commerce of the U.S.S.R.

A 14-knot catamaran of 1,000 dwt was launched at Gorky on the Volga earlier this year. The catamaran will join the riverine fleet, probably transporting fresh fruit and vegetables from the southern ports on the Volga to Moscow, Yaroslavl and Gorky. Larger catamarans are being developed probably for short sea operations. They will almost certainly be used for container freighting, as part of the Comecon countries' 'unified containerisation programme'.

The types of catamaran so far developed at Gorky include a double-hulled floating crane for tending off-shore oil derricks, a catamaran trawler, and an oceanographic research vessel. Catamaran development in the U.S.S.R. is well documented in the Soviet technical journals that are available in the West. *Sudostroyeniye* the main shipbuilding journal, has carried some very interesting articles and technical papers, in particular that by V. A. Anisimov, 'Determination of main dimensions of cargo catamarans', which appeared in the issue for June 1971.

Catamarans and Canals

The construction of a Rhine-Main-Danube trans-European system of waterways, linking the Ukraine with Rotterdam was the subject of an article published in *Pravda* last July. The proposal was made by M. Odinets, the paper's Budapest correspondent. The canal system would, he says, run across, or adjacent to, territories of the Netherlands, West Germany, Austria, Czechoslovakia, Hungary, Yugoslavia, Romania, Bulgaria and the Soviet Union. He said that over 4,000 ships at present sailing on the Danube carry approximately 47 million tons. If the proposed waterway is ever completed he estimates a doubling of this figure. He also reports that official consideration is being given to a Danube-Oder-Elbe canal, which would link the rivers of Poland and the river system of the German Democratic Republic with the river systems of the countries of the Danube region.

If the above projected schemes, together with the plan for linking the Rhine with Lake Geneva, were ever realised, the proposed Soviet moderate deadweight unit-cargo fleet could penetrate as far as the Mediterranean, via the Rhone, thus easing the distribution problem and opening a new era of East-West trade relations. The catamarans discussed above would probably play a large part on the proposed waterways, carrying cargoes up to 3,000 tons.

The Soviet catamaran *Experiment* in port at Kaliningrad on its return from a three-month voyage in the Arctic and Atlantic Oceans. The catamaran was found to be more stable than single hulled vessels in bad weather conditions (*Courtesy Fotokronika Tass*).

SEMI-SUBMERGED VESSELS

The Sea Sulky

A remarkable ship design, claimed to offer high speed with stability and vibration-free sailing, is being developed by A/B Internavia, of Gothenburg. The projected ship, known as the 'Sea Sulky' employs the semi-submerged principle and probably takes it further than any previous designs. The 'Sea Sulky' is mainly conceived as a container carrier or passenger/car ferry, although military and other uses are also envisaged.

The design for the 'Sea Sulky' consists of two submersible pontoons connected to a raised deck by pillars fore and aft on each pontoon. Flexible connections are used to enable the pontoons to move independently for greater stability. The cargo deck is designed to be detached from the rest

of the vessel to allow a faster turnabout time, perhaps allowing a multiple cargo module operation on short voyages.

The twin hulls of the 'Sea Sulky', which are fitted with hydroplanes, allow a variable-draught mode of operation, which in theory cuts wave resistance to a minimum and enables the vessel to operate in adverse weather conditions. Medium speed diesel engines have been suggested for propulsion in smaller classes of vessel, and Rolls-Royce RB 211 gas turbines for larger vessels. Nuclear propulsion units are envisaged for very large vessels.

Experiments are being carried out on the viability of interchangeable types of deck being fitted to one single pontoon section. This would give the 'Sea Sulky'

greater flexibility in any kind of operation. For example the designers envisage any single vessel operating as a container carrier, a bulk carrier, a tanker, a passenger ship or even as a warship.

Specifications of a typical semi-submersible container ship:

Length, pontoon 92·0 m (302 ft)
Breadth, deck 38·0 m (124·5 ft)
Draught, harbour 4·8 m (15·5 ft)
Draught, cruising speed 110· m (36 ft)
Depth, cargo deck double-bottom to waterline in port 13·5 m (44·5 ft)
Output 2 × 24,000 bhp
Speed 35 knots
Container capacity 200 × 20 ft

(A detailed technical report can be found in the September, 1971 issue of *The Motor Ship*.)

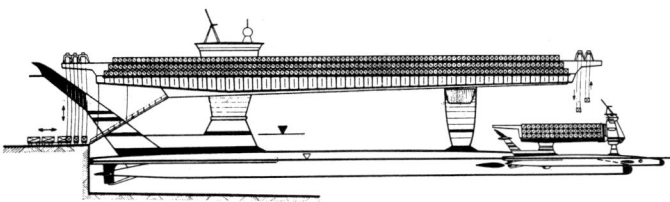

The above drawing shows the 'Sea Sulky' as a 300 m long container-ship attended by its feeder vessel. (*Courtesy The Motor Ship*).

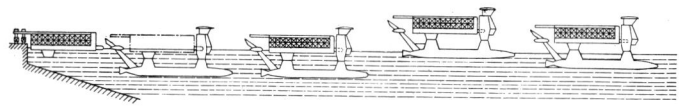

The 'Sea Sulky' in the various stages of docking and voyage preparations. The diagram shows, from the left, the pontoon preparing to take on the cargo deck; the vessel before the water ballast is pumped out; trim control achieved; and the vessel under normal cruising speed (*Courtesy The Motor Ship*).

SUBMARINE CARGO VESSELS

The submarine, traditionally the prerogative of the world's navies since its inception, has only recently entered into the commercial sphere as the main element of a technically feasible sub-sea transport system. This came about by, firstly, the advent of nuclear propulsion, which has made the true submersible possible, and the application of nuclear propulsion in the naval field which resulted in the successful operation of nuclear-powered submarines. The credibility of nuclear submarines operating under the arctic ice was established in 1958 when the U.S. Navy submarine *Nautilus* completed a submerged voyage under the North Polar ice cap. The voyages completed to date include the transit of the North-West Passage and the Kennedy Channel (Nares Strait). Secondly, the growing interest in all the branches of 'oceanography and the 'coming age of hydrospace' has produced a vast range of underwater equipment and a new generation of small research submersibles. With these developments came the ability to service the offshore activities of industry and in particular the oil industry.

The cost of pipelines and large tankers for use in hostile arctic conditions has led many technologists to realise that the submarine is initially the most economic and safe solution. For a submarine would travel far beneath the waves and escape the adverse weather conditions that would be hazardous to many forms of surface transport. Furthermore, sonar sensors strategically placed on the submarine could constantly monitor the underwater environment and provide information on depth, direction, and the existence of possible navigational hazards.

A number of detailed reports on the viability of a submarine transport system have appeared from time to time over the last few years. A few of the more important investigations are listed as follows:

(a) A Japanese proposal for a 30,000 KTDW, 22-knot nuclear submarine for

crude oil transport was made at the second United Nations conference on Peaceful Uses of Atomic Energy ;

(b) An 80,000-ton, 40-knot submarine for the same purpose, also originating from Japan;

(c) A 20,000 dwt, 20-knot and a 40,000 dwt, 40-knot submarine tanker were proposed in a paper presented to U.S. Society of Naval Architects and Marine Engineers.;

(d) Another study from the U.S.A., by F. H. Todd, discusses the hydrodynamic advantages of such craft over conventional cargo ships;

(e) P. R. Crewe and D. J. Handy proposed a 28,000 dwt, 25-knot nuclear submarine bulk carrier for transporting iron ore from Northern Canada to Britain, in a paper read before the Royal Institute of Naval Architects.

In the 1970-71 edition of JANE'S FREIGHT CONTAINERS, investigations and proposals for submarines, semi-submersibles and submersible barges, illustrating the wide interest in cargo vessels of this nature were discussed. The advantages of using these vessels as unit load carriers were mentioned, though most informed technologists doubt the economic sense in this for normal container carrying operations. It is believed, though, that submarines could be developed along the same lines as Lash ships, but no design studies on this mode of operation have yet been done. Therefore, the following report on the General Dynamics proposal has been set out in some detail to illustrate the technical feasibility of an underwater transport system.

General Dynamics

Electric Boat Division
Eastern Point Road
Groton
Connecticut 06340
U.S.A.

In a paper (*Subsea Transport of Arctic Oil—A Technical and Economic Evaluation*) presented at the third annual Offshore Technology Conference in Houston, Texas, in April, 1971, Lawrence R. Jacobsen,

of General Dynamics' Electric Boat Division, proposed a nuclear-powered submarine tanker as the most reliable and flexible means of transporting oil from Alaska's North Slope and the Canadian Arctic islands to North Atlantic and European terminals. It was predicted that these tankers would be in operation by 1975-76. At the same conference Samuel B. Winram, director of General Dynamic's Arctic Transport Systems, announced that proposals had been made to Esso Standard, Standard of Ohio (British Petroleum), Mobil, Atlantic-Richfield and Phillips 66, with regard to their using the tanker for future operations.

The highly detailed paper by Mr. Jacobsen points out that a submerged oil transporter would be superior to, and economically competitive with, other modes of transport for moving oil cheaply and speedily from the hostile Arctic environment to ice-free North Atlantic ports. He went on to say that studies of cargo handling, navigability, operating depth, power and speed, point to vessels in the range of 17,000 dwt to 250,000 dwt.

Specifications for a typical submarine tanker:

Length, between perpendiculars 273·6 m (900 ft)
Beam, moulded 42·7 m (140 ft)
Depth 25·9 m (85 ft)
Deadweight (long tons) 173,900
Oil cargo 1,250,000 barrels
Displacement (long tons):
  Fully loaded, surfaced 241,300 tons
  Submerged 253,340 tons
Normal operating depths 300-400 ft
Crew 49 (accommodation for 57)
Speed, sustained 18·0 knots
Construction time, approximately 4½ years
Life expectancy, about 25 years

The submarine excels in protecting the environment, Mr. Jacobsen believes, 'primarily because it avoids the threat of rupture by sailing below and clear of sea ice. Sophisticated navigation gear will guard against collisions. Moreover, the submarine's cargo-handling and tank-cleaning arrangements will minimise contaminated discharges.'

Other factors affecting submarine tanker economics, Mr. Jacobsen said, are the discovery and location of additional oil reserves, U.S. import policies, routes and terminals, all of which must be brought into a total system before construction decisions can be made.

The submarine tanker has been proposed as a second generation marine transportation system by General Dynamics, who also envisage a future fleet of fifteen 255,000 dwt submarines, requiring an estimated $3,000 million investment.

(The paper by L. R. Jacobsen, No. OTC 1425, can be obtained from: Offshore Technology Conference, 6200 North Central Expressway, Dallas, Texas 75206, U.S.A.)

Samuel B. Winram, Director of Arctic Transport Systems, points out features of the 900-ft, nuclear-powered submarine tanker which General Dynamics displayed for the first time at the third annual Offshore Technology Conference in Houston, Texas.

An artist's impression of the General Dynamics nuclear-powered submarine tanker. Displacing over 250,000 tons when fully loaded, the submarine would traverse the Northwest Passage or the Arctic Ocean, under the ice.

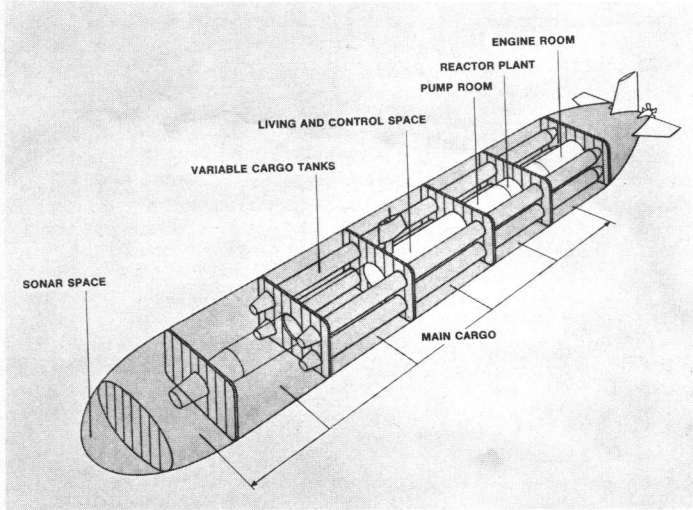

The General Dynamics-designed nuclear submarine tanker would carry as much as 170,000 tons of oil in this 900-ft version. Larger vessels, up to 300,000 tons, could be built from the same design.

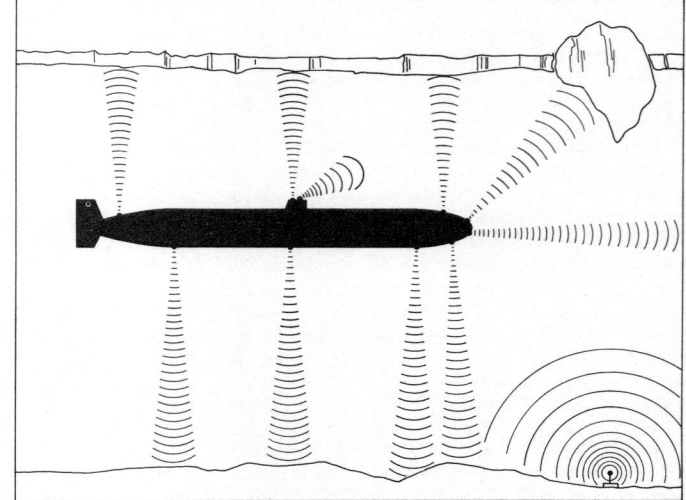

A complete package of sonar, radio, radar and navigation systems would ensure safe passage of the General Dynamics nuclear-powered submarine tanker through the Arctic underwater environment.

NUCLEAR PROPULSION FOR MERCHANT SHIPS

The growing interest in nuclear-powered merchant ships has been highlighted by a symposium on nuclear propulsion held in Hamburg earlier this year. Over five hundred scientists and professional men from more than thirty-three countries took part. Private enterprise was represented for the first time in an event of this kind. The symposium was arranged and sponsored by the International Atomic Energy Agency (I.A.E.A.), the Inter-Governmental Maritime Consultative Organisation (I.M.C.O.) and the Government of the German Federal Republic, in co-operation with a number of private organisations. About fifty-four studies and reports covering all the aspects of nuclear propulsion were read at the symposium.

A general consensus of opinion shows that those taking part in the symposium were quite optimistic about the future prospects of nuclear propulsion. This opinion mainly derives from the view that rising oil prices and the long-term fuel shortage problem necessitates the development of an alternative propulsion system to those in general use. The growing demand for more tonnage in world trade, increasing ship sizes and speed, and the anticipated reduction in the cost of nuclear energy have also helped to make ships with this type of powering a desirable proposition.

A fillip was given to the controversy over nuclear propulsion by Sir David Barran, the chairman of the Shell Transport and Trading Company, when he announced at the annual general meeting that the world consumption of oil during this decade was as much as had been consumed during the last century. He went on to say that by the end of the century the annual world consumption of oil would be approximately 57,000 million tons, which would approach the world reserve level of untapped resources. He clearly indicated that the use of nuclear power would help to conserve the world's oil reserves, and that the break-even point for nuclear-powered high-speed container ships was very close.

Although nuclear-powered ships offer long-term attractions the U.K. Government has reservations about implementing a construction programme for merchant ships. The Government accepted the conclusions of the official nuclear ship study (*Report on the Nuclear Ship Study*, H.M.S.O., 1971), that recommended the commercial development of marine nuclear reactors in the U.K. would be a misuse of resources. On the evidence available, the report could only recommend that work on nuclear propulsion for merchant ships should be limited to reviewing work on marine reactors elsewhere, and any developments in land-based reactors which could substantially improve their performance. Developments in ship propulsion techniques and trends in oil prices were also recommended to be kept under review, as a price rise of 70 to 200 per cent in real terms would make nuclear propulsion for merchant ships competitive with conventional propulsion systems. For the immediate future then, the United Kingdom Atomic Energy Authority and the Department of Trade and Industry will limit their activities to the surveillance of developments in other countries.

Nuclear ship designs are being studied in a number of countries and several nations are at present building and operating nuclear-fuelled ships. A few of the main developments are listed as follows:

U.S.A.: The American Export Isbrandtsen Lines operated the nuclear ship *Savannah*, a cargo/passenger vessel of 9,500 dwt, commercially from 1965 to 1969 for the U.S. Government. Although the ship was not economically self-supporting (Government subsidies amount to $3 million per year), its operation has shown that a nuclear ship could operate safely on international trade routes.

Germany (Federal Republic): The nuclear ship *Otto Hahn*, an ore carrier and research vessel of 15,000 dwt, has been operated by the Gesellschaft für Kernenergieverwetung in Schiffbau und Schiffahrt m.b.H. since 1968. Germany would appear to be taking nuclear propulsion seriously as several shipyards have set up nuclear propulsion research departments.

Japan: The Shipbuilding research Association of Japan has decided to develop a reactor for a nuclear-powered container ship. Another project, the nuclear ship *Matsu Moru* has been built and will be delivered complete with reactor in 1972. The *Matsu Moru* will be mainly used for research and training purposes.

Design and cost studies for nuclear-powered merchant ships have been implemented by research organisations in Belgium, Denmark, Holland, Italy, Norway and Sweden, but Italy is the only country of these nations planning to build a research vessel.

The general opinion held by those who have studied the problem of nuclear propulsion for surface craft is that the high capital cost of both reactors and nuclear fuel would make any commercial ship operation too costly to become competitive until at least a 50 per cent reduction in these costs is effected.

CONTAINERS

CONTAINER LABORATORIES

The entry of the oceanographic research vessel *Le Noroit* into service on 15th June, 1971, has marked the birth of a container with a use other than that of transporting commercial products. *Le Noroit* is equipped with two 'container-laboratories', a unique development in container application, which will probably have far reaching effects on specialised container design and manufacture. However, there has also been a development along similar lines in Iran, where semi-trailers with van bodies and containers have been successfully utilised to provide relatively cheap and highly mobile hospital units. There is also a scheme for equipping small cargo vessels with specially made containers in order to provide the military authorities with cheap hospital ships under development in the German Federal Republic (q.v.).

Le Noroit was built for her owners, the National French Organisation for Oceanic Research (C.N.E.X.O.), by Ateliers et Chantiers du Havre. She was laid down on 18th December, 1969, launched on 16th October, 1970, and delivered to C.N.E.X.O. on 15th June, 1971. She is of the 'Norois' class and can best be described as an oceanographic survey ship, fitted out with non-specialised basic equipment, designed for about three-week long missions from a land base. She owes her high versatility to the employment of 'container-laboratories', each to be equipped according to the mission(s) to be fulfilled. These 'container-laboratories' have been manufactured in accordance with the standards and specifications indicated by the International Organisation for Standardisation (ISO), in their designation 1C, for Cargo Carrying Containers, to enable them to be sent when required, to a remote base by any container transport facilities.

As well as bringing new considerations to bear on future container design, the 'container-laboratory' is expected to be of great benefit to researchers carrying out on-site investigation, on dry land or aboard ship. These containers can be used on either long or short-term missions and will be inexpensive enough to benefit educational institutions, research organisations, and small specialist manufacturing concerns in need of low cost and/or seasonal research facilities. The advantages to be gained by the use of the 'container-laboratories' are expected to be considerable. The most obvious benefits would be:

(a) the provision of a low cost means of transporting scientific equipment in the convenient form of a ready-made laboratory;

(b) the ability to transport the 'container-laboratory' by utilising existing container facilities;

(c) providing fully equipped mobile laboratories, through either a state-run or a private leasing agency, for organisations that could not otherwise afford the high capital expenditure that would be incurred by owning and maintaining specialised apparatus, much of which would be used for relatively short periods each year;

(d) the provision of a ready-made laboratory for research and exploration teams working in remote inland areas, inaccessible to any forms of transport other than hovercraft or helicopter;

(e) safe housing for expensive and delicate instruments, especially in extreme climatic conditions;

(f) a reduction and possible elimination of the damage factor incurred when transporting fragile equipment;

(g) using non-specialised craft with the capability of carrying one or more containers;

(h) the possible provision of specialised facilities afloat, such as a mobile consultancy service for off-shore mineral exploration companies. This would apply mainly to those engaged in the search for hydrocarbons.

One other possible advantageous development that could give immense educational and research benefits to both wealthy and under-developed countries alike, is that a container-ship, with medium capacity, could be employed to carry 'container-laboratories' that have been equipped to accommodate a wide variety of research programmes. This would be an economic and logical method of obtaining international research co-operation, and would allow under-developed countries to participate in research work, as part of an economic and scientific aid programme; or for a modest sum compared to what would have been spent had they provided their own facilities. There is hope that if this scheme were to be adopted as a service on a world-wide basis, a con-siderable saving in time, effort and money would be achieved by eradicating much of the duplication of scientific investigation that must prove so frustrating to those concerned. The costly nature of developing and maintaining a service of this nature, and the use to which it would be put, place it more in the province of an international organisation, such as the United Nations, rather than under the control of any individual government.

One possible disadvantage of using 'container-laboratories' could be the damaging of delicate scientific equipment by excess condensation. This is frequently the cause of damage to goods carried in containers, but it could be reduced, and possibly eliminated, if adequate precautions were taken. The methods used to overcome condensation problems are ventilation, and the operation of a dehydration unit. The latter method is by far the more efficient, and consists of a portable refrigerator which is capable of continuously removing moisture from the air. This system can be coupled to several containers at a time. Condensation Ltd., a London firm, is at present developing a compact unit for dealing economically with individual containers, which could solve any condensation problems with 'container-laboratories'.

A comparison of the main specifications of a non-specialised research vessel like *Le Noroit* with the relatively low cost, for example, of converting a barge, tug or fishing vessel, or in fact any craft with deck space for even one 'container-laboratory', will give a rough guide to the initial expenditure incurred in building and operating a craft of this type, and the advantages of using an alternative. The main characteristics of *Le Noroit* are as follows:

Length overall 50·55 m (165 ft 11 in)
Length between perpendiculars 43·05 m (141 ft 3 in)
Moulded breadth 10·66 m (35 ft)
Depth to main deck 3·91 m (12 ft 11 in)
Depth to upper deck 6·11 m (20 ft 1 in)
Loaded draught aft 4·32 m (14 ft 1 in)
Gross tonnage 499 gt
Loaded displacement 870 tons, approx.
Bunkers 108 tons
Propelling set (engines etc.) Two four-stroke non-reversible supercharged MGO diesels, Mk V 12 ASHR. Declutchable gearbox.

Variable pitch propeller.
Horsepower 2 × 825 HP (1,320 rpm)
Speed 14 knots
Radius 7,500/12
Accommodation (air conditioned) for 30

laboratories and workshops, 1 wet laboratory, 1 scientist's headquarters, 2 container laboratories, 1 electronic shop.
Deck auxiliaries for oceanographic survey,

1 × 6-ton dredging and coring winch, 2 × 1-ton hydrological winches for bathymetric probes, with rotating contacts.

'HOSPITAL CONTAINER' SHIPS

A development commission has been set up in the German Federal Republic to investigate alternatives to orthodox hospital ships, because of the high cost involved in maintaining the latter. The scheme under consideration at the moment is to convert cargo ships by using containers as cabins, operating theatres, etc. Beds for the main ward would be provided by erecting a two-tier framework of modular construction, so that cots could be added to the structure as needed. The great advantage of this scheme is that the vessels used would be profitably employed, performing their normal cargo-carrying duties, until required for conversion. Then specially prepared 'hospital-containers' could be taken out of storage, and used to transform the ships into floating hospitals at very short notice.

A vessel with a large internal area for cargo, that would easily be adapted to the uses and standards required by the development commission, was needed. The ship chosen was of the coaster type, 500 grt, and about 70m in length. There are over a hundred of these sailing under the flag of the Bundesrepublik. The coasters have an adequate main power supply, plenty of storage space for fresh water tanks, and a good air-conditioning system, which means that there is a considerable saving when installing supplementary facilities. Three ships of relatively shallow draught have so far been used; the *Wappen von Hamburg* (since renamed the *Alte Liebe*), the *Bremerhaven* and the *Heligoland*. Plans are going ahead for the adaptation of a fourth vessel.

A specially prepared container measuring 2 m × 2 m × 2 m will serve as a double bunk cabin for the medical staff, and as a hospital bedroom for the patients. Members of the ship's crew would use the accommodation already provided for them. The containers would also be used to provide storage and toilet facilities, etc. Containers measuring 3 m × 6 m × 2 m will provide treatment bays, emergency operating theatres and kitchens. All the containers to be used will be of a light metal double-walled construction, and will be weather-proof. Additionally, they can be transported and handled by all normal freight container methods (though not, we hope, while containing patients).

When loaded into the cargo holds the containers will be strong enough to be double-stacked. A hospital ward arrangement and living accommodation will be provided by placing the containers in two facing rows, with a central gangway in between. The main ward would house the majority of the patients in a modular sleeping arrangement of three rows of beds placed end-to-end, two wide and two high. A space separating the containers from the sides of the ship will enable easy access for any servicing. The containers will be secured to the deck by clamps and rings already fixed in position.

The services essential for safety, hygiene and comfort will be provided by linking the containers to a main power supply, an emergency generator, fresh water supply and to a waste disposal system. A heating and an air-conditioning link for every container, together with a general ventilation system will help to furnish a highly sophisticated medical-care unit.

The first fully operational hospital-container' ship, to be used for experimental purposes, is expected to be ready within two years. It will be capable of caring for about a hundred patients. Should the tests prove successful the West German military authorities are expected to adopt the scheme as a money-saving alternative to the conventional hospital ship.

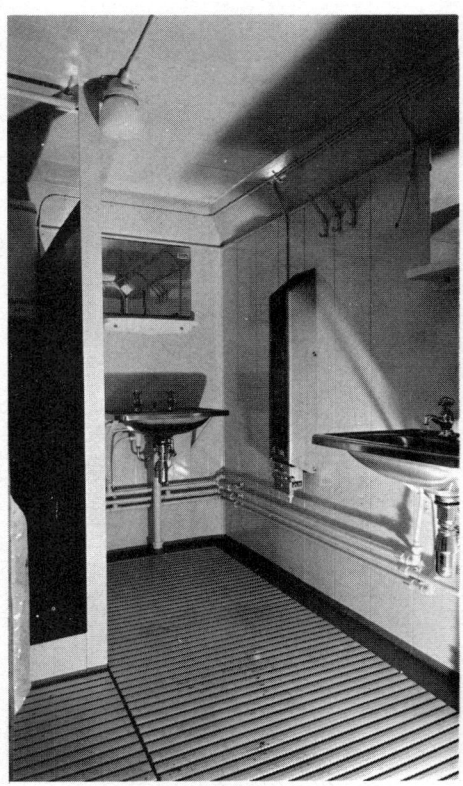

Washing and lighting facilities in a 2 m × 2 m × 2 m toilet container (*Courtesy Marineamt/Gregory*)

A 3 m × 6 m × 2 m container (Behandlungsraum) that can be used as an emergency operating theatre (*Courtesy Marineamt/Gregory*).

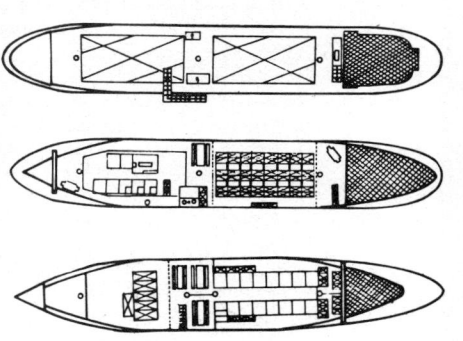

A view of the central gangway showing the container cabins secured below decks (*Courtesy Marineamt/Wehrmed Mtschr*).

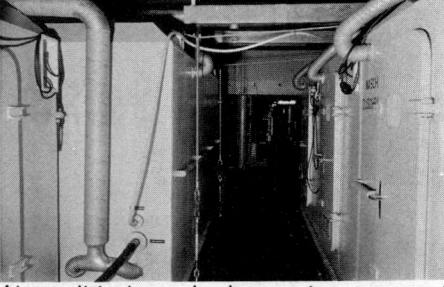

Air-conditioning and other services connected to a large container on the left and smaller containers on the right (*Courtesy Marineamt/Truppenpraxis*).

Loading 2 m × 2 m × 2 m container cabins onto a German coaster (*Courtesy Marineamt/Gregory*).

Container-cabins and fresh-water tanks etc. are constructed in a modular form to facilitate easy storage (*Courtesy Marineamt/Gregory*).

The weather deck, showing the two large hatches with the auxiliary generator situated in between.

The 'tween deck arrangements for the main hospital ward, situated aft, and the toilet facilities in the forward position. The galley and exercise area are indicated amidships. The hot-air units can be seen positioned well aft and forward.

The lower deck showing the cabin-containers and storage space. The fresh water tanks are indicated forward.

AUTOMATED STORAGE SYSTEMS
CONTAINER STORAGE FOR RIJNPOORT

Meeusen Consultants
Barendrecht
The Netherlands

P. Meeusen of Meeusen Consultants has proposed a horizontal container handling and storage system to handle a throughput of over 1,500,000 containers. The proposal has been submitted as a system for inclusion in the Rotterdam-Rijnpoort project. The terminal will be integrated with present types of handling systems and the whole system will be computer controlled. A provisional computer control system has been worked out by H. Nielsen & Son, and Danske Requecentralen A/S, both of Copenhagen. Meeusen Consultants have said that the addition of computer control will enable an error-free operation and make the theft of containers almost impossible.

Meeusen Consultants believe that their container terminal will act as a catalyst in the development of a third generation of large capacity container vessels. In fact Meeusens have prepared ship designs with changes that depart radically from the cellular type of container vessel; instead of the cellular open-deck vessel the new design is for a ship with completely closed decks. The ships will have no vertical cells, but instead, will have horizontal lanes beside each other and above each other, running from the bow to the stern. A system of elevators and conveyor belts assist in providing a continuous stream of containers from the ship into the terminal. The conveyors on the ship, known as 'containoveyors', will be linked with similar conveyors on the dock side. These in turn are to be serviced by overhead

Part of the container handling system projected by Meeusen Consultants.

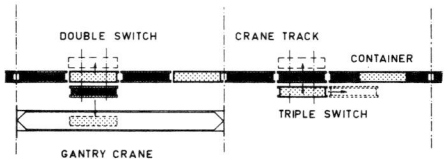

A diagram showing the fully integrated crane and conveyor belt system.

cranes, which will remove the containers to their correct location within the storage area.

Calculations have been made by Meeusen which show that a fully occupied integrated container terminal would be an attractive proposition, paying off investment over a period of three to four years given a reasonably high throughput.

It might perhaps be mentioned that the planned throughput is one and a half million 40 ft boxes on completion of the terminal. The first stage envisages a throughput of half a million units. If the average 40 ft unit contains twenty deadweight tons then the facility will handle ten million tons of general cargo on completion of the first stage, which is more than one third of the total general cargo handled by Rotterdam at present. (1969 figures show 27·9 m tons.) Taking this into consideration together with the technical and financial problems which this scheme would be sure to encounter leads one to draw the conclusion that the very magnitude of the Meeusen project precludes its implementation in toto.

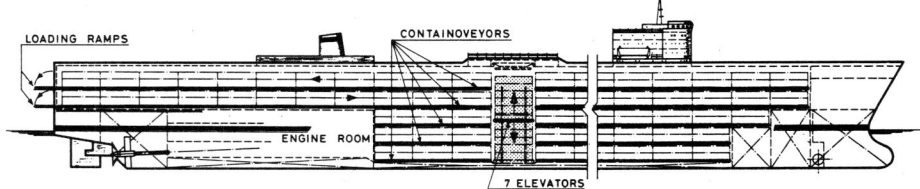

The third generation container vessel projected by Meeusen Consultants, showing the horizontal loading and storage facilities for containers.

KAISER-IHI 'SPEED-TAINER SYSTEM'

Ishikawajima-Harima Heavy Industries Co. Ltd. (IHI) of Japan, have advanced into the field of automatic high-stack container terminal systems through a technical tie-up with Kaiser Engineers International Inc. of the U.S. The technical tie-up concerns engineering for a port terminal system, for marine containers, called the 'speed-tainer system', and the designing and manufacture of various component machinery including the automatic cargo handling system.

IHI have already developed a series of container yard systems of their own; the arrangement with Kaiser Engineers has made it possible for them to supply automatic high-stack container terminal systems suited for any volume of cargo or conditions of location. By making use of systems engineering, IHI is planning to conduct a consulting service for possible users of automated terminal systems.

The container storage system projected by Kaiser Engineers is made up of a dockside crane and an electric rail car loop which links the dockside crane with the container storage building. A stacker crane located in the storage structure will facilitate handling of containers both into and out of store. The whole operation of the terminal system is designed for complete computer control.

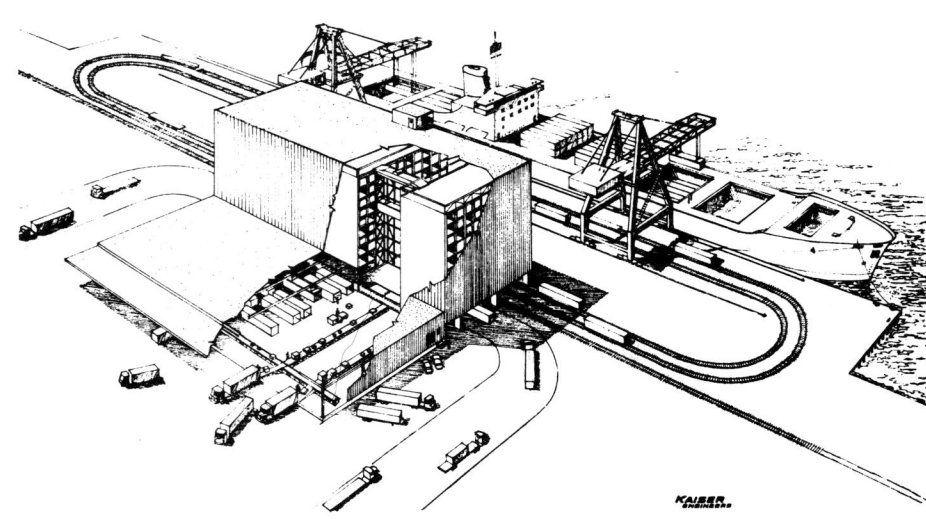

A sketch of the Kaiser-IHI 'speed-tainer system'.

SELECTIVE MULTI-STACKER CONTAINER TERMINAL SYSTEM

Shoosmith, Howe Consultants Limited
Consultant Civil, Mechanical and Marine
Engineers
Pearl House, Bartholomew Street
Newbury, Berkshire
England
Telephone: Newbury 5196
Telex: 847338
DIRECTORS:
G. T. Shoosmith
R. Stedman
J. B. Griffith
T. A. Hughes
G. R. G. Watkins (*Freight Handling Consultant*)

General

The system provides a means of storing incoming and outgoing containers utilising the minimum ground space in such a manner that each container can be located and handled separately.

It is designed to be integrated with existing methods of loading and discharging container vessels.

Method

(*i*) *Transport between ship-shore cranes and terminal storage building:* Dockside tractor/slave trailer units are employed for this purpose in preference to more sophisticated lifter/transporters on account of their cheapness, reliability and flexibility.

(*ii*) *Transport between terminal buildings and inland transport, Road or Rail:* Containers arriving by Road or Rail are transferred to dockside tractor/slave trailer units by means of Goliath–type gantry cranes with top-lifting spreaders for conveyance to the terminal. For containers being discharged from the terminal the reverse procedure takes place.

(*iii*) *The Terminal Storage Buildings:* In the example illustrated, there are two terminal storage buildings containing three alleyways each, each building serving one ship/shore crane. Containers are loaded or discharged into or from the loading platforms at the entrance to each alleyway by overhead gantries carrying top-lifting spreaders. From the loading platforms containers are transferred to stacker-units which load them into designated cells and then select, recover and discharge stored containers if required.

The time cycle for loading one container, stacking it and recovering another from storage and placing it on the exit loading platform is between six and seven minutes depending on the location of the container. Since there are three stacker units feeding one ship/shore crane, this loading cycle is ade-quate to match the loading cycle of the ship/shore crane.

Storage Capacity

The terminal blocks as illustrated show containers stored in cells 8 tiers high and 26 deep per alleyway side; 40 ft and 20 ft cells are shown. The system is designed to store and handle 8 ft or 8 ft 6 in high containers. 40 ft cells can accommodate containers between 20 ft and 40 ft long. As shown the terminal could accommodate 832 × 40 ft containers and 1,664 × 20 ft containers, i.e. one third 40 ft containers.

Area

The terminal blocks occupy approximately four acres whereas a conventional layout employing straddle carriers would need approximately five times as much space.

Control System

A control block is located between the two storage blocks but is placed slightly forward to obtain the best possible field of vision.

The degree of automation and electronic control of the stacker-units to be employed rests with the user but it is considered that the minimum control should include an indication from Control to a stacker-driver as to which cell to load or to unload.

All activities in the terminal areas such as ship/shore cranes, tractor/trailers, Goliath gantries, etc., can be controlled from the control block if the user considers the expense warranted.

Empty Containers

It is proposed that empty containers are handled by front-forklift trucks fitted with the side frame container lifting attachment since this is fast and economical.

Stuffing and Customs Sheds

It is proposed that all handling of containers for stuffing and Customs is carried out by Goliath–type overhead gantries.

Cost

The cost comparison of 'going up' as opposed to occupying more ground space with a conventional two-high container park depends on the cost, the availability and value of land. An S.M-S Container terminal should prove viable in many of the older ports where land is at a premium and might enable valuable dockside land to be used for other purposes.

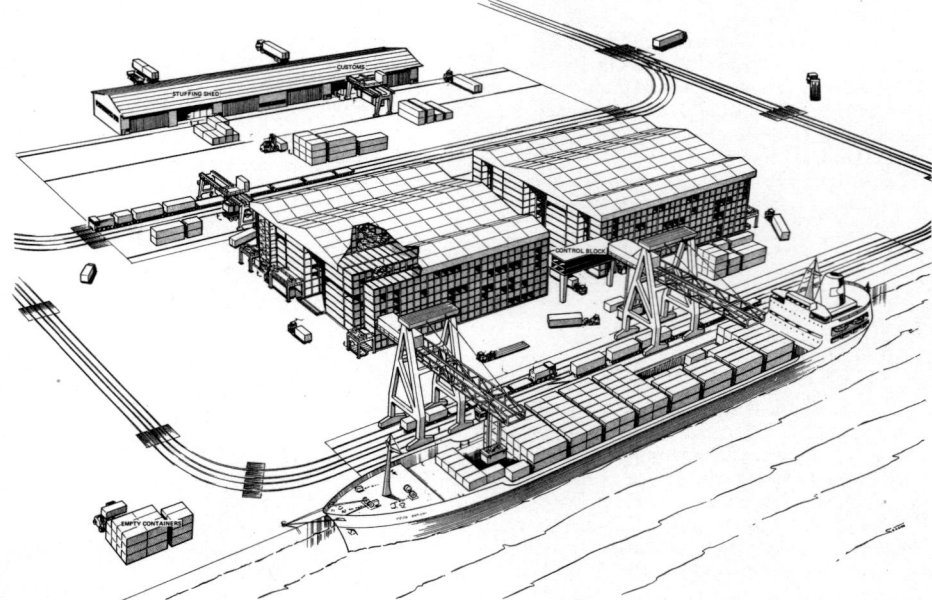

A typical multi-stacker container terminal lay-out, providing individual storage for 823 × 40 ft containers and 1,664 × 20 ft containers. For full details see under Shoosmith Howe.

ADDENDA

ADDENDA

Schindler Carriage & Wagon Co.
4133 Pratteln
Switzerland
TELEPHONE: 061 81 55 11
TELEX: 62 386 SWP
DIRECTORS:
  J. Bonnard
  E. Steiner
  M. Cornelle
  H. Knecht
  P. Piffaretti
  E. Schumacher
PRINCIPLE USERS:
  MAT Transport AG, Basle
  Crowe & Co. AG, Basle
  Container Leasing, Basle
  Danzas AG, Chiasso
  Kirchner & Co. AG, Wien
  Roehlig & Co. Bremen
  Interfrigo, Basle

PRODUCTION:			Quantity manufactured		
Type			20 ft	30 ft	40 ft
Dry goods	1970				
	1971				
Insulated	1970				
	1971				
Refrigerated	1970		15		90
	1971		20		40
Specials	1970		260	280	—
with removable roof	1971		220	250	—

CONTAINERS:
  Dry freight and refrigerated ISO containers made of steel and plastic laminate panels.   The range is as follows:

End door closed top container

DIMENSIONS:		20 ft	30 ft	40 ft
		mm	mm	mm
Exterior	Length	6055 (238$\frac{2}{8}$ in)	9125 (359$\frac{1}{4}$ in)	12190 (480 in)
	Width	2435 (95$\frac{3}{4}$ in)	2435 (95$\frac{3}{4}$ in)	2435 (95$\frac{3}{4}$ in)
	Height	2435 (95$\frac{3}{4}$ in)	2435 (95$\frac{3}{4}$ in)	2435 95$\frac{3}{4}$ in)
Interior	Length	5900 (232$\frac{1}{4}$ in)	8970 (353$\frac{1}{8}$ in)	12035 (473$\frac{3}{4}$ in)
	Width	2325 (91$\frac{1}{2}$ in)	2325 (91$\frac{1}{2}$ in)	2325 (91$\frac{1}{2}$ in)
	Height	2240 (88$\frac{1}{5}$ in)	2240 (88$\frac{1}{8}$ in)	2240 (88$\frac{1}{5}$ in)
OPENINGS FOR LOADING:		mm	mm	mm
	Width	2300 (90$\frac{1}{2}$ in)	2300 (90$\frac{1}{2}$ in)	2300 (90$\frac{1}{2}$ in)
	Height	2130 (83$\frac{1}{5}$ in)	2130 (83$\frac{1}{5}$ in)	2130 (83$\frac{1}{5}$ in)

WEIGHT:	kg	kg	
Weight when empty	1850 (4076 lb)	2500 (5511·6 lb)	3000 (6613·9 lb)
Useful load	18470 (40719·32 lb)	22900 (50486 lb)	27480 (60583 lb)
Total weight	20320 (44798·09 lb)	25400 (55997 lb)	30480 (67197·37 lb)

Container for European standard pallets

This unit which has end and side doors is not made to ISO dimensions. But it is of interest because it is designed to accommodate 1,200 mm and 800 mm European railway pool pallets without waste of space. The four corner castings on the base of the container are designed to be used on a standard ISO container carrying chassis. Top corner castings can similarly be provided to conform to ISO lifting equipment if required.

DIMENSIONS:
Exterior

	mm
Length	7000 (275$\frac{1}{2}$ in)
Width	2500 (98$\frac{1}{2}$ in)
Height	2500 (98$\frac{1}{2}$ in)

Interior

Length	6950 (273$\frac{1}{2}$ in)
Width	2440 (96 in)
Height	2350 (92$\frac{1}{2}$ in)

OPENINGS FOR LOADING:
Front

Width	2430 (95$\frac{1}{2}$ in)
Height	2210 (87 in)

Side

Width	3000 (118$\frac{1}{10}$ in)
Height	2210 (87 in)

WEIGHT:

	kg
Weight when empty	1800 (3968·3 lb)
Useful load	14000 (30865 lb)
Total weight	15800 (34833 lb)

Open sided containers

These units are provided with tarpaulin covers for the openings. Roof may be removable. The containers can be open on all four sides.

DIMENSIONS:	20 ft	30 ft
Exterior	mm	mm
Length	6055 (238$\frac{2}{3}$ in)	9125 (359$\frac{3}{4}$ in)
Width	2435 (95$\frac{3}{4}$ in)	2435 (95$\frac{3}{4}$ in)
Height	2590 (102 in)	2590 (102 in)
Length	5920 (233 in)	8990 (354 in)
Width	2300 (90$\frac{1}{2}$ in)	2300 (90$\frac{1}{2}$ in)
Height	2255 (88$\frac{3}{4}$ in)	2255 (88$\frac{3}{4}$ in)
OPENINGS FOR LOADING:		
Front	mm	mm
Width	2300 (90$\frac{1}{2}$ in)	2300 (90$\frac{1}{2}$ in)
Height	2170 (85$\frac{1}{2}$ in)	2170 (85$\frac{1}{2}$ in)
Side:		
Width	5430 (213$\frac{3}{4}$ in)	8500 (334$\frac{1}{2}$ in)
Height	2200 (86$\frac{1}{2}$ in)	2200 (86$\frac{1}{2}$ in)
WEIGHT:	kg	kg
Weight when empty	2600 (5732 lb)	3450 (7383·9 lb)
Useful load	17720 (39066·09 lb)	21950 (48391·25 lb)
Total weight	20320 (44798·09 lb)	25400 (55997 lb)

Removable roof units

The light metal roof can be removed completely and easily by crane or other lifting device. These containers also have end doors. The roof is locked into place by two rotating bars. Once locked access becomes impossible. The system of locking has been accepted by the Customs. The system is available to order.

Closed top container with one end and one side door

DIMENSIONS:		20 ft	30 ft	40 ft
		mm	mm	mm
Exterior	Length	6055 (238$\frac{5}{8}$ in)	9125 (359$\frac{1}{4}$ in)	12190 (480 in)
	Width	2435 (95$\frac{3}{4}$ in)	2435 (95$\frac{3}{4}$ in)	2435 (95$\frac{3}{4}$ in)
	Height	2435 (95$\frac{3}{4}$ in)	2435 (95$\frac{3}{4}$ in)	2435 (95$\frac{3}{4}$ in)
Interior	Length	5900 (232$\frac{1}{4}$ in)	8970 (353$\frac{1}{2}$ in)	12035 (473$\frac{1}{4}$ in)
	Width	2325 (91$\frac{1}{2}$ in)	2325 (91$\frac{1}{2}$ in)	2325 (91$\frac{1}{2}$ in)
	Height	2240 (88$\frac{1}{5}$ in)	2240 (88$\frac{1}{5}$ in)	2240 (88$\frac{1}{5}$ in)
Front		mm	mm	mm
	Width	2300 (90$\frac{1}{2}$ in)	2300 (90$\frac{1}{2}$ in)	2300 (90$\frac{1}{2}$ in)
	Height	2130 (83$\frac{4}{5}$ in)	2130 (83$\frac{4}{5}$ in)	2130 (83$\frac{4}{5}$ in)
Side	Width	2000 (78$\frac{3}{4}$ in)	2000 (78$\frac{3}{4}$ in)	2000 (78$\frac{3}{4}$ in)
	Height	2130 (83$\frac{4}{5}$ in)	2130 (83$\frac{4}{5}$ in)	2130 (83$\frac{4}{5}$ in)
WEIGHT:		kg	kg	kg
Weight of container		2100 (4269·7 lb)	3100 (6834·3 lb)	3450 (24013 lb)
Useful load		18220 (40168·09 lb)	22300 (49163 lb)	27030 (59591$\frac{1}{4}$ lb)
Total weight		20320 (44798·09 lb)	25400 (55997 lb)	30480 (67197·37 lb)

Container with side doors which open the whole length of the unit

These units also have end doors. They can also have removable roofs. The special hinged doors can be on both sides of the container if required.

DIMENSIONS:	20 ft	30 ft
Exterior	mm	mm
Length	6055 (238$\frac{2}{3}$ in)	9125 (359$\frac{1}{4}$ in)
Width	2435 (93$\frac{3}{4}$ in)	2435 (93$\frac{3}{4}$ in)
Height	2590 (102 in)	2590 (102 in)
Interior:		
Length	5920 (233 in)	8990 (345 in)
Width	2300 (90$\frac{1}{2}$ in)	2300 (90$\frac{1}{2}$ in)
Height	2270 (89$\frac{1}{4}$ in)	2270 (89$\frac{1}{4}$ in)
OPENINGS FOR LOADING:		
Front	mm	mm
Width	2300 (90$\frac{1}{2}$ in)	2300 (90$\frac{1}{2}$ in)
Height	2190 (86$\frac{1}{4}$ in)	2190 (86$\frac{3}{4}$ in)
Side		
Width	5680 (223$\frac{1}{2}$ in)	8750 (344$\frac{1}{2}$ in)
Height	2190 (86$\frac{1}{4}$ in)	2190 (86$\frac{1}{4}$ in)
WEIGHT:	kg	kg
Weight of container	2100 (4269·7 lb)	3450 (7583·9 lb)
Useful load	18220 (40168·09 lb)	21950 (48391$\frac{1}{4}$ lb)
Total weight	20320 (44798·09 lb)	25400 (55997 lb)

End door refrigerated container with space for refrigeration equipment

A space is provided for refrigeration equipment.

Dimensions:	20 ft	30 ft	40 ft
Exterior	mm	mm	mm
Length	6055 (238⅖ in)	9125 (359¼ in)	12190 (480 in)
Width	2435 (95¾ in)	2435 (95¾ in)	2435 (95¾ in)
Height	2435 (95¾ in)	2435 (95¾ in)	2435 (95¾ in)
Interior			
Length	5150 (202¾ in)	7950 (313 in)	1000 (433 in)
Width	2150 (84½ in)	2150 (84½ in)	2150 (84½ in)
Height	2180 (85¾ in)	2180 (85¾ in)	1280 (50⅓ in)
Openings for Loading:	mm	mm	mm
Width	2150 (84½ in)	2150 (84½ in)	2150 (84½ in)
Height	2100 (82½ in)	2100 (82½ in)	2100 (82½ in)
Weight:	kg	kg	kg
Without refrigeration equipment	2800 (6172·9 lb)	3900 (8598 lb)	5200 (11464 lb)
With refrigeration equipment	3600 (7936·6 lb)	5000 (11023·1 lb)	6600 (14550½ lb)
Useful load	16720 (36861·09 lb)	20400 (44974 lb)	23880 (5264⅓ lb)
Total weight	20320 (44798·09 lb)	25400 (55997 lb)	30480 (67197 ⅓ lb)

End and side door refrigerated container

Dimensions:	20 ft	30 ft	40 ft
Exterior	mm	mm	mm
Length	6055 (238⅖ in)	9125 (359¼ in)	12190 (480 in)
Width	2435 (95¾ in)	2435 (95¾ in)	2435 (95¾ in)
Height	2435 (95¾ in)	2435 (95¾ in)	2435 (95¾ in)
Interior			
Length	5150 (202¾ in)	7950 (313 in)	11000 (433 in)
Width	2150 (84½ in)	2150 (84½ in)	2150 (84½ in)
Height	2180 (85¾ in)	2180 (85¾ in)	2180 (85¾ in)

Openings for Loading:			
Weight:	mm	mm	mm
without refrigeration	2150 (84½ in)	2150 (84½ in)	2150 (84½ in)
equipment	2100 (82½ in)	2100 (82½ in)	2100 (82½ in)
With refrigeration			
equipment			
Useful load	2150 (84½ in)	2150 (84½ in)	2150 (82½ in)
Total weight	2100 (82½ in)	2100 (82½ in)	2100 (82½ in)
Front	kg	kg	kg
Width	3400 (7495·7 lb)	4500 (9920·8 lb)	5800 (12786·8 lb)
Height	4200 (9259·4 lb)	5600 (12345·9 lb)	7200 (15873·3 lb)
Side			
Width	16120 (35538·09 lb)	19800 (43652 lb)	23280 (51323·3 lb)
Height	20320 (44793·09 lb)	25400 (55997 lb)	30480 (67197 ⅓ lb)

Tank container

Liquid container within ISO framework for transport of liquids. Made from alloy or stainless steel.

Dimensions:		
	20 ft	30 ft
	mm	mm
Length	6055 (238⅖ in)	9125 (359¼ in)
Width	2435 (95¾ in)	2435 (95¾ in)
Height	2435 (95¾ in)	(2435 (95¾ in)
Volume of Tank:		
	hl	hl
	160	250
	180	280
Weight:	kg	kg
Tank only	5400 (11905 lb)	7000 (15432·4 lb)
Useful load	15000 (33069 lb)	18400 (40565 lb)
Total weight	20320 (44798·09 lb)	25400 (55997 lb)

INDEX

We've come a long way since then

A lot of container makers aren't around any more. York are still very much in business with major shipping and container leasing companies who keep coming back for more. They like the way York steel containers last – they're the only ones with Alchem protection against corrosion. Alchemized containers give you the strength of steel plus longer life and lower maintenance costs. It means extra profitability – at no extra cost. York make 20 ft., 30 ft. and 40 ft. dry freight and refrigerated boxes, open tops and Bulktainers – the ISO containers that double as bulk carriers of powders and granules. Regular 8 ft. height and 8 ft. 6 in. gooseneck tunnel units. Write for our brochure, wherever you are – we've resident salesmen in all maritime countries.

means business

York Trailer Company Limited
Corby, Northants. England.
Phone Corby (05366) 3561 Telex 34516 Cables Yorktra
    York in Canada
Davies Truck Equipment Limited
Phone (416) 247 7421 Telex 06219523
    York in Europe
York Trailer Europa N.V.
Phone 01857-444 or 445 Telex 21510

GBA/4H

SHIPS INDEX

Printed and Bound in Great Britain by
Netherwood Dalton & Co. Ltd., Huddersfield